FOREIGN AND COMMONWEALTH OFFICE

The Commonwealth Yearbook 1992

LONDON : HMSO

First published 1992

Printed in the United Kingdom for HMSO
Dd293544 8/92 C19 G1310 10170

ISBN 0 11 591710 1

HMSO

HMSO publications are available from:

HMSO Publications Centre
(Mail, fax and telephone orders only)
PO Box 276, London, SW8 5DT
Telephone orders 071-873 9090
General enquiries 071-873 0011
(queuing system in operation for both numbers)
Fax orders 071-873 8200

HMSO Bookshops
49 High Holborn, London, WC1V 6HB
(counter service only)
071-873 0011 Fax 071-873 8200
258 Broad Street, Birmingham, B1 2HE
021-643 3740 Fax 021-643 6510
Southey House, 33 Wine Street, Bristol, BS1 2BQ
0272 264306 Fax 0272 294515
9-21 Princess Street, Manchester, M60 8AS
061-834 7201 Fax 061-833 0634
16 Arthur Street, Belfast, BT1 4GD
0232 238451 Fax 0232 235401
71 Lothian Street, Edinburgh, EH3 9AZ
031-228 4181 Fax 031-229 2734

HMSO's Accredited Agents
(see Yellow Pages)

and through good booksellers

ABOUT HMSO's STANDING ORDER SERVICE

The Standing Order service, open to all HMSO account holders* allows customers to receive automatically the publications they require in a specified subject area, thereby saving them the time, trouble and expense of placing individual orders.

Customers may choose from over 4000 classifications arranged in more than 250 sub groups under 30 major subject areas. These classifications enable customers to choose from a wide range of subjects those publications which are of special interest to them. This is a particularly valuable service for the specialist library or research body. All publications will be despatched to arrive immediately after publication date. A special leaflet describing the service in detail may be obtained on request.

Write to PC13A, Standing Order Service, HMSO Books, PO Box 276, LONDON SW8 5DT quoting classification reference O4.02.011 to order future titles in this series.

*Details of requirements to open an account can be obtained from PC21, HMSO Books, PO Box 276, London SW8 5DT.

Preface

This is the sixth edition of *The Commonwealth Yearbook* under its present title.

While every effort has been made to ensure that the information in this volume is correct at the time of going to press the Editor would be grateful if his attention could be drawn to any errors or omissions that may be noticed.

LIBRARY AND RECORDS DEPARTMENT
FOREIGN AND COMMONWEALTH OFFICE

Contents

Page

Readers requiring information on Commonwealth regional organisations and committees, societies and organisations concerned with the Commonwealth should refer to *Directory of Commonwealth Organisations: official and unofficial organisations of the Commonwealth 1991*, compiled by The Information Division, Commonwealth Secretariat.

PART I

The Commonwealth in 1991

The main event during 1991 was the Commonwealth Heads of Government Meeting (CHOGM) in Harare, where leaders of member states reaffirmed their confidence in the Commonwealth. The Harare CHOGM (16–21 October) was one of the most successful meetings of Commonwealth Heads of Government in recent years. The concluding declaration focussed clearly on 'good governance' issues including the promotion of democracy, human rights, market principles and the environment. It also made clear that the "special strength of the Commonwealth lies in the combination of the diversity of its members with their shared inheritance in language, culture and the rule of law. The Commonwealth way is to seek consensus through consultation and the sharing of experience. It is uniquely placed to serve as a model and as a catalyst for new forms of friendship and co-operation to all in the spirit of the Charter of the United Nations".

In February the Committee of Foreign Ministers on South Africa (CCFMSA), met in London and endorsed the process of normalising sporting ties with South Africa on a sport by sport basis. At their September meeting in Delhi, CCFSMA agreed to recommend to CHOGM, a staged dismantling of remaining sanctions.

On March 11th Commonwealth Day in the UK was marked, once again, by a multi-faith Observance at Westminster Abbey, in the presence of Her Majesty The Queen and His Royal Highness The Prince of Wales. High Commissioners in London also attended. The Commonwealth Day theme was "Science and Technology" and children in schools throughout the Commonwealth were encouraged to concentrate Commonwealth Day activities on this subject.

Commonwealth Health Ministers met in Geneva in May at the Pre-World Health Assembly. They reviewed and discussed health issues relevant to Commonwealth countries, including priorities for the work of the Health Programme of the Commonwealth Secretariat. The meeting also discussed plans for the Tenth Commonwealth Health Ministers Meeting in Cyprus in 1992.

In June the 7th meeting of Commonwealth Employment Ministers was held in Geneva. In depth discussions took place on the implications for employment and labour of current trends towards greater attention to the informal sector, self-employment and entrepreneurship.

The Commonwealth Parliamentary Association (CPA) held their 37th Commonwealth Parliamentary Conference from 22nd September to 2nd October in New Delhi, India.

The Commonwealth Finance Ministers met on 9th–10th October in Kuala Lumpur. They noted that economic recovery in both the industrial and developing worlds was still slow and uncertain.

Ministers emphasised that, while recognising the progress already made in dealing with international debt problems, further action was still needed. The importance of adequate financial support for those countries who had so far avoided debt rescheduling was also stressed. Ministers noted the scope for developing countries to help themselves through sound and imaginative economic policies. They observed the improvements in sustainable growth achieved by many developing countries by reducing budget deficits, refocussing the role of government, improving the climate for domestic and foreign investment and developing their human resources. Ministers also welcomed the cut in expenditure on armaments as a result of the diminution in global tensions. It was felt that such reductions could provide a stimulus to the world economy by making resources available for a range of productive, peaceful, purposes.

The High Level Appraisal Group, established at the 1989 CHOGM in Kuala Lumpur to consider roles for the Commonwealth in the 1990's and beyond, met on the eve of the Harare CHOGM. The Group identified several areas, some old, some new, which deserved special emphasis by the Commonwealth in years to come. It also endorsed guidelines for the Commonwealth observance of elections, criteria for Commonwealth membership and a strategy for sharpening the Commonwealth's image.

The Commonwealth Agriculture Ministers meeting took place in November, in Rome. It was their 7th biennial meeting. The agenda reflected major Commonwealth concerns and, in particular, rural poverty and food security within the context of the world food and agricultural situation. Ministers agreed that poverty alleviation was the key to the reduction of hunger, malnutrition and environmental degradation. Agriculture continued to be the main driving force behind economic growth in developing countries.

The year ended with the Commonwealth Group of Distinguished Observers attending the first planary sessions of the Convention for a Democratic South Africa (CODESA) from 20th–21st December. Wide ranging discussions were held with representatives of many of the principal parties and in all cases there was appreciation of the Commonwealth's presence. The Group was delighted that CODESA had met its initial objectives and embarked on a new and peaceful road towards the realisation of a democratic and non-racial South Africa.

The Evolution of the Modern Commonwealth

The modern Commonwealth is a voluntary association of independent sovereign states each responsible for its own policies, consulting and co-operating in their common interests and in the promotion of greater international understanding. As Head of the Commonwealth, HM The Queen underlined the uniqueness of the association when she said in a Christmas broadcast from New Zealand in 1953: *'The Commonwealth bears no resemblance to the empires of the past. It is an entirely new conception built on the highest qualities of the spirit of man: friendship, loyalty and the desire for freedom and peace'.*

Although fundamentally different from the British Empire, the modern Commonwealth can nonetheless trace its origins to the development of British colonial policy from the early nineteenth century. In the 1840s, following Lord Durham's Report, self-government was introduced in Canada and so laid the foundations for the emergence of the first Dominion in 1867. By 1914 the other colonies of settlement had also achieved what became known as Dominion Status ie internal self-government and a considerable degree of freedom in their foreign relations. The 1917 Imperial War Conference recognised that 'the constitutional relations of the component parts of the Empire . . . should be based upon a full recognition of the Dominions as autonomous nations of an Imperial Commonwealth'. Reflecting their newly clarified status all the Dominions (except Newfoundland) and India (an exception amongst the dependencies because of her size and contribution to the recent war effort) had their own representation in the League of Nations and, in 1926, the Inter-Imperial Relations Committee defined their position in what became known as the Balfour Declaration. By this the Dominions (Canada, Newfoundland, Australia, New Zealand, South Africa, and the Irish Free State) were described as:

'autonomous Communities within the British Empire, equal in status, in no way subordinate one to another in any aspect of their domestic or external affairs, though united by a common allegiance to the Crown and freely associated as Members of the British Commonwealth of Nations'.

Formal legal recognition of this fully independent status came with the passage by the British Parliament of the Statute of Westminster in 1931

The sovereign status defined in the preamble of the Statute was conferred upon all the Dominions forthwith. Canada, South Africa and the Irish Free State swiftly took up its provisions. The operation of the Statute was, however, withheld from Newfoundland, Australia and New Zealand at their request until their own Parliaments should determine otherwise. Australia eventually adopted the Statute in 1942 and New Zealand in 1947 (Newfoundland relinquished its Dominion Status in 1934 and became part of Canada in 1949).

During this period pressure was mounting in India for self-government and, in 1947, two new Dominions were created: India and Pakistan. This led to probably the most important single constitutional change in the evolution of the modern post-war Commonwealth in that India's Constituent Assembly decided to adopt a republican constitution and yet expressed the desire to remain within the Commonwealth. The Commonwealth Prime Ministers' meeting of 1949 agreed to India's continued membership on the basis of her expressed 'acceptance of the King as the symbol of the free association of the independent Member Nations and as such Head of the Commonwealth'. This agreement established the precedent both for republican membership and the recognition of the British monarch as Head of the Commonwealth as distinct from his position as Head of State in those countries who wished to retain allegiance to the Crown. No formal functions attach to the title Head of the Commonwealth and it has no strict constitutional significance. However it remains crucial as the symbolic link uniting all member states and is the outward and visible mark of the special relationship which exists between them.

Since 1949 most former British, Australian and New Zealand dependencies have achieved independence and the majority have chosen to join the Commonwealth. Most have done so as republics and in those countries where the Queen remains as Head of State (today called Realms not Dominions) it has become established that the Queen acts as Head of each individual state rather than as monarch of the United Kingdom. This change in practice has also been reflected in what are sometimes called the 'old' Commonwealth countries (Australia, Canada and New Zealand) eg in 1973 the Queen was formally designated 'Queen of Australia'.

Another fundamental characteristic of the modern Commonwealth also dates from the granting of independence in the Indian subcontinent. The South African government had previously (for example at the Imperial Conference in 1930) registered its belief that Dominion autonomy included the right to secede. However, it seems that the position remained ill-defined until 1947 when the British Prime Minister, while discussing the Burma Independence Bill, recognised Burma's wish to become an independent state outside the Commonwealth and said 'it was the duty of His Majesty's Government ... to implement their decision'.

Few states eligible for membership have, in fact, not joined or have left the Commonwealth. Ireland withdrew in 1949 as she had ceased to play an active part and in 1961 South Africa cancelled her application, under the then established convention for readmission upon adopting a republican constitution, because of mounting opposition to apartheid. In January 1972 Pakistan withdrew, giving the reason that Australia, New Zealand and the United Kingdom were about to recognise the independence of East Pakistan which, as Bangladesh, eventually joined the Commonwealth in her own right. Fiji's membership lapsed in 1987 when she did not formally apply for readmission following a military coup d'état which involved the declaration of a Republic and the resignation of the Governor-General.

Certain other territories, formerly British dependencies, mandates, protectorates or protected states, did not become Commonwealth members on achieving independence. Besides Jordan in 1946 and Burma and Palestine in 1948 membership was not taken up by the Sudan (1956), British Somaliland (1960), the South Cameroons (1961), the South Arabian Federation (1967), and the Gulf States (1961–71). The Maldives achieved independence in 1965 but did not join the Commonwealth until 1982. Similarly Western Samoa achieved independence from New Zealand in 1962 but did not join the Commonwealth until 1970. Pakistan established a new precedent in 1989 by rejoining. In 1990 Namibia, a former Mandate and Trust Territory administered by South Africa, joined the Commonwealth on achieving independence.

The contemporary Commonwealth is, therefore, a considerably different body from that which existed in 1931, 1949 or even 1960. It has no formal constitutional structure, its members preferring to rely on largely unwritten conventions and accepted procedures. It imposes no statutory obligations on members and is a voluntary grouping which is still evolving in form. Inter-Governmental consultation is its principal mode of operation, including periodic Commonwealth Heads of Government meetings known until 1966 as Commonwealth Prime Ministers' meetings (see page 25). The main formal official machinery is the Commonwealth Secretariat, established at the 1965 Prime Ministers' meeting to foster closer and more informed understanding between the constituent governments. The Secretariat, jointly supported by all the member governments, has its headquarters in London and its chief official (the Secretary-General) is appointed by the Commonwealth Heads of Government (for details of the Commonwealth Secretariat see page 51). There are, however, a wide variety of professional, educational, parliamentary and other non-official bodies which give substance to the Commonwealth relationship.

Although the Commonwealth does not have a formal constitutional structure its members do subscribe to several sets of principles which reflect the fact that the Commonwealth has grown to be more representative of the world and its diversities. The principles were spelt out at the 1971 Heads of Government Meeting in what has become known as the Declaration of Commonwealth Principles or the Singapore Declaration:

DECLARATION OF COMMONWEALTH PRINCIPLES

The Commonwealth of Nations is a voluntary association of independent sovereign states, each responsible for its own policies, consulting and co-operating in the common interests of their peoples and in the promotion of international understanding and world peace.

Members of the Commonwealth come from territories in the six continents and five oceans, include peoples of different races, languages and religions, and display every stage of economic development from poor developing nations to wealthy industrialised nations. They encompass a rich variety of cultures, traditions and institutions. Membership of the Commonwealth is compatible with the freedom of member governments to be non-aligned or to belong to any other grouping, association or alliance.

Within this diversity all members of the Commonwealth hold certain principles in common. It is by pursuing these principles that the Commonwealth can continue to influence international society for the benefit of mankind.

WE BELIEVE *that international peace and order are essential to the security and prosperity of mankind; we therefore support the United Nations and seek to strengthen its influence for peace in the world, and its efforts to remove the causes of tension between nations.*

WE BELIEVE *in the liberty of the individual, in equal rights for all citizens regardless of race, colour, creed or political belief, and in their inalienable right to participate by means of free and democratic political processes in framing the society in which they live. We therefore strive to promote in each of our countries those representative institutions and guarantees for personal freedom under the law that are our common heritage.*

WE RECOGNISE *racial prejudice as a dangerous sickness threatening the healthy development of the human race and racial discrimination as an unmitigated evil of society. Each of us will vigorously combat this evil within our own nation. No country will afford to regimes which practice racial discrimination assistance which in its own judgment directly contributes to the pursuit or consolidation of this evil policy. We oppose all forms of colonial domination and racial oppression and are committed to the principles of human dignity and equality. We will therefore use all our efforts to foster human equality and dignity everywhere and to further the principles of self-determination and non-racialism.*

WE BELIEVE *that the wide disparities in wealth now existing between different sections of mankind are too great to be tolerated; they also create world tensions; our aim is their progressive removal; we therefore seek to use our efforts to overcome poverty, ignorance and disease, in raising standards of life and achieving a more equitable international society. To this end our aim is to achieve the freest possible flow of international trade on terms fair and equitable to all, taking into account the special requirements of the developing countries, and to encourage the flow of adequate resources, including governmental and private resources, to the developing countries, bearing in mind the importance of doing this in a true spirit of partnership and of establishing for this purpose in the developing countries conditions which are conducive to sustained investment and growth.*

WE BELIEVE *that international co-operation is essential to remove the causes of war, promote tolerance, combat injustice and secure development amongst the peoples of the world; we are convinced that the Commonwealth is one of the most fruitful associations for these purposes.*

In pursuing these principles the Members of the Commonwealth believe that they can provide a constructive example of the multi-national approach which is vital to peace and progress in the modern world. The association is based on consultation, discussion and co-operation. In rejecting coercion as an instrument of policy they recognise that the security of each member state from external aggression is a matter of concern to all members. It provides many channels for continuing exchanges of knowledge and views of professional, cultural, economic, legal and political issues among member states. These relationships we intend to foster and extend for we believe that our multi-national association can expand human understanding and understanding among nations, assist in the elimination of discrimination based on differences of race, colour or creed, maintain and strengthen personal liberty, contribute to the enrichment of life for all, and provide a powerful influence for peace among nations.

Since 1971 Commonwealth governments have sought to harness their diverse experience in collective pursuit of these principles. At their regular meetings, Commonwealth Heads of Government consider issues of global as well as Commonwealth concern, often asking the Commonwealth Secretary-General to set up consultative groups or committees of experts to examine specific problems and suggest practical remedies.

Groups have been set up to consider a broad spectrum of economic, political and other problems. Examples include the committee of experts set up following the 1975 meeting to examine the gap between rich and poor countries, the Commonwealth consultative group established following the 1983 meeting to look into the difficulties confronting small states, and the Expert Group which in 1989 reported on the problems of climate change and sea-level rise.

It has also become a feature of Heads of Government meetings that a Communiqué is issued recording the essence of their discussions which often includes a declaration on a topic of special interest. A persistent concern has been the question of racial equality. Commonwealth opposition to apartheid in South Africa was formally enunciated in the 1977 Gleneagles Agreement, which called on Governments to discourage their citizens from engaging in sporting contacts with South Africa. This concern was reiterated in the 1979 Lusaka Declaration on Racism and Racial Prejudice and the 1985 Nassau Accord on Southern Africa, the 1987 Okanagan Statement and Programme of Action on Southern Africa and the 1989 Kuala Lumpur Statement 'Southern Africa the Way Ahead'.

The 1991 Harare Declaration reaffirmed the 1971 Declaration of Principles and emphasised the importance of Commonwealth co-operation in promoting sound and sustainable development throughout the countries of the Commonwealth.

Important though these governmental or 'official' contacts are, they form only a part of the chronicle of the evolution of the modern Commonwealth. There are literally hundreds of non-governmental and unofficial organisations which draw together the people of the Commonwealth through their activities. These are vital to the development of mutual understanding between peoples from diverse backgrounds which is at the core of this association. (For details of many of these bodies see *Directory of Commonwealth Organisations: official and unofficial Organisations of the Commonwealth 1991*, compiled by the Information Division, Commonwealth Secretariat). All Commonwealth organisations benefit from shared practices and beliefs and from the shared language of English. These qualities often enable the Commonwealth to achieve more than other international organisations in matters where it can draw on such strengths. Secretary-General Anyaoku has described the Commonwealth's central attribute as 'Surely its ability to bridge racial, ideological and economic divides and inequalities, assisted by its common language and common heritage.'

THE EXPANDING COMMONWEALTH

*Denotes Special Members (these have the right to participate in all functional meetings and activities of the Commonwealth, the only limitation being that Special Members do not attend the Commonwealth Heads of Government Meetings).

Country	*Date of Commonwealth Membership*
United Kingdom	
Canada	1931 } under the Statute of Westminster
Australia	1931 } under the Statute of Westminster
New Zealand	1931 } under the Statute of Westminster
India	1947
Pakistan	1947 (left in 1972, rejoined 1989)
Sri Lanka (formerly Ceylon)	1948
Ghana	1957
Malaya	1957 (which became the Federation of Malaysia in 1963)
Nigeria	1960
Cyprus	1961 (independent since 1960)
Sierra Leone	1961
Tanganyika	1961 (which became Tanzania in 1964 upon union with Zanzibar)
Jamaica	1962
Trinidad and Tobago	1962
Uganda	1962
Kenya	1963
Malawi	1964
Malta	1964
Zambia	1964
The Gambia	1965
Singapore	1965 (on secession from Malaysia)
Guyana	1966
Botswana	1966
Lesotho	1966
Barbados	1966
Mauritius	1968
Nauru*	1968
Swaziland	1968
Tonga	1970
Western Samoa	1970 (independent since 1962)
Bangladesh	1972 (on separation from Pakistan)
Bahamas	1973
Grenada	1974
Papua New Guinea	1975
Seychelles	1976
Solomon Islands	1978
Tuvalu*	1978
Dominica	1978
Kiribati	1979
St Lucia	1979
St Vincent and the Grenadines	1979 (joined as Special Member; full member since 1985)
Zimbabwe	1980
Vanuatu	1980
Belize	1981
Antigua and Barbuda	1981
Maldives	1982 (independent since 1965; joined as Special Member; full member since 1985)
St Christopher and Nevis	1983
Brunei	1984
Namibia	1990

Organisation of British Government Relations with Other Commonwealth Countries and Administration of Dependent Territories

Constitutional responsibility to Parliament for British relations with other Commonwealth countries and for the administration of Dependent Territories rests with the Secretary of State for Foreign and Commonwealth Affairs. This follows the amalgamation in 1968 of the former Foreign Office and Commonwealth Office under one Secretary of State. The history of the development of the British government machinery for dealing with Commonwealth and Colonial affairs may be found in earlier editions of the Year Book of the Commonwealth and of the Commonwealth Relations Office List.

Within the Foreign and Commonwealth Office there are departments to advise Ministers on Commonwealth aspects of policy and to administer the remaining Dependent Territories.

Diplomatic representatives exchanged between Commonwealth countries are called High Commissioners instead of Ambassadors, as a mark of the special Commonwealth association. In rank, precedence and immunity, they enjoy a common status with Ambassadors, and their function is broadly similar. Between any two countries of which The Queen is Head of State, the High Commissioner represents his government and not his sovereign. Between countries which have separate Heads of State, the High Commissioner represents his Head of State as well as his government. High Commissioners traditionally deal direct with a wider range of government departments than do their foreign counterparts, and Commonwealth High Commissioners in London have a special relationship with Buckingham Palace which derives from their recognition of The Queen as Head of the Commonwealth and, in the case of The Queen's realms, from Her Majesty being separately their own Head of State.

Except for the specialist advisers, the staff of the Foreign and Commonwealth Office in London and of British High Commissioners and British Embassies overseas are members of H.M. Diplomatic Service, which was formed on 1st January 1965 combining the duties and posts of the former Foreign Service, the Commonwealth Relations Office at home and overseas, and the Trade Commission service.

Matters relating to overseas development and the provision of British aid are the responsibility of the Overseas Development Administration under the overall supervision of the Secetary of State for Foreign and Commonwealth Affairs. Details of the Overseas Development Administration are contained in Part VIII.

Dependent Territories

The administration of each Dependent Territory is executed by its own Government under an Officer Administering the Government. The majority of these are styled Governor and as such are the personal representatives of the Sovereign; the remainder comprise the High Commissioner, British Antarctic Territory; Her Majesty's Commissioner, British Indian Ocean Territory; and the Administrators of Ascension and Tristan da Cunha. Subject to the overriding authority of Parliament, the territorial Governments enjoy a large and increasing measure of autonomy. Each territory has its own legislature and its own civil service, which is paid from local revenue and is not part of the Home Civil Service. The Secretary of State for Foreign and Commonwealth Affairs is responsible for transfers, promotions and discipline of members of Her Majesty's Overseas Civil Service serving in Dependent Territories and appointments of senior officers such as Governors, Senior Administrative, Judicial and Legal Officers.

PART II

Government Offices in London

CAYMAN ISLANDS GOVERNMENT OFFICE
Trevor House, 100 Brompton Road, London SW3 1EX (071-581 9418)
Fax: 071-584 4463
United Kindom Representative: T. Russell, CMG, CBE

The function of the office is to promote Cayman Islands interests in trade and industry, and to carry out liaison duties, particularly in relation to recruitment, Cayman Islands students in the United Kingdom, training and information. The office deals with enquiries about immigration, registrations, and general topics.

FALKLAND ISLANDS GOVERNMENT OFFICE
Falkland House, 14 Broadway, London SW1H 0BH (071-222 2542)
Telex: 8950476 FIGLON
Fax: 071-222 2375
Representative: Sukey Cameron

The main function of the office is to make known the views of the Falkland Islands Government and to promote interests in the development of trade and industry. It also deals with enquiries about immigration and general topics. Liaison with HM Government Departments is maintained on matters of concern to the Falkland Islands.

HONG KONG GOVERNMENT OFFICE
6 Grafton Street, London W1X 3LB (071-499 9821)
Telex: 28404.
Fax: 071-493 1964
Hong Kong Commissioner: John Yaxley, CBE
Deputy Commissioner: Kwong Ki-chi
Assistant Commissioner (Public Affairs): Ms M M L Wong
Senior Administrative Officer (Liaison): Warner Cheuk
Regional Director (Europe), Industrial Promotion: Ian Howard
Head of Commercial Division: Peter Wise
Principal Consultant, Industrial Promotion: Donald Fletcher
Chief Information Officer: Peter Randall
Press Officer: Ranjit Peiris
Chief Community Services Officer: Rupert Cheung

An important function of the office is to liaise with HM Government Departments on matters of concern to Hong Kong. It has sections dealing with Recruitment, Commercial Relations, Industrial Investment, the Hong Kong Chinese Community in Britain, Students from Hong Kong, and the Dissemination of Information.

Government Tourist, Trade and Travel Agencies of Dependent Territories in London

BERMUDA TOURISM
BCB Ltd, 1 Battersea Church Road, London SW11 3LY (071-734 8813)
Fax: (071) 352 6501
Director: Mr Derek R Brightwell
Sales Manager: Miss Rosemary S Wick

The office, which also has information offices in the United States, Canada, and Bermuda, was first established in London in 1925. It is responsible for all tourist activities in Europe with subsidiary offices in Munich and Gothenburg.

The purpose of the office is to assist the development of the tourist trade and to provide intending visitors and travel agents with information and literature about Bermuda. The office is also very active in the promotion of Bermuda as a destination for conferences and incentives.

CAYMAN ISLANDS DEPARTMENT OF TOURISM AND CAYMAN AIRWAYS OFFICE
Trevor House, 100 Brompton Road, Knightsbridge, London SW3 1EX (071-581 9960)
Fax: (071) 584 4463
Regional Sales Manager: Miss Deirdre Kirwan-Taylor

The office function is to promote tourism from the United Kingdom, Europe and Eire and to provide the travel trade and consumer with full information and literature for the Cayman Islands and Cayman Airways.

The office handles all enquiries for conferences and incentives and has a full reservations service for accommodation and Cayman Airways.

The Government Representative, Mr Thomas Russell CMG, CBE, handles all enquiries of a business nature.
See also entry for Cayman Islands Government Office page 13.

GIBRALTAR INFORMATION BUREAU
Arundel Great Court, 179 Strand, London WC2R 1EH (071-836 0777 and 071-240 6611)
Fax: (071) 240 6612
Managing Director: Mr Albert A Poggio

The Gibraltar Information Bureau previously known as the Gibraltar Government Tourist Office, continues to promote tourism and provide literature, advice and assistance to the travel trade and intending holiday visitors to the Rock, as well as general information on Gibraltar.
Its function now also provides for the marketing and promotion of Gibraltar in relation to trade, the financial centre and commercial activities generally.

HONG KONG TOURIST ASSOCIATION
125 Pall Mall, London SW1Y 5EA (071-930 4775)
Telex: 8950160 LUYULOG
Fax: (071) 930 4777
Cable: Luyu London
Director: Mr K W Hayden Sadler

The Hong Kong Tourist Association in London gives assistance to the travel trade and consumer plus advice on: travel to and visitor facilities in Hong Kong; tour operators and travel agents specialising in Hong Kong; and on special interest and study group travel. Its specialist division the Hong Kong Convention and Incentive Travel Bureau also gives advice and information on all aspects of planning and organising conferences and incentives in Hong Kong.

The Hong Kong Tourist Association has 14 offices overseas, and in Europe has offices in London, Paris, Frankfurt, Rome and Barcelona.

HONG KONG TRADE DEVELOPMENT COUNCIL
London Office: Ground floor, Swire House, 59 Buckingham Gate, London SW1E 6AJ (071-828 1661)
Fax: (071) 828 9976
Regional Director, Northern Europe: Mr Joseph K Lee

Hong Kong's statutory trade promotion body providing trade, enquiry, publications, fairs and exhibitions services etc.

TURKS & CAICOS ISLANDS TOURIST OFFICE
3 Epirus Road, London SW6 7UJ (071-376 2981)
Telex: 927533
Fax: (071) 938 4793
Director: Mrs Ruth Buckmaster

The office is responsible for promoting tourism, giving advice and providing literature to intending visitors to the Turks & Caicos Islands. Assistance is also available on other matters concerning the Islands.

Chronological List of British High Commissioners and Representatives in Other Commonwealth Countries

ANTIGUA AND BARBUDA

High Commissioners
1981 (November) J S Arthur, CMG
1982 (September) Viscount Dunrossil, CMG
1983 (August) G. L. Bullard, CMG (later 1985) Sir Giles Bullard, KCVO, CMG)
1986 (October) K F X Burns, CMG
1991 (February) E T Davies, CMG

AUSTRALIA

Representative
1931 (May) E T Crutchley, CB, CMG, OBE

High Commissioners
1936 (March) Sir Geoffrey Whiskard, KCMG. CB
1941 (July) Sir Ronald Cross, Bt., PC, MP
1946 (July) E J Williams, PC (later (1952) Sir Edward Williams, KCMG)
1952 (October) Sir Stephen Holmes, KCMG, MC
1956 (November) Peter Alexander Rupert Carrington, MC, 6th Baron Carrington (later (1958) KCMG)
1959 (November) Lieutenant-General Sir William Oliver, KCB, OBE, DL (later GBE (1965), KCMG (1962))
1965 (June) Sir Charles Johnston, KCMG
1971 (April) The Rt Hon Sir Morrice James, KCMG, CVO, MBE (later (1975), GCMG)
1976 (May) Sir Donald Tebbit, KCMG (later (1980) GCMG)
1980 (April) Sir John Mason, KCMG
1984 (October) Sir John Leahy, KCMG
1988 (March) A J Coles CMG (later (1988), Sir John Coles, KCMG)
1991 (April) B L Barder

BAHAMAS

High Commissioners
1973 (July) C J Treadwell, CMG
1975 (February) P Mennell, CMG, MBE
1978 (August) J S R Duncan, CMG, MBE
1981 (May) A S Papadopoulos, CMG, MVO, MBE
1983 (May) P W Heap
1986 (October) C G Mays (later (1988) CMG)
1991 (July) M E J Gore, CBE

BANGLADESH

High Commissioners
1972 (April) A A Golds, CMG, MVO
1975 (January) B G Smallman, CMG, CVO
1978 (April) F S Miles, CMG
1980 (January) Michael Scott, KCVO, CMG
1981 (October) F Mills, CMG
1983 (December) T G Streeton, CMG (later (1989) Sir Terence Streeton, KBE CMG)
1989 (October) C H Imray, CMG

BARBADOS

High Commissioners
1966 (November) J S Bennett, CVO, CBE
1971 (March) D A Roberts
1973 (November) C S Roberts, CMG
1978 (April) J S Arthur, CMG
1982 (September) Viscount Dunrossil, CMG
1983 (August) G L Bullard, CMG (Later (1985) Sir Giles Bullard, KCVO, CMG)
1986 (October) K F X Burns, CMG
1991 (February) E T Davies, CMG

BELIZE

High Commissioners
1981 (September) F S E Trew (later (1984) CMG)
1984 (October) J M Crosby, MVO
1987 (November) P A B Thomson, CVO
1991 (February) D P R Mackilligin

BOTSWANA

High Commissioners
1966 (September) J S Gandee, CMG, OBE
1969 (November) G D Anderson, CMG
1973 (July) Miss E J Emery, CMG
1977 (May) W Turner, CMG, CVO
1981 (November) W Jones (later (1982) CMG)
1986 (February) P A Raftery CVO, MBE
1989 (February) B Smith, OBE

BRUNEI

High Commissioners
1963 (December) E O Laird, MBE
1965 (July) F D Webber, CMG, MC, TD
1968 (May) A R Adair, CVO, MBE
1972 (January) P Gautrey, CMG, CVO
1975 (January) J A Davidson, OBE
1978 (November) A C Watson, CMG
1983 (August) R F Cornish, MVO
1986 (September) R G Westbrook (later (1990) CMG)
1991 (April) A J Sindall

CANADA

High Commissioners

1928 (September) Sir William Clark, KCSI, KCMG
1935 (January) Sir Francis Floud, KCB, KCMG
1938 (October) Sir Gerald Campbell, KCMG
1941 (April) Malcolm MacDonald, PC, MP
1946 (May) Sir Alexander Clutterbuck, GCMG, MC
1952 (August) Lieutenant-General Sir Archibald Nye, GCSI, GCMG, GCIE, KCB, KBE, MC
1956 (November) Sir Saville Garner, KCMG
1961 (October) Derick Heathcoat-Amory, 1st Viscount Amory, PC, GCMG
1963 (October) Sir Henry Lintott, KCMG
1968 (September) Sir Colin Crowe, KCMG
1970 (October) P T Hayman, CMG, CVO, MBE (later (1971) Sir Peter Hayman, KCMG)
1974 (June) Sir John Johnson, KCMG, KCVO
1978 (April) Sir John Ford, KCMG, MC
1981 (June) Lord Moran, KCMG
1984 (August) Sir Derek Day, KCMG
1987 (December) Sir Alan Urwick, KCVO, CMG
1989 (October) B J P Fall, CMG
1992 (April) N P Bayne, CMG

REPUBLIC OF CYPRUS

High Commissioners

1961 (March) W A W Clark, CMG, CBE (later (1961) Sir Arthur Clark, KCMG)
1964 (April) Major-General W H A Bishop, CB, CMG, CVO, OBE (later (1964) Major-General Sir Alex Bishop, KCMG)
1965 (April) Sir David Hunt, KCMG, OBE
1967 (January) Sir Norman Costar, KCMG
1969 (April) The Hon P E Ramsbottom, CMG
1971 (June) R H G Edmonds, CMG, MBE
1973 (March) S J L Olver, CMG, MBE (later (1975) Sir Stephen Olver, KBE, CMG)
1975 (October) D McD Gordon, CMG
1979 (February) P A Rhodes, CMG
1982 (May) W J A Wilberforce, CMG
1988 (September) The Hon H J H Maud, CMG
1990 (July) D J Dain (later (1991) CMG)

DOMINICA

High Commissioners

1979 (January) J S Arthur, CMG
1982 (September) Viscount Dunrossil, CMG
1983 (August) G L Bullard, CMG (later (1985) Sir Giles Bullard, KCVO, CMG)
1986 (October) K F X Burns, CMG
1991 (February) E T Davies, CMG

THE GAMBIA

High Commissioners

1965 (February) G E Crombie, CMG
1968 (January) J G W Ramage
1972 (February) J R W Parker, OBE
1975 (November) M H G Rogers
1979 (May) E N Smith, CMG
1981 (October) D F B LeBreton, CBE
1984 (November) J D Garner, MVO
1988 (February) A Ibbott (later (1988) CBE)
1990 (October) A J Pover, CMG

GHANA

High Commissioners

1957 (March) Sir Ian Maclennan, KCMG
1959 (September) A W Snelling, CMG (later (1960) Sir Arthur Snelling, KCMG, KCVO)
1961 (December) Sir Geoffrey de Freitas, KCMG
1964 (January) H Smedley, MBE (later (1965) CMG)
1967 (December) H K Matthews, CMG, MBE
1970 (November) H S H Stanley, CMG
1975 (June) F Mills, CMG
1978 (May) J Mellon, CMG
1983 (May) K F X Burns (later (1984) CMG)
1986 (October) A H Wyatt, CMG
1989 (October) A M Goodenough (later (1990) CMG)

GRENADA

High Commissioners

1974 (February) C E Diggines (later (June 1974) CMG)
1977 (August) H S H Stanley, CMG
1980 (March) J S Arthur, CMG
1982 (September) Viscount Dunrossil, CMG
1983 (August) G L Bullard, CMG (later (1985) Sir Giles Bullard, KCVO, CMG)
1986 (October) K F X Burns, CMG
1991 (February) E T Davies, CMG

GUYANA

High Commissioners

1966 (May) T L Crosthwaite, CMG, MBE
1967 (August) K G Ritchie, CMG
1970 (November) W S Bates, CMG
1975 (March) P Gautrey, CMG, CVO
1978 (October) P L V Mallet (later (1980) CMG)
1982 (August) W K Slatcher, CMG (later (1983) CVO)
1985 (April) J D Massingham
1987 (May) D P Small, MBE (later (1988) CMG)
1990 (October) R D Gordon

INDIA

High Commissioners

1946 (November) Sir Terence Shone, KCMG
1948 (October) Lieutenant-General Sir Archibald Nye, GCSI, GCMG, GCIE, KCB, KBE, MC
1952 (October) Sir Alexander Clutterbuck, GCMG, MC

1955 (September) Malcolm MacDonald, PC
1960 (November) Sir Paul Gore-Booth, KCMG (later (1961) KCVO)
1965 (April) The Rt Hon J Freeman, MBE
1968 (October) The Rt Hon Sir Morrice James, KCMG, CVO, MBE
1971 (April) Sir Terence Garvey, KCMG
1973 (December) Sir Michael Walker, KCMG
1977 (January) J A Thomson, CMG (later (1978) Sir John Thomson, KCMG)
1982 (July) R L Wade-Gery, CMG (later (1983) Sir Robert Wade-Gery, KCMG) (KCVO 1983)
1987 (May) Sir David Goodall, KCMG (later (1991) GCMG)

JAMAICA

High Commissioners
1962 (August) Sir Alexander Morley, KCMG, CBE
1965 (May) J D Murray, CMG
1970 (April) E N Larmour, CMG
1973 (March) J D Hennings, CMG
1976 (April) J K Drinkall, CMG
1982 (January) B G Smallman, CMG, CVO
1984 (March) H M S Reid, CMG (later (1987) Sir Martin Reid, KBE, CMG)
1987 (June) A J Payne (later (1988) CMG)
1989 (March) D F Milton (later (1990) CMG)

KENYA

High Commissioners
1963 (December) Sir Geoffrey de Freitas, KCMG
1965 (February) Malcolm MacDonald, PC
1966 (March) Sir Edward Peck, KCMG
1968 (September) E G Norris, CMG (later (1969) Sir Eric Norris, KCMG)
1972 (May) A A Duff, CMG, CVO, DSO, DSC (later (1973) Sir Anthony Duff, KCMG, CVO, DSC)
1975 (October) S J C Fingland, CMG (later (1979) Sir Stanley Fingland, KCMG.
1979 (September) J R Williams, CMG
1982 (September) Sir Leonard Allison, KCVO, CMG
1986 (June) J R Johnson CMG (later (1988) Sir John Johnson, KCMG)
1990 (October) W R Tomkys, CMG (later (1991) Sir Roger Tomkys, KCMG)

KIRIBATI

High Commissioners
1979 (July) D H G Rose
1983 (September) C Thompson (later (1989) OBE)
1990 (January) D L White

LESOTHO

High Commissioners
1966 (October) I B Watt, CMG
1970 (May) H G M Bass, CMG
1973 (September) M J Moynihan, CMG, MC
1976 (January) R H Hobden, DFC
1978 (April) O G Griffith, CBE, MVO
1981 (November) C C Clemens, (later (1983) CMG)
1984 (March) P E Rosling, MVO (later (1987) CMG, MVO)
1988 (May) J C Edwards (later (1989) CMG)
1992 (February) J R Cowling, CMG

MALAWI

High Commissioners
1964 (July) D L Cole, MC (later (1965) CMG)
1967 (October) T S Tull, CBE, DSO
1971 (April) W R Haydon, CMG
1973 (August) K G Ritchie, CMG
1977 (June) M Scott, CMG, MVO (later (1979) Sir Michael Scott, KCVO, CMG)
1980 (February) W Peters, MVO, MBE (later (1981) CMG)
1983 (May) A H Brind, CMG
1987 (August) Dr D G Osborne (later (1990) CMG)
1990 (November) W N Wenban-Smith (later (1991) CMG)

MALAYA

High Commissioner
1957 (August) G W Tory, CMG (later (1958) Sir Geofroy Tory, KCMG) (Malaysia *below*)

MALAYSIA

High Commissioners
1963 (September) Sir Geofroy Tory, KCMG
1963 (November) Anthony Henry Head, 1st Viscount Head, PC, GCMG, MC
1966 (January) Sir Michael Walker, KCMG
1971 (March) Sir John Johnston, KCMG, KCVO
1974 (January) Sir Eric Norris, KCMG
1977 (November) D F Hawley, CMG, MBE (later (1978) Sir Donald Hawley, KCMG, MBE)
1981 (March) W Bentley, CMG
1983 (September) D H Gillmore, CMG
1986 (October) J N T Spreckley, CMG (later (1989) Sir Nicholas Spreckley, KCVO, CMG)
1992 (March) D Slater, CMG

MALDIVES
(Joined the Commonwealth 9 July 1982 as a 'special member' and became a full member on 20 June 1985)

High Commissioners
1982 (July) Sir John Nicholas, KCVO, CMG
1984 (November) J A B Stewart, CMG, OBE
1987 (June) D A S Gladstone (later (1988) CMG)

MALTA

High Commissioners

1964 (September) Sir Edward Wakefield, Bt., CIE
1965 (January) Sir John Martin, KCMG, CB, CVO
1967 (February) Sir Geofroy Tory, KCMG
1970 (March) Sir Duncan Watson, KCMG
1972 (April) J O Moreton, CMG, MC
1974 (June) W R Haydon, CMG
1976 (December) N Aspin, CMG
1979 (October) D P Aiers, CMG
1982 (October) C L Booth, CMG, MVO
1985 (May) S F St C Duncan, CMG
1988 (January) B Hitch, CMG, CVO
1991 (October) P G Wallis, CMG

MAURITIUS

High Commissioners

1968 (March) A Wooller, CBE
1970 (September) P A Carter, CMG
1973 (December) A H Brind, CMG
1977 (June) W A Ward
1981 (January) J N Allan, CBE
1985 (December) R B Crowson, CMG
1989 (August) M E Howell, CMG, OBE

NAMIBIA

High Commissioner

1990 (June) F N Richards

NAURU

High Commissioners

1978 (April) Viscount Dunrossil (later (1981) CMG)
1982 (July) R A R Barltrop (later (1982) CVO) (later (1987) CMG, CVO)
1990 (March) A B P Smart, CMG

NEW ZEALAND

High Commissioners

1939 (March) Sir Harry Batterbee, KCMG, KCVO (later (1945) GCMG)
1945 (July) Sir Patrick Duff, KCB, KCVO
1949 (September) Sir Roy Price, KCMG
1953 (September) General Sir Geoffry Scoones, KCB, KBE, CSI, DSO, MC
1957 (May) H G C Mallaby, CMG, OBE (later (1958) Sir George Mallaby, KCMG)
1959 (December) The Hon F E Cumming-Bruce, CMG (later (1961) The Hon Sir Francis Cumming-Bruce, KCMG)
1964 (March) Sir Ian Maclennan, KCMG
1969 (October) Sir Arthur Galsworthy, KCMG
1973 (January) D A Scott, CMG (later (1974) Sir David Scott, KCMG)
1976 (February) H Smedley, CMG, MBE (later (1978) Sir Harold Smedley, KCMG)
1980 (September) R J Stratton, CMG (later (1982) Sir Richard Stratton, KCMG)
1984 (July) T D O'Leary, CMG
1987 (December) R A C Byatt, CMG
1990 (September) D J Moss, CMG

NIGERIA

High Commissioners

1960 (October) Anthony Henry Head, 1st Viscount Head, PC, CBE, MC (later (1961) KCMG (1963) GCMG)
1964 (February) The Hon Sir Francis Cumming-Bruce, KCMG
1967 (February) Sir David Hunt, KCMG, OBE
1969 (June) Sir Leslie Glass, KCMG
1971 (July) Sir Cyril Pickard, KCMG
1974 (March) C M Le Quesne, CMG (later (June 1974) Sir Martin Le Quesne, KCMG)
1977 (January) Sir Sam Falle, KCVO, CMG, DSC
1979 (January) M Brown, CMG, OBE (later (1981) Sir Mervyn Brown, KCMG, OBE)
1983 (August) W E H Whyte, CMG
1984 (July) (vacant)
1986 (February) M K Ewans, CMG (later (1987) Sir Martin Ewans, KCMG)
1988 (July) B L Barder
1991 (March) A C D S MacRae, CMG

PAKISTAN

High Commissioners

1966 (February) C S Pickard (later (1966) Sir Cyril Pickard, KCMG)
1971 (June) J L Pumphrey (later (1973) Sir Laurence Pumphrey, KCMG)

(*From 30th January 1972, the British High Commission became the British Embassy, then from 1st October 1989 it reverted to the British High Commission*)

1987 (July) N J Barrington (later (1990) Sir Nicholas Barrington, KCMG, CVO)

PAPUA NEW GUINEA

High Commissioners

1975 (September) G W Baker, CBE
1977 (June) D K Middleton (later (1981) CBE)
1982 (January) A J Collins, OBE
1986 (January) M E Howell OBE
1989 (June) E J Sharland
1991 (July) J W Guy, OBE

RHODESIA

(*Following the illegal Declaration of Independence on* 11*th November* 1965, *the High Commission was closed. A residual staff remained, but they were finally withdrawn on* 14*th July* 1969)

High Commissioners

1951 (March) I M R Maclennan, CMG (*see* Federation of Rhodesia and Nyasaland and Zimbabwe *below*)
1964 (January) J B Johnston, CMG

FEDERATION OF RHODESIA AND NYASALAND

(*Formed 3.9.53 Dissolved 31.12.63*)

High Commissioners

1953 (October) I M R Maclennan, CMG (*see* Rhodesia *above* and Zimbabwe *below*)
1955 (August) M R Metcalf, CMG, OBE
1961 (March) Cuthbert James McCall Alport, Baron Alport, PC, TD
1963 (July) J B Johnston, CMG (*see* Rhodesia *above* and Zimbabwe *below*)

SAINT CHRISTOPHER AND NEVIS

High Commissioners

1983 (September) G L Bullard, CMG (later (1985) Sir Giles Bullard, KCVO, CMG)
1986 (October) K F X Burns, CMG
1991 (January) E T Davies, CMG

SAINT LUCIA

High Commissioners

1979 (February) J S Arthur, CMG
1982 (September) Viscount Dunrossil, CMG
1983 (August) G L Bullard, CMG (later (1985) Sir Giles Bullard, KCVO, CMG)
1986 (October) K F X Burns, CMG
1991 (January) E T Davies, CMG

SAINT VINCENT AND THE GRENADINES

High Commissioners

1979 (October) J S Arthur, CMG
1982 (September) Viscount Dunrossil, CMG
1983 (August) G L Bullard, CMG (later (1985) Sir Giles Bullard, KCVO, CMG)
1986 (October) K F X Burns, CMG
1991 (February) E T Davies, CMG

SEYCHELLES

High Commissioners

1976 (June) J A Pugh, OBE
1980 (September) E Young, OBE
1983 (October) C G Mays
1986 (October) A B P Smart
1989 (June) G W P Hart, OBE
1992 (January) E J Sharland

SIERRA LEONE

High Commissioners

1961 (April) J B Johnston (later (1962) CMG)
1963 (September) D J C Crawley, CVO (later (1964) CMG)
1966 (July) S J G Fingland, CMG
1969 (September) S J L Olver, CMG, MBE
1972 (October) I B Watt, CMG
1976 D A Roberts, CMG
1977 (October) M H Morgan, CMG
1981 (May) T D O'Leary (later (1982) CMG)
1984 (September) R D Clift, CMG
1986 (June) D W Partridge (later (1987) CMG)
1991 (May) D K Sprague, MVO

SINGAPORE

High Commissioners

1965 (October) J V Rob, CMG
1968 (January) A J de la Mare, CMG (later (1968) Sir Arthur de la Mare, KCMG)
1970 (December) S Falle, CMG, DSC (later (1972) Sir Sam Falle, KCVO, CMG, DSC)
1974 (May) J P Tripp, CMG
1978 (April) J D Hennings, CMG
1982 (June) Sir Peter Moon, KCVO, CMG
1985 (March) W E H Whyte, CMG (later (1985) Sir Hamilton Whyte KCMG)
1987 (July) M E Pike, CMG (later (1989) Sir Michael Pike, KCVO, CMG)
1991 (January) G A Duggan

SOLOMON ISLANDS

High Commissioners

1978 (June) G J A Slater
1982 (June) G N Stansfield, OBE
1986 (March) J B Noss
1988 (October) D J Young
1991 (May) R F Jones, CBE

SRI LANKA

High Commissioners

1948 (January) Sir Walter Hankinson, KCMG, OBE, MC
1951 (October) Sir Cecil Syers, KCMG, CVO
1957 (December) A F Morley, CMG, CBE (later (1959) Sir Alexander Morley, KCMG)
1962 (November) C M Walker, CMG (later (1963) Sir Michael Walker, KCMG)
1966 (March) F S Tomlinson, CMG (later (1966) Sir Stanley Tomlinson, KCMG)
1969 (March) A M Mackintosh, CMG (later (1972) Sir Angus Mackintosh, KCVO, CMG)
1973 (January) H Smedley, CMG, MBE
1976 (February) D P Aiers, CMG
1979 (October) J W Nicholas, CMG (later (1981) Sir John Nicholas, KCVO, CMG)
1984 (November) J A B Stewart, CMG, OBE
1987 (June) D A S Gladstone (later (1988) CMG)

SWAZILAND

High Commissioners

1968 (September) P Gautrey, CVO (later (1972) CMG)
1972 (January) E G Le Tocq (later (1975) CMG)
1975 (October) J E A Miles, OBE
1979 (August) D M Kerr, OBE
1983 (July) M Reith
1987 (May) J G Flynn
1990 (May) B Watkins

TANGANYIKA

High Commissioner
1961 (December) N Pritchard, CMG (later (1962) Sir Neil Pritchard, KCMG) (*see* Tanganyika and Zanzibar *below*)

TANGANYIKA AND ZANZIBAR
(*United as Tanzania in April 1964*)

High Commissioners
1964 (April) Sir Neil Pritchard, KCMG
1964 (August) R W D Fowler, CMG (*see* Tanzania *below*)

TANZANIA

High Commissioners
1964 (October) R W D Fowler, CMG (later (1966) Sir Robert Fowler, KCMG)
1968 (September) H Phillips, CMG
1973 (January) A R H Kellas, CMG
1975 (January) M Brown, CMG, OBE
1978 (April) P Moon, CMG (later (1979) Sir Peter Moon, KCVO, CMG)
1982 (June) J A Sankey (later (1983) CMG)
1986 (January) C H Imray, CMG
1989 (July) J T Masefield, CMG

TONGA

Representative
1965 (June) A C Reid, CMG, CVO

High Commissioners
1970 (June) Sir Arthur Galsworthy, KCMG
1973 (January) H A Arthington-Davy, MVO, OBE
1980 (November) B Coleman
1984 (January) G F J Rance, MBE
1987 (March) A P Fabian
1990 (March) W L Cordiner

TRINIDAD AND TOBAGO

High Commissioners
1962 (August) N E Costar, CMG (later (1963) Sir Norman Costar, KCMG)
1966 (December) G P Hampshire, CMG (later (1967) Sir Peter Hampshire, KCMG)
1970 (May) R C C Hunt, CMG
1973 (July) C E Diggines (later (1974) CMG)
1977 (September) H S H Stanley, CMG
1980 (April) D N Lane (later (1983) CMG)
1985 (April) M S Berthoud, CMG (later (1985) Sir Martin Berthoud, KCVO, CMG)
1991 (September) B Smith, OBE

TUVALU

High Commissioners
1978 (October) Viscount Dunrossil (later (1981) CMG)
1982 (July) R A R Baltrop (later (1982) CVO) (later (1987) CMG, CVO)
1989 (November) A B P Smart (later (1990) CMG)

UGANDA

High Commissioners
1962 (October) D W S Hunt, CMG, OBE (later (1963) Sir David Hunt, KCMG)
1965 (May) R C C Hunt, CMG
1967 (July) D A Scott, CMG
1970 (March) R M K Slater, CMG
1973 (September) J P I Hennessy, OBE (Acting) (later (1975) CMG, OBE)
(Diplomatic Relations with Uganda were broken off on 28th July, 1976)
1979 (April) R N Posnett, CMG, OBE
1979 (November) B A Flack, CMG
1980 (November) W N Hillier-Fry (later (1982) CMG)
1983 (September) C McLean, CMG, MBE
1986 (June) D M March CBE (later (1988) Sir Derek March, KBE)
1989 (December) C A K Cullimore

VANUATU

High Commissioners
1980 (July) W S Ashford, OBE
1982 (April) R B Dorman
1985 (September) M L Creek, LVO, OBE
1988 (March) J Thompson, MBE
1992 (January) T J Duggan

WEST INDIES ASSOCIATED STATES (ANTIGUA; DOMINICA; ST CHRISTOPHER and NEVIS; ANGUILLA; ST LUCIA; ST VINCENT)

British Government Representatives
1967 (February) C S Roberts
1970 (April) J E Marnham, CMG, MC, TD
1972 (November) E O Laird, CMG, MBE
1975 (November) E G Le Tocq, CMG
1978 (April) J S Arthur, CMG
1982 (September) Viscount Dunrossil, CMG
1983 (August) G L Bullard, CMG (later (1985) Sir Giles Bullard, KCVO, CMG)
1986 (October) K F X Burns, CMG
1991 (January) E T Davies, CMG

WESTERN SAMOA

High Commissioners
1977 (March) Sir Harold Smedley, KCMG
1980 (September) R J Stratton, CMG (later 1982) Sir Richard Stratton, KCMG)

1984 (July) T D O'Leary, CMG
1987 (December) R A C Byatt, CMG
1991 (August) D J Moss, CMG

ZAMBIA

High Commissioners

1964 (October) W B L Monson, CB, CMG (later (1965) Sir Leslie Monson, KCMG)
1967 (January) J L Pumphrey, CMG
1971 (June) J S R Duncan, CMG, MBE
1974 (October) F S Miles, CMG
1978 (February) W L Allinson, CMG, MVO (later (1979) Sir Leonard Allinson, KCVO, CMG)
1980 (June) J R Johnson (later (1981) CMG)
1984 (September) W K K White, CMG
1988 (January) J M Willson (later (1988) CMG)
1990 (June) P R M Hinchcliffe, CMG, CVO

ZANZIBAR

High Commissioner

1963 (December) T L Crosthwaite, MBE (later (1964) CMG)

(*Post terminated with effect from 1st July 1964, see* Tanganyika and Zanzibar *above*)

ZIMBABWE

High Commissioners

1980 (April) R A C Byatt, CMG
1983 (April) M K Ewans, CMG
1985 (February) M R Melhuish, CMG
1989 (August) W K Prendergast (later (1990) CMG)

PART III

Heads of Government Meetings

From 1911 to 1937, Imperial Conferences of the Prime Ministers and other Ministers of Britain and the Dominions were held periodically to discuss matters of common concern, particularly constitutional questions, foreign affairs, defence and economic policy. At the end of each conference full reports of the proceedings and conclusions were published. A brief account of the Imperial Conferences during these years (and of their forerunners, the Colonial Conferences since their inception in 1887), was included in the 1955 *Commonwealth Relations Office List.*

When meetings were resumed in 1944 the old Imperial Conferences gave place to the more informal exchanges of views on issues of first importance provided by the Commonwealth Prime Ministers' Meetings, called Commonwealth Heads of Government Meetings since 1971, and *ad hoc* conferences of other Ministers for the discussion of particular questions. Details of the proceedings of these meetings are not published, but it has generally been the practice for a *communiqué* to be issued at the close of each meeting summarising its results. The *communiqués* issued from 1944 to 1986 may be found in *The Commonwealth at the Summit* published by the Commonwealth Secretariat which has published the 1987 and 1989 *Communiqués* separately.

In 1966 two conferences were held; the earlier of these, at Lagos, was the first to be held in a Commonwealth capital other than London and the first devoted to a single subject (Rhodesia). There were no meetings during 1967 or 1968, but in January 1969 Commonwealth leaders met once again in London, after which the conferences were retitled 'Commonwealth Heads of Government Meetings'.

The first ordinary meeting of Commonwealth Heads of Government to be held outside London (Lagos in 1966 was an extraordinary meeting) was in 1971 in Singapore. From this meeting, Heads of Government issued the *Commonwealth Declaration of Principles,* to which all Commonwealth governments pledged themselves, and the *communiqué,* both published in the 1972 Year Book of the Commonwealth.

Subsequent Commonwealth Heads of Government Meetings were held as follows:
August 1973, Ottawa (communiqué in the 1974 Year Book)
April/May 1975, Kingston, Jamaica (communiqué in the 1975 Year Book)
June 1977, London (communiqué and the Gleneagles Agreement in the 1978 Year Book)
August 1979, Lusaka (communiqué in the 1980 Year Book)
September/October 1981, Melbourne (commmuniqué in 1982 and 1983 Year Books)
November 1983, New Delhi (communiqué in the 1984 and 1985 Year Books)
October 1985, Nassau (communiqué in the 1986 and 1987 Year Books)
October 1987, Vancouver (communiqué in the 1988 and 1989 Year Books)
October 1989, Kuala Lumpur (communiqué in the 1991 Year Book)
October 1991, Harare. The following communiqué was issued at the end of the meeting:

Introduction

1. Commonwealth Heads of Government met in Harare from 16 to 22 October 1991. Of the 47 countries which attended 43 were represented by Heads of State or Prime Ministers. The President of Zimbabwe, Mr Robert Mugabe, was in the Chair.

2. Heads of Government sent a message of felicitation to Her Majesty The Queen as Head of the Commonwealth. They particularly welcomed the opportunity of meeting in Harare at a critical stage in progress towards ending apartheid in South Africa, a long-standing Commonwealth concern. They expressed deep appreciation of the excellent arrangements made for the Meeting and the warm welcome and generous hospitality of the Government and people of Zimbabwe.

3. Recalling the offer of Commonwealth membership extended to Namibia at their Meeting in Kingston in 1975, Heads of Government warmly welcomed their colleague President Sam Nujoma from Namibia whose country had joined the Commonwealth in 1990.

4. Heads of Government expressed their grief at the death of Rajiv Gandhi and observed a minute of silence in his memory.

The Future of the Commonwealth

5. Heads of Government had before them the *Report on the Commonwealth in the 1990s and Beyond* prepared by ten of their number under the Chairmanship of the Prime Minister of Malaysia. The Report formed the centrepiece of their discussions.

6. Heads of Government were unanimously of the view that the fundamental principles enunciated by Commonwealth leaders at Singapore in 1971 remained relevant 20 years later and that the

Commonwealth should reaffirm its full and continuing commitment to those principles. Any appraisal of the Commonwealth's future role should rest on the application of those principles to the contemporary world.

7. They were convinced that, in facing the challenges of the future, the Commonwealth would draw upon its unique strength and character, rooted in its shared ideals, common traditions and language, in its membership which spans nearly one-third of humanity and every corner of the globe and in its ability to fashion a sense of common purpose out of diversity.

8. The discussions of the High-Level Appraisal Group served to identify several areas, some old and others new, which deserved special emphasis on Commonwealth endeavours in years to come. The views of Heads of Government in this regard are contained in a separate document, the *Harare Commonwealth Declaration.* They also endorsed guidelines for the Commonwealth observance of elections, criteria for Commonwealth membership and a strategy for sharpening the Commonwealth image.

9. The High-Level Appraisal reflected the continuing concern of Heads of Government with the situation in South Africa. While recent changes have raised hopes of achieving a free, non-racial and democratic order in South Africa, violence continues to obstruct progress. The Commonwealth has played a leading role in the international campaign against apartheid. Now that the goal is closer than ever before, Heads of Government considered ways in which the Commonwealth should continue to play a significant role in progress towards a non-racial democratic South Africa.

10. Heads of Government also gave consideration to the adequacy of Commonwealth institutions, including the Secretariat, to fulfil the task ahead. They welcomed the Secretary-General's internal review which had identified a measure of existing resources which could be released for redeployment to priorities identified in the Harare Commonwealth Declaration and endorsed his proposal to institute a management audit, to be undertaken by external consultants, designed to enhance the cost-effectiveness and efficiency of the Secretariat. While commending the proposals contained in the Secretary-General's Strategic Action Plan they considered that these should be further examined by senior officials of the High-Level Appraisal Group in the light of the priorities agreed to at the Harare Heads of Government Meeting, taking into account the management audit and the Secretariat's need for adequate resources to implement these priorities. If it emerged that additional resources were still required, after available resources had been matched to needs, Heads of Government agreed to consider making appropriate contributions.

Global Trends and Prospects

11. Heads of Government welcomed the end of the Cold War which had provided new opportunities and greatly improved prospects for international peace, security and economic development. The end of ideological confrontation had made possible more effective internal co-operation in addressing the many problems, old and new, facing humanity. Foremost among these were poverty, hunger, disease and enviromental degradation. They expressed the hope that in a new international order these issues would be of central concern.

12. Heads of Government were particularly encouraged by the resurgence of democratic ideals throughout the world. They undertook to use the Commonwealth's common values and practical means to help advance this hopeful development. Nevertheless the emergence of ethnic chauvinism, racial bigotry, and other forms of intolerance was a cause for serious concern, posing grave threats to peace and communal harmony. Accordingly they agreed to do everything practicable, both within their own societies and internationally, to combat discrimination in all its forms and to promote democracy, human rights, mutual tolerance and the rule of law through processes and institutions which have regard to national circumstances.

13. Heads of Government recognised that opportunities to promote the ideals which inspired the establishment of the United Nations had never been better. Reaffirming their commitment to the world organisation, they agreed to work together to enable it to discharge the role envisaged in its Charter.

Disarmament

14. Heads of Government warmly welcomed the recent dramatic initiative by the United States, matched by the Soviet Union and Britain to reduce their nuclear arsenals which had greatly enhanced the prospects for world peace. They urged these states to continue their efforts and for other nuclear weapons states to do the same. In this context most Heads of Government called for a permanent halt to all further nuclear testing.

15. Heads of Government noted with concern the continuing dangers of regional and local conflicts. These dangers, and the example of the Gulf War, underlined the need to strengthen international regimes limiting weapons of mass destruction and the need to curb the build-up of conventional weapons beyond the legitimate requirements of self-defence. In this context they noted the recent accessions of several states to the Nuclear Non-Proliferation Treaty. They strongly urged all states to redouble efforts to prevent the proliferation of nuclear weapons in all its aspects. They called for the conclusion of a Chemical Weapons Convention in 1992 and endorsed in principle the proposal to establish a register of arms transfers at the United Nations.

Human Rights

16. Heads of Government reaffirmed their strong collective commitment to the principles of justice and human rights, including the rule of law, the independence of the judiciary, equality for women and accountable administrations. They supported the Report and recommendations of the Commonwealth Governmental Working Group of Experts on Human Rights. Recognising that human rights is one of the priorities identified in the Harare Declaration, they requested the Secretariat to give greater impetus to its current activities to promote human rights in all its aspects. Heads of Government recognised the role that non-governmental organisations could play in this area.

17. Believing the International Bill of Human Rights to be the cornerstone of international human rights, Heads of Government reiterated their call to those of their members who have not already done so, to become a party to the International Covenants on Economic, Social and Cultural Rights and on Civil and Political Rights.

South Africa

18. Heads of Government welcomed the important changes that had taken place in South Africa in the last 20 months since the initiatives taken by President de Klerk. These were a vindication of the long years of implacable opposition to apartheid by the democratic opposition forces, and in particular of the tenacity and courage of the liberation movements. These developments had also vindicated the Commonwealth's pre-eminent role in leading international action in support of the struggle to end apartheid. The developments had brought into sight the goal of the eradication of apartheid and the establishment of a non-racial democracy in a united and non-fragmented South Africa.

19. Heads of Government urged all the parties in South Africa to move as quickly as possible to constitutional negotiations. Expressing the hope that the recent tragic escalation of violence would not further set back this process, they strongly condemned this violence and called upon the South African Government as well as on all the parties in South Africa to bring it to an end as a matter of the utmost urgency. In this context they viewed with grave concern both revelations of covert Government funding of political organisations and the mounting reports of the involvement of elements within the security forces in perpetrating acts of violence. They welcomed the Peace Accord and called for its full implementation as quickly as possible.

20. While the terms of a constitutional settlement were for the people of South Africa themselves to determine, Heads believed that the Commonwealth must remain ready to assist the negotiating process in ways that would be found helpful by the parties concerned. They therefore decided to request the Secretary-General to visit South Africa at the earliest possible opportunity in order to explore with the principal parties concerned ways in which the Commonwealth could assist in lending momentum to the negotiating process.

21. On his return, the Secretary-General would report his conclusions to the Ten Heads of Government previously concerned with the High-Level Appraisal, and to the President of Zimbabwe, Chairman of the current Commonwealth Heads of Government Meeting. Heads authorised this Group to consider and determine the necessary follow-up action in the light of the Secretary-General's mission.

Sanctions

22. Heads of Government expressed the hope that the stage would be reached when the situation in South Africa would justify reconsideration of their sanctions policy against South Africa. They recalled that the purpose of sanctions had always been to bring about a peaceful end to apartheid through the promotion of negotiations between the Government and the acknowledged representatives of the black majority. In recognition of the crucial role sanctions had played in bringing about the changes thus far, they agreed to continue to use effective forms of pressure to assure a successful final outcome to the conflict in South Africa. Accordingly (subject to the proviso in the following paragraph) they endorsed the programmed management approach, elaborated by the Commonwealth Committee of Foreign Ministers on Southern Africa, linking any change in the application of sanctions to the taking of real and practical steps to end apartheid. In respect of the different categories of sanctions, subject to the same proviso, Heads of Government agreed as follows:

- **the arms embargo,** applied by the United Nations and supported by a variety of specific Commonwealth measures, should remain in force until a new post-apartheid South African government is firmly established, with full democratic control and accountability;
- the most demonstrably effective of all sanctions – **financial sanctions** — including lending by international financial institutions such as the IMF and World Bank, should be lifted only when agreement is reached on the text of a new democratic constitution, unless a contrary recommendation is made by agreement at the proposed All-Party Conference, or by an interim government;
- other economic sanctions, including **trade and investment measures,** should be lifted when appropriate transitional mechanisms have been agreed which would enable all the parties to participate fully and effectively in negotiations;

- **people to people** sanctions, namely consular and visa restrictions, cultural and scientific boycotts, restrictions on tourism promotion and the ban on direct air links should be lifted immediately in view of progress made in overcoming obstacles to negotiations and the need to give external support and encouragement to democratic anti-apartheid organisations in South Africa and to permit free interaction with them. The ban on air links would be lifted on condition that South African Airways (SAA) and other South African airlines proceed with appropriate affirmative action programmes.

23. The British Prime Minister stressed the importance of foreign investment in restoring growth to the South African economy and the need for decisions now if the current economic decline was to be halted in time for the inauguration of South Africa's first majority government. It is for this reason that, while agreeing with the lifting of "people sanctions" and the maintenance of the arms embargo, he did not agree with the recommendation of the Committee on the time scale for lifting economic and financial sanctions.

Sporting Contacts with South Africa

24. Heads of Government were encouraged by the recent considerable progress in the evolution of a unified and non-racial sports movement in South Africa and welcomed the decision of the International Olympic Committee to grant recognition to the National Olympic Committee of South Africa. They agreed to continue to encourage these developments and, where appropriate, to provide assistance. They stressed the need for each sporting code to provide assistance to sportsmen and women disadvantaged by apartheid. They agreed that restrictions in respect of a particular sport be lifted when the following criteria have been met:

- the formal endorsement of the achievement of unity by the appropriate representative non-racial sporting organisation in South Africa;
- readmittance to the relevant international governing body;
- agreement of the appropriate non-racial sporting organisation within South Africa to resume international competition.

25. Commonwealth governments would continue to be guided in these matters by the National Olympic Committee of South Africa and other appropriate representative non-racial sporting organisations. In particular they welcomed the achievement of cricket in this regard and expressed the strong hope that the International Cricket Conference would accept South Africa's entry in the forthcoming World Cup.

Human Resource Development for a Post-Apartheid South Africa

26. Heads of Government, recognising that the education and training of members of the deprived majority to occupy strategic positions in the transition period and beyond would be crucial to progress, welcomed the Report of the Expert Group on Human Resource Development for a Post-Apartheid South Africa, *Beyond Apartheid.* They looked forward to a significant role for the Commonwealth in addressing the Report's priorities and strategies in partnership with the wider international community. They agreed to assist in meeting the human resource development needs of post-apartheid South Africa on a bilateral and multilateral basis, which could include a voluntary multilateral Commonwealth Programme for Human Resource Development in South Africa. An immediate start should be made to support training and placements within South Africa as well as continuing training and placements outside South Africa.

27. Heads of Government attached importance to an increased role for the Commonwealth network of non-governmental organisations, Skills for South Africa, in the implementation of the Expert Group's recommendations. They called for increased bilateral Commonwealth and other programmes in this area and requested the Secretary-General to bring the Expert Group's Report to the attention of the international community and to explore the possibility of convening, in collaboration with the United Nations, an international donors' conference.

Commonwealth Committee of Foreign Ministers on Southern Africa

28. Heads of Government decided that the Commonwealth Committee of Foreign Ministers on Southern Africa under the continuing Chairmanship of the Canadian Secretary of State for External Affairs should remain ready to meet as and when necessary until the completion of the implementation of their recommendations.

South African Economic Studies

29. Heads of Government recognised the valuable contribution made by the Centre for the Study of the South African Economy and International Finance and looked forward to the continuation of its work.

Namibia

30. Heads of Government welcomed the independence of Namibia and the interim agreement between the Government of Namibia and the Government of South Africa to establish a joint Administration of Walvis Bay and the off-shore islands pending a final settlement. They urged the early reintegration of these territories into Namibia in accordance with United Nations Security Council Resolution 432 (1978). Noting the importance attached by the Government of Namibia to the Enhanced Commonwealth Programme for Namibia, Heads of Government commended the Programme and reaffirmed their support.

Mozambique

31. Heads of Government remained gravely concerned over the continuing conflict in Mozambique which was still claiming human lives and destroying socio-economic infrastructures. They urged an immediate end to all external assistance, material and otherwise, to the MNR. They pledged their support to the search for peace and urged the international community to do everything practicable to advance the peace process. They called upon the parties to the Rome Agreement of 1 December 1990 to honour its letter and spirit, and commended the Government of Mozambique and the mediators in Rome for their persistent efforts to bring about a comprehensive peace settlement and national reconciliation. In this context they further noted that a protocol had been signed on 18 October 1991 which committed both sides to achieving a general peace agreement as soon as possible. Accordingly, they strongly urged the parties to move expeditiously towards the signing of such an agreement.

32. Heads of Government expressed gratitude to those countries hosting the Mozambican refugees who continue to flee from their country and appealed to the international community to continue to render assistance to them. They noted that the plans for the post-war resettlement and rehabilitation of displaced peoples and the normalisation of life in general laid particular emphasis on the strengthening of institutional capacity to guarantee and promote democractic practices. In this context they commended the Special Commonwealth Fund for Mozambique for its contribution to Mozambique's priority needs which is effectively augmenting the significant bilateral contributions of Commonwealth countries, both developed and developing. They recognised that continuing pledges and contributions would be required to enable the Fund to maintain a full five year programme, including assistance in preparations for multi-party elections and in other aspects of institutional development.

Angola

33. Heads of Government also welcomed the signing of a peace accord in Angola between the Government and UNITA, and urged the international community to assist in its implementation, including the democratisation process, and in Angola's reconstruction.

Small States

34. Heads of Government recognised that international developments continued to demonstrate the vulnerability peculiar to small states, and they urged support for initiatives at the bilateral, regional and multilateral levels that would foster an environment conducive to their security and viability. They reaffirmed their view that small states merit special consideration and support because of their particular problems and should continue to have priority in the Secretariat's development assistance. Noting that current trends in official and private financial flows to developing countries and the erosion of trade preferences could make these states even more vulnerable, they urged that the donor community should continue to take into account their special structural problems and needs.

Belize

35. Heads of Government welcomed Guatemala's recognition of Belize as a sovereign, independent state, and looked forward to the speedy conclusion of a formal agreement which would bring an end to the dispute and foster co-operation between the two states for the benefit of both their peoples and the wider region. They reaffirmed that until a satisfactory outcome is reached, the security of Belize will remain a Commonwealth concern.

Cyprus

36. Recalling the position they had adopted at Kuala Lumpur, Heads of Government reiterated their support for the independence, sovereignty, territorial integrity, unity and non-aligned status of the Republic of Cyprus. They stressed the importance of securing compliance with all of the United Nations Resolutions on Cyprus and in particular, Security Council Resolutions 541 (1983), 550 (1984) and 649 (1990). In this connection they emphasised the need for the speedy withdrawal of all foreign forces and settlers from the Republic of Cyprus, the return of the refugees to their homes in safety, the restoration and respect for the human rights of all Cypriots and the accounting for those missing.

37. Heads of Government noted the recent developments on the Cyprus problem contained in the latest report of the United Nations Secretary-General to the Security Council and its respective Resolution 716 (1991) setting out the fundamental principles of a Cyprus settlement. Such a settlement will ensure the well-being and security of all Cypriots, Greek Cypriots and Turkish Cypriots alike. They also expressed the hope that, following the Resolution, obstacles to the current efforts of the United

Nations Secretary-General to find a just and viable solution to the Cyprus problem will be speedily removed and thus the convening of the envisaged international meeting will proceed as planned.

38. Heads of Government agreed that the Commonwealth Action Group on Cyprus should continue to monitor developments within the scope of its terms of reference including, in particular, assisting the efforts of the United Nations Secretary-General.

Mediterranean

39. Heads of Government expressed support for continuing efforts to contribute actively to the elimination of causes of tension in the Mediterranean and to the promotion of a just and lasting solution to the conflicts and crises in the region, in accordance with the United Nations Charter and relevant resolutions. They once again reiterated that security in the Mediterranean is closely linked to European security, as well as to international peace and security. They noted that regional consultations among Mediterranean states are taking place in order to create appropriate conditions for convening a Conference on Security and Co-operation in the Mediterranean.

The Middle East

40. Heads of Government, recalling their statement at Kuala Lumpur on the Middle East and reiterating their concern at the dangerous tensions arising from the unresolved problems of the Middle East, especially the Palestinian issue, welcomed the convening of the Middle East Peace Conference in Madrid on 30 October 1991. They expressed the strong hope that the Conference would lead to a just, comprehensive, and lasting settlement and contribute to peace and security in the Middle East.

Afghanistan

41. Recent developments have increased the prospects of a comprehensive political settlement of the Afghanistan problem and Heads of Government urged that efforts be intensified to restore peace and normalcy in Afghanistan and enable the Afghan refugees to return to their country. They expressed support for the United Nations Secretary-General's five-point proposal of 21 May 1991 and the initiatives of other states to reach a just settlement in Afghanistan and also appealed for continued humanitarian assistance for the Afghan refugees.

South-East Asia

42. Heads of Government welcomed the reconvening of the Paris International Conference on Cambodia (PICC) in Paris from 21 to 23 October 1991 whose objective is to bring about a comprehensive political settlement of the Cambodian problem through the signing of a peace agreement. In this regard, they congratulated the Cambodian parties for demonstrating a spirit of compromise and national reconciliation under the leadership of Prince Sihanouk.

43. As a further means of ensuring peace and stability in the region, Heads of Government noted with approval efforts to establish in South-East Asia a zone of peace, freedom and neutrality and called on all states fully to support these efforts.

Antarctica

44. Recognising that Antarctica has a critical impact on the environment, Heads of Government welcomed the agreement reached in Madrid on a Protocol for the protection of the Antarctic environment, including a prohibition on mining activities in Antarctica. They reiterated their conviction that every effort should be made to protect and conserve the environment of that unique territory and called on all states to co-operate in this regard.

Terrorism

45. Heads of Government reaffirmed their strong condemnation of terrorism in all its forms, including the taking of hostages, as one of the most dangerous and pernicious threats to stability and to human rights. They reiterated their determination to combat terrorism, whether perpetrated by individuals, groups or states, by every means possible through bilateral and multilateral co-operation.

Countering Drug Abuse and Illicit Trafficking

46. Heads of Government expressed deep concern at the increasing menace of drug abuse and illicit trafficking which represents both a serious obstacle to the process of social and economic national development and a threat to the international community. They welcomed the restructuring of the United Nations drug control system, including the establishment of the United Nations International Drug Control Programme to enhance the international campaign against drug abuse and illicit trafficking, and affirmed their support for the Global Programme of Action adopted by the Seventeenth Special Session of the United Nations General Assembly in February 1990.

47. They recognised that imaginative approaches were called for if effective responses were to be developed, particularly to reduce the demand for illicit drugs, and acknowledged that it was imperative for all countries to have appropriate legal frameworks to counter supply. In this regard they undertook to take such steps as might be necessary to become party to the 1988 United Nations Convention Against Illicit Traffic in Narcotic Drugs and Illicit Substances, and to implement the Commonwealth

Scheme for Mutual Assistance in Criminal Matters. They also expressed their support for the Programme of Action adopted by the World Ministerial Summit on Demand Reduction held in London in April 1990.

World Economic Situation

48. Heads of Government reviewed the current world economic situation. They expressed satisfaction that policies pursued by many industrialised countries to keep inflationary forces in check were bearing results, and that many developing countries were maintaining reform policies despite continuing difficult economic circumstances.

49. Heads of Government noted that while the past year had been a difficult one for the world economy, the prospects were now more hopeful in a number of countries. They expressed concern, however, at the external economic conditions which in many respects — for example, high interest rates, depressed commodity prices, low volume of financial flows, onerous debt service burdens, continuing protectionism in major markets and inward-looking regional groupings — remained unfavourable to developing countries. They emphasised the importance of pursuing policies that strengthened the forces of recovery in the world economy; and expressed their determination to work through co-operative international action for a more supportive global environment for development. They agreed that any new world order must comprise enhanced development co-operation.

Global Change and Economic Development

50. Heads of Government noted that they were meeting at a time of dramatic change not only in the world political and economic order, but also in ideas about how societies should be organised. They believed that these changes bring both opportunities and problems for all societies. In this context, they welcomed the Report of the Commonwealth Expert Group, *Change for the Better: Global Change and Economic Development,* which had begun to receive a very favourable international reception. They agreed with its central conclusion that change is resulting in an ever increasing interdependence among nations and that there is a growing mutuality of interest in addressing issues such as poverty, insecurity, environmental degradation, disease and drug trafficking which can be effectively tackled only through development. They also agreed with the Group's view that this required a sustained exercise of political will at national and international levels. They asked the Chairman and the Secretary-General to promote a wide-ranging discussion of the Report, and agreed to take steps at the same time, to promote consideration of the Expert Group's recommendations at high political levels, particularly in specialist economic and regional groupings of which they were members. They also noted that the United Nations Conference on Environment and Development (UNCED) in mid-1992, which will be attended by many Heads of State, would offer a good opportunity for discussion of many of the issues raised.

51. In relation to specific issues, Heads of Government welcomed the emphasis in *Change for the Better* on improved policies to achieve macro-economic stability, reduced budget deficits, reduced military spending, increased savings and investment, more open trade policies, greater reliance on the private sector, market-oriented economies, human resource development, effective population policies, agricultural reform, sound and accountable administration, participatory political processes and the rule of law. They emphasised also the importance of enhanced practical support by the developed countries and international institutions for the developing countries' efforts if they are to succeed. In particular they stressed the need to ensure larger flows of resources including increased aid and debt relief, more open markets, safety nets for vulnerable groups, increased support for structural adjustment, and financial and technological support to make development sustainable.

International Trade and the Uruguay Round

52. Heads of Government deplored the drift towards greater protectionism and further trade discrimination in some industrial countries, particularly when a large number of countries in the developing world as well as in Eastern Europe and elsewhere had embarked on unilateral trade liberalisation programmes. They noted that more protectionism had led to slower growth in world trade which, in turn, had slowed world economic growth. Furthermore export growth in developing countries had been constrained by limited access to markets in developed countries. They noted the inconsistency of developed countries urging developing countries to open their economies to market forces while limiting access to their own markets. The loss to developing countries as a result of these trade barriers more than outweighed the flow of aid monies. Heads of Government called for the multilateral liberalisation of world trade in order to ensure that the world does not repeat the mistakes of the protectionist 1930s; and enlarged access to world markets for developing countries through a liberalised international trading system to help them to expand their exports and to overcome the difficulties caused by constrained inflows of aid and other resources from developed countries.

53. Heads of Government noted that they were meeting at a critical stage in the Uruguay Round. They noted also that there was a growing international momentum for substantial reform of the world trading system. They welcomed the clear commitment by leaders of the Group of Seven industrialised countries at their London Summit to work for an ambitious global and balanced package of results in the Round. Heads of Government called on all governments to show the political will required urgently to translate into action that momentum for reform to achieve a liberalised trading system. They stressed

the critical importance of a successful, substantive and comprehensive outcome to the Uruguay Round, laying particular emphasis on achieving a marked reduction in trade barriers and other distortions in agricultural markets. They drew attention to the dangers of protectionism and inward-looking regionalism and to the great contribution which freer trade and its influence on financial flows can make to sustained and sustainable development. The preservation and enhancement of the integrity of the global trading system is a common interest of developing and industrialised countries. They felt that if the Uruguay Round were to fail, this would increase the dangers of protectionism and very considerably reduce the prospects for economic growth and development in the 1990s and beyond, as well as set back the process of economic liberalisation in many countries.

Regional Economic Co-operation

54. Heads of Government welcomed the increasing efforts in many parts of the world to strengthen and expand regional economic co-operation. They expressed the hope that these efforts would promote trade expansion and strengthen a more open and non-discriminatory multilateral trading system. They called on regional trading groups involving major industrialised countries to give special attention to the impact of their regional trade policies on developing countries, including those not in such groups and to ways in which these countries could take advantage of the opportunities offered. They recognised the need for increased assistance to support regional co-operation among vulnerable countries.

Financial Flows and Debt

55. Heads of Government noted that, despite improvements in financial flows to some developing countries, flows overall remained quite inadequate to support economic recovery in large parts of the developing world, and to address such current concerns as poverty reduction, human resource development and protection of the environment. They therefore called for further debt relief, including cancellation, and increased aid and capital flows, as well as for further measures in developing countries to attract such flows.

56. Heads of Government warmly welcomed the announcement at their Meeting, by the British Prime Minister, the Rt. Hon. John Major, of his Government's decision to press ahead with implementation of the Trinidad and Tobago Terms, providing major relief of the debt of low income countries. They were pleased that Canada endorsed the decision. They expressed the hope that Britain and Canada would be joined in this by other Paris Club members and that this action would lead to speedy adoption by the whole Paris Club. They praised the British Prime Minister for his leadership role in tackling the indebtedness problem of the poorest countries.

57. Heads of Government noted the debt relief extended to Poland and Egypt and welcomed the fact that the Paris Club was continuing to examine the special situations of some other lower-middle income countries. Indebtedness to multilateral financial institutions continues to be a particular problem for some countries and further attention needs to be given to the issue by the donor community. They emphasised also the importance of adequate financial support for those countries in difficult circumstances which have avoided debt rescheduling. They welcomed the British Prime Minister's offer to seek wider eligibility under the IMF's Enhanced Structural Adjustment Facility to include more Commonwealth countries.

58. Heads of Government expressed regret that during the 1980s the aid of most Development Assistance Committee donors had stagnated as a proportion of their gross national product and still fell short of the agreed United Nations target of 0.7 per cent of GNP. They called for renewed efforts to secure expanded official and private flows of finance to developing countries. They welcomed the fact that reduced global tensions are already resulting in cuts in arms expenditure and agreed that this provided significant opportunities for both the industrialised and the developing countries to increase resources for development.

Reforms in Eastern Europe and the Soviet Union

59. Heads of Government welcomed the profound movement that is taking place in Eastern Europe and the Soviet Union towards democracy and market-oriented economies. They stressed the importance of its success for world peace and security. They emphasised, however, that support for reform in that region should not be extended in a manner that is prejudicial to developing countries in terms either of market access or of aid flows.

Investment Funds and Capital Markets

60. Heads of Government welcomed the facilitative role the Commonwealth Secretariat is playing in enhancing portfolio investment in developing member countries. They noted with satisfaction that the Commonwealth Equity Fund had been successfully launched in 1990 and that its operations had made good progress. They looked forward to an early increase of its capital and wider access for its investment in Commonwealth emerging markets.

61. While recognising the importance of tapping external financial flows for their developing efforts, Heads of Government emphasised that the primary source of investment would continue to be domestic. They therefore urged all countries to strengthen their efforts to mobilise domestic savings, which required, among other things, the development of local capital and stock markets.

A Commonwealth Bank for Reconstruction and Development

62. Heads of Government noted the proposal for the establishment of a Commonwealth Bank for Reconstruction and Development and agreed that a preliminary study of the proposal be conducted by the Commonwealth Secretariat.

Least Developed Countries

63. Heads of Government expressed serious concern at the deteriorating socio-economic condition of the least developed countries (LDCs). They noted that these countries faced the most formidable structural constraints to development. They pledged their support for effective implementation of the Programme of Action for the LDCs adopted by the Second United Nations Conference on LDCs in September 1990. They recognised that, while the LDCs bear the primary responsibility for their own development, the developed countries should commit resources to attain the internationally agreed target for Official Development Assistance to these countries as expeditiously as possible.

Agriculture

64. Heads of Government expressed concern at the continuing severe food problems facing developing countries. They stressed the need for these countries to strengthen their policies and incentives for sustainable agricultural development. They urged the developed countries and the international institutions to adopt supportive trade, aid and other policies which would make external conditions more conducive to developing countries' agriculture.

Environment

65. Heads of Government recalled the Langkawi Declaration on Environment, which set out a comprehensive programme of action for the protection of the global environment and the achievement of sustainable development. In that connection they pledged themselves to work for a successful outcome of the 1992 United Nations Conference on Environment and Development (UNCED) which many of them propose to attend.

66. Heads of Government welcomed as important contributions to the UNCED process the Report of the Commonwealth Group of Experts *Sustainable Development: An Imperative for Environmental Protection* and the section on environmentally sustainable development of the Communiqué of the First Commonwealth NGO Forum held in Harare in August 1991.

67. Heads of Government agreed to work actively towards the conclusion at UNCED of an effective framework convention on climate change, of a convention on biological diversity, of a statement of principles for a global consensus on the management, conservation and sustainable development of all types of forest, and appropriate follow-up action thereafter. They agreed that action to tackle these problems would require the participation of all countries. They attached particular importance to achieving consensus on measures to facilitate additional flows of financial resources and environmentally sound and appropriate technologies on fair and favourable terms to developing countries, as a contribution towards the achievement of both national and global environmental and developmental goals. They undertook to co-operate closely in elaborating a realistic and achievable action programme under Agenda 21, which should take account of the different needs, responsibilities and capabilities of developed and developing countries and address action at national, regional and international levels. In all these areas, they stressed the need for effective, democratic and cost-effective institutional arrangements at all levels to deliver the actions agreed at UNCED.

68. Heads of Government took note of the concerns expressed by small states about the adverse consequences for them of climate change, their vulnerability, and the belief that their interests were not receiving adequate attention in the UNCED preparatory process. They agreed that the concerns of these countries should be reflected, as appropriate, in all UNCED's decisions and asked the Commonwealth Secretariat to assist in promoting more effective consideration of the interests of Commonwealth small states by organising consultations and providing them with technical support at important preparatory meetings for UNCED.

69. Heads of Government welcomed the decision that key elements relating to women's critical contributions to sustainable development should be addressed at UNCED as a distinct issue and in the course of all the substantive work, particularly the proposed action programme under Agenda 21. They believed that greater recognition should be given to the vital role played by women in fostering sustainable development and to the need to alleviate the constraints which prevented them from making more effective contributions to environmental management at all levels.

70. Heads of Government also took note of a number of proposals on the environment and related problems. These included: a convention to control dumping of hazardous, toxic and other wastes from ships; measures to protect small island countries against sea-level rise; entrusting the United Nations Trusteeship Council to hold in trust for humanity its common heritage and its common concerns; the setting up of an international environmental tribunal; and the adoption of a code of conduct governing international environmental behaviour.

71. Heads of Government expressed concern at the continuation of large-scale drift-net fishing and the threat this posed to marine resources. They urged all countries to comply with United Nations

General Assembly Resolutions 44/225 and 45/197 and welcomed the prohibition of fishing with long drift-nets in the South Pacific.

Natural Disasters

72. Heads of Government acknowledged the adverse impact of natural disasters on economic growth and development. They welcomed the increasing international attention given to problems posed by disasters and urged better national preparedness and relief measures; the strengthening of international mechanisms with a view to providing timely, adequate and co-ordinated assistance; and the devotion of greater attention to the medium-term implications of disasters in the lending policies of the international financial institutions.

Commonwealth-Government of Guyana Programme for Sustainable Tropical Forestry

73. Heads of Government welcomed progress already made in implementing the Commonwealth-Government of Guyana Programme for Sustainable Tropical Forestry in pursuance of the offer of the President of Guyana to set aside an area of tropical forest for a pilot project, under Commonwealth auspices, on sustainable utilisation and conservation of species. They were pleased at the Commonwealth role being played in this important international project. They were encouraged that several governments, agencies, institutions and non-governmental organisations, inside and outside the Commonwealth, had expressed interest in the Programme, and looked forward, in particular, to early final approval of initial funding for it by the Global Environment Facility. Considering that the Programme had significant potential to benefit the wider international community, they urged all potential donors to mobilise additional resources to facilitate its early implementation. They called on all Commonwealth countries to give urgent consideration to providing further financial and other support to the Programme in order that the Commonwealth could continue to play a major role in it.

Management of Tropical Marine Ecosystems

74. Heads of Government welcomed the Australian Government's initiative to make available its expertise in managing tropical marine environments to assist its Commonwealth partners and other tropical and sub-tropical states in managing these environments.

Women and Structural Adjustment

75. Heads of Government endorsed the Ottawa Declaration on Women and Structural Adjustment which Ministers Responsible for Women's Affairs prepared at their meeting in October 1990. The Declaration is attached as an Annex to this Communiqué.

Child Survival and Development

76. Heads of Government welcomed the Plan of Action for Survival, Protection and Development of Children in the 1990s adopted by the World Summit for Children and committed themselves to the achievement of its goals. These included targeted reduction of infant and maternal mortality; the achievement of health and education for all by the year 2000; sustaining and improving immunisation levels; and ratification and implementation of the United Nations Convention on the Rights of the Child. They stressed that these specific actions for children should be pursued as an essential part of wider national and international development objectives including poverty alleviation, human development and environmental protection. They emphasised that the Commonwealth provided a framework for collaboration to put children first, particularly through co-operation programmes devised to enhance health and literacy levels among children.

77. Heads of Government noted with interest the call by the Organisation of African Unity for the convening of an international donors' conference on assistance to African children in 1992.

AIDS

78. Heads of Government expressed grave concern at the growing impact of AIDS on all countries. This posed a threat to economic progress and human development, particularly in poorer member states, by attacking the most economically productive age group and reversing gains in life expectancy and child survival. The increasing burden on health budgets would stretch national and community resources to the limit, leaving no room for complacency or pretence about the magnitude of the problem. Heads of Government urged all governments to make AIDS prevention a matter of compelling priority, mobilising all relevant resources and sectors to prevent AIDS and to mitigate its socio-economic impact. Measures were required inter alia to develop strong multisectoral national AIDS programmes that would promote education and behaviour change and support action for safer sexual behaviour; combat stigmatisation and discrimination against people with known or suspected HIV infection; ensure the safety of blood and blood products; and co-operate more effectively with scientists in developing vaccines and drugs needed for prevention and therapy. Heads of Government requested Commonwealth Ministers of Health at their annual pre-WHA Meeting to review the matter regularly and keep them informed. They also asked the Seretariat to promote such schemes of Commonwealth co-operation as were practicable in furtherance of these objectives.

Rights of the Disabled

79. Heads of Government noted that there were millions of disabled persons in the world, the majority in developing countries, most of whom faced barriers to education and training, employment, transportation and communications. They welcomed the change in social attitudes towards the disabled fostered by the United Nations Decade of Disabled Persons (1983–92), and agreed to continue to promote measures in their own countries to enable disabled persons to contribute to economic and social life. They asked the Secretariat to keep the matter under review with a view to collating and disseminating information on existing national programmes.

Next Meeting

80. Heads of Government accepted with great pleasure the invitation from the Government of Cyprus to hold their next Meeting in Cyprus in 1993.

COMMONWEALTH FUNCTIONAL CO-OPERATION

1. Heads of Government re-emphasised their commitment to Commonwealth Functional Co-operation which occupies a central place in the association's joint endeavours. They expressed satisfaction with the substantial progress that had been made in various areas of activity under the aegis of the Commonwealth Fund for Technical Co-operation and other Commonwealth Organisations. They agreed that the functional activities of the Commonwealth should reflect the priorities identified in the Harare Commonwealth Declaration.

Commonwealth Fund for Technical Co-operation

2. In reviewing the Commonwealth Fund for Technical Co-operation Heads of Government underlined the importance they attach to the role of the Fund as the operational arm of the Secretariat and the pre-eminent Commonwealth agency for development co-operation. They noted the expansion of CFTC programme services in the two years since their meeting in Kuala Lumpur, and recommended that governments maintain and if possible expand their contributions to the Fund to ensure that it has the capacity to maintain this level of service to governments and is in a position to respond to Commonwealth priorities identified in the Harare Declaration.

Commonwealth Sport

3. Heads of Government endorsed the Report of the Working Party on Strengthening Commonwealth Sport and stressed the special role which sport should play in fostering Commonwealth values particularly in the younger generations. They also welcomed sports development programmes designed to reduce the disparities in available sports facilities and infrastructure between developing and developed countries.

4. Concerned to ensure the strengthening of the Commonwealth Games as a cornerstone of the Commonwealth, Heads of Government called on member governments to make the Commonwealth Games Federation financially self-sufficient and able further to promote the Games and Commonwealth sport generally. To sustain the important role accorded Commonwealth sport by Heads of Government, they requested the Secretary-General to establish an ad hoc committee for a period of four years, with a membership and mandate broadly reflecting those of the Working Party which would meet biennially on the occasion of the Federation's General Assembly. They expressed the hope that in future the hosting of the Games would be shared more equitably among member countries while ensuring that proper standards prevail.

Women and Development: Commonwealth Plan of Action

5. Heads of Government reaffirmed their commitment to the advancement of women, and more particularly to the Plan of Action on Women and Development and its implementation through national and Secretariat initiatives. They welcomed the Secretary-General's Report on the progress achieved by both national governments and the Secretariat, but recognised that much more remained to be done. Heads of Government emphasised that the education and training of women in larger numbers was imperative if the objectives of the Plan of Action were to be realised, and all member governments should make this a matter of the highest priority. They urged member governments to enhance the effectiveness and influence on policy of national women's bureaux, to provide training on gender issues to senior policy makers and planners, and to make the development planning process sensitive to gender considerations. They asked that opportunities for women to work at policy-making levels within national civil services and within the Secretariat should be increased through purposeful action.

Youth Affairs

6. Heads of Government noted that the Review of the Commonwealth Youth Programme's structure and activities had been completed in 1990 and that the Commonwealth Youth Affairs Council (CYAC) had approved the necessary changes to the Programme and its style of work. They enjoined governments to continue to support the Programme financially, and agreed that the CYAC's biennial

meetings should hence-forward be designated as Ministerial Meetings, but held on a triennial basis beginning in 1992.

Scientific Co-operation

7. Heads of Government noted that Commonwealth Ministers Responsible for Science and Technology had met for the first time in Malta in November 1990 and had expressed the wish to meet on a regular basis in future. They acknowledged the important role that such meetings, together with the regular work of the Commonwealth Science Council, could play in enhancing Commonwealth scientific co-operation, promoting new initiatives, and identifying resources for major programmes in science and technology in the Commonwealth. They agreed that ministerial meetings should be held in future on an ad hoc basis in cases where the issues involved so warranted.

Management of Technological Change

8. Heads of Government expressed satisfaction at the establishment of the Commonwealth Consultative Group on Technology Management, a proposal which they had endorsed at their previous meeting. They commended the way in which the Group was undertaking its task of advising governments on techology transfer, adaptation and management, and their integration with economic and environmental policies. In view of the fact that demand for these services was expanding and already exceeded existing resource provision, they requested member governments to give serious consideration to increasing the Group's resources or to financing projects or programmes that the Consultative Group might propose.

Drug Abuse and Illicit Trafficking

9. Heads of Government asked the Secretariat, in close collaboration with the new UN Programme and other relevant agencies including regional organisations, to continue to organise appropriate training and other activities to counter aspects of both supply and demand and to reflect the specific perspectives of the community, in particular of women and young people, in its work. They welcomed the agreement reached at the Commonwealth Law Ministers Meeting in Christchurch in 1990 whereby Commonwealth extradition arrangements could be streamlined, and urged Commonwealth members who had not yet done so to give early consideration to the adoption of the new optional procedures.

Favourable Fee Regime for Commonwealth Students

10. Heads of Government affirmed the fundamental importance of enhanced student mobility for Commonwealth cohesion and for the future of the Commonwealth itself. Enhanced interchange would bring positive benefits for individuals, for educational institutions and for Commonwealth countries themselves. They noted the proposals made by the Secretary-General on the possibility of a favourable fee regime for Commonwealth students with its five main elements of the establishment of an acceptable basis for computation of fees, fee reductions for postgraduate students, expanded scholarship provision, tuition fee scholarships and reciprocal arrangements for fee remission. Acknowledging the divergence of views on the most appropriate measures to be taken, and the requests by some countries for more time to study the implications in more detail, Heads of Government agreed that representatives of interested governments and the Standing Committee on Student Mobility and Higher Education Co-operation should meet early in 1992 to examine the proposals made by the Secretary-General, the policy and operational approaches of developed host countries, and any other proposed measures, with a view to reaching agreement on means of enhancing student mobility in the Commonwealth. They hoped this meeting would be sensitive to the views of many developing member countries on this question.

Commonwealth Higher Education Support Scheme

11. Heads of Government welcomed the establishment of the Commonwealth Higher Education Support Scheme (CHESS) but noted tht only limited progress had been made in developing co-operative projects. To realise the considerable potential of the Scheme for strengthening higher educational quality would require an assured flow of resources from industrialised countries in support of developing countries' own efforts. Heads of Government accordingly urged member countries to make the necessary forward commitments that would permit developing countries to proceed with confidence in preparing and submitting project and programme proposals for funding under CHESS. It would then be possible for the Commonwealth Standing Committee on Student Mobility and Higher Education Co-operation at its next meeting to consider with donor agencies suitable mechanisms and procedures for inviting requests and channelling funds.

The Commonwealth of Learning

12. Heads of Government noted with satisfaction the remarkable progress made by The Commonwealth of Learning since the last meeting of Heads of Government in Kuala Lumpur, and the impressive strides it had taken towards widening educational access and raising educational quality through distance education. They commended the Board, the President and staff of The Commonwealth of Learning on the achievements to date, and on the contribution which the organisation had already begun to make to human resource development in several Commonwealth

countries. They welcomed the new pledges made and urged all member countries to pledge additional financial support as soon as possible, to enable the organisation to develop and expand its services.

Commonwealth Foundation

13. Heads of Government congratulated the Foundation on its 25th Anniversary in 1991. They welcomed the constructive proposals made at the First Commonwealth NGO Forum for NGO-government linkages, NGO collaboration, and the strengthening of NGOs in post-apartheid South Africa. In response to requests by the NGOs present for additional support to cover technical assistance, training, exchanges and regional meetings, they asked the Foundation to proceed to develop such a programme of assistance.

14. Heads of Government expressed satisfaction at the increasing number and range of professional associations, and endorsed recommendations for organisational development, exchange and information-sharing among Commonwealth professionals from the Sydney Conference of Professionals. They commended the proposals of the expert group on culture and accepted the Foundation's plan to introduce a Commonwealth culture desk within existing resources. They believed that more appropriate budgetary procedures were necessary. They invited the Board of Governors to review the position, with a view *inter alia* to ensuring that budgetary questions were no longer taken at Commonwealth Heads of Government Meetings, and to report to the 1992 Senior Officials Meeting. As an interim measure, they recommended a 5 per cent increase for the financial year 1992/93.

15. Heads of Government expressed their appreciation for the services of the retiring Chairman of the Commonwealth Foundation, the Hon. Robert Stanfield and unanimously elected the Rt. Hon. Sir Richard Luce as his successor with effect from 1 January 1992.

Contribution to Commonwealth Budgets

16. Heads of Government welcomed the progress made in reducing the arrears of contributions to Commonwealth budgets, but felt it necessary to draw attention to the importance of eliminating arrears as soon as possible. They also recognised that prompt payment of current contributions was necessary to avoid adverse effects on Commonwealth activities. They welcomed the Secretary-General's intention to hold discussions with the Governments in arrears with a view to agreeing an appropriate schedule of payments and asked Senior Officials to review the position again at their meeting in Kampala, Uganda in 1992.

Commonwealth Institute

17. Heads of Government noted the priority given by the Commonwealth Institute to promoting the ideals and activities of the Commonwealth and its member countries among young people. They particularly welcomed the Institute's new focus on the Commonwealth and Europe, designed to ensure that Commonwealth concerns were better understood throughout Europe.

Commonwealth Non-Governmental Organisations

18. Heads of Government noted the valuable contribution which private individuals, private associations and voluntary bodies of many kinds make to the Commonwealth's well-being. They welcomed the consideration by business groups throughout the Commonwealth of the possibility of establishing a Commonwealth Association of Business Organisations which they thought could help to develop the trade of Commonwealth countries and facilitate their promotion of investment and transfer of technology. Recognising the valuable role played by centres of research and study of Commonwealth affairs, such as the Institute of Commonwealth Studies in London, they welcomed a proposal to establish a Commonwealth Issues Research Network to promote research and information exchanges by academics throughout the Commonwealth on subjects of importance to it.

19. Heads of Government expressed their continuing support for the work of the Commonwealth Trade Union Council and looked forward to the further development of co-operation between the Secretariat and the CTUC.

Report of the Secretary-General

20. Heads of Government received with appreciation the Thirteenth Report of the Secretary-General and commended the record of action outlined in the Report.

HARARE COMMONWEALTH DECLARATION

1. The Heads of Government of the countries of the Commonwealth, meeting in Harare, reaffirm their confidence in the Commonwealth as a voluntary association of sovereign independent states, each responsible for its own policies, consulting and co-operating in the interests of their peoples and in the promotion of international understanding and world peace.

2. Members of the Commonwealth include people of many different races and origins, encompass every state of economic development, and comprise a rich variety of cultures, traditions and institutions.

3. The special strength of the Commonwealth lies in the combination of the diversity of its members with their shared inheritance in language, culture and the rule of law. The Commonwealth way is to

seek consensus through consultation and the sharing of experience. It is uniquely placed to serve as a model and as a catalyst for new forms of friendship and co-operation to all in the spirit of the Charter of the United Nations.

4. Its members also share a commitment to certain fundamental principles. These were set out in a Declaration of Commonwealth Principles agreed by our predecessors at their Meeting in Singapore in 1971. Those principles have stood the test of time, and we reaffirm our full and continuing commitment to them today. In particular, no less today than 20 years ago:

- we believe that international peace and order, global economic development and the rule of international law are essential to the security and prosperity of mankind;
- we believe in the liberty of the individual under the law, in equal rights for all citizens regardless of gender, race, colour, creed or political belief, and in the individual's inalienable right to participate by means of free and democratic political processes in framing the society in which he or she lives;
- we recognise racial prejudice and intolerance as a dangerous sickness and a threat to healthy development, and racial discrimination as an unmitigated evil;
- we oppose all forms of racial oppression, and we are committed to the principles of human dignity and equality;
- we recognise the importance and urgency of economic and social development to satisfy the basic needs and aspirations of the vast majority of the peoples of the world, and seek the progressive removal of the wide disparities in living standards amongst our members.

5. In Harare, our purpose has been to apply those principles in the contemporary situation as the Commonwealth prepares to face the challenges of the 1990s and beyond.

6. Internationally, the world is no longer locked in the iron grip of the Cold War. Totalitarianism is giving way to democracy and justice in many parts of the world. Decolonisation is largely complete. Significant changes are at last under way in South Africa. These changes, so desirable and heartening in themselves, present the world and the Commonwealth with new tasks and challenges.

7. In the last twenty years, several Commonwealth countries have made significant progress in economic and social development. There is increasing recognition that commitment to market principles and openness to international trade and investment can promote economic progress and improve living standards. Many Commonwealth countries are poor and face acute problems, including excessive population growth, crushing poverty, debt burdens and environmental degradation. More than half our member states are particularly vulnerable because of their very small societies.

8. Only sound and sustainable development can offer these millions the prospect of betterment. Achieving this will require a flow of public and private resources from the developed to the developing world, and domestic and international regimes conducive to the realisation of these goals. Development facilitates the task of tackling a range of problems which affect the whole global community such as environmental degradation, the problems of migration and refugees, the fight against communicable diseases, and drug production and trafficking.

9. Having reaffirmed the principles to which the Commonwealth is committed, and reviewed the problems and challenges which the world, and the Commonwealth as part of it, face, we pledge the Commonwealth and our countries to work with renewed vigour, concentrating especially in the following areas:

- the protection and promotion of the fundamental political values of the Commonwealth:

  — democracy, democratic processes and institutions which reflect national circumstances, the rule of law and the independence of the judiciary, just and honest government;

  — fundamental human rights, including equal rights and opportunities for all citizens regardless of race, colour, creed or political belief;
- equality for women, so that they may exercise their full and equal rights;
- provision of universal access to education for the population of our countries;
- continuing action to bring about the end of apartheid and the establishment of a free, democractic, non-racial and prosperous South Africa;
- the promotion of sustainable development and the alleviation of poverty in the countries of the Commonwealth through:

  — a stable international economic framework within which growth can be achieved;

  — sound economic management recognising the central role of the market economy;

  — effective population policies and programmes;

  — sound management of technological change;

  — the freest possible flow of multilateral trade on terms fair and equitable to all, taking account of the special requirements of developing countries;

— an adequate flow of resources from the developed to developing countries, and action to alleviate the debt burdens of developing countries most in need;
— the development of human resources, in particular through education, training, health, culture, sport and programmes for strengthening family and community support, paying special attention to the needs of women, youth and children;
— effective and increasing programmes of bilateral and multilateral co-operation aimed at raising living standards;

- extending the benefits of development within a framework of respect for human rights;
- the protection of the environment through respect for the principles of sustainable development which we enunciated at Langkawi;
- action to combat drug trafficking and abuse and communicable diseases;
- help for small Commonwealth states in tackling their particular economic and security problems;
- support of the United Nations and other international institutions in the world's search for peace, disarmament and effective arms control; and in the promotion of international consensus on major global political, economic and social issues.

10. To give weight and effectiveness to our commitments we intend to focus and improve Commonwealth co-operation in these areas. This would include strengthening the capacity of the Commonwealth to respond to requests from members for assistance in entrenching the practices of democracy, accountable administration and the rule of law.

11. We call on all the intergovernmental institutions of the Commonwealth to seize the opportunities presented by these challenges. We pledge ourselves to assist them to develop programmes which harness our shared historical, professional, cultural and linguistic heritage and which complement the work of other international and regional organisations.

12. We invite the Commonwealth Parliamentary Association and non-governmental Commonwealth organisations to play their full part in promoting these objectives, in a spirit of co-operation and mutual support.

13. In reaffirming the principles of the Commonwealth and in committing ourselves to pursue them in policy and action in response to the challenges of the 1990s, in areas where we believe that the Commonwealth has a distinctive contribution to offer, we the Heads of Government express our determination to renew and enhance the value and importance of the Commonwealth as an institution which can and should strengthen and enrich the lives not only of its own members and their peoples but also of the wider community of peoples of which they are a part.

OTTAWA DECLARATION ON WOMEN AND STRUCTURAL ADJUSTMENT

Submitted by the Third Meeting of Commonwealth Ministers Responsible for Women's Affairs, Ottawa, Canada, 9–12 October 1990

1. We, the Heads of Government of the Commonwealth, believe that the challenges created by the changing world economic environment must be met through sound, equitable and effective adjustment policies at both national and international levels. These policies are vital for achieving the non-inflationary economic growth and sustainable development necessary to enhance human well-being. We endorse the broader approach to adjustment set out in the Commonwealth Expert Group's Report, *Engendering Adjustment for the 1990s*, including its three general principles of an emphasis on social equity and economic growth as well as efficiency; full integration of women into the decision-making processes; and a supportive international environment.

2. We appreciate the determined efforts being made by many governments, inside and outside the Commonwealth, to reform both policies and institutions. Moves towards the creation of a more supportive global economic environment are also greatly valued. But we accept too, that much more needs to be done if women are to regain the advances they lost in the 1980s partly as a result of inappropriate structural adjustment policies.

3. We are convinced that it is both essential and possible to design and implement policies and programmes that will improve the effectiveness, acceptability and sustainability of adjustment efforts. Structural adjustment cannot be sustained, development will be limited and the costs of adjustment will continue to be borne disproportionately by women unless such policies and programmes fully integrate measures to ensure gender equity, greater concern for basic human needs and protection of the physical environment, and are adequately financed.

4. The full potential of the development process can only be reached if its economic and social aspects, including poverty reduction, are recognised as mutually supportive. It is especially important that programmes in primary health care, nutrition, family planning and education and training are not impaired. Greater advances for women in these areas must be maintained. Investment in the nutrition, health and education of a country's population is as crucial to the development of its economy and the well-being of its people as is any investment in physical capital.

5. The structural adjustment process provides important opportunities to re-evaluate the ways in which women and men from all parts of society can best contribute to and benefit from economic and social development. As compared to men, there are considerably more complex demands on women's time from their multiple roles as economic producers, mothers and caregivers, household managers and community organisers.

6. Adjustment programmes must be designed to ensure a more equitable sharing between women and men not only of the programmes' costs but also of the rewards and benefits accruing. It is only in this way that women's active participation and wide-ranging contributions to the economy — too often unrecognised because unpaid — can be brought into the process.

7. Therefore, we commit our governments and commend to others the following programme of action:

(i) To reform social, administrative and legal structures to give women full and effective rights to land, finance and other resources. Such reforms will remove barriers to women's ability to participate in, contribute to and benefit from productive activity in a market economy.

(ii) To invest in enhancing women's productive activities, especially in key areas such as enterprise development, agricultural production and food security. Improved access to appropriate technologies, extension services, transportation and training can increase productivity for women's own benefit and that of the economy as a whole.

(iii) To ensure that incentives to participate in new opportunities and growth sectors do reach women, and that market structures are created which are as open to women as they are to men. Particular support will be provided where necessary to enable women to take advantage of more open and competitive markets, including greater access to and more flexible and innovative terms of credit.

(iv) To ensure that public policy and expenditures are conducive to the provision of basic goods and services to support women's multiple activities. Increased public expenditure on nutrition, education and health programmes that support women is vital in ensuring they have time to make use of new productive capacity and respond to new market incentives. This is necessary for long-run human resource development. A particular priority is to increase access to schooling for girls. This will have positive effects on child health and survival, population growth rates, family well-being and economic productivity. Such emphases must be embodied in programmes that are accountable to women and responsive to their needs.

(v) To integrate women's interests more consistently into public policy, including the design and implementation of structural adjustment policies, through: increasing gender awareness throughout government; ensuring the full involvement of women in decision-making and operational processes at all levels; enhancing the capacity of women's bureaux to contribute effectively to economic analysis and project appraisal; encouraging effective channels for women and women's organisations to express their perspectives and concerns; and establishing steering committees within Ministries of Finance to ensure that gender issues are incorporated into all decisions relating to structural adjustment.

(vi) To improve the collection of data – quantitative and qualitative — and the development of methods and statistical indicators, globally and nationally, that could provide a better understanding of the economic activity of both women and men, and the consequent impact by gender of specific policies, paying particular attention to the possibility of differential impacts within households.

(vii) To encourage the international organisations of which we are members to join us in our endeavour to fully integrate the goal of equity between women and men in the structural adjustment process, to ensure that structural adjustment programmes are growth oriented, more long term, better financed, take account of measures necessary to ameliorate negative social impact, and, in all other ways, including improving market access for developing country exports and increasing external resource flows, to promote a more favourable international economic environment.

Commonwealth Meetings 1991

The Commonwealth Secretariat organises and services meetings of Commonwealth Heads of Government, of Ministers and of Senior Officials as well as specialist conferences, seminars and workshops in areas of functional co-operation. The meetings take place throughout the Commonwealth.

Fourteen meetings of Commonwealth Heads of Government have been organised since the Secretariat was set up in 1965: in Lagos in 1966, London in 1966 and 1969, Singapore in 1971, Ottawa in 1973, Kingston in 1975, London in 1977, Lusaka in 1979, Melbourne in 1981, New Delhi in 1983, Nassau in 1985, Vancouver in 1987, Kuala Lumpur in 1989 and Harare in 1991. Between Heads of Government meetings, the senior officials of governments meet to provide continuity, exchange views on international developments, discuss techniques of government and review the work of the Secretariat. Commonwealth Finance Ministers meet annually (just prior to the World Bank and IMF meetings); Law Ministers meet every two or three years, and Health Ministers and Education Ministers every three years. Ministers of Food and Agriculture held their first full meeting in February 1981. In addition, special ministerial level meetings, for example on trade, youth affairs, industry and rural development, are organised as necessary, and Commonwealth consultations take place at meetings of international bodies.

The meetings, seminars and workshops listed below were among those organised in 1991 by the Commonwealth Secretariat and its affiliated agencies.

JANUARY		
12	Britain	Women Writers' Workshop, at the Commonwealth Institute
14-19	Britain	Course for officers and officials of national medical associations (NMAs) within the Commonwealth, organised by the Commonwealth Medical Association
15-23	Sri Lanka	Seminar on Parliamentary practice and procedure for Asia and SE Asian regions, organised by the Sri Lanka branch of the CPA
21-22	Britain	Meeting of the ten Heads of Government on the High-Level Appraisal of the Commonwealth, organised by ComSec
28-Feb 8	Swaziland	Sixteenth meeting of the Commonwealth Telecommunication's Consultative Committee for Collaborative Arrangements
*	Vanuatu	Commencement of CYP workshop in training trainers for the CYP South Pacific certificate course in youth work, organised by the CYP's South Pacific Centre
*	Vanuatu	Seminar for young Pacific writers, organised by the CYP
FEBRUARY		
11-16	Singapore	Inaugural steering committee meeting of the Association of Commonwealth Workers with the Deaf
13-15	Britain	Second meeting of expert group on the impact of global economic and political change on the development process, organised by ComSec
15-16	Kenya	Seminar on job management and practice matters for architects and allied construction professions in Kenya, Uganda and Tanzania, organised by the CAA in conjunction with the Architects' Association of Kenya and the Royal Institute of British Architects
20-21	Zimbabwe	Seminar on job management and practice matters for architects and allied construction professions in Botswana, Lesotho, Malawi, Namibia, Swaziland, Zambia and Zimbabwe, organised by the CAA in conjunction with the Institute of Architects, Zimbabwe and the Royal Institute of British Architects

20-22	Barbados	ComSec/Carneid planning meeting on a professional development programme for chief education officers in the Commonwealth Caribbean
25-28	Britain	Group meeting to review the activities of the CTO
27-Mar 8	Mauritius	Course on costing of telecommunications services, organised by the CTO and the World Bank
*	Lesotho	Workshop for trainers of traditional birth attendants and village midwives from the Southern African region, organised by Camhadd
*	The Bahamas	Expert group meeting on epidemiology of alcohol and drug abuse, organised by ComSec

MARCH

1-April 25	India	Training programme on environmental assessment and monitoring, organised by the CSC as part of the Langkawi Awards for Environmental Studies Scheme
2	Britain	Sponsored swim for the Commonwealth Society for the Deaf, at the Queen Mother Leisure Centre
4-7	Trinidad & Tobago	Workshop for the Caribbean region on agricultural mechanisation, organised by ComSec
5-16	Britain	Fortieth seminar on parliamentary practice and procedure, jointly organised by CPA headquarters and the UK branch of the CPA
7-8	Nigeria	Conference for heads of African architectural schools, organised by the CAA and the Nigerian Institute of Architects
11	All Commonwealth Countries	COMMONWEALTH DAY
11-16	Trinidad & Tobago	Sixth plenary conference of the Commonwealth Association of Planners and the 4th convocation of the Caribbean Conference for Town and Country Planning on the theme 'Challenges and Opportunities for Planners: The Environment and the New Technologies', jointly organised by the Commonwealth Association of Planners and the Trinidad and Tobago Society of Planners
11-24	Britain	Exhibition of craft from Montserrat, at the Commonwealth Institute
19-21	Ghana	Regional workshop on planning for training to combat drug abuse, organised by ComSec
19-24	Channel Islands	Mid-year executive committee meeting of the CPA
21-23	Britain	Intergovernmental meeting on 'Women and Structural Adjustment', organised by ComSec
23	Britain	Craft Fair, organised by the Manchester Branch, Commonwealth Society for the Deaf
26-28	St Kitts	Symposium on 'Small States: Problems and Opportunities in a World of Rapid Change', organised by ComSec
25-April 19	India	Advanced programme on export market development, organised by ComSec
28	Britain	One day conference on 'Technology Across Cultures', organised by the Commonwealth Institute

APRIL

5-8	Britain	CSC conference on the theme of 'Chemistry and Developing Countries'

6-June 2	Britain	'Kiwi, Kauri and Silver Fern': exhibition showing the development of New Zealand heraldry from the arrival of the Europeans to the present, at the Commonwealth Institute
7	Italy	Meeting of senior Commonwealth fisheries officials, organised by ComSec
8-June 26	Britain	Crown Agents course on customs and excise management
8-June 28	Britain	Crown Agents course on advanced logistics management
9-14	Ghana	Workshop on prevention of birth asphyxia for trainers of traditional birth attendants and nurse midwives from East and West Africa organised by Camhadd with support from the Commonwealth Foundation
12-13	Britain	African writers' conference on the theme of 'African Literature: What shall we read?', jointly organised by the Commonwealth Institute and the Africa Centre
12-May 10	Britain	Crown Agents course on procurement for development projects
15-18	Canada	Meeting of the expert group on human resource development for post-apartheid South Africa, organised by ComSec
15-July 5	Britain	Crown Agents course on trade fraud
17	Britain	Lecture on 'The Impact of Immigrants on British Society', organised by the Royal Society of Arts
17-19	Britain	Meeting of the expert group on environmental concerns, organised by ComSec
22-26	Singapore	RELC regional seminar on second language acquisition
23-28	Zimbabwe	CCGTM workshop on 'Advisory Mechanisms for Science and Technology: the role of a research council'
24	Britain	Lecture on 'Sustainability and the Third World', organised by the Royal Society of Arts
28	Austria	Commonwealth meeting prior to the 34th session of the Commission on Narcotic Drugs, organised by ComSec
29-May 3	Zimbabwe	Seminar on teacher management, organised by ComSec
29-May 3	Bermuda	Seminar on strategic management, organised by ComSec
*	Malaysia	Workshop on geophysical databases, jointly organised by the CSC and UNDTCD
*April/May	Caribbean	Workshop on disaster management (hurricanes), organised by ComSec

MAY

1	Britain	Meeting of the Commonwealth Health Development Programme Steering Group, organised by ComSec
3-June 5	Britain	'A Light from Africa': exhibition of prints showing African people and motifs in a harmonious combination of old and new traditions, at the Commonwealth Institute
5	Switzerland	Pre-WHA meeting of Commonwealth Health Ministers
6-10	Grenada	Second meeting of the working group on eliminating gender stereotyping from primary school textbooks, organised by ComSec
6-10	India	Seminar on 'Efficiency through Competition in utilities', organised by ComSec
8-10	Mauritius	Seminar on island resort development, organised by the CAA with the Mauritius Institute of Architects and the Royal Institute of British Architects
8-24	Britain	Commonwealth parliamentary visit, organised by the UK branch of the CPA

12-14	Pakistan	Regional conference on 'Human Rights in Development', organised by ComSec
12-18	Trinidad & Tobago	Twenty-first parliamentary conference of the Caribbean, the Americas and the Atlantic region, organised by the CPA
13-19	Zambia	Twenty-second CPA African regional conference
14-16	Zimbabwe	CSC Workshop on processing Cassava as an industrial crop
21-23	The Bahamas	ComSec workshop on development of entrepreneurial skills for young women
27-31	Malaysia	CCGTM science advice to governments: participation of CCGTM members with relevant tasks in 10 countries
29-31	Britain	Final meeting of the expert group on the impact of global economic and political change on the development process, organised by ComSec
29-June 5	Papua New Guinea	Meeting of the Operational and Development Group of CTO
*	Uganda	Regional workshop on AIDS and human movement, organised by ComSec
*May/June	Caribbean	CSC evaluation meeting of the Caribbean energy information system

JUNE

3-7	Britain	Round table on 'Public Policy Management and the Changing Role of Government', organised by ComSec
3-Aug 23	Britain	Course on management of training, organised by RIPA
4	Switzerland	Meeting of Commonwealth Employment and Labour Ministers
6-7	Britain	Seminar on 'Human Rights and Development', organised by ComSec, at Cumberland Lodge
8-16	Isle of Man	Third Commonwealth parliamentary seminar, organised by CPA headquarters and the Isle of Man branch
9-15	Malaysia	Workshop for senior women administrators in higher education from the Asia-Pacific region on 'Enhancing Management Skills in Asia', organised by the National University of Malaysia in collaboration with ComSec
10-12	Trinidad & Tobago	Workshop on hazardous wastes, organised by CSC, at the Institute of Marine Affairs
11-12	Britain	Meeting of Heads of Government from Australia, Bahamas, Britain, Canada, India, Jamaica, Malaysia, Nigeria, Singapore and Zambia on the High-Level Appraisal of the Commonwealth, organised by ComSec
12-15	Malta	Workshop on the biodiversity of traditional and under-utilised crops, organised by the CSC
12-16	Channel Islands	Twenty-second CPA British Islands and Mediterranean regional conference
13-14	Britain	Meeting of the Expert Group on Women and Structural Adjustment, organised by ComSec
16	Switzerland	Annual meeting of the Commonwealth Trade Union Council
17-18	Britain	Planning meeting of the Commonwealth Higher Education Support Scheme (CHESS), organised by ComSec
19	Britain	Meeting of the Board of Representatives of the CFTC
21-22	Britain	Annual meeting and conference of the Commonwealth Countries' League

22-23	Britain	Third meeting of the Expert Group on Human Resource Development for a Post-Apartheid South Africa, organised by ComSec
23-25	India	Consultation on Youth Participation in Environment Preservation and Enrichment organised by the CYP Asia Centre
24	Britain	Third Seminar in the series on Mobility and the European Single Market on the theme of 'Student Mobility and the Third World Dimension', organised by ComSec and the Overseas Students Trust
24-26	Zimbabwe	Workshop on human rights training for public officials from the Southern African region, organised by ComSec
24-27	Zimbabwe	CSC workshop on control of Africa's floating water weeds
25	Britain	Lecture by the Rt Hon Lynda Chalker, MP, Minister for Overseas Development, Britain, on 'Aid and Good Government', jointly organised by the ODI and the Royal Institute of Public Administration, at Chatham House
25-July 30	Cook Islands	Course for tutors on distance learning in youth work, organised by the CYP South Pacific Centre
26-28	St Lucia	Evaluation meeting of the Caribbean Energy Information System, organised by the CSC
29-Aug 2	Zambia	Course on training of trainers, organised by the CYP Africa Centre
*	Malaysia or Kenya	CSC/UNDTCD workshop on geophysical databases
June/July	Tonga	Workshop for the South Pacific region on prevention and early intervention of mental handicap and developmental disabilities organised by Camhadd
*	Uganda	Workshop on extension services, organised by ComSec
*		Workshop on ethical and social issues surrounding AIDS, organised by ComSec
*		Workshop on community-based approaches to the prevention of AIDS, organised by ComSec

JULY

5-Sep 7	Guyana	Ninth diploma course in youth and development, organised by ComSec, at the CYP Caribbean Centre
8-12	Vanuatu	Course for tutors in distance learning courses in youth work, organised by the CYP South Pacific Centre
8-Aug 23	Britain	Eleventh international course on applied taxonomy of insects and mites of agricultural importance, organised by the International Institute of Entomology
11-16	Malaysia	CCGTM Science advice to governments: participation of CCGTM members with relevant tasks in 10 countries
14-18	Australia	Workshop on bioresources diversity, ethnobiology, development and sustainability, organised by ComSec in collaboration with the CSIRO International Relations Centre
14-Sep 27	Britain	Course on advanced management training for senior tax officials, organised by the Royal Institute of Public Administration in conjunction with Cata
15-19	Tanzania	Course on basic youth work principles and practice, organised by the CYP Africa Centre
15-Aug 22	Western Samoa	Commencement of six-week regional training programme for senior tax administrators, organised by Cata
29-Aug 2	Tanzania	Workshop on policy formulation for dairy development in Africa, organised by ComSec

31-Aug 2	Britain	Second and final meeting of the Expert Group on Environmental Concerns and the Commonwealth, organised by ComSec
	Kenya	Regional consultation on safe blood and blood products, organised by ComSec

AUGUST

5-9	Zambia	Meeting of the Heads of Paediatric Departments, organised by COL under its East African project on primary health education
6-8	Israel	Biennial conference of the Commonwealth Jewish Council and the Commonwealth Jewish Trust
10-16	Canada	Thirty-first CPA Canadian regional conference
12-16	Britain	Oxford conference on 'International and White Collar Crime', organised by ComSec
12-16	Kenya	Course on youth entrepreneurship development, organised by CYP Africa Centre
18-24	Fiji	Workshop on preparation of AIDS education materials, jointly organised by the CYP, SPC, WHO and UNESCO
19-23	Cyprus	Fourth meeting of law officers of small Commonwealth jurisdictions, organised by ComSec
19-Nov 8	Britain	Course on management of the environment, organised by RIPA
26-29	Canada	Fifth conference of the Commonwealth Pharmaceutical Association
26-30	Malawi	Workshop on youth entrepreneurship development, organised by the CYP Africa Centre
26-30	Zimbabwe	Conference on national chambers of commerce and trade associations, organised by ComSec
26-30	Zimbabwe	Commonwealth-NGO Forum on 'Environmentally Sustainable Development', 'NGO-Government Relations' and 'NGOs and Post-Apartheid South Africa'
28	Canada	Information services steering committee meeting of COL
29-30	Canada	Fifth meeting of COL Board of Governors
*	Caribbean	Regional trade fair management programme for the Caribbean, organised by ComSec
*	Britain, Germany, The Netherlands and Switzerland	Contact promotion programme for Sierra Leone horticultural products, organised by ComSec
Aug/Sept	Guyana	Visit of second advance party of Commonwealth observers in preparation for observance at Guyana general elections

SEPTEMBER

1-7	Malawi	African regional workshop for trainers of teachers on the early intervention programme, organised by Camhadd
2-6	Seychelles	Workshop on youth entrepreneurship development, organised by the CYP Africa Centre
2-6	Zimbabwe	Veterinary conference, organised by the Commonwealth Veterinary Association
3-4	Turks and Caicos Islands	CYP Caribbean Centre regional advisory board meeting
6-9	Fiji	Regional advisory board meeting of the CYP South Pacific Centre

9-13	Nigeria	Workshop on youth entrepreneurship development, organised by CYP Africa Centre
13-14	India	Sixth meeting of the Commonwealth Committee of Foreign Ministers on Southern Africa, organised by ComSec
15-21	Australia	Ninth Commonwealth Magistrates' and Judges' Conference, organised by the Commonwealth Magistrates' and Judges' Association
17	Caribbean	Start of distance learning course, organised by CYP Caribbean Centre
18	Canada	Media seminar on the Canadian economy and the Third World, organised by the International Development Research Centre
19	Asia	Post-conference regional meeting of the Association of Asian Open Universities, organised by COL
19-21	Britain	Veterinary conference, organised by the Commonwealth Veterinary Association
21-23	India	Meeting of the CPA executive committee
22-23	India	Eleventh Commonwealth parliamentary conference of members from small countries, organised by CPA
23-Nov 29	Britain	Crown Agents (diploma) course on site management
23-Nov 29	Britain	Course on legislative drafting, organised by RIPA
23-Dec 13	Britain	Crown Agents courses on supply and materials management, maintenance management, customs and excise enforcement, financial management and immigration management
24-26	Zambia	Regional follow-up to the conference on 'Young People and Drugs', organised by the CYP Africa Centre
24-28	India	Thirty-seventh Commonwealth Parliamentary Conference
28	Britain	Fifty-ninth annual conference of the Commonwealth countries League on 'Education for Development: A Commonwealth Initiative for Young Women'
*	Ghana, Zimbabwe and Botswana	Comparative reviews of science and technology advice, organised by the CCGTM

OCTOBER

1-5	Lesotho	Sub-regional workshop on training for productivity improvement, organised by ComSec, at the Institute of Development Management
1-20	Swaziland	Course on agricultural project analysis and management, organised by ComSec, at the Mananga Agricultural Management Centre
1-Feb	Barbados	Certificate course in climatology, organised by ComSec at the Caribbean Meteorological Institute
2		World Habitat Day on the theme of 'Shelter, Health and the Family'
2-4	New Zealand	Meeting of the Pacific Islands' Law Officers, organised by ComSec
3-6	Uganda	Meeting of the food and nutrition specialists' committee, organised by the Commonwealth Regional Health Secretariat for East, Central and Southern Africa
4-20	Canada	Vancouver International Film Festival
4-29	Hong Kong	Training programme in 'Computer-Aided Design', 'Computer Aided Manufacturing', organised by ComSec in collaboration with the Colombo Plan Staff College for Technician Education

5	Britain	Commonwealth Countries' League Fair, at the Commonwealth Institute
5-Nov 28	Pakistan	Training programme in design of press tools for industrial products, organised by ComSec, at the Pakistan Industrial Technical Assistance Centre
6-11	Pakistan	Workshop on women and literacy, organised by the Commonwealth of Learning in co-operation with Alama Iqbal Open University, Pakistan
6-11	Uganda	Regional workshop on community-based management and control of AIDS, organised by ComSec and the Commonwealth Regional Health Community Secretariat
6-25	Canada	Second international environmental management seminar, organised by ComSec under the Langkawi Awards Programme for Environmental Studies, at Dalhousie University
7-11	Namibia	Workshop on youth entrepreneurship development, organised by the CYP Africa Centre
7-Dec 13	India	Training in Manufacturing and maintenance engineering, organised by ComSec, at the Indian Institute for Foreman Training
7-Dec 13	Britain	Course on manpower budgeting and staff inspection, organised by the Royal Institute of Public Administration
8	Malaysia	Meeting of the Board of Representatives of the CFTC
8	Malaysia	Meeting of Commonwealth Finance Officials organised by ComSec
8-10	Malaysia	Meeting of Commonwealth Finance Ministers
9-18	Malaysia	Course on the costing of telecommunication services, organised by the Commonwealth Telecommunications Organisation and the World Bank
12-Dec 11	Swaziland	Course on management of rural development organised by ComSec at Mananga Agricultural Management Centre
14-18	Cyprus	Thirteenth general assembly and conference of the Commonwealth Association of Architects on the theme of 'Tourism and the Environment'
14-Nov 15	Uganda and Malaysia	Commonwealth Advanced Management programme, organised by ESAMI and ComSec
15	Zimbabwe	Meeting of the Ten Heads of Government of the High-Level Appraisal Group on the 'Commonwealth in the 1990s and Beyond'
16-22	Zimbabwe	Meeting of Commonwealth Heads of Government
16-28	Britain	Exhibition of contemporary Malaysian art, at the Commonwealth Institute
21-24	Hong Kong	Workshop for the Asia-Pacific region on economic crime, and the misuse of legitimate institutions by the illegal narcotics trade, organised by ComSec and the Crown Agents
21-25	Ghana	Workshop on youth entrepreneurship development, organised by CYP Africa Centre
21-Nov 8	Britain	Crown Agents course on corruption prevention at the Crown Agents Management Training Centre
22	Britain	Lecture on 'Economic Prospects for Developing Countries', organised by the ODI, at the Shell Centre
28-31	Tanzania	Curriculum development workshop on anaesthesia, organised by the Commonwealth Regional Health Community Secretariat for East, Central and Southern Africa
*	Barbados	ComSec workshop on consultancy development, at the Caribbean Centre for Development Administration

*	Barbados	ComSec workshop on public enterprises management, at the Caribbean Centre for Development Administration
*Oct-Nov	Britain, Germany and France	Tourism market survey and promotion for countries of the Tourism Council of the South Pacific, organised by ComSec
NOVEMBER		
1-Dec 13	India	Course on computers in financial management organised by ComSec, at the Institute for Financial Management and Research
4-6	New Caledonia	Third regional meeting of heads of rural development services, organised by ComSec
4-8	Sierra Leone	Workshop on youth entrepreneurship development, organised by the CYP Africa Centre
7-12	Ghana	Thirty-first meeting of the Council of the Commonwealth Telecommunications Organisation
8	Italy	Meeting of Commonwealth Agriculture Ministers
10-16	South Pacific	Workshop for young writers from the South Pacific region, organised by the CYP South Pacific Centre
11-15	Tanzania	Ministerial-level seminar on policy issues in the management of the Public Service, organised by ComSec at ESAMI
11-16	Kenya	Conference of Regional Health Ministers, organised by the Commonwealth Regional Health Secretariat for East, Central & Southern Africa
13	Jamaica	Mechanisms for collaboration between Governments and NGOs in the Expanded Programme on Immunisation, organised by ComSec
18-20	Britain	Twenty-seventh executive committee meeting of the CSC
18-23	Jamaica	Third meeting of the International Spice Group, organised by ComSec
19-23	Sierra Leone	CYP Africa Centre regional advisory board meeting
20-29	India	Seminar on introduction to data networks, organised by the Commonwealth Telecommunications Organisation
21-Dec 8	Uganda	Course on reproductive epidemiology, biostatistics and research methodology, organised by the Commonwealth Regional Health Secretariat for East, Central & Southern Africa
27-Dec 3	New Guinea	Fifth general meeting and twelfth technical conference of the Commonwealth Association of Tax Administrators
*	Bangladesh	ComSec course on credit support for smallholder livestock development, at the Central Cattle Breeding Station
*	Bangladesh	SADCC study tour to examine food management systems in Bangladesh, organised by ComSec
*	India	ComSec course on methodology of agricultural sample surveys, crop modelling and computer programmes, at the Indian Agricultural Statistics Research Centre
*	South Pacific	ComSec workshop on management of exclusive economic zones
*	Africa	Workshop on policy incentives and strategies for small farm development in Africa, organised by ComSec
*	Trinidad & Tobago	Regional workshop on maternal and child survival with special reference to the Expanded Programme on Immunisation, organised by ComSec
Nov-Dec	Malaysia	Course on quarantine and biological control methods for quarantine officers from ASEAN countries and other quarantine staff, at the International Institute of Biological Control

Nov-Dec	Cameroon	Course on leadership and management training for NGO women in small-scale enterprises in West Africa, organised by ComSec at the Pan-African Institute for Development

DECEMBER

1	All countries	World AIDS Day on the theme of 'Sharing the Challenge'
1-14	Fiji	CYP/ESCAP regional course for trainers in youth and community development work
3	Britain	Commonwealth Carol Service jointly hosted by the Commonwealth Trust and the Pacific Islands Society at St Martins in the Fields
7	Britain	Symposium on 'Africa, Democracy and the New World Order' at the London School of Economics
9-11	Canada	Dalhousie University conference on the theme of 'Creating a Common Future: University Action for Sustainable Development'
9-13	Britain	'Celebrating Christmas in the Commonwealth': workshops for children showing them how Christmas is celebrated in other Commonwealth countries, at the Commonwealth Institute's Northern Regional Centre
9-13	Nigeria	Judicial Colloquium organised by ComSec
10	All Countries	HUMAN RIGHTS DAY
12	Britain	'Conference on National Curriculum': Conference focusing on multiculturalism issues with particular reference to South Asia, at the Commonwealth Institute

*Precise dates not available

Abbreviations: *CORE: Caribbean Oceanographic Research Expedition*
Cabi: *Commonwealth Agricultural Bureau International*
Camhadd: *Commonwealth Association for Mental Handicap and Developmental Disabilities*
Carneid: *Caribbean Network Educational Information Department*
Cata: *Commonwealth Association of Tax Administrators*
CCGTM: Commonwealth Consultative Group for Technology Management
CFTC: Commonwealth Fund for Technical Co-operation
Cida: *Canadian International Development Agency*
COL: Commonwealth of Learning
CPA: Commonwealth Parliamentary Association
CSC: Commonwealth Science Council
ComSec: *Commonwealth Secretariat*
Commansat: *Commonwealth Strategic Planning and Management of Science and Technology*
CTO: Commonwealth Telecommunications Organisation
CYP: Commonwealth Youth Programme
Casafa: *Inter-Union Commission on the Application of Science to Agriculture, Forestry and Aquaculture*
CSIRO: Commonwealth Scientific Industrial Research Organisation
ESAMI: Eastern Southern African Management Institute
ILO: International Labour Organisation
ODI: Overseas Development Institute
RELC: Regional Language Centre
Ripa: *Royal Institute of Public Administrators*
SADCC: Southern African Development Co-ordination Conference
Satis: *Southern Africa: the Imprisoned Society*
SPC: South Pacific Commission
UNDTCD: UN Department of Technical Co-operation for Development
UNESCO: UN Educational Scientific Cultural Organisation
WHA: World Health Assembly
WHO: World Health Organisation

The Commonwealth Secretariat

Marlborough House, Pall Mall, London SW1Y 5HX (071) 839 3411

Senior staff as at December 1991

Chief Emeka C Anyaoku, CON	Commonwealth Secretary-General	Nigeria
Peter Unwin	Deputy Secretary-General (Economic)	Britain
Sir Anthony M Siaguru	Deputy Secretary-General (Political)	Papua New Guinea
Manmohan Malhoutra	Assistant Secretary-General	India
William H Montgomery	Assistant Secretary-General & Managing Director, CFTC	Canada

Secretary-General's Office

Stuart G Mole	Director	Britain

Administration Division

Prof G R Muhataba	Director	Tanzania
John R Barber	Assistant Director (Personnel)	Britain
R Rickie Sankar	Assistant Director (Finance)	Guyana

Commonwealth Science Council (CSC)

Dr Ulric O'D'Trotz	Science Adviser & Secretary, CSC	Guyana
Dr Raul E Vicencio	Deputy Secretary, CSC	Canada

Economic Affairs Division

Dr B Persaud	Director	Barbados
Ian R Thomas	Asst Director (Primary Products)	Britain
Dr S K Rao	Asst Director (Finance & Economic Co-operation)	India
Dr Indrajit Coomaraswamy	Chief Officer	Sri Lanka

Food Production and Rural Development Division

Joshua K Muthama	Director	Kenya
G L Bailur	Asst Director	India
Dr Chris D Easter	Asst Director	Australia

Information Division

Patsy B Robertson	Director	Jamaica
Clive K Jordan	Asst Director	Britain
Cheryl J Dorall	Asst Director	Malaysia

International Affairs Division

Max Gaylard	Director	Australia
Dr Neville O Linton	Asst Director	Guyana
Amitav Banerji	Asst Director	India
Dr Moses Anafu	Asst Director	Ghana
Human Rights Unit		
Paul LaRose-Edwards	Asst Director	Canada

Legal Division

Jeremy D Pope	Director	New Zealand
Richard Nzerem	Asst Director	Britain
Neroni Slade	Asst Director	Western Samoa
Commercial Crime Unit		
Dr W C Gilmore	Asst Director	Canada

Human Resource Development Group (HRDG)

Commonwealth Youth Programme (HRDG)

Raja G Gomez	Director	Sri Lanka
Warren Feek	Chief Project Officer	Sierra Leone

Education Programme (HRDG)

Peter R C Williams	Director	Britain
J R Swartland	Asst Director	Botswana

Fellowships and Training Programme (HRDG)

Dr Mohan Kaul	Director	India
Carl Wright	Asst Director	Britain
Dr Anita Nazareth	Asst Director	Singapore

Health Programme (HRDG)

Prof Kihumbu Thairu	Director	Kenya
Dr Helen Bichan	Asst Director	New Zealand
Hema Weerasinghe	Adviser, Drug and Substance Abuse	Sri Lanka

Management Development Programme (HRDG)

Dr Mohan Kaul	Director	India
Dr Olu Fadahunsi	Asst Director	Nigeria

Women and Development Programme (HRDG)

Noor Farida Ariffin	Director	Malaysia
Dr Judith May-Parker	Chief Officer	Sierra Leone

Commonwealth Fund for Technical Co-operation (CFTC)

Export Market Development Division (CFTC)

A G Barve	Director	Kenya
P P Kanthan	Asst Director	India

General Technical Assistance Division (CFTC)

Seth Barnor	Director	Ghana
Chris J Bowman	Asst Director	Australia
James B Allie	Asst Director	Sierra Leone

Industrial Development Unit (CFTC)

Keith Maddison	Director (and Head of Unit)	Britain
(Vacant)	Adviser (Technology)	
Dr Olugbenro A Ajayi	Adviser (Industry Promotion)	Nigeria
Anthony Polatajko	Asst Director	Britain
A Vijay	Asst Director	India
P Sinha	Asst Director	India
Dr Chi Amako	Asst Director	Nigeria

Technical Assistance Group (CFTC)

Mr S Sundar	Director (and Head of Group)	India
Carl W Dundas	Special Adviser (Legal)	Jamaica
Mrs Kamala Bhoolai	Special Adviser (Legal)	Trinidad & Tobago
B M J Salleh Amran	Special Adviser (Economic)	Malaysia
Dr Raj Kumar	Special Adviser (Economic)	Malaysia
Dr S Kofi Date-Bah	Special Adviser (Legal)	Ghana

Roger M Nellist	Special Adviser (Economic)	Britain
Constantine F Mutambikwa	Chief Officer	Zimbabwe
L J P Maurel	Chief Officer (Economic)	Mauritius
John R Syson	Co-ordinator, Special, Commonwealth Fund for Mozambique	Britain

Regional Staff (Commonwealth Youth Programme)

Africa Centre (Zambia)		
Joe Massalay	Director	Sierra Leone
Asia Centre (India)		
Devendra Agochiya	Director	India
Caribbean Centre (Guyana)		
Dr B I Henry	Director	Britain
Pacific Centre		
Hannington Alatoa	Director	Vanuatu

The Commonwealth Secretariat is an international body at the service of all member countries of the Commonwealth, providing the central organisation for joint consultation and co-operation in many fields. It was established in 1965 by Commonwealth Heads of Government, who saw it, in the words of the Agreed Memorandum, as 'a visible symbol of the spirit of co-operation which animates the Commonwealth'.

The Secretariat is responsible to Commonwealth governments collectively, and is the main agency for multilateral communication between them. It promotes consultation, and collects and disseminates information for their use. The Secretariat organises meetings and conferences and is responsible for putting into effect decisions for collective action. It also provides technical assistance for economic and social development through the multilateral Commonwealth Fund for Technical Co-operation.

Chief Emeka Anyaoku from Nigeria, one of the Commonwealth's most experienced diplomats, after election by Heads of Government at their 1989 Summit became Secretary-General on 1st July 1990. He succeeded Sir Shridath Ramphal of Guyana (1975–1990). Mr Arnold Smith, of Canada, was the first Secretary-General and served from 1965–1975.

The headquarters of the Secretariat are in London, at Marlborough House, which was made available as a Commonwealth centre by HM Queen Elizabeth II, Head of the Commonwealth.

Finance

The cost of the Secretariat is borne in agreed shares by Commonwealth governments, whose contributions are related to their capacity to pay and are based on their population and national income.

Britain pays the largest contribution (30%) followed by Canada (19.07%), Australia (9.69%), India (3.34%) and New Zealand (2.16%). Malaysia, Nigeria, Pakistan and Singapore each pay 1.6%. Bangladesh, Botswana, Brunei, Cyprus, Ghana, Jamaica, Kenya, Mauritius, Papua New Guinea, Sri Lanka, Tanzania, Trinidad and Tobago, Uganda, Zambia and Zimbabwe each pay 1.17%. The Bahamas, Barbados, Guyana, Lesotho, Malawi, Malta, Namibia, Sierra Leone and Swaziland each pay 0.66%. Antigua and Barbuda, Belize, Dominica, The Gambia, Grenada, Kiribati, Maldives, Seychelles, Solomon Islands, St Kitts and Nevis, St Lucia, St Vincent and the Grenadines, Tonga, Vanuatu and Western Samoa each pay 0.39%. Nauru and Tuvalu, as special members, make annual voluntary contributions.

The Secretariat's annual budget is considered by a Finance Committee composed of Commonwealth High Commissioners in London (or their representatives) and a representative of the British Government. It is then submitted to Commonwealth governments for approval. The approved budget for the financial year 1991/92 is £8,625,870.

The Secretariat also administers the separate budgets of the Commonwealth Fund for Technical Co-operation (CFTC), the Commonwealth Youth Programme (CYP) and the Commonwealth Science Council (CSC).

Staff and Organisation

The Secretary-General is appointed by Commonwealth Heads of Government, and has direct access to them. He is head of the Secretariat.

He is assisted by two Deputy Secretaries-General and two Assistant Secretaries-General. One Assistant Secretary-General is Managing Director of the CFTC, responsible to the Secretary-General for conducting the operations of the Fund.

The Secretariat is organised in divisions and programmes corresponding to its main areas of operation. The Divisions are: international affairs, economic affairs, food production and rural development, information, law and administration, those comprising the CFTC and the Human

Resource Development Group (HRDG). This Group set up in 1983, brings together the programmes concerned with education, fellowships and training (part of the CFTC), health, management development, women and development, and youth, six previously separate programmes whose primary purpose is the development of human resources in Commonwealth countries.

The CFTC's divisions cover general technical assistance, training, export market development, urgent technical consultancy work and industrial development.

Staff in the Secretariat, including the CFTC, the Commonwealth Youth Programme and the Commonwealth Science Council, number some 400. Staff members include nationals of 33 Commonwealth countries.

In addition, the Secretariat has officers appointed to the regional youth development centres in Guyana, the Pacific, India and Zambia.

Economic Affairs

The Economic Affairs Division is the focal point for Secretariat activities in the economic sphere. The Division plays a key role in promoting greater understanding of international economic issues, in identifying possible solutions to economic problems and in helping to achieve an international consensus on these solutions. It engages in research and analysis on economic issues of interest to Commonwealth governments. It organises seminars and conferences involving government representatives as well as experts on important economic questions. It is responsible for organising and servicing the regular meetings of Commonwealth Ministers of Finance and of Employment and Labour, and for assisting in servicing the biennial meetings of Commonwealth Heads of Government.

The Division has serviced a number of expert groups which have met at the request of Commonwealth Heads of Government or Ministers, to make proposals towards the resolution of global economic problems. Their subject matter has tended to mirror the important contemporary preoccupations of the international community. Titles of their reports include: *Towards a New International Economic Order* (1975–77); *The Common Fund* (1977); *Co-operation for Accelerating Industrialisation* (1978); *The World Economic Crisis* (1980); *Protectionism: Threat to International Economic Order* (1982); *The North-South Dialogue: Making it Work* (1982); *Towards a New Bretton Woods: Challenges for the World Financial and Trading System* (1984); *The Debt Crisis and the World Economy* (1984); *Technological Change: Enhancing the Benefits* (1985); *Jobs for Young People: a Way to a Better Future* (1987); *Engendering Adjustment for the 1990s* (1989), *Climate Change; Meeting the Challenge* (1989); *Sustainable Development; An Imperative for Environmental Protection* (1991); and *Change for the Better: Global Change and Economic Development* (1991).

The above reports have been widely used in international debates and negotiations and are generally regarded as making a valuable contribution to discussions on international economic issues. In 1990 the Division published a study entitled *International Economic Issues,* highlighting the contribution of the Commonwealth Expert Group reports to international economic discussion and action.

Work on commodities is an important part of the Division's activities. It continues to undertake studies on issues of commodity policy. A study analysing the causes and effects of depressed prices for many commodities of particular interest to Commonwealth developing countries and considering new approaches to commodity problems was prepared for the consideration of Commonwealth Heads of Government at their Kuala Lumpur meeting (1989); and studies on the impact of technological change on commodities and the relationship between exchange rates and commodity prices have also been completed. The Division continues to publish information on selected commodities of production, trade, consumption, stocks, prices and related policies and developments in its regular publications on wool, fruit, and tropical products. The former is issued under collaborative arrangements with the International Wool Textile Organisation and the International Wool Study Group.

The Division has conducted a number of activities in connection with the Uruguay Round of Multilateral Trade Negotiations. It has undertaken studies geared to identifying areas of negotiating interest to Commonwealth developing countries, and assessing how these interests can best be pursued. The first study, entitled *The Uruguay Round of Multilateral Trade Negotiations: Commonwealth Interests and Opportunities,* was issued in November 1986. Subsequent studies have been concerned with sectoral issues, such as tropical products, agriculture, and trade-related investment measures, trade-related aspects of intellectual property rights, textiles and clothing, and services; or systemic matters, such as the functioning of the GATT system and safeguards. A comprehensive evaluation of the results of the Round, highlighting their policy implications, will be undertaken after its conclusion.

The Division, in collaboration with others, has also held a series of seminars on those aspects of the Round of particular interest to member countries. In addition the Division, in association with the Geneva Office of the Commonwealth Trade Adviser, has circulated to governments periodic bulletins chronicling events in the different negotiating groups of the Uruguay Round. It also provided technical assistance to African, Caribbean and Pacific countries in their re-negotiation of the fourth Lomé Convention with the European Community.

Commonwealth Finance Ministers meet each year on the eve of the annual meetings of the World Bank and the International Monetary Fund. Through these meetings, Ministers have been able to develop an on-going dialogue on international financial issues and have advanced consensus on some of them. Besides servicing these meetings, the Division keeps under surveillance such issues as aid and other financial flows, external debt adjustment problems and the policies of international financial institutions. It has organised symposia to promote exchanges of national experience in such areas as exchange rate management and negotiation of adjustment programmes. The Division is currently paying increasing attention to privatisation issues through analytic work. It also assists in the promotion of contacts between regional organisations.

For some years, the Division has also operated a capital markets programme designed to improve the access of Commonwealth developing countries to international markets. The programme includes circulating a bi-monthly bulletin entitled *International Capital Markets* to member countries. The Division also conducted a number of studies and organised workshops on foreign investment policies and experiences with a view to assisting Commonwealth developing countries in improving policies. Its findings are analysed in a book *Developing With Foreign Investment* published by Croom Helm in 1987. Following the request by Commonwealth Finance Ministers to the Secretariat to examine how Commonwealth developing countries could be assisted in reversing the deterioration in private capital flows to them, a report was prepared which made a number of recommendations including a major proposal for the establishment of a Commonwealth Equity Fund (CEF) — a private, commercially-operated Fund without any government support to enable international portfolio investors to invest in emerging stock markets of Commonwealth developing countries. After further work by the Division, the Hibiscus Issue of the CEF of $56.6 million was launched in September 1990. The Division is currently playing an important facilitative role in promoting regional funds which include a significant venture capital component. It is also beginning to work with Commonwealth governments, through seminars and studies, to broaden the possibilities of domestic and foreign investment through local capital and stock market development and assistance with privatisation. A conference on financing development to discuss financial issues in the Commonwealth Caribbean was held in December 1989, selected papers from which were published by Macmillan in 1991 in the book entitled *Financing Development in the Commonwealth Caribbean.*

More than half of Commonwealth countries have populations of about one million or less. The Division plays a significant role in the Secretariat's programme to assist these countries to overcome the difficulties created by their size. It provided technical support to the Commonwealth Consultative Group set up at the request of Heads of Government in 1983 to examine the special needs of small states. The Group's Report, *Vulnerability: Small States in the Global Society,* published in August 1985, covered both the security and economic needs of these states. The Division has continued to keep small states and others with limited representation at international fora informed of developments on economic and related matters in the United Nations system and other multilateral organisations through its quarterly publication, *International Development Policies.* There is a shortage of published socio-economic data on small states, and since 1980 the Division has been helping to fill this gap by publishing an annual volume of basis statistics on states with populations of less than five million.

The Division plays a lead role in co-ordinating the Secretariat's work on environmental issues. With the completion of the Expert Group's report, *Sustainable Development: An Imperative for Environmental Protection,* the Division is now helping to promote the findings of the report. It also organised Commonwealth consultations and providing technical support, especially for small states, at important preparatory meetings for the United Nations Conference on Environment and Development which is scheduled for June 1992. In 1989, it provided technical support for an international conference held in the Maldives on the consequences for island Commonwealth countries of sea-level rise due to global warming. The Division assisted in coordinating the Secretariat's efforts to mobilise international support for the implementation of a pioneering programme to develop on a sustainable basis nearly a million hectares of tropical forest made available by the Government of Guyana.

The Division has been involved in monitoring developments in the Southern Africa region, and the implementation of economic measures against South Africa by Commonwealth countries. Issues relating to the development of post-apartheid South Africa are now receiving some emphasis in the Division's work.

Education

The Commonwealth Secretariat promotes consultation and cooperation among governments and NGOs on educational issues through its Education Programme (EDP). The Commonwealth Fund for Technical Cooperation (CFTC), through its General Technical Assistance and Fellowships and Training Programmes, helps Commonwealth developing countries meet their need for skilled personnel. The Secretariat's work is complemented by a network of Commonwealth cooperation in education which includes: the Commonwealth of Learning (COL) based in Vancouver and focussing on co-operation in distance education; the Association of Commonwealth Universities (ACU, London); the Commonwealth Council for Educational Administration (CCEA, Australia); the Commonwealth Association of Science, Technology and Mathematics Educators (CASTME, London); the Commonwealth Association for the Education and Training of Adults (CAETA, Zimbabwe); the Commonwealth Association of Polytechnics in Africa (CAPA, Kenya); and the Commonwealth Foundation.

The Education Programme, established in 1960, is now part of the Human Resource Development Group of the Secretariat. It has three main functions. The first is to encourage and sustain contacts between governments, educational institutions, professional associations and individuals. This is supported by extensive correspondence, and by a publications programme including practical handbooks and resource manuals, reports and surveys, directories on educational systems and facilities, a newsletter, *Commonwealth Education News,* and a publications catalogue, *Education Publications 1992.* Professional networks among Commonwealth educators working in various fields are also promoted. The second function is to facilitate member countries' analysis of key policy issues and schemes for developing education and training systems. This is done through meetings, training workshops, consultancies, targeted publications, and support for training attachments and study tours. Programme staff also carry out advisory and consultancy work on request from governments. Finally, the Programme seeks to stimulate and undertake practical activities at regional or national level.

The Secretariat draws authority for its work in education from member governments. Ministers of Education and their senior officials meet every three years to discuss education policy, review cooperative activities and recommend new areas for action. These Conferences, and regular consultations with ministries of education, set guidelines for the work of the Education Programme.

The current five-year programme in education (beginning 1991) highlights three themes: raising the quality of basic education by improving the situation and the effectiveness of teachers in schools, facilitating cooperation among tertiary institutions to strengthen higher education institutions and systems, and addressing the special concerns of ministries of education in the small states of the Commonwealth. The Secretariat, at the request of Ministers, is also giving special consideration to ways in which the quality of education can be protected in the face of conditions of austerity and associated structural adjustment programmes.

Improving the Quality of Basic Education

At their last Conference in Barbados (October 1990), Commonwealth Education Ministers recognised that, while the quantitative expansion of education throughout the Commonwealth during the last 25 years had been impressive, concerns remained about its quality, especially at the basic level. They identified professional development and support for teachers as being key approaches to improving education quality in schools, and mandated the Secretariat to undertake work on these themes. Several areas have been singled out for new initiatives: initial teacher training, teacher's records and personnel information systems, training and support for headteachers, the performance of science teachers, and enhancing the participation of women and girls in science, technology and mathematics.

Higher Education and Student Mobility

Commonwealth student mobility has been threatened by increases in overseas student fees in key host countries. The Commonwealth Standing Committee on Student Mobility and Higher Eduation Cooperation has met regularly since 1982. Its recommendations, and the work of the EDP's Higher Education Unit, have been directed to restraining fee rises for overseas students and resolving other problems associated with international study. Commonwealth Heads of Government continue to demonstrate their concern about constraints which are imposed on the free movement of students within the Commonwealth, and to seek ways to ameliorate the burden of full-cost fees on developing Commonwealth countries.

The Standing Committee has also stressed the complementarity of efforts to build strong higher education systems in countries of the south and enlargement of the network of Commonwealth student exchanges. Its proposal for a Commonwealth Higher Education Support Scheme (CHESS) to improve management procedures, the supply of books and library materials, and staff development programmes in Commonwealth tertiary institutions, was subsequently given flesh by a group of Commonwealth experts, and endorsed by Education Ministers and Heads of Government. CHESS projects are being carried forward jointly by the Education Programme, the ACU and CFTC in consultation with member governments, international development programmes, and institutions.

One of the most widely known of the Commonwealth's cooperative activities in higher education is the Commonwealth Scholarship and Fellowship Plan (CSFP). The target of 1,500 CSFP awards annually, set in 1984, is regularly surpassed. The Plan works through bilateral arrangements, both developing and developed countries offering scholarships to men and women from other Commonwealth countries. Fellowships and other awards enable senior university teachers and administrators to conduct research, teach or familiarise themselves with new developments.

Education Development in Small States

Twenty-seven of the 50 Commonwealth member countries have populations of one and a half million or less. Their educational development, complicated by difficulties related to smallness of scale, has provided a focus for Education Programme work since 1985. Attention has been paid to post-secondary educational provision through the development of national tertiary colleges, the training of educational personnel in archipelago countries, and the organisation and management of ministries of education in small states. Linkages are fostered between ministries and institutions based in the Caribbean, the Indian Ocean, the Mediterranean, and the South Pacific.

Education and Structural Adjustment
At their conference in 1990 education ministers asked the Secretariat to work with them on measures to protect and develop education when structural adjustment limits government budgets. The aim is to increase understanding between ministries of education, ministries of finance, and international donors both by encouraging an informed dialogue between these partners and by ensuring that the economic, social and political case for education is effectively made.

Teaching and Learning About the Commonwealth
Encouragement is given to Commonwealth studies in schools and programmes for the celebration of Commonwealth Day (the second Monday in March). The Programme publishes the *Commonwealth Day Handbook for Schools;* the Secretariat issues a Commonwealth Day poster and other materials. EDP liaises with London's Commonwealth Institute on matters relating to teaching about the Commonwealth.

Information and Publications
The Secretariat collects and disseminates information on innovations, developments, and new publications on education throughout the Commonwealth. The Programme's publications are distributed at low cost, or free to member governments.

Food Production and Rural Development
In the developing Commonwealth, agriculture is the major driving force behind economic growth and an important tool for alleviation of poverty, hunger and environmental degradation. At their meeting in London in 1974, Ministers responsible for agriculture recommended that problems of rural development and food production be treated as an issue of vital concern in allocation of resources, the building-up and strengthening of institutions, the formulation of programmes and policies and the flow of intra-Commonwealth aid. The Food Production and Rural Development Division (FPRD) was established in 1975 to reflect increased emphasis on problems of food production and rural development through the Commonwealth Secretariat's economic studies and technical assistance.

The Division is the focal point in the Secretariat for agriculture defined in the broadest sense to include livestock, fishery and forestry. It provides a medium by which member countries can share experiences in areas of policy formulation, programme planning and management and in sustainable farming methods. Its work programme is based on mandates from Heads of Government and Ministers of Agriculture. It focuses on four programme themes: food and agricultural policy; diversification of agricultural production; agricultural, livestock, fisheries and forestry development services; and conservation for sustainable development. In carrying out this programme, FPRD conducts consultative activities, and provides technical assistance and training in food policy development and food supply information systems and management. It prepares training manuals, facilitates study tours and exchange visits and carries out sectoral investment studies. Specific project activities are initiated in response to bilateral requests from member countries or regional agencies.

The Division uses its inhouse expertise, sometimes supplemented by consultants, to advance consultative activities between countries and to provide country-specific assistance in agricultural project formulation and advisory services. Consultative activities provide exposure to new technologies, and may be carried forward through training, exchange visits, and discussion of policy options.

Exchange visits and study tours have proved particularly successful in Africa and India in relation to land rehabilitation, drought management, social forestry, soil and water conservation and in food supply information and management. In the Caribbean, a regional training programme for middle-level livestock managers has been implemented. Overview of fisheries in the Pacific Region has resulted in identification of investment opportunities and has focussed interest on the role of women in small-scale fisheries. In agricultural services, training programmes to benefit different regions and countries have been organised in: agricultural mechanisation, agricultural credit and dairy development, agricultural statistics, the application of computers in agricultural development, management control and surveillance of Exclusive Economic Zones (EEZs), and food supply information and management. An expert consultation has been held on rural poverty in the Commonwealth. The Division plays a catalytic role in fostering the generation of projects for donor support and especially for the CFTC.

In 1991 Heads of Government expressed concern in their Harare Communiqué at the continuing food problems in developing countries, and pledged to work with renewed vigour to promote sustainable development and the alleviation of poverty. Ministers of Agriculture, at their subsequent meeting in Rome, welcomed the lead thus given and reaffirmed the relevance of FPRD's long-term programme to address rural poverty alleviation; food security; the adoption of appropriate technologies; the diversification of agricultural production; protection of the environment through sustainable management of fisheries, forestry and rangeland resources; appropriate soil and water conservation practices for small farmers; and the enhancement of human resource capabilities for the sustainable management of agricultural services.

FPRD works closely with international and bilateral donor agencies, Commonwealth professional associations and NGOs to ensure complementarity and avoid duplication. Its projects have attracted substantial co-sponsorship funds from these agencies, augmenting CFTC funds to the benefit of developing Commonwealth member countries.

Health

The first Commonwealth Medical Conference took place in Edinburgh in 1965. Health Ministers' meetings have subsequently been held every three years: in Uganda (1968), Mauritius (1971), Sri Lanka (1974), New Zealand (1977), Tanzania (1980), Canada (1983) the Bahamas (1986) and Australia (1989). Mutual assistance in education and training of the health professions, planning and development of health services, community and family health, health education, nutrition, health financing, the supply of medicinal drugs and maintenance of medical equipment are among matters discussed at these ministerial meetings. The work of the Commonwealth Secretariat's Health Programme follows recommendations made at these meetings.

Community approaches to health promotion and disease prevention was the theme of the Ninth Commonwealth Health Ministers Meeting, in Melbourne in 1989. Ministers also focused on training the community and the health team to work together in healthy promotion and disease prevention; community efforts in the prevention and eradication of alcohol and drug abuse; technical co-operation and development assistance in the health field.

Commonwealth Health Ministers have a one-day meeting in Geneva each year, prior to the World Health Assembly, to consider issues before the Assembly and review Commonwealth health activities.

Regional health co-operation between member countries of the Commonwealth is well established. Regional health agencies have been set up in the Caribbean, West Africa and East, Central and Southern Africa, and are responsible to the Health Ministers of their respective regions. They service regional consultations and promote joint projects and the sharing of resources, particularly for education and training. The Commonwealth Secretariat works closely with these regional bodies and provides assistance for their programmes.

In 1986 Commonwealth Health Ministers initiated the Commonwealth Health Development Programme, with the main aim of strengthening the health infrastructure through the development of cadres of health workers with special skills for tackling priority health problems in developing countries. Regional training activities have been developed in each of the five regions covering management of safe blood and blood products in East, Central and Southern Africa; health systems research in the Caribbean; health personnel planning in the Pacific; continuing education of pharmacists in West Africa; and personnel development for primary health care in Asia.

Special studies are commissioned by the Secretariat on a wide range of subjects to assist member governments. The Secretariat also organises meetings on subjects of special concern to member governments. In recent years it has arranged a series of regional workshops on regional maintenance of medical equipment, mechanisms for government/NGO collaboration in health, particularly immunisation, and planning for training to combat drug abuse. Besides publishing the reports of these studies and workshops, the Secretariat has also published a directory of health training resources in the Commonwealth, an inventory on pharmaceutical manufacture and formulation in the Commonwealth and a report on ethical and social aspects of AIDS.

The Commonwealth Secretariat assists the training of health personnel in a wide range of disciplines, which include nursing administration, dentistry, radiography, physiography, pharmacy, speech therapy and operating theatre techniques.

The Commonwealth Nurses Federation, the Commonwealth Pharmaceutical Association, the Commonwealth Medical Association, the Commonwealth Human Ecology Council and the Commonwealth Association for Mental Handicap and Developmental Disabilities link professionals in member countries and promote professional training. All these bodies have received assistance from the Commonwealth Foundation which, in its work to promote professional co-operation and development, supports study and advisory visits and training attachments.

Among Commonwealth voluntary bodies active in the health field are the Commonwealth Society for the Deaf and Sight Savers (the Royal Commonwealth Society for the Blind), which operates the world's largest sight restoration programme, restoring sight to over 100,000 people each year.

Information

The Commonwealth Information Programme was set up in 1971 to increase awareness of the nature, work and value of the Commonwealth. Information material is provided direct to the public and through Commonwealth governments, with the press, broadcasters, educators and NGOs as special targets.

Relations with the media are an important part of the work, based on press briefings, regular news releases, publications and other media material. Direct personal contact is maintained with many Commonwealth journalists both in Britain and in other member countries, and there is a regular supply of material to the print and broadcasting world.

The Secretariat's publications programme comprises a list of some 500 titles. These include the biennial report of the Commonwealth Secretary-General commenting on current issues of

Commonwealth interest and giving an account of the work of the Secretariat. Information publications include *The Commonwealth Today*, an illustrated booklet; *Commonwealth Skills for the 1990s*, a booklet on the work of the Commonwealth Fund for Technical Cooperation; *Racism in Southern Africa: the Commonwealth stand; The Commonwealth Factbook*, giving information on member countries and dependencies; and *Commonwealth Currents*, a bi-monthly magazine. A poster for schools on Commonwealth Day is produced annually. Leaflets in a series of *Notes on the Commonwealth* cover specialised subjects and the declarations of Commonwealth leaders on basic Commonwealth principles, world order, global economic reform, racial justice and South Africa. Up to 50 features a year are sent to about 350 newspapers in the Commonwealth and to selected international news agencies. These cover all aspects of Commonwealth activity, both official and non-governmental. The Secretariat has collaborated with commercial publishers to produce reports commissioned by the Commonwealth Committee of Foreign Ministers on Southern Africa.

Radio material on tape is sent to 75 broadcasting stations and the output averages about 100 Commonwealth current affairs stories a year plus dozens of interviews. Special programmes are also produced and distributed as circumstances dictate. A number of films about the Commonwealth Secretariat, the CFTC and the Commonwealth Science Council have been produced for distribution to television stations in member countries.

Journalists from developing countries are helped to cover major events under a scheme started in 1977. Through the CFTC, the Secretariat provides information specialists and supports institutional training in communications. The Commonwealth Media Development Fund, started in 1980 with funds from Australia and Britain, also supports media training, including projects arranged by the Commonwealth Press Union, the Commonwealth Journalists Association, the Commonwealth Broadcasting Association and other agencies. Recommendations for the development of the media were made by a Commonwealth Committee on Communication and the Media in 1980 and by a further seminar involving members of the committee held in 1982.

As the main source of information about the Commonwealth and its work, the Secretariat handles many oral and written enquiries from the media, other organisations, and individuals.

International Affairs

From its inception in 1965, the Commonwealth Secretariat was envisaged by Heads of Government as helping to promote and facilitate consultation among Commonwealth governments on international issues. To this end, in addition to monitoring international issues and undertaking research on matters of major international importance for dissemination to member governments, the Secretariat was given the specific function of organizing and servicing meetings of Commonwealth Heads of Government and other ministerial and official gatherings. The various standing committees established from time to time by Commonwealth Heads of Government are also serviced by the Secretariat. In recent years these have included the Commonwealth Committee on Southern Africa (formerly the Sanctions Committee), the Commonwealth Committee on Cyprus, and the Commonwealth Ministerial Committee on Belize. This function was extended when Heads of Government, with the exception of Britain, established at their 1987 Vancouver Meeting an eight-member Commonwealth Committee of Foreign Ministers on Southern Africa.

The Division includes a Human Rights Unit set up in 1985. Its mandate is to facilitate the promotion of human rights through educational activity, information sharing, networking and the provision of supportive expertise for those countries undertaking human rights projects.

In certain specific areas of particular Commonwealth concern, such as those concerning Southern Africa, Cyprus and Belize consultation has been supplemented by discussions with representatives of non-Commonwealth governments and leaders of groups directly involved. The Secretariat was granted observer status at the Geneva Conference on Rhodesia convened in October 1976 and was represented at the subsequent Malta Conference held in February 1978. In addition, it provided financial and technical assistance to the African nationalist delegations to these conferences.

Support for the Commonwealth Observer Groups during elections in Zimbabwe from January to March 1980 and in Uganda from November to December 1980, and for the Eminent Persons Group on South Africa established in pursuance of the mandate in the 1985 Nassau Accord, was provided by Secretariat teams. More recently, support teams were provided to the Commonwealth Groups which observed the elections in Malaysia (October 1990), Bangladesh (February 1991) and Zambia (October 1991). Assistance is being provided to Mozambique in its preparations for multi-party elections.

The Secretariat was granted observer status by the United Nations General Assembly in 1976. It also maintains close liaison with a number of UN Agencies in various fields and with other international and regional organizations such as the OAU, the Caribbean Community, the South Pacific Forum Secretariat and the Agence de Co-operation Culturelle et Technique.

There are facilities for trainee Commonwealth diplomats to study the work of an international organization through short attachments or visits to the Secretariat. The Division has been rsponsible for the administration of the expansion of the office facilities in New York which now accommodate on a pan-Commonwealth funded basis, the permanent missions to the UN of eight Commonwealth small states from the Pacific, the Caribbean and Africa.

Law

The Legal Division was established to facilitate the exchange of information among governments on legislation and other legal matters in their respective countries; to act as a central point to bring to the attention of governments information which might be useful to them on particular problems; and to keep them apprised of significant changes in the law of other Commonwealth countries. The quarterly publications, the *Commonwealth Law Bulletin,* is the main vehicle by which the Division performs its primary responsibility: that of keeping member countries aware of legal developments in other parts of the Commonwealth so that they can benefit to the maximum from the experience of others. In 1983 Law Ministers meeting in Colombo invited the Division to develop a wide-ranging scheme for mutual assistance in the administration of justice. This has engaged much of the Division's attention culminating in Senior Officials approving two Commonwealth-wide schemes on mutual assistance in criminal matters and on the transfer of convicted offenders, which Law Ministers considered and adopted in Zimbabwe in August 1986. The two schemes form part of a wider network of Commonwealth mutual co-operation in the administration of justice generally, and the Secretariat has been assisting with their implementation.

Since the creation of the Commonwealth Fund for Technical Co-operation, the work of the Secretariat in the legal field has expanded significantly. Apart from the specialised work of the Technical Assistance Group, the Division has been closely involved with CFTC activities in the legal field under its General Technical Assistance and Education and Training Programmes. The Division has, for example, been responsible for implementing the programme for the training of legislative draftsmen as well as for other training programmes financed by the Fund.

The legislative drafting training courses organised and run by the Division since 1974 under the auspices of the CFTC form a major part of the training activities of the Secretariat in the legal field. By the end of 1991 nearly 400 officers, nominated by over 38 governments, including Namibia which joined the Commonwealth on attaining independence in 1990, had received basic tuition and practical training in drafting. Assistance in the field of legislative drafting has proved to be a priority need of governments, but there are many other areas of developmental importance in which legal expertise has been provided under the CFTC: law reform and revision, international law, taxation, local government, national development and investment, land law and constitutional law. The Secretariat has also been able to help a number of governments to identify candidates for senior posts in the judiciary and in other fields. A Commonwealth Commercial Crime Unit helps to develop liaison to combat international economic fraud and 'white-collar' crime. Its successes have encouraged governments to enlarge and strengthen the service to provide training for law enforcement officers in the fight against organised crime.

Requests for information about legal developments in other Commonwealth jurisdictions continue to increase, and with the co-operation and assistance of Law Ministers and their officers, the Secretariat is able to response promptly and effectively to those requests. The Division helps Law Reform Agencies to collect valuable, and on occasions unique, material when a new reference is referred to them. It has been playing a catalytic role in promoting the idea of regional law development units. Commonwealth Pacific islands law officers now have a unit operating in their region and in September 1983 a unit was established in St Lucia to service members of the Organisation of Eastern Caribbean States.

In the law, as in other fields, the Secretariat has found it increasingly beneficial to co-operate with other organisations: this helps to avoid duplication of work and to ensure the best possible use of limited resources. As well as co-operating with WIPO and ECA in the industrial property field, the Legal Division has actively co-operated with the Asian/African Legal Consultative Committee, of which several Commonwealth governments are members. The Secretariat also enjoys observer status with both UNIDROIT and the Hague Conference on Private International Law. Links have also been developed with ICPO-INTERPOL and the UN agencies concerned with combating the illicit trade in narcotic drugs.

The Commonwealth Legal Education Association, one of the non-governmental organisations built on personal, professional and academic links, operates from within the Legal Division. Its membership includes 79 institutions and 168 individuals in some 38 countries. It aims to foster high but relevant standards of legal education, to encourage training and related research and to assist the spread of information. The Association is able to keep lawyers and teachers in touch with changes and new developments by a modest but informative quarterly newsletter. It publishes lists of Commonwealth law schools and acts as a point of reference. The Division liaises closely with the Commonwealth Magistrates and Judges Association, the Association of Commonwealth Law Draftsmen and the Commonwealth Lawyers' Association under whose auspices the Commonwealth Law Conference—now a major event in the international legal calendar—is held every three years.

Management Development Programme

The Management Development Programme (MDP) is a part of the Human Resource Development Group, focusing on the management and training of human resources. By working closely with the other specialist programmes of the Group, MDP can assist member governments to upgrade their public management systems and practices on a more integrated basis.

MDP responds to problems in public sector management in three ways. First, it works primarily with officials in public administration influential in policy formulation or practical action in national and regional agencies. Second, in view of the importance of promoting national self-reliance, it has concentrated on systems of training and human resources development in both the public and the private sectors. Thirdly, the Programme has sought to identify emerging issues of importance for public servants, and to provide opportunities for them to explore these issues and examine alternative responses.

The Programme organises seminars, workshops and consultations at pan-Commonwealth, regional, sub-regional and national levels on specific areas of public administration. Recent programmes have been in the areas of development management; public administration reforms and modernisation; development and networking of non-governmental organisations; management of technology with special reference to information technology in governments; management of public enterprises; strategies for promoting entrepreneurship and small enterprise development. The programme lays special emphasis on improvement of management training and operates as a clearing house of information on issues in development administration through its publications.

Commonwealth Science Council

The Commonwealth Science Council (CSC) is an inter-governmental body that seeks to increase the capability of Commonwealth countries to apply science and technology for economic and social development. It does so by organising regional programmes, promoting scientific collaboration, providing information and training to Commonwealth scientists and by organising international scientific meetings. Membership of CSC is open to all Commonwealth countries. The organisation has a small secretariat of seven professional staff which is under the directorship of the Secretary. It is based at the Commonwealth Secretariat in London and a special relationship exists between the two organisations through which CSC is the Science Division of the Secretariat and its Secretary serves as Science Adviser to the Commonwealth Secretary-General.

The Commonwealth Science Council's governing body, the Council, determines the programme of work and meets every two years to discuss policy and finance, and to review progress. The last biennial meeting was held in Malta in November 1990. The next meeting is scheduled to take place in Botswana in 1992. An Executive Committee meets once a year to oversee the decisions taken by the Council.

The work programme is built around the following areas of activity: agriculture; biological resources; water and mineral resources; environmental planning; energy resources; industrial support; science management and organisation; and 'awareness of rapid advances in science and technology'.

Member countries are: Australia, Bahamas, Bangladesh, Barbados, Britain, Brunei Darussalam, Canada, Cyprus, Dominica (associate member), Ghana, Grenada, Guyana, India, Jamaica, Kenya, Lesotho, Malawi, Malaysia, Malta, Mauritius, Namibia, New Zealand, Nigeria, Pakistan, Papua New Guinea, Saint Lucia, Seychelles, Sierra Leone, Sri Lanka, Swaziland, Tanzania, Trinidad & Tobago, Uganda, Zambia and Zimbabwe. The current Chairman is Mr J B S Diphaha of Botswana.

Youth

The Commonwealth Youth Programme (CYP) encourages and supports the participation of young people in national development, recognises their contribution to economic, social and cultural development of their societies, and provides opportunities for increasing international understanding among youth. It provides most of its services through the four regional centres based in the Pacific, Guyana, India and Zambia, serving the Pacific, Caribbean, Asia and the Africa regions respectively. These primarily provide training. Residential diploma courses in Youth and Development combine classwork and fieldwork and prepare youth workers and youth affairs personnel to develop youth programmes, formulate youth policies, conduct local training activities, and organise community-based projects. In addition, the Africa, Asia and Caribbean Centres conduct distance learning courses which provide basic training for youth workers throughout the regions.

Short course training, conducted at national level, has concentrated on such topics as programme planning and implementation, training of trainers, methods and techniques of youth work, youth policy development and more recently on youth enterprise and drugs. The courses are run on a cost-sharing basis in collaboration with governments.

The Centres liaise with governments in their regions on a wide range of matters affecting youth policy and serve as resource units on youth and youth programmes. CYP seminars and workshops bring together representatives of government and non-government agencies to discuss problems and issues of concern, to exchange information and to generate new ideas. Commonwealth and regional meetings have focused on such topics as youth enterprise, government youth policies and young people and drugs. In 1989, CYP organised a Commonwealth Conference of young people working in the drugs field in an effort to come up with solutions to tackling the drugs problem. A valuable outcome of the Conference was the development of a set of training materials.

The Programme's priorities for the 1990s, in response to the needs expressed by governments, include youth enterprise and employment, young women and development, youth health and welfare, including drugs and AIDS, environment, literacy and youth policy development. The outcomes of CYP's work in each of these areas will be the development of information and training materials for young people, youth, community and health workers in the form of videos, training manuals, information leaflets and the publication of case studies.

The CYP Youth Project Fund recognises and encourages financially, projects showing youth initiative and innovation in trying to meet community needs. The Commonwealth Youth Service Awards Scheme recognises projects devised and run by young people which are of benefit to the local community and have potential long-term advantages.

The CYP provides an information service on youth programmes and policies. New legislation, policy pronouncements, training programmes, development projects, and the work of governmental and voluntary organisations are monitored and reported widely through the CYP *In Common* newsletter. The CYP regional centres contribute increasingly to the overall CYP information and publications programme.

To facilitate exchanges of experience and information between Commonwealth countries, the programme provides youth study fellowships to enable personnel working with young people or developing policies and programmes for young people to study youth projects and policies in other countries. Assistance is also offered for the planning, establishment and development of national youth programmes through consultancies and commissions.

The CYP is funded on a voluntary basis by Commonwealth governments. The governing body of the CYP is the ministerial-level Commonwealth Youth Affairs Council (CYAC) which comprises members from all Commonwealth countries and meets every three years. A youth caucus is an integral part of CYAC meetings and ensures the active participation of young people in the affairs of CYP. The 1992 meeting will be held in the Maldives.

Women and Development

The Women and Development Programme (WDP), part of the Human Resource Development Group (HRDG), aims at promoting the interests and advancement of women in the Commonwealth. It does so through multi-level activities, within the policy context provided by the Commonwealth Plan of Action on Women and Development, endorsed by Heads of Government in 1987.

The Programme carries out projects on training and policy development with financial assistance from the Commonwealth Fund for Technical Co-operation. Extension services assist member governments in their efforts to integrate women into national development and planning, and to provide training in gender planning techniques to Ministries with responsibility for Women's Affairs.

Training programmes in conservation techniques for rural women will promote the involvement of women in decision-making on the environment. Training manuals have also been developed to teach entrepreneurial skills to young women and to eliminate gender bias from school textbooks.

The Programme's work on women and structural adjustment aims to focus attention on the negative impacts of some structural adjustment policies upon women and to promote a broader approach by policy-makers which takes women's needs, interests and concerns into account. The Ottawa Declaration on Women and Structural Adjustment, which was adopted by Heads of Government in 1991, states Commonwealth principles on the issue and outlines a programme of action.

The Programme acts as a resource to other divisions of the Secretariat. It collaborates in projects, provides training in gender planning and offers advice and assistance to facilitate the pursuit of the Secretariat's policy on women and development as embodied in the Commonwealth Plan of Action.

The Programme is a focal point for information exchange and networking between women's national machineries, women's organisations, NGOs and intergovernmental bodies. A newsletter, *Link-In,* is published twice a year.

The Programme has organised three ministerial meetings. The first was held in Nairobi, Kenya, prior to the World Conference on the United Nations Decade for Women in 1985. A second ministerial meeting was held in Harare, Zimbabwe, in August 1987 and a third took place in Ottawa, Canada, in October 1990.

Development Co-operation

The Commonwealth Fund for Technical Co-operation (CFTC) is a multilateral development fund established in 1971 and administered by the Secretariat. It is an undertaking in mutual self-help, designed to meet the technical assistance needs of developing member countries, associated states, dependent territories and Commonwealth inter-governmental organisations and agencies.

The fund is financed by contributions from all member countries and its controlling board comprises one representative of each participating government. A committee of management with the Commonwealth Secretary-General as chairman supervises general operations and day-to-day management is the responsibility of the Managing Director.

The practical usefulness of the Fund is attested by the increasing demand for its services. Its expenditure has grown from £400,000 in 1971 to £30 million in 1991/92. Currently Canada and Britain provide the largest contributions, followed by Australia, Brunei Darussalam, New Zealand, India and Nigeria.

The CFTC was a pioneer of Technical Co-operation among Developing Countries (TCDC) and this principle illuminates all its work. The majority of its experts come from other developing countries;

most of its training takes place in developing countries, and the experience of one developing country is frequently adapted to the needs of another in its industrial, export or other development projects.

The CFTC provides assistance through five programmes: General Technical Assistance, Fellowships and Training, the Export Market Development Division, the Industrial Development, Unit and the Technical Assistance Group.

General Technical Assistance Programme

At the request of developing member government and regional organisations, this Programme provides experts, or at times consultant expertise, to complement and supplement available local human resources in fields of particular importance to development. The experts work in such areas as economic planning, transport, agriculture, public administration, environmental planning, tourism, legislative drafting, national accounting, statistics, and many others. Experts' assignments range from a few days up to 3 years or more; over 200 CFTC experts are in the field at any one time, and the majority come from other developing countries. Priority is given under the Programme to the needs of small states (about 70 per cent of experts are assigned to small states), the integration of women in the development process and environmental issues.

Each expert not only provides a link in the chain of development, but assists the country towards self-sufficiency by helping with training needs for nationals in his or her particular sphere of expertise. Experts under this Programme have, in addition to meeting normal development needs, been requested by governments at particularly critical times: Guyana, for instance, has called on the Fund's experts to assist in the Government's economic recovery programme; Namibia is receiving special support in its post-independence period, for restructuring its public service, training its expanding diplomatic corps and advising on educational development; while other governments have used its expertise to expand economic planning capabilities, revise and consolidate national legislation, establish and develop information technology systems, and advise on national housing and land use policies. Other international organisations, too, have called on the Fund's expertise in recruiting field experts.

Fellowships and Training Programme

This Programme of the CFTC, part of the Human Resource Development Group, funds training for government and parastatal officials as well as the private sector, in important developmental sectors in the training institutions of other developing countries. It also funds on-the-job training attachments and study visits by staff to countries which have relevant expertise or experience to offer. In 1990/91, it sponsored some 4,100 scholars and supported a further 600 at training seminars and workshops. About 33,000 people have received training awards in the past decade.

The Programme gives preference to middle-level training in those technical and vocational fields which are rated as most important by governments. These include institution-building, public administration and management, advanced technology, environment, entrepreneurship and business development, and sectoral programmes such as health, education and agriculture.

The CFTC supports South African victims of apartheid through the Nassau Fellowships Scheme, for study and short-term training in Commonwealth countries; to date over 500 South Africans have been helped by this scheme. The CFTC is also co-operating with the 'Skills for South Africa' NGO network in arranging training work placements for South Africans and is the major contributor to the Dar es Salaam-based South African Extension Unit under which some 3,000 exiles in Frontline States are undergoing distance education. It is currently considering post-apartheid human resource development including the possibility of training and placements both inside and outside South Africa.

Export Market Development Programme

This specialist programme was established in 1972 to provide technical assistance to help meet member governments' needs for export promotion mechanisms, market intelligence and marketing skills to enable them to compete successfully in the international market place and so earn foreign exchange to finance further economic development. It also complements the work in trade policy of the Economic Affairs Division.

The programme is geared to the specific needs of individual Commonwealth developing countries with widely varying export priorities and industrial infrastructure. The programme helps governments to establish or expand national export promotion bodies, increase production, and meet the standards and requirements of potential buyers through product development and adaptation. It explores new markets and the potential for the expansion of existing markets; and organises buyer-seller meets, contact promotion programmes, integrated marketing programmes, export business intensification programmes and other practical measures to find new buyers and consolidate existing markets for products of member countries.

The buyer-seller meets constitute a particularly important area of activity and provide practical sales and marketing assistance to individual businessmen in a number of member countries. Following intensive preparatory work, a buyer-seller meet provides a major showcase for a single country in an important export market. For example, meets have been held for India in Kuala Lumpur and Milan, for Sri Lanka in Sydney and Los Angeles, for Kenya in London and Tokyo and for Bangladesh, in Dubai,

Chicago and Toronto. The meets have resulted in multi-million dollar earnings for the participating countries in products ranging from textiles and knitwear to light engineering goods.

On a smaller scale, the contact promotion programmes were initiated by the Division to promote commercial contacts between a small group of exporters of one country with importers, wholesalers, retailers and distributors of another. The programmes usually deal with a single product group or small range of products and have been found to be especially useful in promoting contacts in markets which had not previously been tapped.

Another type of project developed by the Division is the Export Business Intensification Programme, which seeks to develop the fullest possible range of experts from one country to another by exploring all aspects of business opportunities, including joint venture possibilities.

The Integrated Marketing Programme aims to provide technical inputs with regard to export design, quality controls and export packaging for a particular product with export possibilities and to follow this up with an aggressive marketing strategy to promote exports from the assisted country to the target market.

The Export Market Development Programme also provides experts from the Commonwealth to help fellow member countries build exportable stocks and find new markets for a wide range of primary and manufactured products. With these experts and with carefully selected consultancy services, the Programme gives advice geared to the recipient country's industrial and infrastructural capacity, on such matters as product development, design and quality control, planning and management of export development and performance, strategies for market penetration and the development of areas leading to greater invisible foreign exchange earnings.

In pursuance of the Commonwealth Plan of Action on Women and Development, the Division initiated an Export Development Programme for women aimed at enhancing the participation of women in export development. The Programme has so far covered Ghana, Kenya, Nigeria and Mauritius in Africa, the Solomon Islands and Papua New Guinea in the Pacific and Jamaica in the Caribbean. The Programme is being extended to other developing member states.

The Division also organises conferences, seminars and symposia and commissions research on trade matters of specific importance to Commonwealth developing countries, such as the international trade in spices, tea and handicrafts, the Multi-Fibre Arrangement and the Generalised System of Preferences, the Multilateral Trade Negotiations and countertrade etc. These conferences, symposia and seminars have enabled developing member countries of the Commonwealth to exchange information and experience on aspects of international trade directly relevant to them and to seek common solutions to problems where appropriate. Training in the concepts and techniques of export marketing is also an important area of the Division's conference and seminar activities.

The Division's emphasis now includes in-house functional activities such as the Commonwealth Conference on Commercial Representation for the benefit of commercial representatives based in London held in June 1987, the Commonwealth Small States Exposition held in Canada in October 1987, an Advanced Programme on Export Market Development organised in India in 1990 and 1991 in collaboration with the Indian Institute of Foreign Trade, and the Commonwealth Roundtable on Export Development Strategies for the 1990s organised for the benefit of Heads of Export Promotion Organisations in London in March 1990. The latest in the series of these activities was the Commonwealth Conference on Commercial Representation in North America, held in Toronto in November 1990; it provided a high-level forum for in-depth discussions on important conceptual and practical aspects relating to the work of commercial representatives in the development of trade, investment, transfer of technology and tourism.

Another important activity recently undertaken by the Division is the publication of guidelines and handbooks for the use of policy-makers and exporters in developing countries. These include *Operational Guidelines for Commercial Representatives of Commonwealth Countries; Guidelines for Exporters of Avocados, Mangoes, Pineapples, Papayas and Passion Fruit to the UK market; Guidelines for Exporters of Selected Vegetables to the UK market; Guidelines for Exporters of Selected Fruits and Vegetables to the German market;* and *Guidelines for Exporters of Cut Flowers to the UK market.*

Industrial Development Unit

The Industrial Development Unit (IDU) provides consultancy services at the request of member governments and regional organisations for key aspects of industrialisation in the development of new industries, or for the reactivation, rehabilitation, expansion or diversification of existing manufacturing resources.

The range of IDU's services includes sector development programming, identification of industrial investment opportunities, preparation of feasibility studies, sourcing of technology and finance, implementation plans, specification of appropriate manufacturing facilities, plant and equipment selection, installation and commissioning, 'on-the-job' training and the promotion of investments.

The Unit also addresses the associated issues of industrial health and safety, pollution control and environmental protection, energy conservation and management.

These services are provided, mainly by its small inhouse professional team of engineers, managers, economists and financial analysts, complemented by external specialists in the full range of manufacturing activities.

With the emphasis on the development and promotion of small and medium-scale industries, special priority is given to the promotion of women entrepreneurs and to manufacturing activities owned, managed and employing women; to the least-developed and most disadvantaged countries; and to the rehabilitation and maintenance of existing manufacturing resources.

During the period 1989–91 IDU was involved with over 170 projects mainly in the categories of agro-industries and food processing, building materials and housing, textiles and clothing, engineering and metal working. A third of the projects assisted were for food and agro-based industries.

Features of IDU's technical assistance are the rapid response to government requests when necessary, and the very practical nature of the assistance in adapting appropriate technologies to suit specific needs to create sustainable industrial operations.

Technical Assistance Group

The Technical Assistance Group (TAG) is the in-house consulting unit of the Commonwealth Fund for Technical Co-operation (CFTC), created to respond quickly and effectively to requests from governments for independent, confidential advice and expertise in areas which have been identified over the years as national priorities. In general, the Group seeks to offer advice in the context of long-term relationships with government.

TAG is staffed by economists, lawyers and computer systems analysts who have considerable practical experience of policy-making and problem-solving in developing countries, and are also accustomed to operating in a commercial environment. TAG's strengths include its ability to field a team of international advisers in a variety of disciplines who are accustomed to working together as colleagues, and its freedom to join the government team at the negotiating table if required. Where highly specialised services are required, TAG makes use of external consultants.

The Group's track record, built up over more than two decades, and its close association with governments ensure a steady demand for its services. The principal areas of activity are natural resources development and macro-economic and financial management, including debt management. TAG's advice in the former area covers assistance in devising and negotiating legal frameworks and appropriate fiscal regimes for natural resources development, while assistance in the latter area includes the establishment of external debt recording and management systems based on TAG's own computer software, the Commonwealth Secretariat Debt Recording and Management System (CS-DRMS), and the formulation of borrowing policies and strategies.

TAG also has a Law of the Sea Programme under which it offers advice to governments on the delimitation of their maritime boundaries and on the negotiation of fisheries access agreements. In addition, TAG's experience with private investment in natural resources has enabled it to provide advice in other sectors where similar legal and economic issues are involved as well as in the promotion of private investment in general, and this has now become an important area of activity.

In the course of its work, TAG seeks to bring about a transfer of skills, and enhances this aspect of its technical assistance with training attachments and courses.

Enhanced Commonwealth Programme of Technical Assistance for Namibia

Since its establishment as a result of a decision of Heads of Government at Kuala Lumpur in October 1989, the Enhanced Commonwealth Programme of Technical Assistance for Namibia has continued to make good initial progress. Experts, provided in a broad range of sectors, have advised on such matters as the Constitution, the establishment of the Foreign Ministry, the restructuring of other ministries, aid coordination, housing, legal drafting, the establishment of a national forensic science laboratory, the media, minerals taxation, import management, the preparation of an indicative industrial plan, the establishment of an investment centre, fisheries development, rural development and the use of distance learning techniques to enhance education opportunities. Over 400 Namibian trainees have been supported in 15 countries in such fields as agriculture, banking, education, environment management, health, marine fisheries, maritime administration and a variety of technical fields. Study visits have been arranged so that Namibian officials can benefit from other Commonwealth countries' experience in rural and agricultural development, managing food systems, game utilization and conservation, hunting laws and tourism. Funds received to date total over £3 million from twelve donors and it is anticipated that the target of £2.5 to £3 million will be achieved. The Namibian Government has expressed its warm appreciation for the assistance which has already been made available and looks forward to its continuation for the remainder of the five-year Programme.

Special Commonwealth Fund for Mozambique

The CFTC manages the Special Commonwealth Fund for Mozambique. This was established in 1987 in recognition of this non-Commonwealth country's special needs and its key position in the Southern African region, largely comprising Commonwealth members, which has suffered from destabilisation by apartheid South Africa and dependency on the apartheid economy. The Fund, which is voluntary, stood at £6.8 million at March 1992, with 17 Commonwealth countries contributing; Australia is the largest contributor. It draws on the whole range of CFTC expertise to promote the development and reconstruction of Mozambique. By March 1992 project disbursements totalled £4.85 million.

The Mozambique Government has named transport, communications and agriculture as priorities for Commonwealth assistance, together with institutional and human resource development. To help develop market structures, Mozambique also draws on the CFTC's specialised programmes in natural resource development, economic and financial management export marketing and industrial rehabilitation and development. The Commonwealth has also been helping Mozambique prepare for multi-party elections.

This assistance provides an integrated response to Mozambique's needs in two major areas. While the CFTC's core technical assistance and training programmes develop skills and institutional capacity, the specialised programmes focus on the productive sector. Efforts are made to ensure that programmes are mutually reinforcing, paying particular attention to counterpart training.

Commonwealth Foundation

Marlborough House, Pall Mall, London SW1Y 5HY
(071-930 3783)

Director
'Inoke Faletau

The Foundation was established in 1966 and registered as a charity in English law, following a decision by Commonwealth Heads of Government at their meeting in London in 1965, to promote closer professional co-operation within the Commonwealth. In February 1983 the Foundation was reconstituted as an international organisation, retaining the objects, autonomous character and organisational arrangements in broadly the same terms as approved earlier, with expanded terms of reference. The Foundation is funded by its Member Governments. The target income is currently £1.7 million.

It makes grants for attendance at small conferences and workshops and for study visits and training attachments within the Commonwealth; provides financial support to Commonwealth professional associations and professional centres; funds short-term fellowship schemes, in co-operation with other organisations, to promote Commonwealth understanding, mid-career training and the widening of professional experience in fields such as agriculture, planning, health, the media and culture; and makes grants to facilitate the flow of professional information through the distribution of publications.

In pursuance of its enlarged mandate from Commonwealth Heads of Government the Foundation has been promoting better understanding of the work carried out by the non-governmental organisations and encouraging the strengthening of information links through facilitating the establishment of NGO Commonwealth liaison units in each Commonwealth country.

Commonwealth Institute

Kensington High Street, London W8 6NQ
(071-603 4535) (Fax: 071-602 7374)

Chairman of Governors
R A Fyjis-Walker, CMG, CVO

Director General
S Cox

Director of Education
G Brandt

The Commonwealth Institute is an educational and cultural agency, set up by Act of Parliament and with all High Commissioners on its Governing Body, to promote awareness of the contemporary Commonwealth.

Its centre in Kensington runs a continuous programme of events for the general visitor, specialists and school children, often built round a single theme (eg Commonwealth Africa in 1984, the Commonwealth Caribbean in 1986 and the Commonwealth Pacific in 1988). Special attractions include seminars for secondary school students, geared to the School Curriculum, and traditional festivals for middle and primary school pupils. There are three floors of permanent exhibitions on the Commonwealth countries and two temporary exhibition spaces which give opportunities for young Commonwealth artists to display their work and for a wide range of thematic exhibitions to be presented. There is a Curriculum Development and Resources Section which works with teachers and pupils on schemes arising from the National Curriculum. The Commonwealth Resource Centre provides information about the Commonwealth and its member countries and supplies books and audio-visual resources for use by teachers and educators. COMPIX, the commercial picture library, provides photographs of Commonwealth countries. There is also a craft, gift and book shop and a restaurant at the Institute. All the Institute facilities, including the theatre, which can be used for conferences, are available for hire.

'What's On', the Institute's bimonthly listing of events is obtainable for an annual subscription of £5.00. Three times a year it also publishes a 'Schools Programme' which is issued free to educational institutions. The Regional Development Section of the Education Division coordinates a significant outreach programme, providing speakers and in-service support for British schools, and the Institute works closely with other Commonwealth and international bodies.

As part of its regionalisation programme, the Institute opened its first regional centre in Bradford on 26th September 1991.

The Institute building is open to the public from 10 am to 5 pm Monday to Saturday, and from 2 pm to 5 pm on Sundays.

A 'Friends' organisation offers benefits in return for an annual membership subscription, and an opportunity to become involved with social events as well as unique study holidays around the world.

The Institute administers a limited fellowship programme in its fields of expertise on behalf of the Commonwealth and Nuffield Foundations.

Commonwealth Institute, Scotland

8 Rutland Square, Edinburgh EH1 2AS
(031-229 6668) Fax: (031-229-6041)

Chairman
Sir Mark Russell, KCMG

Director
C G Carrol

Assistant Director
W N Henderson

Founded in 1956, the Commonwealth Institute, Scotland operates independently of the Commonwealth Institute, London though within the broad policy of its board of governors.

The Institute aims to foster the interests of the Commonwealth and its members by providing information and education services throughout the Scottish education system via conferences, seminars, exhibitions, publications and other related activities.

Commonwealth Parliamentary Association

Secretariat, 7 Old Palace Yard, Westminster, London SW1P 3JY
(071-219 4666 or 799 1460) Fax: (071-222 6073)

President of the Association: Hon Darrell Rolle, MP, Minister of National Security and Leader of the House, The Bahamas.

Chairman of the Executive Committee: Hon Clive E Griffiths, MLC, President of the Legislative Council, Western Australia.

Secretary-General
Hon David Tonkin

An association of parliamentarians, the CPA aims to promote understanding and co-operation among the members of its 121 branches in national and state/provincial legislatures in the Commonwealth, to strengthen parliamentary institutions, and to promote studies in this field.

The Association seeks to meet these goals through annual plenary conferences, regional conferences, parliamentary seminars and the publication of a quarterly journal, *The Parliamentarian*, and regular newsletters on parliamentary and Association affairs. An information service is also offered to members, parliaments, governments and interested students of the parliamentary system.

The principal event in the CPA calendar is the Commonwealth Parliamentary Conference. The 1990 Conference was held in Zimbabwe, the 1991 Conference in India and the 1992 Conference will be held in The Bahamas.

The Association is an organization of parliaments, rather than governments, and its members reflect all shades of political opinion. The annual conference is therefore a unique opportunity for parliamentarians, be they ministers or backbenchers, government or opposition, party representatives or independents, to exchange views on the major political issues of the day and on the systems they use to conduct public business. They are therefore better able to understand the political policies of other nations and the effect of their own policies in the international community, and better able to assess their own parliamentary systems in light of practices and procedures used elsewhere.

The CPA was founded in 1911 as the Empire Parliamentary Association during a visit to London of Dominion MPs at the time of the coronation of King George V. The Association evolved into the CPA in 1948 and celebrated its 75th anniversary in 1986.

Each Branch of the Association is autonomous and equal with all others, regardless of size. Presiding Officers normally serve as Branch Presidents, while the leaders of parliamentary parties usually act as Vice-Presidents. The Clerk of the House customarily performs the duties of Branch Secretary.

CPA affairs are managed by an international committee of parliamentarians, representing each of the eight regions of the Commonwealth, who report to an annual General Assembly. The day-to-day operations are the responsibility of the Secretary-General and an international staff of 11.

Further information may be obtained from the Secretary-General.

Marlborough House

At the Commonwealth Economic Conference in Montreal in September 1958 the British Government offered to provide, for the many Commonwealth activities and meetings which are held in London, suitable premises which might be regarded as a Commonwealth centre. This suggestion was welcomed by the Conference and in February 1959 the Prime Minister announced in the House of Commons that Her Majesty The Queen, who had shown a close personal interest in this project, had placed her Palace of Marlborough House at the disposal of the Government so that it might be available for this purpose.

Few structural alterations were needed but some adjustment and modernisation was required to adapt the building to its new purpose, and new furnishings and equipment were installed. The initial cost of adapting the building was met by the British Government, which also bears the cost of maintenance. The Governments of the twelve countries, then members of the Commonwealth, each presented six chairs for the main conference room.

On 28th March 1962 Marlborough House came into use as a Commonwealth centre.

At their meeting in 1965, Commonwealth Heads of Government decided on the establishment of a body to service The Commonwealth as a whole; as a result in 1966 the Commonwealth Secretariat was formed, and was offered the regular use of parts of Marlborough House as its Headquarters. The Commonwealth Foundation, also established in 1966, is quartered in a wing of the House. The State Rooms on the ground floor, with certain ancillary offices and two conference rooms on the first floor are kept available to accommodate Commonwealth conferences.

Marlborough House stands to the east of St. James's Palace, between the Mall and Pall Mall. Parts of Marlborough House are being renovated in stages, this is expected to take some time. During this time, the occupants are temporarily accommodated in premises in Carlton Gardens. The postal address of the Commonwealth Secretariat, however, continues to be Marlborough House and the cable address, telephone and fax numbers are unchanged.

Commonwealth Membership of United Nations Bodies and Specialised Agencies

	PRINCIPAL ORGANS OF THE UNITED NATIONS	General Assembly	Security Council	Economic and Social Council	Trusteeship Council	International Court of Justice	FUNCTIONAL COMMISSIONS OF ECONOMIC AND SOCIAL COUNCIL	Commission on Human Rights	Commission on Narcotic Drugs	Commission on the Status of Women	Population Commission	Commission for Social Development	Statistical Commission	Sub-Commission on Prevention of Discrimination and Protection of Minorities
Antigua and Barbuda		A												
Australia		A		B				B	B					
Bahamas		A							B	B				
Bangladesh		A		B				B		B	B			
Barbados		A												
Belize		A												
Botswana		A		B							B			
Britain		A	A	B	A	C		B	B		B		B	D
Brunei		A												
Canada		A		B				B		B			B	
Cyprus		A						B		B		B		
Dominica		A												
The Gambia		A						B	B					
Ghana		A						B	B	B		B	B	
Grenada		A												
Guyana		A				C								
India		A	B	B				B		B				D
Jamaica		A		B						B			B	
Kenya		A						B					B	
Kiribati														
Lesotho		A						B						
Malawi		A												
Malaysia		A		B					B	B				
Maldives		A												
Malta		A										B		
Mauritius		A												
Namibia		A												
Nauru*														
New Zealand		A												
Nigeria		A				C		B		B		B		D
Pakistan		A		B				B		B	B	B	B	
Papua New Guinea		A												
St Christopher & Nevis		A												
St Lucia		A												
St Vincent		A												
Seychelles		A												
Sierra Leone		A												
Singapore		A												
Solomon Islands		A												
Sri Lanka		A				C		B						
Swaziland		A		B										
Tanzania		A								B				
Tonga														
Trinidad & Tobago		A		B										
Tuvalu*														
Uganda		A								B	B	B		
Vanuatu		A												
Western Samoa		A												
Zambia		A						B		B	B		B	
Zimbabwe		A	B							B				

A Permanent Member. B Elected Member. C National as Judge. D National as Member. *Special Member of the Commonwealth.

	REGIONAL ECONOMIC COMMISSIONS	Economic Commission for Africa	Economic & Social Commission for Asia & the Pacific	Economic Commission for Europe	Economic Commission for Latin America and the Caribbean	SPECIALISED AGENCIES, the IAEA and GATT	Food and Agriculture Organisation (FAO)	FAO Council	General Agreement on Tariffs and Trade (GATT)	International Atomic Energy Agency (IAEA)	IAEA Board of Governors
Antigua and Barbuda					A		A		A		
Australia			A				A	B	A	A	B
Bahamas					A		A		†		
Bangladesh			A				A		A	A	
Barbados					A		A		A		
Belize					A		A		A		
Botswana		A					A		A		
Britain			A	A	A		A	B	A	A	B
Brunei			A						†		
Canada				A	A		A	B	A	A	B
Cyprus				A			A		A	A	
Dominica					A		A		†		
The Gambia		A					A		A		
Ghana		A					A	B	A	A	B
Grenada					A		A		†		
Guyana					A		A		A		
India			A				A	B	A	A	B
Jamaica					A		A		A	A	
Kenya		A					A	B	A	A	
Kiribati			A						†		
Lesotho		A					A		A		
Malawi		A					A		A		
Malaysia			A				A		A	A	B
Maldives			A				A		A		
Malta				A			A		A		
Mauritius		A					A		A	A	
Namibia		A					A			A	
Nauru			A								
New Zealand			A				A		A	A	
Nigeria		A					A		A	A	
Pakistan			A				A	B	A	A	B
Papua New Guinea			A				A		†		
St Christopher & Nevis					A		A		†		
St Lucia					A		A		†		
St Vincent					A		A		†		
Seychelles		A					A		†		
Sierra Leone		A					A		A	A	
Singapore			A						A	A	
Solomon Islands			A				A		†		
Sri Lanka			A				A		A	A	
Swaziland		A					A		†		
Tanzania		A					A		A	A	
Tonga			A				A		†		
Trinidad & Tobago					A		A	B	A		
Tuvalu			A						†		
Uganda		A					A		A	A	
Vanuatu			A				A				
Western Samoa			A				A				
Zambia		A					A	B	A	A	
Zimbabwe		A					A		A	A	

A Permanent Member. B Elected Member. C Associate Member.

†Applying GATT *de facto* pending final decision as to their future commercial policy.

	International Bank for Reconstruction and Development (IBRD)	International Civil Aviation Organisation (ICAO)	ICAO Council	International Development Association (IDA)	International Finance Corporation (IFC)	International Fund for Agricultural Development (IFAD)	IFAD Executive Board	International Labour Organisation (ILO)	ILO Governing Body	International Maritime Organisation (IMO)	IMO Council	International Monetary Fund (IMF)	IMF Executive Directors	International Telecommunication Union (ITU)
Antigua and Barbuda	A	A			A	A		A		A		A		A
Australia	A	A	B	A	A	A		A	B	A	B	A	D	A
Bahamas	A	A			A			A		A	B	A	A	
Bangladesh	A	A		A	A	A		A	B	A		A		A
Barbados	A	A			A	A		A		A		A		A
Belize	A	A		A	A	A		A		A		A		A
Botswana	A	A		A	A	A		A				A		A
Britain	A	A	B	A	A	A	E	A	A	A	B	A	D	A
Brunei		A								A				A
Canada	A	A	B	A	A	A	E	A	B	A	B	A	D	A
Cyprus	A	A		A	A	A		A		A	B	A		A
Dominica	A			A	A	A		A		A		A		
The Gambia	A	A		A	A	A		A		A		A		A
Ghana	A	A	B	A	A	A		A		A		A		A
Grenada	A	A		A	A	A		A				A		A
Guyana	A	A		A	A	A		A		A		A		A
India	A	A	B	A	A	A	E	A	A	A	B	A	D	A
Jamaica	A	A			A	A		A		A		A		A
Kenya	A	A		A	A	A		A	F	A		A		A
Kiribati	A	A		A	A							A		A
Lesotho	A	A		A	A	A	B	A	B			A	D	A
Malawi	A	A		A	A	A		A	F	A		A		A
Malaysia	A	A		A	A	A		A	F	A		A		A
Maldives	A	A		A	A	A		A		A		A		A
Malta	A	A				A		A	F	A		A		A
Mauritius	A	A		A	A	A		A		A		A		A
Namibia	A				A	A		A				A		A
Nauru		A												A
New Zealand	A	A		A	A	A		A	F	A		A	E	A
Nigeria	A	A	B	A	A	A	B	A	B	A	B	A		A
Pakistan	A	A	B	A	A	A	B	A	F	A	B	A	E	A
Papua New Guinea	A	A		A	A	A		A		A		A		A
St Christopher & Nevis	A			A		A						A		
St Lucia	A	A		A	A	A		A		A		A		
St Vincent	A	A		A		A				A		A		A
Seychelles	A	A			A	A		A		A		A		
Sierra Leone	A	A		A	A	A		A		A		A		A
Singapore	A	A			A			A		A		A		A
Solomon Islands	A	A		A	A	A		A		A		A		A
Sri Lanka	A	A		A	A	A		A		A		A	E	A
Swaziland	A	A		A	A	A		A				A		A
Tanzania	A	A	B	A	A	A		A		A		A		A
Tonga	A	A		A	A	A						A		A
Trinidad & Tobago	A	A	B	A	A	A		A		A		A		A
Tuvalu														
Uganda	A	A		A	A	A	B	A				A		A
Vanuatu	A	A		A	A					A		A		A
Western Samoa	A			A	A	A						A		A
Zambia	A	A		A	A	A		A				A	E	A
Zimbabwe	A	A		A	A	A		A				A		A

A Permanent Member. B Elected Member. D Executive Director.
E Alternate Director/Member. F Deputy Member.

	ITU Administrative Council	UN Educational Scientific and Cultural Organisation (UNESCO)	UNESCO Executive Board	Universal Postal Union (UPU)	UPU Executive Council	World Health Organisation (WHO)	WHO Executive Board	World Intellectual Property Organisation (WIPO)	World Meteorological Organisation (WMO)	WMO Executive Council	United Nations Conference on Trade and Development (UNCTAD)*	United Nations Children's Fund (UNICEF) Executive Board	United Nations Development Programme (UNDP) Governing Council†
Antigua and Barbuda		A		E		A			A		C		
Australia	B	A		A	B	A		A	A	C	B	B	
Bahamas		A		A	B	A	B	A	A		C		
Bangladesh		A		A		A		A	A		A		
Barbados		A		A		A		A	A		C	B	
Belize		A		A					A		C		
Botswana		A		A		A			A		A		
Britain				A	B	A		A	A	D	B	B	B
Brunei				A		A			A		A		
Canada	B	A	B	A	B	A		A	A	D	B	B	B
Cyprus		A		A		A		A	A		B		
Dominica		A		A		A			A		C		
The Gambia		A	B	A		A		A	A		A		B
Ghana		A		A		A		A	A		A		B
Grenada		A		A		A					C		
Guyana		A		A		A			A		C		B
India	B	A	B	A		A		A	A	D	A	B	B
Jamaica	B	A		A		A		A	A		C	B	
Kenya	B	A		A	B	A		A	A	D	A		
Kiribati		A		A		A							
Lesotho		A		A		A		A	A		A		B
Malawi		A		A		A		A	A	D	A		
Malaysia	B	A		A		A		A	A		A		B
Maldives		A		A		A	B		A		A		
Malta		A		A		A		A	A		B		
Mauritius		A		A		A		A	A		A		
Namibia		A		E		A			A		A		
Nauru				A									
New Zealand		A		A	B	A		A	A		B		B
Nigeria	B	A		A	B	A	B	A	A	D	A		B
Pakistan	B	A		A	B	A		A	A		A	B	B
Papua New Guinea		A	B	A		A	B		A		A		
St Christopher & Nevis		A		A		A					C		
St Lucia		A		A		A			A		C		B
St Vincent		A		A		A					C		B
Seychelles		A		A		A	B		A		A		
Sierra Leone		A		A		A	B	A	A		A	B	
Singapore				A		A		A	A	G	A		
Solomon Islands				A		A			A		A		
Sri Lanka		A		A		A		A	A		A	B	B
Swaziland		A		A		A		A	A		A		
Tanzania	B	A	B	A	B	A		A	A		A	B	
Tonga		A		A		A					A		
Trinidad & Tobago		A		A		A		A	A		C		
Tuvalu		A		A									
Uganda		A		A		A		A	A		A		
Vanuatu				A		A			A		A		
Western Samoa		A		A		A					A		
Zambia		A		A	B	A		A	A		A		
Zimbabwe		A		A	B	A		A	A		A	B	B

A Permanent Member. B Elected Member. C Elected Vice President. D Executive Director. G Regional. President. H Secretary-General.

*The UNCTAD groupings are mainly regional: A = Afro Asian States; B = Western European and Other States; C = Latin American & Caribbean States; D = Eastern European States.

†Participation in the Programme (UNDP) is open to any State member of the UN, its specialised agencies and the IAEA.

E Status within the UPU has not yet been regularised.

The British Government is responsible for the international relations of the British Dependent Territories. Some are members of the specialised agencies and United Nations Regional Economic Commissions, viz:

Economic and Social Commission for Asia and the Pacific—Hong Kong (Associate Member).

Economic Commission for Latin America and the Caribbean—Anguilla, British Virgin Islands, Montserrat (Associate Members).

IMO—Hong Kong (Associate Member).

ITU and UPU—Collective Member (known as 'Overseas territories for the international relations of which the Government of the UK is responsible').

UNESCO—British Virgin Islands (Associate Member).

WMO—Territories or groups of territories on behalf of which the *WMO* Convention is applied under Article 3(d) or 3(e) of the Convention: Hong Kong, British Caribbean Dependent Territories.

The British Government may also, when appropriate, include territorial representatives in United Kingdom delegations at meetings of agencies which do not provide for direct territorial representation.

Each member country of the IBRD appoints one Governor. Most of the authority of the Board of Governors for each institution in the World Bank Group (IBRD, IDA, IFC) is delegated to the Executive Directors. Each of the five largest share holders (Japan, Britain, France, Germany, United States of America) appoints a single Executive Director; the remaining 15 Executive Directors are elected for two-year terms. Each Director appoints his own alternate.

Commonwealth Membership of Regional Organisations (Other Than United Nations Bodies)

	GROUP OF 77	NON-ALIGNED	OPEC	ISLAMIC CONFERENCE ORG.	OAU	OAS	RIO TREATY	ASEAN	EC	ACP	OECD	NATO	SOUTH PACIFIC FORUM
Antigua and Barbuda	X					X				X			
Australia											X		X
Bahamas	X	X				X	X			X			
Bangladesh	X	X		X									
Barbados	X	X				X				X			
Belize	X	X				X				X			
Botswana	X	X			X					X			
Britain									X		X	X	
Brunei	X			X				X					
Canada						X					X	X	
Cyprus	X	X											
Dominica	X					X				X			
The Gambia	X	X		X	X					X			
Ghana	X	X			X					X			
Grenada	X	X				X				X			
Guyana	X	X				X				X			
India	X	X											
Jamaica	X	X				X				X			
Kenya	X	X			X					X			
Kiribati										X			X
Lesotho	X	X			X					X			
Malawi	X	X			X					X			
Malaysia	X	X		X				X					
Maldives	X	X		X									
Malta	X	X											
Mauritius	X	X			X					X			
Namibia	X	X			X					X			
Nauru													X
New Zealand											X		X
Nigeria	X	X	X	X	X					X			
Pakistan	X	X		X									
Papua New Guinea	X									X			X
St Christopher & Nevis	X					X				X			
St Lucia	X	X				X				X			
St Vincent	X					X				X			
Seychelles	X	X			X					X			
Sierra Leone	X	X		X	X					X			
Singapore	X	X						X					
Solomon Islands	X									X			X
Sri Lanka	X	X											
Swaziland	X	X			X					X			
Tanzania	X	X			X					X			
Tonga	X									X			X
Trinidad & Tobago	X	X				X	X			X			
Tuvalu										X			X
Uganda	X	X		X	X					X			
Vanuatu	X	X								X			X
Western Samoa	X									X			X
Zambia	X	X			X					X			
Zimbabwe	X	X			X					X			

Diplomatic Representation

Non-Commonwealth Representation in Commonwealth Countries

× Full representation by resident Ambassador

○ Non-resident representation

△ Honorary Consul

■ Consul-General

‡ Chargé d'Affaires

□ Honorary Consul-General

● Resident Representative

∇ Vice Consul

Country: / Represented in	Antigua & Barbuda	Australia	Bahamas	Bangladesh	Barbados	Belize	Botswana	Britain	Brunei Darussalam	Canada	Cyprus	Dominica	The Gambia	Ghana	Grenada	Guyana	India	Jamaica	Kenya	Kiribati	Lesotho	Malawi	Malaysia	Maldives	Malta	Mauritius	Namibia	Nauru	New Zealand	Nigeria	Pakistan	Papua New Guinea	St Christopher-Nevis	St Lucia	St Vincent & The Gren	Seychelles	Sierra Leone	Singapore	Solomon Is	Sri Lanka	Swaziland	Tanzania	Tonga	Trinidad & Tobago	Tuvalu	Uganda	Vanuatu	Western Samoa	Zambia	Zimbabwe
Afghanistan				++				×						○			×														++									○										×
Albania				○						○									×						○		○			○	○									○									○	○
Algeria		×			○		○	×		×	○		○	×		○	×	○	×		○	○	○		○	○			○	×	×						○	○		○	○	×		○		×	○		×	×
Andorra																																																		
Angola							++	×																	○		×			×												×					○		×	×
Argentina	○	×	○		○		○	×		×	○			○	○	○	○	×	×				×		○	○			○	×	×			○	○			×		○				●					○	×
Austria	○	×	◁	○	◁	○	○	×	○	×	○		◁	○	○	○	×	◁	×		○	○	×		◁	○	◁		◁	×	×	◁					○	×		◁	◁	○		○		○	○		×	×
Bahrain								×		◁																																								
Belgium	○	×	◁	×	◁	○	○	×	○	×	○	×	◁	○	○	◁	×	×	×	○	◁	◁	×	○	○	○	○	○	×	×	×				○	□	◁	×	○	×	◁	×	○	○		○	○	○	×	×
Benin								◁		×				×			○													×																				
Bhutan				×													×							○							○																			
Bolivia	○	◁						×		×								++					×										○					○												
Brazil	○	×	○	×	×	○	○	×	○	×	○		○	×	○	×	×	×	×		○		×		◁	○	×		○	×	×		○	○	○		○	×		○	○	●		×		○	○		++	×
Bulgaria		■		×			○	×		×	×		×	×		○	×			○	○			×	○					×						○	○			○					○				×	×
Burkina				○				◁		×				×			○													×	○						○													
Burma		×		×				×									×						×	○		○			○	○	×							○		×							○			
Burundi								◁		×									×																							×				×			○	○
Cambodia																	×														○																			
Cameroon								×		×			○	○					×											×							○					○					○		○	
Cape Verde													○																																				○	
C. African Rep.								○		○				○																×	○																			
Chad								○		○																				×							○													
Chile		×		○				×	○	×			○		○		×		×	○			○		○	○		○	×	○	○	○						×		○	○		○				○	○		
China	++	×		×	×	×	×	×		×	×		++	×		×	×	×	×	++			×	×	×	×	×	○	×	×	×	×		○		++	×	×		×	×	×		×		×	×	×	×	×
Colombia	○	×	○		×			×		×	○				○	++	■	×	×						++				○	○			○	○	○			○						×						
Comoros										○															○	○				○								◁												
Congo								◁		○																	×			○																				○
Costa Rica	○	◁			×	×		×		×							○	×	◁						○															○				○						
Côte d'Ivoire								×		×			◁	×					○											×							++					○				○	○		○	
Cuba		×	○	○	○	○	○	×		×	×			×		×	×	++			○		○	○	○	○	×			×	++						×			×		×		○		×	○		×	×
Czechoslovakia		×		++	○		○	×		×	×			×		○	×	○	×		○		×	×	×				++	×	×						○	○		×		×				○			×	×
Denmark	◁	×	◁	++	◁	◁	▷	×	○	×	○		◁	×	○	◁	×	□	×		◁	○	×		○	◁	++		○	×	×	◁		○	○	◁	▷	×		○	◁	×	○	○		×	○		×	×
Djibouti								○		○									×																			○												
Dominican Rep.		◁	◁		◁			◁		◁	○					○		■																										○						
Ecuador		●			◁			×		◁							○	◁											○															○						

Represented in	Antigua & Barbuda	Australia	Bahamas	Bangladesh	Barbados	Belize	Botswana	Britain	Brunei Darussalam	Canada	Cyprus	Dominica	The Gambia	Ghana	Grenada	Guyana	India	Jamaica	Kenya	Kiribati	Lesotho	Malawi	Malaysia	Maldives	Malta	Mauritius	Namibia	Nauru	New Zealand	Nigeria	Pakistan	Papua New Guinea	St Christopher-Nevis	St Lucia	St Vincent & The Gren	Seychelles	Sierra Leone	Singapore	Solomon Is	Sri Lanka	Swaziland	Tanzania	Tonga	Trinidad & Tobago	Tuvalu	Uganda	Vanuatu	Western Samoa	Zambia	Zimbabwe
Egypt, Arab Rep of		×		×			○	×	○	×	×		○	×	○	○	×	○	×		○	×	×	○	×	×	×	○	○	×	×	○					×	×		×	○	×		○		×		○	×	×
El Salvador						■		×		×																			△									○												
Equatorial Guinea								○		○				○																×																				
Ethiopia		○		○				×		×				×			×		×		○		○							×							○			○		○				○			○	×
Fiji		×						×		○							○			○			×					○	×			△						○					○		○		○	○		
Finland		×		○	□		○	×	○	×	○			○		△	×	△	×			○	×		○	△	×		○	×	‡	△				○		○		×		×		○		○			×	○
France	△	×	△	×	△	○	▽	×	×	×	×	○	△	×	△	△	×	×	×	○	○	×	×	○	×	×	×	○	×	×	×	×	○	×	△	×		×	○	×	○	×	△	×		×	‡	○	×	×
Gabon								×		×				○					△											×																			○	
Germany	△	×	△	×	△	○	×	×	×	×	×		○	×	○	△	×	×	×	○	×	×	×	○	×	○	×	○	×	×	×	×	△	△	△	○		×	△	×	○	×	△	×	○	×	○	○	×	×
Greece	○	×	△	○	○		○	×	○	×	×			○	○	○	×	○	×	○	○	○	○	○	○	○		○	○	×	×	△		○		○	△	○	○	○	○	○	○	○		○	○		■	×
Guatemala		○						×		×								△																										○						
Guinea							○	○		○	○		○	×		○	○	○			○	○	○		○	○				×	○						×			○	○			○		○			○	○
Guinea-Bissau								△		○			■						○																		○													
Haiti		△	‡		△	‡				×								‡												○														○						
Holy See	○	×	○	×	○	○		×		×	×			×	○		×	○	×		○	○			×	○			×	×	×	×						○	○	×		×		○		×			×	×
Honduras		○				×		×		×	○							□							△													○												
Hungary		×		‡	○		○	×		×	×			×		○	×	○	‡				○	○	○				○	×	×						○	○		○		×		○		○			○	×
Iceland		△	△		○			×		○	□						□		○				×	○	△				□	○	○							□				○								
Indonesia		×	○	×				×	×	×			○	○			×	○	×	○			×	○	○	○	‡		×	×	×	×						×	○	×		×		○				○	○	×
Iran		×		×				×	○	×	×		○	×		○	×		×				×	○	○	○	×		×	×	×						×	○		×		×		○					‡	×
Iraq	○	×		×		‡	○		○	×	○		○	○	○	○	×	○	×		○		×	○	○	○			○	×	×			○	○			○	○	×		×		○					×	×
Ireland		×						×	○	×	○			△			×		△		■		×		○				○	×							□	○				●							‡	○
Israel	○	×	△		△	○		×		×	×				○		●	×	×	○	○	×			○				×			○	○	○	○			×			×		○	○				○		
Italy	○	×	△	×	△	○	○	×	○	×	×		○	×	○	△	×	△	×		○	○	×	○	×	○	×		×	×	×	△			○	△	×	×	○	×	△	×	○	○		×	○		×	×
Japan	○	×	△	×	△	○	○	×	×	×	○		○	×	○	△	×	‡	×	○	○	○	×	○	○	○	○	○	×	×	×	×	○	○	○	○	△	×	‡	×	○	×	○	×	○	○	○	○	×	×
Jordan		×		○				×	○	×	○						×	△	△				○	○	○					○	×									○										
Korea, DPR					○		○						○	×		×	×	×				○	×	○	○	○	×	○		×	×			○		○	×	×		○		×		○		×	○		×	×
Korea, Rep. of	○	×	△	×	○	○	○	×	×	×			△	×	○	○	×	×	×	△	○	×	×	○	○	×	×	○	×	×	×	×	○	○	○		×	×	○	×	×		△	×		×	○	○		
Kuwait				×				×	○					○			×		‡				×	○	‡					○	×						○			○							○			
Laos		×						○		○							×						○						○		○									○										
Lebanon		×				△		×		×	×		△	×			×	□	△				○						○	×	×						×			○				○						
Liberia		△						×		×			△	×				▽	×		○				□					×							×	○				○		○					○	
Libya				‡			×			○	×			×			×						×	○	×		‡			×	×									×		×				×	○		×	×
Liechtenstein																																																		
Luxembourg		△						×		○							○		△				×		△													△												
Madagascar		△						△		×									△							×										△	△	○											○	

Represented in	Mali	Mauritania	Mexico	Monaco	Mongolia	Morocco	Mozambique	Nepal	Netherlands	Nicaragua	Niger	Norway	Oman	Panama	Paraguay	Peru	Philippines	Poland	Portugal	Qatar	Romania	Russia	Rwanda	San Marino	Sao Tomé & Prin.	Saudi Arabia	Senegal	Somalia	South Africa	Spain	Sudan	Surinam	Sweden	Switzerland	Syria	Taiwan
Antigua & Barbuda			○						○			○				○			○											○			○	○	○	
Australia			×	△	○	△		△	×	△		×	○	○		×	×	×	×	○	■	×				×	○		×	×			×	×	□	
Bahamas			△	△					△			△				△	○													△			△	△		×
Bangladesh	○				○	×		×	×	○		○	○				×	×		‡	×	×				×	○						×	‡		
Barbados			△						△			△				○			○								○			○		○	△	○		
Belize			×						○	○		○		×																○				○		×
Botswana						○	○		△			■						○	○		○	×						○		○			×	△		
Britain	○		×		×	×	×	×	×	×	○	×	×	×	×	×	×	×	×	×	×	×	○		△	×	×	×	×	×	×		×	×	×	
Brunei Darussalam	○	○						○	○		○	○	‡			○	×									○				○			○	○		
Canada	×	○	×	□	○	×	○	○	×	×	×	×	○	○	○	×	×	×	×	○	×	×	×	□	△	×	×	×	×	×	×	○	×	×	○	
Cyprus			○		○			○	○			○						○	○		×	×								○			○	×	×	
Dominica									△																											‡
The Gambia	△	■	○			○			△			△							○		○	○					×	○		○			△	○		
Ghana	×	○							×		×	○				○	○	×	○		‡	×				‡	○	○		×	○		○	×		
Grenada									△					○					○											○			△	○		×
Guyana			○						△	○		○		○		○		○	○		○	×								○		×	△	○		
India	○		×	○	×	×		×	×	×	○	×	×	×		×	×	×	×	×	×	×	○	□		×	×	×		×	×		×	×	×	
Jamaica			×						‡	○		△		‡		△	○	○			○	×								×		○	△	□		
Kenya	○		×			×	○	○	×		○	×				×	×	×	×		○	×	×			‡	○	×		×	×		×	×		
Kiribati									○							○			○			○														
Lesotho							○		△	○		○							○		○	×								○			‡	○		×
Malawi							×		○			○							○										×	○			○	○		×
Malaysia	○		○		○	×		×	×			×	×			○	×	×	○	○	×	×				×	○	○		×	○		×	×	○	
Maldives								○	○			○					○			○		○				○				○			○	○	○	
Malta	○		○	□		○		○	○			○	○	○			○	○	○	○	○	×				○	○			×	○		○	○	○	
Mauritius			○				○	○	○			△	○					○	○			×								○	○		○	○	○	
Namibia												×							×		×	×	○						‡	×	×		×	■		
Nauru									○										○			○														■
New Zealand	○		○		○			○	×	○		○	○			△	×	‡	○	○		×				○				○			×	×		
Nigeria	○	×	○		○	×		○	×		×	×	○				×	×	×		×	×	○			×	×	×		×	×		×	×	×	
Pakistan	○	○	○		○	×	○	×	×		○	‡	×				×	×	×	×	×	×				×	○	×		×	×		×	×	×	
Papua New Guinea			○						△			△					×	○				×								○			△	△		
St Christopher-Nevis									○			○																		○						‡
St Lucia									△			△				○														○			○			×
St Vincent & The Gren									△						△															○		○		○		‡
Seychelles				△					△													○								△			△	△		
Sierra Leone	△	○				○	○		△		○	△							○		○	×				○	△			△			△	■	△	
Singapore	○		×		○			○	×			×	○	▽		△	×	○	○	○	×	×				‡		○		○			×	×		
Solomon Is									○			○						○												○			○			×
Sri Lanka			○		○	○		○	×			×	○	○			×	×	○	○	×	×				○		○		○	○		×	×	○	
Swaziland							×		△			○							△											○			○	○		×
Tanzania	○		○		○	○	×	○	×	○	○	×	○					‡	○		●	×	×				○			×	×		×	×	‡	
Tonga									○													○								△			△			×
Trinidad & Tobago			○						×			○				○			○	○	○	○					○			○		○	○	○	○	
Tuvalu																																				
Uganda	○					○			○		○	○						○				×	×			×	○	×		○	×		○	○		
Vanuatu			○				○		○	○						○	○	○	○			○								○			○	○		
Western Samoa									○								○					○											○			
Zambia					○		×		×	○	○	■						○	×		‡	×	○			‡	○	×		○	○		×	○	○	
Zimbabwe	○		×				×		×	×	×	×				×		×	×		×	×	○				○		●	×	×		×	×		

Represented in	Antigua & Barbuda	Australia	Bahamas	Bangladesh	Barbados	Belize	Botswana	Britain	Brunei Darussalam	Canada	Cyprus	Dominica	The Gambia	Ghana	Grenada	Guyana	India	Jamaica	Kenya	Kiribati	Lesotho	Malawi	Malaysia	Maldives	Malta
Thailand		×		×				×	×	×	○		△		○		×	○	×				×	○	○
Togo								×		×				‡											
Tunisia		○						×	○	×			○	○			×							○	×
Turkey		×	○	×	△	○	○	×	○	×			○	○	○	○	×	○	×			○	×		□
United Arab Ems.	○			×				×		○			○				×							○	○
USA	‡	×	×	×	×	×	×	×	×	×	×	○	×	×	‡	‡	×	×	×	○	×	×	×	○	×
Uruguay	○	■			○			×		‡	○					○	○							○	
Venezuela	×	×			×	×		×		×		‡		○	×	×	×	×	×				○		○
Vietnam		×		○				×		○	○		○			○	×						×	○	○
Yemen							○	×	○	○	○					○	×		○				○		○
Yugoslavia		×		×	○		○	×		×	×		○	×	○	○	×	△	×		○		×	○	○
Zaire							○	×		×			○	‡			×		×		○	○		○	

Represented in	Mauritius	Namibia	Nauru	New Zealand	Nigeria	Pakistan	Papua New Guinea	St Christopher-Nevis	St Lucia	St Vincent & The Gren	Seychelles	Sierra Leone	Singapore	Solomon Is	Sri Lanka	Swaziland	Tanzania	Tonga	Trinidad & Tobago	Tuvalu	Uganda	Vanuatu	Western Samoa	Zambia	Zimbabwe
Thailand	○			×	×	×	○	○		○		○	×		×				○			○			
Togo					×							×										○			
Tunisia		○			○	×							○		○							○		○	×
Turkey	○		○	○	×	×	△					■	×	○	○	○	○	○	○		○			○	○
United Arab Ems.	○					×						○			○		○								
USA	×	×	○	×	×	×	×	○	○	○	×	×	×	‡	×	×	×	○	×	○	×	○	‡	×	×
Uruguay				○	×	○		○		○									○						
Venezuela		‡		○	×			×	×	×			○						×						
Vietnam				○	○										○							○		○	×
Yemen					○	×							○		○		×								
Yugoslavia	○	‡		‡	×	×						△	○		×		×		○		×	○	○	×	×
Zaire	○	○			×							○	○		○	×	×				×			+	×

Diplomatic Representation

Commonwealth Representation in Other Commonwealth Countries

× Full representation by resident High Commissioner

○ Non-resident representation

△ Honorary Consul

■ Consul-General

‡ Chargé d'Affaires

□ Honorary Consul-General

● Resident Representative

Country: / Represented in	Antigua & Barbuda	Australia	Bahamas	Bangladesh	Barbados	Belize	Botswana	Britain	Brunei Darussalam	Canada	Cyprus	Dominica	The Gambia	Ghana	Grenada	Guyana	India	Jamaica
Antigua & Barbuda		○	○		○	○		×		●		○			○	○		○
Australia	○		○	×	○		○	×	×	×	×	○	○	○	○	○	×	×
Bahamas	○				○			×		×					○	○		○
Bangladesh		×	○		○	○	○	×	○	×	○		○	○	○	○	×	○
Barbados	△	□	△					×		×		○			○	○	△	△
Belize	○							×		×								△
Botswana								×		○						○	×	○
Britain	×	×	×	×	×	×	×		×	×	×	○	×	×	×	×	×	×
Brunei Darussalam		×		○				×		○							○	
Canada	○	×	△	×	×	△	○	×	○		△	○	○	×	○	×	×	×
Cyprus		×	△	○	△			×		△					○	○	×	△
Dominica								×		●							×	△
The Gambia			■					×						△				
Ghana				○				×		×			○			○	×	○
Grenada								×		■						○	○	
Guyana	△		□	○	△		○	×		×	△	△			△		○	△
India	○	×	○	×	○	○	○	×	○	×	×	×	○	×	○	×		×
Jamaica	○	□	△		○	○		×		×		○		○	○	○		
Kenya		×					○	×		×				○			×	
Kiribati		□						△		○								
Lesotho							○	×		×								
Malawi							○	×		×								
Malaysia		×		×				×	×	×	○			●		●	×	●
Maldives																		
Malta		×						×		■	△						△	
Mauritius		×		○				×	○	○							×	
Namibia		○					×	×		×				‡			×	
Nauru		■						●									■	
New Zealand		×		○	○		○	×	○	×	○					○	×	○
Nigeria		×	○	○	○	○	×	×		×	○		×	×		○	×	×
Pakistan		×		×		○	○	×	×	×	○		△	×		□	×	○
Papua New Guinea		×						×		○								
St Christopher-Nevis	○	○	○		○	○		×		×		○			○	○		○
St Lucia								×		■								△
St Vincent & The Grenadines		○			○			×		×						○	○	○
Seychelles		□						×		○							○	
Sierra Leone				○				×		○	△		×	○		○	○	○
Singapore		×		○				×	×	○				○			×	
Solomon Islands										○								
Sri Lanka		×		×				×		×							×	
Swaziland	○	○					○	×	○	×				○		○	○	○
Tanzania					○		○	×		×				○		○	×	○
Tonga		△						×										
Trinidad & Tobago	○	△		○	×			×		×		○		○	○	○	×	×
Tuvalu		○						○		○								○
Uganda								×		○			○				×	
Vanuatu		○		○			○	○		○							○	○
Western Samoa		×								○								
Zambia		×	○	○	○		×	×		×	○		○	○	○	○	×	○
Zimbabwe				○			×	×		×							×	

Country: / Represented in	Kenya	Kiribati	Lesotho	Malawi	Malaysia	Maldives	Malta	Mauritius	Namibia	Nauru	New Zealand	Nigeria	Pakistan	Papua New Guinea	St Christopher-Nevis	St Lucia	St Vincent & The Grenadines	Seychelles
Antigua & Barbuda															○	○	○	
Australia	×	×	○	○	×	○	×	×		×	×	×	×	×	○	○	○	○
Bahamas																		
Bangladesh	×	○	○	○	×	□	○	○	×	○	○	○	×	○		○		○
Barbados												○			○	○	○	
Belize																		
Botswana	○		○	○					×			○						
Britain	×	×	×	×	×	○	×	×	×	○	×	×	×	×	○	×	×	×
Brunei Darussalam					×						○		○	○			○	
Canada	×	○	○	○	×	○	○	○	×		×	×	×	○	○	○	○	○
Cyprus	×				○		△				○	△		△		○		△
Dominica																		
The Gambia												×						
Ghana			○		○		○					×	○					
Grenada																		
Guyana	○												○		○	△	○	
India	×	○	○	×	×	×	×	×	×	○	×	×	×	○	○	○	○	×
Jamaica	○											×			○	○	○	○
Kenya			×	×				△				×	×					
Kiribati					○					○	△			△				
Lesotho	×																	
Malawi	×		○						×			○						
Malaysia		●				●		×			×	×	×	×				
Maldives													○	○				
Malta											○							
Mauritius					×						○		×					
Namibia	×			×							○	×	‡					
Nauru					△						■							
New Zealand	○	×			×	○		△		○		○	○	×				
Nigeria	×		○	○	×		○	○			○		×					○
Pakistan	×		○	○	×	×	○	×			△	‡						
Papua New Guinea		○			×	×					×		○					
St Christopher-Nevis																○	○	
St Lucia																		
St Vincent & The Grenadines																		
Seychelles					△			△					△					
Sierra Leone												×	×					
Singapore					×	○		○			×	○	△	○				
Solomon Islands		○									○							
Sri Lanka	×				×	×					△		×					
Swaziland	×		○	○	○		○		○			○	○					
Tanzania	×		○	○	○							×	○					
Tonga		○																
Trinidad & Tobago	○											×			○	○	○	
Tuvalu		○			○						□			○				
Uganda	×			○				○				×						
Vanuatu		○			○	○				○	○	○	○	○	○			
Western Samoa		○								△	×							
Zambia	×		○	×			○	○			○	×	○					
Zimbabwe	×			×								×	○					

Country: \ Represented in	Sierra Leone	Singapore	Solomon Islands	Sri Lanka	Swaziland	Tanzania	Tonga	Trinidad & Tobago	Tuvalu	Uganda	Vanuatu	Western Samoa	Zambia	Zimbabwe
Antigua & Barbuda								○						
Australia	○	×	×	×	○	×	×	○	○	○	×	×	×	×
Bahamas								○						
Bangladesh	○	×	○	×	○	○	○	○	○	○	○	○	○	×
Barbados								×						
Belize														
Botswana					○	○				○			×	×
Britain	×	×	×	×	×	×	×	×	○	×	×	○	×	×
Brunei Darussalam		×		○			○							
Canada	○	×	○	×	○	×	○	×	○	○	○	○	×	×
Cyprus	△	△		△		△		○		○			■	○
Dominica														
The Gambia	×													
Ghana	×			○	○	○								×
Grenada														
Guyana				○		○		□					×	○
India	○	×	○	×	○	×	○	×	○	×	○	○	×	×
Jamaica	○					○		×					○	○
Kenya				×	×	×				×			×	×
Kiribati			○				○		○		○	○		
Lesotho														
Malawi					○	×				○			×	×
Malaysia		×		×			●	●	○		●	●		
Maldives				×							○			
Malta														
Mauritius				○										
Namibia						○				○			×	×
Nauru							△				○	△		
New Zealand		×	×	○		○	×	○	○		×	×	○	×
Nigeria	×	○		○	○	×		×		×	○		×	×
Pakistan	○	×		×	○	×		△		○			○	×
Papua New Guinea		○	×				×		×		×	×		
St Christopher-Nevis								○						
St Lucia														
St Vincent & The Grenadines								○						
Seychelles		△				△					○			
Sierra Leone						○				○				
Singapore				○		○								
Solomon Islands		○									○			
Sri Lanka		×				○				○	○		○	○
Swaziland						○				○			○	○
Tanzania	○	○		○	○			○		×	○		×	×
Tonga											○			
Trinidad & Tobago	○	○		○		○				×				
Tuvalu			○								○	○		
Uganda	○			○		×							○	○
Vanuatu	○	○	○	○		○	○		○			○		○
Western Samoa											○			
Zambia	○			○	○	×		○		○				×
Zimbabwe		×			○	×					○		×	

Diplomatic Representation

Commonwealth Representation in Non-Commonwealth Countries

× Full representation by resident Ambassador

○ Non-resident representation

△ Honorary Consul

■ Consul-General

‡ Chargé d'Affaires

□ Honorary Consul-General

● Resident Representative

Country: / Represented in	Afghanistan	Albania	Algeria	Andorra	Angola	Argentina	Austria	Bahrain	Belgium	Benin	Bhutan	Bolivia	Brazil	Bulgaria	Burkina	Burma	Burundi	Cambodia
Antigua & Barbuda						○	○		○			○	○					
Australia	○	○			○	×	×	○	×			○	×	○		×		
Bahamas									○									
Bangladesh	‡	○	×		○	○	□	×	×		×	○	×	○		×	○	
Barbados							□		×				△					
Belize									△				○					
Botswana									×									
Britain	×		×	○	×	×	×	×	×	○		×	×	×	○	×	○	
Brunei Darussalam								○	○									
Canada		○	‡	○	○	×	×	○	×	○		‡	×	○	△		△	
Cyprus			○			□	□	□	×			△	△	○		○	△	
Dominica									×									
The Gambia			○				○		×	○			○					
Ghana			×		×				×	×			×	×	×			
Grenada						○	○		‡									
Guyana							○		×				×					
India	×		×		×	×	×	×	×	○	×	○	×	×	○	×	○	×
Jamaica						△	△		×				○	○	○			
Kenya							△		×	○								
Kiribati									○									
Lesotho							○		×									
Malawi							○		×				○					
Malaysia	×					×	×	×	×				×	○		×		
Maldives																		
Malta		○	‡				△	○	×				□	○				
Mauritius						○		○	×				○			○		
Namibia					×				×									
Nauru																		
New Zealand[1]			○			○	○	○	×				○			○		
Nigeria			×		×	×	×		×	×		○	×	×	×	○	○	
Pakistan	‡		×			×	×	×	×				×			×		
Papua New Guinea									×									
St Christopher-Nevis																		
St Lucia																		
St Vincent & The Grenadines						○			○				○					
Seychelles							□		□									
Sierra Leone							○		×									
Singapore						○	○		×				○			×		
Solomon Islands									○									
Sri Lanka	○	○	○			○	○	○	×		○		○	○		×		○
Swaziland			○		○	○	○		×				○	○				
Tanzania			○		×		○	○	×					○			×	○
Tonga									○									
Trinidad & Tobago			○			○	○		×				×					
Tuvalu																		
Uganda									×									
Vanuatu			○		○		○		○				○			○		
Western Samoa																		
Zambia		○	○		×	○	○		×				○	○			○	○
Zimbabwe			×		×				×									

Country: / Represented in	Cameroon	Cape Verde	Central African Rep.	Chad	Chile	China	Colombia	Comoro Islands	Congo	Costa Rica	Côte d'Ivoire	Cuba	Czechoslovakia	Denmark	Djibouti	Dominican Rep.	Ecuador	Egypt, Arab Rep. of
Antigua & Barbuda						○	○			○				○				
Australia					×	×	○	○		○	○		×	×		○	○	×
Bahamas							○					○						
Bangladesh			○	○	○	×	○			○	○	○	○	□	○	○	□	×
Barbados					□		○			○		○		○		△		
Belize										△								
Botswana						‡						○		○				
Britain	×	○	○	○	×	×	×	○	×	×	×	×	×	×	○	○	×	×
Brunei Darussalam																		×
Canada	×	×	○	○	×	×	×	○	‡	×	×	×	×	×	○	△	×	×
Cyprus	△					×	△			△		○	○	□		△	▽	×
Dominica																		
The Gambia	○	○				‡					○			○				○
Ghana						×	○				×	×	×	×				×
Grenada							○							○				
Guyana						×						×						
India	○	○	○	○	×	×	×	○	○	○	×	×	×	×	○		○	×
Jamaica							○			○		○	○	○		○	○	
Kenya						×									○			×
Kiribati					○	○												
Lesotho											○			×				
Malawi														○				○
Malaysia						×						○	×	○				×
Maldives																		
Malta						‡							○	□				×
Mauritius						○						○		○				×
Namibia																		
Nauru					○													
New Zealand					×	×	○			○			○	○			○	○
Nigeria	×	○	×	×	○	×	○		×		×	×	×	×	○		○	×
Pakistan						×				△				‡			□	×
Papua New Guinea						×												
St Christopher-Nevis																		
St Lucia																		
St Vincent & The Grenadines							○							○				
Seychelles						○						○		□				
Sierra Leone						×					○		○					
Singapore					○	×							○	○				×
Solomon Islands																		
Sri Lanka						×						×	○	○				×
Swaziland	○				○								○	×				○
Tanzania						×			○			○	○	○				×
Tonga														○				
Trinidad & Tobago	○						○							○		○	○	
Tuvalu																		
Uganda						×								×				×
Vanuatu	○					○					○	○		○				
Western Samoa																		
Zambia	○				○	×	○		○		○	○	○	○	○	○		×
Zimbabwe						×						×						

Country: / Represented in	El Salvador	Equatorial Guinea	Ethiopia	Fiji	Finland	France	Gabon	Germany	Greece	Guatemala	Guinea	Guinea-Bissau	Haiti	Holy See	Honduras	Hungary	Iceland
Antigua & Barbuda						○		○	○					○			
Australia	○		×	×	○	×	○	×	×	○				×	○	×	○
Bahamas						○		○					‡				
Bangladesh			○	○	□	×		×	□	○	○	○		○	○	○	□
Barbados					△	○		△					○	○			○
Belize	△					○		○							△		
Botswana			○		○	○		○	○								○
Britain	×	○	×	×	×	×	×	×	×	×	○	○	○	×	×	×	×
Brunei Darussalam						×		×									
Canada	‡	○	‡	○	×	×	×	×	×	×	×	○	‡	×	△	×	○
Cyprus			○	○	□	×		×	×					○		×	×
Dominica						○											
The Gambia			○			×		△			○	■		○			
Ghana			×			×		×			×						
Grenada						○		○									
Guyana					○	○		○									
India	○	○	×	×	×	×	○	×	×	○	×	○		×		×	○
Jamaica			×		△	○		×		△			△	○	△	○	
Kenya			×		○	×		×	○							○	○
Kiribati				○		○		○	○								
Lesotho						○		×									
Malawi			×		○	×		×						○			
Malaysia			‡	×	○	×		×	○							○	
Maldives																	
Malta					○	×		×						△		○	
Mauritius					○	×		○	○					○			
Namibia			×														
Nauru				●	○		○	○									
New Zealand				×	○	×		×	○					○	○	○	
Nigeria		×	×	○	○	×	×	×			×	‡	×	×		×	○
Pakistan				△	△	×		×	×							×	
Papua New Guinea				×				×									
St Christopher-Nevis																	
St Lucia														○			
St Vincent & The Grenadines						○		○									
Seychelles					△	×		○	○								
Sierra Leone			×			○		×			×						
Singapore				○	○	×		×	○					○		○	
Solomon Islands								○									
Sri Lanka			○	○	○	×		×	○					○		○	
Swaziland			○		○	○		△	△							○	
Tanzania			×		○	×		×			○	○		○		○	○
Tonga						○		△									
Trinidad & Tobago					○	○		○		○			○				
Tuvalu				×				□									
Uganda			×			×		×									
Vanuatu				○	○	○		○	○								
Western Samoa								○									
Zambia			×		○	×	○	×	○		○		○			○	
Zimbabwe			×			×		×									

Country: / Represented in	Indonesia	Iran	Iraq	Ireland	Israel	Italy	Japan	Jordan	Korea, DFR	Korea, Rep. of	Kuwait	Laos	Lebanon	Liberia	Libya	Liechtenstein	Luxembourg	Madagascar
Antigua & Barbuda			○		○	○	○			○								
Australia	×	×		×	×	×	×	×		×	○	×	×				○	○
Bahamas																		
Bangladesh	×	×	×	○		×	×	□	○	×	×	○	○	○	×		○	○
Barbados					△	○	△										○	
Belize					△		△			△			△					
Botswana						○											○	
Britain	×	×		×	×	×	×	×		×	×	○	×	○		○	×	×
Brunei Darussalam	×			○			×	○		×								
Canada	×	×	×	×	×	×	×	×		×	×	○	○	‡	○	○	△	○
Cyprus				△		×	△	△			△		△		×	△	○	
Dominica																		
The Gambia		○	○			○					○		△	○			○	
Ghana						×	×		○	○				×	×			
Grenada						○											○	
Guyana							△		○	○								
India	×	×	×	×		×	×	×	×	×	×	×	×	○	×	■	○	×
Jamaica					○	△		△		△			△			○	○	
Kenya		×				×	×			○								
Kiribati					○		○			○								
Lesotho						×												
Malawi					○	△				△							○	
Malaysia	×	×	×	×		×	×	○	○	×	×	×	○		×		○	
Maldives																		
Malta			○	△	△	×	△	○	○		○		□		×		△	
Mauritius	○		○			○					○						○	×
Namibia																		
Nauru							●			○								
New Zealand	×	×	×	○	○	×	×	○		×	○	○					○	
Nigeria	×	×	×	×		×	×	○	×	×	○		○	×	×		○	○
Pakistan	×	×	×	□		×	×	×	×	×	×			△	×			
Papua New Guinea	×						×											
St Christopher-Nevis							○			○								
St Lucia																		
St Vincent & The Grenadines			○		○	○	△			○								
Seychelles	△		△			△	○		○				△					△
Sierra Leone														×			○	
Singapore	×	○		○		○	×	○		×							○	
Solomon Islands						○	○			○								
Sri Lanka	×	○	×			×	×	○	○	×	×	○	○		×		○	
Swaziland	○				△	△	△			△							○	
Tanzania	○			○		×	×		○		○			○			○	
Tonga						○	△											
Trinidad & Tobago	○					○	○										○	
Tuvalu							□											
Uganda			×												×			
Vanuatu						○	○		○	○	○				○			
Western Samoa																		
Zambia		○	○	○		×	×		○					○	○		○	○
Zimbabwe							×											

Country: / Represented in	Mali	Mauritania	Mexico	Monaco	Mongolia	Morocco	Mozambique	Nepal	Netherlands	Nicaragua	Niger	Norway	Oman	Panama	Paraguay	Peru	Philippines
Antigua & Barbuda			○						○			△				○	
Australia			×		○	○	○	×	×	○		○	○	○	○	○	×
Bahamas																	
Bangladesh	○		□		○	×	○	×	□	○	○	□	‡	○	○	○	×
Barbados			○						○			○		○		○	
Belize			×						○	○				△			
Botswana			○				○		○			○					
Britain	○	○	×	○	×	×	×	×	×	×	○	×	×	×	×	×	×
Brunei Darussalam		○				○		○				○	×			○	×
Canada	●	○	×	□	○	‡	○	○	×	△	○	×	○	‡	△	×	×
Cyprus			×		○		○	○	△	○	△	△	△	△	△	△	△
Dominica									△								
The Gambia	△	△	○			○			○			△					
Ghana																	
Grenada									○								
Guyana			○				○									○	
India	○	○	×		×	×	×	×	×	○	○	×	×	×	○	×	×
Jamaica			×						○	○		○		■		○	△
Kenya			○					○	×			○					
Kiribati									○							○	
Lesotho							×										
Malawi							×		○			○					
Malaysia	×		○		○	‡		×	×			○	×				×
Maldives																	
Malta			△			○		□	○			○	○				
Mauritius			○					○	○			○	○				
Namibia																	
Nauru									○								■
New Zealand			×				○	○	×	○		○	○			○	×
Nigeria	‡	‡	○		○	×		○	×		×	×			○	○	×
Pakistan			×			×	×	×	×		‡		×	□	△		×
Papua New Guinea																	×
St Christopher-Nevis																	
St Lucia																	
St Vincent & The Grenadines						○			○						○		
Seychelles				△					△			△					△
Sierra Leone									△								
Singapore			○					○	○			○		○			×
Solomon Islands									○								
Sri Lanka			○		○	○		○	○			○	×				○
Swaziland			○			○	×		○			○					○
Tanzania			○				×	○	×			○	○				○
Tonga									○								
Trinidad & Tobago			○						○			○				○	
Tuvalu																	
Uganda																	
Vanuatu			○				○		○	○						○	○
Western Samoa																	
Zambia	○					○	×		○		○	○					
Zimbabwe							×										

Country: / Represented in	Poland	Portugal	Qatar	Romania	Russia	Rwanda	San Marino	Sao Tomé & Principe	Saudi Arabia	Senegal	Somalia	South Africa	Spain	Sudan	Surinam	Sweden	Switzerland	Syria	Taiwan
Antigua & Barbuda		○											○			○	○	○	
Australia	×	×	○	○	×				×	○	○	×	×	○		×	×	×	
Bahamas																			
Bangladesh	×	○	×	×	×	○			×	×	○		□	□	○	×	×	□	
Barbados															○	□	○		
Belize																	△		■
Botswana		○		○	○											×			
Britain	×	×	×	×	×	○	○	△	×	×	×	×	×	×	○	×	×	×	
Brunei Darussalam									×								○		
Canada	×	×	○	‡	×	○	□	×	×	×		×	‡	○	○	×	×	×	
Cyprus	△	△		○	×	△						△	○	○	△	○	△	×	
Dominica																			△
The Gambia			○						×	×	○					△	○		
Ghana					×				×								×		
Grenada													○						
Guyana	○				×										×				
India	×	×	×	×	×	○	■		×	×	×		×	×	×	×	×	×	
Jamaica	○			○	×										○	△	△		
Kenya	○				×	×			×		×			×		×	×		
Kiribati		○																	
Lesotho																			×
Malawi		○		○								×	○			○	○		△
Malaysia	×	○	○	×	×				×	○	×		×	○		×	×	×	
Maldives																			
Malta	○	△	○		‡		○		×				△	○		△	●	△	
Mauritius			○		○				○							○	○		
Namibia					×											×			
Nauru		○																	■
New Zealand	○	○	○	○	×				×				×			○	○		
Nigeria	×	×		×	×	○			×	×	×		×	×	○	×	×	×	
Pakistan	×	×	‡	×	×				×	×	‡		×	‡		×	×	×	
Papua New Guinea																			
St Christopher-Nevis																			○
St Lucia																			
St Vincent & The Grenadines													○		○		△		○
Seychelles					○								□			△	△		
Sierra Leone	○			○	×				×							○			
Singapore		○			×				×				○			○	○		
Solomon Islands													○						○
Sri Lanka	○	○	○	○	×				×				○	○		×	○		
Swaziland	○	○		○					○			●	△			○	△		△
Tanzania	○	○	○	○	×	×			○							×			
Tonga					○												△		
Trinidad & Tobago				○						○					○	○	○		
Tuvalu																			
Uganda					×	×			×					×					
Vanuatu	○	○			○								○			○	○		
Western Samoa																			
Zambia	○	○		○	×	○			○	○	○		○	○		×	○	○	
Zimbabwe					×					×		●				×			

Country: / Represented in	Thailand	Togo	Tunisia	Turkey	United Arab Emirates	USA	Uruguay	Venezuela	Vietnam	Yemen	Yugoslavia	Zaire
Antigua & Barbuda					○	×	○	○				
Australia	×		○	×	○	×	○	×	×	○	×	
Bahamas						×						
Bangladesh	×		○	×	×	×	○	○	○	○	×	○
Barbados						×		×			○	
Belize	△					×	△	△				
Botswana						×					○	
Britain	×	○	×	×	×	×	×	×	×	×	×	×
Brunei Darussalam	×					×						
Canada	×	○	×	×	○	×	○	×	‡	‡	×	×
Cyprus	○					×	△	○	○	○	×	
Dominica						○						
The Gambia	△	○			○	×		○				
Ghana		×				×					×	
Grenada						×		×				
Guyana						×		×				
India	×	○	×	×	×	×	○	×	×	×	×	×
Jamaica						×		×			○	
Kenya		○			×	×					○	×
Kiribati						○						
Lesotho						×						
Malawi						×						○
Malaysia	×			×	×	×			×		×	
Maldives												
Malta	○		○	△	△	×		□		○	○	
Mauritius	○				○	×					○	
Namibia						×						
Nauru						△	○					
New Zealand	×			○	○	×	○	○	○		○	
Nigeria	○	×	○	○	○	×	○	×	○	○	×	×
Pakistan	×		×	×	×	×				×	×	
Papua New Guinea						×						
St Christopher-Nevis						×						
St Lucia						×						
St Vincent & The Grenadines	○					×		○				
Seychelles			△			×						
Sierra Leone						×						
Singapore	×			○		×					○	
Solomon Islands						○						
Sri Lanka	×		○	○	×	×		○	○	○	×	
Swaziland	○			○	○	×		○			○	○
Tanzania	○					×						×
Tonga						■						
Trinidad & Tobago						×		×			○	○
Tuvalu												
Uganda						×						×
Vanuatu	○	○	○			○			○		○	
Western Samoa						×						
Zambia	○	○	○	○	○	×		□			×	×
Zimbabwe						×					×	

PART IV

Member countries of the Commonwealth

Antigua & Barbuda

Capital: St John's

Antigua and Barbuda became an Independent, Sovereign State on 1st November 1981. The country is comprised of the islands of Antigua (80,000 people, 280 sq km), Barbuda (1,500 people, 161 sq km), 40 km north of Antigua, and Redonda (uninhabited, 1.3 sq km) 40 km south-west of Antigua. The country is part of the Leeward Islands in the Eastern Caribbean and lies 17° 3′ N., 61° 48′ W.

The western part of the island of Antigua is composed entirely of volcanic rocks (highest point Boggy Peak 399 m). The eastern and northern parts are of limestone, less than 150 m above sea level, and a central plain stretches diagonally across the island.

The absence of high hills and forest distinguishes Antigua from the rest of the Leeward group. There are no rivers and only a few springs in the island. The mean annual rainfall is about 1,000 mm. The climate is drier than that of most of the West Indies and is delightful from the end of November to the beginning of May, when the north-east trade winds begin to fail. The hot season then sets in, during which the weather is generally rainy. The shade temperature seldom exceeds 88°F.

Barbuda is very flat, with a large lagoon on the west side, and is drier than Antigua. There are excellent beaches of pink and white sand; deer, wildfowl and wild pigs live in the well wooded areas of the north-east.

The capital of Antigua and Barbuda is St John's. The unit of currency is the Eastern Caribbean Dollar. The only town on Barbuda is Codrington.

There is one General Hospital with 220 beds, a privately operated Clinic with 16 beds. There are seven Health Centres and 17 satellite Clinics which are staffed by Public Health Nurses, Family Nurse Practitioners, Nurse/Midwives and visited by District Medical Officers. There are six creches operated by the Government, staffed by creche Aides and two creches operated privately. There is a Mental Hospital. The aged are cared for at the Fiennes Institute.

The main forms of taxation are import duties, excise and consumption taxes. Personal income tax on residents was abolished on 1st January 1977. Company tax is 40 per cent of chargeable income.

Public Finance figures are as follows:

Year	*Revenue*	*Expenditure*
1986 (est)	$159,923,287	$160,599,229
1987 (est)	$181,125,609	$187,036,642
1988 (est)	$217,078,707	$231,779,694
1989 (est)	$236,700,000	$263,579,351
1990 (est)	$249,560,916	$271,730,204

There is a large number of schools and a State College which provides Technical Training and Teacher Training. An off-shore medical college, the University of Health Sciences, Antigua (UHSA) was established in 1982.

The country has a good infrastructure with V C Bird International Airport accommodating large international jet aircraft, a deep water harbour, and an extensive network of roads. The improvement of electricity and water supplies is being pursued with vigour.

Hurricane Hugo hit Antigua and Barbuda in September 1989 causing damage to the infrastructure and to the electricity transmission system. The United Kingdom provided linesmen to help repair the system from the Northern Ireland Electric Company and spare parts for electrical transmission systems.

Sugar was for many years the dominant crop but while its cultivation continues, it is primarily for local consumption. Other agricultural development is in hand including livestock, sea island cotton, corn for cornmeal production, improved vegetable and fruit production.

Antigua with 365 white sand beaches, was one of the first Caribbean islands to attract tourists, and tourism is the main feature of the economy. There are several excellent hotels and a number of others are under construction.

History

The country was discovered by Europeans when Christopher Columbus made his second voyage to the West Indies in 1493. He named Antigua after a church, Santa Maria de la Antigua, in Seville. The Spaniards attempted to settle on the island in 1520 but they found it too dry. The French under d'Esnambue made an abortive attempt at settlement in 1629. Antigua was eventually colonised in the year 1632 by Sir Thomas Warner. In the early years the settlers suffered much from raids by the Caribs. In 1667 under the Treaty of Breda it became a British Colony.

At first the chief crop was tobacco but in the second half of the seventeenth century it was found that sugar was more profitable in the West Indies. This required heavy labour and the defeated armies in the English Civil War were sent to work on the plantations, but when these were found to give indifferent results in the tropical climate the trade in slaves from Africa began and estates became extremely profitable. The wars between the English and French were much concerned with the possession of the sugar islands. Antigua was the only British island to possess a good harbour and English Harbour was the dock-yard for the British West Indies throughout the period. On one occasion the French made a successful landing on Antigua, but the island never passed out of British hands and shows no trace of French influence.

The slaves on Antigua were emancipated in 1834, four years before the general emancipation in British territories. This led at first to some difficulty in obtaining labour for the sugar estates. A disastrous fire in 1841, an earthquake which destroyed the Cathedral in St John's in 1843, and a hurricane which did £100,000 worth of damage in 1847 were serious economic blows. In recent times, particularly between the years 1977 to 1980 the economy has done well averaging 7 per cent growth per annum. This has continued throughout the 1980s.

The Royal Navy used English Harbour in the south of the island during the 17th and 18th centuries and Admiral Nelson, then Captain of HMS *Boreas*, spent 2 or 3 years based there. The Naval Dockyard, commissioned in 1725, was closed in 1854 but during the 1950s considerable voluntary work was done in restoring the Dockyard and it is now an attractive historical monument. English Harbour is also an internationally known yachting centre and is the venue for Antigua Sailing Week, in April every year.

Following decisions taken at a conference in London in February and March 1966, subsequently endorsed by a resolution of the Legislative Council, provision was made in the West Indies Act 1967 under which Antigua assumed a status of association with the United Kingdom on 27th February 1967. The island exercised full internal self government and was accorded executive authority over a wide field of external affairs by the United Kingdom which retained overall responsibility for external relations and defence.

At a Constitutional Conference in London in December 1980 a new Constitution for independent Antigua and Barbuda was worked out by delegations representing the Government of the United Kingdom, the Government of Antigua and Barbuda, the opposition party in the Antigua Parliament and the Barbuda Local Government Council. Antigua and Barbuda became fully independent on 1st November 1981.

Constitution

Under the terms of the Constitution, Antigua and Barbuda remains a Monarchical State with Her Majesty The Queen Elizabeth II as Head of State represented in St John's by a Governor-General. The Constitution also provides for a Government made up of the Prime Minister and Ministers who may be elected members of the Lower House of a bi-cameral Legislature or appointed Senators of the Upper House or Senate. The Constitution also provides for the Attorney-General to be appointed.

General Elections must be held at least every five years, under the Constitution, to elect representatives to the Lower House. Senators are appointed by the Governor-General in his own right and also on the advice of the Prime Minister and Leader of the Opposition.

Arising from the Constitutional Conference, the Barbuda Local Government Council has full autonomy over the internal affairs of Barbuda with the Government retaining control of land and police matters.

A puisne judge of the Eastern Caribbean Supreme Court is resident in Antigua.

Membership of International Organisations

Antigua and Barbuda was a founder-member of the Caribbean Free Trade Association in 1965 which has now expanded to a Caribbean Community and Common Market (CARICOM) embracing 13 English-speaking Caribbean Territories. It is also a founder-member of the Organisation of Eastern Caribbean States (OECS), a grouping of seven Leeward and Windward Islands in the Caribbean. In November 1981, Antigua and Barbuda gained membership of the Commonwealth and became the 157th member of the United Nations. In December 1981, the country also joined the Organisation of American States.

Government

At the General Election on 9th March 1989 the governing Antigua Labour Party won 15 seats, the United National Democratic Party 1 seat and the Barbuda People's Movement the Barbudan Seat. The seven by-elections due in August following electoral petitions were not contested by the opposition parties, leaving the March result unaltered.

HEAD OF STATE
Her Majesty Queen Elizabeth II

GOVERNOR GENERAL
His Excellency Sir Wilfred Jacobs, GCMG, GCVO, OBE, QC

CABINET

Prime Minister, The Rt Hon Dr V C Bird Snr
Attorney General and Minister of Legal Affairs (Appointed): Hon Keith Ford, QC
Minister of Foreign Affairs: Hon Lester Bryant Bird
Minister of Public Utilities, Transport and Energy: Hon Robin Yearwood
Minister of Finance and Trade: Hon Molwyn Joseph
Minister of Education, Culture and Youth Affairs: Hon Bernard Percival
Minister of Labour and Health: Hon Adolphus Freeland
Minister of Home Affairs and Social Services: Hon Christopher M O'Mard
Minister of Agriculture, Fisheries, Lands and Housing: Hon Hilroy Humphreys
Minister of Public Works and Communications: Hon Eustace Cochrane
Minister of Economic Development, Industry and Tourism: Hon Dr Rodney Williams
Minister of Information: Hon John St Luce

Permanent Secretaries
E G K Challenger, CBE, LVO
H A Murdoch, OBE, CVO
C Weston
D Michael
Mrs A Henry, OBE
H Barnes, OBE
E Weston
Mrs E Lynch
M Matthias
R John
E Benjamin
Mrs S Archibald
Mrs I Matthias

Cabinet Secretary
Lounel Stevens, MBE

Financial Secretary
K Hurst

The Commonwealth of Australia

Capital: Canberra

The Commonwealth of Australia derives its name from the Latin *australis,* meaning southern, a name commonly used in early times for regions south of the equator. In the sixteenth century geographers used the name 'Terra Australis' to describe a continent which they thought must exist in the South Pacific. The east coast of Australia was named New South Wales by Captain Cook, but when it was realised that this and New Holland, the name by which the west coast was known, formed one land mass, the word Australia began to be used, and was first given official recognition in April 1817 when Governor Macquarie of New South Wales used the word in his correspondence.

The Commonwealth of Australia comprises the six federated States of New South Wales, Victoria, Queensland, Western Australia, South Australia and Tasmania, each of which has its own Government, and two internal territories: the Australian Capital Territory (ACT), which is the seat of the Commonwealth Government, and the Northern Territory. The ACT has been self-governing since May 1989. The Northern Territory achieved self-government in 1978. Macquarie Island, about 1,600 km south-east of Tasmania, is administered by Tasmania.

Australia's external territories are: Norfolk Island, the Territory of Ashmore and Cartier Islands, the Coral Sea Islands Territory, the Territory of Cocos (Keeling) Islands, the Territory of Christmas Island, the Territory of Heard and McDonald Islands and the Australian Antarctic Territory.

Location, Topography and Climate

The Commonwealth of Australia is situated in the Southern Hemisphere and lies between the parallels of latitude 10° 41′ S. and 43° 39′ S. and the meridians of longitude 113° 9′ E. and 153° 39′ E. It is bounded on the west by the Indian Ocean and on the east by the Coral and Tasman Seas of the South Pacific Ocean, to the north by the Timor and Arafura Seas and to the south by the Southern Ocean.

The total area of the Commonwealth is 7,682,292 sq km (2,966,136 square miles). Almost three quarters of the land mass is a plateau, averaging about 300 m (1,000 feet) above sea level. There is a large portion of lowland less than 150 m (500 feet) high. The third main feature is the eastern highlands belt, comprising a chain of elevated plateaux extending from north to south along the eastern boundary. This chain is known as the Great Dividing Range. The dominating structural division, the Great Western Plateau, has a few high tablelands and ridges such as The Kimberleys Region and the Hamersley, Macdonnell and Musgrave Ranges. The Hamersley Range contains Western Australia's highest peak, Mount Bruce (1,208 m). The Northern Territory's highest point is Mount Zeil (1,485 m) in the Macdonnell Ranges, and South Australia's highest is Mount Woodroffe (1,500 m) in the Musgrave Ranges. Ayers Rock, (330 m), a huge monolith rising from the central Australia desert with a circumference of 9.7 km, is sometimes referred to as the 'largest stone in the world'. The Great Dividing Range stretches from Cape York in Queensland to the southern seaboard of Tasmania, but despite the name the mountains of the Divide are relatively low. In the north and central sections they rarely exceed 1,500 m. The rugged south-eastern area, known as the Australian Alps, is higher with peaks of over 1,800 m. This area contains some of Australia's highest land, together with its highest peak, Mount Kosciusko (2,193 m). The Great Divide also provides the highest points in Queensland, Victoria and Tasmania. These peaks are respectively Mount Bartle Frere (1,587 m), Mount Bogong, (1,956 m) and Mount Ossa (1,592 m).

Australia does not possess any extensive inland river system. The greater part of the continent lies within the southern arid belt between latitudes 15° and 35°S. The largest river system is the Murray River and its tributaries, which drain about 1,072,260 sq km (414,000 square miles), including a large part of southern Queensland, the major part of New South Wales and much of Victoria. The river rises in the Australian Alps and flows westward to form, for 1,931 km (1,200 miles), the boundary between New South Wales and Victoria. After flowing 644 km (400 miles) through South Australia it discharges into the Sea at Lake Alexandrina. With its tributaries (the Darling, the Murrumbidgee, the Lachlan and many smaller rivers in New South Wales, and the Goulburn, Ovens, Campaspe and other rivers in Victoria) the Murray has an estimated flow of some 545 million cubic feet annually. Most of the rivers of the central interior flow only after heavy rains, while the majority of Australia's coastal rivers are short, with moderate rates of flow, although the monsoon season in the north of the country can augment the discharge rate enormously. Australia's largest reservoir is the man-made Ord River Dam in Western Australia with a capacity of 200,560 million cubic feet. Other major reservoirs are Lake Eucumbene, New South Wales, with a storage capacity of 169,450 million cubic feet, Eildon Weir, Victoria, 119,794 million cubic feet, and Hume Reservoir, NSW, 108,916 million cubic feet. Other large lakes include Lake Corangamite, Victoria, 207 sq km in area, Great Lake, Tasmania, and the Gippsland

Lakes, Victoria. The largest lake in Australia is Lake Eyre, which covers an area of about 9,500 sq km (3,668 square miles) with neighbouring Lake Eyre South. However, this lake in central Australia is generally dry, with its bed covered with salt. This is true of many of the lakes of inland Australia, which, although big in area, often contain no water except after infrequent rain.

The four seasons in Australia are: Spring, September to November; Summer, December to February; Autumn, March to May; and Winter, June to August. In most parts January is the hottest month, but in Tasmania and southern Victoria February is hotter, while in the tropical north December is the hottest month (probably because of the cooling monsoon rains occurring in late summer). In northern Australia the year is divided into the usual tropical divisions of dry and wet seasons, with the wet season occurring in summer and the heaviest rain in January, February and March. On the coast, where rainfall is often abundant, the temperature extremes are limited by the moist atmosphere, whereas in the dry inland areas the extremes extend in proportion to the distance from the seaboard. Central and southern Queensland are sub-tropical. Further south there are the warm temperate regions of north and central New South Wales and the cooler areas of Victoria, south-west Western Australia and Tasmania, with rainfall distributed throughout the year and increasing in winter. Australia's coldest regions are the highlands and tablelands of Tasmania and the south-east corner of the mainland. Australia's regular winter snowfalls occur in these areas. Mean maximum and minimum temperatures of the State capitals are: Sydney 21.5C (70.7F)/13.6C (56.5F); Brisbane 25.5C (77.9F)/15.7C (60.3F); Perth 23.2C (73.8F)/13.1C (55.6F); Darwin 31.9C (89.4F)/23.1C (73.6F); Melbourne 19.7C (67.5F)/10.0C (50.0F); Adelaide 22.3C (72.1F)/11.9C (53.4F); 22.4C (72.3F); Hobart 16.8C (62.2F)/8.2C (46.8F); and Canberra 19.4C (66.9F)/6.3C (43.3F). The heaviest rainfall occurs in western Tasmania (up to 2,444 mm/95.3 in) and on the north coast of Queensland (up to 2,224 mm/86.7 in). A vast area of the interior, however, stretching from the far west of New South Wales and south-west Queensland to the western seaboard of Western Australia has a rainfall below 250 mm a year. Between these regions of heavy and very low rainfall are the extensive areas which experience useful to good rains, up to 1,300 mm/50.7 in a year.

Population

Population censuses are held in Australia every five years. At the last census, in 1986, the population totalled 15.2 million, which included some 227,645 persons claiming to be Aborigines or Islanders. By 1991 the population was estimated to be 17,280,000. English is the official language used by the population, except for small minorities of the foreign-born. There are, however, many aboriginal languages; it is believed that at the time of the beginning of white settlement there were about 500. Many attempts have been made in the past to link the Australian languages with other parts of the world, i.e., South India, the Andaman Islands and Africa, but without success. The following are the main groups: the prefixing languages of the Kimberleys and North Australian Regions; the languages of the Western Desert; the Aranda Group of Central Australia; the Victorian languages and the languages of Eastern Australia.

In the 1986 census 73.0 per cent of the population acknowledged the Christian faith; 2.0 per cent were non-Christians; and the balance were either indefinite, had no religion or made no reply.

Health

The direct provision of health services, broadly speaking, is the responsibility of the State governments. The Commonwealth Government is primarily concerned with the formation of broad national policies and influences policy-making in health services through its financial arrangements with the States and the regulation of health insurance. Under the Medicare insurance scheme introduced in 1984 patients obtain refunds of 85 per cent of standard fees authorised for treatment by private medical practitioners and free treatment in hospital. Since 1984 some medical benefits were reduced. At 30th June 1987 there were 1,053 hospitals, with 87,586 beds (5.4 per 1,000 population). In 1989 the major causes of death were diseases of the circulatory system, neoplasms and diseases of the respiratory system. Infectious diseases accounted for relatively few deaths.

Communications

There are about 70 ports of commercial significance in Australia. The largest in terms of annual tonnage loaded (1986/87 figures) are: Dampier (32,099,000), Port Hedland (32,299,000), Newcastle (31,877,000) and Hay Point (29,633,000). The principal shipping companies are: the Australian National Line, the Union Steamship Company of New Zealand, the Associated Steamships Pty Ltd, the Broken Hill Pty Co Ltd, the State Shipping Service of Western Australia, Ampol Petroleum Ltd and Bulkships Ltd.

There are major airports at, or near, all capital cities and most of the larger cities and towns. The principal airports, with distance from the centre of the city in kilometres and length of main runway in metres are: Sydney 18 (3,900); Melbourne 23 (3,600); Brisbane 6 (2,328); Perth 10 (3,090); Darwin 6 (3,300); Adelaide 6 (2,400); Canberra 6 (2,640); Hobart 16 (1,950). Australia's international airline is QANTAS Airways Ltd. The two major domestic airlines are Australian Airlines and Ansett Airlines of Australia.

Railway track totals 38,753 km (24,085 miles) (1986). There are still three gauges, although since 1982 the mainland capitals have been linked by standard gauge.

Australia has 808,379 km (502,411 miles) of highways and roads open for general traffic (1986).

The Economy

A wide range of primary and secondary industry products is made in Australia. The main primary products are wool, wheat and flour, meat, dairy products, sugar, fruit, and a number of minerals including lead, zinc, copper, coal, iron ore, gold, bauxite and uranium. Secondary industry production is diverse and includes engineering products, motor vehicles, chemicals, textiles, domestic appliances, newsprint, petroleum products, food processing, clothing and iron and steel making.

The unit of currency is the Australian dollar.

Total estimated expenditure of the Federal Government for 1989/90 was $86,753 million and estimated receipts were $95,875 million.

Australia has constantly under way a programme of major development schemes. The nation's largest resource project is currently the North West Shelf gas and liquids complex off the West Australian coast.

Education

Primary education is available free throughout Australia and is compulsory between the ages of 6 and 15–16 years; the permissible school-leaving age varies slightly between States. Education is controlled by the State Territory Governments. In addition to the free government schools, there are church and private schools, most of which charge fees. There are special schools, both governmental and non-governmental, for the handicapped. Secondary education throughout Australia is extensive, covering a period of 5 to 6 years (again varying between States) and including High (Grammar) and Technical schools to university entrance, plus numerous specialist schools and colleges in such particular fields as business and commerce, agriculture and home science. University and other tertiary education, including post-graduate institutions, is also extensive. Some newly arrived immigrants know little English, but literacy in their own language is one of the requirements for entry to the country. A special education system helps them adjust to the new language.

Broadcasting

There are 100 national radio stations transmitting the programmes of the Australian Broadcasting Corporation in the medium wave band, together with 6 high frequency and 141 frequency modulation services. There are 144 commercial radio stations broadcasting in the medium wave band and FM. There are 654 television transmitter stations, made up of 366 national and 288 commercial stations (1988 figures).

History

The Aborigines have inhabited Australia for at least 40,000 years. Estimates of the size of the population at the time of the first European landings vary, but some go as high as 750,000. The first known landings were made by the Dutch. In 1606 William Jansz went ashore on the west coast of Cape York Peninsula. A few years later Dirk Hartog sighted the west coast of Australia at Shark Bay and, thereafter, a number of other ships touched on the coast, which was found to be barren and inhospitable. The Dutch named it New Holland. In 1642 Abel Tasman landed on what is now Tasmania, which he named Van Diemen's Land, after the Governor-General in Batavia. A further voyage to the north coast of Australia confirmed the Dutch East India Company's view that no profit was to be obtained from the new land and further exploration was abandoned. The British Admiralty were equally unimpressed by reports of the voyages of Dampier to the west and north-west in 1688 and 1699.

For seventy years no further exploration took place, but on 29th April 1770 Captain James Cook, in command of HMS *Endeavour* and accompanied by the botanist, Sir Joseph Banks, landed at Botany Bay. Subsequently, on 22nd August 1770, Cook took possession of the whole eastern coast, i.e. what now constitutes Victoria and the eastern part of New South Wales and Queensland, in right of King George III. On 18th January 1788 Governor Arthur Phillip and the first party of convicts arrived at Botany Bay and on 26th January moved to Sydney Cove in Port Jackson. A secondary settlement was made at Norfolk Island. (26th January is celebrated as the Australian National Day.) Exploration continued, by Bass and Flinders in particular, and the latter confirmed that New South Wales and New Holland formed part of one continent.

Further settlements were made and these were followed by the advent of free settlers. In 1831 Western Australia became the second Colony, followed in 1836 by South Australia, in 1851 by Victoria, in 1856 by Tasmania and in 1859 by Queensland. (The Northern Territory did not achieve self-government until 1978.) As the rearing of sheep and the wool industry developed (with a ready market in London), and against a background of over-crowding and deprivation in Britain's burgeoning population, emigration to Australia quickened, until by 1850 convicts accounted for less than 15 per cent of the population. Transportation of convicts to New South Wales ceased in 1840, to Tasmania in 1853 and to Western Australia in 1868. Between 1855 and 1890 Westminster-style parliamentary democracy was introduced in all of the colonies.

Meanwhile the economy of Australia had been further strengthened by the discovery of gold and other minerals. Gold, in particular, led to a great inrush of population and to a movement of people within Australia. By 1891 the country had over three million inhabitants. In addition Australia rapidly became one of the leading wheat-producing countries and the invention of refrigeration led to an export trade in dairy products and mutton. The basis of a railway system was laid and as communications improved and the population increased it gradually became apparent that the community of interest between the colonies justified some closer union. After many vicissitudes the Commonwealth of Australia came into existence on 1st January 1901.

Many of the bases of modern Australian social policy and industrial legislation were established between Federation and the First World War, along with a policy of protection, to further national development and maintain full employment. The modern steel industry dates from 1915, when Broken Hill Proprietary started its first blast furnace in Newcastle. This led in due course to the development of other industries, as well as mining. The depression of 1929 severely checked the pace of this development, however, and it did not pick up again until shortly before the Second World War. By 1939 industry accounted for two-fifths of the value of total production, compared with one-fifth in 1911. After the war expansion and diversification accelerated. Immigration was rapidly stepped up (by the end of 1986 an estimated 4,466 new settlers had entered, 41 per cent of them British). The country became virtually self-sufficient in iron and steel in 1958, the car manufacturing industry developed and this in turn encouraged the development of oil refining. The mining of uranium and bauxite was developed, as well as the mining of coal. Commercial oil fields were discovered. Nevertheless agriculture, particularly sheep-rearing, remained the mainstay of the country.

In 1988 celebrations were held, at both national and local level, to commemorate the bicentenary of European settlement.

Constitution

The Commonwealth Parliament

The Commonwealth of Australia Constitution, which was enacted by the Commonwealth of Australia Constitution Act 1900 (UK), established a Federal Parliament called the Parliament of the Commonwealth, consisting of the Queen, the Senate and the House of Representatives. A Governor-General appointed by the Queen is Her Majesty's representative in the Commonwealth. The Constitution requires that a session of the Parliament be held at least once in every year. In 1974 the Queen was pleased to adopt in Australia the style and title of Queen of Australia.

The Senate

As envisaged in the Constitution, the Senate is both a States' House and a House of Review. The present number of Senators is 76, 12 for each of the six States and 2 each for the Australian Capital Territory and the Northern Territory. The Senate is presided over by the President of the Senate, who is chosen by the members from among their number. Senators are chosen for a term of six years. The places of one half of the senators elected by the States become vacant after three years from election, and are then filled for six years (elections of the 4 Senators from the Territories are held at the same time as elections for the House of Representatives). In the event of a double dissolution all Senate places become vacant. The method of electing Senators is by proportional representation.

The House of Representatives

The House of Representatives is at present composed of 148 members, and although the number may be increased or decreased by Parliament such changes must comply with the requirement that the number of members shall, as nearly as practicable, be twice the number of Senators. Unlike the Senate, which has equal representation for each State, the number of Representatives chosen in the respective States is required to be in proportion to the respective numbers of their people. The House of Representatives is presided over by the Speaker, who is chosen by the members from among their number. Every House of Representatives continues for three years from its first meeting, and no longer, but it may be dissolved sooner by the Governor-General. Representatives are elected for Electoral Divisions on an alternative preferential voting system.

To qualify for election to either House a person must be an Australian citizen aged at least 18 and have been a resident of Australia for at least three years.

All persons aged at least 18 and who are citizens of Australia are entitled to vote. (British citizens who were enrolled on or before 25th January, 1984 may also vote).

The Constitution confers on the Parliament two classes of powers: those in respect of which it alone has power to legislate, i.e. exclusive powers, and those in respect of which the States retain power to legislate concurrently, i.e. concurrent powers. When a concurrent State law is inconsistent with a Commonwealth law, the latter prevails and the State law is, to the extent of the inconsistency, invalid. Exclusive powers expressly provided for in the Constitution include the seat of the Commonwealth Government and all places acquired by the Commonwealth for public purposes, the departments of the Commonwealth Public Service, the imposition of customs and excise duties and, subject to limited exceptions, the granting of bounties on the production or export of goods. Concurrent powers given to the Parliament include the power to make laws for the peace, order and good government of the

Commonwealth in respect of international and inter-State trade and commerce, taxation, defence, banking and insurance (other than State banking and insurance), industrial property, immigration and emigration, aliens and naturalisation, marriage, divorce and matrimonial causes, social services, external affairs and conciliation and arbitration for the prevention and settlement of industrial disputes extending beyond the limits of any one State.

With certain exceptions, proposed laws may originate in either House. Proposed laws appropriating revenue or money or imposing taxation may originate only in the House of Representatives and the Senate may not amend them. However, it may return to the House of Representatives such a proposed law requesting the omission or amendment of any item or provision. Should a deadlock occur between the two Houses over a proposed law passed by the House of Representatives and after three months from the disagreement the House of Representatives again passes the proposed law and the Houses again fail to agree, the Governor-General may dissolve both Houses immediately. If, after the double dissolution, the House of Representatives again passes the proposed law and another deadlock occurs, the Governor-General may convene a joint sitting of Representatives and Senators and if the proposed law is passed by an absolute majority of them sitting together it is considered to have been duly passed by both Houses. The first ever joint sitting took place in August 1974 following the double dissolution in May. When a proposed law has been passed by both Houses, it is presented to the Governor-General, who is empowered to assent the Bill in the Queen's name, withhold assent or reserve the law for the Queen's pleasure. Additionally, the Queen is empowered to disallow any law within one year from the Governor-General's assent. These powers of the Queen and the Governor-General are not now exercised.

The executive power of the Commonwealth is vested in the Queen and is exercised by the Governor-General as the Queen's representative. The Governor-General is advised by the Federal Executive Council, the members of which are appointed by him. By convention the Governor-General summons to meetings of the Executive Council only such members as are Ministers of State of the Government of the day. All Ministers of States, of which there are at present 30, are members. By convention the Ministry consists of the leaders of the party or parties which hold a majority of seats in the House of Representatives.

The judicial power of the Commonwealth is vested in the federal courts, i.e. the High Court of Australia and other courts created by Parliament such as the Federal Court of Australia, and the Family Law Court and in certain courts of the States and Territories when exercising federal jurisdiction conferred upon them by Commonwealth law. The High Court of Australia, which is the Federal Supreme Court, consists of the Chief Justice and six other justices, all of whom are, in common with justices of other federal courts, appointed by the Governor-General in Council and are removable by him only on an address by both Houses of Parliament on the ground of proved misbehaviour or incapacity. The High Court has both original and appellate jurisdiction, as envisaged in the Constitution. The Constitution also guarantees that the trial on indictment of an offence against any law of the Commonwealth shall be by jury, and that every such trial shall be held in the State where the offence was committed.

Income tax is levied only by the Commonwealth Parliament and the Commonwealth Government shares the revenue therefrom with the States in proportions agreed each year after consultations with the State Governments. In theory each State can, if it so chooses, legislate to increase its revenue from personal income tax or to give a rebate on personal income tax to residents in the State, but no State has so far done so.

States may not, without the consent of the Commonwealth Parliament, raise or maintain any naval or military forces or impose any tax on property belonging to the Commonwealth; and the Commonwealth in turn is required to protect every State against invasion and, on the application of the Executive Government of the State, against domestic violence, and is not permitted to impose any tax on property belonging to a State. States are required to make provision for the detention in State prisons of persons accused or convicted of offences against the law of the Commonwealth and for the punishment of persons convicted of such offences. The Commonwealth Parliament may admit to the Commonwealth, or establish, new States and in so doing impose such terms and conditions, including the extent of representation in either House of Parliament, as it thinks fit.

The Constitution directed the Commonwealth Parliament to determine the seat of Government, subject to the requirements that it be situated in territory within the State of New South Wales to be granted to, or acquired by, the Commonwealth and that it be situated not less than one hundred miles from the State Capital, Sydney. In 1908 the Parliament chose the area now known as the Australian Capital Territory as the seat of government, although it was not until 1927 that the Parliament first met in Canberra, the national capital situated in the Territory, in a 'provisional' parliament building. (In the interim it had met in Melbourne). A new and definitive parliament building on Capital Hill was opened by the Queen in May 1988, Bicentennial Year.

A proposed amendment of the Constitution must be passed by an absolute majority of both Houses of Parliament and must, not less than two or more than six months after its passage, be submitted in each State to electors qualified to vote for the House of Representatives. It must then be passed by an absolute majority of all electors voting and absolute majorities of the electors in a majority of the States. Since 1901 42 proposals have been submitted to the electors and of these only 8 have been approved.

Government

The last General Election held on 24th March 1990 was won by the Australian Labor Party (ALP) under the leadership of Mr Bob Hawke, who formed the Government. On 20th December 1991 Mr Hawke was succeeded as Prime Minister by Mr Paul Keating, following an ALP leadership election.

HEAD OF STATE
Her Majesty Queen Elizabeth II

GOVERNOR-GENERAL
His Excellency The Hon Mr William Hayden, AC

COMMONWEALTH GOVERNMENT
(First Keating Ministry, December 1991)

**Prime Minister:* The Hon Paul Keating, MP
**Deputy Prime Minister, Minister for Health, Housing and Community Services and Minister assisting the Prime Minister for Social Justice and for Commonwealth-State Relations:* The Hon Brian Howe, MP
**Leader of the Government in the Senate, Minister for Industry, Technology and Commerce:* Senator The Hon John Button
**Deputy Leader of the Government in the Senate and Minister for Foreign Affairs and Trade:* Senator The Hon Gareth Evans, QC, MP
**Attorney-General:* The Hon Michael Duffy, MP
**Minister for Finance:* The Hon Ralph Willis, MP
**Minister for Transport and Communications, and Vice-President of the Executive Council:* Senator The Hon Graham Richardson
**Minister for Employment, Education and Training and Leader of the House:* The Hon Kim Beazley, MP
**Minister for Defence:* Senator The Hon Robert Ray
**Minister for Primary Industries and Energy:* The Hon Simon Crean, MP
**Minister for Social Security:* The Hon Neal Blewett, MP
**Minister for Administrative Services:* Senator The Hon Nick Bolkus
**Treasurer:* Hon John Dawkins, MP
**Minister for the Arts, Sport, the Environment and Territories:* The Hon Ros Kelly, MP
**Minister for Industrial Relations and Minister assisting the Prime Minister for Public Service Matters:* Senator The Hon Peter Cook
**Minister for Immigration, Local Government and Ethnic Affairs and Minister assisting the Prime Minister for Multicultural Affairs:* The Hon Gerry Hand, MP
**Minister for Trade and Overseas Development:* The Hon John Kerin, MP
Minister for Family Support: The Hon David Simmons, MP
Minister for Science and Technology and Minister Assisting the Prime Minister: The Hon Ross Free, MP
Minister for Justice and Consumer Affairs: Senator The Hon Michael Tate
Minister for Veterans' Affairs: The Hon Ben Humphreys, MP
Minister for Aboriginal and Torres Strait Islander Affairs and Minister Assisting the Prime Minister for Aboriginal Reconciliation: The Hon Robert Tickner, MP
Minister for Aged, Family and Health Services: The Hon Peter Staples, MP
Minister for Higher Education and Employment Services: The Hon Peter Baldwin, MP
Minister for the Arts and Territories and Minister assisting the Prime Minister for the Status of Women: The Hon Wendy Fatin, MP
**Minister for Tourism and Minister for Resources:* The Hon Alan Griffiths, MP
Minister for Land Transport: The Hon Bob Brown, MP
**Minister for Shipping and Aviation and Minister Assisting the Prime Minister on Northern Australia:* Senator The Hon Bob Collins
Minister for Defence Science and Personnel: The Hon Gordon Bilney, MP
Minister for Small Business, Construction and Customs: The Hon David Beddall, MP

* Minister in the Cabinet

STATES OF THE COMMONWEALTH AND AUSTRALIAN TERRITORIES

General

In each of the States the Queen is represented by the Governor. All the powers and functions of Her Majesty are exercisable only by the Governor, except when she is personally present in the State. This is now provided for in the Australia Acts which were enacted by the United Kingdom and Commonwealth Parliaments and came into force in March 1986. Under the Acts the Queen, on the advice of the Premier, appoints the Governor. The Govenor acts generally on the advice of the Executive Council or a Minister of the Crown, but also possesses some discretionary powers in certain limited spheres. The Executive Council consists of members of the Ministry formed by the leader of the dominant party in the Legislative, or House of, Assembly and the Governor presides over its deliberations. In practice the pre-eminent policy-making body in each State is the Cabinet, which initiates, directs and coordinates government policy. As the Queen's representative the Governor summons and prorogues Parliament, gives Assent to Bills which have passed all stages in Parliament, with the exception of those required to be specially reserved for the Royal Assent, and exercises the Royal prerogative of mercy.

NEW SOUTH WALES

New South Wales lies in the south eastern portion of the continent and covers about 801,600 sq km (309,418 square miles), a little over two and a half times the size of Great Britain. The estimated population in June 1989 was 5,761,919 of which 3,596,000 lived in the State capital, Sydney. Lord Howe Island in the Tasman Sea is also administered as part of New South Wales.

History

The name New South Wales was given to the eastern portion of Australia (then still called New Holland) on its discovery by Captain Cook in HMS *Endeavour* in 1770. The first European settlement was not formed until 1788, however, when Captain Phillip landed from the First Fleet at Port Jackson near the present day Sydney. New South Wales initially constituted virtually the whole of the eastern continent; Tasmania, Victoria, South Australia and Queensland were eventually separated from it. Population growth was at first slow but accelerated after 1851 when gold was discovered. Responsible government was granted in 1855 and Sydney rapidly expanded to become one of the major commercial and political centres of the country.

Economy

The State economy has important agricultural, manufacturing, mining, mineral and service sectors. Chief exports in 1988/89 were coal and coke, wool, wheat, meat, non-ferrous metal and iron and steel.

The agricultural sector includes major production of cattle (4.9 million), sheep and lambs (54.9 million), pigs, wool (about 240,000 tons in grease), wheat, barley, oats, rice, cotton, sugar cane, tobacco and bananas. Dairying and poultry production are also important. Agriculture employs about 5 per cent of the State's working population.

The State has a relatively broad manufacturing base with the 'other machinery and equipment' being the largest and 'textiles' the smallest sectors. In general manufacturing activity is focused on Sydney, extending to Newcastle in the north and Wollongong in the south. Over 90 per cent of manufacturing employment and value added are in this area. In national terms New South Wales accounts for 34 per cent of employment and 37 per cent of value added in manufacturing.

Mining and minerals are also important activities. The principal minerals are coal, lead, zinc, gold, rutile, copper and zircon. Construction materials such as stone, sand and gravel are also important. About 1.3 per cent of the State's working population are engaged in mining and minerals.

GOVERNOR

HE Rear Admiral Peter Sinclair, AO

STATE MINISTRY

(Liberal Party/National Party Coalition)

Premier, Treasurer, Minister for Ethnic Affairs: The Hon Nicholas Greiner, MP
Deputy Premier, Minister for Public Works, Minister for Roads: The Hon Wallace Murray, MP
Minister for Agriculture and Rural Affairs: The Hon Ian Armstrong, MP
Minister for Transport: The Hon Bruce Baird, MP
Minister for Natural Resources: The Hon Ian Causley, MP
Attorney General, Minister for Consumer Affairs, Minister for Arts: The Hon Peter Collins, MP
Minister for Industrial Relations and Minister for Further Education, Training and Employment: The Hon John Fahey, MP
Minister for School Education and Youth Affairs: The Hon Virginia Chadwick, MLC
Minister for the Environment: The Hon Timothy Moore, MP
Minister for Hospital Management: The Hon Ronald Phillips, MP
Minister for Courts Administration and Corrective Services: The Hon Terence Griffiths, MP
Minister for Local Government, and Minister for Cooperatives: The Hon Gerald Peacock, MP
Minister for Police and Emergency Services, Vice-President of the Executive Council: The Hon Edward Pickering, MLC
Minister for Sport, Recreation and Racing and Minister assisting the Premier: The Hon George Souris, MP
Minister for Housing: The Hon Joseph Schipp, MP
Minister for Planning and Minister for Energy: The Hon Robert Webster, MLC
Minister for Conservation and Land Management: The Hon Garry West, MP
Minister for State Development and Minister for Tourism: The Hon Michael Yabsley, MP
Minister for Health and Community Services: The Hon John Hannaford, MLC
Chief Secretary and Minister for Administrative Services: The Hon Anne Cohen, MP

VICTORIA

Victoria is located in the extreme south east of the continent and covers approximately 227,920 sq km (88,000 square miles). The population was estimated at 4,209,000 in June 1987 of which about 2,931,900 lived in Melbourne, the State capital.

History

The first Europeans to sight Victoria were probably the men of Cook's expedition in 1770. However, the first permanent settlement was not founded until 1834 at Portland: Melbourne followed in 1835. The territory now constituting the State was separated from New South Wales in 1851 to form a new colony of Victoria. Gold was discovered soon afterwards which stimulated a major influx of population. Responsible government was granted in 1855.

Economy

The State economy includes a wide range of activity and has important agricultural, mining, manufacturing and service sectors.

Wheat provides Victoria with its largest single crop and other important agricultural activities include the production of wool, meat and dairy products. Forest products are also important.

The State has a relatively broad manufacturing base and manufacturing remains the most significant single sector in terms of its contribution to the Gross State Product although it has been steadily declining in recent years. Victoria's industries are centred on Melbourne and, apart from smelting and large scale steel making, most types of secondary industry are found in the city. Geelong is the next most important industrial centre. Engineering and metal working remain key industries although they have seen difficult years during the 1980s. Food processing is also significant.

Mining and minerals are important activities. Gold is still mined and the discovery in 1965, and subsequent development of sizeable reserves of oil and natural gas, have contributed to the State's prosperity.

GOVERNOR

HE Dr Davis McCaughey, AC

STATE MINISTRY

(Labor Party)

Premier, Minister responsible for Women's Affairs: The Hon (Mrs) Joan Kirner, MLA

Deputy Premier, Attorney-General, Minister for the Arts, Minister for Major Projects: The Hon James Kennan, QC, MLA

Minister for Manufacturing and Industry Development, Minister responsible for Ports: The Hon David White, MLC

Minister for Tourism, Minister for Water Resources: The Hon Steven Crabb, MLA

Treasurer: The Hon Tony Sheenan, MLA

Minister for Ethnic, Municipal and Community Affairs: The Hon Caroline Hogg, MLC

Minister for Employment, Post-Secondary Education and Training, Minister for Aboriginal Affairs, Minister responsible for Gaming: The Hon Tom Roper, MLA

Minister for Sport and Recreation: The Hon Neil Trezise, MLA

Minister for Transport: The Hon Peter Spyker, MLA

Minister for Finance: The Hon John Harrowfield, MLA

Minister for Planning and Housing: The Hon Andrew McCutcheon, MLA

Minister for Labour, Minister for School Education: The Hon Neil Pope, MLA

Minister for Conservation and Environment: The Hon Barry Pullen, MLC

Minister for Community Services and Minister responsible for Child Care: The Hon (Mrs) Kay Setches, MLA

Minister for Food and Agriculture: The Hon Ian Baker, MLA

Minister for Health: The Hon Ms Maureen Lyster, MLC

Minister for Police and Emergency Services, Minister for Corrections: The Hon Mal Sandon, MLA

Minister for Small Business, Consumer Affairs, Minister for Manufacturing and Industry: The Hon Theo Theophanous, MLC

QUEENSLAND

Queensland occupies the north-eastern portion of Australia, covers almost a quarter of the continent (an area of 1,727,196 sq km (666,871 square miles)), is 7 times the size of the United Kingdom and has a 7,401 km (4,600 mile) coastline. The population was estimated at 2,906,800 in June 1990 of which 1,301,658 lived in Brisbane, the State capital.

History

Captain Cook, in HMS *Endeavour*, discovered Moreton Bay in 1770 but it was 1824 before a settlement was founded. The Darling Downs were explored from 1827 and settlement followed soon afterwards although the territory was not thrown open to colonisation until 1842. In 1859 Queensland was detached from New South Wales and formed as a separate colony with responsible government.

Economy

Queensland is predominantly a primary producer with vast mineral deposits and an important rural sector. The State enjoys a healthy positive balance of trade (exports A$10,901 m; imports A$4,258 m in 1989/90). The strength of the State economy depends on the three major sectors of mining and minerals, agriculture and tourism.

Of Australia's mineral wealth Queensland produces 49 per cent of the black coal, 74 per cent of copper, 47 per cent of silver, and 35 per cent of lead. There are major resources of gold, bauxite, zinc, nickel, tin, magnesite, mineral sands, kaolin and gemstones. Total mineral production is currently valued at A$5,107 m (of which coal accounts for A$2,879 m, and copper A$561 m).

Mining, minerals and related manufacturing contribute 11.7 per cent to the Gross State Product, provide 42 per cent of the State's export revenue and employ 23,000 (half in the coal sector).

Queensland accounts for 20 per cent of Australian primary production, 44 per cent of Australia's meat and virtually all of its sugar. This sector includes the major production of sheep (16.3 m) and beef cattle (8.8 m) pigs, poultry, eggs, milk, wool, cotton, wheat, barley, maize, rice, peanuts, ginger, tobacco, fruit and horticulture. Total agricultural production is currently valued at A$4,723 m.

The newest and fastest growing of the sectors of the Queensland economy is tourism. In the past decade Queensland has recorded twice the growth in tourism than has the rest of Australia. Current earnings represent 7 per cent of Gross State Product and employs 70,000 directly and 145,000 indirectly. The number of overseas visitors catered for in 1989/90 was 961,000. It is currently estimated that 43 per cent of all new investment in the tourism infrastructure in Australia is in Queensland.

Queensland's Gross State Product (at 1985/86 prices)	—A$43,680 m
Exports (1989/90)	—A$10,461 m
Imports (1989/90)	—A$4,258 m
Workforce employed (May 1991)	—1,297,720
Unemployment rate (May 1991)	—10.7%

GOVERNOR

HE The Hon Sir Walter Campbell, AC, QC

STATE MINISTRY

(Labor Party)

Premier, Minister for Economic and Trade Development and Minister for the Arts: The Hon W K Goss, MLA (Wayne)

Deputy Premier, Minister for Housing and Local Government: The Hon T J Burns, MLA (Tom)

Minister for Police and Emergency Services: The Hon T M Mackenroth, MLA (Terry)

Treasurer: The Hon K E De Lacy, MLA (Keith)

Minister for Tourism, Sport and Racing: The Hon R J Gibbs, MLA (Bob)

Minister for Transport and Minister Assisting the Premier on Economic and Trade Development: The Hon D J Hamill, MLA (David)

Minister for Employment, Training and Industrial Relations: The Hon N G Warburton, MLA (Nev)

Minister for Resource Industries: The Hon K H Vaughan, MLA (Ken)

Minister for Primary Industries: The Hon E D Casey, MLA (Ed)

Minister for Health: The Hon K V McElligott, MLA (Ken)

Minister for Education: The Hon P J Braddy, MLA (Paul)

Minister for Environment and Heritage: The Hon P Comben, MLA (Pat)

Attorney-General: The Hon D Wells, MLA (Deane)

Minister for Family Services and Aboriginal and Islander Affairs: The Hon A M Warner, MLA (Anne)

Minister for Justice and Corrective Services: The Hon G R Milliner, MLA (Glen)

Minister for Administrative Services: The Hon R T McLean, MLA (Ron)

Minister for Business, Industry and Regional Development: The Hon G N Smith, MLA (Geoff)

Minister for Land Management: The Hon A G Eaton, MLA (Bill)

The Speaker: Hon D Fouras (Jim)

Leader of the Opposition: T R Cooper, MLA (Russell)

SOUTH AUSTRALIA

South Australia is located in the southern central portion of the continent and has a total area of about 984,381 sq km (380,070 square miles) of which about 37,490 km (23,300 miles) are closely settled (principally near the coast) while the remainder is under sparse occupation, mainly pastoral. The State population in June 1989 was estimated at 1,420,131 of whom 1,036,700 lived in the capital, Adelaide.

History

The south coast was explored by Captain Flinders in 1802 and Captain Sturt in 1830. The colony of South Australia was founded in 1836 on the pattern of colonisation advocated by Edward Gibbon Wakefield; land sales were used to finance emigration into the colony. Control was intially divided between the Colonial Office and a Board of Commissioners for Land Sales and Emigration. The Board was abolished in 1841 and in 1842 a nominated Legislative Council was established. Responsible government was granted in 1856.

Economy

South Australia's economy is relatively diversified. Manufacturing remains a major contributor towards the State's economic base along with primary industries, and the services sector.

Manufacturing employment in South Australia is slightly more significant than for Australia as a whole, and employment in this area remains resilient. A major component of manufacturing includes motor vehicle production. Around 30 per cent of Australia's car manufacturing production occurs in South Australia as well as 40 per cent of the nation's car component production.

The Food and Beverage Industry significantly contributes to manufacturing output employing in excess of 16,000 people. The State's success in the production and export of raw food commodities has led to the development of a large and diversified food processing sector in which the agricultural sector plays an important role. The principal agricultural commodities include wool, wheat, other grain crops, meat, vegetables, fruit and dairy products. Over 50 per cent of Australia's wine is produced in South Australia. South Australia has internationally recognised expertise in dry-land farming techniques, irrigation, soil conservation and watershed management.

Despite the increased competition Adelaide looks set to remain a major whitegoods production centre in Australia. Products made by this group include refrigerators, electric stoves, dishwashing machines, clothes dryers and washers, airconditioners, air coolers and heaters. South Australia possesses some of the most advanced manufacturing plants for electric motors in Australia.

The services sector continues to grow and accounts for around two-thirds of South Australia's production and employment. Areas for potential growth include communications, recreational and personal services, and use of medical and educational facilities.

The State has continued to gravitate towards high technology based industries and is recognised as Australia's most technologically advanced State, with the concentration of the microelectronics and biotechnology industries. More than 500 companies are involved in the production of a range of advanced technology production facilitated by developments at Technology Park, which is renowned world wide as a centre for commercialisation in the information technology and telecommunications field.

South Australia has emerged as the centre for defence related development and production. Construction of submarines for the Royal Australian Navy is based in Adelaide and the State has gained major sub-contracts from the ANZAC Ship Project. The Defence Science Technology Organisation has been responsible for most of Australia's defence and aerospace innovations and is the biggest facility of its kind in the Southern Hemisphere.

South Australia's major export items have traditionally included primary products. However, in recent years the manufacturing sector has become the major export earner for the State accounting for over half of the State's exports. Some of the major elaborately transformed manufactured exports consist of vehicle, vehicle parts, lenses, industry equipment, electrical equipment, glassware, leather, and opal. South Australia's major trading partners include Japan, New Zealand, USA, Singapore and UK.

The Cooper Basin in South Australia's far north provides the State with reserves of liquid petroleum gas and ethane. A hydrocarbon pipeline from the Basin has been completed and opportunities are being evaluated for a substantial petrochemical industry. The world's largest copper, iron, uranium, gold, silver and rare earth mine is located in the State's north at Olympic Dam. South Australia is continuing to capitalise on its mineral resource base and enhance the value of production through developments such as the processing of rare earths to the metal stage. The Steel Industry is concentrated at Whyalla where BHP specialises in long products such as railway lines, structural shapes and sections.

GOVERNOR

HE Dame Roma Mitchell, DBE, CBE

STATE MINISTRY

(Labor Party)

Premier, Treasurer and Minister for State Development: The Hon John Bannon, MP

Deputy Premier, Minister of Health, Community Services and the Aged: The Hon Dr Don Hopgood MP

Attorney-General, Minister for Corporate Affairs and Crime Prevention: The Hon Chris Sumner, MP

Minister of Environment and Planning, Lands and Water Resources: The Hon Susan Lenehan, JP, MP

Minister of Transport, Correctional Services and Finance: The Hon Frank Blevins, MP

Minister of Industry, Trade and Technology, Agriculture and Fisheries, and Ethnic Affairs: The Hon Lynn Arnold, MP
Minister of Mines and Energy, Forests and Emergency Services: The Hon John Klunder, JP, MP
Minister of Education and Children's Services: The Hon Greg Crafter, MP
Minister of Recreation and Sport, Housing and Construction, and Public Works: The Hon Kim Mayes, MP
Minister of Employment and Further Education, Aboriginal Affairs, Youth Affairs and Minister Assisting the Minister for Ethnic Affairs: The Hon Mike Rann, JP, MP
Minister of Labour, Marine, and Occupational Safety and Health: The Hon Bob Gregory, MP
Minister of Tourism, Consumer Affairs and Small Business: The Hon Barbara Wiese, MP
Minister of Arts, Local Government and State Services: The Hon Judith Levy, MP

WESTERN AUSTRALIA

Western Australia covers 2,527,840 sq km (976,000 square miles), nearly one-third of the Australian continent, and is bigger than the combined areas of Great Britain, Japan and Texas. At the end of 1989 the population was estimated to be 1,614,800 of which 1,161,150 lived in Perth, the State capital. Despite its limited population, however, Western Australia contributes substantially to Australia's overall wealth: in the financial year 1988/89 the State accounted for 20.3 per cent of Australian exports by value.

History

The first documented European contact with Western Australia was in 1616. In 1791 Captain Vancouver, in HMS *Discovery*, took formal possession of the area around King George Sound but it was 1826 before a small settlement, subsequently named Albany, was founded. In 1829 Captain Fremantle took formal possession of the territory and in the same year Captain Stirling, who was appointed Lieutenant-Governor, founded the Swan River settlement and the towns of Perth and Fremantle. In 1870 representative government was established whereby the Governor was assisted by an Executive Council of officials and appointed members and a Legislative Council which consisted of three official members of the Executive Council, three unofficial nominees of the Governor and twelve elected members. Responsible government was granted in 1890.

Economy

With a population of only 1.6 million the domestic market in Western Australia is limited. In addition, the State's remoteness from overseas markets has restricted the development of manufacturing industries. Most manufacturing companies are geared to supporting the flourishing mining and offshore industries. A new marine ship-lift and support facility has been constructed and is capable of dry-docking ships and submarines to enable overhauls and servicing to be carried out.

The prosperity of the State is derived from the development of its vast mineral reserves, its flourishing agricultural base, and oil and gas deposits located offshore in the North West Shelf.

Mining and Minerals

The Western Australian mining sector has become highly diversified and four major commodities have now exceeded the A$2 billion mark in terms of total production, namely gold (A$2.794 billion); alumina (A$2.359 billion); iron ore (A$2.343 billion); and petroleum products (A$2.232 billion). Other major mining commodities include nickel (A$558 m); diamonds (A$431 m); mineral sands (A$412 m); coal (A$214 m); salt (A$131 m); and other minerals (A$234 m).

Agriculture

The gross value of Western Australian agricultural production declined by almost 7 per cent in 1989/90 following five successive years of expansion. Even so, the 1989/90 nominal gross value of production was the second highest for the decade.

Wheat production in the State for the 1989/90 season at 4.8 m tonnes was slightly less than the previous year, although comparable to the average for the decade. The area sown increased by 5.4 per cent over 1988/89, but the decline in gross value of wheat production in 1989/90 to A$1 billion reflects the marginal fall in yield from the exceptional level of the previous year.

Other crops also contributed to the State's economy, with the lupin crop providing the second largest contribution to the value of Western Australian grain production and exports. Reduced plantings and yield in 1989/90 resulted in a 27.7 per cent decrease in value of production to A$113 m. Barley production increased by 13.2 per cent in 1989/90 and firm export prices also contributed to the increase in value of the barley crop to A$108 m.

In 1989/90 the Western Australian wool clip increased by 15.9 per cent to 235.6 m kilograms. However, final estimates will show a small decrease in wool returns to around A$1.28 billion. The value of wool exports declined by 34 per cent in 1989/90 to A$779 m. This turnaround in wool trade occurred after successive yearly increases throughout most of the 1980's. As world wool market conditions deteriorated in the second half of 1989/90, the Australian Wool Commission stock accumulated to over

2.5 m bales by the close of the season and the reserve price formed a substantial barrier to clearing the market. For the 1989/90 season only 54 per cent of total offerings were sold to the trade.

Offshore Oil and Gas
The North West Shelf Project is the largest single engineering project in Australia — and one of the largest in the world — and has involved investment of A$14 billion. Natural gas from the North Rankin Field already supplies the domestic market. Export of liquified natural gas to Japan commenced in 1989 under long term contracts and construction of a third LNG Processing Train is on schedule with completion anticipated in 1993. This will correspond with the start of gas production from the Goodwyn A Platform, construction of which is also underway.

In 1989/90 Western Australian crude oil and condensate production enjoyed its largest increase since the period of growth commencing in 1984/85. Crude oil and condensate output rose by 80 per cent and 39 per cent respectively. Values of condensate and crude oil increased by 66 per cent and 122 per cent respectively to A$236 m and A$600 m. Natural gas output increased only slightly, although the higher prices in 1989/90 resulted in a 25 per cent increase in value to A$357 m.

Renewed petroleum exploration activity during 1990 has significantly extended the known reserves of petroleum minerals. Wanaea, Cossack and Griffin (together with associated areas) have total reserves of at least 430 m barrels. Gas reserves have also been upgraded at Barrow Island, Scott Reef, Yodel and Scarborough.

The recent large new petroleum finds indicate that oil and condensate exports would rise to $2 billion by the end of the decade, based on known reserves. In addition, LNG Exports from the North West Shelf could boost total oil and gas exports from Western Australia to $4 billion per annum.

GOVERNOR
HE Sir Francis Burt, AC, KCMG, QC

STATE MINISTRY
(Labor Party)

Premier, Treasurer, Minister for the Family, and Women's Interests: The Hon Dr Carmen Lawrence, MLA
Deputy Premier, Minister for State Development, and the Goldfields: The Hon Ian Taylor, MLA
Attorney-General, Minister for Corrective Services, and Leader of the Government in the Legislative Council: The Hon Joe Berinson, MLC
Minister for Education, Employment and Training, the Arts, and Deputy Leader of the Government in the Legislative Council: The Hon Elsie Hallahan, MLC
Minister for the Environment, and Leader of the Government in the Legislative Assembly: The Hon Bob Pearce, MLA
Minister for Health: The Hon Keith Wilson, MLA
Minister for Transport, Racing and Gaming, and Tourism: The Hon Pam Beggs, MLA
Minister for Agriculture, Water Resources, and the North-West: The Hon Francis Bridge, MLA
Minister for Mines, Fisheries, Mid-West, Minister assisting the Minister for State Development: The Hon Gordon Hill, MLA
Minister for Police, Emergency Services, Sport and Recreation: The Hon Graham Edwards, MLC
Minister for Productivity and Labour Relations, and Consumer Affairs: The Hon Yvonne Henderson, MLA
Minister for Justice, Planning, Lands, Local Government, and the South-West: The Hon David Smith, MLA
Minister for Fuel and Energy, Micro-Economic Reform, and Parliamentary and Electoral Reform, Minister assisting the Treasurer: The Hon Geoff Gallop, MLA
Minister for Aboriginal Affairs, Multi-Cultural and Ethnic Affairs, Seniors; Minister assisting the Minister for Women's Interests: The Hon Dr Judyth Watson, MLA
Minister for Community Services and Disability Services: The Hon Eric Ripper, MLA
Minister for Housing, Construction, Services, and Heritage: The Hon Jim McGinty, MLA
Parliamentary Secretary of the Cabinet: Mr W I Thomas, MLA
Leader of the Opposition: Mr Barry MacKinnon, MLA

TASMANIA

Tasmania, Australia's smallest state, forms an island situated at the south eastern extremity of the continent, and comprises about 68,358 sq km (26,393 sq miles). In December 1989 the population was estimated at 453,600 and is concentrated around Hobart, the State capital, Launceston and the towns of the north-west coast.

History

Tasmania was discovered in 1642 by the Dutch navigator Abel Jansoon Tasman and named Van Diemen's Land. Captain Cook landed in 1777 during his third voyage. Britain took formal possession in 1803 and the island was separated from New South Wales in 1825. Hobart was founded in 1804. Responsible government was granted in 1855 and the name Tasmania formally adopted in 1856.

Economy

Tasmania has developed a relatively diverse economic base, but has a small domestic market.

Sheep for wool and meat form one of the State's oldest industries. The dairy industry is an important part of the rural sector. Beef cattle are also reared. Barley, oats and wheat are grown principally for local consumption while fruit, vegetables and honey are exported widely. Tasmania is the principal source of Australia's hops for brewing. Small quantities of wine are produced. Fishing is also important.

Tasmania has moved beyond primary production into the processing of metal and engineering products, textiles, food and beverages. With 47 per cent of the State covered by trees paper products are also important. The development of hydro-electric power has also been a catalyst for much secondary industrial development.

Mining and minerals have provided a principal source of wealth for the State over the past century. Amongst the minerals produced are iron ore, tin, zinc, tungsten, copper, silver, lead and gold. Renison Bell is the world's largest underground tin mine. A small amount of coal is also mined.

Tasmania has long been a popular destination both for other Australian and overseas visitors and tourism is today a major source of wealth. The natural scenery, unusual wildlife, historic buildings and relatively compact size of the State combine to make an attractive tourist destination.

GOVERNOR
HE General Sir Phillip Bennett, AC, KBE, DSO

STATE MINISTRY
(Liberal Party)

Premier, Treasurer and Minister for Economic Development: Mr Ray Groom
Deputy Premier, Minister for Education and the Arts and Minister for Employment, Industrial Relations and Training: Mr John Beswick
Minister for Construction, Minister for Local Government, Minister for Racing and Gaming, Minister assisting the Treasurer: Mr Ian Lyons
Minister for Environment and Planning, Minister for Parks, Wildlife and Heritage, Minister for Inland Fisheries, Minister for Small Business: Mr John Franklin
Attorney-General, Minister for Justice, Minister for Finance and Budget Management: Mr Ron Braddon
Minister for Primary Industry, Fisheries and Energy: Mr Robin Lyons
Minister for Health, Minister for Community Services: Mr Roger Braddon
Minister for Tourism, Sport and Recreation: Mr Peter Franklin
Minister for Police and Emergency Services, Minister for Roads and Transport: Dr Frank Bass
Minister for Forests, Minister for Mines, Minister assisting the Minister for Economic Development: Mr Tony Braddon
Speaker, House of Assembly: Mr Michael Hodgman
Deputy Chairman of Committees and Whip: Mr John Barker

THE NORTHERN TERRITORY OF AUSTRALIA

The Northern Territory lies in the north central part of the continent and has an area of about 1,346,200 sq km (519,772 square miles). The population was estimated at 157,300 in June 1990 of which 73,300 lived in the administrative centre, Darwin. The Territory has a large number of aboriginal communities in remote areas.

History

The first attempt at European settlement in Northern Australia was made in 1824 and three years later the boundary of New South Wales was moved westwards to include the Territory. In 1863 the Territory was annexed to South Australia and between 1901–11 formed part of that State. In 1911, however, the Territory, together with its adjacent islands, became the responsibility of the Federal Government. In 1978 extended powers of self government were granted. Major powers retained by the Federal Government include rights in respect of aboriginal land, the mining of uranium and certain national parks. With the exception of these powers, the Northern Territory has been treated as a State since 1988.

Economy

The Territory economy depends primarily on mining and tourism although rural activities are also important.

Production of minerals, oil and gas is the Territory's major industry, with oil as the individual commodity of greatest value. Among the minerals, gold now leads in value of production, continued good prices having served to boost exploration and production to their present levels. Output of uranium, bauxite/alumina and manganese is also significant, with substantial quantities of zinc, lead, copper and silver being mined as well.

The Territory's major port is located at Darwin and is operated by the Darwin Port Authority. In addition to these facilities mining companies operate ports at Groote Eylandt and Gove Peninsula.

Pastoral lands are extensive with a wide variety of pasture types. An important part of the Territory's pastoral area consists of tablelands growing high quality rangeland pastures. Rural production is made up of cattle, buffalo, horticulture and field crops. The horticultural crops are mangoes, melons, bananas, pumpkins and grapes. The major field crops include sorghum, maize, mungbean and sesame. There is a substantial fishing industry consisting of the northern prawn, offshore and coastal fisheries.

Tourism is the second largest industry in the Northern Territory; the number of visitors has grown from 411,000 in 1981/82 to 821,000 in 1989/90, representing annual average growth of 9 per cent. By the year 2000 visitor numbers are expected to exceed 2 million.

NORTHERN TERRITORY MINISTRY
(Country Liberal Party)

Chief Minister, Minister Responsible for: Department of the Chief Minister, Police, Fire and Emergency Services, Auditor-General, Ombudsman, Constitutional Development, Women's Affairs, Women's Advisory Council and Northern Territory Remuneration Tribunal: The Hon Marshall Perron, MLA

Treasurer, Minister for Mines and Energy: The Hon Barry Coulter, MLA

Attorney-General, Minister for Health and Community Services: The Hon Daryl Manzie, MLA

Minister for Industries and Development: The Hon Steve Hatton, MLA

Minister for Transport and Works: The Hon Fred Finch, MLA

Minister for Education and the Arts, Minister for Employment and Training: The Hon Shane Stone, MLA

THE AUSTRALIAN CAPITAL TERRITORY

The Constitution adopted in 1901 provided for the selection of a site for a new national capital. Several sites were considered before an area in the Yass-Canberra district was chosen in 1908. The ACT covers 2,395 sq km (934 sq miles) and lies about 320 km (200 miles) south west of Sydney. The ACT became Federal Territory in 1911, and Parliament House was opened by the Duke of York in 1927. New South Wales transferred Jervis Bay to the ACT in 1915 to serve as its port. Today, the city of Canberra occupies the northern section of the ACT and the Territory population totals about 278,700 (June 1989). The workforce of 80,500 is almost equally shared by the public and private sectors. The ACT has had self-government since May 1989.

TERRITORIAL MINISTRY
(Australian Labor Party)

Chief Minister and Treasurer: Rosemary Follett, MLA

Deputy Chief Minister, Minister for Health, Minister for Sport: Wayne Berry, MLA

Minister for Education and the Arts, Minister for the Environment, Land and Planning: Bill Wood, MLA

Attorney-General, Minister for Housing and Community Services, Minister for Urban Services: Terence Connolly, MLA

Commonwealth of The Bahamas

Capital: Nassau

The Commonwealth of the Bahamas comprises an archipelago of about 700 islands and more than 2,000 rocks and cays, lying between latitudes 20° 55′ and 27° 25′ N. and longitudes 72° 35′ and 79° 35′ W.; the total surface area of the islands is 13,934 sq km. The group is separated from Florida on the west by the Straits of Florida and on the south from Cuba by the Old Bahama and Nicholas Channels. About 30 of the islands are inhabited and the more important of these include Abaco, Acklins and Crooked Island, Andros, the Berry and Bimini Islands, Cat Island, Eleuthera, Exuma, Grand Bahama, Long Island, Mayaguana, New Providence, Ragged Island, Rum Cay and San Salvador. Andros is the largest in size, but New Providence, upon which the capital Nassau is situated, is the most important.

The Bahamas lie on a submarine shelf which rises steeply in the east from depths of over 3,600 m, and in the west forms the shallow seas of the Great Bahama Bank. Most of the islands are located on the eastern edge of this shelf and since the seas are coral-bearing the coasts tend to be complex. The islands are composed of coralline limestone and are usually long and narrow, each rising from the shore to a low ridge, beyond which lie lagoons and swamps. The highest point, in Cat Island, is 62 m above sea level, but Grand Bahama barely reaches 12 m. Since the rock is permeable there are no streams and the water supply has to be derived either from shallow wells or from rainwater collected in catchments and cisterns. The shallow soils found in small pockets in the limestone rock afford limited cultivation and suit a variety of sub-tropical vegetables and fruit.

The warm waters of the Gulf Stream render the winter climate agreeably mild and frosts are never experienced. Temperatures during this season average 21°C (70°F), and summer temperatures, although modified by the sea, vary between 27° and 32°C (80° and 90°F). Most of the rain falls in May, June, September and October and thunderstorms are frequent during the summer months. The total rainfall is comparatively slight, averaging 1,100 mm per annum, but it varies between the islands from 750 to 1,500 mm.

Censuses are taken every ten years. The population at the last census (1980) was 254,000. A large proportion, some 60 per cent, of this population resides in New Providence. Freeport, on Grand Bahama, the country's second largest town, has a population exceeding 15,000. The average population density of the islands is only 31 persons per square mile. Abaco, Andros, Eleuthera, Exuma and Cays, Harbour Island and Spanish Wells and Long Island all have more than 3,200 inhabitants. The birth rate in 1988 was an estimated 20.2 per 1,000 and the death rate 5.4 per 1,000. Religion is predominantly Christian, the main denominations being Baptist, Anglican and Roman Catholic. English is the official and spoken language.

The climate is healthy and tropical diseases are absent. Preventive needs are met by child welfare and ante-natal clinics. Immunisation against diphtheria, pertussis, tetanus and poliomyelitis is given in all these clinics and is a requirement for primary school entry. The Ministry of Health, through the Department of Environmental Sanitation, also has health inspectors to advise on hygiene and sanitation. Curative needs are met by the government-operated Princess Margaret Hospital on New Providence, which has 457 beds, full supporting services and full-time consultant specialists in medicine, surgery, anaesthesia, paediatrics, chest diseases, pathology, radiology, obstetrics, gynaecology, neuro-surgery, orthopaedics, ophthalmology and ear, nose & throat. Also situated on New Providence are the government-operated Sandilands Rehabilitation Centre—a mental hospital and rehabilitation unit of 289 beds—and the Geriatric Hospital with 158 beds. Privately operated acute medical care centres are the Lyford Cay Clinic—an emergency facility and plastic surgery centre with 14 beds—and the Doctors' Hospital with 26 beds and medical specialities in general surgery, orthopaedic surgery, obstetrics & gynaecology, ophthalmology, internal medicine, family medicine & paediatrics, an ancillary clinical laboratory, radiology, pharmacy, respiratory and physical therapy departments. On Grand Bahama are the government owned Rand Memorial Hospital—a 74-bed community-type hospital with medical, surgical, obstetrics & gynaecology, paediatrics, accident & emergency, outpatients, clinical laboratories and radiography departments. There are also two private out-patient medical centres offering a wide range of facilities, three government medical clinics, a private holistic-health clinic and a cancer research and treatment centre. On the Family Islands there are 20 government medical officers and approximately 160 private practitioners throughout The Bahamas. On five Family Islands there are government-run cottage hospitals and there are about 57 clinics throughout the islands, the facilities and staff varying somewhat with the clinic. In cases where more medical assistance is needed, the patient is usually flown to Princess Margaret Hospital in Nassau.

Bahamian education is under the jurisdiction of the Ministry of Education. The Ministry has responsibility for all educational institutions in the islands. Primary, secondary, higher, technical and professional schools are maintained or assisted by government funds. Libraries and museums are in the portfolio of the Ministry of Education, while recreation and cultural events such as festivals of music, drama, arts and sports are in that of the Ministry of Youth, Sports & Community Affairs. Schools in the Bahamas are categorized as follows: Primary, ages 5-11 + and Secondary, ages 11-16; All Age, primary and junior high groups or primary, junior and senior groups; Special Schools, all age, catering to students having severe learning disabilities.

Free education is available in the Ministry's New Providence and Family Island schools. Courses lead to the Bahamas Junior Certificate usually after 9-10 years, the General Certificate of Education (GCE) of London University Ordinary Level after 11-12 years. The Bahamas General Certificate of Secondary Education (BGCSE) will be implemented in 1993.

Independent schools also provide education at primary, secondary and higher levels. The term 'college' in their names does not mean university type school, but in English usage connotes a fee-paying school. Several private schools offer clerical, accounting, computer and secretarial training. Evening courses are available. A nursing course is offered at the government-operated Princess Margaret Hospital.

In 1974 the College of the Bahamas was established, providing a two-year programme leading to an Associate Degree in any of seven academic divisions. There is no university in the Bahamas but the country is associated with the University of the West Indies and students may seek admission through the Ministry of Education in Nassau. The University maintains an Extra-Mural Department in Nassau and offers evening courses in several subjects. The College of the Bahamas also maintains a working relationship with several Florida universities.

There are 5 public libraries in Nassau and 25 village libraries on the Family Islands.

The main seaports are Nassau (New Providence), Freeport (Grand Bahama) and Mathew Town (Inagua). Nassau has direct passenger-cargo connections with the United States, Canada, the West Indies and South America. The Bahamas enacted its own shipping register with effect from 31st December 1976, and currently has 1,090 ships registered, totalling 25 m tonnes.

The principal airports are situated at Nassau, 12 miles from the town (runway 3,300 m) and Freeport, Grand Bahama (runway 3,300 m) from which international services are operated; and at West End, Grand Bahama (runway 2,400 m), Treasure Cay, Abaco (runway 2,160 m), Marsh Harbour, Abaco (runway 1,500 m), and Rock Sound, Eleuthera (2,160 m). New international airports recently completed are at Paradise Island (runway 900 m) and at Moss Town, Exuma (runway 2,100 m). There are 50 smaller airports and landing strips designed to facilitate services between the Family Islands. These are operated by Bahamasair, the national flag-carrier, and by various independent charter airline companies. There are more than 386 km of roads on New Providence maintained by the Ministry of Works, 209 km of asphalt roads on Eleuthera, and 156 km on Grand Bahama. There are more than 885 km of paved roads on other Family Islands. New roads are under construction on both New Providence and on many of the smaller islands. There is also a considerable mileage of privately owned and maintained roads, mainly on New Providence. There are no railways in the territory.

The headquarters of the Government owned broadcasting service, operated by the Broadcasting Corporation of the Bahamas, is located in Nassau. It operates on frequencies of 1,240 and 1,540 kHz AM and on frequencies of 107.9 and 107.1 MHz FM and its call signs are Radio New Providence and Radio Bahamas 1 and 2 respectively. It also operates on 104.5 ZNS Radio Bahamas. Radio Bahamas' Northern Service on Grand Bahama broadcasts on a frequency of 810 kHz AM. Commercial broadcasting began in 1950, although a broadcasting station has existed since 1936. Direct television commenced mid-1977.

The principal crops include fresh vegetables, tomatoes, pineapples, bananas, citrus fruits, avocados, mangos, egg-plant, and squash. There are several large-scale, modern pig and poultry farms.

Total exports for 1989 amounted to B$2,487,382; of these the principal exports were: petroleum and petroleum products B$1,931,083, hormones, salt, rum, crawfish and aragonite.

Nearly all the territory's requirements are imported and include foodstuffs, meat, hardware, building materials, clothing, machinery and vehicles, fuel, oil and manufactured goods of a wide variety especially for the tourist industry. The cif value of imports including imports of crude petroleum in 1989 was as follows:

Total	*Crude Petroleum*
B$,000s	B$,000s
3,104,926,392	1,642,393,176

There are three canning plants mainly engaged in canning tomatoes and pineapple and three crawfish freezing factories. Most of the output from the canning plants is consumed locally whereas that from the crawfish factories goes to export markets in the USA. The exploitation of forest products is confined to the yellow pine* forests on Andros and Abaco. Straw products are manufactured as cottage industries and the raw material for this work is chiefly obtained from palm fronds and sisal fibre.

* *Pinus caribaea.*

Electricity production in recent years was (million kWh): 1985, 485; 1986, 477; 1987, 547; 1988, 587; 1989, 638; 1990, 710.

Apart from a tax on real property on a sliding scale on the assessed market value of the land and structure there is no direct taxation or death or estate duties. Government revenue is derived chiefly from import and export duties, excise duty, casino tax, airport departure tax and landing fees, stamp duties, post office services, vehicle tax, company registration fees, banks and trust company fees, immigration fees, hotel occupancy fees, wharf and port dues, business licence fees and other miscellaneous fees and charges. The following figures show details of recurrent revenue and expenditure:

A. Revenue and Expenditure (millions).

	Revenue	*Expenditure*
1986	B$435.55	B$482.25
1987	B$436.1	B$462.0
1988	B$432.6	B$505.1
1989(P)	B$448.1	B$561.6
1990(P)	B$489.1	B$532.1

B. Capital Development (millions).

1986	B$ 41.0
1987	B$ 64.6
1988	B$ 76.7
1989	B$ 90.9
1990(P)	B$ 57.7

The amount of Public Debt outstanding at 31st December 1990 was B$912.3 m.

The prosperity of the Bahamas depends almost wholly on the tourist industry, which now accounts for about two-thirds of the Government's revenue, employing two-thirds of the labour force and supplies half the country's foreign exchange earnings.

	No. of arrivals
1986	3,007,300
1987	3,081,370
1988	3,158,091
1989	3,398,311
1990	3,628,519

The main tourist centres are Nassau, which received 54 per cent of the visitors in 1989, and Freeport on Grand Bahama which received 32.4 per cent. There has been considerable success in opening up the Family Islands to tourism which now accounts for 13.6 per cent of the total numbers.

The absence of any direct taxation, coupled with economic and political stability, has attracted considerable foreign investment and much of this has been used to finance the hotel and resort development, together with related public utilities and communications, essential for a modern tourist industry.

These conditions have also enabled the Bahamas to become one of the world's leading financial centres; and international banking, including Eurodollar and Trust business, is now the second main industry. Over 390 banks and trust companies now operate in the country. The Bahamian dollar has a fixed parity with the US dollar and the rate of exchange, like many other currencies, fluctuates against the floating £ Sterling. In 1973 the Bahamas became the 123rd Member of the World Bank and the 126th Member of the International Monetary Fund. The Queen opened the newly constituted Central Bank of the Bahamas building in February 1975.

Government approval for the establishment of a Free Trade Zone at Nassau, New Providence, was announced in August 1983.

Measures continue to be taken to develop the country's agricultural, fishery and mineral resources and, thereby, to broaden its economic base. To improve agriculture, which is mainly concerned with producing fresh vegetables, fruits and meat and dairy produce for an expanding domestic market, some 182,186 ha of high agricultural potential have been reserved exclusively for farming purposes, and a concerted effort is being made to improve the circumstances of the small farmer. Active measures are also being taken to conserve and develop the country's 323,887 ha of forest and to create, with United Nations assistance, a modern fishing industry. Aragonite, of which there are large reserves, calcium carbonate and salt comprise the country's known mineral wealth and all are being commercially exploited.

Foreign investment has been particularly attracted to the Freeport development on Grand Bahama which began in 1955 with an agreement between the Bahamas Government and a private company financed by American, Canadian and British capital; and which since its inception has benefited from the provision of additional incentives in the form of guaranteed tax holidays and the duty-free import of construction materials and operating equipment. Since 1970 similar incentives have been made available throughout the Family Islands of the Bahamas. There are modern port and bunkering facilities at

Freeport which are among the best in the world and an international airport, an international holiday resort and a commercial centre. It is also the country's leading industrial centre, with a large cement and pharmaceutical plant, and two crude oil trans-shipment terminals. Foreign investment and considerable invisible receipts from the tourist industry have assisted the balance of payments of The Bahamas.

History

San Salvador, so called by Columbus, or Watling's Island, the Amerindian name being Guanahani, one of the islands composing the Bahama chain is generally recognised to be the first land discovered by him on his voyage in 1492. A few years later all the Carib inhabitants, approximately 40,000, called Lucayans who were of the Arawak branch of American peoples were transported to Hispaniola where they perished working the mines operated by the Spanish colonists. It does not appear that the Spaniards had settlements on any of the islands of this group at any time. Early in the 17th century the islands were well known to the settlers of Bermuda and the Carolinas. They were included in the Royal Grant of Sir Robert Heath, the Attorney-General of England, of 30th October 1629. By 1640 the islands had become a well-known place of resort by the inhabitants of Bermuda, and on 9th July 1647 the Company of Eleutherian Adventurers was formed in London for the purpose of making an organised attempt at a systematic colonisation and development of the islands. William Sayle, a former Governor of Bermuda, was the moving spirit of this venture, and associated with him were a number of influential city merchants and Members of Parliament. On 31st August 1649, on the petition of Sayle and others, Parliament passed 'An Act for the Adventurers for the Eleutherian Islands' which constituted Sayle and his associates the 'Proprietors of the Islands'. Notwithstanding the Royal Grant to Heath in 1629 and the Cromwellian Act of 1649, Charles II, on 1st November 1670, granted the islands to six of the Lords Proprietors of Carolina, namely, the Duke of Albemarle, the Earl of Craven, Lord Ashley, Sir George Carteret and Sir Peter Colleton. Before the Royal Grant of 1670 the inhabitants of the islands had organised the settlement, instituted a form of government which included an elective House of Assembly, and chosen Captain John Wentworth as their Governor. Wentworth applied to and received commissions from the Governors of Jamaica. The Lords Proprietors appointed Hugh Wentworth as their first Governor on 24th April 1671, but he did not take up the appointment. They then confirmed in office John Wentworth, the popularly elected Governor, on 26th December 1671. A regular system of government was established including a parliament, the lower house of which was elective, and this was continued with several breaks until the civil and military government of the islands was resumed by the Crown on the surrender of their rights by the Lords Proprietors on 28th October 1717. Thirteen Proprietary Governors were appointed between 1671 and 1715. The settlement on New Providence was sacked by the Spaniards on several occasions between 1680 and 1684. In 1684 nearly all the inhabitants were driven away, and it was not until 1688 that the settlement was re-formed by their return, principally from Jamaica, under the leadership of Thomas Bridges. Bridges was recognised as Governor by the Lords Proprietors on 12th July 1688, and the settlement had reached some importance when it was practically annihilated by the French and Spaniards in 1703. However, a year or so after this the dispersed inhabitants returned to New Providence and another Proprietary Governor was appointed in 1707. But the islands became a regular rendezvous for pirates, and this finally determined the Crown to resume the civil and military government of the place, thus acceding to the numerous petitions which the inhabitants had been making for several years and also carrying out the express wishes of Parliament. Since 1717 there has been a continuous line of Royal Governors. The islands were surrendered to a fleet of the American rebels in 1776 and again to the Spaniards in 1781, but they had been re-taken by a British force under Colonel Deveaux before the conclusion of the war in 1783, when British possession was confirmed.

A significant event in Bahamian history was the influx of Loyalists who had asked to remain under British rule after the Treaty of Versailles. In 1783–84, when the islands' population was 4,058, the Loyalists stated to arrive with their families and slaves. By 1789 the population had risen to more than 11,000. The names of some 630 Loyalist families are to be found widely distributed throughout all sections of the community today. The Loyalists received substantial assistance from England, and on 19th March 1787 the Lords Proprietors surrendered all their proprietary rights to the King for the sum of £12,000, provided by Parliament.

The final abolition of slavery in 1838 caused an important economic and social change. The outbreak of civil war in the United States led to a period of considerable prosperity: between the years 1861 and 1865 the islands became a depot for vessels running the blockade imposed against the Confederate States. However, the boom years were followed by a period of slump during which occurred one of the worst hurricanes in the island's history. The hurricane struck New Providence on 1st October 1866, causing widespread damage. In the latter part of the nineteenth century efforts were made to exploit a number of commercial products, such as sisal, conch shells for cameo broochmaking, and pineapples. The sponge industry was also established and at its height in 1901 employed nearly 6,000 men or roughly one-third of the available labour force. The early 1900s were nonetheless lean years and it was not until 1920, when Nassau became an entrepôt for the American bootlegging trade that some degree of prosperity returned, and remained until the end of the prohibition era. In 1939 the sponge industry collapsed as the result of a fungus disease and the islands' fortunes again appeared to be on a downward trend but since the early 1950s the country has experienced phenomenal growth, based almost entirely on the success of the tourist industry and more recently on the banking industry. Taxation advantages, economic and political stability have encouraged foreign investments; and millions of pounds have poured into the Bahamas during the last two decades.

Up to 1964, representative but not responsible government existed. The executive government was in the hands of the Governor, appointed by the Crown, who had the power of veto and was advised by an Executive Council of not more than nine members. Various executive powers and the right to enact certain subsidiary legislation were vested by law in the Governor in Council. The legislature comprised a Legislative Council (created as a separate Council by Royal Letters Patent in 1841) of eleven members (two ex-officio and nine appointed by the Governor) and an elected House of Assembly with 33 seats (29 until 1960).

The Turks and Caicos Islands (*q.v.*) which are a geographical part of the Bahamas chain and which had often in their early history been claimed both by Bermuda and the Bahamas, were separated from the Bahamas in 1848.

Constitutional Development

Constitutional changes were agreed in 1963. These were embodied in a new constitution which came into effect early in 1964, providing for a ministerial system of government. The bi-cameral Legislature was reconstituted to consist of an Upper House called the Senate and a Lower House called the House of Assembly. The Senate consisted of 15 appointed members. The House of Assembly consisted of 38 members elected under universal adult franchise, 21 representing Family Island constituencies and 17 from New Providence. The Cabinet consisted of a Premier and not less than 8 other Ministers. The Governor appointed as Premier the person who appeared to him to be best able to command a majority in the House of Assembly. The remaining Ministers were appointed by the Governor on the advice of the Premier. As a result of the general election of January 1967, the first held under universal adult suffrage, Mr Lynden O Pindling, the leader of the Progressive Liberal Party (PLP), was able to form a Government with the support of a member of the Labour Party (both major parties having won 18 seats). The United Bahamian Party (UBP) was recognised as the official opposition.

At the next General Election on 10th April 1968 the Progressive Liberal Party won 29 seats and the United Bahamian Party won 7 seats. One representative of the Labour Party and one Independent (the Speaker of the House) were returned as before.

A further Constitutional Conference was held in September 1968. The proposals agreed at this Conference were incorporated in the Bahama Islands (Constitution) Order 1969 which came into operation on 10th May of that year, giving the Bahamas the most advanced form of Constitution possible short of complete independence. This provided for a Governor representing The Queen; a Cabinet consisting of the Prime Minister and not less than 8 other Ministers and a bi-cameral legislature. The Senate was reconstituted to comprise 16 appointed members. The Governor retained special responsibility for certain matters relating to external affairs and defence, but was required to consult Bahamas Ministers through a Security Council on matters which involved the country's political, economic or financial interests. The Governor also retained ultimate responsibility for the Police and internal security, but immediate responsibility was entrusted to a Minister designated on the advice of the Prime Minister.

Independence Conference

Outline proposals for Independence were presented to Parliament by Mr Pindling's Government in March 1972, and in a General Election held in the following September the Progressive Liberal Party, fighting on a platform of early independence, won 29 of the 38 seats in the House of Assembly. The other 9 seats were won by the Free National Movement (formed as a result of an alliance between the UBP and dissident members of the PLP) which, while not opposed to independence, questioned its timing. Subsequently, on 2nd November after a debate on the Government's Independence White Paper, both Houses of the Bahamas Parliament passed, without a dissenting vote, a resolution expressing the desire of the Bahamian people to proceed to Independence in 1973, and requesting that an Independence Conference be convened to implement this wish. The conference met in London from 12th to 20th December 1972 and, in addition to fixing the date of Independence, reached unanimous agreement on a report, subsequently published as a White Paper (Cmnd 5196), setting out the principles on which the Independence Constitution is based. In framing these, the Conference paid particular attention to the need to provide constitutional safeguards ensuring the rule of law, protection of the rights and freedom of the individual, the independence of the Judiciary, the impartiality of the Public Service and the maintenance of the Constitution itself.

The Independence Constitution

Parliament consists of The Queen, whose representative is the Governor-General, a nominated Senate and an elected House of Assembly. The Senate consists of 16 Members appointed by the Governor-General—9 on the advice of the Prime Minister, 4 on the advice of the Leader of the Opposition, and 3 on the advice of the Prime Minister after consultation with the Leader of the Opposition. The House of Assembly consists of 49 elected Members (increased from 38 in 1982). A Constituencies Commission, at intervals of not more than five years, reviews the number of boundaries of the constituencies into which the Bahamas is divided. The life of Parliament is normally limited to five years.

The Cabinet consists of the Prime Minister and not less than 8 other Ministers (of whom one is the Attorney-General) appointed by the Governor-General on the advice of the Prime Minister from among the Members of both Houses of Parliament. The Governor-General is also required to appoint a Leader of the Opposition.

The Constitution provides for a Supreme Court and a Court of Appeal, and appeals are made to the Judicial Committee of the Privy Council.

'Specially entrenched' provisions of the Constitution, such as those relating to the establishment and operation of Parliament, the Cabinet and the Judicial System, may be altered by an Act of Parliament provided the Bill for such an Act has been passed by a three-quarters majority in each House and has been approved by a majority of the electorate voting in such manner as Parliament may prescribe. Certain other provisions ('entrenched') may be altered by a similar process, except that the majority required in Parliament is two-thirds. The remaining provisions may be altered by a simple majority vote in each House of Parliament.

The Commonwealth of the Bahamas became independent and the thirty-third Member of the Commonwealth on 10th July 1973. At the Independence Ceremony, and the accompanying celebrations, The Queen was represented by The Prince of Wales. The first Prime Minister of an independent Bahamas is The Rt Hon Sir Lynden O Pindling, KCMG, MP, Leader of the Progressive Liberal Party, who has been Prime Minister since 1967.

Government

HEAD OF STATE

Her Majesty Queen Elizabeth II

Acting Governor-General: Sir Henry Taylor

CABINET

Prime Minister and Minister of Tourism: The Rt Hon Sir Lynden O Pindling, KCMG, MP

Deputy Prime Minister, Minister of Foreign Affairs & Minister of Public Personnel: The Hon Sir Clement T Maynard, MP

Minister of National Security, and Government Leader in The House of Assembly: The Hon Darrell E Rolle, MP

Minister of Finance: The Hon Paul L Adderley, MP

Minister of Works & Lands: The Hon Philip M Bethel, MP

Minister of Employment and Immigration: The Hon Alfred T Maycock, MP

Minister of Housing and National Insurance: The Hon George W Mackey, MP

Minister of Agriculture, Trade and Industry: The Hon Perry Christie, MP

Attorney General: Senator the Hon Sean G A McWeeney

Minister of Transport: Senator the Hon Peter J Bethel

Minister of Health: The Hon E Charles Carter, MP

Minister of Youth, Sports and Community Affairs: The Hon Dr Norman Gay, MP

Minister of Education: The Hon Dr Bernard J Nottage, MP

Minister of Consumer Affairs: The Hon Vincent A Peet, MP

Minister of Local Government: The Hon Marvin B Pinder, MP

PARLIAMENTARY SECRETARIES

Foreign Affairs: Mr James B Moultrie, MP; Mr Philip Smith, MP

Cabinet Office: Mrs Ruby Ann Darling, MP

Quincentennial Commission: Philip Smith, MP

SENATE

President: The Hon Edwin L Coleby

Vice President: The Hon Frank L Edgecombe

Government Leader, Attorney-General: The Hon Sean A McWeeney

Members: The Hon Mrs Alma A Adams; The Hon Edison M Key; The Hon K Neville W Wisdom; The Hon Mrs Telator C Strachan; The Hon Audley D Hanna; The Hon K Neville Adderley; The Hon Ralph R Hanna

Leader of the Opposition in the Senate: The Hon Miss Theresa Moxey

Members: The Hon Charles Virgill; The Hon V A Knowles; The Hon Keith E Archer; The Hon Brent Symonette

HOUSE OF ASSEMBLY

Speaker: The Hon Sir Clifford Darling, MP

Deputy Speaker: Hon Milo Butler, Jr, MP and 47 other elected Members

MINISTRIES AND GOVERNMENT DEPARTMENTS

Secretary to the Cabinet: Mr Herbert Walkine CMG, OBE

Financial Secretary, Ministry of Finance: Mr Warren Rolle

Chairman, Public Service Commission: Mrs Elizabeth Strachan

Permanent Secretary, Ministry of Housing and National Insurance: Mrs Vylma Thompson Curling

Permanent Secretary, Ministry of Agriculture, Trade and Industry: Mr Basil O'Brien

Permanent Secretary, Ministry of Youth, Sports and Community Affairs: Mr J Edison Deleveaux

Permanent Secretary, Ministry of Works and Lands: Mrs Lois Symonette

Permanent Secretary, Ministry of Tourism: Mrs Williamae Salkey (*Ag*)
Permanent Secretary, Ministry of Transport and Local Government: Mr Colin Deane
Permanent Secretary, Attorney General's Office: Mr Harcourt Turnquest
Permanent Secretary, Ministry of Education: Mr Luther Smith
Permanent Secretary, Ministry of Employment and Immigration: Mr Wendell Major
Permanent Secretary, Ministry of Foreign Affairs: Mrs Mary Sweetnam
Registrar General: Mrs Kelphene Cunningham
Supreme Court Registrar: Mr Nathaniel Dean
Permanent Secretary, Ministry of Health: Mrs Ethlyn Isaacs, OBE
Permanent Secretary, Ministry of Public Personnel: Mr Creswell Sturrup
Director of Legal Affairs: Mr Ricardo Marques
Auditor General: Mr Richard Demeritte
Director of Immigration: Mrs Barbara Pierre
Controller of Customs: Mr Wilfred Horton

JUDICIARY

President of the Court of Appeal: Sir Kenneth Henry
Justice of the Court of Appeal: Mr Vincent Melville
Chief Justice: Mr J C Gonsalves-Sabola
Justices: Mrs Joan Sawyer; Mr Neville L Smith; Mr A C Thorne; Mr Burton P C Hall

Bangladesh

Capital: Dhaka

The People's Republic of Bangladesh, formerly East Pakistan, comprises the old province of East Bengal together with the Sylhet district of Assam. It covers an area of approximately 144,000 sq km. Most of Bangladesh is an alluvial plain, forming part of the Gangetic Delta. It is crossed by a network of navigable rivers, including the eastern arms of the Ganges, the Jamuna (or Brahmaputra) and the Meghna, flowing into the Bay of Bengal.

The climate is tropical and monsoon, hot and extremely humid during the summer and mild and dry during the short winter. The rainfall is heavy, ranging from 1,250 mm in the west to 2,500 mm in the south-east and up to 5,000 mm in parts of Sylhet. The bulk of its falls during the monsoon season (from June to September). The mean temperature during the winter (November to February) is about 16°C (53°F) and during the hot season 25°C (80°F).

The population is estimated to be 108 million. The rate of population increase is currently 2.17 per cent per annum.

The capital of Bangladesh is Dhaka (formerly spelt Dacca). The offices of the Central Government and the Diplomatic Missions are situated there.

The national language is Bangla (Bengali) but English is still widely used. The unit of currency is the Taka.

An estimated 87 per cent of the population is Muslim. Most of the others are Hindu. There are a few Buddhists and Animists, mainly in the Chittagong Hill Tracts and a few small Christian communities.

National Day: 26th March.

Education

Primary education (from 6 to 10) is free, but neither universal nor compulsory. Most primary schools have been nationalised and brought under government management. Secondary education is of 5 years duration (from 11 to 16) followed by 2 years of Higher Secondary Education (17 to 18). This is regarded as a terminal level for the majority of students. The majority of secondary schools and colleges are privately managed, but many of them receive government aid. There are 4 general universities at Dhaka, Chittagong, Jahangirnagar and Rajshahi, an Agricultural University at Mymensingh and a University of Engineering and Technology in Dhaka. The Islamic University about 15 miles north of Dhaka was opened in April 1986. In 1989 literacy was estimated to be at 24.8 per cent of the whole population according to Government statistics.

Transport and Communication

Principal seaports are Chittagong and Chalna. A national Shipping Corporation has been set up by the Bangladesh Government. A new international airport (Zia) was opened in 1980. The other principal airport is at Chittagong. The national airline, Bangladesh Biman, serves 8 internal points and operates internationally to India, Pakistan, Burma, Malaysia, Nepal, Thailand, Singapore, Japan, the Middle East and Europe.

Radio Bangladesh, which is government-owned and operated under the Ministry of Information is the main national broadcasting service. It reaches an estimated audience of 60 million. Bangladesh Television was introduced in Dhaka in 1965. The estimated television audience is 2 million. In 1980 colour transmission was introduced.

The Economy

Eighty per cent of the population live in rural areas. Most are engaged in rice and jute farming, but there are also some 1.2 million fishermen. About 1,172,000 are employed in large and medium scale industry. Of these two-thirds are in the jute, garments, textiles, tea and tobacco industries. Rates of unemployment and under-employment are very high, mitigated slightly by 'food for work' programmes of small-scale rural development projects. Landlessness is increasing.

About 15 million tons of rice is produced each year, over one million tons of wheat, about one million tons of jute, and 7 million tons of sugar cane. Tea production is about 90 million pounds a year. Minor crops include oil seeds, pulses, spices, tobacco, fruits and vegetables, timber and rubber.

Fish is an important source of protein. Consumption is about 750,000 tons a year. Export of frozen shrimps, prawns and frogs legs is growing.

Oil and natural gas have been discovered. Proven reserves of 12.5 trillion cubic feet make natural gas the most important mineral resource. The extent of the oil find has still to be accurately assessed. Small scale extraction has begun and exploration is continuing. Coal reserves are estimated at 553 million tons, limestone at 100 million tons and peat at 142 million tons. Hard rock and quality glass sand deposits have also been discovered. Efforts are being made to exploit all these resources.

Manufacturing output for domestic use includes cotton yarn and cloth, chemicals, fertilizers, pharmaceuticals, steel, cement, sugar, paper and newsprint, tiles, cigarettes, matches and sanitary ware.

Important sectors of the economy are controlled by nationalised corporations. The most prominent of these are the Jute Export Corporation, the Jute Mills, the Textile Mills Corporation, the Chemical Industries Corporation, the Oil, Gas and Minerals Corporation and the Steel and Engineering Corporation. However, industrial development is now being encouraged in the private sector. Nearly half the jute and textile mills previously in public ownership have been returned to the private sector. The Ershad government took important steps towards denationalisation of banks and other financial institutions.

GDP growth is projected to be at best 3.6 per cent in 1990–91 compared with 5.84 per cent in 1989–90. Contributing factors in the slowdown were the Middle East crisis, political uncertainty and the catastrophic storm at the end of April 1991 which wreaked havoc on industrial capacity, infrastructure and agriculture.

Bangladesh is estimated to have lost around US$ 100 million in remittances and US$ 14 million in exports because of the Gulf War.

Prices rose rapidly in the second half of 1990 as a result of speculative trading related to the Gulf crisis. Nevertheless inflation in 1990–91 was kept under control and is expected to remain at under 10 per cent.

Foodcrop production is expected to have increased to a record 19.2 m tons in 1990–91 from 18.7 m tons in 1989–90. This has revived hopes of reaching self-sufficiency in food within the next two years. Jute production rose by 1.31 per cent over the previous year to 4.7 m bales. Industrial production is projected to have grown by 7.86 per cent during 1990–91 compared to 8.35 per cent in 1989–90.

Export earnings rose by 12.9 per cent from US$1.52 bn in 1989–90 to a projected US$1.72 bn in 1990–91. Imports fell from US$3.75 bn in 1989–90 to US$3.6 bn in 1990–91. The narrowing balance of trade deficit is attributed to the expansion in garment exports and higher agricultural productivity.

Garments and garment products account for nearly half of all exports. These goods are rapidly replacing the more traditional exports of tea and jute. There is also a trend towards diversification of export products, encouraged by incentives for the export of non-traditional goods.

Exports 1990–91	(Rate of Exchange) 1US$ = Taka 35 US$m
Garments	742
Jute goods	310
Raw jute	106
Frozen foods (fish, shrimps & frogs legs)	150
Leather	145
Hosiery products	121
Tea	50
Chemical fertilizers	42
Naphtha, furnace oil and bitumen	32
Engineering goods	8
Agricultural products	7
Handicrafts	5
Paper, newsprint & paper goods	3
Others	19
Total Exports	1,740

Net foreign aid fell from US$ 1.507 m in 1989–90 to US$ 1.472 m in 1990–91.

The budget announced in June 1991 targets an economic growth rate of 5.7 per cent. Government revenue receipts are set at Taka 85 bn and expenditure at Taka 80 bn. The budget aims to collect additional revenue through reform of the tax system. The revenue will be used to meet government expenditure and to increase the proportion of the cost of the Annual Development Plan (ADP) met from the country's own resources. Most of the financing of the ADP comes from foreign aid.

Emergence of Bangladesh

Between the termination of British rule in 1947 and the end of 1971, Bangladesh constituted the Eastern Wing of Pakistan. Throughout this period it remained geographically, linguistically and culturally distinct from West Pakistan. In the absence of effective integration between the two wings, the distinctive character of East Bengal became a more potent factor than the common Muslim identity which had led to the partition of India and the creation of Pakistan. The more populous, but less industrialised, East felt itself to be neglected and treated inequitably by the politically dominant West.

These feelings came to the fore in December 1970 when national elections were held for a Constituent Assembly, and for Provincial Assemblies. Since representation in the Constituent Assembly was to be determined on the basis of population, a majority of seats were allocated to East Pakistan. Sheikh Mujibur Rahman, leader of the Awami League, a Bengali nationalist party, campaigned on a Six Point Programme which called for greater autonomy for East Pakistan. He received overwhelming support, winning 167 of the 169 seats in the East, and giving his party an outright majority in the 313 seat Constituent Assembly. The political situation was immediately transformed.

Pakistan's President, Yahya Khan, had intended, following the elections, to abolish martial law and restore democracy under a new Constitution. However, the President postponed convening the Assembly when initial discussions with Sheikh Mujib and Mr Z A Bhutto, leader of the Pakistan Peoples's party (which had won most seats in the West), failed to reach agreement. In response, Sheikh Mujib declared a hartal (political strike), and during the ensuing period of non-co-operation the Awami League assumed effective control of East Pakistan.

On 6th March 1971 President Yahya announced that the Constituent Assembly would meet on 25th March in Dhaka. Sheikh Mujib responded that he would only attend if four conditions were met: the ending of martial law, the return to barracks of troops in East Pakistan, the establishment of an official inquiry into a shooting incident on 2nd March, and the transfer of power to the elected representatives. After consultations in Dhaka from 15th–22nd March between the President, Sheikh Mujib and Mr Bhutto, the President announced, in a broadcast to the nation on Pakistan Day (23rd March), that "the stage was set for the elected representatives to work together for the common goal". However, during the night of 25th–26th March Sheikh Mujib was arrested and flown to West Pakistan to be tried for treason. The Army simultaneously took control of Dhaka and other cities in East Pakistan.

President Yahya then proscribed the Awami League forcing many of its leaders to flee across the border into India. On 17th April they met together in Calcutta and formed a Constituent Assembly of Bangladesh in Exile, and issued a Declaration of Independence proclaiming the sovereignty of Bangladesh. Sheikh Mujib was elected President, and Syed Nazrul Islam as Vice-President of the new nation. The East Pakistan "freedom fighters", the Mukti Fauj (later known as the Mukti Bahini), was formed under the command of Colonel M A G Osman. Composed of the East Pakistan Rifles, the East Bengal Regiment, East Pakistani police, students and other sympathisers, it received Indian support and training.

By August the Pakistan Army was in control of the major towns and main lines of communications. A civilian governor was installed in East Pakistan, and on 12th October President Yahya Khan announced that a new Constitution would be published by 20th December. However, by November, the Mukti Bahini and some 100,000 guerrillas from bases on the Indian border had begun actively disrupting road, rail, and other communications in the province. On 4th December, following rising tension between India and Pakistan, the Indian Army invaded East Pakistan on the side of the Mukti Bahini. Less than two weeks later, on 16th December, the Pakistani military and civilian authorities surrendered.

The Early Years of Independence

With the formation of the People's Republic of Bangladesh prominent Awami League activists set up a provisional government declaring Sheikh Mujib (still imprisoned in Pakistan) as President. Sheikh Mujib returned to Dhaka on 12th January 1972, and was sworn in as first Prime Minister. Justice Abu Sayeed Chowdhury became President.

On 4th November 1972 a Constituent Assembly, comprising the former East Pakistan representatives elected in the 1970 Elections, enacted the country's first Constitution which became effective from 16th December 1972. It provided for a parliamentary system of government based on four principles of state policy: Democracy, Socialism, Secularism and Nationalism. The guerrilla fighters were ordered to surrender their weapons, and many of them were formed into a new force called the Rakkhi Bahini.

The first general elections in Bangladesh were held on 7th March 1973. The Awami League again won a landslide victory with 307 out of 315 seats. Aid had meanwhile poured in from many countries to help relieve poverty, and repair damage to the country's infrastructure inflicted during the independence war.

The early years of independence were marred by administrative difficulties, economic problems, endemic lawlessness, and a series of natural disasters. A State of National Emergency was proclaimed at the end of 1974. On 25th January 1975, the Government passed the 4th Constitutional Amendment Act. Under its terms, Sheikh Mujib became Executive President, Parliament was dissolved and the country moved towards a one-party state. He later replaced the Awami League with a new party: Bangladesh Peasants Workers People's League (BAKSAL) and banned all other parties.

On 15th August 1975, a small group of Army majors assassinated Sheikh Mujib, his wife, three sons, two daughters in law and other relatives at the family home in Dhaka. They then prevailed upon Khondakar Mostaque Ahmed, a former Minister of Commerce, to become President. Ahmed placed the country under martial law and BAKSAL was dissolved, although the Parliament remained. The Army majors settled themselves into the Presidential Palace, and tanks remained at key positions in the city. Nearly three months later Brigadier Khaled Mossh""araf, Chief of General Staff, mounted a second coup, with himself as the new Chief of the Army Staff (replacing Major-General Ziaur Rahman (Zia) who had been COAS under Sheikh Mujib). On the same day four of Sheikh Mujib's former ministers, who were being held in Dhaka Central Prison, were killed. After talks between Brigadier Mosharraf and President Khondakar the latter agreed to step down as President in favour of the Chief Justice, Mr Justice A M Sayem. Only four days later, on 7th November, Mosharraf himself was killed in a counter-coup. Zia returned as Chief of Army Staff. Mr Justice Sayem remained as President, while also assuming the post of Chief Martial Law Administrator (CMLA) through a proclamation on 8th November. The President dissolved parliament, and promised new elections before the end of February 1977.

During 1976 the new Government consolidated its position. Good harvests boosted economic growth and helped revive foreign trade. The Political Parties Regulation Act legalised party politics but the proliferation of parties which emerged (60, of which 22 received official approval) undermined the prospects for an orderly transition to parliamentary rule. On 21st November President Sayem announced the postponement of general elections. Eight days later on 29th November, Zia replaced Sayem as CMLA.

On 21st April 1977, Zia also replaced Sayem as President whilst retaining his military posts. He announced a programme for the restoration of democracy to culminate in a general election in December 1978. In may 1977, Zia held a national referendum to secure a popular mandate for his leadership. This was overwhelmingly successful and was followed by the appointment of Mr Justice Abdul Sattar as Vice-President. In the Autumn, municipal elections were held on a non-party basis.

In June 1978, Zia called a Presidential election on the basis of universal adult franchise. His leading challenger was General (retired) Osman – who was the candidate of an alliance largely dominated by the Awami League. On a turnout of 54 per cent of the electorate, Zia won with approximately 76 per cent of the vote.

On 30th November 1978 President Zia announced that a general election would be held in January 1979. Before it took place, he amended the Constitution to provide for the continuation of a presidential form of government, with the Prime Minister and Cabinet under the President's effective control. Although twelve parties had threatened to boycott the polls unless martial law was lifted, they later agreed to take part in the election which went ahead on 18th February 1979. President Zia's Bangladesh Nationalist Party (BNP), formed in the Autumn of 1978, won 207 out of 300 seats. The Awami League was second with 39 seats. Less than 50 per cent of the total electorate of 38 million voted. The BNP formed a Government, with Shah Mohammad Azizur Rahman as Prime Minister. On 6th April martial law was lifted, after nearly 4 years. On 27th November the Government repealed the 1974 Emergency Powers Ordinance restoring certain parts of the Constitution guaranteeing freedom of movement and other fundamental rights.

On 30th May 1981 President Ziaur Rahman was assassinated by one of his Army Commanders, Major-General Manzoor. The rebellion was confined to Chittagong, and quickly collapsed. Vice-President Sattar took over as Acting President, and announced that Presidential elections would be held. After two postponements it took place on 15th November. Sattar, the BNP candidate, won a landslide victory polling 66 per cent of the votes cast over his nearest rival, Dr Kamal Hossain of the Awami League, who received 26 per cent. The following period was characterised by frequent cabinet changes, during which little progress was made towards achieving political or economic stability. At the same time, the Awami League showed increasing signs of disunity and disarray in the wake of its electoral defeat.

The Ershad Regime

On 24th March 1982 Lt-General H M Ershad, Chief of Army Staff, forced the resignation of President Sattar in a bloodless take-over. He suspended the Constitution and re-imposed martial law, appointing himself as CMLA, and later, in December 1983, as President. The martial law administration embarked on a wide-ranging programme of denationalisation and the decentralisation of the administration with the aim of devolving much of the administrative process to the rural areas. Following several unsuccesful attempts to encourage opposition parties to participate in elections under martial law President Ershad held parliamentary elections on 7th May 1986 with the participation of the Awami League, the Jamaat-e-Islami, and several minor parties. The BNP refused to take part. The Jatiya Party, formed to back President Ershad's policies, won an overall majority in the 330 seat parliament by winning 152 seats, while the Awami League and its allies obtained 104 seats.

The President appointed an all civilian Cabinet immediately before Parliament opened on 10th July. Nearly all the opposition groups with representation boycotted the session in protest at the continuation of martial law, and what they alleged had been an unfair election with blatant vote-rigging. The session lasted for only eight days.

President Ershad joined the Jatiya Party, and was unanimously elected its Chairman in September. He then announced Presidential elections for 15th October. Although there were 12 candidates, none of the major opposition parties participated. President Ershad received 84 per cent of the votes cast, and was duly sworn in. Parliament was summoned on 10th November and adopted an indemnity bill which ratified all the acts of the martial law regime (it became the 7th Amendment to the Constitution). Parliament was then prorogued, and the President lifted martial law and restored the Constitution. A new cabinet was announced at the end of November.

Parliament resumed on 24th January 1987. In addition to the budget it adopted the controversial

District Council Bill which sought to incorporate representatives of the armed forces in the governing bodies of District Councils. It caused widespread dissatisfaction and was returned to Parliament for reconsideration by the President in August. The opposition planned to bring a huge number of people to the capital to put pressure on the government, and to compel the President to step down. Known as the Dhaka siege programme it was thwarted by stern administrative measures, but political developments (including an unprecedented countrywide 72 hours strike) led to the declaration of a State of Emergency by the President on 27th November.

Continuing political unrest prompted Ershad to dissolve Parliament on 6th December and to propose fresh elections. This was rejected by the main opposition parties who reiterated their demand for his resignation, and boycotted the elections which were eventually held on 3rd March 1988. The results thus enjoyed little credibility.

The new Parliament, dominated by the Jatiya Party, convened on 25th April (the State of Emergency having been lifted on 12th April). The District Council Bill, without provision for military representation, was adopted in May. On 7th June the new Parliament passed the Eighth Constitution Amendment Bill which, amongst other provisions, declared Islam to be the State Religion.

In May 1989, following prolonged conflict between the indigenous tribal peoples and Bengali settlers inside the Chittagong Hill Tracts, Parliament passed three bills which established District Councils in the three Hill Tracts districts. These Councils were to be given responsibility for certain issues including land sales and law and order, and to have a majority of tribal members. Elections to these were held on 25th June 1989.

In June Parliament passed the Ninth Amendment to the Constitution providing for an elected Vice-President (previously he had been appointed by the President), and limiting to two consecutive 5-year terms the length of time a person may serve as President.

In March 1990 all parties participated in nationwide upazila (sub-district) elections where 442 seats were at stake. The ruling Jatiya Party won 162 upazilas. The Awami League confirmed its position as the most popular opposition party by winning 104 seats while the BNP did poorly, coming fourth after the Jamaat-i-Islami. Neutral observers commented that the elections were relatively trouble-free, and there were fewer electoral abuses.

Recent Political Developments

Although further Presidential elections were not scheduled until May 1991, opposition forces were again taking to the streets by Autumn 1990 to demand President Ershad's immediate resignation, and the installation of a neutral interim government to prepare the way for "free and fair" elections. The agitation was spearheaded by the All Parties Student Unity, an umbrella movement formed by students in Dhaka and other cities, which steadily widened its appeal to embrace trade unionists, journalists and even civil servants. Imposition of a State of Emergency in late November failed to stem the tide of strikes and demonstrations. On 4th December, President Ershad announced that he was stepping down, his decision reportedly precipitated by a decision of the Army leadership to withdraw support for him.

Two days later, with the backing of all parties, Chief Justice Shahabuddin Ahmed assumed the post of Acting President and appointed a council of advisers, including ex-officials and other technocrats, to administer the country on a caretaker basis. He declared that parliamentary elections would be held on 2nd March 1991 (later brought forward to 27th February). Ershad was placed under house arrest. The Acting President appointed a three man commission, headed by a Supreme Court judge, to investigate allegations of corruption against the deposed leader. Charges of embezzlement, fraud, illegal possession of firearms, and misuse of power were later filed against him.

The elections went ahead on 27th February. Only minor incidents of violence were reported. International observers, including a delegation from the Commonwealth Parliamentary Association, who monitored the polls praised the impartial conduct of the Acting President and his advisers, and agreed that the elections had been the fairest since the early 1970's. Despite expectations of an Awami League victory, the Bangladesh Nationalist Party (BNP) emerged as the largest single party with 138 seats out of a total of 300. The Awami League and its smaller allies won 95 seats and form the main opposition in parliament. Another surprise was the relative success of the former ruling Jatiya Party in taking 35 seats (ex-President Ershad won five seats in his home district of Rangpur). The Jamaat-i-Islami won 18 seats. The acting President asked the BNP leader, Begum Kaleda Zia, to form an Advisory Council of Ministers. On 15th September a national referendum endorsed the 12th Constitution Amendment Bill passed unanimously by Parliament in July, which provided for a return to a parliamentary system of government. Begum Zia formed a new government on 19th September. In October 1991 Acting President Ahmed stepped down, and a new President Abdur Rahman Biswas, took over as a largely ceremonial president.

Government

Prime Minister, Minister of Defence, Establishment and Cabinet Division: Begum Khaleda Zia

CABINET

Minister of Law, Justice and Parliamentary Affairs: Mirza Golam Hafiz

Minister of Agriculture, Irrigation, Flood Control and Water Development: M Majedul Haque
Minister of Foreign Affairs: A S M Mostafizur Rahman
Minister of Finance: M Saifur Rahman
Minister of Local Government, Rural Development & Cooperatives: Barrister Abdus Salam Talukdar
Minister of Communications: Col. (Retd.) Oli Ahmed
Minister of Health and Family Welfare: Chowdhury Kamul Ibne Yusuf
Minister of Industries: Shamsul Islam Khan
Minister of Post and Telecommunications: M Keramat Ali
Minister of Commerce: M K Anwar
Minister of Social Welfare and Women Affairs: Tariqul Islam
Minister of Food: Shamsul Islam
Minister of Information: Nazmul Hudd
Minister of Home Affairs: Abdul Matin Chowdhury
Minister of Energy and Mineral Resources: Dr Khandakar Mosharraf Hossain
Minister of Works: Barrister Rafiqul Islam Miah
Minister of Labour and Manpower: Abdul Mannan Bhuiyan
Minister of Education: Barrister Zamiruddin Sircar
Minister of Environment, Forest, Fisheries and Livestock: Abdullah Al-Noman
Minister of Jute: Hannan Shah
Minister of Planning: A M Zahiruddin Khan

STATE MINISTERS

Education: Principal Md Yunus Khan
Land: Kabir Hossain
Finance: Mujibur Rahman
Religious Affairs: Prof. Abdul Mannan
Youth and Sports: Sadeq Hossain Khoka
Establishment: Md Nurul Huda
Textiles: Major (Retd) M A Mannan
Civil Aviation and Tourism: Abdul Mannan
Relief Affairs: Lutfur Rahman Khan
Culture: Prof. Jahanara Begum
Social Welfare and Women Affairs: Mrs Sarwari Rahman
Shipping: Harun-Al- Rashid
Communications: Iazlur Rahman Patal
Irrigation and Flood Control: Mosharraf Hossain Shahjahan
Environment, Forest, Fisheries and Livestock: Gayeshwar Roy
Law, Justice and Parliamentary Affairs: Mohammad Aminul Huq

DEPUTY MINISTERS

Local Govt., Rural Development and Cooperatives: Abdul Hye
Shipping: A B M Zahidul Huq
Health and Family Welfare: Serajul Haque

Barbados

Capital: Bridgetown

Barbados is the most easterly of the Caribbean islands and lies between latitudes 13° and 14° N. and longitude 59° and 60° W. Its total area is 430 sq km (166 square miles).

It is comparatively flat, rising in a series of tablelands marked by well-defined terraces to the highest point 336 m (1,104 feet) at Mount Hillaby. The north-east corner of the island, the Scotland area, is broken country, much eroded and rather barren. The formation of the rest of the island is coral limestone. There are no rivers but deep gullies, which fill with water during heavy rain, have cut their way through the coral terraces in many places. Indigenous forest covers about 19 hectares (46 acres).

The climate is more equable than the tropical latitude would suggest. North-easterly trade winds blow steadily from December to June but during the remainder of the year, the wet season, the wind moves to the south-east and is less strong, resulting in humid, hotter conditions. The average temperature is 26.5°C (79.8°F). The rainfall is very varied: in the high central district the yearly average is 1,905 mm (75 inches) while in some of the low-lying coastal areas the average is 1,270 mm (50 inches).

The population of Barbados in 1990 was estimated at 257,082. The birth rate in 1990 was 18 per 1,000.

Primary and Secondary education in Government Schools as well as University education is provided free of charge.

Bridgetown is the only sea port but oil is pumped ashore at Spring Garden, at an Esso installation on the West Coast and at Oistins on the South Coast.

The main shipping companies visiting Barbados are Geest Line, Harrison Line, Ned Lloyd, Booth, Caribbean, Hapag-Lloyd, CGM (Compagnie Générale Maritime), TFC Tropical, TMT Bernuth, WISCO (West Indian Shipping Company).

The Grantley Adams international airport is situated at Seawell, 16 km from Bridgetown. British Airways, British West Indian Airways (BWIA), Leeward Islands Air Transport (LIAT), American Airlines, Air Canada, Air Martinique, Guyana Airways, Venezuelan Airways, and Cubana Airlines operate frequent scheduled services connecting Barbados with the major world air routes. These airlines are supplemented by year round charter flights from Europe, North and South America.

The unit of currency is the Barbados Dollar.

There are 1,573 km (965 miles) of roads, of which approximately 1,496 km (917 miles) are paved, 74 km (46 miles) are unpaved and 3 km (2 miles) are four lane highways.

Barbados has a colour television service, six wireless broadcasting services and a wired broadcasting service. The colour television service (Channel 8) and subscription television (American Cable TV—three channels) and two of the wireless broadcasting services are operated by the Caribbean Broadcasting Corporation, a corporate body set up by Order-in-Council of the Barbados Government in 1963. Two other wireless broadcasting services, Voice of Barbados and Yess 104.1, and the wired broadcasting services are operated by Barbados Rediffusion Service Limited. Two further wireless broadcasting services (and the first FM broadcasting station) are the Barbados Broadcasting Service (BBS) which started broadcasting in 1982 and Faith FM set up in 1990.

The economy of the island is based on tourism, sugar and light manufacturing. Domestic exports in 1989 were valued at BDS$248.8m of which BDS$44.7m or 18 per cent went to Britain. Of the domestic exports sugar accounted for BDS$47.1m (18.9 per cent), molasses and syrup BDS$3.5m (1.3 per cent), rum BDS$9.7m (3.9 per cent), electronic components BDS$43.3m (17.4 per cent), clothing BDS$28.4m (11.4 per cent), cement BDS$12.6m (5.1 per cent) and insecticides BDS$10.5m (4.2 per cent).

Imports in 1989 were valued at BDS$1354.3m of which BDS$148.8m (11.0 per cent) came from Britain. Government revenue for the 1990/91 financial year was estimated at BDS$1.3 billion and expenditure BDS$988.0m. Estimated capital expenditure was projected at BDS$227.8m. In 1990 794,703 tourists visited the island.

Per capita GNP was BDS$11,274.00 at December 1989.

Barbados National Day is Independence Day, which commemorates the achievement of independence on 30th November 1966.

History

The first inhabitants of Barbados were Arawak Indians but the island was uninhabited when the first British landings took place sometime between 1620 and 1625.

The first British settlements in the island were established between 1625 and 1628. The first group of settlers was led by Captain Henry Powell, representing the interests of Sir William Courteen. Other groups were sponsored by the Earl of Carlisle who in 1628 was granted a patent by King Charles I in respect of all Barbados settlements. This was subsequently leased by Carlisle's son to Lord Willoughby of Parham who during the Civil War became Governor of the island and continued to hold it in the Royalist interest until 1652, when he capitulated to a Cromwellian fleet. The terms of this capitulation, however, guaranteed the rights of the settlers and became known as the Charter of Barbados.

At the Restoration, the Carlisle/Willoughby interests were renewed, but the patent was surrendered to the Crown in exchange for a provision entitling Lord Willoughby and his heirs to a duty of $4\frac{1}{4}$ per cent on Barbados exports. Although this agreement marked the end of proprietary rule, the export duty was sorely resented by the islanders and remained a source of grievance until it was abolished by Act of Parliament in 1838.

Constitutional development

The island has one of the oldest constitutions in the Commonwealth. The office of Governor and a Legislative Council were established in 1627. The House of Assembly was formally constituted in 1639, with the 350th Anniversary of Parliament being celebrated in 1989 (June 26th having been designated as a public holiday). A distinctive feature of the constitutional development of Barbados was that it progressed and was regulated largely by convention, rather than by formal legislation. It is nevertheless convenient to trace, by reference to the latter, the steps by which the island progressed through widening forms of representation and suffrage and through modifications of policy-making and legislative powers, successively to a ministerial form of government, to a cabinet system and finally, through full internal self-government, to independence.

The first of these steps was the creation in 1876 of an Executive Council which in 1881 became the nucleus of an Executive Committee, some of whose functions and powers developed into forms analogous to those of Ministerial government.

A widening of the franchise in 1944 was to prove the start of a quickening process towards full internal self-government; a party political system and a modified form of ministerial government in 1946; universal adult suffrage in 1951; a full ministerial system in 1954; cabinet government in 1958.

By the end of 1957, Barbados had in practice progressed to virtual self-government. This status was formally achieved in 1961, when the post of Chief Secretary was abolished, nominated members ceased to sit in the Executive Committee and provisions were made under which the Governor, subject to one reference back, was bound to accept the advice of the Ministers in the Executive Committee. At the same time, the powers and responsibilities of Ministers were widened and the island assumed control over its own public service. Arrangements were made for appeals on matters of discipline, which formerly went to the Secretary of State, to be dealt with by the Executive Council, which was re-named the Privy Council.

The final stage of constitutional advance before Independence was reached in 1964, when the Executive Committee was abolished and its powers and functions transferred entirely to the Cabinet. Among other changes, the Legislative Assembly was also abolished and replaced by a Senate.

Barbados had been a member of the Federation of the West Indies, which was set up in 1958 but which was dissolved in 1962. In August 1965 the Barbados Government announced its intention to seek separate independence. At a conference held in London in June/July 1966, arrangements were agreed under which Barbados became an independent Sovereign State within the Commonwealth on 30th November 1966.

Constitution

The Constitution of Barbados, contained in the Barbados Independence Order 1966, provides for a Governor-General appointed by Her Majesty The Queen and for a bi-cameral Legislature. The Senate consists of 21 Senators appointed by the Governor-General, 12 on the advice of the Prime Minister, two on the advice of the Leader of the Opposition and seven by the Governor-General acting in her own discretion. The House of Assembly consists of 28 elected members but provision is made for a greater number of members as may be prescribed by Parliament. The President and Deputy President of the Senate and Speaker and Deputy Speaker of the House of Assembly are elected, respectively by the Senate and the House of Assembly from within their own membership.

The normal life of Parliament is five years. The Cabinet consists of the Prime Minister who must be an elected Member of Parliament and such other ministers as the Governor-General, acting on the advice of the Prime Minister, appoints from among the Senators and elected Members of Parliament. The Member of Parliament, who in the judgement of the Governor-General is the Leader of the party commanding the support of the largest number of Members in the elected House of Assembly in opposition to the Government, is appointed by her as Leader of the Opposition.

Apart from the entrenched provisions, the Constitution may be amended by an Act of Parliament passed by both Houses. The entrenched provisions which relate to citizenship, rights and freedom, the establishment of the office of the Governor-General, her functions, the composition of the two Houses of Parliament, Sessions of Parliament, the Prorogation and Dissolution of Parliament, General

Elections, the appointment of Senators, the executive Authority of Barbados, the Judicature, the Civil Service and Finance, can only be amended by a vote of two-thirds of all the members of both Houses.

There is a Supreme Court of Judicature consisting of a High Court and a Court of Appeal, and in certain cases a further appeal lies to the Judicial Committee of Her Majesty's Privy Council. The Chief Justice and the Puisne Judges are appointed by the Governor-General acting on the recommendation of the Prime Minister after consultation with the Leader of the Opposition.

The Constitution also contains provisions relating to citizenship and the fundamental rights and freedoms of the individual.

Historical List

GOVERNOR-GENERAL

Sir John Montague Stow, GCMG, KCVO, from 30th November 1966 to 15th May 1967

Sir Winston Scott, GCMG, GCVO, from 15th May 1967 to 9th August 1976 (deceased)

Sir Deighton Ward, GCMG, GCVO, KA, from 17th November 1976 to 9th January 1984 (deceased)

Sir Hugh Springer, GCMG, GCVO, CBE, from 24th February 1984 to 30th April, 1990

Dame R Nita Barrow, GCMG, DA, from 6th June 1990

Government

The last general election took place on 22nd January, 1991, and as a result the composition of the political parties in the House of Assembly was: Democratic Labour Party 18; Barbados Labour Party 10.

The Budget of April 1988 led to the breakaway of four members of the Democratic Labour Party, and their formation of the National Democratic Party in February 1989.

The NDP is headed by Dr Richie Haynes, former finance minister in the DLP government, and one of the four who left the DLP.

The official opposition party is the Barbados Labour Party led by Henry Forde, QC

HEAD OF STATE

Her Majesty Queen Elizabeth II

GOVERNOR-GENERAL

Her Excellency Dame R Nita Barrow, GCMG, DA

CABINET

Prime Minister, Minister of Finance and Economic Affairs, Minister for the Civil Service: The Rt Hon L Erskine Sandiford, MP

Deputy Prime Minister, Minister of Public Works, Communications, Transportation, Leader of the House of Assembly: The Hon Philip M Greaves, QC, MP

Attorney General, Minister of Foreign Affairs: The Hon Maurice A King, QC, MP

Minister of State, Finance and Economic Affairs: The Hon Harold Blackman, MP

Minister of Health: The Hon Branford M Taitt, MP

Minister of Education: The Hon Cyril V Walker, MP

Minister of Tourism and Sports: The Hon Wesley 'Wes' W Hall, MP

Minister of Labour, Consumer Affairs and Environment: The Hon Warwick Franklin, MP

Minister of Trade, Industry and Commerce: Senator The Hon Dr Carl D Clarke

Minister of Housing and Lands: The Hon E Evelyn Greaves, MP

Minister of Agriculture, Food and Fisheries and Leader of the Senate: Senator The Hon L V Harcourt Lewis

Minister of Justice and Public Safety: The Hon Keith Simmons, MP

Minister of Community Development and Culture: The Hon David Thompson, MP

PARLIAMENTARY SECRETARIES

Ministry of the Civil Service: Senator Mrs Maizie Barker-Welch

Minister of Public Works, Communications and Transportation: Senator Anderson Morrison

SPEAKERS

Speaker: His Hon Lawson A Weekes, MP

Deputy Speaker: His Hon Tyronne Estwick, MP

Chairman of Committee: The Hon Leroy Braithwaite, MP

Clerk of Parliament: Mr George Brancker

JUDICIARY

Chief Justice: Rt Hon Sir Denys A Williams, KB, GCM

Chief Magistrate: Miss Shirley Bell

Puisne Judges: Mr Justice Elliott Belgrave, QC

Mr Justice Clifford Husbands

Mr Justice Frederick Waterman

Mr Justice Errol DaCosta Chase

Registrar to the Supreme Court: Ms Marie McCormack

MINISTRIES AND GOVERNMENT DEPARTMENTS

PRIME MINISTER'S OFFICE

Cabinet Secretary: Luther Bourne

Permanent Secretary and Head of the Civil Service: Brazane Babb

DIRECTOR OF FINANCE AND ECONOMIC AFFAIRS: Dr George Reid

MINISTRY OF FINANCE AND ECONOMIC AFFAIRS
Permanent Secretary, Finance: E Griffith
Permanent Secretary, Economic Affairs: R Carvallo

MINISTRY OF FOREIGN AFFAIRS
Permanent Secretary: Dr Peter Laurie

MINISTRY OF HEALTH
Permanent Secretary: Carl Yard

MINISTRY OF EDUCATION
Permanent Secretary: Carlisle Carter (*Ag*)

MINISTRY OF TOURISM AND SPORTS
Permanent Secretary: Edward Layne

MINISTRY OF PUBLIC WORKS, COMMUNICATIONS AND TRANSPORTATION
Permanent Secretary (International Transport and Communications Division): Harcourt Williams

MINISTRY OF JUSTICE AND PUBLIC SAFETY
Permanent Secretary: R O 'Frankie' Jordan

PRIME MINISTER'S OFFICE
Permanent Secretary (Special Assignments): Albert Brathwaite

MINISTRY OF TRADE, INDUSTRY AND COMMERCE
Permanent Secretary: Leroy Roach

MINISTRY OF PUBLIC WORKS, COMMUNICATIONS AND TRANSPORTATION
Permanent Secretary: Lionel Weekes (*Ag*)

MINISTRY OF HOUSING AND LANDS
Permanent Secretary: Owen Estwick

MINISTRY OF LABOUR, CONSUMER AFFAIRS AND THE ENVIRONMENT
Permanent Secretary: Fozlo Brewster

MINISTRY OF AGRICULTURE, FOOD AND FISHERIES
Permanent Secretary: Ruall Harris

MINISTRY OF CIVIL SERVICE
Permanent Secretary, Training Division: V C Alleyne
Chief Personnel Officer, Personnel Administration Division: H Richards
Permanent Secretary: L Moe

MINISTRY OF COMMUNITY DEVELOPMENT AND CULTURE
Permanent Secretary: Denis Smith (*Ag*)

SOLICITOR GENERAL
Woodbine Davis

Belize

Capital: Belmopan

Belize is situated on the east coast of Central America bounded on the north and part of the west by Mexico and by Guatemala on the remainder of the west and south. In length the country extends 280 km from the Rio Hondo in the north to the Sarstoon River in the south. In breadth the widest part (Belize City to Benque Viejo del Carmen) is 109 km. Its land area is about 22,962 sq km which includes a number of islets (known as cayes) lying off the coast.

The coastline is for the most part flat and swampy but the country rises gradually towards the interior. The Maya Mountains and the Cockscombs, which reach a height of 1,140 m (Victoria Peak), form the backbone of the southern half of the territory. All the Western (Cayo) District is hilly and includes the Mountain Pine Ridge most of which lies between 300 and 600 m above sea level but rises in parts to around 900 m. The northern districts are also hilly except towards the coast but contain considerable areas of low tableland. There are seventeen principal rivers, of which the Belize River is the most important. None is navigable by vessels over five feet draught and few for any distance.

The coastal waters are shallow for 16-32 km to the east. This shallow sea is dotted with cayes and is bounded by a coral encrusted reef second only in size to the great barrier reef off the eastern coast of Australia. Three separate reef areas lie still further to the east and the most easterly islet is more than 97 km to the east of Belize City.

The climate is sub-tropical and on the whole agreeable. In the largest city, Belize City, the temperature averages 24°C (75°F) from November to January and 27°C (81°F) from May to September. The mean annual temperature is 26°C (79°F). Day temperatures often reach 32°C-35°C (90°F-96°F) and night temperatures may very occasionally fall to the fifties. Most of the year the heat and humidity are tempered by sea breezes. This description applies with small variation along the whole coastal area. Inland, the day temperatures during the dry season tend to be higher, but drop considerably at night. Rainfall increases from north to south:

	Annual average rainfall (mm)
Corozal	1,275
Belize City	1,575
San Ignacio	1,300
Dangriga (formerly Stann Creek)	3,675
Punta Gorda	4,375

There are two dry seasons, the main one from March to May and the other in August and September (called the Maugre Season).

Belize has been struck from time to time by hurricanes. On 10th September 1931 a hurricane struck Belize City causing heavy loss of life and property; on 27th September 1955 hurricane 'Janet' struck the northern part of the country completely destroying the town of Corozal and damaging dozens of villages in the Corozal and Orange Walk Districts; on 15th July 1960 hurricane 'Abby' struck the area of the Sittee River, south of Dangriga, causing some damage to crops and dwellings; on 24th July 1961 hurricane 'Anna' wrought fairly extensive damage in the villages of Seine Bight and Placentia and almost completely destroyed banana plantations in the Stann Creek district; on 31st October 1961 hurricane 'Hattie' caused 262 deaths and most serious damage to Belize City, Dangriga and other parts of the country. In 1974 Belize was struck by hurricanes 'Carmen' and 'Fifi' but suffered only one fatality. Crops, bananas and corn, were the main victims. In 1978 hurricane 'Greta' caused extensive damage to crops and communications in the centre of the country but only four fatalities.

In May 1991 the population of Belize was recorded as 190,792. In 1989 the birth rate was 37.2 per 1,000 population; the death rate was 4.2 per 1,000. The infant death rate per 1,000 live births was 20.4. The main racial groups are Creoles, Mestizos (Maya-Spanish) and Caribs. There are also a number of persons of East Indian and Spanish descent. The races are, however, now heavily inter-mixed and a great many persons would have considerable difficulty in deciding to which group they belong. There are about 6,000 Mennonites farming at Spanish Lookout, Shipyard and the Blue Creek area of Belize.

The great majority of the population belong to one or other of the Christian churches: Catholic 62 per cent; Anglican 12 per cent; Methodist 6 per cent; Mennonites 4 per cent and Others 16 per cent. In addition to a large contribution in the field of education a few of the denominations, notably the Mennonites and Nazarenes, operate health clinics, and many provide social and family welfare services.

Until 1st August 1970 Belize City was the capital, where almost one third of the country's population live (59,220—1991 census). The new capital of the country is Belmopan, some 81 km inland on the Western Highway with a population of 4,000.

English is the official language. In certain areas, for instance Corozal and Cayo districts, the mother tongue of many people is Spanish and in the southern districts, Stann Creek and Toledo, there are ethnic groups whose first language is Garifuna, Maya or Ketchi. But everywhere English is, from the beginning, the medium of instruction in schools. Spanish is taught in secondary schools but a start has now been made in introducing the teaching of Spanish in primary schools and bi-lingualism is the objective. Nearly everyone speaks an English dialect known as 'creole'. It is the most popular vernacular of the country.

Health

After a recent resurgence in the incidence of malaria, fewer cases were reported in 1988 than in 1987. Any new, or suspect, case is tackled by the Eradication Service. The total hospital bed strength in the country is now 583 in a total of 10 hospitals and similar institutions. Construction of a new hospital in Belize City is due to start in 1992, providing a further 200 beds.

Communications

The international airport has now been renamed the Philip S W Goldson International Airport and is situated 14.4 km north-west of Belize City. It is the principal airport and from it international air services are operated by Transportes Aereos Centro Americano SA (TACA International Airlines), Transportes Aereo Nacionales SA (TAN Airlines) and Servicio Aereo de Honduras SA (SAHSA), Continental Airlines, Belize Trans Air and American Airlines to and from all parts of Central America and to Miami, Houston and New Orleans in the United States. The runway, at present 2,190 m long and 45 m wide, is capable of handling up to DC9, Boeing 707, 727, 737, and 767 Lockheed Electra, BAC 111, and VC10 aircraft. A new airport terminal building with modern airport control facilities, was completed and officially opened on 27th July 1990 at a cost of nearly BZ$14m. The Belize Meteorological Department provides weather information through its radar system, and its equipment has been upgraded to connect with the Universal Weather Satellite system. Maya Airways and Tropic Air maintain a scheduled internal passenger air service to the principal towns throughout the country using a variety of light aircraft. At present there are 21 government owned or privately licensed airfields suitable for light single or twin engined aircraft.

The main port is Belize City. A new pier was constructed in 1977 financed by the Caribbean Development Bank (at a cost of about BZ$22m), which caters for vessels drawing up to 5 m. Vessels drawing over 6 m anchor a mile off shore. Cargoes have to be lightered ashore. A regular 12-day cargo service from Europe is maintained by the Caribbean Overseas Lines (consisting of Harrison, Hapag-Lloyd, Nedlloyd and CGM). The main regional service from the United States (Miami) is provided by The Tropical Line. The port handles some 1.5 million tons of cargo annually. Commerce Bight pier, south of Dangriga, has been improved and lengthened to accommodate medium-size vessels required to handle increased shipments of citrus products. Construction of a new port at Big Creek for the shipment of bananas was opened on 16th October 1990.

The country possesses four main highways, the Northern Highway connecting Belize City with Chetumal on the Mexican frontier, the Western Highway connecting Belize City with the capital of Belmopan and continuing on to the Guatemalan frontier, the Hummingbird Highway running from Belmopan to the east of Dangriga and the Southern Highway linking the Stann Creek and Toledo districts to the rest of Belize. Most of the main highways with the exception of the Hummingbird and Southern Highways have a tarmacadam surface. In all, there are 3,001 km of road in the country made up of 592 km of main roads, 827 km of feeder and sugar roads, 805 km of forest roads and 651 km of bush trails and cart roads. There are no railways.

The Economy

Approximately 44 per cent of the working population is engaged in agriculture, of which about a third are working on their own account. The estimated numbers engaged in the principal wage-earning occupations in 1985 were as follows: services 6,512; Government 6,268; agriculture, forestry and fisheries 13,065; manufacturing 4,192; construction 1,974; trade and commerce 4,558; transport 2,035 and others 5,902. The last category includes a rapidly increasing number of people involved in the expanding tourist industry. Construction has also grown in the last few years.

Corn (maize), rice and red kidney beans are the main food crops cultivated. Root crops such as yams, cassava and sweet potatoes, as well as a wide variety of fruit trees are also grown. Maize production increased from 29.0 million pounds in 1985 to 50.9 million pounds in 1988. Red kidney bean production increased from 2.3 million pounds in 1985 to 4.97 million pounds in 1988.

The main agricultural exports are sugar, citrus and bananas. With the privatization of the banana industry, production has expanded, and in 1989 earned Belize BZ$18.1m. Sugar continues to do well and in 1989 earned Belize BZ$68.1m. Exports of citrus products earned BZ$38.8m in 1989. In addition to cacao planting by Hershey Corporation of USA, there is a market in the US for winter vegetables, and in the first quarter of 1988 exports earned BZ$0.75m. Mango production in 1988 was 2,330 pounds whole fruit earning BZ$6,000 and 34,224 gallons of concentrate, which earned BZ$775,000.

Cattle, pigs and poultry are raised throughout the country. The country is more or less self-sufficient in fresh beef and fresh pork, but continues to import processed beef and pork products. The domestic demand for poultry meat and eggs is met from local production. The domestic dairy industry continues to expand, with the Western Dairies and Macal Dairy in Cayo District supplying the Belize City and Belmopan markets with fresh milk. Imports of dairy products, which were valued at over BZ$18.7m in 1981, were reduced to BZ$0.4m by 1988.

The production of honey dropped drastically in 1988 to 510,000 pounds, of which 474,000 pounds were exported, earning some BZ$380,000. In 1988 there were approximately 475 bee-keepers operating a total of 7,906 hives.

Timber production for 1989 was 3.6 million board feet. Exports from this were valued at BZ$4.9m. Mahogany continues to be the main contributor. Lobster, conch, shrimps and scale fish continued to attract importers from the United States and marine exports (fish products) during 1989 totalled 1.68m lbs valued at BZ$17.1m. The value of clothing exported in 1988 was BZ$37.3m compared with BZ$31.2m in 1987.

Fishing on the barrier reef and the ruins of the ancient Maya civilisation continued to attract tourists, and during 1988 an estimated 142,000 tourists visited Belize, and contributed BZ$44.7m to the national economy, an increase of BZ$8.2m over 1987.

The drilling of exploratory wells in search of oil continues, but none has yet been found in commercial quantities.

In 1985 the total value of domestic exports was BZ$128.8m increasing to BZ$145.4m in 1986, BZ$173.0m in 1987 and BZ$190.34m in 1988. Goods to the value of BZ$36.3m were re-exported in 1986, BZ$28.0m in 1987 and BZ$48.0m in 1988.

The provisional figure for Government recurrent revenue in 1988/89 was BZ$132.2m and for recurrent expenditure it was BZ$131.3m. The figures for 1989/90 are BZ$158.6m and BZ$132.9m respectively. Capital expenditure depends largely on overseas aid flows. The Government of Belize has economic co-operation programmes with the United Kingdom, the United States, Canada, the Commonwealth Development Corporation, the Caribbean Development Bank, the World Bank and the European Development Fund, with smaller programmes being run by UNDP, UNICEF and the UNHCR.

Belize strengthened her economic ties with the Commonwealth Caribbean when on 1st May 1974 she joined the Caribbean Community and Common Market.

Education

Education is compulsory from the age 5 to 14 years. Only about 7 per cent of the population over the age of 10 years is illiterate. In 1990, primary education was provided by some 233 state and grant-aided schools almost entirely run by the churches under a denominational system. The total enrolment, free of cost in government and government-assisted primary schools and private schools was about 45,000 pupils. Secondary education is provided by some 35 institutions and has an enrolment of 8,546 pupils. The primary and secondary schools were staffed in 1988 by 2,188 teachers, certificated and uncertificated. The Government also maintains two special schools for the mentally retarded and physically handicapped. There are 5 post secondary institutions. The Belize Teachers' College, the Belize Technical College, St. John's Junior College, University College of Belize and the Belize College of Agriculture. Training is provided at the Vocational Training Centre in Belize City for primary school leavers who do not enter technical college: in addition vocational training is afforded to adults. It is now possible to obtain a Bachelor's Degree in certain subjects at the University College of Belize. Places are limited at present, however, and there is still the need for students to go abroad for both Bachelor and higher level university education. Scholarships are awarded by the Government to attend the University of the West Indies and other universities in Britain, Canada and the USA. The number of scholarships to universities and other institutions abroad in 1989 was about 220. Recurrent expenditure on education is estimated at BZ$23.9m for 1988/89.

There are three government training institutions, one each for teachers, nurses and the police. The University Centre of UWI is a new institution recently opened and operated by the Extra-Mural Department of the UWI and conducts courses and seminars in a range of academic, professional and cultural areas. There are other Adult Evening Institutes such as St John's College Extension Department, Belize Technical College Evening Institute, the YWCA, the Christian Social Council and a School of Dancing.

The Baron Bliss Institute, which opened in 1974, is maintained and operated by the Government for the encouragement of cultural activities. The National Library Service, the headquarters of which are housed in a section of this institute, has established 80 service points all over the country.

The Media

The Government operates a radio broadcasting service (Belize Radio) which transmits programmes from Belize City in both English and Spanish for some 120 hours per week. The service, which is semi-commercial, is radiated on the medium and short wave bands and covers most of the country, aided by transmitters in Belmopan, Punta Gorda, Corozal, and San Ignacio. There are educational programmes for primary and secondary schools. The first stage of a new VHF FM service has been implemented giving better quality of reception to a larger area of the country.

There is no official television service in the country at present, but a number of private operators retransmit United States satellite programmes.

Belize Telecommunication Limited acts both as an agent for the Government for the regulation of internal telecommunications including the assignment of radio frequencies and as the operator of internal and external telephone services. The automatic external services are operated under licence from the Government of Belize through an earth satellite station. There are also overland microwave circuits through Mexico to the United States which are now held in reserve.

History

Little is known of the early history of the area which is now Belize but the numerous ruins throughout the territory indicate that for hundreds of years it was heavily populated by Maya Indians. The Maya civilisation appears to have reached its apogee about the 8th century. It then collapsed and many of the people migrated.

In 1502 Columbus discovered and named the Bay of Honduras though he did not actually visit that part of the coast which later became British Honduras. The present settlement was established in 1638 but British sea rovers frequented the bay long before that and there is some evidence that a settlement was formed in or about 1603. From then on the coast was visited by buccaneers and logwood cutters, logwood being in great demand in Europe for the manufacture of dyes. The British settlement of 1638 (known as the Bay Settlement), augmented intermittently by sea rovers and particularly disbanded British sailors and soldiers after the capture of Jamaica in 1665, had a troubled history during the next 150 years. It was subjected to repeated attacks from neighbouring Spanish settlements, for Spain, with papal sanction, claimed sovereignty over the whole of the New World except the regions of South America assigned to Portugal.

By the Treaty of Madrid of 1670 Spain accorded recognition to the *de facto* British possessions in the Caribbean area but did not accept Britain's contention that the terms of the treaty included the Bay Settlement and Spanish attacks on the settlers continued. During the 18th century the status of the logwood cutters remained an issue between the two powers and it was not until 1763 under the Treaty of Paris that Spain, while retaining sovereignty over Belize, conceded to the British settlers the right to engage in the logwood industry. This was reaffirmed by the Treaty of Versailles in 1783, and by a further treaty of 1786—the Convention of London—the area of the logwood concession was extended while Britain gave up her claim to the Mosquito Coast further south on the mainland of Central America. Despite these concessions, the Spaniards continued their attacks, while the settlers protested that the extended limits of the logwood concession were insufficient. In September 1798, years after the outbreak of war between England and Spain, a strong Spanish attack was launched in a naval engagement off St George's Caye. The Baymen, although badly underarmed and heavily outnumbered, resisted and after several days of skirmishing the forces met in a sea battle off St George's Caye. Supported by HM sloop *Merlin* the Baymen fought with such determination that the Spaniards were forced to retreat. This was their last attempt to dislodge the Baymen by force of arms. British *de facto* control over the area gradually increased as Spanish power over the West Indies and Central America declined, and in 1862 Belize was designated by Britain as a British Colony and called British Honduras.

Until 1786 the Baymen governed themselves. In that year, after many petitions, Britain appointed and sent out a Superintendent, but the office was allowed to lapse in 1791. In 1797 Colonel Thomas Barrow was appointed Superintendent and also was given the title of Commander-in-Chief (held by the Governors of the Colony thereafter) to enable him to organise a defence against the obviously impending Spanish attack. Thereafter the office of Superintendent continued until 1862 when it was replaced by that of a Lieutenant-Governor under the Governor of Jamaica and the settlement raised to the status of a Colony; the Baymen resented being subordinated to Jamaica and in 1884 the Colony was detached and a Governor was appointed.

Constitutional development

From a very early date the settlers achieved a primitive form of democratic government by Public Meeting, at which all free settlers were eligible to vote and voice their opinions. Each year the Public Meeting elected members of the community to be unpaid magistrates empowered to make laws, levy taxes, dispense justice and carry out many other duties.

In 1765 Admiral Sir William Burnaby, who had been sent to the territory to enquire into the fulfilment of treaty obligations by Spain, codified the laws and granted, in the King's name, a constitution founded on the then existing form of government. In 1786, in the face of opposition from the settlers, the first Superintendent abolished this system of government by elected magistrates. In 1790 however, with further changes in relations with Spain, the Burnaby Code was restored in its entirety and started functioning again after the Superintendent left the settlement in 1791. It continued to be enforced without material change until about 1825 when the Public Meeting's privilege of choosing subjects for discussion was curtailed. Seven years later the annual election of the magistracy by the Public Meeting was superseded in favour of appointment by the Superintendent; and in 1840 the whole of what remained of the Burnaby Code was replaced by the law of England. An Executive Council was then created and in 1853 the Public Meeting, which had become something of a closed oligarchy, was finally displaced by a Legislative Assembly of 18 elected and three nominated members, with the Superintendent as chairman.

The quality of the members of the Legislative Assembly deteriorated during the nineteenth century and by 1870 it was realised that the old system had become unworkable and unrepresentative of the people as a whole. In 1871 the elected Legislative Assembly was replaced by a nominated Legislative Council with an official majority and the Lieutenant-Governor as President. An attempt to re-introduce elected members in 1890 was turned down but in 1892 an unofficial majority was created in the Legislative Council, and this constitution, with only minor modifications, continued until 1935 when the elective principle was once again introduced.

Following a disastrous hurricane in 1931, Belize became dependent on financial aid from Britain and found it necessary to raise a reconstruction loan. The British Government would only guarantee this on condition that reserve powers for the governor were incorporated into the constitution. This was done by the Belize Constitution Ordinance of 1935 under which the Legislative Council was reconstituted to comprise five official and seven unofficial members, with the Governor as President with casting vote and reserve powers. Of the seven unofficial members, two were nominated by the Governor and five elected by secret ballot of the registered voters from four constituencies. Men and women, without distinction of race, colour or creed, were entitled to vote subject to a small income qualification or a small property qualification and to being sufficiently literate to write the date and to sign their name on an application form. Amendments were made to this Ordinance in 1938 when the number of elected members on the Legislative Council was increased by one, owing to the formation of a fifth constituency. In 1945 the constitution was again amended when the proportion of unofficial members was considerably increased. The executive government devolved on the Governor and an Executive Council, composed of three *ex-officio* members (the Colonial Secretary, the Attorney-General and the Financial Secretary) and four nominated unofficial members. The Legislative Council was reconstituted to consist of the Governor as President, the same three *ex-officio* members and ten unofficial members, of whom four were nominated by the Governor and six were elected from the constituencies.

In 1954 the Legislative Council was replaced by a Legislative Assembly composed of nine elected members, three *ex-officio* members and a Speaker and three unofficial members nominated by the Governor. The status of the Executive Council was changed to that of chief instrument of policy and it was composed of the Governor, as Chairman, three *ex-officio* members and six members of the Legislative Assembly. The latter were elected by the Assembly but included not less than two of the nominated unofficial members of that body. Universal adult suffrage was also introduced in 1954, and the first general election under the new constitution was held on 28th April 1954. The only fully organised party, the People's United Party, gained eight of the nine elected seats. The principle of Steering Members, appointed by the Governor from among the unofficial members of the Executive Council as the first step towards full ministerial status, was adopted in 1955. At the general elections which took place on 20th March 1957 the People's United Party gained all nine of the elected seats.

In February 1960 a conference was convened in London to consider proposals for further development of the constitution of British Honduras. The conference decided to adopt a ministerial form of government based on a revised Legislative Assembly and Executive Council. This revised constitution was introduced in March 1961 following a general election. The new Legislative Assembly, presided over by a Speaker, consisted of 18 members elected by the general public, five nominated members and two *ex-officio* members (the Chief Secretary (formerly known as Colonial Secetary) and the Attorney-General). The normal life of the Assembly was four years. The revised Executive Council under the chairmanship of the Governor, consisted of two *ex-officio* members (the Chief Secretary, responsible, *inter alia,* for defence, security and external affairs, and the Attorney-General) and six unofficial members holding various departmental portfolios as Ministers, of whom at least one was a nominated member of the Legislative Assembly. The leader of the political party obtaining a majority at a general election for the Legislative Assembly seats was appointed First Minister and the remaining five unofficial members of the Executive Council were elected by the unofficial members of the Legislative Assembly from among their own number. The Governor appointed the five nominated members of the Legislative Assembly, after consultation with the First Minister in respect of two seats and after consultation with the leader of the minority party in respect of one seat, the remaining two seats being filled by the Governor after consultation with the leaders of both the majority and minority parties.

At the general election held in March 1961, the People's United Party, led by Mr George Price, won all the 18 elected seats in the Legislative Assembly. Mr Price was thereupon appointed First Minister.

Constitution

At a Constitutional Conference held in London in July 1963 a Ministerial system of internal self-government with a two-chamber legislature was agreed. Under this new constitution introduced on 6th January 1964, the Governor had special responsibilities for defence, external affairs, internal security and the safeguarding of the terms and conditions of service of public officers. Further, for so long as the Government of British Honduras continued to receive money from the United Kingdom Government in the form of Grant-in-Aid of the current revenues, the Governor had a special responsibility for maintaining or securing the financial and economic stability of British Honduras and for ensuring that any condition attached to any financial grant or loan made by Her Majesty's Government was complied with. This latter responsibility came to an end on 31st December 1966 when the Grant-in-Aid ceased.

The Executive Council was replaced by a Cabinet consisting of a Premier and other Ministers. Ministers were appointed by the Governor on the advice of the Premier. Under the Independence Constitution the Governor-General appoints as Prime Minister the person who appears to her to be likely to command the support of the majority party in the House of Representatives.

The bi-cameral legislature is known as the National Assembly and comprises a House of Representatives and a Senate. The House of Representatives consists of 28 members elected under the system of universal adult suffrage. The Speaker may be elected by the House from among its own number or from outside the House but the Deputy Speaker is elected by the House from amongst its own number. The Senate consists of eight members appointed by the Governor-General. Five are appointed on the advice of the Prime Minister, two on the advice of the Leader of the Opposition and one after consulting such persons as the Governor-General considers appropriate. The President may be elected by the Senate from amongst its own number, or from outside the Senate, but the Vice-President is elected by the Senate from amongst its own number.

Independence

The Belize Government's desire for independence was expressed on many occasions after the dependency gained internal self-government in 1964. Britain's aim to bring Belize to independence as soon as possible in line with successive United Nations General Assembly resolutions was, however, hampered by the Guatemalan territorial claim. Belize finally achieved independence on 21st September 1981.

Territorial claim

Guatemala claims to have inherited sovereignty over Belize from Spain. In 1859, however, it signed and ratified a treaty with Britain recognising the boundaries between the two countries. The treaty also contained an article calling upon both parties to use their best efforts to build a means of communication between Guatemala City and the Caribbean coast. Guatemala denounced the 1859 Treaty in 1939, claiming that Britain had not fulfilled its obligations under this article.

Numerous unsuccessful attempts were made, particularly in the 1960's and 1970's to resolve the problem by negotiation. Talks in 1980-81 led to the signature in March 1981 of 'Heads of Agreement' setting out a framework for resolving Guatemala's territorial claim.

Discussions designed to finalise a treaty based on the 'Heads of Agreement' took place in May and July 1981, but were suspended without agreement. However, in January 1986 a civilian government came to power in Guatemala, committed to pursuing a peaceful settlement to the dispute, and the Guatemalan Constitution was amended appropriately. There were now prospects of substantial improvement in the relations between Guatemala and Belize and on 19th May 1988 the two Governments announced the establishment of a permanent Joint Commission of representatives of Belize and Guatemala, to work towards the preparation of a comprehensive draft Treaty which would provide "a just and honourable solution" to the difficulties between the two countries. Such a draft Treaty would be submitted to both electorates in referenda before signature.

The first meeting of the Joint Commission was held in Miami in May 1988, and subsequent meetings were held in July and October of 1988, in February 1989 and in July 1990.

Following the election to office, in January 1991, of the new Guatemalan President, Jorge Serrano Elias, further bilateral talks in Miami and London led to agreement on a rapid series of moves towards a settlement. On 16th August Belize introduced legislation to delimit its southern territorial sea in such a way as to allow Guatemala access to the Caribbean. On 5th September Guatemala recognised Belize as an independent sovereign state and on 11th September full diplomatic relations were established between the two countries. Their governments have issued a joint statement expressing their determination to find a solution to their outstanding differences and anticipating a new era of peaceful co-existence and mutual benefits to their peoples.

Land Policy

The alienation of Crown land is carefully controlled to prevent, as far as possible, the acquisition of such land for purely speculative, non-productive purposes. During 1953 and 1954 a land use survey was carried out. A land policy, based on the findings and recommendations of the Survey Team, was formulated and published by Government in 1958. In order to encourage the economic development of the country a tax on undeveloped rural land was introduced in January 1966. In 1971 land tax was doubled on holdings over 60 acres. In 1973 The Aliens Land Holding Ordinance was passed to prevent foreign speculation in land, a practice which had been growing in recent years. Land prices had been forced up artificially and to such an extent that investment and development were impeded. Non-nationals seeking to buy land for serious development will have no difficulty in obtaining licences, and certain tax concessions are available for this purpose.

Government

At the 1963 Constitutional Conference it was agreed that the next general election should be held when it became due in the ordinary course, ie. not later than March 1965. As the members of the legislature at that time were elected on the basis of the 1961 constitution, the conference agreed that the alterations in the legislature should not take place until after the next General Election, except that the two official seats in the legislature should be abolished when the new constitution was introduced. The constitution was introduced on 6th January 1964 and at the election held on 1st March 1965 the People's United Party (PUP) secured 16 seats and the National Independence Party (NIP) two seats. The House of Representatives elected a Speaker from outside the House. In the Senate a President was elected outside the Senate. The second election under the 1963 Self Government Constitution was held on 1st December 1969. The People's United Party won 17 out of 18 seats under the leadership of Premier George Price. The third election was held on 30th October 1974 to fill the 18 seats in the Belize House of Representatives. Of these 12 were won by the People's United Party and 6 were won by the United Democratic Party. The representation in the House changed in 1976 when the opposition representative in Toledo South resigned his party and joined the People's United Party who then held 13 seats.

The General Election held on 21st November 1979 resulted in 13 seats for the People's United Party (whose leader Mr Price retained the Premiership) and 5 seats for the United Democratic Party led by Dr Theodore Aranda.

In 1983 Dr Aranda was replaced as Leader of the UDP by Mr Manuel Esquivel (then a Senator) with Mr Curl Thompson as leader of the Opposition.

At the General Election held on 14th December 1984 the UDP won 21 of the 28 seats in the enlarged House of Representatives, while at the General Election held on 4th September 1989, the PUP under Mr George Price won 15 of the 28 seats, with the UDP winning the remaining 13. A subsequent change of allegiance by a UDP member increased Price's majority by 2 seats.

GOVERNORS
1972 Mr R N Posnett, CMG, OBE
1976 Mr P D McEntee, CMG, OBE
1980 Mr J P I Hennessy, CMG, OBE
(*See 1978 Edition for full historical list*)

GOVERNOR-GENERAL
HE Dame Minita E Gordon, GCMG, GCVO

THE CABINET
Prime Minister and Minister of Finance, Home Affairs, Defence, Trade and Commerce: Rt Hon George Price
Deputy Prime Minister and Minister of Natural Resources and Industry: Hon Florencio Marin
Minister of Foreign Affairs, Economic Development and Education: Hon Said Musa
Minister of Energy and Communication: Hon Carlos Diaz
Minister of Agriculture and Fisheries: Hon Michael Espat
Minister of Housing and Co-operatives: Hon Leopoldo Briceno
Minister of Social Services and Community Development: Hon Remijio Montejo
Attorney General, Minister of Tourism and Environment: Hon Glen Godfrey
Minister of Health and Urban Development: Hon Theodore Aranda
Minister of Works: Hon Samuel Waight
Minister of Labour, Local Government and Public Service: Hon Valdemar Castillo

MEMBERS OF THE SENATE
Hon Ralph Fonseca
Hon Conrad Lewis
Hon Rolando Perdomo
Hon Santiago Rosado
Hon Winston Smiling
Hon Mrs Jane Usher
Hon Gregorio Aleman
Hon Solomon Lewis
Hon Rita Salazar

MINISTRIES AND GOVERNMENT DEPARTMENTS

PRIME MINISTERS OFFICE
Ministers of State: Hon Ralph Fonseca (Finance); Hon Daniel Silva (Trade and Commerce)
Financial Secretary: Keith Arnold
Cabinet Secretary: Anthony Sylvester
Permanent Secretary, Home Affairs and Defence: Bernard Bevans (Acting)
Permanent Secretary, Trade and Commerce: Cresencio Sosa

MINISTRY OF NATURAL RESOURCES AND INDUSTRY
Minister of State: Hon Guadalupe Pech
Permanent Secretary: David Gibson

MINISTRY OF FOREIGN AFFAIRS, ECONOMIC DEVELOPMENT AND EDUCATION
Minister of State: Hon Vildo Marin
Permanent Secretary, Foreign Affairs: Joseph Bulwer (Acting)
Permanent Secretary, Economic Development: Mr Joe Waight
Permanent Secretary, Education: Mrs Sandra Hall

MINISTRY OF ENERGY AND COMMUNICATION
Minister of State: Miguel Ruiz
Permanent Secretary: Patrick Bernard

MINISTRY OF AGRICULTURE AND FISHERIES
Permanent Secretary: Rodney Neal

MINISTRY OF HOUSING AND CO-OPERATIVES
Permanent Secretary: William Tillett

MINISTRY OF SOCIAL SERVICES AND COMMUNITY DEVELOPMENT
Permanent Secretary: Orlando Puga

ATTORNEY GENERAL, MINISTRY OF TOURISM AND ENVIRONMENT
Permanent Secretary: Dr Victor Gonzalez
Solicitor General: Gian Gandhi

MINISTRY OF HEALTH AND URBAN DEVELOPMENT
Permanent Secretary: Fred Smith

MINISTRY OF WORKS
Permanent Secretary: Gerald Henry

MINISTRY OF LABOUR, LOCAL GOVERNMENT AND PUBLIC SERVICE
Permanent Secretary: Ernest Castro

Botswana

Capital: Gaborone

The Republic of Botswana lies between latitudes 18° and 27° S. and longitudes 20° and 28° W. The area of the country, which has not yet been wholly surveyed, is estimated to be 569,800 sq km (220,000 square miles), about the size of France, and has a mean altitude of 990 m (3,300 feet). Entirely landlocked, its neighbours are the Republic of South Africa to the south and east, Zimbabwe to the north-east, Zambia and the Caprivi Strip (part of Namibia) to the north, and Namibia to the west.

A ridge at a height of about 1,200 m (4,000 feet), which forms the watershed between the Molopo and Notwane Rivers in the south and swings northeast from a point about 32 km (20 miles) west of Kanye all the way to the border of Zimbabwe, divides the country into two dominant topographical regions, characterised by two drainage systems. To the east of the ridge, streams flow into the Marico, Notwane and Limpopo Rivers; to the west is an inactive internal system, which at one time drained this tableland into the great Makgadikgadi pans. Within this flat region there are three sub-regions: the Kalahari Desert, the Okavango Delta and the Northern State Lands area.

Eastern Botswana is broken by a series of rocky hills and is covered, particularly along its eastern margin and over its northern half, by relatively dense bush, but its rainfall is sufficient to produce good pasturage. The existence of grasses of high food value in many parts, the easily tapped underground watertable and the presence of water at shallow depths in the sand beds of the rivers and streams for most of the year, combine to make this an excellent cattle-rearing region. Most of the arable land is also situated in this area, where a mean annual rainfall of 500 mm (20 inches) is normally sufficient for the production of sorghum, maize and wheat. Eighty per cent of the population lives in this region.

West of the ridge which marks the boundary of Eastern Botswana the ground falls to the great expanse of the Kalahari Desert, a level tract closely covered with thorn bush and grass, extending 483 km (300 miles) to the west and bounded by the Makgadikgadi pans and the Botete River in the north. Rainfall in the Kalahari Desert varies from 500 mm (20 inches) in the east to a scant 225 mm (9 inches) in the south-west. Precipitation, however, tends to be erratic and is frequently of a local nature. Surface water is absent except for limited accumulations in flat, clay-floored depressions in the sandveld, known as pans, and in dams built as a result of tribal initiative or the provision of post-war development funds. Along the eastern margin of this region, where the sand mantle thins out, and in the north-west on the Ghanzi ridge which extends into the desert from Namibia, potable underground water supplies have been developed. Elsewhere underground water tends to be saline and sweet water supplies are rare. Where potable water is found in the desert small Bakgalagadi communities gather with their cattle, but there is virtually no arable land. Some bands of bushmen are to be found in this area.

The 16,835 sq km (6,500 square miles) of the Okavango delta lie in the remote northwestern corner of Botswana known as Ngamiland. Apart from the Limpopo and Chobe Rivers, this area is the only source of permanent surface water in the country. The Okavango River, which flows into the delta, is estimated to have an average flow of 9,000 cubic feet per second at Shakawe, but most of this flow is either trapped in the *sudd*-like swamps where it evaporates, or disappears in the sand beds of the Botete and Thamalakane Rivers. Some parts of the delta are infested with tsetse fly which is harboured by the shade trees and dense undergrowth, and is spread beyond the margins of the swamp by wild game. However, an eradication programme is being conducted by the Government. The perimeter of this area is inhabited by the Batswana and allied tribes, numbering around 100,000. They are chiefly pastoralists and the cattle population of the district is estimated as over 150,000, but crops can be produced utilising the residual moisture of the soil in areas which are subject to seasonal flooding, or in other areas under normal rainfall conditions.

The Kalahari Desert extends north of the Botete River and the Makgadikgadi depression into the Northern State Lands where it gives way to belts of indigenous forest and dense bush sustained by the higher rainfall of the region. Valuable stands of *mukwa* (Zimbabwean teak) and *mukusi* cover extensive areas, whilst in other parts, where poorer soils are found, *mopane* forest predominates. The availability of ground water resources, particularly in the southern and eastern sections, and the existence of suitable soils and reliable rainfall in the north-eastern corner of this sub-region indicates a favourable development potential. The remaining areas are populated only by vast herds of game, in whose migratory path the Northern State Lands lie. Elephant numbers alone are estimated at about 55,000 and are increasing at four to five per cent a year. As in the case of the Kalahari Desert, the human population is sparsely scattered around the perimeter.

The climate of the country is generally sub-tropical, but varies considerably with latitude and altitude. The Tropic of Cancer passes through Botswana, and the northern part therefore lies within the tropics.

The southern and south western areas vary between hot steppe with summer rains to desert or semi-desert climate.

During the winter the days are pleasantly warm and the nights cold, with occasional frosts in the north, and heavy frosts in the semi-desert areas. The summer is hot but tempered by a prevailing north-easterly breeze.

The annual seasonal winds from the West Coast begin in August and with every drop of humidity extracted during the Kalahari crossing, sweep across the country raising dust and sandstorms. The normally dry atmosphere helps to mitigate the high temperatures throughout the year, though this consistent dryness and constant glaring sunlight added to the effect of altitude can prove trying, particularly to those whose occupation is sedentary. The whole territory lies in the summer rainfall belt, the rains generally beginning in late October and ending in April. May to September are usually completely dry months.

The mean maximum temperature at Gaborone, the capital, which is 1,002 m (3,339 feet) above mean sea level, is about 32.5°C (90.5°F). The mean annual rainfall at Gaborone is 506 mm (20.24 inches.)

The country's population is estimated at 1,300,000 of whom around 20,000 are non-citizens. Approximately 40,000 Botswana citizens are outside the country, of whom some 22,000 are employed in the mining industry in the Republic of South Africa. Overall population density is 4.40 persons per square mile, but the rural population densities vary from less than one person per square mile over much of the country to more than 60 persons per square mile in parts of the North East District. The natural rate of population growth is currently estimated at 3.4 per cent.

The main business centres are Gaborone (138,000), Francistown (60,000), Lobatse (29,000) and Selebi Phikwe (55,000).

In January 1974 Air Botswana was incorporated. It now operates flights to Lusaka, twice weekly, and to Johannesburg daily and throughout the SADCC region (often in conjunction with other SADCC national airlines). South African Airways, Zambia Airways and Air Zimbabwe also have scheduled services to Botswana. British Airways operate twice weekly flights to and from Heathrow via Johannesburg. There are over 44 government owned and 109 private landing strips in Botswana. The new International Airport in Gaborone has a 3,000 metre runway and can cope with aircraft of up to 747 standard, with weight limitations.

The main railway line from Cape Town to Zimbabwe passes through Botswana running practically due north, entering at Ramatlabama 1,393 km (866 miles) from Cape Town, and leaving at Ramokgwebane 643 km (394 miles) further north. The single track runs parallel to the eastern boundary of Botswana at an average distance from it of about 80 km (50 miles). The gauge of the track is 3ft 6 in. The line is owned and operated by Botswana Railways.

During 1990, a 175 km line was opened between Francistown and the newly built Sowa Town to serve the recently opened Soda ash plant.

In 1966 there were only 12 km of bitumenised roads in Botswana. Since then the expansion of the road network has been rapid, particularly in the years after 1976. By 1989 there were approximately 2,500 km of paved roads in the country of which about 90 per cent were classified as trunk/main roads. In addition, there are about 790 km of gravel roads and 5,000 km of earth and sand tracks.

Since the eastern part of Botswana is the most populated part of the country, initially road construction concentrated on linking the main centres there.

The Government's policy is to provide a high standard bitumenised main road network linking national and international centres. The policy also provides for linking district centres with an all-weather engineered and preferably bitumenised road network which is supplemented by feeder roads of appropriate standard.

Radio Botswana is the only broadcasting service in the country. It broadcasts from Gaborone in the 41, 49, 60 and 90 metre bands, short wave and also in the medium wave band on VHF. There are plans to develop Botswana's own TV service within the next few years.

Botswana's principal exports are diamonds, nickel/copper matte, beef (and beef products) and their primary respective export earnings in 1990 were P2,613 million, P260 million and P138 million.

Botswana's beef industry has suffered considerably from the six years of drought now ended, that has resulted in poor grazing and water conditions, increased offtake and a decline in calving rates. As a result the size of the national herd fell from over 3 million before the onset of drought to around 2.3 million in 1986 but by 1989 had returned to 2.5 million.

Botswana is now one of the large producers of uncut diamonds in the world. Production is now levelling off at about 15.2 million carats per annum.

Copper/Nickel export earnings also increased (by a very small percentage) in 1989, but from the third quarter of 1989 there was a marked decline in this sector's export contribution due to a deterioration in the quality of ore mined.

Preliminary figures for economic performance in 1990 show that export earnings declined by 11 per cent whilst imports grew by 25 per cent. This resulted in a negative trade balance of some P220 million. Foreign exchange reserves are now equivalent to about 21 months of import cover.

In 1976 a central bank, the Bank of Botswana, was established and Botswana's own currency was introduced to replace the rand. The pula was originally tied to the US dollar but since June 1980 has been pegged to a basket of currencies, but principally the rand.

Britain maintains a substantial aid programme to Botswana which consists of manpower training and a small amount of technical assistance. Aid is provided to many sectors but education and engineering receive the greatest share. Other main bilateral aid donors to Botswana include Sweden, Norway, the United States, Germany and the European Community.

The first schools were established by the London Missionary Society during the first half of the last century. As the number of schools increased so did administrative problems and in 1910 the Society and the Chief of the Bangwaketse tribe formed a committee to administer schools in that tribal area. This committee included representatives of the tribe, the Mission and the District Administration. Other tribes followed suit and the system of committee management proved so useful and popular that it was extended to cover practically all educational work being done in tribal areas. Local District Councils were formed in 1966 and today most primary schools are controlled by the local authorities. All professional matters are controlled by the Ministry of Education.

There are now over 550 local authority, aided mission and unaided primary schools; 98 community junior secondary schools and 23 government and government aided schools. Considerable progress has been made towards the target of universal primary education—over 85 per cent in 1985, while in the move towards universal access to junior secondary education the government launched a massive expansion of secondary education in 1984. When this has been completed primary and secondary education will constitute a basic education system lasting nine years and open to all. Senior secondary education will be extended from two to three years and will remain selective, its scale being related to modern sector manpower requirements. The Ministry of Education is also responsible for the administration of four primary teacher training colleges, and one for secondary teachers; the Botswana Polytechnic which offers full-time residential courses in mechanical, civil and electrical engineering and is linked to a network of vocational training centres; and the non-formal education sector which is promoting three main programmes—a system of correspondence courses, a National Literacy Programme, and involvement with Village Development Committees. The University of Botswana was inaugurated on 1st July 1982 as the national university, with faculties of education, humanities, science and social science, and a National Institute of Development Research and Documentation.

History

The picture presented by most parts of Southern Africa in the first quarter of the 19th century was one of tribal wars, pillage and bloodshed, caused mainly by the expansion of the Zulus under Chaka. This warrior chief had succeeded in welding his people into a disciplined and warlike nation who fell upon everyone unfortunate enough to be within their reach. Their neighbouring tribes therefore fled to all points of the compass, despoiling on their way the peoples in their path and thereby setting up a general movement of destructive migration.

Among these migratory bands were the followers of an amazon called Mma-Ntatisi and her son Sekonyela, who came from tribes living in the neighbourhood of what is now Lesotho. They united to form a kind of cohesive army, and advanced northwards and westwards, attacking the tribes along their way.

In a different category were the Matabele. These were originally a group of Chaka's people under Mzilikazi, one of Chaka's principal captains. On one of his raids it is said that Mzilikazi embezzled the booty and decided not to return home. He moved north-westwards and, after a destructive march, established himself near what is now the town of Zeerust, from where he made warlike raids on the tribes within his reach.

Among the victims of Mzilikazi's onslaughts were those known as Batswana, of Western Sotho stock—and hence related to the people of what is now Lesotho—who lived in the western Transvaal and westwards towards the Kalahari. Like other Sotho peoples, their early history is shrouded in legend.

The generally accepted tradition is that the principal tribes of the group are descended from a people ruled by a chief named Masilo who lived about the middle of the 17th century. Masilo had two sons, Mohurutshe and Malope. The former founded the line of the chiefs of the Bahurutshe, while the latter had three sons, Kwena, Ngwato and Ngwaketse. Ngwato and Ngwaketse at different times broke away from Kwena's tribe and went with their followers to live at a distance from each other. The Bahurutshe were set upon first by Mma-Ntatisi's people and then by the Matabele. The home of the Bahurutshe is in the western Transvaal but scattered elements have attached themselves to the present tribes of Botswana. The Bangwaketse, after several migrations, finally settled in their present country around Kanye, while the Bamangwato founded a colony in the vicinity of Shoshong in the area occupied by the tribe today. The descendants of the Kwena section now live around Molepolole. Among the Bamangwato a further split occurred; Tawana, one of the Chief Mathiba's sons seceded at the end of the 18th century and formed a settlement in Ngamiland. The Batswana are still the ruling community in that area.

The Barolong, the greater number of whom today live in the Republic of South Africa, trace the genealogy of their chief to one Rolong, who lived at a time even more remote than did Masilo. The Barolong are settled along the southern border of Botswana and round Mafeking.

Other important tribes of the Batswana are the Bakgatla, the Bamalete, and the Batlokwa. These arrived in Botswana from the Western Transvaal in the 19th century, driven out by the Westward movement of the Boers.

The years between 1820 and 1870 saw a number of intertribal disputes. These were complicated by the impact of the Boer trekkers, who did, however, rid the Zeerust area of the Matabele: after losing several engagements with the Boers, Mzilikazi trekked northwards in 1838, attacking the less warlike Batswana and Makalanga on the way. Few of the Batswana chiefs were able to make effective resistance, but in 1840 Chief Sekgoma of the Bamangwato defeated several Matabele raiding parties. About this time, David Livingstone established a mission among the Bakwena, where he stayed until the early fifties.

In 1872 one of the most remarkable Africans of his time succeeded to the chieftainship of the Bamangwato. This was Khama III (the son of Sekgoma), whose youth had been much troubled by dissensions within the tribe and by the ever-present peril of the Matabele. During the first few years of his reign Khama greatly enhanced the standing of his tribe. He was a capable general, and formed a small but well-trained army. With this he earned the respect of Lobengula, son of Mzilikazi, thus obtaining immunity from the depredations of the Matabele. A lifelong and firm adherent of Christianity, Khama introduced many reforms into the life of the tribe, of which the most important, and the one on which he himself set most store, was the total prohibition of alcoholic liquor. A capable if occasionally a harsh administrator, he devoted himself with energy to the organisation of his people.

Though the weaker tribes still suffered at the hands of Lobengula's Matabele, by the middle 1870's there was some stability and order in the life of the Bamangwato and the other Batswana tribes.

At this time, the Batswana had seen little of the white man. A few traders and hunters had penetrated into their territories, but, except at centres like Shoshong, no permanent relations had been established. The only Europeans who had lived among the Batswana were the missionaries, men like Moffat and Livingstone. Now began the exploration of Africa and the division of the continent among the European Powers. Embittered relations between the Boers from the Transvaal and the Batswana people (particularly the Barolong and the Batlhaping) prompted the latter to address appeals for assistance to the Cape authorities, while Khama, shortly after his accession, also asked for his country to be taken under British protection.

The British Government showed no anxiety to assume such new responsibilites, and it was not until 1884 that the missionary John Mackenzie was sent to Bechuanaland as Deputy Commissioner. Finally in 1885 Sir Charles Warren, with the concurrence of Khama and the other principal chiefs, proclaimed the whole of Bechuanaland to be under the protection of the Queen.

The part of the Territory to the south of the Molopo River, which included Mafeking, Vryburg and Kuruman, was constituted a Crown Colony, called British Bechuanaland, in 1885, and became part of the Cape Colony (now the Cape Province of the Republic of South Africa) in 1895. The northern part, the Bechuanaland Protectorate, remained under the protection of the British Crown. The colony and the protectorate were at first both administered from Vryburg; but on the incorporation of the Colony in the Cape, the headquarters of the protectorate were moved to Mafeking, the nearest convenient centre to the protectorate.

The British expansion northwards continued, under the powerful inspiration of Cecil John Rhodes, who had in 1889 obtained a Royal Charter for his British South Africa Company organised 'for the development of the Bechuanaland Protectorate and the North'. With the occupation in 1895 of what is now Zimbabwe, Rhodes's description of Botswana as the 'Suez Canal to the North' was seen to be an apt one.

In 1894 the British Government showed itself in favour of handing the administration of the protectorate to the British South Africa Company. Chiefs Khama of the Bamangwato, Bathoen of the Bangwaketse and Sebele of the Bakwena went to England to protect against the suggested transfer. A compromise was reached whereby the tribal lands would be demarcated, with the understanding that all other lands not specifically reserved would come under the control of the British South Africa Company and a strip of land on the eastern side of the protectorate would be ceded for the building of a railway. In the event, the diminution of Rhodes's influence which followed the failure of the Jameson Raid in December 1895, led to postponement and eventual abandonment of the plan to hand over the administration of the non-tribal lands of the protectorate to the British South Africa Company.

The South Africa Act of Union of 1909, which established the Union of South Africa, included provisions for the possible inclusion in South Africa of the three territories of Basutoland, Bechuanaland and Swaziland, which were administered by the High Commissioner for South Africa.

When the South African Constitution was being drawn up the Chiefs in Basutoland, Bechuanaland and Swaziland objected to any scheme which would bring their territories under the rule of South Africa. Assurances were given that no immediate change would be made in the administration of these territories, but provision was made for the possible eventual transfer subject to certain conditions for the protection of African rights embodied in the Act. From 1909 onwards successive South African Governments asked for the implementation of the transfer, which was understood to be provided for by the Schedule to the South African Act of Union. The British Government reiterated that it alone bore the ultimate responsibility in the question of a decision about transfer and that no such transfer could take place until the wishes of the inhabitants had been ascertained and considered. For many years past the records of the African Advisory Council, African Council, and Legislative Council have left no doubt of the opposition of the African people of Botswana to any such transfer. The question of handing over the administration of the three countries to South Africa ceased to be a serious issue in 1960. In February 1965 the headquarters of the Administration was transferred from Mafeking in the Cape Province of South Africa, which had been its home since 1895, to Gaborone.

Constitutional development

From 1891 to 1960, the constitutional position of the protectorate was governed by various Orders in Council and Proclamations of which the most important was the Order in Council of Queen Victoria dated 9th May 1891 which empowered the High Commissioner to exercise on her behalf all the powers and jurisdiction of the Queen, subject to such instructions as he might receive from Her Majesty or through a Secretary of State.

Since about the mid-thirties necessary intervention in tribal affairs by the central authority, financial and economic development, the growth of export and import trade, technical advances and ever-increasing demands for more and better services brought about an inevitable and intensifying extension of central government activity. The expansion of central authority was accompanied by the steady evolution of local tribal government. In 1934, the promulgation of the African Courts and African Administration Proclamation set out to regularise the position of the Chiefs, to provide for the proper exercise of their powers and functions, to define the constitution and functions of the Courts and to establish their powers and jurisdiction on a proper legal footing. The actions of African Authorities and African Courts were consequently henceforward governed by law.

In 1960 a new constitution was introduced providing for an advisory Executive Council consisting of the Resident Commissioner (or the High Commissioner), three *ex-officio* members (The Government Secretary, the Finance Secretary and the Attorney-General), two official members appointed by the High Commissioner, and four nominated members appointed by the High Commissioner who were members of the Legislative Council not holding any public office, two of them African and two Europeans; a representative Legislative Council, consisting of the Resident Commissioner as President, the three *ex-officio* members of the Executive Council, seven official members holding public office appointed by the High Commissioner, twenty-one elected members, and not more than four nominated members, not holding any public office, appointed by the High Commissioner, who had to be either one African and one European or two Africans and two Europeans; and an advisory African Council partly official, partly *ex-officio,* and partly elected. The Constitution also established a judicature consisting of a High Court comprising a Chief Justice and puisne judges.

By Order in Council signed on 27th September 1963 the territory was made independent of High Commission rule by the transformation of the post of Resident Commissioner into that of Her Majesty's Commissioner, with the status and rank of a Governor. Her Majesty's Commissioner assented to laws and was directly responsible to the Secretary of State for the Colonies. Certain powers retained by the High Commissioner ceased to exist when the office was abolished on 1st August 1964. During 1963 and early in 1964 a series of constitutional discussions took place to determine the form of further constitutional advance.

Unanimously agreed proposals for internal self-government based on universal adult suffrage and a ministerial form of government were put forward to Her Majesty's Government and were accepted in June 1964.

The new Constitution contained in the Bechuanaland Protectorate (Constitution) Orders 1965 (S.I. 1965 Nos. 134 and 1718) as modified by the Bechuanaland Protectorate (Constitution) (Amendment) Order 1965 (S.I. 1965 No 1718) and by Her Majesty's Commissioner's order in terms of section 12(7) of the Bechuanaland Protectorate (Constitution) Order 1965 (G.N. No. 99 of 1965), came into effect on 3rd March 1965. This Constitution granted to the country a form of responsible government upon which the present Constitution is based.

The executive government of Bechuanaland was controlled by a Cabinet presided over by the Prime Minister, consisting of the Deputy Prime Minister and six other members chosen by the Prime Minister from the Legislative Assembly. Under the Constitution, the Prime Minister was the member of Legislative Assembly who appeared to Her Majesty's Commissioner to command the support of the majority of the Members of the Assembly, i.e. the leader of that political party which obtained the largest number of seats in the General Election.

The National Day of the Republic of Botswana is 30th September, commemorating the achievement of independence in 1966.

Constitution

The President of Bctswana is Head of State, in whom is vested the executive power of the Republic. The Vice-President is appointed by the President from among members of the National Assembly and is the principal assistant to the President and leader of Government business in the National Assembly. The Cabinet, which advises the President on Government policy, consists of not more than ten ministers, appointed by the President.

The Botswana Parliament consists of the President and the National Assembly. The Assembly is made up of 34 elected members and four specially elected members, the Attorney-General, who does not have a vote in the Assembly and the Speaker. The Assembly is elected on the basis of universal adult suffrage.

The House of Chiefs consists of eight *ex-officio* members, who are the chiefs of the eight principal Batswana tribes, four members elected from among their own number by the Sub-Chiefs who reside in the State Land areas, and three specially elected members, elected by the *ex-officio* and elected members. The House of Chiefs considers draft bills which are referred to it by the National Assembly, and which if enacted would alter any of the provisions of the Constitution or affect a defined range of subjects relating to tribal matters. The House of Chiefs is also entitled to discuss any matters affecting the tribes and tribal organisations and may make representations to the President, and through him to the Cabinet, and may send messages to the National Assembly.

Government

For the first general election in the Bechuanaland Protectorate, roughly 80 per cent of the potential electorate registered as voters in 1964; of those nearly 5/6ths actually voted in 1965. The result was an overwhelming victory for the Bechuanaland Democratic Party led by the late Sir Seretse Khama, who won 28 seats in the National Assembly. The remaining 3 seats went to the Bechuanaland People's Party led by the late Mr Philip Matante.

Sir Seretse Khama became the first Prime Minister of Bechuanaland and subsequently the first President of the Republic of Botswana on 30th September 1966.

On 18th October 1969, the first general elections since the achievement of Independence in 1966 were held, and about one-half of the registered voters of Botswana went to the polls. The result was a victory for the Botswana Democratic Party, led by Sir Seretse Khama, which won 24 seats in the National Assembly. The Botswana People's Party and the Botswana National Front won 3 seats each, and the Botswana Independence Party gained 1 seat.

A Presidential Candidate who is supported by more than one-half of elected MPs is automatically declared as President. As his party had a clear majority Sir Seretse Khama therefore retained the Presidency and was sworn in by the Chief Justice on 22nd October 1969.

Sir Seretse Khama died on 13th July 1980 and was succeeded as President by Dr Q K J Masire.

In the General Election held on 7th October 1989 almost two-thirds of the registered voters went to the polls and returned to power the Botswana Democratic Party with 31 of the 34 seats in the National Assembly. The remaining seats are held by the Botswana National Front led by Dr Kenneth Koma.

HEAD OF STATE

President: The Hon Dr Q K J Masire, LL.D, PH, JP, MP

CABINET

Vice-President and Minister of Local Government and Lands: The Hon P S Mmusi, MP

Minister of Presidential Affairs and Public Administration: The Hon Lt Gen M S Merafhe, MP

Minister for External Affairs: The Hon Dr G K T Chiepe, MBE, MP

Minister of Health: The Hon K P Morake, MP

Minister of Labour and Home Affairs: The Hon P K Balopi, MP

Minister of Agriculture: The Hon D K Kwelagobe, MP

Minister of Works, Transport and Communications: The Hon C J Butale, MP

Minister of Commerce and Industry: The Hon P H K Kedikilwe, MP

Minister of Education: The Hon R M Molomo, MP

Minister of Mineral Resources and Water Affairs: The Hon A M Mogwe, MBE, MP

Minister of Finance and Development Planning: The Hon F G Mogae, MP

Assistant Minister, Local Government and Lands: The Hon M R Tshipinare, MP

Assistant Minister, Local Government and Lands: The Hon R K Sebego, MP

Assistant Minister, Finance and Development Planning: The Hon D N Magang, MP

Assistant Minister of Agriculture: The Hon G M Oteng, MP

JUDICIARY

Chief Justice: Elsen Livesey-Luke

Registrar: K Yoganathan

NATIONAL ASSEMBLY

Speaker: The Hon M P K Nwako, MP

MINISTRIES AND DEPARTMENTS

PRESIDENT'S OFFICE

Permanent Secretary to the President and Secretary to the Cabinet: E Legwaila

Administrative Secretary: T D Mogami

Secretary for External Affairs: G G Garebamono

Commissioner of Police: S A Hirschfeld, DPM

Director of Public Service Management: M Modise

Director of Information and Broadcasting: P Makgekgenene

MINISTRY OF LOCAL GOVERNMENT AND LANDS

Permanent Secretary: Miss P Venson

Director of Surveys and Lands: B Morebodi

MINISTRY OF FINANCE AND DEVELOPMENT PLANNING
Permanent Secretary: B Gaolathe
Accountant-General: M C Monthsiwa

MINISTRY OF HEALTH
Permanent Secretary: E T Maganu
Director of Health Services: Dr J Mulwa

MINISTRY OF LABOUR AND HOME AFFAIRS
Permanent Secretary: K M Masogo
Commissioner of Prisons: B F W Lekoko

MINISTRY OF AGRICULTURE
Permanent Secretary: Dr M M Mannathoko
Director of Veterinary Services: Dr M Mosienyane

MINISTRY OF WORKS, TRANSPORT AND COMMUNICATIONS
Permanent Secretary: M C Tibone
Director of Civil Aviation: J Moatshe
Director of Postal Services: D Gabaraane

MINISTRY OF COMMERCE AND INDUSTRY
Permanent Secretary: M L Mokone

MINISTRY OF EDUCATION
Permanent Secretary: P Molosi

MINISTRY OF MINERAL RESOURCES AND WATER AFFAIRS
Permanent Secretary: C M Lekaukau
Director of Geological Survey: T Machacha
Director of Water Affairs: M Sekwale

ATTORNEY-GENERAL
The Hon M P Mokama, MP

AUDIT DEPARTMENT
Auditor-General: E P S Letsididi

BOTSWANA DEFENCE FORCE
Commander: Lt-General S K I Khama

Brunei

Capital: Bandar Seri Begawan

Negara Brunei Darussalam is situated on the north-west coast of Borneo and lies between latitudes 4°2′ and 5°3′ North and longitudes 114° and 115° 22′ East. It has an area of 5,765 sq km (2,226 square miles) and has a coast line of approximately 161 km (100 miles). It is divided into two parts by Sarawak. To the west are the districts of Brunei-Muara, Tutong and Belait, and to the east is the district of Temburong. Brunei lies on a narrow coastal plain intersected by several rivers descending from the hilly hinterland. To the east, in Temburong District, the coastal plain reaches up to more mountainous regions surrounding Brunei's highest point, Bukit Pagon, which is 1,812 m (6,040 ft) above sea level.

The climate is tropical and is characterised by a uniform temperature throughout the year, a high humidity and heavy rainfall, varying from 2,500 mm (100 inches) a year at the coast to over 5,000 mm (200 inches) in certain parts of the interior. There is no distinct wet season but there is a tendency for heavier rainfall from November to January. Much of the rain falls in sudden thundery showers.

The vegetation in the interior consists mainly of primary and secondary tropical rain forest which is dense in places. Along the coastal plains there are mangrove swamps and sandy beaches.

In early 1991 the population was estimated at 265,000. Annual growth rate is estimated at 3 per cent. Brunei's largest racial group is Malay but there are approximately 70,000 non-Malays, including some 43,000 Chinese. The non-Malay indigenous people are mainly Ibans and Dusuns, but there are several other minor tribal groupings. Europeans make up a small part of the population, holding some posts in teaching, the Armed Forces, commerce and the oil industry.

The official language of Brunei is Malay but English is widely understood. Other languages spoken include Chinese, Iban and a number of native dialects.

The unit of currency is the Brunei dollar (freely exchangeable at par with the Singapore dollar). In August 1991 the Brunei dollar was equal to approximately £0.34.

The principal towns are Bandar Seri Begawan, the capital, and Seria and Kuala Belait which are situated in the centre of the oil and gas industry at the western end of the State. Other main towns include Tutong and Bangar. The State's only deep water port capable of taking oceangoing ships is at Muara, 27 km (17 miles) from the capital and on the mouth of the Brunei River. There is a small port at Kuala Belait which handles shallow draught vessels.

The largest proportion of Brunei's income is derived from participation royalties and taxes on crude oil from Brunei Shell Petroleum's oil fields at Seria, which produces an estimated 150,000 barrels per day. Although the first field was established onshore, most of Brunei Shell's production is now from offshore wells.

Brunei Shell also sells natural gas to the Brunei Liquidfied Natural Gas company. The gas is liquified at Lumut, one of the biggest plants of its kind in the world, and shipped to Japan. Brunei LNG is a joint venture between the Brunei Government, Shell and Japanese interests.

The favourable trade balance in 1990 was B$2.4 billion.

Gross Domestic Product (GDP) for 1990 at current prices, B$7.15 billion.

Brunei possesses one of Asia's finest health care systems. Medical services are heavily subsidised by the Government and generally free of charge. Of the eight hospitals in the country, four are government, three are military and one is operated by Brunei Shell Petroleum. In addition there is a highly efficient 'Flying Doctor' service, mobile dispensaries and various clinics. Brunei is the only region of Borneo where malaria has been completely eradicated, while cholera is virtually non-existent.

There are some 350 schools in Brunei and education to sixth form level is provided free by the Government for all Brunei citizens. The University in Bandar Seri Begawan opened on 26th October 1985 with 120 students in the first year, mainly in the Arts and Social Sciences. Degrees were awarded at the first Convocation Ceremony held in September 1989. The literacy rate for young people is estimated at 95 per cent.

Land tenure in Brunei is governed by the Land Code. All land belongs to the nation but may be allotted to individuals by the Sultan. Except for fish and poultry, fruit and vegetables, Brunei imports most of its food requirements. Agriculture mainly consists of small-scale subsistence farms growing rice, sago, vegetables and fruit, but there are a number of agricultural stations developing hydroponics and propagation techniques. There are also plans to develop forestry and fisheries.

The main road in Brunei connects the two principal towns of Bandar Seri Begawan and Kuala Belait, but there are a few secondary roads which run inland. There is no road link between Temburong District to the east and the districts of Belait, Tutong and Brunei/Muara to the west. There are no railways in Brunei.

Brunei International Airport has recently been redeveloped and expanded. It is served by the state-owned airline, Royal Brunei Airlines, and by a number of regional airlines. Regular scheduled services operate between Brunei and Singapore, Malaysia, Thailand, Australia, Indonesia, Hong Kong, Philippines, Taipei, the UK and Dubai. Air Service Agreements were signed in November 1990 with Bangladesh and the Federal Republic of Germany.

Radio Television Brunei broadcasts an all-colour television service and two FM stereo and MW radio channels from a modern well-equipped complex in the centre of Bandar Seri Begawan. It transmits a wide range of programmes from Brunei and overseas.

Brunei is a Sultanate and the present Ruler, the twenty-ninth of his line, succeeded to the throne on 4th October 1967 following the abdication of his father. The Constitution, promulgated on 29th September 1959 provides for a Privy Council, a Council of Ministers, a Religious Council and a Council of Succession. Executive authority is vested in the Sultan to be exercised by him either directly or through officers subordinate to him.

Brunei is one of the most ancient kingdoms in Asia and records show that it was first settled in the 8th century, becoming an Islamic state as early as the 13th century. Its power and influence reached a peak during the rule of Sultan Bolkiah from 1473 to 1521 when it was the centre of an empire covering the whole of Borneo and stretching as far as Java, Malacca and the Philippines. The voyages of exploration by the Portuguese, Spanish and Dutch expanded Brunei's trading links. However, Brunei's power gradually declined as rampant piracy, wars and the expansion of the colonial empires of the Dutch and British led to the break up of Borneo into new states.

Relations with Britain. In 1847 the Sultan entered into a Treaty with Britain for the furtherance of commercial relations and for the suppression of piracy. By a further Treaty in 1888 Brunei was placed under British protection and the Sultan agreed that the foreign relations of the State should be conducted by Her Majesty's Government. In 1905–1906 a supplementary agreement was entered into, whereby the Sultan undertook to accept a British Officer, to be styled as Resident, who should be the agent and representative of the British Government under the High Commissioner for the Malay States. The Governor of Sarawak was High Commissioner for Brunei from 1948 until 1959.

On 29th September 1959 a further agreement was concluded between Her Majesty The Queen and His Highness the Sultan replacing the 1905–1906 Agreement, under which the British Government continued to be responsible for the defence and external affairs of the State. The Agreement provided for the appointment of a High Commissioner, resident in Brunei.

In November 1971, the Sultan and the British Government signed an agreement amending the 1959 Agreement. Under the Amending Agreement Brunei ceased to be a Protected State but the British Government continued to be responsible for her external affairs and undertook to consult with the Brunei Government in the event of external attack or threat of such attack. As a result of negotiations in June 1978, the Sultan and the British Government signed a new Treaty on 7th January, 1979 under which Brunei became a fully sovereign and independent State on 31st December 1983.

HEAD OF STATE

Kebawah Duli Yang Maha Mulia Paduka Seri Beginda Sultan Haji Hassanal Bolkiah Mu'izzaddin Waddaulah DKMB, DK, PSSUB, DPKG, DPKT, PSPNB, PSNB, PSLJ, SPMB, PANB, GCMG, DMN, DK(KELANTAN) DK(JOHOR), DK(NEGERI SEMBILAN), Sultan dan Yang Di-Pertuan Negara Brunei Darussalam

MINISTERS

Prime Minister and Minister of Defence
His Majesty Sultan Haji Hassanal Bolkiah Mu'izzaddin Waddaulah, Sultan and Yang Di-Pertuan of Brunei Darussalam

Minister of Foreign Affairs
His Royal Highness Prince Mohamed Bolkiah

Minister of Finance
His Royal Highness Prince Jefri Bolkiah

Special Adviser to His Majesty The Sultan and Yang Di-Pertuan of Brunei Darussalam in the Prime Minister's Office cum Minister of Home Affairs
Yang Berhormat Pehin Orang Kaya Laila Setia Bakti Di-Raja Dato Laila Utama Haji Awang Isa bin Pehin Datu Perdana Menteri Dato Laila Utama Haji Awang Ibrahim

Minister of Education
Yang Berhormat Pehin Orang Kaya Laila Wijaya Dato Seri Setia Haji Awang Abdul Aziz bin Begawan Pehin Udana Khatib Dato Seri Paduka Haji Awang Umar

Minister of Law
Yang Amat Mulia Pengiran Laila Kanun Di-Raja Pengiran Bahrin bin Pengiran Haji Abas

Minister of Industry and Primary Resources
Yang Berhormat Pehin Orang Kaya Setia Pahlawan Dato Seri Setia Haji Awang Abdul Rahman bin Dato Setia Haji Awang Mohammad Taib

Minister of Religious Affairs
Yang Berhormat Pehin Orang Kaya Ratna Di-Raja Dato Seri Utama Dr. Ustaz Haji Awang Mohammad Zain bin Haji Serudin

Minister of Development
Yang Berhormat Pengiran Dato Seri Laila Jasa Dr. Haji Ismail bin Pengiran Haji Damit

Minister of Culture, Youth and Sports
Yang Berhormat Pehin Jawatan Luar Pekerma Raja Dato Seri Paduka Haji Awang Hussein bin Pehin Orang Kaya Di-Gadong Seri Di-Raja Dato Laila Utama Haji Awang Mohammad Yusof

Minister of Health
Yang Berhormat Dato Paduka Dr. Haji Johar bin Dato Paduka Haji Nordin
Minister of Communications
Yang Berhormat Dato Seri Laila Jasa Haji Awang Zakaria bin Datu Mahawangsa Haji Awang Sulaiman

DEPUTY MINISTERS
Deputy Minister of Defence
Yang Amat Mulia Pengiran Sanggamara Di-Raja Major General Pengiran Haji Ibnu bin Pengiran Datu Penghulu Pengiran Haji Apong
Deputy Minister of Foreign Affairs
Yang Mulia Dato Paduka Haji Awang Mohammad Ali bin Haji Mohammad Daud
The Deputy Minister of Finance
Yang Mulia Dato Paduka Seri Laila Jasa Haji Awang Ahmad Wally Skinner
Deputy Minister of Home Affairs
Yang Mulia Dato Paduka Haji Awang Abidin bin Orang Kaya Periwara Abdul Rashid
Deputy Minister of Education
Yang Mulia Dato Seri Laila Jasa Haji Awang Ahmad bin Jahi Jumat
Deputy Minister of Religous Affairs
Yang Dimuliakan Pehin Si-Raja Khatib Dato Paduka Seri Setia Ustaz Haji Awang Yahya bin Haji Ibrahim
Deputy Minister of Culture, Youth and Sports
Yang Mulia Dato Paduka Haji Awang Selamat bin Haji Munap

Canada

Capital: Ottawa

Canada occupies the northern half of the North American continent with the exception of Alaska, which is part of the United States, Greenland which is part of the Kingdom of Denmark, and the small islands of St Pierre and Miquelon off the coast of Newfoundland which belong to France. In latitude the country stretches from Middle Island in Lake Erie, at 41° 41′ N., to Cape Columbia on Ellesmere Island, at 83° 07′ N. It thus includes the islands immediately north of the mainland such as Victoria Island and Baffin Island as well as those in the extreme north known collectively as the Queen Elizabeth Islands. Other islands of importance are Vancouver Island and the Queen Charlotte Islands off the west coast; the island of Newfoundland forming part of the Province of Newfoundland; the Province of Prince Edward Island; Cape Breton Island forming part of the Province of Nova Scotia; Grand Manan and Campobello Islands forming part of the Province of New Brunswick; Anticosti Island and the Magdalen group included in the Province of Quebec. Canada is the largest country in the western Hemisphere and the second largest country in the world, comprising an area computed at 9,976,185 sq km (3,851,809 square miles) of land and fresh water, over forty times the area of Britain.

The predominant geographical feature is the Great Cordilleran Mountain System which contains many peaks over 3,000 m (10,000 feet) in height. The highest peak in Canada is Mount Logan, in the St Elias Mountains of Yukon Territory, which rises 5,955 m (19,850 feet) above sea level. The highest elevations in the country are to be found in Yukon (19 other peaks over 3,000 m (10,000 feet)), Alberta (32 peaks over 3,000 m (10,000 feet) in the Rockies) and British Columbia (32 peaks over 3,000 m (10,000 feet)).

Another geographical feature of note is the area known as the great Canadian Shield. This is a vast area of ancient rocks occupying the greater part of the territory north of the River St Lawrence. It consists of plateau-like highlands, made up of a great mass of ancient, very hard rocks, which present a rough, broken surface strewn with lakes and varying in height from 300 m to 900 m (1,000 to 3,000 feet) above sea level with a few higher peaks. It contains rich mineral deposits, and its vast forest and water power resources contribute much to the wealth of the country.

Canada's inland waters are very extensive, constituting about 7.6 per cent of the total area of the country. The Great Lakes are the outstanding lakes of the country, their total Canadian area being almost 93,240 sq km (36,000 square miles). Other large lakes ranging in area from 24,605 to 31,857 sq km (9,500 to 12,300 square miles) are Lake Winnipeg, Great Slave Lake and Great Bear Lake. In addition there are innumerable lakes scattered over that major portion of Canada lying within the Canadian Shield; in an area of 15,783 sq km (6,094 square miles) south and east of Lake Winnipeg there are 3,000 lakes. Eastern Canada is dominated by the Great Lakes—St Lawrence system which drains an area of about 1,756,020 sq km (678,000 square miles) and forms an unequalled navigable inland waterway through a region rich in natural and industrial resources. From the head of Lake Superior to the entrance to the Gulf of St Lawrence the distance is 3,668 km (2,280 miles). In the mid-west two main branches of the Saskatchewan River, tributary to the Nelson flowing into Hudson Bay, drain one of Canada's great agricultural regions and are now the bases of important irrigation projects. North-westward, one of the world's largest rivers, the Mackenzie, flows 4,239 km (2,635 miles) to the Arctic Ocean and drains an area in the three westernmost provinces of approximately 1,813,000 sq km (700,000 square miles).

There are great differences in the weather throughout Canada at any given time, as there are many climates. Because Canada is situated in the northern half of the hemisphere, most of the country loses more heat annually than it receives from the sun. The general atmospheric circulation compensates for this and at the same time produces a general movement of air from west to east. Migrant low pressure areas move across the country in this 'westerly zone', producing storms and bad weather. In intervals between storms there prevails the fair weather associated with high pressure areas. The physical geography of North America also contributes greatly to the climate. On the west coast, the western Cordillera limits mild air from the Pacific to a narrow band along the coast, while the prairies to the east of the mountains are dry and have extreme temperatures. The prairies are part of a wide north-south corridor open to rapid air flow from either north or south which often brings sudden and drastic weather changes. On the other hand, the large water surfaces of eastern Canada produce a considerable modification to the climate. In south-western Ontario winters are milder with more snow, and in summer the cooling effect of the lakes is well illustrated by the number of resorts along their shores. On

For further information about Canada see *Canada Year Book*, published by Statistics Canada.

the east coast the Atlantic Ocean has considerable effect on the immediate coastal area where temperatures are modified and conditions made more humid when the winds blow inland from the ocean. The following figures give some indication of the varying mean temperatures (Fahrenheit): Newfoundland (Gander) January 21.1, July 61.7; Nova Scotia (Halifax) January 26.0, July 65.3; Quebec (Montreal) January 16.0, July 70.8; Prairie Provinces (Regina) January 0.9, July 66.0; British Columbia (Vancouver) January 36.3. July 63.4; Smith River, January 11.4, July 57.4; Yukon (Whitehorse) January 2.0, July 57.3.

The Canadian federal state was established by the British North America Act, 1867, now known in Canada as the Constitution Act 1867, and now consists of ten Provinces and two Territories. The Provinces, with the year in which they joined the Confederation, are: Ontario (1867), Quebec (1867), Nova Scotia (1867), New Brunswick (1867), Manitoba (1870), British Columbia (1871), Prince Edward Island (1873), Saskatchewan (1905), Alberta (1905) and Newfoundland (1949). The Territories are the Northwest Territories (1870) and the Yukon Territory (1898). The Northwest Territories were divided in 1920 into the Districts of Mackenzie, Keewatin and Franklin.

The population of Canada according to the 1986 census is 25,354,064. Of the total population 28.9 per cent are 0–19 years of age, 60.4 per cent are 20–64 years of age, and 10.7 per cent are 65 years and over. The birthrate for 1989 was 14.5 per 1,000 population and the death rate 7.3 per 1,000. According to the 1986 census of Canada, the two basic language groups in the Canadian population, based on single mother tongue, are English and French, with 15,334,085 and 6,159,740 respectively. The next largest are Italian 455,820, German 438,680 (includes Alsacian in 1986) and Chinese (266,560).

Canada, over the years 1981–1986, experienced an increase of 4.2 per cent in population growth. Newfoundland 0.1 per cent, Prince Edward Island 3.4 per cent, Nova Scotia 3.0 per cent, New Brunswick 2.0 per cent, Quebec 1.6 per cent, Ontario 5.7 per cent, Manitoba 4.4 per cent, Saskatchewan 4.3 per cent, Alberta 6.1 per cent, British Columbia 5.3 per cent, Yukon 1.5 per cent and Northwest Territories 14.2 per cent.

Birth, death, immigration and emigration are the components of population change. The high mean annual birth rate (28.0 per thousand in 1951–56) and mean annual rate of natural increase (19.6 per thousand) are representative of the rapid growth that occurred in the early postwar period, which peaked to record highs in the mid-1950s. Lower rates of growth in succeeding years resulted mainly from falling birth rates beginning in the early 1960s and continuing on to 1976. Death rates, though declining slightly, have remained relatively stable compared to other components of growth. Net international migration (total emigration subtracted from total immigration) during the early and mid-1950s (7.9 per thousand in the period 1951–56 and 5.6 per thousand in 1956–61) has also had a strong influence on Canada's population growth.

Canada had a mean population density of 2.8 persons per square kilometre in 1986; still one of the lowest population densities in the world. However, this figure takes into account the whole land area of the country and it should be kept in mind that vast spatial variations exist. Over 80 per cent of the total population is concentrated in Quebec, Ontario, Alberta and British Columbia which have larger land areas than other provinces. Alberta, British Columbia and Ontario were the only provinces whose annual population increases exceeded the national average in the past. Prince Edward Island, Nova Scotia and New Brunswick are the smallest provinces in terms of land area, but have population densities (22.4, 16.5 and 9.9 persons per square kilometre, respectively) well above the national average of 2.8 persons per square kilometre, whereas the Yukon and the Northwest Territories, with vast land areas, have markedly low densities of 0.05 and 0.02 persons per square kilometre, respectively.

In 1986, over 50 per cent of Canada's total population resided in 25 census metropolitan areas. Population figures show that Toronto (3,427,168) and Montreal (2,921,357) were Canada's largest metropolitan areas, while Vancouver had grown to 1,380,729. In terms of growth rate, the big winners among Canada's census metropolitan areas for the 1981–86 period were Saskatoon with 14.6 per cent, Ottawa-Hull 10.1 per cent, followed by Toronto with 9.5 per cent and Oshawa 9.2 per cent.

Interprovincial migration has always played an important role in provincial population growth.

Between 1971–76, Alberta and British Columbia had the most important migratory gains. On the other hand, Prince Edward Island, Nova Scotia and New Brunswick, some of the provinces that traditionally presented negative migratory balances, experienced over this 5 year period, positive migration.

However, results for the 1976–81 period were very different. Only Alberta and British Columbia experienced positive migration during this 5 year period.

Between 1981–86 Ontario had its first positive migration balance since the 1966–71 period. At the same time Alberta experienced negative migration for the first time since 1961–66. More significantly, Ontario represented the only province that showed a positive net interprovincial migration in 1985–86. Between 1987–90, British Columbia and Prince Edward Island were the only provinces with a positive net interprovincial migration. Since 1987, Saskatchewan was the only province to see its population fall while the rest of the provinces experienced population growth.

The combined population of native people of Canada (including registered Indians and Inuit) is 498,179 (1990 estimates). There are 466,337 Indians living in 596 bands. Approximately 260,760 Indians live on Indian reserves; 18,911 live on Crown leased land and some 186,666 live outside reserves (figures of December 1989). In the northern and outlying areas, hunting, fishing and trapping remain an

1 **Trinidad:** Morne Catherine Radar Tower, Chaguaramas/*Bill Preston, British High Commission, Port-of-Spain*

2 **Hong Kong:** A Hong Kong tram/*Gillian Allen, FCO*

3 **Namibia:** Herdsmen and horses/*Compix*

4 **Canada:** Satellite Network Operations Centre, Telesat Headquarters, Ottawa/*Telesat Canada*

5 **Belize:** Milling rice/*Compix*

6 **Nigeria:** Frangipani/*Compix*

7 **Botswana:** Magope, East of Selebi-Phikwe/ *Mr R White, Gaborone*

8 **New Zealand:** View towards the Bluff on Ninety Mile Beach, North Cape/*Compix*

9 **Pakistan:** Lahore Fort/*High Commission for Pakistan, London*

10 **St Helena:** Man and Horse Cliffs/*Compix*

11 **Zambia:** Rural bus near Chingola/*Compix*

12 **Kenya:** Longonot Satellite Station/*Compix*

13 **Zimbabwe:** Bat-Eared Fox, Hwange National Park/*Jane Wildash, British High Commission, Harare*

14 **Australia:** View West from Cape Patton Lookout, Otway Range, Great Ocean Road, Victoria/ *Norman Fryer, FCO*

15 **Western Samoa:** Aggie Grey's Hotel, Apia/*Bob Setterfield, British High Commission, Wellington*

16 **Falkland Islands:** Stanley Harbour in early morning from Ross Road/*Graham France, Government House, Stanley*

17 **Seychelles:** Seychelles Domestic Satellite System/ *Russ Covey, Cable and Wireless, Seychelles*

18 **Papua New Guinea:** The Port Moresby Show, June 1991/*Susan Farrent, British High Commission, Port Moresby*

19 **Jamaica:** Devon House, Craft and Entertainment Centre, St Andrew/*Jill Roberts, British High Commission, Kingston*

20 **Malta:** The Blue Grotto/*David Cooke*

3

4

6

8

9

11

12

13

14

15

18

19

20

important means of livelihood for them but in the more settled areas many Indians have fitted into the economy of the communities in which they live in a wide range of occupations.

Subject to special provisions in the Indian Act, all laws of general application are applicable to Indians, and they may vote in federal elections on the same basis as other citizens and in provincial elections where the electoral laws of the provinces permit. Indian affairs are administered by the Federal Government and are conducted in a manner that will enable the Indians to participate fully in the social and economic life of the country. A wide range of programmes has been brought into effect in the fields of education, economic development, social welfare and community development; 87,907 Indians were enrolled in schools in the provinces in 1989–90.

There are approximately 27,840 Canadian Inuit living in the Northwest Territories, northern Quebec and Labrador. While many of them still hold to the traditional way of life, an ever-increasing number are making the change from a nomadic existence to regular wage employment. Continued development in the north, coupled with a decrease in some types of game, is resulting in more and more Inuits settling in modern communities with schools, health and transportation facilities and wage employment opportunities. The Canadian Government is helping this transition by providing such forms of assistance as education and welfare services, vocational training and economic development programmes.

Figures based on the official languages from the 1986 census of Canada, showed that 16,716,905 persons spoke English only, 3,957,730 spoke French only, 4,056,160 spoke English and French and 291,215 spoke neither English nor French.

The main religious denominations (1981 census of Canada) were: Roman Catholic 11,210,390; United Church of Canada 3,758,700; Anglican Church of Canada 2,436, 375; Presbyterian 812,105; Lutheran 702,905; Baptist 696,850 and Jewish 296,425.

Primary education is free and universal. School enrolment for 1989–90 is: Grades 1–6 Public: 2,209,005, Private: 81,649; Grades 7–13 Public: 2,103,237, Private: 131,074. The latest figures available for university education are for the year 1989–90 which showed 425,533 enrolled for Bachelor and first professional degrees; 34,955 for Masters degrees and 17,268 for Doctoral (these data are based on full-time enrolment).

Exports and re-exports for the calendar year 1990 were valued at $148,170 million and imports at $135,921 million.

Canada's top 10 airports registered 81 per cent of all flight take-offs and landings in scheduled services, 89 per cent of all passengers travel and 94 per cent of all cargo movement. Among these, the Pearson International, Vancouver International and Montreal International airports accounted for 48 per cent of flights, 60 per cent of passengers and 63 per cent of cargo; Mirabel International contributed another 15 per cent to the cargo volume.

The scheduled international routes of the two largest Canadian air carriers—Air Canada and Canadian Airlines International Ltd. (formed in 1987)—form a vast network connecting Canada to every major continent. Canadian airlines also fly charters to destinations around the world.

From 1987 to 1988, Canada's major air carriers reported increases of 9 per cent in the number of passengers carried and 15 per cent in passenger-kilometres. Many short-haul domestic routes were dropped in order to concentrate on long-haul markets. These short-haul routes are now serviced by regional carriers. Considerable growth was experienced by Canada's other air carriers, including regionals, as passengers carried increased by 21 per cent and passenger-kilometres increased by 55 per cent over the same period. Consumption of turbine fuel increased by 12 per cent to 4,500 million litres, in 1988, for all carriers.

While the net operating profit for the major carriers dropped from $259 million in 1987 to $160 million in 1988, Canada's other carriers maintained a consistent performance, with the equivalent financial result reported at $104 million in 1987 and $100 million in 1988.

There are two continent-wide railways, Canadian National and Canadian Pacific. Inter-city pasenger services are provided by VIA Rail Canada. In 1987, there were 94,184 km of railway track.

In 1986, there was a total of 280,251 km (174,177 miles) of highway in Canada, not including municipal streets. Of these 266,445 km (165,597 miles) or 95.0 per cent were provincial highways and 13,806 km (8,580 miles) or 4.9 per cent were federal highways. Of the overall length of 280,251 km (174,177 miles) at least 160,840 km (99,963 miles) or 57 per cent were surfaced with pavement.

One hundred and twenty-seven originating Television Stations and their 1,319 rebroadcasting stations in Canada reach at least 99 per cent of the population. The originating stations include the Crown Corporation CBC English network made up of 29 owned and operated stations plus 29 private affiliates, and the CTV English network, which is privately owned and financed and made up of 26 privately owned affiliates. The remaining 15 English language stations are Independent and Educational. The CBC French language network has 12 owned and operated stations plus 5 affiliates. The TVA French network has 10 stations and Radio Quebec (Educational) has 1 originating and 19 rebroadcasting stations while Le Réseau Quatre Saisons has 8. There are 2,082 cable television undertakings in Canada all privately owned and operated, serving some 7 million subscribers. Basically these are cable delivery systems which make it possible for subscribers to receive Canadian and U.S. transmissions, many of which would not normally be available.

There are 710 originating and 990 rebroadcasting AM and FM radio stations in Canada which reach 95 per cent of the population. Of these, 322 AM and 173 FM are privately owned radio stations.

CBC owns and operates 33 AM and 32 FM originating stations.

All commercial stations accept advertising.

The National Day of Canada is 1st July, Canada Day.

History

Discovery and Exploration. The original inhabitants of North America migrated from Asia across the Bering Strait over twenty-five thousand years ago, gradually dispersing themselves throughout the continent. The first Europeans known to have landed on Canadian shores were the Vikings under Leif Ericson who founded short-lived settlements, probably in Newfoundland or Labrador, about A.D. 1000. Thereafter contact was lost between Europe and the New World.

The re-discovery of North America by Columbus encouraged other mariners to sail westward, among them John Cabot who, in the service of King Henry VII, made a landing in the Gulf of St Lawrence in 1497. Cabot's reports of the abundance of fish off Newfoundland attracted French, Spanish, Portuguese and English fishermen, who have continued to frequent these fishing grounds ever since. As early as 1534 Jacques Cartier, in the service of France, visited the Gulf of St Lawrence and in 1535 sailed up the St Lawrence River, where he visited Indian villages on the sites of present-day Quebec and Montreal. The name 'Canada' may be derived from the Indian word *kanata,* meaning a town, applied to one of these villages.

Seeking a north-west passage to the Orient, Frobisher in 1576 and Davis in 1585 penetrated into the Frobisher and Davis Strait, and in 1602 Hudson Strait was discovered, and Hudson himself explored Hudson Bay in 1610. But the explorations of Baffin and others eventually persuaded the explorers that there was no suitable north-west passage. It was not until the nineteenth century that the explorations of Parry, Ross and Franklin enabled the passage to be passed by Roald Amundsen in 1906. The Pacific coast of Canada was explored by the Russians from Siberia, and by the Spaniards from Mexico, in the eighteenth century. It was left to Captain Cook to make a more thorough survey in 1778–79 and to Captain George Vancouver to complete his work in 1792–94.

The exploration of the interior of northern North America was impelled by the requirements of the fur trade. Samuel de Champlain of France reached the shores of Lake Huron in 1615 and laid the basis for the exploration of the Great Lakes. Other French traders turned south to the Mississippi or traversed the wilderness north of the Great Lakes to reach the western prairies. The Hudson's Bay Company also sent explorers into the Saskatchewan country. Alexander Mackenzie, a Montreal fur trader, was the first man to travel overland across northern North America. He reached the Pacific Coast in 1793.

Settlement. The main English settlements in North America were those along the Atlantic seaboard which later became the United States. Settlements in the northern part of the continent emerged through the need for bases for the fisheries and the fur trade. The English settlements were centred in Newfoundland, but the Hudson's Bay Company, founded by Royal Charter in 1670, claimed trading rights over Rupert's Land, defined as the area whose rivers drained into Hudson Bay. The father of the French empire in North America, Samuel de Champlain, founded Quebec at the narrows of the St Lawrence in 1608. A riverine colony, New France or Quebec became the base for a chain of fur trading posts that reached south to the Gulf of Mexico (to the landward of the English Atlantic colonies) and westward to the Rocky Mountains.

Until 1663 Quebec was governed autocratically by a trading company; in that year it became a Royal Province, under a Governor to whom was entrusted the general policy of the colony, the direction of its military affairs and its relations with the Indian tribes. A Superior Council also existed with certain administrative powers more formal than real. This system continued until the end of the French régime.

Meanwhile the English North American colonies established along the Atlantic seaboard was growing in population and wealth. Economic rivalry in the fishing and fur trades between the two European empires was reinforced by dynastic struggles in Europe. Four major wars were fought between 1689 and 1763, each with its North American sphere of operations. By the Treaty of Utrecht which, in 1713, ended the second of these wars, France surrendered all claims to Rupert's Land, to Acadia 'within its ancient limits' and to her settlements in Newfoundland, retaining, however, two small islands, St Pierre and Miquelon (which she still possesses) and some controversal fishing rights which remained in dispute until 1904. France, however, only surrendered that part of Acadia which is now Nova Scotia, keeping that part which is now New Brunswick as well as Isle St Jean (Prince Edward Island) and Isle Royale (Cape Breton Island) on which was constructed the fortress of Louisburg.

That part of Acadia which was surrendered was renamed Nova Scotia, and possessed few British settlers until the strategic base at Halifax was established in 1749. The fourth war, the Seven Years war, reached its North American culmination in Wolfe's victory at the Plains of Abraham outside Quebec (1759), which led to the conquest of Quebec and Montreal and the fall of the French empire in North America. By the Treaty of Paris of 1763 New France ceased to exist and all French territory east of the Mississippi was transferred to British sovereignty.

From 1763 until the outbreak of the American War of Independence in 1775, the whole of North America to the east of the Mississippi was held by Britain, the various colonies having a population of nearly 2,000,000 persons. In the north was Rupert's Land, under the jurisdiction of the Hudson's Bay Company; Newfoundland, still sparsely inhabited by fishermen; Nova Scotia, including Cape Breton Island and what is now New Brunswick and Prince Edward Island; and the Province of Quebec, comprising the area of the former French settlements along the St Lawrence and the Great Lakes.

The final partition of North America occurred as a result of the American War of Independence, which in some respects reflected the old economic rivalry between French and English in North America. An attempt by the American colonies to invade Quebec was unsuccessful and the Treaty of Paris, 1783, established what was to become the definitive boundary in eastern North America from the St Croix River in the Bay of Fundy to the Lake of the Woods. Various adjustments were, however, later made in the boundary, notably the Maine-New Brunswick boundary settlement (the Webster-Ashburton Treaty) of 1842.

From 1763 to 1774 Quebec was governed in the main by military authority. In the latter year the Quebec Act, passed by the British Parliament, secured for the French colonists the right to retain their language, religion and civil law. Roman Catholics were allowed the free exercise of their religion and were relieved of all civil disabilities. An appointed Council was created to advise the Governor. The Quebec Act laid the legal basis for the survival of French culture and institutions in North America. Its embodiment of the principle of toleration for non-British elements in the colonies represented the emergence of a policy that was to be highly significant for the later Commonwealth.

The British character of the remaining North American colonies was strengthened as a result of the American Revolution. A considerable migration of Loyalists, perhaps 35,000 in number, moved north to remain under the rule of the Crown. Many of these people went to Nova Scotia, from which Prince Edward Island had been detached in 1769, while others settled in Cape Breton Island (a separate colony from 1784 to 1820 when it again became part of Nova Scotia) or established the new colony of New Brunswick. Still others entered Quebec, the majority settling in the western reaches of the colony. Objecting to the authoritarian rule of the Quebec Act, the Loyalists and other British residents petitioned for representative institutions. In 1791 Parliament passed the Constitutional Act to meet their wishes. Quebec was divided along the Ottawa River into two provinces: Upper Canada (now Ontario) and Lower Canada (Quebec). An elected Assembly was provided for each province, though the Governors, appointed by the Crown, and the nominated Legislative Councils retained control. Thus the Canadas followed Nova Scotia, which had been granted an Assembly in 1758, in taking the first step towards democratic institutions. Assemblies were also authorised for New Brunswick and Prince Edward Island but Newfoundland, with its large transient fishing population, did not gain a legislature until 1832.

The economic life of the British North American colonies in the early nineteenth century was based on several great staple trades. Fishing, the oldest of these activities, continued to be pursued all along the coasts of the Maritime colonies and Newfoundland and around the Gulf of St Lawrence. The Napoleonic Wars produced a great demand for timber and a flourishing export in square timbers and naval stores grew up in New Brunswick and Quebec. All the Maritime colonies, but particularly Nova Scotia, built wooden ships for sale or for their own carrying trade. The Canadas exported wheat to Britain and, under the protection of the British preferential system, engaged in a large milling industry. The fur trade continued to be the dominant activity in the vast interior, where the Hudson's Bay Company (which by absorbing rival Montreal fur trading interests in 1821 monopolised trade throughout the West to the Pacific) exercised semi-governmental powers over the traders and the Indian population. Efforts were made to improve the transportation system of the Great Lakes—St Lawrence route, first by canals and then by railways, in an attempt to channel the export trade of the American mid-West through British North American ports.

The British North American colonies gained a considerable increase in population through the waves of immigration that flowed out from Europe in the 1830s '40s and '50s. By 1851, the year of the first decennial census, the population of the colonies stood at 2.4 million. The colonies suffered economic dislocation in 1846, when Britain embarked upon the policy of free trade, and in 1849, when the Navigation Laws were repealed. The search for assured markets turned their eyes to the south, where the United States economy was advancing rapidly during this period. The Governor-General of British North America, Lord Elgin (8th Earl of Elgin and Kincardine), was successful in negotiating a Reciprocity Treaty (the Elgin-Marcy Treaty) in 1854. This provided for the free exchange of natural products and opened the Maritime inshore fisheries to American vessels. Although the treaty was abrogated by the United States in 1866, the demands of the Civil War created a large interchange of goods under it and brought prosperity to British North America.

In Upper and Lower Canada the constitution of 1791 did not prove a success. A struggle soon developed between the elected Assembly and the executive composed of the Governor and his advisers; this conflict was exacerbated in Lower Canada by friction between the French-speaking majority, who dominated the assembly, and the English minority, whose representatives surrounded the Governor. Disputes over the control of finance led to a small and ineffectual rebellion in Upper Canada in 1837 and to more serious uprisings in Lower Canada which lasted into 1838. The Melbourne government in Britain sent Lord Durham to the Canadas to investigate and report on the situation.

Durham was in North America for only five months, but his *Report on the Affairs of British North America* is one of the great landmarks in the history of Britain's relations with her colonies. His solution of the problem of how to preserve the relationship between Britain and her empire was to urge that the colonies be given self-government in all matters except those, such as foreign relations, regulation of commerce, the disposal of public lands and the determination of constitutions, which then appeared essential for the maintenance of imperial unity. At the same time he recommended the union of Upper and Lower Canada under one government in the hope that this might help to assimilate the French population. His recommendations were partly embodied in the Union Act of 1840, which set up a single Province of Canada. The common government was to consist of the Governor, a nominated Legislative Council and an Assembly of 84 members, 42 to be elected from each part. The new constitution did not correct what Durham saw as the basic weakness of government in British North America—the lack of conformity between the executive and the legislature.

The struggle to establish the practice of responsible or cabinet government in British North America continued for the next eight years. The principle was first achieved in Nova Scotia, following instructions sent to Sir John Harvey, the Lieutenant-Governor, by Lord Grey (3rd Earl Grey), the Colonial Secretary: 'It cannot be too distinctly acknowledged that it is neither possible nor desirable to carry on the government of any of the British provinces in North America in opposition to the opinion of the inhabitants'. As a result Nova Scotia witnessed the accession to office, early in 1848, of a reform ministry which enjoyed the confidence of the majority of the legislature. In Canada the principle was affirmed in 1849 when Lord Elgin, despite riots and the burning of the Parliament buildings, refused to veto an unpopular bill which had been sponsored by the Baldwin-Lafontaine ministry and passed by the legislature. The Governor-General's decision to withdraw from meetings of his cabinet was a further confirmation of the principle. New Brunswick gained responsible government more peacefully in 1854; Newfoundland in 1855.

For the first century after the English victory at Quebec the British colonies shared the continent uneasily with their expanding neighbour, the United States. The War of 1812 marked a renewal of the American efforts of 1775–83 to expel Britain from the continent. The Canadas were invaded during each of the three years of the war.

The war was followed by two notable events which pointed the way towards a permanent settlement in North America. One was the Rush-Bagot Agreement of 1817, by which Britain and the United States limited naval vessels on the Great Lakes. This agreement removed a source of friction, even if it did not apply to land fortifications. These continued to be built until the Civil War, and it was not until 1871 that there can be said to have been 'an undefended border' between the United States and Canada. A second agreement, the Convention of 1818, fixed the international boundary along the 49th parallel of latitude from the Lake of the Woods to the Rockies. The Oregon territory, lying between the Rocky Mountains and the Pacific, was left in joint ownership at this time. However, the migration of American settlers into the southern part of the territory determined its political disposition. The Treaty of Washington (1846) confirmed a continuation of the 49th parallel as the boundary west to the Pacific.

Relations between the United States and British North America were strained again during the American Civil War when border troubles, ship seizures, privateering and smuggling were rife. After the war the victorious North assumed an expansionist attitude, which expressed itself in threats and pressures on Canada. There was concern in Canada that the Hudson's Bay Company territories might be occupied by the same process that had determined the fate of Oregon. There was also fear that the United States might insist on the cession of Canada in the post-Civil War settlement with Britain. These anxieties were intensified by the withdrawal of the British garrisons from the North American colonies, a process which had been temporarily interrupted by the Civil War emergency. With Britain reducing her commitments in North America it seemed as if the colonies would have to look to each other for more of their security. Thus the Civil War, and the mood which followed it, provoked the discussions for a union of the British North American colonies.

The initiative for the confederation of British North America came from the province of Canada, where the mechanism of government had broken down by 1864. Neither Canada East nor Canada West had been happy in the union, and each had given support to political groups which found it impossible to co-operate for common purposes. The prospect of a wider union offered an escape from this political deadlock. Thus a coalition was formed in Canada to explore a plan of federation with the Maritime colonies. At a conference in Charlottetown in 1864 delegates from the colonies met to consider the practicability of union. The discussion was resumed at the Quebec conference in October, where a scheme of union, the Seventy-Two Resolutions, was drafted. Accepted by the British government and modified by later meetings, the Seventy-Two Resolutions became the basis of the British North America Act, 1867. Under this imperial statute the three colonies of Canada, Nova Scotia and New Brunswick were 'federally united' to form 'One Dominion under the name of Canada'. Self-government and union had produced the first colonial state and given rise to yet another line of growth that led to the Commonwealth.

In 1867 Canada consisted of only four provinces: Quebec and Ontario (the historic divisions of the Province of Canada), New Brunswick and Nova Scotia. It was imperative that steps be taken to secure the annexation of the West, still a fur trader's preserve under the authority of the Hudson's Bay Company. In 1869 the Company formally relinquished its charter, under compensation, to the Crown; and the whole of the vast territory over which the Company had exercised trading rights, known as Rupert's Land and the North-Western Territory, was in 1870 transferred to the Dominion of Canada.

This territory did not include Alaska, purchased by the United States from the Russians in 1867. The transfer was opposed by some of the settlers, the Métis, who succeeded in having a new province, Manitoba, created in the lower Red River valley. Manitoba entered the Dominion in 1870 to become Canada's fifth province.

Beyond the Rockies existed the Crown colony of British Columbia, with a history extending from the days of the maritime fur trade in the last part of the eighteenth century. Vancouver Island had been created as a colony in 1849, while the mainland area, British Columbia, was made a colony in 1858, as a means of maintaining order during the troubled period of a gold rush. The two jurisdictions were joined in 1866 under the name of British Columbia. However, the decline of the gold fields rendered the new colony's financial position precarious and in 1871 it was induced to become part of the Canadian union. The little colony of Prince Edward Island, which had held aloof from the earlier scheme of union, also cast in its lot with the new Dominion in 1873. Thus Canada extended from the Atlantic to the Pacific, the interior prairie region being administered as a federal territory. Sovereignty over the Arctic archipelago was formally transferred from Britain to Canada in 1880, giving the Dominion jurisdiction to the Pole.

The growth of settlement on the prairies led, in 1905, to the creation of two new provinces, Alberta and Saskatchewan. Their northern boundary was set at the 60th parallel, so that north of them the federal government still retained control of two regions, the Yukon Territory and the North-West Territories. Newfoundland, obliged to give up its powers of self-government in 1934 because of the impact of the world depression, voted to join Canada in 1948. Together with its dependency of Labrador, it became Canada's tenth province a year later. The inclusion of Newfoundland fulfilled the original design of the Canadian confederation.

Since 1867 the history of Canada has been a record of steady and substantial progress. Population growth, while slow in the last three decades of the nineteenth century, increased rapidly during a period of active immigration and Western settlement lasting from 1896 to the outset of the First World War. A similar period of rapid growth, this time associated with industrial advance, followed the Second World War, leading to a Canadian population of over 20 millions by 1961. Transportation, the sinew of Canada, has shown a continuous development since 1867. The country's first transcontinental railway, the Canadian Pacific Railway, was completed in 1885; by the First World War two other transcontinental lines were in operation. Air routes and gas and oil pipe lines now span the country and the opening of the St. Lawrence Seaway in 1959 allowed ocean-going vessels to sail into the heart of the continent. New resources—pulp and paper, base metals, oil, uranium and iron—have joined the traditional export staples of Canada. Secondary industry has advanced rapidly, particularly around Canada's largest cities, Montreal and Toronto.

The Treaty of Washington, 1871, ended the American hopes of Canada eventually becoming part of the United States. Although Canadians rejected a comprehensive offer of trade reciprocity with the United States in 1911, favourable commercial arrangements in the 1930s allowed a growing measure of economic interdependence to develop between the two countries. The Boundary Waters Treaty of 1909 created an International Joint Commission for the solution of border problems of all kinds. Association in two world wars has strengthened the mutual confidence across the border, which is now symbolized by such military arrangements as the Permanent Joint Board on Defence (1940), the North Atlantic Treaty Organization (1949) and the North American Air Defence Command (1958).

Constitutional development

The machinery of government set up by the British North America Act of 1867 has remained basically unchanged to the present day; the principal change being the introduction of universal adult franchise in 1921. But the area over which the Canadian government exercises jurisdiction has greatly increased not only by the addition of new Provinces, increasing the number from 4 to 10, but by the transfer to the Canadian Government of vast areas which it rules directly. This increase in the area of Canadian governmental jurisdiction has resulted in an increase in the number of the Members both of the Senate and of the House of Commons.

The Constitution Act, 1867, included within its provisions lists of subjects over which the Canadian Federal Parliament and Provincial Legislatures respectively had exclusive legislative authority. Broadly speaking the Federal Government was given jurisdiction over all subjects of general interest and the Provincial Governments jurisdiction over subjects of local concern. But the lists were not comprehensive and there have, over the years, been jurisdictional disputes between the two levels of government.

After 1867 there still remained a number of limitations on the internal self-governing powers of the Canadian Government. By section 55 of the Act, the Governor-General had the power, at his discretion, to withhold consent to Bills passed by the Canadian Parliament. In fact he was instructed to do so if the Bills were repugnant to the laws of Britain or if they concerned certain subjects which were reserved to the British Parliament. However, these powers ceased to be used after 1875, and the Governor-General became less and less the representative or agent of the British Government. In 1926 it was finally confirmed that his status was only that of personal representative of the Crown and that he was bound to act on the advice of his Canadian Ministers. British garrisons remained on Canadian soil until 1906, and Canadian troops served under British generals up to the 1914 war. Another restriction on Canadian internal self-government was the appellate jurisdiction of the Judicial Committee of the Privy Council, and this was abolished in 1949. Yet another restriction arose from the fact that the British North America Act was an Act of the British Parliament and could only be amended by another Act of that Parliament. The British Parliament only acted at the request of the Canadian Government. The right to amend the Act in respect of certain internal matters was granted to the Canadian Parliament by the British North America Act (No. 2) of 1949. Except for the restriction on the power to amend its constitution, all the remaining legal and other restrictions on Canadian sovereignty were swept away as a result of the Imperial Conferences of the 1920s and the Statute of Westminster of 1931. Although there was repeated consideration in the Canadian Parliament and in Federal/Provincial conferences and meetings over the last few decades of procedures for amending the constitution in Canada, no solution satisfactory to both the Federal and Provincial governments was reached until 1981.

In 1980, following the breakdown of Federal-Provincial talks, the Ottawa Government presented proposals to the Canadian Parliament for the transfer to Canada of those residual rights still remaining at Westminster, an amending formula and for a Canadian Charter of Rights and Freedoms. Initially the constitutional proposals were opposed by the Parliamentary Opposition and eight of the Provinces. The issue went to the Canadian Supreme Court which in September 1981 announced that the Federal Government could, on technical grounds, proceed with its proposals but to do so without provincial agreement would violate constitutional convention. Agreement was reached at a First Ministers' Conference in November 1981 between the Federal Government and nine of the ten provinces (all except Quebec). A new resolution, incorporating the compromises, was approved by the Federal Parliament in December 1981 and the Canada Bill, giving effect to the Canadian Legislation, was introduced into the British House of Commons shortly afterwards. The Canada Act received Royal Assent on 29th March 1982, and the new Canadian constitution was proclaimed by the Queen in Ottawa on 17th April 1982. Section 15 of the Charter of Rights, which asserts the right to legal equality without discrimination on any grounds, came into effect on 17th April 1985 as did section 28 which further states that, notwithstanding any other clause in the Charter, 'the rights and freedoms referred to in it are guaranteed equally to male and female persons.' Both sections had been delayed for three years so the Federal government and each province would have time to bring their statutes into line.

It was in the matter of the conduct of her foreign affairs that Canada from 1867 had the least self-government. The British North America Act which, since 1982, has been renamed The Constitution Act 1867, left foreign affairs to the British Foreign Office, which was responsible for the conduct of foreign affairs of the Empire as a whole. Canada was not, in the eyes of Britain and the world, a sovereign state. Although Canadian representatives might sit with their British colleagues in discussions with foreign countries on matters concerning Canada, the resultant agreements or treaties were at first signed only by Britain. Until 1877 Canada was bound by British commercial treaties, but from that year she could choose whether to be bound or not; and from 1899 could withdraw from a commercial treaty. Later she was permitted to make her own commercial treaties, but the first non-commercial treaty to be made and signed by the Canadian Government was the Halibut Fishery Treaty with the United States in 1923. Although permitted to appoint to Britain in 1880 a semi-diplomatic representative, named a High Commissioner, Canada had no foreign affairs department until 1909, and did not appoint diplomatic representatives to other countries until 1927. As the population of Canada increased and as her influence grew, her subordinate status became more irksome to her, and the 1914–18 war, in which half a million Canadians took part, brought a realisation to Britain and to other countries that Canada had an independent part to play in world affairs. That the organisation of the Empire was based on equality of manhood was recognised in 1917 by the Imperial War Cabinet, on which Canada was represented, and Canada played an important and independent part in the Peace Conference, signed the Peace of Versailles, and became a member not only of the International Labour Organization but of the League of Nations, to whose Council she was elected for 1927.

Finally the Balfour formula of 1926, endorsed by the Statute of Westminster in 1931, set the seal on Canada's complete independence within the Commonwealth and on her status as a sovereign country.

Constitution

The Executive Government is vested in the Crown and is exercised by a Governor-General appointed by the Queen on the recommendation of the Prime Minister of Canada. The Governor-General exercises the executive powers on the advice of the Cabinet, which is formed of the Ministers of the Government, chosen by the Prime Minister and responsible to the Parliament of Canada. The Cabinet is a Committee of the Queen's Privy Council for Canada, and has at present 38 Members. Membership of the Privy Council is for life, so that Privy Councillors include both former and present Ministers of the Crown as well as a number of persons who have been, from time to time as an honour, sworn as Privy Councillors; these include members of the Royal Family, past and present provincial premiers, and former Speakers of the Senate and of the House of Commons of Canada. Although no reference to the Cabinet is to be found in the Constitution Act, it is the body in which executive power is vested. All its members with the exception of one Senator who is styled 'Leader of the Government in the Senate', are elected members of the House of Commons.*

The Supreme legislative power in the area of federal jurisdiction is vested in Parliament, consisting of the Queen (represented by the Governor-General), Senate and House of Commons. The Senate of Canada is represented provincially with 24 Senators representing Ontario, 24 Quebec, 10 Nova Scotia, 10 New Brunswick, 6 Manitoba, 6 British Columbia, 6 Saskatchewan, 6 Alberta, 6 Newfoundland, 4 Prince Edward Island, 1 the Yukon and 1 the Northwest Territories. The normal full complement for the Senate is thus 104. In the Fall of 1990, eight extra Conservative Senators were appointed in accordance with section 26 of The Constitution Acts 1867 to 1982 to pass a new tax law. Membership at that time was 112, but is declining due to retirements. Until 1965, Senators were appointed for life, but in accordance with an amendment to the Constitution passed on 2nd June 1965, Senators appointed after that date are obliged to retire on reaching 75 years of age. The qualifications for Senator include the possession of property with a net worth of at least $4,000, age not less than 30 years and residency within the province for which he or she is appointed. The House of Commons consisted originally (1867) of 181 elected members; this number has been increased to 295 by additions on the accession of new provinces and as the result of increase in population. Representation in the House is reviewed decennially. There is no property qualification; the age qualification is 18 years. A Parliament lasts five years if not sooner dissolved.

The Parliament of Canada has exclusive legislative power in certain specified matters; these include external affairs, the regulation of trade and commerce, navigation and shipping, defence, postal service, currency and coinage, banking, bankruptcy, patents, copyrights, Indian affairs, naturalization, and marriage and divorce. It also has the general power to make laws for the peace, order and good government of Canada. Exclusive provincial powers include education, municipal institutions, property and civil rights in the province and the administration of justice in the province. Concurrent powers include agriculture, immigration and various areas of social policy.

The majority of the judges are appointed by the Governor-General on the advice of the Federal Government.

The Government

The Progressive Conservative Party under Mr Brian Mulroney retained power, albeit with a reduced majority, in the Federal Election of 21st November 1988. The current distribution in the 295 seat House of Commons is:

Progressive Conservatives	158	New Democratic Party	44
Liberals	81	Independent	12

Mr Mulroney has been leader of the Progressive Conservative Party since June 1983. His party's landslide victory in the September 1984 General Election brought to an end 21 years of almost continuous Liberal Government under Mr Trudeau, broken only when the Progressive Conservatives, under Mr Joe Clark, were in power between April 1979 and February 1980.

HEAD OF STATE
Her Majesty Queen Elizabeth II

GOVERNOR-GENERAL AND COMMANDER-IN-CHIEF
His Excellency the Rt Hon Ramon John Hnatyshyn, PC, QC, LLB, BA
Secretary to the Governor-General: Ms Judith La Rocque

CABINET (in order of precedence)
Prime Minister: The Rt Hon Brian Mulroney
Deputy Prime Minister and Minister of Finance: Hon Donald Mazankowski
President of the Queen's Privy Council for Canada: Rt Hon Joseph Clark
Minister of Fisheries & Oceans: Hon John Crosbie
Minister of Public Works: Hon Elmer MacIntosh
Minister of Energy, Mines & Resources: Hon Jake Epp
Secretary of State: Hon Robert R de Cotret
Minister of Industry, Science & Technology and Minister for International Trade: Hon Michael Holcombe
Minister of National Defence: Hon Marcel Masse
Minister of Communications: Hon Perrin Beatty
Minister of State: Hon Harvie Andre
Minister of National Revenue: Hon Otto Jelinek
Minister of Indian Affairs & Northern Development: Hon Thomas Siddon
Minister of Western Economic Diversification and Minister of State (Grains & Oilseeds): Hon Charles Mayer
Minister of Agriculture: Hon William McKnight
Minister of National Health & Welfare: Hon Benoît Bouchard

* The Governor-General, the Prime Minister and the Chief Justice of Canada enjoy the style 'Right Honourable' for life. Otherwise in Canada the prefix 'Rt. Hon.' indicates membership of the British Privy Council and the suffix 'PC', if used, indicates membership of the Canadian Privy Council. In the historical lists in this section of the Year Book the suffix 'PC' denotes membership of the British Privy Council. Elsewhere in the section it indicates membership of the Canadian Privy Council.

Secretary of State for External Affairs: Hon Barbara McDougall
Minister of Veterans Affairs: Hon Gerald Merrithew
Minister of State (Employment & Immigration) and Minister of State (Seniors): Hon Monique Vézina
Minister of Forestry: Hon Frank Oberle
Minister of Supply & Services: Hon Paul Dick
Minister of State (Fitness & Amateur Sport) and Minister of State (Youth): Hon Pierre Cadieux
Minister of the Environment: Hon Jean J Charest
Minister of State (Small Businesses & Tourism): Hon Thomas Hockin
Minister for External Relations and Minister of State (Indian Affairs & Northern Development): Hon Monique Landry
Minister of Employment & Immigration: Hon Bernard Valcourt
Minister of Multiculturalism & Citizenship: Hon Gerry Weiner
Solicitor General of Canada: Hon Douglas Lewis
Minister of Consumer & Corporate Affairs and Minister of State (Agriculture): Hon Pierre Blais
Minister of State (Finance & Privatization): Hon John McDermid
Minister of State (Transport): Hon Shirley Martin
Associate Minister of National Defence: Hon Mary Collins
Minister for Science: Hon William Winegard
Minister of Justice & Attorney General of Canada: Hon Kim Campbell
Minister of Transport: Hon Jean Corbeil
President of the Treasury Board and Minister of State (Finance): Hon Gilles Loiselle
Ministry of Labour: Hon Marcel Danis
Minister of State (Environment): Hon Pauline Browes
Leader of the Government in the Senate: Hon Lowell Murray

LEADER OF THE OPPOSITION
The Hon Jean Chretien, PC

SENATE OF CANADA
Speaker: Hon Senator Guy Charbonneau
Leader of the Government in the Senate: Hon Senator Lowell Murray
Leader of the Opposition in the Senate: Hon Senator Allan J MacEachen
Deputy Leader of the Government: Hon C William Doody
Deputy Leader of the Opposition: Hon Royce Frith
Clerk of the Senate and Clerk of the Parliaments: Hon Gordon Barnhart
Gentleman Usher of the Black Rod: Réné Gutknecht
Clerk Assistant of the Senate: Richard Greene
Law Clerk and Parliamentary Counsel: Raymond du Plessis, QC
Parliamentary Librarian: E J Spicer

HOUSE OF COMMONS
Speaker: Hon John Fraser MP
Clerk of the House of Commons: R Marleau
Sergeant-at-Arms: Major-General M G Cloutier

SUPREME COURT OF CANADA
Chief Justice of Canada: Rt Hon Antonio Lamer
Puisne Judges: Hon Madam Claire L'Heureux-Dube
Hon G La Forest
Hon John Sopinka
Hon Charles Gonthier
Hon P de Carteret Cory
Hon Madam B McLachin
Hon William Stevenson
Hon Frank Iacobucci
Registrar: Anne Roland

FEDERAL COURT OF CANADA
Chief Justice: Hon F Iacobucci
Associate Chief Justice: Hon James A Jerome

COURT OF APPEAL JUDGES
The Hon Mr Justice Louis Pratte
The Hon Mr Justice Darrel Verner Heald
The Hon Patrick M Mahoney PC
The Hon Louis Marceau
The Hon James K Hugessen
The Hon Arthur J Stone
The Hon Mark MacGuigan
The Hon Robert Décary
The Hon Madame Alice Desjardins
The Hon Allen M Linden

TRIAL DIVISION JUDGES
The Hon Mr Justice F U Collier
The Hon Mr Justice J E Dubé, PC
The Hon Mr Justice U C Rouleau
The Hon Mr Justice Francis Muldoon
The Hon Mr Justice Barry L Strayer
The Hon Mr Justice John McNair
The Hon Madame Justice Barbara J Reed
The Hon Mr Justice Pierre Denault
The Hon Mr Justice Yvon Pinard, PC
The Hon Mr Justice Louis Marcel Joyal
The Hon Mr Justice Bud Cullen, PC
The Hon Mr Justice Leonard A Martin
The Hon Mr Justice Max M Teitelbaum
The Hon Mr Justice A McKay
Administrator of the Court: Robert Biljan

COURT MARTIAL APPEAL COURT
The Chief Justice: The Hon Mr Justice Patrick M Mahoney, PC
Judges:
The Hon Mr Justice Louis Pratte
The Hon Mr Justice Darrel V Heald
The Hon Mr Justice Frank U Collier
The Hon Mr Justice David M Dickson
The Hon Mr Justice Gordon L S Hart
The Hon Mr Justice Alphonse Barbeau

The Hon Mr Justice James K Hugessen
The Hon Mr Justice Yves Forest
The Hon Mr Justice Jean-Eudes Dube, PC
The Hon Mr Justice Louis Marceau
The Hon Mr Justice Benjamin Hewak
The Hon Mr Justice Alexander M MacIntosh
The Hon Mr Justice William J Trainor
The Hon Mr Justice Robert C Rutherford
The Hon Mr Justice Charles C Locke
The Hon Mr Justice Lloyd G McKenzie
The Hon Mr Justice Hugh P Legg
The Hon Mr Justice James A Jerome
The Hon Mr Justice Lawrence A Poitras
The Hon Mr Justice John Watson Brooke
The Hon Mr Justice N H A Goodrige
The Hon Mr Justice Jacques Vaillancourt
The Hon Mr Justice D Gordon Blair
The Hon Mr Justice Francois Chevalier
The Hon Madam Justice Mary J Batten
The Hon Mr Justice Louis-Philippe Landry
The Hon Mr Justice Paul U C Rouleau
The Hon Mr Justice Francis C Muldoon
The Hon Mr Justice Edward C Malone
The Hon Mr Justice Arthur J Stone
The Hon Mr Justice Barry L Strayer
The Hon Madam Justice Barbara J Reed
The Hon Mr Justice Yvon Pinard
The Hon Mr Justice Joseph H Potts
The Hon Mr Justice J S G Bud Cullen PC
The Hon Mr Justice L Marcel Joyal
The Hon Mr Justice Pierre Denault
The Hon Mr Justice Mark R MacGuigan
The Hon Mr Justice A L Sirois
The Hon Mr Justice Leonard A Martin
The Hon Max M Teitelbaum
The Hon Mr Justice W Andrew MacKay
The Hon Madame Justice Alice Desjardins
The Hon Mr Justice Melvin E Shannon
The Hon Mr Justice David C McDonald
The Hon Madame Justice Elizabeth A McFadyen
The Hon Madame Justice Joanne B Veit
The Hon Mr Justice Robert Decary
The Hon Mr Justice Allen M Linden

Administrator of the Court: Robert Biljan

GOVERNMENT DEPARTMENTS

PRIME MINISTER'S OFFICE
Chief of Staff: Hugh Segal

PRIVY COUNCIL OFFICE
Clerk of the Privy Council and Secretary to the Cabinet: Paul Tellier
Secretary to the Cabinet for Federal/Provincial Relations: Paul Tellier

TRANSPORT CANADA
Deputy Minister: Hugette Labelle

DEPARTMENTAL OF EXTERNAL AFFAIRS CANADA
Under-Secretary of State for External Affairs: Reid Morden
Associate Under-Secretary of State for External Affairs: Raymond Chretien
Deputy Minister (International Trade): Donald W Campbell

CANADIAN INTERNATIONAL DEVELOPMENT AGENCY
President: Marcel Masse

SOLICITOR-GENERAL CANADA
Deputy Solicitor-General: Joseph S Stanford, QC
Commissioner of Correctional Services: O M Ingstrup

PUBLIC WORKS CANADA
Deputy Minister: R J Giroux

DEPARTMENT OF ENERGY, MINES AND RESOURCES CANADA
Deputy Minister: Bruce Howe

DEPARTMENT OF EMPLOYMENT AND IMMIGRATION CANADA
Deputy Minister: Arthur Kroeger

TREASURY BOARD
Secretary: Ian D Clark

DEPARTMENT OF FINANCE CANADA
Deputy Minister: Frederick W Gorbet

NATIONAL DEFENCE CANADA
Deputy Minister: R R Fowler
Chief of Defence Staff: General John de Chastelain

OFFICE OF THE AUDITOR-GENERAL CANADA
Auditor-General: Denis Desautels

REVENUE CANADA
Deputy Minister (Customs and Excise): R Hubbard
Deputy Minister (Taxation): P Gravelle

DEPARTMENT OF JUSTICE CANADA
Deputy Minister and Deputy Attorney-General of Canada: J C Tait, QC

DEPARTMENT OF INDIAN AND NORTHERN AFFAIRS CANADA
Deputy Minister: H Swain

LABOUR CANADA
Deputy Minister: Gerald Capello

AGRICULTURE CANADA
Deputy Minister: Jean-Jacques Noreau

VETERANS' AFFAIRS CANADA
Deputy Minister: David P Broadbent

DEPARTMENT OF CONSUMER AND CORPORATE AFFAIRS
Deputy Minister and Deputy Registrar General: Nancy Hughes-Anthony

SUPPLY AND SERVICES CANADA
Deputy Minister (Supply and Services) and Deputy Receiver-General for Canada: Nick Mulder

DEPARTMENT OF COMMUNICATIONS
Deputy Minister: Alain Gourd

CANADA POST CORPORATION
Chairman: Sylvain Cloutier

CANADIAN INTERNATIONAL TRADE TRIBUNAL
Chairman: John Coleman

ATOMIC ENERGY CONTROL BOARD
President: Dr R J A Levesque

ATOMIC ENERGY OF CANADA LTD
President: S R Hatcher

CANADA COUNCIL
Director: Ms Joyce L Zemans

CANADIAN BROADCASTING CORPORATION
President: Gerard Veilleux
Chairman: Patrick Watson

CANADIAN RADIO-TELEVISION AND TELECOMMUNICATIONS COMMISSION
Chairman: Keith Spicer

NATIONAL TRANSPORTATION AGENCY OF CANADA
President: Hon E Nielsen

HEALTH AND WELFARE CANADA
Deputy Minister: Margaret Catley-Carlson

SECRETARY OF STATE OF CANADA
Under-Secretary of State: Jean T Fournier

ENVIRONMENT CANADA
Deputy Minister: Dr Len Good

DEPARTMENT OF SCIENCE AND TECHNOLOGY
Deputy Minister: H G Rogers

OFFICE OF SUPERINTENDENT OF FINANCIAL INSTITUTIONS
Superintendent: M MacKenzie

ECONOMIC COUNCIL OF CANADA
Chairman: Judith Maxwell

EXPORT DEVELOPMENT CORPORATION
President: Robert Richardson

IMMIGRATION AND REFUGEE BOARD
Chairman: Gordon Fairweather

INTERNATIONAL DEVELOPMENT RESEARCH CENTRE
President: Ivan Head

INTERNATIONAL JOINT COMMISSION
Chairman (Canadian Section): Hon E Davie Fulton, PC, QC

MEDICAL RESEARCH COUNCIL OF CANADA
President: Dr Pierre Bois

NATIONAL ARTS CENTRE
Director-General: Yvon Desrochers

NATIONAL CAPITAL COMMISSION
Chairman: Jean Pigott

STATISTICS CANADA
Chief Statistician of Canada: Ivan Fellegi

NATIONAL ENERGY BOARD
Chairman: Roland Priddle

NATIONAL FILM BOARD
Chairperson and Government Film Commissioner: Joan Pennefather

NATIONAL GALLERY OF CANADA
Director: Dr Shirley Thomson

NATIONAL RESEARCH COUNCIL CANADA
President: Pierre Perron

PUBLIC SERVICE COMMISSION OF CANADA
Chairman: Robert Giroux

PUBLIC SERVICE STAFF RELATIONS BOARD
Chairperson: Ian Deans

ROYAL CANADIAN MOUNTED POLICE
Commissioner: N D Inkster

CANADIAN SECURITY INTELLIGENCE SERVICE
Director: Raymond Protti

SCIENCE COUNCIL OF CANADA
Chairperson: Janet E Halliwell

THE PROVINCES OF CANADA

Canada consists of ten Provinces and two Territories. The Provinces comprise the Atlantic Provinces of Newfoundland, Prince Edward Island, Nova Scotia and New Brunswick; the Provinces of Quebec and Ontario; the Prairie Provinces of Manitoba, Saskatchewan and Alberta; and the Pacific Province of British Columbia.

Prior to the Constitution Act 1867, British North America consisted of the Colonies of Canada (the provinces of Ontario and Quebec), New Brunswick, Nova Scotia, Prince Edward Island and Newfoundland in the east, the Colony of British Columbia in the west, the vast central and northern territory being known as Rupert's Land (the territory which drained into the Hudson Bay) and the North-Western Territory. There were also lands to the north which were virtually unexplored.

In 1867 the Constitution Act divided Canada into the two Provinces of Quebec and Ontario and joined these with the colonies of New Brunswick and Nova Scotia to form a confederation, to which was given the name of Canada. This Act was brought into force on 1st July 1867 by Royal Proclamation dated 22nd May 1867.

By Order in Council dated 23rd June 1870, following the introduction of the Rupert's Land Act, 1868, Rupert's Land and the North-Western Territory were transferred to Canada with effect from 15th July 1870. The combined territories were designated as The North-West Territories.

On the date of the transfer a part of the North-West Territories, by the Manitoba Act 1870, was formed into a new province called the Province of Manitoba (its boundaries being later extended in 1881). On the same day the new Province was admitted separately into the Union of Canada. A Lieutenant-Governor was appointed to govern Manitoba, and by a separate commission the Governor of Manitoba was appointed as the Lieutenant-Governor of the North-West Territories.

By Order in Council dated 16th May 1871 the Colony of British Columbia was admitted into the confederation on 20th July 1871.

Prince Edward Island was admitted by Order in Council of 26th June 1873 on the 1st July of that year.

On 31st July 1880, in compliance with the prayer of an Address from the Parliament of Canada dated 3rd May 1878, Her Majesty issued an Order in Council annexing to Canada from 1st September 1880 all British Territories in North America not already included within Canada and all islands adjacent thereto, with the exception of the Colony of Newfoundland and its dependencies. These additional territories were formally included in the North-West Territories.

The Keewatin Act, 1876, provided for the formation of a separate district of the North-West Territories, to be known as the District of Keewatin, to the north of Manitoba. By Order in Council of 8th May 1882 the southern part of the North-West Territories was divided into the provisional Districts of Assiniboia, Saskatchewan, Alberta and Athabasca and by Order in Council of 2nd June 1895 further provisional Districts of Ungava, Franklin, Mackenzie and Yukon were created in the north of the Territories, the boundaries being redefined by Order in Council of 18th December 1897. Yukon was created a separate Territory, distinct from the North-West Territories, by the Yukon Territory Act, 1898.

On 1st September 1905, by the Alberta Act, and the Saskatchewan Act, the Provinces of Alberta and Saskatchewan were formed from the provisional Districts of Alberta, Assiniboia, Saskatchewan and Athabasca, the dividing line running north and south.

The remainder of the North-West Territories were re-designated the Northwest Territories in 1906.

By a Federal Act of 1912 the boundaries of the Provinces of Ontario, Quebec and Manitoba were extended, the whole of Ungava being transferred to Quebec and parts of Keewatin to Ontario and Manitoba. However, the Newfoundland Government objected to the transfer of the whole of Ungava to Quebec. By the decision, on 1st March 1927, of the Judicial Committee of the Privy Council, Newfoundland was confirmed in the ownership of the Atlantic watershed of the Labrador peninsula, including the basin of the Hamilton River, an area of about 112,000 square miles. The decision was the outcome of a dispute between Canada and Newfoundland as to the ownership of this region which had lasted for 25 years and was ultimately by agreement submitted to the arbitration of this Tribunal.

In 1949 Newfoundland, including Labrador, was joined by the Newfoundland Act with the existing nine Provinces as a tenth Province after the people of Newfoundland had by a majority voted in favour in a referendum held in 1948.

For each province there is a Lieutenant-Governor, appointed by the Governor-General in Council and holding office during pleasure, but not removable within five years of appointment except for cause assigned.

Each province has a Legislative Assembly. The Provincial Legislatures possess the power of altering their own constitutions. The territory not comprised within any province (Yukon and the Northwest Territories) is very thinly inhabited. The Yukon Territory is governed by an appointed Commissioner (under instructions from the Governor-General in Council or the Minister of Northern Affairs and National Resources) and an elective legislative council of seven members. The Northwest Territories are similarly governed by a Commissioner and nine councillors, of whom four are elected and the rest appointed by the Governor-General in Council.

The Provincial Legislatures have powers to legislate in respect of certain specified subjects, of which the chief are property and civil rights, the alteration of their own constitutions, direct taxation within the province and provincial loans, the management of provincial public lands, provincial and municipal offices, hospitals, gaols, licenses, local works, and the general civil law and procedure. Over education they have full powers, subject only to certain provisions to secure protection to religious minorities. In agricultural, quarantine and immigration matters they possess concurrent legislative powers with the Parliament of Canada.

Under various legislative provisions, the Federal Government makes financial payment to the individual provinces. These payments include equalisation payments (to the less wealthy provinces) and contributions to shared cost programmes.

NEWFOUNDLAND AND LABRADOR

Situation and population

The Province of Newfoundland and Labrador consists of the island of Newfoundland and the mainland of Labrador. The island, with an area of 112,299 sq km (43,359 square miles), lies between the Gulf of St Lawrence and the Atlantic Ocean. It is triangular in shape, each side being about 514 km (320 miles) long. The mainland consists of that part of the Ungava peninsula which drains into the Atlantic Ocean as distinct from Hudson Bay or the Gulf of St Lawrence; its area is 405,720 sq km (156,649 square miles).

The population of Newfoundland in 1990 (including Labrador) was 572,600. The capital is St John's with a population of 96,216 (city proper).

History

The island of Newfoundland, according to the Icelandic saga, was sighted in AD 1001 by a merchant of Iceland, voyaging in search of trade. John Cabot discovered the island in 1497, but no permanent settlement resulted. The interior was explored by Anthony Parkhurst in 1578, but the first attempt at formal annexation, made by Sir Humphrey Gilbert in 1583, had no direct effect on subsequent history. In 1610 a Charter was granted to the 'Treasurer and Company of Adventurers and Planters for the Colony or Plantation in Newfoundland', and colonists were established by the company in Conception Bay, mainly for the purpose of improving the fishing industry. The first permanent colony was founded by Sir David Kirke, who was granted two Patents in 1637 for the colonisation of the whole of Newfoundland, and by 1774 a true colony had grown up, after which the island proceeded to develop more normally as compared with its previously amphibious character as 'a great English ship moored near the Banks during the fishing season for the convenience of fishermen'.

By the Treaty of Utrecht in 1713, subsequently ratified by the Treaty of Paris, the French, who in 1662 had established a base at Placentia, acknowledged British sovereignty over the whole of Newfoundland. Certain rights were granted to French fishermen under the Treaty, the extent of which long remained in dispute until settled by the Anglo-French Convention of 1904, by which France renounced her privileges under Article XIII. The Convention was of great benefit to Newfoundland, since it removed an obstruction to local development, to mining and other industrial enterprises, over some two-fifths of the whole coast-line. French sovereignty over the islands of St Pierre and Miquelon 15 miles off the tip of the Basin peninsula remains, however, and this now gives rise to the question of demarcation of undersea mineral rights, a matter of growing importance with the upsurge of off-shore oil explorations.

Constitutional development

Newfoundland has had a Legislature since 1832, but it was the last of the old North American Colonies to which responsible government was conceded, in 1855. The Constitution Act, 1867, made provision for the accession of Newfoundland to Canada, but Newfoundland voted against confederation in 1869.

Owing to the world depression and inability to meet the interest charges on the Public Debt, the Legislature in 1933 requested His Majesty The King to suspend the constitution and to appoint six Commissioners who, with the Governor as Chairman, would administer the government under the supervision of the British Government until Newfoundland became self-supporting again. His Majesty thereupon appointed three Commissioners from Newfoundland and three drawn from Britain, who took office in 1934.

The issue was decided by referendum in 1948 when the final votes were 78,323 in favour of confederation with Canada and 71,334 for responsible government. A delegation of seven was sent to Ottawa to discuss the terms of union with Canada, and agreement was reached on 11th December 1948.

The union of Newfoundland and Canada took effect immediately before the expiration of the thirty-first day of March 1949 (Newfoundland Act).

Constitution

Under the Terms of Union the Province of Newfoundland (embracing Labrador and the island of Newfoundland, with their existing boundaries) became part of Canada with provision for the application of the Constitution Acts, 1867 to 1946, to Newfoundland as if the latter had been one of the Provinces originally united, but subject to the modifications mentioned in the terms of agreement and to the omission of such provisions as were specially applicable to or only intended to affect one or two but not all of the original Provinces. By an Act passed in 1964 the name of the province was changed to 'Newfoundland and Labrador'. Provision was made for Newfoundland to be represented in the Senate of Canada by six members and in the House of Commons by seven, subject to subsequent readjustment in accordance with the provisions of the Constitution Acts.

The present Government of Newfoundland consists of a Lieutenant-Governor, an Executive Council and a House of Assembly of 52 members, elected for a term of five years.

The Government
The last General Election was held on 21st April 1989. Present party standings are Liberal Party 33 seats, Progressive Conservatives 18 seats, New Democratic Party 1 seat.

LIEUTENANT-GOVERNOR
Hon James McGrath, PC

EXECUTIVE COUNCIL
The Premier and Minister responsible for Intergovernmental Affairs: The Hon Clyde Kirby Wells
President of the Executive Council and President of the Treasury Board: The Hon R Winston Baker
Minister of Municipal and Provincial Affairs: The Hon Eric A Gullage
Minister of Forestry and Agriculture: The Hon Graham F Flight
Minister of Education: The Hon Dr Philip J Warren
Minister of Employment and Labour Relations: Hon Patricia A Cowan
Minister of Finance: The Hon Dr Hubert W Kitchen
Minister of Fisheries: The Hon Walter C Carter
Minister of Health: The Hon Christopher R Decker
Minister of Justice: The Hon Paul David Dicks
Minister of Mines and Energy: The Hon Dr Rex V Gibbons
Minister of Environment and Lands: The Hon Otto P Kelland
Minister of Development: The Hon Charles J Furey
Minister of Works, Services and Transportation: The Hon David Samuel Gilbert
Minister of Social Services: The Hon Reuben John Efford

SUPREME COURT OF NEWFOUNDLAND AND LABRADOR
Chief Justice of Newfoundland (Appeal Division): Hon Noel Goodridge, QC
Chief Justice of Trial Division: Hon T Alex Hickman, QC

HOUSE OF ASSEMBLY
Speaker: Hon Tom Lush
Deputy Speaker: Lloyd Snow
Clerk of the House: Miss Bettie Duff

PRINCE EDWARD ISLAND

Situation and population
Prince Edward Island lies in the southern part of the Gulf of St Lawrence. Its area is 5,659 sq km (2,185 square miles). The Provincial population in 1990 was 130,200 of whom 15,776 (city proper) live in Charlottetown, the capital city.

History and constitutional development
Prince Edward Island, formerly the Isle St Jean and a dependency of Cape Breton Island (Isle Royale), formed part of the French province of Acadia. It was ceded to Britain in 1763 by the Treaty of Paris and formed part of the colony of Nova Scotia. It was separated from Nova Scotia and formed into a separate colony in 1769 and shared in the influx of Loyalists from the American colonies during and after the Revolutionary War. The problem of absentee proprietors bedevilled the relations of Governor and Assembly for the next 60 years, but responsible government was established in 1851. The colony was not one of the original provinces of Canada but joined the federation in 1873.

Constitution
The Government of the Province of Prince Edward Island consists of a Lieutenant-Governor, an Executive Council and a Legislative Assembly of 32 members, elected for a statutory term of five years.

The Government
The last General Election was held on 29th May 1989. The Party standings are: Liberals 30, Progressive Conservatives 2.

LIEUTENANT-GOVERNOR
Hon Marion Reid

EXECUTIVE COUNCIL
Premier, President of the Executive Council and Minister of Justice and Attorney General: The Hon Joseph A Ghiz, QC
Minister of Finance and Environment: The Hon Gilbert R Clements
Minister of Energy and Forestry: The Hon Barry Hicken
Minister of Industry: The Hon Robert Morrissey
Minister of Community and Cultural Affairs, Fisheries and Agriculture: The Hon Leonce Bernard
Minister of Labour: The Hon Roberta Hubley
Minister of Transportation and Public Works: The Hon Gordon E MacInnis
Minister of Education: The Hon Paul Connolly
Minister of Agriculture: The Hon Keith W Milligan
Minister of Tourism and Parks: The Hon Nancy Guptill
Minister of Health and Social Services: The Hon Wayne D Cheverie, QC
Clerk of the Executive Council and Secretary to the Cabinet: Diane I Blanchard

SUPREME COURT

Chief Justice (Appeal Division): The Hon Norman H Carruthers

Chief Justice (Trial Division): Kenneth R MacDonald

NOVA SCOTIA

Situation and population

Nova Scotia consists of the peninsula of Nova Scotia and the island of Cape Breton, both lying between the Gulf of St Lawrence and the Atlantic Ocean. The area is 55,490 sq km (21,425 square miles). The population of the province in 1990 was 890,200 of whom 113,577 (city proper) live in Halifax the capital city.

History and constitutional development

Nova Scotia was first discovered by the Norsemen and rediscovered by John Cabot in 1497; it was colonised by the French in 1598; was taken by the English, and a grant of it made to Sir W Alexander by James I in 1621. In 1632 it was restored to France, with Quebec, by the Treaty of St Germain-en-Laye, but again ceded to England at the Peace of Utrecht in 1713. After the Peace of Aix-la-Chapelle in 1748, a settlement for disbanded troops was formed there by Lord Halifax, and the city which now bears his name is the capital of the province. Cape Breton Island was not finally taken from the French until 1758, in which year the first Assembly was summoned. Many Loyalists moved to Nova Scotia from the former American colonies to the south when the independence of the latter was recognised in 1783 and the last British troops withdrawn. In 1769 Prince Edward Island became a separate colony and in 1784 New Brunswick and Cape Breton Island were also separated from the rest of Nova Scotia to which Cape Breton Island was later reunited. In 1848 responsible government was established, and in 1867 Nova Scotia was one of the three colonies which united to form Canada, of which it became a Province.

Constitution

The Government of Nova Scotia consists of a Lieutenant-Governor, an Executive Council and a House of Assembly. The Legislature has 52 members elected for a maximum term of five years.

The Government

The last Provincial election was held on 6th September 1988. Present party standings are Progressive Conservatives 26, Liberal 22, New Democratic Party 3, Independent 1.

LIEUTENANT-GOVERNOR

The Hon Lloyd R Crouse

EXECUTIVE COUNCIL

Premier, President of the Executive Council, Minister responsible for the Cabinet Secretariat, Chairman of the Policy Board: The Hon Donald W Cameron

Deputy Premier, Minister of Industry, Trade and Technology and Minister of Small Business Development: The Hon Thomas J McInnis

Minister of Health and Fitness: The Hon George C Moody

Minister of Agriculture & Marketing: The Hon George Archibald

Minister of Transportation and Communications: The Hon Kenneth Streach

Minister of Lands and Forests, Minister of Mines and Energy: The Hon Charles W MacNeil, MD

Attorney General and Solicitor General: The Hon Ranci Matheson

Minister of Education and Minister of Advanced Education and Job Training: The Hon Ronald C Griffin, QC

Minister of Municipal Affairs: The Hon Brian A Young

Minister of Consumer Affairs: The Hon Donald P McInnes

Minister of Government Services, Minister of Intergovernmental Affairs, chairman of the Management Board: The Hon Neil J Leblanc

Minister of Community Services, Minister Responsible for Acadian Affairs: The Hon Marie P Dechman

Minister of Tourism and Culture: The Hon Terance R B Donahoe

Minister of Finance: The Hon Greg Kerr

Minister of Fisheries and Minister responsible for the Status of Women: The Hon Guy J Leblanc

Minister of the Environment: The Hon John G Leefe

Minister of Labour: The Hon Joseph L Legeve

Secretary to the Executive Council: Michael Kontak

Clerk of the Executive Council: Harold F G Stevens, QC

HOUSE OF ASSEMBLY

Speaker: Hon Arthur Donahoe

Clerk of Assembly: R K MacArthur

SUPREME COURT

Appeal Division: The Hon Chief Justice Lorne O Clark

Ombudsman: Dr Guy MacLean

NEW BRUNSWICK

Situation and population

New Brunswick consists of the mainland between Quebec and Nova Scotia. The area of the Province is 73,439 sq km (28,355 square miles) and the Provincial population in 1990 was 722,900. The Provincial capital is Fredericton, with a population of 44,722 (city proper).

History and constitutional development

New Brunswick was part of the ancient French Province of Acadia and was ceded to England by the Treaty of Utrecht in 1713. Great Britain, however, did not obtain full possession of the country until after the fall of Quebec in 1759. It was first colonised by British subjects from New England in 1761, and in 1783, at the close of the Revolutionary War, it received a large body of Loyalists from the Thirteen Colonies. In 1784 it was separated from Nova Scotia, of which it had formed a part, and given a separate Governor and Assembly. The colony remained quiet and prosperous, largely free from the conflicts between Executive and Legislature which vexed the other North American colonies until 1837. In 1854 responsible government was established, and in 1867 New Brunswick was one of the colonies which agreed to form the Dominion of Canada, of which it became an original Province.

Constitution

The Government of New Brunswick consists of a Lieutenant-Governor, an Executive Council and a House of Assembly. The Legislature has 58 members who are elected for a statutory term of five years.

The Government

The last General Election was held on 23rd September 1991. Present party standings are: Liberal Party, 46 seats; Confederation of Regions (COR), 8 seats; Progressive Conservatives, 3 seats; New Democrats, 1 seat

LIEUTENANT-GOVERNOR
The Hon Gilbert Finn

Premier, Minister responsible for the Advisory Council on the Status of Women and Minister responsible for the Regional Development Council: Hon Frank McKenna
Speaker: Hon Shirley Dysart
Minister of Intergovernmental Affairs, Attorney General and Minister of Justice: Hon Edmond Blanchard QC
Solicitor General: Hon Bruce Smith
Minister of Finance and Chairman of the Board of Management: Hon Allan Maher
Minister of Supply & Services: Hon Laureen Jarrett
Minister of Transportation: Hon Sheldon Lee
Minister of Natural Resources & Energy: Hon Alan Graham
Minister of Agriculture: Hon Gerald Clavette
Minister of Health & Community Services: Hon Russell King
Minister of Income Assistance, Minister of State for Literacy: Hon Ann Breault
Minister of Advanced Education and Labour: Hon Vaughan Blaney
Minister of Education: Hon Paul Buffie
Minister of Municipalities, Culture and Housing: Hon Marcelle Mersereau
Minister of the Environment: Hon Jane Barry
Minister of Economic Development and Tourism: Hon Denis Lasier
Minister of Fisheries and Aquaculture: Hon Camille Theriault
Chairman of New Brunswick Power: Hon Raymond Frenette
Minister of State for Mines and Energy: Hon Doug Tyler
Chief Justice of New Brunswick: Hon Stuart G Stratton

QUEBEC

Situation and population

Quebec lies on both sides of the Lower St Lawrence and extends from the New England states of the USA to the Davis Strait. Its area is 1,540,674 sq km (594,855 square miles). The population of the Province in 1990 was 6,790,100. The provincial capital is Quebec, with a population of 164,580 (city proper). In 1986, 81 per cent of the provincial population reported French as their only mother tongue (single responses). Montreal, which is among the world's largest inland ports, is located at the confluence of the Ottawa and St Lawrence rivers 1,609 km (1,000 miles) from the Atlantic Ocean.

History

(For the history of Quebec see page 154 *et seq.*)

Constitution

The Government of Quebec consists of a Lieutenant-Governor, an Executive Council and since 1969, a uni-cameral legislature, called the National Assembly. The Legislative Council was abolished by the legislature at the end of 1968, and the name of the Assembly changed. The National Assembly has 125 elected members.

The Government

The last General Election was held on 25th September 1989. Present party standings are: Liberal Party 92 seats, Parti Québecois 29 seats and Equality Party 4 seats.

LIEUTENANT-GOVERNOR

Hon Martial Asselin, PC, QC

EXECUTIVE COUNCIL

Prime Minister: Robert Bourassa

Deputy Premier; Minister for Energy and Resources: Lise Bacon

Minister of Finance: Gérard D Levesque

Minister of Municipal Affairs; Minister for Public Security; responsibility for implementing the Language Law: Claude Ryan

Minister of Education; Leader of the House: Michel Pagé

Minister of Agriculture, Fisheries and Food; responsibility for Regional Development: Yvon Picotte

Minister of International Affairs: John Ciaccia

Minister of Health and Social Services; assigned to Electoral Reform: Marc-Yvan Côté

Minister of the Environment: Pierre Paradis

Minister for the Administration and the Public Service; President of the Treasury Board: Daniel Johnson

Minister of Manpower, Income Security and Professional Training; responsibility for the Montérégie: André Bourbeau

Minister of Justice, Attorney General and Minister assigned to Canadian Intergovernmental Affairs: Gil Rémillard

Minister of Tourism: André Vallerand

Minister of Supply and Services: Robert Dutil

Minister of Immigration and Cultural Communities: Monique Ganon-Tremblay

Minister of Recreation, Hunting and Fishing: Gaston Blackburn

Minister of Industry, Commerce and Technology: Gérald Tremblay

Minister of Transport: Sam Elkas

Minister of Cultural Affairs: Liza Frulla-Hébert

Minister of Higher Education and Science: Lucienne Robillard

Minister of Revenue; responsiblity for implementing laws relating to professions: Raymond Savoie

Minister of Labour; Junior Minister for Cultural Communities: Normand Cherry

Minister of Communications; Vice-President of the National Assembly: Lawrence Cannon

Minister assigned to Forestry: Albert Côté

Junior Minister for Finance: Louise Robic

Minister assigned to la Francophonie: Guy Rivard

Minister assigned to the Status of Women; Minister with responsibility for the Family: Violette Trépanier

Junior Minister for Agriculture, Fisheries and Food, and Regional Development; responsibility for Fisheries: Yvon Vallières

Junior Minister for Transport: Robert Middlemiss

Minister assigned to Native Affairs: Christos Sirros

COURT OF APPEAL

Chief Justice: Hon Claude C Bisson

SUPERIOR COURT QUEBEC

Chief Justice: Hon M Alan B Gold

COURT OF QUEBEC

Chief Justice (Montreal): Albert Gobeil

Associate Chief Justice (Quebec): Yvon Mercier

ONTARIO

Situation and population

The Province stretches 1,000 miles from east to west, from Quebec to the Prairies, and 1,050 miles from south to north, from the Great Lakes to Hudson Bay. Its area is 1,068,577 sq km (412,578 square miles), the population in 1990 was 9,698,500. The provincial capital is Toronto, with a population of 612,289 (city proper).

History

(For the history of Ontario see page 154 et seq.)

Constitution

The Government of Ontario consists of a Lieutenant-Governor, an Executive Council and a House of Assembly. The House of Assembly, the single-chamber Legislature of the province, is composed of 125 members elected for a statutory term of five years.

Government

The last General election was held on 7th September 1990. Present distribution of seats is Liberal Party 36 seats, New Democratic Party 74, Progressive Conservative Party 20.

LIEUTENANT-GOVERNOR

The Hon Lincoln Alexander, PC, QC

EXECUTIVE COUNCIL

Premier, Minister of Intergovernmental Affairs: Bob Rae

Deputy Premier, Treasurer of Ontario and Minister of Economics: Floyd Laughren

Minister of Education: Marion Boyd

Minister of Colleges and Universities, Skills Development: Richard Allen

Minister of Environment, Minister responsible for the Greater Toronto Area: Ruth Grier
Attorney General: Howard Hampton
Government House Leader and Minister of Municipal Affairs: Dave Cooke
Minister of Financial Institutions: Brian Charlton
Minister of Transportation, Minister responsible for Francophone Affairs: Gilles Pouliot
Minister of Industry, Trade and Technology: Ed Philip
Minister of Health, Minister responsible for Anti-Drug Secretariat: Frances Lankin
Minister of Northern Development and Mines: Shelley Martel
Minister of Energy: Will Ferguson
Minister of Agriculture and Food: Elmer Buchanan
Minister of Government Services: Fred Wilson
Minister of Natural Resources, responsible for Native Affairs: Bud Wildman
Minister of Labour: Bob Mackenzie
Minister of Citizenship: Elaine Ziemba
Minister of Revenue: Shelley Wark-Martyn
Minister without Portfolio responsible for Women's Issues: Anne Swarbrick
Solicitor General and Minister of Correctional Services: Allan Pilkey
Minister of Culture and Communications: Karen Haslam
Minister of Community and Social Services: Zanana Akande
Minister of Tourism and Recreation: Peter North
Minister Without Portfolio, Government Whip: Shirley Coppen
Minister of Consumer and Commercial Relations: Marilyn Churley
Minister of Housing: Evelyn Gigantes
Chairman of Management Board of Cabinet: Tony Silipo
Secretary of the Cabinet and Clerk of the Executive Council: Peter Barnes
Chief Justice of Ontario: Hon Charles L Dubin
Chief Justice of the High Court: Hon Frank Callaghan

MANITOBA

Situation and population

Manitoba was the first of the Prairie Provinces to be formed, and when created in 1870 included only a small area south of Lake Winnipeg. In 1912 it was increased to its present size of 649,947 sq km (250,945 square miles). The population of the Province in 1990 was 1,089,900 and Winnipeg, the provincial capital, was 618,300 (city proper).

History

Manitoba was formed from the territory, including the Red River Colony, which formed part of Rupert's Land, granted to the Hudson's Bay Company when it received a Royal Charter in 1670. It became a Province of the Canadian Federation by legislative enactments taking effect on 15th July 1870.

Constitution

The Government of Manitoba consists of a Lieutenant-Governor, an Executive Council, at present composed of 13 members, and a Legislative Assembly of 57 members elected for a term of five years.

The Government

The last General election was held on 11th September 1990. The present distribution of seats is Progressive Conservative Party 30 seats; Liberal Party 7 seats; New Democratic Party 20 seats.

LIEUTENANT-GOVERNOR
His Hon George Johnson

MANITOBA EXECUTIVE COUNCIL MEMBERS IN ORDER OF PRECEDENCE
Premier; President of the Council; Minister of Federal-Provincial Relations: The Hon Gary Albert Filmon
Minister of Northern Affairs, Deputy Premier; Minister responsible for Native Affairs: The Hon James Erwin Downey
Minister of Health: The Hon Donald Warder Orchard
Minister of Highways and Transportation; Minister of Government Services: The Hon Albert Driedger
Minister of Finance, House Leader: The Hon Clayton Sidney Manness
Minister of Family Services: The Hon Harold Gilleshammer
Minister of Environment: The Hon (James) Glen Cummings
Minister of Justice and Attorney General; Keeper of the Great Seal; Minister responsible for Constitutional Affairs, Corrections: The Hon James Collus McCrae
Minister of Co-operative, Consumer and Corporate affairs: The Hon Linda McIntosh
Minister of Industry, Trade and Tourism, Sport: The Hon Eric Stefanson
Minister of Agriculture: The Hon Glen Marshall Findlay
Minister of Education and Training: The Hon Leonard Derkach
Minister of Urban Affairs; Minister of Housing: The Hon James A Ernst
Minister of Culture, Heritage and Recreation, Minister responsible for Multicultural Affairs, and for the Status of Women: The Hon Bonnie Elizabeth Mitchelson

Minister of Natural Resources: The Hon Harry John Enns
Minister of Energy and Mines: The Hon Harold John Neufeld
Minister of Labour: The Hon Darren Praznik
Minister of Government Services and Minister responsible for Seniors: Hon Gerald Ducharme
Chief Justice of Manitoba: The Hon A M Monnin

SASKATCHEWAN

Situation and population
Saskatchewan lies between Manitoba and Alberta. It has an area of 652,327 sq km (251,864 square miles). The population in 1990 was 1,000,400 of whom approximately 175,064 live in the provincial capital, Regina (city proper), and 177,641 live in Saskatoon (city proper).

History
Rupert's Land and the Northwest Territories, the vast area under the jurisdiction of the Hudson's Bay Company, in 1870, extended from Labrador to the Rockies and from the headwaters of the Red River to Chesterfield Inlet on Hudson Bay. When the Province of Manitoba was established in 1870, the Hudson's Bay Company surrendered to the Government of Canada its territorial rights to the entire area. In 1882, the provincial districts of Assiniboia, Saskatchewan, Alberta and Athabaska were created from the southern portion of the Northwest Territories. Population in the districts increased rapidly during the last two decades of the nineteenth century and with it the desire for provincial status. This was achieved in 1905 when approximately four-fifths of the district of Assiniboia and Saskatchewan and one half of the district of Athabaska were merged to form the present Province of Saskatchewan.

Constitution
The Government of Saskatchewan consists of a Lieutenant-Governor, an Executive Council and a Legislative Assembly of 64 members, elected for a statutory term of five years.

The Government
The last General election was held on 21st October 1991. Present party standings are: New Democratic Party, 55 seats; Progressive Conservative Party, 10 seats; Liberals, 1 seat.

LIEUTENANT-GOVERNOR
Hon Sylvia O Fedoruk, OC, MA, DSC, FCCPM

EXECUTIVE COUNCIL
Premier: Hon Roy J Romanow QC
Deputy Premier & Finance: Hon Ed Tchorzewski
Agriculture & Food, Highways and Transportation: Hon Berny Wiens
Community Services, Environment and Public Safety: Hon Carol Carson
Economic Diversification & Trade: Hon Dwain Lingenfelter
Education & Family: Hon Carol Teichrob
Energy & Mines: Hon John Penner
Health and Public Service Commission: Hon Louise Simard
Human Resources, Labour & Employment, Indian and Metis Affairs and Minister for Justice: Hon Bob Mitchell QC
Parks and Renewable Resources and Rural Development: Hon Darrel Cunningham
Saskatchewan Property Management Corporation: Hon Carol Carson
Social Services: Hon Janice MacKinnon
Speaker: Hon Arnold Tusa
Chief Justice of Saskatchewan: Hon E D Bayda
Chief Justice of Queen's Bench: Hon Donald K MacPherson
Chief Judge of Provincial Court: Hon B Patrick Carey

ALBERTA

Situation and population
Alberta lies between Saskatchewan and British Columbia. Its area is 661,188 sq km (255,285 square miles), and the population in 1990 was 2,459,200 of whom 583,872 (city proper) live in the provincial capital, Edmonton.

History
Alberta was created a Province by an enactment of the Parliament of Canada on 1st September 1905 out of territory that previously had formed part of the North-West Territories.

Constitution
The Government of Alberta consists of a Lieutenant-Governor, an Executive Council and a Legislative Assembly of 83 members, elected for a maximum period of five years.

The Government
The last General election was held on 20th March 1989. Present distribution of seats is: Progressive Conservative Party 59 seats, New Democratic Party 16 seats, Liberals 8 seats.

LIEUTENANT-GOVERNOR
The Hon Gordon Towers

EXECUTIVE COUNCIL
Premier, President of Executive Council: The Hon Donald R L Getty
Deputy Premier and Minister of Federal and Intergovernmental Affairs, Government House Leader: The Hon James D Horsman
Minister of Economic Development and Trade: The Hon Peter Elzinga
Provincial Treasurer: The Hon Dick Johnston
Minister of Energy: The Hon Rick Orman
Minister of Technology, Research and Telecommunications, Deputy House Leader: The Hon Fred Stewart
Minister of Transportation and Utilities: The Hon Al Adair
Solicitor General, responsible for Native Affairs: The Hon Dick Fowler
Minister of Forestry, Lands and Wildlife: The Hon LeRoy Fjordbotten
Minister of Environment: The Hon Ralph Klein
Minister of Family and Social Services: The Hon John Oldring
Associate Minister of Family and Social Services: The Hon Roy Brassard
Minister of Tourism: The Hon Don Sparrow
Minister of Career Development and Employment: The Hon Norman Weiss
Minister of Public Works, Supply and Services: The Hon Ken Kowalski
Minister of Agriculture: The Hon E D (Ernie) Isley
Associate Minister of Agriculture: The Hon Shirley McClellan
Minister of Culture and Multiculturalism: The Hon Doug Main
Minister of Municipal Affairs and Public Safety Services, responsible for Housing: The Hon Ray Speaker
Minister of Recreation and Parks: The Hon Dr Steve West
Minister of Labour: The Hon Elaine McCoy
Minister of Health: The Hon Nancy Betkowski
Attorney-General: The Hon Ken Rostad
Minister of Consumer and Corporate Affairs: The Hon Dennis Anderson
Minister of Education: The Hon Jim Dinning
Minister responsible for Occupational Health and Safety, Workers Compensation Board: The Hon Peter Trynchy
Minister of Advanced Education, Deputy House Leader: The Hon John Gogo

COURT OF APPEAL
Chief Justice of Alberta: Hon J H Laycraft

COURT OF QUEENS BENCH
Chief Justice: Hon K W Moore

CLERK OF THE LEGISLATIVE ASSEMBLY
Dr W J David McNeil

BRITISH COLUMBIA

Situation and population
British Columbia is the westernmost Province in Canada and lies between the Rocky Mountains and the Pacific Ocean. The area (including Vancouver Island and Queen Charlotte Islands) is 947,794 sq km (365,944 square miles). The provincial population in 1991 was 3,200,400 of whom 68,671 (city proper) live in Victoria, the provincial capital.

History
British Columbia is an amalgamation of four Colonial jurisdictions. Vancouver Island was granted to the Hudson's Bay Company by Royal Charter in 1849, at which time the Crown Colony was established. In 1852 the Queen Charlotte Islands were established as a Lieutenant-Dependency of Vancouver Island. In consequence of a large migration on the discovery of gold on the Fraser and Thompson Rivers in 1858, the mainland Crown Colony of British Columbia was constituted, comprising roughly the southern half of the mainland. In 1862 the northern half of the mainland, including part of the present Yukon Territory, was established as the Territory of Stikine. In 1863 the Queen Charlotte Islands, British Columbia and the Stikine Territory were united under the name of British Columbia. In 1866 this colony of British Columbia and Vancouver Island were united under the former name and in 1871 British Columbia became a province of Canada.

Constitution
The Government of British Columbia consists of a Lieutenant-Governor, an Executive Council and a Legislative Assembly of 69 members elected for a term not to exceed five years.

The Government
The last General Election was held on 17th October, 1991. Present distribution of seats is: New Democratic Party, 51 seats; Liberals, 17 seats; Social Credit Party, 7 seats.

LIEUTENANT-GOVERNOR
The Hon Dr David See-Chai Lam

EXECUTIVE COUNCIL
Premier: Hon Michael Harcourt
Finance & Corporate Relations and House Leader: Hon Glen Clark
Attorney General: Hon Colin Gablemann
Deputy Premier, Education & Minister responsible for Multiculturalism and Human Rights: Hon Anita Hagen
Labour and Consumer Services and Minister responsible for Constitutional Affairs: Hon Moe Sihota
Environment, Land and Parks: Hon John Cashore
Health & Minister responsible for Seniors: Hon Elizabeth Cull
Advanced Education, Training and Technology: Hon Tom Perry
Social Services: Hon Joan Smallwood
Aboriginal Affairs: Hon Andrew Petter
Government Services: Hon Lois Boone
Tourism & Minister responsible for Culture: Hon Darlene Marzari
Agriculture, Fisheries & Food: Hon Bill Barlee
Energy Mines & Petroleum Resources: Hon Anne Edwards
Economic Development, Small Business & Trade: Hon David Zirnhelt
Municipial Affairs, Recreation and Housing: Hon Robin Blencoe
Forests: Hon Dan Miller
Women's Equality: Hon Penny Priddy
Transportation and Highways: Hon Art Charbonneau
Court of Appeal: Chief Justice Allan McEachern
Supreme Court: Chief Justice William A Esson

THE TERRITORIES OF CANADA
The areas over which the Hudson's Bay Company had trading rights, known as Rupert's Land and the Northwest Territory, were transferred by Britain to the Dominion of Canada with effect from 15th July 1870 and were administered by the Federal Government. To this was added on 1st September 1880 all the remaining British territories to the north, including the polar islands. As set out on page 157, several Provinces were formed from the vast area, and other parts of it were transferred to existing Provinces. However, one third of the area of Canada still lies outside the Provinces, and is divided into two Territories, each administered directly by the Canadian Government.

YUKON TERRITORY

Situation and population
The Yukon Territory covers 483,449 sq km (186,660 square miles). The population of the Territory in 1990 was 29,886 of whom 21,112 (city proper) live in the capital city, Whitehorse.

Administration
The Yukon was created a separate Territory in June 1898 as the result of development in the mining industry, the Klondike gold strike and the consequent influx of population. The Territorial Government consists of a Federal Government Commissioner, who in practice functions as a Lieutenant-Governor, (that is, accepts the advice of the government leader), and an elected Legislature consisting of sixteen members with a four-year tenure of office. The leader of the party with a majority in the Legislature becomes the Premier. The Legislative Assembly exercises power delegated by the Federal Government of Canada over a host of matters of a local or regional nature. While territorial rights and responsibilities are derived from the federal government, they have been incrementally increased, especially since 1979. There is an assumption on the part of both the Yukon and the Federal Government that the Yukon will continue its evolution towards provincial status. Federally, the Yukon is represented by one member each in the Senate and House of Commons of the Parliament of Canada.

Commissioner: Ken McKinnon

EXECUTIVE COUNCIL
Premier, Minister of the Executive Council, Minister of Finance: Hon Tony Penikett
House Leader, Minister of Education, Minister of Government Services, Minister responsible for the Public Service Commission, Minister responsible for the Workers' Compensation Board: Hon Piers McDonald
Minister of Justice, Minister responsible for the Women's Directorate, Minister responsible for the Yukon Liquor Corporation: Hon Margaret Joe
Minister of Renewable Resources, Minister of Tourism: Hon Art Webster
Minister of Community and Transportation Services, Minister of Economic Development, Mines and Small Business, Minister responsible for the Yukon Development Corporation: Hon Maurice Byblow

Minister of Health and Social Services, Minister responsible for the Yukon Housing Corporation: Hon Joyce Hayden

LEGISLATIVE ASSEMBLY MEMBERS

Government Members—New Democrat Caucus: Danny Joe, Sam Johnston, Norma Kassi

Official Opposition Members—Progressive Conservative Caucus: Dan Lang (Acting Leader of the Official Opposition), Willard Phelps, Bill Brewster, John Devries, Doug Phillips

Independent: Alan Nordling, Bea Firth

SUPREME COURT

Judge H C B Maddison

TERRITORIAL COURT

Judge: Heino Lilles

COURT OF APPEAL

Chief Justice of British Columbia,
Justices of Appeal of British Columbia,
Judges of the Territorial Courts of the Northwest Territories and the Yukon Territory

NORTHWEST TERRITORIES

Situation and population

The Northwest Territories comprise those parts of former Rupert's Land and the Northwest Territories which remained after the formation of the Yukon Territory, the provinces of Manitoba, Alberta and Saskatchewan, and the expansion of British Columbia, Ontario and Quebec. It consists of the greater part of Canada which lies to the north of 60°N. latitude and includes the principal islands in Hudson and James Bays, the Canadian Archipelago and the Queen Elizabeth Islands, which stretch to 83°N. latitude. The total area is about 3,426,311 sq km (1,322,900 square miles), one third of all Canada. The population in 1990 was 54,000. Yellowknife is the capital city, with a population of 11,753 (city proper).

Administration

By an Order in Council which became effective on 1st January 1920, the Northwest Territories was subdivided into the Districts of Mackenzie (the western mainland), Keewatin (the central and eastern mainland) and Franklin (the northern islands). Under the Canadian Northwest Territories Act (RSC 1952, c. 331 as amended in 1966 and 1970) the Government of the Northwest Territories is administered by a Commissioner, appointed by the Governor-General in Council, aided by a Legislative Assembly of twenty-two elected members as at October 1979. Prior to the autumn of 1967, the seat of Government was in Ottawa, but in September of that year the Commissioner, Deputy Commissioner and the nucleus of what is now the Northwest Territories administration moved to Yellowknife. At that time, the administration was responsible for all those provincial-type services except education, welfare, engineering, legal services, health services and natural resources. By a process of transfer of responsibility from the federal to territorial jurisdictions, the Government of the Northwest Territories assumed responsibility for the western (Mackenzie area) region of the Territories in 1967 and for the whole (central and eastern Arctic regions) on 1st April 1970. During this transitional period, the Territorial Administration gradually assumed control of the major provincial-type programmes and services, with the exception of some services to indigenous native persons which are federal responsibility, all natural resources and certain renewable resources. Management of resources and of certain programmes for indigenous people remain under the control of the Department of Indian and Northern Affairs, who maintain administrative offices centrally in Yellowknife and at various other locations in the Territories. Other Federal Government departments and agencies including the RCMP, Energy, Mines and Resources, Justice, Employment and Immigration, National Defence, Health and Welfare, Public Works, Communications, Environment, Fisheries and Marine Services and the Ministry of Transport also maintain offices in the Northwest Territories.

Commissioner: John H Parker

EXECUTIVE COUNCIL:

Government Leader and responsibility for Energy Mines and Resources and the NWT Power Corporation: Nellie Cournoyea

Finance, Economic Development and Tourism, Public Utilities and Government House Leader: John Pollard

Intergovernment and Aboriginal Affairs: Stephen Kakfwi

Justice, Municipal and Community Affairs, Safety and Public Services, Workers Compensation Board: Dennis Patterson

Health, Social Services, Science Institute: Tony Whitford

Renewable Resources, Government Services, Women's Directorate: John Ningark

Public Works, Housing Corporation: Don Morin

Education, Culture and Communications Transportation: Titus Allooloo

Speaker: Hon Richard Nerysoo

LEGISLATIVE ASSEMBLY

Hudson Bay (Charloe Crow); Baffin South (Joe Arlooktoo); Yellowknife North (Hon Michael

Ballantyre); Inuvik (Thomas H Butters); Aivilik (Peter Ernerk); Nunakput (Nellie J Cournoyea); Baffin Central (Ipeelee Kilabuk); Yellowknife Centre (Brian Lewis); Pine Point (Bruce McLaughlin); Mackenzie Delta (Richard W Nerysoo); Iqaluit (Dennis G Patterson); High Arctic (Ludy Pudluk); Nahendeh (Nick G Sibbeston); Yellowknife South (Tony Whitford); Rae-Lac la Martre (Henry Zoe); Natilikmiot (John Ningark); Amittuq (Titus Allooloo); Sahtu (Steve Kakfwi); Slave River (Jeannie Marie-Jewell); Dehcho (Sam Gargan); Tu Nede (Don Morin); Kitik Meot West (Red Pedersen); Hay River (John Pollard); Kivallivik (Gordon Wray).

Officers of the Council
Clerk: W H Remnant
Legal Adviser: S Lal

SUPREME COURT OF THE NORTHWEST TERRITORIES
Judges: Hon Mark de Weerdt, Hon T D Marshall, J E Richard

TERRITORIAL COURT
Chief Judge: Hon R W Halifax

COURT OF APPEAL
Chief Justice of Alberta,
Justices of Appeal of Alberta,
Judges of the Supreme Court of the Northwest Territories and the Yukon Territory

Republic of Cyprus

Capital: Nicosia

Location, Topography and Climate
The island of Cyprus, latitude 35° N., longitude 33° 30′ E., lies in the eastern Mediterranean and has an area of 9,251 sq km. It is the third largest island in the Mediterranean stretching 225 km at its greatest length (south-west to north-east) and 97 km at its greatest breadth (north to south). There are two mountain systems; the 161 km Kyrenia range along the northern coast, rising to 1,003 m at its highest point and the Troodos Massif in the south-west, with Mount Olympus at 1,921 m as the highest peak. Cyprus has an intense Mediterranean climate with a hot dry summer and a variable winter. July and August are the hottest months with a maximum temperature of 44.5°C (112°F) while December and February are the coldest with a minimum temperature of –5.5°C (22°F). The annual rainfall varies between 678 mm maximum and 243 mm minimum.

The territory of the Republic of Cyprus comprises the whole of the island with the exception of the two Sovereign Base Areas of Akrotiri and Dhekelia in the south, retained under British sovereignty, which have a combined area of 256 sq km. Since August 1974 (see under 'Events of July and August 1974' below) some 37 per cent of the territory of the Republic has been under Turkish military occupation, and exists at present as a Turkish Cypriot area (entitled as the so-called 'Turkish Republic of Northern Cyprus', 'TRNC') with its own unrecognised administration, outside the control of the Government of the Republic. Under this military and political division of the island there is hardly any access between the two sides.

Population
At the last full census in 1960 the population was 576,615, consisting of the two major communities: the Greek Cypriots 441,656 and the Turkish Cypriots 104,942. The remaining groups are: Armenians 3,378, Maronites 2,752 and other nationalities 23,887. At mid 1989 the population of the (Greek Cypriot) Government-controlled area was estimated at 565,400, including 9,000 resident aliens. According to Turkish Cypriot statistics the figure for their area at mid 1990 was 171,000, including 1,000 resident aliens. (Both sets of figures exclude foreign military personnel.) In addition to the Greek and Turkish Cypriot populations in the island, probably as many as one-third more are resident abroad, with the largest communities being in Britain.

Rapid urban growth in the South has carried the main towns well beyond their earlier limits. The largest centres are Nicosia (168,800), Limassol (132,100), Larnaca (60,900) and Paphos (27,800). In the Turkish Cypriot area the biggest urban centre is the Turkish part of Nicosia (37,000).

The official languages are Greek and Turkish, though English is also widely used. The predominant religion is Greek Orthodox in the South, and Muslim in the Turkish Cypriot area.

Education
Primary education is free and universal, and the extent of secondary education is also very wide. Although they have to obtain their higher education abroad (the biggest number in Greece), the proportion of university graduates in the Greek Cypriot population is among the highest in the world.

Communications
Following the closure in 1974 of the former international airport outside Nicosia (which lies between the military ceasefire lines), an airstrip at Larnaca was rapidly developed to international standards by the Government as the new principal airport. A second international airport was opened near Paphos in 1984. In the Turkish Cypriot area, Tymbou (Ercan) has been developed as the main airport, with an alternative at Lefkoniko (Gecitkale); but these are not recognised for international traffic except by Turkey. Limassol, followed by Larnaca, is the main commercial seaport in the South; and Famagusta in the North. There are no railways. The network of paved roads on both sides is reasonably good, but under continuous development, especially in the South, to meet heavily increasing traffic needs. At present the only two routes of near motorway standard are from Nicosia to the west side of Limassol and from Nicosia to Larnaca. The Greek Cypriot telecommunications network is highly advanced and has been a factor in making Cyprus an alternative business and communications hub for the Middle East in place of Beirut.

The Economy
Until July 1974 the Greek Cypriot economy was developing vigorously, particularly the agricultural, tourism and light industry sectors. The events of that year hit it hard, transferring some 37 per cent of

the island, including almost three-quarters of the existing tourist hotel accommodation and the most productive agricultural land and many businesses and factories, to the Turkish Cypriot sector.

With about one-third of the population displaced from their property and employment, the recovery of the Greek Cypriot economy by 1979 to the 1973 level of activity for the whole island was in truth an 'economic miracle'. A good rate of growth has been maintained during the 1980s, with per capita GNP rising during 1979–1990 from C£1,300 to C£4,500 and total trade from C£640m to C£1,600m. Given the high standard of living, and the lack of indigenous energy and raw material resources, a substantial trade deficit has been inevitable, despite agricultural and light industrial exports, and the entrepreneurial skills of Cypriot construction firms in Middle East markets. The major balancing factor in the current account has been provided by the remarkable creation of a new tourist industry along the South coast, with annual visitors increasing from 264,000 in 1973 to 1,500,000 in 1990. External debt financing has been well managed, but a reform of the taxation system, including the introduction of VAT, is expected in order to reduce the excessive fiscal deficit.

Britain remains the leading trading partner of Cyprus, with UK statistics for 1990 showing UK exports of sterling £204m and UK imports of sterling £164m. Despite the importance to Cyprus of some Middle East markets, her essential economic and cultural orientation towards Western Europe was demonstrated by the conclusion, and entry into force in 1988, of a unique Customs Union Agreement with the European Community, originally foreseen under the 1972 Association Agreement at the time of Britain's EC entry. Cyprus applied for EC membership in July 1990.

The unit of currency is the Cyprus pound, at a premium to sterling, whose rate is fixed by the Central Bank in relation to a basket of currencies, and which is still subject to exchange controls. In the 'TRNC', where the Turkish lira (TL) is in use, economic recovery after 1974 lagged far behind that in the Government-controlled area. The small-scale and isolated economy remains heavily dependent on Turkey, particularly for development projects. Turkish Cypriot statistics show that during 1979–1990 per capita GNP increased from TL57,269 to TL9,000,000 and total trade from TL1,982.5m to TL1,300,000m.

History

Extensive archaeological finds going back to the fifth millenium BC testify to the existence of cultures in Cyprus in the earliest times. By the beginning of the first millenium, Greek speaking Achaean colonies had been established, and in the 8th century BC the island appears to have been divided into a series of independent Greek and Phoenician kingdoms, tributaries of the Assyrian Empire.

From the Assyrians, Cyprus passed successively to the Egyptians and the Persians. In 391 BC Evagoras of Salamis, having made himself master of almost the whole of Cyprus, raised the island to a position of virtual independence, but was unable to sustain his position for long. On the division of the Empire of Alexander the Great, Cyprus passed to the Ptolemaic Kingdom of Egypt. It became a Roman province in 58 BC, was soon converted to Christianity and, on the partition of the Roman Empire, fell under the rule of the Byzantine Emperor. From an early date the Church of Cyprus has been autocephalous. In 478 AD following the discovery of the remains of St Barnabas, the Emperor bestowed certain privileges on the Archbishop of Cyprus which have been retained to this day. From the 7th to the 10th centuries Cyprus was ravaged intermittently by the Arabs. Only in 965 AD was Byzantine rule re-established, but it endured for another 200 years, a period marked by much church building.

In 1185 Isaac Comnenos usurped the Governorship of Cyprus and proclaimed his independence. In 1191 ships of the fleet of Richard Coeur de Lion, who was on his way to take part in the Third Crusade, were wrecked on the coast of Cyprus and their crews maltreated by Isaac. To avenge the wrongs done to his bride and his men, Richard attacked and defeated Isaac and conquered the island. Shortly afterwards he celebrated his marriage to Berengaria of Navarre at Limassol. Richard sold Cyprus after a few months to the Knights Templar, but they found the task of government beyond their powers and the next year with Richard's agreement, it was transferred to Guy de Lusignan, the dispossessed King of Jerusalem. Thereafter Kings of the House of Lusignan ruled Cyprus until 1489, although from 1373 to 1464 the Genoese Republic held Famagusta and exercised suzerainty over a part of the country.

The 300 years of Frankish rule were a great epoch in the history of Cyprus. The little kingdom played a distinguished part in several aspects of mediaeval civilization. Its constitution, inherited from the Kingdom of Jerusalem, was the model of that of a mediaeval feudal state. In the Abbey of Bellapais and in the cathedrals of Nicosia and Famagusta it could boast examples of Gothic architecture without equal in the Levant. But such achievements were only attained through the introduction of an alien nobility and the ruthless subjugation of the Greek Church to a Latin hierarchy. The fall of Acre in 1291 left Cyprus the outpost of Christendom in the Levant. With the diversion of the Syrian trade to its ports, Cyprus prospered for a period and under King Peter I Alexandria was sacked and towns on the Turkish coast were occupied. But towards the end of the 14th century, with the Black Death and plagues and the Genoese invasion of 1373, the power of the Lusignans began to wane. In 1489 control of Cyprus passed to the Republic of Venice, which held it until it was conquered by the Turks in 1571. The Venetian administration was elaborate, but often inefficient and corrupt. The population increased to about 200,000, but the former prosperity did not return.

The Turkish conquest was welcomed by many Cypriots, particularly since the liquidation of the Latin Church ensued. Serfdom disappeared, the Orthodox Archbishop was restored after having been in abeyance since about 1275, and the Christian population was granted a large measure of freedom. The power and authority which passed into the Archbishop's hands were particularly significant. As time went on, the Church acquired much influence. In 1821 the Archbishop, Bishops and leading personages of the Orthodox community were arrested and executed on a charge of conspiring with the insurgents in Greece.

In 1878, in exchange for a promise of British assistance to Turkey against Russian encroachment on her eastern provinces, Cyprus passed under the administration of Britain, although nominally it was still Ottoman territory and its inhabitants Ottoman subjects. At the outbreak of war with Turkey in 1914 Cyprus was annexed to the British Crown. The annexation was recognised by Greece and Turkey under the Treaty of Lausanne and in 1925 Cyprus became a Crown Colony.

The movement among the Greek population in Cyprus for the union (*Enosis*) of Cyprus with Greece was a constant feature of local political life during the British period. In 1915 Britain offered Cyprus to Greece on condition that Greece went forthwith to the aid of Serbia. Greece declined the offer, which subsequently lapsed. In October 1931 the Enosis movement led to widespread disturbances. The Greek Government's action in 1954 in taking the question of self-determination for Cyprus to the United Nations and Her Majesty's Government announcement in July of the same year that it was intended to introduce a constitution as a first step towards self-government, gave added impetus to local political activities. The Church and local politicians advocated a boycott of the plans for introducing self-governing institutions, which they stigmatised as a betrayal of Enosis. In April 1955 the Greek Cypriot underground organisation, EOKA (*Ethniki Organosis Kyprion Agoniston*—National Organisation of Cypriot Combatants) launched an armed campaign under the clandestine leadership of General Grivas in support of the demand for Enosis. This led to the declaration of a State of Emergency, which was to last four years.

The Emergency ended only on the signature in February 1959 of the Agreements of Zürich and London regarding the establishment of the Cyprus Republic. A further eighteen months of preparation for independence and of detailed negotiations (particularly over the provisions of the Treaty concerning the Establishment of the Republic) led to the transfer of power by Britain and to the declaration of the Republic on 16th August 1960. In February 1961 following a resolution by the House of Representatives, the Republic applied to become a Member of the Commonwealth; and at the Meeting of Commonwealth Prime Ministers on 13th March 1961 Cyprus was welcomed as a Member of the Commonwealth.

Constitution

The English text of the Constitution of the Republic of Cyprus is contained in the July 1960 White Paper on Cyprus (Cmnd. 1093). The Constitution was based on the document setting out the basic structure of the Republic of Cyprus which was initialled by the Prime Ministers of Greece and Turkey at Zurich on 11th February 1959, and provided for executive authority vested in the President, who must be a Greek Cypriot, and the Vice-President, who must be a Turkish Cypriot. Both were to be elected by universal suffrage by the members of their respective communities and work through a Council of Ministers consisting of ten members, of whom seven must be Greek Cypriots and three Turkish Cypriots. The Ministry of Foreign Affairs or the Ministry of Defence or the Ministry of Finance was to be entrusted to a Turkish Cypriot. Legislative authority other than in matters expressly reserved for the Communal Chambers was vested in the House of Representatives, whose 50 members were to be elected for a period of five years by universal suffrage, there being provision for 35 Greek Cypriot members and 15 Turkish Cypriot members, elected separately. The President and Vice-President of the Republic, separately and conjointly, had the right of veto on any law or decision of the House concerning foreign affairs, and certain questions of defence and security, and might also return all laws and decisions to the House of Representatives for reconsideration. In matters where laws and decisions of the House were considered by the President or Vice-President as discriminating against either of the two communities, the Supreme Constitutional Court might annul, confirm or return the measures to the House for reconsideration in whole or in part.

Other provisions of the Constitution concerned fundamental rights and liberties, the Communal Chambers, the Judiciary, the Public Service (to be composed of 70 per cent Greek Cypriots and 30 per cent Turkish Cypriots) the establishment of separate Greek Cypriot and Turkish Cypriot municipalities in the main towns, the use of Greek and Turkish as official languages, the right of Greek Cypriot and Turkish Cypriot communities to celebrate the Greek Cypriot and Turkish national holidays, and the constitutional validity of the Treaty of Guarantee concluded between the Republic, Greece, Turkey and Britain and the Treaty of Alliance concluded between Greece, Turkey and Cyprus. The Constitution provided further that the territory of the Republic should be one and indivisible and excluded the integral or partial union of Cyprus with any other state. The basic articles of the Constitution could not be amended, although other articles might be modified by a majority of two-thirds of each of the representatives of the two communities in the House of Representatives.

Despite the breakdown of these arrangements in 1963/64, the 1960 Constitution remains, in the Government-controlled area, the Constitution of the Republic. Based, however, on the "doctrine of necessity" and in the absence of Turkish Cypriot participation, some departures from the 1960 arrangements have been adopted by the Greek Cypriots acting alone. In the Turkish Cypriot area, on the other hand, separate arrangements have been adopted, currently under a new constitution approved by referendum following the illegal declaration of the 'TRNC' in November 1983.

The Breakdown of Law and Order, December 1963

Throughout 1963 there was a steady deterioration in political relations between the Greek Cypriot and Turkish Cypriot communities in Cyprus and it was apparent that the constitutional settlement resulting from the Zürich and London Agreements was in danger of breaking down. The provisions regarding municipal government in the main towns were a principal source of contention. Events were precipitated by the rejection in early December by the Turkish Government of proposals for constitutional reform which were presented by Archbishop Makarios to Dr Kutchuk on 30th November 1963. These proposals were designed to give the Greek Cypriots a greater control over the Government of the Republic.

Following a succession of violent incidents, particularly in Nicosia, armed fighting broke out on the island on 22nd December. Four days later the Cyprus Government accepted an offer that the forces of the United Kingdom, Greece and Turkey, stationed in Cyprus, and placed under British Command, should assist them to secure the preservation of a ceasefire and the restoration of peace. A Joint Force Headquarters under British Command was established forthwith in Nicosia and carried out peace-keeping operations.

In January 1964 the London Conference, attended by delegates of Greece, Turkey, the United Kingdom and representatives of the Greek and Turkish communities in Cyprus, met to find a solution to the problem. No agreement was reached. Meanwhile the island remained in a very disturbed state and there were fresh outbreaks of fighting. The problem was eventually referred to the Security Council of the United Nations. On 4th March the Security Council passed a Resolution to set up a United Nations Peace-keeping Force in Cyprus for three months, and this replaced the British Command on 27th March (UNFICYP has had to remain in Cyprus ever since). Meanwhile, the United Nations Secretary-General appointed a United Nations Mediator in Cyprus to attempt to evolve a satisfactory solution to the constitutional problem. The eventual report of Senor Galo Plaza on 26th March 1965 recorded the views of the interested parties and expressed the Mediator's personal opinion that settlement should be on the basis of an independent unitary state with a new constitution in which guarantees for the Turkish Cypriots would be incorporated. The Turkish Government declared that the Mediator had exceeded his mandate and the mediation effort lapsed.

In November 1967 a long dispute about the right of the Cyprus police to patrol two Turkish villages in the Larnaca District came to a head and Greek Cypriot forces under General Grivas attacked the villages, inflicting more than twenty casualties. Turkey reacted vigorously and a full-scale international crisis resulted. Forceful intervention by Mr Cyrus Vance, the Special Representative of President Johnson, was successful in preventing a Turkish invasion. Following the crisis General Grivas was recalled to Athens and several thousand Greek mainland soldiers in excess of the National contingent laid down in the Treaty of Alliance were withdrawn. Greek mainland officers serving with the unconstitutional Greek Cypriot Militia (National Guard) remained.

At a meeting of the Security Council held in December 1967, U Thant offered his good offices in helping to bring about a political settlement. The UN peacemaking effort has remained limited to this formula of a 'good offices mission', as distinct from the earlier effort at 'mediation'. Contacts subsequently took place between the communities and in June 1968 Mr Denktash and Mr Clerides (President of the House of Representatives) began unofficial talks aimed at finding a basis for a new constitution for Cyprus. The talks continued, albeit intermittently, until July 1974.

The Events of July and August 1974

On 15th July 1974, mainland Greek officers of the Greek Cypriot National Guard launched a coup d'état against President Makarios. The leaders of the coup attempt claimed that President Makarios was dead and appointed a former EOKA member, Mr Nicos Sampson, in his place. The following day, President Makarios was rescued by an RAF helicopter from Paphos in western Cyprus and was flown from the British Sovereign Base at Akrotiri to Malta and thereafter to London. The Turkish Government viewed the coup as threatening the security, rights and interests of the Turkish Cypriots.

On 17th July the Turkish Prime Minister, Mr Ecevit, arrived in London for consultations under Article 4 of the 1960 Treaty of Guarantee. The British Foreign and Commonwealth Secretary, Mr Callaghan, stated that the best interests of stability in the Middle East would be served—and the legal position restored—if Archbishop Makarios were recognised and returned to the island in his full capacity and with his full powers. Having failed to enlist British support for military intervention, Turkish forces invaded northern Cyprus on 20th July. Mr Callaghan, while recognising that the coup d'état had precipitated the invasion, expressed strong disapproval of the Turkish action and asked that senior Greek and Turkish Government Representatives should meet to discuss the problem in London. On the same day UN Security Council Resolution No. 353 called for a ceasefire, and the British Government undertook intense diplomatic activity to prevent hostilities from spreading or escalating. Following agreement by the Greek and Turkish Governments on 22nd July to a ceasefire in Cyprus, Mr Callaghan obtained Greek and Turkish agreement for talks between the guarantor states in Geneva, describing Britain's aims as being to restore constitutional rule in Cyprus.

On 23rd July the Greek Military Government resigned and handed over power to a civilian government headed by Mr Karamanlis. Mr Sampson was subsequently replaced by Mr Glafkos Clerides as acting President of Cyprus. The first stage of the Geneva Conference ended on 30th July with an interim agreement that (i) the ceasefire line should be that held by Turkish forces at the time of the agreement; (ii) the three guarantor Powers reserved their rights and obligations as formulated by the 1960 Treaty of Guarantee; (iii) the talks would reconvene on 8th August when representatives of Greek and Turkish Cypriots would join the guarantors in considering the wider issues involved in a lasting solution of the Cyprus problem. On 1st August UN Security Council Resolution No. 355 authorised UNFICYP to undertake new duties in patrolling the buffer-zone between the Turkish and Greek Cypriot forces and policing mixed Greek/Turkish Cypriot villages. On 7th August the Turkish Cypriot leader, Mr Rauf Denktash, advocated a bicommunal independent Cyprus, the two communities living in separate areas. The following day the Geneva talks resumed with Greek Cypriot and Turkish Cypriot representatives present. Mr Callaghan expressed disappointment that the terms of the 30th July Declaration had not been fully implemented. A UN report acknowledged that while some progress had been made, only the first steps had been taken to implement Security Council Resolutions Nos. 353 and 355. On 12th August the Turkish delegation in Geneva demanded a constructive reply to their proposal for a clearly-defined Turkish Cypriot zone covering a third of the island, and the Turkish President announced a deadline on 13th August for a successful conclusion to the Geneva talks. The Turkish Government refused to extend its deadline and the Geneva talks broke down. Turkish forces subsequently moved to extend their control over northern Cyprus, and Turkish aircraft attacked targets in Nicosia.

UN Security Council Resolution No. 357 of 14th August called for an immediate ceasefire and for resumption of the peace talks. The Turkish Foreign Minister declared that Turkey was prepared to conform with Security Council Resolution No. 357 and would be prepared to accept further talks in Geneva in a few days, when its forces had reached their final positions in Cyprus. On 15th August the UN Security Council unanimously adopted resolution No. 358 deeply deploring non-compliance with its resolution No. 357 and insisted on the full implementation of this and previous resolutions by all parties with the immediate and strict observance of the ceasefire. On 16th August the UN Security Council adopted resolution No. 359 deeply deploring casualties inflicted on the UN Peace-keeping force (UNFICYP) and demanded that all parties should refrain from action which might endanger the lives and safety of its members. The Turkish Government subsequently announced a second ceasefire in Cyprus, on achieving their declared objectives, and again stated their readiness to resume negotiations in Geneva.

Subsequent Developments

The Turkish military intervention, and the regrouping of population which followed from it, transformed the character of the political and security problems in Cyprus. In place of an existence since 1964 in enclaves within a State dominated by the Greek Cypriots, the Turkish Cypriots were regrouped into an homogeneous zone of their own (of roughly twice the size to which their population ratio would entitle them). There followed, on 13th February 1975, the declaration of a 'Turkish Federated State of Cyprus' in the area of Cyprus under Turkish military occupation. On 12th March 1975 the UN Security Council adopted a resolution No. 367 regretting that a part of the Republic of Cyprus would become a 'federated Turkish state' and calling for new efforts to be undertaken to assist the resumption of negotiations between representatives of the two communities with a view to reaching freely a mutually acceptable political settlement. In its resolution the Security Council asked the UN Secretary-General, Dr Waldheim, to undertake a new mission of good offices and to place himself personally at the disposal of the parties.

No progress could be made, however, until negotiations between the two communities were resumed in January 1977, when President Makarios and Mr Denktash met in Nicosia for the first time in 13 years. This was followed by a second meeting in Nicosia in February, under the chairmanship of Dr Waldheim. Agreement was reached on a set of four principles or guidelines for future negotiations including Greek Cypriot acceptance for the first time of a bicommunal federation as the basis for a settlement. Nothing came, however, of the follow-up intercommunal talks.

On 3rd August 1977 President Makarios died. Mr Spyros Kyprianou, President of the House of Representatives, was the unopposed candidate as interim President (to complete the remaining six months term of office of the late President) and was elected unopposed in February 1978 for a full 5 year period as the second President of the Republic. He secured re-election again in 1983.

In January 1978, President Kyprianou and Mr Denktash met for the first time, under the aegis of Dr Waldheim. The Turkish Cypriots agreed to produce detailed proposals on both the constitutional and territorial issues. They did so in April and Dr Waldheim passed them to the Greek Cypriots, who declared them to be totally unacceptable as a basis for negotiation. Following an initiative by the United States, Britain and Canada in the Autumn of 1978, and subsequent renewed efforts by Dr Waldheim, a further meeting between President Kyprianou and Mr Denktash took place in May 1979. The meeting concluded with a 10 point agreement providing for a resumption of full intercommunal negotiations. The two High Level Agreements (Makarios-Denktash, and Kyprianou-Denktash) of 1977 and 1979 still constitute the main element of common ground on the substance of a settlement. But, as before, the 1979 Agreement led to no significant progress in follow-up intercommunal talks, which were interrupted in April 1983 when the Cyprus Government initiated a further recourse to the UN General Assembly.

On 15th November 1983 the Turkish Cypriots issued a declaration purporting to establish an independent state in the north called the 'Turkish Republic of Northern Cyprus'. UN Security Council Resolution No. 541, which was passed unanimously on 18th November, deplored the declaration, called for its withdrawal and asked all states not to recognise any Cyprus State other than the Republic of Cyprus. Only Turkey has recognised the 'TRNC', and exchanged Ambassadors in April 1984. This was condemned by Security Council Resolution No. 550.

In August 1984 the UN Secretary-General Mr Perez de Cuellar, after a series of 'proximity talks' in New York with President Kyprianou and Mr Denktash, launched a new initiative which held promise. But a High-Level Meeting with the two leaders in January 1985 failed to reach agreement; and by mid-1986 the possibility of getting both sides to agree on the text of the draft framework agreement under discussion appeared to have been exhausted.

In the Greek Cypriot Presidential election of February 1988, Mr Kyprianou was replaced as President of the Republic by the independent candidate, Mr George Vassiliou. In August 1988 Mr Perez de Cuellar arranged a meeting in Geneva between President Vassiliou and Mr Denktash, who committed themselves to an intensive series of negotiations in Nicosia, with the target of reaching agreement by June 1989. However, this deadline was passed without an agreement being reached. Since the breakdown of the last round of talks between the two leaders in March 1990, the UN has continued its efforts to narrow the differences between the two sides. Some progress was made in intensive consultation from July-September 1991 but considerable problems remain.

UNFICYP

The UN Force in Cyprus (UNFICYP) was set up by UN Security Council Resolution 186 of 4th March 1964. In recent years its mandate has been renewed every six months, in June and December. In December 1990 its strength stood at 2,151 personnel. Britain supplies the largest contingent (742 in May 1990) and the logistic support for the whole Force. In addition, the Force comprises military contingents from Austria, Canada and Denmark and civilian police from Australia and Austria all under the command of Major-General Clive Milner of Canada.

British Aid

In addition to a contribution to the cost of the UNFICYP, estimated at £24m in 1990/91, Britain has spent over £2½ million on refugee relief, including donations given in response to international appeals by the United Nations High Commissioner for Refugees.

Britain runs a small co-operation programme (£250,000 per annum) which includes scholarships and technical aid to both Turkish and Greek Cypriot Communities. There is also a Scholarship Scheme for students studying in the UK.

Historical List

PRESIDENT*

Archbishop Makarios from 16th August 1960
Mr Spyros Kyprianou from 3rd August 1977
Mr George Vassiliou from 1st March 1988

VICE-PRESIDENT*

Dr Fazil Kutchuk from 16th August 1960
Mr Rauf Denktash from 28th February 1973

HEAD OF STATE

The President: His Excellency Dr George Vassiliou

VICE-PRESIDENT

His Excellency Mr Rauf Denktash†

MINISTERS

Minister of Foreign Affairs: Mr George Iacovou
Minister of Interior: Mr Christodoulos Veniamin
Minister of Defence: Mr Andreas Aloneftis
Minister of Education: Mr Christoforos Christofides
Minister of Finance: Mr George Syrimis
Minister of Commerce and Industry: Mr Takis Nemitsas
Minister of Communications and Works: Mr Renos Stavrakis
Minister of Agriculture and Natural Resources: Dr Andreas Gavrielides
Minister of Health: Mr Panikos Papageorgiou
Minister of Labour and Social Insurance: Mr Iacovos Aristidou
Minister of Justice: Mr Nicos Papaioannou

MINISTRIES AND GOVERNMENT DEPARTMENTS

MINISTRY OF FINANCE

Permanent Secretary: M Erotokritos
Permanent Secretary, Planning Bureau: G Hadjianastassiou

* The President and Vice-President of the Republic have had no common dealings since December 1963.

† Mr Denktash no longer considers himself to be Vice-President of the Republic of Cyprus, notwithstanding his election to the office in 1973, and has adopted the style 'President of the Turkish Republic of Northern Cyprus'.

MINISTRY OF FOREIGN AFFAIRS
Permanent Secretary: T Panayides

MINISTRY OF THE INTERIOR
Permanent Secretary: Mr Hadjipanayiotou

MINISTRY OF DEFENCE
Permanent Secretary: L Shakallis

MINISTRY OF AGRICULTURE AND NATURAL RESOURCES
Permanent Secretary: Mr Christodoulou

MINISTRY OF HEALTH
Permanent Secretary: A Louca

MINISTRY OF EDUCATION
Permanent Secretary: Achilleas Patzinakos

MINISTRY OF COMMERCE AND INDUSTRY
Permanent Secretary: K Christophi

MINISTRY OF COMMUNICATIONS AND WORKS
Permanent Secretary: N Symeonides

MINISTRY OF LABOUR AND SOCIAL INSURANCE
Permanent Secretary: G Anastassiades

MINISTRY OF JUSTICE
Permanent Secretary: Antonis Malaos

PRESS & INFORMATION OFFICE
Director: Andreas Sofocleous

CYPRUS BROADCASTING CORPORATION
Director-General: D Kyprianou

PRISONS
Chief Superintendent of Prisons: G Anastassiades (Ag)

CULTURAL SERVICES DEPARTMENT
Director: Yiannis Katsouris

Commonwealth of Dominica

Capital: Roseau

Dominica lies in the Windward Islands group between the French islands of Guadeloupe to the north and Martinique to the south, near to the intersection of the parallels 15°N. and 61°W.

The island is 46 km (29 miles) long and 25 km (16 miles) wide with an area of 751 sq km (290 square miles). It is roughly rectangular in shape with rounded projections at each end and is very mountainous, picturesque and well-watered. A central ridge with lateral spurs runs from Cape Melville in the north to terminate in cliffs in the extreme south, where is found the largest concentration of high land. Morne Diablotin 1,447 m (4,747 feet) in the north is the highest point.

During the cool months of the year—December to March—the climate is particularly pleasant. The dry season lasts from about February to May; June to October are generally the wettest months and the period during which hurricanes may occur. The annual temperature ranges from 26°C (78°F) to 33°C (90°F) in the hottest month—generally July. The rainfall is heavy, especially in the mountainous areas, where the average figure is 6,250 mm (250 inches) as compared with 1,750 mm (70 inches) along the coast. There are numerous rivers but none is navigable.

At the end of 1988 the population was estimated at 81,300. The population of Roseau, the capital, is approximately 22,000 and Portsmouth 5,000.

The unit of currency is the East Caribbean Dollar.

The population is composed of people of African descent, people of mixed descent, Europeans, Syrians and Caribs, the last three groups in small numbers, English, the official language, is very widely spoken and almost universally understood but a French patois persists as the medium of conversation among the masses. Religious adherence is predominantly Roman Catholic but the Church of England and the Methodist Church have also been long established. There are about 15 other religious denominations operating in the State.

The health system in Dominica has four levels. These are as follows, in order of ascending complexity of care and service being offered:

(i) Type I Clinics
(ii) Type II Health Centre
(iii) a Polyclinic
(iv) The National Referral Hospital

Type I clinics provide basic services to villages as small as 600 in population. These clinics are staffed by Primary Care Nurses, a new level of health worker introduced into the health care system to meet the specific community health needs of Dominica. They have two years of training in the delivery of primary health care services including basic Maternal and Child Health Services (MCH) (including midwifery), sanitation, health education, monitoring diabetics and hypertensives and referral of serious problems to the next higher level in the system.

The second level of care is provided by seven Type III main Health Centres. These facilities provide primary health care services to a population of 2,000 to 3,000 while providing a higher level of service to the total population in the district, usually about 6,000–8,000 people. There is one Type III Health Centre in each Health Centre district. Care at the centre covers the following services: limited maternity in-patient service, out-patient referral service, dental service, supervision and support to level I and environmental health services.

The third level of care is a Polyclinic at the Princess Margaret Hospital. This provides improved out-patient care made available to all Type III Health Centres.

The fourth level of care is delivered by the Princess Margaret Hospital. It has 136 beds and provides a broad range of specialised services including full diagnostic, laboratory and radiological services. The Princess Margaret Hospital is the referral point in the island's health system for most cases requiring hospitalisation.

The Portsmouth Hospital with 50 beds provides care for the inhabitants of the second town, but the major cases are referred to the general hospital. Cottage hospitals are situated at Marigot (6 beds) and Grand Bay (4 beds).

Agriculture is the principal occupation, but road and building construction, secondary industries, transport, commerce and tourism absorb a large number of the working population. The estimated labour force in 1981 was 25,253 of whom 16,602 were males and 8,921 females. The umemployment rate is generally regarded as between 10–20 per cent. There are five registered trade unions.

The main crops are bananas, coconuts, limes, grapefruit, oranges, cocoa, mangoes, plantains, avocado pears, coffee, patchoulin and various ground provisions for domestic use and for exports. The main products are oil and soap from coconut, bay oil, copra and rum. Bananas account for 70 per cent of total domestic exports and most of these go to the UK. Dominica is the second largest exporter of bananas in the Windward Islands. In all some 40,000 hectares (100,000 acres) are under cultivation by some 9,000 farmers.

Forest resources in merchantable timber are considerable and efforts have been made to get the timber industry restarted with the help of the British Government through a British financed Forestry Industry Development Corporation.

There is a Government-controlled fisheries scheme which in its present form provides, as one of its main features, interest loans to fishermen through a co-operative to purchase outboard motors and fishing boats. Fuel and lubricating oil used for fishing is obtainable free of duty. Workshop facilities for maintenance and repair of the motors are provided under the scheme.

The only commercially exploitable mineral found on the island is pumice, a light-weight concrete aggregate of volcanic origin used chiefly for building purposes. It was recently mined under licence by a group of American investors, but is now being mined by a local concern. Substantial limestone and clay deposits are also prevalent.

The principal manufactures and other exports are household soaps, cigarettes, cigars, handicrafts and canned citrus juices. Household soaps account for 17 per cent of Dominica's exports. Coconut meal, cloves and crude oil are also produced.

Other manufactures include pepper sauce, foam mattresses, ground coffee from roasted local coffee beans, preserves and wooden furniture.

There were 65 registered co-operatives in mid-1986, of which 23 were Credit Unions. Credit Unions had a share capital of 17 million EC dollars and a combined membership of 36,000 representing 42.5 per cent of the population. Of the other co-operatives, 21 were agricultural. Their membership in 1983 was 1,608, with sales of around 2 million dollars. The Government is vigorously promoting co-operatives and has decided that co-operative education be included in the primary schools' curriculum.

Roseau is the principal port but the banana boats of Geest Industries Ltd, the marketing company, call regularly at Portsmouth, the second town, to collect the bananas of the northern district. A new deepwater harbour has been constructed at Woodbridge Bay near Roseau.

Dominica is served by LIAT, Air Guadeloupe, Air Martinique and Nature Island Airways which provide air services between Dominica and other Caribbean islands. CARICARGO, Seagull Enterprises and Seagreen Air Transport provide air cargo services. Melville Hall Airport is situated in the north-east of the island approximately 54 km (34 miles) from Roseau. A 609 m (2,000 ft) airstrip has been constructed at Canefield three miles north of Roseau with funds from the British Government, and has been extended by the French government.

The following steamship services call at Dominica: the West Indies Shipping Service, Harrison Line, Lamport Grimaldi and Holt Line, Siosi Lines, Seaway and Booker Steamship Co., Saguenay Shipping Ltd, Compagnie Générale Transatlantique Ltd, Royal Netherlands Steamship Ltd, Geest Lines, Atlantic Lines and Caribbean Shipping Line. In addition there are many small sailing craft and several West Indian-owned motor vessels, ranging between 23 tons and 130 tons, which connect Dominica with other islands of the Eastern Caribbean.

In 1984 there were 370 km (230 miles) of class I (surfaced roads), 259 km (161 miles) of class II (all weather part-sealed roads), 115 km (72 miles) of class III (dry weather roads) and 453 km (282 miles) of tracks suitable only for pedestrians. A major road rehabilitation programme financed by the US, Canadian, UK and other donors was completed in 1986.

Current expenditure in 1988/89 financial year is estimated at EC$98,700,000 while capital expenditure is estimated at EC$55,500,000.

The main heads of taxation are income tax and customs and excise duties. No income tax is paid on the first EC$12,000 earned. Those earning between EC$12,000–25,000 pay 25 per cent income tax, EC$25,000–50,000 will pay 35 per cent and EC$50,000 and over 45 per cent. Customs duties on goods imported into the territory are generally specific in regard to foodstuffs and ad valorem on other commodities. The rate of ad valorem duty varies between 5 per cent and 40 per cent. Export duty, at varying rates, is payable on the principal agricultural products. Consumption tax is payable except on zero rated items such as live animals, books, textiles, insecticides, farming tools and certain vehicles including tractors. Another form of taxation is estate duty. There is provision for double income tax relief in respect of Britain, Canada, the United States, Sweden, Denmark and Norway.

There are 66 Primary Schools and 10 Secondary Schools of which one is for boys, two for girls and the others are co-educational. There are 63 pre-schools in Dominica for the 3 to 5 year age group. Among those, 11 are private and self-supporting and 5 are supported by Government. Secondary education is provided up to a university-admission level. The secondary schools prepare pupils for the Cambridge GCE and CXC examinations. On the results of the GCE 'A' level examination an annual Government scholarship is awarded. An increasing number of opportunities for higher education by way of scholarships, bursaries and training courses have been made available in recent years mainly by the United Kingdom, United States, Canada, France and the University of the West Indies. There are two tertiary institutions and a Nursing School.

There is one central free library in Roseau, with branches at Portsmouth in the north which is the second town, Grand Bay in the south and Marigot in the north-west. There is a commercial cinema, the Carib and one arts centre, the Arawak, both in Roseau.

There are three radio stations: D.B.S. which is managed by the Dominica Broadcasting Corporation, and Voice of Life, a Religious radio broadcasting service managed by Racom International and Voice of the Islands run by the Roman Catholic Church. A Cable TV Company, Marpin TV, provides a 12 channel service to residents of Roseau and the immediate surrounding villages. Marpin programmes are beamed via satellite from American TV Networks. Video One also provides TV services. The New Chronicle, founded in 1909 is the main newspaper.

Hurricane David struck Dominica on 29th August 1979. Wind speeds reached in excess of 140 mph. The winds lasted six hours from 10.00 am to 4.00 pm. The whole country was declared a disaster area by the Government. The country's agricultural economy was virtually ruined, with 75 per cent of the agricultural crop destroyed. The banana export earnings have yet to reach pre-1979 figures.

Immediate help and rescue operations were mounted by a number of countries and international organisations. The task of reconstruction and rehabilitation of the country's infrastructure and the patient uphill struggle of restoring the country's economy received a further setback in August 1980 when agriculture was severely affected by Hurricane Allen and again in 1989 when a large proportion of the banana crop was laid to waste by Hurricane Hugo.

History

Dominica was discovered by Columbus on Sunday (*dies dominica*) 3rd November 1493. It was then a stronghold of the Caribs, who had arrived in the Antilles from the mainland of South America and were in the course of driving out the less warlike Arawaks. The Spaniards made no attempts to establish settlements on the island either then or later, probably because of the strength of the Caribs and the forbidding terrain.

English associations with Dominica did not begin until 1627, when it was included in a grant of sundry islands in the Caribbean made to the Earl of Carlisle; several attempts to take possession, however, proved abortive.

Under the treaty of Aix-la-Chapelle, 1748, Great Britain and France agreed to treat the island as neutral ground and to leave it to the Caribs. Nevertheless, French planters continued to settle and establish plantations and Dominica came to be regarded as a *de facto* French colony. In 1759 the English captured it from the French and the conquest was acknowledged in the ninth article of the Peace of Paris 1763. The French settlers were generously secured in their possessions on condition of taking the oath of allegiance and paying a small quit rent. In 1775, by Royal Proclamation, a House of Representatives was established.

In 1778, the French in Martinique, attracted by the fertility of Dominica and encouraged by some of their countrymen on the island, launched a military and naval assault under the Marquis de Bouillé. They captured Dominica on 7th September after an obstinate resistance. Marquis Duchilleau, a cruel and tyrannical officer, was appointed Governor. Trade failed and great distress followed.

In 1783 the island was again restored to the English and Sir John Ord, Bart. was appointed Governor.

In 1795 another invasion of the island was attempted by Victor Hugues, the French Republican leader who had previously forced the British troops to evacuate Guadeloupe. The brave and well-directed resistance of the inhabitants, under the command of Governor Hamilton, forced part of the enemy to flee, and the rest to surrender.

In 1805 the French again landed at each flank of Roseau. The regular troops and the militia fought gallantly, but unfortunately the capital was set on fire accidentally and was obliged to capitulate, paying the enemy £12,000 to quit; whilst the Governor, Sir George Prévost, and the troops (regular and militia) proceeded across the island to the superior position of Prince Rupert, near the town of Portsmouth. The French withdrew and made no further attempt to capture the island.

In 1833 the island was, with Antigua and the other Leeward islands, formed into a general government, under a Governor-in-Chief, resident at Antigua.

In 1871 Dominica and the other British islands to the north were formed into the Federation of the Leeward Islands Colony to which Dominica remained attached until 1939. In 1940 the island became a unit of the Windward Islands group. In January 1960 the post of the Governor of the Windward Islands was abolished and the Windwards Group was dissolved as an administrative unit.

Constitutional Development

In March 1967 Dominica assumed a status of association with the United Kingdom. The island exercised full internal self government and was accorded executive authority over a wide field of external relations by the United Kingdom, which retained responsibility for external and defence affairs.

On 3rd November 1978 Dominica became an independent republic governed by a President and democratically elected Parliament. On independence the island took the name of Commonwealth of Dominica.

Soon after internal disturbances in May 1979 all members of the Cabinet of Prime Minister Patrick John resigned except the Prime Minister himself. A Committee of National Salvation representing the majority group was then formed. The Committee proposed the formation of an interim Government led by Mr Oliver Seraphin, which was sworn in on 21st June. At General Elections held on 21st July 1980, the Dominica Freedom Party led by Miss Mary Eugenia Charles secured 17 of the 21 seats.

The Dominica Freedom Party retained office in general elections held in July 1985 and again in May 1990 winning 11 seats, a majority of only one. The Dominica United Workers Party, formed in July 1988 and contesting for the first time, won 6 seats. Led by Edison James it is the official opposition party.

Constitution

Under the Constitution executive authority is vested in the President elected by the House of Assembly for not more than two terms of five years. He acts on the advice of his Cabinet except where otherwise required by the Constitution.

The Cabinet, which is presided over by the Prime Minister, advises the President and is collectively responsible to Parliament for any advice given to the President. The Cabinet consists of the Prime Minister and other ministers and the Attorney General. The President appoints as Prime Minister the elected member of the House who commands the support of a majority of its elected members and other ministers on the advice of the Prime Minister. Not more than three ministers may be from among the senators appointed to Parliament. The President has the power to remove the Prime Minister if after a resolution in the House of no confidence he does not resign or advise the dissolution of Parliament within three days. The President appoints as Leader of the Opposition the elected member who appears to him to command majority support among elected members who do not support the Government.

Parliament consists of the President and the House of Assembly made up of elected representatives and nine Senators. The latter may be appointed by the President—five on the advice of the Prime Minister and four on the advice of the Leader of the Opposition—or elected, in accordance with the wishes of Parliament.

The life of Parliament is five years. It is elected by universal adult suffrage in single member constituencies. The qualifying age for voters is 18.

Parliament may make laws for the peace, order and good government of Dominica. The Constitution contains safeguards for fundamental rights and freedoms. Special provisions relate to a Bill to alter the Constitution or the law establishing the West Indies Associated States Supreme Court or the law relating to appeals to the Privy Council. The West Indies Associated States Supreme Court is now known in Dominica as the Eastern Caribbean Supreme Court.

A puisne Judge is resident in Dominica.

The appointment, dismissal and disciplinary control of public officers is, with certain exceptions, vested in the Public Service and Police Service Commissions, the members of which are appointed by the President in accordance with the advice of the Prime Minister, one from amongst persons selected by the appropriate representative body. There is provision for appeal in disciplinary cases to a Public Service Board of Appeal.

Land Policy

The freehold system remains the predominant form of land tenure. Alienated Crown Lands have been sold to residents without any preconditions since 1962. Aliens must first obtain a licence from the Government, to which certain conditions are attached, before being able to purchase lands in the territory. The leasehold system still exists on estate lands and the relations between landlords and tenants are governed by the Agricultural Small Tenancy Ordinance, 1953 (Cap 74). The State occupies approximately 40 per cent of the total land area.

PRESIDENT: His Excellency Sir Clarence A Seignoret, GCB, OBE

CABINET

Prime Minister and Minister for Finance, Economic Development, Establishment and Security: Hon Miss M Eugenia Charles

Minister for External Affairs (and OECS Unity): Hon Brian Alleyne

Attorney-General and Minister for Legal Affairs: Hon Jenner B M Armour

Minister for Trade, Industry and Tourism: Hon Charles Maynard

Minister for Community Development, Social Affairs, and Women's Affairs: Hon Henry George

Minister for Communications, Works and Housing: Hon Alleyne Carbon

Minister for Immigration and Labour: Hon Heskeith Alexander

Minister for Agriculture, Lands and Forestry: Hon Maynard Joseph

Minister for Education and Sports: Hon Rupert Sorhaindo

Minister for Health: Allan Guye

Minister Without Portfolio: Dermott Southwell

HOUSE OF ASSEMBLY

Speaker: Hon Crispin Sorhaidoo

Clerk of the House: Mrs Albertha Jno Baptiste

Leader of the Opposition: Hon Edison James

CIVIL ESTABLISHMENT

Cabinet Secretariat

Secretary to the Cabinet: Julian Johnson

MINISTRY OF EXTERNAL AFFAIRS
Permanent Secretary: Justinian Coipel

MINISTRY OF FINANCE AND TRADE
Fiscal Adviser: Alick Lazare
Financial Secretary: Gilbert Williams

MINISTRY OF COMMUNITY DEVELOPMENT, HOUSING AND LABOUR
Parliamentary Secretaries: Johnson Boston; Hon Jacklyn Hurtult
Permanent Secretary (Agriculture): Eliud Williams
Permanent Secretary (Trade): Wolsey Louis

MINISTRY OF TRADE, INDUSTRY AND TOURISM
Parliamentary Secretary: Hon Ossie Walsh

MINISTRY OF LEGAL AFFAIRS:
Permanent Secretary: Mrs Adora Benjamin

MINISTRY OF LABOUR AND IMMIGRATION:
Permanent Secretary: Mrs Rhona Fingal

MINISTRY OF EDUCATION, YOUTH AFFAIRS AND SPORTS
Permanent Secretary: Mrs Judith Pestaina

MINISTRY OF HEALTH
Permanent Secretary: Mrs Doreen Nicholas

MINISTRY OF COMMUNITY DEVELOPMENT, HOUSING AND SOCIAL AFFAIRS:
Permanent Secretary: Arden Shillingford

MINISTRY OF COMMUNICATIONS AND WORKS
Permanent Secretary: Osbourne Symes
Parliamentary Secretary: Hon Clem Shillingford
Chief Establishment Officer: Mrs Jennifer Astaphan

The Gambia

Capital: Banjul

The Gambia lies on the west coast of Africa between latitudes 13° and 14° north of the equator. Surrounded by Senegal except at the coast, it is called after the River Gambia which it straddles for over 322 km (as the crow flies) eastwards from the Atlantic Ocean to longitude 13° 90′W. At the estuary its northern and southern boundaries are 48 km apart, but from about 145 km inland these narrow to enclose two ribbons of land, each only about 10 km wide, which follow the course of the river along the north and south banks. The country's total area, land and water, is just over 10,360 sq km. The land is very flat, with only some low laterite ridges rising to about 20 metres. There are extensive mangrove swamps along the river and its creeks.

The river, one of the finest waterways in Africa, is The Gambia's principal geographical feature and indeed the background to its history and the source of its life. The capital and seaport of Banjul (formerly Bathurst), situated at the mouth of the river, can accommodate ocean-going vessels of up to 28 feet draught, while smaller freighters of up to 18 feet draught can sail 193 km upstream to the township and port of Kaur, from which groundnuts are shipped. Shallow-draught river craft ply to Basse, 418 km upriver. The river rises in the Futa Jallon highlands in the Republic of Guinea.

The Gambia's climate has two seasons, and is similar to that of the southern Sahel across to northern Nigeria. It is cool and dry from late November to April/May, with temperatures down to 15°C (60°F), but during the other half of the year it is hot and humid, the thermometer at midday up-river often going well beyond 38°C (100°F). The rain falls almost exclusively between June and October in the hot season, the annual country average being about 925 mm although considerable fluctuations occur both from year to year and from place to place. The harmattan wind blows from January–March bringing fine dust and often thick haze from the Sahara.

The total population in the 1983 census was 695,886. In 1988 it was estimated to have risen to about 780,000 and to be increasing at almost 3.2 per cent per annum. Banjul (1983 census population 44,536) has a City Council. The adjacent district of Kombo St Mary (population 102,858) has its own Council too. The rest of the country is divided for administrative purposes into five Divisions each with a Commissioner. The Divisions are sub-divided into Districts. Each Division has an Area Council responsible for some local services. These Divisions, with their headquarter towns (in brackets) and their populations (1983 census) are:—

Western Division (Brikama)	138,504
North Bank Division (Kerewan)	111,411
Lower River Division (Mansakonko)	55,630
MacCarthy Island Division (Georgetown)	130,041
Upper River Division (Basse)	112,916

There are a number of tribes, the main ones being (in descending order of size) the Mandinka, Fula, Wollof, Jola, and Serahuli. In Banjul the Wollofs form the largest element. An influential community is that of the Akus or Creoles, mainly descended from detribalised Africans liberated in the early nineteenth century during the campaign against the slave trade.

The official language is English and all State education, both at primary and secondary level, is in English, but each tribe has its own language. The principal vernacular languages are Mandingo and Wollof. The predominant religion is Islam.

A free, non compulsory six-year primary education programme is provided by 238 primary schools with a total enrolment of 75,000, representing about 60 per cent of the primary school-age population. Secondary education is provided by 28 secondary technical schools and high schools, the latter offering candidates for West African Examinations Council 'O' and 'A' level examinations. The Government Technical Training Institute offers craft and technician level training in a variety of technical and commercial subjects while vocational training is provided by a number of small, mainly rural institutions run by non government organisations. Post secondary education is available at the Gambia College constituent Schools of Education, Agriculture, Public Health and Nursing. No degree courses are currently available locally.

There are numerous Muslim schools in which Arabic is taught for the better understanding of the Koran. The Christian Mission schools are Roman Catholic, Methodist and Anglican.

Banjul International Airport is at Yundum, 27 km from the city; the main runway is 3,600 metres long. Airlines flying scheduled services are Nigeria Airways, Ghana Airways, Sabena, Air Gambia and

Gambia Airways. In the high tourist season (November–March/April) there are numerous charter flights from several European countries.

Internal communications are by road and river. There are approximately 3,100 km of motorable roads, of which 950 km rank as all-season. There is no railway.

The principal sea port at Banjul serves ocean-going and coastal ships, as well as fishing vessels and river craft. Construction of a new larger jetty and an increased port area were completed in 1985.

The Gambia's main export is groundnuts, groundnut-oil and groundnut-cake. The 1990/91 groundnut crop was about 74,500 tonnes. Gambian farmers also grow sorghum, millet, maize, rice and cotton. Fishing and livestock industries are being developed. There is also a growing tourist industry, with about 71,500 visitors in the 1990/91 season. There are no significant mineral deposits, and industry is still small scale. Gambian trade includes a high proportion of foodstuffs, textiles and other goods imported for re-export to neighbouring countries in the sub-region.

The unit of currency in The Gambia is the dalasi, which was introduced in 1971, replacing the Gambia pound. In August 1991 D15 = £1 sterling. In 1990/91 total imports were valued at D1,569 million and total exports D1,239 million (of which 1,023 million were re-exports).

The Government's financial year runs from July to June.

History

The banks of the Gambia River have been inhabited for many centuries and a number of stone circles of ancient origin exist, but there is insufficient archaeological or written evidence to throw much light on the early history of the country.

During the fifth to eighth centuries AD most of the Sene-Gambian area was part of the empire of Ghana, whose rulers were of the Serahuli tribe, still strongly represented in The Gambia, and had their seat north of the Upper Niger (not in the country now known as 'Ghana', of which only a small sector was an outlying part of the empire). The Ghana empire was gradually superseded by the kingdom of the Songhais, based on the bend of the Niger south of Timbuktu. The Songhai rulers were also of the Serahuli tribe. They became Muslims and vigorously promoted Islam.

About the thirteenth century AD tribes of Mandinka and Susus from the Futa Jallon plateau of Guinea shook off Songhai rule and established themselves in what is now Mali, from Bamako to Timbuktu. They assumed overlordship over the whole Gambia basin. What is now The Gambia was then probably mainly inhabited by Wollofs on the north bank and by Jolas on the south bank. The Mali rulers' names, Keita and Sonko, are still prominent names among Gambian Mandinkas.

The Mali empire declined by about AD 1500 and its Mandinka leaders retired to their former lands in Futa Jallon, but they held influence over The Gambia as recently as the early eighteenth century. Later in that century the area was penetrated by Fula invaders, whose ancestors had come from North Africa and who went on to found the Emirates of Northern Nigeria.

The first Europeans to visit the River Gambia were a Venetian and a Genoese, commissioned by Prince Henry the Navigator of Portugal to lead an expedition along the African coast to the south of Cape Verde. They arrived in the River Gambia in 1455, but only proceeded a short way upstream. In the following year they proceeded farther up the river and got in touch with some of the native chiefs. When they were near the river's mouth 'they cast anchor at an island in the shape of a smoothing iron, where one of the sailors, who had died of fever, was buried. As his name was Andrew, being well loved, they gave the island the name of St Andrew'. For some three centuries afterwards the history of the European occupation of The Gambia was largely the history of this island.

This discovery was followed by attempts on the part of the Portuguese at settlement along the river banks. The number of settlers never appears at any time to have been large and such few as there were intermarried with the local people. The European strain in their descendants rapidly diminished, but Christian communities of Portuguese descent continued to live on the banks of the Gambia in separate villages well into the middle of the eighteenth century.

In 1580 a number of Portuguese took refuge in England, one of whom piloted two English ships to the Gambia and returned with a profitable cargo of hides and ivory in 1587. Thereafter certain London and Devon merchants purchased the exclusive right to trade between the Rivers Senegal and Gambia; this grant was confirmed to the grantees for a period of 10 years by letters patent of Queen Elizabeth. The patentees reported that the Gambia was a river of secret trade and riches, concealed by the Portuguese. In 1612 another attempt by the French to settle in The Gambia ended disastrously owing to sickness and mortality.

Letters patent were subsequently granted to other adventurers, but no attempt was made by the English to explore the river until 1618. The expedition in that year had for its objective the opening of trade with Timbuktu. Leaving his ship in the estuary the commander proceeded with a small party in boats. During his absence the crew of his ship were massacred by the Portuguese, but some of the party managed on their return to make their way overland to Cape Verde and thence to England. In the meantime a relief expedition had been sent out under the command of Richard Jobson, who gave a glowing account of the commercial potentialities of the River Gambia in his *Golden Trade*. But his expedition had resulted in considerable losses and a subsequent voyage, which he made in 1624, proved a complete failure. The patentees made no further attempt to exploit the resources of The Gambia.

In 1651 Cromwell granted a patent to certain London merchants who established a trading post at Bintang. Members of the expedition proceeded as far as the Barokunda Falls in search of gold, but Prince Rupert entered the Gambia with three Royalist ships and captured the patentees' vessels. After this heavy loss the patentees abandoned any further enterprise in The Gambia.

In the meantime, James, Duke of Courland had obtained from various chiefs the cession of St Andrew's Island and land which is now the Half-Die quarter of Banjul. Settlers, merchants and missionaries were sent out by Courland and forts were erected.

After the Restoration, English interest in The Gambia was revived as the result of information which Prince Rupert had obtained in 1652 regarding the reputed existence of gold. A new patent was granted to a number of persons, who were styled the 'Royal Adventurers Trading to Africa' and of whom the most prominent were James, Duke of York and Prince Rupert. The Adventurers sent an expedition to The Gambia which arrived in the river at the beginning of 1661. It occupied what is now 'Dog Island' and erected a temporary fort there. This expedition seized St Andrew's Island from the Courlanders and gave it the name of James Island, which it retains.

In 1677 the French seized the island of Gorée near Dakar, and the history of the next century and a half is the history of a continuous struggle between Britain and France for political and commercial supremacy in the regions of Senegal and The Gambia. By 1681 the French had acquired a small enclave at Albreda opposite James Island. Except for short periods, during which trouble with the natives of Barra or hostilities with Britain compelled them temporarily to abandon the place, they retained their foothold there until 1857.

During the wars with France, James Fort was captured on four occasions by the French—in 1695, 1702, 1704 and 1708, but no attempt was made by them to occupy the fort permanently. At the treaty of Utrecht in 1713 they recognised the right of the British to James Island and their settlements in the River Gambia. During the war of the Spanish Succession, James Fort, Gorée and Saint-Louis were captured on several occasions by British or French forces, and the short lived British province of Senegambia came into existence in 1765. The Treaty of Versailles in 1783 returned Gorée and Saint-Louis to France, leaving James Island to Great Britain and the colony ceased to exist. The Gambia was once more entrusted to the care of the Africa Company which, however, made no attempt to administer it.

When the African slave trade was abolished by Act of Parliament in 1807, the British were in possession of Gorée. With the co-operation of the Royal Navy, the garrison of that fort made strenuous efforts to suppress the traffic in the River Gambia which was being carried on by American and Spanish vessels, but the slavers offered stubborn resistance.

At the close of the Napoleonic Wars Gorée was returned to France. On the recommendation of Sir Charles MacCarthy, the Governor of the British Colony in Sierra Leone, and in order to suppress the traffic in slaves, Captain Alexander Grant of the African Corps was despatched to establish a military post in The Gambia. James Island was found to be unsuitable, and on 23rd April 1816 Grant entered into a treaty with the Chief of Kombo for the cession of the island of Banjul. It was renamed St Mary's Island, and the settlement, which was established there, was called Bathurst (now Banjul) after the then Secretary of State for the Colonies. In 1821 The Gambia was placed under the Government of Sierra Leone and was administered from Freetown until 1843, when it was created a separate colony. Again in 1866 The Gambia and Sierra Leone were united under a single administration until 1888.

Groundnuts first appear as an export from Banjul in 1835. Thereafter they rapidly replaced the beeswax, ivory and skins, which had hitherto formed the main items of external trade.

From the late eighteenth century and throughout the early and middle nineteenth century there was bitter and protracted religious dissension in the rural areas, cutting across tribal groups, between the Marabouts, strict followers of Islam, and the Soninkis, who were not prepared to abjure animist customs and liquor. As a consequence of this civil strife various chiefs sought protection from the British established at Bathurst and treaties between the British and the chiefs were concluded. In 1826 a strip along the north bank of the River opposite Bathurst was ceded to Britain by the Chief of Barra. In 1823 Grant had acquired Lemain Island, about 170 miles up the River, to be made into a settlement for liberated African slaves. He renamed it MacCarthy Island and it became the headquarters of a Wesleyan Mission. In 1840 and 1853 areas of the mainland adjoining St Mary's Island were obtained from the Chief of Kombo for the settlement of discharged soldiers of the West India Regiment and of liberated Africans. In 1857 Albreda, the French enclave in The Gambia which had proved a constant source of friction, was handed over to Britain in return for concessions up the coast. The British Government was at this period desiring to reduce its liabilities and consolidate its areas of influence in West Africa. In 1870, and again in 1876, it entered into negotiations with the French for the exchange of The Gambia for territory further down the coast, but the proposal aroused such opposition in Britain and in The Gambia that it was decided to drop the scheme.

The modern history of The Gambia dates from 1888, when the administration was once again separated from Sierra Leone and a Gambian legislature was established. In the following year delimitation of the boundaries between The Gambia and Senegal was put in hand. For several years thereafter much of the country was unsettled but gradually the Government negotiated treaties of British protection with all the principal chiefs along the River. The last, and most important, was the treaty concluded in 1901 with Musa Mullah, Chief of Fulladu. Thereby it became possible to pass the

Protectorate Ordinance of 1902, under which the whole of The Gambia was brought under the 'protectorate system' except Banjul and Kombo St Mary, which continued to be termed the 'Colony'. Between 1902 and the end of the war in 1945 the history of The Gambia was uneventful. There were years of booming trade during and directly after the 1914–18 war and a period of deep depression during the 1930s, but the general picture was one of political tranquillity and very gentle economic advance. The pattern of the single cash crop, the busy 'trade season', and the wet season, slack in business but devoted to farming, soon became established and has remained very much unchanged ever since.

The political tranquillity associated with the country came to a sudden end on 30th July 1981 when rebels, including dissident members of The Gambia's para military Field Force attempted to take over the country whilst President Jawara was absent in Britain. With Senegalese army help the rebellion was put down.

The attempted coup gave momentum to the longstanding idea of a confederation between Senegal and The Gambia. A joint communique was issued in November 1981 and the Confederation of Senegambia was formally established on 1st February 1982. The Foundation Agreement, while stating that each confederal state should maintain its independence and sovereignty, called for the integration of the armed and security forces, economic and monetary union, co-operation in the fields of communications and external relations and the establishment of joint institutions (ie President, Vice President, Council of Ministers and a Confederal Parliament). While some agreement was reached, there were differing views on the aim of confederation. Senegal saw it as a means towards eventual federation, while Gambia regarded confederation as an end in itself. As a consequence of these fundamental differences of view, the Confederation was dissolved in September 1989. It is proposed that new methods of cooperation be agreed and in May 1991 a Treaty of Cooperation and Friendship was signed by Senegal and The Gambia.

Constitutional development

When the small British settlements on the Gambia River were again formed into a separate Colony in 1888, the usual form of Crown Colony government was set up, with an Executive Council and a Legislative Council. The Executive Council consisted of the Administrator and three other officials; the Legislative Council consisted of the Administrator as President, the three other members of the Executive Council and two nominated unofficial members. In 1893, after the creation of an administration in the Protectorate, the Legislative Council of the Colony was empowered to make rules by Ordinance for the government of the Protectorate, subject to the understanding, as expressed in the Protectorate Ordinance of 1894, that 'all native laws and customs in force in the Protected Territories which are not repugnant to natural justice nor incompatible with any laws of the Colony which applies to the Protectorate shall have the same effect as regulations made under Colony Ordinances'. However the Protectorate did not at first have any representative on the Legislative Council.

The title of 'Administrator' was changed to that of 'Governor' in 1901. By 1902 the only settlement remaining under direct Crown Colony government was the Island of St Mary, of about five square miles, the remaining territories of what was then known as the Colony being administered under the Protectorate system together with the rest of the Protectorate. In 1915 the Legislative Council was enlarged, there being in addition to the Governor, four officials and three nominated unofficial members, one of whom was to be a person to represent the business community and the other two were to be African Christians from Banjul. In 1921 one of the latter was replaced by an African Muslim. In 1932 the Council was further enlarged by the inclusion of an African member nominated by the Banjul Urban District Council (formed in 1931) and by the inclusion also of one of the Commissioners from the Protectorate. Thus the Protectorate was represented for the first time on the Council. Until the end of the 1939/45 war, the Legislative Council continued to consist of the Governor, the Colonial Secretary, five official members (one of whom was a Commissioner from the Protectorate), and four unofficial members.

Under a new Constitution agreed in 1946 the principle of election was introduced for the first time, the Legislative Council consisting of the Governor, the Colonial Secretary, three official members, six unofficial nominated members and one elected member to represent Banjul and Kombo St Mary, which now together formed the Colony for administrative purposes. Of the six unofficial members, two were to represent the Colony and four the Protectorate. There was thus an unofficial majority. In 1947 the membership of the Executive Council was also enlarged to consist of the official members of the Legislative Council and three nominated unofficial members, of whom one was normally the elected member for the Colony. A second elected member was added in 1951.

The first Gambian political party, the Democratic Party, was formed in 1951 by the Reverend John C Faye, and two others, the Muslim Congress Party and P S N'Jie's United Party, in 1952. Under a new constitution in 1954 the Legislative Council was composed of the Governor, five *ex officio* members, two nominated unofficial members, seven elected members from the Colony (four directly and three indirectly elected) and seven elected members from the Protectorate, four of these being chosen by the Divisional Councils and three by the Chiefs. For the first time there was also an unofficial majority on the Executive Council, and three of the six unofficial members were appointed to act as Members to head Ministries.

There was criticism of this Constitution because it gave too much power to the District Commissioners and Chiefs of the Protectorate; and in 1959 representatives of the political parties made proposals which resulted in the 1959 Constitution which came into operation in 1960. The Legislative Council was replaced by a House of Representatives of thirty-four persons, with four *ex-officio* members, three nominated members, seven directly elected members from the Colony, twelve directly elected members from the Protectorate and eight representatives of the Chiefs. There was an elected Speaker and Deputy Speaker. At the same time all six of the unofficial members of the Executive Council were given Ministerial posts. The elections which took place in May 1960 saw the rise of the People's Progressive Party under the leadership of D K (now Sir Dawda) Jawara. Dissatisfaction with the continuing influence of the chiefs, and also with the appointment of the Governor of P S N'Jie as Chief Minister in 1961, resulted in further constitutional changes in April 1962. The office of Premier was created, and the Executive Council consisted of the Governor as Chairman, the Premier and eight other Ministers. The House of Representatives had seven elected members from the Colony and twenty-five from the Protectorate, two members nominated by the Governor after consultation with the Premier (without voting rights), the Attorney-General (also without voting rights) and four members elected by the Chiefs. Finally, in October 1963, The Gambia attained full internal self-government, with a Prime Minister and Cabinet of eight other Ministers. On 18th February 1965 the People's Progressive Party led the country to independence.

Constitution

At Independence, The Gambia had a monarchical constitution with The Queen being represented by a Governor-General. A new Republican Constitution was introduced in April 1970 after a national referendum. This provides for a President, with both executive and ceremonial functions. Since 1982 the President has been elected directly, at an election held together with the General Elections. The Vice-President and other Cabinet Ministers are chosen by the President from among elected MPs. The Vice-President is also leader of the House. Sir Dawda Jawara, who had held chief executive authority initially as Premier and then as Prime Minister since 1962, became the first President of the Republic on 24th April 1970. He was re-elected (indirectly) in 1972 and 1977, and directly in 1982 and 1987.

The Gambia is one of the few countries in Africa having multi-party political activity and Parliamentary representation. The House of Representatives consists of a Speaker and the following other members; 36 'elected members' who are elected on the basis of universal adult suffrage in 36 single-member constituencies of roughly equal populations; five Chiefs' Representative Members who are elected by the Head Chiefs from among their own number by secret vote; the Attorney-General (*ex officio*); and 8 'nominated members' who are appointed by the President but who do not have a vote. Members must have attained the age of 21 years, and be able to speak English well enough to take part in the proceedings of the House. All except the nominated members must be citizens of The Gambia. The Speaker of the House of Representatives is elected from among the members of the House or from persons who are qualified to be elected as members; and when elected from among the former, must vacate his seat in the House. The Speaker has no vote. A voting member must vacate his seat in the House, if in the case of an elected member, he ceases to be registered as a voter in elections of elected members to the House of Representatives or ceases to be qualified to vote in such election; in the case of a Chiefs' Representative Member, if he ceases to be a Head Chief; or in the case of the Attorney-General (unless he is an elected member) if he is removed from office.

The Constitution can be amended by a vote of two-thirds of all the voting members of Parliament. Certain provisions have also to be submitted to and be approved at a referendum by a majority vote of the whole electorate or by two-thirds of all the votes validly cast at the referendum.

The President may at any time prorogue or dissolve the Parliament. Parliament is also dissolved after passing a resolution of no confidence in the Government. The life of a Parliament is not more than five years (extendable in time of war).

There is a Supreme Court which has unlimited original jurisdiction to hear and determine any civil or ciminal proceedings under any law. The Court consists of the Chief Justice and Puisne Judges. The Chief Justice is appointed by the President, and the Puisne Judges are also appointed by him, but acting on the advice of a Judicial Service Commission. In addition there is a Court of Appeal and various subordinate courts.

The Judicial Service Commission consists of the Chief Justice as Chairman, the Chairman of the Public Service Commission and a member appointed by the President. The Public Service Commission consists of a Chairman, Deputy Chairman and four other members appointed by the President.

The Constitution contains provisions for the protection of fundamental rights and freedoms. It provides that a person charged with a criminal offence shall be presumed innocent until proved guilty and shall be given full facilities for defending himself. If any person alleges that any of the provisions of the Constitution relating to these matters are being or are likely to be contravened in relation to him, he has the right of application to the Supreme Court to seek redress.

Government

The House of Representatives comprises 36 elected members, 8 non-voting nominated members, the Attorney-General and 5 Chiefs' Representative members. The People's Progressive Party forms the

Government, with 31 elected members (after 1987 general election). The opposition National Convention Party has 5 seats. Two new opposition parties (The Gambia People's Party and the People's Democratic Organisation for Independence and Socialism) were formed in 1986 and another party (the Gambian People's Democratic Party) in September 1991. Presidential and parliamentary elections will be held in 1992.

HEAD OF STATE

President and Minister of Defence:
His Excellency Alhaji Sir Dawda Kairaba Jawara, GMRG, GCMG

THE CABINET

Vice-President and Minister of Education, Youth, Sport and Culture: The Hon Bakary B Darbo, GORG, MP
Minister of Justice and Attorney General: The Hon Hassan B Jallow, CRG, MP
Minister of Agriculture: Alhaji, The Hon Omar Amadou Jallow, MP
Minister of Trade, Industry and Employment: The Hon Mbemba Jatta, MP
Minister of External Affairs: Alhaji, The Hon Omar Sey, CRG, MP
Minister of Finance and Economic Affairs: Alhaji The Hon Saihou Sabally, CRG, MP
Minister of Health, Labour and Social Welfare: The Hon Mrs Louise N'Jie, CRG, MBE, MP
Minister of Information and Tourism: The Hon Alkali James Gaye, MP
Minister of the Interior: Alhaji The Hon Lamin Kiti Jabang, CRG, MP
Minister of Local Government and Lands: The Hon Landing Jallow Sonko, MP
Minister of Natural Resources, Forestry and Fisheries: The Hon Sarjo Touray, MP
Minister of Works and Communications: The Hon Matthew Yaya Baldeh, MP

HOUSE OF REPRESENTATIVES

Speaker: Alhaji The Hon M B N'Jie
Clerk of the House: Mr R Sowe

JUDICIARY

Chief Justice: The Hon E Olayinka Ayoola

MINISTRIES, PERMANENT SECRETARIES ETC

President's Office:
Secretary General—Alhaji Abdou Janha, CRG
Secretary to the Cabinet—Mr G Gorrie-N'Diaye
Permanent Secretary—Mr Baba Jange
Vice President's Office:
Permanent Secretary—Mr Bernard Baldeh
Agriculture
Permanent Secretary—Mr Yaya Jallow
Defence:
Permanent Secretary—Mr Abdoulie Sallah
Trade, Industry and Employment:
Permanent Secretary—Mr Mamour Jagne
Education, Youth, Sport and Culture:
Permanent Secretary—Mr Kalim Bayo
External Affairs:
Permanent Secretary—Mr Sulayman Jack
Finance and Economic Affairs:
Permanent Secretary—Mr Alieu N'Gum
Health, Labour and Social Welfare:
Permanent Secretary—Mr Lamin Samateh
Information and Tourism:
Permanent Secretary—Mr Ebraima Manneh
Interior:
Permanent Secretary—Mr Sulayman Ceesay
Justice:
Solicitor General and Legal Secretary—Mrs Amie Bensouda
Local Government and Lands:
Permanent Secretary—Mr Amadou Taal
Personal Management Office:
Permanent Secretary—Mr S A R N'Jai
Natural Resources, Forestry and Fisheries:
Permanent Secretary—Mr Bolong Sonko
Works and Communications:
Permanent Secretary—Mr Phoday S Jarjussey

Ghana

Capital: Accra

Ghana, named after the ancient African Empire in which, it is thought by some historians, the people of the country had their origins, comprises the area in West Africa formerly known as the Gold Coast (the Gold Coast Colony, Ashanti and the Northern Territories) together with that part of Togoland which had been administered by the British Government under United Nations trusteeship. Its area is 237,873 sq km, almost the same as that of the United Kingdom of Great Britain and Northern Ireland. The whole area lies in the tropics. In the Northern Territories, the country is open and undulating and the climate is warm and fairly dry. The flat eastern coastal belt is hot and humid. In most areas the mean maximum temperature is highest in March (absolute maximum 109°F) and lowest in January or August (absolute minimum 51°F). Coastal regions normally experience temperatures between 24°C (75°F) and 35°C (95°F) throughout the year. Annual rainfall varies in the different regions from 700 mm to 2,150 mm. The Harmattan wind affects the climate of various parts of Ghana from November to April. The principal river system in the country is formed by the Black, White and Red Voltas which merge to form the River Volta on which is situated the Volta Lake, some 402 km long and 8,482 sq km in extent, created by damming the river at Akosombo. Other major rivers are the Pra and the Ankobra. There are no high mountains but several ranges of hills rise to a maximum of about 900 m. The central forest area is broken up into heavily wooded ridges and valleys.

Agriculture forms the basis of the economy. Crops include cocoa—the largest single source of revenue—palmoil, cassava, yams, rice, maize, millet, groundnuts, coconut, fruit and vegetables. Cattle are reared in the north and there are extensive fisheries. Timber, gold, diamonds, manganese and bauxite are the principal natural resources.

At the time of the census taken in 1960 the population was estimated to be 6,726,815 and at June 1966 7,945,000. A further census was held in 1970 and the published figure was 8,545,561. A census taken in March 1984 gave the population as 12,205,574. The country is divided into ten regions: Greater Accra, Ashanti, Brong Ahafo, Central, Eastern, Northern, Upper East, Upper West, Volta and Western. Ghana's population is estimated to be 15 million.

English is the official language and is used for instruction in schools from Primary Class II upwards. The principal indigenous language group is Akan, of which Twi and Fanti are the most commonly used forms. Ga is spoken in the Accra Region and Ewe in Volta. The Mole-Dagbani language group is one of a number spoken in Northern Ghana. The principal religions are: Christian 42 per cent; Animist 38 per cent; Islam 12 per cent; others 7 per cent. Primary education is free and universal.

The cedi is the unit of currency, reaching 378 = $1 in October 1991.

The capital city of Ghana is Accra. The 1984 census provisional population total for the Greater Accra Region (including Tema) was 1,420,066. For the other Regions, the 1984 population figures were: Western 1,116,930; Central 1,145,520; Volta 1,201,095; Eastern 1,677,483; Ashanti 2,089,083; Brong Ahafo 1,179,407; Northern 1,162,645; Upper East 771,584; Upper West 439,161. The principal ports are Tema in the Greater Accra Region (approximately 32 km from Accra) and Takoradi in the Western Region (approximately 225 km from Accra). The main shipping line is the Black Star Line. The only international airport is at Accra, ten km from the city centre (length of runway 2,880 m) and the country's national airline is Ghana Airways Corporation. There are also internal airports at Takoradi (runway 1,710 m); Kumasi (runway 1,350 m); Tamale (runway 1,260 m). There are 965 route km of 3ft 6ins gauge railway, and the mortorable road is 32,180 km of which 3,757 km are bitumenised and 5,775 km gravel truck road. Broadcasting and television facilities are provided by the Ghana Broadcasting Corporation. There are two State-owned daily newspapers and an increasing number of independent newspapers. Ghana is provided with electricity by hydro-electricity schemes at Akosombo on the Volta river and at Kpong where a new power station came on stream in 1981.

History

The oral traditions of the tribes at present occupying the country indicate that their arrival there was only comparatively recent, historically speaking. They appear to have originated to the north of the present boundaries of Ghana and to have migrated southwards, roughly over the period A.D. 1200 to 1600. The identity of the previous inhabitants can only be conjectured; it is certain, however, that the country had been occupied by peoples of Negro stock. The discovery of neolithic and, more rarely, palaeolithic relics points to the country having been occupied at an even earlier date by peoples of a different race; but no clues have been found to the physical type of these prehistoric inhabitants.

The Gold Coast first became known in Europe through Portuguese navigators who visited the country in the second half of the 15th century in search of gold, ivory and spices. The first recorded

English trading voyage to the Coast was made by Thomas Windham in 1553 and in the course of the next three centuries the English, French, Danes, Swedes, Dutch, Germans and Portuguese all controlled various parts of the Coast at different periods. By 1750 only the English, the Dutch and the Danes had settlements on the Coast. In 1821 the British Government assumed control of the British trading settlements and on 6th March 1844 the Chiefs in the immediate neighbourhood agreed to adhere to a Bond from which British power and jurisdiction were generally derived. The British Settlements were at that time controlled from Sierra Leone. The Danes relinquished their settlements in 1850 and in 1871 the Dutch ceded theirs to the British. Under a new Charter in 1874 the Colony was still limited to the forts and settlements, but other territory under British influence was declared a Protectorate. In 1896 treaties of trade and protection were concluded with several tribes north of Ashanti and a Protectorate over the area now constituting the Northern, Upper West and Upper East Regions was established in 1898. Boundary Commissions in 1898 and 1899 delimited the borders of the Gold Coast and neighbouring French and German African territories, and the area of British jurisdiction was clarified in 1901 by Orders in Council which declared as a Colony by settlement all territories in the Gold Coast south of Ashanti, declared Ashanti a Colony by conquest, and the Northern Territories a Protectorate under the Foreign Jurisdiction Act of 1890. It was thus not until 1901 that Britain assumed full responsibility for the government of the Gold Coast and its hinterland. In 1922 a part of the adjoining German territory of Togoland was placed under British administration by a League of Nations Mandate and after the Second World War was placed by agreement under the trusteeship system of the United Nations. From that time it was administered by Britain as part of the Gold Coast up to the date of independence in 1957.

Constitutional development

The first Legislative Council was set up in 1850 in what was then the Colony Area; the first African unofficial members were appointed to the Legislative Council the same year and by 1916 the unofficial side of the Council consisted of three Europeans, three Paramount Chiefs and three other Africans. In 1925 a new Constitution was promulgated which introduced the principles of direct election in municipalities and indirect election in the provinces of the Colony area.

The next major development was the Burns Constitution of 1946. Until then Ashanti, and until 1951 the Northern Territories, were administered directly by the Governor; the 1946 Constitution brought in the first Legislative Council in British Africa to have a majority of African members. In 1948 disturbances occurred in the southern parts of the country and a Commission of Enquiry (the Watson Commission) was set up to make a thorough investigation into the general conditions in the country. As a result an all-African Committee was established to deal with the whole structure of government machinery from village area councils to the Executive Council and the Governor's reserved powers. The proposals of the Coussey Committee were generally accepted by the British Government and in 1951 elections took place under a new Constitution based on its recommendations. This provided for an Executive Council or Cabinet with the Governor as President, and a Legislative Assembly with some members representing special interests and 75 elected members with a fixed ratio between the Colony, Ashanti and the Northern Territories. In 1952 the office of Prime Minister was created; in 1953 proposals for further constitutional reform were submitted to the British Government and a new Constitution was introduced in 1954 with an all-African Cabinet and a Legislature of 104 members elected by direct suffrage. This was the Constitution in force up to the date of Independence. The Governor retained only certain reserved powers, including responsibility in his discretion for external affairs (including Togoland under United Kingdom trusteeship) defence and the police. On 11th May 1956 the Colonial Secretary announced that if a general election were held in the Gold Coast the British Government would be prepared to accept a motion calling for independence within the Commonwealth passed by a reasonable majority in a newly elected Legislature, and then to declare a firm date for the attainment of independence within the Commonwealth. A general election was accordingly held in July 1956, and Dr Nkrumah's Party (the Convention People's Party) was returned with a majority of over two-thirds of the Legislative Assembly. The new assembly approved a motion requesting the British Government to initiate the legislation. In May 1956 a plebiscite was held under United Nation's auspices in the Trust territory of Togoland as a result of which the United Nations agreed that the Trusteeship Agreement should end on the attainment of Independence by the Gold Coast. On the 6th March 1957 Ghana attained independence as a fully self-governing Member of the Commonwealth with the Queen as Sovereign (the first British dependency in Sub-Saharan Africa to do so). It has since remained non-aligned.

Following a plebiscite held in April 1960 a Republican Constitution was adopted by the National Assembly on 29th June 1960. Ghana became a republic on 1st July 1960. On 21st February 1964, Ghana formally became a one-party state, the national party being the Convention People's Party. A general election was held in June 1965 and all 198 candidates nominated by the CPP were returned unopposed.

On 24th February 1966 a *coup d'état* by the army and the police overthrew President Nkrumah while he was visiting Peking. The National Liberation Council consisting of four representatives each from the army and police was set up under the chairmanship of Major-General J A Ankrah, subsequently appointed Lieutenant-General. (Lieutenant-General E K Kotoka, one of the members of the NLC was killed on 17th April 1967 in an abortive coup. He was not replaced on the NLC). The NLC dissolved the National Assembly and the CPP and repealed the Constitution. On 18th November 1966, the NLC appointed a Constitutional Commission, headed by the Chief Justice, to draft a new Constitution. This finished its work in January 1968, and the draft Constitution was published the next month. In December of that year the NLC set up a Constituent Assembly to amend and approve the draft.

In April 1969 General Ankrah, resigned from the NLC and was replaced as Chairman by Brigadier A A Afrifa.

The ban on political activity was lifted on 1st May 1969 and in the general elections held on 29th August 1969, Dr K A Busia's Progress Party won 105 seats, and the National Alliance of Liberals, led by Mr K A Gbedemah 29, the remaining 6 seats being won by minority parties. Dr Busia was sworn in as Prime Minister.

A new constitution was promulgated by the Constituent Assembly on 22nd August 1969, and the NLC formally handed over to the civilian Government on 1st October 1969. A three-man presidential commission was inaugurated on 3rd September 1969. It was dissolved on 30th July 1970. A month later Mr E Akufo-Addo was chosen as president by the Presidential Electoral College.

On 13th January 1972, during a period of increasing economic difficulty, the Busia administration was ousted in an army *cop d'état* led by Colonel I K Acheampong. The Constitution was withdrawn, the National Assembly and political parties proscribed and the Presidency abolished. The supreme governing body from 1972 until 9th October 1975 was the National Redemption Council, composed mainly of military personnel. On 19th April 1972 Colonel Acheampong, Commander in Chief of the Armed Forces, became Head of State, On 9th October 1975 a new seven-man Supreme Military Council was established by decree. It consisted of the Head of State, Inspector General of Police, Commander Border Guards and service commanders. The NRC was reconstituted as a second tier body, including the members of the SMC, Central Government Commissioners (Ministers) and the Commanders of the First and Second Infantry Brigades. Rule was by decree. On 7th April 1976 the SMC promoted Colonel Acheampong to the rank of full General.

On 5th July 1978 General Acheampong was forced to resign as Head of State and Chairman of the SMC. He also retired from the Armed Forces. He was succeeded by Lt General (later General) F W K Akuffo, Chief of Defence Staff. General Akuffo recognised that the greatest challenge facing the nation was the perilous state of the economy and undertook to tackle economic problems as a first priority. The government changed from the old to a new cedi in March 1979.

On coming to power General Akuffo promised a return to civilian rule in July 1979. On 31st July 1978 he made his second broadcast to the nation and announced that the SMC would hand over power in 1979 to a transitional national Government which would be fully representative on the basis of free elections with no institutional representation of the armed forces or the police in the Government. Activity by political parties was reintroduced at the beginning of January 1979. A constitutional Committee (set up under General Acheampong) was reconstituted and worked out a new Constitution. Elections for both Parliament and President were set for 18th June 1979.

On 4th June 1979 *a coup d'état* by junior officers and other ranks of the Armed Forces took power from General Akuffo. An Armed Forces Revolutionary Council was formed, chaired by Flight Lieutenant Jerry Rawlings. Civilian commissioners of the Akuffo regime were confirmed in office but a number of senior figures of the two previous governments, including Generals Acheampong, Akuffo and Afrifa were executed. Elections for a civilian government were allowed to proceed as planned on 18th June but the return to civilian rule was postponed to 1st October 1979. The People's National Party (PNP) won a majority of the Parliamentary seats and Dr Hilla Limann of the PNP was elected President-designate. Dr Limann took up office on 24th September 1979.

On 31st December 1981, the Government of Dr Limann was overthrown in a *coup d'état* which brought back into power Flight Lieutenant Jerry Rawlings. The Constitution was suspended and political parties banned. A new ruling body called the Provisional National Defence Council (PNDC) was formed, and Secretaries were appointed to head the Ministries and Regions. The principal themes of the new Government were the need for a greater degree of participatory democracy to be achieved through People's and Workers' Defence Committees, renamed Committees for the Defence of the Revolution in December 1984; and a campaign against corruption and profiteering. The new Government was also faced with deep and potentially destabilising economic problems. In 1983 the PNDC introduced an austerity budget and a 4-year economic recovery programme (ERP). The International Monetary Fund subsequently agreed to loan Ghana approximately US$360m Special Drawing Rights over twelve months. At a meeting of the World Bank Consultative Group in November 1983 donors pledged $150m in new aid. There was a second austerity budget in 1984, accompanied by further devaluations. A second IMF Stand-by Agreement of $150m was negotiated in August 1984 and at a World Bank Consultative Group meeting in December 1984 donors pledged $450m. The 1985 budget was somewhat less austere but the cedi was devalued further, the Government continued to take the line that more sacrifice was needed. At the World Bank Consultative Group meeting in November 1985 donors pledged $517m in new aid. The PNDC then launched a medium-term policy framework for 1986/88 which is now being implemented. At the World Bank Consultative group meetings in May 1987 donors pledged $818.6m in new aid. In November 1988, a three year arrangement under the IMF Enhanced Structural Adjustment Facility was approved in an amount equivalent to SDR 368.1 million.

This agreement secured in March 1989 $971m of aid, with $500m from bilateral donors and over $400m from multilateral donors including the World Bank.

Ghana hosted the 1991 Summit Conference of Foreign Ministers of the Non-Aligned Movement from 2nd to 9th September.

The PNDC has announced a programme to return the country to constitutional rule. Presidential and Parliamentary elections are to be held in November/December 1992, according to a programme outlined by the Government. A national referendum on a draft constitution, being prepared by a Consultative Assembly is scheduled for 28th April. The ban on party politics is expected to be lifted on 18th May 1992.

Historical List

(A full detailed list is shown in the 1978 Edition)

CHAIRMAN OF PRESIDENTIAL COMMISSION

Brigadier (later Lt-Gen) A A Afrifa, DSO, 3rd September 1969 to 30th July 1970

PRESIDENTS

Mr E A Akufo-Addo, MV, 31st August 1970 to 13th January 1972

Dr H Limann 24th September 1979 to 31st December 1981

CHAIRMAN OF THE NATIONAL REDEMPTION COUNCIL

General I K Acheampong from 19th April 1972 to 9th October 1975

CHAIRMAN OF THE SUPREME MILITARY COUNCIL

General I K Acheampong from 9th October 1975 to 5th July 1978

Lt General F W K Akuffo 5th July 1978 to 3rd June 1979

CHAIRMAN OF THE ARMED FORCES REVOLUTIONARY COUNCIL

Flt Lt J J Rawlings 4th June 1979 to 24th September 1979

PRIME MINISTER

Dr K A Busia, MP, 25th September 1969 to 13th January 1972

CHAIRMAN OF THE PROVISIONAL NATIONAL DEFENCE COUNCIL

Flt Lt J J Rawlings, 31st December 1981 to date

The Government

THE PROVISIONAL NATIONAL DEFENCE COUNCIL

Chairman: Flt-Lt J J Rawlings

Members: Mr Justice D F Annan, Mr Ebo Tawiah, Alhaji Mahama Iddrisu, Mr P V Obeng, Captain Kojo Tsikata (Rtd), Lt-Gen A Quainoo, Dr Mary Grant.

SECRETARIES IN CHARGE OF MINISTRIES

Foreign Affairs: Dr Obed Asamoah

Chieftaincy Affairs: Nana Akuoko Sarpong

Finance and Economic Planning: Dr Kwesi Botchwey

Defence: Alhaji Mahama Iddrisu

Energy (Formerly Fuel & Power): Mr Ato Ahwoi

Local Government: Mr Kwamena Ahwoi

Education and Culture: Dr Mary Grant (also PNDC member)

Youth and Sports: General Arnold Quainoo (also PNDC member), special responsibility

Transport and Communications: Mr Kwame Peprah

Works and Housing: Col Kenneth Ampratwum

Industries, Science and Technology: Naval Captain K A Butah

Justice & Attorney General: Mr E G Tanoh (Acting)

Health: Commodore Steve Obimpeh

Information: Mr Kofi Totobi Quakyi

Lands and Natural Resources: Mr J A Danso

Roads and Highways: Colonel Richard Commey

Mobilisation and Social Welfare: Mr D S Boateng

Interior: Colonel (rtd) E M Osei-Owusu

CDR (Committees for the Defence of the Revolution) Affairs: Mr Huudu Yahaya

Trade: John Bawa

Education: Ibrahim Adam (Acting)

SECRETARIES IN CHARGE OF REGIONS

Western: Mr J R E Amenlemah

Northern: Mr Thomas Ibrahim

Upper West: Mr Yelibora-Antumini

Greater Accra: Nii Okaija Adamafio

Eastern: Mr Fred Ohene-Kena

Volta: Dr Francis Agbley

Central: Mr Ato Austin

Upper East: Mr Lionel Kukundab Mollrila

Brong-Ahafo: Mr Owusu-Acheampong

Ashanti: Mr J Y Ansah (Acting)

Grenada

Capital: St George's

Most southerly of the Windward Islands, Grenada lies approximately 144 km (90 miles) north of Trinidad and 109 km (68 miles) south-south-west of St Vincent. The Island is about 33 km (21 miles) in length and 19 km (12 miles) in breadth at its extremes and has an area of 310 sq km (120 square miles). Between it and St Vincent lie the islets known as the Grenadines, some of which are included in the territory of St Vincent and some in that of Grenada. The largest of the latter is Carriacou, 33 sq km (13 square miles) in area.

Grenada is mountainous and very picturesque, its ridges of hills covered with thick forest and brushwood. The mountains are chiefly volcanic, running off in spurs from a central backbone range which extends along the entire length of the island. The highest peak is Mount St Catherine, 840 m (2,756 feet). The terrain slopes gradually to the east and south-east coast.

The island contains a number of mineral and other springs and is well watered by quick-flowing streams. A small lake, the Grand Etang, lies at a height of 530 m (1,740 feet) above sea level in an old crater near the summit of a mountain and is one of the most remarkable features of the island.

The climate is good with a dry season from January to May and a wet season for the rest of the year. During the dry season when the trade winds prevail the climate is especially agreeable, the temperature falling as low as 18°C (65°F) at night. During the wet season, when the temperature rises to as high as 32°C (90°F) on the low lands, there is little variation between night and day. Although this season is oppressive, it is not unhealthy. The rainfall varies considerably, the average for the coastal districts being about 1,500 mm (60 inches) and in the mountainous interior as much as 3,750 mm (150 inches). The average for Carriacou is above 1,125 mm (45 inches).

Population

The population in the middle of 1991 was estimated to be 97,000. The birth rate in 1989 was 33 per thousand of population and the death rate was 8.3 per thousand. The majority of the population are of African and mixed descent. There is a small European population, a number of Indians and a small community of the descendents of early European settlers. The people are predominantly Roman Catholic, although there is a substantial Anglican minority. English is universally spoken. St George's, the principal town, lies in the south-west of the island and has a fine natural harbour. The town of St George's has an estimated population of 7,500. The other towns are Gouyave, Victoria, Grenville, Sauteurs, and Hillsborough in Carriacou.

Health

Located in St George's and operated by the Ministry of Health are the General Hospital (242 beds), a sanatorium and homes for handicapped children and geriatric patients. At St Andrew's the Princess Alice Hospital provides 60 beds and the Princess Royal Hospital at Carriacou 40. There are six main health centres at St George's, Gouyave, Sauteurs, Grenville, St David's and Carriacou. Maternity and Child Welfare work is carried out at 30 District Medical Stations, each of which is in the charge of a Nurse-Midwife and is visited by one of the territory's 11 District Medical Officers who hold general and specialist clinics. There is also a midwifery unit attached to the Gouyave Health Centre and another in Sauteurs. A dental clinic operates in six of the parishes. Medical and dental treatment in Government hospitals and clinics is free. There are 50 doctors, 6 dentists, 37 district nurses/midwives, 120 nurses, 41 nurse assistants and 140 student nurses.

The insect control programme, launched in 1953, appeared to eradicate malaria in the island but there was a small outbreak in 1978; it has not reappeared since. By 1956 *Aedes aegypti* (the yellow fever mosquito) was firmly under control but it has since reappeared. After susceptibility studies a new programme to eradicate the *Aedes aegypti* was started with assistance from PAHO/WHO in 1970. This is having some success and there has been a lowering of the *aegypti* index.

Communications

The well-sheltered natural harbour of St George's is the territory's chief port. The inner harbour possesses a 240 m (800 ft) long pier with a minimum depth of 9 m (30 ft) alongside. The eastern side of the pier can accommodate two ocean-going vessels with a length of 120–150 m (400–500 ft), whilst the western side provides berths for small craft. The portion of the harbour known as the Lagoon affords ideal anchorage for yachts and facilities for repairs and careenage. Prickly Bay on the south-east coast is also a port for yachts. A marina with slipway, chandlery and some repair facilities is located in Prickly Bay, where there is a marine travel lift capable of lifting 35 tons. A modern marina is operated by the

Grenada Yacht Services with Syncro lifts capable of lifting ships up to 230 tons. A new yachting marina has been built at Secret Harbour, south of St George's. Several international shipping lines provide regular cargo services from British, European, Canadian and US ports. The ships of Geest Industries which call every other week carry 12 round-trip passengers between Wales and Grenada. Three hundred and forty cruise ships visited Grenada during the 1990/1991 season.

Passenger and cargo services between the territory and neighbouring islands are provided by numerous small motor vessels and auxiliary schooners.

An international airport at Point Salines in the south west of the island with a runway of 2,940 m (9,800 feet) became operational at the end of 1984. Leeward Islands Air Transport (LIAT) operates daily scheduled services to other parts of the Caribbean. British Airways operates a weekly service to London via Antigua and BWIA fly to Trinidad, London via Trinidad and to the USA. A daily American Airlines flight to San Juan began in June 1990. A small airstrip, restricted to aircraft of maximum permissible weight not exceeding 12,000 lbs, is located at Lauriston in Carriacou. LIAT operates daily scheduled services linking Carriacou with Grenada and St Vincent. These services are in the process of being extended.

The island has a good network of more than 965 km (600 miles) of all types of roads. Grenada is crossed by a main road and another runs completely round the island. Ongoing road improvement programmes since 1984 have provided first class roads linking the new airport in the south west with St George's and Grenville. There are no railways in the territory. As from 1st November 1988 Grenada Telecommunications Ltd. was formed, jointly owned by the Government of Grenada and Cable and Wireless (WI) Ltd (28 per cent/72 per cent). It operates 9 fully automatic exchanges connected by trunk lines and digital and analogue radio links. About 12,000 telephones are in use. The company also provides telex, telegraph and facsimile services. International telecommunications services are provided by a modern digital microwave system interconnecting with the Eastern Caribbean Microwave System which is owned and operated by Cable and Wireless (WI) Ltd. There are 6 district Post Offices and 44 Postal Agencies.

The Economy

All towns on the island and many villages are served by a piped water supply. The Island's electricity is generated and distributed by Grenlec, a company formed in 1961 between the Government and the Commonwealth Development Corporation. The Government now owns the company.

The major crops are cocoa, nutmegs and bananas. A wide variety of other crops can be grown and efforts are being made to increase the production of fruit and vegetables for local consumption and export.

There is limited livestock production on the island and most meat and dairy products are imported.

Recently priority has been given to the development of the fishing industry and diversification.

The territory has few manufacturing industries. The Grenada Sugar Factory Ltd. produces unrefined sugar for local consumption. Sugar cane is grown primarily by small farmers. Rum is beginning to be exported. There is a flour and feed mill, a food canning factory, a cigarette factory, soft drinks factories, a brewery, garment manufacturers, a coffee processing plant, a fruit, juice and vegetable canning plant, a fish processing plant, and a spice grinding plant. A small industrial park has been set up in Frequente and a new park is under construction in St Andrews.

There are eight major trade unions and marketing and trading co-operatives.

The Government owns approximately 75 per cent of Grenada's estimated 4,000 ha (10,000 acres) of rain forest. The Government reserves are located chiefly in the water catchment area in the Central Highlands and exploitation is confined to not more than 40 ha (100 acres) annually. Since 1957, approximately 320 ha (800 acres) of Government forest lands have been reafforested with Blue Mahoe, Teak and Honduras Mahogany and other species. *Pinus caribaea var. hondurensis* is undergoing intensive research with good promise.

The unit of currency is the East Carribean Dollar.

Principal domestic exports by value and quantity for 1989 are as follows:

Commodity	*Value* *EC$ in millions*	*Quantity* *'000 lbs*
Cocoa	6.75	2.9
Nutmeg & mace	37.6	4.3
Banana	10.8	16.4
Fresh fruit	4.6	—

Total value of imports in 1989 was EC$316 million, total exports EC$84.24 million.

Education

Although school attendance is not compulsory, a total of 19,988 children received primary education in 1988 at 57 primary schools. The Island has 17 secondary schools with a total enrolment of 5,457 pupils at the end of 1988.

In July 1989 the Grenada National College for Post-Secondary education was formed by amalgamating the Institute of Further Education, the Technical and Vocational Institute, the Teacher Training College, the Domestic Arts Institute, the National Handicrafts Institute, the Science and Technology Institute, and the Continuing Education Programme. The Mirabeau Agricultural school, the School of Nursing and the School of Pharmacology will be incorporated in due course.

There are 24 handicraft or housecraft centres. There is a free public library in St George's. A private University School of Medicine has been established in St George's.

The Media

Following the demise of the Windward Islands Broadcasting Service in 1971 the Government-owned Radio Grenada came into being on 1st January 1972. It was known as Radio Free Grenada from 13th March 1979 until 25th October 1983. The radio station was destroyed during the military action and returned to the air from temporary premises as Spice Island Radio. It resumed the name Radio Grenada in early 1984. The Government-owned Grenada Television broadcasts throughout the island.

History

Discovered by Christopher Columbus on 15th August 1498, the island now known as Grenada was given the name of Conception. In 1609 a company of London merchants attempted to form a settlement, but were so harassed by the Caribs that they were compelled to abandon the attempt. In 1650 Du Parquet, Governor of Martinique, purchased the island from a French company and established a settlement at St George's. Finding the venture did not pay, Du Parquet sold the island in 1657 to the Comte de Cerrillac and in 1674 it was annexed to France, the proprietors receiving compensation for their claims.

Following surrender to a British squadron under Admiral Rodney in 1762, the island passed under British dominion, and was formally ceded to the British Crown by the Treaty of Paris on 10th February 1763. Sixteen years later it was retaken by the French under the Comte D'Estaing, only to be restored to Great Britain by the Treaty of Versailles in 1783. In 1795–6 it was the scene of a rebellion against the British rule by a French colonist. The Lieutenant-Governor and 47 other British subjects were massacred by the rebels. Sir Ralph Abercromby suppressed the uprising in June 1796 and the ringleaders were executed

Grenada joined the Federation of the West Indies as an independent member on its formation on 3rd January 1958, and remained a member until its dissolution following an Order in Council dated 23rd May 1962.

Following decisions taken at a conference in London in April and May 1966, subsequently endorsed by a Resolution of the Legislative Council, provision was made in the West Indies Act 1967, under which Grenada assumed a status of association with the United Kingdom on 3rd March 1967. Grenada became fully self-governing in all internal affairs; the United Kingdom remained responsible for defence and external affairs.

At a General Election held in Grenada in February 1972 the Premier made the proposal to seek early independence the first item on his party's programme. His party won 13 out of 15 seats in the House of Representatives. He then asked the British Government to recommend that by Order in Council made under S10(2) of the West Indies Act 1967 Her Majesty terminate the status of association of Grenada with the United Kingdom. Following a Constitutional Conference in May 1973, Grenada became an independent nation within the Commonwealth on 7th February, 1974. Grenada became a member of the UN on 17th September, 1974.

On 13th March 1979 the government of Sir Eric Gairy was ousted in his absence in the United States by the New Jewel Movement led by Mr Maurice Bishop, the Leader of the Opposition. Mr Bishop became Prime Minister of the People's Revolutionary Government (PRG).

In October 1983 disagreements within the PRG gave rise to violence and the death of Mr Bishop, whose government was replaced by a Revolutionary Military Council. These events prompted the intervention of Caribbean and United States forces. The Governor-General as the sole remaining constitutional authority installed an Advisory Council to act as a provisional government with a remit to administer the country and to set in train elections for a new parliament and government. At the general election held on 3rd December 1984 the New National Party won 14 of the 15 seats, and its leader, Mr Herbert Blaize, became Prime Minister. Defections, for various reasons, from the NNP had reduced the number of their seats in Parliament to 9 by April 1987. The other 6 MPs, led by George Brizan, formed the National Democratic Congress in October 1987.

At the NNP Annual Convention in January 1989 Mr Blaize lost the leadership of the party to his Minister of Works Dr Keith Mitchell. In July 1989 the Prime Minister dismissed Dr Mitchell from Government. Two NNP Ministers resigned in protest. Subsequently Mr Blaize formed his own Party, The National Party (TNP) taking with him his six remaining Ministers.

Prime Minister, Mr Blaize died on 19th December 1989. He had been ill for some time. Mr Blaize's deputy, Mr Ben Jones, was sworn in as Prime Minister. A General Election was held on 13th March 1990 which resulted in the NDC, led by Nicholas Brathwaite, winning 7 of the 15 seats. After defections from the 3 opposition parties, the NDC now holds a comfortable 11–4 majority

Constitution

The constitution at independence provided for a Governor-General appointed by Her Majesty The Queen and for a bicameral legislature. The Senate consisted of 13 Senators, 7 of whom were appointed on the advice of the Prime Minister, 3 on the advice of the Leader of the Opposition and 3 on the advice of the Prime Minister after he had consulted interests which he considered Senators should be selected to represent. The Constitution did not specify the number of elected members of the House of Representatives, but the country is divided into 15 constituencies.

The Cabinet consisted of a Prime Minister, who had to be a member of the House of Representatives, and such other Ministers as the Governor-General appointed on the advice of the Prime Minister

Following the Revolution of 13th March 1979, the government suspended the Constitution on 28th March 1979, made provision for HM the Queen to remain Head of State represented in Grenada by the Governor-General, established a Supreme Court of Grenada, provided for the continuity of laws, and established a People's Revolutionary Army. The PRG issued a series of People's Laws.

Under the provisional government instituted in November 1983 the 1974 independence constitution was partially reinstated. Some of the PRG's People's Laws were revoked. The provisional government issued a number of ordinances. The 1974 Constitution was almost fully reinstated following the December 1984 elections

CABINET (MARCH 1990)

Prime Minister, Minister of Finance, External Affairs, National Security, Carriacou & Petit Martinique Affairs and Political Unity: Rt Hon Nicholas A Brathwaite

Minister of Agriculture, Fisheries, Forestry, Lands, Trade, Industry, Production and Energy: Hon George I Brizan

Attorney General and Minister of Legal Affairs, Local Government: Hon Francis R Alexis

Minister of Works, Communications and Public Works: Hon Phinsley St Louis

Minister of Health, Community Development, Physical Planning and Co-operatives: Hon Michael Andrew

Minister of Tourism, Civil Aviation, Women's Affairs, Culture, Youth Affairs and Sport: Hon Joan Purcell

Minister of Labour, Employment, Social Security: Hon Edzell Thomas

Minister of State, Ministry of Finance: Sen The Hon Tillman Thomas

Minister of Education and Information: Hon Carlyle Glean

PARLIAMENTARY SECRETARIES

Parliamentary Secretary for Agriculture and Fisheries: Sen Denis Noel

Parliamentary Secretary for Health, Community Development: Sen Norton Noel

Parliamentary Secretary for Tourism: Sen Godfrey Ventour

Parliamentary Secretary for Labour: Sen Alleyne Walker

Guyana

Capital: Georgetown

Guyana lies on the north-east shoulder of the South American continent between latitudes 1° and 9° N. and longitudes 56° and 62° W. It is 214,970 sq km in area. The Atlantic sea-coast stretches for 434 km; from it the land extends southwards into the interior for about 724 km. Its borders are with Venezuela to the west, Brazil to the south and Surinam to the east. The country has three distinct geographical areas—the coastal belt, the forest area and the savannah zone. The narrow coastal belt, which is generally about 16 km in width (though it runs inland for up to 64 km along the banks of the main rivers), and which accounts for only 4 per cent of the total area, is intensively cultivated and contains 90 per cent of the population. It lies 1 to 1.5 m below sea level at high tide and is dependent upon an elaborate system of dams, walls and groynes to protect it from the sea. The flatness of the coast necessitates an equally elaborate system of drainage canals.

Behind the coastal zone the land rises, gently at first, to an area of dense rain forest and mountains, Minerals are found in this area, the most valuable being bauxite, diamonds, gold and manganese. In the south-west the forest gives way to some open savannah country, usually known as the Rupununi, although the Rupununi District is much more extensive than the savannah area. The highest point is Mount Roraima (2,728 m) in the Pakaraima range. The sparse population of this area is predominantly Amerindian.

Guyana is notable for its mighty rivers, the four best known being the Demerara, Berbice, Essequibo and Corentyne, of which the Essequibo is by far the largest. They are of limited navigational value because of the many rapids, bars and falls. Georgetown, the capital, lies at the mouth of the Demerara. The left bank of the Corentyne forms the boundary with Surinam. The most spectacular of the numerous waterfalls and rapids is Kaieteur Fall on the Potaro River which has a drop of 222 m, nearly five times the height of Niagara Falls. In the north-west several rivers flow north-east towards the mouth of the Orinoco while part of the Rupunini district lies in the Amazon basin.

The climate is tropical, and there is very little temperature variation at the coast, where temperatures above 32°C (90°F) or below 24°C (75°F) at any time of the day or night are rare. There are greater temperature variations inland. Annual rainfall at the coast averages 2,250 mm. It is generally less in the interior but varies with altitude.

The last full census of the country took place in May 1980 when the total population was 793,000 (est). Guyanese of East Indian descent account for over half the population, those of African descent for about a third; the remainder are composed of Amerindians (the aboriginal inhabitants of the country), Portuguese, Chinese and people of mixed race. Guyanese of African descent provide most of the urban and industrial community while those of East Indian descent provide most of the labour force in the sugar and rice industries. The Amerindian people live mainly in the west and south and there are a number of reserved areas for their protection.

Communications throughout the country are difficult. As mentioned above, the rivers are obstructed by rapids and falls not far from the coast. They are therefore of very limited value for communication though they do provide some sort of link with the timber and mining areas of the interior. There are asphalt roads along the coast from Charity on the Pomeroon to Crabwood Creek on the Corentyne, broken by ferry crossings of the Essequibo (4 hours) and Berbice ($\frac{1}{2}$ hour) Rivers, and from Georgetown to Linden (formerly Mackenzie). There are dirt roads running further inland, but there is no road link between the coast and the Rupununi. A road to Brazil is under construction. Air transport is the easiest means of communication between the coast and the interior. There are no public railways.

Georgetown is the main seaport, followed by New Amsterdam, Bauxite ships sail up the Demerara river as far as Linden, and Everton on the Berbice.

Education is free and universal, up to and including University level. The literacy rate is about 90 per cent. The University of Guyana has a total enrolment of about 1,800. Guyana has two radio broadcasting stations operated by the Guyana Broadcasting Corporation, Voice of Guyana and Radio Roraima; there is a fledgling television service provided by the Guyana Television Corporation and by two private firms which rebroadcast satellite TV.

The Guyanese dollar is the unit of currency. Since March 1991 the Official Exchange rate has been calculated weekly as an average of market rates prevailing at local licensed 'cambios'. As at 30th November 1991 the rate was G$220 to £1.

Guyana's economy is based almost entirely on sugar, bauxite and rice but there is in addition some production of gold, diamonds, timber and rum, and some cattle ranching. There is also some small scale industrial development and an expanding fishing industry (mostly shrimp).

Total exports in 1986 were provisionally valued at US$210.0 million, which included, in millions of US dollars:

Bauxite	82.4
Sugar	83.4
Rice	10.5

History

Guyana is an Amerindian word meaning Land of Waters. This name was originally given to the territory on the north east of the South American continent which is drained by several large rivers, the most important being the Amazon, Orinoco, Demerara, Berbice, Essequibo and Corentyne. From this territory five Guianas emerged: Spanish Guiana (now Venezuela), Portuguese Guiana (now Brazil), French Guiana, Dutch Guiana (now Surinam) and British Guiana (now Guyana).

The coastline was first traced by Spanish sailors in 1499 and 1500 and the first European settlements were almost certainly Spanish or Portuguese. The Dutch established a settlement on the Pomeroon in 1581 but were evicted by Spanish and Amerindians about 1596, after which they retired to a settlement up the Essequibo River. In 1627 Dutch merchants settled on the Berbice River. The Dutch West India Company, formed in 1621, controlled these settlements.

British attempts at settlement were made in 1604, 1609 and 1629, but no permanent settlements were established. A British settlement was founded in Surinam in 1651 but this was captured by the Dutch in 1667. In October of the same year it was recaptured by a British expedition. The Dutch finally obtained possession of Surinam in mid-1668 in accordance with the Treaty of Breda.

Meanwhile, the Dutch were in possession of that part of the area which is now Guyana. Although yielding intermittently to Britain, France and Portugal, they retained their hold on the territory until 1796 when it was captured by the British. It was restored to the Dutch in 1802, but in the following year was retaken by Great Britain. At that time the territory comprised the separate colonies of Essequibo, Demerara and Berbice. These were finally ceded to Great Britain in 1814.

The Courts of Policy and the Combined Courts, the legislature and executive bodies created by the Dutch remained in operation under British rule for another century. In 1831 the three Colonies merged to become British Guiana.

Constitutional development

A new Constitution with universal adult suffrage at the age of 21, two Chamber Legislature and a ministerial system was introduced in 1953 and a General Election was held, at which the People's Progressive Party (PPP) won a majority. Later in 1953, Her Majesty's Government suspended the Constitution in circumstances which were subsequently analysed in a report by a Constitutional Commission consisting of Sir James Robertson, GCVO, GCMG, KBE, Sir Donald Jackson (then Chief Justice of the Windward and Leeward Islands) and Mr George Woodcock, CBE (then Assistant General Secretary of the Trades Union Congress).

After the Commission's report was published in November 1954 Her Majesty's Government accepted its recommendation for a period of 'marking time' in the advance towards self-government. In the meantime the Colony continued to be administered in accordance with the British Guiana (Constitution) (Temporary Provisions) Order in Council of 22nd December 1953, which provided for an Executive Council of three *ex officio* Members and not more than seven Nominated Members; and a Legislative Council of a Speaker, the same three *ex officio* Members and not more than twenty-four Nominated Members.

Constitutional changes were introduced by the British Guiana (Constitutional) (Temporary Provisions) (Amendment) Order in Council 1956, providing for a Legislative Council of not more than 28 Members (excluding the Speaker) comprising three *ex officio* Members, not less than 14 Elected Members and not more than 11 Nominated Members. At the first election held under the amended constitution in August 1957 the number of Elected Members was 14, and six other Members were nominated by the Governor.

As a result of a resolution passed by the Legislative Council in June 1958, a Constitutional Conference was convened in London in March 1960. Following the decisions of this Conference, the British Guiana (Constitution) Order in Council, 1961 was passed, providing for a new constitution giving full internal self-government to British Guiana.

The new constitution, which came into effect on 18th July 1961, provided for a bi-cameral Legislature—a Legislative Assembly of 35 members, elected by universal adult suffrage, and a nominated Senate of 13 members, eight appointed on the advice of the Premier, three after consultation with such persons as could speak for the differing political views of opposition groups in the Assembly, and two by the Governor in his discretion. The life of the legislature was to be for four years unless dissolved before. The Legislative Assembly was presided over by a Speaker who was not a member of the Assembly. The Senate was presided over by a President chosen by members from among their own number.

The Council of Ministers consisted of a Premier and not more than nine other Ministers and the Governor was required to exercise all his powers in accordance with the advice of the Council except where otherwise expressly stated (the notable exception being defence and external affairs).

In the elections under the new constitution held on 21st August 1961, the People's Progressive Party under Dr Cheddi Jagan obtained twenty seats and formed a government.

In January 1962, Her Majesty's Government announced its willingness to hold a Constitutional Conference to discuss the date and arrangements to be made for the achievement of independence by British Guiana. The Conference was held in October but was unable to reach agreement and was adjourned to allow for further discussions between the parties in British Guiana. Since these discussions did not lead to agreement the Secretary of State reconvened the Conference in 1963.

At the resumed Conference the leaders of the three parties reported that they had failed to reach agreement between themselves on the terms of a constitution for independence and asked the British Government to settle on its own authority all the outstanding political issues. The then Secretary of State for the Colonies (the Right Honourable Duncan Sandys, MP) announced his decisions on 31st October 1963 at the closing session of the Conference. The most important item was that elections would be held on a new basis as soon as possible under a system of proportional representation.

In spite of renewed disturbances in the course of 1964 the elections were duly held under the proportional representation system in December 1964 as a result of which Mr L F S Burnham, Leader of the People's National Congress (PNC), formed a Government in coalition with the United Force (UF).

A final Constitutional Conference was held in London in November 1965 when agreement was reached on the outline of a Constitution under which British Guiana should become independent under the name of Guyana on 26th May 1966 (Cmnd. 2849, December 1965). The Leader of the People's Progressive Party (PPP), Dr Cheddi Jagan declined to attend the Constitutional Conference or to be associated with its conclusions.

The British Parliament gave effect to the decisions of the Constitutional Conference in the Guyana Independence Act (1966 Ch. 14) of 12th May 1966. The Act gave power to provide a constitution for Guyana by Order in Council. An Order in Council was accordingly made on 16th May 1966 (SI 1966 No 575) containing in a Schedule the Constitution of Guyana. The country became independent on 26th May 1966, and became a Republic within the Commonwealth on 23rd February 1970.

On 10th April 1978 the Constitution Amendment Bill was passed in the National Assembly. The Bill sought to amend Article 73 of the 1966 Constitution so as to remove the requirement for the holding of a Referendum and to enable provisions of that kind to be amended by a Bill which has been supported by the vote of not less than two-thirds of all the elected members of the National Assembly. After the Constitution had been so amended it would be competent for the Assembly to repeal the existing Constitution and to replace it by another without the necessity for a Referendum. A Referendum permitting the Assembly so to act was held on 10th July 1978. A Constituent Assembly was established to draw up the new Constitution, providing for an Executive President, for submission to the National Assembly for approval. The life of the Assembly elected in 1973 which was extended until October 1979 for this purpose, was further extended for a period of twelve months. A new Guyanese Constitution was enacted on 20th February 1980.

The new constitution was promulgated on 6th October 1980 and Prime Minister Burnham assumed office as Executive President on that date. At the General Election held on 15th December 1980, President Burnham's party was returned to office with an increased majority. President Burnham died on 6th August 1985 and was succeeded by President Hoyte. The People's National Congress retained office in General Elections held in December 1985. The Constitution was amended to allow postponement of the General Election due by 2nd May 1991. Elections announced for 16th December were subsequently postponed until 1992.

The Constitution

The Constitution provides for a uni-cameral Legislature, which is referred to throughout the Constitution as the National Assembly but is now more usually known simply as Parliament. Members of Parliament are elected under a system of proportional representation by which those qualified to vote may cast a single vote in favour of lists of candidates. The seats in Parliament are then allocated between the lists in proportion to the numbers of votes cast. There is universal adult suffrage.

The normal life of Parliament is five years. The Cabinet consists of the President, the Prime Minister, who must be an elected Member of Parliament, the Deputy Prime Ministers and such other Ministers as the President may appoint. Provision is made for the appointment of Ministers who have not been elected. Such Ministers become Members of Parliament but have no right to vote. There is an office of Leader of the Minority to which appointments are made by the President.

The constitution also provides for a National Congress of Local Democratic Organs responsible for the interests of local government and a Supreme Congress of the People consisting of all members of the National Assembly and all members of the National Congress of Local Democratic Organs to meet as appointed by proclamation by the President.

There is a Court of Appeal and High Court. The Judges of the Court of Appeal are the Chancellor, who is President, the Chief Justice and such number of Justices of Appeal as Parliament prescribes. The Judges of the High Court are the Chief Justice and such number of Puisne Judges as Parliament prescribes. The Constitution provides for an Ombudsman to investigate actions taken by Government departments or other authorities.

The Constitution also contains provisions relating to human rights, citizenship, the functions of the executive, Parliamentary procedure and elections, and procedures for appointments in the Judicature, Public Service and Police. Parliament has power to alter the Constitution but certain provisions are entrenched.

Historical List

GOVERNORS-GENERAL

Sir Richard Luyt, GCMG, KCVO, DCM, 26th May 1966 to 31st October 1966

Sir Kenneth Stoby, 1st November 1966 to 15th December 1966

Sir David Rose, GCMG, CVO, MBE, 16th December 1966 to 10th November 1969

Sir Edward Luckhoo, QC, 11th November 1969 to 22nd February 1970

PRESIDENTS

Mr Arthur Chung, 17th March 1970 to 5th April 1980

Cde L F S Burnham, OE, SC, 6th October 1980 to 6th August 1985

HEAD OF STATE

President: H E Cde H D Hoyte, SC

Government

At the elections on 9th December 1985, the People's National Congress (PNC) won 42 seats; the People's Progressive Party (PPP) 8 seats; The United Force (UF) 2 seats and the Working People's Alliance (WPA) one seat. Opposition members resigned in May 1991.

CABINET

President and Minister of Foreign Affairs: Cde Hugh Desmond Hoyte, SC

MINISTERS IN THE CABINET

Executive President of the Cooperative Republic of Guyana: HE Hugh Desmond Hoyte, SC

Prime Minister and Minister of Health: Hamilton Green, MP

Attorney-General and Minister of Legal Affairs: *Keith Stanislaus Massiah, OR, SC, MP

Deputy Prime Minister, Public Works, Communications and Regional Development: Robert Corbin, MP

Deputy Prime Minister, Trade, Tourism and Industry: Winston Murray, CCH, MP

Minister of Finance: *Carl Greenidge, MP

Minister of Agriculture: *Dr Patrick McKenzie, AA, MP

Minister of Education and Cultural Development: *Deryck Bernard, MP

Minister of Labour and Social Services: *Rabbian Ali-Khan, MP

SENIOR MINISTERS (Not in the Cabinet)

Minister in the Ministry of Public Works, Communications and Regional Development: *Jules Kranenburg, MP

Senior Minister in the Office of the President: Gowkarran Sharma, AA, JP, MP

OTHER MINISTERS

Minister in the Ministry of Trade, Tourism and Industry: Sharandeo Sawh, MP

Minister in the Ministry of Agriculture: *Vibert Parvattan, MP

Minister in the Ministry of Health: J T Kissoon, MP

Minister in the Office of the President, Minister of Public Services: Dr Faith Harding, MP

Minister of Home Affairs: Stella Odie-Alli, MP

Minister in the Ministry of Labour and Social Services: Jean Persico, AA, MP

NATIONAL ASSEMBLY

Speaker: Cde Sase Narain, OR, SC, JP, MP

Deputy Speaker: (Vacant)

Clerk of the National Assembly: Cde F A Narain, AA

Leader of the Minority in the National Assembly: (Vacant)

JUDICIARY

Chancellor: Cde K M George

Chief Justice: Cde R Harper

MINISTRIES AND GOVERNMENT DEPARTMENTS

OFFICE OF THE PRESIDENT

Head of the Presidential Secretariat and Head of the Public Service: Dr Tyrone Ferguson

Permanent Secretary: Cde P Mohamed

Deputy Permanent Secretary: Cde R Sivanand

ADVISERS TO THE PRESIDENT

Special Advisers: Cde Dr P A Reid, OE

Economic Adviser: Cde D Harris

Head of Political and Press Division: Cde H Majeed

Adviser on Investment and Administrative Matters: Dr K King

Consultant on Communications: Cde Kit Nascimento

ATTORNEY GENERAL'S CHAMBERS

Solicitor-General: Cde J C Nurse, SC

SUPREME COURT

Registrar: Cde P Killikelly

DIRECTOR OF PUBLIC PROSECUTION

Cde George Jackman

MINISTRY OF AGRICULTURE

Permanent Secretary: Cde C Gopaul

* Non-elected member

MINISTRY OF PUBLIC WORKS, COMMUNICATIONS AND REGIONAL DEVELOPMENT
Permanent Secretary: Cde G Sahai
Deputy Permanent Secretary: Cde C Abrams

MINISTRY OF FOREIGN AFFAIRS
Permanent Secretary: Cde David Hales

MINISTRY OF TRADE, TOURISM AND INDUSTRY
Permanent Secretary: Cde N Gravesande
Deputy Permanent Secretary: Cde H Khan

MINISTRY OF LABOUR AND SOCIAL SERVICES
Permanent Secretary: Cde C Moore

MINISTRY OF HOME AFFAIRS
Permanent Secretary: Cde Fairbairn Liverpool, MSM

MINISTRY OF HEALTH
Permanent Secretary: Cde E Lee

MINISTRY OF EDUCATION AND CULTURAL DEVELOPMENT
Permanent Secretary: Cde N Adonis

GUYANA PUBLIC COMMUNICATIONS AGENCY
Executive Chairman: Cde C Nascimento

PUBLIC SERVICE COMMISSION
Secretary: Cde J S M Worrell, AA

DEPARTMENT OF INLAND REVENUE
Commissioner: Cde E Heyliger, AA

MINISTRY OF LEGAL AFFAIRS
Permanent Secretary: Cde C Profitt

MINISTRY OF FINANCE
Head of Department of International Economic Cooperation: Dr B Scotland
Comptroller of Customs and Excise: Cde A Christopher
Deputy Comptroller of Customs and Excise: Cde Clarence Chue
Accountant General: Cde E Jayme
Secretary to the Treasury: Cde H O Thompson
Deputy Secretary to the Treasury: Cde C Herbert

GUYANA FORESTRY COMMISSION
Commissioner of Forests: Mr D Black

CIVIL DEFENCE COMMISSION
Chief Executive Officer: Cde F Cumberbatch

OFFICE OF THE AUDITOR GENERAL
Auditor General: Cde A Goolsarran

India

Capital: New Delhi

Location, Topography, Climate

India is bounded to the north-west by Pakistan, to the north by China, Nepal and Bhutan, and to the northeast by Bangladesh and Burma; Sri Lanka lies off the south-east coast. India also includes the Andaman and Nicobar Islands in the Bay of Bengal and the Lakshadweep islands in the Arabian Sea. The mainland can be divided into three well-defined regions: (*a*) the mountain zone of the Himalayas; (*b*) the Indo-Gangetic Plain and (*c*) the Southern Peninsula. The main mountain ranges are the Himalayas in the north (over 8,700 m), the Aravallis and Vindhyas (up to 1,200 m) in central India and the Western and Eastern Ghats (over 2,400 m). The most important rivers are the Ganges, Jamuna, Brahmaputra, Indus, Godavari, Krishna, Mahanadi, Narmada and Cauvery which are all navigable in parts.

There are four distinct seasons: (i) the cold season (December-March); (ii) the hot season (April-May); (iii) the rainy season (June-September); and (iv) what is known as the season of the retreating SW monsoon (October-November). The mean temperatures range at Delhi from 10°C (50°F) to 33°C (92°F), at Calcutta from 18°C (65°F) to 30°C (86°F) and at Madras from 25°C (75°F) to 32°C (89°F). Maximum temperatures of about 38°C (100°F) and 45°C (115°F) are reached during May in Madras and Delhi respectively. Annual rainfall varies widely; as little as 100 mm falls in the Thar desert, but parts of Assam experience more than 7,500 mm.

Population

India is the world's second most populous country. A census is taken every ten years and at the time of the 1991 census the population was estimated to be 844 million. The birth rate is about 30.5 per 1,000 and the death rate about 10.2 per 1,000. The numbers of adherents to the main religions practised in India at the time of the 1991 census were: Hindus 697 million; Muslims 96 million; Christians 20 million; Sikhs 16 million.

Information about the division of the country into States and about the various languages used in India will be found in the sections dealing with Constitutional Development and Constitution below. New Delhi is the capital of the country with an estimated population in 1991 of 9.4 million. Other principal cities are Calcutta (10.9 million), Greater Bombay (12.6 million) and Madras (5.4 million). The states with the largest population are Uttar Pradesh (about 138.8 million), Bihar (about 86.3 million), Maharashtra (78.7 million), West Bengal (68 million), Andhra Pradesh (66.3 million), Madhya Pradesh (66.1 million) and Tamil Nadu (55.6 million).

Education

The constitution provides for free and compulsory education until the age of 14, although not all States have yet managed to achieve this. In Government schools secondary education is free in some States and Territories. The first modern universities were established in India in 1857. In 1948 there were 21 universities; by 1990 there were 142 universities and 28 other institutions deemed to be universities.

Communications

Major ports in India are: Bombay, Kandla, Marmugao, New Mangalore and Cochin on the west coast, and Madras, Tuticorin, Visakhapatnam, Paradip and Calcutta-Haldia on the east coast. A total traffic of 147 million tonnes was handled by all the major ports during 1989/90. The principal shipping lines are: Shipping Corporation of India, Scindia Steamship Navigation Company, Great Eastern Shipping Company and India Steamship Company. The main airports are: Delhi (Indira Gandhi International Airport), Bombay (Sahar and Santa Cruz). Calcutta (Dum Dum) and Madras (Meenambakkam). The main airlines are: Indian Airlines (internal) and Air India (international). In 1989/90, road kilometreage was 960,000 (surfaced) and 1,010,000 (unsurfaced). There are 62,210 kilometres of railway. Radio services are provided for the whole country by All India Radio; a national network of television stations is operated by Doordarshan.

The Economy

India's main crops are rice, wheat and other cereals (millet, sorghum, maize, etc), chick peas and other pulses, sugar cane, jute, cotton and tea. Other agricultural products include oil seeds, spices, groundnuts, tobacco, rubber and coffee. Among principal manufactures are textile, jute goods, sugar, cement, paper, industrial and consumer goods. Industries include iron and steel, heavy and light engineering, drugs and chemicals, fertilisers, oil and petroleum products, coal and lignite. Among other minerals produced are iron, manganese, copper, gold, limestone, mica and salt.

The budget estimates for 1992/93 give Government Revenue as Rs756,880 million excluding States' share of tax revenue and expenditure at Rs895,700 million. There are also substantial receipts and expenditures on capital account. Gross aid receipts for 1991/92 were estimated at Rs77,831 million but external debt service for 1991/92 was estimated at Rs61,067 million. In the Seventh Five Year Plan (1985/86–1989/90) an annual average growth rate of 5.2 per cent in GDP was achieved. It is expected that the growth of GDP in real terms during 1990/91 will be about 5 per cent. The Eighth Five Year Plan (1990/91–1994/95) is yet to be finalised.

Agriculture is the mainstay of the economy, providing employment to nearly 70 per cent of the workforce and generating 33 per cent of national income. Overall economic growth remains closely tied to progress in this sector which, in the period 1950–84, showed average growth of 2.2 per cent per annum. India's Gross Domestic Product in the same period grew by an average 3.56 per cent per annum, dubbed "the Hindu rate of growth" by one Indian Economist.

With irrigation available for only about one third of cultivated land Indian agriculture depends to a considerable degree on good monsoon rains. In 1987 a severe drought in many areas led to a significant fall in foodgrain production but a good monsoon in 1988 brought a sharp increase in production. After three years of record agricultural output, current indications are that agricultural production in 1991/92 experienced little or no growth, or possibly declined. This is mainly because the 1991 monsoon rainfall although only slightly below average was distributed very unevenly.

India has substantial energy reserves in the form of coal, oil and gas. Natural gas production doubled in the period 1980-85 and indigenous crude oil production, much of it from offshore fields near Bombay, now provides some two-thirds of the country's requirements. However demands for petroleum and petroleum products is growing rapidly and the government has sanctioned ambitious exploration plans. As a result of exploiting new discoveries it is now estimated that total crude production could be raised to around 51 m tons in 1994/5 against estimated demands of 7 m tons. Electricity shortfalls continue to constitute a significant bottleneck for industry. There are five nuclear reactors now in operation, providing 3 per cent of electricity generating capacity. Private sector participation in power generation has now been approved, subject to various conditions. In 1991 India's first coal fired 1,000 m ton power station was completed at Rihand Lake.

Steel production in India is mainly in the hands of the public sector. There are five integrated public sector steel plants with an annual ingot capacity of 14 m tonnes; the only private sector plant has a capacity of 3 m tonnes. The Government is planning to set up two coastal steel plants.

The engineering industry in India has made considerable progress. The heavy engineering industry is primarily in the hands of the public sector. Some major firms are the Heavy Engineering Corporation, Ranchi, which has a heavy machine building plant, foundry forge plant, and heavy machine tools plant. Heavy electrical machinery is manufactured by the Bharat Heavy Electricals Ltd. Hindustan Machine Tools Ltd manufacture a number of machine tools in Punjab, Karnataka, Kerala and Andhra Pradesh. India has also enlarged its manufacturing facilities for chemicals, fertilisers and petrochemicals. The automobile and commercial vehicles industries have also grown fast during the last twenty years. India's export of engineering goods in the 1980s grew by 26 per cent per annum and chemicals by 30 per cent per annum.

Constitutional development

Under the Indian Independence Act, power was transferred to the first government of the new Dominion of India on 15th August 1947: on that day Lord Mountbatten relinquished the office of Viceroy and was appointed, on the advice of the Indian Government, first Governor-General of independent India. Since then, the principal constitutional developments in India have been the integration of the Indian Princely States, the adoption of a Republican Constitution and the reorganisation of State boundaries.

The Princely States. One of the major problems involved in the transfer of power was the future of the Indian Princely States which numbered about 560 and comprised two-fifths of the area of the sub-continent. During the period of British rule, the Princely States had preserved a large measure of internal autonomy subject only to the paramountcy of the British Crown expressed in the form of many separate treaties and agreements entered into with the Rulers concerned. Under the Indian Independence Act this paramountcy was declared to have lapsed and with it the existing treaties between the Rulers and the Crown.

During the final preparations for the transfer of power, the Rulers of the States were advised by the Viceroy to accede to one or other of the two successor Dominions. In the event nearly all the Rulers accepted this advice; and, by the date of the transfer, practically all the States whose territory lay within or contiguous to the boundaries of the new Dominion of India had signed Instruments of Accession, the only major exceptions being Kashmir and Hyderabad. In October 1947 the Maharaja of Kashmir signed an Instrument of Accession to India. Pakistan did not accept the validity of this accession and fighting broke out between the two countries in 1948 and again in the latter part of 1965. Hyderabad was occupied by Indian forces in September 1948 after a long dispute between the Government of India and the Nizam (ruler).

The Instruments which the Princes signed provided for accession in a limited number of subjects only. The larger and more important States (about 140 in all) acceded in respect of External Affairs, Defence and Communications; but in the case of the smaller States (which had had less autonomy under British rule), other subjects were added to the list. During the two years following the transfer of power, the Indian Government energetically pursued a policy of persuading the Rulers to agree to the complete integration of their States with the body politic of India and the consequent surrender of their remaining Princely powers. This aim was successfully achieved, and by the end of 1949 all the 554 States which had acceded to India (with the exception of Jammu and Kashmir which retained a special status) had been integrated with India. The Rulers signed individual agreements under which, in return for giving up their States, the Indian Government agreed to pay them privy purses for life and to grant certain other personal privileges. These purses and privileges were abolished by a Presidential order in September 1970 which 'de-recognised' the former Rulers. In December 1970 this Presidential Order was struck down by the Supreme Court of India as being *ultra vires* of the Constitution. However, in 1971 the Constitution itself was amended by the Constitution (Twenty-sixth Amendment) Act which abolished the privy purse and extinguished all rights, liabilities and obligations in respect of them.

The constitutional arrangements for administering the Princely States after integration varied according to geographical and other circumstances. Some were incorporated in the former British Provinces; others were grouped into new composite political units (Rajasthan, Madhya Bharat, Patiala and East Punjab States Union, Saurashtra, Travancore-Cochin, Vindhya Pradesh, and Himachal Pradesh); and others retained their separate identities (Mysore, Hyderabad, Bhopal, Kutch, Manipur, Tripura, and Bilaspur). The larger States or groups of States in the two latter categories (Rajasthan, Madhya Bharat, PEPSU, Saurashtra, Travancore-Cochin, Mysore and Hyderabad) eventually became, under the 1950 Constitution, Part B States, with parliamentary institutions on the same lines as those possessed by the former British Provinces (Part A States), except that they had at their head a senior Princely Ruler–a Rajpramukh—rather than a Governor. The smaller units became Part C States and as such were placed under various forms of central administration.

The States Reorganisation Act, 1956.

Soon after the Constitution (*see below under* 'Constitution') came into force in 1950 a movement gathered impetus for the redrawing of State boundaries on a more rational and in particular on a linguistic basis. (In several of the existing States the population was divided into two or three major language groups.) The first fruit of the linguistic campaign was the decision in 1953 to separate the Telugu-speaking areas of Madras to form a new State called Andhra; this came into being in October 1953. In December 1953 the first official move towards a more comprehensive reorganisation of the States was made with the appointment by the Government of a States Reorganisation Commission which was charged with a detailed examination of the whole problem. In its Report, submitted in September 1955, the Commission recommended a radical re-drawing of State boundaries. In September 1956, after prolonged public and parliamentary debate, the decisions of the Government on this Report, incorporated in the States Reorganisation Bill and the consequential Constitution (Seventh Amendment) Bill, were passed by the Indian Parliament, and the reorganisation of States became effective on 1st November 1956.

Under the new Acts, the former categories of States and with them the office of Rajpramukh were abolished, and the component parts of the Indian Union were reduced to 13 States (apart from Jammu and Kashmir) and 6 Union Territories, the revised division being mainly on a linguistic basis. Perhaps the most striking territorial change was the disappearance of Hyderabad and the incorporation of its parts in Andhra, Bombay and Mysore. Another major change was the re-shaping of Bombay which, as a bilingual Marathi-Gujarati-speaking State, lost its Kannada-speaking areas in the south to Mysore, but acquired Saurashtra, Kutch and extensive territories from Madhya Pradesh and Hyderabad. Travancore-Cochin, enlarged to include the Malabar District of Madras, was renamed Kerala. The union of former Punjab Princely States known as PEPSU was merged with Punjab. Madhya Pradesh (the former Central Provinces) was extensively reshaped, losing a large area to Bombay, but incorporating Madhya Bharat, Vindhya Pradesh and Bhopal, all of which were former Princely States or unions of such States. Mysore was substantially enlarged to include Coorg and parts of Bombay and Hyderabad. Thus, under this comprehensive reorganisation, the political map of India was radically changed and in many places (with important exceptions like the States of Uttar Pradesh and Bihar) the old boundaries of the major Princely States and provinces of British India were no longer recognisable. In March 1960, following persistent agitation against its bilingual structure, Bombay State was, by the terms of the Bombay Reorganisation Act, 1960, divided into the separate unilingual States of Maharashtra and Gujarat. In 1961 Nagaland (comprising the Naga Hills area of Assam and the Tuensang area of the North East Frontier Agency) was accorded the status of a separate State of the Indian Union.

One bilingual State which the States Reorganisation Commission had left untouched was the Punjab, where both Hindi and Punjabi were joint official languages. In 1966, following prolonged pressure from some Punjabi-speakers, the Indian Government decided to split the Punjab on a linguistic basis. Part of its territory was incorporated into the Union Territory of Himachal Pradesh, and the remainder divided between a greatly contracted area which preserves the name Punjab, and a new Hindi-speaking State, Haryana. Since then the following territories have been granted full statehood: Himachal Pradesh in January 1971, Manipur, Tripura and Meghalaya in January 1972, Sikkim in May 1975, Mizoram in August 1986, Arunachal Pradesh in February 1987 and Goa in May 1987.

India and the Commonwealth

The relationship between India and the other Members of the Commonwealth was settled at the Prime Ministers' Meeting held in London in April 1949. This Meeting had been arranged to consider the constitutional issues arising from the decision of the Indian Constituent Assembly to adopt a republican form of Government. The final *communiqué* stated that 'The Government of India have informed the other Governments of the Commonwealth of the intention of the Indian people that under the new Constitution which is about to be adopted, India shall become a sovereign independent Republic. The Government of India have, however, declared and affirmed India's desire to continue her full membership of the Commonwealth of Nations and her acceptance of the King as the symbol of the free association of its independent member-nations and as such the Head of the Commonwealth. The Governments of the other countries of the Commonwealth, the basis of whose membership of the Commonwealth is not hereby changed, accept and recognise India's continuing membership in accordance with the terms of this declaration'.

Constitution

The Indian Independence Act (*see above under* 'Constitutional Development') provided that the Government of India Act, 1935, should remain in force in the two new Dominions as their Constitutions, subject to any modifying Orders made by their Governors-General. Under this latter provision, the Governor-General of India made the India (Provisional Constitution) Order, 1947, to serve as a Constitution for India until a fresh Constitution had been drafted and put into force.

Meanwhile a Constituent Assembly, elected in 1946 from the existing Provincial Legislatures and intended to serve also as a Provisional Parliament, had begun drafting a Constitution. This one, which described India as a 'Union of States' and as a 'Sovereign Democratic Republic' with a President as its constitutional head, was adopted in November 1949, and came into force on 26th January 1950. On that day the last Governor-General of India (Mr C Rajagopalachari) relinquished his office and Dr Rajendra Prasad assumed office as the first President. Broadly speaking the Constitution provides, both at the Centre and in the States, for a system of Parliamentary and Cabinet government though in a republican form. In December 1976 a further Constitutional amendment altered the description to 'Sovereign Socialist Secular Democratic Republic'.

Under the Constitution, the executive power is vested in the President, acting on the advice of the Prime Minister, who is elected for a period of five years by an electoral college consisting of the elected members of the Union and State Legislatures, the voting strength of the Central Legislature in the college being equal to that of all the States put together. In his absence his functions are performed by the Vice-President, who at other times acts as Chairman of the Rajya Sabha (the Upper House). The President is 'aided and advised' in his functions by a Council of Ministers (the Cabinet). He appoints the Prime Minister and, on the latter's advice, the other Ministers and can dismiss them. The Council of Ministers is collectively responsible to the Lok Sabha (the Lower House) and all Ministers must be or become within six months Members of Parliament.

The legislative power vests in Parliament which comprises the President, the Rajya Sabha and the Lok Sabha. The Rajya Sabha consists of not more than 250 members, 12 nominated by the President, the rest elected by the members of the State legislatures or representing the Union Territories (*see below*) on a population basis; they hold office for six years, one-third retiring every two years. The Lok Sabha originally consisted of not more than 500 members, but this figure was adjusted in 1956 to take account of the reclassification of States and Territories and it now consists of not more than 544 members, of whom 525 represent territorial constituencies in the States, 17 represent the Union Territories and two are nominated members of the Anglo-Indian community. The members from the States are chosen by direct election under universal adult franchise; those from the Union Territories are chosen 'in such manner as Parliament may by law provide'. In December 1976 the Lok Sabha's term was extended from five to a maximum of six years. It was later reduced once again to five years. Approximately one-fifth of the seats in the Lok Sabha are reserved for the Scheduled Castes and Scheduled Tribes.

There is a Supreme Court comprising the Chief Justice, not more than 25 other judges appointed by the President and only removable by his order following an address passed by each House of Parliament. The Court has sole jurisdiction in all disputes between State and Union or between State and State. It is also the final Court of Appeal from other Courts.

The Constitution laid down that after 1965 Hindi should be used for all official purposes. The Official Languages Act, 1963, however, provided for the continued use after 1965 of English, in addition to Hindi, for all official purposes of the Union and for the transaction of business in Parliament. Under this Act a Parliamentary Committee was set up in 1975 to review the progress made in the use of Hindi. Article 345 of the Constitution provided for the adoption by States Legislatures, for official purposes of the State, of any of the fourteen regional languages listed in the Eighth Schedule to the Constitution. These are Assamese, Bengali, Gujarati, Hindi, Kannada, Kashmiri, Malayalam, Marathi, Oriya,

Punjabi, Sanskrit, Tamil, Telugu and Urdu. A fifteenth, Sindhi, was subsequently added. Sanskrit, which is a scholarly language used primary in religious or poetic contexts has not been adopted for official use by any State. Urdu, although not adopted officially by any State, is spoken in the Punjab, Uttar Pradesh, Bihar, Delhi and Himachal Pradesh. The areas in which the other regional languages are used are indicated in the notes on the States and Territories of the Union at the end of this chapter.

The Constitution can be (and has on sixty-three occasions already been) amended by a Bill passed in each House of the Union Parliament by a majority of its total members and by a majority of not less than two-thirds of its members present and voting. Amendments to certain Articles must, however, also be ratified by the legislatures of a majority of the States.

HISTORICAL LIST
(For full Historical List see the 1978 Edition)

Heads of States

GOVERNORS-GENERAL (Dominion of India)

Louis Francis Albert Victor Nicholas Mountbatten, 1st Earl Mountbatten of Burma, KG, PC, GCSI, GCIE, GCVO, KCB, DSO (*later* GCB), 15th August 1947 to 20th June 1948

Chakravarti Rajagopalachari, 21st June 1948 to 26th January 1950

PRESIDENTS (Republic of India)

V V Giri from 24th August 1969 to 24th August 1974

F A Ahmed from 24th August 1974 to 11th February 1977

B D Jatti, 11th February 1977 to 25th July 1977 (Acting President)

N Sanjiva Reddy from 25th July 1977 to 25th July 1982

Zail Singh from 25th July 1982 to 24th July 1987

Ramaswamy Venkataraman from 25th July 1987

PRIME MINISTERS

Mrs Indira Gandhi from 24th January 1966 to 24th March 1977

Morarji Desai from 24th March 1977 to 28th July 1979

Charan Singh from 28th July 1979 to 14th January 1980

Mrs Indira Gandhi from 14th January 1980 to 31st October 1984

Rajiv Gandhi from 31st October 1984 to 3rd December 1989

Vishwanath Pratap Singh from 3rd December 1989 to 10th November 1990

Chandra Shekhar from 10th November 1990 to 6th March 1991

P V Nasasimha Rao from 21st June 1991

Government

The first general elections based on universal adult franchise in accordance with the new Constitution were held in 1952 and resulted in a sweeping victory for the Congress Party which won 75 per cent of the seats in the Lok Sabha (Lower House of the Central Parliament). The main opposition comprised the Communist Party and its allies, with some 30 seats, and the Praja Socialist Party (formed by the merger of two other left wing parties) with 26 seats.

The second series of elections to the Lok Sabha and the Vidhan Sabhas (State Assemblies) were held in 1957. In the Lok Sabha the Congress Party maintained their position with another decisive victory, securing 371 of the 494 seats filled by direct election and increasing their share of the poll by 3 per cent to 48 per cent. The position of the Communist Party and its allies was virtually unchanged and they remained the largest single opposition group. The Praja Socialist Party won only 19 seats.

In the Vidhan Sabhas the Congress Party won absolute majorities in 11 out of the 13 States and formed governments in 12 of them. In Orissa they formed, in May 1959, a coalition government with the Ganatantra Parishad, the largest opposition party. In Kerala, the Communist Party with 60 of the 126 contested seats in the State Assembly, governed with the support of 5 Independents until July 1959 when their administration was dismissed by the President under his emergency powers (*see above* under "The Constitution") pending fresh elections in the State. In mid-term elections to the Assembly in February 1960 the main non-communist parties formed an alliance and secured 94 of the 126 seats, and the Congress Party and Praja Socialist Parties who controlled 83 of them formed a coalition which lasted until October 1962 when the Praja Socialists withdrew leaving Congress to govern Kerala by themselves.

In the third general elections in February 1962, the Congress Party won another victory, although slightly less decisive. Their number of seats declined by 10 to 361 and their share of the poll to 45 per cent. The Communist Party gained a further seat to total 30, but the Praja Socialist Parties were reduced to only 12 seats. A new party, the Swatantra Party won 22 seats, and the Jan Sangh won 10 more than in 1957 to total 14.

In 162 simultaneous elections to the Vidhan Sabhas were held in all States except Kerala and Orissa, where there had been mid-term elections (*see above*). The Congress retained their majority in 10 out of 12 States, but lost an overall majority in the other two, Rajasthan and Madhya Pradesh, although they continued to form the Governments there. In 1964 first elections were held in the new State of Nagaland. Congress did not contest the elections, which were won by the Naga Nationalist Organisation.

Mr Jawaharlal Nehru, who had been the Prime Minister of India since Independence, died on 27th May 1964. On 9th June Mr Lal Bahadur Shastri, who had been unaminously elected as leader by the Congress Party, was sworn in as Prime Minister. Following his death at Tashkent on 11th January 1966 the Congress Parliamentary Party elected Mrs Indira Gandhi daughter of Jawaharlal Nehru as its new leader, and she was sworn in as Prime Minister on 24th January 1966.

General Elections held in February 1967 were a setback for Congress, which was returned to power with 280 seats out of the 521 contested. The Swatantra and Jan Sangh increased their seats to 44 and 35 respectively. The Communist Party had split in 1964 into a Right (CPI) and Left (CPI (Marxist)) Party, and the CPI won 22 seats, and the CPI (M) 19. The Samyukta Socialist Party increased their number of seats from 6 to 23, and the Praja Socialists won 13. The Dravida Munnetra Kazhagam (DMK) —a regional party based in Tamil Nadu (the former Madras State) —increased their seats from 7 to 25.

In the simultaneous 1967 elections to the Vidhan Sabhas, the Congress party won an absolute majority in only eight States, failing in Uttar Pradesh, Bihar, West Bengal, Rajasthan and Punjab, and being defeated in Orissa, Madras and Kerala.

In November 1969 the Congress Party split into two wings, the Congress (Ruling) and the Congress (Opposition). The former, led by Mrs Gandhi, had 228 seats in the Lok Sabha, the latter, led by Dr Ram Subhag Singh and Mr Morarji Desai, 64.

In December 1970 the President, on the advice of Mrs Gandhi, dissolved the Lok Sabha. In the ensuing General Election, held a year early in March 1971, Congress (R) obtained more than two-thirds of the seats in the Lok Sabha with 350 out of 521. The opposition parties were largely routed and only the CPI (Marxist) increased its seats to 25. The CPI and DMK got 23 each; the Jana Sangh 22; the Congress (O) 16 and the Swatantra 8.

In November 1971 the Supreme Court ruled that the pro-Mrs Gandhi Congress (R) could be recognized as the Indian National Congress and the suffix "Ruling" was dropped.

Vidhan Sabha elections were held in March 1972 and Congress won and formed State Governments in 14 of 16 States.

On 26th June 1975 a State of Emergency was declared throughout India on the grounds of deteriorating law and order. Twenty-six opposition groups were banned and press censorship was imposed. In December 1976 the Constitution 42nd Amendment Act was passed giving the centre wide-ranging powers over the judiciary and the States. The normal parliamentary term was extended from 4 to 6 years.

In January 1977 the President, in a surprise move, again dissolved the Lok Sabha on the advice of Mrs Gandhi. General elections were held in March 1977 and resulted in a decisive victory for the Janata front (270 seats), with the Congress for Democracy (CFD), a breakaway party headed by Jagivan Ram, obtaining 27 seats. Congress itself was badly beaten (153 seats), the CPI was almost totally routed, but the CPI (Marxist) were comparatively successful with 22 seats.

Elections were held in 10 States and 3 Union Territories in June 1977. Janata governments were returned to power in all except Goa, Pondicherry, Tamil Nadu and Jammu and Kashmir (where local parties formed the government), in the Punjab where the Akali Dal and Janata formed a coalition, and in West Bengal where the Marxists won a decisive victory. In Tripura differences between the CPI (M) and Janata coalition government led to its fall and the imposition of President's rule in November. When fresh elections were held on 31st December 1977, the CPI won outright and formed a government.

Following its defeat in the 1977 elections the Congress (R) party split again into two groups. The first became known from February 1978 as Congress (I) and was led by Mrs Gandhi. The second group eventually became known from November 1979 as Congress (U) after its leader Devraj Urs.

On 25th February 1978 elections were held in a further 5 states and also in the Union Territory of Arunacha Pradesh. Mrs Gandhi's Congress (I) won landslide victories in Andhra Pradesh and Karnataka, and formed a coalition government in Maharashtra with Congress (S). A coalition government was also formed in Assam with Janata and the CPI (M). Janata only gained an absolute majority in Arunachal Pradesh.

In July 1979 the ruling Janata Party split and the Prime Minister, Morarji Desai, resigned. The Deputy Prime Minister, Charan Singh, leading a faction of the coalition known then as Janata (Secular) and later as Lok Dal, took over as Prime Minister on 26th July. However, the anticipated support from Congress (I) was withdrawn and he had to resign and dissolve Parliament.

A General Election, held in January 1980, saw an overwhelming victory for Mrs Gandhi whose Congress (I) Party gained 352 out of 544 seats, with no opposition parties gaining enough seats to constitute the official opposition. In February President's rule was imposed on 9 States with ruling governments of opposition parties and their assemblies dissolved. Elections took place in May and Congress (I) governments were elected in Bihar, Gujarat, Madhya Pradesh, Maharashtra, Orissa, Punjab, Rajasthan and Uttar Pradesh. In Tamil Nadu the regional party, DMK, was elected.

The Indian political scene was significantly affected in June 1980 by the death in an air accident of Mrs Gandhi's elder son, Sanjay, General Secretary of Congress (I) and the MP for Amethi. In June 1981 her surviving son, Rajiv, formerly an Indian Airlines pilot, was elected to succeed his brother as the Member for Amethi.

A Presidential Election took place in July 1982 in which MR Zail Singh, the Congress (I) candidate, won with a large majority. In November, after elections in Nagaland, a Congress (I) Government was formed with the help of independents.

In 1983 Congress lost control of the State Governments of Andhra Pradesh and Karnataka, but formed a Government in Assam. Dr Farooq Abdullah's National Conference Party retained power in Jammu and Kashmir.

In June 1984 the Army was deployed in Punjab, after the instigation of President's rule, and instituted military action against Sikh extremists occupying a number of shrines, including the Golden temple at Amritsar. In July, the National Conference Government in Jammu and Kashmir split and was dismissed by the State Governor. A breakaway group led by Mr G M Shah, formed a new government with support from outside from Congress (I).

In August 1984 Parliament approved legislation to introduce a system of Special Courts to try people charged with terrorist offences. In Vice-Presidential elections the Congress (I) nominee, former Defence Minister Mr R Venkataraman, was elected by a large majority of Parliament.

On 31st October 1984 Mrs Gandhi was assassinated by two Sikh members of her bodyguard outside her residence in New Delhi. Rajiv Gandhi was immediately sworn in as Prime Minister, and called the scheduled parliamentary elections for 24th and 27th December 1984.

The elections resulted in an overwhelming majority for Congress (I) which won 401 of the 508 seats at stake. The Party was only checked by the National Conference in Kashmir, Telugu Desam in Andhra Pradesh and the DMK Party in Tamil Nadu.

In Provincial elections held in March 1985 Congress (I) was again successful in the States of Uttar Pradesh, Bihar, Himachal Pradesh, Rajasthan, Maharashtra, Orissa, Madhya Pradesh and in Pondicherry but lost to Janata in Karnataka and to Telugu Desam in Andhra Pradesh. The only change was in Sikkim where Mr N B Bhandari's Sikkim Sangram Parishad came to power.

In July 1985 Prime Minister Rajiv Gandhi signed the Punjab Accord with Akali Dal leader, Sant Longowal. Despite Longowal's subsequent assassination, state elections were held in Punjab in September and the Akali Dal formed the State Government.

In Jammu and Kashmir, Governor's rule was imposed following the fall of the National Conference (K) Government in March 1986, and in September that year President's rule was imposed for the first time. After twenty years of insurrection by the Mizo National front a peace accord was signed on 30th June 1986 and as a result Mizoram became a full State of the Indian Union in August 1986 governed by a coalition of the Mizo National Front under its leader Laldenga and of the Congress (I) Party.

In March 1987 President's rule was lifted in Jammu and Kashmir following state elections where the National Conference Party and the Congress (I) formed the State government, but was re-imposed in May in Punjab due to a breakdown in law and order. The Lok Sabha had previously adopted in March legislation empowering the Government to impose emergency rule in Punjab, and approved on 6th May an extension of President's rule there for six months.

In a major operation, codenamed "Black Thunder", security forces around the Golden Temple complex in Amritsar on 15th May succeeded in forcing 146 people, many of them terrorists, to surrender.

On 6th August 1988 seven opposition parties formed themselves into the National People's Front. The parties were the Lok Dal, the Janata Party, the Congress (S), the DMK, the Assam Gana Parishad and the Jan Morcha. A new centrist party, the Janata Dal, was also formed in Bangalore on 11th October.

The Supreme Court confirmed the death sentences on the assassins of Mrs Indira Gandhi, Satwant Singh and Kehar Singh, who were both hanged on 6th January 1989.

Compensation of $470 million was agreed when the Bhopal gas tragedy was settled in the Supreme Court on 14th February 1989.

On 21st April 1989 opposition leaders forced the President to impose President's rule in Karnataka.

The Government announced a new scheme on 28th April, the "Jawahar Rozgar Yojna", intended to provide rural jobs to at least one member of each poor rural family and to reach out to the 4.4 million families living below the poverty line. The 64th Constitution Bill 1989, introduced on 15th May, concerning the Panchayati Raj, aimed to empower people at district, block and village level to create democratically elected bodies to run local administration, levy taxes, and run public welfare schemes.

The General Elections of 22nd–26th November 1989 allowed the National Front Coalition led by the Janata Dal to take power. They won 141 out of 525 Parliamentary seats and were supported by the Bharatiya Janata Party (BJP) who gained 86 seats to total 88, and the Communists with 51. The Janata leader, V P Singh, became Prime Minister. Congress (I), with 193 seats remained the largest party, having gained most support in the South. In the simultaneous State Assembly elections Congress (I) was successful in Andhra Pradesh and Karnataka, and Janata Dal in Uttar Pradesh.

Assembly elections were held on 12th February in Manipur, and on 27th February in eight States and the Union Territory of Pondicherry. All had been controlled by Congress (I), but they only managed to retain power in Maharashtra and Arunachal Pradesh. BJP governments were formed in Himachal Pradesh, Madhya Pradesh and Rajasthan (the last in coalition with Janata Dal); and Janata Dal governments in Orissa, Gujarat and Bihar (the last two in coalitions with the BJP). A United Legislature Front Coalition was formed in Manipur, and a coalition in Pondicherry.

During 1990 internal tensions surfaced within the Janata Dal and the Hindu nationalist BJP withdrew its support for V P Singh's government following the arrest of their leader in connection with a Hindu/ Muslim dispute over a disused mosque. The Janata Dal split, a minority faction forming round Devi Lal and Chandra Shekhar, and in November 1990 the government lost a vote of confidence in Parliament. The Congress (I) agreed to support a new minority government formed by the breakaway Janata Dal (S), and its leader, Chandra Shekhar, became Prime Minister on 10th November 1990.

India exchanged with Pakistan on 27th January 1991 instruments ratifying the agreement on the prohibition of attack on each other's nuclear installations and facilities, which had originally been signed on 31st December 1988.

In February 1991 Congress (I) threatened to withdraw its support from the Government on the issue of re-fuelling American military aircraft involved in the Gulf War, and eventually boycotted Parliament demanding action against those responsible for ordering surveillance of Rajiv Gandhi's home. Chandra Shekhar resigned on 6th March. On 13th March the President, Mr R Venkataraman, ordered the dissolution of the ninth Lok Sabha and called for elections before 5th June.

The Electoral Commission announced on 12th April that polling for elections to the tenth Lok Sabha and State Assemblies of Haryana, Kerala, Tamil Nadu, Uttar Pradesh and West Bengal plus the Union Territory of Pondicherry would be on 20th, 23rd and 26th May. Polls in Assam and Punjab were postponed to 6th and 8th June respectively.

The Elections were interrupted by the assassination of the Congress Party leader and former Prime Minister, Rajiv Gandhi, on 21st May. Gandhi, campaigning in Tamil Nadu, was killed by a bomb attached to his assassin. Police later discovered that the murder had been the result of a conspiracy by Sri Lankans with apparent links to the Tamil extremist group, the LTTE. The police investigation was suspended when the principal suspect committed suicide. Gandhi's widow, Sonia, was initially nominated to succeed him as party leader but she declined. Narasimha Rao, veteran Congress politician and former Foreign Minister, was subsequently elected acting party president.

The Election campaign was the most violent since Independence. Due to the violence there was no voting in Kashmir and polling was postponed in Punjab. Voter turnout was low and polling was marred by allegations of ballot-rigging. Although Congress improved on its 1989 performance, and emerged as the largest party with an increase of 31 seats to a total of 226 out of 545, its share of the poll fell from 39.5 to 37 per cent. The Hindu supremacist Bharatiya Janata Party (BJP) meanwhile established itself as the main national opposition party increasing its share of seats from 88 to 117. The main loser was the Janata Party who secured only 59 seats, a loss of 81.

Narasimha Rao became Prime Minister in June and his minority congress administration was confirmed in office (with his chief rival, Sharad Pawar, as Defence Minister) on 15th July with the support of Janata and left-wing MPs.

The new Government introduced new financial and industrial policies to deal with India's serious economic problems. It also faced continuing law and order problems in Assam, Kashmir and Punjab. Despite a boycott and intimidation by the main Sikh parties, elections were held in Punjab in February 1992. On a low turn-out Congress won 87 of the 117 seats in the State Assembly and strengthened its position in the Lok Sabha by winning 12 of the 13 seats being contested. Separatist extremist violence continues in Punjab and also in Kashmir where Muslim militants are seeking to detach Kashmir from India. This has led to increased tension with Pakistan and India's accusations that Pakistan is conducting a proxy-war by supporting the militants.

HEAD OF STATE

President: Mr Ramaswamy Venkataraman

VICE-PRESIDENT

Dr S D Sharma

CABINET MINISTERS

(October 1991)

Prime Minister (also Minister of Personnel, Public Grievances, Science and Technology, Ocean Development, Electronics, Atomic Energy, Space, Chemicals and Fertilizers, Civil Supplies and Public Distribution System (Additional Charges) and Industry): Mr P V Narasimha Rao

Human Resource Development: Mr Arjun Singh

Agriculture and Rural Development: Mr Balram Jakhar

Home Affairs: Mr S B Chavan

Health and Family Welfare: Mr M L Fotedar

Parliamentary Affairs: Mr Ghulam Nabi Azad

Railways: Mr C K Jaffer Sharief

Urban Development: Mrs Sheila Kaul

Welfare: Mr Sitaram Kesri

Law, Justice and Company Affairs: Mr K V Bhaskar Reddy

Civil Aviation and Tourism: Mr Madhav Rao Scindia

Petroleum and Natural Gas: Mr B Shankaranand

Water Resources: Mr V C Shukla

Finance: Dr Manmohan Singh

External Affairs: (Vacant)

Defence: Mr Sharad Pawar

MINISTERS OF STATE (INDEPENDENT CHARGE)

Planning and Programme Implementation: Mr H R Bharadwaj

Commerce: Mr P Chidambaram

Steel: Mr Santosh Mohan Deb

Textiles: Mr Ashok Gehlot

Food: Mr Tarun Gogoi

Food Processing Industries: Mr Giridhar Gomango

Environment and Forests: Mr Kamal Nath

Information and Broadcasting: Mr Ajit Kumar Panja
Communications: Mr Rajesh Pilot
Power and Non-Conventional Energy Sources: Mr Kalpnath Rai
Labour: (Vacant)
Coal: Mr P A Sangma
Surface Transport: Mr Jagdish Tytler
Mines: Mr Balram Singh Yadav

MINISTERS OF STATE
Civil Supplies and Public Distribution: Mr Kamaluddin Ahmed
Personnel, Public Grievances and Pensions: Mrs Margaret Alva
Urban Development: Mr M Arunachalam
Human Resource Development (Dept. of Youth Affairs Sports, Women and Child Development): Ms Mamta Banerjee
External Affairs: Mr Eduado Faleiro
Civil Aviation and Tourism: Mr M O H Farook
Parliamentary Affairs and Home Affairs: Mr M M Jacob
Health and Family Welfare: Mrs Tara Devi
Parliamentary Affairs and Law, Justice & Company Affairs: Mr R Kumaramangalam
Defence, Petroleum and Natural Gas: Mr S Krishna Kumar
Industry: Mr P J Kurien, Mr P K Thungon
Agriculture: Mr K C Lenka
Railways: Mr M Mallikarjun
Chemicals and Fertilizers: Mr Chinta Mohan
Rural Development: Mr M Ramachandran, Mr G Venkat Swamy
Finance: Mr Shantaram Potdukhe, Mr Dalbir Singh, Mr Rameshwarthakor

DEPUTY MINISTERS
Labour: Mr Paban Sing Ghatowar
Welfare: Mrs K Kamala Kumari
Commerce: Mr Salman Khursheed
Communications: Mr P V Rangaya Naidu
Home Affairs: Mr Ram Lal Rahi
Information and Broadcasting: Ms Girija Vyas
Coal: Mr S D Gowda

PRESIDENT'S STAFF
Principal Secretary: Mr P Murari
Military Secretary: Rear Admiral S Ramsagar

VICE-PRESIDENT'S STAFF
Secretary: Mr S S Sohoni

RAJYA SABHA (COUNCIL OF STATES)
Chairman: Dr S D Sharma
Deputy Chairman: Dr (Mrs) Najma Heptulla
Secretary General: Mr S Agarwal

LOK SABHA (HOUSE OF THE PEOPLE)
Speaker: Mr Shivraj V Patil
Secretary General: Mr K C Rastogi

PRIME MINISTER'S OFFICE
Principal Secretary: Mr A N Verma
Information Adviser: I Rammohan Rao

CABINET SECRETARY
Secretary: Mr Naresh Chandra

JUDICIARY
Supreme Court of India
Chief Justice of India: Justice Rangnath Mishra

Each State has a separate High Court, the judges on which are appointed by the President.

PLANNING COMMISSION
Chairman: Mr P V Narasimha Rao
Deputy Chairman: Mr Pranab Mukherjee
Secretary: Mr Nitish Sengupta
Members: Dr Chitra Naik, Dr D Swaminathan, Mr V Krishnamurthy, Dr C Rangarajan, Dr S Z Qasim, Prof J S Bajaj, Dr Jayant Patil, Mr Sharad Pawar (Defence Minister), Mr Manmohan Singh (Finance Minister), Mr Balram Jakhar (Agriculture Minister)

MINISTRIES AND GOVERNMENT DEPARTMENTS

MINISTRY OF SCIENCE AND TECHNOLOGY, ATOMIC ENERGY, ELECTRONICS, OCEAN DEVELOPMENT AND SPACE
Secretary: Mr V R Gowariker
Secretary (Biotechnology): Dr S Ramachandran
Secretary (Space): Prof U R Rao
Secretary (Science and Technology): Dr P Rama Rao
Secretary (Atomic Energy): Dr P K Iyenger
Secretary (Electronics): Mr N Vittal
Secretary (Ocean-Development): Dr V K Gaur

MINISTRY OF FINANCE
Secretary: Mr K P Geetakrishnan
Secretary (Expenditure): Mr K V R Nair
Secretary (Revenue): Mr K P Geetakrishnan
Secretary (Economic Affairs): Mr M S Ahluwalia

MINISTRY OF EXTERNAL AFFAIRS
Foreign Secretary: Mr J N Dixit
Secretary (West): I P Khosla
Secretary (East): Mr L L Mehrotra

MINISTRY OF DEFENCE
Secretary: Mr N M Vohra
Secretary (Production and Supplies): Mr N Raghunathan
Secretary (Research and Development): Dr V S Arunachalam
Secretary (Defence Finance): Mr B V Adavi

MINISTRY OF HOME AFFAIRS
Secretary: Mr M D Godbole

MINISTRY OF RAILWAYS
Chairman and Secretary (Railway Board): Mr R D Kitson

MINISTRY OF POWER AND NON-CONVENTIONAL ENERGY SOURCES
Secretary (Power): Mr S Rajagopal
Secretary (Department of Non-Conventional Energy Sources): Mr R K Sharma

MINISTRY OF PETROLEUM AND NATURAL GAS
Secretary: Mr Ashok Chandra

MINISTRY OF INDUSTRY
Secretary (Industrial Development and Company Affairs): Mr Suresh Mathur
Secretary (Small Scale and Rural Industry): Mr R Vasudevan
Secretary (Public Enterprises): Mr S Sharma

MINISTRY OF LAW, JUSTICE AND COMPANY AFFAIRS
Attorney-General: Mr G Ramaswami
Secretary (Legal Affairs): Dr P C Rao
Secretary (Legislative Department): Ms V S Ramadevi
Secretary (Department of Company Affairs and Industry): Mr Suresh Mathur

MINISTRY OF LABOUR
Secretary: Mr V P Sawhney

MINISTRY OF PARLIAMENTARY AFFAIRS
Secretary: Mr R Srinivasan

MINISTRY OF AGRICULTURE
Secretary (Agriculture and Co-operation): Mr R C Kapila
Secretary (Rural Development): Mr S R Sankaran

MINISTRY OF FOOD PROCESSING INDUSTRIES
Secretary: Mr M M S Srivastava

MINISTRY OF FOOD
Secretary: Mr P Tripathy

MINISTRY OF CIVIL SUPPLIES AND PUBLIC DISTRIBUTION SYSTEM
Secretary: Mr B K Goswami

MINISTRY OF CHEMICALS AND FERTILIZERS
Secretary (Chemicals): Mr M S Gill
Secretary (Fertilizers): Mr P V Krishnaswamy

MINISTRY OF COMMERCE
Secretary (Commerce): (Vacant)
Secretary (Supply): Mr K C Sivaramakrishnan

MINISTRY OF HUMAN RESOURCE DEVELOPMENT
Secretary (Human Resource Development): J Veeraroghavan
Secretary (Education): Mr Anil Bordia
Secretary (Culture): Mr B Ghose
Secretary (Women and Child Development): Ms Meera Seth
Secretary (Sports and Youth): Mr M Rajendran

MINISTRY OF INFORMATION AND BROADCASTING
Secretary: Mr Mahesh Prasad

MINISTRY OF STEEL AND MINES
Secretary (Steel): Mr R Vasudevan
Secretary (Mines): Mr V Krishnan

MINISTRY OF PLANNING AND PROGRAMME IMPLEMENTATION
Secretary (Programme Implementation): Mr S K Lal

MINISTRY OF TEXTILES
Secretary: Mr K Aradhanareswaran

MINISTRY OF WATER RESOURCES
Secretary: Mr M A Chitale

MINISTRY OF COAL
Secretary: Mr R C Jain

MINISTRY OF PERSONNEL, PUBLIC GRIEVANCES, PENSIONS
Secretary: Mr M Dandapani

DEPARTMENT OF SURFACE TRANSPORT
Secretary: Mr P M Abraham

MINISTRY OF CIVIL AVIATION AND TOURISM
Secretary (Civil Aviation): Mr A V Ganesan
Secretary (Tourism): Mr M Bahl

MINISTRY OF HEALTH AND FAMILY WELFARE
Secretary: Mr R L Misra
Secretary (Family Welfare): Mr K K Mathur

MINISTRY OF COMMUNICATIONS
Secretary: Mr S G Pitroda

MINISTRY OF URBAN DEVELOPMENT
Secretary: Mr R K Bhargava

MINISTRY OF WELFARE
Secretary: Mrs Ushavohra

MINISTRY OF ENVIRONMENT AND FORESTS
Secretary: Mr R Rajamani

ARMED FORCES HEADQUARTERS
Chief of Army Staff: General S F Rodrigues
Chief of Naval Staff: Admiral L Ramdas
Chief of Air Staff: Air Chief Marshal N C Suri

Comptroller and Auditor-General: Mr C G Somiah

THE STATES AND TERRITORIES OF THE UNION

The Executive of each State consists of a Governor appointed by the President and normally holding his office for a period of five years, and a Council of Ministers who must be, or within six months become, members of the Legislature of the State. In some States the Legislature consists of a single House only, the Legislative Assembly, but in other States there is an Upper House as well, the Legislative Council.

Each assembly is elected directly by adult suffrage and has a maximum life of five years and strict limits as to maximum and minimum membership.

The legislative field is divided explicitly between the Union and the States, the residual powers belonging to the Union. In case of conflict, Union law overrides State law. Subject to the provisions of the Constitution, the Union Parliament may make laws for the whole or any part of the territory of India, and the Legislature of a State may make laws for the whole or any part of the State. The Union Parliament has exclusive powers to make laws with respect to matters grouped under 97 headings in the Constitution, including, *eg*, foreign affairs, defence, citizenship, currency, banking, railways, aviation, shipping, communications and trade and commerce with other countries. The State Legislatures have exclusive power to make laws for their own States with respect to matters grouped under 66 headings in the Constitution, *eg*, public order and police, education, public health, the administration of justice, elections to the Legislature, excise and taxes, water, land and forests. The Union Parliament and, subject to the exclusive powers referred to above, the State Legislatures have concurrent powers to make laws with respect to certain matters which are grouped under 47 headings in the Constitution, including criminal law and procedure, marriage and divorce, civil procedure, social security, labour, trade and commerce.

The Judges of the High Court of a State are appointed by the President, not by the Governor.

The President may proclaim an emergency which empowers the Union Government to assume executive and financial control of any State, but the proclamation must be approved subsequently by the Union Parliament. For up to three years the President may, if satisfied that the State cannot be governed in accordance with its constitution, himself assume the functions of Government subject to his proclamations (each valid for six months) receiving the subsequent approval of the Union Parliament.

The Union Territories are administered, save as otherwise provided by Parliament, by the President acting through an Administrator or other authority appointed by him.

Population figures mentioned below are based on the 1981 census.

STATES

ANDHRA PRADESH

The State of Andhra was formed in 1953 out of the Telugu-speaking parts of Madras State. Under the States Reorganisation Act, 1956, its size was almost doubled by the incorporation of the Telugu-speaking areas of the former Princely State of Hyderabad and its name was changed to Andhra Pradesh. Its area is about 274,540 sq km and its population 53.4 million. The State capital is Hyderabad. The Congress (I) Party forms the Government.

Governor: Krishna Kant
Chief Minister: Janardhan Reddy
Chief Secretary: G R Nair

ARUNACHAL PRADESH

In January 1972 the North East Frontier Agency (part of Assam but administered by the Union Government) was made into the Union Territory called Arunachal Pradesh. Its area is over 82,800 sq km and the population is about 6,320,000. Arunachal Pradesh became a full State of the Indian Union in February, 1987. The State capital is Itanagar. It was granted a Legislative Assembly in 1975. The Assembly was dissolved and President's rule imposed on 3rd November, 1979. This was lifted when elections were held in January 1980, which resulted in a victory for the Congress (I). Congress (I) was again victorious in the December 1984 and February 1990 elections.

Governor: S N Dwivedi
Chief Minister: Gegong Apang
Chief Secretary: Matin Dai

ASSAM

The State of Assam comprises the former Province of Assam, and a number of small Princely States. Its borders were affected by the States Reorganisation Act, 1956, and in 1972 Meghalaya (*q.v.*) and Arunachal Pradesh (*q.v.*) were cut out of Assam. Its principal language is Assamese. Its area is about 99,197 sq km and the population is nearly 20 million. The State capital is Dispur.

President's rule was imposed in November 1990. It was lifted when State elections were held in June 1991, resulting in a victory for Congress (I).

Governor: Loknath Misra
Chief Minister: Hiteshwar Saikia
Chief Secretary: P C Mishra

BIHAR

The State of Bihar comprises the former Province of Bihar and the two small Princely States of Kharsawan and Seraikella. Under the States Reorganisation Act, 1956, it lost some territory to the neighbouring State of West Bengal. Its principal language is Hindi. Its area is about 173,530 sq km and its population is about 70 million. The state capital is Patna. President's Rule was imposed in February 1980 and Advisors to the Governor appointed. It was lifted when State elections were held in May 1980, resulting in a victory for Congress (I). The Congress (I) lost to the Janata Dal (122 of 324 seats) following elections in February 1990.

Governor: M S Qureshi
Chief Minister: L P Yadav
Chief Secretary: Arun Pathak

GOA

Goa, Daman and Diu became a territory of the Indian Union according to the provisions of the Constitution (Twelfth Amendement) Act, 1962. Goa became a full State of the Indian Union in May 1987. The State has an area of 3,610 sq km and the population is about one million. The State capital is Panaji. The Congress (I) lost to the Progressive Democratic Front following elections in January 1990. (Daman and Diu remain Union Territory).

Governor: Bhanu Pratap Singh
Chief Minister: Ravi Naik
Chief Secretary: P V JayaKrishnan

GUJARAT

Established on 1st May 1960, following the division of the bi-lingual Bombay State, Gujarat comprises the former States of Saurashtra and Kutch and the Gujarati-speaking area in the north of the former Bombay State reaching as far south as Surat. The area of the State is about 186,480 sq km and its population about 34 million. The state capital is Gandhinagar. President's Rule was imposed in February 1980 but was lifted when State elections were held in May 1980, resulting in a victory for Congress (I). Congress (I) lost to the Janata Dal following elections in February 1990.

Governor: Dr Sarup Singh
Chief Minister: Chimanbhai Patel
Chief Secretary: H K Khan

HARYANA

Haryana was established as a separate State in 1966 following the reorganisation of the Punjab (of which it was previously a part) on linguistic lines. Its principal language is Hindi. Its area is about 44,030 sq km and its population almost 13 million. The town of Chandigarh, part of a separate Union Territory forms the State capital of Punjab as well as Haryana. The award of exclusive control of the city to Punjab remains to be implemented. The State elections were held in June 1991 resulting in the defeat of Janata Dal. The Congress (I) forms the State Government.

Governor: D L Mandal
Chief Minister: Bhajan Lalh
Chief Secretary: B Sojha

HIMACHAL PRADESH

The State of Himachal Pradesh comprises a number of former Princely States in the Punjab Hill area, plus six districts formerly belonging to the Punjab but allotted to Himachal when the Punjab was reorganised in 1966. Himachal Pradesh was a Union Territory until January 1971 when it acquired full Statehood. The State's area is about 50,505 sq km and its population about 4.3 million. Its capital is Simla. The Bharatiya Janata Party (46 of 68 seats) won the elections held in March 1990.

Governor: Virendra Verma
Chief Minister: Shanta Kumar
Chief Secretary: M S Mukherjee

JAMMU & KASHMIR
The State of Jammu & Kashmir has a claimed area of over 222,740 sq km although a large part of this is occupied by China and Pakistan. Its population is 6 million. Capital, Srinagar (summer), Jammu (winter). State elections were held in March 1987. The Chief Minister, Dr Farooq Abdullah resigned on 18th January 1990, Governor's rule was imposed on 19th January 1990 and President's rule since 19th July 1990.

Governor: G C Saxena
Chief Secretary: V K Kapur

KARNATAKA
The state of Karnataka comprises the former Princely State of Mysore, more than doubled in size in 1956 by the addition of the Kannada-speaking areas of Bombay, Hyderabad, Madras and Coorg. Its area is about 191,660 sq km and its population about 37 million. The State capital is Bangalore. The state was brought under the President's rule on 21st April 1989. State elections were held in November 1989. The Congress (I) Party forms the State Government.

Governor: K A Khan
Chief Minister: S Bangarappa
Chief Secretary: M Shan Karanarayanan

KERALA
The State of Kerala was formed in 1956 out of most of the former Malayalam-speaking State of Travancore-Cochin (originally a Union of Princely States) together with the Malabar District of Madras, also Malayalam-speaking. Its area is about 38,850 sq km and its population about 25.4 million. The state capital is Trivandrum. The Congress (I) led United Democratic Front forms the State Government following elections in June 1991.

Governor: B Rachiah
Chief Minister: K Karanakalau
Chief Secretary: S Narayanaswamy

MADHYA PRADESH
The State of Madhya Pradesh originally comprised the former Central Provinces, Berar and 15 Princely States. In 1956 its borders were substantially redrawn. It lost territory in the south-west (Berar) to Bombay and acquired the former States of Bhopal, Madhya Bharat and Vindhya Pradesh, all originally Princely States or unions of such States. Its principal language is Hindi. Its area is about 442,890 sq km and its population about 52.1 million. Its capital is Bhopal. Bharatiya Janata Party won the State elections in March 1990 (220 of 320 seats).

Governor: Kanwar Mahmood Ali
Chief Minister: Sunderlal Patwa
Chief Secretary: R P Kapoor

MAHARASHTRA
Established on 1st May 1960 following the division of the bi-lingual Bombay State, Maharashtra comprises the area of the former Bombay State south and east of Surat District (including Vidarbha). The area of the State is about 306,915 sq km and its population about 62.7 million. The principal language is Marathi. The State capital is Bombay City. Congress (I) won state elections in May 1980 and March 1985 (162 of 285 seats). It was re-elected in March 1990 (142 of 288 seats).

Governor: C Subramaniam
Chief Minister: Sudhakar Naik
Chief Secretary: D M Sukthankar

MANIPUR

Manipur was formerly a Princely State and then a Part C State of the same name. It was granted full statehood in January 1972. Its area is about 22,274 sq km and its population is about 1 million. Its capital is Imphal. The State elections were held in February 1990. The six party United Legislature Front (33 of 60 seats) forms the State Government.

Governor: C Panigrahi
Chief Minister: R K Ranbir Singh
Chief Secretary: B R Basu

MEGHALAYA

In April 1970 Meghalaya was formed as a sub-state within the State of Assam from the two Assam hill Districts of Garo and United Khasi and Jaintia Hills. Meghalaya attained full statehood in January 1972. Its capital is Shillong. Its area is about 20,720 sq km and its population just over 1 million. Meghlaya United Parliamentary Party forms the State Government. The next election is due in February 1993.

Governor: Madhukar Dighe
Chief Minister: B B Lyngdoh
Chief Secretary: V Ramakrishnan

MIZORAM

In January 1972 the Mizo Hills Area of Assam was made into a Union Territory called Mizoram. Its capital is Aizawl. Its area is about 20,720 sq km and its population about 0.5 million. Mizoram became a full State of the Indian Union in August 1986. The Mizo National Front won 24 of the 40 Assembly seats in the February 1987 elections and formed the state government. Mr Laldenga's government fell in September 1988 and Mizoram was brought under President's rule. In fresh elections in January 1989 the Congress (I) was victorious.

Governor: Swaraj Kaushal
Chief Minister: Lal Thanhawla
Chief Secretary: M Lalmanzuala

NAGALAND

Under the Constitution (Thirteenth Amendment) Act 1962, the areas comprised in the Naga Hills-Tuensang Area, known by the name of Nagaland, became a separate State of the Indian Union. The State has an area of 16,151 sq km and the population number about 775,000. The State capital is Kohima.

The Congress (I) was returned to power in elections in January 1989. S C Jamir was elected Chief Minister. However, his Ministry was reduced to a minority on 14th May 1990 as 12 party MLAs left the party. A 14-member United Legislature Front Ministry, headed by K L Chisi, was sworn in on 15th May 1990 following the dismissal of the Congress (I) Ministry headed by S C Hamir. K L Chisi resigned on 19th June 1990 and Mr Vamuzo, leader of the 42-member Joint Legislature Party was sworn in as the new Chief Minister.

Governor: M M Thomas
Chief Minister: Vamuzo
Chief Secretary: T C K Lotha

ORISSA

The State of Orissa comprises the former Province of Orissa and 24 former Princely States. Its borders were unaffected by the States Reorganization Act, 1956. Its principal language is Oriya. Its area is about 155,400 sq km and its population about 26 million. The State capital is Bhubaneshwar. Janata Dal won the elections in February 1990 (123 of 147 seats).

Governor: Y D Sharma
Chief Minister: Biju Patnaik
Chief Secretary: R K Mishra

PUNJAB

The Punjab lost its strict claim to the name (which means 'Five Rivers') when it was partitioned in 1947. In 1956 it was enlarged by the incorporation of a group of former Princely States. In 1966 it was reorganised and divided on linguistic lines. The present Punjab, the main language of which is Punjabi, thus represents only a small portion of the original Punjab. Its area is about 50,505 sq km, and its population about 16.7 million. The State capital is Chandigarh. In July 1985 Prime Minister Rajiv Gandhi signed the Punjab Accord with Akali Dal leader Sant Longowal. Despite Longowal's assassination, state elections were held in Punjab in September 1985 and the Akali Dal formed the State Government. Due to complete breakdown of law and order in the State, the Barnala Ministry was dismissed and President's rule was imposed on 11th May 1987. The Punjab Assembly was dissolved on 6th March 1988. President's rule continues to apply in the state.

Governor: Gen O P Malhotra
Chief Secretary: Tejinder Khanna

RAJASTHAN

The State of Rajasthan was formed by the union of 18 minor and four major Princely States, including Jaipur, Bikaner, Jodhpur and Udaipur. It was enlarged in 1956 by the addition of Ajmer. Its principal language is Hindi. Its area is about 341,880 sq km and its population about 34.1 million. The State capital is Jaipur. Bharatiya Janata Party won the elections in February 1990. BJP(85) JD(54) Coalition forms the State Government.

Governor: Dr M Channa Reddy
Chief Minister: B S Shekhawat
Chief Secretary: V B L Mathur

SIKKIM

The area of the Himalayan State of Sikkim is 7,110 sq km and its population about 0.3 million. Its capital is Gangtok. Sikkim became an 'associated state' of the Indian Union, with the right to have representatives in the Union Parliament, by a constitutional amendment (1974). The Chogyal (ruler) lost his control over the administration, and Sikkim became a full State of the Indian Union in May 1975 under a further constitutional amendment. President's Rule was imposed on 25th May 1984 and the 32-member State Assembly dissolved in the face of a deepening political crisis following the resignation of 17 Congress (I) legislators from the party that reduced the Gurung Ministry, inducted into office less than a fortnight earlier, to a minority. In fresh elections in March 1985 N B Bhandari's Sikkim Sangram Parishad was victorious (31 of 32 seats)

Governor: Admiral R H Tahiliani
Chief Minister: N B Bhandari
Chief Secretary: K C Pradhan

TAMIL NADU

The State of Madras was re-named Tamil Nadu in 1968 and comprises the large Tamil-speaking remnant of the former Province of Madras. In 1953 it lost its northern areas to Andhra and in 1956 some of its western districts to Mysore and Kerala. It acquired, however, in 1956 a small Tamil-speaking portion of Travancore-Cochin. Its area is about 129,500 sq km and its population about 48.4 million. The State capital is Madras. The All India Anna DMK Party was victorious in state elections in May 1980 and again in March 1985, when it fought in alliance with the Congress (I) (133 of 235 seats). The Chief Minister, Mr M G Ramachandran died on 24th December 1987. An eight-member cabinet was formed by V N Janaki Ramachandran (wife of the late Chief Minister) on 7th January 1988 but Tamil Nadu was brought under President's rule on 30th January 1988. In elections held in January 1989 Mr Karunanidhi's DMK party was victorious, winning 147 seats. President's rule was imposed again on 30th January 1991. President's rule was lifted following elections in June 1991. AIADMK Party forms the State Government.

Governor: B N Singh
Chief Minister: Miss Jayalalitha
Chief Secretary: T V Venkataraman

TRIPURA
Tripura was formerly a Princely State and then a Part C State of the same name. It was granted full statehood in January 1972. Its area is about 10,360 sq km and its population about 2.1 million. Its capital is Agartala. A Left Front headed by the Communist Party (Marxist) camc to power in 1977 and was re-elected in 1982 (37 of 60 seats). The most recent elections were held in February 1988. A 16-member two-tier Congress (I)—TUJS coalition forms the state government.

Governor: Raghunath Reddy
Chief Minister: S R Majumdar
Chief Secretary: I P Gupta

UTTAR PRADESH
The State of Uttar Pradesh comprises the former United Provinces and the Princely States of Benares, Tehri-Garhwal and Rampur. Its boundaries were unaffected by the States Reorganisation Act, 1956. Its principal language is Hindi. Its area is about 292,670 sq km and its population is about 111 million. The State capital is Lucknow. Janata Dal won the elections held in December 1989 (209 of 426 seats). Following elections in June 1991, the Janata Dal government was defeated. The BJP (211 of 404 seats) forms the State Government. Elections in 21 constituencies were countermanded.

Governor: B Satya Narain Reddy
Chief Minister: Kalyan Singh
Chief Secretary: Dr V K Saxena

WEST BENGAL
The State of West Bengal comprises the western part of the former Bengal Province and the Princely State of Cooch Behar. Under the States Reorganisation Act, 1956, it was enlarged to include certain contiguous areas of Bihar. Its principal language is Bengali. Its area is about 88,060 sq km and its population about 54.5 million. The State capital is Calcutta. The Communist Party (Marxist) is the major party in the Left Front State Government, following elections in June 1991 (242 of 294 seats).
The next election is due in June 1996.

Governor: Prof Nurul Hasan
Chief Minister: Jyoti Basu
Chief Secretary: N Krishnamurthi

UNION TERRITORIES

THE ANDAMAN AND NICOBAR ISLANDS
This chain of islands, with an area of 8,327 sq km, lies in the eastern part of the Bay of Bengal about 1,287 km to the east and south-east of Madras. The total population is about 200,000 of whom two thirds are to be found in the Andamans, where the majority live within a radius of 24 km of Port Blair, the capital.

Lieutenant Governor: Lt Gen (Rtd) R S Dyal
Chief Secretry: Gorakh Ram

CHANDIGARH
The Union Territory of Chandigarh came into being in 1966, in accordance with the Constitution (Eighteenth Amendment) Act, providing for the linguistic reorganisation of the Punjab. It has an area of 114 sq km and a population of about 0.5 million.

Chief Administrator: Gen O P Malhotra

DADRA AND NAGAR HAVELI
The area became a Union Territory, under the terms of the Constitution (Tenth Amendment) Act, 1961, on 11th August 1961. It has an area of 490 sq km, and a population of 100,000. Its capital is Silvassa.

Administrator: Bhanu P Singh
Chief Secretary: K M Sahni

DAMAN AND DIU

Goa, Daman and Diu became a territory of the Indian Union according to the provisions of the Constitution (Twelth Amendment) Act, 1962. Goa became the 25th State of the Indian Union on 30th May 1987. The area of Daman and Diu is about 96 sq km and its population is 51,602.

Administrator: Bhanu P Singh
Chief Secretary: K M Sahni

DELHI

The Territory of Delhi (formerly a Part C State) comprises the cities of Old and New Delhi and the area immediately surrounding them. Its area is 1,484 sq km and its population about 6 million. Delhi Metropolitan Council and the Executive Council were dissolved on 13th January 1990.

Lieutenant Governor: Markandey Singh
Chief Minister: Jag Parvesh Chandra
Chief Secretary: R K Takkar

LAKSHADWEEP

(formerly known as The Laccadive, Minicoy and Amindivi Islands)
This group of very small islands lies between 161 and 322 km off the south-west coast of India. The islands were, prior to 1956, administered by the State of Madras. The total area of the group is 28 sq km and the population about 40,000. The Administrative Headquarters is at Kavaratti.

Administrator: W Habibullah

PONDICHERRY

The Government of India, in agreement with the Government of France, took over the administration of the French Establishments in India (Pondicherry, Karaikal, Yanam and Mahe) in 1954, and a Treaty ceding these territories was signed in 1956 and ratified by the French Assembly in 1962. The total area is 482 sq km and the population 600,000. The former French settlements now form one Territory of the Union under the collective name of Pondicherry. The Assembly was dissolved on 24th June 1983 and President's Rule was imposed for six months. President's Rule was extended for the third time on 23rd June 1984. In elections in March 1985 the Congress (I) fighting in alliance with the AIADMK was victorious. DMK won the elections held in February 1990. Pondicherry has been under President's rule since 12th January 1991. President's rule was lifted following elections in June 1991 resulting in victory for the Congress (I).

Lieutenant Governor: Harswarup Singh
Chief Minister: V Vaithilingam
Chief Secretary: P M Nair

Titles in India

Prefixes to Indian names

Indian prefixes (to be used instead of, and not in addition to, Mr, Mrs, and Miss) are for men, Shri; for married women, Shrimati; and for unmarried women, Kumari. In the case of Sikhs the prefixes are Sardar, Sardani and Biba respectively. In Tamil Nadu for men it is Thiru, for married women Thirumathi and unmarried women Selvi.

The suffix 'ji' is frequently added to Indian names as a term of respect. This can either be to the first name (Indiraji) or to the last name (Gandhiji).

Indian Honours

The practice of giving awards was abolished by the Janata Government in July 1977 but was later revived.

Titles

Under the Indian Constitution, 'no title, not being a military or academic distinction, shall be conferred by the State'.

Titles received before Independence, or hereditary titles, may be retained, but they are not used in official communications.

Jamaica

Capital: Kingston

Location, Topography and Climate

Christopher Columbus named the island Jamaica on his first visit in 1494, taking the word from the Arawak 'Xaymaca', the meaning of which is obscure. Lying in the tropics (between 70° 11′ and 78° 21′ W and 17° 43′ and 18° 32′ N), Jamaica is 160 km (100 miles) west of Haiti and 144 km (90 miles) south of Cuba (nearest point to nearest point). The island is 234 km (146 miles) long and about 82 km (51 miles) wide at the widest point, with a total area of 11,469 sq km (4,411 square miles) making it the third largest island in the Caribbean, and the largest Anglophone.

Jamaica is mountainous; the main range runs from east to west and the highest point is Blue Mountain Peak 2,221 m (7,402 ft). There are no large waterways but many small rivers and streams which can cause flash floods after heavy rain. The coastline is indented with many bays and harbours, the most important being Kingston Harbour, one of the finest in the world. On the north coast the main ports (and resorts) are Montego Bay and Ocho Rios. Port Antonio on the east coast and Negril at the Western tip of the island are growing centres for tourism.

On the coast daytime temperatures are high, maximum 34°C (94°F) minimum 22°C (70°F), but are mitigated by sea breezes; higher up it is markedly cooler. Jamaica lies in the hurricane zone; in 1988, Hurricane Gilbert raged the length of the island causing widespread damage. Rainfall is greater in the latter half of the year, and on the north coast, averaging 1,500 mm (60 inches) in Kingston but 3,850 mm (154 inches) in Port Antonio.

Population

The population of Jamaica (official figure: December 1990) is 2,415,100, not including the substantial communities of Jamaican citizens in the UK, USA and Canada. The birth rate in 1987 was 24.8 per thousand and the death rate was 5.1 per thousand while life expectancy at birth was 68.1 years for males and 72.6 for females. The 1990 figures give the annual rate of increase of population as 1.0 per cent. English is spoken everywhere, although visitors may find it difficult to understand the local patois dialect.

Some 75 per cent of Jamaicans are members or adherents of Christian churches and there are also Hindu, Moslem and Jewish communities. Of the Christians about half belong to the 'established' churches (notably Anglican, Methodist, Baptist and Roman Catholic), the others to churches in the North American Pentecostal tradition.

Health

Apart from sickle cell disease the pattern of illnesses corresponds more or less to that of the developed world. Diabetes, hypertension and venereal diseases are the most prevalent; malaria, yellow fever, rabies and bilharzia do not exist. Government medical services and hospital care are subsidised and, at their best, are of a high standard but shortage of funds makes the service patchy. There are several private clinics and hospitals.

Communications

Passenger transport to and from Jamaica is almost entirely by air. There are two international airports, Norman Manley (length of runway 2,627 m (8,616 ft)) some 22 km (14 miles) from the centre of Kingston and Donald Sangster (length of runway 2,668 m (8,751 ft)) at Montego Bay. British Airways and other European, North and South American airlines operate scheduled services. Jamaica's international carrier is Air Jamaica. Flights both regular and charter are available to smaller domestic airfields.

The 11 berths at Newport West, which comprise a part of the Port of Kingston, handle most of Jamaica's imports. Two private companies, Kingston Wharves Ltd and Western Terminals Ltd operate 7 of the 11 berths and the other 4 which comprise a transhipment container port, are operated by the Port Authority of Jamaica.

At the Port of Kingston, there are also dedicated sufferance wharves to handle bulk cargoes such as petroleum, flour, cement, gypsum and lumber. Other ports in the island handle sugar, banana, bauxite/alumina among others.

The major shipping lines providing regular service to the Port of Kingston are: Zim Israeli, Carol Consortium, Evergreen and Sealand.

There are 4,740 km (2,944 miles) of main roads, 11,695 km (7,264 miles) of subsidiary roads and 1,497 km (930 miles) of road in the Kingston Metropolitan area.

The Economy

Jamaica has a large and diversified economy by regional standards but one which is particularly sensitive to changing external factors.

During most of the 1970's Jamaica was the world's largest exporter of bauxite and alumina which in 1981 accounted for 78 per cent of visible exports. But in the early 1980's, recession in Jamaica's main markets (North America and the UK) led to a sharp decline in earnings from these exports. This led to a difficult period of adjustment, during which Jamaica's economic and industrial development was financed through increased borrowing from the IMF and other financial institutions. The country has an external debt of some US $4.5 billion, the servicing of which consumes over 45 per cent of foreign exchange earnings.

In September 1991 the Government announced the lifting of the remaining foreign exchange controls.

Tourism is now the principal foreign exchange earner although the industry is susceptible to changing market trends and faces fierce competition from other holiday destinations such as Barbados and Dominica. It recovered fully after Hurricane Gilbert in 1988.

From time to time hurricanes are a threat to Jamaica's main agricultural exports—bananas, sugar, coffee. Prices for these products are also susceptible to market fluctuations.

Education

Jamaica's educational system is based on the British pre-war pattern. The State provides primary schooling throughout the island. Entry to secondary education, also free, is by the 'Common Entrance' (11 plus) examination. There are a number of independent preparatory schools and two independent high schools in Kingston. All high school students sit the CXC (Caribbean Examination Certificate) before graduating and most high schools offer GCE Advanced Level courses.

Entry to university or technical college is also by competition. The University of the West Indies at Mona is the principal of three campuses the others being in Trinidad and in Barbados. The University College Hospital was opened in 1953 and its degrees are recognised by the General Medical Council of England. Unable to compete on salary, Jamaica loses many of its graduates by emigration, especially to the United States.

The Media

There are currently six broadcasting companies in Jamaica. The Jamaica Broadcasting Corporation operates the only television station. Programmes are broadcast in colour. A new television station CVM–TV is due to begin broadcasting.

JBC and RJR (Radio Jamaica Ltd) broadcast radio programmes on both AM and FM frequencies. Three other stations broadcast only on the FM band. They are KLAS (Island Broadcasting Services Ltd) from Mandeville, Radio WAVES from Montego Bay and Radio IRIE from Ocho Rios.

There are two national daily newspapers in Jamaica—*The Daily Gleaner* and *The Jamaica Record.* Both produce weekend editions and the Gleaner company also produces an afternoon daily, The Star.

History and Constitutional Development

When Columbus arrived in Jamaica in 1494, the indigenous Arawak Indians are thought to have numbered about 60,000. Columbus took possession of the island for Spain and a Spanish governor was appointed in 1509 but, because it lacked gold, Jamaica was never regarded as important and served mainly as a staging post for ships bound for the isthmus. The first small capital, Sevilla la Nueva, near St Ann's Bay on the North coast was soon abandoned in favour of Vila de la Vega, now Spanish Town. The Arawak Indians soon died out.

In 1655 an English expedition under Admiral Penn and General Venables, having failed to accomplish Cromwell's 'Grand Design' of capturing Hispaniola, sailed on to Jamaica and occupied the capital, meeting only light resistance. The Spanish Governor with some followers and slaves held out in the rugged Cockpit country in the west of the island until escaping in 1660 to Cuba. Slaves whom they left behind formed the nucleus of what came to be known as the Maroons.

General Edward D'Oyley was appointed the first civil Governor in 1661, and was succeeded in 1662 by Lord Windsor, who brought with him a Royal Proclamation giving the settlers of Jamaica the rights of citizens of England and the right to make laws. This first colonial constitution, which lasted for two centuries, provided for an Executive (the Governor and a nominated Council) and a Legislature (the Governor, the Council and a Representative Assembly).

Although Port Royal was the first capital, much of the administration was removed in 1664 to Spanish Town, where the first elected members of the Representative Assembly, comprising 20 freeholders, met that year.

In the early years colonisation proceeded slowly, the island proving very unhealthy. Settlers included special groups from Nevis and Barbados and later from Surinam. Using slaves from Africa, they developed estates producing sugar, cocoa, indigo, and later coffee. Buccaneers made Port Royal prosperous on their plunder of Spanish ships and ports, but an earthquake destroyed the town in 1692, the date from which Kingston developed. During these years the Maroons, reinforced by fugitive slaves, continued to resist British authority, until in 1739 and 1740 agreements were signed on honourable terms guaranteeing the Maroons liberty and property rights.

Port Royal recovered from the earthquake to become a British naval base, steadily more important in the face of the growing threat of French attack, which was not finally laid to rest until Trafalgar.

During the eighteenth century many thousands of slaves were imported from Africa and were essential to the prosperity of the estates. Their ownership was regulated by Slave Laws which, though at first concerned with the owner's interests, eventually gave some protection to the slaves. Opposition to slavery and the slave trade developed in Jamaica in the latter half of the eighteenth century especially under the influence of Baptist missionaries, in parallel with the campaign in Britain led by Wilberforce and others.

The complete abolition of slavery in 1838 led to a shortage of labour on the estates which was not compensated for by the import of Chinese and Indian workers. At the same time the price of sugar was kept low by British free trade policy and Jamaica's strategic importance was declining. All this, combined with the social change which followed from the decline of the estate as the basic social unit, caused increasingly bitter feeling between whites, the blacks and the 'brown' middle class which had grown up between them.

Another cause of discontent was misuse of power by the whites under the terms of the old colonial constitution. By this time the Governor's Council, known as the Privy Council, consisted of a number of persons holding senior office, such as the Chief Justice and the Bishop, and representatives of the Legislative Council and Assembly. The latter was effectively limited to whites, who were mainly concerned with promoting their own interests.

All this led to the 1865 Morant Bay rebellion which, together with its ruthless suppression, shocked opinion in Britain and was the direct cause of the establishment of a Crown Colony giving much greater control to London. The new constitution gave legislative power to a Governor acting with the advice and consent of a Council, a majority of whose members were nominated. With a number of revisions in 1884 and 1895 this constitution lasted until 1944 and, paradoxically, was to pave the way for future political independence.

The economy revived in the latter half of the nineteenth century. Overseas markets were developed for Jamaican bananas, communications were improved and the country benefited from the general prosperity of the British Empire at the summit of its power, symbolised by Jamaica's Great Exhibition of 1891 opened in Kingston by the future King George V.

A disastrous earthquake in 1907 damaged every building in Kingston, destroyed the lower part of the town and killed 800 people.

After the First World War the rapid increase in population, banana disease and a series of storms increased economic distress caused by world recession; the political consequences were riots, a great increase in trade union activity and the beginnings of political parties. The People's National Party (PNP) was formed in 1938 under the leadership of Norman Manley to campaign for independence within the Commonwealth. The Jamaica Labour Party (JLP) was founded in 1943 by Manley's cousin Sir Alexander Bustamante. Both parties were trade union based.

It was at this time, in 1944, that the next big change in the constitution was initiated. The functions of the Privy Council were transferred to an Executive Council, half of whose members, now known as Ministers, had to have been elected by universal adult suffrage. The term Privy Council was retained for the body of senior people who also advised on the use of the Royal Prerogative. Self-government grew closer in 1953 when Ministers took charge of a majority of portfolios and Bustamante became Chief Minister, followed by Manley in 1955.

Jamaica joined the West Indian Federation in 1958. By this time the Jamaican Government had full responsibility for all internal affairs. The Council was now called the Cabinet, the Legislative Council became more and more like an Upper House or Senate, and the Legislative Assembly like the House of Representatives, a lower house where the real power lay. Service commissions on familiar lines were established. The Privy Council retained its limited role.

Jamaica was mainly responsible for the break-up of the Federation and thereafter sought full independence, which took effect on 6th August 1962. Sir Alexander Bustamante became the first Prime Minister.

While these political developments were taking place, there were important trends in the economy. Jamaica's bauxite industry, first established in the Second World War when supplies in large quantities from safe accessible places were essential, expanded greatly after the war so that by 1957 Jamaica was the world's largest producer; bauxite and alumina accounted for more than half of exports. The banana industry revived and Jamaica became a popular tourist destination. In spite of all this, unemployment persisted, aggravated by the growth of population. Large numbers of Jamaicans emigrated to Britain and North America.

Norman Manley's son Michael won the elections of 1972 and remained in office until 1980 when the JLP under Edward Seaga was returned to power with fifty-one seats to Manley's nine. The PNP boycotted the elections called by the JLP in 1983, but returned to fight and win the general election of 1989 which was delayed by the devastation caused by Hurricane Gilbert.

Constitution

The Constitution provides for a Governor-General appointed by The Queen and for a bi-cameral Legislature. The Senate consists of 21 Senators appointed by the Governor-General, 13 on the advice of the Prime Minister and 8 on the advice of the Opposition. The House of Representatives consists of 60 elected members.

Apart from certain entrenched provisions, the Constitution may be amended by a majority of all the members of each House. There are ordinarily entrenched and specially entrenched provisions. The first group may be amended by an affirmative vote of not less than two-thirds of all the members of each House, provided that there shall be a period of three months between the introduction of the Bill seeking to amend the Constitution and the commencement of the debate on it in the House of Representatives and a further period of three months between the conclusion of that debate and the passing of the Bill by the House. The specially entrenched provisions (which relate to the legal force of the Constitution, Parliament, Sessions of Parliament, the Prorogation and Dissolution of Parliament, General Elections and the appointment of Senators, and the Executive Authority of Jamaica, and which include the section providing for the alteration of the Constitution) may be amended by the same procedure as that required for the ordinarily entrenched provisions with the additional requirement that such amendment shall be approved by the electorate by referendum. Should the Senate not approve a Bill amending any of the specially entrenched provisions by a two-thirds majority of all its members the matter may be referred to the electorate by referendum in which case a majority of two-thirds of the electorate voting shall be required before the Bill may be presented to the Governor-General for assent. As regards any ordinarily entrenched provision the required majority is three-fifths of the electorate voting.

The Privy Council consisting of six members appointed by the Governor-General after consultation with the Prime Minister, of whom at least two are persons who hold or have held public office, advises the Governor-General on the exercise of the Royal Prerogative of Mercy and on appeals on disciplinary matters from the three Service Commissions.

The Governor-General appoints as Prime Minister the member of the House of Representatives who, in his judgement, is best able to command the support of the majority of the members of the House. The Governor-General also appoints the Leader of the Opposition.

Executive responsibility rests with a Cabinet consisting of the Prime Minister and not less than eleven other Ministers of whom not less than two nor more than four shall be members of the Senate. In addition any number of Parliamentary Secretaries may be appointed from the Senate.

The Governor-General is required to act on the advice of the Cabinet except in respect of any function conferred upon him in his discretion or any function exercisable on the advice or recommendation of, or after consultation with, persons or authorities other than the Cabinet.

Provision is made for the appointment of an Attorney-General, a Director of Public Prosecutions, an Auditor-General, a Public Service Commission, a Police Service Commission and a Judicial Service Commission.

There is a Supreme Court and a Court of Appeal. The President of the Court of Appeal and the Chief Justice of the Supreme Court are appointed by the Governor-General on the advice of the Prime Minister after consultation with the Leader of the Opposition.

HISTORICAL LIST OF GOVERNORS-GENERAL

Sir Kenneth Blackburne, GBE, KCMG (later GCMG), 6th August 1962 to 30th November 1962

Sir Clifford Campbell, GCVO, GCMG, from 1st December 1962 to 26th June 1973

Hon Florizel Glasspole, ON, CD, from 27th June 1973 to 1st August 1991

Hon Howard Felix Hanlan Cooke, CD, MJIM, from 1st August 1991

HISTORICAL LIST OF PRIME MINISTERS

Hon Sir Alexander Bustamante (Rt Hon Sir Alexander Bustamante from January 1964, GBE January 1967), 6th August 1962 to 21st February 1967

Hon D B Sangster (Sir Donald Sangster, KCMG, from 7th April 1967), 22nd February 1967 to 11th April 1967

Hon H L Shearer from 11th April 1967 (Rt Hon H L Shearer, from 6th January 1969) to 29th February 1972

Hon Michael N Manley, from 1st March 1972 to 1st November 1980

Hon Edward P Seaga from 2nd November 1980 to 9th February, 1989

Government

At the General Election on 9th February 1989 the People's National Party obtained 45 seats and the Jamaica Labour Party 15 seats.

HEAD OF STATE

Her Majesty Queen Elizabeth II

GOVERNOR-GENERAL

His Excellency the Most Honourable Howard Felix Hanlan Cooke, CD, MJIM

CABINET

Prime Minister: The Rt Hon P J Patterson, MP

Minister of Finance and Planning: The Hon Hugh Small, QC, MP

Minister of Agriculture: The Hon Seymour Mullings, MP

Minister of Production Mining and Commerce: Sen The Hon Carlyle Dunkley

Minister of Public Utilities, Transport and Energy: The Hon Robert Pickersgill, MP

Minister of Tourism and the Environment: The Hon John Junor, MP

Minister of Foreign Affairs and Foreign Trade: Sen The Hon David Coore

Minister of Education and Culture: The Hon Burchell Whiteman, MP
Minister of Health: The Hon Easton Douglas, MP
Minister of Labour, Welfare and Sport: The Hon Portia Simpson, MP
Minister of Construction: The Hon O D Ramtallie, MP
Minister of Public Service and Information: Sen The Hon Paul Robertson
Minister of Local Government, Youth and Community Development: The Hon Desmond Leakey, MP
Minister of National Security and Justice: The Hon K D Knight, MP
Minister without Portfolio: Sen The Hon Peter Phillips

MINISTERS OF STATE
Prime Minister's Office: Sen The Hon Maxine Henry-Wilson
Ministry of Agriculture: The Hon Ruddy Lawson, MP; The Hon Roger Clarke, MP
Ministry of Production, Mining and Commerce: The Hon Dean Peart, MP
Ministry of Public Utilities, Transport and Energy: The Hon Bobby Jones, MP
Ministry of Foreign Affairs and Foreign Trade: The Hon Ben Clare, MP
Ministry of Labour, Welfare and Sport: The Hon Marjorie Taylor, MP
Ministry of Construction: The Hon Terry Gillette, MP
Ministry of Local Government, Youth and Community Development: The Hon Donald Buchanan, MP
Ministry of Finance and Planning: The Hon Errol Ennis, MP

PARLIAMENTARY SECRETARIES
Ministry of Local Government, Youth and Community Development: Mr Horace Dalley, MP
Ministry of Education and Culture: Mr A J Nicholson, MP; Dr Karl Blythe, MP
Ministry of National Security and Justice: Mr Carl Miller, MP
Ministry of Local Government, Youth and Community Development: Mr Derrick Kellier, MP
Ministry of Health: Miss Violet Neilson, MP

LEADER OF THE OPPOSITION
The Rt Hon Edward P G Seaga, MP

PRESIDENT OF THE SENATE
(Vacant)

DEPUTY PRESIDENT OF THE SENATE
Senator Courtney Fletcher

HOUSE OF REPRESENTATIVES
Speaker: Hon Headley Cunningham, MP
Deputy Speaker: Mr Emerson Barrett, MP

OMBUDSMEN
Hon J S Kerr
Mr E G Green
Mr O G Marsh

JUDICIARY
Chief Justice and Keeper of the Records: Hon Edward Zacca

JUDGES OF THE COURT OF APPEAL
President: Mr Justice Ira Rowe

JUDGES OF APPEAL
B M Carey
U V Campbell
M L Wright
I X Forte
H E Downer

MINISTRIES AND GOVERNMENT DEPARTMENTS

KING'S HOUSE
Governor-General's Secretary: Carlton Scott
Auditor-General: A P Strachan

SECRETARY TO THE CABINET
Mr R Williams

PERMANENT SECRETARIES
Office of the Prime Minister: Ambassador Anthony Hill
Ministry of Foreign Affairs: Ambassador Glaister Duncan, CD
Ministry of Construction (Works): Mr Ronald Brown
Ministry of Construction (Housing): Mr Joseph Shako
Ministry of Public Utilities: (vacant)
Ministry of Agriculture: Mr Clarence Franklin, CD
Ministry of National Security: Mrs Clair Kean
Ministry of Justice: Mrs Sandra Mitchell
Ministry of the Public Service: Dr G Marshalleck
Ministry of Education: Dr Rae Davis
Ministry of Health: Mr Rupert Ramcharan
Ministry of Local Government: Mr Maisie Oreggio Alexander
Ministry of Youth and Community Development: Mr Horace Edwards
Ministry of Tourism: Mr Oswald Leake
Ministry of Labour, Welfare and Sport: Mr Alvin McIntosh
Ministry of Finance, Development and Planning: Mrs Shirley Tyndall
Ministry of Industry, Production and Commerce: Mrs Charmaine Constantine
Ministry of Mining and Energy: Mr Godfrey Perkins
Ministry of Information and Culture: Mrs Merle Brown
Ministry of Labour, Welfare and Sports: Mr Tony Irons

Kenya

Capital: Nairobi

Kenya has a total area of about 582,646 sq km, including 11,230 sq km of water. The territory lies astride the equator and extends from the Indian Ocean in the east to Uganda in the west, from Tanzania in the south to Ethiopia and Sudan in the north, while the north-east frontier runs with Somalia.

Physically, Kenya may be divided into four areas. The north-east is an arid plain, mostly covered with thorn bushes, less than 2,000 feet above sea level, with a small nomadic population; the south-east is similar but practically uninhabited except along the banks of the Tana River and in the coastal strip and the Taita Hills, which rise to 7,000 feet above sea level, and where the rainfall is adequate. The north-west is also generally low and arid, but includes Lake Turkana (formerly Rudolph) 160 miles long, and many mountains, including Nyiru (9,203 feet). The south-west quarter, in which 85 per cent of the population and practically all the economic production is concentrated, comprises a plateau rising to 10,000 feet, and includes Mount Kenya (17,058 feet), Mount Elgon (14,178 feet) and the Aberdare Range (13,104 feet). Much of the area between 7,000 and 11,000 feet above sea level (some 5,000 square miles) is forest. The plateau is bisected from north to south by a part of the Great Rift Valley, thirty to forty miles wide and 2,000 to 3,000 feet below the plateau on either side. The Rift floor rises from 1,280 feet above sea level at Lake Turkana to 7,000 feet near Naivasha, and falls again to 2,000 feet at Lake Natron. West of the Rift the plateau falls to Lake Victoria (3,720 feet above sea level) and eastward the Tana (length 425 miles) and Athi (length 329 miles) rivers flow to the Indian Ocean. The Athi River changes its name to the Galana at Tsavo. Neither river is navigable except by local craft.

Rainfall in Kenya ranges from a mean annual figure of 6 inches at Lodwar to 58 inches at Kisumu. There is a fairly close inverse correlation between altitude and temperature: at Mombasa, 53 feet above sea-level, the mean annual temperature is 27°C (80°F); at Nairobi, the capital, 5,495 feet, 19°C (67°F); on the equator at 9,062 feet, the mean temperature is 13°C (56°F). Glaciers are found on Mount Kenya down to 15,000 feet above sea level.

Comparative figures for population by race in 1969 and 1979, and the number of Kenyan citizens in each category in 1979 were:—

	1969 Census	*1979 Census*	*Citizens (1979)*
African (including Somali)	10,733,202	15,101,540	15,029,722
Asian	139,037	78,600	32,554
European	40,593	39,901	4,445
Arab	27,886	39,146	18,861
Other (covers all those who did not supply particulars of race)	1,987	67,874	57,318
TOTAL	10,942,705	15,327,061	15,142,900*

The current rate of population growth is in the region of 3.6 per cent per annum. In AD 2000 the total population is expected to reach 37 million.

Tribes and tribal groupings remain significant. Many sub-tribes also still exist and tribal languages are still spoken. The official languages are English and Swahili. The latter is much used in the towns but not universally spoken elsewhere. At the 1979 census the Kikuyu, Embu, Meru group comprised 27.9 per cent of the population, of which the Kikuyu were 21 per cent. The Luhya were 14 per cent and had overtaken the Luo (12.9 per cent) since the previous census. The Kamba (11.4 per cent) were followed by the Kalenjin group (10.9 per cent) who were previously counted separately and included the Kipsigis, Nandi, Tugen and Elgeyo tribes, all Kalenjin-speaking. The other significant tribes were the Kisii (6.2 per cent), the Mijikenda group of Coastal tribes (4.8 per cent), the Masai (1.6 per cent), the Turkana (1.3 per cent), the Somali and the Taita (each about 1 per cent).

Christianity is the major religion and is very widespread. There are many Muslims on the coast. The Asians include Hindus, Sikhs, Jains, Ismailis and Muslims.

Kenya is divided into eight provinces (Central, Coast, North-Eastern, Eastern, Western, Nyanza, Rift Valley and Nairobi).

* (now estimated to be about 20 million)

The capital of Kenya is Nairobi with a fast-growing population of well over 1 million.

The main port is Mombasa. Principal international airports are at Nairobi and Mombasa. Several air charter companies operate within Kenya. There are about 2,092 km (1,300 miles) of railway open for traffic.

Broadcasting services are provided by the parastatal Kenya Broadcasting Corporation. Radio services in English, Swahili, Hindustani and 15 African languages cover 80 per cent of the country. TV covers Nairobi and a belt west of Nairobi as far as Kisumu and Mombasa.

The economy of Kenya is essentially agricultural but secondary industry is being encouraged and tourism is the major foreign exchange earner with over 400,000 visitors a year.

Kenya's Development Plan for 1984–88 set a monetary GDP growth target expanding from 3.9 per cent in 1984 to 5.7 per cent in 1988. In a foreword, the Minister for Finance and Planning points out that the Plan has been made against a background of world recession which has spilt over into Kenya in terms of her balance of payments crisis and serious debt service ratio. From 1976/77, when the debt service ratio stood at 2.8 per cent of GDP, it has now risen to more than 24 per cent of GDP. This represents a major strain on the economy and has led to the theme of the mobilisation of domestic resources for equitable development, which underlines the Plan.

Kenya recorded a balance of payments surplus of K£73 million during 1986. The total value of exports grew by 22 per cent from K£811 million in 1985 to K£987 million in 1986 while the value of imports increased by 12 per cent from K£1,196 million in 1985 to K£1,338 million in 1986. This was due in part to a rapid growth of exports, which was mainly attributed to high coffee earnings, and to a modest rise in imports brought about in part by a lower energy bill following lower petroleum prices during most of 1986. The result was a decline in the trade deficit. This reduced deficit plus higher capital inflows resulted in a balance of payments surplus.

The terms of trade improved appreciably in 1986. Coffee prices rose considerably early in the year following fears of a shortfall in coffee production in Brazil. The sharp increase in the price of coffee led to the abolition of coffee quotas. On the other hand, there was a dramatic fall in the prices of petroleum products in 1986. The buoyant coffee and low oil prices contributed to an increase of 12 per cent in the terms of trade in 1986. Exports to the EC rose significantly, while those to the African region also continued to increase.

Reserve holdings improved in 1986, with a record level of K£395 million being registered in April 1986. The reserves rose partly as a result of the better performance of the export sector, and also partly as a result of the decline in the Kenya Shilling vis-à-vis the foreign currencies in which Kenya's reserves are held. Overall the Kenya Shilling depreciated by 6 per cent in trade weighted terms. Against the SDR the Shilling depreciated by 8 per cent despite its appreciation by slightly over 1 per cent against the US dollar. The Shilling remained at almost the same level against the Pound Sterling, but declined considerably against the German Mark.

Britain is Kenya's leading trading partner. Principal imports from Kenya are tea and coffee, fruit and vegetables, crude animal and vegetable material. Britain's main exports to Kenya are machinery, road vehicles, power generating machinery and telecommunications equipment.

Public holidays

Jamhuri Day, 12th December, celebrates both the attainment of Independence in 1963 and the adoption of a republican constitution in 1964. Kenyatta Day, 20th October, is the anniversary of the detention of President Kenyatta in 1952. Moi day, 10th October, marks the accession of President Moi to power in 1978. KANU Day, 11th June, first celebrated in 1990, marks the anniversary of the registration of the KANU Party in 1960. Madaraka Day on 1st June marks the anniversary of the attainment of internal self-government. 1st May is a holiday celebrating Labour Day, and the Muslim festival of Id-ul-Fitr, Christmas, Easter, and New Year's Day are also observed as public holidays.

Pre-independence history

Apart from knowledge of successive tribal migrations, little information is available regarding the early history of Kenya's interior. The coastal area has, however, been known for at least 2,000 years to Arabian merchants, who during the 7th century AD began to settle it with trading posts. The Portuguese explorer Vasco da Gama landed at Malindi, at the mouth of the Sabaki river, in 1498, after sailing round the Cape, and was welcomed by the Sultan. Subsequently the Portuguese established trading posts and gained for a time a monopoly of coastal trading. The Arabs appealed for help and their kinsmen from Oman drove out the Portuguese; Fort Jesus, in Mombasa, being taken in 1698. Although all important Portuguese possessions had gone by 1740, stability did not return to the coast until the rule of Seyyid Said (1806–1856).

The interior remained largely unknown to the West until the arrival of the first explorers in the middle of the 19th century.

Following German interest in East Africa, Britain and Germany concluded an agreement in 1886 regarding their respective spheres of influence. Britain was not, however, prepared to intervene directly, so in 1887 the British East Africa Association obtained from the Sultan of Zanzibar a concession of the mainland between the Umba and Tana Rivers. In 1888 the Imperial British East Africa Company was incorporated under Royal Charter.

Difficulties of administration in, and communication with, Uganda led to the construction of a railway linking the port of Mombasa with Kisumu on Lake Victoria. Construction commenced in 1895, and Kisumu was reached by 1901. During 1895 a Protectorate was declared over what is now Kenya and Uganda, the properties of the Imperial British East Africa Company being bought up.

European settlement took place between 1897 and the start of the First World War, following a survey made by Lord Delamere. Conditions of land alienation were laid down in 1902. There was also a large influx of Asians, in particular to work on the construction of the railways.

In 1905 the Protectorate was transferred from the authority of the Foreign Office to that of the Colonial Office, and a Governor and Commander-in-Chief, and Legislative and Executive Councils, were appointed in 1906. The Protectorate developed steadily prior to the First World War, settlement making good progress and exports of coffee, wool and wheat seemed promising.

The Germans in East Africa took the offensive at the start of the First World War, and penetrated Kenya's southern border. The British forces, under General Smuts, counter-attacked in 1916 and by 1917 much of German East Africa had been invaded and captured.

Many more settlers arrived after the War, special schemes being launched for ex-soldiers. The early 1920s were marked by financial and economic crises, and Kenya was still on the road to recovery when the effects of the world depression of the early 1930s were felt. Economically, the story of the later 1930s is one of gradual recovery.

The defence forces in Kenya were strengthened after the Italian occupation of Ethiopia in 1936. Italy entered the Second World War in 1940, and British forces, under General Cunningham, took the offensive in 1941. Italian resistance in East Africa ceased when Gondar fell in November 1941.

Between October 1952 and January 1960 a State of Emergency existed, during the period of the Mau Mau uprising. This rebellion was caused by discontent, particularly among the Kikuyu, over land and colonial rule. About 13,000 Africans were killed but less than 100 Europeans. The Kenya African Union party was banned and its leader, Mr Jomo Kenyatta, imprisoned. By 1956 the rebellion had been largely suppressed with the aid of British forces when the last remnants of the Mau Mau fighters were driven into the mountain forests and their leader, Dedan Kimathi, was captured. Over 80,000 people were detained during the emergency which also contributed to constitutional advance in other colonial territories by its effects on the policies of the British Government.

National political activities resumed when the State of Emergency was ended in preparation for independence. Two parties, the Kenya African National Union (KANU) and the Kenya African Democratic Union (KADU) were formed. On his release from restriction in August 1961 Mr Jomo Kenyatta became President of KANU. KADU which favoured a regional form of government was led by a Mr Ronald Ngala and Mr Daniel arap Moi.

Constitutional development

The first Legislative and Executive Council were appointed in 1906 following the transfer of the Protectorate from Foreign Office to Colonial Office authority.

In 1919 Europeans were elected to the Legislative Council and the number of Nominated Unofficial Europeans was increased from four to eleven. This led the more numerous Asian community to demand equal privileges. But in the Devonshire White Paper of 1923 it was laid down that Kenya was primarily an African territory and where African interests conflicted with those of the immigrant communities African interests should prevail. In the administration of Kenya His Majesty's Government regarded themselves as exercising a trust on behalf of the African population. At this time the African population was some two hundred times larger than the European population and one hundred times larger than the Asian population.

Although this White Paper led initially only to the nomination of one European missionary as an Unofficial Member to represent African interests it limited Asian representation to only five seats with one for Arabs whereas Europeans still had eleven seats. These statements stimulated African political activity but although Local Native Councils were established in 1925 it was only in 1944 that the first African, Mr Eliud Mathu was nominated to the Legislative Council.

Further changes occurred after the Second World War. In 1951 the Council was changed to comprise twenty-six Government and nominated members, fourteen European elected members and six Asian elected members plus six African and one Arab nominated representative members. In 1954 a Council of Ministers was introduced with six official and six unofficial Ministers including one African. In 1956 it was decided to replace the six African representative members by eight African elected members. Elections for these seats on a restricted franchise took place in 1957. In March 1958 elections for a further six African seats were held.

In 1960 it was agreed in London that the Constitution should be further amended and in February of 1961 elections were held for thirty-three open seats and twenty reserved seats on a common roll. The reserved seats were allocated ten for Europeans, eight for Asians and two for Arabs. A further twelve members were then specially elected by the Council. Although KANU won more seats than any other party, it declined to form a Government because Mr Kenyatta had not been released. KADU therefore formed a Government with the support of non-African members.

Mr Kenyatta was released in August 1961 and in January 1962 elected unopposed to the Legislative Council. Further constitutional talks in London led to a national coalition government of KANU and

KADU in which each party leader had equal status and there was no Chief Minister. In May 1963 following further amendments to the constitution general elections were held for 117 seats in a New House of Representatives and for 41 seats in a Senate, one for each district. Elections were also held for 176 seats in seven regional assemblies. KANU won 66 seats and its ally the Northern Province United Alliance NPUA 3, KADU won 31, the African Peoples Party (APP) 8 and Independents 4. The five seats in the North Eastern region were boycotted due to the Somali dispute. In the Senate KANU won 19 seats and NPUA 1, KADU 16 and APP 2. In the Regional Assemblies KANU won 88 seats to KADU's 51. This Parliament lasted until 1969.

On 1st June 1963 Kenya attained full internal self-government with Mr Kenyatta as Prime Minister of a KANU Government. On 12th December 1963 Kenya attained full independence as a Member of the Commonwealth.

Post independence history and the Constitution

The Independence Constitution provided for a Governor-General to be appointed by Her Majesty The Queen and a Parliament consisting of Her Majesty and a bi-cameral legislature, the National Assembly, comprising a Senate and a House of Representatives. The Constitution also provided for Regional Assemblies for each of the seven regions, each with a President and a Vice-President elected from within their own membership. The Regional Assemblies were given exclusive legislative competence in some matters and concurrent legislative competence with Parliament in others.

The Constitution (Amendment) Acts 1964 and 1965 provided for Kenya to become a Republic with a President as Head of State, Head of the Cabinet and Commander-in-Chief of the Armed Forces, choosing his Vice-President and Cabinet from among the members of the National Assembly to whom they are collectively responsible. The President would also appoint the Chief Justice, Chief Commissioner of Police and most senior civil servants. The first President was to be the Prime Minister in office immediately before 12th December 1964 (ie Mr Kenyatta) and was thereafter to be chosen by a majority of members of the House of Representatives. These acts also drastically reduced the powers and financial resources given to the Regional Assemblies by the Independence Constitution. These became Provincial Councils and were eventually abolished altogether by a further amendment in July 1967. During the passage of the 1964 Amendment Act the KADU opposition party, which had favoured the regional constitution, dissolved itself and joined the governing party KANU.

A further amendment in May 1965 reduced the majorities needed in the House of Representatives and the Senate to amend any clauses of the Constitution to a 65 per cent majority of all members of each House and provided that thenceforth no clauses should be specially entrenched as certain clauses had been in the Independence Constitution.

Following the resignation in April 1966 of the Vice-President, Mr Oginga Odinga, and his formation of a new Opposition Party, the KPU (Kenya People's Union), a Constitutional Amendment Act was passed requiring those members who changed their party allegiance to seek re-election. In the 'Little General Election' held in June 1966, KANU gained a majority of the contested seats but Mr Odinga was returned to lead the KPU, later recognised as the official Parliamentary Opposition.

Another Constitutional Amendment Act was passed in December 1966 to enable the Senate to be amalgamated with the House of Representatives as a unicameral National Assembly with 158 elected constituency members and 12 specially elected members elected by the constituency members. The Constituency boundaries were redrawn to give each Senator a constituency including at least a part of his former district and remained unchanged until 1988 when the number was increased to 188.

In June 1968 the Constitution was further amended to provide that both Presidential and Parliamentary candidates had to be nominated by a registered political party and, if opposed, elected by a popular vote. The amendment also provided that should a President die or become incapacitated in office, elections for a new President should be held within 90 days during which time the Vice-President, or failing him, such Minister as might be chosen by the Cabinet would act as President. It further provided that the 12 non-constituency members would henceforth be nominated by the President. A bill to consolidate these amendments with the remaining clauses of the Independence Constitution was passed in December 1968.

In August 1969 a system of primary elections for the selection of party candidates by universal suffrage was introduced and later extended to local elections.

In October 1969 the sole Opposition Party, the KPU, was banned and Kenya became a *de facto* one-party state. Thus in December 1969 only the primary elections to select one KANU candidate in each constituency were held, the successful candidate then being returned unopposed in the General Elections. The President, as the Presidential candidate of KANU, was also returned unopposed. President Kenyatta died on 22nd August 1978. The Vice-President, Mr Moi, acted as President during an interim period. He was subsequently elected President of KANU on 6th October and President of the Republic on 10th October (both unopposed). President Moi was sworn in as Kenya's second President on 14th October 1978 and was returned unopposed in November 1979, September 1983 and in March 1988.

In 1974 the Electoral Act was amended to make the primary elections more like General Elections with tighter control of voting arrangements. Local elections under the revised system were held on 17th August 1974 and national elections on 14th October 1974. Successful candidates in the primary elections were formally returned unopposed on 28th October and the new government announced on 31st October. The Third Parliament was sworn in on 6th November. It was dissolved in October 1979 and primary elections held on 8th November. Members were formally returned unopposed on 22nd November 1979. Following constitutional amendments in July 1974 and February 1975, the National Assembly debated in Swahili though bills and other documents were still in English. A further amendment in 1978 allowed debate to be in either Swahili or English. The Constitution was amended in June 1982 to make Kenya a *de jure* one party state. General elections were held in September 1983. The General Elections in March 1988 were preceded by party preliminary elections conducted by queuing in public, and 65 candidates receiving over 70 per cent were declared elected unopposed in the General Election. The election in the remaining 123 constituencies was conducted by secret ballot.

In December 1990 KANU changed its rules to abolish queuing and reintroduced the secret ballot in party preliminary elections. The 1982 Amendment to the Constitution making Kenya a one-party state was revoked in December 1991. Multi-party elections are due to take place before March 1993.

Land transfer and settlement schemes

From 1961 onwards several schemes for the transfer of mixed farming land from Europeans to Africans were begun to encourage African farming and agricultural development.

A programme known as the Million Acre Settlement Scheme, financed almost entirely by British loans and grants, was agreed. About one million acres of European-owned mixed farming land was to be divided into smallholdings and transferred to African farmers. Parallel with the million acre scheme the Agricultural Finance Corporation and Land Bank operated schemes to assist African farmers to buy European owned farms. The land transfer and settlement programme ended on 31st March 1979, by which time British grants and loans of £49 million had been made available.

Historical List

PRIME MINISTER

The Hon Mzee Jomo Kenyatta, MP, 12th December 1963 to 11th December 1964

PRESIDENT

His Excellency The Hon Mzee Jomo Kenyatta, CGH, MP (Died 22nd August 1978)

Government

HEAD OF STATE

President of the Republic of Kenya, Commander in Chief of the Armed Forces: His Excellency Daniel Toroitich arap Moi, CGH, MP, from 14th October 1978

Ministers of State: Hon Jackson Angaine, EGH, EBS, MP, Hon Maalim Mohamed, EBS, MP, Hon Joseph Ngutu, MP, Hon Nahashon Kanyi, MP

Vice-President and Minister for Finance: Hon Prof G Saitot, EGH, EBS, MP

Minister of Planning and National Development: Hon Dr Zachary Onyonka, EGH, MP

Minister for Water Development: Hon John Okwanyo, MP

Minister for Co-operative Development: Hon John Cheruiyot, MP

Minister for Agriculture: Hon Elijah Wasike Mwangale, MP

Minister for Livestock Development: Hon James Muregi, MP

Minister for Local Government and Physical Planning: Hon William ole Ntimama, MP

Minister for Information and Broadcasting: Hon Burudi Nabwera, MP

Minister for Foreign Affairs and International Co-operation: Hon Dr Wilson Ndolo Ayah, EGH, MP

Minister for Lands and Housing: Hon Darius Mbela, MP

Minister for Energy: Hon John Kyalo, EBS, MP

Minister for Public Works, Planning: Hon Timothy Mibei, MP

Minister for Commerce: Hon Arthur Magugu, MP

Minister for Industry: Hon Francis O Kaparo, MP

Minister for Culture and Social Services: Hon James Njiru, MP

Minister for Tourism and Wildlife: Hon Noah Katana Ngala, MP

Minister for Transport and Communications: Hon Dalmas A Otieno, EBS, MP

Minister for Environment and Natural Resources: Hon Dr Philip Leakey

Minister for Education: Hon Joseph Kamotho, MP

Minister for Research, Science and Technology: Hon Kirugi M'Mukindia

Minister for Labour: Hon Philip J W Masinde, MP

Minister for Health: Hon Jeremiah Nyagah

Minister for Supplies and Marketing: Hon Wycliffe Musalia Mudavadi, MP

Minister for Technological Training and Applied Technology: Hon Sam K Ongeri, MP

Minister for Manpower Development and Employment: Archbishop Stephen Ondiek

Minister for Regional Development: Hon Mathews Midika, MP

Attorney General: Hon Justice Amos Wako, MP

Minister for Reclamation and Development of Arid and Semi-Arid Wasteland: Mr George Mutua Ndotto, MP

MINISTRIES AND GOVERNMENT DEPARTMENTS

PRESIDENT'S OFFICE

Permanent Secretary and Head of the Civil Service: Professor Philip Mbithi

OFFICE OF THE VICE-PRESIDENT AND MINISTRY OF FINANCE
Permanent Secretary: Dr Karuga Koinange

MINISTRY OF PLANNING AND NATIONAL DEVELOPMENT
Permanent Secretary: Mr Joseph Mureria Hungu

MINISTRY FOR WATER DEVELOPMENT
Permanent Secretary: Mr S M Mbova

MINISTRY FOR CO-OPERATIVE DEVELOPMENT
Permanent Secretary: Mr R Adero

MINISTRY FOR AGRICULTURE
Permanent Secretary: Mr J M Magari

MINISTRY FOR LIVESTOCK DEVELOPMENT
Permanent Secretary: Mr Leonard Sawe

MINISTRY FOR LOCAL GOVERNMENT AND PHYSICAL PLANNING
Permanent Secretary: Mr A Wasike

MINISTRY FOR INFORMATION AND BROADCASTING
Permanent Secretary: Mr David K Andere

MINISTRY FOR FOREIGN AFFAIRS
Permanent Secretary: Dr Sally Kosbey

MINISTRY FOR RECLAMATION AND DEVELOPMENT OF ARID AND SEMI-ARID WASTELAND
Permanent Secretary: Mr Davies Mboya

MINISTRY OF HOME AFFAIRS
Permanent Secretary: Mr Andrew Ligale

MINISTRY OF MANPOWER DEVELOPMENT
Permanent Secretary: Mr Ben Mwangi

MINISTRY OF PUBLIC WORKS
Permanent Secretary: Mr P Wambura, CBS

MINISTRY OF REGIONAL DEVELOPMENT
Permanent Secretary: Mr Eliakim Masale

MINISTRY FOR LANDS AND HOUSING
Permanent Secretary: Mr Josiah Sang

MINISTRY FOR COMMERCE
Permanent Secretary: Mrs Margaret Githinji, SS

MINISTRY FOR INDUSTRY
Permanent Secretary: Mr P Munene

MINISTRY FOR CULTURE AND SOCIAL SERVICES
Permanent Secretary: Mr Philip Mulei

MINISTRY FOR TOURISM AND WILDLIFE
Permanent Secretary: Mr Philemon Mwaisaka

MINISTRY FOR ENERGY
Permanent Secretary: Mr C N Mutitu

MINISTRY FOR EDUCATION
Permanent Secretary: Mr B Kipkulei

MINISTRY FOR RESEARCH, SCIENCE AND TECHNOLOGY
Permanent Secretary: Mr S Arasa

MINISTRY FOR TRANSPORT AND COMMUNICATIONS
Permanent Secretary: Mr Simon Lesirma

MINISTRY FOR ENVIRONMENT AND NATURAL RESOURCES
Permanent Secretary: Mr Michael Okeyo

MINISTRY FOR LABOUR
Permanent Secretary: Mr F I Abuje

MINISTRY FOR HEALTH
Permanent Secretary: Mr David Mbiti

MINISTRY FOR SUPPLIES AND MARKETING
Permanent Secretary: Mr Philemon Mwaisaka

PROVINCIAL COMMISSIONERS
Nairobi: Mr F Waiganjo
Central: Mr V Musoga
North Eastern: Mr A arap Bore
Eastern: Mr A Oyier
Coast: Mr Simon Mung'ala, EBS
Western: Mr F Lekolool
Nyanza: Mr J Kobia
Rift Valley: Mr Y M Haji

Kiribati*

Capital: Tarawa

Kiribati (formerly the Gilbert Islands) became independent as a republic within the Commonwealth on 12th July 1979. Kiribati comprises 33 islands—the Gilbert Group (17) including Banaba (Ocean Island), the Phoenix Islands (8) and the Line Islands (8)—situated in the Central Pacific around the point where the International Date Line cuts the Equator. Although the total land area is only 684 sq km (264 square miles) it is scattered over more than 5.2 million sq km (two million square miles) of ocean, and distances between extreme points are enormous. Christmas Island in the east is 3,218 km (2,000 miles) from Banaba in the west, and the latitude of Washington Island in the north is 1,126 km (700 miles) from the latitude of Gardner Island in the south. Furthermore, the islands are remote from large centres of civilisation, and Tarawa, the capital, is about 4,023 km (2,500 miles) from Sydney and 2,196 km (1,365 miles) from Suva. The scattered nature of the territory and its remoteness cause many difficulties in administration, transport and communications.

With the exception of Banaba, the islands are atolls composed of coral reefs built on a submerged volcanic chain. In most of the atolls the reef encloses a lagoon, on the eastern side of which are long narrow stretches of land varying in length from a few hundred metres to some 80 km (50 miles), and in width from one or two hundred metres to nearly a mile. The surface of these islands seldom rises more than 4 metres above sea level.

Tempered by the prevailing easterly trade winds, the climate of Kiribati is generally sunny and pleasant without uncomfortable high temperatures or excessive humidity. From November to April, however, the climate is more unsettled with occasional periods of heavy rain, high humidity and strong to gale force winds and tends to be rather enervating. Over most of the Gilbert Group, the average annual rainfall is about 1,200–1,500mm but to the north of Tarawa the average increases rapidly to about 3,000mm over Butaritari and Makin. Rainfall varies considerably from year to year and annual totals may be 15–200 per cent of the average. Throughout the Gilbert Group the wettest months are usually December to April. Situated within the equatorial dry zone, Christmas Island has an annual average rainfall of only 782mm; the period from September to December has an average total of only 142mm. Severe droughts occur from time to time in all the islands. The mean annual temperature varies from 27°C (81°F) on Fanning Island (Line Islands) to 29°C (84°F) on Arorae. There is less than one degree variation between the coolest months and the warmest months. On average, temperatures range from 25°C (77°F) just before sunrise to 31–32°C (88°F) in the early afternoon. The highest temperature on record is 36°C (97°F) and the lowest is 18°C (65°F). All the islands are outside the tropical cyclone belt but strong or gale force winds are sometimes experienced; these disturbances are usually brief, however, and are very infrequent from May to September. Tornadoes are not unknown. The relative humidity is generally between 70 per cent and 90 per cent, and there is little monthly variation. Days with high humidity are more common, however, from November to March.

The Australian dollar is the unit of currency.

Population

The people are of Micronesian stock. The last census of the population of the islands was held in November 1990. The results show a total population of 72,298.

The languages spoken are I-Kiribati and English. The official language is English, but on the outer islands away from the headquarters at Tarawa it is seldom used. The population is predominantly Christian, with a slight preponderance of Roman Catholics over Protestants with a number of other sects also represented.

The islands of the territory are divided into administrative districts which are (with their headquarters islands in brackets); Banaba, Northern Gilbert Islands (Butaritari), Central Gilbert Islands (Abemama), Southern Gilbert Islands (Tabiteuea), South-Eastern Gilbert Islands (Beru), Line Islands (Christmas Island) and The Phoenix group (Kanton). The Phoenix group and the Central and Southern Line Islands are largely uninhabited. Tarawa is the capital. Government offices are on South Tarawa at Betio, Bairiki, and Bikenibeu. Bairiki and Bikenibeu are connected by causeways. Betio, the port area and scene of the bitter struggle between the United States Marines and the Japanese in 1943, lies two miles west of Bairiki and was connected to Bairiki by a causeway in mid-1987.

* pronounced Kiribass

Health

The Ministry of Health, Family Planning and Social Welfare, has its headquarters at Bikenibeu, Tarawa, where the Central Hospital (160 beds) is also situated. Kiribati is divided into four medical districts. Each island has a dispensary with a medical assistant or nursing officer in charge.

The principal endemic diseases are infantile diarrhoea, chicken pox, amoebiasis, bacillary dysentery, tuberculosis, hookworm, giardiasis, hepatitis A and B. There are a few cases of leprosy and typhoid and regular outbreaks of dengue fever occur. Tuberculosis remains one of the most serious public health problems. There was a cholera outbreak in 1977. The first AIDS case was reported in Tarawa in 1991.

Communications

The principal port is at Betio Islet (Tarawa). Small ships of up to 10 feet draught may enter the harbour at Betio, whilst larger vessels drawing up to 28 feet anchor in the lagoon and are serviced by barges. At Christmas Island vessels anchor or lie at buoys outside the lagoon.

The airports at Christmas Island and Bonriki on Tarawa are used for scheduled overseas commercial flights. Air Marshall Islands operates a twice weekly flight between Majuro, Tarawa and Nadi (Fiji). All the islands of the Gilbert group have airstrips and a regular internal service is operated.

The Economy

Agriculture is virtually non-existent in the islands due to the poor quality of the soil, which is composed largely of coral sand and rock fragments. The major part of all islands, except Banaba and some of the Phoenix and Line group, is covered with coconut palms which provide the islands with an important source of food and drink, and with copra, which is their only cash crop. Sea fishing is an important source of revenue from the export of fish and the sale of fishing licences. The cultivation and export of seaweed is a developing industry. Phosphate of lime was mined on Banaba by the British Phosphate Commissioners until the exhaustion of the reserves in 1979. Livestock is limited to pigs and poultry. There is little useful timber.

The people of the territory maintain a reasonable standard of subsistence living by intensive exploitation of the sea and the very limited resources of their infertile atolls, and by sending their young men abroad to work. The main outlets are to the phosphate industry on Nauru (the neighbouring republic), many of them accompanied by their families, and as seamen working on overseas ships, based mainly in German ports. At mid 1991 there were approximately 870 men at sea.

The only major exports are copra, fish and seaweed. The value of imports in 1990 was A$34,446 compared with A$28,596 in 1989.

Main exports from 1986–1990 were in A$:—

	Copra	*Fish*	*Seaweed*	*Total Exports (inc. re-exports)*
1986	459,000	1,797,000	21,000	2,496,000
1987	1,173,000	839,000	62,000	2,869,000
1988	4,203,000	1,606,000	15,000	6,670,000
1989	3,127,000	2,600,000	85,000	6,435,000
1990	1,023,000	964,000	723,000	3,681,000

Most imports and sales of retail goods are handled by the co-operative and the Government Supplies Division. The volume of private trading is small but growing.

Income tax is levied on chargeable income on a sliding scale. PAYE was introduced in January 1975. Companies pay tax at a flat rate of 25 per cent on all chargeable income. With the end of taxation from phosphate mining on Banaba in 1979 the main sources of revenue to government are investment income from the Reserve Fund (built up from past phosphate taxation surpluses and now worth around A$220m), import duties, fees from overseas tuna fishing fleets and philatelic sales. Island Councils have a wide range of rating powers and also levy a landowners tax (based on area and fertility), licence fees and other dues.

A Development Plan for the years 1991–94 was published in late 1991. The plan is supported by development aid and technical assistance from the United Kingdom, by the international agencies, by Australia and New Zealand who operate regional aid Programmes, by Japan, by loans from the Asian Development Bank, which Kiribati (then the Gilbert and Ellice Islands Colony) joined in 1974 and from the European Development Fund operated by the EEC. Kiribati also benefits from the EC Stabex scheme in respect of copra exports. Canada, USA, Germany, South Korea and the Peoples Republic of China have also started small aid programmes. With the end of surplus revenue from phosphate, contributions from local funds to the development programme have been greatly reduced.

Education

On 7th November 1990 there were 15,500 children attending 113 registered primary schools. The Government Secondary School teaching up to Form 7 has 500 students. The school has changed from Cambridge Overseas School Certificate to the New Zealand School Certificate, except for technical subjects in Home Economics and Industrial Art. Kiribati National Certificate is in the process of being changed. Another 1,800 students attended six church secondary schools. A Government Teacher Training College provides courses for primary school teachers and the Tarawa Technical Institute conducts technical and vocational education for a wide range of students. The Rural Training Centre for appropriate technology is part of the Tarawa Technical Institute. The Marine Training Centre provides a one and half year course, with two intakes a year, for deck, engine room, and catering staff destined for employment in merchant shipping lines overseas. Kiribati participates in the University of the South Pacific.

The Media

Radio Kiribati (call sign T3K1) operated by the Broadcasting and Publications Authority transmits daily on 354.6 metres (846 KHz) in the medium waveband (10 KW) from 1800 to 2000 hours, 2400–0200 and 0600–1000 GMT Monday to Friday, 1800 to 0200 and 0600 to 1000 GMT on Saturdays and 2300 to 0200 and 0600 to 1000 GMT on Sundays. A 1 KW short wave transmitter operating on 16433 KHz relays programmes to Christmas Island using the Lower side-band. Morning and lunchtime programmes mainly consist of news, information and music with feature and interview programmes in the evenings. With the exception of a news bulletin in English and a few imported programmes from the UK, Australia and New Zealand, the whole output is in I-Kiribati.

The Broadcasting and Publications Authority also publishes a weekly newspaper Te Uekera which is mainly in I-Kiribati, but with main news items also in English.

History

The I-Kiribati, who are a Micronesian people, appear to have two separate stories about the origin of their race which, although interwoven by the passage of time and the handing down of oral traditions, are easily distinguishable. The earlier of the two tells of a creator, Nareau, and a pantheon of gods and goddesses created by him from the void. This tradition appears to have become interwoven with a 'Tree of Life' myth, based upon Samoa, with stories of a cannibal race practising skull-worship on the sacred mountain of Maungatabu. The Tree had its own pantheon of heroes and heroines and they, as well as those of the Nareau creation story, are the sub-deities of traditional beliefs. These stories tell of civil disturbances in Samoa; of the breaking of the 'Tree of Life' and the disposal of its people to Kiribati; and of their meeting there with a people of similar ancestry. They create the impression that the I-Kiribati believe their islands to have been inhabited before their arrival from Nipe by a people holding related traditions. Efforts to trace any substantial reference to the Samoan deity Tangaroa have been unsuccessful. This seems to indicate that the disposal preceded his rise to pre-eminence in Samoan religion, which would place the migration to Kiribati somewhere between AD 1000 and 1300.

From the earliest days the I-Kiribati have waged a dour fight against starvation. Their islands are infertile coral atolls, periodically ravaged by droughts, and the coconut is the ubiquitous provider, together with laboriously-cultivated coarse edible tubers, pandanus, and breadfruit. This simple subsistence agriculture has always been a grim task, one which made land the prize of love and war. But while this struggle went on ashore they were able, in their swift, well-constructed canoes, to fish their lagoons and ocean shores, and their limited navigation served them well enough on their occasional inter-island voyages of depredation. From this background the cautious character of the people grew.

The European discovery of Kiribati dates from the 16th century; it is thought that Christmas Island and Nonouti in the Gilbert group were sighted in 1537 by Grijalva's mutinous crew on their disastrous voyage across the Pacific to New Guinea. Quiros is thought to have discovered Butaritari in the Northern Gilberts in 1606.

After the probable early Spanish sightings, further discovery had to await the latter part of the 18th century and the first quarter of the 19th century. After Captain Byron's visit, in HMS *Dolphin* in 1765, the remaining islands in the group were discovered largely as an unintended result of increasing commercial activity in the Pacific. The last islands to be discovered were Onotoa and Beru in 1826.

From the early days of their discovery until about 1870, the waters of Kiribati were a favourite sperm-whaling ground and the crews of these whalers occasionally deserted and settled ashore. One of the first Europeans to settle in Kiribati landed about 1837 and the number steadily grew. Trading ships began to visit the islands regularly from 1850 onwards. Although at first trade merely consisted of bartering curios for European luxuries, trade in coconut oil began about 1860 and in ten or twenty years gave way to the sale of copra.

In 1900, by chance, Sir Albert Ellis noticed in a Sydney office a sample of rock from German-annexed Nauru and identified it as a piece of valuable phosphate. An expedition was speedily sent by the Pacific Islands Company to the neighbouring Ocean Island to see whether this island also contained the same rock. Although, by agreement with Germany, Ocean Island was at this time within the British sphere of influence, it had not yet been annexed. The representatives of the Pacific Islands Company discovered that the soil of Ocean Island was almost pure phosphate rock and they were able to obtain from the inhabitants a concession to mine it.

Dr Hiram Bingham of the American Board of Foreign Missions landed at Abaiang in 1857 and began to spread Christianity through the Northern Gilberts. In 1870 the London Missionary Society placed Samoan pastors at Arorae, Tamana, Onotoa and Beru. By agreement in 1917, the American Board withdrew from the Colony, handing over the cause of Protestant Christianity to the London

Missionary Society. Roman Catholic missionaries landed in the Gilbert Islands in 1888, and Roman Catholicism has now spread to all the Gilberts except the two most southerly, Tamana and Arorae, which are still Protestant strongholds.

In 1892, Captain Davis of HMS *Royalist,* on behalf of Queen Victoria, proclaimed at Abemama a British protectorate in the Gilberts; HMS *Royalist* then visited other Gilbert Islands to raise the flag. The headquarters was established at Tarawa and district magistrates were assigned to the various islands. A simple code of laws was drawn up based on earlier mission legislation, and the councils of old men were transformed into native courts to administer them. With peace in the groups the people were gathered into orderly villages and an era dawned of simple administration through the Native Governments guided by a very small number of European officers. In 1915, after consultations and at the wish of the Native Governments, the Gilbert and Ellice Islands were annexed by an Order in Council which came into effect on 12th January 1916.

From 1942 to 1943 the Gilberts were occupied by the Japanese. The Administration established a temporary headquarters at Sydney, Australia, which was transferred to Funafuti when United States forces occupied the Ellice group. From there, the Government controlled a war-time administration over the Ellice, Phoenix and Line Islands until, in November 1943, the United States forces drove the Japanese from the Gilberts. Officers of the Administration accompanying the military forces set up headquarters on Tarawa. On 1st October 1975 the Ellice Islands separated by agreement from the territory to form a separate dependency called Tuvalu (independent from 1978).

Internal self-government was introduced in the Gilbert Islands on 1st January 1977. At a Constitutional Conference held in London in November/December 1978 it was agreed that the Gilbert Islands should become fully independent as a republic in early July 1979 (subsequently agreed on 12th July 1979). On independence Kiribati became the 41st member of the Commonwealth.

Land policy

Since 1917 the sale of land to non-natives has been prohibited. Before 1892 there was, of course, no legal restriction on alienation and between 1892 and 1917 limited alienation was permitted. Fortunately, there was no serious loss of land to the islanders during these periods. An insignificant area now remains alienated. Most of this is owned by Missions and is used for social purposes. Fanning and Washington Islands (in the Line Group) belonged to a private company and were operated as commercial copra plantations until March 1983 when they were purchased by the Government. Christmas Island is owned by the State.

Constitution

The Gilbert and Ellice Islands Colony came under the jurisdiction of the High Commissioner for the Western Pacific until 1st January 1972, when a Governor was appointed. An Order in Council in October 1971 withdrew the Colony from the High Commissioner's jurisdiction except for certain judicial matters.

Constitutional advance began in 1963, when by an ordinance enacted by the High Commissioner an Advisory Council was established whose function was to advise the then Resident Commissioner on matters relating to administration. The Advisory Council consisted of the Resident Commissioner as President, the Assistant Resident Commissioner as *ex-officio* Member, not more than four Official Members and not less than eight and not more than twelve Unofficial Members. The Gilbert and Ellice Islands Order in Council 1963 provided for an Executive Council consisting of the Assistant Resident Commissioner as *ex-officio* Member, not more than three Official Members and not more than four Unofficial Members.

The Gilbert and Ellice Islands Order 1967 made provision for the government of the territory. It established a Governing Council consisting of the Assistant Resident Commissioner and the Attorney-General, *ex-officio;* not more than three appointed members; and five elected members. The Governing Council replaced the Executive Council and had legislative as well as executive functions. The Order also established a House of Representatives consisting of the Assistant Resident Commissioner and the Attorney-General *ex-officio;* up to five appointed members and 23 elected members. The Resident Commissioner presided over both the House and the Council. The elected members of the House selected from among their own members five members (one of whom was elected as Chief Elected Member) to the Governing Council. The House advised the Governing Council on proposed legislation and other public matters referred to it by the Council or raised by individual members of the House.

In 1970 the next step of constitutional development was approved. The Gilbert and Ellice Islands Order 1970 made new provision for the government of the territory. It established a Legislative Council, Executive Council to replace the House of Representatives and Governing Council. The Legislative Council consisted of 3 *ex-officio* members, 2 public service members and 28 elected members, elected under the principle of universal adult suffrage. The Executive Council comprised the *ex-officio* and public service members of the Legislative Council, a Leader of Government Business elected by members of the Legislative Council and 4 appointed members from the Legislative Council.

Ministerial government was introduced on 1st May 1974. The Legislative Council was replaced by a House of Assembly with 28 elected and 3 *ex-officio* members. The House of Assembly elected the Chief

Minister who advised the Governor on the appointment of not less than four and not more than six ministers, one of whom had to be an Ellice Islander. The Governor presided in the Council of Ministers which consisted of the Chief Minister, the other ministers and the Deputy Governor, Attorney-General and Financial Secretary. The Governor was obliged to consult the Council of Ministers on all matters but retained special responsibility for external affairs, defence, security and the public service.

On 1st October 1974 the result of the referendum held to determine the future of the Ellice Islands revealed that the vast majority of Ellice Islanders were in favour of separation and the establishment of a new colony. The Government of the Gilbert and Ellice Islands subsequently confirmed that the wishes of the majority of Ellice Islanders would be respected and separation of the administration was effected on 1st October 1975 with the formation of Tuvalu.

The number of elected members in the Gilbert Islands House of Assembly was reduced from 28 to 21 with 3 *ex-officio* members. The provision that there also had to be an Ellice Island Minister now fell away.

On 1st January 1977, the Gilbert Islands (Amendment) Order 1976 brought into effect the next major constitutional change—Internal Self Government. This specifically made provision for an additional minister (not less than 5 and not more than 7 ministers) in order to facilitate the appointment of a Minister of Finance. The *ex-officio* appointments of the Deputy Governor and Financial Secretary fell away.

In 1977 two further constitutional amendments were introduced. The Gilbert Islands (Amendment) Order 1977 increased the number of elected members of the House of Assembly to 36 with one *ex-officio* member (the Attorney-General); and enabled the Governor, acting upon the wishes of the House, to provide for the national election of the Chief Minister in place of his election by the House. The Gilbert Islands (Amendment) (No 2) Order 1977 reduced the number of elected members of the House to 35; and allowed for the other seat to be occupied by the nominee of the Rabi Council of Leaders.

In February 1978 a General Election was held and on 17th March the Chief Minister was elected in a separate national election. On independence on 12th July 1979 the Chief Minister, Mr Ieremia Tabai became the first President of Kiribati. He was re-elected following a General Election in April 1982. On 10th December 1982 President Tabai's government fell after defeat in a vote of no-confidence. The House of Assembly was dissolved and a Council of State assumed charge. Elections were held in January 1983 and in February Ieremia Tabai was re-elected President. He was re-elected in May 1987.

Teatao Teannake, the former Vice-President, was elected President in 1991. The Constitution precluded the former President Tabai from standing for a further term. At the General Election in 1991 the Government was returned to power.

Under the Independence Constitution Kiribati became a sovereign and democratic republic with an elected House of Assembly (Maneaba ni Maungatabu). The President (Beretitenti*) is Head of State and Head of Government and is elected nationally, following elections for the House of Assembly, from not less than three and not more than four candidates, all of whom must be members of the House and nominated by it.

Executive authority is vested in a Cabinet collectively responsible to the House and consisting of the President, Vice-President, the Attorney-General and not more than eight other ministers. The ministers are appointed by the President from members of the House. The Attorney-General, the Government's principal legal adviser, is also appointed by the President.

The House of Assembly is composed of 39 Members plus the Attorney-General and the nominated member from the Banaban community in Rabi. An Electoral Commission administers elections and referenda and is responsible for reviewing the number and boundaries of electoral districts.

The constitution also protects fundamental human rights and freedoms and contains special provisions for Banaba and the Banabans. The superior court is a High Court with a Chief Justice and other judges and provision is included in the Constitution for the establishment of a Court of Appeal.

CABINET

(as at September 1991)

President & Minister of Foreign Affairs & International Trade: Hon Teatao Teannaki

Vice-President & Minister of Finance: Hon Taomati T Iuta

Minister of Home Affairs & Rural Development: Hon Binata Tetaeka

Minister of Health & Family Planning & Social Welfare: Hon Baitika Toum

Minister of Transport, Communication & Tourism: Hon Inatoa Tebania

Minister of Commerce, Industry & Employment: Hon Remuera Tateraka

Minister of Works & Energy: Hon Teaiwa Tenieu

Minister of the Environment & Natural Resource Development: Hon Ieremia T Tabai GCMG

Minister of Education, Science & Technology: Hon Anterea Kaitaake

Minister of Line & Phoenix Development: Hon Boanarike Boanarike

Attorney-General: Hon Michael Takabwebwe

HOUSE OF ASSEMBLY

The Speaker: Hon Beretitara Neeti

Clerk: Atiera Tatoa

* pronounced Beresitence

CIVIL ESTABLISHMENT

JUDICIARY

Chief Justice: Hon Faqir Muhammad
Attorney-General: Hon Michael Takabwebwe

PERMANENT SECRETARIES

Secretary to the Cabinet: Peter Timeon
Secretary for Foreign Affairs: Mrs Margaret Baaro
Ministry of Home Affairs & Rural Development: Baraniko Baaro
Ministry of Health, Family Planning & Social Welfare: Dr Tetaua Taitai
Ministry of Transport, Communications & Tourism: Teken C Tokataake
Ministry of Finance & Economic Planning: Ntiua Tetinaniku
Ministry of Works & Energy: Ratintera Beriki
Ministry of Education, Science & Technology: Meita B Bakeea
Ministry of Line & Phoenix Development: Kaiarake Taburuea
Ministry of Commerce, Industry & Employment: T Nauan Bauro
Ministry of Environment and Natural Resource Development: Nakibae Teuatabo

Lesotho

Capital: Maseru

Lesotho lies between latitudes 28° 35′ and 30° 40′ S. and longitudes 27° and 29° 30′ E. It is a mountainous country wholly surrounded by South Africa, with Natal to the east, Cape Province to the south and the Orange Free State to the north and west. Out of the total area of 30,344 sq km (11,716 square miles), about one third lying along the western and southern boundaries, is classed as 'lowland' and is between 1,500 m (5,000 feet) and 1,800 m (6,000 feet) above sea level. The remainder of the country, the 'highlands', is mostly between 2,100 m (7,000 feet) and 2,700 m (9,000 feet) above sea level. The two main mountain ranges are the Maluti Mountains and the Drakensberg range, which run from north to south. The Maluti, in the central part of the country, are spurs of the main Drakensberg range, which they join in the north forming a high plateau. The highest mountains are in the Drakensberg range, which forms the border with Natal, where Cathkin Peak, Giant's Castle and Mont-aux-Sources are all over 3,000 m (10,000 feet) high. The highest mountain is Thabana Ntlenyana, 3,427 m (11,425 feet) high.

Two of the largest rivers in the Republic of South Africa, the Orange and its tributary the Caledon, have their sources in the mountains of Lesotho. The climate is generally healthy and pleasant. Rainfall is variable and averages about 725 mm (29 inches) a year over the greater part of the country. Most of the rain falls during the summer months between October and April but there is normally no month which has less than half an inch of rain. The winters are normally dry with heavy frosts in the lowlands. Temperatures in the lowlands vary from about 32.2°C (90°F) in summer to a minimum of −6.7°C (20°F) in winter. In the highlands the range is much wider and temperatures below freezing point are common. Snow falls frequently in the highlands in winter but only rarely in the lowlands.

The language of the Basotho is Sesotho (or southern Sotho). Some small tribal units speak also vernaculars of the Nguni group, including Zulu and Xhosa. The official languages are English and Sesotho. About 80 per cent of the population are Christians. The non-Christians hold to their traditional beliefs.

Lesotho is divided into ten districts, Maseru is the capital, each with the same name as the district town. The latest population figures available are as follows:

	De Jure Population (1986)
Butha-Buthe	100,644
Leribe	257,988
Berea	194,631
Maseru	311,157
Mafeteng	195,591
Mohale's Hoek	164,392
Quthing	110,376
Qacha's Nek	63,984
Mokhotlong	74,676
Thaba Tseka	104,095
Total	1,577,534

Current population growth is estimated at 2.6 per cent per annum.

There are daily scheduled air flights from Johannesburg to Maseru and back and other scheduled international flights to Maputo and Gaborone. Apart from the Moshoeshoe I international airport just outside Maseru, there are some thirty airstrips in Lesotho, the main ones being at Mokhotlong, Sehonghong, Semonkong and Qacha's Neck. Most of the latter are suitable only for the lightest type of aircraft. The country is linked for goods services with the rail system of South Africa by a short line (gauge 3 feet 6 inches) from Maseru to Marseilles on the Bloemfontein–Natal main line. One mile of the line is in Lesotho. Elsewhere goods are transported by road to and from the nearest station across the frontier. There are some 2,091 km (1,300 miles) of gravelled and earth roads and vehicle tracks, and a few miles of bitumenised roads in urban areas. A tarred road links Maseru to several of the main lowlands towns in Lesotho, and this is being extended in sections around the southern perimeter of the country. Tarred access roads have been built into the mountains to supply the Highland Water Project.

The unit of currency is the Loti (plural Maloti) which is interchangeable with the South African Rand.

Radio Lesotho is a broadcasting station operated by the Government Department of Information and Broadcasting.

The economy is based on agriculture and animal husbandry, and the adverse balance of trade (mainly consumer and capital goods) is offset in part by the earnings of the large numbers of Basotho who work in South Africa. Apart from some diamonds, the mining of which has now largely ceased, no mineral deposits have so far been discovered. Lesotho has few natural resources and industrial development is still on a small scale. The Lesotho National Development Corporation, which exists to initiate, promote and facilitate the development of projects in manufacturing and processing industries, mining, trade and tourism is having some success in gradually expanding the industrial base of the country. Industrial exports are now more valuable than traditional exports such as wool and mohair.

Following a satisfactory feasibility study, work commenced in 1986 on the Highlands Water Project—a project which will gain revenue for Lesotho by diverting the flow from the Maluti mountains of the Senqui (or Orange) river northwards by means of a series of dams and tunnels to the Vaal basin industrial area of South Africa, while at the same time generating hydroelectric power for Lesotho. Work on the main dam and water transfer tunnel began early in 1991. The project is scheduled for completion by 2020 at a cost of over R4 billion, though the first water and electricity is planned to flow in 1996.

British financial assistance towards the economic and social development of Lesotho has included both capital aid and budgetary grants. Under the Colonial Welfare and Development (CD&W) Acts grants totalling £4.9 million were provided between 1945–1946. Until 1956 the increasing recurrent expenditure incurred by the expansion of social services, and even some development capital, was provided out of the country's revenues. From 1957 onwards the recurrent budget ran into deficit and in 1960 Britain began giving budgetary aid. This continued until 1973 when increasing revenue arising from the renegotiation of Lesotho's Customs Pool Agreement with South Africa became sufficient to obviate the need.

Since 1966 Britain has offered aid to Lesotho in the total amount of over £82 million, a proportion of which until 1973 was employed for supplementation of the current budget. The current annual development aid allocation is approximately £6 million.

Lesotho's well developed education system owes much to missionary work. Most schools are mission-controlled, the Government providing grants for salaries and buildings. There are more than 1,000 recognised primary schools in Lesotho. Despite the mountainous countryside, few areas lack a school, a fact reflected in the high literacy rate of approximately 70 per cent. There are over 100 secondary schools, approximately 35 of which offer a full five-year course leading to the Cambridge Overseas School Certificate. There is an increasing stress on agricultural and vocational education. The National University of Lesotho at Roma, 22 miles from Maseru, was established on 20th October 1975. Before that the campus at Roma was a constituent part of the University of Botswana, Lesotho and Swaziland.

History

In the early nineteenth century some of the leading tribal groups which were later to form part of the Basotho nation were settled along the present-day north-western borders of Lesotho near Leribe. Among these were the Bakwena, led by Moshoeshoe, then a young man who, though only a minor chief, had shown outstanding qualities of leadership and gathered a following from other tribes. This was the period of the 'Wars of Calamity' when Chaka's Zulu *impis* raided across the Drakensburg from Natal, driving before them the remnants of other tribes. In 1824 Moshoeshoe, who now was the leader of some 5,000 persons, sought refuge at Thaba Bosiu, a virtually impregnable flat-topped hill near Maseru. From this base he was able, by a judicious mixture of firmness and diplomacy, to avert further Zulu and Matabele attacks. By 1831 he had become the acknowledged chief of the local Basotho clans and had gained the allegiance of other tribal groups.

Within a few years, however, an even greater threat to Moshoeshoe's people arose in the form of the emigrant Boers of the Great Trek of 1834. These Voortrekkers, seeking homes and grazing for their herds, encroached on the level lands around the Caledon river where the Basotho were already established.

From then on, until his death in 1870, Moshoeshoe was engaged in a struggle involving both border warfare and negotiation to preserve the territorial integrity and independence of the Basotho homeland. In this he was ably assisted by the French Protestant missionary Eugene Casalis, who from his arrival in 1833 with two companions identified himself with the Basotho and acted as Moshoeshoe's adviser in relations with the outside world.

For over 30 years the western and southern marches of the customary lands of the Basotho were in a state of constant unrest. While the Boer farmers continually encroached into Moshoeshoe's territory, the Basotho retaliated by raiding their cattle. By adopting the horse as a means of transport and by acquiring firearms the Basotho were able to inflict severe reverses on the Boer commandos, but the creation of the independent Orange Free State (OFS) in 1854 led to increased pressure and in 1858 to inconclusive warfare.

Advised by Casalis, Moshoeshoe had from as early as 1842 sought the protection of the British Crown; in the following year he signed an agreement by which he became a 'friend and ally' of the Cape Colony, but this agreement was later cancelled. In 1861, under further pressure from the OFS, Moshoeshoe again petitioned the British High Commissioner in South Africa, saying that his country could only be secure if the Basotho were to be recognised as the Queen's subjects. The British

Government continued to be unwilling to assume further responsibilities in South Africa until renewed hostilities between the OFS and the Basotho from 1865 onwards, which seemed likely to result early in 1868 in the complete defeat of the Basotho and the total annexation of their country, led to a change of policy. On 12th March 1868 the British High Commissioner issued a proclamation declaring the Basotho to be British subjects and their territory to be British territory.

There remained the immediate cause of the conflict, the lack of a defined and accepted frontier between the OFS and the Basotho. The Convention of Aliwal North, concluded on 12 March 1869 confirmed to the OFS the recently conquered lands west of the Caledon river but restored to the Basotho other lands east of the Caledon which had been lost in the recent fighting. The frontier laid down by the convention has remained substantially unchanged to the present day.

For three years Basutoland was administered by the High Commissioner, but in 1871 it was formally annexed, with the agreement of Britain, to Cape Colony which had recently been granted responsible government. Although material conditions quickly improved under a rule of law and order, there was a legacy amongst the minor chiefs of insubordination to the Paramount Chief (as Moshoeshoe's successors were entitled) and of apprehension amongst the people about the future. Much of the proceeds of the sales of their livestock or from their earnings by service in the Kimberley diamond fields (which from about 1870 began to provide a market for expatriate Basotho labour) were invested in firearms. An attempt by the Cape Colony Government in 1880 to enforce a policy of disarmament on the Basotho tribesmen, led to several years of desultory and inconclusive fighting—the so-called Gun War. In 1883 the Cape Government asked Britain to be relieved of the charge of Basutoland. The British Government thereupon offered the Basotho the choice of returning to the position they had occupied before being taken under the protection of the Crown or of coming under direct British rule. In November 1883 the major Basotho chiefs signified their wish to become British subjects 'under the direct rule of the Queen'. In March 1884 Basutoland was brought by proclamation and Order in Council under the direct control of the Crown, through the High Commissioner in South Africa.

Constitutional development

When the four provinces of South Africa came together in 1908 to discuss the possibility of a federation or union, the Basotho chiefs sent a deputation to England asking that Basutoland should not be incorporated in any future union. Accordingly when the Act of Union was passed Basutoland remained a British colony.

In 1910 an advisory body known as the Basutoland Council consisting of the Resident Commissioner as President, the Paramount Chief as Chief Councillor and 99 Basotho members (94 nominated by the Paramount Chief and 5 by the Resident Commissioner) was constituted by proclamation of the High Commissioner. Later on, the constitution of the 99 Basotho members was changed: 42 were elected, 52 were nominated by the Paramount Chief and five were nominated by the Resident Commissioner. In 1944 the High Commissioner formally declared that it was 'the policy of His Majesty's Government to consult the Paramount Chief and the Basutoland Council before proclamations closely affecting the domestic affairs and welfare of the Basotho people or the progress of the Basotho Native Administration are enacted'. At the same time, the Paramount Chief confirmed that it was the policy of the Paramountcy 'to consult the Basutoland Council before issuing orders or making rules closely affecting the life or welfare of the Basotho people and the administration of the Basotho'. In 1945 a small elected standing committee was created to deal with important matters between sessions of the full Council. In 1946 a Basotho National Treasury was established and a new system of some 122 courts, held by Basotho stipendiary magistrates, replaced the 1,340 courts previously held by chiefs in their own name. Fines and fees from these courts now went to the National Treasury. By 1949 the number of these courts had been further reduced to 107. In 1960 a legislature—the Basutoland National Council—and an Executive Council were formed. In 1962 a Constitutional Commission was appointed by the Paramount Chief to formulate proposals for the amendment of the 1960 Constitution. The Commission reported in 1963 and its report was adopted in February 1964 by the National Council as a basis for negotiation with the British Government. A Constitutional Conference was held in London in 1964 and agreement was reached on a new Pre-Independence Constitution on lines recommended by the Constitutional Commission. The new Constitution was brought into operation on 30th April 1965. The Paramount Chief became the Queen's Representative. The legislature became bi-cameral; the Senate consisting of 22 Principal and Ward Chiefs and 11 other persons nominated by the Paramount Chief and the National Assembly consisting of 60 elected members. The Resident Commissioner became the British Government Representative retaining responsibility for defence, external affairs, internal security and the public service and for proper financial administration. At the 1964 Conference, the Secretary of State gave a formal undertaking that if at any time not earlier than one year after the new elections the people of Basutoland should ask for independence the British Government would seek to give effect to their wishes as soon as possible.

The first elections took place on the 29th and 30th April 1965 and were narrowly won by the National Party (BNP) which won 31 of the 60 seats giving it a majority of two over the combined strength of the Congress Party (BCP) (25 seats) and the Marema Tlou Freedom Party (four seats). The deputy leader of the National Party held office as Prime Minister until 1st July 1965 when he was succeeded in office by Chief Leabua Jonathan who had entered the National Assembly after winning a by-election.

At further talks held in London in November 1965, between the British and Basutoland Governments, the Basutoland Prime Minister confirmed that a formal request for independence would be submitted immediately after 29th April 1966 and asked the British Government to accept that the conditions attached to the Colonial Secretary's undertaking of 24th April 1964 were likely to be fulfilled. The British Government accepted the Prime Minister's statement of intention and his assurances on the fulfilment of the stipulated conditions.

On the 18th and 19th April 1966 the Basutoland Government moved resolutions in the Senate and the National Assembly asking the British Government to grant independence to Lesotho in the terms of the agreement reached in London in 1964 and in terms of a White Paper of the 8th March 1966 in which the Basutoland Government had set out the conditions under which it proposed to seek independence. The resolutions were eventually passed and the Basutoland Independence Conference was held in London from the 8th to 17th June 1966 under the chairmanship of the Secretary of State for the Colonies. At the conclusion of the Conference the Colonial Secretary confirmed that the British Government accepted the independence resolutions of the Basutoland Government and that it would take the necessary steps to grant independence to Basutoland in accordance with the undertaking given at the 1964 Conference. The Conference agreed that Basutoland should become an independent kingdom under the name of Lesotho on the 4th October 1966. Parliament gave effect to this decision by the Lesotho Independence Act 1966, enacted on 3rd August.

Constitution

On 10th February 1970 the Prime Minister, Chief Leabua Jonathan, suspended the Constitution granted on independence. An interim National Assembly with a nominated membership was set up in April 1973. The suspended Independence Order was subsequently replaced by the Parliament Act 1983, as amended in 1984, and by the Human Rights Act 1983, which came into force in July 1984. The Interim National Assembly was dissolved on 1st January 1985 and elections were announced for an unspecified date in 1985. Opposition parties did not nominate candidates for elections proposed for 17th/18th September 1985. Candidates of the Basotho National Party were, therefore, declared duly elected members of the National Assembly, and the elections were cancelled.

On 20th January 1986, the Lesotho Paramilitary Force (LPF) subsequently renamed the Royal Lesotho Defence Force (RLDF) took control of Lesotho and established a Military Council under the Chairmanship of Major-General Lekhanya, Commander of the LPF. Lesotho Order No. 3 of 1986, vested all legislative and executive authority in the King, who remained Head of State. The King was advised by the Military Council and assisted in the administration of the country by a Council of Ministers.

The division of power between King Moshoeshoe and the Military Council generated tensions between the royalist faction and those who supported General Lekhanya. Little progress had been made towards the avowed aim of returning Lesotho to a form of representative democracy, when, in February 1990 General Lekhanya approved the arrest of half the Military Council and the dismissal of nine Ministers, all close to the King. When the King refused to approve these changes the executive powers conferred on him in 1986 were assumed by General Lekhanya and the King went into exile in London.

In June 1990 the government set up a National Constituent Assembly whose principal task was to prepare a new draft Constitution for multiparty elections in 1992. They used the 1966 Independence Constitution as the basis for their recommendations. The Draft Constitution was submitted in June 1991. The Government plans to set up a Constitutional Commission to explain the Constitution to the people. Their report will be considered by the Government before confirming the final version of the Constitution. Party political activity was legalised in May 1991 and preparations for elections the following year have begun. The indications are that BCP and BNP will again be strong challengers for the elections.

Meanwhile the division between King Moshoeshoe and the government had not been healed, although it appeared at one point that the King might agree to return to Lesotho with the power of constitutional monarch only. The King's very public criticisms of the government from London eventually persuaded General Lekhanya to depose him and the new King, Letsie III, the former Crown Prince and eldest son of Moshoeshoe, was sworn in in November 1990 with the power of Constitutional Monarch.

Government

HEAD OF STATE

His Majesty King Letsie III

MILITARY COUNCIL

Defence and Internal Security and the Public Service: HE Major General E P Ramaema

Employment, Works, Transport and Communications: HE Colonel T M Lehohla

Agriculture, Cooperatives and Marketing, Trade and Industry, Youth and Women's Affairs, Water, Energy and Mining: HE Lieutenant-Colonel E M Mothibeli

Health, Highlands Water: HE Brigadier B M Lerotholi

Law, Constitutional and Parliamentary Affairs, Justice and Prisons, Education, Printing: HE Colonel J M Jane

Interior, Chieftainship Affairs and Rural Development, Tourism, Sports and Culture: HE Lieutenant-Colonel E M Mokete

Chief Justice: Hon D P Cullinan
President of the National Constituent Assembly: Hon J T Kolane

COUNCIL OF MINISTERS

Minister of Information and Broadcasting: The Hon Mr P J Molapo
Minister of Works, Transport and Communication: The Hon Colonel V M Mokone
Minister of Employment and Social Security: The Hon Colonel P L Mothakathi
Minister of Lesotho Highlands Water and Energy Affairs: The Hon Major R Habi
Minister of Foreign Affairs: The Hon Captain P Molapo
Minister of Law and Justice: The Hon Mr K A Maope
Minister of Health: The Hon Colonel M Khuele
Minister of Water, Energy and Mining: The Hon Colonel L Jane
Minister of Finance and Planning: The Hon Mr A L Thoahlane
Minister of Interior Chieftainship Affairs and Rural Development: The Hon Chief M Matete
Minister of Trade and Industry: The Hon Chief M Mokoroane
Minister of Education: The Hon Dr L B B J Machobane
Minister of Tourism, Sports and Culture: The Hon Chief L Mathealira
Minister of Agriculture Cooperatives and Marketing: Major-General J L Dingiswayo

ASSISTANT MINISTERS

Education: The Hon Mr P 'Mabathoana
Youth and Women's Affairs: The Hon Mrs 'Matlelima Hlalele

PRINCIPAL SECRETARIES

Principal Secretary, Ministry of Works: Mr P K Moonyane
Principal Secretary, Ministry of Transport and Communications: Mr T L Makhakhe
Principal Secretary, Ministry of Employment, Social Welfare and Pensions: Mr C T Thamae
Principal Secretary, Ministry of Lesotho Highlands Water and Energy Affairs: Mr W T Van Tonder
Principal Secretary, Ministry of Foreign Affairs: Mr M Mathibeli
Principal Secretary, Ministry of Information and Broadcasting: Mr P L Ntholi
Principal Secretary, Ministry of Justice and Prisons: Mr F Maema
Principal Secretary, Ministry of Law, Constitutional and Parliamentary Affairs: Mr M Pholo
Principal Secretary, Ministry of Health: Mr L S Makhaola
Principal Secretary, Ministry of Water, Energy and Mining: Mr T Tsietsi
Principal Secretary, Ministry of Finance: Mr L T Tuoane
Principal Secretary, Ministry of Planning, Economic and Manpower Development: Mr T M Thokoa
Principal Secretary, Ministry of the Interior, Chieftainship Affairs and Rural Development: Mr B A Sekhonyana
Principal Secretary, Ministry of Trade and Industry: Mr P Magoaela
Principal Secretary, Ministry of Education: Mr K Matete
Principal Secretary, Ministry of Tourism, Sports and Culture: Mr O T Maphasa

Malawi

Capital: Lilongwe

Malawi is the modern spelling of 'Malavi', the name of widespread groups of closely associated Bantu people who lived in Central Africa, including present-day Malawi and parts of Zambia and Mozambique. Etymologically, the word has associations with a meaning of reflected light or bright haze. The name Malawi was adopted at independence; previously the country had been known as Nyasaland.

Location, Topography, Climate

Malawi is a land-locked country, lying between latitudes 9°45′ and 17°16′ south and between longitudes 33° and 36° east. It is 900 km long and varies in width from 80 km to 160 km. It covers an area of 118,485 sq km. The southern half of the country is surrounded by Mozambique, the northwest is bordered by Zambia, the northeast by Tanzania.

Malawi is dominated by plateaux of varying heights, bordering the deep rift valley trench which averages 80 km in width. The northern two thirds of the rift valley floor is occupied by Lake Malawi while the southern third is traversed by the Shire river, which flows from the Lake to join the Zambezi in Mozambique. Plateaux on either side of the rift valley rise to about 760–1,370 m, but greater altitudes are found: west of the Lake are, from north to south, the Nyika and Viphya plateaux, the Dedza mountains and the Kirk range, which rise to 1,500–2,440 m in places. South of the Lake are the Shire highlands, the Zomba plateau and Mulanje mountain. The last, at 3,000 m, is the highest mountain in Central Africa.

Lake Malawi, Africa's third largest lake, is 568 km long and 16 to 80 km wide. It is 470 m above sea level, and at the northern end is 700 m deep. A number of rivers flow into the lake, and the Shire out of it. None are navigable, but they are utilised for hydro-electricity and irrigation.

Variations in latitude and altitude and the influence of the Lake are responsible for a wide range of climatic and vegetation conditions for the size of the country. There are three seasons: (a) a cool dry season from May to August with mean temperatures of 15–18°C on the plateaux and 20–25°C in the valley; (b) a warm dry season from September to November, with mean temperatures of 22–24°C on the plateaux and 27–30°C in the valley; (c) a rainy season from December to April. Ninety per cent of the annual rainfall occurs in this season. Most of the country receives 800–2,500 mm, but some areas in the higher plateaux receive over 3,500 mm, while some rain shadow areas receive less.

Population

Malawi is one of the most densely populated countries of Africa. The 1987 census showed 85 persons per sq km, compared with 59 persons per sq km in 1977. The population is unevenly distributed, with over half of it in the southern region, 35 per cent in the central and 11 per cent in the northern regions.

The vast majority of the population live in the rural areas. The only large towns are Blantyre (332,000), Lilongwe (234,000), Zomba (43,000) and Mzuzu (44,000).

Many people of Malawi origin live in neighbouring countries. In the past few years there has been a large influx of displaced persons from Mozambique—over 800,000. The number is still increasing.

Over 99 per cent of the population is African. The largest grouping is the Chewa, whose ancestors came from Zaire. Other groups are the Ngoni, whose forebears came from northern Natal in the mid 19th century, and the Yao, whose ancestors come from Mozambique.

The official language is English. The national language is Chichewa.

The majority of the population follow traditional beliefs. About a third of the inhabitants are Christians—Roman Catholic, Church of Central Africa Presbyterian, and Anglican. There are a number of Muslims, particularly among the Yao people. There are three regions: the northern (capital Mzuru) the Central (capital Lilongwe) and the Southern (capital Blantyre). Lilongwe became the national capital in 1975.

Health

The common tropical diseases—malaria, dysentery, bilharzia—prevail, as well as measles, tuberculosis and hepatitis. There has been a successful campaign against leprosy. As in many other countries, AIDS is a growing problem.

There are two central hospitals, in Lilongwe and Blantyre, supported by a network of district hospitals, one general hospital in Zomba, primary health centres and dispensaries. The majority of these are run by the Government, but some by the Private Hospitals Association of Malawi.

Communications

There are 789 km of railway track. The principal line runs northwards from Nsanje in the south via Blantyre to Salima on Lake Malawi, then turns west through Lilongwe to Mchinji on the Zambian border. Another line branches east from Nkaya to Nayuli. From Nsanje and Nayuli there are rail connections through Mozambique to the ports of Beira and Nacala respectively.

These were the traditional routes to the sea for Malawi exports and imports. However, both lines in Mozambique have in recent years worked only spasmodically, and Malawi has had to seek other, more costly, routes for her trade, either through Tanzania to Dar-es-Salaam, or through Zambia and Botswana or Mozambique and Zimbabwe to South African ports. This has reduced export earnings and increased the cost of imports particularly in the case of goods which are bulky in relation to their value.

Attempts are being made to improve external transport. The Northern Corridor project aims to improve the route to Dar-es-Salaam, while the Beira Corridor project in Zimbabwe/Mozambique should benefit Malawi.

Malawi Railways operate both passenger and freight services on Lake Malawi.

There are 12,192 km. of roads, 2,671 of them main roads. The country is covered by a reasonable network of tarred roads. These are connected by a network of secondary roads, most of them usable except at the time of the most heavy rains.

A modern international airport was opened in Lilongwe in 1983, capable of handling all types of aircraft. The national airline is Air Malawi. It operates regular internal flights to Blantyre, Mzuzu, Mangochi and Karonga. There are external flights by Air Malawi and other airlines to southern, central and east Africa, and to Western Europe.

The Economy

Malawi has one of the lowest gross domestic products of countries in Africa at $160 per head in 1986. It has no minerals which have been exploited on any scale, while industrial development is hindered by the country's shape, its land-locked position and distance from foreign markets. However, there has been economic progress since independence. The late '60s and '70s saw a growth in GDP, considerable agricultural expansion, particularly in the smallholder sector, a growth in literacy and an increase in life expectancy. Development in the '80s has been more patchy, because of deterioration in the terms of international trade and a substantial increase in debt servicing (taking over 40 per cent of export earnings in 1987), compounded by disruption of the traditional transport routes. The Malawi Government has taken measures to deal with these problems: debts have been rescheduled, a tight curb kept on government expenditure, close liaison maintained with the World Bank and the IMF, and an attempt to diversify crops and transport routes.

In mid 1988, Malawi became the first recipient of an IMF Enhanced Structural Adjustment Facility (ESAF) worth about £73m, to accompany an economic reform programme including, among its aims, a reduction of the budget deficit, a more market oriented foreign exchange allocation system and the reorganisation of the Agricultural Development and Marketing Corporation (ADMARC).

Trade and Finance

Malawi's main imports are plant and machinery, petroleum products and manufactured goods. Her most important trading partners are South Africa, the UK, West Germany, USA, Zimbabwe, Zambia, the Netherlands and Mozambique.

The unit of currency is the kwacha, divided into 100 tambala. The exchange rate to the £ in December 1990 was K5.11 = £1. It is aligned to a basket of currencies of the country's major trading partners.

Agriculture

Just over half the country's land area is considered suitable for cultivation. Agriculture accounts for 90 per cent of Malawi's export earnings, and more than 90 per cent of the working population is engaged in agricultural pursuits. There are two sectors—the estates and the smallholder. The former accounts for almost 80 per cent of export earnings, but the latter for 78 per cent of the cultivated area and nearly 80 per cent of agricultural production.

Maize, the main food crop, is mainly grown by smallholders. Other food crops include cassava, millet, sorghum, groundnuts, rice and fruit.

The principal agricultural exports are tobacco, tea and sugar. Tea and sugar, and to a lesser extent tobacco, are produced mainly on estates.

In recent years estate production has increased more rapidly than smallholder's, but the Government is attempting to increase the smallholder contribution, through pricing policies and the expansion of extension services. New export crops, such as coffee and macadamia nuts, are also being encouraged, with reasonable success.

Education

The formal education system consists of 8 years of primary education, 4 years of secondary education, 3 or 4 years of tertiary education, depending on whether a diploma or degree course is being followed. Education is not compulsory, and despite a large expansion in the number of school places, particularly in secondary schools, many children, especially in the remoter areas, receive no formal education.

In the academic year 1985/86, almost one million pupils were attending some 2,500 primary schools, with a teaching staff of 16,000; 25,000 pupils were attending 75 secondary schools with a teaching staff of 1,300. The University of Malawi has nearly 2,000 students, it has 4 constituent colleges: Chancellor College in Zomba for arts and pure science, the Polytechnic in Blantyre for engineering and business studies, Bunda College near Lilongwe for agriculture, and the Kamuzu College of Nursing in Lilongwe and Blantyre.

The Media

There is no television in Malawi. The Malawi Broadcasting Corporation broadcasts for 133 hours a week. Twenty-nine per cent of their programmes are educational, 17.5 per cent are devoted to news and current affairs. About 40 per cent of the programmes are in English, 60 per cent in Chichewa.

There is one daily newspaper, the *Daily Times*, one weekly, the *Malawi News*, and a fortnightly *Odini*, all privately owned. The Government Information Department produces a monthly newspaper in Chichewa, *Boma Lathu*, and a monthly magazine, *This is Malawi*. Monthly magazines, in English and Chichewa, are also published by private organisations. The Malawi News Agency, operating under the Department of Information, covers the whole country.

History

Present day Malawi was occupied by succeeding Stone Age cultures from about 50,000 BC who were moving in a generally north to south direction. The earliest settlement by Bantu speaking people appears to have been about the first century AD.

The area is mentioned in early Arab writings and in Portuguese writings of the 17th to 18th centuries. David Livingstone visited Lake Nyasa in 1859, and was followed by British missionaries, traders and planters in succeeding decades. This was an unsettled period, with widespread slave raiding.

A British Consul, accredited to the 'Kings and Chiefs of Central Africa', was appointed in Blantyre in 1883, and a British Protectorate was proclaimed over the southern part of present day Malawi in 1889. An Anglo-Portuguese convention subsequently defined the spheres of influence of the two countries, and on 15th June 1891 a British Protectorate was declared over the 'Nyasaland districts'—the modern Malawi. The territory was renamed the British Central Africa Protectorate in 1893, and the Nyasaland Protectorate in 1907. The last decade of the 19th century saw the pacification of the areas affected by slave raiding, and the establishment of an administration. The first Governor was appointed in 1897, Legislative and Executive Councils were established in 1907.

Constitutional Development

The question of associating Nyasaland with one or more of its neighbours was considered several times, and in 1953 the Federation of Rhodesia and Nyasaland came into existence. This resulted in a number of spheres of government being transferred to the control of the Federal Government. The Federation was not popular in Nyasaland, and the Nyasaland African Congress invited Dr H Kamuzu Banda, who had lived abroad for over 30 years, to return to lead the fight against it. He arrived on 6th July 1958, reorganised the Congress Party, and held a series of mass meetings criticising the Federation. In an attempt to control a deteriorating situation, the Government declared a state of emergency in 1959, followed by the detention of Dr Banda and other members of the Congress Party.

Following his release in 1960, a series of Constitutional Conferences were held, as were elections. Internal self-government was achieved in 1963, the Federation was dissolved at the end of that year, and Malawi attained complete independence as a full member of the Commonwealth on 6th July 1964.

Constitution

Two years after independence Malawi became a Republic, with Dr Banda as President. The present constitution, subsequently amended, came into force on 6th July 1966. In 1971 Dr Banda was made Life President.

The constitution provides that should there be a vacancy in the office of President, or should the President be incapacitated, the functions of the office would be performed by a Presidential Commission, consisting of the Secretary General of the Malawi Congress Party (vacant since 1983) and two Cabinet ministers who are also members of the National Executive Committee of the Party. When the Presidency falls vacant, the Constitution provides for a large, broadly based Electoral College to nominate a candidate for election to the office.

There is a National Assembly, most of whose members are elected by universal adult suffrage, as well as some nominated members. The Speaker is appointed by the President. The Assembly usually has two sessions a year.

The Constitution gives the President, who is also Commander-in-Chief of the Armed Forces, widespread powers. President Banda also holds a number of ministerial portfolios, including External Affairs, Agriculture, Justice and Works.

Historical List

GOVERNOR-GENERAL
Sir Glyn Jones, KCMG (later GCMG), MBE, from 6th July 1964 to 5th July 1966.

PRIME MINISTER
Dr H Kamuzu Banda, from 6th July 1964 to 5th July 1966

PRESIDENT
Dr H Kamuzu Banda, from 6th July 1966 and Life President from March 1971

THE HEAD OF STATE
His Excellency the Life President Ngwazi Dr H Kamuzu Banda—
Minister of External Affairs, Minister of Works, Minister of Agriculture, and Minister of Justice

THE CABINET
Minister Without Portfolio: Hon M Pashane, MP
Minister of Labour: Hon W B Deleza, MP
Minister of Health: Hon Dr Heatherwick Ntaba
Minister of Trade, Industry and Tourism: Hon R W Chirwa, MP
Minister of Finance: Hon L J Chimango, MP
Minister of Forestry and Natural Resources: (Vacant)
Minister of Transport & Communications: Hon D S Katopola, MP
Minister of Community Services: Hon M M Mwakikunga, MP
Minister of Education and Culture: Hon M U K Mlambala, MP
Minister of Local Government: Hon E C Katola Phiri, MP
Deputy Minister of Agriculture: Hon Francis M Kangaude
Deputy Minister of Works: Hon J R Kangere

NATIONAL ASSEMBLY
Speaker: The Hon M M Lungu, MP
Deputy Speakers: Mr D G Chimutu Nkhoma, MP (1st) Mr W V Binali, MP (2nd)
Clerk of National Assembly: Mr R L Gondwe

JUDICIARY
Chief Justice: The Hon F L Makuta

AUDIT DEPARTMENT
Auditor General: Mr Kamphambe Nkhome

MINISTRIES AND GOVERNMENT DEPARTMENTS

PRINCIPAL SECRETARIES
Office of the President
Comptroller of State Residences: Mr N Collins
Office of the President and Cabinet: (Vacant)
Principal Secretary (Administration): (Vacant)
Principal Secretary (Finance): Mr E F Matingwi
Principal Secretary (Media Services and Public Affairs): (Vacant)
Principal Secretary (Personnel Management and Training): Mr W W Mamon'ga
Principal Secretary (Chitukuko cha Amayi 'm' Malawi (CCAM)): Mrs H G Kawalewale
Principal Secretary (Youth and Malawi Young Pioneers): Mr M B Chimutu
Principal Secretary (District Administration): (Vacant)
Regional Administrator (North): Mr B B Mwambakulu
Regional Administrator (Centre): Mr B S Phangaphanga
Regional Administrator (South): Mr S Winga

Ministry of Agriculture
Principal Secretary: Mr B M Ndisale

Ministry of Community Services
Principal Secretary: Mrs E Kalyati

Ministry of Education and Culture
Principal Secretary: Dr I C Lamba

Ministry of External Affairs
Principal Secretary: (Vacant)

Ministry of Finance
Secretary to the Treasury: Mr G B Chiwaula
Accountant General: Patrick Chilambe

Ministry of Foresty and Natural Resources
Principal Secretary: Dr S S Kamvazina

Ministry of Health
Principal Secretary: Mr R P Dzanjalimodzi

Ministry of Justice
Attorney-General: Mr J B Villiera

Ministry of Labour
Principal Secretary: Mr B B Mawindo

Ministry of Local Government
Principal Secretary: Mr B M Phiri

Ministry of Trade, Industry and Tourism
Principal Secretary: Mr T I M Vareta

Ministry of Transport and Communications
Acting Principal Secretary: Mr J L Kalemera

Ministry of Works
Principal Secretary: (Vacant)

NATIONAL EXECUTIVE COMMITTEE OF MALAWI CONGRESS PARTY

Administrative Secretary: Mr M P Pashane, MP
Treasurer General: Mr John Z U Tembo

Mr R W Chirwa, MP
Mr B J Bisani, MP
Mr W B Deleza, MP
Vice-administrative secretary: Mr E C Katola Phiri, MP
Mr M M Mwakikunga

Central Regional Chairman: Hon L J Chimango, MP
Speaker of the National Assembly and Northern Regional Chairman: Mr M M Lungu
Southern Regional Chairman: (Vacant)

Malaysia

Capital: Kuala Lumpur

Location, Topography and Climate
Malaysia is a federation consisting of the eleven States of Peninsular Malaysia, namely Johore, Kedah, Kelantan, Malacca, Negeri Sembilan, Pahang, Penang, Perak, Perlis, Selangor and Terengganu and the two States of Sabah and Sarawak on the north coast of the island of Kalimantan. The States of Peninsular Malaysia are situated in that part of the Malay Peninsula which lies to the south of the Isthmus of Kra between latitudes 1° and 7° North and longitudes 100° and 105° East. They are bordered on the north by Thailand, on the west by the Straits of Malacca, on the east by the South China Sea and to the south by Singapore. Sabah and Sarawak are situated on the North and West coasts of Northern Borneo being bounded by the South China Sea to the West, the Sulu and Celebes Sea to the East and Indonesia to the South. Sabah lies between latitudes 4° and 7° North and longitudes 115° and 120° East, while Sarawak lies between latitudes 1° and 5° North and longitudes 109° and 116° East.

The total area of Malaysia is about 330,434 sq km, divided as follows:—

	sq km
Peninsular Malaysia	131,587
Sabah and Sarawak	198,846

Malaysia includes a number of islands, none of which is far distant from its shores. In addition to the large island of Penang, the most important are the Langkawi Islands which are administratively part of Kedah, the Pangkor Islands off the coast of Perak, the Tioman Islands off the coast of Pahang and Labuan off the coast of Sabah.

The greater part of Malaysia is covered by dense tropical jungle, the only generally cleared areas being in the west and north-east of Peninsular Malaysia and along the principal river valleys. Large areas of Pahang are gradually being cleared. In Peninsular Malaysia the mountain range runs along the spine of the country from the north-west to the south-east, the highest mountain being Gunong Tahan (2,156 m). The main rivers are the Perak and the Pahang. In Sabah the central range rises to heights of from 1,200 m to 1,800 m and culminates in Mount Kinabalu (4,037 m), the highest mountain in the region. The principal river is the Kinabatangan. The highest mountain in Sarawak is Murud (2,385 m), and the main river the Rejang.

Both Peninsular Malaysia and Sabah and Sarawak are open to maritime influences and are subject to the interplay of the wind systems which originate in the Indian Ocean and the South China Sea. The year is divided into the south-west and north-east monsoon seasons which in time correspond roughly with the summer and winter of northern latitudes. In Peninsular Malaysia the months between the two monsoon periods are generally the wettest, though on the east coast the period of the north-east monsoon brings the greatest amount of rain. In Sarawak, from the beginning of October until nearly the end of February, the north-east monsoon brings heavy rainfall, particularly in the coastal belt. From April to July there is a mild south-east monsoon and during the period rainfall often occurs in the form of afternoon thunderstorms. In Sabah the north-east monsoon lasts from late November and December until March and April, and the south-west monsoon from May to August with interim periods of indeterminate winds between the two monsoons. On the west coast the wetter seasons occur during the south-west monsoon period and the interim periods, while on the east coast the heaviest rainfall occurs during the north-east monsoon. Humidity is generally high.

Throughout Malaysia average daily temperature varies from about 21°C (70°F) to 32°C (90°F) though in higher areas temperatures are lower and vary more widely. In the Cameron Highlands in Pahang the extreme temperatures recorded are 26.5°C (79°F) and 2°C (36°F). Rainfall averages about 2,500 mm throughout the year, though the annual fall varies from place to place and from year to year. The driest part of Peninsular Malaysia is Jelebu in Negeri Sembilan with an average of 1,625 mm, and the wettest place Maxwell's Hill in Perak with 4,950 mm a year. A large area of Sarawak receives between 3,000 mm and 4,000 mm of rain. In Sabah rainfall varies from 250 mm to 4,000 mm.

Population
Malaysia is a multi-racial state. The principal racial groups are the Malays, followed by the Chinese and various communities from the Indian sub-continent and Sri Lanka. Other numerically significant groups are: the indigenous races of Sarawak and Sabah, of whom the Dayaks, Kadazans (Dusuns),

Bajaus, Melanaus and Muruts are the most numerous; the aboriginal peoples who live in Peninsular Malaysia; Europeans and Eurasians.

The languages mainly spoken are Malay (Bahasa Malaysia), English, Chinese (various dialects) and Tamil. There are a few indigenous tongues spoken widely in Sabah and Sarawak. Hokkien and Cantonese are the main Chinese dialects.

Malay which is the national language of Malaysia is the sole official language.

Islam is the official religion of Malaysia, but Confucianism, Buddhism, Taoism, Hinduism and Christianity are also widely and freely practised.

The population is increasing rapidly and the population figures based on the 1990 estimates are:

MALAYSIA—total population: 17,756,200

1990	PENINSULAR MALAYSIA		
	Malays	8,507,000	
	Chinese	4,581,000	
	Indians	1,436,000	
	Others	93,000	
			14,617,000
	SABAH		
	Bumiputera and others	1,267,800	
	Chinese	202,400	
			1,470,200
	SARAWAK		
	Bumiputera and others	1,186,500	
	Chinese	482,500	
			1,669,000

The following is a list of the States and their capitals with population figures (1990 estimate):

State	*Capital*	*Total population*
Johore	Johore Baru	2,106,500
Kedah	Alor Setar	1,412,800
Kelantan	Kota Baru	1,221,100
Malacca	Malacca	583,500
Negeri Sembilan	Seremban	723,800
Pahang	Kuantan	1,054,800
Penang	Georgetown	1,142,200
Perak	Ipoh	2,222,200
Perlis	Kangar	187,200
Sabah	Kota Kinabalu	1,470,200
Sarawak	Kuching	1,669,000
Selangor	Shah Alam	1,978,000
Terengganu	Kuala Terengganu	752,000
Federal Territory	Kuala Lumpur	1,232,900

The capital of Malaysia is Kuala Lumpur situated in Peninsular Malaysia half-way between Penang and Johore and 43 km inland from Port Klang. The town was founded in 1857, succeeded Klang as the capital of Selangor in 1895 and became the capital of the Federated Malay States. In 1948 it became the capital of the Federation of Malaya and in 1963 the capital of Malaysia. Under the Federal Capital Act of 1960 the previously elected Municipal Council was abolished and Kuala Lumpur is now a Federal Territory, being administered on behalf of the Malaysian Government by a Mayor with an Advisory Board of six official and five unofficial Members. The Federal Territory itself was formed in 1972.

Communications

The principal sea ports in Peninsular Malaysia are Port Kelang, Penang, Pasir Gudang in Johore and Kuantan. In East Malaysia work in Sabah was completed on the extensions to existing port facilities at Kota Kinabalu and Sandakan.

In Sarawak a new port is planned at Kuching and the expansion of port facilities at Sibu has been completed.

The principal airports are at Subang, 23 km from Kuala Lumpur, (runway 3,990 × 46 metres); Penang 15 km from town (runway 3,354 × 46 metres); Labuan (runway 1,945 × 46 metres); Kota Kinabalu, 6 km from town (runway 2,987 × 46 metres); Sandakan, 11 km from town (runway 2,134 × 46 metres); Tawau (runway 1,707 × 30 metres); Kuching, 11 km from town (runway 2,454 × 46 metres); Sibu, (runway 1,372 × 30 Metres); Miri (runway 1,981 × 61 metres); Senai outside Johore Bahru (runway 3,354 × 46 metres); Kuantan (2,804 × 46 metres). There are many others suitable for small aircraft. All parts of Malaysia are linked by air services provided at present by the Malaysian national airline called Malaysian Airline System (MAS) which also operates international air services. There are 2,681 km of main running railway lines and 2,156 km of loops, sidings and yard lines. Metalled roads total 28,753 km in Peninsular Malaysia.

The Economy

The worldwide recession and the fall in commodity prices in the mid 1980's shook Malaysia's economy badly and the Government became determined to reduce the country's vulnerability to such external factors. Emphasis was placed on industrialisation and the economy of Malaysia is now moving away from its traditional reliance on primary commodity exports towards a greater concentration on manufactured goods. In 1990, almost 60 per cent of Malaysia's exports were manufactured goods, with commodities (rubber, palm oil etc.) contributing 22 per cent and minerals (particularly petroleum) around 18 per cent.

Since 1988, the economy has grown by over 8 per cent per annum and in 1991 it grew by 8.8 per cent. Projections for 1992 and 1993 show slowing but very respectable growth rates of 8 per cent plus. The Government continues to put emphasis on attracting foreign investment and this is proving very successful; foreign investment increased by over 100 per cent in 1990. The privatisation programme continues.

The future outlook for the Malaysian economy remains favourable but labour constraints and a rising inflation level are beginning to cause some concern.

Education

Formal education comprises 6 years primary, 3 years lower secondary, 2 years upper secondary and 2 years post secondary education. Education is not compulsory. It is free at the primary level and also at secondary level for classes conducted in Malay—11 years of education.

Primary education begins at age 7. There were 437,331 new pupils enrolled for primary education in 1991. Schooling is available in all the three major languages: Bahasa Malaysia, Chinese and Tamil. All schools use a common content curriculum. Promotion is automatic but national assessment tests are carried out at Standard 6.

Admission to lower secondary school is automatic. Pupils from Malay medium schools enter Form 1 whereas those from Chinese and Tamil schools enter a remove year before proceeding to Form 1. The new curriculum encourages students to develop a range of abilities in academic and pre-vocational areas. Promotion is automatic until Form 3, at the end of which pupils sit a national examination to select for Form 4.

On the basis of results in the Form 3 examination, students may be channelled into Academic, Technical or Vocational Schools. In 1990 185,496 students enrolled into upper secondary. Out of this, 28,615 proceeded to post-secondary. At the end of 2 years students in the Academic and Technical Schools sit for the Malaysian Certificate of Education (MCE) while those from the Vocational Schools sit for the Malaysian Certificate of Vocational Education (MCVE).

Students with good results in the MCE and MCVE are selected for entry to 6th Forms, which offer a two-year course for the Higher School Certificate, or to other post secondary institutions such as the MARA Institute of Technology, the Tunku Abdul Rahman College or the Polytechnics at Kuantan, Ipoh and Batu Pahat. These offer a range of certificate, pre-university, diploma and degree level courses of from 2 to 5 years duration in the full range of professional and technical subjects. There are also 25 teacher training colleges offering a 2-year course for intending primary and lower secondary teachers.

There are seven universities: namely the University of Malaya, National University, University of Agriculture, University of Science, University of Technology, the International Islamic University and the Northern University of Malaysia. They offer a wide range of first degree courses lasting 3 or 4 years, except for medicine, dentistry and veterinary medicine courses which take longer. Masters and doctorate degrees are also awarded.

A number of private institutions provide education mainly at kindergarten, upper secondary and post secondary levels. They are subject to registration with the Ministry of Education. Other Ministries are involved in both formal and non-formal training of skilled manpower.

Secondary and post-secondary education has converted from the medium of English to Bahasa Malaysia except for certain post graduate courses.

The overall national planning of the country is spelt out in the National Development Policy (NDP) of June 1991 which has superceded the New Economic Policy (NEP). The NDP aims to consolidate Malaysia's economic growth, devoting greater resources to training and education and removing barriers to inward investment. The Prime Minister has called for Malaysia to be a fully developed country by 2020.

The cost of education, both capital and recurrent is financed almost entirely from public revenue with only a small contribution from Education Rates. Expenditure on education constitutes a significant proportion of the total national budget. Under the Sixth Malaysia Plan (SMP) 1991–1995, a total of M$8,501,000 million was allocated for education expenditure.

There is a large programme of school building at primary and secondary level and increasing emphasis is placed on the provision of facilities for science and technical education including the construction of Special Science Schools with residential facilities. It has been necessary to maintain a balance between the various races in access to higher education.

The Media

The Department of Broadcasting includes Radio Malaysia and T.V. Malaysia (RTM) which were integrated on 1st October 1969. It is located in a modern and up-to-date complex at Angkasapuri. Radio Malaysia broadcasts programmes in Malay, English, Chinese and Tamil and operates six domestic networks. The national service broadcasts around the clock in Peninsular Malaysia; the other services broadcast a total of 293 hours 30 minutes a week, in English, Chinese (Mandarin, Amoy, Hakka and Cantonese) and Tamil. The department also provides a local radio service for Kuala Lumpur, Capital City Broadcast, which was launched in November 1973. An FM Stereo Service was launched in June 1975.

Programmes are also broadcast in the two main aboriginal languages, Semai and Temiar, 14 hours weekly for 45,000 aborigines in the country. Radio Malaysia Sarawak broadcasts a total of 396 hours a week in Malay, Iban, Chinese, English, Bidayuh, Melanau and Kayan/Kenyah, Murut and Bisayas.

Suara Malaysia or 'The Voice of Malaysia' is the Overseas Service of Radio Malaysia. Formed in 1963, this service broadcasts in eight languages—Indonesian 63 hours, English 17½ hours, Mandarin 14 hours, Filipino (Tagalog) 17½ hours, Thai 10½ hours, Arabic 10½ hours, Burmese 7 hours and Malay 14 hours.

Facilities are now provided for commercial advertising to the whole of Malaysia. Commercial radio emanating from Kota Kinabalu, Sabah, began in February 1972 while Sarawak launched its commercial radio broadcasting in May 1972. It is estimated that there are more than 762,011 licensed radio receivers in Malaysia today.

Television was introduced in Kuala Lumpur in December 1963, with coverage progressively extended to the whole of the West Coast of Malaysia. Likewise, all main centres of population on the East Coast of Peninsular Malaysia began to receive a two-network television service at the end of 1971 with new television transmitting stations installed at Kuantan, Dungun, Kuala Terengganu and Kota Bharu. Direct transmissions to Sabah and Sarawak commenced in August 1975. Colour transmission to all parts of the country began in December 1978. The Director General of the Department is Datuk Jaafar Kamin.

In addition to RTM, Rediffusion (M) Sdn Bhd, a private commercial enterprise, operate a wired service in the major urban areas of Peninsular Malaysia, viz Kuala Lumpur, Petaling Jaya, Ipoh and Penang, and provide advertising facilities in each of the three main languages, English, Malay and Chinese (Cantonese, Hokkien, Mandarin, Hakka, Teochew, Hainanese).

Malaysia's first private television network, TV3, started transmission in June 1984. It is run by Sistem Telivisyen Malaysia Berhad (STMB), a company in the Fleet Group.

History

Peninsular Malaysia

Archaeological research in Peninsular Malaysia, although far from complete, has furnished proof of occupation of the peninsula at least five thousand years ago. Enough has been uncovered to show that the peninsula was one of the routes by which the pre-historic populations of Indonesia, Melanesia and Australia travelled on their way south to their ultimate homes. Evidence of a later Bronze Age culture dating from about 250 B.C. has also been found.

From very early in the Christian era trading ships were sailing between India and China, some of which touched at river mouths in the Malay peninsula. The Chinese traders made no attempt to settle but Indian traders opened trading posts on the Merbok estuary in Kedah and elsewhere on the west coast, bringing with them both the Buddhist and Hindu religions. From the 7th to the 13th centuries the Indo-Malay empire of Sri Vijaya centred on south-east Sumatra controlled both sides of the Straits of Malacca. It was destroyed by the expanding Thais and Javanese. It is probable that settlers from Sri Vijaya founded Temasek (Tumasik) (later known as Singapore). Between 1331 and 1351 the whole of the Malay peninsula was temporarily overrun by the Javanese.

Malacca rose as a result of the destruction of Temasek, receiving large numbers of fugitives, amongst them Parameswara, exiled ruler of Temasek, who became ruler of Malacca. The conversion of the Malays to Islam also began in the early 15th century. Parameswara, although a Hindu when he came to Malacca, embraced the Muslim faith late in life, about 1411, and was known as Megat Iskander Shah. His example was rapidly followed and Malacca soon became an important Muslim missionary centre. Malacca's growth was rapid and, in the reign of the fourth Sultan, Kedah, Kelantan and Patani (now in Thailand) came under its rule.

In 1509 the first European fleet sailed into Malacca under the Portuguese flag but it was not until 1511 that Malacca became a Portuguese possession, which it stayed for 130 years. The Portuguese did not attempt to administer their conquered territory but held trading suzerainty and allowed a wide measure of self-government. Malcacca was conquered by the Dutch in 1641.

During the period of the Portuguese possession of Malacca the Malay Kingdom of Johore held suzerainty over the remainder of the peninsula. From 1722 Bugis chiefs from the Celebes held a dominant position in the Riau-Johore Kingdom and later in Selangor and Perak. Although temporarily ousted from power in Riau by an alliance of the Dutch and the Johore Sultan and his chiefs, the Bugis continued to rule in Selangor and to exercise control in Kedah. As Dutch influence declined, however, the Bugis became once again the dominant power. The Malay kingdom of Riau-Johore now consisted of little more than the Riau-Lingga group of islands. The former capital of Johore was abandoned and the territories of Johore and Pahang were each normally supervised by a major chief on behalf of the Sultan. Selangor was an independent state under a Bugis ruler and Minangkabau settlers from Sumatra created a new territorial unit, south of Selangor, later to be known as Negeri Sembilan.

The history of the British connection with Peninsular Malaysia began with the establishment of three British trading settlements at Penang, Malacca and Singapore. The earliest was established on Penang Island in 1786, when Capt Francis Light obtained for the East India Company a grant of the island from the Sultan of Kedah; in 1800 Province Wellesley on the mainland was added. Until 1806 the settlement was governed by Superintendents and Lieutenant-Governors under the Presidency of Bengal. In 1806 Penang was made a Presidency of equal rank with Madras and Bombay.

Malacca, which had been occupied by the Portuguese from 1511 and then by the Dutch from 1641, came into British hands in 1795 during the Napoleonic Wars, but was returned to the Dutch by the Convention of London of 1814. It was finally ceded to Britain (in exchange for the East India Company's settlement at Bencoolen on the west coast of Sumatra) by the Anglo-Dutch Treaty of London of 17th March 1824.

It was the temporary loss of Malacca and the transfer back to the Dutch of Java in 1814 which caused Stamford Raffles to found a trading post on the sparsely inhabited island of Singapore as a rival to Malacca. In return for support for his claim to the disputed throne, the Temenggong of Johore signed a Treaty in 1819 granting Raffles permission to establish a settlement, and in 1824 the island of Singapore was transferred to Britain. As a free port, Singapore at once began its phenomenal development as a centre of *entrepôt* trade. From 1819 to 1824 Singapore was subordinate to the East India Company's settlement at Bencoolen but in the latter year it was placed under the Presidency of Bengal.

In 1826 Singapore and Malacca were incorporated with Penang to form the Straits Settlements. The seat of Government remained at Penang until 1832 when it was transferred to Singapore. With the reorganisation of the government of Bengal and the creation of the office of Governor-General of India on 22nd April 1834 the Straits Settlements came under the direct control of the Governor-General. On the same day the 'United Company of Merchants of England Trading to the East Indies' officially became 'The East India Company' and it was ordered that their exclusive trading with China and the tea trade were to cease. Act 29 & 30 Vict cap 115 of 1866 provided for the separation of the Straits Settlements, comprising Prince of Wales Island (Penang), the island of Singapore, the town of Malacca, and their dependencies, from Indian control and by virtue of an Order in Council dated 28th December 1866 the Straits Settlements became a Crown Colony in 1867. The extension of British authority into the peninsula was hastened by unsettled conditions in the Malay States which had deteriorated in some cases into civil war. In 1873 the new Governor of the Straits Settlements went out with authority for more active intervention. The first result was the Treaty of Pangkor with Perak in 1874, and in the next decade there followed agreements with Selangor, with the States of Negeri Sembilan and with Pahang. In 1909 Siam transferred to Britain her rights in Kedah, Perlis, Kelantan and Terengganu by the Treaty of Bangkok. In 1910 agreements were concluded with Kelantan and Terengganu (the latter amended in 1919); in 1914 with Johore; in 1923 with Kedah, and in 1930 with Perlis. All these treaties were similiar in their main features. The Malay States agreed to accept British protection and to have no dealings with foreign powers except through Britain, and were in turn guaranteed protection against attack by foreign powers; to each State there was appointed, as Resident or Adviser, a British Officer whose advice the Rulers agreed to follow in all matters except those of the Muslim religion or Malay custom. The foundations of good government and friendly relations laid by such early Residents as Sir Hugh Low and Sir Frank Swettenham made possible the great economic development of this century, when European and Chinese capital built up the rubber and tin industries and made of the Malay Peninsula one of the most prosperous territories in the Commonwealth. On 1st July 1896 Perak, Selangor, Negeri Sembilan and Pahang became a Federation (the Federated Malay States) with a Resident-General as chief executive officer, and a system of centralised government was inaugurated. This system lasted in varying forms until 1932, when there was a measure of decentralisation by which legislative powers were to some extent restored to the States and the authority of the Rulers and Residents was reinforced. The Federated Malay States, being Protected States, did not form part of the Colony of the Straits Settlements, but the Governor of the Colony was concurrently the High Commissioner of the Federated Malay States. The remaining five Malay States did not join the Federation and were hence known as the Unfederated Malay States. In addition to Penang, Malacca and Singapore, the Straits Settlements included the mainland opposite Penang Island, known as Province Wellesley (ceded in 1796), the

Dindings, including Pangkor Island, ceded by the Treaty of Pangkor in 1874 and returned to Perak in 1935, Labuan in what is now Sabah (from 1905) and the Indian Ocean islands of Christmas Island and Cocos (Keeling) Islands (from 1882 and 1888 respectively).

In December 1941 progress and prosperity of all the territories which now form part of Malaysia were interrupted by the Japanese invasion and subsequent occupation, which lasted until the unconditional surrender of the Japanese and the British re-occupation in 1945. In September a British Military Administration was established in Malaya and Singapore. This was followed by the publication in January 1946 of a British Government White Paper setting out proposals for a Malayan Union which would unite Malaya, including the four Federated Malay States, the five Unfederated Malay States and the Settlements of Penang and Malacca, but excluding Singapore, Labuan, Christmas Island and the Cocos (Keeling) Islands, under a Governor and a strong unitary government. Because of opposition throughout the country, principally by the Malays organised under Dato Onn's leadership in the United Malays National Organisation, the Malayan Union, which was established on 1st April 1946, was soon abandoned. In its place the Federation of Malaya Agreement, which was concluded in January 1948, created the Federation of Malaya, consisting of the same territories as the Malayan Union.

An attempt by Dato Onn in 1951 to widen the membership of the UMNO in the Federation of Malaya by admitting members of other races led to his displacement as President of the party by Tunku Abdul Rahman, who became the Chief Minister of the first elected government in 1955, and led the negotiations with the British which culminated in the attainment of independence by the Federation of Malaya in 1957.

The Emergency in Malaya. During the Japanese occupation, the Malayan Communist Party had carried on guerrilla warfare in the jungle, and had been able to build up a powerful organisation and to collect quantities of arms and equipment. These arms and equipment were not given up after the defeat of the Japanese. In June 1948, after a period of legal and semi-legal activity, the Party decided to resort to armed terrorism, and a State of Emergency was declared by the Federation Government. The communist terrorists failed, however, to disrupt the economy of the country, and the Federation's armed forces and police, assisted by overseas Commonwealth forces from Britain, Australia, New Zealand, Fiji, and elsewhere, gradually eliminated them, with the result that the Federation Government was able to declare the Emergency officially over on 31st July 1960. By that time virtually the sole remaining communist terrorists on Malayan soil were a few scattered bands in the neighbourhood of the Thai border.

Sabah

The earliest artefacts so far discovered in Sabah date from the mesolithic period about 8,000 years ago. Later neolithic tools have been found in relative abundance and are kept as charms by the Dusuns and Bajaus of the Kota Belud district. Fragments of Ming, Sung and other pottery indicate that there was trade with China from the seventh century onward.

Early in the fifteenth century the Sultan of Brunei was the overlord of most of Sabah but the Sultan of Sulu may have exercised the rights of suzerainty over some of the northern parts. The area was visited by the Portuguese, the Spaniards and by the Dutch, who eventually became the most important European nation in the East Indies. The British first visited Borneo in 1609. The Sultan of Sulu later ceded to the East India Company all the territory obtained from the Sultan of Brunei and shortly afterwards the Company opened a trading station in Balembangan Island. This settlement existed from 1773 until 1775 and from 1803 to 1804. Although the Dutch never occupied the whole of the island, European intervention weakened the power of the Sultan of Brunei, and there was much lawlessness and piracy. After the founding of Singapore, British interest in north Borneo revived, mainly because of the need to protect the trade routes from the pirates. Sir James Brooke established himself in Sarawak and in 1847 the island of Labuan was ceded to Britain by the Sultan of Brunei. In 1872 the Labuan Trading Company was established in Sandakan; and in 1878 the Sultan of Sulu again ceded his territory in North Borneo in perpetuity to Mr (later Sir Alfred) Dent and his associates, who also obtained certain areas from the Sultan of Brunei. In 1881 a Company was formed and was granted a Royal Charter. In 1882 the British North Borneo (Chartered) Company was formed and took over all the sovereign and territorial rights ceded by the original grants, and proceeded to organise the administration of the territory. The territory of the Company was subsequently extended by further grants from the Sultan of Brunei, and, by agreement, was made a British Protectorate in 1888, remaining, however, under the administration of the Company until January 1942, when it fell to the Japanese. Labuan was put under the jurisdiction of the Company in 1890 but was removed from that jurisdiction in 1905 and transferred to the Straits Settlements. The British North Borneo Company was the last of the Chartered Companies to administer British territory. When British North Borneo was liberated by the Australians who landed in June 1945 it was first placed under Military Administration, but on 15th July 1946 it became a Crown Colony. Labuan was also incorporated in the new colony to form the Colony of North Borneo.

Sarawak

Archaeological excavations in the Niah Caves, in the Fourth Division, have produced artefacts dating from the Middle Palaeolithic period of about 40–50,000 B.C. Other sites have produced ceramics and stone and metal objects dating from the first millenium of this era; but few objects which can be dated from between A.D. 1450 to modern times have been discovered.

When the ships of Magellan reached Brunei in 1521, after the death of their leader in the Philippines, they found a rich and powerful Brunei Sultanate controlling most of Borneo including what is now Sarawak. Islam had reached this Sultanate in the previous century. But the history of Sarawak as an integral state began in 1839, when the Malays and Land Dayaks of the southern province of Brunei were in revolt against the Sultan of Brunei. James Brooke intervened in this dispute and brought about a settlement, being rewarded for his services by being installed in 1841 as Rajah of the territory from Cape Datu to the Samarahan River. Thereafter Rajah Brooke devoted himself to the suppression of piracy and head-hunting, often with the assistance of ships of the Royal Navy. Sarawak was recognised as an independent state by the United States of America in 1850 and by Britain in 1864. In 1861 the territory was enlarged by the cession by the Sultan of Brunei of all rivers and lands from the Sadong River to Kidurong Point.

At his death in 1868 Sir James Brooke bequeathed to his nephew and successor Charles Brooke a country paternally governed with a solid foundation of mutual trust and affection between ruler and ruled. In 1882 the frontier was advanced beyond the Baram River; in 1885 the valley of the Trusan River was ceded; and in 1890 the Limbang River was annexed at the request of the inhabitants. In 1905 the Lawas River area was purchased from the British North Borneo Company, with the consent of the British Government. British protection was accorded to Sarawak in 1888.

The third Rajah, Sir Charles Vyner Brooke, succeeded his father in 1917 and progress continued in all spheres. In 1941, the centenary year of Brooke rule, the state was in a sound economic position with large reserves. To celebrate the centenary, the Rajah enacted a new constitution, and set his people on the first stage of the road to democratic government.

During the Japanese occupation social services and communications were neglected; education ceased; health precautions were ignored; sickness and malnutrition spread throughout the country. After the surrender of Japan the Australian forces entered Kuching on 11th September 1945 and Sarawak was for seven months under a British Military Administration, which began the rehabilitation of the country. On 15th April 1946 the Rajah resumed the administration; but it was evident to him that greater resources and more technical and scientific experience were needed to restore to Sarawak her former prosperity, and he therefore decided to hand over the country to the British Crown. A Bill for this purpose was introduced into the Council Negeri in May 1946 and passed by a small majority. By an Order in Council the State became a British Colony on 1st July 1946.

Constitutional development of the Federation of Malaya

Under the Federation of Malaya Agreement, 1948, between the British Crown and the Rulers of the nine Malay States, the Federation of Malaya, comprising the nine Malay States of Johore, Pahang, Negeri Sembilan, Selangor, Perak, Kedah, Perlis, Kelantan and Terengganu and the two British Settlements of Penang and Malacca, was constituted on 1st February 1948. The Agreement, as from time to time amended, provided for an Executive Council presided over by the High Commissioner, and for a Legislative Council presided over by a Speaker with a majority of elected members. Because of the outbreak of the communist terrorism in 1948, it was not practicable to hold the first Federal Elections until 27th July 1955. These were based on the principle of universal adult franchise for all Federal citizens on a common electoral roll. The Alliance Party, formed by the combination of the United Malays National Organisation, the Malayan Chinese Association and the Malayan Indian Congress, won 51 out of 52 elective seats. In each of the Malay States there was a State Executive Council and a Council of State, which was the legislative body, and in the two Settlements a Settlement Executive Council and a Settlement Council. Elections to these Councils were held also in 1955, the elected members, together with unofficial members, being in a majority in each Council. In all of them the overwhelming majority of elected seats were held by members of the Alliance Party.

At a Conference held in London in January/February 1956, attended by representatives of the British Government, of the Rulers of the Malay States and of the elected Government of the Federation, agreement was reached on certain changes in the Constitution of the Federation and also on the appointment of an independent Constitutional Commission to make recommendations for the constitution of the Federation of Malaya after independence, which was to be achieved, if possible, by 31st August 1957. The Commission, under the chairmanship of Lord Reid and including three members from other Commonwealth countries, began work in Malaya in July 1956. A further conference held in London in May 1957 broadly accepted the recommendations in the Commission's report. Thereafter steps were taken to bring the new Constitution into effect on 31st August 1957, on which day the Federation of Malaya gained independence. The Federation was, with the agreement of the other Members, recognised as a Member of the Commonwealth. The Queen relinquished sovereignty of the two former Settlements of Penang and Malacca, each of which became a State on a parity with the other nine States.

The Malaysia Arrangements

The idea of political association between the Federation of Malaya, Singapore and the British territories in Borneo (the Colonies of North Borneo and Sarawak and the Protected State of Brunei) had been mooted for some years. It was not, however, until 1961 that it became a practicable proposition when in May the Prime Minister of the Federation of Malaya, in a public speech, spoke favourably about the possibility of such an association. His proposals were welcomed by the British Government. In November the Malayan Government reached an agreement with the Government of Singapore on the broad terms for their countries' merger. Soon afterwards, following talks in London, the British and Malayan Prime Ministers issued on 22nd November a joint statement to the effect that they had agreed that Malaysia was a desirable aim but that before coming to a decision it would be necessary to ascertain the views of the people of North Borneo and Sarawak. A joint Anglo-Malayan Commission was to be set up to ascertain these views and to make recommendations; and the views of the Sultan of Brunei were sought.

The Commission, under Lord Cobbold's chairmanship, spent two months travelling widely throughout the two territories and made careful enquiries amongst all sections of the population, interviewing not only large numbers of individuals but also many associations and organisations of all types. The Commission's report concluded that a substantial majority of the people in both territories were in favour of Malaysia in principle, given suitable conditions and safeguards, that it was in the interests of both territories to join, and that an early decision to proceed with Malaysia was essential.

On 1st August 1962 the British and Malayan Governments announced their acceptance of the Cobbold Report and their agreement in principle to the arrangements for Malaysia coming into force by 31st August 1963. The detailed constitutional arrangements, including safeguards for the special interests of North Borneo and Sarawak, were to be drawn up by Inter-Governmental Committee, with representatives of the Governments of Britain, Malaya, North Borneo and Sarawak, under the chairmanship of Lord Lansdowne (Minister of State at the Colonial Office). The Committee was charged with the task of working out the detailed terms under which North Borneo and Sarawak would join Malaysia. The British and Malayan Governments informed the Sultan of Brunei of their agreement and made it clear that their Governments would welcome the inclusion of the State of Brunei in Malaysia.

In September 1962 a referendum was held in Singapore resulting in a decisive majority in favour of accepting the broad terms agreed in 1961 for merger with the Federation of Malaya. In the same month the general concept of joining Malaysia was debated by the legislatures of Sarawak and North Borneo and both passed resolutions (unanimously in the case of North Borneo: without dissentient vote in Sarawak) welcoming the decision in principle to establish Malaysia by 31st August 1963 provided that their interests could be safeguarded. The Legislative Council of Brunei had previously also adopted a resolution supporting Brunei's entry in principle, but negotiations between the Brunei Government and the Malayan Government on this were broken off temporarily by a revolt which broke out in Brunei on 8th December. They were resumed later in 1963 but agreement did not prove possible.

The detailed proposals made by the Lansdowne Committee were approved in February by the Legislatures of North Borneo and Sarawak which had unofficial majorities. In London on 9th July 1963 Britain, the Federation of Malaya, North Borneo, Sarawak and Singapore signed the Malaysia Agreement. In accordance with this Agreement, Britain would relinquish sovereignty over the Colonies of North Borneo and Sarawak and the State of Singapore, and these would thereupon be federated with the existing States of the Federation of Malaya as the States of Sabah, Sarawak and Singapore, the federation thereafter being called Malaysia. The Agreement also provided that the federation of the new States would be in accordance with draft constitutional instruments annexed to the Agreement, of which the principal ones were new constitutions for Singapore, Sabah and Sarawak (Sabah being the new name for North Borneo) and a draft Bill to be enacted by the Malayan Parliament amending the constitution of the Federation of Malaya. In another annex, Annex J, were set out the terms of an agreement between the Federation of Malaya and Singapore on common market and financial arrangements, providing *inter alia* for the progressive establishment of a common market within Malaysia for local manufacturers for local consumption. A Malaysia Act, providing for the relinquishment of sovereignty, was passed by the British Parliament in July 1963; the Federation of Malaya enacted its legislation during August; and an Order in Council containing the constitutions of Sabah, Sarawak and Singapore was made on 29th August.

However, at a meeting held in Manila from 30th July to 6th August, the Presidents of Indonesia and of the Philippines and the Prime Minister of Malaya agreed to invite the Secretary-General of the United Nations Organisation to send working teams to North Borneo and Sarawak to ascertain, in the light of the United Nations Resolution on Self-Determination, whether the people of North Borneo and Sarawak wished to join Malaysia. To enable this enquiry to be carried out, the date of the coming into force of the Malaysia arrangements was postponed from 31st August until 16th September. The Secretary-General said that a sizeable majority of the peoples of each territory wished to join.

On 7th August 1965 the Prime Ministers of Malaysia and Singapore concluded an agreement of the separation of Singapore from Malaysia as an independent sovereign state from 9th August. On 9th August the Malaysian Parliament passed the Constitution and Malaysia (Singapore Amendment) Act, 1965, providing for Singapore to become independent on that date.

Constitution

The Constitution is to be found in the original constitution for Malaya as set out in the Schedule to the

Federation of Malaya Independence Order in Council 1957 as subsequently amended, in particular by the *Malayan* Malaysia Act, 1963. A consolidated version of the Constitution was published in 1985.

The Head of the State is the Yang Di Pertuan Agong who is elected for a period of five years from among their own number by the nine hereditary Malay Rulers of Peninsular Malaysia. These nine Rulers also elect, in similar manner, a Timbalan Yang Di Pertuan Agong (Deputy Supreme Head of State). The present Yang Di Pertuan Agong (the Sultan of Perak) was sworn in on 26th April 1989.

There is a Conference of Rulers consisting of the nine Malay Rulers already mentioned and the Yang Di Pertuan Negeri (Governors) of Malacca, Penang, Sarawak and Sabah. The Conference of Rulers has the power to elect the Yang Di Pertuan Agong and the Timbalan Yang Di Pertuan Agong, and to agree or disagree the extension of any religious acts, observances or ceremonies (except in Sabah and Sarawak), to consent or withhold consent to any law and to make, or give advice on, certain appointments; but only the nine Malay Rulers attend those meetings of the Conference which deal with matters directly relating to Their Royal Highness the Rulers themselves (including the election of the Yang Di Pertuan Agong and Timbalan Yang Di Pertuan Agong).

There is a federal form of government with a bi-cameral legislature, residual legislative power resting with the States. The Malaysian Parliament consists of the Yang Di Pertuan Agong and two Houses of Parliament, known as the Senate (Dewan Negara) and the House of Representatives (Dewan Rakyat). The Senate consists of 68 members of whom 2 are elected by the Legislative Assembly of each State and 42 are nominated by the Yang Di Pertuan Agong. The House of Representatives consists of 180 members, 133 being from Peninsular Malaysia, 20 from Sabah and 27 from Sarawak. The maximum life of the House of Representatives is five years. Bills have to be passed by both Houses and assented to by the Yang Di Pertuan Agong. A bill may originate in either House, with the exception of a money bill which may not be introduced in the Senate. A money bill, which has been passed by the House of Representatives and which the Senate fails to pass without amendment within a month, is presented to the Yang Di Pertuan Agong for his assent unless the House of Representatives otherwise directs. The Senate has the power to hold up for one year a bill which is not a money bill and which has been passed by the House of Representatives. The term of office of members of the Senate is six years and is not affected by the dissolution of Parliament.

The Yang di Pertuan Agong appoints as Prime Minister a member of the House of Representatives, who, in his judgement, is likely to command the confidence of the majority of the members of that House. On the advice of the Prime Minister he appoints other Ministers from among the members of either House of Parliament. Every member of the Cabinet has the right to take part in the proceedings of either House of Parliament, but may not vote in the House of which he is not a member. The Yang Di Pertuan Agong exercises his functions generally in accordance with the advice of Ministers. Cases in which he may act at his discretion include the appointment of a Prime Minister and the withholding of consent to a request for the dissolution of Parliament.

The Malaysian Constitution can only be altered by a two-thirds majority in each of the two Houses of Parliament.

On 15th May 1969 after disturbances in the capital a State of Emergency was declared and a National Operations Council set up. Its Director was given supreme power to administer the country. The Council contained civil, police and military representatives and was paralleled by State and District Operations Councils at the lower level. Parliament and State Assemblies were suspended at the same time, although an interim emergency Cabinet and the State Executive Councils remained in being. The State of Emergency was brought to an end and the National Operations Council dissolved in February 1971. Parliament was reconvened and executive power returned to the Cabinet.

Islam is the official religion of Malaysia, but the Constitution provides that other religions may be practised in peace and harmony. The Ruler is the Head of the Muslim religion in his State. In States not having a ruler the Yang Di Pertuan Agong holds that position.

The judicial power is vested in two High Courts of co-ordinate jurisdiction and status, namely:—

The High Court in Peninsular Malaysia, with its principal Registry in Kuala Lumpur.

The High Court in Sabah and Sarawak with its principal Registry in Kuching.

There is also a Federal Court, with its principal Registry in Kuala Lumpur, which is the Court of Appeal from the High Courts, and also has certain original and consultative jurisdiction. In particular the Federal Court has jurisdiction to determine whether any law made by Parliament or a State Legislature is invalid as being *ultra vires*, and to determine disputes between States or between the Central Government and a State.

Judges are appointed by the Yang Di Pertuan Agong on the advice of the Prime Minister after consulting the Conference of Rulers, but before tendering his advice, the Prime Minister is required to consult the Lord President of the Federal Court, and, in certain cases, the Chief Justices of the High Courts and the Chief Ministers of Sabah and Sarawak.

There is a Judicial and Legal Service Commission whose jurisdiction extends to all members of the judicial and legal service. There is also a Public Services Commission.

Historical List of Prime Ministers

Tunku Abdul Rahman Putra Al-Haj, KOM, CH, 31st August 1957 to 16th April 1959
Tun Abdul Razak bin Datuk Hussein, SMN, 16th April 1959 to 19th August 1959

Tunku Abdul Rahman Putra Al-Haj, KOM, CH, from 19th August 1959 to 22nd September 1970
Tun Haji Abdul Razak bin Datuk Hussein, SMN, from 22nd September 1970 to 14th January 1976
Tun Hussein bin Onn, DKI, SPMJ, SIMP, SPDK, from 14th January 1976 to 16th July 1981.
Datuk Seri Dr Mahathir bin Mohamad, SSDK, SPMJ, SPMS, SSAP, DP, DUPM, from 16th July 1981.

The last general elections were held on 21st October 1990 in Peninsular Malaysia to contest for 180 Parliamentary and 351 State Assembly seats. (2 Parliamentary and 8 State seats were won uncontested on nomination day). In Sabah and Sarawak elections were held from 20th–21st October 1990.

The state of the parties in the 180-seat Parliament as at December 1990 is:—

National Front	
United Malays National Organisation (UMNO)	71
Malaysian Chinese Association (MCA)	18
Malaysian Indian Congress (MIC)	6
Malaysian People's Movement (GERAKAN)	5
Total (Peninsular Malaysia)	100
Partai Pesaka Bumiputra Bersatu (PBB)	10
Sarawak United People's Party (SUPP)	4
Sarawak National Party (SNAP)	3
Parti Bangsa Dayak Sarawak (PBDS)	4
Total (Sarawak)	21
USNO	6
Total (Sabah)	6
Grand Total:	127
Independent	4
Opposition	
Parti Islam (PAS)	7
Democratic Action Party (DAP)	20
Semangat 46	8
PBS	14
Total	53

Government

HEAD OF STATE

The Yang Di Pertuan Agong, The Sultan of Perak His Majesty Sultan Azlan Muhibuddin Shah Ibni Al-Marhum Sultan Yussuf Izzuddin Ghafarullahu-lahu Shah DK, DMN, PMN, SSM, PSM, SPCM, SPTS, SPMP, SMP

CABINET

Prime Minister and Minister of Home Affairs: Datuk Seri Dr Mahathir bin Mohamad

Deputy Prime Minister and Minister of National and Rural Development: Encik Abdul Ghafar bin Baba

Minister in the PM's Department and Minister of Justice: Tuan Syed Hamid Syed Jaafar Albar

Minister in the PM's Department: Datuk Abang Abu Bakar Datu Mustapha

Minister of Works and Public Utilities: Datuk Leo Moggie anak Irok

Minister of Transport: Datuk Seri Dr Ling Liong Sik

Minister of Science, Technology and the Environment: Encik Law Hieng Sing

Minister of Primary Industries: Datuk Dr Lim Keng Yaik

Minister of Land and Co-operative Development: Tan Sri Haji Sakaran Dandai

Minister of National Unity and Social Development: Datuk Napsiah Omar

Minister of Foreign Affairs: Datuk Abdullah Ahmad Badawi

Minister of Housing and Local Government: Dr Ting Chew Peh

Minister of Education: Datuk Dr Sulaiman Daud

Minister of Finance: Datuk Seri Anwar Ibrahim

Minister of Youth and Sports: Senator Annuar Musa

Minister of Health: Datuk Lee Kim Sai

Minister of Agriculture: Datuk Seri Sanusi Junid

CABINET—*continued*

Minister of Information: Datuk Mohamed Rahmat

Minister of Human Resources: Datuk Lim Ah Lek

Minister of Culture, Arts and Tourism: Datuk Haji Sabaruddin Chik

Minister of Public Enterprises: Datuk Dr Mohd Yusuf Noor

Minister of Energy, Telecommunications and Post: Datuk Seri S Samy Vellu

Minister for International Trade and Industry: Datuk Seri Rafidah Aziz

Minister of Defence: Datuk Seri Najib Tun Razak

Minister of Domestic Trade and Consumer Affairs: Datuk Abu Hassan Omar

THE SENATE (DEWAN NEGARA)

President: YB Dato Tan Choon Tak

Clerk to the Senate: Haji Mohd Salleh Abu Bakar

HOUSE OF REPRESENTATIVES (DEWAN RAKYAT)

Speaker: Tan Sri Datuk Mohd Zahir bin Ismail

Clerk to the House: Datuk Wan Zahir bin Abdul Rahman

THE JUDICIARY

THE SUPREME COURT

Lord President of Supreme Courts: Tun Abdul Hamid Haji Omar

Chief Justice of Malaya: Tan Sri Hashim Yeop Sani

Chief Justice of Borneo: Datuk Mohamed Jemuri Sarjan

Judges:

Tan Sri Datuk Hashim bin Yeop Abdullah Sani

Tan Sri Haji Mohd Azmi bin Datuk Haji Kamaruddin

Tan Sri Datuk Eusoffe Abdoolcader

Datuk Syed Agil bin Syed Barakbah

Datuk Harun bin Hashim

Datuk Ajaib Singh

Datuk Edgar Joseph Jr

INDUSTRIAL COURT

President: Encik Tam Kam Weng

Judges

Mr Justice Encik Mustapha Hussain (Alor Star)

Mr Justice Abdul Razak bin Datuk Abu Samah (Kuala Lumpur)

Mr Justice Datuk Mohd Eusoff Chin (Kuala Lumpur)

Mr Justice Gunn Chit Tuan, JSM (Kuala Lumpur)

Mr Justice Datuk Wan Yahya bin Pawan Teh, DPMS, JSM (Melaka)

Mr Justice Datuk Annuar bin Datuk Zainal Abidin, JMN, ASDK, SMP (Ipoh)

Mr Justice Wan Mohamed bin Haji Wan Mustapha (Kuala Terengganu)

Mr Justice Chan Nyarn Hoi (Kuala Lumpur)

Mr Justice Peh Swee Chin (Seremban)

Mr Justice Mohamed Dzaiddin Bin Haji Abdullah (Penang)

Encik Dr Zakaria bin Mohamed Yatim (Kuala Lumpur)

Datuk Siti Norma Yaacob (Kuala Lumpur)

Encik Shak Daud bin Haji Mohd Ismail (Kuala Lumpur)

Datuk Mohamed Yusof bin Mohamed (Johore Bharu)

Encik Mahadev Shankar (Johore Bharu)

Datuk Idriss bin Yusoff (Kuantan)

Tuan Haji Abdul Malek bin Haji Ahmad (Ipoh)

Datuk Mohd Ariff bin Datuk Othman (Alor Star)

Datuk Tan Chiaw Thong (Kuching)

Encik John Chong Yik Liong (Kuching)

Datuk Chong Swee Fai (Sibu)

Datuk Charles Ho Nyen Cheung (Kota Kinabalu)

Datuk Haji Abu Mansor bin Ali (Kota Kinabalu)

Datuk Mohtar Abdullah (Kuala Lumpur)

Encik Faiza Thamby Chik (Kuala Lumpur)

Datuk Ahmad Fairuz Sheik Abdul Halim (Kuala Lumpur)

FEDERAL MINISTRIES AND GOVERNMENT DEPARTMENTS

PRIME MINISTER'S DEPARTMENT

Chief Secretary to the Government and Secretary to the Cabinet: Tan Sri Datuk Ahmad Sarji bin Abdul Hamid

MINISTRY OF INTERNATIONAL TRADE AND INDUSTRY

Secretary General: Datuk Haji Shaharuddin bin Harun

MINISTRY OF DEFENCE

Secretary General: Datuk Nasarudin bin Bahari

Chief of Armed Forces Staff: General Tan Sri Datuk Hashim bin Mohamed Ali

Chief of Army: Tan Sri Dato' Mohamad Yaacob Mohd Zain

Chief of Air Staff: Lt-General Datuk Mohd Yunus Tasi

Chief of Naval Staff: Vice-Admiral Datuk Mohd Shariff Ishak

MINISTRY OF PRIMARY INDUSTRIES

Secretary General: Tan Sri Dato' Wong Kum Choon

MINISTRY OF FOREIGN AFFAIRS

Secretary General: Datuk Ahmad Kamil Jaafar

MINISTRY OF FINANCE

Secretary General: Datuk Mohd Sheriff Mohd

MINISTRY OF HOME AFFAIRS

Secretary General: Datuk Zainol Mahmud

Inspector General of Police: Tan Sri Mohd Haniff bin Omar

MINISTRY OF HOUSING AND LOCAL GOVERNMENT
Secretary General: Dato Ahmad Hassan Osman

MINISTRY OF WORKS AND PUBLIC UTILITIES
Secretary General: Haji Mohamed Khalil Mohamed Noor

MINISTRY OF NATIONAL UNITY AND SOCIAL DEVELOPMENT
Secretary General: Dr Johari Mat

MINISTRY OF TRANSPORT
Secretary General: Datuk Dr Mohd Nor Ghani

MINISTRY OF PUBLIC ENTERPRISES
Secretary General: Datuk Amiruddin Kaharuddin

MINISTRY OF ENERGY, TELECOMMUNICATIONS AND POSTS
Secretary General: Dato Helmi Mohd Noor

MINISTRY OF LAND AND CO-OPERATIVE DEVELOPMENT
Secretary General: Datuk Haji Zainal Abidin Haji Nordin

MINISTRY OF INFORMATION
Secretary General: Dr Mazlan Ahmad

MINISTRY OF HUMAN RESOURCES
Secretary General: Encik Nik Mohd Amin Nik Abu Bakar

MINISTRY OF EDUCATION
Secretary General: Dato' Abdul Latif bin Sahan

MINISTRY OF AGRICULTURE
Secretary General: Datuk Wan Jaafar Abdullah

MINISTRY OF HEALTH
Secretary General: Datuk Mohd Ramli Mat Wajib

MINISTRY OF SCIENCE, TECHNOLOGY AND THE ENVIRONMENT
Secretary General: Datuk Mohamed Nordin Hassan

MINISTRY OF NATIONAL AND RURAL DEVELOPMENT
Secretary General: Dato' Ismail Mansur

MINISTRY OF JUSTICE
Secretary General: Puan Maimun Bte Din

MINISTRY OF YOUTH AND SPORTS
Secretary General: Encik Ahmad Zabri Ibrahim

MINISTRY OF CULTURE, ARTS AND TOURISM
Secretary General: Encik Khalid Ismail

MINISTRY OF DOMESTIC TRADE AND CONSUMER AFFAIRS
Secretary General: Dr Shamsuddin Mohd Kassim

PUBLIC SERVICES DEPARTMENT
Director General: Tan Sri Datuk Mahmud Taib

ECONOMIC PLANNING UNIT
Director General: Datuk Mohd Sheriff Mohd Kassim

PUBLIC SERVICES COMMISSION
Secretary: Dato' Shahbuddin Bin Imam Mohamad

NATIONAL UNITY BOARD
Director General: Encik Mohd Jawhar Hassan

LEGAL SERVICES COMMISSION
Chairman: Tan Sri Sheikh Abdullah bin Sheikh Abu Bakar

ELECTION COMMISSION
Chairman: Datuk Harun Din

THE STATES OF MALAYSIA

Each State has its own constitution, which must be compatible with the constitution of Malaysia. The constitutions of all the States are similar. In the East Malaysia States there are certain differences in nomenclature, and these are also mentioned in the articles on those States.

In each of the States there is a Head of State. In nine of the States of Peninsular Malaysia (those nine which were originally the Federated and Unfederated Malay States) the Head of State is a Malay Ruler. The Malay Rulers are either chosen or succeed to their position in accordance with the custom of the particular State. In other States the Head of State is appointed by the Yang Di Pertuan Agong acting in his discretion but after consultation with the Chief Minister of the State. In Sarawak and Sabah the Head of State is the Yang Di Pertuan Negeri. They hold office for four years.

The executive authority in a State is vested in the Head of the State but he is advised by an Executive Council (Cabinet in Sabah and Supreme Council in Sarawak) in the exercise of his functions. The Executive Council consists of a Chief Minister (Mentri Besar) who is a Member of the State Legislative Assembly and who is likely to command the confidence of the majority of the Members of that Assembly; not more than eight or less than four other Members (in the case of Sarawak the number of other Members is fixed at five), appointed by the Head of State from among the Members of the Assembly on the advice of the Chief Minister. Portfolios may be allotted to members of the Supreme Council in Sarawak or Cabinet in Sabah as 'ministers'. The Head of State is required to act in accordance with the advice of the Executive Council (or Cabinet or Supreme Council) except in certain matters. These exceptions include the appointment of the Chief Minister and the withholding of consent to a request for the dissolution of the Legislative Assembly. A Malay Ruler may also act otherwise than in accordance with the advice of the Executive Council in matters which fall within his purview as head of the Muslim Religion or relate to the customs of the Malays.

The Legislature of the State consists of the Head of State and one House, known as the Legislative Assembly (in Sarawak the Council Negeri). The Legislative Assembly (Dewan Negeri) consists of a Speaker, elected Members and Members nominated by the Head of State. The maximum life of the Assembly is five years.

The distribution of legislative powers between the Central Government and the States is set out in a Federal List, a State List and a Concurrent List. Any matter not enumerated in any of the Lists falls to the States. The main subjects in the Federal List are external affairs, defence, internal security, civil and criminal law, citizenship, finance, commerce and industry, shipping communications, education, health and labour. The most important general State subject is land. Some matters such as religion, language, immigration and citizenship, are subject to special constitutional safeguards in their application to Sabah and Sarawak. The Malaysian Parliament may make laws with respect to any matter in the State List for the purpose of promoting uniformity of the laws of two or more States, and may legislate on any State subject if so requested by the Legislative Assembly of the State.

Each of the States of Peninsular Malaysia receives from the Federal Government an annual capitation grant at the rate of M$15 per person for the first 50,000 persons, M$10 for the next 200,000 and M$4 per person for the remainder. Each State also receives a State road grant. Sources of revenue assigned to the States include revenue from land, mines and forests, from certain licences, court fees and receipts from land sales of State property. In the case of Sabah and Sarawak sufficient revenues are secured to them to meet the cost of State services at the level existing immediately before joining Malaysia and to provide for their reasonable expansion. Consequently certain revenues additional to those assigned to the States of Peninsular Malaysia are assigned to the two East Malaysia States, such as customs duties on petroleum products, timber and minerals, and revenue from State sales taxes and port dues. In the case of Sabah 30 per cent of all other customs revenue is assigned for as long as responsibility is retained by the State for medical and health expenditure. In addition to these assignments, a number of different grants from federal funds are made to Sabah and Sarawak. These grants are to be subject to review.

The Malaysian Parliament may, by a simple majority, admit other States to the Federation.

JOHORE

The most southerly State of Peninsular Malaysia, Johore is separated from Singapore by the Straits of Johore which are crossed by a causeway carrying a road and railway. Its area is about 19,400 sq km. Total population 1990 (estimate): 2,106,500. The capital is Johore Bahru.

The composition of the State Legislative Assembly, is now as follows:—

National Front	32
DAP	3
Semangat 46	1

Ruler: His Royal Highness Sultan Mahmood Iskandar Al-Haj ibni Al-Marhum Sultan Ismail DK, SPMJ, SPDK, DK (Brunei), SSIJ, PIS, BSI

Mentri Besar (Chief Minister): Tan Sri Haji Muhyiddin Mohd Yassin, PSM

KEDAH

This State lies on the north-west coast of Peninsular Malaysia and includes the Langkawi group of islands. It has a common frontier with Thailand and was subject to Thai suzerainty from 1511–1909 when an Anglo-Siamese Treaty transferred suzerainty from Thailand to Britain. The total area is 9,479 sq km. Its population as at 1990 was 1,412,800. The capital is Alor Star.

The composition of the State Legislative Assembly is now as follows:—

National Front	26
Parti Islam	1
DAP	1

Ruler: His Royal Highness Tuanku Haji Abdul Halim Muadzam Shah ibni Al-Marhum Sultan Badlishah, DK, DKH, DKM, DMN, DUK, DK (Kelantan), DK (Pahang), DK (Perlis), DK (Selangor), DK (N. Sembilan), DK (Sarawak)
Mentri Besar (Chief Minister): Tan Sri Datuk Paduka Haji Osman Aroff, SSDK, SPNK

KELANTAN

This State lies in the north-east of Peninsular Malaysia bordered on the north by Thailand. Its total area is about 14,763 sq km. It population as at 1990 was 1,220,100. The capital is Kota Bahru.

The composition of the State Legislative Assembly is now as follows:—

Parti Islam	24
Semangat 46	14
Berjasa	1

Ruler: His Royal Highness Al-Sultan Ismail Petra Ibni Al-Marhum Sultan Yahya Petra, DK, DMN, DK (N. Sembilan), SPMK, SSMK, SPSK
Mentri Besar (Chief Minister): Haji Nik Aziz Nik Mat

MALACCA

This States lies on the west coast of Peninsular Malaysia bounded to the north by Negeri Sembilan and to the east by Johore. It was one of the two former British Straits Settlements which were incorporated in the former Federation of Malaya. Its area is 1,658 sq km. Its population as at 1990 was 583,500. The capital is Malacca.

The composition of the State Legislative Assembly is now as follows:—

National Front	17
Democratic Action Party ..	3

Yang Di Pertuan Negeri: His Excellency Tun Syed Ahmad bin Syed Mahmud Shahabuddin
Chief Minister: Tan Sri Datuk Rahim Tamby Chik, AMN, PJK, PSM

NEGERI SEMBILAN

This State also lies on the west coast of Peninsular Malaysia and is bordered to the north by Selangor and to the south by Malacca and Johore. Its total area is about 6,500 sq km and its population as at 1990 was 723,800. The capital and seat of government is Seremban but the principal Royal Palace is at Sri Menanti about 40 km to the east. In Negeri Sembilan (which is in itself a confederation of six states) the Ruler is elected from the male issue of the Royal Family.

The composition of the State Legislative Assembly is now as follows:—

National Front	24
Democratic Action Party ..	4

Ruler: His Royal Highness the Yang Dipertuan Besar, Tuanku Ja'afar Al-haj ibni Al-Marhum Tuanku Abdul Rahman Al-Haj, DMN, DK (Brunei), DK (Kelantan), DK (Selangor), DK (Kedah)
Mentri Besar (Chief Minister): Datuk Mohd Isa Haji Abdul Samad, DSNS

PAHANG

This is the largest State in Peninsular Malaysia. It has a coastline of 209 km on the east coast. Its area is about 35,700 sq km. Its population as at 1990 was 1,054,800. The seat of Government is Kuantan on the east coast but the Sultan's residence is at Pekan, about 32 km to the south.

The composition of the State Legislative Assembly is now as follows:—

National Front	31
Democratic Action Party ..	1
PAS	1

Ruler: His Royal Highness Sultan Haji Ahmad Shah Ibni Al-Marhum Sultan Abu Bakar, DKM, DKP, DK, SSAP, SIM, DMN, DK (Perak), DK (Johore), DK (Kelantan), DK (Terengganu), DK (Perlis), DK (Kedah), DK (Brunei), SPCM, SPMS
Mentri Besar (Chief Minister): Tan Sri Haji Mohd Khalil Yaakub, PSM

PENANG

This consists of the Island of Pennang and Province Wellesley on the mainland of Peninsular Malaysia. It was one of the British Straits Settlements which were incorporated in the former Federation of Malaya. Its area is 1,005 sq km. Its population as at 1990 was 1,142,200.

The composition of the State Legislative Assembly, following the 1990 General Election and the July 1991 By-Election is now as follows:—

National Front	20
Democratic Action Party ..	13

Yang Di Pertuan Negeri: His Excellency Tun Haji Hamdan Sheikh Tahir, SMN, PSM
Chief Minister: Dr Kah Tsu Koon

PERAK

This State, lying on the west coast to the north of Selangor and to the south of Kedah and the Thai border, has some of the richest tin deposits in Peninsular Malaysia, particularly in the Kinta district. Its total area is 20,720 sq km. Its population as at 1990 was 2,222,200. The capital of the State is Ipoh but the seat of the Ruler is Kuala Kangsar about 48 km to the north-west.

The composition of the State Legislative Assembly is now as follows:—

National Front	33
Democratic Action Party ..	13

Ruler: His Royal Highness Sultan Azlan Muhibbudin Shah Ibni Al-Marhum Sultan Yusof Izuddin Ghafarullahu-Lahu
Regent: His Royal Highness Raja Nazrin Shah Ibni Sultan Azlan Muhibbudin Shah
Mentri Besar (Chief Minister): Tan Sri Ramli Ngah Talib

PERLIS

This is the smallest State in Peninsular Malaysia. It lies in the north-west tip of the country bounded by the sea, Thailand and Kedah. Its total area is 818 sq km. Its population as at 1990 was 187,700. The capital is Kangar.

The composition of the State Legislative Assembly is now as follows:—

National Front	14

Ruler: His Royal Highness Raja Tuanku Syed Putra ibni Al-Marhum Syed Hassan Jamalullail, DK, DKM, DMN, SMN, SPMP, DK (Brunei), SPDK
Mentri Besar (Chief Minister): Dr Abdul Hamid Pawanteh, ANP, JP

SABAH

Formerly known as North Borneo, Sabah became a State of Malaysia on 16th September 1963. The name Sabah is an old one, but apparently was originally the name for only the northern part of the area, being commonly used for the whole only after the beginning of the British occupation. The State, which occupies the north eastern corner of Borneo and also the island of Labuan, is largely covered by tropical jungle and contains the highest mountain in the region, Mount Kinabalu (4,034 m). The most extensive plain is that on the east coast irrigated by the Kinabatangan River. In the interior are the Keningau and Tambunan plains which are traversed by the Pelangan River. The Keningau plain consists of wide stretches of grassland while Tambunan maintains a large rice-producing population.

Sabah is divided into four Residencies: Sandakan, Tawau, Interior and West Coast. The capital is Kota Kinabalu (formerly known as Jesselton). Its population as at 1990 was 1,470,000.

Constitutional development

At first the Colony of North Borneo was administered by the Governor with the aid of an Advisory Council, but Executive and Legislative Councils were established in October 1950.

During 1960 the Royal Instructions and Orders in Council were amended to provide for an unofficial majority in the Legislative Council and in 1961 they were further amended to provide an increased unofficial majority.

Elections to District Councils and Town Boards under a franchise of universal adult suffrage subject to a residence qualification took place between December 1962 and May 1963. These Councils formed the basis of an electoral college system which in July 1963 elected the eighteen unofficial Members of the Legislative Council.

With the establishment of Malaysia, a Head of State, the Yang Dipertuan Negeri, was appointed. There is a State Cabinet which is headed by a Chief Minister and has up to eight members. The State Cabinet is collectively responsible to the Legislative Assembly which comprises 48 elected members and up to six members nominated by the Yang Di Pertuan Negeri.

The composition of the State Legislative Assembly following the July 1990 State elections and December 1990 and May 1991 by-elections is now as follows:—

PBS	36
USNO	11

Head of State: Yang Di Pertuan Negeri: His Excellency Tun Mohd Said bin Keruak, PMN, SPDK
Chief Minister: Datuk Joseph Pairin Kitingan, PGDK, PNBS, JES

SARAWAK

Sarawak became a State of Malaysia on 16th September 1963. The State consists of a coastal strip 724 km long and varies from 64 to 193 km wide. The State is divided into three main zones, firstly an alluvial and coastal plain in which isolated mountains and mountain groups rise to 600 m or more; then rolling country of yellow, sandy clay intersected by ranges of mountains; and finally a mountainous area in the interior. The Rejang and Sarawak Rivers are navigable for ocean-going ships for 274 and 35 km respectively. For administrative purposes, the State is divided into nine Divisions, known as Kuching Division, Sri Aman Division, Sibu Division, Miri Division, Limbang Division, Sarikei Division, Kapit Division, Samarahan Division and Bintulu Division. The capital is Kuching. Its population as at 1990 was 1,669,000.

Constitutional development

Sarawak became a Crown Colony in 1946 at the end of a century of rule by the Brooke ('White Rajah') family.

A new constitution was granted in 1956 and came into force on 1st April 1957. This provided for a reformed legislature of forty-five Members of whom twenty-four were to be elected, fourteen to be *ex officio* Members, four were to be nominated by the Governor, and three were to be Standing Members for life. The Supreme Council was to consist of three *ex officio* Members, two Nominated Members and five Elected Members.

Orders in Council made in 1962 and 1963 provided for the Supreme Council to consist of a Chief Minister, three *ex officio* Members and five Members appointed on the advice of the Chief Minister from among the Members of the Council Negeri, and for the Council Negeri to consist of a Speaker, three *ex officio* Members, thirty-six elected Members and not more than three nominated Members and one standing Member. The latter seat was abolished in September 1963, on the establishment of Malaysia.

In May and June 1963 direct elections were held to the District and Municipal Councils, which in turn elected representatives to the five Divisional Councils. The latter in July 1963 acted as electoral colleges for the Council Negeri. Direct elections to the Council Negeri which were suspended in May 1969, were held in June 1970.

The results of the election of September 1991 are as follows:

National Front	49
PBDS	7

Head of State: Yang Di Pertuan Negeri: His Excellency Tun Datuk Patinggi Haji Ahmad Zaidi Adruce bin Mohamed Noor
Chief Minister: YAB Datuk Patinggi Tan Sri Haji Abdul Taib Mahmud, DA, SPMJ, PGDK, PSM

SELANGOR

This west coast State of Peninsular Malaysia is bounded on the north by Perak, on the east by Pahang and on the south by Negeri Sembilan. Its area is 8,184 sq km. Its population as at 1990 was 1,978,000. The State capital is Shah Alam. The State contains Malaysia's port of Port Klang.

The composition of the State Legislative Assembly is now as follows:—

National Front	35
Democratic Action Party ..	6
Semangat 46	1

Ruler: His Royal Highness Sultan Salahuddin Abdul Aziz Shah ibni Al-Marhum Sultan Hisammuddin Alam Shah Al-Haj, DMN, DK, SPMS, DK (Brunei), SPDK, DP
Mentri Besar (Chief Minister): Tan Sri Mohamad bin Mohamad Taib, PSM, SPMS

TERENGGANU
This State lies on the east coast of Peninsular Malaysia bordered to the north by Kelantan and to the south by Pahang. Its area is about 12,950 sq km. Its population as at 1990 was 752,000. The capital is Kuala Terengganu.

The composition of the State Legislative Assembly is now as follows:—

National Front	22
Parti Islam	8
Semangat 46	2

Ruler: His Royal Highness Sultan Mahmud ibni Al-Marhum Tuanku Al Sultan Ismail Naziruddin Shah, DK, DMN, SPMT, SPCM, DKT
Mentri Besar (Chief Minister): Tan Sri Datuk Seri Amar di-Raja Haji Wan Mokhtar bin Ahmad, AMN, JP, PJK, SPMT, PSD, KMN, PSM

MALAYSIAN TITLES, ORDERS, DECORATIONS AND MEDALS
A detailed list of Malaysian titles, orders, decorations and medals may be found in the *Commonwealth Relations Office Year Book*, 1966.

Republic of Maldives

Capital: Malé

The Maldive Archipelago is situated in the Indian Ocean about 645 km (400 miles) south west of Sri Lanka. It consists of a chain of about 20 coral atolls comprising over 1,200 islands, 202 of which are inhabited. The climate is hot and humid and the average temperature is 27°C (80°F) with little daily or seasonal variation. The islands are small; the capital Malé (population 46,334) is only one mile long and half a mile across.

The population of 200,000 is of mixed descent but largely of Dravidian stock speaking an Indo Aryan language (Divehi) akin to mediaeval Sinhala. Islam is the state religion and the Maldivians are Sunni Muslims.

The Maldives has always been a maritime nation and fishing remains a major industry, joined now by shipping and tourism. 'Maldive fish' a dried preparation made from bonito, was the main export until recently, when the country switched to exporting fresh fish. Coconut palms, millet and fruit grow in abundance on the islands and are also exported. Other occupations include coir and lace making. Tourism is the new growth industry, however, and with the opening of the Malé International Airport in 1981, the Maldives can now receive wide-bodied aircraft bringing passengers direct from Europe. This has boosted the tourism industry on the islands.

Until 31st December 1952 the islands were a Sultanate under the protection of Her Majesty. The Sultanate was elective after 1932. As from January 1953 a Republic was inaugurated, but the following year it was decided to revert to Sultanate Government under a new consitution. Following a referendum in 1968, a Republic was again declared, which provides for election of an executive President every five years. There is a Parliament (the Majlis) with representatives elected from all the atolls. Presidential Elections were held in September 1988. President Abdul Gayoom was re-elected for a third term of office. Elections to the Majlis were held in November 1989.

Relations with Britain

The Islands long enjoyed the protection of the British Crown and this was formally recorded in an exchange of letters between the Sultan and the Governor of Ceylon (now Sri Lanka) in December 1887. On the independence of Ceylon in 1948, a new agreement dated 24th April 1948 was signed between the Sultan and the British Government. This provided that the Islands would remain under the protection of the Crown; that their external affairs would be conducted by, or in accordance with the advice of, the British Government; that the British Government would refrain from any interference in the internal affairs of the Islands; and that the Sultan afford such facilities to HM Forces as the British Government might, after consultation, consider necessary for the defence of the Islands or of the Commonwealth. Relations between the Maldive Islands and Britain were to be conducted through the British High Commissioner in Ceylon. These provisions were reaffirmed in a new agreement of 1st January 1953.

A revised agreement was signed on the 14th February 1960 making certain changes in the agreement of 1953, allowing the Maldivian Government to conduct relations with other Governments in certain economic and cultural fields, and providing for the establishment of a British airfield on Gan Island in Addu Atoll.

In 1964 further negotiations took place between the British and Maldivian Governments resulting in a new Agreement dated 26th July 1965 (Cmnd 2749). Under this Agreement and on that date the Maldive Islands became a fully independent state and Britain ceased to be responsible for defence and for the conduct of foreign affairs. Britain continued to use the facilities at Gan which had been accorded under the 1960 Agreement, until withdrawal in 1976 and the termination of the 1965 Anglo-Maldivian Agreement. Britain sponsored the Republic of Maldives for United Nations admission in 1965.

The Republic of Maldives became a 'special' member of the Commonwealth on 9th July 1982 and a full member on 20th June 1985. The National Day of the Maldives is 26th July.

President Gayoom reshuffled his Cabinet on 30th May 1990.

HEAD OF STATE

The President, Commander-in-Chief of the Armed Forces, Minister of Defence and National Security and Minister of Finance: HE Maumoon Abdul Gayoom

CABINET

Minister of Justice: Hon Mohamed Rasheed Ibrahim

Minister of Home Affairs and Sports: Hon Umar Zahir

Minister of Education: Hon Abdulla Hameed
Minister of Health and Welfare: Hon Abdul Sattar Moosa Didi
Minister of Fisheries and Agriculture: Hon Abbas Ibrahim
Minister of Transport and Shipping: Hon Ahmed Zahir
Minister of Tourism: Hon Abdulla Jameel
Minister of Public Works and Labour: Hon Abdulla Kamaludeen
Minister of Foreign Affairs: Hon Fathulla Jameel
Minister of Planning and Environment: Hon Ismail Shafeeu
Minister at the President's Office: Hon Mohamed Zahir Hussein
Minister of Atolls Administration: Hon Ilyas Ibrahim
Minister of Trade and Industries: (Vacant)
Minister at the President's Office: Hon Mohamed Zahir Hussain
Attorney-General: Hon Mohamed Hussain
Chief Justice: Hon Moosa Fathy
Speaker of the Citizens' Majlis: Hon Ahmed Zaki
Minister of State for Finance: Hon Ismail Fathy
Minister of State for Presidential Affairs: Hon Abdul Rasheed Hussain

Republic of Malta

Capital: Valletta

Location, Topography and Climate
Malta lies in the Mediterranean, latitude 35° 8′ N., longitude 14° 5′ E., 92 km (50 miles) south of Sicily and approximately 290 km (181 miles) east of Tunisia. The Maltese archipelago consists of the islands of Malta 245 sq km (95 sq miles), Gozo 67 sq km (26 sq miles) and Comino 3 sq km (1 sq mile) together with four uninhabited islets, Cominotto, St Paul's Islands and Filfla. The name Malta is derived from the Roman name for the Island, Melita.

The highest point in Malta is just over 244 metres (800 feet) above sea level. The islands enjoy an average winter temperature of 13°C (55°F) while in summer the average is 27°C (81°F). The mean annual rainfall is 508 mm (20 ins), falling mainly between October and March.

The islands are rocky with some magnificent limestone cliffs along the western coasts. The soil is limey and shallow except in low-lying areas and good agricultural land is scarce. There are 13,227 hectares (132 sq km) of arable land, the main crops being potatoes, onions, tomatoes, grapes, wheat, barley, oranges and flowers.

Population
The last population census took place in 1985. The estimated population of the Maltese Islands in 1990 was 355,910. Substantial emigration took place in the post-war years, mostly to Australia, but also to Canada and Britain. The main centres of population lie around Valletta and the two harbours on either side of the capital—Grand Harbour and Marsamxett. Over 100,000 people live in this inner harbour area which covers the districts of Floriana, Sliema, Gzira, Hamrun and Paola. Another 98,000 live in the outer harbour region embracing the districts of Birkirkara, Qormi and Zabbar. The only towns of any size outside these conurbations are Rabat (pop. 13,028), Mosta (pop. 12,408) and Zejtun (pop. 11,691). The capital of Gozo is Victoria (pop. 6,025).

The population is predominantly European and Roman Catholic. The national language is Maltese but both English and Maltese are official languages. Italian is also widely spoken. Parliamentary business is conducted in Maltese which is also the language of the courts.

Health
Malta enjoys a Mediterranean climate and poses few health problems. People with chest allergies may, however, suffer from dust in the dry summer months. The *scirocco,* a sand-bearing wind from North Africa, which blows occasionally in summer, can also cause difficulties for asthmatics. Mosquitoes are not malarial.

The government provides a comprehensive range of free health services. These are largely carried out by Polyclinics situated in different towns and villages and include ante-natal services, free immunisation, a school medical service, a food and drink industry inspectorate, a general practitioner service, community nursing and midwifery.

There is a large general hospital in Malta and a smaller one in Gozo. There are also psychiatric and geriatric hospitals.

Port health is maintained by Port Medical Officers and Port Health Inspectors.

Environmental services include pollution control and monitoring, public cleansing, waste disposal and pest control.

The birth and death rates in 1988 were 15.8 and 8.4 per thousand respectively.

Communications
The Grand Harbour is the main port. Traffic handled was 2,169,903 tonnes in 1989. Anchorage facing the south east is provided at Marsaxlokk Bay and anchorage facing the north east is provided at St Paul's Bay. A yachting centre is established at Marsamxett Harbour. The airport at Luqa (runway 4,000 metres) is 8 kilometres from Valletta. A new terminal will open in 1992. The principal airlines are Air Malta, Alitalia, Libyan Arab Airlines, Tunisavia, Balkan Airlines, Yugoslavia Airlines, Lufthansa and Aeroflot. Scheduled services are operated between Malta and U.K., Germany, France, Italy, Libya, Tunisia, Netherlands, Switzerland, Belgium, Austria, Denmark, Egypt, Bulgaria, Yugoslavia, Greece and the USSR. Sea Malta Company Ltd is the national shipping line. There are regular car ferry services from Sicily and the Italian mainland. There are no railways. There are 1,398 km of surfaced road. The Telemalta Corporation is responsible for overall management of the telephone, telex and cable services as well as the broadcasting services.

There are three daily and eight weekly papers in Malta, belonging to four main groups: Progress

Press, whose papers are all in the English language, Union Press, Independence Press and the Media Centre. These latter are mainly in Maltese and owned by the General Workers' Union, the Nationalist Party and the Church respectively.

The radio and TV stations, known collectively as Xandir Malta, are state-owned. The Voice of the Mediterranean is run jointly by the Maltese and Libyan Governments, broadcasting in English and Arabic.

A Broadcasting Bill was passed in 1991 ending the state monopoly. Cable TV will be introduced in 1992.

Economy

The rundown in dockyard activity and the final closure of the British base in 1979 accelerated the requirement to diversify the economy in a country possessing no minerals and limited raw materials. Total direct production now accounts for over 42.9 per cent of GDP and employs 52.4 per cent of the workforce. Malta produces a wide range of commodities including food, textiles, building materials and furniture. Clothing and footwear constitute the leading exports. The European Community is Malta's main trading partner providing 64 per cent of her imports and absorbing 68 per cent of her exports. West Germany takes 28 per cent of total exports followed by Italy (15 per cent) and Britain (13 per cent).

Tourism also assumes primary importance and accounts for 22 per cent of GDP. Malta received over 871,776 visitors in 1990; over half of these were from Britain. Total capacity for tourist accommodation rose to over 41,639 beds in 1990. Agriculture accounts for only 4 per cent of GDP.

The Malta Development Corporation was set up in 1967 to assist and finance development projects. The deepwater container transhipment harbour constructed at Marsaxlokk has been converted into a Freeport area. A grain silo with a storage capacity of 86,000 tons has been built in Valletta Grand Harbour and a shipbuilding industry established at Marsa. It is also planned to develop the whole of Marsamxett Harbour as a yachting centre where there is already stern to quay berthing facilities for 800 yachts.

Further improvements to the infrastructure are being made by the Government including the construction of a new power station, desalination plants, a new airport terminal, a new by-pass and tunnel, and the complete modernisation of the Maltese telecommunications network. These major infrastructural projects are showing considerable progress.

The present government have announced the setting up of a National Council for Economic Development to formulate a new development plan consistent with a strategy of private sector-oriented growth.

The unit of currency is the Maltese lira. The exchange rate is pegged to a basket of currencies reflecting both trade and invisible transactions.

Education

Education in Malta is compulsory from the ages of 6 to 16 and free in Government schools. The school system starts at the kindergarten/nursery level, i.e. at age 3 (earlier in private schools) and by age 5, when the primary school course begins, virtually all children are enrolled. The primary school course lasts 6 years. This may be extended by 1 or 2 years of post-primary (preparatory secondary) education in the case of lower ability children.

Secondary education is available for all. This may be obtained in selective fee-paying private schools, most of which are operated by the Catholic Church, selective Government Junior Lyceums, or area government secondary comprehensive schools. The course lasts 5 years at the end of which students may sit for the General Certificate of Education (London or Oxford) at 'Ordinary' level, or the Malta Matriculation. There exist government trade schools for students who wish to transfer to vocational trade courses from the end of Form II Secondary. Trade school courses are of 4 years duration. There are also craft centres for boys whose attainment is too low for them to benefit from an academic or trade school curriculum.

Post-secondary education facilities are of three kinds: a) Advanced level studies in Government New Lyceums under a system which includes work periods, or in private school VIth Forms, b) full time craft and technician courses in technical institutes and certain specialised technical schools and c) an Extended Skill Training Scheme for students who have successfully finished their trade school courses and certain technical institute courses. There is also a government higher secondary school which provides GCE 'O' and/or 'A' level courses for school leavers (Fifth Formers).

The University of Malta provides courses leading to degrees in Law, Medicine and Surgery, Engineering and Architecture, Dental Surgery, Education and Management Studies, Arts and Science. An Academy for Diplomatic Studies was opened in 1991 and the University also hosts the International Maritime Organisation's Maritime Law Institute (IMLI).

Other educational facilities available in Malta are evening courses for adults, summer schools for the teaching of English to foreign students, a School of Art, a School of Music, the Manoel Theatre Academy of Dramatic Art, The Institute for Tourism Studies, the Nursing School, and a number of part-time commercial schools. There are also private ballet schools, keep fit schools, music schools and adult schools in economic and political studies.

History

There are notable stone-age survivals in Malta, but its history begins with settlement by the Phoenicians. After Phoenicia was conquered by the Persians, Carthage became the capital of the Punic Empire, and from Carthage Malta was colonised and received the earliest known form of its language. Malta remained under Carthaginian control until Hamilcar's surrender to the Roman Consul, Titus Sempronius, in 216 B.C.

The best known event during Malta's occupation by the Romans was St Paul's shipwreck in 60 A.D. in the bay which now bears his name, and the conversion of the Maltese to Christianity. After the collapse of the Western Roman Empire, Malta remained within the jurisdiction of the Byzantine Emperors in Constantinople until it was taken by the Arabs in 870. The Arabic occupation, which lasted for two centuries, served to introduce into the Maltese language a vocabulary of contemporary Arabic words which did not, however, destroy the earlier related Punic words. This produced a blend which still forms the core of modern Maltese and into this framework fresh words, mostly English or Italian, have been fitted.

After the expulsion of the Arabs by Roger the Norman, Malta remained in the hands of successive Sicilian rulers until it passed to the Holy Roman Emperor Charles V, who, in 1530, gave it as a sovereign fief to the Order of the Hospital of St John of Jerusalem, which had been homeless since its eviction by the Turks from Rhodes in 1523. The gift was conditional on the Knights of the Order assuming the defence of Tripoli as a Christian outpost in North Africa. Tripoli was lost to the Turks in 1551, but when the Turks tried to capture Malta itself they were eventually repelled in 1565, after the Great Siege. Soon after this victory, the Knights set about building Valletta within an impressive system of fortifications. At first Malta flourished as a bastion of Christendom and developed as a centre of trade and communications; but its importance declined after the Ottoman sea-power was broken at the battle of Lepanto in 1571. Thenceforth the Knights turned their activities to politics, and by the eighteenth century the Order had declined and become an anachronism, dependent on the support of other countries rather than on its own resources.

Napoleon Bonaparte regarded Malta as a vital link in a route to the East and in his designs on Egypt and India. The French met with no resistance when they landed at Valletta in June 1798 and Bonaparte departed for Egypt leaving a force of 6,000 troops on the island. The Maltese, however, soon rose against the French, offended by their pillaging of churches and encouraged by the defeat of Bonaparte at the Nile. In response to an appeal from the Maltese people for help Admiral Nelson set up a blockade and on 9th September 1798 sent Captain Ball, RN, to assume responsibility for the administration of the island. The French were driven into the fortified towns where they remained until they capitulated in 1800 whereupon they were evicted from the island. In May 1801 the administration of Malta was divided between the British Military Commander and a British Civil Commission. In 1802 the Treaty of Amiens provided for the Maltese administration to revert to the Knights of St John but the Maltese people petitioned Britain to place the island under British sovereignty and protection. The first British Governor was appointed in July 1813 and Malta formally became British by the Treaty of Paris in 1814.

Recognising Malta's strategic importance, Britain introduced a garrison which not only protected the islands but provided a source of income for their inhabitants. British trade with the Near East and the Adriatic began to pass through Malta, which was made a free port; and by 1812 there were some 60 British and 20 Maltese middlemen in business there. The port services required by ships engaged in this trade provided additional employment and with increasing prosperity agriculture was also stimulated.

Thenceforth Malta depended on shipping, military and civil. In 1827 the British Mediterranean Fleet was based on Malta and in 1832 the Admiralty started a packet service to the Island. A few years later the ships of the P and O Shipping Company and other Companies began to use Malta as a port of call on their runs to Egypt and the Levant. The volume of shipping greatly increased with the opening of the Suez Canal in 1869: by 1882 some 80 per cent of the recorded tonnage in Malta had cargoes for other than Mediterranean ports.

The boom in shipping caused a movement to the towns, and in the decade 1871–80 urban employment increased by 6,000, mainly in the docks. However, as larger merchant ships were introduced, the boom declined, for their longer range made it less necessary for them to call at Malta. But British Government expenditure bridged the gap, and by 1905 over 9,000 men were employed in the Naval Establishments in Malta. The Naval Dockyard and the income from the Defence services became the mainstay of Malta's economy.

Malta was an important base in the First World War; and in the Second World War the heroic garrison and the indomitable people of Malta were exposed to frequent and heavy air attacks and to an intense blockade. In recognition of their courageous resistance and of the exceptional hardships and privations which they endured, Malta was awarded the George Cross in 1942. A representation of this decoration appears in the National Flag of independent Malta.

In 1960 as a consequence of the decline in the use of Malta for British naval repair work, the Naval Dockyard was converted to commercial use and finally nationalised in 1968. At the time of Malta's independence on 21st September 1964 two Agreements were signed with Britain providing for British forces to remain in Malta for ten years and for financial aid to assist Malta to diversify her economy.

At the General Election in 1966 the Nationalist Party led by Dr G Borg Olivier was returned to power but the following election in 1971 was won by the Labour party led by Mr Dom Mintoff. Mr Mintoff requested a renegotiation of the terms of the Defence Agreement and a new one was concluded in March 1972. This agreement expired on 31st March 1979 when all British forces left the island. The Labour government remained in office for 16 years until its defeat by the Nationalist Party led by Dr E Fenech Adami in the 1987 elections. A general election is expected to be held before October 1992. Malta formally applied to join the EC on 16th July 1990.

Constitutional Development

During the period that Malta was a Crown Colony, the usual Advisory Councils to the Governor had contained a number of Maltese Members. In 1921 a constitution was introduced which established a limited form of self-government. A dyarchical system of government was set up in which the Maltese Government, composed of a bi-cameral legislature and Ministry, was responsible for local affairs while the Maltese Imperial Government, composed of the Governor advised by a nominated Council, had full control of reserved matters including, in particular, defence, foreign affairs and language questions. In the Maltese Government, ten of the seventeen Senators were nominated or elected to represent special classes, and the others were returned by the general electorate. Members of the Legislative Assembly were elected by proportional representation, each voter having a single, transferable vote. However, owing to political crises, the constitution was suspended in 1930 and 1933 and finally revoked in 1936. Crown Colony rule was resumed in 1939 and self-government restored in 1947.

The constitution of 1947 provided for a uni-cameral legislature of 40 Members, elected under a system of proportional representation, with a Prime Minister and a Cabinet. The Assembly was empowered to legislate for the peace, order and good government of Malta, but certain matters, including defence, civil aviation, currency, immigration and nationality, were reserved to the Maltese Imperial Government under the Governor.

In 1953 the Nationalist Coalition Government then in power, put forward proposals for Dominion status for Malta. Because of Malta's strategic importance and inability to be financially self-supporting, these proposals were unacceptable to the British Government, which suggested that Malta's status might be improved if responsibility for the islands were transferred to the Home Office. In 1955 a Labour Administration was formed by Mr Dom Mintoff and arrangements were made for a Round Table Conference in December of that year. Representatives of all the Maltese political parties and the Archbishop of Malta attended the Conference, and all accepted that the British Government needed to retain ultimate responsibility for Defence and foreign affairs. All wished to enhance the status of the Maltese Parliament and Government, and agreed that the position of the Roman Catholic Church should not be diminished; but the Maltese Government and Opposition were unable to agree on what should be Malta's ultimate constitutional status. The Labour Party wanted representation at Westminster, whereas the Nationalists wanted independence within the Commonwealth.

In a referendum held in February 1956, 76 per cent of the votes cast (44 per cent of the electorate) favoured integration with Britain and Maltese representation at Westminster. This was accepted in principle by the British Government but the consequent negotiation as to details broke down in March 1958, both the governing Malta Labour Party and the Opposition demanding independence. In the ensuing crisis the British Government felt compelled to institute direct rule once again. In 1959 an interim constitution was introduced under which executive authority was vested in the Governor who was advised by a nominated Executive Council which included Maltese non-official members, an arrangement similar to that which had been in force between 1936 and 1939.

As a result of the report of the Malta Constitutional Commission, 1960, which was appointed under the Chairmanship of Sir Hilary Blood, a new constitution giving internal self-government was put into operation in March 1962. Foreign Affairs and Defence remained the ultimate responsibility of the British Government, which was represented in Malta by a United Kingdom Commissioner. A Consultative Council was established to provide for consultation between the Governments on matters of mutual concern. The Legislative Assembly consisted of 50 members elected under the single, transferable vote system. A Cabinet, consisting of a Prime Minister and not more than seven other ministers, was appointed from the Legislative Assembly, and was collectively responsible to it. The Governor was appointed by the Crown and generally acted on the advice of the Maltese Ministers

In 1962 the Nationalist Party under the late Dr Borg Olivier was successful at the polls, and after talks with the Colonial Secretary constitutional amendments were made giving wider powers to the Maltese Government. But this constitution was acceptable to neither of the major parties both of whose electoral programmes had included independence for Malta. After further discussions a Malta Independence Conference took place in London in July 1963. This broke up without settling the final details of an Independence constitution. After further talks in London and Malta Dr Borg Olivier produced a new Constitution which was approved by the Malta Legislative Assembly and later by an island-wide referendum.

Malta became independent on 21st September 1964. In December 1974 following the passing of certain constitutional amendments, she became a Republic.

In January 1987 the principles of neutrality and non-alignment were entrenched in the Maltese constitution. The electoral provisions in the constitution were also amended to ensure that the political party which secured a majority of votes also formed the Government.

In August 1987 a Select Committee was established to recommend changes to the Constitution. Consideration is being given to changing the role of the Presidency and to including protection for the Courts and broadcasting under the Constitution.

Constitution

The Maltese Constitution is based on the Malta Independence Constitution as set out in the Malta Independence Order 1964 (SI Number 1398) and as subsequently amended. It describes Malta as a democratic republic and as a neutral state adhering to a policy of non-alignment. Such a status is to imply that no foreign military base will be permitted on Maltese territory and that no military facilities will be allowed to be used by any foreign forces except at the request of the Malta Government. More specifically, Malta shipyards are denied to the military vessels of the two super-powers.

The Parliament of Malta consists of the President and the House of Representatives. The House of Representatives is elected by the single transferable vote system of proportional representation. However, where in a general election a political party obtains more than 50 per cent of the votes on the first count but secures fewer than 50 per cent of the seats the party's representation is increased by as many members as may be necessary to provide it with a majority of one over all other parties. The conduct of elections is under the direction and supervision of an Electoral Commission, which is also required to review the boundaries of the Electoral Divisions from time to time. Parliament, unless previously dissolved, has a life of five years.

Executive authority is vested in the President who is appointed by the House of Representatives for five years. The President is required to act in accordance with the advice of the Cabinet except in certain specific cases. The Prime Minister is appointed by the President and must be a member of the House of Representatives who in the judgement of the President is able to command the confidence of the majority of the members of the House. The Ministers are also appointed by the President on the advice of the Prime Minister and portfolios are allocated to them by the President on the same advice.

The leader of the Opposition is appointed by the President, who appoints to this post either the Leader of the main opposition party, or if there are two or more opposition parties, the person who, in his judgement, commands the support of the largest single group of members of the House in opposition to the Government.

The Constitution provides for Superior Courts, one of which is known as the Constitutional Court and which has the jurisdiction to hear and determine disputes over membership of the House of Representatives and appeals from other courts on constitutional, electoral and certain other matters and to consider cases referred to it by the Electoral Commissioner where an election has been suspended because of corrupt practices. The Chief Justice, Judges and the Attorney General are appointed by the President on the advice of the Prime Minister

The Constitution states that the religion of Malta is the Roman Catholic Apostolic religion and requires that Roman Catholic Apostolic faith is taught in all state schools.

Historical List

GOVERNORS-GENERAL

1964–1971 Sir Maurice Dorman
1971–1974 Sir Anthony Mamo

PRESIDENTS

1974–1976 Sir Anthony Mamo
1976–1981 Dr Anton Buttigieg
1981–1982 (Acting) Dr Albert V Hyzler
1982–1987 Miss Agatha Barbara
1987–1989 (Acting) Mr Paul Xuereb
1989– Dr Vincent Tabone

PRIME MINISTERS

1962–1971 Hon Dr G Borg Olivier
1971–1984 Hon Dom Mintoff
1984–1987 Hon Dr C Mifsud Bonnici
1987– Hon Dr E Fenech Adami

Government

HEAD OF STATE

President: The Hon Dr Vincent Tabone, MD, DO (Oxon), DOMS (Lond), DMJ FRCS (Edin), MP

CABINET

Prime Minister: The Hon Dr Eddie Fenech Adami, BA, LLD, MP

Minister of Foreign Affairs, Parliamentary Affairs, Justice and Deputy Prime Minister: The Hon Professor Guido De Marco, BA, LLD, MP

Minister of Education and the Interior: The Hon Dr Ugo Mifsud Bonnici, BA, LLD, MP

Minister for Social Policy: The Hon Dr Louis Galea, BA, LLD, MP

Minister of Finance: The Hon Dr George Bonello du Puis, LLD, MP

Minister for Economic Affairs: The Hon Dr John Dalli FCCA, CPA, MBIM, MP

Minister for the Development of the Infrastructure: The Hon Mr Michael Falzon BARCH, A&CE, MP

Minister of Agriculture and Fisheries: The Hon Mr Lawrence Gatt BARCH, A&CE, MP

Minister for the Development of the Tertiary Sector: The Hon Dr E Bonnici, BA, LLD, MP

Minister for Gozo: The Hon Mr Anton Tabone, MP

Parliamentary Secretary for the Environment, Local Government, Public Cleansing and Lands: Dr Stanley Zammit MD

Parliamentary Secretary for Youth, Sport, Consumer Protection, Broadcasting, Theatre and Culture: Dr Michael Frendo LLM LLD

Parliamentary Secretary for Health: The Hon Dr George Hyzler, MD, MP
Parliamentary Secretary for the Elderly: The Hon Dr John Rizzo Naudi, MD, BSC, FRCP, MP
Parliamentary Secretary for Housing: The Hon Dr Joe Cassar, BA, LLD, MP
Parliamentary Secretary for Energy: The Hon Ninu Zammit, BARCH, A&CE, MP
Parliamentary Secretary for Telephone & Telecommunications, Postal Services, Public Transport, Civil Aviation and Air Terminal Management: Dr Francis Zammit Dimech LLD
Parliamentary Secretary for Tourism: The Hon Dr Michael Refalo, BA, LLD, MP
Parliamentary Secretary for Maritime Affairs: The Hon Dr Joe Fenech, BA, LLD, MP

HOUSE OF REPRESENTATIVES
Speaker: The Hon Dr Lawrence Gonzi BA, LLD
Clerk to the House of Representatives: P Muscat Terribile

LEADER OF THE OPPOSITION
Dr Carmelo Mifsud Bonnici

JUDICIARY
Chief Justice:
The Hon Prof G Mifsud Bonnici

MINISTRIES AND GOVERNMENT DEPARTMENTS

OFFICE OF THE PRIME MINISTER
Secretary-General and Secretary to the Cabinet: G W Borg
Chief Electoral Commissioner: C Callus
Director of Civil Aviation: S Fenech
Director of Information: Lewis Portelli

MINISTRY OF JUSTICE
Attorney General: Dr A Borg Barthet
Registrar of the Superior Courts: E Grech
Director of the Public Registry: M Said
A/Chief Notary to Government: Dr F Pellegrini
Commissioner of Land: A Gouder

MINISTRY OF FOREIGN AFFAIRS
Secretary: V Gauci

MINISTRY OF EDUCATION AND THE INTERIOR
Commissioner of Police: A Calleja
Commander Armed Forces of Malta: Brig J Spiteri
Director of Prisons: J Psaila (Acting)
Secretary: G de Marco
Director of Education: F Fearne

MINISTRY OF FINANCE
Secretary: E Wadge
Commissioner of Inland Revenue: V Galea
Director of Audit: L Spiteri
Comptroller of Customs: J Portelli
Accountant General: C Portelli

MINISTRY OF DEVELOPMENT OF THE INFRASTRUCTURE
Director of Public Works: J Mizzi
Manager, Waterworks: C Delia

MINISTRY FOR SOCIAL POLICY
Director of Labour: E Cilia Debono
Director of Social Services: C de Degabriele
Chief Government Medical Officer: Dr A Vassallo

MINISTRY OF DEVELOPMENT OF THE TERTIARY SECTOR
Secretary: J F X Muscat
Director of Trade: L Coppini

Independent Statutory Bodies

ENEMALTA CORPORATION
Chairman: L Ciantar

THE MALTA DEVELOPMENT CORPORATION
Chairman: J Bannister

THE MALTA DRYDOCKS
Chairman: S Meilaq

THE PUBLIC SERVICE COMMISSION
Chairman: Dr A G Camilleri

TELEMALTA CORPORATION
Chairman: J A Scicluna

CENTRAL BANK OF MALTA
Governor: A P Galdes
Deputy Governor: H C Degabriele

AIR MALTA
Chairman: A Mizzi

SEA MALTA
Chairman: C J Mallia

Mauritius

Capital: Port Louis

Mauritius owes its name to the Dutch settlers who landed there in 1598 and named the island after their ruler, Prince Maurice of Nassau. The territory includes Rodrigues Island, 563 km (350 miles) to the east, with an area of 104 sq km (40 square miles) and a population of some 37,700, and lesser dependencies.

Location, Topography, Climate

Mauritius lies about 805 km (500 miles) off the east coast of the Democratic Republic of Madagascar between latitudes 19° 58′ and 20° 32′ south and longitudes 57° 17′ and 57° 46′ east. It is 5,125 km (3,185 miles) from Perth, Australia, 3,369 km (2,094 miles) from Colombo and 2,496 km (1,551 miles) from Durban.

The island, roughly pear-shaped, is 61 km (38 miles) long by 47 km (29 miles) broad. From the north an undulating plain rises gently towards the central plateau, where it reaches a height of about 660 m (2,200 feet) before dropping sharply to the southern and south-western coasts. The mountains are a striking feature of the landscape, rising abruptly from the plain, with their lower slopes covered in dense vegetation, sugar cane or tea and their upper slopes ending in precipitous rocky peaks. The three main groups of mountains are: the Moka range, running in an east-north-easterly direction; the Black River Savanne group, massed north to south; and the Bambous group, with an east-west trend. The highest peaks are Piton de la Riviere Noire (815 m), Pieter Both (810 m) and Le Pouce (799 m). The main watershed runs northwards across the central plateau; the rivers consequently tend to run westward or eastward. Most are short (the longest being 39.4 km) and fast-flowing, generally at the bottom of deep ravines and interrupted by waterfalls. None is navigable, but some have been harnessed for hydro-electric purposes. True crater lakes are found at Grand Bassin and Bassin Blanc, but in general water conservation is achieved by man-made reservoirs, of which there are at present eight, the largest being Mare aux Vacoas.

The island is almost completely encircled by coral reefs, within which lagoons and a succession of beaches of near-white coral sand offer tempting attractions to the tourist.

Mauritius enjoys a sub-tropical maritime climate. The considerable variation in rainfall and temperature between different parts of the island helps to avoid monotony, as does the difference between summer and winter. The summer season runs from December to April and the winter from June to September. April to June and September to November are transitional periods and tend to be the most pleasant of the year. In Port Louis the daytime Summer maximum and night-time minimum temperatures average 31°C (87.8°F) and 24°C (75°F) respectively; in winter they average 25°C (77°F) and 20°C (68°F). The highest and lowest recorded are 36°C (96.8°F) and 12°C (53.6°F). At Curepipe, 555 m above sea level, the maximum recorded is 32°C (89.6°F) and the minimum 7°C (44.6°F).

The southeast trade winds blow for most of the year and the climate is generally humid. Rain falls mainly in the summer. The uplift of moisture-laden maritime air caused by the mountains results in an annual rainfall ranging from 875 mm (35 inches) on the west coast, 1,000 mm (40 inches) around Port Louis and 1,500 mm (60 inches) on the south-east coast to 5,000 mm (200 inches) on the central plateau. Variations from year to year significantly affect the size of the sugar crop. Mauritius lies in the Indian Ocean cyclone belt; the cyclone season normally extends from December to April. Occasional intense cyclones, such as Carol in 1960 and Gervaise in 1975, can cause widespread devastation. More frequent moderate ones may cause some damage but bring essential rain at a critical time for the sugar cane.

Population

The last census (July 1983) showed a population of 1,000,432 including 33,569 for the smaller islands. By the end of March 1991 the population of Mauritius was estimated to be 1,088,200 and has stabilized at just over a million, thanks to a successful family planning programme. The census showed a population of approximately 52 per cent Hindus; 17 per cent Muslims; 3 per cent Sino-Mauritians and 28 per cent General population, ie people of African or European descent or of mixed descent. Most of the General population are Christians—mainly Roman Catholics but with significant numbers of Anglicans and members of other denominations.

The official language is English, but French is more widely spoken and may be used in the Legislative Assembly and the lower courts of law. It is also used by the press. Creole is the lingua franca. Other languages in use include Hindi, Tamil, Urdu, Telegu, Marathi and Chinese (Hakka or Cantonese).

Health

The pattern of disease resembles more a developed country than a tropical African nation. Cardiovascular diseases are the leading cause of death; other main causes include diabetes, bronchial diseases and cancer. Malaria has nearly been eradicated. AIDS has not so far seriously affected the island. Measures have been taken to alert the population to its dangers. There are still some cases of leprosy in Rodrigues.

A national health service provides free medical care for all, through government hospitals, dispensaries and health centres. Private doctors and clinics are also readily available, as are dentists and opticians, as well as a range of traditional Chinese and Indian medicines.

Communications

The island is served by the modern facilities of the Sir Seewoosagur Ramgoolam International Airport at Plaisance in the southeast. A number of international airlines offer frequent scheduled services to London, Paris and other European cities and to various points in Asia, Africa (including South Africa), the Middle East and the Indian Ocean region.

Port Louis is the only significant port. It can accommodate eleven ocean-going and six smaller ships. There are regular sailings between the island of Mauritius and Rodrigues and the outer islands.

There are now no railways but there is a good network of tarred roads, including some with dual-carriageway.

The Economy

The development of the Mauritian economy since the early 1980s has been a remarkable success.

The three main pillars of the economy are sugar, light manufacturing industry (mainly for export) and tourism. An Export Processing Zone (EPZ), covering the whole country, was established in November 1970 and offers attractive duty and other concessions to local and overseas investors who set up factories manufacturing for export. Gross revenues from EPZ exports have overtaken those from the traditional export, sugar. EPZ industries at the end of March 1991 were employing 89,908 workers. Most are in the textile and garment sectors, with particular emphasis on wool sweaters — Mauritius is the third largest producer in the world. Other sectors include leatherware, spectacle frames, printing and finishing, diamond cutting and polishing, etc. A wider variety of goods is produced principally for domestic consumption.

Tourism has been increasing steadily in recent years registering 292,000 arrivals in 1990. Mauritian hotels aim mainly at the upper sectors of the market. Tourists come principally from France (including Reunion Island), Germany, Britain, Italy, Switzerland and South Africa, but an attempt is being made to tap the Far Eastern and South-East Asian markets. New hotels continue to be built, but it is intended to limit further development in order to prevent the island from becoming overcrowded with tourists. Charter tourists are discouraged.

The development of the EPZ and of tourism has transformed a comparatively recent situation of chronic unemployment into one of virtually full employment. Largely as a result, there has been some pressure on wage levels. Inflation, from under 2 per cent in 1988, was 10.7 per cent in 1989/90 and has risen to 13.4 per cent for the 12 months ending March 1991. The relative prosperity brought about by economic success has substantially raised living standards for large numbers of the population. Environmental pollution poses an increasing problem and is largely a result of economic success. Steps are now being taken to tackle it.

Trade and Finance

Under the provisions of the Lomé Convention, Mauritian manufactured exports enjoy duty and quota-free access to the markets of the European Community. There are quotas on the export of garments to the USA. Mauritius is a member of the African Preferential Trade Area.

Mauritius still imports most of her requirements of manufactured goods, as well as raw materials, oil and many foodstuffs. Principal suppliers include France, Britain, South Africa, Germany, Japan, Taiwan and oil producing states in the Middle East. Mauritius trades freely with all countries, but Commonwealth preference applies to many categories of goods.

The economic boom has enabled Mauritius to build up monetary reserves equal to the cost of several months imports and to repay loans to the IMF ahead of time. Her credit-worthiness is consequently high. She continues to receive aid from multilateral bodies, including the World Bank and the African Development Bank, as well as from bi-lateral donors. The Commonwealth development Corporation opened an office in Port Louis in 1989 and is investing in several sectors of the economy.

Mauritius hopes to develop as an offshore financial centre. Legislation has recently been passed to provide for the development of offshore banking; in 1989 Barclays Bank plc was the first bank to be granted a licence for this type of business and six other banks have now opened offshore units.

The unit of currency is the Mauritian rupee, whose value is determined each business day against a basket of currencies. In 1989 the average exchange rate was about 25 rupees to one pound sterling and in 1991 it reached 27 rupees to one pound sterling.

Agriculture

Sugar has long been the principal crop. The total area harvested in 1989 was around 77,000 ha (190,000 acres). More than half the crop is grown by large plantations, which also operate the mills and process the cane produced by the many smaller planters, mainly Indo-Mauritian families. Under the Sugar

Protocol of the Lomé Convention, some 510,000 tonnes of the crop are exported to the European Community (in practice mainly to Britain) at guaranteed prices currently some four times those obtainable on the open world market. A bulk sugar terminal with an automated loading system can handle the whole crop. In 1989 total sugar exports reached 636,000 tonnes but fell in 1990 to 578,000 tonnes. Domestic consumption amounts to some 36,720 tonnes.

Current policy is to maintain approximately the present level of sugar production from a somewhat reduced acreage by using improved varieties and production techniques. Land thus released becomes available for growing food crops, thereby reducing imports. This country is virtually self-sufficient in many kinds of vegetables and in tropical fruits.

Tea and tobacco are also produced and processed but on a much smaller scale than sugar. The tobacco crop is mainly for domestic consumption, but much of the tea is exported.

Education

The education system is, in many respects, modelled on the British pattern. Free primary education is available to all. Free secondary education at government or subsidised private schools is available to those who do sufficiently well at the primary level. Pupils take the Cambridge School Certificate and Higher School Certificate (equivalent to 'O' and 'A' levels). Those with the most outstanding results — currently 18 in number — become 'laureates' and are eligible for scholarships at British universities funded by the British and Mauritian Governments. Others may go on to study at the University of Mauritius which has schools (faculties) of Agriculture, Industrial Technology, Administration and Law and is expanding into other disciplines; or they may take up scholarships offered by other countries, including France, India, Australia, the USA and the USSR.

The Mauritius Institute of Education provides teacher training courses and the Mauritius College of the Air offers distance learning. The Mahatma Gandhi Institute provides opportunities to study certain specialised subjects, including in particular those relating to Asian cultures.

The Media

The Mauritius Broadcasting Corporation, an independent body, offers radio and colour television services. It has a monopoly in the country, but programmes broadcast from the neighbouring French island of Reunion can also easily be received.

There is a free and lively press. Several daily and weekly newspapers are published in French (often with some articles in English) and in a number of Asian languages

History

Mauritius was probably first visited by Arab and Malay sailors during the Middle Ages. Portuguese sailors came to the island several times during the early sixteenth century, but it remained uninhabited (and the home of many distinctive species of fauna and flora, including the dodo) until the Dutch landed in 1598 and established settlements from 1638 onwards. In 1710, however, they abandoned the island. In 1715 the French took formal possession and in 1721 sent a small contingent of colonists from the neighbouring island of Bourbon (now Reunion), followed in 1722 by another sent on behalf of the French East India Company, which governed the island until about 1767. From then until 1810 (apart from a brief period of independence under the Colonial Assembly during the French Revolution), it was in the charge of officials appointed by the French Government. The French renamed the island Isle de France. Slaves were imported from Madagascar, Mozambique and other parts of Africa.

During the Napoleonic wars, French men-of-war and privateers based in Mauritius, frequently attacked British merchant vessels. The British Government accordingly resolved to capture the island. After defeating a small British force at the battle of Grand Port in 1809, the French surrendered to a stronger British expedition in 1810.

The British restored the name of Mauritius. The island, together with its dependencies including Seychelles and Rodrigues, was formally ceded to Britain under the Treaty of Paris in 1814.

The British Government abolished slavery in Mauritius in 1835 and paid substantial compensation to the former slave owners. Thereafter indentured labourers were recruited, mainly from India, to work on the sugar plantations. It is principally their descendants who form the present Indo-Mauritian community.

Constitutional Development

From 1810 to 1903 Mauritius and Seychelles were administered as a single British colony by a Governor and a number of British officials. In 1825 a Council of Government was established consisting of the Governor and four officials nominated by him. In 1832 an equal number of officials and non-officials were appointed.

The Constitution was amended in 1885 and in 1886 elections were held on a limited franchise for a Council of Government in which there were 8 officials, 9 other members (including some officials) chosen by the Governor, and 10 members elected by the various districts of the island. Elections were subsequently held every five years until 1936. Seychelles became a separate colony in 1903.

In 1947 a new Constitution granted a wide measure of enfranchisement on the basis of a simple literacy requirement. After a general election in August 1948 the first Legislative Council met on 1st

September. In 1957 a ministerial system was introduced. In 1958 the constitution was amended to provide for universal adult suffrage.

At a Constitutional conference held in London in September, 1965, the Secretary of State for the Colonies stated that it was right for Mauritius to become independent. It was decided that after a general election had been held and a new Government formed, HM Government would be prepared to take the necessary steps to declare Mauritius independent after a period of six months of full internal self-government, provided that the Legislative Assembly passed a resolution to that effect. The General Election was held on 7th August, 1967. In spite of considerable local opposition to the idea of independence, the Alliance Independence Party under Sir Seewoosagur Ramgoolam won the election and with it a mandate to proceed to independence. A new Constitution granting full internal self-government was introduced and on 22nd August 1967 the Legislative Assembly passed the independence motion. The country duly became independent on 12th March, 1968.

The Constitution

The Constitution guarantees the protection of the fundamental rights and freedoms of the individual and defines Mauritian citizenship.

On 12th March 1992 Mauritius became a Republic within the Commonwealth and Sir Veerasamy Ringadoo became President. There is a single-chamber Legislative Assembly consisting of 62 directly elected members (including 2 for Rodrigues) and up to 8 'best losers' appointed to redress any imbalance of representation between the ethnic communities without disturbing the balance between the political parties. The New Constitution provides for the appointment of a President and Vice-President. It also provides for the appointment of a Speaker and a Deputy-Speaker, a Prime Minister, a Deputy Prime Minister and a Cabinet of ministers as well as up to 10 Parliamentary Secretaries. Provision is further made for an Attorney-General, a Secretary to the Cabinet, a Commissioner of Police, a Director of Public Prosecutions and a Leader of the Opposition.

The Judicature includes a Supreme Court and a Court of Appeal, from which there is a right of appeal in certain cases to Her Majesty in Council. After March 1992 appeals will be possible to the Judicial Committee of the Privy Council. Other sections of the Constitution relate to Service Commissions and the Public Service; the Ombudsman; and Public Finance.

HEAD OF STATE

President: His Excellency Sir Veerasamy Ringadoo, GCMG, QC

CABINET

Prime Minister, Minister of Defence and Internal Security, Minister of Information, and Minister of Internal and External Communications, and the Outer Islands: The Right Honourable Sir Anerood Jugnauth, PC, KCMG, QC

Deputy Prime Minister and Minister of Health: Dr The Hon Paramhamsa Nababsing

Minister of Trade and Shipping: The Hon Anil Kumar Bachoo

Minister of Women's Rights, Child Development and Family Welfare: The Hon Mrs Sheilabhai Bappoo

Minister of External Affairs: The Hon Paul Raymond Berenger

Minister of Arts, Culture, Leisure, and Reform Institutions: The Hon Mookhesswur Choonee

Minister for Rodrigues: The Hon Louis Serge Clair

Minister for Housing, Lands, and Town and Country Planning: The Hon Jaya Krishna Cuttaree

Minister of Economic Planning and Development: The Hon Jean Claude Gervais Raoul De L'Estrac

Minister of Agriculture, Fisheries, and Natural Resources: The Hon Murlidas Dulloo

Minister of Local Government: The Hon Jean Regis Finette

Minister of Labour and Industrial Relations: The Hon Dharmanand Goopt Fokeer

Attorney-General and Minister of Justice: The Hon Alan Ganoo

Minister of Youth and Sports: The Hon Michael James Kevin Glover

Minister of Cooperatives, Handicraft, and Small Scale Industries: The Hon Jagdishwar Goburdhun

Minister of Works: The Hon Dwarkanath Gungah

Minister of Manpower Resources, and Vocational and Technical Training: The Hon Ramduthsing Jaddoo

Minister of the Environment and Quality of Life: Dr The Hon Ahmud Swalay Kasenally

Minister of Tourism: The Hon Noe Ah-Qwet Lee Cheong Lem

Minister of Social Security and National Solidarity: The Hon Karl Auguste Offmann

Minister of Education and Science: The Hon Armoogum Parsuraman

Minister for Civil Service Affairs and Employment: The Hon Keerteecoomar Ruhee

Minister of Finance: The Hon Ramakrishna Sithanen

Minister of Energy, Water Resources, and Postal Services: The Hon Mahyendrah Utchanah

Minister of Industry and Industrial Technology: The Hon Cassam Uteem

Legislative Assembly

Speaker: The Hon C Daby Ajay, MLA

Clerk: Rivaltz Quenette

Namibia

Capital: Windhoek

Location, Topography, Climate

The territory of the Republic of Namibia lies between latitudes 17°S and 28°S and between longitudes 12°E and 21°E for the most part, with an extension of a narrow strip of land, the Caprivi Strip, in the extreme north east taking its longitude there to just beyond 25°E. It is bounded by the South Atlantic Ocean on the west, Angola to the north, Zambia, (connected via the Caprivi Strip), to the north east, Botswana to the east and South Africa to the south. The name 'Namibia' is derived from the Nama/Damara word 'Namib' meaning enclosure, which also gives its name to the Namib desert along the coast. The name was formally adopted on 12th June 1968 by the United Nations General Assembly (UNGA) to replace its former name, South West Africa.

The area of Namibia is 824,269.59 sq km, a figure which includes Walvis Bay (1,124 sq km). Sovereignty over both Walvis Bay and the offshore Penguin Islands remains in dispute with South Africa. The country is divided into three broad zones, with the Namib Desert to the west and the Kalahari Desert to the east enclosing the Central Plateau in between. The Namib Desert, constituting 15 per cent of the total land area extends some 1,600 km along the Atlantic seaboard forming a narrow coastal plain varying in width from 80 to 130 km. Its relief is made up of long lines of sand dunes, some up to 300 metres high, interspersed with rocky outcrops, the whole virtually devoid of vegetation. Behind the coastal plain the Great Escarpment rises to the Central Plateau, which covers over 50 per cent of the land area, and which has an average altitude of 1,100 metres. Toward its centre mountain ranges rise up to 2,440 metres. Windhoek stands at an altitude of 1,833 metres above sea level. The landscape of the plateau is made up of rugged mountains, rocky outcrops, sand filled valleys and gently undulating upland plains. The land slopes eastward to the Kalahari Basin and northwards to the large Etosha Pan. A near total lack of surface water is typical of the Kalahari zone.

The climate is characterised by the sparseness and irregularity of the rainfall. A large part of the territory is either arid or semi-arid, making it one of the driest countries on earth. The rainfall increases from the south west to the north east with least (less than 50 mm per annum) on the coastal arid zone, while the semi-arid central plateau averages between 200 and 400 mm per annum, and the north eastern border with Angola and the Caprivi Strip, considered to be a sub-humid zone, may receive rainfall in excess of 600 mm annually. Prolonged periods of drought, as suffered in the years 1979–85, are characteristic of the climate.

Population

Despite Namibia's vast size the population is small, a reflection of the harshness of much of the environment. The most recent estimate (1989) gives a total of 1.5 million. Current projections based on a 2.8 per cent annual growth rate forecast a population of just under 2 million by the year 2000. The largest group, with 50 per cent of the total, is the Ovambo, agro-pastoralists who have lived in the north of the country since the mid-16th century. The Kavango, with 9.3 per cent, are also agro-pastoralists who have traditionally supplemented their diet with fish from the Okavango River. The Herero, with 7.5 per cent, represent the most exclusively pastoral group of all the Bantu-speaking peoples of the area. They entered Kaokoland around 1550 but gradually moved into the north central and central parts of the country. The Dama (or Damara), with 7.5 per cent, are not directly related to the Bantu, also pastoralists, and are among the earliest inhabitants of the country. The Nama, with 4.8 per cent, are a section of the Khoi people, pastoralists whose language, like that of the Bushmen, is characterised by clicks. The Caprivians, with 2.9 per cent, are also agro-pastoralists and share a similar economic base with the Ovambo and the Kavango. The San (Bushmen) with 2.9 per cent, are the earliest known inhabitants of the territory, having lived there for over 11,000 years, and they are some of the oldest surviving hunter-gatherers in the world. The Basters, with 2.5 per cent, who settled in Rehoboth in 1870, are descendants of people stemming from mixed marriages between white farmers and Khoi mothers in the north west of Cape Province. They are mainly Afrikaans speakers. The Coloureds, with 4.1 per cent of the total, also relatively recent immigrants from South Africa, are mainly Afrikaans speaking, and tend to live in the urban areas. The White group comes from European stock, and with 78,000 they represent about 6.6 per cent of the country's population. About half are South African by origin, one quarter of German ancestry, one fifth are Boer 'sudwesters' who migrated there at the turn of the century, and a few thousand are of British ancestry. The official language of Namibia is English. Windhoek, by far the largest town, has a population of over 110,000. Only 29 per cent of the population is urban. The distribution of the rural population was affected by the implementation of the Odendaal Plan which created 'homelands' for the various ethnic groups. Ninety per cent of the population live in the subsistence sector, with the highest densities in the north. Elsewhere the country is sparsely populated.

Communications

Namibia has a well developed transport infrastructure, which is largely linked to the South African network, with little or no connections to other neighbouring states. The railway network, largely built during the German colonial period, comprises 2,349 km of narrow gauge track. The main line runs from the border with South Africa through Windhoek to Walvis Bay. A northern branch connects with the mining area centred on Tsumeb, and two other branches connect Windhoek with Gobabis, an important cattle centre, and link Luderitz port to the main line south of Keetmanshoop. Nearly all the major centres are connected by over 4,000 km of tarred roads. Most roads in the north and east are untarred. The total road network, mostly gravel or dirt, totals about 42,000 km. Road construction is costly, due to climatic conditions, and the nature of the terrain. Namibia is served by ports, Walvis Bay and Luderitz, but the former handles most of the country's freight, and has marine engineering and ship repair facilities as well as container quays. There is a national airline, recently renamed Air Namibia from Namib Air.

The Economy

Namibia's economy is based on the commercial exploitation and export of vast and accessible mineral deposits, diamonds, uranium and base metals, and commercial agriculture based on cattle ranching and karakul sheep farming, the latter for their pelts for the fur trade. The two sectors have traditionally accounted for over 50 per cent of GDP and 90 per cent of total exports.

Diamonds are mined by Consolidated Diamond Mines (CDM), a wholly owned De Beers subsidiary, from alluvial coastal deposits north of the Orange River. Output in 1987 was over one million carats. Uranium output from the Rossing mine, which began in 1976, in which Rio Tinto Zinc (RTZ) has a 46.5 per cent equity interest, reached its full current capacity of 5,000 tons in 1980, though there have been subsequent substantial reductions in output and employment following a sustained fall in the world uranium price. Seventy per cent of the base metal production is by Tsumeb Corporation Ltd (TCL), which operates 4 mines and the territory's only copper smelter and lead refinery. It is 80 per cent owned by Gold Fields of South Africa (GFSA).

Eighty to ninety per cent of the overall value of commercial agricultural production is derived from 4,000 large cattle ranches, owned by white farmers, on the central and south plateaux, or from karakul sheep ranches in the semi-arid south. White farmers farm just under half the land area, and earn 93 per cent of the agricultural income, with 150,000 small farm families making up the rest. Millet production is of growing importance and is the staple food of the north of the country. Namibia is almost self-sufficient in maize. Commercial farmers have enjoyed heavy state subsidies in the past, while there has been little investment in the 'communal areas' in the north where most people live.

Namibia's coastal waters are rich in fish both demersal (bottom feeding, eg Hake) and pelagic (surface-feeding, eg pilchards). Rock lobster is also found. But the stocks have been subject to overfishing in the past by foreign fleets. The new government has declared a 200-mile exclusive economic zone, which if properly protected, should give fish stocks the opportunity to recover. There is also potential for a revival of fish processing.

The manufacturing base is rudimentary largely because it was not developed during the 75 years of South African rule. Manufactured goods have always been readily available from South Africa. Namibia is a highly import-dependent economy, with up to 90 per cent of its needs, including food, imported.

The economy is and will remain in the short to medium term influenced by its historic links with the South African economy. Namibia will remain in the Rand monetary area for the meantime, but a Central Bank has been established which is planning the introduction of a new currency regime. Namibia has become a full member of the Southern African Customs Union (SACU). Its only natural deep water harbour, Walvis Bay, which handles 95 per cent of the country's seaborne trade and 85 per cent of all its trade, is South African territory. Budget deficits are projected in the next few years. This shortfall reflects the end of South African budgetary support and the need to increase expenditure in certain areas, particularly on the social infrastructure, to meet the expectations generated by independence and to start to redress the unequal allocation of resources inherited from the pre-independence period. A first donors' conference took place in June 1990, which provided pledges of some $200 million, for the first year of the reconstruction programme, and a further $150 million each for the following two years much on concessional terms. Namibia's membership of the Lomé Convention, of the World Bank and IMF, and of the Southern African Development Coordination Conference (SADCC) should soon provide additional sources of aid funds. Namibia will also benefit from a beef quota under Lomé arrangements and Karakul pelt sales will be protected by the Stabex scheme.

According to UN estimates, the economically active population is about 500,000, of which some 240,000 are engaged in subsistence agriculture, 56,500 in commercial ranches, 20,000 in mining, 7,500 in fishing, 28,500 in the secondary sector and 148,000 in the tertiary sector, of which about half are in domestic service. One of the most pressing development problems for the government is employment creation, with unemployment running at over 30 per cent.

There are no available statistics on Namibia's energy resources, although this is a potential growth area. There are known reserves of gas and coal, none of which has yet been developed, as well as a possible major source of hydro-electric power from the Cunene River Basin in co-operation with Angola. But development of these resources will require heavy capital investment.

History

In the pre-colonial phase, European explorers and traders first made contact with Namibia in the 15th century. The Portuguese arrived first in 1485 followed by the Dutch in 1652 and the British in 1786. But the inhospitable Namib desert along the Atlantic Coast proved an effective barrier to the interior until the beginning of the 19th century, when Rhenish and British missionaries first ventured inland. At the same period the south and central parts of the country were subject to immigration by various Oorlam (Khoi) families from Cape Province who had refused to subject themselves to European control. They settled among the Nama. This was followed by an influx of Baster migrants who crossed the Orange River in 1868, settling in Rehoboth in 1870. The first permanent influx of Boers started during the period 1889–1894, reaching a total of nearly 900 settlers by 1900.

Continual group conflict in the 19th century between the indigenous Herero and Nama tribes over land grazing and water rights caused the missionaries to ask the British government in the Cape for protection. Although Britain did not extend its protection beyond the Orange River, it did annex the Penguin Islands to Cape Colony in 1866 and later the harbour, settlement and surrounding area of Walvis Bay on 12th March 1878, which was transferred to Cape Colony in 1884. The rest of the country was annexed by Germany which formally declared a protectorate in April 1884 over a 20 km wide belt of land from the port of Luderitz southwards to the Orange River. This land had been purchased from Nama chiefs by an agent of Adolf Luderitz, a Bremen merchant, who had earlier established a commercial outpost in the area. The land boundaries of the territory which in 1890 became the colony known as German South-West Africa were subsequently laid down in agreements concluded in 1886 with Portugal and in 1890 with Britain. The Anglo-German Treaty of 1890 also recognised the status of both the Penguin Islands and Walvis Bay as part of the Cape Colony.

The land policies implemented by the German settlers and concession companies were contested by the Nama and Herero who rebelled in the years 1902–1907. As early as 1898 the German authorities sought to displace the indigenous population who were relegated into 'native reserves'. By 1903 the Herero had lost one quarter of their best grazing land to this policy and on 26th December 1905 the Kaiser signed a decree expropriating all Herero land and prohibiting them from keeping cattle. The Nama and Herero numbers were drastically reduced by the German military in the course of quelling the rebellions. Pass laws were introduced in 1907, as was the institutionalisation of migrant contract labour. It was during this period that the foundations of Namibia's export economy based on mining and stock farming were laid. Diamond and copper mining began in 1908/9, while the karakul sheep was first introduced in 1908.

With the outbreak of the 1st World War, troops from the Union of South Africa entered German South West Africa with the full agreement of the British government. On 15th July 1915 German forces surrendered. For the next 5 years the territory was under military occupation and martial law. During this period English and Dutch became the official languages, Roman Dutch law was introduced to replace German law and, after the signing of the Treaty of Versailles, over 6,000 Germans (military, police and officials) were deported leaving a German community of just under 8,000 in the country.

At the end of the 1st World War Germany relinquished all its former colonial possessions, including German South West Africa, by Article 119 of the Treaty of Versailles. It then became known as South West Africa (SWA). At the peace conference General Smuts for South Africa had argued for outright annexation by South Africa of the territory and its incorporation as the 'fifth province' of the Union of South Africa. This was not acceptable to the Allied Powers. Instead a class 'C' mandate was established for it in terms of Article 22 Part I of the Covenant of the League of Nations. The Mandate Agreement was signed on 17th December 1920. Under its terms South Africa was the designated mandatory power. Article 2 allowed it to administer the territory '... as an integral portion of the Union of South Africa' and enabled it to '... apply the laws of the Union of South Africa ...' to the territory, but demanded of the mandatory power the promotion of '... the material and moral well-being and the social progress of the inhabitants ...'. Under Article 6 South Africa was obliged to submit annual reports on its fulfilment of these obligations to the Permanent Mandates Commission (PMC) of the League of Nations.

Following the founding of the United Nations in 1945 as successor to the League of Nations, South Africa again attempted to incorporate SWA into the Union. But the United Nations General Assembly (UNGA) rejected this on 14th December 1946. The trusteeship system replaced the mandates system but South Africa refused to enter into a trusteeship agreement for SWA. It argued that the mandate had lapsed on the dissolution of the League and that it was in no way accountable to the UN for its administration of the territory, but that it would continue to administer it '... in the spirit of the mandate'. In July 1949 the South African government informed the UN that it would discontinue its annual reports. In December 1949 the UNGA decided to seek an Advisory Opinion from the International Court of Justice (ICJ) on the legal status of SWA—since by this stage South Africa claimed that sovereignty resided in the Union as the mandatory power. In 1950 the ICJ ruled that South Africa had no obligation to conclude a trusteeship agreement, that the mandate remained in force but that South Africa had no right to change unilaterally the international status of SWA. South Africa repudiated the Opinion, and in 1954 went ahead with the transfer of the administration of 'native affairs' to the Union Government. In 1955 and 1956 the UNGA obtained two further Advisory Opinions from the ICJ. The ICJ upheld the right of the UN Permanent Committee on SWA (1953–1960) to supervise the administration of the territory and confirmed *inter alia* that the UNGA had the right to adopt resolutions on SWA and the right to grant oral hearings. A series of petitions to the UN from black leaders in SWA followed, all of which sought to end South African rule and to achieve self government leading to independence.

Because of the UN's failure thus far to settle the legal dispute with South Africa, further legal action was taken by the UN between 1960 and 1966.

In the meanwhile black nationalist movements began to spring up in the territory. The first, SWA National Union (SWANU), was set up in 1959 with the support of the Herero Chiefs Council, and, in 1960 SWA People's Organisation (SWAPO) was founded, based largely among the Ovambo migrant workers. In the meanwhile, in June 1960, Liberia and Ethiopia, announced that they were instituting action against South Africa through the ICJ. They asked the Court to find that the policy of 'apartheid' failed to promote '. . . the material and moral well being and the social progress of the inhabitants . . .' of SWA as provided for in the Mandate. This legal battle lasted 6 years. Finally, on 18th July 1966 the ICJ produced a controversial Opinion advising that it could not rule on the substance of the case because Ethiopia and Liberia had not established any legal right or interest in the matter. By this stage SWAPO had launched its guerilla campaign inside Namibia, and its first clash with the South African police occurred in August 1966. Thus began the militarisation of Ovamboland which came to be known as the 'operational area' subject to martial law.

Two months later the General Assembly, in its Resolution 2145 (XXI) of 27th October 1966, terminated the mandate and declared that henceforth SWA was under the direct responsibility of the UN. In 1967 an Ad Hoc Committee for SWA was created to recommend means by which the territory should be administered to enable the inhabitants to exercise their right of self-determination and independence. This Committee's recommendations led to the creation by the UNGA of the UN Council for SWA to administer the territory until independence. It was renamed the UN council for Namibia in 1968.

In April 1968 the UN Council for Namibia tried to enter the country to take over its administration as mandated by the UNGA. But South Africa refused them landing rights. This led to the direct intervention of the Security Council in the dispute when, by its Resolution SCR 264 of 20th March 1969, it upheld the UNGA's termination of the Mandate, and by its Resolution SCR 269 on 12th August 1969 required South Africa to withdraw its administration from Namibia no later than 4th October 1969. South Africa refused to comply.

As a result the dispute was transferred back to the ICJ, which delivered an Advisory Opinion on 21st June 1971 on 'The Legal Consequences for States of the Continued Presence of South Africa in Namibia'. The ICJ ruled that the mandate had been lawfully terminated, that South Africa's presence was therefore illegal, and that member states should refrain from any dealings with South Africa which would lend support to their presence and administration in Namibia. The Security Council accepted the Opinion by its Resolution SCR 301 of 20th October 1971. South Africa rejected the Opinion.

In March 1972 the UN Secretary-General visited South Africa and Namibia to open negotiations with all the relevant parties on the political future of Namibia. In August 1972 the Security Council authorised the appointment of a Personal Representative of the UN Secretary-General on Namibia who visited South Africa and Namibia from 12th–28th October 1972 to pursue the UN's dialogue with South Africa.

Action in the UN continued. On 17th December 1974 SCR 366, adopted unanimously by the Security Council, demanded that South Africa abolish the 'homelands' (set up in terms of the Odendaal Commission's recommendations of 1964) and remove all discriminatory legislation and practices in Namibia. In June 1975 the South African Prime Minister conceded that the peoples of SWA should be allowed to decide their own future. On 30th January 1976 the Security Council adopted unanimously Resolution SCR 385 calling on South Africa to transfer power to the peoples of Namibia and allow free elections under UN supervision leading to independence for the territory.

A 5-nation 'Contact Group' was established in early 1977 comprising the then 5 western members of the Security Council—UK, France, USA, Canada and West Germany—to negotiate directly with South Africa a plan which would be internationally acceptable for Namibia's independence. To this end the 'Contact Group' held several rounds of talks with South Africa and with SWAPO out of which emerged a detailed Proposal for an independence settlement which was submitted to the Security Council on 10th April 1978.

The Contact Group's Proposal for a Settlement of the Namibian Situation (Document S/12636) provided for free and fair elections for a Consituent Assembly to draw up and adopt an independence constitution prior to the installation of an independent Namibian Government during 1978. It also provided for the establishment by the Security Council of a UN Transition Assistance Group (UNTAG) led by a UN Special Representative.

On 25th April 1978 South Africa announced its acceptance of the Proposal. A setback to the prospects of a peacefully negotiated settlement occurred on 4th May when South African forces raided SWAPO bases in Southern Angola, at Cassinga, leaving 600 dead. The Proposal was endorsed by the Security Council in its Resolution 431 of 27th July 1978 to which South Africa announced its qualified acceptance on 31st July 1978. Following the visit of his newly appointed Special Representative for Namibia, Mr Marti Ahtisaari, to Namibia in August the Secretary General submitted a Report to the Security Council (Document S/12827) on the implementation of the UN Plan (as it was henceforth known). The Security Council approved the Report by Resolution SCR 435 on 29th September 1978.

For the next 10 years discussions continued with all parties on the details of the implementation process, with South Africa raising one problem after another, questioning, *inter alia,* the size of UNTAG (a supervisory UN mixed military-civilian force), the issue of UN impartiality, and the problem of monitoring SWAPO forces at their bases in neighbouring states. The negotiations were often deadlocked, and the date for implementation slipped further and further into the distance. In 1981, following the failure of pre-implementation meeting held in Geneva, South Africa decided that it would not agree to the implementation of the UN Plan until there was agreement on the withdrawal of Cuban troops from neighbouring Angola. South Africa made it clear that this linkage was non-negotiable, although outside the UN Plan *per se*. This issue dominated the subsequent discussions with South Africa until 1988. Throughout this period South African attacks against SWAPO bases in Angola continued. The only substantive advances made during this period was the agreement by all parties in July 1982 of a set of Constitutional Principles designed to guide the Constituent Assembly in drawing up the independence constitution (Document S/15287, Annex B), the negotiation of a Confidential Impartiality Check List in August 1982 (subsequently made public in S/20635 in May 1989), and, in November 1985, the agreement by South Africa on proportional representation as the appropriate system for elections to the Constituent Assembly (S/17658).

It was not until 1988 that sufficient common purpose was established by the principal parties in the Namibia/Angola linkage to allow a regional solution. From May to November 1988 the USA (with the blessing of the USSR) mediated a series of direct talks between South Africa, Angola and Cuba, which culminated in the signature of two agreements in December 1988: a tripartite agreement between South Africa, Angola and Cuba creating the conditions for the implementation of the UN plan and a bilateral agreement between Angola and Cuba setting out a timetable for the staged and total withdrawal of Cuban troops from Angola by July 1991. The Security Council endorsed the two agreements and on 16th February 1989 passed the Enabling Resolution establishing UNTAG and setting the date for the beginning of the transition process at 1st April 1989.

The transition period lasted 10 months, during which the process was supervised by 4,486 military personnel and 1,500 police monitors from 20 countries and some 1,700 civilian election monitors, while the UNHCR supervised the return of over 40,000 exiles. Elections to a 72 member Constituent Assembly took place between the 7th and 11th November 1989. Within 3 months the independence constitution had been drafted. Independence was achieved on 21st March 1990.

Constitutional Development

Following the grant in 1920 of the Mandate, the territory was developed to a certain extent along its own separate constitutional lines. Initially an Advisory Council was constituted consisting of 6 white nominated members to advise the South African-appointed Administrator. In 1925 the SWA Constitution Act No 42 of 1925 was adopted. This gave some limited legislative power to an all-white 18 member Legislative Assembly, but the Governor-General of the Union held an overall veto on the legislative programme. Key functions remained centralised in the South African government, including powers to pass laws on black affairs. The first elections (for the white electorate only) under the 1925 Act were held on 25th May 1926.

The German policy of providing reserves for the indigenous population was gradually extended by South Africa and by 1939, 17 reserves had been established, covering some 59,570 sq km. They were administered in a variety of ways, provided for under the Ovamboland Affairs Proclamation No 27 of 1929, the Okavango Native Territory Proclamation No 32 of 1937, while the Natives Trust Funds Proclamation No 23 of 1939 established the Herero Tribal Trust Fund and authorised the local administration to establish the same for the Dama and Nama peoples. The position of the Eastern Caprivi Strip was different. It was administered up to 1929, under Proclamation No 12 issued by the Governor-General in 1922, by the British High Commissioner of South Africa as if it were a part of the Bechuanaland Protectorate, then from 1929 to 1939 by the Administrator of SWA, and from 1939 to 1977 by the South African Ministry of Bantu Administration and Development. The Rehoboth Baster community had yet another form of government. By Proclamation No 28 of 1923 a limited form of self-government was granted by South Africa, but cancelled in 1924 by the Administrator who transferred all the powers of the Rehoboth 'Kaptein' to the Magistrates of Rehoboth. Several petitions were sent to the League of Nations between then and 1932 calling for the independence of Rehoboth based on their 1885 treaty with the Germans, who had recognised their claim to independence. In 1928 a partly elected Advisory council was established under the overall authority of the Magistrates.

In 1932 the 1925 Constitution Act was amended to extend the powers of the local Legislative Assembly to include education, the police and postal services. A further Amendment of 1939, gave white women in SWA the Vote for the first time. The territory's constitution was further amended by the SWA Affairs Amendment Act, No 23 of 1949, which gave whites direct representation in the South African Parliament.

In 1962 the South African Government appointed the Odendaal Commission of Enquiry to investigate the social, economic and politial conditions in SWA. It reported in 1964. Its recommendations influenced all subsequent constitutional developments in the territory up to independence. The Odendaal Plan recommended the creation of 'homelands' for the various black ethnic groups, with the ultimate intention of leading these homelands to their separate independence. Black reserves were accordingly enlarged from about 26 per cent to nearly 40 per cent of the total land area. The system of government for the whites was to stay as it was although some functions would be transferred to the South African government. Accordingly the proposed areas for the Rehoboth Basters and Namaland were to be administered by the Department of Coloured Affairs in South Africa while the black 'homelands' were to be administered by its Department of Bantu Administration and Development. The system of government for the 'homelands' (Okavangoland, Ovamboland, Kaokaveld, Damaraland, Hereroland, East Caprivi and Namaland) was to consist of a Legislative Council with limited political autonomy, these Councils to comprise a majority of ex-officio chiefs and headmen and a minority of elected representatives, and Executive Councils elected by the Legislative Councils. The Odendaal Plan was only partially implemented, but was finally abandoned, unfinished, in 1977.

Ovamboland was the first to be declared a 'self-governing' area and elections were held to a 56 member Legislative Council (although SWAPO did not take part in the election); Kavango was the second; while a Proclamation of 22nd October 1974 provided for 'self-government' for Eastern Caprivi with effect from 1st April 1976. At the same time, a section of the Bantu Laws Amendment Act, No 7 of 1973, provided for further land to be reserved for the indigenous population groups, the land to be vested in the South African Bantu Trust for this purpose. Namaland received a measure of local autonomy when an Advisory Council for Namaland was instituted in 1976 and in May 1976 Rehoboth was granted full self-government. The Rehoboth Self-Government Act, No 56 of 1976, provided for the return of an elected Volksraad and Kapteinsraad. Under elections held there in 1977, Dr Ben Africa was elected the first Baster Kaptein in over 70 years, and in 1979 Hans Diergaardt was elected in a re-run. Rehoboth was the only 'homeland' to reach this advanced stage.

At the same time as these steps towards self-government in the 'homelands' were being undertaken, South Africa established in 1973 the Prime Minister's Advisory Council for SWA. Each population group sent 1–2 representatives to this body where the future of the territory was discussed. About 40 delegates attended its meetings through 1973/74. This body was the direct predecessor of the Turnhalle Constitutional Conference, which opened in Windhoek on 1st September 1975 and ran until November 1977, whose purpose was to draft a Constitution for the territory. It brought together 156 delegates representing all 11 recognised ethnic groups, including whites (SWAPO did not participate). Some 18 months later, in March 1977, a draft constitution was completed. It provided for a 3 tier system of ethnic government.

The SWA Constitution Act was further amended by Amendment No 95 of 1977 which gave the State President of South Africa powers to pass laws for the territory, significantly, '. . . with a view to the eventual independence . . .' of the country and provided for the appointment of an Administrator-General (AG) for SWA/Namibia as the direct representative of the State President. The 1977 Amendment also dealt with Walvis Bay, transferring its administration back to the Cape Province. (From 1884 to 1922 it was administered from the Cape, whence for practical reasons its administration was transferred to SWA until 1977). The 1977 Amendment also abolished direct representation in the South African Parliament of 6 MPs from SWA, a situation which had prevailed since 1949. The AG abolished many discriminatory laws including significantly the pass laws, influx control (except in the military 'operational area' in the North), and the prohibition on mixed marriages. Other petty apartheid laws were also gradually abolished while responsibility for several government departments, notably the departments of Bantu Administration, Development and Education, and the Coloured, Rehoboth and Nama Relations, were transferred to the AG's office from Pretoria.

Following the final meeting of the Turnhalle Constitution Conference in November 1977 a political movement was formed known as the Democratic Turnhalle Alliance (DTA) an alliance of all the groups, except the National Party of SWA, who had attended the Turnhalle talks. The DTA fundamentally objected to the ethnic basis of the Turnhalle draft constitution, and it produced its own anti-discriminatory constitutional proposals. South Africa then organised internal elections between the 4th and 8th December 1978, to test the Turnhalle proposals, in spite of its acceptance earlier in 1978 of the UN Plan. The DTA won 82 per cent of the vote (in a poll of 80.3 per cent of the registered electorate) in the first ever one-man-one-vote election in the territory. (SWAPO did not participate). Thus the DTA received the majority of the seats (41 out of 50) in the Constituent Assembly. This body was transformed into a National Assembly in May 1979, and it received executive powers with the creation of a 12 member Council of Ministers on 1st July 1980. This 'internal government' subsequently abolished all the remaining aspects of the formal apartheid laws.

In 1980 second tier Representative Authorities for 9 ethnic groups were created in terms of an umbrella decree issued by the AG, the Proclamation AG8 of 1980. The created Representative

Authorities for Whites, Coloureds, Ovambos, Kavangos, Caprivians, Damaras, Namas, Tswanas and Hereros. Rehoboth was not covered because it had its own government since 1976. Elections were held between 11th and 13th November 1980 to most of the second tier Authorities—except those in the 'operational area'. The second tier Authorities each had a small Executive Committee, a Legislative Assembly and an Administration responsible for the running of functions which had been delegated to them—limited to welfare, agriculture, education and community services.

In January 1983 the Council of Ministers resigned in a dispute with the AG of the time. This resulted in the return of direct rule by the AG. This remained the position until 17th June 1985 when South Africa appointed, without further elections, a Transitional Government of National Unity (TGNU). Established by Proclamation R101 of the State President, executive authority was vested in an 8 member 'Cabinet', and legislative authority was vested in a 62 member 'National Assembly', whose members were nominated by 6 political groups, including the DTA, which had participated in a further constitution-making exercise, as the Multi-Party Conference (MPC), from 12th November 1983 to June 1985. The MPC had drawn up a Bill of Fundamental Rights, which was adopted by the TGNU. Although the TGNU was given fairly wide legislative powers, the AG, and ultimately the South African President, retained the power of veto over bills. The TGNU was formally dissolved in February 1989 in preparation for the beginning of the implementation of the UN Plan for independence on 1st April 1989.

The Constitution

The Constitution entered into force on independence day. It provides for a multi-party democracy, in a unitary state. It includes 25 entrenched clauses providing for a wide range of fundamental human rights and freedoms. There is no death sentence nor detention without trial, and the practice and ideology of apartheid is expressly forbidden.

The President is Head of State and Government and Commander-in-Chief of the Defence Force. He jointly exercises executive power with the Cabinet. Elected by direct, universal and equal suffrage, he must receive more than 50 per cent of the votes cast to be so elected, and he is limited to two terms of 5 years each. The Prime Minister is the leader of Government business in Parliament. Although the President has the power to appoint the Prime Minister and Cabinet Ministers, the National Assembly has the power to revoke any appointment by a majority vote.

Legislative Power is vested in the National Assembly, which comprises 72 elected members and up to 6 nominated but non-voting members. Each serves for a maximum term of 5 years.

There is provision for an upper house, the National Council (yet to be established), which will consist of 2 members from each of the 13 regions (delimited in June 1991) to be elected from amongst their members by Regional Councils (yet to be elected). The term of office of upper house members is 6 years.

The constitution guarantees the independence of the Judiciary.

Below national level the constitution provides for the establishment of regional and local government structures. The regional boundaries were determined on a geographical basis by a Delimitation Commission (established by the National Assembly on 8th August 1990) and which reported in June 1991. Elections on a constituency basis, on a first-past-the-post system, will be held in 1992 to elect the Regional Councils, who will then elect members to serve on the National Council.

Apart from the entrenched clauses on fundamental rights amendments to the Constitution can only be made by two thirds majorities of the membership of both houses. This provision is entrenched. There is also provision for a referendum in the event of the National Council failing to meet the required two thirds vote. Under the Transitional Provisions the Constituent Assembly became the first National Assembly with effect from the date of independence. Until a National Council is elected, the National Assembly has the sole legislative making power. The Delimitation Commission reported to the President with proposals for boundaries of regions and local authorities in June 1991. Elections for Local Authories are expected to be held early in 1992, with elections to Regional Councils due one month later, and lastly elections to the first National Council one month later again. On the basis of this prescribed timetable, elections to all levels should be completed by mid-1992.

Government

After over 25 years of exile, SWAPO officials began to return to Namibia from mid-June 1989. Ten political parties, including SWAPO, registered to take part in the UN supervised elections which were held between 7th and 11th November 1989. Over 96 per cent or 676,000 out of a registered total of 701,433 voters (including 240,096 in Ovamboland) voted in the election. On the basis of proportional representation, SWAPO gained 41 seats out of the 72 in the Constituent Assembly (with 57.33 per cent of the vote), the DTA 21 seats (with 28.55 per cent), the United Democratic Front (UDF) 4 seats (with 5.65 per cent), Action Christian National (ACN) 3 seats (with 3.54 per cent), National Patriotic Front (NPF) 1 seat (with 1.59 per cent), and the Namibia National Front (NNF) 1 seat (with 0.80 per cent). The remaining three parties—Christian Democratic Action (CDA), SWAPO Democrats (SWAPO-D) and the Namibia National Democratic Party (NNDP) did not get sufficient votes to gain any seats (the quota required to secure a seat being 9,317 votes).

Dr Sam Nujoma was elected on 16th February 1990 by the Constituent Assembly to be the first President of an independent Namibia and the Constituent Assembly was transformed into the country's first National Assembly on independence. SWAPO, as the majority party, named the Cabinet Ministers to form the first Government on independence.

HEAD OF STATE

The President: His Excellency Dr Sam Nujoma

THE CABINET

Prime Minister: Hon Hage Geingob
Minister of Foreign Affairs: Hon Theo-Ben Gurirab
Minister of Defence: Hon Peter Mueshihange
Minister of Information & Broadcasting: Hon Hidipo Hamutenya
Minister of Wildlife, Conservation & Tourism: Hon Nico Bessinger
Minister of Trade & Industry: Hon Ben Amathila
Minister of Lands, Resettlement & Rehabilitation: Hon Marco Hausiku
Minister of Home Affairs: Hon Hifikepunye Pohamba
Minister of Labour, Public Service & Manpower Development: Hon Hendrik Wootbooi
Minister of Mines & Energy: Hon Andimba Toivo ya Toivo
Minister of Education and Culture: Hon Nahas Angula
Minister of Health & Social Services: Hon Dr Nicky Iyambo
Minister of Local Government & Housing: Hon Dr Libertine Amathila
Minister of Finance: Hon Dr Otto Herrigel
Minister of Agriculture, Water & Rural Development: Hon Gert Hanekom
Minister for Security: (Vacant)
Minister of Works, Transport & Communications: Hon Richard Kapelwa
Minister of Justice: Hon Dr Ngarikutuke (Ernest) Tjiriange
Minister of Fisheries and Marine Resources: Hon Helmut Angula
Minister of Youth and Sports: Hon Ms Pendukeni Ithana

DEPUTY MINISTERS

Foreign Affairs: Hon Ms Netumbo Ndaitwah
Defence: Hon Phillemon Malima
Information and Broadcasting: Hon Daniel Tjongarero
Wildlife Conservation and Tourism: Hon Ben Ulenga
Trade and Industry: Hon Anton von Wietersheim
Lands, Resettlement and Rehabilitation: Hon Marcus Shivute
Home Affairs: Hon Nangolo Ithete
Labour, Public Service and Manpower Development: Hon Hadino Hishongwa
Mines and Energy: Hon Jesaya Nyamu
Education and Culture: Hon Buddy Wentworth
Local Government and Housing: Hon Jerry Ekandjo
Agriculture, Water and Rural Development: Hon Dr Kaire Mbuende
Security: Hon Peter Tsheehama
Works, Transport and Communications: Hon Klaus Dierks
Justice: Hon Reinhard Rukoro
Fisheries and Marine Resources: (Vacant)
Youth and Sports: Reggie Diergaardt
Finance: Rick Kukuri
Health and Social Services: Dr Iyambo Indongo

MINISTRIES AND GOVERNMENT DEPARTMENTS

CABINET SECRETARY

Nangolo Mbumba

PRESIDENT'S OFFICE

Permanent Secretary: Eddie Amkongo

PRIME MINISTER'S OFFICE

Permanent Secretary: Petrus Damaseb

FOREIGN AFFAIRS

Permanent Secretary: Andreas Guibeb

DEFENCE

Permanent Secretary: Frans Kapofi

INFORMATION AND BROADCASTING

Permanent Secretary: Vezera Kandetu

WILDLIFE, NATURE CONSERVATION AND TOURISM

Permanent Secretary: Hanno Rumpf

TRADE AND INDUSTRY

Permanent Secretary: Tsudao Gurirab

LANDS, RESETTLEMENT AND REHABILITATION

Permanent Secretary: Ms Vlitala Hiveluah

HOME AFFAIRS

Permanent Secretary: Ndali Kamati

LABOUR, PUBLIC SERVICE AND MANPOWER DEVELOPMENT

Permanent Secretary: Tuli Hiveluah

MINES AND ENERGY

Permanent Secretary: Dr Leake Hangala

EDUCATION, CULTURE AND SPORT

Permanent Secretary: Vitalis Ankama

HEALTH AND SOCIAL SERVICES

Permanent Secretary: Dr Solomon Amadhila

LOCAL GOVERNMENT AND HOUSING

Permanent Secretary: Nghidimondjila Shoombe

FINANCE
Permanent Secretary: Godfrey Gaoseb

AGRICULTURE, FISHERIES, WATER AND RURAL DEVELOPMENT
Permanent Secretary, Fisheries and Marine Resources: Calle Schlettwein
Permanent Secretary, Agriculture Water and Rural Development: Vilho Nghipondoka

WORKS, TRANSPORT AND COMMUNICATIONS
Permanent Secretary: Dr Peingeondjabi Shipoh

SECURITY
Permanent Secretary: (Vacant)

JUSTICE
Permanent Secretary: Dr Albert Kanawa

Republic of Nauru

The Republic of Nauru consists of a single island of approximately 2,130 hectares lying 42 km south of the equator at 0°32′S. and 166°56′E. Nauru's nearest neighbour, 305 km to the east, is Ocean Island, part of the Republic of Kiribati. The island is 4,000 km from Sydney, 4,100 km from Honolulu, and 4,800 km from Tokyo. Nauruan time is 12 hours in advance of GMT.

Approximately oval and about 20 km in circumference, the island is surrounded by a coral reef, which is exposed at low tide, and by a sandy beach from which the ground rises forming a fertile belt between 150 and 300 metres wide encircling the island. Inland coral cliffs rise to a height of up to 30 metres and merge with the central plateau, the highest point of which is 65 metres above sea level. The plateau is largely composed of phosphate rock and, where this has been removed, there is a rugged terrain of coral pinnacles up to 15 metres high.

The climate is tropical but is tempered by sea breezes. Average annual rainfall since 1950 has been 2,060 mm but there have been marked deviations from this average; as many as 4,572 mm and as few as 305 mm have been recorded since 1940. The only fertile areas are the narrow coastal belt where coconut palms and pandanus trees grow and the land surrounding Buada lagoon where bananas, pineapples and some vegetables are grown. Erratic rainfall and the highly porous nature of the soil severely restrict cultivation and local requirements of fruit and vegetables are mostly met by imports from Australia and New Zealand. Some sparse secondary vegetation grows over the coral pinnacles left by the removal of phosphate. There are few indigenous animals and birdlife is not plentiful. At times fish are abundant in the deep waters surrounding the island.

The Nauruan people are mainly of mixed Polynesian, Micronesian and Melanesian origin but are most closely related to the Polynesians. The Nauruan language provides no information about the origin of the people. English is understood by all Nauruans. At the last census, which was held on 13th May 1983, the Nauruan population was 4,964; other Pacific Islanders were 2,134; Asians 682 and Caucasians 262, making a total of 8,042.

Economy

The economy of Nauru is heavily dependent upon the extraction of phosphate from what is one of the world's richest deposits (averaging 38 per cent phosphorus pentoxide (P_2O_5) with few impurities). 1,500 of the island's 2,130 hectares are classified as phosphate bearing and represent a total of more than 96 million tonnes. Between 1922 and 30th June 1984, 64,186,586 tonnes of phosphate was exported. It has been estimated that some 32 million tonnes of phosphate remains to be worked of which about 1.5 million tonnes of phosphate are mined each year. The Nauru Phosphate Corporation was established to run the industry from 1st July 1970 and provides employment for Nauruans, Kiribati and Tuvaluan Islanders, Chinese and Europeans as well as some Filipinos. The majority of Nauruans not employed in the phosphate industry are employed in either the Public Service or by the Nauru Local Government Council and the Nauru Corporation. Phosphate revenues give Nauru one of the highest per capital incomes in the world.

Considerable investment has been made since independence in the development of international communications. Nauru Pacific Line owned by the Local Government Council owns six ships and Air Nauru, owned by the Government since 1971, operates scheduled services to several South Pacific islands and destinations on the Pacific run. At the end of 1975 a Satellite/Earth telecommunications station was established augmenting the existing VHF radio facilities.

Nauru formed its own insurance corporation in November 1974. The Corporation is the sole licensed insurer on Nauru and underwrites all classes of general insurance including aviation and marine. Nauru Insurance Corporation is constituted under an Act of Parliament and all liabilities incurred by the Corporation are guaranteed by the Republic of Nauru. The government hopes to develop a local fishing industry and the Nauru Fishing Corporation was formed in 1979. It is owned by Nauru Local Government Council. Also, considerable investments have been made abroad to provide for the period when phosphate production begins to decline.

History

The first European to visit Nauru was Captain John Fearn of the whaling ship *Hunter* in 1798. He called it Pleasant Island and noted that it was 'extremely populous' with 'houses in great number'. During the 19th century various traders, beachcombers, etc., established themselves on the island without it coming under the formal control of any of the European powers. By the Anglo-German Convention of 1886 the island was allocated to the German sphere of interest and reverted to its native name of Nauru. German occupation began on 1st October 1888 when the gunboat *Eber* arrived carrying a German Commissioner, whose initial task was the restoration of peace between the twelve tribes living on the island. The earlier arrival of firearms and alcohol had upset the balance between the tribes and precipitated a ten year war which reduced the population to little over 900 in 1888 compared with the figure of 1,400 observed in 1843. Apart from banning alcohol and restoring order the Germans did little to foster the development of Nauru until after the arrival of the Reverend Delaporte, who initiated education alongside Christianity (which had been introduced a few years earlier).

During World War I the Germans surrendered Nauru to an Australian Expeditionary Force on 6th November 1914 and the island passed under British administration. The Germans formally renounced their title to Nauru by the Treaty of Versailles in 1919 and in 1920 Nauru became a British mandated territory under the League of Nations. Although Britain, Australia and New Zealand accepted the Trustee Mandate jointly, the administration of the island was conducted on their behalf by Australia. The three Governments established the British Phosphate Commissioners, who bought out the existing Pacific Phosphate Company and ran the industry.

Nauru was extensively damaged in World War II. While the allies still controlled the island in 1940, the installations were damaged by German naval gunfire and, following the Japanese occupation, the allies bombed the airfield. 1,200 Nauruans were deported by the Japanese to Truk in the Carolines where 463 died of starvation, disease, bombing and brutality. Only 591 Nauruans remained on Nauru when the Japanese surrendered on 13th September 1945 and the 737 survivors from Truk were returned to Nauru on 31st January 1946, which is remembered in Nauru as the 'Day of Deliverance'. On 1st November 1947 the General Assembly of the United Nations approved a Trusteeship Agreement for the Territory of Nauru submitted by the Governments of Australia, New Zealand and the United Kingdom on the same lines as the Mandate under the League of Nations.

Constitutional Development

The first elections to be held on Nauru took place on 15th December 1951 for the Nauru Local Government Council, which elected Timothy Detudamo as Head Chief. The Council was, however, advisory only and in 1953 the United Nations Mission to the territory pressed for Nauru to have increased self-government.

In the period from 1951 until 1964 discussion of Nauru's future centred on the possibility of resettling the island's population on another island, whose economic future would not be clouded by the eventual exhaustion of the phosphate deposits. Many locations, including sites on the Australian mainland near Brisbane and Sydney, Prince of Wales Island and Fraser Island off Marysborough in Queensland, and, later, Curtis Island in Gladstone Harbour, were discussed as sites for possible resettlement. The proposal was abandoned in 1964 because the Nauruans under the leadership of Hammer DeRoburt, who had been elected head Chief in 1955, were unhappy about a solution under which they did not retain some measure of sovereignty.

After 1964 discussions of Nauru's future were closely bound up with the Nauruan efforts to gain control of the phosphate extraction industry. In June 1967 the British, Australian and New Zealand Governments reached agreement in principle with the Nauruans for the sale to Nauru of the assets of the British Phosphate Commissioners. The details were subsequently incorporated in the Nauru Phosphate Agreement, 1967, which provided for payment over the three years ending June 1970. The price was later agreed at about $A21 million, which was paid by April 1969. Earlier, in December 1965, the Australian Parliament passed legislation establishing the Nauru Legislative Council, the first elections for which were held on 25th January 1966 and whose first session was held on the 20th anniversary of Nauru's Day of Deliverance from the Japanese, 31st January 1966. In October 1967 agreement was reached for Nauru to become an independent Republic on 31st January 1968. The UN General Assembly agreed to terminate the Trusteeship Agreement the same day. A Parliament of 18 members was elected and Hammer DeRoburt was elected the Republic's first President on 31st January 1968 for a term of three years, and was re-elected in January 1971 and December 1973. Mr Bernard Dowiyogo was elected President after the general elections of December 1976 and November 1977. He was succeeded by Mr Lagumot Harris in April 1978. Mr Hammer DeRoburt was re-elected President on 11th May 1978, he resigned as President on 7th December 1978, and was re-elected President on 8th December 1978. He was re-elected President after elections in 1980, 1983, 1986 and 1987. Mr Kenas Aroi was elected President on 17th August 1989 following a vote of no confidence. Mr Aroi was not able to stand for re-election in December 1989 after a stroke in November and Mr Bernard Dowiyogo returned to the Presidency.

Nauru has not applied for membership of the United Nations, but plays an active part in several United Nations agencies.

Nauru is a member of the South Pacific Commission, the South Pacific Forum, the Universal Postal Union, the International Telecommunication Union and the Economic and Social Council for Asia and the Pacific.

Nauru and the Commonwealth

In November 1968, in response to a request by the Government of Nauru, Commonwealth Heads of Government agreed that Nauru should be accorded the status of a special member of the Commonwealth. This 'special membership' was devised in close consultation with the Government of

Nauru; under it Nauru has all the benefits of Commonwealth membership, except that it does not participate in full regular (as distinct from regional) meetings of Commonwealth Heads of Government.

Government

HEAD OF STATE
President: His Excellency The Hon Bernard Dowiyogo, MP

GOVERNMENT CABINET
Minister for External Affairs, Minister for Internal Affairs, Minister for Island Development and Industry, Minister for Civil Aviation Authority and Minister responsible for the Public Service: His Excellency the Hon. Bernard Dowiyogo, MP
Minister of Works and Community Services and Minister assisting the President: The Hon Vinson Detenamo, MP
Minister for Justice: The Hon Pres Nimes Ekwona
Minister for Health and Education: The Hon Vinci Clodumar, MP
Minister for Finance: The Hon Kinza Clodumar, MP
Attorney-General, Secretary for Justice: Mr William Halm

JUDICIARY
Chief Justice: Sir Gaven John Donne, KBE
Presidential Counsel: Mr Leo Keke

GOVERNMENT DEPARTMENTS

CHIEF SECRETARY'S DEPARTMENT
Chief Secretary: Mr Kelly Emiu (Acting)

DEPARTMENT OF EXTERNAL AFFAIRS
Secretary: Mr Obeira Menke (Acting)

DEPARTMENT OF FINANCE
Secretary: Mr R R Ghambir (Acting)

DEPARTMENT OF AUDIT
Director: Mr J Ganesan

DEPARTMENT OF ISLAND DEVELOPMENT AND INDUSTRY
Secretary: Mr Felix Kun

DEPARTMENT OF HEALTH AND EDUCATION
Secretary: Dr Ludwig Keke (Acting)

DEPARTMENT OF JUSTICE
Secretary: Mr William Halm

DEPARTMENT OF WORKS
Secretary: Mr Creswick Agogenang

DIRECTORATE OF CIVIL AVIATION
Director: Mr Barry Cranston

DIRECTORATE OF THE NAURU POLICE FORCE
Director: Insp Alf Itsimaera

New Zealand

Capital: Wellington

THE ISLAND TERRITORY OF TOKELAU AND THE ROSS DEPENDENCY

The boundaries of New Zealand were defined in 1863 as lying between 33° and 53°S. latitude and 162°E. and 173°W. longitude. New Zealand therefore consisted of the North Island and the South Island together with the smaller and sparsely-populated Stewart Island, which lies south of the South Island. The boundaries included the Chatham and Pitt Islands, some 850 km east of Christchurch, and the Auckland Islands, which are south of the South Island. Other islands lying within this group were Three Kings Islands, Great Barrier Island, Solander Island, The Snares, Campbell Island, Bounty Island and the Antipodes Islands. The North Island, the South Island and Stewart Island extend over a distance of more than 1,600 km. Wellington was declared the capital of New Zealand in 1865.

By Proclamation dated 21st July 1887 the group of islands called the Kermadec Islands, lying between 29° and 32°S. latitude and 177° and 180°W. longitude, was annexed to New Zealand. The principal islands are Raoul Island or Sunday Island, and Macauley Island. The other islands are Curtis Island and L'Esperance Rock. Raoul Island, comprising an area of 28 sq km, rises to a height of 517 m and is covered with forest.

The coasts of the Ross Sea and adjacent islands, south of 60°S. latitude and between 160°E. and 150°W. longitude, were brought within the jurisdiction of New Zealand by Order in Council on 30th July 1923.*

The total area of New Zealand, exclusive of the Island Territories and the Ross Dependency, is 268,808 sq km (North Island 114,829 sq km, South Island 153,979 sq km). Less than one quarter of the land surface lies below 200 m. In the North Island the mountain system runs generally in a south-westerly direction parallel to the coast. Approximately one-tenth of the surface is covered by mountain ranges. Except for the volcanic peaks Egmont (2,518 m), Ruapehu (2,797 m), Ngauruhoe (2,290 m) and Tongariro (1,968 m) the mountains do not exceed 1,830 m. In the South Island the Southern Alps run almost the entire length of the island. Mount Cook (3,764 m) is in the centre and 19 peaks are over 3,000 m. There are numerous swift flowing rivers but most are useless for navigation. In the North Island the main rivers are the Waikato, Wanganui, Rangitikei, Rangitaiki and Manawatu; in the South Island the Clutha, Taieri, Mataura, Waiau, Clarence, Waitaki and Oreti. There are numerous lakes, mostly at high altitude in remote and rugged country. The most important are Lake Taupo (606 sq km) in the North Island and Lake Wakatipu (293 sq km) and Te Anau (344 sq km) in the South Island. The islands of New Zealand are part of the unstable circum-Pacific mobile belt, a region where volcanoes are active and where the earth's crust has long been buckling and breaking at a geologically rapid rate of change. The Rotorua area of the North Island is world famous for its geo-thermal activities, boiling lakes, boiling mud, geysers, etc.

The climate is temperate and changeable, very similar to that in Britain except that there is a higher average level of sunshine. Normal temperatures range from 6.44°C in June to 16.2°C in January. The average rainfall for the greater part of the country is from 600–1,500 mm, but because of the mountain ranges it can vary from as much as 8,000 mm to 300 mm.

There are 17.7 million hectares (June 1988) of occupied farmland. In June 1988 there were 64.60 million sheep, 3.2 million dairy cattle and 4.86 million beef cattle.

A census of population is taken every five years, the last being in March 1991 when the population was 3,429,364. In 1990 the birth rate was 17.8 per thousand and the death rate was 7.85 per thousand.

English is the official language and used by all; but a proportion of the Maori population of 404,775, comprising 12 per cent of the total population, are bilingual in English and Maori.

Christianity is the main religion and the 1986 census showed the chief groups to be Church of England 24.7 per cent, Presbyterian 18.3 per cent, Roman Catholic 15.5 per cent and Methodist 4.8 per cent. Other denominations and sects include Ratana (Maori).

Primary and secondary education is free and universal. University education is accessible to all holders of the University Entrance Examination and about one-tenth of pupils leaving Secondary Schools go to Universities. Technical institutes have also been established. There is no illiteracy.

The urban centres which have the main concentrations of population are in the North Island, Auckland (885,400), Wellington (324,800), Hamilton (123,200), Napier/Hastings (109,900), Tauranga

* The Ross Dependency, see page 298.

For further information about New Zealand, see *New Zealand Official Year Book*.

(70,700), and Palmerston North (70,800) and in the South Island, Christchurch (306,900) Dunedin (109,400) and Invercargill (52,400).

The main airports are Auckland International Airport at Mangere with 3,291 metres of runway, Christchurch with 2,442 metres and Wellington with 1,935 metres. The major domestic and international airlines have been merged to form one company known as Air New Zealand. In 1989 there were about 93,000 km of road and about 4,300 km of 1067 mm gauge railway.

The unit of currency is the New Zealand dollar.

The principal products and their export values in the year ended June 1991 were: meat (NZ$2,585.0 million); dairy products (NZ$2,015.0 million); wool (NZ$962.7 million); hides, skins and leather (NZ$559.0 million); forest products (NZ$1,510.5 million); fruit and vegetables (NZ$1,068.4 million) and fish (NZ$537.5 million). In 1990 manufactured exports were valued at NZ$2,189.3 million. New Zealand is one of the largest exporters in the world of meat, dairy produce and wool and is heavily dependent on the export of pastoral products. There are probably more farm animals in proportion to population than in any other country. The value of goods exported forms a much higher percentage, about 21 per cent, of GDP than for most countries.

The bulk of New Zealand's electricity is generated from hydro resources with the remainder coming from thermal stations all of which are in the North Island. The largest of these is a 1,000 MW gas and coal-fired thermal station at Huntly.

Four natural gas fields are in operation producing a light crude oil (condensate) as a joint product with the gas. The onshore field at Kapuni has produced natural gas and associated hydrocarbons since 1970 while the much larger offshore Maui field was commissioned in May 1979. Recoverable gas reserves are estimated at 2,934 billion cubic feet (1988) from the two fields. Recoverable oil reserves were estimated at 146.32 million stock tank barrels (1988).

In 1988 it was estimated that the total recoverable reserves of coal of all types was 117,620 petajoules (PJ). This includes 96,450 PJ of lignites, assuming 50 per cent of the reserves to be economically recoverable. Studies are being made about the possible development of a liquid fuel industry based on lignite deposits.

New Zealand has concluded an agreement on Closer Economic Relations with Australia which became effective on 1st January 1983 and which will eventually remove all barriers to trade between the two countries.

History

New Zealand was first discovered and settled by the ancestors of its present Polynesian inhabitants some time before AD 1000. Over the centuries further immigrants arrived; and as their numbers increased they spread over the North Island until the whole island was divided up among a number of tribal communities, each under its own chief, each claiming descent from one or other of the crews of the canoes which had brought their ancestors from overseas. The South Island, where the climate was less congenial, was more sparsely inhabited; but at the time when contact with Europe began, it is estimated that the total population may have been more than 100,000 persons. The name Maori, meaning 'normal' (indigenous) person, used to describe these peoples, did not come into use until the nineteenth century.

The first European to sight New Zealand, on 13th December 1642, was the Dutchman Abel Janszoon Tasman. An employee of the Dutch East India Company, he was searching on behalf of the Company in Java for the legendary southern continent which geographers then believed must exist in the southern hemisphere. He charted part of the west coast of the South Island, and, hoping that he had found part of the continent he was seeking, named it Staaten Landt, that being the name of the land discovered south of South America and believed to be part of the same continent. When the latter land was found to be an island, the new land was renamed Niew Zeeland, after the Dutch province. Although he did not land, Tasman found the inhabitants hostile and the land poor; no further European visitor touched its shores for over a century.

The next visitor was Lieutenant, later Captain, James Cook, preceding the Frenchman de Surville by only two months. Cook, who was sailing under the auspices of the Royal Society and the Admiralty, with the scientist Joseph Banks on board, had made a further search for the southern continent before sailing west to look for the land which Tasman had discovered. On 7th October 1769 he sighted the eastern shores of the North Island, and in the months that followed circumnavigated the country and brilliantly charted its shores, proving that it consisted of two main islands. He was followed later by other explorers, Marion de Fresne, Crozet, d'Entrecasteaux and Vancouver, among others.

Cook found the inhabitants generally friendly; and his reports of good harbours, of the abundance of seals, and of the existance of timber and flax later attracted the attention of sealers and traders. Many of these came from the newly established community of Sydney across the Tasman Sea; but the existence of whales also brought whalers from America, Britain and France. Among the first settlers were the missionaries, organized initially by the Reverend Samuel Marsden from New South Wales, who aimed to assist the Maoris and to introduce European farming. At the end of the 1830s a slump in New South Wales increased the inflow of settlers, and by 1839 it was estimated that there were 2,000 of them, and that 130 ships were calling annually at the Bay of Islands.

The arrival of sailors, traders, missionaries and settlers in a land lacking an established administration and a rule of law, and their inter-relationship with the Maoris, whose traditional customs began to break down under the impact of association with the West, gave rise to problems which the British Government were at first reluctant to face. Cook's declarations of British sovereignty in 1769 and 1770 were repudiated; and as late as 1828 New Zealand was named in a British Act as a place not under British sovereignty. However, the need for action led the Governor of New South Wales to take, or be given, powers to try to maintain order. In 1814 Thomas Kendall, a missionary, was made a Justice of the Peace to assist in bringing British offenders to justice in the courts of New South Wales; and the Reverend John Gare Butler was made a Magistrate in 1819 with jurisdiction over the British settlements. In 1828 the jurisdiction of the courts of New South Wales was extended to deal with all kinds of offences committed by British subjects within the islands of New Zealand. In 1832 James Busby was appointed as British Resident at the Bay of Islands. His appointment indicated that the British Government still looked upon New Zealand as an independent country, but legislation to give him authority failed on the grounds that it was not lawful to legislate for an independent country. Two years later, in 1835, as a counter to the activities of the French Baron de Thierry, Busby convened an assembly of chiefs who signed a Declaration of Independence which was recognised by the Crown. Finally, pressure by settlers, traders and missionaries, and the clear need to protect the Maoris and to control the settlers, who were about to be re-inforced by additional emigrants sent by Edward Gibbon Wakefield's New Zealand Association, together with a suspicion that other nations had become interested, led the British Government to intervene more directly. Letters Patent of 5th June 1839 authorised the Government of New South Wales to include within the boundaries of that Colony any territory in New Zealand that might be acquired in sovereignty; and Captain Hobson landed in the Bay of Islands on 29th January 1840 and assumed the office of Lieutenant-Governor. Hobson was instructed to treat with the Maoris as an independent nation for recognition of the Queen's sovereignty over the whole of the country or over any parts which they might be willing to cede. A meeting of Chiefs was held at Waitangi on 5th February, and on the 6th February 1840 forty-six chiefs signed the Treaty of Waitangi ceding sovereignty to Queen Victoria; and their example was followed by many others. Finally, on 21st May, Hobson issued two proclamations, one declaring British sovereignty over the North Island by virtue of the cession of the Treaty of Waitangi, and the other over all the islands of New Zealand from 34° 30′N. to 47° 10′S., and from 166° 5′E. to 179°E. by virtue of the right of discovery by Cook. This strip in fact included not only Fiji but the Marshall Islands and even Wake. New Zealand remained as part of New South Wales until 16th November 1840, when Letters Patent made it a separate colony. The boundaries were corrected by the charter of April 1842.

The signing of the Treaty of Waitangi is commemorated annually on 6th February.

The date on which Queen Victoria assumed the sovereignty of New Zealand also marked the beginning of the 'hungry forties' in Britain where many of those displaced by the industrial revolution felt that their only hope for the future was to emigrate. The propaganda of the New Zealand Company, which had obtained a Royal Charter in 1840, turned attention to the opportunities which might exist in the new Colony with its temperate climate; and the stream of immigrants into New Zealand was such that by 1858 the newcomers had begun to outnumber the Maoris. Many of these settlers were assisted by the New Zealand Company until it lost its Charter in 1850. These European New Zealanders pressured the Maoris, not all of whom wished to sell land under the crown pre-emption system inaugurated by the Treaty of Waitangi. Disputes arose, resulting in greater unity among the Maoris, in a stiffening of their resistance to encroachment and finally in the Maori wars from 1860 to 1872. The defeat of the Maoris appeared likely at first to be disastrous for them; but the realisation by the now much more populous race that both had their part to play in the future of the country led to improved relations, to the greater integration of the Maori people into the life of the country, to returning pride in their Maori heritage and to an increased birthrate.

The hopes of quick prosperity held out to its settlers by the New Zealand Company were not at first realised. Timber and flax remained important articles of export, but wool soon became still more important. Meat was exported to the gold miners in Australia; and the discovery of gold in Otago in 1865 not only itself increased prosperity but led to an influx of miners to provide an additional market for the farmers. The slump of the 1880s was lightened by the departure to England in 1882 of the first ship carrying refrigerated meat, and this was the herald of a prosperity built on wool, meat and dairy produce which, with an interval during the great slump, has continued until the present.

The development of the country was furthered during the 1870s by the financial policy of Julius (later Sir Julius) Vogel who borrowed on a large scale to develop government-controlled communications and to double the population through immigration schemes; but this policy, while bringing the provinces closer together, also aggravated the effects of the slump. During the 1890s R J Seddon brought in a series of laws dealing among other things with land, income tax, old age pensions, factory conditions, and industrial arbitration; laws which were to make New Zealand for a time probably the most socially progressive state in the world. The Boer War and the First World War brought New Zealand on to the world stage and to a full realization of her nationhood. The development of New Zealand into the first Welfare State gained momentum from 1936. The Second World War brought New Zealand still more into the world arena, and the war with Japan stressed the importance of her role in East Asia and the Pacific. This was reinforced by participation in military operations in Korea, Malaysia, and Vietnam. In

1951 she concluded an important defensive alliance with Australia and the United States (ANZUS). New Zealand has taken a full part in both the Commonwealth and United Nations.

Constitutional Development

By the Proclamation of 21st May 1840 New Zealand became British Territory. On 16th June 1840 the laws of New South Wales were, so far as they were applicable, extended to New Zealand by Act of the New South Wales Legislative Council. However, by Letters Patent of 16th November in the same year, made under a Statute passed on 17th August, New Zealand became a separate colony, although the laws of New South Wales remained temporarily in force. The North Island, the South Island and Stewart Island (named after an unsuccessful flax planter) were renamed New Ulster, New Munster and New Leinster; an Executive Council, consisting of the Governor, the Colonial Secretary, the Attorney-General and the Treasurer was formed; and the Governor was authorised to set up a Legislative Council to make laws and ordinances for the peace and good government of the Colony. This Charter was promulgated on 3rd May 1841, and the Legislative Council was duly formed, consisting of three officials and three senior Justices of the Peace. The Council met on twelve occasions, and passed a total of one hundred and twenty-nine ordinances.

When Captain (later Sir George) Grey became Governor in 1845 there was pressure for a greater measure of popular representation, and a new Charter, dated 23rd December 1846, proposed to divide the Colony into two Provinces, one being named New Ulster, consisting of the whole of the North Island other than the district around Wellington, and the other New Munster, which covered the rest. It was the intention to appoint Lieutenant-Governors to each Province and to set up not only a central General Assembly, with an elected House of Representatives, but also Provincial Councils, which too, would have elected Houses of Representatives. In 1848 a suspending Act of the Imperial Parliament delayed the creation of both General and Provincial assemblies for a period of five years. The Colonial Legislative Council was therefore revived and in 1848 passed the Provincial Legislative Councils Ordinance, setting up nominated Provincial Councils with unofficial majorities. Since the composition of the New Ulster Provincial Legislative Council was almost the same as that of the Colonial Legislative Council, the former never met. That of New Munster met once, in 1849.

On 30th June 1852 the British Parliament passed an Act to 'Grant a Representative Constitution to the Colony of New Zealand'. The number of Provinces was increased from two to six, the Provinces being Auckland, New Plymouth, Wellington, Nelson, Canterbury and Otago. At the centre, the General Assembly consisted of the Governor, a nominated Legislative Council and an elected House of Representatives. In each of the Provinces there was an elected Superintendent and an elected Provincial Council with defined, if limited, powers. The General Assembly, and the Provincial Councils, were expressly debarred from regulating Crown Lands or lands in the possession of the Maoris; and the laws, customs and usages of the Maoris were 'for the present to be maintained for the Government of themselves, in all their Relations to and Dealings with each other, and that particular Districts should be set apart within which such Laws, Customs and Usages should be observed'. There were also a number of other restrictions on the legislative capacity of the General Assembly; and the laws passed by it required the Royal Assent and were not to be repugnant to the laws of England. Thus the constitutional picture of New Zealand as a result of this Constitution was that of six small scattered European settlements each with its own Provincial Government and a central Parliament; the Maori-occupied country between the settlements, having no part in this representative Government, governed itself according to Maori custom, subject to the overriding authority of the Governor in Council. In 1867 four Maori seats were established in the General Assembly on the basis of manhood suffrage.

No provision was made in the Constitution for a responsible Executive, and although three Members of the House of Representatives and two Members of the Legislative Council took office without portfolio, effective power remained in the hands of the three officials, who, with the Governor, still continued to sit in the Executive Council. This arrangement led to disputes between the legislature and the executive, the resulting deadlock only being resolved when, on 7th May 1856, Henry Sewell took office as the first Premier of a fully responsible administration. The title of Prime Minister, although in common use from that date, was not officially assumed until 1899.

The name of the Province of New Plymouth was changed in 1858 to Taranaki, and new Provinces of Hawke's Bay, Marlborough, Southland and Westland were formed in 1858, 1859, 1861 and 1864 respectively. Southland, however, was re-united with Otago in 1870. The system of having both central and provincial governments led, as the Provinces developed, to friction between them; and in 1875 the Provincial organisation was brought to an end by the Abolition of Provinces Act, which became operative in 1876.

Some of the restrictions placed on the powers of the New Zealand General Assembly were removed by the New Zealand Constitutional Amendment Act of 1857, which gave power to the Assembly to amend, alter, suspend or repeal the majority of the provisions of the Act of 1852. Responsibility for Maori affairs remained with the Governor until 1864, when it was finally handed over to the New Zealand Government; and from that date the New Zealand central Government was responsible for the whole of New Zealand. By a Royal Proclamation of 9th September 1907 it was declared that after 26th September 1907 the Colony of New Zealand should be known by the title of the Dominion of New

Zealand. A few restrictions on the powers of the New Zealand Parliament to change the constitution remained, and were confirmed by Section 8 of the Statute of Westminster (1931). This Statute was, however, fully adopted by New Zealand in 1947, when the New Zealand Statute of Westminster Adoption Act was passed, to be followed by the New Zealand Constitution (Request and Consent) Act, which, after implementary legislation had been passed by the British Parliament, finally removed the last restrictions on the right of the New Zealand Parliament to amend the New Zealand constitution.

As originally provided, the Legislative Council which formed the Upper House, had a maximum of 15 members, but this number was slowly increased until 1885 when it had 53 members, which included two Maori Members from 1871. From that time the maximum number of Councillors was generally kept at half the membership of the House of Representatives. Legislative Councillors were at first appointed for life, by the Governor. In 1891 their term of appointment was reduced to five years, but they were eligible for re-appointment. In 1914 it was proposed that Councillors should become elective, but although an Act to this effect was passed it was never brought into force. Women were entitled to be Councillors from 1941.

In 1950 the Legislative Council was abolished by the Legislative Council Abolition Act; and the New Zealand Parliament thenceforth consisted of a single chamber only.

The first House of Representatives had only 40 Members, but the number slowly increased until 1881, when it had 95 Members. In 1887 the number was reduced to 74 and in 1900 increased to 80. Since the passing of the Maori Representation Act in 1867 four Maori Members have been elected by the Maori people. More seats were added in 1969, 1972, 1978, 1983 and 1987. The membership of the House now stands at 97. Women have been eligible for election since 1919. Under the 1852 Constitution a vote could be exercised by any male person over the age of 21 years who possessed certain property qualifications. By the Qualification of Electors Act of 1879 every male person over the age of 21 years was entitled to vote, and women's suffrage was introduced in 1893. By the Legislative Act of 1908 the second ballot was introduced to ensure that elected Members have an absolute majority of the votes polled; but this was repealed in 1913. By the constitution of 1852 the House of Representatives was elected for five years, but this period was reduced to three years in 1879. In 1934 it was increased to four years, but reduced again to three years in 1937. The Electoral Amendment Act 1974, reduced the voting age to 18 years.

During the 1984–87 first term of the Lange ministry, many departments of State, or parts of departments, engaged in trade or business activities were formed into state owned enterprises. After the 1987 election ministerial responsibilities were rearranged to take account of the change and one minister was appointed to oversee most SOEs.

Historical List

GOVERNORS GENERAL SINCE 1967

Sir Arthur Porritt, BT, GCMG, GCVO, CBE, 1st December, 1967 to 7th September, 1972

Sir Denis Blundell, GCMG, GCVO, KBE, QSO, from 27th September 1972 to 5th October 1977

Sir Keith Holyoake, KG, GCMG, PC, CH, QSO, from 26th October 1977 to 27th October 1980

Sir David Beattie, GCMG, GCVO, QSO, QC, from 6th November 1980 to 10th November 1985

The Most Reverend Sir Paul Reeves, GCMG, GCVO, QC, from 20th November 1985 to 29th November 1990

Dame Catherine Tizard, GCMG, DBE, from 13th December 1990

PRIME MINISTERS SINCE 1960

Sir Keith Holyoake, GCMG, CH, 12th December 1960 to 7th February 1972

Sir John Marshall, GBE, CH from 7th February 1972 to 8th December 1972

Norman Kirk, from 8th December 1972 to 31st August 1974

Sir Wallace Rowling, KCMG, from 6th September 1974 to 12th December 1975

Sir Robert Muldoon, GCMG, CH, from 12th December 1975 to 26th July 1984

David Lange from 26th July 1984 to 8th August 1989

Geoffrey Palmer from 8th August 1989 to 4th September 1990

Mike Moore from 4th September 1990 to 27th October 1990

Jim Bolger from 27th October 1990

A complete Historical List is included in the 1976 edition of the Year Book.

Government

At the General Election in October 1990, the National Party gained 67 seats, the Labour Party 29 seats and the New Labour Party 1 seat

HEAD OF STATE

HM The Queen

GOVERNOR-GENERAL

Her Excellency Dame Catherine Tizard, GCMG, DBE

CABINET (October 1991)

Prime Minister, Minister in Charge of the Security Intelligence Service: The Right Hon Jim Bolger

Deputy Prime Minister, Minister of External Relations and Trade, Minister of Foreign Affairs, Minister of Pacific Island Affairs: The Hon Don McKinnon

Minister of Labour, Minister of State Services, Minister of Employment, Minister of Immigration: The Hon Bill Birch, MP
Minister of Finance: The Hon Ruth Richardson, MP
Attorney General and Leader of the House, Minister of Crown Health Enterprises: The Hon Paul East, MP
Minister of Agriculture, Minister of Foresty: The Hon John Falloon, MP
Minister of Maori Affairs and Minister of Fisheries: The Hon Doug Kidd, MP
Minister of Commerce, Minister for Industry, Minister for Trade Negotiations: The Hon Philip Burdon, MP
Minister of Health, Minister of Research, Science and Technology, Minister of Crown Research Institutes: The Hon Simon Upton, MP
Minister of Police, Minister of Tourism, Minister of Recreation and Sport: The Hon John Banks, MP
Minister of Social Welfare, Minister of Women's Affairs: The Hon Jenny Shipley, MP
Minister of Defence, Minister of Local Government: The Hon Warren Cooper, MP
Minister of Justice, Minister of Disarmament and Arms Control, Minister of Culture: The Hon Doug Graham, MP
Minister of Education: The Hon Dr Lockwood Smith, MP
Minister of State-owned Enterprises, Minister of Railways, Minister of Works and Development: The Hon Maurice McTigue, MP
Minister of Transport, Minister of Lands, Minister for the Environment: The Hon Rob Storey, MP
Minister of Conservation: The Hon Denis Marshall, MP
Minister of Housing, Minister of Energy: The Hon John Luxton, MP
Minister of Revenue, Minister for Senior Citizens: The Hon Wyatt Creech, MP
Minister of Communications, Minister of Broadcasting, Minister of Statistics: The Hon Maurice Williamson, MP

MINISTERS NOT IN CABINET

Minister of Consumer Affairs: The Hon Katherine O'Regan
Minister of Youth Affairs: The Hon Roger McClay
Minister of Internal Affairs, Minister of Civil Defence: The Hon Graeme Lee
Minister of Business Development: The Hon Roger Maxwell
Minister of Customs: The Hon Murray McCully

LEADER OF THE OPPOSITION
Rt Hon M K Moore, MP

HOUSE OF REPRESENTATIVES
Speaker: Hon Robin Gray, MP
Chairman of Committees: Jim Gerard, MP
Clerk of the House: D McGee

JUDICIARY
Chief Justice: Rt Hon Sir Thomas Eichelbaum, GBE

COURT OF APPEAL
President: Rt Hon Sir Robin Cooke, KBE
Rt Hon Sir Ivor Richardson
Rt Hon M Hardie-Boys
Rt Hon M E Casey
Hon T M Gault

JUDGES OF THE HIGH COURT
Hon Justice Barker
Hon Justice Jeffries
Hon Justice Greig
Hon Justice Sinclair
Hon Justice Holland
Hon Justice Thorp
Hon Justice Wallace
Hon Justice Tompkins
Hon Justice Gallen
Hon Justice Henry
Hon Justice Heron
Hon Justice Ellis
Hon Justice Williamsom
Hon Justice Smellie
Hon Justice Wylie
Hon Justice Doogue
Hon Justice McGechan
Hon Justice Tipping
Hon Justice Anderson
Hon Justice Robertson
Hon Justice Fisher
Hon Justice Neazor
Hon Justice Thomas
Hon Justice Fraser
Hon Justice Penlington
Hon Justice Temm

GOVERNMENT DEPARTMENTS

PRIME MINISTER AND CABINET
Director: (Vacant)

MINISTRY OF AGRICULTURE AND FISHERIES
Director-General: R Ballard

AUDIT OFFICE
Controller and Auditor General: B H C Tyler

COMMERCE
Secretary: J Belgrave

CONSERVATION:
Director General: W Mansfield

CROWN LAW OFFICE
Solicitor-General: J J McGrath QC

CULTURAL AFFAIRS
Chief Executive: C Blake

CUSTOMS DEPARTMENT
Comptroller: G W Ludlow (Acting)

MINISTRY OF DEFENCE
Secretary: G Hensley

DEPARTMENT OF EDUCATION
Director-General: Dr M O'Rourke

MINISTRY FOR THE ENVIRONMENT
Secretary: Dr R W G Blakely

MINISTRY OF EXTERNAL RELATIONS AND TRADE
Secretary: R Nottage

MINISTRY OF FORESTRY
Secretary: Dr J Valentine

DEPARTMENT OF HEALTH
Director-General: I Miller (Acting)

HOUSING CORPORATION OF NEW ZEALAND
Director-General: R Henderson (Acting)

DEPARTMENT OF INLAND REVENUE
Commissioner: D Henry

DEPARTMENT OF INTERNAL AFFAIRS
Secretary, Clerk of the Writs and Secretary for Local Government: P Cameron

DEPARTMENT OF JUSTICE
Secretary: D Oughton

DEPARTMENT OF LABOUR
Secretary: J McKenzie

MINISTRY OF MAORI AFFAIRS
Secretary: J Clarke

OMBUDSMAN
Chief Ombudsman: J F Robertson

MINISTRY OF PACIFIC ISLAND AFFAIRS
Chief Executive: A Rohgo-Raea

PARLIAMENTARY COUNSEL OFFICE
Chief Parliamentary Counsel and Compiler of Statutes: W Iles

POLICE DEPARTMENT
Commissioner: J A Jamieson

MINISTRY OF RESEARCH, SCIENCE AND TECHNOLOGY
Chief Executive: Dr B Walker

RESERVE BANK
Governor: Dr D Brash

DEPARTMENT OF SCIENTIFIC AND INDUSTRIAL RESEARCH
Director-General: M A Collins

DEPARTMENT OF SOCIAL WELFARE
Director-General: A Kirkland

STATE SERVICES COMMISSION
Chairman: D K Hunn

DEPARTMENT OF STATISTICS
Government Statistician: S Kuzmicich

DEPARTMENT OF SURVEY AND LAND INFORMATION
Director-General/Surveyor General: W Robertson

NZ TOURISM DEPARTMENT
General Manager: W N Plimmer

MINISTRY OF TRANSPORT
Secretary: Mrs M C Bazley

TREASURY
Secretary: Dr G C Scott

MINISTRY OF WOMEN'S AFFAIRS
Secretary: J Aitken

TOKELAU

This group consists of three islands, or group of islets, Atafu (2.03 sq km), Nukunonu (5.46 sq km) and Fakaofo (2.63 sq km), and lies about 4° due north of Apia, Western Samoa. According to the 1986 census the total population was then 1,690, an increase of 118 as compared to 1981. There were 603 inhabitants on Atafu, 426 on Nukunonu and 661 on Fakaofo. The constraints of atoll subsistence and population pressure have led some 3,000 Tokelauans to settle abroad, mainly in New Zealand and Samoa.

The three islands became a British Protectorate in 1877, and formal declarations were made at each atoll in 1889. At the request of the inhabitants, Britain annexed the islands (then known as the Union Islands) in 1916 and included them within the boundaries of the Gilbert and Ellice Islands Colony. In 1925, at the request of the British Government, New Zealand assumed responsibility for the administration of the Group, and as a result the islands were separated from the Gilbert and Ellice Islands Colony. In 1946 the Tokelau Nomenclature Ordinance officially designated the Group as the Tokelau Islands. The islands were included within the territorial boundaries of New Zealand by the Tokelau Islands Act, 1948.

The islands, now known as Tokelau, are administered by an Administrator in whom all administrative and executive functions are vested. From 1st January 1962 until December 1970, the High Commissioner for New Zealand in Western Samoa held the office of Administrator of the Tokelau Islands and was charged with all administrative and executive functions in the Tokelau Islands subject to the authority of the Minister of Island Affairs. The Tokelau Islands Administration Regulations 1971, which came into force on 1st January 1972, transferred the office of Administrator to the Secretary of Maori and Island Affairs. With the abolition of the Islands Affairs portfolio in 1974 the New Zealand Secretary of Foreign Affairs became the Administrator, responsible to the Minister of Foreign Affairs; under the Tokelau Administration Regulations 1980, the offices of Secretary of Foreign Affairs and Administrator may be held by separate persons (as is the case at present).

In practice, most of the powers of the Administrator are exercised by the Official Secretary of the Office for Tokelau Affairs, which, by agreement with the Government of Western Samoa, is based in Apia. The Office itself co-ordinates the activities of the members of the Tokelau Public Service (TPS) working on the atolls. Increasingly, the Administrator and the Official Secretary in his rôle as Administrator's representative, act in a supervisory capacity only, with the TPS operating under the overall director of the village representatives.

Atoll affairs are run by Village Councils (one for each atoll) of which the two elected local government representatives, the *faipule* and *pulenuku,* are leading members. The *pulenuku* may be described as the village mayor; the *faipule* represents the village at large in its dealings with the administering power and the public service, he is customarily the village magistrate (Commissioner) and heads his atoll's delegation to the General *Fono* (joint sessions of representatives from the three atolls).

THE ROSS DEPENDENCY

The Antarctic territory known as the Ross Dependency was brought within the jurisdiction of the New Zealand Government by Order in Council of 30th July 1923, under the British Settlements Act, 1887. It is defined as 'all the islands and territories between the 160th degree of east longitude and the 150th degree of west longitude which are situated south of the 60th degree of south latitude'. The land area is estimated at 413,540 sq km and permanent shelf ice at 336,770 sq km. There are no permanent inhabitants, but scientific stations are staffed all the year round.

Laws for the Dependency have been made by regulations promulgated by the Governor-General of New Zealand. Administrative powers are vested in the Governor-General of New Zealand, and Administrative Officers (commonly referred to as Administrators) have been appointed from time to time since 1923.

Many famous explorers visited the area during the last century, including Sir James Ross, Captain R F Scott, RN, Sir Ernest Shackleton, Roald Amundsen and Richard E Byrd.

New Zealand is a party to the Antarctic Treaty (1959) which reserves the Antarctic for peaceful purposes. Recent New Zealand legislation enforces measures for the conservation of Antarctic flora and fauna which were adopted under Article IX of the Treaty and gives effect to the Convention for the Conservation of Antarctic Marine Living Resources which was adopted in 1980.

The New Zealand Antarctic Expedition established Scott Base on Ross Island in January 1957. In March 1958 the New Zealand Government appointed the Ross Dependency Research Committee to co-ordinate and supervise all New Zealand activity in the Dependency, with particular reference to the scientific and technical programme. A continuing programme of field work and research has since been carried out, under the auspices of the New Zealand Antarctic Research Programme.

Scott Base remains the centre of New Zealand's operations in the Ross Dependency although a summer scientific station has also been established near Lake Varda. Scientific field parties travel extensively throughout the Dependency during the summer research season.

Federal Republic of Nigeria

Capital: Lagos

Location, Topography, Climate

Nigeria, which takes its name from the Niger, or 'great', river which flows through it to the sea, is situated on the west coast of Africa on the shores of the Gulf of Guinea and lies between 4° and 14°N. latitude and 2° and 15°E. longitude. It is bounded on the west by the People's Republic of Benin, on the north by the Republic of Niger and on the east by the United Republic of Cameroon. It includes part of Lake Chad on the north-east. The total area is 923,772 sq km, (356,669 square miles). It is 1,045 km (650 miles) from the coast to the farthest point on the northern border and its greatest width is 1,126 km (700 miles). It is not a mountainous country: the only high ground is the plateau area near Jos and along the eastern border. There is one other major navigable river of importance, apart from the Niger, The River Benue. There are two well-marked seasons, the rains lasting from April to October, and the dry season from November to March. Temperatures at the coast seldom rise above 32°C (90°F) but the humidity is high. Farther north the climate is drier and the temperature range greater, the extremes being 43°C (110°F) and 10°C (50°F) although it is occasionally lower in certain areas.

Population

Nigeria is the most populous state in Africa. At the time of the 1952–53 census the population stood at 30,417,000; the census held in late 1963 recorded a total population of 55,654,000. The last census was held from 26th–28th November 1991. Estimated population exceeds 90 million. The census results are due in 1992.

There are approximately 250 ethnic groups, the main ones being Hausa/Fulani, Yoruba and Ibo to which nearly three-quarters of the population belong. The non-African population does not exceed 40,000. The principal languages in Nigeria are English, Hausa, Yoruba and Ibo.

The two main religions are Muslim, concentrated in the north and west and Christian, concentrated in the south.

Movement to the site of the new Federal Capital at Abuja began in 1982 but for the time being the Federal Capital remained in Lagos until 1991 when Abuja was finally so designated. The movement of government offices and foreign embassies to the new capital may take several years to complete.

Health

Nigeria suffers from a range of tropical and other diseases, including malaria, dysentry and hepatitis. Cholera epidemics occur from time to time. Leprosy is largely under control. AIDS exists, but does not seem to be widely prevalent. There is some malnutrition. There is a nationwide spread of hospitals and other health facilities, both publicly and privately run. Current Government policies are focused on primary health care.

Communications

The principal seaports are served by a number of shipping lines including the Nigerian National Shipping Lines, Elder Dempster and Palm Lines. Several international airlines operate frequent services to the main international airports at Lagos, Kano and Port Harcourt. Regular internal air services by Nigeria Airways and several private companies connect these airports with Ibadan, Benin City, Calabar, Abuja, Jos, Kaduna, Maiduguri, Sokoto, Enugu, Yola, Ilorin and Makurdi. Passenger and freight services are operated by the Nigerian Railway Corporation over a total of 2,680 route miles. The country has an extensive network of tarred roads, with dirt roads covering more remote areas. Traffic is also carried on the main rivers.

The Economy

During the 1970s and 1980s the structure of the Nigerian economy changed. The process is still continuing. Agriculture and manufacturing were as important as oil as generators of wealth in the early 1970s. But the balance shifted towards greater dependence on oil, and hence greater vulnerability to changes in world oil prices. The rise in oil prices in the 1970s had a swift, large and wide ranging impact on Nigeria. Consumption and production based on imports became more important. Industry grew behind protective barriers. External debts were contracted.

Then the oil price fell. Trade and external balance problems became pressing. The Government tried to tackle them by administrative means, but failed to halt càpital flight, to deal with an overvalued exchange rate, or encourage the efficient use of resources.

In 1986 the Babangida Government launched a programme of economic reform under the title SAP—Structural Adjustment Programme. The exchange rate was devalued and allowed to be determined more by market forces, import and export licences were abolished, as were most price controls.

Faced with mounting unemployment problems the Government attempted to stimulate growth by reflating the economy in 1988. It succeeded but at the price of stoking up inflation and widening the fiscal deficit. Corrective action was taken in the 1989 Budget. This paved the way for a new agreement with the IMF, made possible debt rescheduling deals with the Paris and London Clubs, and helped Nigeria to attract aid support from the international community.

In 1990 the Budget introduced a three year rolling plan. This replaced a series of five year plans of public expenditure. Private investment was also made easier with a reform of rules governing ownership of companies—the Enterprises Decree. Now all bar 40 areas of industrial activity are open to 100 per cent foreign ownership, and even the restricted areas are open under prescribed circumstances.

The Nigerian economy remains dominated by the oil sector. Production, at around 1.6 million barrels per day, generates over 90 per cent of export earnings. Among other exports cocoa, rubber and palm kernels are of importance, even if less so than in pre oil price boom days.

Nigeria's main imports are capital goods, manufactures, and chemicals. Her main trading partners are Britain, Germany, France, USA and Japan.

The unit of currency is the Naira; one Naira is divided into 100 Kobos.

Education

A programme aimed at achieving universal primary education was introduced in September 1976. Although given a high priority by successive Nigerian Governments (including the present one), standards in education have suffered through cuts in Government spending. Reliable figures are not available, but the projected figures for educational establishments in 1982/83 were: 15.4 m primary school pupils, 3.5 m in secondary school; 53,766 in polytechnics and 88,636 in universities.

The Media

A nationwide TV and radio network has been developed under the control of the Nigerian Television Authority and the Federal Radio Corporation of Nigeria. Each State has its own radio station and many States are developing their own TV station. A wide range of daily, weekly and periodical publications is produced in Lagos and other Nigerian towns. Most states now publish their own newspaper and there has been something of a 'media explosion' following the years of newsprint shortage.

History

The Nigerian plateau in the area around Jos is now regarded as a focal point in early Nigerian history: it was the meeting point for influences from the upper Niger valley, where agriculture had been independently developed around 5000 BC, and from the civilisation of Egypt. We know that the Plateau people practised agriculture by 3000 BC and it would seem that increased food supplies allowed the development of more complex societies which pushed their way southward. The Bantu, who subsequently conquered most of eastern and southern Africa with their iron weapons, are thought by some authorities to have originated on the Plateau. By 500 BC the remarkable Nok culture had emerged, controlling an area around the Plateau of some 400 square miles, a culture characterised by terra-cotta heads and figurines of a high technical and artistic standard, which reveal an agricultural people, who knew iron-working and had developed a specialised society. These heads show that a tradition of terra-cotta sculpture existed within what are now the boundaries of present-day Nigeria well before the city of Ife was founded.

Nigerian history is characterised by the pressure of northern peoples on the southern forest belt. The northerners exploited geographical advantages, for their climate allowed them to domesticate cattle and horses and grow cotton and cereals, so that textiles, leather-working and smithing were able to develop. In the southern tropical forest agriculture depended on root crops and palm products until the later entry of Indonesian and American crops. The north was also in contact with Egypt and North Africa, and strong political state systems, often based on the concept of divine kingship, emerged early in the Christian era. Two main systems emerged in the north. In the area around Lake Chad the shadowy Zaghawa kingdom had by the eleventh century become the Kanem-Bornu empire, the Bornu section of which later became a separate state. The Hausa Bokwoi dominated the area further west as a loose confederation of several states which probably originated at different times between AD 100 and the tenth century. These two powers, Kanem-Bornu and Hausa Bokwoi dominated the politics of the north until the nineteenth century. Both were profoundly, though not exclusively, influenced by Islam, brought in by desert traders and later by Fulani immigrants. Both developed extensive foreign trade across the Sahara in leather goods, salt, cloth, slaves and gold. They were intermittently torn by internal civil wars, they fought each other, were invaded from outside (parts of Hausaland were forced to submit to the Songhai empire in the sixteenth century) and menaced by the Jukun state, centred upon Ibi on the River Benue, during the sixteenth century.

As yet little is known of events in the south in mediaeval times. Of the Ibo, the dominant linguistic group in eastern Nigeria, we know little beyond shadowy legends indicating struggles with invaders from north and west. Though without centralised monarchical institutions, the Ibo survived and multiplied, developing agriculture to support a dense population which by the eighteenth century became a magnet for slave traders. Rather more is known of the Yoruba, the predominant group in the west. Their cultural history originated in the founding before AD 1000 of Ife, still the spiritual centre of Yorubaland, despite the fact that its political control was eclipsed in the fourteenth century by Oyo, which was in turn displaced by Ibadan and Abeokuta in the nineteenth century. The origins of Benin are also connected with Ife, and the claim of both upon the attention of historians lies in their magnificent sculpture, now regarded by some authorities as a major contribution to mankind's artistic heritage; its humanism and naturalism reflect a highly developed and sophisticated society. The bronze sculptures demonstrate great technical aptitude by the mastery of the complicated 'lost wax' process of casting.

Contact with Europe began in the fifteenth century with the Portuguese, and at first this contact seemed likely to have profound results, for it brought missionaries to Benin, who introduced the art of writing, and made converts among the royal family. Benin's territory expanded when the lucrative spice trade allowed her to purchase firearms, and, after the discovery of America, new plants revolutionised the diet of all the forest peoples. But by the seventeenth century the Portuguese began to lose interest, developing instead the richer trade of the Indian Ocean. Moreover, with the development of plantations in America and the West Indies, the demand for slaves from West Africa rapidly began to overshadow all other activities. The slave trade was developed from existing forms of slavery, using African middlemen. It needed no technical innovations, and as the slaves were bought from coastal states without the buyers penetrating inland there was very little external influence of new ideas. The firearms which were exchanged for the slaves strengthened the southern states; Benin expanded to extend from Lagos to Bonny, and her influence on the Niger was felt as far north as Onitsha; and Oyo fought her Yoruba brothers to carve a way to the sea.

In this trade Britain had by the eighteenth century secured the major share, yet this had resulted in no colonial activity in Nigeria. Paradoxically it was the movement in Britain against the slave trade which began to involve the British in Nigerian affairs. In 1807 the slave trade was made illegal for British subjects, the Royal Navy began to patrol the coast, and the Sierra Leone colony became the resettlement area for slaves liberated at sea, the majority of whom were Nigerians. The anti-slavery groups, however, were sceptical of the blockage, and pressed instead for the development of missionary work and 'legitimate commerce' to check the trade at its source in the interior. At the same time the rise of the British chemical and soap industries created a demand for palm oil and other vegetable oils capable of providing a substitute traffic. Missionaries settled in Abeokuta in the 1840s to begin a 'sunrise within the tropics' through 'the Bible and the Plough'. Africans liberated at sea from the slave ships played a major rôle in this process. Samuel Adjai Crowther, a liberated Yoruba, accompanied the British Niger Expedition of 1841, later returning to found a chain of Anglican missions on the Niger, staffed entirely by liberated Africans. In 1846 he became the first African Bishop of the Anglican communion. Such African Christians may be described as the first modern Nigerian nationalists; they had a vision of a united Christian country, transcending tribal divisions. In the valley of the Niger, Crowther, though a Yoruba, worked for most of his life among the Efik, Ibo, Ijaw, Ibibio and Nupe people.

Commercial involvement proceeded alongside missionary penetration of the Niger. After 1854, when W B Baikie demonstrated that quinine could reduce European mortality from malaria, shallow-draught trading steamboats annually ascended the river.

Meanwhile events had occurred in the north profoundly affecting the history of modern Nigeria. In May 1804 Shehu Usman dan Fodio, a Fulani religious teacher, declared a jihad or holy war upon the Hausa state of Gobir. Giving flags to his generals he succeeded during the next thirteen years of his life in overthrowing most of the Hausa rulers, replacing them with Fulani Emirs. The impulse of the movement was Muslim reforming zeal, and it led to the creation of an empire composed of city states with many features of Islamic administrative character, the lasting value of which was proved in the subsequent history of the area. When Usman died his son Bello was left as Sultan of Sokoto, with his brother Abdullahi as Emir of Gwandu, twin suzerains of the state. The effects of this revolution might well be compared to those of the Norman Conquest of England. A state-system was created with a common religious and judicial basis, an aristocratic *lingua franca* and a system of education through Koranic schools. Though some Hausa states, notably Gobir, resisted successfully, the Fulani movement spread beyond Hausaland; a new Emirate in Adamawa was established, the Nupe were conquered, the Yoruba state of Ilorin made Muslim, and the Yoruba capital of Oyo destroyed. The Yoruba might well have been crushed between the Fulani in the north and Dahomey in the west had not Ibadan and Abeokuta beaten them off with the help of liberated slaves and European weapons.

With missionaries and traders moving into the south and up the Niger, it was inevitable that the British Government should become involved. British Consuls were appointed, and in 1861, after ten years of fitful interference in its affairs, Lagos was annexed partly at the behest of the Christian party in Abeokuta, who desired a docile and friendly port. Thereafter it was impossible to keep out of local politics, despite the Parliamentary Select Committee of 1865, which decreed no more expansion but eventual withdrawal. Further involvement arose on the Niger from the opposition of African middlemen to British trade in the palm oil-producing regions, and naval expeditions on the river became annual from the 1860's.

Before 1880, however, the British were reluctant to extend political control; the climate was still deadly to European officials, and trade and missions seemed to flourish without the expense of a colonial régime. After 1880, the situation changed rapidly with the arrival of missionaries, traders, and treaty-making explorers in the service of both France and Germany. The British responded with three methods of extending control; Lagos, ruled by the Colonial Office was expanded by treaties with Yoruba states; areas under consular rule were transformed by treaties into the Oil Rivers Protectorate in 1884; and on the Niger, where Sir George Goldie had amalgamated the British traders and bought out the French firms, his company was given a Royal Charter granting administrative powers in 1886. Renamed the Royal Niger Company it was placed under the somewhat sketchy control of the Foreign Office. From these bases British control was extended gradually in the next 20 years. The rule of the African middlemen in the Oil Rivers was broken by the deposition of rulers like King Jaja of Opopo, who opposed the penetration of British traders and missions into his markets. Force was used against Benin in 1897, and by the Niger Company against Ilorin and Nupe in the same year. The Ijebu were conquered by force in the 1890s, but elsewhere in Yorubaland treaties were the more usual method of control. A renewed period of rivalry with France resulted in the creation of much more direct control during the Colonial Secretaryship of Joseph Chamberlain (1895–1902). The frontiers were settled by agreements with France, the West African Frontier Force was established under Colonel (later Lord) Lugard, the Royal Niger Company was deprived of its administrative powers in 1900 and northern and eastern Nigeria placed under Colonial Office supervision. Lugard was made Governor of Northern Nigeria, and gradually occupied the Emirates militarily. Similar military moves led to the gradual conquest of the Ibo people.

Despite this forceful assertion of control, the British rejected, where they could, the idea of ruling directly, and thereby destroying indigenous political institutions. 'Indirect rule' had been practised by both the Royal Niger Company and the Lagos authorities, and it was cheaper, more economical in men and less likely to provoke opposition than direct administration. The classic system was developed by Lord Lugard in the north, where the area continued to be ruled by the Fulani Emirs, with their systems of justice and taxation reformed from their more unsatisfactory characteristics and developed to suit the colonial régime. In Yorubaland a similar policy was attempted, especially after 1914 when Nigeria was united administratively into one dependency. In the west, however, the system was more difficult to administer for the chiefs were not feudal rulers and did not fit easily into the hierarchical system. Among the Ibo indirect rule was almost impossible, and the British resorted to the expedient of creating warrant chiefs, a policy which contributed to widespread rioting in the 1920s. Among many educated Africans indirect rule became unpopular for its emphasis on preserving traditional culture, excluding them from administration and the native courts. Probably the policy was maintained after it had served its purpose; yet it did protect Africans; its corollary was the British refusal to allow white settlement or plantations such as those demanded by Lord Leverhulme in the 1920s. This protective element allowed economic development, especially in agriculture, to take place through Nigerian enterprise. Transported by a new network of railways, or carried in Nigerian-owned lorries on a vastly extended road system, a large export trade in cocoa, groundnuts, leather, cotton and vegetable oils developed.

After the 1914–1918 War, part of the adjacent German colony of Kamerun was placed under British mandate by the League of Nations, and renamed the British Cameroons. It was administered as an integral part of Nigeria. On the formation of the United Nations, the Cameroons became a Trust territory. At a plebiscite held in the Northern Cameroons in November 1959 the territory voted to defer a decision on its own future and did not therefore achieve independence in 1960 as part of Northern Nigeria. The Cameroons ceased to be a part of Nigeria when Nigeria became independent but a plebiscite was held in February 1961 to decide whether the Cameroons should join Nigeria or the Cameroon Republic. At this second plebiscite the Northern Cameroons voted to become part of Nigeria and formally became part of the Federation on the 1st June 1961 and now forms part of Gongola and Borno States. The Southern Cameroons at the same plebiscite opted to join the Republic of Cameroon and did so on 1st October 1961.

From 1960 to 1967 Nigeria was a Federation of three and subsequently four regions (after the creation of Mid-Western Nigeria following a referendum held on 13th July 1963). On 27th May 1967, regions were abolished and 12 states were created, increased to 19 in February 1976. Two new states were created by President Babangida in September 1987, bringing the total to 21.

Constitutional development

When in 1914 Northern and Southern Nigeria were amalgamated, a Nigerian Council, consisting of six African and 30 European members, but without executive or legislative authority, was set up alongside the Lagos Executive Council. The Governor was not bound to give effect to any Resolution of the Council unless he thought fit to do so.

In 1922 a new constitution was introduced, providing for a Legislative Council of 46 members, of whom 10 were Africans, four of these being elected. The Council was empowered to legislate for the Colony and for the Southern Provinces of Nigeria, while the Governor continued to legislate by proclamation for the Northern Provinces.

No further changes in the Constitution were made until 1947, when the 'Richards Constitution' was introduced (so-called after the Governor, Sir Arthur Richards, later Lord Milverton). A Legislative Council was set up for the whole of Nigeria, with 45 Members, of whom 28 were Africans (four elected and 24 nominated) while the Executive Council was still composed mainly of official members. But the biggest change brought about by the 1947 Constitution was the setting up of Regional Houses of Assembly in Eastern, Western and Northern Nigeria, with a House of Chiefs for the Northern Region. Executive functions were not provided for, but their recommendations were considered by the Governor-in-Council and were placed before the Central Legislative Council. The importance and uniqueness of the 'Richards Constitution' was its introduction of the policy of regionalisation which was subsequently developed in successive constitutions. In 1951 a further constitution was introduced under Governor Macpherson. This provided for a Council of Ministers of 18 members (12 Africans and six officials), a House of Representatives of 142 members (136 Africans and six officials) and for a House of Assembly in each of the three Regions and a House of Chiefs in Northern and Western Nigeria. Increased legislative powers were given to the Regional Houses subject to reference to the Governor-in-Council. There was equal representation for each Region in the Council of Ministers.

Throughout its life of 27 months the 1951 Constitution was subject to stresses and strains and in March 1953 a crisis developed which made it clear that further constitutional revision had become necessary.

In August 1953 and in January 1954 delegates of all Nigerian political parties met to consider the problems involved in creating a new constitution. On 1st October 1954 a new constitution was brought into operation which recognised to a limited extent the autonomy of Regional Governments for their internal administration and affairs. The 1954 Constitution retained the framework of its predecessor but carried regionalisation a stage further by declaring Nigeria a Federation. It also gave responsibilities to Nigerian Ministers for the formulation and execution of policy.

The review of the 1954 Constitution, scheduled for 1956, was deferred until May and June 1957. The delegates, pressed for a firm date for the granting of full independence; and an undertaking was given by the British Government that sympathetic consideration would be given to this after a new Federal House had been elected in 1959. In August 1957 the first Federal Prime Minister was appointed, and formed a coalition Government of the principal political parties. A Federal Council of Ministers was composed of the Governor-General, as President, the Prime Minister and ten other Ministers. Internal self-government was granted to the Eastern and Western Regions in August 1957, and to Northern Nigeria in March 1959.

In September and October 1958 the Constitutional Conference was resumed in London and the British Government agreed to grant independence to the Federation of Nigeria as from 1st October 1960, if the Federal House of Representatives, to be elected at the end of 1959, so requested.

New elections to the Federal House of Representatives were held in December 1959. At its first meeting in January 1960 the new House passed a resolution requesting Her Majesty's Government to introduce the necessary legislation to enable Nigeria to become an independent sovereign state with effect from 1st October 1960, and seeking the support of Britain for Nigeria's request that she should be accepted as a Member of the Commonwealth on Independence. The Senate endorsed the resolution a few days later.

The Independence Act was passed by both Houses of the British Parliament in July 1960 and received the Royal Assent on 29th July. Accordingly the Federation of Nigeria achieved independence and became a Member of the Commonwealth on 1st October 1960. In 1963 it was decided that Nigeria should become a republic within the Commonwealth. The Federal Republic of Nigeria was duly inaugurated on 1st October 1963 with Dr Nnamdi Azikiwe as the first President.

Post Independence History and the Constitution

The Constitution of the Federation Act was passed by the Nigerian Parliament on 19th September 1963 and provided for a Federal Government at Lagos and for Regional Governments in the four regions.

The First Republic came to an end on 15th January 1966 when a *coup d'état* was staged by a small group of Army officers, and Major-General J T U Aguiyi-Ironsi, at the time General Officer Commanding the Nigerian Army, was invited to head a Military Government.

On 24th May he published a decree abolishing the Federation and the Regions and establishing a unitary state. On 29th July a second army *coup d'état* was staged, this time by troops of the Northern Army, in which Major-General Aguiyi-Ironsi was killed. Lt-Col Y Gowon was subsequently invited by the majority of the surviving members of the Supreme Military Council to become Supreme Commander. One of his first acts was to abolish the unitary Decree of 24th May and to re-establish Nigeria as a Federation.

In September 1966 a Constitutional Conference began in Lagos with representatives from each of the Regions, to try to reach agreement on a new Constitution acceptable to all Nigerians. No agreement had been reached by November 1966 when the Conference was adjourned, and in May 1967, Lt-Col Gowon—later promoted to General—announced the abolition of the regions and the creation of 12 states in their place. He incorporated civilians within the Federal Executive Council and reaffirmed his intention to restore civilian rule as soon as practicable.

On 30th May 1967 the Military Governor of Eastern Nigeria, Lt-Col Ojukwu, declared the Region an independent sovereign state under the name of the Republic of Biafra. The Federal Government declared this step illegal and took immediate steps to bring the secession attempt to an end. Fighting broke out in July. Various peace initiatives under Commonwealth and OAU auspices having achieved no results, the secessionist forces were eventually defeated in early January 1970. Former secessionist officers formally surrendered to the FMG on 15th January 1970 and Lt-Col Ojukwu went into exile.

On 29th July 1975 General Gowon's government was overthrown in a bloodless *coup d'état* and Brigadier (later General) Murtala Muhammed became Head of State. In October 1975, Brigadier Muhammed announced a programme for a return to civilian rule, phased over four years. A Constitutional Drafting Committee was established in October 1975. A panel was set up to advise on the creation of new States; and on the basis of its report, 19 new States were created on 4th February 1976. On 13th February, the Head of State was assassinated in an abortive *coup d'état*. His successor, Lt General Olusegun Obasanjo, appointed on 14th February 1976, pledged himself to continue the late Head of State's policies. In September 1978 a new Constitution (providing for a system of government on the US pattern) was formally promulgated and the ban on political activity lifted. Five parties were registered to contest elections which took place in July and early August 1979. The National Party of Nigeria (NPN) was returned as the largest party with the widest spread of support and its Presidential candidate, Alhaji Shehu Shagari, was sworn in as President of the Federal Republic on 1st October 1979, on which day the new constitution came into effect.

On 1st October 1981 President Shagari announced the granting of a pardon to General Gowon and on 18th May 1982, to the former Biafran 'Head of State', Emeka Ojukwu, who subsequently returned to Nigeria. Further elections were held in August and September 1983 and President Shagari was returned to office for a second four year term.

On 31st December 1983, the Government of Alhaji Shehu Shagari was displaced in a virtually bloodless *coup d'état* and Major General Mohammadu Buhari was declared Head of State. The Supreme Military Council (SMC) was the policy-making body. Subordinate to it was a Federal Executive Council (FEC) of military and civilian Ministers, the two bodies comprising the Federal Military Government. The Military took power, in their words, to eliminate corruption, reduce the profligacy of the previous administration and restore order and discipline both into the Nigerian economy, and into Nigerian life. The FMG sharply tightened up the previous government's austerity programme with further cuts in government spending, restrictions on the expenditure of foreign currency, and retrenchment throughout the public service. As part of the drive against corruption, the Government pursued a 'War Against Indiscipline' (WAI) with severe penalties for those deemed guilty of idleness or self-enrichment. Former politicians thought to have corruptly used their offices for personal gain were vigorously pursued; some receiving heavy jail sentences and fines.

The apparent failure of these measures to resolve Nigeria's economic problems, however, provided the main impetus for the subsequent *coup d'état* on 27th August 1985 which displaced Major General Buhari and brought Major General Babangida (later General) to power as President and Commander-in-Chief of the Armed Forces. Again, the *coup d'état* was virtually bloodless. In announcing his new government, President Babangida retained the structure of the previous administration, except that the SMC was expanded and renamed the Armed Forces Ruling Council (AFRC) and the FEC was renamed the National Council of Ministers. The government announced its respect for civil rights and overturned a number of controversial decrees passed by its predecessor, releasing many of those detained under Buhari. Babangida's government is committed to restoring civilian rule and a programme for the return to civilian administration by 1992 was announced on 1st July 1987. A Constituent Assembly was appointed in May 1988 and in April 1989 presented a draft Constitution to the President. The latter announced the new Constitution in May 1989 and the ban on political parties was lifted simultaneously. In February 1989 the AFRC was disbanded and reconstituted as a smaller body, and in June 1989 a 265-member Armed Forces Consultative Assembly was appointed. Thirteen political associations applied for registration to become political parties; but the AFRC decided all were ineligible for registration on the grounds that they lacked widespread and non-partisan grassroots support and had no clearly defined policies. In October 1989 President Babangida announced the formation of two new political parties—the National Republican Convention and the Social Democratic Party, who will contend for power in 1992, and laid down their contributions and manifestos. Elections for the National Executive for each party were held in July 1990. Elections for local government took place peacefully on 8th December 1990.

Elections for the State Assemblies and Governors were held on 14th December 1991, after the number of states had been increased, on 27th August 1991, from 21 to 30. The new Governors were sworn in on 2nd January 1992. The transition to a wholly civil government is due to be completed by general elections for the Federal Senate and House of Representatives on 7th November 1992, and concluded after presidential elections on 5th Decmber 1992.

Historical List
(A full historical list is shown in the 1978 edition)

HEADS OF THE FEDERAL MILITARY GOVERNMENT AND COMMANDERS-IN-CHIEF OF THE ARMED FORCES
General Y Gowon from 1st August 1966 to 29th July 1975
General M R Muhammed from 29th July 1975 to 13th February 1976
General O Obasanjo from 14th February 1976 to 30th September 1979
Major General Muhammadu Buhari from 31st December 1983 to 27th August 1985

PRESIDENT OF THE FEDERAL REPUBLIC AND COMMANDER-IN-CHIEF OF THE ARMED FORCES
Alhaji Shehu Shagari from 1st October 1979 to 31st December 1983

Membership of the Armed Forces Ruling Council, National Council of Ministers and State Governors is as follows:

ARMED FORCES RULING COUNCIL (AFRC) (January 1992)
President and Commander in Chief: General I B Babangida, CFR, FSS, MNI
Vice-President: Admiral A Aikhomu (Rtd)
Chief of Defence Staff and Minister of Defence: General S Abacha
Chief of Army Staff: Lieutenant General S E Ibrahim, FSS, PSC, FHWC
Chief of Naval Staff: Vice Admiral M A H Nyako, FSS, RCDS, MRIN
Chief of Air Staff: Air Marshal N O O Yussuff, FSS, PSC, MNI
Inspector General of Police: Alhaji Aliyu A Attah
Commandant, Nigerian Defence Academy: Major General Garba Duba
Director of Training Operations Defence Headquarters: Major General J N Dogonyaro
Flag Officer Commanding (Western N N Command) (NN): Rear Admiral M A B Elegbede
Chief of Logistics (NN): Rear Admiral C O Kaja
Chief of Policy and Planning, Defence Headquarters: Major General A A Abubakar
Chief of Logistics, Defence Headquarters: Major General R M Kupolati
Director Administration, Defence Headquarters: Major General A Mohammed
GOC, 2 Mechanised Division, Ibadan (NA): Brigadier J M Inienger
GOC, 3 Armoured Division, Jos (NA): Brigadier A I Olurin
GOC, 82 Division, Enugu (NA): Brigadier C A Garuba
Air Officer Operations: Air Vice Marshal C A Dada
Air Officer Logistics: Air Vice Marshal A Daggash

NATIONAL COUNCIL OF MINISTERS
Agriculture, Water Resources and Rural Development: Alhaji A Hashidu
Commerce and Tourism: A V M Yahaya (Rtd)
Defence (and CDS): General Sani Abacha, FSS, MNI
Education and Youth Development: Professor Aliyu B Fafunwa
Federal Capital Territory: Maj Gen N G Nasko (Rtd)
Finance: Alhaji Abubakar Alhaji
Foreign Affairs: Maj Gen I O S Nwachukwu (Rtd), FSS, MNI GCMG, PSC, LLD
Minister of State for Foreign Affairs: Ambassador Zakari Y Ibrahim
Health and Human Services: Professor Olikoye Ransome-Kuti
Information and Culture: Professor Sam Oyovbaire
Internal Affairs: Dr T Olagunju
Industry and Technology: Maj Gen A B Mamman (Rtd)
Justice: Mr Clement Akpangbo
Labour and Productivity: Alhaji Bunu Sherif Musa
Power and Steel: A V M Nura M Iman (Rtd), FSS, PSC, USAWC
Petroleum and Mineral Resources: Professor Jibril Aminu
Transport and Communications: Mr Olawau Ige
Works and Housing: Maj Gen M T Kontagora (Rtd)
Police Affairs: Alhaji Isma'ila Gwarzo, MNI
Establishment and Management Services: Mr Senas Ukpanah
Special Duties and National Planning Commission: Dr Chu Okongwu

STATE GOVERNORS
Abia: Dr Ogbonaya Onu (NRC)
Adamawa: Alhaji Sule Michikai (NRC)
Akwa Ibom: Obong Akpan Isemin (NRC)
Anambra: Dr Chukwuemeka Ezeife (SDP)
Bauchi: Alhaji Dahiru Mohammed (NRC)
Benue: Rev Fr Moses Adasu (SDP)
Borno: Maina Ma'aji Lawan (SDP)
Cross River: Clement David Ebri (NRC)
Delta: Chief Felix Ibru (SDP)
Edo: Chief John Oyegun (SDP)
Enugu: Dr Okwi Nwodo (NRC)
Imo: Chief Evans Enwerem (NRC)
Jigawa: Alhaji A S Birinkada (SDP)
Kaduna: Alhaji Dabo Lere (NRC)
Kano: Alhaji Kabiru Ibrahim Gaya (NRC)
Katsina: Alhaji Saidu Barda (NRC)
Kebbi: Alhaji Abubakar Musa (NRC)
Kogi: Alhaji Abubakar Audu (NRC)
Kwara: Alhaji Mohammed Shaaba Lafiagi (SDP)
Lagos: Chief Michael Otedola (NRC)
Niger: Dr Musa Inuwa (NRC)
Ogun: Chief Segun Osoba (SDP)
Ondo: Bamidele Isola Olumilua (SDP)
Osun: Adetunji Isiaka Adeleke (SDP)
Oyo: Chief Kolapo Isola (SDP)
Plateau: Fidelis Tapgun (SDP)
Rivers: Rufus Ada George (NRC)
Sokoto: Alhaji Yahaya Abdulkarim (NRC)
Taraba: Rev Jolly Toro Nyame (SDP)
Yobe: Bukar Abba Ibrahim (SDP)

Pakistan

Capital: Islamabad

Location, Topography, Climate

The Islamic Republic of Pakistan is situated in the North West of the Indian sub-continent between Latitude 23° 45′ and 36° 50′ North and Longitude 60° 55′ and 75° 30′ East covering an area of 803, 943 sq km excluding territory in Jammu and Kashmir whose status is in dispute.

Pakistan is bounded to the West and North West by Iran and Afghanistan, to the North East by a short frontier with China, to East and South by Jammu and Kashmir and India and to the South West by the Arabian Sea. Pakistan is separated from the Soviet Union by a short panhandle of Afghan territory called the Wakhan Corridor.

A part of the Indo-Gangetic Plain, fed by the five rivers of the Punjab: Indus, Jhelum, Chenab, Ravi, and Sutlej, runs 1,609 km (1,000 miles) North East from Karachi to Lahore and Rawalpindi. In the North East are the high Himalaya, Karakoram and Pamir ranges, containing three of the world's highest peaks (K2, Nanga Parbat and Rakaposhi). In the North and West are lower mountain ranges and plateaux inland from the Afghan and Iranian borders. To the South the Thar desert borders India.

The climate is arid and semi arid. The Plains have three seasons. The cool season lasts from November to February (12°C in January but warmer at the coast (18°C)). In the hot season from March to August temperatures range between 32°C and 49°C. From June to September the South West Monsoon brings wind and rain (average 440 mm in the Plains to 1,750 mm in the Northern Hills). The mountains have long and severe winters; the snow melt is a vital element of the country's water supply.

Population

Pakistan is the world's ninth most populous country, the estimated population by 1990 was around 110 million. There are 5 towns with populations of over 750,000: Karachi, Lahore, Faislabad, Hyderabad and Multan. Annual rate of population growth is around 3.1 per cent. Ninety-five per cent of the population are Muslim (mainly Sunni but with a substantial Shia minority), the remainder are Hindu, Christian and some Parsis (Zoroastrians). The major ethnic groups are Punjabi, Sindhi, Pushtun, Muhajr (Urdu speaking refugees from India after 1947 and Bangladesh after 1971, mainly settled in Sindh province) and Baluch. Another ethnic group, the Seraikis, are to be found in southern Punjab and northern Sindh. The official language is Urdu, but English is widely used in both government and business. The ethnic groups use their own languages locally.

Health

Average annual birth rate is estimated in 1980–1985 at 41.6 per 1,000 and the Death Rate at 96 per 1,000. The infant mortality rate is 110 per 1,000 births. Tropical diseases found in Pakistan include malaria and dysentery. Leprosy has been successfully controlled. Illicit drug consumption has become a serious problem in recent years and a few cases of Aids have been reported. There are both public and private hospitals in the major towns; the major teaching hospital is the Aga Khan Hospital in Karachi.

Communications

Communications, both internal and international are by air, road, railway and by sea from Karachi and Bin Qasim. River transport is impossible in the mountainous areas and rarely used even in the plains.

Pakistan International Airlines is State-owned and flies from Karachi and Islamabad to North America, Europe, China, the Soviet Union and the Middle and Far East with a fleet of 747s.

Internally, a fleet of Fokker aircraft serves the major towns and are particularly important to the Northern Regions where mountain roads are hazardous.

There were 8,775 km of rail track in 1990 serving the length of the country through the Indus Plain and linking the port of Karachi with the hinterland via Lahore up to Peshawar. A line serves Baluchistan through the Bolan pass. Rail links to India exist but are currently severely restricted. Freight and passengers are carried and the stock is in need of modernisation.

There were over 111,000 km of main and secondary roads in 1990. They are heavily used, especially by a fleet of 130,000 buses and lorries. Pakistan has one road link with India which is open to traffic, as well as road links to Iran, Afghanistan (affected however by the Afghan war) and China. The latter is by the Karakoram Highway, open to international travellers since 1986, which passes over the Khunjerab Pass (5,000 m) in the Karakoram Range into Xinjiang Province.

Karachi is the main port, handling some 17.8 million long tons of goods in 1988/89. A second port Mohammed Bin Qasim is in partial operation (over 3 million tons handled in 1988/89) and efforts are also being made to develop Gwador in Baluchistan as a mini-port.

Media

Radio and television are state-owned and run by the Pakistan Broadcasting Corporation and Pakistan Television respectively. There are five radio stations. The National Service broadcasts in a number of the regional languages and in Urdu and there is an external service in 17 languages. There are two Television Channels broadcasting news, religious, educational and entertainment programmes mainly in Urdu but also in English.

There is a wide variety of newspapers, mainly in Urdu or English. The Urdu press comprises almost 800 newspapers of which twelve are published on a national basis. The biggest is Daily Jang which also produces an edition in the UK. There are several English language papers including *The Dawn* (Karachi), *The News* (Karachi, Lahore and Islamabad), *The Nation* (Lahore), *The Muslim* and the State-owned *Pakistan Times*. There are numerous weekly, fortnightly and monthly periodicals. Although the English language press is numerically small and reaches only a minority of the population, it is influential in political, academic, professional and business circles.

During the martial law period the media was subject to some censorship and guidance. With the installation of a democratic government in 1988 freedom of the press has improved.

The Economy

The Pakistan Economy is regulated in accordance with a series of 5 year plans. The Seventh (1988–93) projecting a total expenditure of Rs 616.000 m: Public Sector investment accounting for Rs 350.000 m and the Private Sector Rs 266.000 m. The plan gives priority to enlarging the Private Sector role in industry, education, energy, development and employment. Target GDP growth is 4.5 per cent in real terms; this averaged 6.7 per cent during the 1970s but declined to 4.8 per cent in 1988/9 recovering to 5.8 per cent in 1989/90. Per capita income is increasing at about half GDP rate. Pakistan's strong growth rate is affected by an annual population growth of 3.1 per cent accompanied by a low literacy rate of 29 per cent; by world commodity prices and international quotas; and by weather conditions affecting both exports and imports, especially cotton, as well as rice, wheat, sugar, edible oils and energy. Recently, the economy has been hit by the effects of the Gulf crisis. Steep rises in energy costs and the loss of around $300 million in remittances following the repatriation of some 70,000 migrant workers from Kuwait and Iraq have boosted short term domestic inflation and increased the projected trade deficit to an estimated $2.1 billion although Pakistan's export performance has been better than expected since this estimate was made. The new Government responded with an austerity programme, including increases in utility prices and widening the scope of sales tax to cover both the manufacturing and the retail sectors.

Agriculture is the most important industry accounting for 23 per cent of GDP and employing 50 per cent of available labour. It is widely supported by irrigation which also poses problems of waterlogging and of salinity, 60 per cent of all agricultural land being affected in some degree. Cotton is the main crop and chief foreign exchange earner followed by rice, wheat and sugar cane.

Manufacturing industry accounts for 20 per cent of GDP and employs 13 per cent of the labour force. Major industries are textiles, cotton yarn, cement, fertilisers, sugar, vegetable oil, iron and steel. Major exports based mostly on local commodities are cotton textiles and yarn, leather goods, sports goods and carpets. Production of the manufacturing sector increased by an annual average of over 7 per cent. In his first parliamentary speech as Prime Minister, Nawaz Sharif identified the liberalisation of the economy and, in particular, the privatisation of State owned industries, banks and insurance companies as a key priority. Two State companies have since been privatised and the Government has taken measures to liberalise for example foreign exchange dealings.

Total energy requirements are met by consumption of oil (around 41 per cent), gas (around 36 per cent) and coal (6 per cent). Natural gas (over 400 million cu ft per annum) covers domestic consumption but only around one-third of domestic oil requirements are produced locally (60,000 bpd). Hydropower supplies about 45 per cent of totalled installed power capacity (8,430 MW); new dams at Kalabagh and Busha are planned to boost capacity further but construction is subject to resolution of inter-provincial disputes. Power from new plants using open cast coal mining is expected to become available in 1992. Nuclear provides only a small percentage of energy requirements but the proportion will rise in the late 1990's. A 300 MW second atomic reactor is under construction at Chasma, and negotiations are taking place with France for a possible new 900 MW plant at Islamabad. Shortage of energy remains a major constraint on industrial expansion.

Pakistan has received aid from the World Bank, IMF, Asian Development Bank and a number of bilateral donors notably the US and Japan, although US aid is currently suspended under the Pressler Amendment. A Donor's Consortium in May 1991 pledged US$2.3 bn for 1991/92 and in September 1991 the IMF released the final tranche of a US$850 m facility agreed in December 1988 to support a three year economic adjustment programme which includes tax reforms, liberalisation of external trade and the encouragement of domestic investment. The programme envisaged an annual growth rate of between 5.2 and 5.5 per cent, a reduction of the annual rate of inflation to 6 per cent although some of these Conditions were relaxed in subsequent negotiations with the IMF. The new government has pledged to maintain the adjustment programme and has sought increased support to cope with the impact of the Gulf crisis.

The USA and Japan are Pakistan's principal trading partners each providing around 15 per cent of imports and accounting for 10 per cent of exports, followed by Germany, the UK and Saudi Arabia.

Education

Universal free primary education is a constitutional right but it is not compulsory. Primary education begins at the age of 5 and lasts for 5 years. Secondary education lasts for up to a further 7 years. Total primary and secondary education reaches 30 per cent of all school age children. Higher education is provided by Vocational Institutes, Professional Colleges and Universities with a total of over 600,000 students. UNESCO adult literacy figures for 1985 were 30.9 per cent men and 19.6 per cent women, an average of 29.6 per cent.

History

Pakistan, created in August 1947 by the partition of British India, was founded on the inspiration of the poet Mohammed Iqbal and on the political leadership of Mohammed Ali Jinnah who were determined to establish a national home for the Muslims on the subcontinent. At Independence, Pakistan consisted of a West Wing, now the Islamic Republic of Pakistan, and an East Wing, now Bangladesh. It proved impossible to maintain the unity of these two economically and ethnically distant wings separated by 1,000 miles of Indian territory. Jinnah, revered as founder of the State and the first Governor-General died in September 1948. Pakistan's first Prime Minister, Liaquat Ali Khan, was assassinated in 1951. A Constitution adopted in 1956 and establishing a Federal Republic of the two wings and a parliamentary form of Government was abrogated in 1958 when Martial Law was declared. The Commander-in-Chief General Ayub Khan later assumed the Presidency. The 1962 Constitution provided for a Presidential system of Government with a largely indirect system of elections. However, serious disturbances beginning in late 1968 forced Ayub Khan to hand over power in March 1969 to Field Marshall Yahya Khan, who in turn abrogated the 1962 Constitution and declared Martial Law. In Pakistan's first General Elections in December 1970 the Awami League led by Sheikh Mujibur Rahman advocating provincial autonomy captured virtually all seats in East Pakistan giving it an overall majority in the National Assembly. The Pakistan People's Party (PPP) led by Z A Bhutto won a substantial majority in West Pakistan. Attempts to form a coalition between the two parties and agree upon a Constitution failed, with the Awami League increasing their demands for complete autonomy for East Pakistan. In November President Yahya Khan reimposed Martial Law. The Awami League declared a political strike and civil war broke out. Fighting continued in East Pakistan until December 1971 when India intervened forcing the Pakistan Army to surrender and securing the independence of Bangladesh.

Following Bangladeshi independence on 16th December 1971 Yahya Khan was replaced by Mr Bhutto as President and civilian Chief Martial Law Administrator who aimed to restructure Pakistan's institutions and redirect its economic and social development to provide a more equitable social order on which to base political stability. Major structural reforms of the Civil Service, Judiciary and Armed Forces were enforced as were wide reaching agrarian reform, an enlarged Government role in economic policy and large scale nationalisation of financial institutions and basic industry. In 1972 Pakistan withdrew from the Commonwealth, although relations with India were restored by the Simla Agreement. In 1973 a Constitution approved by Parliament gave wide powers to the Prime Minister, a post assumed by Mr Bhutto. In 1977 the PPP won handsomely in national and provincial elections but was accused by the opposition of election rigging. In response a grouping of opposition forces, the Pakistan National Alliance, launched a nationwide agitation. The Army Chief of Staff General Zia-ul-Haq staged a bloodless coup on 5th July 1977 'to avert chaos and a more serious crisis.' Martial law was imposed and Mr Bhutto was arrested and tried for conspiring to murder a political opponent. His conviction and death sentence was later confirmed by the Supreme Court and despite international appeals for clemency, he was hanged on 4th April 1979.

Although initially promising fresh general elections General Zia-ul-Haq moved to align the country's institutions with Islamic law and to find a political formula allowing a return to a degree of civilian and democratic rule without, as he saw it, losing the efficiency of military order or suffering divisive party politics. In 1979 new Islamic penal and fiscal laws were introduced, planned elections were scrapped, political parties were banned and until 1985 Zia ruled through a series of cabinets containing technocrats, army officers and politicians who forsook party affiliations. In 1981 a 300 member Federal Council nominated by Zia was established under a Provisional Constitutional Order (PCO), and a special committee of the Council, asked to advise on Pakistan's future political system, recommended a restoration of parliamentary government. Meanwhile the deposed PPP, reorganised under the leadership of Mr Bhutto's daughter Benazir, accused Zia of seeking to perpetuate his own power and together with other opposition forces, formed the Movement for the Restoration of Democracy in 1981. In 1983 the MRD launched a major uprising which caused casualties in the Sindh but failed to unseat the government. In December 1984 a national referendum on the official Islamisation programme was held, the affirmative vote was taken to endorse Zia as President until 1990. In February 1985 elections took place as promised but on a non-party basis. An indirectly elected Senate together with the newly elected National Assembly replaced the Federal Council. Zia then nominated Mohammed Khan Junejo as Prime Minister. Following the passage of legislation putting the past actions of military rule beyond legal challenge and legalising political parties, martial law was lifted and fundamental rights restored on 30th December 1985.

With elections now scheduled for 1990 Miss Benazir Bhutto returned from exile in April 1986 to a rousing reception and called for Zia's resignation, and the restoration of full party democracy. The

Junejo government faced increasing law and order problems, especially in the Sindh where serious communal strife occurred in late 1986/early 1987. Accusing the Prime Minister of ineffectiveness, General Zia in May 1988 dismissed the government and dissolved the National and Provincial assemblies. Sharia, the Islamic legal code was declared the superior law of Pakistan.

New non-party elections were announced for November 1988, but in August President Zia was killed in an aircrash (for which neither cause nor responsibility have yet been established). An emergency National Council assumed power and declared that the elections should proceed. At the elections the PPP emerged as the largest party in the National Assembly, while the party speaking for Muslim immigrants from India (MQM) established itself as a major third force in urban Sindh. An alliance between the PPP, MQM and Independents secured Miss Bhutto's appointment as Prime Minister (the first woman leader of a Muslim country). The Islamic Democratic Alliance became the main opposition party. The Emergency was lifted, the National Council dissolved, and a new cabinet appointed.

Although the new government soon released political prisoners, lifted the ban on trade unions, and reduced state control of the press it did not undertake a major legislative programme. Its freedom of manoeuvre was limited by having to contend with an inherited economic crisis. A cautious but well-balanced budget was passed in April 1989, abiding by the terms of an IMF Agreement entered into by its predecessor government. Domestic budget deficits were reduced but inflation and the worsening balance of payments remained causes for concern.

Miss Bhutto's government achieved foreign policy successes including the hosting of the summit of the South Asian Association for Regional Co-operation (SAARC) leaders in December 1988, obtaining an extra $3 billion of assistance from the Western Aid Consortium in July 1989, and by returning Pakistan into the Commonwealth from 1st October 1989. No progress was made, however, on resolving two key external issues: the Kashmir problem with India, and the crisis in Afghanistan which left over 3m refugees on Pakistan soil.

The task of Miss Bhutto's government was made difficult by the Opposition dominance of the Senate and control of two of the country's four provinces. The Chief Minister of Punjab province, Nawaz Sharif, was instrumental in assembling a wide ranging alliance of opposition forces, the Combined Opposition Party (COP). In October 1989 the MQM broke with the PPP and joined the COP prompting the tabling of a vote of no-confidence which was only defeated by 12 votes.

Recent Political Developments

On 6th August 1990 President Ghulam Ishaq Khan, using powers granted to him under the 1973 Constitution, dismissed the Bhutto Government and dissolved the National Assembly. He did so on the grounds that the PPP Administration had been corrupt and had not dealt adequately with the country's problems—especially the ethnic violence in the Sindh. He appointed a caretaker Cabinet, with COP leader Ghulam Mustapha Jatoi as caretaker Prime Minister, and announced that general elections would be held on 24th October.

The caretaker administration declared that officials of the previous government who were suspected of having misused their positions would be tried under special "accountability" tribunals under legislation dating from General Zia's government. Anyone convicted could be debarred from holding political office for seven years. Among those charged were five former federal ministers (one was later acquitted) and Miss Bhutto herself pleaded not guilty to seven charges of corruption.

The elections were held as scheduled and, although the difference in actual votes was small, the IDA won decisively in terms of seats—mainly due to a landslide triumph in the largest province, Punjab. The IDA secured 105 seats in the National Assembly against 45 by the PPP. In the provincial elections the PPP lost power in both the North West Frontier Province and its traditional heartland of Sindh and also remained an opposition party in the Punjab Assembly. Of the third parties the MQM retained its predominance in the cities of Karachi and Hyderabad and emerged as the largest component in a new coalition government in Sindh. Other regional parties, such as the Awami National Party, also fared well, but the smaller religious parties lost ground.

With the additional support of independents, minor parties and non-Muslim representatives, the IDA leader (and former Punjab Chief Minister), Nawaz Sharif, was elected as Prime Minister by the National Assembly on 6th November.

Initially Nawaz Sharif achieved notable agreements on longstanding issues such as the distribution of water and financial resources between the four provinces. He also successfully maintained Pakistan's position of support for UN-sponsored action against Iraq during the Gulf conflict in face of considerable domestic pressures. A former industrialist, he has pursued free market reforms to reduce budget deficits and attract foreign investment and has also introduced a privatisation programme involving 100 companies. The passing of a Shariat (Islamic Law) in May 1991—designed to pave the way for an "Islamic Welfare State"—was greeted with alarm by liberal and secular forces. Law and order has continued to be a problem, with an upsurge in organised crime, riots in Baluchistan involving Afghan refugees and, above all, ethnic violence in Sindh between urban Muhajirs (Urdu-speaking refugees from India) and native Sindhis.

Problems of internal security have been compounded by financial scandals linked to the collapse of BCCI and several co-operative banks. This has led to some doubts over the credibility of the new government. In August the PPP joined with 20 other opposition groups to demand the government's resignation and fresh elections. The Prime Minister was also accused with other Ministers of corruption and abuse of power. The allegations have been denied but a judicial commission of investigation has been set up. The crisis caused the Prime Minister to postpone local elections due in November until April 1992.

Although Miss Bhutto has consistently claimed that the result of the October 1990 elections were fraudulent the PPP continues to participate in the National and Provincial Assemblies, and Miss Bhutto herself is facing charges of corruption.

Nawaz Sharif expanded his cabinet to a record size in September 1991 involving 12 new Ministers and 17 more Ministers of State embracing associates and relatives of chief rivals within the ruling Islamic Democratic Alliance.

Relations with India are currently stable—with Kashmir a continuing stumbling block to substantial improvement. A more pressing problem has been the suspension of further military and economic aid by the USA (although funds from earlier commitments are still being disbursed) because of the perceived direction of Pakistan's nuclear programme, but both sides appear willing to have discussions to resolve this issue in a regional context.

Constitution

The constitution in force was promulgated on 10th April 1973; and amended in 1985. Much of it was suspended following the imposition of Martial Law in 1977 and restored on 30th December 1985.

The Constitution proclaims Pakistan to be Islamic and Democratic with fundamental rights guaranteed, including the freedoms of thought, speech, religion and worship, assembly, association and the Press, as well as equality of status.

Pakistan consists of four provinces, Baluchistan, North West Frontier Province (NWFP), Punjab and Sindh as well as the Tribal Areas in the NWFP that are federally administered. The Provinces are autonomous units with their own Provincial Assemblies and Cabinets.

The Head of State is the President, who must be Muslim and who is elected by the Federal Legislature for a term of five years. The Federal Legislature consists of a Lower House, the National Assembly, of 207 members directly elected on the basis of universal suffrage (adults over 21) plus 20 women members and 10 members representing minorities. The Prime Minister is elected by the National Assembly. The Senate or Upper House consists of 87 members elected by the Provincial Assemblies (19 each), 8 returned from the Tribal Areas and 3 from the Federal Capital. The Assembly has sole authority for Money Bills. Otherwise Bills may be originated in either House.
(See also 1972 edition)

Government
(October 1991)

HEAD OF STATE
President: His Excellency President Ghulam Ishaq Khan

MINISTERS
Prime Minister (also holds Foreign Affairs Portfolio): Mohammad Nawaz Sharif (IJI)
Interior: Choudhry Shujaat Hussain (IJI)
Industries and Culture: Sheik Rashid Ahmed (IJI)
Narcotics Control: Rana Chandar Singh (Minority Seat)
Environment and Urban Affairs: Anwar Saifullah Khan (IND)
Commerce: Malik Mohammad Naeem Khan (IJI)
Food and Agriculture: Lt Gen (Rtd) Abdul Majid Malik (IJI)
Production: Islam Nabi (MQM)
Finance, Economic Affairs: Sartaj Aziz (IJI)
Communications: Ghulam Murtaza Jatoi (IND)
Railways: Ghulam Ahmed Bilour (IJI)
Petroleum and Natural Resources: Choudhry Nisar Ali Khan (IJI)
Science and Technology: Illahi Bukhsh Soomro (IND)
Health: Syed Tasneem Nawaz Gardezi (IJI)
Housing and Works: Syed Tariq Mahmood (MQM)
Labour, Manpower, Overseas Pakistanis: Mohammad Ijaz-ul-Haq (IJI)
Education: Syed Fakhar Imam (IJI)
Minister for Kashmir and Northern Areas and Minority Affairs: Sardar Mehtab Ahmed Khan (IJI)
Parliamentary Affairs and Youth Affairs: Choudhry Amir Hussain (IJI)
Advisor to the Prime Minister: Roedad Khan (Non-elected)
Advisor to the Prime Minister: Mohammed Asad Ali Junejo (Non-elected)
Advisor to PM on Population Welfare: Syeda Abida Hussain (Non-elected)
Religious Affairs: Maulana Sattar Niazi (IJI)
Local Government and Rural Development: Ghulam Dastagir Khan (IJI)
Defence: Syed Ghous Ali Shah (IJI)
Information and Broadcasting: Abdus Sattar Lalika (IJI)
Law and Justice: Choudhry Abdul Ghafoor (IJI)
Water and Power: Shahzada Mohammad Yousaf (IND)
Inter-Provincial Co-ordination: Mohammad Aslam Khan Khattak (IND)
Defence Production: Mir Hazar Khan Bijarani (IJI)
State and Frontier Region: Sardar Yaqub Khan Naseer (IJI)
Planning and Development: Chandhry Hamid Nasir Chattha (IJI)

The Independent State of Papua New Guinea

Capital: Port Moresby

Papua New Guinea extends from the equator to Cape Baganowa in the Louisiade Archipelago at 11° south latitude and from the border with Irian Jaya to 160° east longitude. The total area of Papua New Guinea is 461,693 sq km (178,260 square miles).

The central core of the mainland is a massive cordillera which forms a complex system of ranges often separated by broad upland valleys. The central cordillera is bordered on north and south by an extensive zone of foothills, drained to the north by the Sepik and Ramu rivers and to the south by the Fly.

The main islands in Papua New Guinea are the Bismarck Archipelago, a portion of the Solomon Islands, the Trobriands, the D'Entrecasteaux Islands and the Louisiade Archipelago. The Bismarck Archipelago comprises New Britain, New Ireland and Manus. Bougainville is the largest of the Solomon Islands within Papua New Guinea.

Papua New Guinea lies wholly within the tropics between the continents of Asia and Australia and has a typically monsoonal climate. Atmospheric temperature and humidity are uniformly high throughout the year with the mean maximum seldom exceeding 33°C (92°F) and the mean minimum rarely falling below 22°C (72°F). The Highland valleys have a more temperate climate. The average rainfall is about 2,000 mm per year but there are wide variations from 1,175 mm at Port Moresby to over 5,000 mm in the mountainous western areas.

Population

In 1989 the estimated population of Papua New Guinea was 3.7 million. Papua New Guineans comprise a great diversity of physical types and over 700 linguistic groups. They may, in general, be grouped with the Melanesians who occupy the greater part of the Western Pacific. The population is increasing by approximately 2.3 per cent annually.

Economy

Although most of the population engage in traditional subsistence agriculture, there are important commercial cash crops: copra, coffee, cocoa, timber, palm oil, rubber, tea, sugar and cardamom are grown on substantial modern estates, long established plantations or smallholdings. The economy (and the balance of payments) has been much influenced in recent years by the development of mineral wealth. The world's largest known deposits of low grade copper were mined at Panguna, North Solomons Province. But Separatist insurgent activity caused the closure of the mine in May 1989. Gold has been mined in small quantities for many years and the development at Ok Tedi in Western Province is yielding large deposits of gold as well as copper. Gold has also been found in significant quantities in Porgera, Misima, Lihir and Mount Kare.

Petroleum has been discovered in workable quantities at Kutubu and is expected to come on stream, via a pipe-line to the Gulf of Papua, in 1992. Natural gas has been discovered in Hides, close to Porgera, and will be used to provide electricity to the mine.

The limited industrial sector, originally orientated towards processing primary products, now also partly meets local needs. Examples are brewing, bottling and packaging, paint, plywood, printing, metal manufacturing and the construction industries.

The unit of currency is the Kina. The rate is computed daily against a basket of international currencies.

History

New Guinea was sighted by Portuguese and Spanish navigators in the early part of the sixteenth century. Following occasional visits by navigators of several countries, some limited exploration and occasional European small settlements took place from the mid-nineteenth century. In 1884 Germany formally took possession of those areas which later came to be known as German New Guinea. Administration was placed in the hands of a chartered company, the German New Guinea Company, but in 1889 the German Government assumed control. In 1914 German New Guinea was occupied by Australian troops and remained under military administration until 1921.

On 6th November 1884 a British Protectorate was proclaimed over the southern coast of New Guinea and the adjacent islands lying between 141st and 155th meridians of east longitude and the 5th and 12th parallels of south latitude. British New Guinea, as the Protectorate was called, was annexed outright on 4th September 1888.

In 1902 the Territory of British New Guinea was placed under the authority of the Commonwealth of Australia; under the Papua Act 1905 it became the Territory of Papua. This Act came into force on 1st September 1906 and Australian administration began from that date.

In 1920 the League of Nations conferred on the Australian Government a mandate for the government of German New Guinea. The New Guinea Act 1920 provided for the governing of the Territory in accordance with Article 22 of the Covenant of the League.

Former German New Guinea was administered under the mandate and Papua was administered under the Papua Act until the invasion by the Japanese in 1942, when the civil administration was suspended and an Australian Military Government established for the parts not occupied by the Japanese.

With the return of peace civil administration was progressively restored, under the provisions of the Papua–New Guinea Provisional Administration Act 1945–46. This Act and the subsequent Papua and New Guinea Act 1949 approved the placing of New Guinea under the International Trusteeship System of the United Nations and provided for the government of New Guinea in an administrative union with Papua with the title of the Territory of Papua and New Guinea.

The Act also provided for a Legislative Council (established at Port Moresby on 26th November 1951) and also for a judicial organisation, a public service and a system of local government. The Legislative Council consisted of the Administrator and 28 other members, 16 of whom were official members, three were elected and nine appointed. At least three of the nine appointed members were to be Papua New Guineans.

The Papua and New Guinea Act 1960 increased the size of the Legislative Council to 37 members who were to include the Administrator, 12 elected members, of whom six were to be Papua New Guineans elected by the Papua New Guinea people; 10 appointed members, of whom at least five were to be Papua New Guineans; and 14 official members.

The Papua and New Guinea Act 1963 replaced the Legislative Council by a House of Assembly. The first House of Assembly opened on 8th June 1964 and had 64 members who included an elected Papua New Guinean majority and only 10 nominated official members.

In May 1965 the House of Assembly appointed a Select Committee on constitutional development.

The Papua and New Guinea Act 1967 implemented the recommendations contained in the first report of the Select Committee by increasing the number of elected members of the House of Assembly to 84. The Papua and New Guinea Act 1968 implemented the recommendations of the Select Committee concerning the executive government, including a new ministerial system and an Administrator's Executive Council. The Act provided for seven Ministerial Members and eight Assistant Ministerial Members with departmental functions. The Administrator's Executive Council comprised the seven Ministerial Members, three Official Members, the Administrator, and at his discretion a Councillor chosen from the elected members who were not holding office as Ministerial Members. A spokesman of the Administrator's Executive Council was appointed in 1970 and he was acknowledged as the leader of Government Business in the House.

From 1970 there was a gradual assumption of powers by the Papua New Guinea Government. In March 1971 the Select Committee on Constitutional Development had made its final report which recommended that the Territory should take steps during the period 1972–76 to prepare for self-government and recommended changes in the composition of the Legislature.

Elections held in April 1972 returned a House of Assembly which had 100 elected members; there were only four official and three appointed members. A coalition government was formed with Mr Michael Somare as Chief Minister; formal self-government was achieved in December 1973. Final reserve powers held by Australia over defence and foreign relations were largely relinquished in March 1975.

Papua New Guinea achieved full independence on 16th September 1975, with HM Queen Elizabeth II as Head of State, and Sir John Guise, a Papua New Guinean, as the first Governor-General.

Michael Somare again formed a coalition government after the elections of June 1977. In November 1978 the People's Progress Party withdrew from the Coalition Government and the Pangu Party, the major partner, continued in government with the United Party as its coalition partner.

In March 1980 Michael Somare suffered a Parliamentary defeat and was succeeded by Sir Julius Chan as Prime Minister. The Chan Government was a coalition of the People's Progress Party, the National Party, the United Party, Papua Besena and the Melanesian Alliance. Following a general election in June 1982, Michael Somare was again elected Prime Minister by Parliament and formed a coalition government from the Pangu and United Parties. In 1985 the Melanesian Alliance and National Party joined the Government, which however lost some of its own supporters to the Opposition. In March 1985 the former Deputy Prime Ministry Paias Wingti resigned from Pangu and founded the People's Democratic Movement. In November 1985, Paias Wingti with support from the People's Progress Party and National Party successfully tabled a motion of no-confidence in the Government and became the first Prime Minister from the Highland region. The election in July 1987 resulted in a coalition government headed by Paias Wingti, which was defeated on a no-confidence motion in July 1988 and succeeded by a Pangu-led coalition under Mr Rabbie Namaliu as Prime Minister; Mr Namaliu had succeeded Michael Somare when the latter resigned as Leader of the Pangu Party in May 1988.

The island of Bougainville, in the North Solomons Province, declared its independence from Papua New Guinea in 1990. Bougainville's independence has, however, been acknowledged by no other country. After a military operation failed to end the secessionist claims, a blockade was imposed on the island by the Papua New Guinea Government. Talks are currently taking place, and the blockade has been lifted, but the question of Bougainville's sovereignty has not yet been resolved.

Sir John Guise resigned as Governor-General in February 1977 and Sir Tore Lokoloko was appointed for a six-year term. He was succeeded in 1983 by Sir Kingsford Dibela, and by Sir Ignatius Kilage in 1989. Sir Ignatius died in office on 31st December 1989 and was succeeded by Sir Serei Eri. Sir Wiwa Korowi succeeded Sir Serei Eri on 18th November 1991.

Papua New Guinea became a member of the Commonwealth on 16th September 1975 and of the United Nations on 10th October 1975. Prior to independence Papua New Guinea had become an associate member of UNESCO, ESCAP, IMF, IBRD, IDA and the International Telecommunications Union. Papua New Guinea became a full member of the IMF and FAO in 1975. Papua New Guinea is also a signatory of the Lomé Convention; has observer status with ASEAN, NAM, and is a member of both the South Pacific Forum and Commission.

HEAD OF STATE
Her Majesty Queen Elizabeth II

GOVERNOR-GENERAL
The Hon Sir Wiwa Korowi, GCMG, KStJ

SPEAKER OF NATIONAL PARLIAMENT
Mr Dennis Young CMG

The distribution of portfolios at October 1991 was:

Prime Minister: Rabbie Namaliu, CMG
Deputy Prime Minister: Akoka Doi, KBE
Minister for Public Service: Jacob Lemeki
Foreign Affairs: Sir Michael Somare GCMG, CH
Finance and Planning: Paul Pora
Trade and Industry: John Giheno
Provincial Affairs: Father John Momis
Justice: Bernard Narokobi
Forests: Jack Genia
Labour and Employment: Tony Ila CMG
Civil Aviation: John Wauwia
Defence: Benais Sabumei MBE
Home Affairs: Mathew Bendumb CMG
Education: Utula Samana
Minerals and Energy: Patterson Lowa CBE
Agriculture and Livestock: Tom Pais
Works: Lukus Waka
Administrative Services: William Wi
Environment and Conservation: Michael Singan
Corrective Institutions: Tenda Lau
Communications: Brown Sinamoi CMG
Police: Mathias Ijape
Transport: Anthony Temo
Fisheries: Akoka Doi KBE
Culture and Tourism: Gerald Beona
Lands and Physical Planning: Sir Hugo Berghuser
Health: Galeva Kwarara
Housing: Bob Bubec
Minister of State: Akoka Doi KBE

St Christopher and Nevis

Capital: Basseterre

The two islands of St Christopher (St Kitts) and Nevis lie in the northern part of the Leeward group of the Lesser Antilles in the Eastern Caribbean. St Kitts and Nevis are separated by a channel some two miles in width.

St Kitts (17° 20′ N., 62° 48′ W.) is roughly oval in shape, with a narrow neck of land extending like a handle from the south-eastern end. The total length of the island is 37 km (23 miles) and its area is 168 sq km (65 square miles). The central part of the main body consists of a rugged mountain range whose highest point is Mount Liamuiga (formerly Mount Misery) (1,138 m). A branch of the range encloses a spacious and fertile valley, on the seaboard of which lies the capital, Basseterre, with a population of about 15,000. This valley and the circle of land formed by the skirts and lower slopes of the mountain constitutes most of the arable and cultivated portion of the island. The higher slopes are covered with short grass, affording excellent pasturage, and the summits of the range are crowned with forest. The dominant crop is sugar cane. St Kitts is of volcanic formation and most of the beaches are of black volcanic sand but the best, fringing the peninsula (known as Frigate Bay and Salt Ponds) which reaches out towards Nevis, are golden.

Nevis (17° 10′ N., 62° 35′ W.) has an area of 93 sq km (36 square miles). Like St Kitts, it was discovered by Columbus in 1493. It was first colonised by English settlers from St Kitts in 1628. The island's peak, which appears perfectly conical from some angles, its tip usually encircled by clouds, rises gradually to 970 m, giving Nevis a spectacularly beautiful appearance from the sea. There are long stretches of golden sandy beaches. Most of the inhabitants are peasant farmers. The main crops are vegetables and coconuts, but whereas the soil of St Kitts (except in the mountains) is light and porous that of Nevis is stiff clay studded with volcanic boulders. The only town, Charlestown, has a population of about 1,200.

The climate of St Christopher and Nevis is pleasant and healthy. The islands lie on the path of the north-east trade winds and there is a steady cooling breeze throughout the year. The highest temperature recorded in this century is 33°C (92°F) and the lowest 17°C (62°F). Humidity is low and there is no rainy season. Average annual rainfall on St Kitts is about 1,375 mm. Tropical diseases are virtually non-existent.

On St Kitts, sugar remains the main employer of labour, on 30 estates, in the Sugar Factory and in ancillary services. Within the Federation the other main employers are Government, electronic plants, garment factories, food processing plants, the tourist industry, offices, stores and the construction industry. Most of the garment and electronics factories manufacture products for the United States market.

The total population in St Kitts and Nevis is estimated to be 45,100 (St Kitts 35,700, Nevis 9,400).

In January 1975 the House of Assembly passed the Sugar Estates' Lands Acquisition Act 1975, by which all the sugar estate lands were purported to be vested in the Crown on behalf of the people. Government also purchased the sugar factory from private ownership in 1976.

The take-over and control of the land provided the opportunity to introduce an improvement to the field side of the industry. The National Agricultural Corporation began operation in January 1976. Ten years later it was merged with the St Kitts Sugar Manufacturing Company which now deals with all crops.

There are 34 Government, 14 Private and 6 Denominational Schools in St Kitts and Nevis. Primary education is compulsory for all children between the ages of 5 to 14, but no pupil is required to leave school until the age of 16 years.

Agriculture in Nevis is almost exclusively on a peasant small-holding basis and more than half the small farms in the territory are on this island. There are, however, five large coconut estates and some privately-owned livestock farms. The main crops are cotton and vegetables.

Government revenue and expenditure figures for 1983 to 1989 are as follows:–

Year	*Revenue*	*Expenditure*
1986	EC$62,673,190	EC$66,312,977
1987	EC$73,127,680	EC$72,683,244
1988	EC$74,307,180	EC$72,948,635
1989	EC$86,966,000	EC$86,973,000
1990 (est)	EC$99,000,000	EC$93,200,000

Airports in the State are: Golden Rock, St Kitts, runway length 2,400 m, about 2.4 km from

Basseterre and Newcastle airfield; Nevis, runway length 810 m, 12 km from Charlestown. St Kitts has approximately 97 km of road, Nevis 101 km.

The Golden Rock Airport accommodates direct flights from the United States of America and Canada. Both this and the residential and tourist development of the Frigate Bay area are making a significant impact on the country's development. Several new hotel condominiums are currently being constructed in this zone, which contains two large hotels, some condominium villages, an 18-hole golf course and private homes. Construction was completed in December 1989 of a South-East Peninsula Road, which has opened up the previously uninhabited peninsula of St Kitts for development purposes. The Basseterre harbour contains a deepwater port, which has greatly facilitated cruise ship arrivals and the operations of cargo vessels since 1982–3.

In September 1989 Hurricane Hugo caused damage to housing and disruption of the electricity supply system. The United Kingdom helped in repairs to housing and rehabilitation of the electricity transmission supply in the country.

History

St Christopher, discovered by Columbus on his second voyage in 1493, was the first island in the West Indies to be colonised by the English, when Sir Thomas Warner took settlers there in 1623. In 1624 the French, under d'Esnambuc, also colonised part of the island

Intermittent warfare between the French and British settlers during the seventeenth century ravaged the economy of the island. It was, however, ceded to Britain by the treaty of Utrecht in 1713. The last fighting on the island took place in 1782 when the French captured Brimstone Hill after a memorable siege and once more took possession of St Christopher. The island was finally restored to Britain by the Treaty of Versailles in 1783.

Nevis, also sighted by Columbus on his voyage, was settled by the English in 1628 and soon became one of the most prosperous of the Antilles. Although it suffered from French and Spanish attacks in the seventeenth and eighteenth centuries, it maintained a sound economic position until the middle of the nineteenth century.

The former colony of St Kitts, Nevis and Anguilla assumed the status of association with the United Kingdom on 27th February 1967. The de facto separation of Anguilla from the state soon after was formally effected on 19th December 1980 leaving St Kitts and Nevis to move towards complete independence.

Following the Constitutional Conference in London in December 1982 it was agreed that the islands should become independent as a sovereign democratic federal state as the Federation of St. Christopher and Nevis (or St Kitts and Nevis). The state would be a monarchy with Her Majesty The Queen as head represented by a Governor General.

Independence Day was 19th September 1983.

Constitution

The Independence Constitution is basically the same as that in operation immediately before Independence.

The Governor-General is required to act in accordance with the advice of the Cabinet or a Minister acting under the general authority of the Cabinet which is collectively responsible to the National Assembly. The Cabinet consists of the Prime Minister, the other Ministers and at any time when his office is a public office, the Attorney-General *ex-officio*. The Governor-General appoints as Prime Minister a member of the National Assembly who appears to him likely to command a majority in that Assembly. The other Ministers are appointed from among the members of the Assembly on the advice of the Prime Minister. There is provision for the appointment of Parliamentary Secretaries.

Parliament consists of Her Majesty and the National Assembly. The National Assembly consists of a Speaker, eleven members elected in single member constituencies under universal adult suffrage (minimum age 18), one of whom may be the Speaker, and three nominated members (known as senators) or, if a nominated member is Attorney-General, four.

The main difference from before Independence is that Nevis has its own legislature, Premier and administration. The Legislature consists of Her Majesty The Queen and a Nevis Island Assembly. The Assembly consists of five elected and three nominated members. The Nevis Administration has exclusive administrative responsibility within Nevis for certain specific matters such as airports and seaports, education, extraction and processing of minerals, fisheries, health and welfare, labour and licensing of imports and exports. The Central Government retains responsibility for formulation of policy and Parliament has the power to legislate in these fields.

The Constitution makes provision for the seccession of Nevis from the federation subject to six months notice in the Nevis Assembly of full and detailed constitutional proposals for a separate state and to a two thirds majority vote in the Nevis Assembly followed by a two thirds majority for the bill in a referendum on the island.

A Puisne Judge of the Eastern Caribbean Supreme Court is resident in St Kitts.

The appointment, dismissal and disciplinary control of public officers are, with certain exceptions, vested in the Public Service and Police Service Commissions. There is provision for appeals to the Public Service Board of Appeal.

Land Policy

Aliens cannot own land except under licence from the Government.

Government

At the General Election in St Christopher and Nevis on 21st March 1989 the ruling People's Action Movement (PAM) retained its six seats to the Labour Party's two. The Nevis Reformation Party (NRP) won two of the island's seats, losing one to the Concerned Citizens Movement (CCM). The Federal Government is a coalition between PAM and NRP. In the Nevis Island Assembly four of the elected seats are held by the NRP and one by the CCM.

HEAD OF STATE

Her Majesty Queen Elizabeth II

GOVERNOR-GENERAL

H E Sir Clement Arrindell, GCMG, KCVO, KB, QC

MINISTERS

Prime Minister and Minister of Finance, Home Affairs and Foreign Affairs: Rt Hon Dr Kennedy S A Simmonds

Deputy Prime Minister and Minister for Labour and Tourism: Hon Michael O Powell

Minister in Prime Minister's Office: Hon Joseph Parry

Minister for Education, Youth and Community Affairs, and Communications, Works and Public Utilities: Hon Sydney Morris

Special Assistant in Ministry of Communications, Works and Public Utilities: Royden Benjamin

Special Adviser in Ministry of Communications, Works and Public Utilities: Uriel Swanston

Minister of Agriculture, Lands, Housing and Development: Hon Hugh Heyliger

Assistant to Minister of Agriculture, Lands, Housing and Development: Roosevelt Caines

Minister for Trade and Industry: Hon Fitzroy Jones

Minister for Women's Affairs and Health: Hon Constance V Mitcham

Minister in the Ministry of Finance: Hon Richard L Caines

Attorney-General (ex officio): Hon S W Tapley Seaton

St Lucia

Capital: Castries

St Lucia, in the Windward Island group, lies 39 km (24 miles) to the south of Martinique and 34 km (21 miles) north-east of St Vincent, latitude 14° N., longitude 61° W. The island is pear-shaped and measures 43 km by 23 km (27 miles by 14 miles). Its circumference is 241 km (150 miles) and its area about 616 sq km (238 square miles).

The island is mountainous, with magnificent scenery. The highest peak is Mt Gimie (944 m); the most spectacular are the Gros Piton (786 m) and the Petit Piton (738 m) which are old volcanic forest-clad cones rising sheer out of the sea. Petit Piton, the steeper of the two, stands guard like a sentinel over the harbour of Soufrière, while Gros Piton, one mile away as the crow flies, is actually in the parish of Choiseul. A few miles away from Petit Piton in an ancient crater are hot, sulphurous springs, the potential of which as a source of cheap energy for generating electricity is now under investigation. The mountains are intersected by numerous short rivers. In places, these rivers debouch into broad, fertile and well cultivated valleys. The scenery is of outstanding beauty, even when compared with other Caribbean islands, and in the neighbourhood of the Pitons it has the less common element of grandeur.

There is a dry season roughly from January to April, and a rainy season from May to November. Towards the end of the year it is usually wet. The island lies in latitudes where the north-east trade winds are an almost constant influence. The mean annual temperature is about 27°C (80°F). Rainfall varies (according to altitude) in different parts of the island from 1,500 mm to 3,450 mm.

The population of St Lucia by 1989 was estimated at 148,000. The population of the capital, Castries, is about 57,300.

National Motto: The land, the light, the people. National Bird: The St Lucia Parrot (Amazona Versicolor).

The unit of currency is the East Caribbean Dollar (EC$2.70 = US$1.00).

There are 13 secondary schools with a total enrolment of 7,239 students. The Sir Arthur Lewis Community College is the newest educational complex with 165 students at the Division of Technical, Education and Administrative Section, 276 students at the Division of Technical Education and Management Studies, 274 students at the Division of Arts and Science and General Studies and 34 students at the Nursing Education and Health Science Division.

There are 83 primary schools with a total student population of 32,639. In the education system there is an Adult Education Officer supporting the Saint Lucia Literacy Programme.

Community Centres, of which there are 30 distributed throughout the island, serve as meeting places for the discussion of community affairs as well as centres of recreation and for the holding of social and cultural activities.

Medical services are provided by eleven district medical officers, one Chief Medical Officer and one Medical Officer for Health. There are eight dental surgeons, one Consultant Psychiatrist and twelve specialists based at Victoria Hospital including two General Surgeons, three obstetricians and gynaecologists, one physician, three paediatricians, one radiologist, one pathologist and two anaesthetists. The Consultants are supported by Registrars and five House Officers and there are five Casualty Officers responsible to a Medical Superintendent giving a 24 hour service. There are 167 available beds, laboratory, x-ray and physiotherapy departments. A small private suite is available. Psychiatric cases are treated at the Golden Hope Hospital with 152 beds and there are two 'cottage' hospitals at Dennery and Soufriere. A privately run partially Government funded hospital operates in Vieux Fort managed by a religious order, providing 108 beds, and a complement of visiting short term specialists. Nurses are trained (approximately 20 per year) at the Nursing Department of the Community College.

There are two airfields—Vigie Airport and Hewanorra International Airport (formerly Beane Field)—owned and operated by the Government of St Lucia for scheduled and charter service. The runway at Hewanorra, which is located in the Vieux Fort District, was lengthened from 1,500 m to 2,700 m, enabling it to accommodate large jets like the Lockheed Tristar and Boeing Jumbo jets. Air services with other territories are maintained by British West Indian Airways (BWIA), American Airlines, Leeward Islands Air Transport (LIAT), Air Canada, American Eagle, Air Martinique, British Airways, Alitalia, and Carribbean Air Cargo, as well as various Charter Airlines.

There are about 965 km (600 miles) of roads.

The island is served by the following shipping lines: Burmuth, Tec Marina, Tropical, West Indies Shipping Company (WISCO), Nedlloyd, CTMT, CGM Inter-line, and Geest—cargo and passenger vessels.

Radio Caribbean International St Lucia, a commercial radio station with a power output of 10 kW, broadcasts daily in English. There is also a Government-owned station, Radio St Lucia, which was formerly a sub-station of the Windward Islands Broadcasting Service. There are two commercial television services, Helen Television System and Daher Broadcasting Service. A cable service is also run by Cable and Wireless (WI) Ltd offering 13 channels to 2,700 subscribers.

The main crops are bananas, cocoa, mangoes, avocado pears, breadfruit, spices, root crops, such as cassava and yams, and citrus fruits. There is a fair amount of fishing, most of it handled by the Fisheries Complex with cold storage facilities.

The principal manufactures are beer, coconut products, (copra, edible oils, and soap), cigarettes, rum, mineral water, textiles, cardboard cartons and furniture. Principal exports are coconut oil, bananas, clothing, paper and cardboard.

The main form of direct taxation is income tax, based on the following table:—

Income Year	*Rate of Tax*	
1988	On the first $6,000 and under	10%
	On the next $6,000 viz. 6,001–12,000	20%
	On the next $5,000 viz. 12,001–17,000	30%
	On the remainder	40%
1989	On the first $8,000 and under	10%
	On the next $7,000 viz. 8,001–15,000	15%
	On the next $5,000 viz. 15,001–20,000	25%
	On the remainder	30%
1990	On the first $10,000 and under	10%
	On the next $10,000 viz. 10,001–20,000	15%
	On the next $10,000 viz. 20,001–30,000	20%
	On the remainder	30%

On the chargeable income, on every dollar thereof, of—
(a) companies existing before the commencement of this Act*
(i) for the income year 1988—40%
(ii) for the income year 1989—35%
(iii) for the income year 1990—33⅓%
(b) new small business enterprises—
(i) for the income year 1988—25%
(ii) for the income year 1989—30%
(iii) for the income year 1990—33⅓%

* Income Act no. 1 of 1989 which came into force on 1st January 1989.

Company tax is at the rate of 45 per cent on chargeable income.

The economy is based on the tripod of agriculture, tourism and industry.

Diversification of the economy is continuing, much emphasis being placed on industrialisation. Exploration for geothermal energy in the region of the Soufrière Sulphur Springs is in progress.

The St Lucia National Bank opened in January 1981 and the St Lucia Development Bank came into being in February 1981. The Amerada Hess Corporation of America have built an oil terminal storage facility (10 million barrels) in Cul-de-Sac Bay which is now operational.

History

Neither the date of discovery nor the discoverer of St Lucia is known, for according to the evidence of Columbus's voyage, he appears to have missed the island. As early as 1605, 67 Englishmen en route to Guiana, touched at St Lucia and made an unsuccessful effort to settle. The island at the time was peopled by Caribs and continued in their possession until 1635, when it was granted by the King of France to MM. de L'Olive and Duplessis. In 1638 the first recorded settlement was made by English colonists from Bermuda and St Kitts but they were murdered by the Caribs about three years later.

In 1642 the King of France, still claiming a right of sovereignty over the island, ceded it to the French West India Company, who in 1650 sold it to MM. Honel and Du Parquet. After repeated attempts by the Caribs to expel the French, the latter concluded a treaty of peace with them in 1660.

In 1664 Thomas Warner, son of the Governor of St Kitts, made a descent on St Lucia. The English continued in possession till the Peace of Breda in 1667, when the island was restored to the French. In 1674 it was re-annexed to the Crown of France, and made a dependency of Martinique.

After the Peace of Utrecht, in 1713, the rival pretensions of England and France to the possession of St Lucia resulted in open hostility. In 1718 the Regent, d'Orleans, made a grant of the island to Marshal d'Estrées, and in 1722, the King of England made a grant of it to the Duke of Montague. In the following year, however, a body of troops, despatched to St Lucia by the Governor of Martinique, compelled the English settlers to evacuate the island and it was declared neutral.

In 1743 the French took advantage of the declaration of war to resume possession of St Lucia, which they retained till the Treaty of Aix-la-Chapelle in 1748, when it was again declared neutral. In 1756, on the renewal of hostilities, the French put the island in a state of defence; but in 1762 it surrendered to the joint operations of Admiral Rodney and General Monckton. In the following year, by the Treaty of Paris, it was assigned to the French, who continued in peaceable possession till 1778, when effective measures were taken by the British for its conquest, but by the Peace of Versailles, St Lucia was once more restored to France.

In 1793, on the declaration of war against revolutionary France, the West Indies became the scene of a series of naval and military operations which resulted in the surrender of St Lucia to the British on 4th April 1794. In 1796 the British Government despatched to the relief of their West Indian possessions a body of troops, 12,000 strong, under the command of Sir Ralph Abercromby, supported by a squadron under Admiral Sir Hugh Christian. On 26th April these forces appeared off St Lucia, and after an obstinate and sanguinary contest, which lasted till 26th May, the Republican party, which had been aided by Victor Hugues and his guerilla band, laid down their arms and surrendered as prisoners of war. The British retained possession of St Lucia till 1802, when it was restored to France by the Treaty of Amiens; but on the renewal of hostilities it surrendered by capitulation to General Grinfield on 22nd June 1803, and was finally ceded to Britain in 1814 by the Treaty of Paris.

St Lucia became independent on 22nd February 1979 after 12 years as an Associated State with full internal self government.

In the two general elections held in April 1987 the United Workers Party retained power and enjoys a 10 to 7 seat majority in the House of Assembly.

Constitution

St Lucia is a constitutional monarchy with the Queen as Head of State, represented in the Island by a St Lucian Governor-General. The bicameral Parliament consists of a House of Assembly of 17 members elected by universal adult suffrage and a Senate of 11 members, six of whom are appointed on the advice of the Prime Minister, three on the advice of the Leader of the Opposition and two by the Governor-General after consultation with economic, social and religious bodies. The Constitution also provides for a Parliamentary Commissioner, an Electoral Commission and a Constituency Boundaries Commission. The maximum life of each Parliament is five years.

The Eastern Caribbean Supreme Court (formerly known as the West Indies Associated States Supreme Court) operates from St Lucia. There is an itinerant Court of Appeal consisting of a Chief Justice and three Justices of Appeal; a High Court with a resident judge, a senior magistrate and four other resident magistrates. The other Eastern Caribbean states which share the Supreme Court are Antigua, British Virgin Islands, Dominica, Montserrat, St Kitts and St Vincent. There is a High Court with one resident judge in each of the states.

The Constitution contains safeguards for fundamental rights and freedoms. Special provisions relate to a Bill to alter the Constitution or the law establishing the West Indies Associated States Supreme Court or the law relating to appeals to the Privy Council.

The appointment, dismissal and disciplinary control of public officers is, with certain exceptions, vested in the Public Service Commission, appointed by the Governor-General in accordance with the Advice of the Prime Minister. There is provision for appeals to the Public Service Board of Appeal.

There is also a Teaching Service Commission with powers to appoint persons into the teaching service.

HEAD OF STATE
Her Majesty Queen Elizabeth II

ACTING GOVERNOR-GENERAL
His Excellency Stanilaus James, CMG, OBE, JP

MINISTRIES
Prime Minister, Minister of Finance, Planning, Development and Home Affairs: Rt Hon John G M Compton, PC
Deputy Prime Minister, Minister of Trade, Tourism and Industry: Hon William George Mallet, CBE
Minister for Foreign Affairs: Hon Neville Cenac
Minister of Communications, Works and Transport: Hon Gregory Avril
Minister of Health, Housing and Labour, and Information and Broadcasting: Hon Romanus Lansiquot
Minister of Youth, Community Development, Social Affairs, Sport: Hon Stephenson King
Attorney General, Minister for Legal Affairs: Senator The Hon Parry Husbands
Minister of Agriculture, Lands, Fisheries and Cooperatives: Hon Ferdinand Henry
Minister of Education and Culture: Hon Louis George
Minister of State in the Ministry of Labour: Senator Hon Winhall Joshua
Minister of State in the Office of the Prime Minister: Hon Desmond Brathwaite

MINISTRIES AND GOVERNMENT DEPARTMENTS

Cabinet Secretary: Victor Girard, OBE
Permanent Secretary, Ministry of Health: Percival McDonald
Permanent Secretary, Ministry of Works: Gregory St Helene

Permanent Secretary, Ministry of Education and Culture: Dr Nicholas Frederick
Permanent Secretary, Ministry of Trade, Industry and Tourism: Anthony Severin
Permanent Secretary, Ministry of Agriculture: Cosmos Richardson
Permanent Secretary, Ministry of Youth, Community Development, Sport and Social Affairs: Joseph Alexander
Permanent Secretary, Planning, Establishment and Training: Ausbert D'Auvergne
Permanent Secretary, Ministry of Foreign Affairs: Johannes Leonce
Director of Finance: Bernard La Corbiniere

St Vincent and the Grenadines

Capital: Kingstown

St Vincent lies at the lower end of the Caribbean chain, about 97 km (60 miles) north of Grenada. The territory includes the northern Grenadines, some of the larger islands of which are: Bequia, Canouan, Mayreau, Mustique, Isle D'Quatre and Union Island. The island lies between latitudes 13°6′ and 14°35′N and longitudes 61°6′ and 61°20′W at a distance of 34 km (21 miles) to the south-west of St Lucia and 161 km (100 miles) west of Barbados. Including the Grenadines the territory comprises 389 sq km (150.3 square miles), ie approximately 38,851 ha (96,000 acres).

The main island, St Vincent, is 29 km (18 miles) by 18 km (11 miles) at its extremities and has an area of 344 sq km (133 square miles) (34,448 ha) of which 16,107 ha are forested.

The most striking natural feature of St Vincent is the Soufrière, a volcano, situated at the northernmost extremity of the island and rising to 1,159 m above sea level. After a violent eruption in 1812, it remained dormant for a period of ninety years and then broke into violent eruption again on 7th May 1902, when the entire northern half of the island was devastated and nearly 2,000 lives were lost. The eruption synchronised with that of Mont Pélée in Martinique which destroyed the town of St Pierre. The Soufrière was intermittently active throughout 1902 and there was a further eruption in 1903. The volcano again became active during October 1971 to April 1972. This eruption was a mild one and involved the growth of a volcanic dome which gradually rose in the Crater Lake forming an island. Further volcanic activity resumed in April 1979 causing the evacuation of the northern part of the island and damage to agriculture.

The whole island is of volcanic origin. A backbone of densely wooded and almost impassable mountains traverses it from the Soufrière at its northern end to Mount St Andrew (750 m) dominating the Kingstown valley in the south. The range sends off spurs on each side, cutting up the island into a series of valleys trending east and west from the central range to the coast. There is a somewhat level tract called the Carib Country at the north-east of the island between the Soufrière and the sea. The second highest point in the range is Richmond Peak (1,062 m). The streams are numerous but, except after heavy rains, small. None of them is navigable.

Average temperatures range from 18–32°C (64–90°F) and the maximum rarely exceeds 34°C (93°F) in the shade. At Kingstown the mean temperature in 1984 was 28°C (82°F) and the total rainfall 1,519 mm. From January to May there is a pronounced dry season. From May or June the rains start in earnest and continue to the end of the year. Annual rainfall ranges from 1,500 mm in the extreme south to 3,750 mm in the interior of the island.

The up-dated census of 1980 shows a 1987 population of 112,589.

The island is divided into five parishes: Charlotte, St George, St Andrew, St David and St Patrick. The thirteen political divisions are North Leeward, Central Leeward, South Leeward, East Kingstown, West Kingstown, East St George, West St George, Marriaqua, South Windward, South Central Windward, North Central Windward, North Windward and the Grenadines.

Kingstown, the capital and principal port and suburbs, has an estimated population of 28,936. The other principal towns are Georgetown, Calliaqua, Layou, Barrouallie and Chateaubelair. The working population is estimated to be 30,000, about 40 per cent of whom are engaged in agriculture, forestry and fishing.

The unit of currency is the Eastern Caribbean Dollar.

English is the only language in general use. The main religious denominations are Methodist, Anglican and Roman Catholic.

Primary education is free but not compulsory. Secondary education is offered free in two Government Senior Secondary Schools and in ten fee paying Assisted Secondary Schools. There are several primary schools which are conducted under private ownership but their number is not known. The literacy rate is estimated at 85 per cent. In 1990 there was an enrolment of 24,366 students at 62 primary schools and 6,822 at government and government assisted secondary schools.

The crude death rate in 1990 was 6.0 per thousand and the birth rate was 22.3 per thousand.

Health measures and health education continue to be directed at the control of infantile malnutrition and gastro-enteritis. Insect-borne diseases are not prevalent. There are 35 Government clinics and dispensaries throughout the State and over 500 hospital beds of which 207 are located in the Central General Hospital.

Approved estimates for Government medical and health services in 1990/91 were EC$18,184,969.

The airstrip is located at Arnos Vale, two miles south-east of the capital, Kingstown. The runway is 1,395 m long by 45 m, lying in a strip 150 m wide. Scheduled daily services are operated by Leeward Islands Air Transport (LIAT) Antigua, Air Martinique and Aero Services. There are also three airstrips in the Grenadines, viz. Mustique, Union Island and Canouan. The present schedules and services provide daily flights to all Caribbean islands stretching from St Martin to Trinidad, and connections are possible the same day to Europe and North America.

There are 346 km of all-weather roads, 378 km of rough roads, and 386 km of tracks and by-ways.

The main shipping lines calling at St Vincent are the Ned Lloyd, West Indies Shipping Co (WISCO), Saguenay Shipping, the Geest Line, Bernuth Line, TMT and TEC Lines.

A fully automatic internal telephone system serving St Vincent, Union Island, Bequia, Mustique, Prune Island and Petit St Vincent is operated by Cable and Wireless (WI) Ltd., with the main exchange building at Kingstown. Public call boxes have been installed at strategic points throughout the island. International direct dialling, telegraph and telex services are also provided by Cable and Wireless (WI) Ltd. International Aeradio (Caribbean) Ltd provide radio facilities for aircraft.

There is a broadcasting station on St Vincent, which relays regional news. It relays BBC World Service news and sport periodically each day. The station provided local programming but has now expanded to full time programming. Television reception of the Trinidad and Barbados programmes is possible in some localities and there is a local television station which relays local and US programmes.

The main crops in order of importance are bananas, tropical vegetables, plantains, sweet potatoes, arrowroot, peanuts, coconuts, ginger, tobacco, nutmegs and mace.

Livestock slaughtered in Kingstown in 1990: 868 cattle, 987 pigs, 1,165 sheep and 277 goats.

Sales of timber on Crown Lands are restricted to a minimum so as to avoid excessive exploitation at the expense of soil and water conservation.

Both in-shore and off-shore fishing is carried on. An ice-making and cold storage plant has been installed in the Kingstown Market and commenced operations in 1969. The Marketing Board took over the marketing of fish in Kingstown in 1969.

Industry is based on agriculture, mainly bananas. There is an arrowroot factory, Owia, providing starch. Two privately-owned plants for processing copra commenced operation during 1968. There is a small cigarette factory, which produces annually over two million packets of 10 cigarettes from imported tobacco. Other small industries include a box-making plant, a rum distillery based on molasses produced locally, three plants producing aerated drinks, two tyre-recapping plants and several furniture-making concerns. There is also a newly developed Industrial Site at Campden Park which comprises several small factories, manufacturing ready made garments, linens etc. A flour mill (Canadian/Vincentian Project) produces 2,200 bags of flour per day. A new dairy plant is at present producing long-life milk and juices from imported products. Milk products are exported to neighbouring islands. The 'Hairoun' brewery was officially opened on 15th November 1985. It produces lager, Malta, stout and other soft drinks.

Exports include bananas, arrowroot and various root crops and spices. Carrot production has declined to almost nil over the last ten years due to nematodes. Traffickers who travel weekly between St Vincent and Trinidad now deal in sweet potatoes since the breakdown of the agricultural marketing protocol. There is also a good trade in plantains with Barbados and Trinidad. The main imports are foodstuffs, manufactured goods, machinery and transport equipment, chemicals and miscellaneous manufactured articles.

A statutory Marketing Board mainly handles sweet potatoes but a substantial trade has also been built up in other starchy roots, mainly with the United Kingdom, the United States of America and Trinidad. The Board assists in the marketing of pasteurised milk.

Expenditure in agriculture is aimed at both the diversification and increase in yields of agricultural products. An Agricultural and Co-operative Bank to facilitate credit to farmers commenced operation on 15th February 1969. While it is recognised that the economy will still remain largely dependent on agriculture in the foreseeable future, provision has been made for establishing light industries to utilise local produce through the Development Corporation of St Vincent, which was established in 1970.

Apart from agriculture, tourism is the main field in which the economy is expanding. The number of visitors arriving in the State in 1990 was 157,532. It is recognised that tourism is the sector with great growth potential in the future and accordingly investment is devoted to the development of the infrastructure.

A graduated income tax is imposed on individuals, ranging from 10 cents to 55 cents on every dollar of chargeable income. The present scale of allowances is a 10 per cent reduction of earned income up to a maximum of EC$500, personal allowance for a single man of EC$1,200 and for a married man of EC$1,900, for each child EC$400, for a widower or widow a housekeeper allowance of EC$200 and a similar allowance for a dependent relative. There is also relief for life assurance. Instead of itemised claims a flat rate of EC$10,000 is allowed on income from employment. A simplified non-cumulative PAYE system is in operation for employees. Companies pay at a flat rate of 45 per cent.

History

St Vincent was included in a patent given by Charles I to the Earl of Carlisle in 1627. In 1660 England and France agreed that the island should be neutral, but in 1672 Charles II granted it to Lord Willoughby. In 1673 the first people of African origin arrived, a party of slaves shipwrecked in the Grenadines who eventually reached St Vincent and intermarried with the Carib inhabitants. Later, French settlements were made along the leeward coast including the site of the present capital. By the

Treaty of Aix-la-Chapelle, St Vincent was declared neutral but was captured by the British in 1762. After the conclusion of peace in 1763, European settlers began to arrive. During the American War of Independence, France declared war on Britain and St Vincent fell into the hands of the French in 1779. With the signing of the Treaty of Versailles in 1783 it was restored to Britain. In March 1795 the Caribs, aided by the French residents, threatened to master the whole island, but they were finally subdued in June 1796 when Sir Ralph Abercromby arrived with further reinforcements. The majority of the Caribs were deported to the island of Rattan in the Bay of Honduras and peace was restored.

In 1812 the Soufrière erupted and devastated the greater part of the island. In 1848 due to the shortage of local labour, Portuguese were imported in fairly large numbers from Madeira to work on the sugar estates, and a little over a decade later East Indians arrived for the same purpose. Both the Portuguese and the East Indians are now respected members of the island community.

In the second half of the nineteenth century the price of sugar fell and a serious depression set in which lasted until the end of the century. Before prosperity returned, the island suffered a great calamity in the hurricane of 1898 which killed about 300 people and damaged a large number of buildings. This was followed in 1902 by the disastrous volcanic eruption mentioned at the beginning of this chapter.

In 1951 universal adult suffrage was granted, and in 1956 elected members were given a majority in the Executive Council and elected Ministers took office for the first time.

A conference was held in 1966 on further constitutional change; its decisions were endorsed by a resolution in the Legislative Council. Provision was made in the West Indies Act 1967 for St Vincent to assume a status of association with the United Kingdom by 1st June 1967. Due to political problems within St Vincent this date was delayed. Following a further Constitutional Conference in London in June 1969 St Vincent became an Associated State with full internal self government on 27th October 1969. The United Kingdom retained responsibility for defence and external affairs.

Following preliminary talks in April 1978 a draft independence constitution was discussed at a Constitutional Conference in September 1978. A report with proposed amendments was published in St Vincent and debated in the House of Assembly in February 1979. With the addition of further amendments it was passed by 10 votes to nil. In May a number of amendments proposed by the opposition were incorporated, after talks in St Vincent between a British Minister and Government and Opposition leaders. St Vincent and the Grenadines became independent on 27th October 1979, a special member of the Commonwealth in the same year and a full member on 20th June 1985.

Constitution

The Constitution provides for a Vincentian Governor-General appointed by The Queen and a unicameral legislature. The House of Assembly is composed of 15 Representatives elected in single member constituencies, and six Senators, appointed by the Governor-General, four on the advice of the Prime Minister and two on the advice of the Leader of the Opposition. Each Parliament has a maximum life of five years. The Prime Minister is appointed by the Governor-General who designates the Representative who is likely to command majority support among the other Representatives. Other ministers are appointed on the advice of the Prime Minister. No more than two ministers may be senators.

Under the constitution the St Vincent legislature may make laws for the peace, order and good government of the territory. The Constitution contains safeguards for fundamental rights and freedoms. There are special provisions relating to the Bill to alter the Constitution or the Supreme Court Order. St Vincent retains its connection with the West Indies Associated States Supreme Court, which is known in St Vincent as the Eastern Caribbean Supreme Court. It consists of a Court of Appeal and a High Court. There is at present one puisne judge of the Eastern Caribbean Supreme Court resident in St Vincent. The Judicial Committee of the Privy Council remains the final Court of appeal.

Land Policy

All land, other than Crown Land, is freehold. Individual ownership is recognised, but aliens may purchase land only with the approval of the Government.

Government

At the General Election on 16th May 1989 the New Democratic Party was returned to power, winning all 15 seats in an expanded parliament. Prior to the election the NDP held 10 seats to the 3 held by the St Vincent Labour Party.

HEAD OF STATE
Her Majesty Queen Elizabeth II

GOVERNOR-GENERAL
His Excellency Sir David Jack, GCMG, MBE

MINISTRIES
Prime Minister and Minister of Finance, and Foreign Affairs: The Rt Hon James F Mitchell

Attorney General and Minister of Justice and Information: Hon Parnel R Campbell, CVO

Minister of Agriculture, Industry and Labour: Hon Chiefton A Cruickshank

Minister of Education, Youth, Women's Affairs and Culture: Hon Alexander John-Clark Horne

Minister of Communication and Works: Hon Jeremiah C Scott

Minister of Trade and Tourism: Hon Herbert G Young
Minister of Health and Environment: Hon Burton Bernard Williams
Minister of Housing, Local Government and Community Development: Hon Louis Jones
Minister of State in the Ministry of Education, Youth, Women's Affairs and Culture: Hon Yvonne Francis-Gibson
Parliamentary Secretary in the Ministry of Trade and Tourism: Hon Stuart Nanton
Parliamentary Secretary in the Ministry of Communication and Works: Hon Monty Roberts
Parliamentary Secretary in the Ministry of Housing, Local Government and Community Development: Hon Bernard Wyllie
Parliamentary Secretary in the Ministry of Health and Environment: Hon Alpian Allen
Minister of State in the Prime Minister's Office: Hon Jonathan Peters

HOUSE OF ASSEMBLY

Speaker: Monty Maule
Deputy Speaker: Mrs Mary Hutchinson
Member for East St George: Louis Jones
Member for South Central Windward: Allan Cruickshank
Member for North Windward: Monty Roberts
Member for North Central Windward: Jonathan Peters
Member for South Windward: Burton B Williams
Member for Marriaqua: Bernard Wyllie
Member for West St George: Yvonne Francis-Gibson
Member for East Kingstown: Carlyle Dougan
Member for Central Kingstown: Parnel Campbell, CVO
Member for West Kingstown: John A Horne
Member for South Leeward: Jeremiah C Scott
Member for Central Leeward: Herbert G Young
Member for North Leeward: Alpian Allen
Member for the Northern Grenadines: James F Mitchell
Member for the Southern Grenadines: Mary Hutchinson
Senator Stephanie Browne
Senator Robert S Nanton
Senator Owen Walker
Senator St Clair Robinson

CIVIL ESTABLISHMENT

Director of Finance and Planning: Maurice Edwards
Cabinet Secretary/PS to Premier's Office: Mrs Young
Permanent Secretary, Ministry of Trade and Tourism: H Phillips
Permanent Secretary, Ministry of Communications, Works and Labour: Mrs J A Leigertwood
Permanent Secretary, Ministry of Agriculture, Industry and Labour: J Venner (Ag)
Permanent Secretary, Housing, Labour and Community Development: O Cuffy
Permanent Secretary, Ministry of Education: A Soso
Permanent Secretary, Ministry of Health: Cecil John
Director of Planning/Planning Unit: R Cato (Ag)
Comptroller of Customs and Excise: B Bailey (Ag)
Senior Medical Officer: Dr H Rampersaud
Labour Commissioner: Noel Cooke
Commissioner of Police: R Toussaint, OBE, LVO, CPM
Port Manager: P Kirby
Chief Personnel Officer: P Griffith
Chief Statistician: W G Ollivierre
Chief Technical Officer: J Cato (Ag)
Chief Agricultural Officer: Reuben Robinson
Chief Education Officer: McCauley Peters (Ag)
Veterinary Officer: Dr N Raninga
Manager, Central Water Authority: D Cummings (Ag)
Accountant General: Miss C Jack
Superintendent of Airports: A Alexander
Director of Audit: F B D Providence
Government Information Officer: Jimmy Prince (Ag)
Chief Surveyor: C E R Williams
Postmaster: M James
Comptroller of Inland Revenue: I Bailey (Ag)
Superintendent of Prisons: B T Marksman (Ag)

JUDICIARY

Puisne Judge, St Vincent circuit: Miss Monica Joseph
Magistrates: Clifton-Mounsey, F Bruce Lyle and Raymond-Cadette
Registrar, Supreme Court: T Browne

Seychelles

Capital: Victoria

The Seychelles became an independent Republic within the Commonwealth on 29th June 1976.

The Seychelles archipelago consists of 115 islands, some 41 of which are granitic and the remainder coralline, scattered over about 1,036,000 sq km (400,000 square miles) of Western Indian Ocean. The estimated total land area of the islands is 455 sq km (175 square miles.)

The granitic islands, which rise steeply from the sea and are all of great beauty, form a relatively compact group within the archipelago. Mahé, the largest and most populated of this group, lies about 1,609 km (1,000 miles) due east of Mombasa. It is 27 km (17 miles) wide, and has a long central ridge which at its highest point, Morne Seychellois, reaches nearly 900 m. The capital, Victoria, (population 23,000) is situated on Mahé and is the only town of any size in Seychelles. Praslin, second largest island in the group, is 43 km (27 miles) north east of Mahé and the other granitic islands are within a radius of 56 km (35 miles). The coral islands are reefs in different stages of formation, rising only a few feet above sea level and are only sparsely populated.

The climate is tropical but for islands so close to the Equator not unpleasant. Maximum shade temperature at sea level averages 29°C (84°F) and during the coolest months, the average minimum temperature drops to 24°C (75°F). At higher levels temperatures are rather lower and the air fresher. There are two seasons, hot from December to May and cooler from June to November while the south-east trade winds are blowing. Rainfall varies over the group; the greater part falls during the hot months when the north-west trade winds blow and the climate then tends to be humid and somewhat enervating. The mean annual rainfall in Victoria taken over the past 68 years is 2,360 mm (93 inches) and the mean average temperature nearly 27°C (80°F). All the granitic islands lie outside the cyclone belt. High winds and thunderstorms are rare.

Population

The mid-year estimate of the population for 1990 was 67,378. The annual rate of increase is 1.0 per cent there having been 1,617 births and 543 deaths and net emigration of 430 in 1990. The infant mortality rate for 1990 was 13.0 per 1,000 live births.

The Seychellois people have a variety of ethnic origins—African, European, Chinese and Indian. More than 90 per cent of the population is Roman Catholic and nearly 8 per cent Anglican with very small minorities adhering to other sects. Their diet consists mainly of rice, fish and lentils; meat, primarily chicken and pork, is eaten occasionally and local fruit and vegetables are available.

Education

All education in Seychelles is public and free. Government directs the formulation of educational policy. As Seychelles is a tri-lingual (Creole, English and French) society, each language is accorded a position of importance in the education system. (Creole is used in primary Schools as a medium of instruction with English replacing it at advanced levels. French is studied and used as a language of support). The basis of the education system is free universal primary education available to all children between six and fifteen years. After completing their primary education students enter the voluntary National Youth Service, which is an innovative secondary education programme which links academic teaching with training for social and political development. A sixth-form-level Polytechnic was inaugurated in 1982 regrouping vocational schools and expanding vocational training into new fields. Voluntary pre-school creches in 1982 involved more than 80 per cent of the four to six year old population. Adult education courses focus mainly on functional literacy and numeracy.

In 1991 3,228 children were in creches; 10,078 students in primary schools; 7,397 in secondary schools and 1,604 at Seychelles Polytechnic.

Broadcasting Services

Radio and television services are run by Radio-Television Seychelles, an organisation formed in January 1983 and consisting of RTS-Radio and RTS-TV.

Radio Seychelles broadcasts both local and international news and various political, educational, agricultural and cultural programmes on both a national and international level.

RTS-TV was launched on 1st January 1983 as a Weekend Service. From 1st July 1989 the Service expanded to cover 7 days. Programmes feature news, feature films, documentaries, educational and musical topics and sports. There is a mobile TV Unit and a studio at Hermitage.

Radio and television programmes are presented in Creole, English and French. The introduction of television is indicative of the government's emphasis on the role of non-formal education and information in national development.

Seychelles has few of the diseases usually associated with tropical climates. There is no malaria. No cases of yellow fever have ever been reported although there are aedes mosquitoes on most of the islands. Bilharzia does not exist in Seychelles. There is a decline in the number of notified cases of tuberculosis, leprosy and filariasis. Intestinal parasites are prevalent, notably hookworm, roundworm, amoebiasis, giardia lambia and strongyloid stercoracis.

There is a Public Health Service and most children are immunised against whooping cough, tetanus, diphtheria, poliomyelitis, measles, rubella (german measles), smallpox and tuberculosis. In the last three years no cases of measles, poliomyelitis or diphtheria have been reported. There is one general hospital in Seychelles (with 248 beds out of a total of 421 hospital beds) which serves as the referral centre. Basic health services are decentralized and organised in the districts.

There are three small hospitals in the district totalling 130 beds. A doctor is permanently stationed on the islands of Praslin and La Digue and a nurse/midwife is stationed on Silhouette.

There are 113 professional medical and dental officers, 282 nurses, 435 para-medical staff and 35 student nurses. Private medical practice has almost completely been phased out.

The Economy

Following the opening of the International Airport on Mahé, tourism has proved a major industry in Seychelles. The number of visitors arriving in 1990 was 103,770 compared to 89,093 in 1989, an increase of 21 per cent over the previous year. The number of beds available during 1990 was 3,590, and the bed occupancy was 67 per cent; 78.3 per cent of visitors came from Europe. In 1990, the average length of stay was 10.1 nights per visitor and SR646m was earned in foreign exchange.

The greater number of visitors are accommodated in the larger hotels on Mahé, with lesser accommodation on other inner islands such as Praslin and La Digue, and outer islands of Denis, Bird Island and Desroches.

The Government policy is to encourage the development of the more distant islands while at the same time protecting their natural assets.

In early 1983 the Government launched a new tourism promotion programme, together with a plan to improve the tourism product offered to visitors.

The main links with Europe are by Air Seychelles, British Airways and Air France (all direct). Air Seychelles also flies to Singapore. Domestic flights are operated by Air Seychelles.

The Port of Victoria, which is protected by a chain of islands and coral reefs, consists of approximately one square mile of deep water roadstead for ships of all sizes and an inner harbour of about half that area. Up to six ocean-going ships can be accommodated at any one time in the outer harbour depending on their size. The inner harbour can accommodate two vessels berthed alongside Mahé quay, which became operational from 1st March 1975. There are two berths, both of which have fuel, fresh water and telephone connections and a maximum depth of water of 10 metres, and 13½ metres. Three tugs are now available and vessels of up to 225 metres in length are able to berth alongside. A separate fishing port, catering almost exclusively for the tuna industry, has 2 quays totalling 198 metres with a maximum draught of 7.5 metres. Vessels of up to 115 metres in length are able to berth alongside. The number of vessels entered and cleared from Victoria in 1990 was 953 (excluding yachts). The tonnage handled was 11,200 m tonnes loaded and 347,700 m tonnes unloaded in 1990. Transhipment amounting to 161,100 m tonnes was handled in the same year.

The road system in Seychelles is quite extensive; on Mahé 68 per cent of the 285 km of motorable road is surfaced; on Praslin 41 per cent of the 55 km is surfaced. On La Digue less than 30 motor vehicles together with the traditional ox-carts and bicycles use the 16 km of unsurfaced roads.

La Gogue dam costing £6m and associated works, including the new water treatment plant, was opened in June 1979. These works will provide raw water storage and treated water facilities for the larger proportion of the population of Mahé into the next decade. Associated with that project are reticulation extensions which are undertaken by direct labour and 1982 saw facilities of a treated water main around the northern tip of the island serving the majority of the population and most popular tourist areas. Work on a new scheme to extend and improve the water distribution is expected to begin shortly.

Electricity services continue to be extended throughout Mahé and a seventh generator, of 5 MW capacity, will increase the installed capacity to 27 MW in 1991. The present maximum demand is about 15 MW but is increasing as the industrial load develops. There is a 33 kV transmission line on Mahé and an 11 kV distribution system on Mahé, Praslin and La Digue where new consumers continue to receive electricity services via small extensions or low voltage schemes.

The priority given in the past to plantation agriculture as the traditional mainstay of the Seychelles' economy has meant that the country has had to import most of the food it needs for its resident and tourist populations. It is now Government policy to realise the full potential of the country's agricultural land for the growing of food crops and the rearing of livestock. Farmers are being encouraged to diversify into these sectors through loans, grants, extension and a comprehensive land reform programme. But the lack of extensive arable land, poor soils, unpredictable weather and pests and diseases make it difficult for Seychelles to reach sustainable self sufficiency in agricultural products.

The Government is developing the national forestry resources in order to supply the domestic market with more home-grown timber. The outer islands of the Seychelles group are now being brought into the mainstream of economic development, and have considerable potential for both agriculture and forestry.

The Seychelles fishing industry has traditionally revolved round small, open boats using traditional methods and operating close to the islands. A fleet of larger boats, using the same methods, now operate further afield and has given rise to a modest export industry. Seychelles' fish resources, particularly of tuna, can support a substantially larger industry. With this in mind the Government has established the basic organs of a larger tuna fishery with the completion of a large 1,000 tonne capacity cold store, a new quay and a tuna canning factory. The Government now aims to acquire its own tuna fishing vessels. Natural stocks of marine shellfish are believed to be small but potential exists for farming certain species such as oysters, and prawns.

Other industries include the Seychelles brewery, Amalgamated Tobacco, a plastics factory, a UHT milk production plant and soap and detergent factories, enterprises which have successfully established themselves in the last few years. There are several small bakeries and a range of small scale manufacturing industries including tailoring, boat building, furniture-making, printing and local handicrafts.

Currency is the Seychelles rupee (SR) divided into 100 cents. Prior to 5th November 1979, the currency was tied to sterling at the rate of 7½p to one rupee. Since 16th March 1981 the Seychelles rupee is pegged to the Special Drawing Right at the rate of SR 7.2345.

Visitors brought SR 646m in foreign exchange on the current account during 1990. Domestic exports were valued at SR 73.2m, re-exports at SR 139.8m in the same year, while total imports amounted to SR 991.5m. Details of visible exports in 1990 were as follows:

	SR (m)
Copra	1.6
Cinnamon bark	0.4
Fish (fresh)	11.2
Fish (canned)	55.3

Details of the main items imported in 1990 are as follows:

	SR (m)
Food, beverages and tobacco	182.1
Mineral fuels, lubricants and related materials including chemicals	191.4
Manufactured goods	276.4
Machinery and transport equipment	261.5
Other	80.1

Government Finance and Taxation

Estimates of recurrent revenue for 1990 are SR 989.2m and of recurrent expenditure the same year SR 891.3m. There is also a continuing programme of capital projects which are being financed from foreign aid and loans.

From 1st January 1988, the government abolished Income Tax on the earnings of all employees in formal employment. From that date employees were subject only to a single statutory deduction for contributions to social security (remaining at the rate of 5 per cent of their new gross salaries). Salary earners continued to receive about the same take-home pay. What they used to pay in income tax was, thenceforth, paid by their employers to Social Security.

Again with effect from 1st January 1988, a new Business Tax was introduced to tax the profits of all corporations, companies and businesses, incorporate or otherwise, on a pay-as-you-earn basis. The Business Tax also applies to all individuals not in formal employment who earn profits from business activities.

History

There is some evidence to suggest that the Seychelles Islands were known and visited in the Middle Ages by traders from Arabia and the Persian Gulf sailing to and from ports in East Africa with the monsoons; they are clearly associated with the great Portuguese voyages in the Indian Ocean. The Amirantes group was sighted by Vasco da Gama on his second voyage to India in 1502. The first map showing what is thought to be the main group of islands was drawn at about the same time. However, the first well-documented visit to the archipelago was made by the English seaman Alexander Sharpeigh. Commissioned by the East India Company on a trading expedition to Aden and Surat in 1609 Sharpeigh's party came accidentally upon the main granitic group. Mahé and nearby islands were visited thus ante-dating by almost a century and a half the first French exploration led by Picault in 1741. A circumstantial account of Sharpeigh's voyage is to be found in the *Journal of John Jourdain*, published by the Hakluyt Society.

It was that greatest of all French Governors of Mauritius, the Vicomte Mahé de Labourdonnais, who briefed Picault in 1741 to explore Seychelles. Had Labourdonnais not fallen victim to naval base intrigues, it is possible, even probable, that he would have turned Mahé into a formidable base against Britain at a time when French and British interests were clashing in India. For fifteen years Seychelles remained forgotten and then, on intelligence that the British were seeking uninhabited islands in the Indian Ocean, France decided to annex Mahé and seven other islands of the group. To that end Captain C N Morphey was despatched with orders to set up on Mahé a 'Stone of Possession' engraved with the arms of France. He did so on 1st November 1756, whereafter he set sail leaving the islands still uninhabited.

By 1763 the French East India Company, owing to mismanagement and military setbacks, had lost most of its possessions in India and disrupted the economy of Mauritius. It was wound up and its remaining assets, including Mauritius and its dependencies, lapsed to the King of France. The transfer was not completed till 1767 when two official Administrators were sent to Mauritius—Jean Dumas in charge of naval and political affairs, and Pierre Poivre in charge of finance and agriculture—to develop the islands and prepare for further hostilities with Britain in the East. Both men soon turned their eyes to Seychelles. Dumas' interests were to find a cheap and reliable source of timber for his naval dockyards, and he despatched an expedition in 1768. Poivre, trying to introduce into Mauritius the cultivation of spices to offset the Dutch monopoly in the Far East, extended this operation to Seychelles, and a garden was started, as well as a small settlement on St Anne's Island in 1770.

After the first failure, the Administrators of Mauritius repeatedly urged that the responsiblity of administrating any future settlement in Seychelles should rest directly with representatives of the King and not with private entrepreneurs as had been the case with the first settlements. The plan they put forward was to station on Mahé a small garrison and to accept the offer of a number of inhabitants of Mauritius and Réunion to settle there with their slaves. The function of the settlers was to grow food for the garrison and passing ships. Two years later Lieutenant Romainville, with 15 soldiers and 12 slaves, was sent to set up an Administrative Headquarters on the site around which Victoria was later to arise. Thereafter settlers with parties of slaves began to arrive.

These settlers in the main came from previously well-to-do families who had fled France in face of financial disaster and threatening revolution, or had quit India after the collapse of French supremacy there in 1761. All were faced with the necessity of starting life afresh. Though the official role allotted to them was that of farmers, their primary ambition was to rebuild their shattered fortunes, and they found it quicker and vastly more lucrative to traffic in the island's natural and abundant resources—tortoises and timber. Between 1784 and 1789 alone it was estimated that more than 13,000 giant tortoises had been shipped from Mahé, while many others were slaughtered for home consumption. Damage to the island's magnificent forests had been on much the same scale. Appalled by this devastation, the French authorities in Mauritius sent M Malavois in 1789 with orders to end it. The granting of land was regulated and attempts made to regulate the indiscriminate exploitation of the Island's natural resources.

In 1790 following the French Revolution, the colonists set up a Permanent Colonial Assembly and a Committee for Administration. The control of a distant administration on their economic activities had never been popular with the colonists and they saw the Revolution as a golden opportunity to cut the link with Mauritius. They repudiated all links with Mauritius, and invested the Assembly with judicial and other powers of internal self-government, thus anticipating by 113 years the status of Crown Colony granted to Seychelles by Britain in 1903.

Their hope for a permanent separation from Mauritius, however, evaporated with the arrival of a Republican Commandant who proclaimed, among other changes, the abolition of slavery without compensation. Almost to a man the colonists boycotted him. He was succeeded by the Chevalier de Quincy, who brought news that the edict concerning slavery had been revoked, and Seychelles once more settled down as a dependency of Mauritius.

For a number of years serious depredations to British shipping in the Indian Ocean had been caused by French privateers. Several of the marauding ships were owned by Seychellois, and it was partly to put an end to such activities that in 1794 a British squadron appeared off Victoria, demanding the unconditional surrender of the island. de Quincy had no forces to repel an attack but managed to obtain a deed of capitulation favourable to the islanders. In 1802 the Peace of Amiens was signed but hostilities broke out again in 1803. With a view to weakening the British hold on India, Napoleon determined to station a strong fleet on the main trade route in the Indian Ocean. To this end, Mauritius was made the naval and military headquarters, Réunion and Madagascar the depots of food and stores, and Seychelles an advanced outpost. Britain's reply was to place a naval blockade on all these islands. In 1804 Seychelles was forced to capitulate for the second time. Again de Quincy managed to obtain a concession whereby ships of Seychelles flying a certain flag could pass through the blockade unmolested. The many ships calling at Mahé for supplies and a virtual monopoly of trade secured by the Seychelles under the terms of the capitulation, brought considerable wealth to the colony. However, with the fall of Mauritius to British forces in 1810, when Britain made it clear that slavery was to be abolished, a number of colonists with their slaves, estimated at nearly half the population, left Seychelles.

During the *pourparlers* to the Treaty of Paris, Britain offered to restore Mauritius and its dependencies to France if that country would renounce all claims to its small remaining possessions in India. France refused and so in 1814 all these islands were formally ceded to Britain. Although all previous undertakings to respect French ownership of property, law and customs were omitted from the treaty, these continued to be honoured in deed. As a further proof of good-will, the Chevalier de Quincy was invited by the British Government to become *Juge de Paix* in Seychelles. He accepted and served in that office until his death 13 years later.

From the date of its foundation until 1903, Seychelles was regarded as a dependency of Mauritius. A series of Civil Commissioners under the tutelage of Mauritius administered Seychelles from 1811 to 1888. Some degree of separation was effected in 1872 when a Board of Civil Commissioners was appointed with financial autonomy. The powers of this Board under a Chief Civil Commissioner were extended by another Order in Council of 1874. In 1888 the importance of the islands warranted a further change in the constitution, and an Order-in-Council was passed creating an Administrator with a nominated Executive and Legislative Council as from 1889. In 1897 the separation from Mauritius became more marked when the Administrator was endowed with the full powers of Governor. Six years later, by Letters Patent of 31st August 1903, separation was completed and Seychelles became a Crown Colony with a Governor and Executive and Legislative Councils.

Constitution

A Constitutional Conference was held at Marlborough House in March 1975, at which the principles of an Interim Constitution and a number of points for an Independence Constitution were agreed.

As agreed at the March 1975 Constitutional Conference the Interim Constitution, which provided for a larger measure of internal self-government, was introduced in September 1975. At the second session of the Constitutional Conference held in London in January 1976, an Independence Constitution was agreed which provided for Seychelles to become a sovereign republic. Following the approval of Parliament, the Constitution came into effect at midnight on 28/29th June 1976. There was a coup d'etat early in the morning of 5th June 1977 and Mr F A René became President of the Republic. The Constitution was immediately suspended but re-introduced a few days later with certain amendments. Provisions relating to the Prime Minister, the National Assembly and the Public Service Commission were deleted. Following the report of a Constitutional Commission under the Chairmanship of Mr Telford Georges, a distinguished lawyer from Dominica, a new Constitution was brought into force on 5th June 1979. It recognises that Seychelles is a sovereign socialist republic with one party and the guarantee of fundamental human rights.

The executive power lies with the President, who is elected for five years by universal suffrage. The legislative power lies with the President and the Assembly.

The legislative body is a People's Assembly of 23 elected members and two members designated by the President to represent outer and inner islands.

On 4th December 1991 President René announced that an extraordinary Congress of the Seychelles People's Progressive Front had adopted unanimously his proposal to transform Seychelles from a single-party popular democracy to a pluralist democratic system. The President outlined a process under which the Constitution would be amended to allow the registration of other political parties, a Constitutional Commission to be established on a proportional party basis and a new Constitution to be put to a national referendum.

An Office for the Registration of Political Parties opened on 27th January 1992 and a number of opposition parties have formed.

Government

PRESIDENT

Mr France Albert René

COUNCIL OF MINISTERS

Minister of Administration and Manpower: Joseph Belmont

Minister of Agriculture and Fisheries: Jeremie Bonnelame

Minister of Community Development: Esme Jumeau

Minister of Education: Mrs Simone Testa

Minister of Employment and Social Affairs: William Herminie

Minister of Finance: James Michel

Minister of Health: Ralph Adam

Minister of Information, Culture and Sport: Ms Sylvette Frichot

Minister of Planning and External Relations: Mrs Danielle de St Jorre

Minister of Tourism and Transport: Jacques Hodoul

JUDICIARY

Chief Justice: Isaac Abban

Sierra Leone

Capital: Freetown

Sierra Leone lies on the west coast of Africa between 6° 55′ and 10° N. latitude and 10° 16′ and 13° 18′ W. longitude. Its 338 km (210-mile) sea coast extends from the border of Guinea to the border of Liberia, these two countries enclosing Sierra Leone inland. The total area of Sierra Leone is 72,326 sq km (27,925 square miles). Because of the hills of the Freetown peninsula Sierra Leone is the only West African country with a hilly coastline; the very name of the country is a derivation of the Portuguese for 'Lion Mountain Range'. It was given to this part of the coast by Pedro de Cintra in about 1462. De Cintra's expedition was one of the last great Portuguese voyages of discovery carried out under the direct influence and authority of Don Henry (Henry the Navigator) who died the following year.

The highest mountains are inland and include Bintumani (also known as Loma Mansa) in the Loma mountain range near the Guinea border to the north-east, 1,917 m, and Sankan-Biriwa, 1,824 m. The main estuaries navigable by ocean vessels are the Sierra Leone river and the Sherbro river, while small craft can travel certain distances on the Great and Little Scarcies, Bangru, Jong, Sewa, Waanje and Moa rivers. The source of the Niger which runs into the sea at Port Harcourt, Nigeria, is just within the north-eastern boundary.

There are two distinct seasons: the dry season from approximately November to May and the rainy season for the rest of the year. The heaviest rainfall is on the coast from July to September. The annual rainfall ranges from 1,875 mm to more than 3,250 mm, with 6,250 mm at Guma Valley, 16 km (10 miles) south of the capital, Freetown. The mean temperature is 26.7°C (80°F) with little variation. During the dry season the country experiences the *harmattan,* a dry, sand-laden wind from the Sahara.

The last census held in December 1985 put the population of Sierra Leone at 3.7 million with the capital, Freetown, having a population of 470,000.

The unit of currency is the Leone. The country's financial year runs from 1st July to 30th June.

The official language is English while the main local languages are Mende, Temne and Krio, the lingua franca. There are, however, at least thirteen tribes living in Sierra Leone, each of which has its own language.

The University of Sierra Leone was created in 1967. It consists of four constituent colleges—Fourah Bay College, the oldest institution of higher education in West Africa, founded in 1827, Njala University College founded in 1964, the Institute of Public Administration and Management founded in 1980, and the College of Medicine and Allied Health Sciences founded in 1988. The Milton Margai Teachers Training College near Freetown caters for secondary school teachers, and there are six primary teacher training colleges situated throughout the country.

At the moment there are 215 secondary schools, and 2,042 primary schools operating in Sierra Leone. It is estimated that just under 15 per cent of the population are literate, though the Western Area has up to 45 per cent literacy. The main religions are Islam and Christianity.

Outside the Freetown peninsula, which is officially known as the Western Area, the country is divided into the Southern, Eastern and Northern Provinces, and the provinces are further divided into twelve districts. The Southern Province includes the Districts of Bo, Bonthe, Moyamba and Pujehun, with headquarters of the administration located at Bo, The Eastern Province includes the Districts of Kenema, Kailahun and Kono, with provincial headquarters at Kenema. The Northern Province comprises the Districts of Bombali, Kambia, Koinadugu, Port Loko and Tonkili and the headquarters of the provincial administration are at Makeni.

In each of the three provincial headquarter towns is a Provincial Secretary's Office headed by a Provincial Secretary. There are 149 Chiefdoms in Sierre Leone and in each of these the Chiefdom Councillors elect a Paramount Chief.

Sierra Leone has four ports—Freetown, Bonthe, Niti and Pepel. The most important of these is Freetown, which is one of the largest natural harbours in the world. Sierra Leone Ports Authority handled 403,372 tons of cargo in 1990 during which period 146,092 tons of crude oil were discharged and 15,962 containers were handled. In the same period the port of Freetown was visited by 503 vessels. Berthing facilities for six ships are available at Queen Elizabeth II Quay in Freetown. Freetown is the only port for imports and it also exports agricultural produce. It is now assuming increasing importance as a trans-shipment container centre. Rutile and bauxite are exported from Niti in the Moyamba district, whilst Pepel iron ore exports ceased in March 1985. Freetown International Airport, Lungi is on the northern bank of the Sierra Leone River opposite Freetown. Passengers are taken by ferry and bus to the airport. In 1990 the airport handled 130,150 passengers and 2,269 tons of freight. There are smaller airfields at Hastings (Freetown), Kenema, Yengema, and Bonthe. There are no internal air services.

Since the phasing out of the railway system in 1974 Sierra Leone's road network has been developed considerably. About 1,215 km of the 7,107 km of road in Sierra Leone are surfaced.

Radio is operated by the Sierra Leone Broadcasting Service. Two 10 KW short wave transmitters were recently installed which will improve audibility and extend services to all parts of the country.

The Sierra Leone economy depends very largely on the export of minerals, in particular diamonds which are mined by the National Diamond Mining Company (SL) Ltd (DIMINCO), in which the Government has a 51 per cent shareholding. DIMINCO has concessions in the Yengema, Kono, and Tongo districts. Outside these concessions individual Sierra Leone diggers are licensed under the alluvial diamond mining scheme. Total export of diamonds in 1990 amounted to Le1,905.6 million.

The production of bauxite by the Sierra Leone Ore and Metal Company Ltd (SIEROMCO) at Mokanji in the Southern province commenced in 1963 and exports of bauxite in 1990 amounted to Le3,915.4 million. Reserves of up to 100 million tonnes are located in the Port Loko district and development of these reserves is being discussed.

A comparatively new development is the mining of rutile, the deposits of which are reported to be among the largest in the world. In 1972 a US owned company, Sierra Rutile Ltd was formed which instituted a comprehensive prospecting programme and mining of rutile began in 1979 at Gbangbama. The value of exports for 1990 was estimated at Le11,911.4 million. The production of rutile ceased for several months in 1982 because of a decrease in world demand, but following the sale of Bethlehem Steel's shareholding to Nord, production started up again in 1983.

Gold has been discovered in commercial quantities. Exports of gold in 1990 amounted to Le23.8 million. Early in 1984 the Sierra Leone Government concluded an agreement with a consortium of companies for off-shore oil exploration to be carried out over the following two years. Amoco (SL) Exploration Co Ltd, a member of the Standard Oil of Indiana Group has carried out a series of seismic surveys. Drilling of two off-shore exploration wells have so far showed positive signs of hydrocarbons, and in 1986 the company had its agreement extended to a further six years.

According to forecast figures for 1990, total imports (Le23,606.8 m) exceeded exports (Le20,915.2 m) by Le2,691.6 m. Agricultural exports include coffee, cocoa, palm kernel oil and cake, ginger, kola nuts and cassava. The main imports are machinery and plant, vehicles, electrical equipment, foodstuffs and mineral fuels. Rice, fish and cassava are the staple foods of the population but, rice imports have increased dramatically in recent years. In December 1986 the government launched the Green Revolution programme with subsidies and loans given to farmers to increase and extend their production. In June 1989 government removed all export taxes on agricultural products as a further incentive to farmers.

In 1986 the government adopted a new structural adjustment programme, but the IMF declared Sierra Leone ineligible for special grants in April 1988. Since then the Fund has been considering restoring the country's eligibility.

In November 1987 the government declared a 'state of economic emergency' to enable it to apprehend economic saboteurs. This was extended for a further twelve months in March 1988. The state of economic emergency ceased to exist in June 1989.

The Mano River Union was established between Sierra Leone and Liberia in 1973 to promote a customs union and economic co-operation between the two countries. It was extended to include Guinea in 1980.

The total budgeted revenue and grants for 1991/92 amounts to Le33,906 million.

The total budgeted expenditure for 1991/92 amounts to Le59,038 million.

History

Before Independence, Sierra Leone consisted of the Colony, which was broadly identical with the peninsula on which Freetown stands, and the Protectorate on the mainland.

The history of modern Sierra Leone dates from 1787 when Granville Sharp and other British abolitionists, acting on a scheme proposed by Dr Henry Smeatham, purchased from a local chief named Naimbana a strip of land on the peninsula and settled on it 400 freed slaves. In 1791 a Royal Charter was granted to a Sierra Leone company, of which both Sharp and William Wilberforce were directors, and, despite difficulties with local tribesmen and with the French, more settlers were introduced, many being freed slaves from Jamaica and Nova Scotia. In 1800 the peninsula was granted to the charterred company by letter patent; and the court of directors was empowered to appoint a Governor and Council, the former having powers to make laws. In 1807, when Britain outlawed slave trading, a naval station was established at Freetown, and slaves freed in operations by the ships stationed there were brought back to the settlement. Finally in 1808 Freetown became a colony, and the jurisdiction of the company was assumed by the Crown. From 1816 to 1843 the Gambia was governed from Sierra Leone; and the Gold Coast was a dependency from 1843 to 1850.

In 1862 a large tract of coastal area including Sherbro Island was added to the colony, and as the century progressed treaties were made with neighbouring Chiefs to protect the trade of the colony with the hinterland, and British influence was thus extended. To define the geographical extent of this influence, an agreement on boundaries was made with Liberia in 1885 and with France in 1895; and in 1896 a protectorate was declared over the territories so defined. Although British law and taxation procedure were introduced, the people of the protectorate still continued to be administered indirectly through their own rules.

Constitutional development until independence in 1961

Until 1863 the Government of Sierra Leone consisted of a Governor and an Advisory Council comprising *ex officio* members and one or two appointed members.

In 1863 an Executive Council and Legislative Council were created. In 1866 Sierra Leone was joined with The Gambia, the Gold Coast and Lagos to form the West Africa Settlements with a Governor in Chief in Freetown. In 1874 Lagos and the Gold Coast jointly became a separate colony and The Gambia was separated as a colony from Sierra Leone in 1888.

In 1924, by Order in Council dated 16th January, a new and considerably enlarged Legislative Council was set up providing for elected members, and also providing for direct representation of Protectorate interests for the first time.

An Order in Council in 1951 provided for a Legislative Council of thirty-two members, consisting of seven *ex officio* members, seven members elected from the Colony districts, twelve members elected from the Protectorate district council, two members elected from the Protectorate Assembly and two members nominated by the Governor, together with the Governor as President and a Vice-President. Provision was made by Royal Instruction for an Executive Council of four *ex officio* members and not less than four unofficial members appointed from among the elected members of the Legislative Council.

In 1953 a Ministerial system was introduced and in the next year the title of Chief Minister was accorded to the leader of the majority party in the Legislative Council.

Under a new constitution in 1956 the Legislative Council became the House of Representatives and was enlarged to consist of a Speaker, four *ex officio* members, fifty-one elected members and two nominated members (the last had no voting powers). In the General Election of 1957 virtually all adult males and all adult female taxpayers or property owners were eligible to vote. The Constitution was further altered in 1958 by the exclusion of *ex officio* members from the Executive Council and House of Representatives. The new Executive Council included eleven Ministers appointed from among the elected members of the House of Representatives. Dr (late Sir Milton) Margai, who had been Chief Minister under the previous constitutional arrangements, was appointed Prime Minister.

At the Constitutional Conference held in London from 20th April to 4th May 1960 the constitutional changes necessary before Sierra Leone became independent were agreed. Sierra Leone attained complete independence as a fully self-governing Member of the Commonwealth with Her Majesty The Queen as Sovereign on 27th April 1961.

Constitutional development from independence to March 1967

The Constitution of Sierra Leone, contained in the Sierra Leone (Constitution) Order in Council 1961, included provision for a Governor-General appointed by Her Majesty The Queen and for a House of Representatives consisting of not less than sixty members with a Speaker elected by the members from among their own number or from persons who were qualified to become members. For an interim period until a new House of Representatives was elected the House as established by the previous Constitution remained the legislative body.

To qualify for election to the House of Representatives a person had to be a citizen of Sierra Leone, had to have attained the age of twenty-five and had to speak English well enough to be able to take an active part in the proceedings of the House. Provision was made for the establishment of an Electoral Commission of a chairman and up to four members.

Provision was made for questions coming before the House of Representatives to be determined by a majority vote of the members present and voting, except in the case of certain constitutional amendments which required a two-thirds majority of all members in two successive sessions of the House, one before and the other following a dissolution. Finance Bills could only be introduced by a Minister of the Government. The House had a normal life of five years, unless sooner dissolved, and had to meet at least once a year.

Executive responsibility rested with a Cabinet of Ministers drawn from among the members of the House of Representatives. The Cabinet was presided over by a Prime Minister appointed by the Governor-General as the person likely to command the support of a majority of the members of the House. Other Ministers were appointed on the advice of the Prime Minister.

The first general elections following Independence were held in May 1962 when the Sierra Leone People's Party (SLPP) was returned to form a government. The next elections, in March 1967, resulted in a small majority for the other main political party, the All People's Congress (APC), led by Dr Siaka Stevens, but the election results were disputed.

The National Reformation Council and the return to civilian rule

After the second of two army *coups* in March 1967, a National Reformation Council was formed which ruled the country until April 1968 when it was overthrown by a third *coup* led by non-commissioned officers of the army and police. Dr Stevens was recalled from Guinea where he had taken refuge, to form a National Government in May 1968.

On 11th September 1970 two senior Cabinet Ministers resigned from the government and went into opposition. Following disturbances in the provinces a State of Emergency was declared and a reshuffled Cabinet was announced. A group of leading opposition personalities formed a new political party called the United Democractic Party (UDP) on 19th September. The UDP was banned on 8th October and its leaders were detained. By early 1971 most of them had been released.

On 23rd March 1971 in the course of an abortive military *coup* two attempts were made to kill the Prime Minister. On 28th March the Prime Minister signed a defence agreement with Guinea.

The Governor-General, Sir Banja Tejan-Sie, was relieved of his office and departed on leave with effect from 5th April 1971. On 19th April 1971 Sierra Leone became a Republic under a Constitution which provided for a Ceremonial President and the Acting Governor-General, Mr Christopher Cole, was sworn in as President. On 21st April the Constitution was again amended to provide for an Executive President and the Prime Minister, Dr Siaka Stevens, was sworn in. The amendments provided that the President should hold office for 5 years and that no President should hold that office for more than two consecutive terms.

A General Election was held in two stages on 11th and 15th May 1973. The Sierra Leone People's Party withdrew its nominations and the All People's Congress were returned unopposed.

In August 1974, during the absence abroad of President Stevens, a bomb attack was made on the house of the then Acting Vice-President, Mr C A Kamara-Taylor. After a trial in November 1974 eight people were executed for this crime in July 1975.

On 26th March 1976 President Stevens was nominated and re-elected unopposed by a special session of Parliament for a further term of office. Following demonstrations by students, the President on 1st February 1977 declared a State of Emergency. He later prorogued Parliament and called a General Election for May. The General Election on 6th May 1977, which took place a year early amid unrest, resulted in a victory for the All People's Congress with 72 MP's returned to Parliament against the Sierra Leone People's Party's 15. In Bo, violence on and before polling day resulted in voting being postponed until 6th October when the only candidates nominated represented the All People's Congress Party; all 8 being returned unopposed. As a result of subsequent by-elections there were only 11 SLPP Members of Parliament by May 1978. A new constitution, establishing a one-party state (with the All People's Congress the single recognised party) was approved by Parliament in May 1978 and confirmed by referendum in June 1978. Dr Stevens became the first President under the new constitution with the presidential term of office having been extended from five to seven years. General elections, the first under a one party system, were held on 1st May 1982. They were marked by violence and election irregularities which caused the cancellation of elections in 13 out of 85 constituencies. Under the terms of the 1978 Constitution (as amended by an Act of Parliament in June 1985) a Presidential Election had to be held before the end of 1985. On 2nd August the chief of the armed forces, Major-General Joseph Momoh was the only candidate nominated for the October presidential election by the All People's Congress. He was duly elected, and his inauguration took place on 26th January 1986. General Elections followed in May 1986 and were marked by the absence of violence.

In March 1987 the government announced it had foiled an attempted coup. A number of people were arrested including Francis Minah, the First Vice-President, who was dismissed from office. In the following October after a five-month trial, Minah and 15 other defendants were sentenced to death for plotting to assassinate President Momoh and to overthrow the government. In September 1988 the Appeal Court dimissed the appeal of Minah and 11 others who subsequently appealed to the Supreme Court.

On 29th September 1989 the Supreme Court rejected all 12 appeals. On 7th October 1989 Minah, Gabriel Kai-K'ai (the Coup leader) and four others were executed. President Momoh exercised his prerogative of mercy for the remaining 6 defendants who are now serving life sentences.

In October 1990, after repeated calls for Constitutional reform, the Head of State appointed a Constitutional Review Commission to review the 1978 Constitution of Sierra Leone and make recommendations thereon. In March 1991 the Constitutional Review Commission submitted its recommendations to the Government advocating a return to multi-party politics. A referendum was held in August 1991, the result of which was an overwhelming vote in favour of a multi-party democratic system. In September 1991, following the said referendum, a new Constitution reintroducing multi-party democracy was passed. A number of political parties have now been registered, and elections are due before September 1992. However, since March 1991, there have been repeated border-incursions in the Southern and Eastern provinces by liberation rebels. Sierra Leone forces, with assistance of units from Nigeria and Guinea, have recaptured several towns, but while rebel activity continues, the elections are unlikely to take place.

Historical List

GOVERNORS GENERAL

Sir Maurice Dorman, GCMG, GCVO, 27th April 1961 to 5th May 1962

H J Lightfoot Boston, CMG, JP (later Sir Henry Lightfoot Boston, GCMG) 5th May to 11th July 1962 (acting)

Sir Henry Lightfoot Boston, GCMG, JP, from 11th July 1962 to May 1967

HEAD OF STATE

President: His Excellency Major-General Dr Joseph Saidu Momoh

MEMBERS OF THE CABINET

Minister of Defence and Establishment: His Excellency the President

First Vice-President, Minister of Internal Affairs and Rural Development: Hon Dr Abdulai Conteh

Second Vice-President, Attorney-General and Minister of Justice: Hon Joseph Bandabla Dauda

Minister of Finance, Development and Economic Planning: Hon Dr James S A Funna

Minister of Foreign Affairs: Hon Dr Ahmed Dumbuya

Minister of Trade, Industry and State Enterprises: Hon Dr Tom Kargbo

Minister of Works: Hon A N D Koroma

Minister of Mineral Resources: Hon Abu Aiah Koroma

Minister of Transport, Communications and Tourism: Hon Dr Raymond Kamara

Minister of Labour, Energy and Power: Hon Ibrahim Barrie

Minister of Information, Broadcasting and Culture: Hon Robert Sam Kpakra

Minister of Health and Social Services: Hon Mrs Agnes Taylor-Lewis

Minister of Agriculture, Forestry and Fisheries: Hon Dr George Carew

Minister of Education, Youth and Sports: Hon Dr William Conton

Minister of Lands, Housing and the Environment: Hon Dr Bu-Buake Jabbie

Minister of State and Leader of the House: Hon J D Sandy

Minister of State and Force Commander: Hon Major-Gen Mohamed Sheku Tarawalli

Minister of State and Inspector-General of Police: Hon James Bambay Kamara

DEPUTY MINISTERS OF STATE (NOT IN THE CABINET)

Office of the President: Hon Dr Alimamy Kaba Turay

Office of the First Vice-President, Minister of Internal Affairs and Rural Development: Hon Emadu Rogers

Ministry of Finance, Development and Economic Planning: Hon Leonard Fofanah; Hon Thaim Kamara

Ministry of Foreign Affairs: Hon Dr Augustine Stevens

Ministry of Transport, Communications and Tourism: Hon Mrs Matilda Conteh

Ministry of Agriculture, Forestry and Fisheries: Hon Daniel Koroma; Hon Mrs Emma Clay-Simbo

Ministry of Education, Youth and Sports: Hon Yembeh Mansaray

Ministry of Trade, Industry and State Enterprises: Hon B M Koroma

RESIDENT MINISTERS

Southern Province: Hon Ernest Ndomahina

Eastern Province: Hon James Musa Gendemeh

Northern Province: Hon S B Saccoh

Singapore

Singapore is an island to the south of the Malay Peninsula from which it is separated by a narrow channel crossed by a causeway 1.2 km long. Included within its boundaries are a number of smaller islands. A few miles to the south are islands belonging to Indonesia. Singapore is situated just north of the equator, its central point being about 1°20′N. latitude and 103°40′E longitude. The area is 636 sq km (including the smaller islands) and the highest point, Bukit Timah, is 165 m above sea level. The name is derived from the Sanskrit 'Singa pura' or 'City of the Lion'.

The climate of Singapore is similar to that of Peninsula Malaysia being hot and humid with no clearly defined seasons. Rainfall averages 2,369 mm annually and the average daytime temperature is 26.6°C (78°F) dropping to an average minimum of 23.8°C (74°F) at night.

The 1990 Census gave the population of the Republic as 3 million, approximately 300,000 of whom were non-residents. Racial groups comprised:

Chinese	2.09 million	(77.7%)
Malays	380,600	(14.4%)
Indians	191,000	(7.1%)
Other races (Europeans, Eurasians etc)	29,200	(1.1%)

The annual rate of population growth in 1990 was 1.7 per cent.

The unit of currency is the Singapore dollar.

Malay, Mandarin, Tamil and English are official languages, but English is the language of administration, and the most commonly used. At least eight different Chinese dialects are used. However, an increasing number of Chinese speak Mandarin in addition to their own dialect and many speak English. The Chinese written language is common to all Chinese. The principal Indian language is Tamil, but many others are spoken.

Primary education is almost universal with emphasis on bi-lingualism.

The main religions are Islam, Buddhism, Taoism, Hinduism and Christianity. Many Chinese follow the Confucian system of ethics.

Singapore's traditional means of livelihood is entrepôt trade, including the processing of primary produce from neighbouring countries, but since independence its economy has grown rapidly and it has become a manufacturing, service and oil-refining centre. Singapore is one of the busiest ports in the world, with a modern container port, deep water wharves and ship repairing facilities. Total cargo handled in 1990 was 188 million tonnes.

Singapore Airlines is the national airline of Singapore. The international airport at Changi became operational in July 1981 and a second terminal was completed in late 1990. It is 20 km from the centre of the city with a runway length of 4 km. There are 26 km of metre gauge railway, the railway crossing the Straits of Johore by causeway and forming part of the Malaysian system. In addition eight miles of railway were completed in November 1965, to connect with the industrial area at Jurong. In 1990 there were 2,882 km of roads. The Mass Rapid Transit (MRT) railway system, begun in October 1983, opened in December 1987 and was completed in 1990. It consists of three lines totalling 67 km.

Radio Singapore together with Television Singapore became the Singapore Broadcasting Corporation, an autonomous statutory body on 1st February 1980. Radio broadcasts are on 9 channels and in Chinese, English, Malay and Tamil and provide facilities for commercial advertising. The number of radio and TV licence holders in 1990 was 124,031 and 550,829 respectively.

In addition, Rediffusion Services (S) Pte Ltd, a private commercial enterprise, operate a wired service, providing advertising facilities in Mandarin and English.

Television, introduced in 1963, operates on three channels, programmes being in Chinese, Malay, Tamil and English.

Singapore's Gross National Product (GNP) increased in 1990 to S$63.9bn, a 13.5 per cent increase over 1989. The 1991/92 budget estimates show S$3,700 million will be spent on defence; S$2,437 million on education and S$987 million on health. The estimated revenue for 1991/92 amounts to S$17.2 billion (an increase of S$300 million over 1990/91).

Having a limited land space and no natural resources, Singapore's prosperity was built up on entrepôt trade with the Port of Singapore, one of the busiest in the world in terms of annual shipping tonnage, as the keystone of the economy. To broaden the base of the economy and provide for more rapid growth an industrialisation programme was launched in 1960 which was accelerated in view of the pullout of British forces by the end of March 1976. Singapore actively encourages foreign private investors by offering tax and other incentives and free repatriation of profits and capital.

The recession of 1985/86 was overcome by determined Singapore government action to cut employers' costs. GDP growth in 1990 was 8.3 per cent, compared with 9.2 per cent in 1989. GDP growth in 1991 was 6.7 per cent.

The transport and communications sector grew by 8.8 per cent in 1990 while the financial and business services sector managed a 15 per cent growth. The commerce sector (which includes wholesale and retail trades, hotels and restaurants) grew by 7.8 per cent, while the construction sector registered positive growth of 7.2 per cent after a turning point in 1989 following four consecutive years of decline. The manufacturing sector grew by 10.5 per cent.

The Jurong Town Corporation is charged with the development and management of industrial estates in Singapore. It manages 30 industrial estates, including Jurong, the largest estate. There are in all some 4,950 companies, employing a total of 290,000 workers, in these estates.

Singapore is the third largest refining centre in the world, after Houston and Rotterdam. The oil refineries operate at almost their full capacity of one million barrels per day.

By the end of 1990 there were 142 hotels providing 24,167 rooms to cater for all categories of visitor. In 1990, the number of tourists who visited Singapore was 5.3 million, an increase of 10 per cent over 1989.

The majority of visitors to Singapore in 1990 were from ASEAN countries (27 per cent), Japan (18.3 per cent), Australia (8.6 per cent), the UK (5.6 per cent) and the US (4.9 per cent).

In addition, because of its location and high reputation for efficient communications and financial facilities, Singapore has become the region's logistical and supply centre for the off-shore oil exploration activities in South East Asia. It is being called upon to provide a wide variety of goods and support services.

Singapore's external trade in 1990, including trade with Peninsula Malaysia, was S$205 billion, an increase of 11.4 per cent over 1989. Imports were worth S$109.8 billion and exports S$95.2 billion.

History

The history of Singapore prior to 1948 is outlined in the history of Malaysia. Singapore's rapid development from the time of Sir Stamford Raffles was due in part to the farsightedness of Raffles himself in choosing an island lying, with its magnificent natural habour, not only on the trade routes to the Far East but also placed so as to be the natural trading centre for all the surrounding territories. Over the years Singapore flourished as a free port, living on its trade, its docking facilities and its processing of imported raw materials. It was not until 1921, with the emergence of Japan as the third naval power in the world, that a decision was made to construct there, in the channel between the island and the State of Johore, a first-class naval base with graving and floating docks to take the largest ships afloat. This base was completed in 1938. The defences of the island were, however, designed for resistance to attack by sea and in February 1942 it fell to a Japanese land attack down the Malay Peninsula and across the Johore Strait. On the liberation of Singapore in 1945, the island was detached from the other Straits Settlements and established as a separate Colony in 1946. At the same time Labuan was detached from Singapore and became part of the Colony of North Borneo; and the Cocos (Keeling) Islands (which were never occupied by the Japanese) and Christmas Island were transferred to Australia in 1955 and 1958 respectively. The Colony remained a free port and still continued to handle much of the trade of Malaya and to a lesser extent that of Indonesia. At the same time local industries were developed. A new constitution conferring full internal self-government and the title 'State of Singapore' was introduced in 1959. Singapore became a State of Malaysia on 16th September 1963. On 9th August 1965, it was separated from Malaysia and became an independent sovereign state.

Since independence, Singapore has increasingly become a well-respected member of the international community. In 1965, she became a member of the United Nations and, in 1967, was a founder member of the Association of South-East Asian Nations (ASEAN), along with Malaysia, Thailand, Indonesia and the Philippines.

Constitutional Development

After the end of the war with Japan, a short period of military administration was followed by the restoration of civil government on 1st April 1946. By Order in Council of 27th March 1946 Singapore was established as a separate Colony and a provisional Advisory Council was created pending the establishment of fully representative Executive and Legislative Councils.

The Advisory Council met for the first time on 11th April 1946 and set up a Committee to make recommendations as to the form of the Legislative Council. As a result of their recommendations, a partly elected Council met on 1st April 1948, with six Members elected from territorial constituencies. For the elections in 1951 the number of elected Members was increased to nine. In 1953 a Commission under the chairmanship of Sir George Rendel was set up to advise on a new constitution; and by Order in Council which came into force on 8th February 1955 Singapore was given a large measure of internal self-government. A Council of Ministers was formed, responsible collectively to a Legislative Assembly of thirty-two Members, of whom twenty-five were elected from single-member constituencies, three were *ex-officio* Members and four were Nominated Unofficial Members. The Governor ceased to preside over the Assembly and was replaced by a Speaker. There was a Council of Ministers consisting of the Governor, three *ex-officio* Members and seven Ministers appointed from among the elected and nominated Members of the Assembly. Mr David Marshall became Singapore's first Chief Minister, but was succeeded by Mr Lim Yew Hock in the following year.

In 1957, after discussions in Singapore and London, an Agreement was signed in London providing for the constitution of a State of Singapore with full internal self-government and the creation of a Singapore citizenship. The new constitution provided for a Head of State to be known as the Yang di-Pertuan Negara, a Cabinet presided over by a Prime Minister, and a fully elective Legislative Assembly of fifty-one Members with a Speaker and Deputy Speaker. On the coming into force of this Constitution in 1959 the Governor, Sir William Goode, became the first Yang di-Pertuan Negara of the State of Singapore and the first United Kingdom Commissioner; but he relinquished the former post six months later, Enche Yusof bin Ishak being appointed in his place. The first Prime Minister was Mr Lee Kuan Yew. One of the first acts of the new Government was to abolish the Singapore Municipal Council and to assume its functions. The United Kingdom Commissioner remained responsible for Defence and External Affairs but certain responsibilities in respect of the latter were delegated to the Government of Singapore. The Singapore Government was responsible for internal security subject to the oversight of an Internal Security Council consisting of three British Representatives, three Singapore representatives and one representative of the Federation of Malaya.

On Singapore's entry into Malaysia the Internal Security Council ceased to exist, internal security becoming the responsibility of the Malaysian Government. The office of United Kingdom Commissioner was also abolished, the senior British representative being the Deputy High Commissioner who was responsible to the British High Commissioner in Kuala Lumpur. After the separation from Malaysia, a British High Commissioner was appointed to Singapore.

On 7th August 1965 the Prime Ministers of Malaysia and Singapore concluded an agreement on the separation of Singapore from Malaysia as an independent sovereign state from 9th August. The Malaysian Government agreed to enact constitutional instruments to give effect to the separation. On 9th August the Malaysian Parliament passed the Constitution of Malaysia (Singapore Amendment) Act, 1965, providing for Singapore to become independent on that date and Singapore became a Member of the Commonwealth. By legislation passed in December 1965, with retrospective effect to 9th August, the island became a Republic, the Yang di-Pertuan Negara was re-styled President and the Legislative Assembly renamed Parliament. Singapore established a Presidential Council by legislation passed in December 1969. The Council, chaired by the Chief Justice, exists to examine legislation to see whether it contains elements which differentiate between racial or religious communities or contains provisions inconsistent with the fundamental liberties of Singapore citizens, and to report and advise the Government thereon.

There are currently 81 elected members in Singapore's Parliament, which operates along Westminster lines. In 1984, the Government passed legislation providing for up to six "non-constituency" MPs (NCMPs), to be drawn from those unsuccessful opposition candidates who polled the most votes in the General Election. After the 1984 election, the Government offered three seats to NCMPs, none were accepted. However, after the 1988 election, two NCMP seats were taken though one of these NCMPs was subsequently disbarred from Parliament. No NCMP seats were offered by the Government after the 1991 General Election as four opposition candidates were elected. In 1990, the Government passed legislation providing for up to six "nominated MPs" (NMPs). These are non-elected MPs who have the right to speak and vote in Parliament on non-financial or constitutional bills.

In 1986, three Town Councils were introduced on an experimental basis, and by 1991 all constituents had been given their own Town Councils. Their powers are, however, restricted and are largely confined to the management of public housing estates.

In 1988, "Group Representational Constituencies" (GRCs) were introduced. These are represented by four MPs from the same party, one of whom must be from an ethnic minority. Ater the 1991 General Election there were 15 GRCs, accounting for 60 of the 81 MPs in Parliament.

In January 1991, the Government passed legislation providing for an Elected Presidency, and the first Presidential Election will be held in 1993. Besides having veto powers over the use of the national reserves and the appointment of key public officials, the Elected President will also be empowered to prevent the Government from abusing its powers to curb subversion, religious extremism and corruption.

Government

The People's Action Party has held uninterrupted power since 1959. In November 1990, Prime Minister Lee Kuan Yew handed over the premiership to his First Deputy Prime Minister, Goh Chok Tong, thus completing the transition to the "second generation leadership". Although no longer Prime Minister, Lee Kuan Yew stayed on in the Cabinet as Senior Minister in the Prime Minister's Office.

In August 1991, after only 9 months as Prime Minister, Goh Chok Tong called a General Election to seek a mandate from the electorate both for his more consultative style of government, and for spending some of the national reserves on a number of health and education programmes he wished to implement. On nomination day, 41 of the 81 seats were uncontested by opposition candidates, and the

PAP was automatically returned to power. However, in the elections for the uncontested seats, 4 were lost to Opposition candidates, 3 to the Singapore Democratic Party and 1 to the Workers' Party, and the PAP's share of the vote dipped from 63.2 per cent in 1988 to 61 per cent. There are now more opposition MPs in Parliament than at any time since 1966.

HEAD OF STATE
President: Mr Wee Kim Wee

CABINET
(At March 1992)
Prime Minister: Goh Chok Tong
Senior Minister, Prime Minister's Office: Lee Kuan Yew
Deputy Prime Minister: Ong Teng Cheong
Deputy Prime Minister and Minister for Trade & Industry: Lee Hsien Loong
Minister for National Development: S Dhanabalan
Minister for Education: Lee Yock Suan
Minister for the Environment: Ahmad Mattar
Minister for Defence: Yeo Ning Hong
Minister for Law and Minister for Home Affairs: S Jayakumar
Minister for Finance: Richard Hu Tsu Tau
Minister for Labour: Lee Boon Yang
Minister for Foreign Affairs: Wong Kan Seng
Minister for Health and Minister for Community Development: Yeo Cheow Tong
Minister for Information and the Arts and Second Minister for Foreign Affairs: George Yeo Yang Boon
Minister for Communications: Mah Bow Tan

PARLIAMENT
Speaker: Tan Soo Khoon
First Deputy Speaker: Abdullah Tarmugi
Second Deputy Speaker: Lim Boon Heng
Clerk of Parliament: A Lopez
Leader of the House: Wong Kan Seng
Government Whip: Lee Boon Yang
Deputy Government Whip: Ho Kah Leong

THE JUDICIARY—THE SUPREME COURT OF SINGAPORE
Chief Justice of the Supreme Court of Singapore: The Hon Justice Yong Pung How
Attorney-General: Tan Boon Teik

MINISTRIES AND GOVERNMENT DEPARTMENTS

PRIME MINISTER'S OFFICE
Political Secretary: Tan Guan Seng
Permanent Secretary: Ngiam Tong Dow
Permanent Secretary (Special Duties): Dr Andrew G K Chew
Secretary to the Cabinet and to the Prime Minister: Wong Chooi Sen

MINISTRY OF FINANCE
Permanent Secretary: Ngiam Tong Dow
Public Service Division: Dr Andrew G K Chew
Accountant-General: Chris Liew Peng Fook
Auditor-General: Chee Keng Soon

MINISTRY OF FOREIGN AFFAIRS:
Parliamentary Secretary: Yatiman Yusof
Permanent Secretary: Peter Chan Jer Hing

MINISTRY OF HEALTH
Minister of State: Dr Aline Wong
Permanent Secretary: Dr Kwa Soon Bee

MINISTRY OF LABOUR
Parliamentary Secretary: Ong Chit Chung
Permanent Secretary: Moh Siew Meng

MINISTRY OF NATIONAL DEVELOPMENT
Minister of State: Lim Hng Kiang
Senior Parliamentary Secretary: Lee Yiok Seng
Permanent Secretary: J Y Pillay

MINISTRY OF INFORMATION AND THE ARTS
Minister of State: Ker Sin Tze
Senior Parliamentary Secretary: Ho Kah Leong
Parliamentary Secretary: Mohamad Maidin Packer Mohd
Permanent Secretary: Goh Kim Leong

MINISTRY OF COMMUNICATIONS
Permanent Secretary: Tan Guong Ching
Director of Marine: Teh Kong Leong
Director-General of Civil Aviation: Lim Hock San

MINISTRY OF DEFENCE
Second Minister for Defence: Lee Boon Yang
Parliamentary Secretary: Matthias Yao Chih
Permanent Secretary: Lim Siong Guan
Permanent Secretary: Koh Yong Guan

MINISTRY OF COMMUNITY DEVELOPMENT
Senior Minister of State: Ch'ng Jit Koon
Permanent Secretary: Koh Cher Siang

MINISTRY OF LAW
Permanent Secretary: Cheong Quee Wah

MINISTRY OF THE ENVIRONMENT
Permanent Secretary: Cheong Quee Wah

MINISTRY OF HOME AFFAIRS:
Parliamentary Secretary: Ong Chit Chung
Political Secretary: Harun Ghani
Permanent Secretary: B G (Res) Tan Chin Tiong
Controller of Immigration: Lim Ek Hong
Commissioner of Police: Goh Yong Hong
Director of Prisons: Tee Tua Ba
Director, Central Narcotics Bureau: Sim Poh Heng

MINISTRY OF EDUCATION
Senior Minister of State: Tay Eng Soon
Ministers of State: Sidek bin Saniff; Ker Sin Tze
Permanent Secretary: Er Kwong Wah
Director of Education: Dr John Yip Soon Kwong

MINISTRY OF TRADE AND INDUSTRY
Senior Minister of State: Lim Boon Heng
Permanent Secretary: Lam Chuan Leong

Solomon Islands

Capital: Honiara

Solomon Islands were so named by the Spanish navigator Alvaro de Mendaña following his discovery of the archipelago in 1568. The territory consists of a double chain of mountainous islands—the South Solomons—situated between the parallels of 5° and 13° 06′S. and the meridians of 155° and 170°E., and includes the islands of Guadalcanal, Malaita, Makira, New Georgia, Santa Isabel, Choiseul, Mono (or Treasury), Shortlands, Vella Lavella, Ranongga, Gizo, Rendova, Kolombangara, Russell, Florida, Nendo, Rennell, and numerous small islands. The total land area is approximately 28,370 square km. The highest named mountain is Mount Makarakombou 2,293 m (7,644 feet) on Guadalcanal. There are no navigable rivers.

The climate is equatorial with small seasonal variations defined by the trade winds. The south-east season lasts from April to November when the minimum temperatures are recorded. The highest mean and maximum temperatures and the highest rainfall are, as a rule, recorded in the north-west season from November to April. The mean annual temperature at the capital, Honiara (Guadalcanal) is about 27°C (80°F). The average annual rainfall at Honiara over a 10 year period is 2,145 mm (85.8 inches). Elsewhere it is nearer 3,000 mm (120 inches).

The first attempt at a census was carried out in 1931 and resulted in an estimated total population figure of 94,066. A sample census in 1959 gave an estimated total of 124,000. The first full census of the territory was held on 1st February 1970. The population at this time was found to be 160,998. Six years later in 1976 the population had risen to 196,823. The most recent census gives a population of 306,000.

The largest concentration of population is in the capital, Honiara, where the November 1986 census gave a total of 30,499 persons, with 16,727 males and 13,772 females. This compared with 3,548 in 1959, 6,684 in 1965, 11,191 in 1970 and 18,346 in 1979. Elsewhere population density varies although nowhere could be called overcrowded. Densities vary from 292 persons per square km on Tikopia to 3 persons per square km on Rennell. The population is currently increasing at 3.5 per cent per year.

The official language is English, in which language all teaching is carried out except at lowest primary level, but each tribe has its own language and there are numerous dialects. A form of English consisting of an English derived vocabulary based on a typically Melanesian syntax and known as pidgin is widespread and serves as a *lingua franca* to a considerable degree in the towns and coastal areas. There are some 86 dialects, not all in common use.

Education

The national system is wholly financed by the central government. Private educational agencies are at liberty to operate outside the national system but, if they opt to do so, they can expect to receive very limited financial help from the central government.

The central government gives grants to primary schools for equipment and it pays teachers' salaries. Secondary schools under the control of local authorities receive grants for boarding, equipment, building maintenance and pupils' travel costs. Capital aid is available for both primary and secondary schools. In line with its policy of decentralisation the central government has handed over responsiblity for running primary and certain secondary schools to provinces. The government recognises and encourages pre-schooling for children but, because of its limited resources, it is unable to assist financially at present. However several pre-school centres are run privately in urban areas.

There are 463 primary schools within the national system operated by provinces and 42 primary schools administered by independent education agencies. Total enrolment in primary schools in 1990 was 44,019.

The secondary school system is composed of national and provincial secondary schools operating on different lines. The national secondary schools run a five-year course for children who complete six years of primary schooling and are selected for secondary education by means of examination at primary standard six. The provincial secondary schools form the basis of rural education and as such have been slowly absorbing rural training centres. The emphasis is on equipping school leavers with the knowledge and know-how that is likely to be useful to them in a rural environment. The provincial secondary schools introduced a three year course taking 'core' academic subjects together with technical subjects. At the end of this period pupils sit a national examination to select a few pupils to move across to form four of the national secondary schools. There are six aided national secondary schools and two administered privately. The existing twelve provincial secondary schools adopted the three year course from 1979. Total enrolment in secondary schools in 1987 was 5,551. The first Solomon Islands Schools Certificate examination was introduced in September 1978. This replaced the Cambridge School Certificate examination which had been taken by secondary form five pupils since 1950. Primary and secondary school teachers are trained at the Solomon Islands College of Higher Education. Two government-administered schools, KGVI in Honiara and Wiamapura on Malaita and a church-administered secondary school in Honiara run a one year sixth form to prepare about 120 students a year for university study abroad.

Solomon Islands College of Higher Education offers technical subjects for skilled and semi-skilled manpower at middle level in the public and private sectors as well as having an intake from Form 3 and upwards in National Secondary Schools.

Health Services

Central Hospital, with 264 beds, acts as a national hospital besides acting as provincial hospital for Guadalcanal, Central Islands and Honiara Municipal Authority. Central Hospital provides consultant services in surgery, obstetrics and gynaecology, paediatrics, anaesthetics and dental surgery and is the main referral hospital for all hospitals in the provinces. Central Hospital provides a high standard of medical care with the availability of supportive services such as laboratory, pharmacy, X-ray, physiotheraphy and dental therapy.

The provincial hospitals are situated at Auki (Malaita) 216 beds, Buala (Isabel) 34 beds, Gizo (Western) 94 beds, Kira Kira (Makira) 100 beds, and Lata (Temotu) 46 beds. In addition, the Seventh Day Adventist Church runs a 93 bed hospital at Atoifi in East Malaita. Improvement is being undertaken of the facilities and supportive services. The main purpose of improving the facilities is to improve the supportive services for referral cases from the rural clinics.

Outside hospitals, health services are provided through a network of health centres, clinics aid posts and satellite clinics operated by government. Altogether there are 6 hospitals, 5 area health centres, 93 clinics and 36 aid posts run by government and in provinces there are two church hospitals, 19 church clinics, 12 industrial clinics and 19 privately run aid posts.

The principal endemic diseases are malaria and tuberculosis with gastrointestinal and upper respiratory diseases prevalent in the country. Malaria has always been regarded as the major health threat in Solomon Islands and a full-scale eradication programme was brought into operation in 1970 but was never fully successful and the incidence of malaria, including a chloroquine resistant strain is on the increase again. As a result of early efforts with new effective drugs leprosy is no longer a major threat to Solomon Islanders as it used to be in past years. In 1980 the number of cases reported was 36, by 1986 the number was down to 3.

The Economy

The dramatic rise in copra prices in 1974 followed by a drop in 1975/76 and coupled with a decline in the world market for timber, resulted in some employment shifts. The labour force consists largely of unskilled men, with a keen shortage of skilled islanders for supervisory posts. Employers engaging overseas workers are urged to train locals at the same time. Efforts at localisation have led to the number of expatriates in employment falling markedly.

Most workers in the cash economy are now represented by one of several trade unions which negotiate wage settlements and housing facilities on their behalf. In the event of a breakdown in negotiations between trade unions and an employer the matter may be referred to a Trade Disputes Panel. The decision of the Panel is legally binding on both parties. Unskilled daily paid workers employed by the government in January 1987 received a basic wage of SI$6.64 per day for a five-day week of 40 hours. Skilled daily paid government workers received up to SI$11.20 per day. Annual salaries of Public Service established staff ranged from SI$2,637 to SI$19,697 as at January 1987.

The report of the Foresty Policy Review Committee was approved, with some government reservations, by the Legislative Assembly in September 1975. The revised policy aims to spread the benefits from working the country's timber resources, both by extension of new concessions to new areas of customary land, after the government land is worked out, and also on a smaller scale by co-ordinating timber working with road and agricultural programmes. Timber working is largely done by some 10–12 private companies but some small scale sawmilling by local people is being sponsored.

Copra is still produced by small holders and by private plantations, the largest being owned jointly by Lever Solomon Limited (60 per cent) and government (40 per cent). The level of copra production fluctuates from year to year for smallholders, but production from the plantations was, until recently, relatively stable at about 10,000 tonnes per annum. Reaction to reduced world prices caused a 30 per cent drop in production in both smallholder operations and plantations during 1986.

Oil palm production was badly hit by cyclone Namu in May 1986, which killed or seriously damaged two-thirds of the SIPL plantation's trees. The 3,918 planted hectares, which yielded 92,251 tonnes of fruit in 1985, produced only 68,743 during 1986. That they recovered to this extent was due largely to the creditable work of rehabilitation by the company and its employees. SIPL is a joint venture between the Commonwealth Development Corporation and the Government. Cocoa exports in 1986 overtook the value of copra for the first time, at SI$6.5 million. Spices are grown on a small scale. The cattle industry was seen as a potential growth area, but plans to increase the cattle population in the first half of the 1980's have not been successful. Efforts are being made to improve production of chickens and pigs.

Timber is one of the three major export earners, most of it being exported as logs. In 1984 approximately 392,000 cubic metres were exported at a total value of SI$14.7 million. In 1986 this had risen to 433,900 cubic metres at a value of SI$33.9 million. In 1987 this dropped to 280,280 but increased in value to SI$35.1 million. The annual cut nominal figure is a little over 400,000 cubic metres. The joint venture fishing company Solomon Taiyo Limited exported 44,200 tonnes of fresh/frozen fish in 1986 at a value of SI$47 million but dropped to 26,478 tonnes and SI$43 million in 1987. The fishing base at Tulagi is well established and a second base at Noro is under construction. Fishing methods are pole and line and purse seine and longline. Other exports of particular importance to the rural dweller are marine shells and beche-de-mer. Local industries include the manufacture of twist tobacco, some of which is exported, biscuits, mineral water, nails, fibreglass products and furniture. Efforts are being made to widen the range of industries and promote exports. Total exports (FOB) in 1983 were SI$71.2 million, 1984 SI$118.6 million, 1985 SI$103.8 million, 1986 SI$114.9 million and 1987 SI$124.4 million. Total imports (FOB) in 1983 were SI$70.6 million, 1984 SI$83.8 million, 1985 SI$102.7 million, 1986 SI$104.3 million and 1987 SI$134.9 million.

	1986		1987		1988	
	Volume	Value SI$M	Volume	Value SI$M	Volume	Value SI$M
Timber (logs)	434,000	33.9	280,280	35.1	291,440	37.6
Timber (sawn)	5,810	1.8	5,370	2.1	4,660	2.2
Fresh/Frozen Fish	39,565	49.9	26,478	43.0	35,660	66.5
Canned Fish	1,040	4.8	1,200	7.1	1,205	8.9
Copra	32,431	5.9	27,903	10.2	27,228	15.7
Palm oil	14,490	5.6	11,562	6.9	13,591	12.3

Three trading banks are operating in Solomon Islands—the National Bank of Solomon Islands, the Australia and New Zealand Banking Group, and Westpac Bank.

There are four main ports: Honiara, Gizo, Noro and Yandina. Other ports are used exclusively for the export of fish or timber and there are numerous landing-places throughout the islands which are used by local vessels. Honiara has a deep water berth 70.5 m long with a minimum depth of 9 m alongside, capable of taking vessels up to 195 m in length. Yandina has a steel and concrete wharf with 52.8 m of face and a minimum depth of 7.5 m alongside. Gizo has a jetty with a depth alongside of 3.6 m. Sheltered anchorage is available there in 16 fathoms.

There are 14 international flights a week carrying international mail and passengers. International air services are provided by Qantas, Air Niugini and Solomon Islands Airlines. Solomon Islands Airlines also provides internal air services within the Solomons.

There are no railways. There are 467 km of main roads and 885 km of secondary rural roads in the country.

In addition to the General Post Office in Honiara post offices are established at Gizo, Munda, Yandina, Tulagi, Auki, Kira Kira, Santa Cruz and Taro. There are also 95 postal agencies operating throughout the country and 124 licensed stamp dealers. All mail is normally sent by air throughout the country. Where this is not possible inter-island shipping is used. Eighteen international flights a week carrying international airmail and overseas shipping is used for international surface mail as and when such vessels call at Solomon Islands.

A Philatelic Bureau operates from the General Post Office and arrangements can be made to open a deposit account from which stamps and First Day Covers will automatically be issued against standing instructions. Information about the facilities available and details of future and current issues can be obtained by writing to: The Philatelic Bureau, GPO, Honiara, Solomon Islands.

Solomon Islands Broadcasting Corporation, which is a statutory body established on 1st January 1977, broadcasts for 16 hours a day and includes a commercial advertising service. The daily programme service is transmitted from Honiara on 1035 kHz (medium wave) and on short wave frequencies 5020 kHz and 9545 kHz. Transmission hours were reduced on grounds of economy in 1987 and the regional stations closed but SIBC restored a full service in 1988. The transmitter output is 10 Kw. SIBC broadcasts from 0600 to 2300 daily, mainly in pidgin.

Solomon Islands introduced its own currency on 24th October 1977. Both Solomon Islands and Australian dollars were legal tender for the transitional period that ended on 30th September 1978. At the end of August 1990 the exchange rate was SI$1.0 = A$0.50.

The main domestic sources of internal revenue are import and export duties and income tax. Important provisions designed to encourage investment in the territory—including in certain circumstances a tax holiday for pioneer industries—are incorporated in the tax law.

History

The origin of the present Melanesian inhabitants is uncertain.

The era of European discovery opened in 1568 when Mendaña sighted land at Santa Isabel. Mendaña spent six months exploring in the group before returning to South America. Though he reported evidence of gold he was unable to produce proof and in consequence he lost favour in the Court and his achievements were belittled. Mendaña however was convinced of the potential of the islands and partly to impress his countrymen called them the Isle of Solomon, in the hope that they would be connected with the source of King Solomon's wealth. In 1595 Mendaña led another expedition to re-discover the archipelago. This time he did not reach the Solomons proper, but discovered the Santa Cruz Group. In Graciosa Bay he founded a short-lived colony which was totally abandoned soon after his death there. Tasman discovered Ontong Java in 1643, but for two centuries the main islands of the group remained lost to the sight of Europeans. It was not until 1767 that Carteret re-discovered what Mendaña had seen. Thereafter, European explorers sailed through Solomon Islands with increasing frequency—Bougainville in 1768, de Surville in 1769, Maurelle in 1781, Shortland in 1788 and d'Entrecasteaux in 1799.

The European explorers had, however, still made no impression on the lives of the indigenous inhabitants. These lived in very small groups, most of them having an anarchical attitude to authority. Gradually, however, here and there, some powerful personality began to assert himself and to gain adherents from other groups of people. Succession and rule were matters of challenge, contest and victory, and life was a pattern of very small communities living in fear of each other; a pattern of internecine warfare, headhunting and cannibalism, lived in such exclusive isolation that even dialects had changed to an extent where adjacent villages had difficulty understanding each other. The pattern remained unaltered until regular visits by Europeans began in the nineteenth century.

The inauguration of sugar plantations in Queensland and Fiji, the arrival of missionaries and traders and the more regular (even if very intermittent) patrols of naval ships began a new era. Labour needed for the sugar plantations was combed from the Solomons as well as other island groups. Some of the recruiters used methods which shocked the outside world and in return provoked reprisals. Massacres of Europeans and natives steadily mounted until Great Britain, in an effort to stem the mounting tide of savagery, declared a Protectorate in 1893 over the Southern Solomons, comprising Guadalcanal, Savo, Malaita, San Cristobal and the New Georgia group. In 1898 and 1899 the islands of the Santa Cruz group were added to the Protectorate, and in 1900 the islands of the Shortland groups, Santa Isabel, Choiseul and Ontong Java were transferred by treaty from Germany to Great Britain.

The copra industry began in 1908, three years after the last worker had been returned from the overseas plantations. The acreage under coconuts continued to expand until the price of copra fell in the early nineteen-twenties. The greater part of the copra produced was in the hands of companies, at least until the Japanese invasion in 1942. The copra industry made a special mark on social life in those parts of the Solomons which provided the labour for the plantations. Young men began to regard it as natural to go away for a couple of years at a time, to earn money and bring back trade goods for their family in the villages, and this became part of family life.

The effect of the spread of Christianity and desire for gainful employment was to check inter-clan warfare and raids on other villages and islands. Missionary societies started schools and began to teach some of the boys various trades; efforts were also made to teach hygiene in the home and child welfare, and to produce staff useful to the churches.

The 1914–18 war had little effect on the islands, but in 1942 there came invasion, occupation by the Japanese, counter-attack and battle, air-raids, and finally occupation by United States and Allied forces, mainly in the Central and Western Districts.

For nearly three years there had been a state of havoc, fear, and uncertainty, and added to this the revelation of material resources, profligately expended or generously shared, such as Solomon Islanders had never seen before. The loyalty of the islanders was remarkable. Many joined the Defence Force, the combat unit of the Protectorate that took part in active battle, often in the spearhead of the attack where they were employed as guides, or in patrolling behind the enemy lines. They earned military distinction and a number of decorations. In the areas occupied by the enemy, Government headmen carried on, protecting British coast-watchers from capture, rescuing allied airmen shot down behind enemy lines and helping them when the American and British forces landed.

After the war a political movement, known as Masina Ruu, started in Malaita, and for over six years its leaders endeavoured to dominate native affairs in Malaita while their influence spread to other parts of the Protectorate. At the outset the movement preached a policy of improved agriculture, concentration into large villages and non-co-operation with Government and missionary societies. These teachings were coupled with a policy of fostering rumours of an earthly paradise to come, promises which were earnestly believed and which formed part of the psychological background of the movement.

The year 1952, however, saw a decided lessening of the political tension which had handicapped development and administration during the post-war years. A severe epidemic of poliomyelitis may fortuitously also have shaken confidence in the new settlements and in the wisdom of rejecting formal medical attention. Strenuous efforts to bring about a rapprochement between the Government and the leaders of Masina Ruu on Malaita culminated in the formation of a properly organised Council (now Provincial Assembly) for the whole of Malaita for the first time. The Malaita people, through their representatives on this Council, like the people of other islands, thereafter had a progressively increasing amount of responsibility for the management of their own local affairs. Similar local government councils were established in the years immediately following the war, and the number was gradually increased until in 1966 the whole Protectorate except Tikopia and Anuta was covered by these councils, all the members of which are elected by universal adult suffrage.

There are now seven Provincial Assemblies in addition to the Honiara Town Council. It is Government policy progressively to allocate more functions to local government while ensuring that national interests are safeguarded and developed, and substantial responsibility has been devolved for education, agriculture, works and health services.

The islands became independent in July 1978 under the government of Sir (then Mr) Peter Kenilorea, who was returned to power in the elections of 1980. His coalition government fell, however, in August 1981 and Mr Solomon Mamaloni became Prime Minister until November 1984 when Sir Peter Kenilorea was elected Prime Minister of a coalition government for the second time. In December 1986 Sir Peter Kenilorea was succeeded by his deputy Mr Ezekiel Alebua. After the elections of February 1989 Mr Mamaloni again became Prime Minister.

Constitution

The British Solomon Islands Order 1974, came into effect in the territory in August of that year, thereby revoking the British Solomon Islands Order 1970. The new Constitution was drafted in accordance with the recommendations of a Special Select Committee on Constitutional Development appointed by the former Governing Council of the Protectorate. In accordance with the new Constitution, the office of High Commissioner for the Western Pacific was redesignated so far as the Solomons were concerned.

The Constitution thus established a new office of Governor of the Protectorate, and introduced a new Legislative Assembly whose 24 elected members chose a Chief Minister. It replaced the former Governing Council in its executive capacity (and the Committees which assisted in this capacity) by a Council of Ministers whose members were collectively responsible to the Legislative Assembly for any advice given to the Governor in the exercise of their functions under the Constitution. In accordance with The British Solomon Islands (Amendment) Order 1975, which came into effect in the territory in July 1975, there are eight Ministers appointed by the Governor on the Chief Minister's advice. The expatriate Financial Secretary was replaced by a local Minister of Finance, also in accordance with The British Solomon Islands (Amendment) Order 1975.

The British Solomon Islands (Name of Territory) Order 1975 changed the official name of the Protectorate to 'Solomon Islands' though its Protectorate status remained unchanged.

Under the Solomon Islands (Amendment) Order 1975, Solomon Islands received Internal Self Government on 2nd January 1976, The Order provided for the Chief Minister to be President of the Council of Ministers, in place of the Governor, who was bound henceforth to act in accordance with advice given to him by the Council of Ministers in most internal matters. The Governor, however, retained responsibility for defence, external affairs, internal security and the Public Service, and certain discretionary powers. These several constitutional démarches came as a result of direct discussions between British and Solomon Islands ministers in May 1975, which produced a programme for Solomon Islands to attain independence. A general election was held in June 1976 and 38 candidates were returned, the increased number provided by The Solomon Islands (Amendment) Order 1976. A Constitutional Conference was held in September 1977 to draw up an Independence Constitution, in the light of the Report of a Constitutional Committee which met during 1975/76 and was composed entirely of Solomon Islands legislators, local council members and other leaders. This report was debated twice by the new Legislative Assembly, which then adopted certain 'Principles' in February 1977 in readiness for the Conference. In addition to setting out the broad principles of an independence constitution, the Constitutional Conference agreed that on independence Solomon Islands should become a constitutional monarchy with the Queen as Head of State. A resolution in support of the Conference's decisions was approved by the Legislative Assembly on 18th November 1977. At the same time it approved 7th July 1978 as Independence Day.

The Solomon Islands Bill was given the Royal Assent on 25th May. The Independence Order in Council incorporating the new Constitution for Solomon Islands was made at a meeting of the Privy Council on 31st May and laid before the British Parliament on 8th June 1978.

In July 1982 it was announced that a working party would review the Constitution with the object of adopting a 'quasi-federation or domestic union between the Central and Provincial governments'. Following the General Election of 1984, however, the Provincial Ministries were abolished.

Government
(October 1991)

THE GOVERNOR-GENERAL
HE Sir George Lepping, GCMG, MBE

CABINET
Prime Minister: Hon Solomon Mamaloni
Minister for Agriculture and Lands: Hon George Luilamo
Minister for Home Affairs and Deputy Prime Minister: Hon Sir Baddeley Devesi, GCMG, GCVO, K ST J
Minister for Commerce and Primary Industries: Hon Michael Maina
Minister for Education and Human Resources Development: Hon Sam Alasia
Minister for Finance and Economic Planning: Hon Christopher Abe
Minister for Foreign Affairs and Trade Relations: Hon Sir Peter Kenilorea, KBE
Minister for Health and Medical Services: Hon Nathaniel Supa
Minister for Housing and Government Services: Hon Allen Kemakeza

21 **Bermuda:** Aloe/*Bermuda Government Information Services, Hamilton*

22 **Sri Lanka:** Mahout and elephant, Mahaweli Ganga/*Compix*

23 **Cayman Islands:** Cayman Islands National Museum, George Town/*Cayman Islands Government Information Services, George Town*

24 **British Virgin Islands:** Farmer working on a Government-funded plant project/*Department of Agriculture, Tortola*

25 **Seychelles:** Pitcher plants/*Robert Jenner, British High Commission, Victoria*

26 **Bangladesh:** Cotton dyeing/*Compix*

27 **Mauritius:** Children fishing/*Compix*

28 **St Lucia:** Soufrière Bay/*Compix*

29 **Malaysia:** Mouse Deer/*Compix*

30 **Canada:** Writing-on-Stone Provincial Park, staff conducting a guided hike/*Alberta Recreation and Parks*

31 **Grenada:** St George's Harbour/*Compix*

32 **India:** Benares Observatory/*Compix*

33 **Belize:** Supreme Court, Belize City/*Compix*

34 **Hong Kong:** View from Victoria Peak/*Gillian Allen, FCO*

35 **Namibia:** Bushman women, Tsumkwe/*Compix*

36 **New Zealand:** Wellington from Mount Victoria/*Compix*

37 **India:** Jaipur/*Compix*

38 **Pakistan:** A busy street in Karachi/*High Commission for Pakistan, London*

39 **Trinidad:** Scarlet Ibis, Pointe-à-Pierre Wildfowl Trust/*Bill Preston, British High Commission, Port of Spain*

22

23

24

26

28

29

32

33

34

37

38

39

Minister for Natural Resources: Hon Job Dudley Tausinga
Minister for Police and Justice: Hon Albert Laore
Minister for Post and Communications: Hon Ben Gale Fa'aitoa
Minister for Provincial Government: Hon Allan Qurusu
Minister for Tourism and Aviation: Hon Victor Ngele
Minister for Transport, Works and Utilities: Hon Alfred Maetia

Leader of the Opposition: Hon Andrew Nori

Other Members of the National Parliament:
E Alebua, E Andressen, A Bartlett, J Fisango, B Foukona, A Kapei, Mrs H Kari, G Kejoa, Rev C Kotali, A Laore, R Lilo, R Mara, A Paul, D Philip, J Piasi, F J Saemala, D Sitai, J F Sukina'a, P Tovua, J Tuhanuku, N Waena.

Speaker of the National Parliament:
Hon Waita Ben.

CIVIL ESTABLISHMENT
Chairman Public Service Commission: Dennis Lulei
Permanent Secretary for Office of Prime Minister: Wilson Ifunaoa
Permanent Secretary for Agriculture and Lands: Geoffrey Siapu
Permanent Secretary for Education and Human Resources: Mostyn Habu
Permanent Secretary for Finance and Economic Planning: Leonard Maenu'u, OBE
Permanent Secretary for Foreign Affairs and Trade Relations: Mrs Phyllis Taloikwai
Permanent Secretary for Health and Medical Services: Daniel Ho'ota
Permanent Secretary for Home Affairs: Walter Ramo
Permanent Secretary for Housing and Government Services: Mathias Pepena
Permanent Secretary for Natural Resources: Snyder Rini
Permanent Secretary for Police and Justice: Benjamin Newyear
Permanent Secretary for Post and Communications: Richard Kohata
Permanent Secretary for Provincial Government: Patteson Oti
Permanent Secretary for Tourism and Aviation: James Saliga
Permanent Secretary for Transport, Works and Utilities: Stephen Danitofea
Permanent Secretary for Commerce and Primary Industries: Allan Arafoa

JUDICIARY
Chief Justice: Hon Gordon Ward
Attorney General: F Kabui

Sri Lanka

Capital: Colombo

Location, Topography and Climate

The island of Sri Lanka lies in the Indian Ocean off the southern extremity of the Indian sub-continent, between latitudes 5° 55′ and 9° 50′N and longitudes 79° 42′ and 81° 53′E. It is separated from Cape Cormorin by the Palk Strait. The maximum length of the island from north to south is 434 km (270 miles) and its greatest width is 225 km (140 miles). Its area is 65,610 sq km (25,332 square miles), about half the size of England.

From the coastal plains, broadest in the north, the land rises to a central massif of mountains of almost solid gneiss which is of outstanding scenic beauty. The highest peak is Pidurutalagala 2,484 m, but the most famous and spectacular is Adam's Peak 2,208 m. It is a place of pilgrimage, revered by Buddhists, Hindus and Muslims; a mark on the summit resembles a human footprint, variously claimed to be that of the Buddha, Vishnu or Adam when cast down from Paradise.

Rivers radiate in all directions from the central massif; the longest is the Mahaweli Ganga (over 322 km), a major source of hydro electric power, which drains into Trincomalee Bay. None of the rivers is navigable to ocean-going vessels. Trincomalee Bay is an excellent natural deep water harbour, used as a major naval base up to the end of the Second World War, but overshadowed as a commercial port by Colombo.

The climate is hot in the low country, particularly from March to May. The average mean temperature is 26°–28°C (79°–82°F) and the humidity in the wet zone (the South-Western plain and the Southwest side of the hill country together with the area around Matale) is high. In the hills it is pleasantly temperate, and at resorts such as Nuwara Eliya there is on rare occasions frost at night in December and January. There are two main seasons, that of the south-west monsoon from mid-May to September and that of the north-east monsoon from November to March. The short dry season lasts from March to mid-May. The average temperature in Colombo throughout the year is 27°C (80°F) ranging to a maximum of 35°C (95°F) with high humidity. The annual rainfall ranges from 1,075 mm in the dry Northern Province to 5,450 mm in the central massif. The island average is 2,487 mm.

Population

At the last national census in March 1981 the total population was 14.8 million. By mid 1988 government estimates put the figure at around 16.5 million. The distribution of the main ethnic groups was:

	per cent
Sinhalese	73.98
Ceylon Tamils	12.60
Indian Tamils	5.66
Ceylon Moors	7.12
Malays	0.29
Burghers	0.26

Some 70 per cent of the population are Buddhists, 15.5 per cent Hindus, 7 per cent Roman Catholics and other Christians and 7.5 per cent Muslims. The official languages are Sinhala and Tamil, while English is widely used in the commercial and government sectors.

Health

Apart from the normal European illnesses malaria has still not been eradicated and dengue fever remains a hazard. There is a free health service with island-wide hospitals and clinics, staffed by well-qualified doctors, though nursing standards are not high, and the service inevitably suffers from shortage of funds. There are several private hospitals and clinics in Colombo.

Communications

Passenger traffic to and from Sri Lanka is almost entirely by air. The regular ferry service from Mannar to Tamil Nadu in India has been interrupted for several years due to the security situation in the Northeast. The international airport is at Katunayake, 31 km north of Colombo; the terminal buildings were extended and modernised in 1988. There are a number of airstrips around the island, but no regular internal air service.

Internal transport is by road and rail. The Government-owned bus company, which is in the process of being privatised, runs services throughout the island on the extensive road system (25,560 km), supplemented by privately owned buses and mini-buses, especially in the area around Colombo. The Ceylon Government Railways has 1,453 km of broad gauge line; the system radiates from Colombo south to Matara, north to Jaffna, east to Trincomalee and Batticaloa and up-country via Kandy to Nanu Oya near Nuwara Eliya. Rail links to the north and east have been restricted for some time because of the security situation.

Due to the fighting in the north and east of the island there are some restrictions on travel within these areas. Colombo is the principal port, handling 8,676,892 metric tons of cargo in 1989, Trincomalee and Galle are subsidiary ports.

The Economy

A significant upsurge in economic growth, assisted by a resilient agricultural sector and a buoyant manufacturing sector, enabled the Gross Domestic Product to increase in real terms by 6.2 per cent, nearly three times the 1989 rate. Agriculture, forestry and fishing account for 26 per cent of GDP. Export crops of tea, rubber and copra are produced on large estates, mainly Government owned, and still provide a substantial part of the country's export earnings. Tea production in 1990 reached an all time record of 233 million kgs. Spices and gems are also important export earners.

Over the last eleven years manufacturing has played a larger part in the economy: in the two Free Trade Zones near Colombo the assembly of garments and electronic equipment for export is a major activity. A third Free Trade Zone was recently opened at Koggala, near Galle, in the Southern Province. Textile and garment products now account for 31.7 per cent of the country's total exports.

Balance of payment results for 1990 were encouraging, with an overall surplus for the first time in five years and a narrowing of the current account deficit. The value of merchandise exports recorded a growth of 27.6 per cent whilst imports grew by 20.8 per cent. Receipts from workers abroad rose by 26 per cent in rupee terms compared to 1989. Tourism increased by 65 per cent, with 297,000 arrivals generating foreign exchange earnings of US$115 million. Reserves at year end stood at US$423 million. In line with maintaining its tight monetary policy the Government was successful in containing the budget deficit to within the target of 10 per cent of GDP. Domestic savings increased from 12.2 per cent of nominal GDP in 1989 to 14.8 per cent in 1990. Inflation however was one negative feature of performance, fuelled by elimination of subsidies on wheat, flour, rice and fertilisers.

Steps are currently being taken to streamline and modernise a number of public sector enterprises with the aim of eventually privatising them. In 1990 the Colombo Stock Exchange also had a watershed year with the abolition of the penal tax levied on foreigners investing in Sri Lanka stocks, encouraging rising share prices and brisk trading.

EXPORTS

Commodity:	*Value (Rs. m.) 1990*
Tea	19,823
Rubber	3,080
Coconut and Coconut Products	2,783
Other products	44,675
Precious Stones/Other Mineral Exports	3,484
Unclassified	5,635
	79,480*

IMPORTS

Commodity	*Value (Rs. m.) 1990*
Consumer Goods	28,004
of which:—	
(a) Food & Drink	16,566
(i) Rice	1,758
(ii) Flour	1,388
(iii) Sugar	5,173
(b) Textiles	10,977
(c) Other Consumer Goods	11,438
Intermediate Goods	58,672
Investment Goods	19,129
Unclassified	1,923
	107,728*

Sri Lanka's three major trading partners are Japan, the USA and the United Kingdom.

* All figures provisional

Tourism developed rapidly in the early 1980s as a foreign exchange earner with large investments on hotel buildings on the south-west coast, on the east coast and in Colombo. In 1982 over 450,000 tourists visited the island. Owing to the continued civil disturbances less than 185,000 arrived in 1989, but levels recovered with 297,000 arrivals in 1990. Gross foreign exchange earnings in 1989 were estimated by the Ceylon Tourist Board at Rs. 2,750 million.

Education

Education is free from primary to University level and compulsory from grade 1 (age 6) to grade 9. Some 40 per cent of the relevant age groups attend secondary school. There are several Universities throughout the island, with some 20,000 students.

The Media

With a very high level of literacy, there is a wide range of Sinhala and Tamil language newspapers, and two daily newspapers in English. The Government-owned radio station broadcasts throughout the island in the three languages. There are two Government-owned television stations: the Rupavahini Corporation provides an island-wide network, mainly in the Sinhala and Tamil languages, while the Independent Television Network provides a service, mainly in English, in the greater Colombo area.

History

The earliest known inhabitants of Sri Lanka were aborigines who migrated about five thousand years ago from the pre-Dravidian tribes which populated the Deccan. Their descendants, the primitive Veddhas, are still to be found in small numbers in the remote forests of the interior.

According to the Mahavamsa chronicle, the sequence of the earliest Sinhalese kings began with Vijaya I, the traditional founder of the Great Dynasty in 543 BC. Expelled from Bengal for lawlessness, Vijaya landed in the island and soon became the King of Sri Lanka. Vijaya's followers were called Sihala, or Sinhala (lion race) after Vijaya's father, Sinha Baleu.

The civilization of Sri Lanka from the earliest times up to the twelfth century was centred on the dry zone in the north. The whole surface of the northern plains was converted to cultivated land by means of an extensive irrigation system, which was to last for fifteen centuries, and the remnants of which exist today.

Buddhism was introduced into Sri Lanka during the reign of Tissa, circa 247–207 BC, by the son of the Emperor Asoka, Prince Mahinda.

The country flourished for several centuries until it was invaded from southern India. The history of Sri Lanka thereafter is largely a succession of invasions from southern India and of internal strife fomented by Sinhalese chiefs who employed Tamil mercenaries in their conflicts with the royal line. From the seventh century onwards the Tamils came in increasing numbers and they filled all the principal offices, including that of Prime Minister. In the eighth century the king was forced to leave Anuradhapura, which had been the Sinhalese royal seat for almost a thousand years, and the capital was moved to Polonnaruwa. In 1017 the whole of Sri Lanka was subdued by a great invasion from the Chola Empire but sixty years later a Sinhalese prince of the exiled royal house succeeded in restoring part of the Sinhalese kingdom. The exploits of a successor, King Parakrama Bahu I, who became ruler of the entire island and reduced the Chola and Pandya Empires to the position of tributaries, are among the most notable in the history of Sri Lanka. Thirty years after his death invaders from Kalinga in southern India appeared. Under their leader Magha, the north of Sri Lanka became a Tamil kingdom. Magha's invasion compelled the Sinhalese rulers to move south and a new capital was eventually established in 1410 at Kotte, near Colombo.

The Sinhalese kings who followed Parakrama were weak and exercised little control over their semi-independent chiefs. This led, at the end of the fifteenth century, to the rise of an independent kingdom of Kandy, dividing the inhabitants into low-country and up-country Sinhalese. The up-country kingdom of Kandy originally comprised the present North-Central and Eastern Provinces and Hambantota District. The low-country kingdom of Kotte covered the present North-Western, Western and Sabaragamuwa Provinces and the Galle and Matara Districts.

The Colonial Period

The Portuguese first came to the island in 1505, and in 1517 the Sinhalese king at Kotte submitted to Portuguese protection. The last legitimate king of Sri Lanka ruling from Kotte was Dharmapala, who, on his death in 1597 bequeathed Sri Lanka to King Philip I of Portugal (Philip II of Spain). Portugal thus gained control of the island except for the Tamil kingdom of Jaffna, which was taken in 1621, and the territory of the king of Kandy. The Portuguese introduced Roman Catholicism, which today has more than three quarters of a million adherents in Sri Lanka.

The Dutch from 1602 began to take an interest in the island and from 1634, with help from the king of Kandy, gradually overran the Portuguese possessions. In 1656 the Portuguese capitulated and the Dutch became masters of the whole island except for the kingdom of Kandy.

Throughout the Dutch occupation there was constant trouble with the king of Kandy, but in 1766 he was complelled to sign a treaty relinquishing to the Dutch not only the settlements they already held but also the remaining districts bordering the coast, the Kandyans being thus cut off from the outer world. The Dutch divided their settlements between Colombo, Jaffna and Galle, building a track round the coast. Roman-Dutch law, the forts and the Burghers, who are the descendants of the Dutch colonists, are the principal legacies of Dutch rule in Sri Lanka.

France declared war on Britain and Holland on 1st February 1793 and during the next two years overran Holland. In January 1795 the Dutch Stadtholder, William IV of Orange, fled to England and called upon the Dutch overseas possessions to seek British protection. Disobeying the orders of the Stadtholder, the Dutch in Sri Lanka refused British protection. An expedition from Madras in 1798 captured Trincomalee and other Dutch posts including Colombo were placed under siege. By the terms of the capitulation, signed on 15th February 1796, Colombo and the remaining Dutch settlements were surrendered to Britain; this was confirmed at the Peace of Amiens in 1802. Difficulties with the Kandyan kingdom of the interior continued up to 1815 when the king was deposed and the whole island came under the control of Britain.

Improvements in communications, coupled with reforms in the ancient Sinhalese systems of land tenure, contributed to the transformation of the economy. The British introduced plantation crops, coffee, coconuts, rubber and, after coffee was wiped out by disease in the 1870s, tea, with such success that by the end of the 19th century the export of these crops formed the mainstay of the economy, as they still do.

The British brought with them to Sri Lanka their system of justice and the English common law, although some difficulty was encountered at first in assimilating this with the legacy of Roman-Dutch law left behind by the Dutch. In 1801 a Supreme Court of Justice and a High Court of Appeal were established from both of which appeal lay to the Privy Council.

Independence

Following the Report of The Colebrook Commission in 1832 Executive and Legislative Councils were established in 1833. Ceylonese were admitted to the Civil Service and the educational system was developed. The first Legislative Council consisted of 9 official and 6 unofficial members but in response to increasing demands over the next decades the composition in 1924 had become 12 official and 37 unofficial members of whom 34 were elected. Political consciousness among the Ceylonese grew and in 1908 the Ceylon National Association was formed, becoming the Ceylon National Congress in 1918.

The practical working of the Constitution was examined by the Donoughmore Commission in 1927–28. As a result the new Constitution promulgated in 1931 provided for universal suffrage and a 50 member Legislature (the State Council), included 8 members nominated by the Governor and 3 officials. Groups from the Legislature formed seven executive Committees, the Chairmen of which constituted the Board of Ministers.

In 1944, the Soulbury Commission recommended a new Constitution granting internal self-government which was introduced in 1946, and was followed in 1948 by full independence within the Commonwealth.

Post Independence Politics

From 1948 to 1956 Sri Lanka was governed by the United National Party, (UNP), which had its origins in the National Congress, supported by the Tamil Congress. At first the Opposition consisted of the (Trotskyist) Marxist Lanka Sama Samaja Party (LSSP) and the Communists; from 1951 onwards its ranks were augmented by the Sri Lanka Freedom Party (SLFP) led by Mr S W R D Bandaranaike who had, with several others, broken away from UNP. The first Prime Minister was Mr D S Senanayake who had been prominent in the Ceylonese independence movement from its earliest days. In 1952. Mr Senanayake died and was succeeded in the premiership by his son, Mr Dudley Sananayake. Dudley Senanayake resigned on grounds of ill health in 1953 and the reins of office passed to Sir John Kotelawala.

In the 1956 General Election Mr Bandaranaike joined hands with Mr Philip Gunawardena and Mr W Dahanayake, to form the Mahajana Eksath Peramuna (MEP) or People's United Front with a socialist and Sinhalese nationalist programme. Assisted by dissension among the Marxist groups, and by the fact that the Tamil constituencies in the north and north-east of Sri Lanka were contested almost entirely on a communal basis between the Tamil Congress and the Federal party, the MEP won a sweeping victory, reducing the UNP to 8 seats in the House of Representatives. The year marked a watershed in Ceylonese politics. The policies of the UNP Governments had been moderately conservative in internal and economic affairs, and western-aligned in foreign affairs. The policies of the MEP Government were based upon the three pillars of linguistic and racial nationalism in internal affairs, socialism in economic affairs and non-alignment in foreign affairs. One of the first acts of Mr Bandaranaike's Government was to negotiate with the British Government for the handing over to Sri Lanka of the naval base at Trincomalee and the airfield at Katunayake which had been retained under a Defence Agreement entered into on Indendence.

In September 1959 Mr Bandaranaike was assassinated. He was succeeded in the Premiership by Mr Dahanayake who called a General Election in March 1960. This returned to power the UNP under Mr

Dudley Senanayake's leadership. Although the UNP was the largest single party, however, it was outnumbered by the Opposition parties and defeated immediately on the Vote on the Address. A further General Election was held in July 1960.

At this stage Mrs Sirimavo Bandaranaike assumed the leadership of her late husband's original Party, the SLFP. Assisted by a no-contest pact with the Trotskyist LSSP and the orthodox Communist Party, the SLFP won an overall majority in the House of Representatives. In June 1964 Mrs Bandaranaike entered into a coalition with the Lanka Sama Samaja Party led by Dr N M Perera to strengthen her administration and to combat mounting industrial unrest. The policies of the Coalition Government, however, aroused considerable uneasiness both within the SLFP and in the country at large. This culminated in December 1964 in the defection of a section of the SLFP, which led to the Government being defeated in the House of Representatives. Parliament was dissolved and a General Election was called for March 1965, at which the United National Party emerged the largest single party with 66 seats. Mr Dudley Senanayake was able to form a government with the support of the two Tamil Parties (17), the breakaway group of the SLFP (5) and other groupings. Although losing the support of the Tamil Party in 1969, Mr Senanayake remained in power until the General Election of May 1970 when the SLFP, together with its allies the LSSP and the Communist Party, was returned to power, with the UNP winning only 18 seats.

In 1972 Ceylon adopted a new constitution as the Republic of Sri Lanka, within the Commonwealth. The new constitution provided for a unicameral legislature, renamed the National State Assembly, with the former Governor-General, Mr William Gopallawa as the first President and Head of State. Mrs Bandaranaike continued as Prime Minister.

The Government pursued strong socialist policies, including the nationalisation of the major tea estates, a great extension of state-owned Corporations, and welfare projects. Nevertheless, the Government faced a serious internal crisis in 1971 when there was an uprising by Janatha Vimukti Peramuna (JVP), a Che Guevaraist inspired organisation of youth. The continued decline in the economy led in 1975 to a major split in the United Front coalition. The 3 LSSP Ministers were removed from office in September and the Communist Party Ministers resigned in February 1977, thus ending the coalition. Parliament was prorogued and the General Election, held on 21st July 1977, resulted in a landslide victory for the UNP, now under Mr J R Jayewardene's leadership.

The new Government introduced liberal economic policies, undertook major new development projects supported by Western aid, and encouraged the private sector and foreign investment.

In 1978, a new Constitution brought in a Presidential form of government and a system of proportional representation. Mr J R Jayawardene became the first Executive President. In 1982, at the first Presidential Election, Mr Jayawardene was elected for a second term. In December 1982, a national referendum extended the life of the 1977 Parliament for a further 6 years, without recourse to a General Election.

Under the Government's new economic policies, the country made substantial economic progress in the years up to 1983. In that year, however, a problem, which had long been faced by previous Governments, developed to an extent which has subsequently endangered the structure of the State and its economic progress. The Ceylon Tamils had since independence had their own political parties, aligning themselves as they saw fit in the interests of their minority community. In the mid-1970s, however, the militant youth wing of the Tamil Congress, demanded 'Eelam', or independence for the north and east, which they claimed to be the Tamil homelands. In the early 1980s the militant groups made an increasing number of terrorist attacks on politicians, the police and the army in the north. In July 1983 there was a Sinhalese backlash and in Colombo and the southwest Tamils were attacked and murdered and their houses and shops looted. The militant groups greatly increased their strength. Many thousands of Tamils fled to the north and to Tamil Nadu in India. India made several attempts to mediate between the Sri Lankan government and the Tamil groups. The situation continued to deteriorate until, in July 1987, the Indian Prime Minister, Rajiv Gandhi, signed an agreement with President Jayewardene which offered Indian forces to oversee a ceasefire and surrender of weapons by the Tamil groups. In return the Sri Lankan Government agreed to set up a temporarily merged elected Provincial Council for the north and east districts (and similar Councils throughout the island) with a degree of autonomy, not to allow any foreign power the use of Trincomalee and to re-examine the use of broadcasting facilities by the Voice of America relay station. While some Indian-supported Tamil groups cooperated, winning the elections to the North East Provincial Council, the Liberation Tigers of Tamil Eelam (LTTE or "Tamil Tigers") continued their militant campaign. Indian forces, initially intended only to supervise the ceasefire, found themselves heavily engaged in military operations against the Tamil Tigers; their forces increased to well over 50,000 men.

Meanwhile, the JVP in the south strongly opposed the settlement and the presence of Indian troops on the island, and conducted a terrorist campaign which at the height reduced the country to a state of near anarchy. The new Government under President Premadasa, elected in December 1988, entered into negotiations with the Tamil Tigers and secured India's commitment to the withdrawal of its forces by the end of March 1990. At the same time vigorous operations by the security forces in the south led to the deaths of the JVP leadership in late 1989 and their terrorist campaign petered out. Negotiations with the Tamils broke down in June 1990, when the Tamil Tigers renewed their violent campaign. Although the Sri Lankan security forces gained control of the main towns in the east and hold some bases in the

North, much of the north including Jaffna remains largely under Tamil Tiger control. Major military operations continue.

The Constitution

The 1978 Constitution provides for a strong executive President elected by the people and for a single chamber Parliament. The President appoints all Ministers and chairs Cabinet meetings. Voting is by a system of proportional representation. MPs who resign, die, or leave the party are replaced by a nominee of the party. The Constitution can be amended, but with major amendments, if so ruled by the Supreme Court, subject to a national referendum. The judiciary, appointed by the President, are independent of the Executive.

The Constitution has been amended a number of times. The Sixth Amendment required MPs to swear allegiance to a sovereign unitary state; this led to the withdrawal of Tamil MPs from Parliament and exacerbated the ethnic problems. The Thirteenth Amendment instituted Provincial Councils and devolved certain powers from the central government.

Government

In December 1988, the second Presidential elections were held. Mr Ranasinghe Premadasa, who succeeded Mr J R Jayewardene as UNP leader, won the election with 50.43 per cent of the votes cast. At the general election in February 1989, the UNP were again returned to power winning 125 seats in the enlarged parliament of 225 seats. The SLFP under Mrs Bandaranaike won 67 seats.

HEAD OF STATE

President: His Excellency President Ranasinghe Premadasa

THE CABINET

(July 1991)

President, Minister of Buddha Sasana, Minister of Policy Planning & Implementation, Minister of Defence, Minister of Education and Higher Education: His Excellency Mr R Premadasa

Prime Minister, Minister of Finance, Minister of State for Defence, Minister of Labour and Vocational Training: The Hon D B Wijetunge MP

Minister of Transport & Highways: The Hon Wijayapala Mendis MP

Minister of Justice: The Hon A C S Hameed MP

Minister of Environment & Parliamentary Affairs: The Hon M Vincent Perera MP

Minister of Public Administration, Provincial Councils & Home Affairs: The Hon Festus Perera MP

Minister of Tourism & Rural Industrial Development: The Hon S Thondaman MP

Minister of Industries, Science & Technology: The Hon Ranil Wickramasinghe MP

Minister of Lands, Irrigation & Mahaweli Development: The Hon Gamini Athukorale MP

Minister of Fisheries & Aquatic Resources: The Hon Joseph Michael Perera MP

Minister of Cultural Affairs & Information: The Hon W J M Lokubandara MP

Minister of Posts & Telecommunications: The Hon A M S Adhikari MP

Minister of Youth Affairs & Sports: The Hon C Nanda Mathew MP

Minister of Trade & Commerce: The Hon A R Munsoor MP

Minister of Handlooms & Textiles Industries: The Hon U B Wijekoon MP

Minister of Health & Women's Affairs: The Hon Renuka Herath MP

Minister of Reconstruction, Rehabilitation & Social Welfare: The Hon P Dayaratne MP

Minister of Housing & Construction: The Hon B Sirisena Cooray MP

Minister of Plantation Industries: The Hon Rupa Karunatilleke MP

Minister of Foreign Affairs: The Hon Harold Herat MP

Minister of Food & Co-operatives: The Hon Weerasinghe Mallimarachchi MP

Minister of Agricultural Development & Research: The Hon Dharmadasa Banda MP

Minister of Power & Energy: The Hon K D M Chandra Bandara MP

Minister of Ports & Shipping: The Hon Alick Aluvihare MP

MINISTERS OUTSIDE THE CABINET

(PROJECT MINISTERS)

Minister of Higher Education: The Hon A C S Hameed, MP

Minister of Education Service: The Hon Sunethra Ranasinghe, MP

Minister of Energy Conservation: The Hon Sarath Chandra Rajakaruna, MP

Minister of Science & Technology: The Hon E P Paul Perera, MP

Minister of Plantation Services: The Hon M L M Aboosally, MP

Minister of Indigenous Medicine: The Hon H B Wanninayake, MP

Minister of Coconut Industries & Crop Diversification: The Hon Indradasa Hettiarachchi MP

Minister of Minerals & Mineral Based Industries: The Hon Ariyaratne Jayatilleke, MP

Minister of Human Resource Mobilisation: The Hon Dayananda Wickremasinghe, MP

Minister of Mahaweli Development: The Hon H M A Lokubanda, MP

Minister of Legal & Prison Reform: The Hon Tyronne Fernando, MP

Minister of Telecommunication Development: The Hon Harindra Corea, MP
Minister of Socio-Cultural Integration: The Hon P B Kaviratne, MP
Minister of Handloom Industry: U B Wijekoon
Minister of Livestock Development & Milk Production: The Hon Mahendra Wijeratne, MP
Minister of Export Development: The Hon Senaraja Samaranayake, MP
Minister of Home Affairs: The Hon A Piyaseeli Ratnayake, MP
Minister of Agricultural Production & Marketing: The Hon J G Wijeratne Banda, MP
Minister of Provincial Councils: The Hon John A E Amaratunga, MP
Minister of Up-country Peasantry Rehabilitation: The Hon Chandra Karunaratne, MP
Minister of Lands & Land Alienation: The Hon Asoka Wadigamangawa, MP
Minister of Construction & Building Materials: The Hon Chandra Ranatunga, MP
Minister of Environment: The Hon Dr Wimal Wickremasinghe, MP

MINISTERS OF STATE

Minister of Defence: The Hon D B Wijetunge, MP
Minister of Finance: The Hon Harold Herat, MP
Minister of Foreign Affairs: The Hon John A E Amaratunga, MP
Minister of Policy Planning & Implementation: The Hon Dr Wimal Wickramasinghe, MP
Minister of Rural Industrial Development: The Hon H G P Nelson, MP
Minister of Ports & Shipping: The Hon M E H Maharoof, MP
Minister of Health: The Hon Jabir A Cader, MP
Minister of Agricultural Development & Research: The Hon H M A Loku Banda, MP
Minister of Trade & Commerce: The Hon Rohan Abeygunasekara, MP
Minister of Power & Energy: The Hon Mervyn J Cooray, MP
Minister of Fisheries & Aquatic Resources: The Hon P S L Galappatthy, MP
Minister of Tourism: The Hon Gamini Lokuge, MP
Minister of Highways: The Hon K Ananda Kularatne, MP
Minister of Labour & Vocational Training: (Vacant)
Minister of Re-construction, Rehabilitation & Social Welfare: The Hon M Samantha Karunaratne, MP
Minister of Buddha Sasana: The Hon Lal Dharmapriya Gamage, MP
Minister of Housing: The Hon Abdul Bakeer Markar Imthiaz, MP
Minister of Food & Co-operatives: The Hon Ravindra Samaraweera, MP
Minister of Sports: The Hon D M Ariyadasa, MP
Minister of Hindu Religious & Cultural Affairs: The Hon P P Devaraj, MP
Minister of Information: The Hon A J Ranasinghe, MP
Minister of Industries: The Hon M S Sellasamy, MP
Minister of Transport: The Hon U L M Farook, MP
Minister of Irrigation: The Hon Sarath Welagedera, MP
Minister of Women's Affairs: The Hon (Mrs) A Chandra Karunaratne, MP
Minister of Education: The Hon R Pulendran, MP
Minister of Parliamentary Affairs: The Hon G Tissakutti Arachchi, MP
Minister of Muslim Religious & Cultural Affairs: The Hon A H W Azwer, MP
Minister of Textile Industries: The Hon M D A Gunatillake, MP

SECRETARIES TO MINISTRIES

President: Mr K H J Wijayadasa
Prime Minister: Mr K H Abeysinghe
Cabinet of Ministers: Mr M A G Perera
Ministry of Buddha Sasana: Mr D M P B Dassanayake
Ministry of Policy Planning & Implementation: Mr R Paskaralingam
Ministry of Defence: General S C Ranatunga
Ministry of Foreign Affairs: Mr B P Tilakaratna
Ministry of Lands, Irrigation & Mahaweli Development: Mr A A Wijetunge
Ministry of Food & Co-operatives: Mr T P G N Leelaratne
Ministry of Agricultural Development & Research: Dr Dixon Nilaweera
Ministry of Fisheries & Aquatic Resources: Mr N V K K Weragoda
Ministry of Public Administration, Provincial Councils & Home Affairs: Mr R Abeyaratne
Ministry of Finance: Mr R Paskaralingam
Ministry of Trade & Commerce: Mr R A B Goonetileke
Ministry of Plantation Industries: Mr R S Jayaratne
Ministry of Industries, Science & Technology: Mr A S Jayawardena
Ministry of Power & Energy: Mr Akiel Mohamed
Ministry of Transport & Highways: Mr A R M Jayawardene
Ministry of Justice: Mr S Y M P B Herat
Ministry of Cultural Affairs & Information: Mr K A S Gunasekera
Ministry of Health & Women's Affairs: Dr Joe Fernando
Ministry of Education & Higher Education: Mr M D D Peiris
Ministry of Labour & Vocational Training: Mr Shyamon Jayasinghe
Ministry of Environment & Parliamentary Affairs: Dr D Nessiah
Ministry of Housing & Construction: Mr W D Ailapperuma

Ministry of Tourism & Rural Industrial Development: Mr Dharmasena Wijesinghe
Ministry of Posts & Telecommunications: Mr Asoka de Z Gunasekera
Ministry of Youth Affairs & Sports: Col V S Kudaligama
Ministry of Handloom & Textile Industries: Mr A P Hapudeniya
Ministry of Ports & Shipping: Mr T K Dassanayake
Ministry of Reconstruction, Rehabilitation & Social Welfare: Mr Charita Ratwatte

Swaziland

Capital: Mbabane

Swaziland takes its name from the Swazi tribe, a composite people of various clan origins who have existed as a distinct tribe since the beginning of the nineteenth century. The country lies to the east of the Transvaal Province of the Republic of South Africa, which bounds it on the north, west and south. On the east it borders Mozambique and the South African province of Natal. Most of the country is between latitudes 26° and 27°S. and longitudes 31° and 32°E. The area is 17,366 sq km (6,705 square miles).

Swaziland has four well-defined topographic regions. These extend longitudinally north and south throughout the country in roughly parallel belts. The Highveld (westernmost), Middleveld and Lowveld are of more or less equal breadth and the Lubombo is a narrower strip along the eastern border. The Highveld is a north-eastward continuation of the Natal Drakensberg. The average elevation is 1,050 m to 1,350 m (3,500 to 4,500 feet), with the highest altitudes at the summits of Emlembe (1,830 m) and Ngwenya (1,800 m). The area is 5,180 sq km (2,000 square miles). The Middleveld is rolling tall grass country of an average altitude of 600 to 750 m (2,000 to 2,500 feet). Its area is 4,921 sq km (1,900 square miles). The Lowveld or Bushveld is a gently undulating lowland but seldom a true plain. Isolated knolls and ridges rise above the general level of 150 m to 300 m (500 to 1,000 feet) to more than 690 m (2,300 feet). It covers some 5,698 sq km (2,200 square miles). the Lubombo is an impressive escarpment which rises along the whole length of the eastern Lowveld, terminating it seaward and interrupted only by the gorges of the Ingwavuma, Usutu and Mbuluzi Rivers.

In their journey to the sea Swaziland's major rivers traverse all four regions. The mean discharge where the rivers leave the country would be about two million gallons a minute if no water was taken from them. However, the Lowveld and Middleveld increasingly draw on their reaches of river for supplies of irrigation water. Nearly all Highveld streams are perennial. In contrast, the water courses of the Lowveld, other than the trunk rivers, are only filled after heavy rainstorms, and at other times are dry channels or wadis. From the Highveld, the Lomati, Komati, Mbuluzi, Usushwana (or Little Usutu), Usutu (or Great Usutu), Ngwempisi, and Mkhondo (or Assegaai), fed by countless minor streams, flow in a generally eastward direction towards the Indian Ocean. None of the rivers is navigable in the true sense of the word.

The Highveld region has a humid near-temperate climate, with 1,000 to 2,250 mm (40 to 90 inches) mean annual rainfall, while the Middleveld and Lubombo are sub-tropical and less humid (750 to 1,125 mm). The Lowveld is near-tropical but drier, receiving 500 to 875 mm (20 to 35 inches) of rain in an average year. Most of the rain falls in the summer—from October to March. The winter period, April to September, is comparatively dry throughout the country. The mean annual temperature on the Highveld is just over 16°C (60°F), and in the Lowveld it is about 22°C (72°F). Seasonal and daily ranges of temperatures are considerable in all areas but greatest in the Lowveld. There is a low incidence of frost, but it can be expected for a few days in most years on much of the Highveld and Middleveld and in valley bottoms throughout the country.

Population censuses take place at intervals of 10 years, the most recent being in January 1986, when a de jure population figure of 712,131 was arrived at. Over 95 per cent of the population is Swazi, the remainder being Africans from other countries, Europeans, and people of mixed race. English and siSwati are the official languages.

In 1976 it was estimated that about 40 per cent of adult Africans hold indigenous beliefs. Almost all the rest of the adult population are Christians.

At the time of the last census the birth rate was estimated to be 52.5 per thousand of the total population and the death rate about 18.5 per thousand; the population is increasing at the rate of about 3.5 per cent per year.

Government provides curative and preventive medical services, aided in both fields by the missions, certain industrial concerns and by private practitioners. Diarrhoea disease is the major health problem. Tuberculosis, especially pulmonary tuberculosis, is also a health problem, but efforts are being made to improve diagnosis and treatment. Malnutrition and associated diseases are still a major cause of morbidity and mortality in children.

Food supplements received from the World Food Programme are distributed to the under five year olds at maternity and child welfare centres to help reduce protein deficiency. Typhoid and para-typhoid fevers are prevalent and are likely to remain so until rural hygiene can be undertaken on a larger scale. No cases of cholera have been notified in Swaziland in the past five years. Malaria, while still present in the Lowveld, has been controlled and does not present a widespread public health problem. The incidence of bilharzia is increasing and the position will not improve until a relatively cheap and efficient molluscicide and a cheap therapeutic agent are disovered. Immunisation against typhoid fever, diphtheria, whooping cough, tetanus, poliomyelitis and cholera is offered at all hospitals, clinics and health offices. The number of beds at Government and subsidised mission hospitals in 1991 was 2,000.

The Christian festivals are observed as Public Holidays in Swaziland, including Easter Monday and Ascension Day. Boxing Day and New Year's Day are also celebrated. Other Public holidays are the King's birthday (19th April), National Flag Day (25th April), Umhlanga (Reed Dance) Day (variable Mondays in August and September), Independence Day (6th September), and Newala Day (to be appointed each year).

The majority of Swazis who migrate in search of employment are recruited for work in the gold mines of South Africa. In 1991 over 20,000 Swazis were employed in the gold mines. Such recruitment is controlled under the Employment Proclamation 1962. At present Swaziland has 19 registered trade unions of which only 13 are active; works councils, made up of representatives of employer and labour force, have been established in many companies. These councils provide a forum for discussion and have been successful in promoting Swaziland's tradition of good management and labour relations.

The sugar industry in Swaziland is a key sector in the country's economy and is one of the most modern and efficient in the world, with some 34,800 hectares under cane. Sugar exports are approximately 34 per cent of total export revenue. There are three sugar mills in Swaziland—at Big Bend, Mhlume and Simunye and they have a capacity to process just over 500,000 tonnes annually.

Citrus fruit is the other main crop grown under irrigation.

Maize is the staple food of Swaziland and occupies over half of the arable utilised land area.

Cotton is the main dry land crop and is widely grown in the Lowveld. There are 6,500 registered growers and 20,000 registered hectares. There is one cotton ginnery currently operating in Swaziland, Cotona Ginnery Company Limited in Matsapa. Other important dry land crops are pineapples, avocados and bananas. Most of the major crops are grown commercially for export. The sole fruit processing factory in the country (Swaziland Fruit Canners) at Malkerns processes mainly pineapples and citrus fruit. Swaziland also has large numbers of cattle and goats.

The forestry sector accounts for about 19 per cent of the total value of exports. There are 127,000 hectares of man made and natural forests which provide exports principally of woodpulp, also of sawn timber for construction and other industrial purposes. About three-quarters of the commercial forests are of pines, which mature in 16 years compared with 40 years in northern Europe; the remainder is made up of gum trees and wattle. The industry is dominated by two large foreign owned companies—for woodpulp, the Usutu Pulp Company which is a joint venture of SAPPI (RSA) and the Commonwealth Development Corporation, and for industry and commercial timber, Peak Timbers Company which is part of the Anglo-American Mining Company group.

Asbestos, coal and more recently diamonds are the country's most important minerals. Asbestos is produced at the VHL Bulembo Mine at Piggs Peak. The country's only coal mine at Mpaka started production in 1964 and is now operated by Gencor of South Africa. Substantial reserves estimated at 2 billion tonnes have been discovered in the northern part of the country, but are yet to be exploited.

Swaziland's manufacturing industries are mainly concerned with the processing of agricultural livestock and forestry products. There is a brewery in Matsapa. A textile mill began operation in 1986.

The only international airport, Matsapa, 8 km from the town of Manzini, has a new 2,600 metre runway. Improvements to the terminal, communications and safety facilities have been made.

The only airline in Swaziland, the Royal Swazi National Airways Corporation was inaugurated in August 1978. There are flights each day of the week to and from Johannesburg by Royal Swazi Air and Comair. Royal Swazi Air also have four flights a week to Durban, one flight a week to Lusaka, Maseru, Maputo, and Harare and two flights per week to Dar es Salaam and Nairobi.

Swaziland's railway, which has a 3 feet 6 inches gauge, and which is for goods traffic only, runs from Kadake through the middle of the country to Goba on the eastern border, where it connects with the Mozambique railway to the port of Maputo. A rail link was connected with RSA at Gollel from Phuzumoya in November 1978. Swaziland Railways have constructed a 55 Km heavy duty rail line from Mpaka in central Swaziland to the Swazi border with South Africa, to join up with a new 65 Km line laid by the South African Railways from Komatipoort in the Eastern Transvaal. The line opened in 1986. The line provides a direct link from the Eastern Transvaal to Richards Bay for South African Railways (saving the 300 Km journey around Swaziland) and gives Swaziland a direct link to Zimbabwe and points north via Beit Bridge.

The trans-territorial highway from Oshoek, on the Transvaal border, to Lomahasha on the Mozambique border is completely tarred as is the road from Manzini to Layumisa via Big Bend. The road from Mbabane via Piggs Peak to the northern border with South Africa at Jeppes Reef is also tarred. Thirty miles of tarred road link Mhlambanyati and Bunyua with the trans-territorial highway. Most other roads in the country have gravel surfaces.

A Government-operated broadcasting station transmits programmes in siSwati and English for three hours each morning, three hours at lunchtime and 5½ hours each evening on weekdays. Programmes are broadcast from 6.00 am to 10.30 pm at weekends and on public holidays. Programmes for schools are broadcast for four hours each school day. There is a 10 kW transmitter in Mbabane along with a 100 W FM transmitter and also a 20 W FM transmitter in Manzini. The station opened in April 1966. The Swaziland Television Broadcasting Corporation (STBC) commenced a colour television service in

February 1978. To date they have an audience of over 5,500 television receivers and provides coverage over the whole of Swaziland (and some adjacent parts of South Africa). STBC broadcasts in English and siSwati. Viewing hours are generally from 1800 hours to 2230 hours. The service is owned by the Swaziland Government but run on commercial lines with revenue being earned from advertisers and the rental of television sets.

Since 1910, Swaziland (with Botswana and Lesotho) has been in a customs and currency union with the Republic of South Africa. In 1974, Swaziland introduced its own currency, Emalangeni (singular Lilangeni) E1 = R1. The original Customs Union Agreement was renegotiated in 1969 and the revised agreement came into force on 1st March 1970. In addition to changing the formula for the distribution of the pool of customs, excise, additional duties and sales tax the new Agreement deals with other matters of commercial importance to the four signatory governments. The new formula is no longer a fixed percentage (as it was under the 1910 Agreement) but fluctuates according to the actual value of imports into each of the four countries. In the case of Swaziland, the immediate consequences of the new Agreement have been very favourable: customs and excise receipts have now displaced income tax as the main source of Government revenue. In 1990/91 Customs Union receipts totalled 45.3 per cent of estimated revenue or 50.5 per cent of tax revenue. Income tax is payable by all persons with incomes exceeding E10,000 and is collected on the PAYE system. Personal income tax contributes only a small amount to the total, however, and the major source is company tax (37.5 per cent). Non-residents are liable to a withholding tax of 15 per cent on dividends and 10 per cent on other interests. In 1969, a single graded tax ranging from E4.20 to E18 and payable by persons over 18 years of age, was introduced to replace the former poll tax, Swazi tax and the Swazi national levy. Licensing exists for many trades. A double taxation agreement with Britain was signed in 1968.

A 5 per cent sales tax introduced in 1984 and increased to 10 per cent in 1986, is levied on both imported and locally manufactured goods. Food and certain other essential items have been exempted from sales tax.

Primary education is not yet universal. There are no tuition fees but pupils pay a nominal E50 per year to the school funds and also pay for their books. There are three teacher training colleges in Swaziland the most recent being completed in 1982 at Nhlangano with European Development Fund funding. There is also a Swaziland College of Technology (SCOT) and a Staff Training Institute. The Swaziland Agricultural College and University Centre at Luyengo is now part of the University of Swaziland and offers a 2-year University diploma course in Agriculture as well as shorter certificate courses. In 1972 the University moved into a new university complex financed by Britain, Canada and the United States on land provided by the King at Kwaluseni. The 1966 census revealed that 68.7 per cent of the men and 72.5 per cent of the women had had less than four effective years of schooling but the situation is improving and in the younger age groups the comparable figure is probably less than 50 per cent. There is a national library with its headquarters in Mbabane and in addition, clubs and associations run small libraries in the main centres. A Swaziland National Library Service has been established in Manzini, which runs mobile services for outlying districts.

History

Swaziland remained nominally independent until 1890. From 1890 to 1894 the United Kingdom and the Transvaal (South African Republic) Governments established a species of condominium which was replaced in 1894 by an arrangement under which the South African Republic was given powers of protection and administration without actual incorporation. After the Anglo-Boer War, the administration of Swaziland was transferred to the Governor of the Transvaal, who was also the High Commissioner of South Africa, but in 1907 responsibility for Swaziland was transferred from the Governor to the High Commissioner for South Africa. Swaziland therefore remained under the control of the United Kingdom when the Transvaal became a province of the Union of South Africa in 1910. Swaziland became an independent Member of the Commonwealth on 6th September 1968.

Constitutional development

In May 1963 the Secretary of State for the Colonies published a White Paper (Cmnd 2052) outlining a constitution for Swaziland. This Constitution was established by the Swaziland Order in Council 1963, which was made on 20th December. Under this Constitution, Swaziland was administered by Her Majesty's Commissioner, a post equivalent to that of Governor. The Commissioner assented to legislation and was directly responsible to the Secretary of State. The Constitution made provision for an Executive Council of eight members (four official and four unofficial) and a Legislative Council of four official members, 24 elected members and up to three members nominated by Her Majesty's Commissioner. In August 1965 the number of unofficial members in the Executive Council was increased from four to six and in October 1966, to seven.

Of the 24 elected Legislative Council members, eight were Swazi or Eurafricans certified by the Ngwenyama (the Paramount Chief) in Council as having been elected in accordance with Swazi traditional methods; eight were Europeans or Eurafricans, of whom four were elected by voters registered on a 'European roll' and four elected by voters registered on a 'national roll'; and eight were persons of any race elected by voters registered on the national roll. Election on the national roll was virtually by universal adult suffrage.

The country was divided into four national roll constituencies to correspond with the four administrative districts. Each constituency returned three members, one of whom must be European or Eurafrican. The European roll constituency was the whole of Swaziland.

The elections for the first Legislative Council took place in June 1964. The Imbokodvo National Movement won 10 national roll seats and the United Swaziland Association gained two national roll seats and the four European roll seats. Five other political parties contested the elections but failed to win a seat. Her Majesty's Commissioner nominated one person to the Legislative Council.

In August 1965 a local committee was set up to review the Constitution and make detailed recommendations on the form of a new one to the Secretary of State for the Colonies. The committee comprised 12 unofficial members chosen from the membership of the Legislative Council, and two officials. The Queen's Commissioner was chairman. The committee's proposals on a constitution which would give the country Internal Self Government were sent to the Secretary of State in March 1966. The British Government had informed the committee that it proposed to grant Swaziland Internal Self Government and was willing, subject to the approval of Her Majesty The Queen, to change the territory's status to that of a Protected State with the Ngwenyama recognised as King and Head of State. Britain's protection would continue until Swaziland attained independence not later than the end of 1969.

Constitution

Following further discussions with the Swaziland Government, the Secretary of State for the Colonies published a White Paper (Cmnd 3119) in October 1966 containing a draft of the proposed Agreement which would turn Swaziland into a Protected State and an outline of the proposed Internal Self Government constitution. This Constitution was contained in a schedule to the Swaziland Constitution Order 1967, made on 22nd February 1967. The Constitution, which came into operation on 25th April 1967, provided that:

(i) the Ngwenyama was recognised as King of Swaziland and Head of State;

(ii) Her Majesty's Commissioner, who was also the representative of Her Majesty's Government in Swaziland, retained responsibility for external affairs, defence and internal security and also certain responsibility in the fields of finance and the public service; and there was a Consultative Council consisting of local representatives of Her Majesty's Government and of the Swaziland Government, for consultation on the exercise of these responsibilities;

(iii) there was a Parliament comprising a House of Assembly (consisting of a Speaker, 24 members elected by adult suffrage in 8 three-member constituencies, 6 members appointed by the King, and the Attorney-General (who had no vote)), and a Senate (consisting of 6 members elected by the members of the House of Assembly and 6 members appointed by the King);

(iv) subject to the powers of Her Majesty's Commissioner referred to in (ii) above, executive authority was vested in the King and exercised through a Cabinet consisting of a Prime Minister, a Deputy Prime Minister and up to six other Ministers; the Attorney-General normally attended Cabinet meetings in an advisory capacity;

(v) there was a Public Service Commission and a Judicial Service Commission, which became executive on 1st April 1968;

(vi) the Constitution provided for citizenship of Swaziland, which until Independence had a purely local significance;

(vii) Her Majesty retained general power to amend the Constitution but it was open to the Swaziland Government to request amendments provided that certain specified procedures had been carried out;

(viii) all minerals were vested in the Ngwenyama in trust for the Swazi nation, and the right to make grants in respect of minerals was vested in the King, who in exercising the power to make such grants acted in accordance with the advice of the Cabinet, but before giving its advice the Cabinet was required to consult a committee appointed by the King after consultation with the Swazi National Council.

The Agreement whereby Swaziland became a Protected State was signed by the Queen's Commissioner and the Ngwenyama on 24th April 1967 and came into force on 25th April.

In September 1967 the House of Assembly and the Senate approved motions authorising the Swaziland Government to ask Her Majesty's Government to grant Swaziland independence on 6th September 1968. Two months later Britain announced that she agreed to this request.

The 1967 Constitution was designed to take the country into Independence with only a few alterations, and these were agreed by both Her Majesty's Government and the Swaziland Government at an Independence Conference held in Marlborough House, London, in February 1968. The Constitution was contained in a schedule to the Swaziland Independence Order, 1968 which was made on 26th August 1968 and came into operation immediately before Independence on 6th September 1968. The major difference in the Independence Constitution compared with the 1967 Constitution apart from the abolition of the office and powers of Her Majesty's Commissioner, the abolition of the power of Her Majesty to amend the Constitution, and the lifting of the restriction on the number of Cabinet Ministers, is the provision regarding the control of minerals. Under the Independence Constitution, minerals and mineral oils are vested in the Ngwenyama, who is advised by a Minerals Committee (instead of the Cabinet) appointed by him after consultation with the Swazi National Council.

On 12th April 1973, King Sobhuza II repealed the 1968 Constitution by proclamation and he assumed supreme powers. All political parties were dissolved and prohibited and the Parliament provided for under the constitution became non-existent.

On 12th October 1978, the King announced that elections would be held on 27th October and that a new Constitution had been produced. It was announced that an Electoral College, comprising eighty members elected by the Tinkhundla (tribal or community committees), would elect, by secret ballot, forty persons to serve as members of the House of Assembly, Parliament would consist of a Senate and a House of Assembly. The Senate would have twenty members, ten elected by the House of Assembly and the remaining ten appointed by the King.

King Sobhuza II died on 21st August 1982 having reigned for 61 years. At his death the King was widely regarded as being the world's longest reigning monarch. King Sobhuza's Diamond Jubilee was celebrated on 4th September 1981 when a number of Heads of State and their representatives attended a national ceremony. Her Majesty Queen Elizabeth II was represented by HRH The Princess Margaret.

The Crown Prince HRH Prince Makhosetive became HM King Mswati III at his coronation on 25th April 1986. Her Majesty Queen Elizabeth II was represented by HRH Prince Michael of Kent.

King Mswati dissolved Parliament in September 1987, and elections to the Electoral College which elected the 40 members of the new House of Assembly took place in November 1987. The Assembly also elected 10 members of the new Senate, the other 10 being appointed by the King.

Land policy

The complex pattern of land ownership in Swaziland is largely the result of historical events which occurred before the establishment of the British Administration in 1902. Between the years 1875 and 1889 the Swazi ruler Mbandzeni granted numerous concessions to Europeans which included grants and leases of land for grazing and agricultural purposes. The concessions covered almost the whole extent of the Territory and many of the deeds contained clauses which reserved to the Ngwenyama his sovereign rights and forbade the concessionaires from interfering with the rights of the Swazi living within the area of the concessions. In terms of the Swaziland Convention of 1890, a Chief Court was established to undertake an enquiry into the validity of disputed concessions. It did, in fact, examine the initial validity of the majority of concessions and its decisions were adhered to by the British Administration. The Swaziland Administration Proclamation (No 3 of 1904) provided for the establishment of a commission which was, *inter alia,* required to examine each land and grazing concession and cause their boundaries to be defined and surveyed. On the completion of the commission's work, a Special Commissioner was appointed in terms of the Swaziland Concessions Partition Proclamation (No 28 of 1907) to set aside areas for the sole and exclusive use and occupation of the Swazi. He was empowered to expropriate one third of the area of each concession without compensation, but should more than this be required, compensation was payable. The remaining concessions were freed from any rights of use and occupation possessed by the Swazi, and the owners of concessions who held title to the ownership of the land or leases of not less than 99 years' duration, with or without rights of renewal, were granted freehold title. The reversionary rights to land and mineral concessions were vested in the Crown in terms of the Swaziland Crown Lands and Minerals Order in Council of 1908 as amended by a subsequent Order in Council in 1910. Following the partition of the Territory, further legislation was passed to secure the rights of the Swazi in the areas that had been set aside for them (Proclamation No 39 of 1910), also to define the conditions under which the Crown could sell, lease or otherwise dispose of Crown Land (Proclamation No 13 of 1911). Proclamation No 2 of 1915 made provision for securing for the benefit of the Swazi any land acquired on behalf of the Swazi Nation.

Abortive efforts were made by the Swazi in 1922 and 1923 to set aside the Partition Proclamation of 1907; but a petition to King George VI in 1941 was more successful and resulted in the introduction of the Swazi Land Settlement Scheme (see below). The land question was raised at the independence conference in 1968, and at subsequent post-independence talks in November/December 1968 the British Government stated their willingness to examine the matter on strictly economic grounds. This offer was accepted by the Swaziland Government and a working party under the independent chairmanship of Mr R E T Hobbs and consisting of two nominees each of the British and Swaziland Governments was appointed. The Working Party presented its Report ('The Hobbs Report') on 14th March 1969, and its conclusions were accepted in principle by both Governments. On 22nd April 1970, the Minister of Finance in Swaziland was able to announce that a substantial part of British development aid to the agricultural sector would be earmarked for a land purchase and development programme 'aimed at restoring a considerable acreage to Swazi ownership'. This continues to be the policy today.

At the end of 1967, some 56 per cent of the total area of the Territory, which covers 4,290,944 acres, was reserved for occupation by the Swazi. This comprised Swazi Area, land purchased by the Swazi

Nation and Swazi Land Settlement areas. Swazi Area, which was set aside by the Concessions Partition Commissioner for occupation by the Swazi in 1910, is vested in the Ngwenyama as Swazi Nation Land in trust for the Swazi Nation. It is scattered throughout the Territory in blocks of varying size and covers 1,639,687 acres or 38.2 per cent of the total area of the country. The purchase of land by the Swazi Nation started initially as a reaction to the partition of the Territory. The Swazi were encouraged by the Chief Regent to go to the Transvaal in order to earn money with which to purchase land from European holders. Purchases continued to be made with monies raised locally by collections or levies until the start of the Lifa Fund in 1946. The purposes of this fund were to reduce overstocking and to purchase additional land. Under an order made by the Ngwenyama in Libandla (Council), cattle were culled from the herds of those Swazi who owned more than 10 head. The animals thus acquired were auctioned and a levy on the proceeds credited to the Lifa Fund. By the end of 1964, the area of land purchased in this way amounted to some 268,000 acres. The Lifa Fund was wound up in 1968.

Swazi Land Settlement areas, which consist of farms purchased from European owners and Crown Land set aside for the purpose by Government, were defined in 1946 and are generally contiguous with the existing Swazi areas. This land, some 316,700 acres in extent, is now vested in the Ngwenyama as Swazi Nation Land in trust for the Swazi Nation.

Land owned by individual Africans, missions, Europeans, Coloured (mixed race) and others covers about 36 per cent of the total area of the Territory. Of this privately-owned land, less than 10 per cent now consists of land concessions, held in perpetuity or on leases of more than 99 years' duration. In order to avoid the complications which have persisted because of differing forms of title, the owners of these concessions have been requested to exercise their option under the provision of Proclamation No 28 of 1907 and convert their title to freehold. Farms which are purchased by individual Africans are registered in their own names. The area owned by individual Swazis totals 30,000 acres. Missions own 21,100 acres and the extent of farms owned by Europeans, Coloured (mixed race) and others or of land situated in proclamation townships, is 1,873,400 acres. The remaining area of the Territory comprises Government-owned land some 101,900 acres in extent and this, excluding land required for public purposes (schools, police posts, townships, etc), is being transferred to the Ngwenyama as Swazi Nation Land in trust for the Swazi Nation.

On Swazi Area a system of communal land ownership is practised. One of the most important rights exercised by the chiefs is the allocation of residential and ploughing land. The Ngwenyama is recognised as having overall control of Swazi Area but in practice he defers to local chiefs in all matters of rights of occupancy, except in areas which, by tradition, belong to the Swazi ruling house. An individual obtains rights to use and occupy land from the chief of an area. Such rights once granted are firm and can only be extinguished by the individual concerned relinquishing them or by his being arraigned before a chief for a misdemeanor, such as witchcraft or adultery, sufficiently serious to justify banishment. An appeal against such an order would lie to the Ngwenyama. As might be expected, however, from a contact of over 50 years with European systems of land tenure and an increasing scarcity of the land, the traditional system of land ownership is gradually acquiring a more clearly defined individual emphasis in many areas.

The principles of the Roman-Dutch law of land ownership, which apply to land owned in freehold, embody the Roman Law conception of absolute ownership of land in contradistinction to the English law of tenure which, in theory holds that all land is held by the Crown. Freeholders and, if their concessions do not prohibit this, concessionaires occasionally grant occupation or grazing leases, and, in a few instances, land is farmed on a crop share basis. Outside urban areas, some freehold and concession land is subject to the payment of quitrent, generally of a small amount. Township stands are subject to a fixed quitrent of one rand per annum.

In 1971 the Government passed a Land Speculation Control Act making it impossible to sell land or immovable property to non-Swazi without the permission of a Control Board.

HEAD OF STATE

HM King Mswati III

GOVERNMENT

Prime Minister: HE The Rt Hon Obed Dlamini, MP

Minister for Foreign Affairs: Senator The Hon George Mamba, GCVO

Minister for Labour & Public Service: Senator The Hon David Motsa

Minister for Justice: Sen The Hon Dr A Zonke Khumalo

Minister for Education: The Hon Prince Khuzulwandle

Minister for Agriculture & Co-operatives: The Hon Themba Masuku

Minister for Finance: The Hon Barnabas Sibusiso Dlamini, MP

Minister for Commerce, Industry, Mines & Tourism: Senator The Hon Nkomeni Douglas Ntiwane

Minister for Natural Resources, Land Utilization & Energy: The Hon Senzenjani Shabalala

Minister for Interior & Immigration: The Hon Prince Sobandla

Minister for Health: Senator The Hon Dr Fanny Friedman

Minister for Works & Construction: The Hon Prince Mbilini

Minister for Housing and Township Development: The Hon Thomas Stephens

Minister for Economic Planning: The Hon Solomon Dlamini

Minister for Transport and Communications: The Hon Albert Shabangin
Minister for Broadcasting, Information and Tourism: The Hon Barnabas Mhlongo

GOVERNMENT DEPARTMENTS

PRIME MINISTER'S OFFICE
Secretary to the Cabinet: Alphus Shabangu

MINISTRY OF FOREIGN AFFAIRS
Principal Secretary: Philemon Dlamini

MINISTRY OF LABOUR & PUBLIC SERVICE
Principal Secretary: Mrs Futhi Kuhlase

MINISTRY OF DEFENCE & YOUTH
Principal Secretary: Mr Joshua T Mkhatshwa

MINISTRY OF JUSTICE
Principal Secretary: The Rev Percy Mngomezulu

MINISTRY OF EDUCATION
Principal Secretary: Mr M E Vilakazi

MINISTRY OF AGRICULTURE & CO-OPERATIVES
Principal Secretary: Mr Frank Buckham

MINISTRY OF FINANCE
Principal Secretary: Mr Isaac Shabangu

MINISTRY OF COMMERCE, INDUSTRY, MINES & TOURISM
Principal Secretary: HRH Prince Sulumlomo

MINISTRY OF NATURAL RESOURCES, LAND UTILIZATION & ENERGY
Principal Secretary: Mr Sandile Ceko

MINISTRY OF INTERIOR & IMMIGRATION
Principal Secretary: Mr Enos Mavuso

MINISTRY OF HEALTH
Principal Secretary: Mr Christopher Mkhonza

MINISTRY OF WORKS & COMMUNICATIONS
Principal Secretary: Mr Norman Malinga

DEPARTMENT OF ECONOMIC PLANNING AND STATISTICS
Principal Secretary: Mr Elliott Bhembe

United Republic of Tanzania

Capital: Dodoma

The United Republic of Tanzania was formed on 26th April 1964 by the union of that part of the East African mainland known as Tanganyika, which included Mafia and a number of other small off-shore islands, and Zanzibar, which included not only the island of Zanzibar itself but also the islands of Pemba and Latham. The name Tanzania was adopted on 29th October 1964. The total area of the country is 942,004 sq km (363,708 square miles).

The area of the mainland (Tanganyika) is approximately 939,393 sq km (362,700 square miles), including some 51,800 sq km (20,000 square miles) of inland water. It is bounded on the east by the Indian Ocean, on the north by Kenya, Lake Victoria and Uganda; on the west by Rwanda, Burundi, Lake Tanganyika (across which is Zaire); and on the south by Zambia, Malawi, Lake Malawi and Mozambique.

The mainland contains the two extremes of topographical relief of the whole continent of Africa: Kilimanjaro, with a permanent ice-cap rising to 5,802 m above sea level, and the deep trough-like depression filled by Lake Tanganyika, the world's second deepest lake. Mount Meru, 80 km (50 miles) west of Kilimanjaro, rises to 4,492 m. The Mbulu Range of mountains (highest point Mount Hanang, 3,365 m) lies 241 km (150 miles) S.W. of Mount Kilimanjaro, and the Mbeya Range (highest point Mount Rungwe, 2,915 m) and the Livingstone Mountains (2,880 m) and other large mountains are just north of the Mbulu Range and include Loolmalasin (3,591 m) and the still active volcano Oldonyo Lengai.

The main rivers are the Pangani or Ruvu, the Wami, the Ruvu (Kingoni), the Rufiji, the Great Ruaha, the Matandu, the Mbwemkuru, the Lukuledi and the Ruvuma, which drain the central plateau and flow into the Indian Ocean; and the Mori, Mara and Kagera, the Malagarasi, the Songwe and Ruhuhu which feed the great lakes.

The climate is very varied and not typically tropical; rainfall can be anything between 358 mm and 3,085 mm a year. There are three climatic zones: the hot and humid coastal area; the drier central plateau with a great deal of seasonal variations of temperature; and the semi-temperate mountain areas.

Zanzibar consists of Zanzibar Island and Pemba Island. Zanzibar Island is situated in the Indian Ocean in latitude 6°S and longitude 39°E. It is separated (36 km) from the mainland by the Zanzibar Channel and is the largest island off the coast of East Africa, being 85 km (53 miles) long and 39 km (24 miles) wide, with a total area of 1,658 sq km (640 square miles). The eastern and central parts, comprising two-thirds of the island, consist of low-lying coral country covered by bush and grass plains, largely uninhabited except for fishing settlements on the east coast. The western side of the island is fertile and densely populated, with several ridges rising to over 60 m above sea level; the highest ridge, the Masingini Ridge, is 117 m above sea level. In this area coconuts and to a lesser extent cloves are extensively grown. The island of Pemba lies 40 km (25 miles) to the north-east, in latitude 5°S and longitude 39°E. It is 68 km (42 miles) long and about 23 km (14 miles) wide, with an area of 984 sq km (380 square miles). The west and centre of the island consists of a flat-topped ridge about 10 km wide, deeply intersected by streams. The coastline is deeply indented especially in the west and the inlets are mostly filled with mangrove swamps. Apart from the narrow belt of coral country in the east the island is fertile and densely populated, clove growing being the major industry. Cloves account for a large part of Zanzibar's exports, and at one time Zanzibar produced over 80 per cent of the world's total supply, but the Islands share of the world market has declined rapidly due to competition from Indonesia and Brazil in particular. Pemba provides about 90 per cent of Zanzibar's cloves.

Mafia Island is situated 129 km (80 miles) south of Dar es Salaam and has excellent deep-sea fishing grounds.

The climate of Zanzibar is tropical, tempered throughout the year with constant sea breezes except during the rainy seasons. The heavy rains fall in April and May with lesser rains in November and December. The main maximum and minimum temperatures for Zanzibar town are 29°C (84.4°F) and 24.8°C (76.6°F) respectively and for Wete, in Pemba, 30.2°C (86.3°F) and 24.5°C (76.1°F). The annual rainfall for Zanzibar town averages 1,548 mm and for Wete 1,923 mm.

The total at the last census in August 1988 of the population was 23,174,336 of whom 22,533,758 lived on the mainland and 640,578 in Zanzibar and Pemba. Since the previous census in August 1978 there had been an annual growth rate of 2.8 per cent.

There are some 120 tribes on the mainland, none of which exceeds 10 per cent of the population. The largest is the Sukuma tribe and others include the Nyamwezi; Ha; Makonde; Gogo; Haya; Masai and Chagga. Swahili is the official language. The main religions are Islam and Christianity of many denominations.

For administrative purposes the mainland is divided into 20 regions under Regional Commissioners, namely Arusha, Coast, Dar es Salaam, Dodoma, Kigoma, Kilimanjaro, Lindi, Mara, Morogoro, Mtwara, Mwanza, Rukwa, Ruvuma, Shinyanga, Iringa, Mbeya, Tabora, Tanga, Singida and Kagera. The regions are further divided into Districts under District Commissioners.

The economic and administrative centre is Dar es Salaam with a population of approximately one million. Leading towns include Zanzibar, Mwanza, Arusha, Moshi, Tanga, Morogoro, Dodoma, Iringa, Tabora, Kigoma, Mtwara, Songea and Mbeya. Dodoma was named as the official capital of Tanzania in 1973 and is being developed to become the administrative centre.

Dar es Salaam is the principal port, other ports include Tanga, Mtwara, Zanzibar and Wete together with Mwanza, Musoma and Bukoba on Lake Victoria and Kigoma on Lake Tanganyika. Coastal shipping services connect the mainland and Zanzibar and lake services are operated on Lake Tanganyika and Lake Malawi with neighbouring countries.

The principal airports are Dar es Salaam and Kilimanjaro.

There are two railway systems. The metre gauge system formerly operated by East African Railways has two main lines, one from Dar es Salaam to northern Tanzania and Kenya and one to Lake Tanganyika and Victoria. The other system, completed in 1975, is the 3 foot 6 inch gauge line of the Tanzania-Zambia Railway Authority from Dar es Salaam to Zambia.

Radio services are operated by Radio Tanzania in Dar es Salaam and Zanzibar. Zanzibar also has a colour television service.

Overall economic and development policy has been governed by the precepts of the 1967 Arusha Declaration in emphasising self-reliance and the equitable distribution of economic resources. Recent development plans have been hampered by adverse economic and other factors.

Major exports are coffee, cotton, sisal, cloves, tea, tobacco, cashew nuts, pyrethrum and diamonds. The principal imports are manufactured goods, machinery, transport equipment and oil fuels. Since the late 1970s, a fall in world commodity prices, adverse weather conditions and structural problems led to a fall in crop production and hence foreign exchange earnings. Tanzania has suffered acute balance of payments difficulties. In 1986 a three-year Economic recovery Programme (ERP) designed to revive production, particularly in the agricultural sector was announced. Measures included a devaluation of the shilling, increased producer prices on all export crops, and trade liberalisation. Agreement was reached with the IMF in August 1986, resulting in the IMF stand-by arrangement, substantial support from aid donors and a major rescheduling of Tanzania's public and private sector debt at the Paris Club. From October 1987 the ERP was supported by a 3-year IMF Structural Adjustment Facility, and in June 1991 agreement was reached between the Tanzanian Government and the IMF on an Enhanced Structural Adjustment Facility which will be effective for a further three years.

History

It is known that the East African coast had trade connections with Arabia and India before the beginning of the Christian era.

In the first century AD the coast, including Zanzibar, was, and had long been, under the control of the ruler of south-western Arabia; the geography and products of the area were known to the Greeks of Alexandria and the most southerly market-town known to the ancients, Rhapta, must have been situated somewhere on the coast within a hundred miles of Dar-es-Salaam. From the eleventh century onwards the Sultanate of Kilwa came into prominence, attaining its greatest prosperity in the fourteenth and fifteenth centuries when its rulers controlled the trade of a long stretch of the coast, extending down to Sofala, near the present Beira in Mozambique.

In 1498 the arrival of Vasco da Gama off the coast of East Africa heralded a period of Portuguese predominance over the coasts and waters of East Africa. Though very few of the Portuguese settled in the country, the civilisation of the coastal towns suffered a severe decline. Towards the end of the sixteenth century, however, the Portuguese began to give way to the Turks and Arabs, notably the Imams of Oman. But Arab influence declined during the eighteenth century and the allegiance to Muscat became more and more shadowy until 1832 when the fifth ruler of the Albusaidi dynasty, Seyyid Said, moved his capital from Muscat to Zanzibar. The second period of Arab domination was the great period of the slave trade. Bagamoyo, Sadani and Pangani on the Tanganyika coast were the usual points of departure and Tabora the most important inland centre. After Seyyid Said's death in 1856 his territories were divided between his two elder sons, and Zanzibar, with the adjacent coast, became an independent sultanate.

The country later known as Tanganyika came under German influence largely through the initiative of Dr Karl Peters, who in 1884 journeyed into the interior and in six weeks concluded twelve treaties with chiefs, whose chiefdoms were then declared to be German territory. In 1885 the land which Peters had acquired, including 60,000 square miles of territory over which the sultan of Zanzibar claimed suzerainty, was placed under the protection of the Imperial German Government. A ten-mile belt along the coast was regarded as belonging to Zanzibar but in 1888 Germany acquired the right of collecting duties on the coast and in 1890 took over the coastal strip on payment of £200,000 to the Sultan of Zanzibar. Later the same year the supremacy of British interests in Zanzibar and Pemba was recognised by France and Germany and on 4th November the islands were proclaimed a British Protectorate,

Zanzibar affairs being handled by the Foreign Office. In 1891 a constitutional government was established in Zanzibar and the Sultan appointed a British subject, Lloyd Mathews, as his First Minister. The British Representative at that time was the Consul-General, Sir Gerald Portal.

Soon after the outbreak of the 1914–18 War clashes took place between British and German forces on the northern frontier of Tanganyika, but the main campaign to occupy the country did not begin until 1916. By the end of that year all the country north of the Central Railway was occupied by British or Belgian forces and a provisional Civil Administration was established for that area on the 1st January 1917. In November 1917 the German forces were driven across the Ruvuma River into Portuguese East Africa and the occupation of the whole of the territory was then completed.

By Article 119 of the Treaty of Peace with Germany, signed at Versailles on the 28th June 1919, Germany renounced in favour of the Principal Allied and Associated Powers all her rights over her overseas possessions, including her East African colony. The Principal Allied and Associated Powers agreed that His Britannic Majesty should exercise a mandate to administer this former German colony, except for the areas of Rwanda and Burundi for which the mandate was given to the Belgian Government. The administration of Tanganyika continued to be carried out under the terms of the mandate until its transfer to the Trusteeship System under the Charter of the United Nations by the Trusteeship Agreement of 13th December 1946.

TANGANYIKA

Constitutional development

The Legislative Council was first constituted by the Tanganyika (Legislative Council) Order in Council, 1926, and consisted of the Governor as President, 13 Official members and not more than ten Unofficial members. The full quota of Unofficials was not filled until 1935, when seven Europeans and three Asians were nominated. In the same year changes were made in the Official membership and a further revision took place two years later.

In 1945 the Legislative Council was enlarged to consist of the Governor as President, 15 Official and not more than 14 Unofficial members. As a result of these changes the 14 Unofficial Members included, from 1948 onwards, four Africans (two appointed in 1945, a third in 1947 and a fourth in 1948) and three Asians. In 1949 the Governor appointed a Committee including African, Asian and European representatives to review the country's constitutional structure. Its report was published in 1951 and recommended equal representation of the territory's three main races in the unofficial membership of an enlarged Legislative Council with the retention of an official majority. After further examination the recommendations were put into effect in 1955. The new Council was presided over by a Speaker and had 31 Official members and 30 Unofficials (comprising ten Africans, ten Asians and ten Europeans).

From 1948 onwards the Executive Council, which assisted the Governor in an advisory capacity, was remodelled on the 'Member' system, whereby groups of Government Departments were the responsibility of certain individual members of the Executive Council. By the end of 1954 the Executive Council consisted of the Governor as President, three *ex officio* members, five nominated Official members and six Unofficial members (of whom two were Europeans, two Asians and two Africans). In 1957 the Official members of the Executive Council were redesignated as Ministers and at the same time six Assistant Ministers (four Africans, one European and one Asian) were appointed. The Assistant Ministers became *ex officio* members of the Legislative Council with the duty of speaking for the departments assigned to them but they were not, however, members of the Executive Council although they might attend meetings and take part in discussions when matters affecting their departments came before it.

The first General Election in Tanganyika was held in 1958–59 in two phases, because of the administrative and other problems involved in holding this first series of elections in such a large country.

After the elections the Governor announced that it was proposed to set up a Council of Ministers in which Unofficials, including Africans, would for the first time be appointed to Ministerial office. The new Council which took office in July 1959 had 12 Ministers, five of whom were elected Unofficials (three African, one Asian and one European), and it advised the Governor on constitutional and legislative matters. The Executive Council was still in existence but only advised the Governor on a limited range of subjects.

The Governor announced in December 1959 that there would be new elections followed by important constitutional changes.

The second General Election, which brought in an elected majority in both the executive and the legislative spheres, was held in August 1960. The elected side of the Legislature comprised 71 seats and of this figure 50 seats were open to contest by all races and 21 reserved for minority communities, 11 Asians and 10 Europeans. Although there were 71 seats in fact there were only 13 contests in 11 constituencies because 58 candidates, 17 of whom were former members of Legislative Council, were returned unopposed.

Only two Parties contested the election, the Tanganyika African National Union and the African National Congress. There were, however, a number of independent candidates.

The election resulted in an overwhelming victory for the Tanganyika African National Union under the leadership of Mr Julius Nyerere, which obtained 70 of the 71 elected seats. The single successful non-TANU candidate stood as an Independent.

On the new government taking office certain changes took place in the constitutional framework of the executive, the principal of which was the abolition of the office of Chief Secretary and the creation of the new office of Deputy Governor, who was a member of the Council of Ministers but not of the Legislative Council. With this change came the abolition of the Executive Council and the introduction of the office of Chief Minister.

After the Constitutional Conference held in Dar es Salaam in March 1961, under the chairmanship of the Secretary of State for the Colonies, the British Government announced that it had agreed to grant internal self-government to Tanganyika from 1st May 1961 and full independence from 28th December 1961. The latter was later altered to 9th December 1961.

During the period 1st May to 9th December 1961 the Governor continued to be responsible for Defence and External Affairs. On 1st May 1961 Mr Nyerere, formerly Chief Minister, became the country's first Prime Minister, at the head of a Cabinet of 12. On the same day the Legislative Council was re-named the National Assembly, its composition remaining unchanged. The post of Deputy Governor was abolished from 1st July 1961.

In June 1961 the Tanganyika National Assembly unanimously passed a motion asking other member governments of the Commonwealth to join with the British Government in supporting Tanganyika's desire to become a Member of the Commonwealth. All Commonwealth Governments agreed to this and Tanganyika became a Member of the Commonwealth on achieving independence on the 9th December 1961. At the same time the Trusteeship Agreement was terminated by the United Nations.

On 15th February 1962 the Tanganyika National Assembly unanimously adopted a government motion that the Constitution be amended to provide for Tanganyika to become a Republic within the Commonwealth. At the Meeting of Commonwealth Prime Ministers held in London on 10th September 1962 the Prime Minister of Tanganyika was informed by the Heads of Delegations of the other member countries of the Commonwealth that the present relations between their countries and Tanganyika would remain unaffected by this constitutional change and that they would be happy to recognise Tanganyika's continued membership of the Commonwealth.

The Republic of Tanganyika was inaugurated on 9th December 1962. Its Constitution provided for a President who was executive Head of State and Commander-in-Chief of the Armed Forces; he was empowered to appoint a Vice-President and Ministers of his Cabinet, though he was not bound to act on their advice. The first President, Mr Nyerere, was directly elected by universal suffrage. The Constitution provided for the election of subsequent Presidents by the National Assembly at five-yearly intervals or on the dissolution of Parliament. The Constitution was changed in 1965, however, to establish a Democratic One Party State. The election of the President (the sole party candidate) is by universal suffrage: the voters having the right to confirm or reject the Presidential candidate.

ZANZIBAR

Constitutional development

On 1st July 1913 the control of Zanzibar passed from the Foreign Office to the Colonial Office, and by a Zanzibar Order in Council of 1914 the offices of British Consul-General and the Sultan's First Minister were merged in the newly-created post of British Resident, who was appointed, subject to the control of the Governor of the British East Africa Protectorate, as High Commissioner. A Protectorate Council was constituted as an advisory body with the Sultan as President and the British Resident as Vice-President. In 1925 the office of High Commissioner was abolished and the British Resident was made directly responsible to the Colonial Office. Executive and Legislative Councils were constituted in 1926 in place of the old advisory Protectorate Council. In 1960, following recommendations made by Sir Hilary Blood who had been appointed Constitutional Commissioner, a degree of responsible government was granted. Elected Ministers, one of whom was Chief Minister, formed the majority in the Executive Council, and in the Legislative Council there was a large elected majority.

In 1962 the franchise was extended to provide for universal adult suffrage, and a Delimitation Commission recommended an increase in the number of elected members in the Legislative Council. On 24th June 1963 internal self-government was introduced. After a General Election in July a Government was formed from a coalition between the Zanzibar Nationalist Party and the Zanzibar and Pemba People's Party, which had won a majority of seats (though not of votes) over the Afro-Shirazi Party headed by Sheikh Abeid Amani Karume. At the Independence Conference held in London in September 1963 arrangements were agreed for the final transfer of power, and Zanzibar attained full sovereign independence on 10th December 1963 under the Sultan as Head of State.

Establishment of The People's Republic of Zanzibar

On 12th January 1964 the Sultan's Government was overthrown. Zanzibar was proclaimed a People's Republic, with Mr Karume as President. The former constitution was abrogated, but other existing laws continued in force. A Revolutionary Council of 32 members was declared the Supreme Authority in the Republic. A Cabinet of Ministers was appointed to exercise executive power on behalf of, and with the advice of, the Revolutionary Council. Under a Presidential Decree made in February 1964 the

Revolutionary Council was to enact constitutional Decrees which were to form the basic law of the Republic, and a Constituent Assembly was to be convened to consider these basic provisions which, after having received the Assembly's assent, were to be the Constitution of Zanzibar. A further Presidential Decree of 11th May 1965 established the Afro-Shirazi Party as the sole party and supreme authority in Zanzibar.

UNION OF TANGANYIKA AND ZANZIBAR

After meetings between President Nyerere and President Karume it was decided that Tanganyika and Zanzibar should form one Sovereign State. Articles of Union were signed on 22nd April 1964 and on 25th April 1964 legislation ratifying these Articles was enacted by both the Tanganyika Parliament and the Revolutionary Council of Zanzibar. By this legislation the United Republic of Tanganyika and Zanzibar was created as a single sovereign state, as from 26th April 1964, under President Nyerere. President Karume was declared 1st Vice-President of the United Republic, while retaining the style of President of Zanzibar as head of the separate Legislature and Executive for Zanzibar. There were 18 members from Zanzibar in the National Assembly of the United Republic and some of these became Ministers and Parliamentary Secretaries in the United Republic Government.

The legislation provided for an interim constitution which laid down that the United Republic should be governed in accordance with the provisions of the existing Tanganyika Constitution suitably modified to provide for a separate Legislature and Executive in Zanzibar with exclusive authority over matters other than reserved matters. Reserved matters were: external affairs; defence; police; emergency powers; citizenship; immigration; external trade and borrowing (but see below); the Public Service of the United Republic; income tax, corporation tax, customs and excise duties; harbours, civil aviation, posts and telegraphs.

The main subjects which remained within the competence of the Zanzibar Government and for which there were separate ministries or departments included agriculture and fisheries; education and national culture; health and social insurance; information and broadcasting; labour; prisons; roads, power, works and justice. In practice Zanzibar has also retained control of her external trade.

The United Republic of Tanganyika and Zanzibar became the United Republic of Tanzania on 29th October 1964.

On 5th July 1965 the National Assembly passed the Interim Constitution Act which formally declared Tanzania to be a one-party state. A revised TANU constitution formed the first schedule of the Act, which looked forward to the union of TANU and the Afro-Shirazi party which took place with the formation of the new Chama Cha Mapinduzi (CCM) 'Revolutionary Party' on 5th February 1977.

The CCM is the supreme political organ in Tanzania, formulating policy for the country's development. The Government is charged with the day to day implementation of the policy and is accountable to both President and Party. The legislatures (the National Assembly and the House of Representatives, Zanzibar) are simultaneously the Parliamentary Committees of the CCM. President Mwinyi took over the chairmanship of the Party on President Nyerere's retirement in August 1990.

Elections

There have been six Presidential Elections in Tanzania, in 1965, 1970, 1975, 1980, 1985 and 1990. In each election the sole Presidential candidate was elected by a large majority of affirmative votes. Concurrent General Elections were held in mainland Tanzania in which the ruling party nominated two candidates in each constituency. These were selected by party district primary elections and approved by the party National Executive Committee. Elections for the Presidency of Zanzibar were held in 1980, 1984 and 1985 and the first national constituency elections in 1977. The Zanzibar House of Representatives was established in 1979 but full constituency elections were not held there until 1985. Elections for the CCM are also held every 5 years at local, regional and national level. The last national party elections were held in November 1987. The last Presidential and General Elections were held on 28th October 1990. President Mwinyi was elected for a second and final term.

Separate elections were held on 21st October 1990 to elect members of the Zanzibar House of Representatives and the President of Zanzibar, Dr Salmin Amour, was elected President by a large majority.

Constitution

Revised constitutions for both the United Republic and for Zanzibar came into force for the 1985 elections. Zanzibar's position in the Union is more clearly defined and its Government democratically elected. As before the mainland has no separate Government. Presidents may now serve only two terms. There are two Vice-Presidents, one of whom is also Prime Minister and the other President of Zanzibar. When a Zanzibari is President of the United Republic his Prime Minister, whom he appoints along with other Ministers from the National Assembly, is First Vice-President and the elected President of Zanzibar is Second Vice-President. When the President of the United Republic comes from the mainland the President of Zanzibar is the First Vice-President and the Prime Minister the Second Vice-President. The current 1985 Union Constitution includes a Bill of Rights and increases the proportion of constituency MPs in the National Assembly of 255 members. There are now 180 constituencies of which 50 are in Zanzibar. The Assembly also includes the 25 Regional Commissioners, 15 MPs elected by the Assembly to represent women and 15 similarly elected to represent the Party mass organisations plus 5 elected by the Zanzibar House of Representatives and 15 nominated by the President. Under the 1985 Constitution of Zanzibar the House of Representatives of 75 members has 50 constituency members, 5 Regional Commissioners, 10 Presidential Nominees and 10 elected by the House to represent Party mass organisations and women. The Party mass organisations represent women, youth, trade unions, co-operatives and parents. But in August 1991 the CCM's trade union organisation, JUWATA, was replaced by the Organisation of Tanzanian Trade Unions (OTTU) which will be independent of it's ruling party. Other mass organisations are similarly planned to become independent. The President of Zanzibar appoints a Chief Minister and 18 other members of the Zanzibar Revolutionary Council which constitutes the Cabinet of Zanzibar together with himself as chairman.

In March 1991 a Presidential Commission began work to examine further revision of the Constitution, including the question of a multi-party State and is due to report in 1992.

Tanzania's principal National Days are:—
12th January, Zanzibar Revolution Day;
5th February, Founding date of Chama Cha Mapinduzi;
26th April, Union Day (Anniversary of the Union of Tanganyika and Zanzibar in 1964);
9th December, Independence Day and Republic Day.

Historical List

(A full historical list is shown in the 1978 edition)

PRESIDENT

Mwalimu Julius K Nyerere, from 26th April 1964 to 5th November 1985

PRESIDENTS OF ZANZIBAR

Sheikh Abeid Amani Karume, from 26th April 1964 to 7th April 1972
Aboud Jumbe, from 12th April 1972 to 23rd January 1984
Ali Hassan Mwinyi, from 22nd April 1984 to 17th October 1985
Idris Abdul Wakil, from 17th October 1985 to 28th October 1990.

Government

HEAD OF STATE

The President: His Excellency Ali Hassan Mwinyi (from 5th November 1985)
First Vice-President and Prime Minister: Hon John Samuel Malecela, MP
Second Vice-President: Hon Dr Salmin Amour

MINISTERS

Foreign Affairs: Hon Hassan Diria
Agriculture and Livestock Development and Cooperatives: Hon Amran Mayagila
Communications and Transport: Hon Jackson Makwetta
Works: Hon Nalaila Kiula
Defence: Hon Ali Hassan Mwinyi
Education: Hon Charles Kabeho
Energy, Minerals and Water: Hon Lt Col Jakaya Kikwete
Finance: Hon Steven Kibona
Health: Hon Prof Philemon Sarungi
Home Affairs: Hon Augustine Mrema
Industries and Trade: Hon Cleopa D Msuya
Information and Broadcasting: Hon Benjamin Mkapa
Labour and Youth Development: Hon Joseph Rwegasira
Lands, Housing and Urban Development: Hon Marcel B Komanya
Regional Administration and Local Governments: Hon Anna Abdallah
Community Development, Women and Children: Hon Anna Makinda
Tourism, Natural Resources and Environment: Hon Abubakar Mugumia
Science, Technology and Higher Education: Hon Dr William Shija
Minister Without Portfolio and CCM Vice Chairman: Hon Rashid M Kawawa

PLANNING COMMISSION

Chairman: Hon Ali Hassan Mwinyi
Vice-Chairman: Hon Prof Kighoma Malima
Commissioners: Mr Mustafa Nyang' anyi; Mr Pius Msekwa; Mr Damas Mbogoro; Mr Nsa Kaisi
Commissioner of the Budget: Mr George Chisanga
Principal Secretary: Mr Fulgence Kazaura
Deputy Principle Secretary: Mr Raphael Mhagama

MINISTERS OF STATE

President's office
Defence: Hon Lt Col Abdul Rahman Kinana
Planning: Hon Prof Kighoma Malima
Civil Service: Hon Mrs Fatma Said Ali
Prime Minister and First Vice Presidents' office: Hon Edward Lowassa

DEPUTY MINISTERS

Foreign Affairs and International Cooperation: Emmanuel Mwambulu Kutu
Agriculture and Livestock Development and Cooperatives: Frederick T Sumaye
Water, Energy and Minerals: Hon Ernest Nyanda
Finance: Hon Juma Hamad Omar
Industries and Trade: Dr Nicas Mahinda
Home Affairs: Judge Edward Mwesiumo

Defence and National Service: Ramadhani Ditopilemzuzuri
Works: Major Sigela Nswima

MINISTRIES AND GOVERNMENT DEPARTMENTS

PRESIDENT'S OFFICE
Chief Secretary: Paul Rupia
Principal Secretary (Planning Commission): Fulgence Kazaura
Principal Secretary (Civil Service): William H Shellukindo
Deputy PS: Dio Trephes Mmari

PRIME MINISTER AND FIRST VICE PRESIDENT'S OFFICE
Principal Secretary: Peter Ngumbulu
Deputy PS: Joshua Doriye
Deputy PS: Vincent Mrisho

SECOND VICE PRESIDENT'S OFFICE
Principal Secretary: Muhammed A Muhammed

DEFENCE AND NATIONAL SERVICE
Principal Secretary: Frank Kejo

FINANCE
Principal Secretary: Prof Simon Mbilinyi
Deputy PS: Raphael O S Mollel
Deputy PS: ?
Deputy PS: Dr Jonas Kipokola

FOREIGN AFFAIRS
Principal Secretary: Crispin Mbapila

COMMUNICATIONS AND TRANSPORT
Principal Secretary: F Mujuni

REGIONAL ADMINISTRATION AND LOCAL GOVERNMENTS
Principal Secretary: Rogarian Shirima
Deputy PS: Bernard Mchomvu

AGRICULTURE AND LIVESTOCK DEVELOPMENT AND COOPERATIVES
Principal Secretary: Dr Ben Moshi

LABOUR AND YOUTH DEVELOPMENT
Principal Secretary: Ali M Vuai

TOURISM, NATURAL RESOURCES AND ENVIRONMENT
Principal Secretary: Paul Mkanga

HOME AFFAIRS
Principal Secretary: Martin Lumbanga

ENERGY, MINERALS AND WATER
Principal Secretary: Prof Mwandosya

INDUSTRIES AND TRADE
Principal Secretary: S L Adel

EDUCATION
Principal Secretary: Kenya Hassan

HEALTH
Principal Secretary: Wilfred Mwambulambo

INFORMATION AND BROADCASTING
Principal Secretary: Richard Mariki

JUSTICE
Attorney-General: Damian Lubuva
Deputy Attorney-General: Thomas Mkude

WORKS
Principal Secretary: Dr George Mlingwa
Deputy PS: Raynold M Minja

COMMUNITY DEVELOPMENT, WOMEN AND CHILDREN
Principal Secretary: Rose Lugembe

SCIENCE, TECHNOLOGY AND HIGHER EDUCATION
Principal Secretary: Dr Mohammed Bilal

SPEAKER'S OFFICE
Speaker: Chairman of Electoral Commission: Hon Chief Adam Sapi Mkwawa, OBE, MP
Deputy Speaker: Hon George Nhigula, MP
Clerk of National Assembly and Director of Elections: Mohamed Mwindadi

CIVIL SERVICE COMMISSION
Chairman: Bernard Mulokozi

JUDICIARY
Chief Justice: Mr Justice F Nyalali

REGIONAL COMMISIONERS
Mainland
Arusha: Lt Col Anatoli Tarimo, MP
Coast: Maj Gen Lupogo, MP
Dar es Salaam: Mrs Mary Alice Chipungahelo, MP
Dodoma: Athuman S Kabongo, MP
Iringa: Mr Stephen Wassira, MP
Kagera: Paul Kimiti, MP
Kigoma: Chrisant M Mzindakaya, MP
Kilimanjaro: Samuel Sitta, MP
Lindi: Edgar Maokola-Majogo, MP
Mara: Maj Joseph Butiku, MP
Mbeya: Azan Said Al-Jabri, MP
Morogoro: Yusuf Makamba, MP
Mtwara: Col Ferdinand Swai, MP
Mwanza: Philip Mangula, MP
Rukwa: Dr Mayanja Kiwannuka, MP
Ruvuma: Major-General James Luhanga, MP
Shinyanga: Nicodemus Banduka, MP
Singida: Galus Abeid, MP
Tabora: Lawrence Mtazama Gama, MP
Tanga: Ms Halima Hamisi, MP

Islands
Zanzibar North: Said Rashid Mohammed, MP
Zanzibar South: Ali Mzee Ali, MP
Zanzibar Urban/West: Prof Ishau A Khamis, MP

Pemba North: Mohamed Mahmoud, MP
Pemba South: Hassan Takrima, MP

ZANZIBAR GOVERNMENT LIST

**The President:* Hon Dr Salmin Amour

CABINET

**Chief Minister:* Hon Dr Omar Ali Juma, MP
**Agriculture, Livestock Development and Natural Resources:* Hon Seif Rashid Seif, MP
**Communications and Transport:* Hon Rufeya Juma Mbarouk, MP
Education: Hon Omar Ramadhan Mapuri
Finance: Hon Amina Salum Ali, MP
**Health:* Dr Msim Abdulrahman Hassan, MP
**Information, Culture, Tourism and Youth:* Hon Ramadhan Abdalla Shaaban, MP
Trade, Industry and Marketing: Hon Amaan Karume, MP
Water, Energy, Construction: Hon Salum Hashim Rajab, MP

MINISTERS OF STATE

Planning: Hon Issack Sepetu
Regional Administration and Security: Hon Iddi Pandu Hassan
**Special Duties:* Hon Taimur Saleh Juma
**Minister Without Portfolio:* Said Iddi Babuai
Minister of State in Chief Minister's Office: Said Bakari Jecha

---

*Member of Zanzibar Revolutionary Council

Tonga

Capital: Nuku'alofa

The Kingdom of Tonga comprises a group of islands situated in the south-west Pacific between latitudes 15° and 23° 30'S. and longitudes 173° and 177°W. The group, known as the Tonga or the Friendly Islands, is divided into three main sub-groups: Vava'u, Ha'apai and Tongatapu. The total estimated area, including inland waters, is 747.3 sq km (288.55 square miles). Tongatapu, the largest island, has an area of 256.9 sq km (99.2 square miles). The islands on the eastern side are of coral formation, those on the west are volcanic. There are active volcanoes on four of the islands.

The climate is healthy, though hot and humid from January to March with temperatures of 32°C (90°F); during the rest of the year it is pleasantly cool with temperatures as low as 9°C (48°F) on Tongatapu. The mean annual temperature is 23°C (73°F); the mean annual rainfall is 1,750 mm on Tongatapu and 2,750 mm on Vava'u.

The population, as recorded in the 1986 census was 94,535. It is now estimated to be 100,000.

The administrative capital is Nuku'alofa on Tongatapu, the population of which was 28,899 in the 1986 census.

The unit of currency is the Pa'anga (T$), which is tied to a basket of currencies.

Primary Education is compulsory, commencing at 6 years with 92 per cent attending government schools and 8 per cent church schools. For secondary education 90 per cent attend church schools. The budget allocation for expenditure on education in 1991/92 is T$8,763,000.

The Government of Tonga Medical Department operates three public hospitals one in each of the three main islands, and a number of dispensaries. Government expenditure on medical services (exclusive of buildings and building maintenance) is estimated to be T$5,395,000 in 1991/92.

There is an international airport at Fua'amotu, 21 km from Nuku'alofa. Air Pacific (in which Tonga is a minor shareholder) operates 6 flights a week to Nandi, Air New Zealand two a week to Auckland and one to Nandi, Polynesian Airlines two a week each way to Auckland and back, one to Apia and back and one from Apia and Hawaiian Air two flights a week to and from Honolulu via Pago Pago. Through Fiji there are connections to Australia, the US, Canada and Japan.

Tonga's airline, Royal Tongan, flies once a week to Auckland return and also, operates internal services to all the main islands: 'Eua, Ha'apai, Vava'u, Niuatoputapu and Niuafo'ou.

There are approximately 198 km of metalled road in Tongatapu and 74 km in Vava'u suitable for motor traffic. There are some 94 km of unsealed roads which can be used by motor traffic only in dry weather.

Regional shipping services operate to the two main ports of entry, Nuku'alofa and Neiafu (Vava'u). Pacific Forum Line operates a fully containerised service from Australia via Fiji; there are regular although infrequent services from Auckland, Japan and Hawaii, while Bank Line and Columbus Line operate a joint cargo service from Europe.

Broadcasting is administered by the Tonga Broadcasting Commission. The studios are situated at Nuku'alofa and the transmitter at Popua, about one mile away. The station A3Z, known as Radio Tonga, was opened by the late Queen Salote Tupou on 4th July 1961. The station broadcasts for 16 hours daily from Monday to Saturday and a minimum 5½ hours on Sundays, in English and Tongan. Transmissions are on medium wave on a frequency of 1,017 kc/s, and can also be heard in New Zealand, Fiji, Norfolk Islands, Samoa and Niue. Commercial advertising is accepted in English and Tongan. The output of the station largely consists of locally originated programmes including traditional Tongan music and spoken word, news bulletin and weather forecasts. They also retransmit BBC, American, New Zealand and Australian news broadcasts. A local English language service on the FM channel opened in July 1988.

There is a small, privately owned television station which transmits videos.

Tonga is essentially an agricultural country with a large percentage of the population involved in subsistence farming, although employment opportunities in Government and commerce are increasing.

The Government's Sixth Development Plan, implemented in July 1991 gives priority to continued development through the private sector although the public sector will have an important role to play in the economy by providing adequate infrastructure.

The main crops are coconuts, bananas, vanilla, pumpkins, kumalas, yams, targo, cassava, groundnuts, maize, watermelons, pineapples, tomatoes, kava and capsicum. The main export crops are now vanilla and pumpkins. Coffee has recently been introduced.

The fishing sector is relatively undeveloped. The Government has therefore given emphasis to its expansion with assistance to fishermen through custom duty concessions, boat purchase assistance and Tonga Development Bank loan finance.

Tourism as a sector now forms an important part of the economy. The Kingdom has the potential for the development of tourism and this could become an important source of foreign exchange earnings and income. Government policies since 1982 have led to increased development in this sector but much is yet to be done. The establishment of domestic flights on a regular basis within the Kingdom has assisted the development of tourism as well as commerce, as have improvements to airports, and the provision of international telephones to Tongatapu, Ha'apai, Vava'u and in 'Eua in August 1988, extension of electricity to all villages in Tongatapu, 'Eua, Ha'apai (Lifuka and Foa) and to major parts of Vava'u in 1988. The Government will continue to strive for improvement of the infrastructure required to promote tourism, such as Fua'amotu's new airport, the improvement of international flights to and from Tonga, the encouragement of new industry and the establishment of new hotels in the Kingdom under the approved incentive policies which grant a 5 year tax holiday with possible extension to 10 years, no duty on capital goods and 50 per cent of the Port and Service tax rate on capital goods for building the project.

Limited areas of forest land are found in the islands of 'Eua and Vava'u.

The main manufacturing industries in Tonga are the production of concrete blocks, small excavators, clothing, furniture, sports equipment including small boats and coconut oil. Handicrafts are produced for local sale to tourists and for export. A brewery came into production in 1987.

The chief imports are textiles, flour, preserved meat, fresh meat, beverages, cigarettes and tobacco, fuel oils, machinery and transport equipment, building supplies and materials.

Several seeps of crude oil have been found in Tonga. Oil is to be found in the Tonga Trench, but so far its exploitation has not been commercially viable.

There has been renewed interest in gold exploration in the South Pacific and two Mineral Exploration licences, covering most of the islands in the Kingdom, were awarded in 1987. One of the licences was renewed in 1988.

Revenue and expenditure during the years 1987/88–1991/92 were:

	Revenue T$	*Recurrent Expenditure* T$	*Development Expenditure* T$(m)
1987–88	to balance	29,846,266	31.2
1988–89	to balance	33,500,000	41.6
1989–90	to balance	43,719,880	29.0
1990–91	48,056,655	47,853,896	48.0
1991–92	51,715,000	51,429,000	69.0

About 56 per cent of revenue accrues from customs duty. The main areas of expenditure are public works, medical services, education and agriculture. The financial year begins on 1st July.

In 1986, the Government undertook a major tax reform by moving away from direct to indirect taxes through the reduction for all personal and non-company business taxes from a maximum of 40 per cent to a flat 10 per cent, the reduction of resident companies tax by 5 per cent and the introduction of a tax on the sales of goods and services. The objective of the changes was to make the Kingdom more attractive to business. Income tax for resident companies is 15 per cent on the first T$100,000 of net profits and 30 per cent thereafter.

Indirect taxation includes import duties (tariff 15 per cent—45 per cent according to the commodities ad valorem CIF) and a port and service tax on imports of 17½ per cent.

Foreign reserves in March 1991, excluding more than US$30 m held in a trust fund in the US stood at a record T$39.3 m.

History

During the first half of the nineteenth century civil wars were rife in the islands. They were finally checked during the reign of King George Tupou I (1845–93) who had by conquest gathered all power in his own hands.

Wesleyan missionaries landed on Tonga in 1826 and by the middle of the century practically all the chiefs and people had been converted to Christianity. Not until the last decade of the century, however, were questions regarding freedom of worship and the relationship of Church and State peaceably settled. Britain and Tonga concluded a Treaty of Friendship in 1879 and in 1900, by a Treaty of Friendship and Protection, Tonga became a British Protected State. There were several subsequent revisions of the Treaty reflecting changes which occured during the 20th century. Under the latest, by an exchange of letters on 19th May 1970, it was agreed that the United Kingdom Government should, as from 4th June 1970, cease to have any responsibility for the external relations of the Kingdom of Tonga. The provisions of Articles II, III, IV and V of the 1968 Revised Treaty accordingly ceased to have effect. At the same time Tonga became a full member of the Commonwealth and accepted The Queen as a symbol of the free association of independent member nations and as such The Head of the Commonwealth. The British High Commissioner in New Zealand was appointed concurrently United Kingdom High Commissioner (non-resident) in Tonga, while the former resident post of Commissioner and Consul became Deputy High Commissioner. In 1973 the Resident Deputy High Commissioner was appointed High Commissioner.

Constitution

The present constitution is based, with relatively little amendment, on that granted in 1875 by King George Tupou I. It provides for a Government consisting of the Sovereign (at present King Taufa'ahau Tupou IV, GCMG, GCVO, KBE), a Privy Council and Cabinet, a Legislative Assembly and a Judiciary. The Legislative Assembly consists of the Prime Minister and Ministers of the Crown (including the Governors of Vava'u and Ha'apai), nine representatives of the nobles elected by their peers, and nine representatives of the people elected by popular franchise, every male Tongan of 21 years of age who pays taxes and can read and write, being qualified to vote. In 1960 for the first time women were included, and held a vote, in the election of Legislative Assembly members. Several women also stood for election but were defeated at the polls. The first Lady Member was elected in 1975. Elections are held every three years. The President of the Legislative Assembly is the Speaker, appointed by the Sovereign. The courts consist of a Supreme Court, a Magistrate's Court and a Land Court.

Land Policy

According to the Constitution every male Tongan on reaching the taxable age of 16 years is entitled to 8¼ acres of land for cultivation in addition to a small village allotment for his dwelling. Because of the shortage of land about two-thirds of eligible males have not received their allotments. Land may not be leased to non-Tongans without the consent of the Government. Immigrant settlement is not encouraged owing to the increasing shortage of land available.

HEAD OF STATE

HM King Taufa'ahau Tupou IV, GCMG, GCVO, KBE

Government (January 1992)

Prime Minister and Minister of Agriculture Marine, Forestry and Fisheries: Hon Baron Vaea

Deputy Prime Minister and Minister of Education, Works and Civil Aviation: Hon Dr S Langi Kavaliku

Minister of Labour, Commerce and Industry: Hon Tutoatasi Fakafanva

Minister of Health: Hon Dr S Tapa

Minister of Finance: Hon Cecil Cocker

Minister of Education, Works and Civil Aviation: Hon Dr Hu'akavameiliku

Minister of Police and Prisons: Hon Akau'ola

Minister of Foreign Affairs and Defence: HRH Crown Prince Tupouto'a

Minister of Justice and Attorney General: Hon Tevita Tupou

Minister without Portfolio: Hon Ma'afu Takui'aulahi

Acting Minister for Lands, Survey and Natural Resources: Hon Dr Ma'afu Tupou

Governor of Ha'apai: Hon Fakafanua

Acting Governor of Vava'u: Hon Tu'i'afitu

Speaker of the House: Hon Fusitu'a

Chief Secretary and Secretary to Cabinet: Taniela Hoko'ila Tufui

Chief Justice: G Ward

Puisne Judge: Ramsey Dalgety, QC

Solicitor-General: ' A H Taumoepeau

The Republic of Trinidad and Tobago

Capital: Port of Spain

The islands of Trinidad and Tobago are the most southerly of the West Indian islands. They lie between latitudes 10° 2′ and 11° 2′ North and between longitudes 60° 30′ and 61° 56′ West and are in close proximity to the north coast of South America with the nearest point being Venezuela, just 11.2 km away. Trinidad is about 80 km in length at its longest point and 59.2 km in width at its widest point with an area of 4,828.5 sq km. Tobago is 41.9 km long and 12 km wide, with an area of 300 sq km. Trinidad is traversed by three mountain ranges—the Northern Range, running across the northern width of the island from west to east, the Central Range running diagonally across the island and the Southern Range running along the southern coast from Guayaguayare to Icacos. Between the Northern and Central Ranges the land is flat and comprises the Caroni Plain; south of the Central Range the land is undulating rising to the Southern Range. Apart from small areas in the Northern Range of which the main peaks are Cerro de Aripo (925.5 metres) and El Tucuche (921.6 metres), and in the central range of which Mount Tamana (302.7 metres) is the highest peak, all the land on the island is below 300 metres. In Tobago, a main ridge of hills, 28.96 km in length extends nearly two-thirds of the island from its north-eastern extremity. The highest point is 576.07 metres. Forest Reserves and state lands amount to 1,264.93 sq km, approximately 24 per cent of the total land surface. Lying just north of the equator, this country has a warm tropical climate with mean air temperatures of 22° Celsius (minimum) and 30.7° Celsius (maximum) and an average annual rainfall of 185.8 mm. The dry season is from January to May and wet season from June to December, with a short dry sunny spell called the Petit Careme, from September to October.

Population
Based on the statistics of Central Statistical Office, Trinidad and Tobago's population by mid 1988 was estimated at 1,235,395. Population distribution for the main administrative areas in 1987 were:—

Port of Spain	591,173
San Fernando	33,601
Arima (Borough)	28,970
St. George	442,332
Caroni	169,806
Nariva/Mayaro	33,727
St. Andrew/St. David	58,621
Victoria	222,001
St. Patrick	142,196
Tobago	44,968

Religious groupings include Anglican, Baptist, Jehovah Witness, Methodist, Pentecostal, Presbyterian, Roman Catholic, Seventh Day Adventist, Hindu and Muslim. The major religions are Roman Catholicism 33.6 per cent, Hinduism 25.6 per cent, Anglicanism 15.0 per cent, Islam 5.9 per cent.

English is the official language, but some Spanish, French patois, Chinese and Indian dialects are spoken mainly by the descendants of these cultures.

Communications
The principal sea ports are Point Lisas, a deepwater port serving not only the needs of the energy-based industries in operation on the Point Lisas Industrial Estate, but also now the main sea port; Port of Spain; Scarborough in Tobago, a deepwater harbour; Chaguaramas; Point-a-Pierre and Point Fortin Oil Terminals; and Brighton, an asphalt and oil loading point.

Trinidad and Tobago is serviced by the national shipping line SCOTT (Shipping Corporation of Trinidad and Tobago), as well as WISCO (West Indies Shipping Corporation) jointly owned by Trinidad & Tobago, Jamaica, Barbados, Guyana and the Windward and Leeward Islands. It is also served by other European lines such as Harrison Line and Hapag-Lloyd.

The national airline is Trinidad & Tobago Airways Corporation (British West Indian Airways—BWIA). The international airport of Trinidad is Piarco with a runway length of 3,201.2 metres (10,500 feet) which is located 25.7 kilometres south-east of Port of Spain. The Crown Point International Airport in Tobago which also links the twin-islands by air, has just had its runway lengthened to take wide-bodied jets, and now measures 2,743 metres (9,000 feet) for landing and 2,438 metres (8,000 feet) for takeoff.

Passenger transportation throughout the twin islands is conducted by the state-owned Public Transport Service Corporation which operates the public bus service throughout the islands, by privately-owned route taxis consisting of maxi-taxis and hired motor-cars and by private cars. Transportation between the two islands is by air, from Piarco to Crown Point Airport and by sea from Port-of-Spain to Scarborough. The twin islands have a road network of about 6,435.4 km of which approximately 2,000 km are national highways.

The Economy

Despite the fall of oil prices on the international market in recent years, the economy continues to be dominated by the oil and gas sectors. Government policy is to use the country's proven and probable natural gas reserves of 17.5 trillion cubic feet, (or over 100 years at present production rate) to develop a base of energy intensive industries and to seek new extra-regional export markets for these new areas of production. However, the Government is also trying to diversify into other areas including agriculture and agro-processing, light manufacturing for export, and tourism.

On the west coast of the sugar belt, in county Caroni, Point Lisas has developed into the Caribbean's largest industrial port. Here the Point Lisas Industrial Estate under the direction of the Point Lisas Industrial Port Development Co (PLIPDECO) in which Government is the major shareholder, is the setting for industries producing iron and steel, anhydrous ammonia, urea, and methanol. Also located here is the Point Lisas Power Station fired by natural gas, to supply the energy for the major industries on the estate.

The Iron and Steel Co of Trinidad and Tobago (ISCOTT) as it used to be known was leased to an Indian-owned company for a period of 10 years from 1st May 1989. It is now known as Caribbean ISPAT Ltd. Other major companies situated here, are Fertilisers of Trinidad and Tobago Ltd (FERTRIN), The Trinidad and Tobago Methanol Co Ltd, The Trinidad and Tobago Urea Co Limited, Agro Trinidad Nitrogen Limited and Phoenix Park Gas Processors, and Trinidad Nitrogen Limited.

The Petroleum sector continues to be the most vital sector of the economy. In 1990 the petroleum sector accounted for 30.5 per cent of GDP. The non-petroleum sectors collectively accounted for 69.5 per cent of output, but no individual sector contributes as much as petroleum. In 1990 the petroleum sector accounted for 27.4 per cent of GDP.

Gross Domestic Product fell by 0.4 per cent in 1990 compared to a fall of 2.4 per cent in 1989 (and an average annual decline of 4.6 per cent over the period 1983–1988). This is a real reduction in the rate of contraction of the domestic economy. This achievement was due primarily to an enhanced performance of the petroleum sector, helped by increases in refinery production and stability of domestic crude production.

An IMF Standby Agreement was put in place in January 1989, with a second Agreement in March 1990. A third arrangement is now being sought. Trinidad and Tobago's public debt was also rescheduled in 1989 with a 5-year moratorium and a 10-year repayment period. A US$40m Structural Adjustment Loan was agreed by the IBRD in January 1990.

During 1990, crude oil production was 150,792 barrels per day. This represents a 1.0 per cent increase in output compared with 1989. Marine production continues to be the larger proportion of total production. Although in general decline since 1985, the year 1990 has shown an increase from 74.8 per cent to 75.7 per cent. Land production, though, fell by 2.9 per cent in 1990.

The increase in exploratory drilling activity in 1989 has continued into 1990 in both marine and land areas, amounting to an increase of 11.1 per cent in 1990. An important development in 1989 was the implementation of the Lease Operatorship Programme by one of the State-owned oil companies, and the commencement of another such scheme by a second State-owned company in 1990. The Southern Basin Consortium involved two and three dimensional seismic surveys and two other oil recovery projects—the Trintoc heavy oil project and the Trinmar waterflood project.

Amoco continues to be the largest single producer of crude oil accounting for 49.8 per cent of total production in 1989. Of the other producers, Trinmar produced 22.8 per cent, Trintoc produced 12.4 per cent, Trintopec produced 12.7 per cent and Premier Consolidated Oilfields the other 2.3 per cent.

Refinery output in 1990 increased by 21.2 per cent to approximately 89,600 barrels per day. Much of this stemmed from an agreement with the Venezuelan Company, Maraven, for the processing of Venezuelan crude. A refinery upgrading project continued in 1990 with the undertaking of preparatory work, and pre-investment studies. Funding for the upgrading costing US$260m is being sought from the Inter-American Development Bank.

Natural gas production declined by 7.7 per cent in 1990. Work continued in 1990 to expand the supply of natural gas with production starting in early 1990 from three wells in the Pelican field.

The joint venture company, Phoenix Park Gas Processor, formed to construct a plant at Point Lisas to recover natural gas liquids is on schedule to start production in 1991. This should extract an average of 8,000 bpd of liquids from gas supplied by the National Gas Company.

The manufacturing sector increased by 2.3 per cent in 1990 to a value of TT$1285.2m. The services sector continues to be the largest contributor to the GDP. Its contribution is estimated to fall marginally from 65.2 per cent in 1989 to 63.9 per cent in 1990.

Agricultural production grew by 15.3 per cent to register the second consecutive year of strong growth. Sugar and domestic agriculture performed well with real value added increasing by 11.6 per cent and 18.3 per cent respectively. Export agriculture grew by 0.4 per cent. Production of raw sugar amounted to 116,000 tonnes, a 23 per cent increase in output over the 1989 level. Both cocoa and coffee production and export improved in the first half of 1990. As a result of the rise in production levels, exports of cocoa increased by 484,000 kilograms, while exports of coffee increased to 523,000 kilograms from a level of zero exports the previous year. Meat production declined by 12.1 per cent in the first six months of 1990 compared with the corresponding period in 1989. Citrus production fell sharply by 45.9 per cent due mainly to the unusually cold weather of December 1989 which prevented the crop maturing.

The Iron and Steel Company, Caribbean ISPAT Ltd, increased production of billets and direct reduced iron. Production of direct reduced iron reached 681,000 tonnes and output of wire rods was 252,000 tonnes. Output of billets was 364,000 tonnes.

The construction industry declined yet again, this time by 8 per cent following declines of 7.4 per cent in 1988 and a decline of 12.7 per cent in 1989. Consistent with this trend was a fall of 9.7 per cent in sales of cement on the domestic market after a decline of 10.5 per cent in 1989.

Unemployment in Trinidad and Tobago fell to 20.4 per cent in 1990. Inflation for 1990 was 11.0 per cent. The 1990 Government fiscal operations were conducted within the framework of an IMF supported adjustment programme. During the year the Government implemented the final phase of the tax reform programme begun in 1989. The effects of this, combined with increases in international oil prices resulted in higher Government revenue. Thus a fiscal surplus of TT$210m or 1.0 per cent of GDP was recorded; the first positive balance since 1985. The overall deficit remained, but narrowed to TT$88.2m. Government revenue grew by 13.5 per cent in 1990 to TT$5,645m. Government expenditure on wages and salaries declined marginally to TT$1,997.8m. The 10 per cent cut in the salaries of all public service employees imposed in 1989 was restored in January 1991, as announced in the 1991 Budget presented to Parliament in December 1990.

Trinidad and Tobago joined the Organisation of American States on 23rd February, 1967 and is a member of the Caribbean Economic Community (CARICOM) which was established on 1st August, 1973 with headquarters in Guyana.

Located in Trinidad are the Citrus Research Unit (shared by Belize, Jamaica, Dominica and Trinidad and Tobago); the Regional Research Centre (Agricultural and Soils Research); the Regional Virus Laboratory; the Seismic Research Unit; the Standing Advisory Committee for Medical Research in the Caribbean; and Commonwealth Regional Organizations such as the Regional Shipping Council, the West Indies Shipping Service, the Commonwealth Institute of Biological Control and the Caribbean Meteorological Organization.

Education

The education system is based on the British model and includes primary and secondary school level education and university. In addition, pre-school education is provided by the Government pre-school Centre at 50 community centres (1988) throughout the country and by private institutions. The system ensures that free education is available at all state-owned and government-assisted denominational schools and at certain faculties at the University of the West Indies. Selection for free secondary education is by the Common Entrance Examination (11+ exams) at 11 years. Alternatives to free secondary education include the private secondary schools and the vocational schools e.g. Youth Camps, Trade Centres. The literacy rate was 96.3 per cent in 1980.

The Media

Three companies operate radio stations while a fourth operates the only television station. These companies are: the National Broadcasting Company of Trinidad and Tobago Limited (Radio 610) nationalised in 1969, which transmits three services on the 610 kHz (AM) frequency, 98.9 MHz (FM) frequency and 100 MHz (FM) frequency; the Trinidad Broadcasting Company Limited, which operates two services—Radio Trinidad with the same programming on 730 kHz (AM) frequency and on 105 MHz (FM) frequency, and Radio 95 on 95 MHz (FM) frequency; Caribbean Communication Network Group of Companies operates service on the 106 MHz (FM) frequency and began broadcasts on Channel 6 in 1991; while the state-owned Trinidad and Tobago Television Company broadcasts on two channels.

An additional television production company, AVM, is expected to commence transmitting its broadcasts in the near future.

TRINIDAD

The aboriginal name for the island was Iere (widely interpreted as 'Humming Bird' though one source refers to it as an Arawak word meaning 'Island'). Columbus landed on the island on his third voyage in 1498 and took possession of it on behalf of the Crown of Spain, naming it Trinidad.

No Governor was appointed by the King of Spain until 1532 and even then, and for many years afterwards, the Spanish colonists had the greatest difficulty in maintaining a footing on the island. In

1595 Sir Walter Raleigh destroyed the newly-founded town of St. Joseph. In 1640 it was raided by the Dutch, and in 1677 and 1690 by the French.

Towards the end of the seventeenth and the beginning of the eighteenth centuries, cocoa was largely and successfully cultivated, but in 1725 a blight fell upon the plantations. Thereafter Trinidad made scarcely any progress until 1783 when, upon representations made to the Court of Madrid as to Trinidad's exceptional fertility, a royal proclamation was issued offering extraordinary advantages to Roman Catholics of all nations friendly with Spain to settle there. This resulted in a large influx of population, including many French families driven from Santo Domingo (Haiti) and elsewhere by the events of the French Revolution so that there was a large French element in a colony which never belonged to France.

In 1797, during the Revolutionary War, a British expedition sailed from Martinique for the reduction of Trinidad. The expedition resulted in the surrender of the island to His Majesty's Forces. In 1802 Trinidad was ceded to the British Crown by the Treaty of Amiens.

Emancipation of slaves in 1834 and the adoption of free trade by Britain in 1846 resulted in far-reaching social and economic changes. To meet the labour shortage immigration was encouraged. Between 1845 and 1917 there arrived over 150,000 immigrants from India, China and Madeira. The fall in the price of sugar and the general decline of the sugar industry, which dominated the island's history in the nineteenth century, stimulated the search for substitute crops; by the latter part of the century cocoa had been resuscitated and for a time replaced sugar as the most important industry.

After its cession to Britain in 1802 Trinidad became a Crown Colony. By the terms of the capitulation, the Spanish constitution and laws were maintained and the Governor ruled with the help of a newly-created Council of Advice and the existing Cabildo, a corporate body elected annually by the taxpayers, which combined the functions of a parish vestry, a municipal council, an ecclesiastical council and a council of government. The Council of Advice evolved in 1831 into an Executive Council and a Council of Government, which later became the Legislative Council. In 1840 the Cabildo became the Port of Spain Town Council. By the middle of the nineteenth century English procedure and legislation had displaced Spanish law.

TOBAGO

Tobago was discovered by Columbus in 1498, at which time it was occupied by Caribs. It was visited in 1596 and found to be uninhabited. The island remained unoccupied until 1632 when 300 Zealanders were sent out by a Company of Dutch merchants who styled it New Walcheren. After a residence of about two years these settlers were all killed or expelled by the Indians and Spaniards from Trinidad. In 1641 James, Duke of Courland, obtained a grant of the island from Charles I and in 1642 two vessels arrived with a number of Courlanders who settled on the north side. These were followed by further Dutch colonists in 1654 who, having effected a compromise with the Courlanders, established themselves on the southern coast; but in 1658 the Courlanders were overpowered by the Dutch, who remained in possession of the island until 1662 when the Dutch company resigned their right to it. In this year Cornelius Lampsius procured Letters Patent from Louis XIV creating him the Baron of Tobago and proprietor of the island under the crown of France.

In 1664 the grant of Tobago to the Duke of Courland was renewed by Charles II. The Dutch refused to recognise the Duke's title but in 1667 they themselves were compelled by the French to evacuate the island. Louis XIV restored the island to the Duke of Courland who, in 1681, made over his title to a company of London merchants. In 1748, by the Treaty of Aix-la-Chapelle, Tobago was declared neutral; the subjects of all European Powers were at liberty to form settlements or carry on commerce but not to place garrisons upon it. At the peace of 1763, by the Treaty of Paris, Tobago was ceded by France to England in perpetuity.

In 1781 Tobago was captured by the French after a gallant defence by the colonists. In 1783 it was surrendered by treaty to the French Crown. On 15th April 1793 it was captured by British Forces under Admiral Lefrey and General Cuyler. It was once more restored to the French by the Treaty of Amiens in 1802 and again re-conquered in 1803. In 1814 it was ceded in perpetuity to the British Crown.

Tobago continued to keep its old institutions, its House of Assembly, its Legislative Council, its Privy Council and its numerous Law Courts until 1874, when the House of Assembly was abolished and a one-Chamber Legislative Council formed. The abolition of slavery, the great storm of 1847 when most of the sugar works were damaged, the introduction of beet sugar in Europe, the lack of capital and many other factors had by this time resulted in a depressed state of trade. Tobago became a Crown Colony in 1877 at the request of the Legislative Council following the disastrous Belmanna riots. The Government was then administered by a resident administrator, subordinate to the Governor-in-Chief of the Windward Islands at Grenada, and a Legislative Council was established by an Order in Council on 7th February 1877, to consist of not less than three persons designated by Her Majesty The Queen.

The fall in the price of sugar gave the final blow to Tobago's status as a separate colonial unit, and in 1888 Tobago was amalgamated with Trinidad.

TRINIDAD AND TOBAGO

By Order in Council dated 17th November 1888 Tobago was amalgamated with Trinidad, the name of the new Colony being Trinidad and Tobago. The latter island was then administered by a

Commissioner appointed by the Governor of the United Colony, who was *ex officio* a member of the Legislative Council. One unofficial member of the Council represented Tobago. The Commissioner was assisted by a financial board of five members, two nominated by the Governor, and three elected. The revenue, expenditure and debt of the islands remained distinct, but there was a freedom of commercial intercourse between them and the laws of Trinidad were, with some specified exceptions, the laws of both.

By an Order in Council of 20th October 1898 the Order in Council of November 1888 was almost entirely revoked and it was provided that the Island of Tobago should become a Ward of the United Colony of Trinidad and Tobago; that the revenue, expenditure and debt of Tobago should be merged with those of the United Colony; that the debt due from Tobago to Trinidad should be cancelled; that (with some specified exceptions) the laws of Trinidad should operate in Tobago, and those of Tobago cease to operate so far as they conflicted with the laws of Trinidad; that all future Ordinances of the Legislature of the Colony should extend to Tobago, with the proviso that the Legislature should be able to enact special and local ordinances and regulations applicable to Tobago as distinguished from the rest of the Colony. This Order in Council was brought into effect on 1st January 1899 by a Proclamation of the Governor. The post of Commissioner for the island of Tobago then ceased to exist and the post of Warden was created instead.

In 1924 the elective principle was introduced for the formation of the Legislative Council. Adult suffrage and further steps towards self-government and independence then followed (*see* Constitutional Development *below*).

The discovery of oil in the south of Trinidad and its exploitation after 1910 made it the most important industry but agriculture continued to play a major role. In 1931 sugar regained its lead over cocoa as the most important agricultural industry and today oil, sugar (with its by-products, molasses and rum), cocoa, asphalt, chemicals, coffee and fertilisers constitute the main exports. There has been a steady expansion of the manufacturing industry since 1950, assisted by pioneer aid legislation.

Constitutional development

The Trinidad and Tobago (Legislative Council) Order in Council 1924 (subsequently amended by Orders in Council of 1928, 1941, 1942 and 1945) was the authority for the 1924 Constitution. It was history-making as it introduced for the first time limited elected representation in Trinidad (Tobago had had elections before) and for the first time for Trinidad and Tobago as a united country. This Constitution provided for seven elected members, twelve official members and six nominated members.

The 1945 amending Order in Council brought into effect universal adult suffrage and reduced the qualifications for election as a member of the Legislative Council. In February 1947, following a resolution moved by one of the elected members of the Legislative Council, a Committee was appointed to consider the reform of the Constitution; its report, and subsequent discussions, led to the introduction of the Constitution of 1950.

The Constitution of 1950, subsequently amended in 1956 and 1959, provided for a unicameral legislature (Legislative Council) with an elected majority, the composition being three *ex-officio* members, five nominated members and eighteen elected members, presided over by a Speaker, with neither an original nor a casting vote, appointed by the Governor from outside the Council. Other provisions were: an Executive Council, which was the chief instrument of policy, comprising three *ex-officio* members, one nominated member and five elected members elected by the Legislative Council; a quasi-ministerial system in which members of the Executive Council were associated with the administrative work of Government Departments; reserve powers of the Governor to be exercisable with the consent of the Executive Council, but in the event of their refusing to give such consent, with the approval of the Secretary of State; a Public Service Commission.

After further changes introduced by Orders in Council in 1956, 1958 and 1959, the Constitution in 1959 provided for a Legislative Council consisting of a Speaker elected by the members; two *ex-officio* members (the Chief Secretary and the Attorney-General), five members nominated by the Governor and twenty-four elected members. The Cabinet consisted of nine Ministers including the Premier, who were elected members of the Legislative Council, and two *ex-officio* members (the Chief Secretary and the Attorney-General), neither of whom was entitled to vote. The Governor did not normally preside at Cabinet meetings, but had the power to call special meetings of the Cabinet and, if he did so, to preside over them. With certain exceptions, the Governor had to consult with the Cabinet in the exercise of his powers and act in accordance with its advice. At this stage, the Constitution also contained provisions for the establishment of a Judicial and Legal Service Commission and a Police Service Commission, as well as a Public Service Commission. The Governor was bound to accept the recommendations of these Commissions on appointments and promotions, except in respect of a few special posts.

In elections held on 24th September 1956, under the 1950 Constitution, as amended, the People's National Movement (PNM) gained thirteen seats and formed a Government under the leadership of Dr Eric Williams. The People's Democratic Party (now the Democratic Labour Party—DLP) gained five seats; the Home Rule Party two seats; the Trinidad Labour Party two seats and Independents two seats.

After further Constitutional discussions held in London in November 1959 and June 1960, the Secretary of State for the Colonies announced agreement on a new Constitution providing for full internal self-government with a bicameral legislature consisting of a nominated Senate and an elected

House of Representatives. This new Constitution was brought fully into operation following the General Election held on 4th December 1961, at which the PNM was again returned to power, winning twenty of the seats in the House of Representatives and polling 58 per cent of the total votes cast. The DLP won the remaining ten seats polling 39.7 per cent of the total votes cast. The 1960 Constitution provided that of the twenty-one nominated members of the Senate, twelve should be appointed on the advice of the Premier, two on the advice of the Leader of the Opposition and seven by the Governor at his discretion to represent special interests. The Cabinet was to consist of the Premier (as the Chief Minister was now called) and not more than eleven other Ministers (of whom one would be the Attorney-General). There was a wholly-elected House of Representatives of 30 members which was later increased to 36 members. The People's National Movement was again returned at the General Election held on 7th November 1966, winning 24 of the 36 seats in the Lower House and polling 52 per cent of the votes cast. The Democratic Labour Party, which won the remaining 12 seats and polled 34 per cent of votes cast, again formed the Opposition.

In 1958 the Federation of the West Indies was formed with a membership consisting of Trinidad and Tobago, Jamaica, Barbados and the Leeward and Windward Islands. Agreement had been reached in principle on a Constitution under which the Federation would proceed to Independence on 31st May 1962; but in September 1961 the Jamaican Government held a referendum on the question of membership of the Federation which resulted in a vote in favour of withdrawal. The British and Jamaican Governments subsequently agreed that Jamaica would withdraw from the Federation and would proceed to Independence on its own. As a consequence, on 14th January 1962, the General Council of the People's National Movement unanimously approved a resolution that Trinidad and Tobago should also proceed forthwith to independence without prejudice to the possibility of the territory's future association in a unitary state with other territories in the East Caribbean. The resolution also requested the Government to take the initiative in proposing the maximum possible measure of collaboration between the former members of the Federation of the West Indies regarding common services, and to declare their willingness to take part in and work for a Caribbean economic community. This resolution was endorsed at a special convention of the party held towards the end of January and the Government accepted the terms of the resolution as their policy in this matter. In April the Secretary of State for the Colonies, in reply to a despatch from the Governor, agreed that Trinidad and Tobago should become independent as early as practicable in 1962, and proposed that, provided the necessary steps could be taken in time, an independence conference should be held in London towards the end of May to agree upon a constitution and the date of independence.

Meanwhile, in February, the Government of Trinidad and Tobago had published the first draft of an independence constitution: this was distributed widely in the territory, and organisations and the general public were invited to submit written comments on it by 31st March. Over 160 memoranda were received, and from 25th to 27th April the Government held meetings with those who had submitted memoranda, at which the draft constitution was considered. The draft constitution, as amended in the light of these consultations, was considered by a Joint Select Committee of the Senate and House of Representatives, after which it was debated and, on 11th May, approved by a majority of 16 to 9 in the House of Representatives.

The revised draft of the independence constitution, as approved by the Legislature, formed the basic document at the Trinidad and Tobago Independence Conference held in London between 28th May and 8th June 1962. At this Conference, at which the Trinidad and Tobago delegation unanimously expressed the wish that an independent Trinidad and Tobago should be accepted as a member of the Commonwealth, it was agreed that Trinidad and Tobago should become independent on 31st August 1962. On 1st August 1976 Trinidad and Tobago became a Republic within the Commonwealth. The first President was His Excellency Ellis Clarke, who was formerly Governor-General. He was elected by an electoral college for a second term of five years in 1981. In September 1980 the Tobago House of Assembly Bill was passed, the provisions of which afforded Tobago a certain degree of self-administration. The House of Assembly is composed of 12 elected members and 3 Councillors elected by the former. The Prime Minister of Trinidad and Tobago is responsible for Tobago.

Constitution

The Constitution of the Republic of Trinidad and Tobago provides for the election of a President by an electoral college comprising all members of the Senate and House of Representatives. The President holds office for five years. The Senate (Upper House) consists of 31 Senators, 16 of whom are appointed on the advice of the Prime Minister, 6 on the advice of the Leader of the Opposition and 9 by the President from economic, social or other fields of endeavour. The House of Representatives (Lower House) has 36 seats. There is universal adult suffrage. The normal life of Parliament is 5 years.

The Cabinet consists of the Prime Minister, who must be a member of the House of Representatives, and such other Ministers as the President, acting on the advice of the Prime Minister, appoints from the Senators and members of the House of Representatives. The Attorney-General must be a member of the Cabinet. The President appoints as leader of the Opposition the member of the House of Representatives who, in his judgement, is the leader in the House of the party commanding support of the largest number of members of the House in opposition to the Government.

The principal provisions of the constitution are entrenched and, of these, the most important are specially entrenched. The ordinary entrenched provisions can only be amended by a vote of two-thirds of all the members of both Houses; these include the provisions relating to human rights and freedoms, prorogation of Parliament, appointment, etc, of judical officers, the various Service Commissions and the office and functions of the Auditor-General. Specially entrenched provisions can only be altered by a vote of three-quarters of all the members of the House of Representatives and two-thirds of the Senate. The specially entrenched provisions included among other things those concerning the office of the President, the establishment of Parliament and the composition of the two Houses, general elections and the appointment of Senators, the establishment of boundaries and election commissions and matters affecting the Judiciary.

There is a Supreme Court of Judicature, consisting of a High Court and a Court of Appeal, and in certain cases a further appeal lies to the Judical Committee of Her Majesty's Privy Council. The Chief Justice is appointed by the President acting on the advice of the Prime Minister. Puisne Judges are appointed by the President acting in accordance with the advice of the Judicial and Legal Service Commissions.

The Constitution also contains provisions relating to citizenship; an amendment to the Constitution in 1965 provided for a limited category of dual nationality.

Government

At the general election in December 1991 the People's National Movement won 21 seats, the United National Congress Party 13 seats and the National Alliance for Reconstruction 2 seats.

HEAD OF STATE

President: His Excellency Mr Noor Hassanali

THE CABINET

Prime Minister: The Hon Patrick Manning, MP

Minister in the Office of the Prime Minister: Senator The Hon Gordon Draper

Minister of Planning and Development and Minister in the Office of the Prime Minister: Senator The Hon Dr Lenny Saith

Minister of Finance: The Hon Wendell Mottley, MP

Minister of Local Government and Minister in the Ministry of Finance: The Hon Kenneth Valley, MP

Minister of National Security: Senator The Hon Russel Huggins

Attorney General and Minister for Legal Affairs: The Hon Keith Sobion, MP

Minister of Foreign Affairs: The Hon Ralph Maraj, MP

Minister of Trade, Industry and Tourism: Senator The Hon Brian Kuei Tung

Minister of Energy and Energy based Industries: Senator The Hon Barry Barnes

Minister of Labour and Cooperatives: The Hon Kenneth Collis, MP

Minister of Education: The Hon Agustus Ramrekersingh, MP

Minister of Health: The Hon John Eckstein, MP

Minister of Works and Transport: The Hon Colm Imbert, MP

Minister of Public Utilities: The Hon Morris Marshall, MP

Minister of Agriculture, Lands and Marine Resources: The Hon Dr Keith Rowley, MP

Minister of Housing and Settlement: The Hon Dr Vincent Lasse, MP

Minister of Community Development, Culture and Women's Affairs: Senator The Hon Joan Yuille-Williams

Minister of Sport and Youth Affairs: The Hon Jean Pierre, MP

Minister of Consumer Affairs and Social Services: The Hon Dr Linda Baboolal, MP

Minister of Information: Senator The Hon Camille Robinson-Regis

PARLIAMENTARY SECRETARIES

Ministry of Sport and Youth Affairs: Mr Edward Hart, MP

Ministry of Agriculture, Lands and Marine Resources: Mr Andrew Cassimire, MP

Ministry of Works and Transport: Mr Jarette Narine

Ministry of Labour and Cooperatives: Senator Stanford Callender

MINISTRIES AND GOVERNMENT DEPARTMENTS

PRIME MINISTER'S OFFICE

Permanent Secretaries: John Andrews (Head of the Public Service); Ronald Cuffy; Mrs Lenore Dorset; Mrs Katherine Boswell-Inniss

OFFICE OF THE ATTORNEY-GENERAL

Permanent Secretary: Kemchan Ramdath

MINISTRY OF FOOD PRODUCTION AND MARINE EXPLOITATION

Permanent Secretary: Winston Rudder

MINISTRY OF LABOUR, EMPLOYMENT AND MANPOWER RESOURCES

Permanent Secretary: Louis McShine

MINISTRY OF EXTERNAL AFFAIRS AND INTERNATIONAL TRADE

Permanent Secretaries: Trevor Spencer; David Punch

MINISTRY OF WORKS, INFRASTRUCTURE AND DECENTRALISATION

Permanent Secretaries: Joseph Allard; Rene Wilkie

MINISTRY OF PLANNING AND MOBILISATION
Permanent Secretary: Carlyle Greaves

MINISTRY OF HEALTH
Permanent Secretary: Errol Pilgrim

MINISTRY OF JUSTICE AND NATIONAL SECURITY
Permanent Secretaries: Ainsley Tim Pow; Dr B August

MINISTRY OF ENVIRONMENT AND NATIONAL SERVICE
Permanent Secretary: Derek Commissiong

MINISTRY OF SOCIAL DEVELOPMENT AND FAMILY SERVICES
Permanent Secretary: Louis J Bryan

MINISTRY OF YOUTH, SPORT, CULTURE AND CREATIVE ARTS
Permanent Secretary: Annette des Isles

MINISTRY OF EDUCATION
Permanent Secretary: Hart Edwards

MINISTRY OF INDUSTRY, ENTERPRISE AND TOURISM
Permanent Secretaries: Neville Blake; Harold Atwell

MINISTRY OF FINANCE
Permanent Secretary: Reynold Rampersad

MINISTRY OF SETTLEMENTS AND PUBLIC UTILITIES
Permanent Secretary: Ainsworth Harewood

SERVICE COMMISSIONS
Public Service Commission Chairman: Kenneth Lala
Police Service Commission Chairman: Kenneth Lala
Elections and Boundaries Commission Chairman: Sir Isaac Hyatali
Judicial and Legal Service Commission Chairman: Chief Justice, The Hon Mr Clinton Bernard

TEACHING SERVICE COMMISSION
Chairman: Trevor Lee

PUBLIC UTILITIES COMMISSION
Chairman: Edward Beckles

Tuvalu

Capital: Funafuti

Tuvalu, which is the name taken by the former Ellice Islands in October 1975 when they separated from the Gilberts, comprises nine islands situated in the South West Pacific between 5° and 11°S. and 176° and 180° E. The total land area is only 26 sq. km (10 square miles), and the islands lie in a chain running in a North West to South East line some 595 km (370 miles) in length. The islands are remote from large centres of civilisation: Suva is 1,046 km (650 miles) from the capital Funafuti and Sydney is 4,025 km (2,500 miles) away.

The islands are atolls composed of coral reefs built on the outer arc of the ridges formed by pressure from the central Pacific against the ancient core of Australia. In five of the atolls the reef encloses sizeable lagoons, but in the case of the remaining four, the islands comprise only pinnacles of land rising sheer from the ocean bed. Only at Funafuti and Nukufetau can ships enter the lagoons. Elsewhere in all but the calmest weather there are no anchorages. The surface of the islands seldom rises more than 4.5 m above sea level.

The climate of Tuvalu is pleasant but monotonous. There are no marked wet and dry, or hot and cold seasons. The country is situated North of the recognised hurricane belt though the islands have been struck three times in modern times by severe cyclones in 1894, 1972 and 1990. The mean temperature is 30°C (86°F) and the heat is moderated by trade winds which blow from the East for much of the year. Rainfall averages 3,535 mm per annum.

A census of the population was held in 1985 and showed 8,229 Tuvaluans living in the country at the time. It was estimated that approximately a further 700 were overseas on census day, mainly working in the phosphate industry on Nauru or employed in overseas ships. The total number, thus, who call Tuvalu their home is now about 9,000. The people are almost entirely of Polynesian stock and have close ties with the Samoans and Tokelauans to the south and east. Population density in the islands is extremely high with an average of 317 persons per square kilometre.

The main languages spoken are Tuvaluan and English. Almost the entire population is Christian and predominantly Protestant.

Agriculture is virtually non-existent on the islands due to the poor quality of the soil which is composed largely of coral sand and rock fragments. The major part of all islands is covered with coconut palms which provide an important source of food and drink, and with copra the only cash crop. Sea fishing is excellent. Vessels from Japan, South Korea and Taiwan are currently allowed to fish under licence within Tuvaluan waters. Early in 1982 a fishing vessel, Te Tautai, was presented to Tuvalu as part of the Japanese aid programme. Crewed mainly by Tuvaluans, the vessel undertakes commercial fishing both inside and outside Tuvalu's territorial waters. In 1987 Tuvalu together with country members of the Forum Fisheries Agency finalised a multilateral Fisheries Agreement with the Government of the United States of America through which American fishing vessels could fish under licences inside EEZ's of the countries. Tuvalu signed the agreement in mid 1987, and expects to receive substantial income from licences under this agreement. There is little useful timber. The main food crops, apart from coconuts are pulaka, a species of taro, pandanus fruit, bananas and occasionally pawpaws.

The people of the territory maintain a reasonable standard of living by intensive exploitation of the sea, reefs and atolls, and by sending their young men out to work. Substantial numbers are employed in the phosphate industry on Nauru. Others work as seamen in overseas ships. All are intensely loyal to their families at home remitting on average about 70 per cent of their wages.

The value of imports into Tuvalu in 1989 was A$5,170,307 (FOB) and of exports from Tuvalu A$79,116.

The only real export is copra. Hurricane Bebe in 1972 had a very adverse effect upon the amount of copra produced in the following years. In 1979 the territory exported 528 tonnes, valued at A$226,521; by 1982 production had fallen to 243 tonnes and in 1983 copra production was 340 tonnes, valued at A$103,250. Since 1st January 1976, a copra co-operative has been responsible for purchasing copra from producers for sale overseas. The low price of copra on the commodity markets has meant that producers are currently receiving very low prices.

Postage stamps have been an important source of foreign exchange, accounting for 48 per cent and 70 per cent of export for the years 1984 and 1985 respectively, but this has recently fallen dramatically.

The only port is Funafuti, the capital. Vessels up to 30 feet draught can enter the lagoon and berth at the new deepwater wharf, completed in October 1980.

The only airfield is again on Funafuti. It is a grass strip unsuitable for jets. Fiji Air used to operate three flights a week using a Heron aircraft but this service terminated in May 1990 pending Fiji Air's acquisition of a suitable alternative aircraft. The Airline of the Marshall Islands runs a twice weekly service using HS–748.

Funafuti, the former district centre, although devastated by hurricane Bebe in 1972, was selected as capital of the new territory on separation from the Gilberts. The headquarters of the five Ministries and the Governor-General's Office are situated there, together with almost all organs of government and commerce in the country. Only the agricultural division was based elsewhere—on Vaitupu which is the island with the largest land area and the site of the secondary school, before it was moved to Funafuti. There is a hospital at Funafuti with 30 general beds, four maternity beds and two public wards. All islands are served by a dispensary, wireless station, post office, government's executive office and primary school.

Filarial fever was common but a WHO scheme completed in 1975 has virtually eliminated the disease. Mosquito-borne dengue fever is occasionally present, but there is no malaria. Health in the islands is generally good.

In 1989 there were 1,381 children receiving primary education in 9 schools and 294 children were undergoing secondary courses at Motufoua School. Motufoua School at Vaitupu, previously a church school is now run by the Government. There is only one training institution, a Maritime Training School opened at Funafuti in 1979. Teachers, nurses, technicians, and trainees for Government service are sent to suitable institutions in Fiji, New Zealand, Australia or other Pacific countries.

The Tuvalu Broadcasting Service (call sign T2U2) transmits daily in the medium wave band 621 (kHz) from (local time) 0630 hrs to 0745 hrs and 1130 hrs to 1300 hrs everyday except Saturday and from 1800 hrs to 2100 hrs Monday to Sunday.

As from 1st January 1983 Government introduced a Sales Tax of 5 per cent on the landed cost of all goods. At the same time, the rates of income tax and personal allowances were changed in a move away from direct taxation. There is now a standard rate of 30 cents in the dollar on all income of an individual in excess of A$1,900. Companies taxation was revised upwards in 1984 to 40 per cent on the net chargeable profit. Island Councils have a wide range of rating powers and also levy a head tax, landowners' tax (based on area and fertility), licence fees and other dues, import duties, income tax, sales tax, fisheries licence fees and philatelic sales which are the main source of revenue.

The budget for 1991 estimates total expenditure of some A$5,413,579 of which A$4,432,500 will be financed from local sources and the remainder by contributions from the Tuvalu Trust Fund. The Development Budget provides for expenditure of some A$1.3 m from Australia, A$1.5 m from New Zealand, A$1.5 m from the United Kingdom, A$2.34 m from Taiwan, A$900,000 from the EDF, A$900,000 from the UNDP, A$500,000 from Japan, A$250,000 from France and A$200,000 from the United States. Other aid donors, including Canada, Germany, South Korea CFTC and Forum Secretariat account for a further A$687,000 of planned project expenditure.

History

The Tuvaluans are a Polynesian people and their language shows strong affinities with those of Tonga, Niue and Samoa. Tradition speaks of Samoa as their original home and it is probable that the islands were settled accidentally by parties drifting westwards with the prevailing wind from the larger Polynesian islands in the central Pacific. The islands have ample rain which provides a much more luxuriant vegetation than is found in the neighbouring Gilberts and life is reasonably carefree. Existence seems always to have been peaceful apart from comparatively rare stories of marauders coming to their shores from the Gilberts and Tonga, blackbirders and World War II.

It is thought that the first time Europeans set eyes on Tuvalu was when Mendana sighted Nui in 1568 and Niulakita in 1595. Following these early Spanish sightings further contact was not made until the latter part of the 18th and first quarter of the 19th century. The last islands to experience contact with Europeans were Niutao and Vaitupu in 1826.

The Reverend A W Murray of the London Missionary Society visited the islands from Samoa in 1865. He placed Samoan pastors on the islands. The new faith was universally embraced and all aspects of island life not conforming with the strict tenets of these pastors were cast aside. The territory still remains predominantly Protestant though there are small Catholic communities on Nanumea and Nui, and lately the Bahai'is, Jehovah's Witnesses and Seventh Day Adventists have gained a footing in Funafuti. The island people are staunch Church goers and religion is a powerful factor in everyday life for a large majority.

In 1892 after Captain Davis had proclaimed the Gilbert islands to be a British Protectorate, Captain Gibson of HMS *Curacoa*, having ascertained the wishes of the inhabitants, declared a protectorate in the Ellice Islands and the British flag was hoisted. The headquarters of the Gilbert and Ellice Islands Protectorate was established at Tarawa and district magistrates were assigned to the various islands. A simple code of laws was drawn up based on earlier mission legislation, and the councils of old men were transformed into native courts to administer them. The people were gathered into orderly villages and an era dawned of simple administration through the Native Governments guided by a very small number of European officers. In 1915, after consultations and at the wish of the Native Governments, the Gilbert and Ellice Islands were annexed by an Order in Council which came into effect on 12th January 1916.

From 1942 to 1943 the Gilbert Islands were occupied by the Japanese. The Administration established a temporary headquarters at Sydney, Australia, which was transferred to Funafuti when United States forces occupied the Ellice group. From there, the Government controlled a war-time administration over the Ellice, Phoenix and Line Islands until, in November 1943, the United States forces drove the Japanese from the Gilberts. Officers of the Administration accompanying the military forces set up headquarters on Tarawa.

The Gilbert and Ellice Islands Colony came under the jurisdiction of the High Commissioner for the Western Pacific until 1st January 1972, when a Governor was appointed. An Order in Council in October 1971 withdrew the Colony from the High Commissioner's jurisdiction except for certain judicial matters.

The steps towards the present system of Government began in 1963, when by an Ordinance enacted by the High Commissioner, an Advisory Council was established whose function was to advise the then Resident Commissioner on matters relating to administration. The Advisory Council consisted of the Resident Commissioner as President, the Assistant Resident Commissioner as *ex-officio* Member, not more than 4 Official Members and not less than 8 and not more than 12 Unofficial Members. The Gilbert and Ellice Islands Order in Council 1963 provided for an Executive Council consisting of the Assistant Resident Commissioner as *ex-officio* member, not more than 3 Official Members and not more than 4 Unofficial Members.

The Gilbert and Ellice Islands Order 1967 made provision for the government of the territory. It established a Governing Council consisting of the Assistant Resident Commissioner and the Attorney-General, *ex-officio;* not more than 3 appointed members; and 5 elected members. The Governing Council replaced the Executive Council and had legislative as well as executive functions. The Order also established a House of Representatives consisting of the Assistant Resident Commissioner and the Attorney-General *ex-officio;* up to 5 appointed members and 23 elected members. The Resident Commissioner presided over both the House and the Council. The elected members of the House selected from among their own members 5 members (one of whom was elected as Chief Elected Member) for the Governing Council. The House advised the Governing Council on proposed legislation and other public matters were referred to it by the Council or raised by individual members of the House.

In 1970 the next step on the path of constitutional development was approved. The Gilbert and Ellice Islands Order 1970 made new provision for the government of the territory. It established a Legislative Council and Executive Council to replace the House of Representatives and Governing Council. The Legislative Council consisted of 3 *ex-officio* members, 2 public service members and 28 elected members, elected under the principle of universal adult suffrage. The Executive Council comprised the *ex-officio* and public service members of the Legislative Council, a Leader of Government Business elected by members of the Legislative Council and 4 appointed members from the Legislative Council.

On 1st May 1974 a Ministerial system of government was introduced. A House of Assembly with 28 elected and 3 *ex-officio* members replaced the Legislative Council. A Chief Minister was elected by Assembly members and he advised the Governor on the appointment of not less than 4 and not more than 6 ministers 2 of whom had to be Ellice Islanders. The Governor presided in the Council of Ministers which consisted of the Chief Minister, the other Ministers, the Deputy Governor, Attorney-General and Financial Secretary. The Governor, obliged to consult the Council of Ministers on all matters of importance, retained special responsibility for external affairs, defence, security and the public service.

After separation from the Gilbert Islands (see below) a General Election was held on 29th August, 1977 for 12 members of the House of Assembly which became the House of Parliament at the time of Independence. This Parliament was dissolved in July 1981. On 8th September 1981 a General Election was held again returning 12 members of Parliament, and Dr Puapua defeated the incumbent Prime Minister Mr Toaripi Lauti.

In September 1985 a further General Election was held and Dr Puapua was subsequently re-elected as Prime Minister.

Tuvalu most recently went to the polls in September 1989; Mr Bikenibeu Paeniu then became Prime Minister.

A very important recent step has been the establishment on 16th June 1987 of the Tuvalu Trust Fund totalling A$27 m with contributions from the Governments of Australia, New Zealand, the United Kingdom, Japan, Republic of Korea and Tuvalu itself; in aid terms, a great innovation.

The Fund is invested through commercial fund managers and the net income each year paid to Tuvalu for its recurrent budget, giving it a degree of financial independence which it has not previously experienced.

Land policy

Since 1917 the sale of land to non-natives has been prohibited. Before 1892 there were, of course, no legal restrictions on alienation and between 1892 and 1917 limited alienation was permitted. Fortunately, in Tuvalu there was no serious loss of land to the islanders during these periods.

Constitution and Separation of GEIC

On 1st October 1974 the result of a referendum held to determine the future of the Ellice Islands revealed that the majority of Ellice Islanders were in favour of separating from the Gilbert Islands and forming a new Colony. The Government of the Gilbert and Ellice Islands subsequently confirmed that the wishes of the majority of the Ellice Islanders would be respected. New separate constitutions for the Ellice, which was renamed Tuvalu, and the Gilberts came into force on 1st October 1975 and administrative separation was implemented on 1st January 1976.

Tuvalu came into being at the same level of constitutional development as had obtained in the former Colony, with a Chief Minister, 2 other Ministers, and 5 Members of the House of Assembly. The Queen's representative, responsible to the Secretary of State in London for foreign affairs, defence, internal security and finance, was styled Her Majesty's Commissioner and presided over the Cabinet. The Attorney General and Financial Secretary were both *ex-officio* members of Cabinet and the House of Assembly,

Between separation and independence, Tuvalu saw further constitutional changes, with an increase in the number of Members of the House of Assembly to 12 (2 from each of the 4 most highly populated islands, and one each from the remainder—for electoral purposes Niulakita is regarded as part of Niutao) and in May 1978 a move to full internal self government with one additional Minister and the Chief Minister becoming Chairman of Cabinet and responsible for finance.

As the result of the Constitutional Conference in London in February 1978, Tuvalu became independent on October 1st 1978, with a Governor-General, Prime Minister, 4 other Ministers, and 7 Members of Parliament. The Attorney-General, although not an *ex-officio* member of Parliament or Cabinet, is required by law to attend meetings of both bodies, and also fulfils the functions of Director of Public Prosecutions. Eight island courts are constituted under Island Courts Act (Cap 3) by which island courts have limited jurisdiction, in respect of both Tuvaluans and non-Tuvaluans, in civil and criminal matters, and a similar group of courts has jurisdiction in respect of land matters. A Senior Magistrate visits Tuvalu two or three times each year to hear more serious cases and appeals, and there is a High Court of Tuvalu with a Chief Justice who also comes twice a year for court sessions. There is a police force of 32 men. At independence Tuvalu joined the Commonwealth as a Special Member.

A new Constitution was established and came into effect on 1st October 1986, the eighth anniversary of independence. This was adopted after thorough consultation with all the island communities and maneapas (meeting houses). While retaining many of the features of the Independence Constitution, it introduces changes to take account throughout of the special Tuvaluan values of interdependence among the people on small coral atolls spread across hundreds of miles of the South Pacific Ocean, often completely isolated for long periods; and of their ways of agreement and consensus rather than confrontation.

On all islands except Niulakita local government councils have been established under the Local Government Act (Cap 19), which provides the framework for a policy aimed at developing local government authorities able to accept responsibility for, and to finance, the local services required at island level. These local government councils have power, subject to the approval of the responsible Minister, to make bye-laws on a wide range of subjects and are charged with the duty of providing services for the general health, security and well being of the inhabitants of their respective islands.

HEAD OF STATE

Her Majesty Queen Elizabeth II

GOVERNOR GENERAL

H E The Rt Hon Sir Toaripi Lauti, PC, GCMG

THE CABINET

Prime Minister (also Minister for Foreign Affairs and Economic Planning): The Rt Hon Bikenibeu Paeniu, PC, MP

Deputy Prime Minister and Minister of Finance and Commerce: Hon Dr Alesana Seluka, MP

Minister of Home Affairs and Natural Resources: Hon Tomu Sione, MP, OBE

Minister of Works and Communications: Hon Ionatana Ionatana, MP, CVO, OBE

Minister for Health, Education and Community Affairs: Mrs Naama Maheu Latasi, MP

CHIEF JUSTICE

Hon Sir Gaven Donne, KBE

HOUSE OF PARLIAMENT

The Speaker: Hon Kokea Malua, MP

CIVIL ESTABLISHMENT

Attorney General: Hon David Ballantyne

Secretary to Government: Mr Tauaasa Taafaki, MBE

Deputy Secretary to Government: Mr Amasone Kilei

Secretary for Foreign Affairs and Economic Planning: Mr Ehele Sopoaga (Acting)

Secretary for Finance and Commerce: Mr Panapasi Nelesone

Ambassador to Fiji: (Vacant)

Secretary, Works and Communications: Mr Kelese Kolone

Secretary, Natural Resources Development: Mr Pokia Tihala

Secretary, Health, Education and Community Affairs: Mr David Cottingham

Secretary, Home Affairs and Rural Development: Mr Simeti K Lopati

Chief of Police: Mr Uaelesi Taafaki (Acting)

Principal Auditor: Mr Lotoala M Tealofi

Senior Medical Officer: Dr Falesene Salesa

Senior Magistrate: (Vacant)

Resident Magistrate: Mr Mavaega Kaua

Uganda

Capital: Kampala

Uganda is near the centre of the continent of Africa. It is bounded on the east by Kenya, on the south by Tanzania and Rwanda, on the west by Zaire and on the north by the Sudan. The distance from north to south of the country is about 644 km (400 miles) and from east to west about 563 km (350 miles).

The total area is 235,887 sq km (91,076 square miles), of which 42,383 sq km (16,364 square miles) are open water. This area of open water consists of parts of Lakes Victoria, Mobuto Sese Seko (Albert) and Edward and all of Lakes George and Kyoga. From Lake Victoria at Jinja the Nile begins its 6,114 km (3,800 miles) journey to the Mediterranean.

Lake Victoria is 1,116 m above sea level; in the north at the Sudan frontier the altitude is only 600 m. The ground rises towards Mount Elgon (4,253 m) in the east and towards the Ruwenzori Mountains in the west. The highest peak of the snow-capped Ruwenzori range is 5,038 m, the third highest mountain in Africa. Uganda has thus great variety of landscape and vegetation. There are hot, dry deserts in the north-east, rain forests in the west and south-east, the remainder being mostly tree-savannah with extensive swamps. Wildlife is varied but numbers have diminished considerably as a result of years of armed strife.

Over most of the country the weather is that of a perpetual summer, with hot sunshine, cool breezes and showers of rain. Temperature ranges at Entebbe are about 17.5°C (62°–64°F) minimum and 26°–27°C (77°–81°F) maximum. The mean annual rainfall at Entebbe is 1,586 mm.

The principal towns are Kampala, the capital (population including suburbs 800,000), Jinja (population 50,000), Mbale (population 28,000) and Masaka (30,000).

In 1961 the population was estimated to number some 6,845,000 of whom 6,751,000 were Africans, 11,600 Europeans, and the remainder mostly Asians. In mid-1965 it was estimated that the population was 7,551,000. The 1980 census put the population of Uganda at 12,636,179. The largest tribe was the Baganda with about three and a half million members. Other large tribes are the Basoga and Banyankole with over a million members each, but precise figures are unobtainable as the census results were not broken down by tribe. The provisional January 1991 census estimate is 16,583,000. The annual growth rate since 1980 has declined to 2.5 per cent from 2.8 per cent in the previous decade. Since the expulsion of Asians and foreigners, in and after 1972, the Asian and expatriate community has been of negligible size, though it has increased since the war of 1979 which deposed the military government. Twenty-four languages in various groups (Bantu, Nilotic and Hamitic) are spoken but English is the official language. No statistics are available giving information about the main religions but it is believed that one-third of the people are Roman Catholic, one-third Protestant, one-sixth Muslim and a sixth not conforming to any organised religion.

In 1989 Uganda had 8,041 primary schools with an enrolment of 2,522,800 children and 88,639 teachers; 238,467 students were enrolled in 854 secondary schools with 12,919 teachers. There were 15,166 students in teacher training colleges, 6,941 students in technical schools and institutes and 4,388 students in teacher, technical and commercial colleges.

In 1989 there were 6,318 students at Makerere University College, Kampala, having 600 teachers/lecturers. This institution opened as a technical school in 1921, became Makerere University College, a constituent college of the University of East Africa in 1963, and a separate national university in its own right on 1st July 1970. First degree courses are offered at Makerere in agriculture, arts, education, medicine, science, social administration, commerce, law, engineering, forestry, veterinary medicine and librarianship, and there are also postgraduate courses.

Having no sea coast, Uganda is dependent principally upon the railway line and road to Mombasa, Kenya, and a ferry and rail route to Dar es Salaam, Tanzania, for her imports and exports, although for cargoes of high value air freight is also becoming important. There are 1,237 km of mainline railways in Uganda between Tororo and Kasese and Tororo and Pakwach, though much of the track in the north and west is currently scarcely used. There are 27,536 km of roads and highways in varying states of disrepair, most of which are being renovated under the NRM government's Economic and Rehabilitation Programme.

Uganda's international airport is situated at Entebbe, 34 km from Kampala. The main runway is 3,600 m in length. There are also landing grounds at Tororo, Jinja, Soroti, Gulu, Arua, Kasese, Pakuba and Mbarara.

Radio Uganda and Uganda Television are both State controlled, as is the principal newspaper, New Vision which replaced the Uganda Times in 1986. There are also a number of private and independent newspapers and publications.

Britain's imports from Uganda in 1989 were £20.30 million, and Uganda imported from Britain in the same period goods to the value of £39.22 million.

Uganda Independence Day is 9th October.

History

Archaeological evidence points to human occupation of the area which is now Uganda from the earliest times. The pursuit of agriculture may have originated in the first millenium BC, probably coincidentally with Bantu settlement. For a time the earlier stone-age inhabitants and the agriculturalists continued to exist side by side, the former being gradually absorbed. The working of iron was learned perhaps a thousand years ago.

The fertility of the south and west of the country favoured the development of political institutions, and in those areas there grew up a number of highly coherent, centrally controlled units. Up to the nineteenth century the most powerful of these was Bunyoro, but in that century Buganda took the lead. In the north, different conditions had favoured the development of small tribal organisations.

During the nineteenth century, the first British traders, explorers and missionaries reached Uganda. Speke and Grant penetrated from the east coast of Africa in 1862; Baker from the north in 1864. In the 1870s there were unsuccessful attempts by Egypt to obtain control. In the late 1870s the first missionaries reached Buganda.

In 1888 British interests in East Africa were assigned by Royal Charter to the Imperial British East Africa Company, and in 1890 Captain (later Lord) Lugard was sent to represent the Company in Uganda. He concluded a treaty with the Kabaka of Buganda and established the Company's influence.

The cost of the Company's operations was, however, prohibitive, and in 1893 an Imperial Commissioner, Sir Gerald Portal, assumed the obligations and rights of the Company on behalf of the British Government. Buganda was formally declared a Protectorate in 1894; Bunyoro, Toro, Ankole and Busoga followed in 1896. New agreements were negotiated with Buganda, Toro and Ankole in 1900 and 1901.

The basic pattern of Uganda's economic development was laid down before the First World War, in spite of the Administration's pre-occupation with the suppression of an outbreak of sleeping sickness which devastated the country. Cotton growing by peasant farmers, introduced in 1904, flourished, and the development of this sector of the economy stimulated the growth of transport and communications. The construction of a network of all-weather roads was begun, and a connection with the coast was obtained by a shipping service across Lake Victoria to Kisumu in Kenya, which was linked to Mombasa by rail in 1901. In 1913 the Busoga Railway was completed, and this, with the system of waterways radiating from the Nile basin, helped the development of the area of fine cotton-growing soil in the eastern part of the country.

The 1914–18 War made considerable demands on manpower, and checked Uganda's economic progress, especially in the context of world depression in the early 1920s. Coffee was developed as an alternative cash crop, and the first sugar refinery was opened in 1924. By 1928 the railway from the coast had been extended as far as Jinja, and the completion of a bridge over the Nile in 1931 finally linked Kampala with the Indian Ocean.

Under British administration land policy prohibited acquisition by non-Africans of freehold title to land. As a result European settlement did not become a feature of Uganda's development; and in Buganda, where title to land was held almost exclusively by Africans, indiscriminate purchase and exploitation by non-Africans was eliminated. This was an important factor in the development of harmonious race relations in Uganda.

The war of 1939–45 also made great demands on Uganda's resources and the emphasis of Government policy in the immediate post-war period was upon economic rehabilitation and development, a programme which was greatly helped by the high prices obtainable for cotton and coffee.

Constitutional development

The Uganda Order in Council 1902 made provision for the government of the protectorate, and control was passed from the Foreign Office to the Colonial Office in 1905. By 1914 a series of boundary commissions had established the country's boundaries which remained unchanged until the present day except for the transfer of Rudolph Province to Kenya in 1926. In 1921 Executive and Legislative Councils were created, and the latter was expanded in 1953 to make it more representative. The Legislative Council was further increased in 1955, half the membership then being African. At the same time a ministerial system was introduced, a number of the ministers being non-officials. In 1958 direct elections of African Representative Members to the Legislative Council were held in a number of Districts. Buganda, however, did not take part and was consequently not represented in the new Council. The year 1960 saw further constitutional advance, with the general objects of broadening the composition of the Legislative Council and restricting its membership almost entirely to elected members, and of converting the Governor's Executive Council into a Council of Ministers. A Commission under Lord Munster considered the relationships between the Kingdoms and the Central Government.

A general election under the new arrangements was held in March 1961 and resulted in a majority for the Democratic Party, led by Mr Benedicto Kiwanuka, who became Chief Minister. Following a constitutional conference in London later the same year, Uganda attained internal self-government in March 1962 and Mr Kiwanuka became the first Prime Minister.

The new Constitution provided for a Legislature of a single Chamber, styled the National Assembly, consisting of a Speaker, 82 Elected Members and nine Specially Elected Members. Of the Elected Members, 21 were elected within Buganda (excluding the Municipality of Kampala) and the Buganda Lukiiko (Legislative Assembly) had the power to declare before each General Election that these Members should be elected by the Lukiiko itself. The executive power was to be exercised on behalf of Her Majesty by the Governor but, except in regard to certain reserved functions, he could assign responsibilities to Ministers and was normally required to act on the advice of the Cabinet which was collectively responsible to the National Assembly. Buganda's relationship with Uganda was defined as a federal one.

A general election held in April 1962 resulted in a majority for the Uganda People's Congress, supported until 24th August 1964 by the Kabaka Yekka, a Buganda political organisation. Mr Milton Obote, leader of the UPC, because Prime Minister.

At the opening of the new Parliament the Governor announced that his Ministers desired that Her Majesty should be Queen of independent Uganda and that Uganda would seek membership of the Commonwealth.

Following a further Constitutional Conference in London in June 1962 Uganda became an independent sovereign country and a Member of the Commonwealth on the 9th October 1962.

In 1963 the Uganda Parliament amended the Constitution so that from 9th October 1963 (the anniversary of Independence) Her Majesty The Queen would no longer be the Head of State of Uganda and instead would be a sovereign independent country with a citizen of Uganda as Head of State, to be known as 'President of Uganda'. The first holder of this office was the Kabaka of Buganda, Sir Edward Mutesa. At the same time Uganda expressed a desire to continue as a Member of the Commonwealth of which the Queen is the Head.

On 24th February 1966, the Prime Minister, the Hon Dr A M Obote, MP, announced that the Constitution had been suspended, except for certain specified subjects. On 2nd March 1966 it was announced that Dr Obote acting with the advice and consent of the Cabinet had declared that the executive authority of Uganda should be vested in the Prime Minister (instead of the President) and that the duties, powers and other functions performed or exercisable by the President or Vice-President should be vested in the Prime Minister. On 15th April in the National Assembly, Dr Obote announced the abrogation of the 1962 Constitution and moved a motion for the introduction of a new Constitution which was adopted by 55 votes to four. Dr Obote was then sworn in as President.

Under the 1966 Constitution, the President was both Head of State and Head of the Executive, advised by a Cabinet of Ministers of which he was a member. The National Assembly consisted of 82 elected members, all directly elected, including 21 from Buganda (exclusive of Kampala) and nine specially elected members. Parliament was to continue for five years unless sooner dissolved by the President, acing on the advice of the Cabinet.

In June 1967 the National Assembly resolved itself into a Constituent Assembly to consider proposals submitted to it by the Government for the amendment of the 1966 Constitution. After due consideration the proposals, as modified following debate, were adopted, and a new Constitution under which Uganda became a Republic was proclaimed on 8th September 1967. The main changes from the previous constitution were the abolition of the old kingdoms and the dissolution of Buganda into four districts for administrative purposes; and provision for specially elected members in number related to the strength of the party having greatest numerical strength in the National Assembly in order to give that party a majority of not more than 10. The number of elected members remained at 82. The powers of the President were defined and the rights and freedoms of the individual prescribed. It was decided that subject to the provisions of the Constitution for dissolution, the life of the Parliament should be five years from the introduction of the preceding constitution, *viz* 15th April 1966.

On 25th January 1971 the Commander of the Armed Forces, Major-General Idi Amin, mounted a successful *coup d'état* against Dr Obote. A military government was set up headed by General Amin as President. Parliament was dissolved and those Sections of the 1967 Constitution dealing with executive and legislative powers suspended. The President ruled by decree. The Cabinet remained in existence and a Defence Council, consisting of the Commanders of the Armed Forces and such other officers as might be co-opted from time to time, was set up.

Her Majesty's Government broke off diplomatic relations with Uganda in 1976; relations were restored only on the fall of Amin in 1979.

The increasing disregard for human rights which characterised Amin's government led to its unpopularity.

On 30th October 1978 Ugandan forces occupied the Kagera Salient, part of Tanzania and the area was then annexed to Uganda. Tanzanian and Ugandan exile forces counter-attacked and after a long campaign captured Kampala on 11th April 1979. Meanwhile Ugandan exile groups united at a conference held at Moshi in Tanzania from 23rd-25th March 1979 to form the Uganda National Liberation Front which pledged to hold free elections as soon as possible. A former Principal of Makerere University College, Professor Y K Lule was elected Chairman of the Front's Executive

Council. After the capture of Kampala, Professor Lule was sworn in on 13th April 1979 as President of Uganda together with his new government. On 20th June 1979, Professor Lule was replaced by Mr Godfrey Binaisa as President of the Republic of Uganda. On 10th May 1980 President Binaisa was replaced by a Presidential Commission as Head of State and by the Chairman of the Military Commission of the Uganda National Liberation Front, Mr Paulo Muwanga, as Head of Government.

Preparations for elections were put in hand and, at the request of the Ugandan authorities and of the leaders of the four contesting parties, the Commonwealth Secretary-General agreed on 21st November to send a team of observers drawn from nine Commonwealth countries (Australia, Barbados, Botswana, Canada, Cyprus, Ghana, India, Sierra Leone, and the UK) to monitor the elections. The elections were held on 10th–11th December 1980 and resulted in a victory for the Uganda People's Congress. The results were Uganda People's Congress 74 seats, Democratic Party 51 seats, Uganda Patriotic Movement one seat, Conservative Party nil. Twenty further members were nominated by Government, including 10 from the Uganda National Liberation Army (UNLA). Dr Milton Obote was sworn in as President of the Republic of Uganda on 15th December 1980.

President Obote's government was overthrown by a military coup on 27th July 1985. A ruling military council was formed headed by the Army Commander General Tito Okello who appointed the former Vice-President Paulo Muwanga to form a Cabinet. On 26th August Muwanga was replaced by Abraham Waligo. The same day talks began between the Government and the National Resistance Movement led by Yoweri Museveni, under the auspices of the President of Kenya, in Nairobi and concluded on 17th December 1985 with an agreement for a ceasefire and the formation of a new military council. However, a month later this agreement had not been implemented. Renewed fighting led to the capture of Kampala by the National Resistance Army and the installation of a new government headed by Yoweri Museveni who was sworn in as President on 29th January 1986 with the pledge to restore democratic rule by 1990. On 30th January Dr Samson Kisekka was appointed Prime Minister and some other ministerial appointments were announced. A National Resistance Council was also formed. President Museveni subsequently appointed a civilian cabinet including representatives from all four main political parties and most of the larger tribes. Wherever possible, Resistance Committees were set up as a new form of grassroots local government. Overt party political activity was suspended but party structures remain.

Constitutional development and economic recovery were impeded by renewed fighting which began in the North and North East later in 1986 when supporters of the former regime returned. However, in February 1989 a decree was promulgated dissolving the 1986 Military Council and introducing a new structure of Government built on the Resistance Council which had been set up in some parts of the country.

Elections were then held in most parts of the country for 8,096 Village Resistance Councils by universal adult suffrage through an open voting system. These Village Councils formed the first of a six-tier Resistance Council System in which the Councils of each tier elected Resistance Committees which in turn elected the Councils in the tier above. At level two there are 3,778 Parish Councils, at level three 750 Sub-County or 'Gombolola' Councils, at level four 149 County Councils and at level five 36 District Councils. The top tier is the National Resistance Council which functions as a National Parliament and itself elects a National Executive Committee as a national policy-making body distinct from the executive of the Present and Government Ministers.

The National Resistance Council comprises 58 members appointed by the President, comprising the 38 original members of the 1986 National Resistance Army, 20 others recommended by them, 10 members of the separate National Resistance Army Council elected by that body, one representative from each county elected by the sub-counties within each county meeting as an electoral college, a woman's representative elected by each of the 34 District Councils, three workers' representatives and five from youth representatives elected from Kampala and 14 from other towns; 278 members in all. The National Executive Committee, a standing Committee of the National Resistance Council, has the 38 original members of the National Resistance Army, 34 District elected members, 10 Presidentially appointed members and can have other members co-opted but without voting rights. This National Resistance Council structure remains non-party, though many individual members still retain party loyalty. The National Resistance Army Council comprises members of the High Command and senior army officers and has an advisory role but also takes part with the National Resistance Council in the election of the president and can intervene in other matters including the Constitution.

In February 1989 a Constitutional Commission was appointed to report within two years on a new political framework including the procedures for Presidential elections. As a result the Government was not able to meet the four-year target set in 1986 and in October 1989 a bill to extend the term of the present Government by up to five years from 25th January 1990 was approved. Further Constitutional developments now await the report of the Constitutional Commission, now expected in mid-1992.

Historical List

PRESIDENTS

Sir Edward Mutesa, 9th October 1963 to 24th February 1966

Dr A Milton Obote, from 15th April 1966 to 15th January 1971

Field Marshal Al-Hajji Dr Idi Amin Dada, from 20th February 1971 to 13th April 1979

Prof Y K Lule from 13th April 1979 to 20th June 1979
Mr Godfrey Binaisa from 20th June 1979 to 13th May 1980
Presidential Commission from 13th May to 15th December 1980
Dr A Milton Obote from 15th December 1980 to 27th July 1985
Lt-General Tito Okello from 27th July 1985 to 29th January 1986
Mr Yoweri K Museveni from 29th January 1986 to date

Government (July 1991)

MINISTERS

President & Minister of Defence: Lt-Gen Yoweri Kaguta Museveni
Vice-President & Minister of Internal Affairs: Mr Sansom Babi Kisekka
Prime Minister: Mr George Kosmos Adyebo
1st Deputy Prime Minister & National Political Commissar: Mr Eriya Kategaya
2nd Deputy Prime Minister & Minister of Foreign & Regional Affairs: Mr Paul Kawanga Ssemogerere
3rd Deputy Prime Minister & Minister of Justice/Attorney General: Mr Abubakar Mayanja
Minister of Agriculture, Animal Industry & Fisheries: Mrs Victoria Ssekitoleko
Minister of Commerce, Cooperatives and Marketing: Mr Richard Kaijuka
Minister of Education and Sports: Mr Amanya Mushega
Minister of Energy, Minerals & Environment Protection: Mr Henry Kajura
Minister of Finance: Dr Crispus Kiyonga
Minister of Health: Dr James Makumbi
Minister of Land, Housing & Urban Development: Dr Eric Adriko
Minister of Industry & Technology: Mr James W Wapakhabulo
Minister of Information & Broadcasting: Mr Paul Etiang
Minister of Tourism, Wildlife & Antiquities: Mr Sam Sebagereka
Minister of Labour & Social Welfare: Mr Ateker Ejalu
Minister of Local Government: Mr Jaberi Bidandi Ssali
Minister of Planning & Economic Development: Mr J S Mayanja-Nkangi
Minister of Public Service: Mr Tom Rubaale
Minister of Works, Transport & Communications: Dr Ruhakana-Rugunda
Minister of Women in Development, Culture & Youth: Dr Kazibwe Wandira Specioza

MINISTERS OF STATE

Office of the President (Karamoja): Mr Anthony Butele
Office of the President (Security): Mr Balaki Kirya
Office of the President (Presidential Affairs): Mr Kinto-Musoke
Office of the Prime Minister (Resident in the North): Mrs Betty Bigombe
Ministry of Defence: Maj-Gen David Tinyefuza
Ministry of Finance (Responsible for Custodian Board): Mr Moses Kintu
Ministry of Foreign & Regional Affairs: Mr Kirunda Kivejjinja
Ministry of Internal Affairs: Mr Tom Butime
Ministry of Justice & Constitutional Affairs: Mr Sam K Njuba
Ministry of Planning & Economic Development: Mr Matthew Rukikaire

DEPUTY MINISTERS

Ministry of Agriculture, Animal Industry & Fisheries: Mr Ojok Obwangamoi
Ministry of Commerce, Cooperatives & Marketing: Mr Gerald Ssendaula
Ministry of Education & Sports: Mr David Pulkol
Ministry of Labour & Social Welfare: Mrs Betty Okwir
Ministry of Land, Housing & Urban Development: Mr Besweri Mulondo
Ministry of Local Government: Dr Steven Chebrot
Ministry of Finance: Mr Abbey Kafumbe-Mukasa
Ministry of Industry & Technology: Mr Bart Katureebe
Ministry of Public Service & Cabinet Affairs: Mr Charles Alai
Ministry of Foreign & Regional Affairs: Mr Agard Didi

The United Kingdom of Great Britain and Northern Ireland

Capital: London

The House of Commons is composed of 651 Members representing 524 constituencies in England, 72 in Scotland, 38 in Wales and 17 in Northern Ireland. The Speaker and his three deputies do not by custom vote for their parties in the House. At 28th April 1992 the distribution of seats by party is:— Conservative 334, Labour 269, Liberal Democrats 20, Ulster Unionists 9, Ulster Democratic Unionist Party 3, Scottish National Party 3, Plaid Cymru 4, Ulster Popular Unionist 1, Social Democratic and Labour Party 4, The Speaker 1, Deputy Speakers 3.

HEAD OF STATE
Her Majesty Queen Elizabeth II

HER MAJESTY'S GOVERNMENT

(Formed by the Right Hon John Major, MP, April 1992)

THE CABINET

Prime Minister, First Lord of the Treasury and Minister for the Civil Service: The Rt Hon John Major, MP
Lord Chancellor: The Rt Hon The Lord MacKay of Clashfern
Secretary of State for Foreign and Commonwealth Affairs: The Rt Hon Douglas Hurd, CBE, MP
Chancellor of The Exchequer: The Rt Hon Norman Lamont, MP
Secretary of State for the Home Department: The Rt Hon Kenneth Clarke, QC, MP
President of the Board of Trade (Secretary of State for Trade and Industry): The Rt Hon Michael Heseltine, MP
Secretary of State for Transport: The Rt Hon John MacGregor, OBE, MP
Secretary of State for Defence: The Rt Hon Malcolm Rifkind, QC, MP
Lord Privy Seal and Leader of the House of Lords: The Rt Hon Lord Wakeham
Lord President of the Council and Leader of the House of Commons: The Rt Hon Antony Newton, OBE, MP
Minister of Agriculture, Fisheries and Food: The Rt Hon John Gummer, MP
Secretary of State for the Environment: The Rt Hon Michael Howard, QC, MP
Secretary of State for Wales: The Rt Hon David Hunt, MBE, MP
Secretary of State for Social Security: The Rt Hon Peter Lilley, MP
Chancellor of the Duchy of Lancaster: The Rt Hon William Waldegrave, MP
Secretary of State for Scotland: The Rt Hon Ian Lang, MP
Secretary of State for National Heritage: The Rt Hon David Mellor, QC, MP
Secretary of State for Northern Ireland: The Rt Hon Sir Patrick Mayhew, QC, MP
Secretary of State for Education and Science: The Rt Hon John Patten, MP
Secretary of State for Health: The Rt Hon Virginia Bottomley, JP, MP
Secretary of State for Employment: The Rt Hon Gillian Shephard, MP
Chief Secretary to the Treasury: The Rt Hon Michael Portillo, MP

LAW OFFICERS

Attorney General: The Rt Hon Sir Nicholas Lyell, QC, MP
Lord Advocate: The Rt Hon Lord Rodger of Earlsferry, QC
Solicitor-General: Sir Derek Spencer, QC, MP
Solicitor-General for Scotland: Thomas Dawson, Esq, QC

MINISTERS NOT IN THE CABINET

Parliamentary Secretary to the Treasury: The Rt Hon Richard Ryder, OBE, MP
Minister for Overseas Development: The Rt Hon Baroness Chalker of Wallasey
Ministers of State, Foreign and Commonwealth Office: The Rt Hon Douglas Hogg, QC, MP; The Rt Hon Tristan Garel-Jones, MP; The Rt Hon Alistair Goodlad, MP
Financial Secretary to the Treasury: Stephen Dorrell, Esq, MP
Paymaster General: The Rt Hon Sir John Cope, MP
Ministers of State, Home Office: The Rt Hon Earl Ferrers, DL; Peter Lloyd, Esq, MP; Michael Jack, Esq, MP
Ministers of State, Department of Trade and Industry: Minister for Industry: The Rt Hon Tim Sainsbury, MP; *Minister for Energy:* Tim Eggar, Esq, MP; *Minister for Trade:* Richard Needham, Esq, MP
Ministers of State, Department of Transport: Minister for Public Transport: Roger Freeman, Esq, MP; *Minister for Aviation and Shipping:* Earl of Caithness

Ministers of State, Ministry of Defence: Minister of State for the Armed Forces: The Rt Hon Archibald Hamilton, MP; *Minister of State for Defence Procurement:* Jonathan Aitken, Esq, MP

Minister of State, Ministry of Agriculture, Fisheries and Food: David Curry, Esq, MP

Ministers of State, Department of the Environment: Minister for Housing and Planning: Sir George Young, BT MP; *Minister for Local Government and Inner Cities:* John Redwood, Esq, MP; *Minister for the Environment and Countryside:* David Maclean, Esq, MP

Minister of State, Welsh Office: The Rt Hon Sir Wyn Roberts, MP

Minister of State, Department of Social Security: Minister for Social Security and Disabled People: The Rt Hon Nicholas Scott, MBE, MP

Minister of State, Scottish Office: The Rt Hon Lord Fraser of Carmyllie, QC

Ministers of State, Northern Ireland Office: Robert Atkins, Esq, MP; Michael Mates, Esq, MP

Minister of State, Department of Education and Science: Baroness Blatch, CBE

Minister of State, Department of Health: Minister for Health: Dr Brian Mawhinney, MP

Minister of State, Department of Employment: Michael Forsyth, Esq, MP

DEPARTMENTS OF STATE AND MINISTERS

AGRICULTURE, FISHERIES AND FOOD

Minister: The Rt Hon John Gummer, MP

Minister of State: David Curry, Esq, MP

Parliamentary Secretaries: Earl Howe; Hon Nicholas Soames, MP

CHANCELLOR OF THE DUCHY OF LANCASTER (OFFICE OF THE MINISTER FOR THE CIVIL SERVICE)

Prime Minister and Minister for the Civil Service: The Rt Hon John Major, MP

Chancellor of the Duchy of Lancaster: The Rt Hon William Waldegrave, MP

Parliamentary Under-Secretary of State: Robert Jackson, Esq, MP

DEFENCE

Secretary of State: The Rt Hon Malcolm Rifkind, QC, MP

Ministers of State: Minister of State for the Armed Forces: The Rt Hon Archibald Hamilton, MP

Minister of State for Defence Procurement: Jonathan Aitken, Esq, MP

Parliamentary Under-Secretary of State: Lord Cecil

EDUCATION AND SCIENCE

Secretary of State: The Rt Hon John Patten, MP

Minister of State: Baroness Blatch, CBE

Parliamentary Under-Secretaries of State: Eric Forth, Esq, MP; Nigel Forman, Esq, MP

EMPLOYMENT

Secretary of State: The Rt Hon Gillian Shephard MP

Minister of State: Michael Forsyth, Esq, MP

Parliamentary Under-Secretaries of State: Patrick McLoughlin, Esq, MP; Viscount Ullswater

ENVIRONMENT

Secretary of State: The Rt Hon Michael Howard, QC, MP

Ministers of State: Minister for Housing and Planning: Sir George Young, BT MP

Minister for Local Government and Inner Cities: John Redwood, Esq, MP

Minister for the Environment and Countryside: David Maclean, Esq, MP

Parliamentary Under-Secretaries of State: Tony Baldry, Esq, MP; Robin Squire, Esq, MP; Lord Strathclyde

FOREIGN AND COMMONWEALTH AFFAIRS

Secretary of State: The Rt Hon Douglas Hurd, CBE, MP

Minister for Overseas Development: The Rt Hon Baroness Chalker of Wallasey

Ministers of State: The Rt Hon Douglas Hogg, QC MP; The Rt Hon Tristan Garel-Jones, MP; The Rt Hon Alistair Goodlad, MP

Parliamentary Under-Secretary of State: The Hon Mark Lennox-Boyd, MP

HEALTH

Secretary of State for Health: The Rt Hon Virginia Bottomley, JP MP

Minister of State: Dr Brian Mawhinney, MP

Parliamentary Under-Secretaries of State: Baroness Cumberlege, CBE; Timothy Yeo, Esq, MP; The Hon Tom Sackville, MP

HOME OFFICE

Secretary of State for the Home Department: The Rt Hon Kenneth Clarke, QC, MP

Ministers of State: The Rt Hon Earl Ferrers DL; Peter Lloyd, Esq, MP; Michael Jack, Esq, MP

Parliamentary Under-Secretary of State: Charles Wardle, Esq, MP

LAW OFFICERS' DEPARTMENT

Attorney-General: The Rt Hon Sir Nicholas Lyell, QC, MP

Solicitor-General: Sir Derek Spencer, QC, MP

LORD ADVOCATE'S DEPARTMENT

Lord-Advocate: The Rt Hon Lord Rodger of Earlsferry, QC

Solicitor-General for Scotland: Thomas Dawson, Esq, QC

LORD CHANCELLOR'S DEPARTMENT

Lord Chancellor: The Rt Hon Lord Mackay of Clashfern

Parliamentary Under-Secretary of State: John M Taylor, Esq, MP

NATIONAL HERITAGE
Secretary of State: The Rt Hon David Mellor, QC, MP
Parliamentary Under-Secretary of State: Robert Key, Esq, MP

NORTHERN IRELAND OFFICE
Secretary of State for Northern Ireland: The Rt Hon Sir Patrick Mayhew, QC, MP
Ministers of State: Robert Atkins, Esq, MP; Michael Mates, Esq, MP
Parliamentary Under-Secretaries of State: Jeremy Hanley, Esq, MP; Earl of Arran

OVERSEAS DEVELOPMENT ADMINISTRATION
Minister for Overseas Development: The Rt Hon Baroness Chalker of Wallasey

PRIVY COUNCIL OFFICE
Lord Privy Seal and Leader of the House of Lords: The Rt Hon Lord Wakeham
Lord President of the Council and Leader of the House of Commons: The Rt Hon Antony Newton OBE, MP

SCOTTISH OFFICE
Secretary of State for Scotland: The Rt Hon Ian Lang, MP
Minister of State: The Rt Hon Lord Fraser of Carmyllie, QC
Parliamentary Under-Secretaries of State: Lord James Douglas-Hamilton, MP; Allan Stewart, Esq, MP; Sir Hector Monro, JP, DL, MP

SOCIAL SECURITY
Secretary of State for Social Security: The Rt Hon Peter Lilley, MP
Minister of State for Social Security and Disabled People: The Rt Hon Nicholas Scott, MBE, MP
Parliamentary Under-Secretaries of State: Lord Henley; Ann Widdecombe, MP; Alistair Burt, Esq, MP

TRADE AND INDUSTRY
President of the Board of Trade (Secretary of State for Trade and Industry): The Rt Hon Michael Heseltine, MP
Ministers of State: Minister for Industry: The Rt Hon Tim Sainsbury, MP; *Minister for Energy:* Tim Eggar, Esq, MP; *Minister for Trade:* Richard Needham, Esq, MP
Parliamentary Under-Secretaries of State: Parliamentary Under-Secretary of State for Technology: Edward Leigh, Esq, MP; *Parliamentary Under-Secretary of State for Consumer Affairs and Small Firms:* Baroness Denton of Wakefield, CBE; *Parliamentary Under-Secretary of State for Corporate Affairs:* Neil Hamilton, Esq, MP

TRANSPORT
Secretary of State for Transport: The Rt Hon John MacGregor, OBE, MP
Ministers of State: Minister for Public Transport: Roger Freeman, Esq, MP; *Minister for Aviation and Shipping:* The Rt Hon Earl of Caithness:
Parliamentary Under-Secretaries of State: Minister for Roads and Traffic: Kenneth Carlisle, Esq, MP; *Minister for Transport in London:* Steven Norris, Esq, MP

TREASURY
Prime Minister and First Lord of the Treasury: The Rt Hon John Major MP
Chancellor of the Exchequer: The Rt Hon Norman Lamont, MP
Chief Secretary: The Rt Hon Michael Portillo, MP
Financial Secretary: Stephen Dorrell, Esq, MP
Paymaster General: The Rt Hon Sir John Cope, MP
Economic Secretary: Anthony Nelson, Esq, MP
Parliamentary Secretary to the Treasury: The Rt Hon Richard Ryder, OBE, MP
Lords Commissioners: Greg Knight, Esq, MP; Irvine Patnick, Esq, OBE, MP; Nicholas Baker, Esq, MP; Timothy Wood, Esq, MP; Timothy Boswell, Esq, MP
Assistant Whips: Timothy Kirkhope, Esq, MP; David Davis, Esq, MP; Andrew Mackay, Esq, MP; Robert G Hughes, Esq, MP; James Arbuthnot, Esq, MP

WELSH OFFICE
Secretary of State for Wales: The Rt Hon David Hunt, MBE, MP
Minister of State: The Rt Hon Sir Wyn Roberts, MP
Parliamentary Under-Secretary of State: Gwilym Jones, Esq, MP

HER MAJESTY'S HOUSEHOLD
Lord Chamberlain: The Rt Hon Earl of Airlie, KT, GCVO
Lord Steward: Viscount Ridley, KG
Master of the Horse: Lord Somerleyton
Treasurer: David Heathcoat-Amory, Esq, MP
Comptroller: David Lightbown, Esq, MP
Vice-Chamberlain: Sydney Chapman, Esq, MP
Captain of the Honourable Corps of Gentlemen-at-Arms: The Rt Hon Lord Hesketh
Captain of the Queen's Bodyguard of the Yeomen of the Guard: Earl of Strathmore and Kinghorne
Lords in Waiting: Viscount Long, Viscount Astor, Viscount St Davids, Viscount Goschen
Baroness in Waiting: The Rt Hon Baroness Trumpington
Second Church Estates Commissioner, representing Church Commissioners: The Rt Hon Michael Alison, MP

LEADER OF THE OPPOSITION
The Rt Hon Neil Kinnock, MP

House of Commons
The Speaker: The Rt Hon Betty Boothroyd, MP
Chairman of Ways and Means: The Rt Hon Michael Morris, MP

First Deputy Chairman of Ways and Means: Geoffrey Lofthouse, MP
Second Deputy Chairman of Ways and Means: Dame Janet Fookes, MP
Speaker's Secretary: P J Kitcatt, Esq, CB
Clerk of the House of Commons: Sir Clifford Boulton, KCB
Serjeant at Arms: Sir Alan Urwick, KCVO, CMG

House of Lords
Lord Privy Seal and Leader of the House of Lords: The Rt Hon The Lord Wakeham
Lord Chancellor: The Rt Hon The Lord MacKay of Clashfern
Chairman of Committees: The Rt Hon The Lord Aberdare, KBE
Principal Deputy Chairman of Committees: The Baroness Serota
Clerk of the Parliaments: Michael Wheeler-Booth

NORTHERN IRELAND

Northern Ireland is a constituent part of the United Kingdom but for 50 years until 1972 was administered by a devolved government. The Northern Ireland Constitution Act 1973 and the Northern Ireland Act 1982 continue to provide for a measure of devolved government, mainly in social and economic matters. Before devolution can be implemented, Parliament must be satisfied that any new arrangements command widespread acceptance throughout the community. In the present absence of such agreement, the Secretary of State for Northern Ireland is responsible for the government of Northern Ireland under the Northern Ireland Act 1974. The Northern Ireland Assembly elected in 1982 was dissolved in June 1986. It performed only scrutinising, deliberative and consultative functions.

The Anglo-Irish Agreement, signed in 1985, contained an affirmation by both the UK and Irish Governments that any change in the status of Northern Ireland would only come about with the consent of a majority of the people of Northern Ireland, and that such consent was not at present forthcoming. It also established an Intergovernmental Conference, through which the Government of the Republic of Ireland may put views or proposals on certain specified matters to the UK Government, and which provides a framework for co-operation between the two Governments on security, economic, cultural and social matters.

THE CHANNEL ISLANDS AND THE ISLE OF MAN

The Channel Islands and the Isle of Man do not form part of the United Kingdom, but have a special status as Crown dependencies. They have their own legislative assemblies and legal and administrative systems, their laws depending for their validity on their receiving Royal Assent. Her Majesty's Government is responsible for the defence and international relations of the Islands and the Crown is ultimately responsible for their good government.

In fulfilling its role towards the Islands, the Crown acts through the Privy Council, on the recommendation of Ministers of Her Majesty's Government, acting in their capacity as Privy Counsellors. The Home Secretary is the Privy Counsellor charged with particular responsibility for matters relating to the Islands; that responsibility derives from his special role in the Privy Council rather than from his membership of Her Majesty's Government.

While Parliament at Westminster has a residual power to legislate for the Islands, it would be contrary to constitutional convention for that power to be used in matters that are domestic to the Islands, particularly where taxation is concerned. On such matters each Island enacts its own legislation.

The broad effect of special terms applicable to the Channel Islands and the Isle of Man is that they are included in the European Community solely for customs purposes and for certain aspects of the common agricultural policy. They neither contribute to, nor benefit from Community funds.

The Channel Islands consist of two Bailiwicks: Jersey constituting one, and the other comprising Guernsey and the adjacent islets of Herm and Jethou, together with Alderney and Sark, the two latter having their own legislative assemblies. The Sovereign is represented in each Bailiwick by a Lieutenant Governor, who is the official channel of communication between Her Majesty's Government in the United Kingdom and the Island administrations. In Jersey and Guernsey, the Bailiff, who is appointed by the Crown, presides over the Royal Court and the representative assembly (the States) and is the head of the Island administration.

The Queen is similarly represented by a Lieutenant Governor in the Isle of Man, where the legislative assembly is the Court of Tynwald, which comprises the Legislative Council and the popularly elected House of Keys. The President of Tynwald presides over the Court of Tynwald and the Legislative Council. The House of Keys is presided over by the Speaker. The Council of Ministers comprises a Chief Minister (elected by members of Tynwald) and nine Ministers chosen by the Chief Minister from members of Tynwald.

BAILIWICK OF JERSEY

Lieutenant-Governor and Commander in Chief: His Excellency Air Marshal Sir John Sutton, KCB

Secretary and ADC to Lieutenant-Governor: Lieutenant Colonel A J C Woodrow, OBE, MC, QGM

Bailiff: Sir Peter Crill, CBE
Deputy Bailiff: V A Tomes
HM Attorney-General: P M Bailhache, QC
HM Solicitor-General: T C Sowden, QC
Greffier of the States: R S Gray
Finance and Economics Committee: Senator P Horsfall
Defence Committee: Deputy M Wavell
Harbours and Airport Committee: Senator B T Binnington
Public Services Committee: Deputy J Le Gallais
Education Committee: Connétable Mrs Iris Le Feuvre
Public Health Committee: Deputy J Roche
Committee of Agriculture and Fisheries: Senator J Rothwell
Tourism Committee: Senator R Shenton
Social Security Committee: Deputy T Le Sueur
Island Development Committee: Connétable J P Le Sueur
Housing Committee: Deputy L Norman
Telecommunications: Deputy R Rumboll
Etat Civil: Connétable A P Querée
Legislation: Deputy E Becquet
Cottage Homes: Deputy Mrs Margaret Beadle
Prison Board: Senator Mrs Anne Baal
Establishment: Senator R J Shenton
Rayner Fund: Senator P Horsfall
Gambling Control: Deputy R Blampied
Sports and Recreation: Senator T Le Main
Policy and Resources: Senator R R Jeune, OBE
Overseas Aid: Deputy Mrs Anne Bailhache
Postal: Senator Mrs Corrie Stein
Broadcasting: Connétable Mrs Enid Quénault
Committees and States Relationship (Special Committee): Senator R R Jeune, OBE
Industrial Relations: Deputy T Jordan
House: Deputy G Huelin
Occupation and Liberation: Senator J Le Maistre

BAILIWICK OF GUERNSEY

Lieutenant-Governor and Commander in Chief: His Excellency Lieutenant General Sir Michael Wilkins, KCB, OBE

Secretary and ADC to the Lieutenant-Governor: Captain D P L Hodgetts

GUERNSEY
Bailiff: G M Dorey
Deputy Bailiff: de V G Carey
HM Procureur (Attorney-General): A C K Day, QC
HM Comptroller (Solicitor-General): G R Rowland
HM Greffier: K Tough
Advisory and Finance Committee: Conseiller R J Falla
Board of Administration: Conseiller R C Berry
Board of Health: Conseiller R M Chilcott
Board of Employment, Industry and Commerce: Deputy D Evans
Agricultural and Milk Marketing Board: Conseiller P L de Garis
Committee for Horticulture: Conseiller R H Marquis
Education Committee: Conseiller L L Guille
Housing Committee: Conseiller J E Langlois
Income Tax Authority: Deputy D Evans
Insurance Authority: Conseiller L Morgan
Island Development Committee: Conseiller J E Langlois
Home Affairs Committee: Conseiller M Torode
Sea Fisheries: Deputy R J Le Moignan
Tourist Board: Conseiller R J Ozanne

ALDERNEY
President of the States: J Kay-Mouat
Chairman of the Court: Jurat H G Smith

SARK
Seigneur de Serk: J M Beaumont
Senechal: L P de Carteret

ISLE OF MAN

Lieutenant Governor: Air Marshal Sir Laurence Jones, KCB, AFC, FBIM
Chief Secretary: J F Kissack
Chief Minister: Hon M R Walker, CBE, MHK

COUNCIL OF MINISTERS
Treasury: Hon D J Gelling, MHK
Agriculture, Fisheries and Forestry: Hon J Corma, MHK
Education: Hon H Hannan, MHK
Health and Social Security: Hon B May, MHK
Highways, Ports and Properties: Hon D North, MHK
Home Affairs: Hon A A Callin, MLC
Industry: Hon A R Bell, MHK
Local Government and Environment: Hon J A Brown, MHK
Tourism, Leisure and Transport: Hon A R Bell, MHK
Minister Without Portfolio: Hon E G Lowey, MLC

TYNWALD
President of Tynwald: The Hon Sir Charles Kerruish, OBE, CP
Clerk: Professor T St J N Bates

LEGISLATIVE COUNCIL
President of the Legislative Council: The Hon Sir Charles Kerruish, OBE, CP
Clerk: T A Bawden

HOUSE OF KEYS

Speaker: Hon J C Cain, FCA, SHK

Secretary and Counsel to the Speaker: Professor T St J N Bates

JUSTICE

First Deemster and Clerk of the Rolls: His Honour Deemster J W Corrin

Second Deemster: His Honour Deemster H W Callow

HM Attorney-General: T W Cain, QC, MA

Vanuatu

Capital: Vila

Vanuatu, formerly the Anglo-French Condominium of the New Hebrides, lies in the South-west Pacific between 13° and 21° S. and 166° and 171° E., forming an irregular Y-shaped chain of islands with a total land area of about 14,763 sq km (5,700 square miles). They were named the New Hebrides in 1774 by Captain Cook, and there are some 65 inhabited islands and islets, the larger of which are Espiritu Santo, Malekula, Efate, Ambrym, Tanna, Erromango, Epi, Aoba, Pentecost and Maewo.

The islands are of coral and volcanic origin, with active volcanoes on several islands including Tanna, Lopevi and Ambrym. Most are forested and mountainous, Santo Peak and Tabwemasana on Espiritu Santo rising to over 1,800 m (6,000 feet). The group is generally well-watered. The climate is oceanic tropical and moderated by the south-east trade winds which blow between the months of May and October. During the remainder of the year winds are variable and cyclones may occur. High humidity occasionally leads to enervating conditions. Temperatures in Port Vila, the capital, vary between 16°C(60°F) and 33°C(92°F) and average rainfall ranges from about 2,250 mm in the south to 3,875 mm in the north, with a mean figure of 2,275 mm for Vila.

The 1989 estimate of the population of Vanuatu gave a total of 142,944, the most populous islands being Efate (30,868), Santo (25,581), Malekula (19,298) and Tanna (19,825). About 95 per cent of the population are Melanesian, with small numbers of Europeans, Polynesians and Micronesians making up the rest.

The population of Port Vila in 1989 was 19,311. The population of the only other town, Luganville, on the island of Santo, was 6,983.

Many languages and dialects are spoken. Most belong to the Melanesian family, and are related to those of Fiji and New Caledonia. A New Hebrides form of pidgin, known as Bislama or Bichelama, is the *lingua franca,* while English and French are also official languages. Bislama is used in debate in the Parliament and records of parliamentary proceedings are produced in Bislama as well as in English and French.

The unit of currency is the Vatu, which replaced at parity the New Hebrides franc (FNH).

The Anglican, Presbyterian and Roman Catholic churches began missionary work in the New Hebrides in the 19th century. More recently other religions, including the Seventh Day Adventist Church, have become active in various parts of the Group. The Presbyterian Church has the largest number of adherents, followed by the Anglican and Roman Catholic churches. Most religious denominations have now handed over their schools to government-supervised and assisted bodies, and in the case of certain English-language secondary schools and primary schools, to Boards of Management set up under government authority.

The health services previously under British and French control have been unified since independence, and medical care is now provided through a network of government hospitals, health centres and dispensaries. The Central Hospital at Port Vila and the hospital at Luganville are the two major hospitals, and there is a well established Nurses Training School in Port Vila. Increasing emphasis is being placed on preventive medicine. Malaria is widespread and is the most serious endemic disease, but tuberculosis is also a considerable problem.

Principal exports are copra, meat, fish, cocoa and timber.

Total exports in million vatu

1985	*1986*	*1987*	*1988*	*1989*	*1990*
3,262	1,841	1,942	2,114	2,563	2,202

Most of the population is employed on plantations or in subsistence agriculture. The most important cash crops are copra, cocoa and coffee. The principal subsistence crops are yams, taro, manioc, sweet potato and breadfruit. Large numbers of cattle are kept on the plantations and efforts continue to develop an export trade in meat (frozen, tinned and chilled) and to expand the local meat industry. Small amounts of timber are felled and milled for local use, and export.

In view of the absence of direct taxation a Finance Centre has developed in Port Vila. This is served by eight Trust Companies, four commercial and merchant banks, six firms of accountants and four firms of lawyers. Over six hundred offshore companies and banks are registered in Port Vila. Vanuatu also operates as a port of open registry.

Tourism is important to the economy and Vanuatu now boasts three international-style hotels and a number of smaller but comfortable ones of good standard. A number of good restaurants serve French, Chinese and Vietnamese food.

The principal ports of Vanuatu are Port Vila (Efate) and Luganville (Espiritu Santo).

The principal airports are Bauerfield (Efate) and Pekoa (Espiritu Santo). Bauerfield is about three miles from Vila, and Pekoa the same distance from Santo Town. Both are 6,000 ft long. Bauerfield was re-surfaced and upgraded in 1986 to take wide-bodied jet aircraft such as the 767. It was extended in 1990 by an extra 600 metres. There are 26 smaller airfields, on Malekula, Aoba, Pentecost, Epi, Tongoa, Efate, Erromango, Tanna, Aneityum, Emae, Vanua Lava, Mota Lava, Torres, Maewo, Aniwa and Futuna. Three further air fields are also planned for Gaua, Paama, and North Ambrym.

External air services are provided by Air Vanuatu, Air Pacific, Solomon Airlines and Air Caledonia, linking Port Vila with Australia, Fiji, Solomon Islands, New Caledonia and New Zealand. The internal airline, Vanair, operates regular services to almost all parts of Vanuatu.

There are about 1,130 kms of road or track, of which some 54 kms are paved.

Regular shipping services to and from New Caledonia, Australia, New Zealand and Europe are maintained by Compagnie Generale Maritime, Sofrana Unilines, and the Bank Line. It is also possible to arrive or depart by many of the cruise ships which are frequent callers. Small vessels give an inter-island service.

Radio Vanuatu, established in 1966, broadcasts daily in English, French and Bislama.

There are international telephone and telex links through Noumea, Hong Kong and Sydney. These have been complemented since mid-1979 by the establishment of a satellite earth station.

Vanuatu's First National Development Plan ran from 1982 to 1986. A Second Plan covers the years 1987–1991. Implementation of development projects is largely dependent on international aid, supplied by the multilateral agencies and by bilaterial donors including Britain, Australia, France, New Zealand and Japan.

Revenue derives from indirect taxation: import duties account for a large proportion of total recurrent revenue, and export duty is levied on the territory's primary products: copra, frozen fish and meat, coffee, cocoa and shells. There is no direct personal tax or company tax.

For the past few years Vanuatu has had an adverse balance of trade and this has worsened in recent years as the cost of imports has risen more rapidly than exports. In 1988 imports totalled Vatu 7,361 million while the value of exports was Vatu 2,114 million. In 1989 the figures were Vatu 8,218 million for imports and Vatu 2,563 million for exports and in 1990 imports totalled Vatu 10,768 million whilst exports were Vatu 2,202 million. The deficit was offset by earnings from tourism and from overseas aid.

Primary education is not free but only nominal fees are charged. Primary schooling is available for almost all children. Exceptions are the relatively few populated inland areas where changes in patterns of living are taking place for the first time and a desire for education is only now springing up.

Full secondary education is available at a number of schools.

The national education system is at present under review, the aim being to introduce a unified system, at least at the primary level.

No statistics on literacy are available but it is fairly widespread amongst persons under 35–40 years. Above 40 years it is often limited to pastors, elders, and teachers. Many Ni-Vanuatu are literate in their own language, although there is practically no secular reading matter in the many vernaculars. Many Ni-Vanuatu speak either English or French, and almost all speak Bislama. It is common for Ni-Vanuatu to speak two or three native languages.

History and Constitution

The New Hebrides were discovered by the Spanish explorer, de Quiros, in 1606. He was followed by the French navigator, de Bougainville, in 1768 and in 1774 Captain Cook visited and charted the greater part of the chain of islands which comprise the group. Other early visitors were La Perouse who is believed to have passed through in 1788, and d'Entrecasteaux who came in search of Captain Bligh in the course of his open-boat voyage to Timor after the mutiny on the *Bounty*. Last century, before any government showed any interest in the New Hebrides, a number of British and French missionaries, planters and traders had established themselves and in 1887, by the Anglo-French Convention of 16th November, the two nations appointed a Joint Naval Commission charged with the protection in the New Hebrides of the lives and properties of British and French subjects.

In 1902 the British and French Governments each appointed a Resident Commissioner for the territory. In February 1906 an Anglo-French conference took place in London. A draft convention was prepared to provide for settlement of land claims and for an arrangement to end the difficulties arising from the absence of jurisdiction over the indigenous inhabitants. This was confirmed on 20th October 1906, and an Anglo-French Condominium was established. A Protocol, drawn up in London in 1914 to replace the Convention of 1906, was ratified in 1922. From the 1960's the local inhabitants began to feel increasing concern over the European impact, especially the alienation of land, and this led to their first political initiatives.

At a meeting between the Metropolitan Governments in London in November 1974, it was agreed that a Representative Assembly with new powers and responsibilities would, before the end of 1975, replace the former Advisory Council. The first national elections were held in November 1975 to elect 29 members to the Assembly by universal suffrage, and 9 members to represent economic interests, the latter elected by electoral colleges representing the Chamber of Commerce and the two Co-operative Federations. Disagreements and difficulties between the four chiefs representing traditional interests prevented the election from being held on Schedule, and eventually, after an Exchange of Notes, the first meeting of the Representative Assembly took place in June 1976, without chiefs. When the election of the four chiefs was completed, the second meeting of the Assembly took place at the end of the year.

However, in February 1977, the Assembly was halted by a Vanua'aku Party boycott. The party, which originally demanded Independence in 1977 and which, with its supporters held 21 of the 42 seats in the Assembly, was particularly opposed to the inclusion of the six Chamber of Commerce members in the Economic Interests section, already mentioned.

The High Commissioners of Britain and France held talks with political parties and traditional chiefs in Vila in March, as a result of which they recommended a ministerial conference in Europe in July, and the setting up of a provisional council to advise the Resident Commissioners on the running of the country during the period before elections for a Representative Assembly based entirely on universal suffrage.

Later the Vanua'aku Party demanded three assurances as a pre-condition to its attending the ministerial talks. The points were: that elections should be held in 1977; that the next Assembly should mark the stage of self-government, and that the majority party in the Assembly should form the government.

The government's reply indicated that they were not unsympathetic to these points, but wished them to be discussed by all parties concerned at the talks. This reply failed to satisfy the Vanua'aku Party, and it refused to attend.

At the talks, held in Paris, it was agreed that elections be held before 1st December 1977, that internal self-government should come in the first months of 1978, and that there would be further elections, and a referendum on the independence issue, in the second half of 1980. Independence would follow, if that was what people wanted. The Ministers also said they would go to Vila in December, or January 1978, for further talks.

In September, the Vanua'aku Party threatened to boycott the elections unless: only native New Hebrideans could vote or stand as candidates; the voting age was lowered to 18; the party with the elected majority formed the government; full internal self-government was granted immediately after the elections, and there was a referendum on independence before the end of 1977.

The Metropolitan powers replied that their difficulties were more of timing than of principle, and that it was impractical in the time available, to implement the Party's demands.

The Party said it would not take part in the elections, and later said it would proclaim its own 'People's Provisional Government' on election day, 29th November.

As a result of this non-participation, independent or opposition party candidates were declared elected unopposed for 38 of the 39 seats, with one seat remaining vacant.

At its first meeting early in December, the new Assembly elected its own chairman, to replace the Resident Commissioners. The Council of Ministers was formally set up at a special session during a visit by the High Commissioners in January 1978. The Chief Minister announced the names and portfolios of six ministers, and also offered a further three ministries to the Vanua'aku Party, which refused them.

Following a visit by the French Minister concerned in August, 1978 'meetings of understanding' were held between the Government and the Vanua'aku Party in December in an attempt to set up a 'government of National Unity' in which the two sides would have an equal number of ministers to lead the country until the 1979 elections.

A Government of National Unity was formed in December 1978 under the leadership of Father Gerard Leymang. Its major task was to draw up an Independence Constitution acceptable to all the people of the New Hebrides. A Constitutional Committee was formed, assisted by constitutional advisers provided by Britain and France, and a Constitutional Conference was held in September 1979. The new Constitution was formally adopted by the British and French Governments in an Exchange of Notes signed in Paris on 23rd October 1979. The Exchange of Notes provided for the New Hebrides to become independent in 1980.

Elections were held on 14 November 1979 as a result of which the Vanua'aku Party won 26 of the 39 seats in the Representative Assembly and majorities in both the regional councils of Santo and Tanna, Father Walter Lini, the VP President, became the Chief Minister and a nine-man Council of Ministers was established.

In May 1980 a largely francophone group based on the island of Santo attempted to break away from the rest of the archipelago and declared the so-called independent 'Government of Vemarana', which encompassed the custom party known as Nagriamel led by Jimmy Stevens. Attempts were made throughout June and early July to resolve the differences between the central government and the Vemarana rebels. This, however, proved impossible and British and French troops were finally sent to Luganville on 24th July.

Despite this convulsion, the New Hebrides attained independence on 30th July, 1980. Renamed Vanuatu, the territory became an independent Republic within the Commonwealth with Father Lini as Prime Minister.

In mid-August the British and French troops were replaced on Santo by forces of Papua New Guinea who, assisted by local elements of the mobile police force, put down the rebellion on Santo and arrested the ringleaders. Of those arrested all have now been released and peace has returned to the islands.

At the first general election since independence, in November 1983, the Vanua'aku Party were returned to power with 24 of the 39 seats in Parliament. Father Lini was re-elected Prime Minister. At the second general election in November, 1987, the Vanua'aku Party was again elected, this time with 26 of the 46 seats in Parliament. Father Lini was again re-elected as Prime Minister.

In December 1988, the then President Sokomanu purported to dissolve Parliament and set up an 'interim' Government. This attempt failed and the President, and several others were jailed. Following an appeal against their sentences they were released but the Appeal Court confirmed that the action had been illegal. President Sokomanu was deprived of office in January 1989 by an overwhelming majority of the Electoral College. He was replaced by President Timakata.

In August 1991, after growing dissension and a prolonged political struggle within the Vanua'aku Party, an extraordinary Party Congress elected Donald Kalpokas as the new party President to replace Father Lini. A Parliamentary motion of no confidence was lodged against Father Lini and, on 6th September, he was voted out of office. Donald Kalpokas was elected as Vanuatu's second Prime Minister since Independence. Parliament was dissolved on 14th October and General Elections held on 2nd December 1991. These resulted in a coalition government led by the Union of Moderate Parties (UMP) and including members of the party of the former Prime Minister, Father Lini—the National United Party (NUP).

HEAD OF STATE

President: His Excellency Frederick Karlomoana Timakata

Speaker of Parliament: Alfred Maseng (UMP)

THE COUNCIL OF MINISTERS

Prime Minister: Hon Maxinne Carlot (UMP)

Minister of Justice, Culture and Women's Affairs and Deputy Prime Minister: Hon Sethy Regenvanu (NUP)

Minister of Finance, Commerce, Industry and Tourism: Hon Willie Jimmy (UMP)

Minister of Agriculture, Livestock, Forestry and Fisheries: Hon Onneyn Tahi (NUP)

Minister of Transport, Public Works, Urban Water Supply, Ports and Marine: Hon Amos Bangabiti (UMP)

Minister of Education: Hon Romain Batick (UMP)

Minister of Health and Rural Water Supply: Hon Hilda Lini (NUP)

Minister of Land and Natural Resources: Hon Paul Telukluk (UMP)

Minister of Postal Services, Meteo and Communications: Hon Dr Edward Tambisari (NUP)

JUDICIARY

Acting Chief Justice: E P Goldsbrough

Western Samoa

Capital: Apia

Western Samoa lies in central Polynesia in the South West Pacific Ocean between latitudes 13° and 15° south and longitudes 171° and 173° west. The Samoan group lies 4,183 km (2,600 miles) south-west of Hawaii, 4,344 km (2,700 miles) from Sydney, 2,896 km (1,800 miles) north-east of New Zealand. The islands are formed mainly of volcanic rock, and coral reefs surround much of Western Samoa's coastline. Fresh water is plentiful in rivers and lakes. More than half of the total land in Upolu which is suitable for cultivation is around the three-to-four mile limit inland from the coast where most of the population is also settled. It is estimated that an area of 699 sq km (270 square miles) is under cultivation.

Nine islands make up Western Samoa and the total land area is some 2,823 sq km (1,090 square miles). Of this area, some 1,709 sq km (660 square miles) form the island of Savai'i and 1,113 sq km (430 square miles) the island of Upolu. The other islands are Apolima, Manono, Fanuatapu, Namua, Nuutele, Nuulua and Nuusafee. The climate is tropical, temperatures normally ranging from 22°C (72°F) to 30°C (86°F). The cooler months are from May to November when the fresh trade winds blow and the rainy season extends from December to April. The rainfall is uneven in territorial distribution and the northern coast of Upolu normally receives less than the southern and the western less than the eastern coast. The annual figures for rainfall are 2,800 mm (112 inches) for the northern coast and 2,750 mm (110 inches) for the western end. An analogous distribution occurs on Savai'i. Hurricanes are not unknown in Western Samoa, occasionally causing great damage to property and crops.

The Samoans are a Polynesian people akin to the Maori of New Zealand and the Tongans. Since 1960 people residing in Western Samoa have been classed either as Western Samoan citizens or as foreigners; citizens travel on Western Samoan passports. The pre-requisite for Samoan citizenship is to be born in the country or to have five years residence. Other racial groups in Samoa include Euronesians, other Pacific Islanders, Chinese and Europeans.

There has been a steady increase in Samoan population from 33,478 in 1906 when the first census was taken. At the census of November 1966 the population was 131,377 and in 1976 it was 151,150. The 1981 census recorded a population of 158,130 and according to an estimate it was 162,000 in 1988. The population of Apia, the capital, on the island of Upolu, is 35,000.

The annual natural population growth rate is about 3 per cent, but due to emigration the actual population growth rate in recent years is estimated to have been about 0.6 per cent.

The Samoans are Christian by religion and have assimilated religious observances into the pattern of village life. Among the Christian missions which have established themselves in Western Samoa are the Congregational, the Roman Catholic, the Methodist, the Latter Day Saints and the Seventh Day Adventists.

The main languages spoken in Samoa are Samoan and English.

The Economy

The unit of Currency is the Western Samoan $ (tala).

Land tenure in Samoa is of considerable importance. Since 1961 all land in Western Samoa has been held as:

(i) customary land held from the State in accordance with Samoan custom;

(ii) freehold land which is held from the State of Western Samoa in fee simple; and

(iii) public land (formerly crown land) being land that is free from customary title and from any estate in fee simple.

Of the 2,823 sq km (1,090 square miles) that make up the land of Western Samoa some 80.5 per cent cent is 'customary land' controlled by the matai or chiefs and held in accordance with Samoan custom and usage. The matai is in effect the trustee of the extended family group. The control of the land does not necessarily pass from the chief to his son as there is an election of a new matai when the former matai dies. Customary land can be leased but not purchased. At independence, of a total 290,000 ha (725,000 acres) in the islands of Western Samoa, 12,800 ha (32,000 acres) were Trust Estate land, 224,424 ha (561,062 acres) were indigenous land and 10,908 ha (26,953 acres) were freehold land. The remainder was crown land, now called public land.

Agriculture has formed the basis for Western Samoa's economy and seems likely to continue to play a most important role. Agriculture has largely been of a subsistence type with little money income accruing to the average Samoan planter. The land and the sea have provided food and the means for shelter for the Samoans and until recently there has been little intensive agriculture.

The major crops are coconuts (copra), cocoa, bananas, passion fruit and taro.

Copra is marketed through the Copra Board and the Western Samoa Coconut Products Limited which operates the coconut crushing mill. Coconut oil exports have replaced copra exports in importance and copra is followed by cocoa and bananas as major export earners. Other agricultural exports include coffee, timber, tropical fruits and seeds.

As far as fisheries are concerned, marine products are gathered by the Samoans mainly for personal consumption and commercial fishing is not yet of any significance. Efforts are, however, being made to develop marine resources generally.

As a result of Government encouragment under the Enterprises Incentives Act, there has been a steady increase in the number and scope of manufacturing activities. The Contribution of the manufacturing sector to GDP was estimated at about 10 per cent in 1987. The new industries now include those engaged in the production of foodstuffs and beverages, saw milling and woodwork operations, light metal work and engineering, garment and footwear manufacture, and a wide range of other related activities. Prospects for development of a food processing industry, particularly tropical fruit and juice for export, appear good. Further growth in this industry is expected to be greatly helped by the establishment of a modern food processing laboratory.

Western Samoa's approach to tourism reflects its concern to preserve the Samoan way of life. The economic benefits of tourism are, however, recognised and a policy of positive development is now being pursued. Expansion of hotel facilities is being undertaken together with the upgrading of Western Samoa's airport and roads. The number of tourists visiting Western Samoa has increased steadily over recent years.

The pattern of Western Samoa's exports reflects the situation in a country where, with very little secondary industry, the main emphasis is on agriculture. The most important purchasing countries are New Zealand, Germany, The Netherlands, American Samoa, Australia, other Pacific countries and Britain.

An analysis of Western Samoa's imports shows a concentration of foodstuffs, most of which are imported from New Zealand, Australia and Japan.

There are some 2,100 km of roads in Western Samoa and priority has been given to a programme of upgrading and the provision of low grade access roads for village plantations. As far as shipping services are concerned, a regular fortnightly service operates to New Zealand via Fiji, Tonga and Niue. A daily service links Apia and Pago Pago in American Samoa. There are also shipping connections with Australia, direct line services with Britain approximately once every six weeks, with Japan every three months and with the Pacific coast of America once a month. Western Samoa has provided a roll on-roll off ship, built with German aid, for the Pacific Forum Line, which has its headquarters in Apia. Western Samoa's main airport is situated at Faleolo, thirty-five kilometres west of Apia. Extension work on the airport runway has enabled aircraft up to 747 size to come to Western Samoa. The national airline is Polynesian Airlines. Other carriers serving Western Samoa include Air New Zealand, Air Pacific, South Pacific Airways and Hawaiian Airlines, with direct connections to New Zealand, Tonga, Australia, Fiji, Cook Islands, American Samoa and Hawaii. There are also inter-island daily air services between Upolu and Savai'i operated by Polynesian Airlines. A deep water wharf at Apia was opened in April 1966. A second port for ocean-going vessels at Asau on the island of Savai'i was opened in 1972.

The problems of economic development in Western Samoa differ little from those experienced in other developing countries. Broadly stated, the difficulty is to sustain a policy of rational economic growth against the background of a rapidly increasing population, limited agricultural exports and the relatively wide fluctuations in the prices paid on the international market for these products. Special circumstances in Western Samoa, however, tend to sharpen and accentuate the effect of these difficulties. These include geographical isolation, an absence of mineral resources, the lack of nearby markets and of a large domestic market, and the low level of productive efficiency in the agricultural sector of the economy.

New Zealand in particular has sought to assist in the economic development of the country and provides technical and capital assistance to Western Samoa in a number of fields including health, education, civil aviation, meteorological services, labour and economic development. Lately, a number of other countries including Japan, and Germany, have provided financial and technical assistance towards selected development projects. Technical assistance is also provided under various United Nations programmes with UNDP providing a number of experts in planning, statistics, forestry and engineering. A number of Commonwealth countries assist Western Samoa by making teacher training awards for Western Samoan students. Australia in addition provides expert personnel, machinery and equipment. The New Zealand volunteer Service Abroad, the US Peace Corps and Japanese Overseas Volunteers have a number of volunteers serving in Western Samoa. Other development partners include the EC, CFTC, OPEC Fund, ADB and the World Bank.

In February 1990 Western Samoa was hard hit by Cyclone Ofa. The severe damage to houses, roads, water supply and agricultural crops represented a serious setback to the country's development efforts. The Government sought help from the United Nations, World Bank and ADB, as well as from New Zealand, Australia and other bilateral donors.

In December 1991 the island was devastated by Cyclone Val which caused widespread damage and 13 deaths.

The Social Services

Samoa is fortunate in that most of the worst tropical diseases are unknown in the islands. There is a Department of Health and there are fourteen health districts with Medical Officers responsible for health activities in each district. The Apia General Hospital is being expanded as are the district hospitals at Tuasivi and Aleipata. There are programmes for assisting in tuberculosis control and combating filariasis and yaws. The 1984 estimate for payments for the Health Department was WS$5 million.

Samoa participates in the South Pacific Health Service, a regional organisation with its headquarters and Director-General at Suva in Fiji; through this the country is involved in the regional planning in the area. For both training and treatment the universities and teaching hospitals in New Zealand play an important role for the whole region.

Education in Western Samoa is a Government responsibility carried out through a Department of Education, but several missions also operate schools. The education system is divided into three divisions: primary, intermediate and secondary, and all are based on the New Zealand system. There are also a Trades' Training Institute, Teachers' Training College and a college for tropical agriculture in Western Samoa. Western Samoa has joined other Governments in the area in establishing the regional University of the South Pacific and a Samoan served as the first pro-Chancellor.

Labour matters in Western Samoa are governed by a Labour Ordinance. There are probably 19,000 people in the country who could be classed as wage earners and at least half of them are employed by the Government or the Trust Estates Corporation. It is calculated that another 22,000 are employed in village agriculture. There are no trade unions and the Government works on the basis of a 40-hour week which is generally followed by private enterprise. There is a substantial annual migration to New Zealand. Some thousands have migrated in this way on a permanent or semi-permanent basis.

History

Little is known of Samoan history before the 13th century but some archaeological evidence indicates that Samoa could have been settled as far back as 1000 BC. After 1250 AD, genealogies of important titles, legends and charts provide a reasonably clear outline of the main events of Samoa's political history. Fijian nobles feature in many Samoan legends, indicating connection with and knowledge of Fijian peoples and customs. This applies also to the Tongans. Throughout this early period there was intermittent contact both friendly and hostile between the three groups of islands.

The first European contact with Samoa came in 1722 with a visit by the Dutch navigator, Jacob Roggeveen. In 1830, the missionary John Williams, landed in Savai'i and Samoan society has been in contact with the Western world from that time onwards. But it has largely retained its traditional organisation, modifying and adapting intrusive elements to suit its needs.

Towards the end of the 19th century, Germany, Britain and the United States obtained privileges in Western Samoa for themselves and their nationals. Rivalry between these three powers reached a climax in 1889 when a special conference was called to solve the three-way power struggle. The resultant Berlin Treaty established an independent government in Samoa but also granted authority to the United States, German and British Consuls to supervise local affairs. The agreement, however, proved to be cumbersome and unsatisfactory. By the Samoa Convention of 1899, therefore, Germany was permitted to annex western Samoa, the United States eastern Samoa and Britain withdrew its claims. Germany administered Western Samoa until 1914 when New Zealand military forces occupied it. In 1919, New Zealand was granted a League of Nations Mandate for Samoa. Shortly after the end of the Pacific War in 1946, Western Samoa was made a UN Trust Territory with New Zealand as the administering power. The Samoan people requested independence but were not granted it at that stage.

Constitutional development

From 1947 to 1961 there was a series of constitutional advances which brought Samoa from a dependent status to self-government and independence. In 1947 a Legislative Assembly was established. In March 1953, New Zealand proposed to quicken the pace of political and economic development and in 1954 a Constitutional Convention, representing all sections of Samoan society, met to study proposals for political development. Its recommendations were in the main adopted by the New Zealand Government and these set the pattern for evolution towards constitutional government. From this time members of the Legislative Assembly assumed an increasingly greater role in the conduct of Government affairs culminating in the appointment of the Hon E F Paul as Leader of Government business in 1959. In January 1959, a committee on self-government was established and empowered to work out a draft constitution. Cabinet Government was inaugurated in October 1959 and the late Fiama Mata'afa became the first Prime Minister. In August 1960, a Constitutional Convention met and formally adopted the Constitution. This was an instrument combining the cherished elements of traditional Samoan society and the needs of a modern state. A plebiscite was held in May 1961 under the auspices of the United Nations and an overwhelming majority of the Samoan people voted for independence on the basis of the Constitution. In October 1961, the UN General Assembly at the request of New Zealand and on the claim of Western Samoa to independence, voted unanimously to end the Trusteeship Agreement. The New Zealand Parliament then passed the Independence (State of Western Samoa) Act, formally ending New Zealand's powers over the country.

Foreign relations

Western Samoa is an independent and sovereign state; under a Treaty of Friendship between Western Samoa and New Zealand, signed eight months after Western Samoa became independent, New Zealand agreed to assist in the independent state's foreign relations 'in such a manner as will in no way impair the rights of the Government of Western Samoa to formulate its own foreign policies'. In other words, the New Zealand Government merely acts as the agent of the Western Samoan Government when requested to do so. Western Samoa became a member of the UN in 1976 and has joined ECAFE, WHO, ADB, IMF, the South Pacific Commission and the South Pacific Forum. Following consultation with Commonwealth governments, it was agreed that pending a decision by the Western Samoan Government on whether to seek membership, Western Samoa would be treated for most purposes as if it were a member of the Commonwealth.

The Western Samoan Government decided in 1970 to seek membership and following consultations with Commonwealth Governments became a full member of the Commonwealth in August 1970. In 1977 Western Samoa established its first diplomatic mission overseas: a High Commission in Wellington, New Zealand. The Western Samoan representative in Brussels is accredited as High Commissioner to London.

The Government

Western Samoa has a strong, stable, and democratic system of parliamentary government which is a blend of Polynesian and British practices. The Constitution which came into force on 1st January 1962, provides for a Head of State to be elected by the Legislative Assembly for a term of five years. In the first instance, however, it was decided that two of the four Paramount chiefs should jointly hold the office of Head of State for life. On 5th April 1963, one of the Paramount Chiefs died and in accordance with the provisions of the Constitution, Malietoa Tanumafili II became the holder of the office of Head of State for life. The Head of State, whose functions are analogous to those of a constitutional monarch, appoints the Prime Minister who has the support of a majority of the elected members of the Assembly and is himself an elected member. Executive government is carried out by the Cabinet consisting of a Prime Minister and eight other Ministers, selected by the Prime Minister. All legislation passed by the Legislative Assembly must have the assent of the Head of State before it becomes law. The Head of State also has other powers such as the granting of pardons and reprieves or suspending sentences.

Prior to 1991 the voting system had as its basis the 'aiga' (extended family) unit headed by a 'matai' who spoke for the entire 'aiga'.

Early in 1991 the Government of Tofilau Eti Alesana introduced universal adult suffrage for all persons over 18. However, it remains the case that only the 'Matai' can stand for election.

The Constitution also provides for a Council of Deputies to consist of not more than three persons. The function of the Council is to act in place of the Head of State if a vacancy exists in that office or the holder of that office is incapacitated or absent from the country.

Local government is based on the matai system through meetings of family heads in the village.

The Constitution provides for a Public Service Commission which determines salaries and other conditions of service in Western Samoan Public Service.

HISTORICAL LIST OF PRIME MINISTERS

Fiame Mata'afa Faumuina Mulinu'u II, CBE, 1962 to 1970
Tupua Tamasese Lealofi IV, 1970 to 1973
Fiame Mata'afa Faumuina Mulinu'u II, CBE, 1973 to 1975
Tupua Tamasese Lealofi IV, 1975 to 1976
Tupuola Efi from 1976 to 1982
Vaai Kolone, April 1982 to September, 1982
Tupuola Efi from September 1982
Tofilau Eti Alesana from December 1982
Vaai Kolone from December 1985 to February 1988

HEAD OF STATE

His Highness Malietoa Tanumafili II, GCMG, CBE

CABINET

Prime Minister (inc. responsibility for Foreign Affairs): Hon Tofilau Eti Alesana
Minister of Finance: Hon Tuilaepa Sailele
Minister of Agriculture: Hon Jack Netzler
Minister of Education: Hon Fiame Naomi Mata'afa
Minister of Justice: Hon Fuimaono Lotomalu
Minister of Posts and Telecommunications: Hon Toi Aukuso
Minister of Works: Hon Leafa Vitale
Minister of Health: Hon Salo Vaimili II
Minister of Lands and Environment: Hon Faasootauloa Pati

In the General Election of 5th April 1991, the first to be held under universal suffrage, the Government of Prime Minister Tofilau Eti Alesana retained power. The new Government was sworn in on 14th May 1991. The Human Rights Protection Party holds 30 seats, the Samoan National Development Party has 14, and there are 3 Independent MPs.

Zambia

Capital: Lusaka

Zambia lies between latitudes 8° and 18° S., and longitudes 22° and 34° E. The country is land-locked and its neighbours are Angola on the west, Namibia (via the Caprivi Strip), the Republic of Botswana and Zimbabwe on the south, Mozambique and Malawi on the south-east and east, the United Republic of Tanzania on the north-east and Republic of Zaire on the north and north-west. The name Zambia is derived from Zambesi, the river which flows through the country and provides the boundary with Zimbabwe.

The area of Zambia is 752,620 sq km, which is well over five times the size of England. It consists mostly of a high plateau from 1,067 to 1,372 metres above sea level except where on the Malawi border it rises to over 1,807 metres, or where the plateau is deeply entrenched by the Zambesi river and its tributaries, the Kafue and the Luangwa Rivers, or by the Luapala River, which forms part of the headwaters of the River Zaire (previously Congo), in the north-west. The Mafinga Mountains, the highest in the country, form part of the great escarpment running down the eastern edge of the Luangwa River valley, with peaks rising to just over 1,807 metres. There are three great lakes: Lake Mweru on the northern boundary with Zaire; Lake Tanganyika on the northern boundary with Tanzania; Lake Bangweulu and its swamps, in the north of the country covering an area of approximately 9,842 sq km. Along the southern border stretches Lake Kariba, a man-made lake, covering approximately 5,180 sq km. There are three seasons: a cool dry season from May to August, a hot dry season from September to November, and a wet season from December to April. In the hot season day temperatures may vary from 27°–38°C (80°–100°F), but at night there is a very distinct drop in the temperature. At times in the cool season frost occurs in some areas. The rainfall range is 508 mm–1,270 mm (20 inches–51 inches) a year.

The population of Zambia as recorded in the 1990 census was 7,818,447. This represents a 38 per cent increase over the total of 5,661,801 recorded at the previous census in 1980 and an annual growth rate of 3.2 per cent. There are 73 tribes of which the largest are: Bemba, Ngoni, Chewa, Bisa, Lozi, Tonga, Luvale, Lenje, Ila, Senga, Lala, Lunda. English is widely spoken throughout the territory and is the official language. There are six main vernacular languages, viz—Nyanja, Bemba, Tonga, Lozi, Lunda and Luvale. Primary education is free but is not yet universal. About 85 per cent of the children in the age groups concerned attend primary school, and of these about 20 per cent to 25 per cent go on to take the five-year course in secondary schools. The University of Zambia was established in 1965 and the first students were admitted in March 1966. In 1984 enrolment was 4,330 including part-time and correspondence students. Christianity is the main religion.

For administrative purposes, Zambia is divided into nine provinces: Central, Lusaka, Copperbelt, Eastern, Luapula, Northern, North-Western, Southern and Western.

The latest census was conducted in 1990. The projected population of Lusaka, the capital, and other main centres were as follows:

Lusaka (city only)		982,362
Kabwe (town only)		166,619
Kitwe	Copperbelt	348,571
Ndola (urban only)	Copperbelt	376,311
Mufulira	Copperbelt	175,025
Luanshya	Copperbelt	147,747
Chingola	Copperbelt	186,769
Chililabombwe	Copperbelt	86,637
Kalulushi	Copperbelt	90,630
Livingstone		84,116

Zambia Railways was established in 1967 and took over the former North West Region of Rhodesia Railways. The gauge is three feet six inches, and the main line runs from Livingstone via Lusaka to the Copperbelt where it links with the Zairian railway system. The Tazara railway line from Dar es Salaam via Kasama and Mpika links up with the main line at Kapiri Mposhi. The main roads from Livingstone and Chirundu to Lusaka and on to the Copperbelt are tarmac. The Great East Road to Malawi, and the Great North Road to Tanzania are also tarmac. The principal airports are at Lusaka, Livingstone and Ndola, with runway lengths of 13,000; 7,500 and 8,240 feet respectively. In addition there are 12 secondary airports, 31 minor airports and 34 privately owned and operated airstrips. The main airlines are: Zambia Airways, British Airways, UTA, Kenya Airways, Air Malawi, Aeroflot, Air India, South African Airways and Air Zimbabwe. The Zambia National Broadcasting Corporation (ZNBC) is headed by a board of directors, but is government controlled through the Zambia Industrial and Mining Corporation (ZIMCO) which administers all state-controlled companies. The television service covers Lusaka, the Copperbelt, Livingstone, Chipata, Mongu and Kasama.

Copper mining is the economic mainstay of Zambia and provides approximately 85 per cent of Zambia's export earnings, generally 7.5 per cent of government revenue. The total sales of minerals for the year ending 31st March 1990 was as follows:

	tonnes	*Value*
Copper	634,486	28,853 (K million)
Zinc	12,243	368 (K million)
Lead	3,704	47 (K million)
Coal	na	na
Cobalt	4,304	1,415 (K'000)

Zambia is self-sufficient in sugar production. Other main crops are maize, cassava, tobacco and groundnuts. Small quantities of cotton, coffee, rice, pulses, citrus, potatoes, tropical fruits, vegetables, wheat, oilseed and beeswax are also produced.

The budget revenue for 1990 was K23,142 million and budget expenditure was K29,926.3 million. Total proposed expenditure for 1991 was K58,304.8 million.

The two-tier Foreign Exchange System introduced in February 1990 has been abandoned. The rate of exchange to 1$US is K70.

History

The early history of Zambia is fragmentary, being based on tribal oral tradition and on accounts of early European explorers such as Dr Lacerda who led an expedition to Lake Mweru in 1798, and Livingstone who travelled from Bechuanaland through Barotseland to Luanda in 1853 and returned to Mozambique in 1855.

During the early part of the nineteenth century the country was invaded by Arabs, who established a slave trade on a route via Lake Malawi to the east coast. This flourished until 1893 when British forces put a stop to it. The territory was also invaded by the Ngoni branch of the Zulus and by the Makololo, migrating from Basutoland, who established themselves as the dominant tribe in Barotseland and neighbouring districts until they were defeated by the indigenous Lozi, under their leader Chief Lewanika. Meanwhile British influence had been spreading north from the Cape, and the Africa Order in Council in 1889 included the area of Northern Rhodesia as one that was subject to Her Majesty's protection. But administration, when it came to Northern Rhodesia, was administration not by the Colonial Government in the Cape but by the British South Africa Company which had in 1889 received a Royal Charter which empowered it to exercise complete administrative and legislative control over Southern Rhodesia and northern Bechuanaland, subject to a requirement that it must pay attention to the wishes of the British High Commissioner in Cape Town. From 1889 onwards the British South Africa Company extended its activities to Northern Rhodesia and within a few years had stamped out the Arab slave-trading in the territory.

The Barotseland-North Western Rhodesia Order in Council dated 28th November 1899 provided for the administration of the western half of Northern Rhodesia by the British South Africa Company under an Administrator nominated by the Company and appointed by the British High Commissioner in South Africa. A similar Order, The North-Eastern Rhodesia Order in Council dated 29th January 1900, provided for the administration of the eastern half of Northern Rhodesia by an Administrator nominated by the Company and appointed by the Consul-General and Commissioner for the British Central Africa Protectorate. Both these orders were revoked in 1911 by the Northern Rhodesia Protectorate Order in Council (S.I. 438) by which the two territories were combined to form the Protectorate of Northern Rhodesia, under the control of the British High Commissioner in South Africa. The British South Africa Company, however, continued to exercise administrative and legislative control. The Company was empowered to administer the country in accordance with its Charter and the Order in Council. The Secretary of State reserved the right to appoint a Resident Commissioner who would report to the British High Commissioner in South Africa on any proclamation issued by the Administrator nominated by the Company. The High Commissioner was empowered to alter or repeal any proclamation for the administration of justice and the raising of revenue and generally to provide for the peace, order and good government of the territory.

In July 1923 a settlement was arranged of the various outstanding problems relating to the Company's position in Northern Rhodesia. The Company surrendered its buildings and assets and its land and monopoly rights, other than mineral rights, but retained freehold land in north-eastern Northern Rhodesia. In return the Company received a cash payment on 1st October 1923 from the British Government.

Constitutional Development

The office of Governor of Northern Rhodesia was created in 1924 by the Northern Rhodesia Order in Council dated 20th February 1924, and Executive and Legislative Councils were established. On this date the High Commissioner in Cape Town ceased to have any jurisdiction in Northern Rhodesia. Until 1935 the capital was at Livingstone but in that year it was moved to Lusaka.

The first Executive Council consisted of the Governor as President, the Chief Secretary, the Attorney-General, the Treasurer, the Secretary for Native Affairs and the Principal Medical Officer. The Legislative Council was composed of the Governor, as President, members of the Executive Council *ex officio*, four nominated members, and five unofficial members who were to be nominated until such time as provision could be made for election. The first elected members took their seats in 1926. In 1928 an unofficial member, nominated by the Governor to represent African interests, was appointed to the Council. The number of unofficial members was increased to seven in 1929 and to nine in 1938.

In 1945 the number of unofficial members was increased from nine to thirteen, of whom eight were elected and five nominated by the Governor. Of the nominated members three were nominated to represent African interests.

In 1948 further changes took place. The Executive Council was composed of the Governor, as President, the Chief Secretary, the Financial Secretary, the Secretary for Native Affairs, the Administrative Secretary, the Economic Secretary, the Director of Development, and four unofficial members of whom three were elected members of the Legislative Council and one a nominated member of the Legislative Council representing African interests. In the Legislative Council a Speaker was appointed to replace the Governor. In addition there were nine official members and fourteen unofficial members (consisting of ten elected European members, two European members to represent African interests and two African members).

As a result of a series of conferences held in 1951, 1952 and 1953 to consider the closer association of Northern Rhodesia, Southern Rhodesia and Nyasaland, a draft Federal scheme was prepared setting out the details for the Constitution of the Federation of Rhodesia and Nyasaland. Whether or not to participate in this was the subject of a referendum in Southern Rhodesia in April 1953 and in the same month the proposals were approved by the Legislative Councils of Northern Rhodesia and Nyasaland. The appropriate Order in Council received Royal Assent on 14th July 1953 and the Federation of Rhodesia and Nyasaland came into existence on 3rd September 1953. The Constitution Order in Council defined the functions and responsibilities of the Federal and Territorial legislatures.

In December 1953 the composition of the Northern Rhodesia Legislative Council consisted of a Speaker and twenty-six members, comprising eight official and eighteen unofficial members. Four of the official members were *ex officio* and the eighteen unofficial members consisted of twelve elected members, four African members (appointed by the Governor on the advice of the African Representative Council), and two members nominated to represent African interests. The Executive Council consisted of the four *ex officio* official members of the Legislative Council, three elected members and one of the nominated unofficial members of the Legislative Council, presided over by the Governor.

In 1959 the elected membership of the Legislative Council was increased to provide a majority of 22 out of 30 seats. At the same time an unofficial majority was introduced in Executive Council and the number of officials was reduced.

Under the Constitution which came into force on 11th September 1962, the Executive Council comprised ten Ministers of whom four were *ex officio* members. The Legislative Council consisted of a Speaker, forty-five elected members, six official members, including the four *ex officio* Ministers and one or two unofficial members nominated by the Governor.

As a result of the dissolution of the Federation of Rhodesia and Nyasaland, on 31st December 1963, the territorial Government of Northern Rhodesia re-assumed the functions which were transferred to Federal responsibility by the Federation of Rhodesia and Nyasaland Constitution Order in Council of 1953.

A new Constitution giving the country internal self-government came into effect in January 1964. The final form of Northern Rhodesia's independence constitution was settled at a conference held in London in May 1964. Northern Rhodesia, under the name of the Republic of Zambia, became independent and a Member of the Commonwealth on 24th October 1964.

The 1964 Constitution was amended in December 1972 to provide for the introduction of a One Party State and a new Constitution was adopted in August 1973. The Constitution was amended in December 1990 to permit the formation of other political parties. A new Constitution for the Third Republic was given presidential assent on 24th August 1991. It took effect on 30th August 1991.

Constitution

Under the Constitution the Head of State of Zambia is the President who is also Commander-in-Chief of the Armed Forces and who has executive powers. No individual may hold the office of President for more than 2 terms, each of 5 years. The Vice President and the Cabinet are appointed by the President from the National Assembly. Cabinet is responsible for formulating policy and for advising the President on policy and it is accountable to the National Assembly.

The legislative powers of the Republic are vested in Parliament consisting of the President and the

National Assembly of 150 members elected from single member constituencies. The President has the power to nominate eight persons as special members of the National Assembly, five of whom can serve in the Cabinet. The Constitution provides for the formation of an upper house but debate on the matter has been referred to the incoming National Assembly.

The franchise is based on universal suffrage for all persons aged 18 years and over who are citizens of Zambia. The Election Regulations are drawn up by an Electoral Commission which may also prescribe and review the delimitation of constituency boundaries.

The Constitution contains a Bill of Rights, setting out the fundamental rights and freedoms of the individual and providing protection from discrimination on grounds of race, tribe, sex, place of origin, marital status, political opinions, colour or creed.

The Government

The first General and Presidential elections under the new Constitution for the Third Republic were held on 31st October 1991. The composition of the political parties in the National Assembly was as follows:

MMD (Movement for Multi-Party Democracy) 125 seats; UNIP (United National Independence Party) 25 seats. None of the other contesting parties gained any seats.

The newly-elected President, Frederick T. Chiluba, was sworn in on 2nd November 1991, having secured over 73 per cent of the total votes cast, compared to just over 23 per cent for the outgoing President, Kenneth Kaunda.

President Chiluba announced the new government team on 7th and 9th November 1991, as follows:

CABINET

The President: His Excellency Frederick T. Chiluba
Vice President: Levy Mwanawasa
Minister without Portfolio (party/govt liaison): Gen Godfrey Miyanda
Ministry of Finance: Emmanuel Kasonde
Ministry of Defence: Ben Mwila
Ministry of Foreign Affairs: Vernon Mwaanga
Ministry of Home Affairs: Newstead Zimba
Ministry of Local Government: Michael Sata
Ministry of Health: Dr Boniface Kawimbe
Ministry of Education: Arthur Wina
Ministry of Legal Affairs: Dr Rodger Chongwe
Ministry of Community Development and Social Welfare: Gabriel Maka
Ministry of Labour and Social Security: Dr Ludwig Sondashi
Ministry of Communication and Transport: Andrew Kashita
Ministry of Agriculture, Food and Fisheries: Dr Guy Scott
Ministry of Lands: Dawson Lupunga
Ministry of Energy and Water Resources: Alfeyo Hambahi
Ministry of Information and Continued Education: Stan Kristafor
Ministry of Mines and Minerals: Humphrey Mulemba
Ministry of Technical and Vocational Education: Dr Akashambatwa Mbikusita-Lewanika
Ministry of Environment: Keli Walubita
Ministry of Commerce, Trade and Industry: Ronald Penza
Ministry of Sports, Youth and Children: Baldwin Nkumbula
Ministry of Tourism: Gen Christon Tembo
Ministry of Works and Supply: Ephraim Chiwe

DEPUTY MINISTERS

In Presidency for Environment: Simon Zukas
In Presidency: Dean Mungomba
Ministry of Finance: Derick Chitala
Ministry of Defence: Major Celestino Chibamba
Ministry of Foreign Affairs: Dr Remmy Mushota
Ministry of Home Affairs: Lt Col Chonda Sosala
Ministry of Local Govt and Housing: Falentine Kayope
Ministry of Health: Dr Katele Kalumba
Ministry of Education: Dr Kabunda Kayombo
Ministry of Community Development and Social Welfare: Chitala Sampa
Ministry of Labour and Social Security: Dr Peter Machangwa
Ministry of Communication and Transport: Gilbert Mululu
Ministry of Agriculture, Food and Fisheries: Dr Chinulu Kalima and Gibson Nkasusu
Ministry of Lands: Edward Shimwande
Ministry of Energy and Water: Edith Nawakwi
Ministry of Information and Continued Education: Bishop Danny Pule
Ministry of Mines and Minerals: Dr Mathias Mpanda
Ministry of Technical and Vocational Education: Suresh Desai
Ministry of Commerce, Trade and Industry: Dipak Patel
Ministry of Sport, Youth and Children: Katongo Maine
Ministry of Tourism: Princess Nakatini
Ministry of Works and Supply: Syacheye Madynkuku

DEPUTY MINISTERS (for individual Provinces)

Southern: Peter Munga
Eastern: Hosio Soko
Lusaka: Elias Chipimo
Northern: David Kapapa
Luapula: Edward Mungo
Central: Wendy Sinkala
Copperbelt: Kangwa Nsuluka
North Western: Vacant
Western: Vacant

Zimbabwe

Capital: Harare

The country takes its name from 'Zimbabwe' (buildings of stone or venerated buildings), the impressive and ancient ruins near Masvingo. Prior to Independence it was known as Southern Rhodesia, deriving that name from Cecil John Rhodes (1853–1902).

Zimbabwe extends from the Zambezi River (latitude 15° 50′ S.) to the Limpopo River (latitude 22° 25′ S.) and from Botswana in longitude 25° 14′ E. to Mozambique in longitude 33° 4′ E. Entirely land-locked, its neighbours are Zambia on the north and north-west, Botswana on the south-west, the Republic of South Africa on the south, and Mozambique on the east and north-east. Part of the boundary to the north with Zambia runs through Lake Kariba which was formed by the damming of the Zambezi in the Kariba Gorge, and was completed in 1959. The Lake is 282 km (175 miles) long, up to 32 km (20 miles) wide, and covers 5,180 sq km (2,000 square miles).

The area of Zimbabwe is 390,624 sq km (150,820 square miles), which is about three times the size of England. Although Zimbabwe lies within the tropics the climate is not typically tropical owing to the elevation of much of the country, particularly in the central plateau or Highveld areas where the majority of the population lives. Of the total area 21 per cent lies over 1,200 m above sea-level. Temperatures range from a mean minimum of 5°C (40°F) to a mean maximum of 30°C (85°F) on the central plateau. The central plateau traverses the country in a north-easterly direction until it links up with a narrow belt of mountainous country striking north and south along the eastern border. There are two important offshoots from the main plateau to the north-west and north of Harare. On either side of the main plateau is the Middleveld which lies between 600 m and 1,200 m above sea-level. The lowveld region, below 600 m, is found along a narrow strip in the Zambezi valley and in a broader tract in the basin of the Limpopo and Sabi Rivers. The lowest point is 198 m above sea-level where the Limpopo River leaves the country. The greatest rainfall occurs in the mountainous country along the eastern border where considerable areas have an annual mean of over 1,200 mm. In the centre of the country annual rainfall varies from a mean of 825 mm in the Harare area to a mean of 600 mm in the Bulawayo area.

The highlands are in two main portions. The northern portion is generally about 1,800 m high, rising at the highest point to 2,555 m above sea-level. The southern portion forms the Vumba Mountains, the Chimanimani Range, which has peaks rising to a height of over 2,400 m and the Chimanimani Uplands. Between them is the Mutare gap through which runs the road and railway to Beira, the nearest outlet to the sea.

The total population is estimated at about 10 million, over 98 per cent of whom are Africans. The remainder of the population is composed of Europeans, Asians and persons of mixed race. The African population is composed mainly of the Shona and Ndebele and their related tribes. No reliable figures are available of the breakdown into tribes but in the country as a whole the Shona are in the majority. The official language is English, but Shona and Ndebele are important vernaculars. Numerous Christian missions of various denominations including Anglican, Roman Catholic and nonconformist are active throughout the country, but the majority of Africans are non-Christian, adhering to traditional beliefs. There are small Muslim, Hindu and Jewish communities.

The capital of Zimbabwe is the city of Harare (formerly Salisbury). Since its foundation in 1890, the city has become the centre of a large urban complex with a population of about one million. Harare and Bulawayo, the second largest city and the railway centre, possess the two largest concentrations of secondary industry in Zimbabwe.

The other areas of greatest industrial development are situated in the Midlands (Gweru, Kwekwe and Kadoma) and at Mutare, near the border with Mozambique.

Harare Airport, 13 km by road from the city, is the centre of Zimbabwe's internal and external civil air communications. The other principal civil airport in Zimbabwe, Woodvale Airport, is 16 km from the city of Bulawayo.

In 1984 there were 18,432 km of state roads. All the main centres of population are also served by National Railways of Zimbabwe, which are connected with the South African, Botswana, Zambia, Mozambique and Angola railway systems. In 1991 Zimbabwe had 2,759 km of 1.067 m (3ft. 6in) gauge railway line. The Harare–Gweru stretch (313 km) is now electrified.

The Zimbabwe Broadcasting Corporation broadcasts from Harare and Bulawayo using short and medium wave and frequency modulation transmitters which, with the help of booster stations, provide countrywide coverage. Television is available in many districts.

The unit of currency is the Zimbabwe dollar. The rate of exchange was £1 = Z$5.99 as at August 1991.

In 1990/91 the Government's total expenditure and net lending amounted to Z$8,355 million, about 54 per cent of GDP.

In contrast with most countries in sub-Saharan Africa, Zimbabwe has an efficient and diverse agricultural sector. It is self-sufficient in food production. In normal years it is able to export substantial amounts of tobacco, sugar, maize and meat. This part of the economy represents the basic means of support for approximately 70 per cent of the population.

Zimbabwe is the most industrialised country in the Southern African Development Co-ordination Conference (SADCC) region. It has a well-established mining industry. Leading minerals are gold, ferrochrome, nickel, copper, tin and asbestos. It also has the ability to be self-sufficient in energy having substantial deposits of coal and the potential for further development of hydro-electric power.

Manufacturing industry was first established in the 1920s. It has experienced a period of almost uninterrupted growth over the past 20 years. The most important areas of production are metals, metal products, chemicals, foodstuffs and textiles.

Zimbabwe, with the encouragement of the World Bank/IMF and other donors, has embarked upon a programme of economic structural adjustment. In the short term this will lead to higher rates of inflation and unemployment but in the longer term it is expected to result in a more efficient dynamic and export orientated economy.

History

It is thought that Zimbabwe was first settled by peoples of Bantu stock between 1,000 and 1,500 years ago, during a great southward migration which also led to the Bantu colonisation of Natal. These immigrants, who are believed to have been the ancestors of the tribes now collectively known as the Shona, found the country inhabited by the Bushmen, the last representatives of a succession of Stone Age cultures of which remains have been discovered 500,000 years old. The Bushmen, hunting peoples who possessed a highly developed artistic sense, were gradually displaced by the Bantu agriculturalists and have now almost disappeared from Zimbabwe.

The second great movement of Bantu peoples into Zimbabwe occurred in 1830, when off-shoots of the Bantu who had reached Natal, and who had by then combined to form the Zulu nation, moved northwards. The most important of these were the Ndebele, under Mzilikazi, who eventually settled in the south-west of the country, in the area known as Matabeleland.

As a result of their attempts in the sixteenth century to open up south central Africa from the east coast of Africa, the Portuguese were the first Europeans to explore what is now Zimbabwe. In 1514 Antonio Fernandez reached the region of Kwekwe, and nearly half a century later the Jesuit priest Gonzalo da Silveira reached Mount Fura where he was murdered after visiting and baptising the Emperor Monomatapa. In 1569 Francesco Barreto led a large military expedition into the interior with the primary object of exploiting the reputed goldfields. The expedition failed and Barreto died at Sena on the Zambezi River.

For some three hundred years there was no further European contact with the hinterland until the coming of the missionary explorers, the hunters, traders and gold-seekers, who between them opened up much of Africa to European influence. David Livingstone first sighted the Zambezi river in 1851 and reached the Victoria Falls in 1855. In 1857 the missionary, Robert Moffat, visited Mzilikazi in Matabeleland, and this led to the establishment in 1859 of the first mission to the Matabele by the London Missionary Society. A second mission was established in 1870 at Hope Fountain.

In 1887 Cecil Rhodes was instrumental in the despatch of J S Moffat to Matabeleland. On 11th February 1888 Lobengula, son and successor to Mzilikazi, signed a treaty pledging not to cede territory without leave of the British High Commissioner at the Cape. Later in the same year, on 30th October, Lobengula granted the Rudd Concession over the minerals in his kingdom. This led to the formation of the British South Africa Company which was granted a Royal Charter on 29th October 1889 in the region of Southern Africa lying immediately to the north of British Bechuanaland (subsequently annexed to the Cape Colony in 1895) and to the north and west of the then South African Republic, and to the west of the Portuguese Dominions. The pioneer column and its escort of police set out from Bechuanaland in 1890 and after skirting Matabeleland reached the present site of Harare on 12th September 1890, and established an administration in Mashonaland. The Anglo-Portuguese Agreement of 1891 which was finally confirmed by Signor Vigliani's award in 1897, settled the boundary disputes with the Portuguese on the eastern border.

In 1893 an Ndebele raid led to the first Matabele War which terminated in the destruction of the Ndebele power and the flight of Lobengula from Bulawayo. Matabeleland then came under the Chartered Company's civil administration. The territories under the Company's administration adopted the name 'Rhodesia' in 1895 and this was formally approved by the Colonial Office in 1897.

The second Matabele War broke out in 1896. The War ended in August 1896 when Cecil Rhodes and a small party met the Ndebele leaders in the Matopos Hills near Bulawayo and arranged a settlement. Risings by the Shona peoples, however, lasted until 1897.

Constitutional development

The territory was administered by the British South Africa Company from the commencement of European colonisation in 1890 until the grant of responsible government in 1923.

In 1922, however the local Legislative Council (on which there was an elected majority) passed a resolution requesting the establishment of responsible government 'forthwith'. The issue was put to the electorate (almost entirely white) as one of two choices, responsible government or entry into the Union of South Africa as the fifth province, and at a referendum in 1922 8,744 votes were cast for self-government and 5,989 for the alternative.

After the 1922 referendum Southern Rhodesia was formally annexed to His Majesty's Dominions as a Colony on 12th September 1923 and was granted full self-government with the exception that legislation affecting African interests, the Rhodesia Railways and certain other matters were reserved to the Secretary of State. Except for those concerning differential legislation affecting the African population, these reservations fell away in time so far as internal affairs were concerned. The British Government conducted formal international relations on behalf of Southern Rhodesia: Commonwealth relations, trade relations, and relations with Colonial territories in Africa were mainly conducted by the Southern Rhodesian Government direct.

The constitutional and other developments in the territory over the next 35 years—the numerous constitutional conferences, the establishment and dissolution of the Central African Federation 1953–63, the illegal declaration of independence by Mr Ian Smith on 11th November 1965, the British assertion of the Six Principles, the imposition of sanctions, the Pearce Commission of 1972, the growing guerrilla war, the abortive Geneva Conference of 1976, the equally abortive Anglo-American Proposals of 1977–78, the successful Lancaster House conference of September/December 1979, and the brief period of direct British rule under Lord Soames as Governor from December 1979 to April 1980—are recorded in some detail in earlier editions of this Yearbook. Suffice it to say that in February 1980, elections were held in preparation for independence, supervised by the British Election Commission and observed, inter alia, by the Commonwealth Observer Group.

Mr Mugabe's ZANU (PF) party won 57 seats; Mr Nkomo's PF-ZAPU won 20 seats, and Bishop Muzorewa's UANC party won 3 seats. In their interim reports, both the British Election Commissioner and the members of the Commonwealth Observer Group had indicated that the elections had been held in the fairest conditions possible under the circumstances and that their results would reflect the wishes of the majority of the Rhodesian electorate. Over 90 per cent of the electorate voted at the elections.

On 4th March the Governor invited Mr Mugabe, as the leader of the party with an outright majority, to form a Government. In doing so, Mr Mugabe invited ZAPU to join with him in a broadly-based administration.

Rhodesia came to independence as Zimbabwe on 18th April 1980.

Fresh general elections to the House of Assembly (Lower House) were held in June/July 1985. Mr Mugabe's ZANU (PF) party won 64 seats, Mr Nkomo's Patriotic Front (ZAPU) won 15 seats, and Mr Sithole's ZANU party won 1 seat. CAZ party won 15 of the separate 20 white roll seats, Independents the remaining 5.

These twenty seats reserved for white parliamentarians were abolished, along with the separate white roll, in constitutional amendments introduced in September 1987. The remaining 80 members acted as an electoral college to vote in non-constituency members selected from amongst party nominations to fill the vacated seats in October 1987. A senate (Upper House) of 40 members was abolished in 1990.

The last general elections (to form the Third Parliament of Zimbabwe) were held in March 1990.

ZANU (PF) and PF-ZAPU signed a unity accord in December 1987 and the formal unification of the two parties was completed in December 1989. As at September 1991, the united ZANU (PF) had 117 of the 120 constituency seats in Parliament. The Zimbabwe Unity Movement had 2 seats, ZANU one.

Constitution

The present Constitution of Zimbabwe is contained in the Zimbabwe Constitution Order (S.I. 1979 No 1600) together with its 11 amendments. Executive authority is vested in the President, who may exercise it directly or through the Cabinet, the two Vice-Presidents, a Minister or Deputy. The President is elected by voters registered on the common roll and holds office for a period of six years. The last Presidential elections were held in March 1990.

Parliament has a life of five years and consists of 120 elected members, 8 Provincial Governors (who are appointed by the President), 10 Chiefs (who are elected by the Council of Chiefs) and 12 non-constituency members who are appointed by the President.

The Constitution contains a fully justiciable Declaration of Rights and provides for the protection of civil service pensions as well as for an ombudsman.

Historical List

Prime Ministers of Southern Rhodesia (*A full Historical List is shown in the 1978 edition*).

HEAD OF STATE (PRESIDENT)
The Hon Robert Gabriel Mugabe

GOVERNMENT
Vice President: The Hon Simon Vengayi Muzenda, MP

Vice President: The Hon Dr Joshua Mqabuko Nkomo, MP

Senior Minister in the President's Office and Minister of Local Government, Rural and Urban Development: The Hon Joseph Msika, MP

Senior Minister of Political Affairs: The Hon Didymus Noel Edwin Mutasa, MP
Senior Minister of Finance, Economic Planning and Development: Dr The Hon Bernard Thomas Chidzero, MP
Attorney-General: The Hon Patrick Anthony Chinamasa
Minister of Foreign Affairs: Dr The Hon Nathan Marwirakuwa Shamuyarira, MP
Minister of Justice, Legal and Parliamentary Affairs: The Hon Emmerson Dambudzo Mnangagwa, MP
Minister of State for National Security: Dr The Hon Sydney Tigere Sekeramayi, MP
Minister of Defence: The Hon Richard Chemist Hove, MP
Minister of Home Affairs: The Hon Moven Enock Mahachi, MP
Minister of State for Local Government, Rural and Urban Development: Dr The Hon Swithun Tachiona Mombeshora, MP
Minister of Lands, Agriculture and Rural Resettlement: Dr The Hon Witness Pasichigara Magunda Mangwende, MP
Minister of Information, Posts and Telecommunications: The Hon Victoria Fikile Chitepo, MP
Minister of Labour, Manpower Planning and Social Welfare: The Hon John Landa Nkomo, MP
Minister of Industry and Commerce: The Hon Kumbirai Manyika Kangai, MP
Minister of State for the Public Service: Dr The Hon Eddison Jonas Mudadirwa Zvobgo, MP
Minister of Energy and Water Resources and Development: Dr The Hon Herbert Sylvester Masiyiwa Ushewokunze, MP
Minister of Mines: The Hon Jonas Christian Andersen, MP
Minister of Transport and National Supplies: The Hon Dennis Norman, MP
Minister of Health: Dr The Hon Timothy Stamps, MP
Minister of Community and Co-operative Development: The Hon Joyce Teurai Ropa Mujuru, MP
Minister of Public Construction and National Housing: The Hon Enos Chamunorwa Chikowore, MP
Minister of Environment and Tourism: Dr The Hon Herbert Muchemwa Murerwa, MP
Minister of Higher Education: The Hon David Ishemunyoro Karimanzira, MP
Minister of Education and Culture: The Hon Fay Chung, MP
Minister of State in the President's Office (Regional and International Co-operation): The Hon Simbi Veke Mubako, MP
Minister of State in the President's Office for Sports Co-ordination: The Hon David Kwidini, MP
Minister of State for National Scholarships: The Hon Joseph Culverwell, MP
Minister of State for Finance, Economic Planning and Development: Dr The Hon Tichaendepi Robert Masaya, MP
Minister of State for Political Affairs: The Hon Welshman Hadane Mabhena, MP
Minister of State for Political Affairs (National Service): Brigadier Dr The Hon Felix Muchemwa, MP
Deputy Minister of State for Political Affairs (Youth): Norman Zikhali, MP

ZANU (PF)

President and First Secretary: R G Mugabe
Vice-Presidents and Second Secretaries: S V Muzenda and J M Nkomo
National Chairman: J Msika
Secretary for Administration: D N E Mutasa
Secretary for Finance: E D Mnangagwa
Secretary for Foreign Affairs: S J Nkomo
Secretary for Commissariat and Culture: M E Mahachi
Secretary for National Security: S T Sekeramayi
Secretary for Transport and Welfare: W H Mabhena
Secretary for Information and Publicity: N M Shamuyarira
Secretary for Production and Labour: J L Nkomo
Secretary for Women's Affairs: Mrs S Mugabe
Secretary for Youth: (Vacant)
Secretary for Economic Affairs: N K Ndlovu
Secretary for Legal Affairs: E J N Zvobgo
Secretary for Education: Mrs J T R Mujuru
Secretary for Health: H S M Ushewokunze
Committee Members: Mrs T V Lesabe, B T G Chidzero, R C Hove, N C Makombe

MINISTRIES AND GOVERNMENT DEPARTMENTS

MINISTRY OF LANDS, AGRICULTURE AND RURAL SETTLEMENT
Secretary: Dr Boniface Ndimande

MINISTRY OF COMMUNITY AND CO-OPERATIVE DEVELOPMENT
Deputy Minister: Kenneth Bute, MP
Secretary: Dr Langford Chitsike

MINISTRY OF PUBLIC CONSTRUCTION AND NATIONAL HOUSING
Secretary: Mr Paul Kodzwa

MINISTRY OF DEFENCE
Secretary: Mr Willard Chiwewe

MINISTRY OF HIGHER EDUCATION
Secretary: Dr Elijah John Chanakira

MINISTRY OF EDUCATION AND CULTURE
Deputy Minister: Gabriel Machinga, MP
Secretary: Mr Isaiah Sibanda

MINISTRY OF ENERGY AND WATER RESOURCES AND DEVELOPMENT
Secretary: Mr James Chitauro

MINISTRY OF FINANCE, ECONOMIC PLANNING AND DEVELOPMENT
Secretary: Dr Elisha Mushayakarara

MINISTRY OF FOREIGN AFFAIRS
Deputy Minister: Stephen Jege Nyongolo Nkomo, MP
Secretary: Dr Tichaona Jokonya

MINISTRY OF HEALTH
Secretary: Dr Godfrey Sikipa

MINISTRY OF HOME AFFAIRS
Deputy Minister: Dumiso Dabengwa, MP
Secretary: Dr Job Whabira

MINISTRY OF INFORMATION, POSTS AND TELECOMMUNICATIONS:
Deputy Minister: Chenhamo Chakazha Chimutengwende, MP
Secretary: Mrs Sarah Letty Kachingwe

MINISTRY OF JUSTICE, LEGAL AND PARLIAMENTARY AFFAIRS
Secretary: Mr Paddington Garwe

MINISTRY OF LABOUR, MANPOWER PLANNING AND SOCIAL WELFARE
Deputy Minister: Mrs Florence Chitauro, MP
Secretary: Mr July Moyo

MINISTRY OF LOCAL GOVERNMENT, RURAL AND URBAN DEVELOPMENT
Secretary: Dr Mariyo Mariyawanda Nzuwah

MINISTRY OF MINES
Secretary: David Edgar Murangari

MINISTRY OF ENVIRONMENT AND TOURISM
Deputy Minister: Mrs Thenjiwe Virginia Lesabe, MP
Secretary: Mr Tichafa Eneas Mundangepfupfu

MINISTRY OF POLITICAL AFFAIRS (ADMINISTRATION)
Deputy Minister: Miss Tsungirirayi Hungwe, MP
Deputy Minister of State (External Affairs): Mrs Oppah Chamu Rushesha, MP
Deputy Minister of State (Women's Affairs and the Commissariat): Mrs Shuvai Taderera, MP
Secretary: Dr Isaac Mudenge

PUBLIC SERVICE
Secretary: Dr Samuel Agere

MINISTRY OF INDUSTRY AND COMMERCE
Deputy Minister: Moton Dizzy Paul Malianga, MP
Secretary: Dr Mudziviri Nziramasanga

MINISTRY OF TRANSPORT AND NATIONAL SUPPLIES
Deputy Minister: Mrs Amina Hughes, MP
Secretary: Mr Sam Geza

PART V

Dependent Territories of Commonwealth Countries

DEPENDENT TERRITORIES OF THE COMMONWEALTH

United Kingdom

The remaining dependent territories of the United Kingdom differ widely in social, economic and political circumstances. It is impossible, therefore, to apply a uniform policy and the problems of each territory are considered in relation to its own particular requirements and aspirations, (see below pp 416–475): The dependent territories retain their connection with the United Kingdom by virtue of the wishes of their inhabitants and there is no intention either to delay independence for those territories which desire it nor force it on those which do not.

The inhabited territories have already assumed a very substantial measure of responsibility for the conduct of their own affairs. Governors are appointed by the Crown on the advice of the British Government which retains responsibility for external affairs, defence and, usually, internal security and the public service. The organs of local self-government are provided by Executive Councils and Legislative Assemblies (or their equivalents).

Australia

The Australian External Territories are also of diverse character and are governed in a number of different ways. (see below pp 476–480). The connection of the inhabited territories with Australia is also a reflection of the wishes of their inhabitants.

New Zealand

The New Zealand dependent territories fall into two broad categories: those directly administered by New Zealand and those enjoying full self-government but in association with New Zealand, (see below pp 481–482.

Anguilla

Anguilla is the most northerly of the Leeward Islands in the Eastern Caribbean. It lies approximately 18° north latitude and 63° west longitude. It is approximately 8 km (5 miles) from the Dutch and French Island of St Martin. The territory of Anguilla includes some offshore islets and cays such as Scrub Island to the north east, Dog Island, Prickly Pear Cays and Sandy Island to the north west. There is also Sombrero Island (where there is a lighthouse station manned and operated from Anguilla on behalf of Trinity House) some 61 km (38 miles) to the north west. Anguilla is long and flat. The highest elevation at Crocus Hill is about 64 m above sea level. It is a dry island with for the most part a thin layer of soil over rock and in some places there are pockets of fertile soil. A large part of the island is covered with scrub. The island has about 30 white coral sand beaches. There are no rivers but there are some salt ponds. The island itself is about 91 sq km (35 square miles) in area not including the offshore cays. It stretches from north east to south west and is about 26 km (16 miles) long by a maximum of 5 km (3 miles) wide.

The tropical marine climate is generally pleasant and healthy. The hottest months are July to October, and the coolest December to February. Rainfall is low and erratic—ranging from 550 to 1,250 mm per annum with an average of about 875 mm. Rain may fall at any time of the year but the wettest months are usually September to January and sometimes April to May. During the hurricane season from July to October, sudden squalls and occasional thunder showers can be expected.

The unit of currency is the Eastern Caribbean dollar.

The last census in 1984 showed a population of about 7,000. Religion is Christian, the main denominations being Anglican, Methodist and Seventh Day Adventists. English is the official and spoken language.

There are six government primary schools and a comprehensive school. The total school population in 1990 was over 2,200 pupils. Tertiary education is provided at regional universities and similar institutions.

The standard of housing in Anguilla is high compared to elsewhere in the Caribbean. Most houses are built of concrete and are often spacious in design.

The main seaports are Road Bay and Blowing Point, the latter serving passenger traffic to and from St Martin. Wallblake Airport has a surfaced runway length of 1,080 m and a new terminal building was opened in November 1988.

There are about 65 km of tarred road and 40 km of gravel and earth public roads serving all parts of the island. Electricity distribution is island-wide.

There is a modern internal telephone service with 1,300 exchange lines, and international telegraph, telex and telephone services, all operated by Cable and Wireless. The Government operates a radio broadcasting service (Radio Anguilla) for about 14 hours a day. It operates on a frequency of 1505 KHZ (200 metres) with a power of 1,000 watts.

There is a 24-bed cottage hospital and a new 36-bed hospital is presently under construction on a new site and should be completed in 1992. There are, at present, four government Medical Officers. Specialist medical treatment is obtainable from neighbouring islands. There is a government Dental Surgeon and a modern dental clinic.

Because of low rainfall agriculture potential is limited. The chief crops are pigeon peas, corn and sweet potatoes. Livestock consists of sheep, goats, pigs, cattle and poultry. Fishing is carried out inshore and on the reefs. Lobsters are exported live to neighbouring islands.

There are hotels, guest houses and apartments offering tourism facilities for visitors to enjoy the beaches and various marine attractions. Several of the hotels are of international standard.

Most of the land registered in Anguilla is privately owned. There is also a system of Aliens Land Holding Licences devised to protect the long term interest of the local population.

Government revenue in 1991 is estimated at EC$33.1 million, recurrent expenditure at EC$30.1 million and capital expenditure from local funds EC$2.9 million. In addition further capital expenditure is financed from aid funds mainly provided from the United Kingdom.

History

Anguilla was given its name by the Spaniards or the French because of its eel-like shape. Its Carib name was Malliouhana. Archaeological evidence shows that Anguilla was inhabited by substantial numbers of Arawaks for several centuries prior to the arrival of European colonists. Anguilla was colonised in 1650 by English settlers coming from St Kitts. It has remained a British territory ever since, though the Dutch did construct and maintain a fort for a few years in Anguilla in 1631. In 1688 the island was attacked by a party of Irishmen who stayed to settle and eventually left descendants with Irish names that have been carried to the present day.

Anguilla was attacked by the French twice in the eighteenth century. In 1745 a force of about 700 men landed on the north coast near Crocus Bay but was beaten off. In 1796 a force of 400 men landed on the south coast at Rendezvous Bay and drove the Anguillan defenders eastwards across the island until a fierce battle took place at Sandy Hill at which they were repelled.

After British colonisation in the seventeenth century Anguilla was administered as part of the Leeward Islands. From 1825 Anguilla became more closely associated with St Kitts. In 1872 a petition was sent to the Colonial Office asking for separate status and direct rule from Britain. This was not granted. In 1958 the islanders formally petitioned the Governor requesting a dissolution of the political and administrative association with St Kitts. It was to no avail. From 1958 until 1962 Anguilla was, along with St Kitts and Nevis, a unit of the short-lived Federation of the West Indies.

In 1967 there was opposition to the continuance of rule from St Kitts with the coming of Associated State status. On 30th May 1967 the St Kitts policemen in Anguilla were evicted from the island and Anguilla refused to recognise the authority of the State Government any longer. This decision was endorsed in a referendum held in July 1967. There were numerous attempts from outside to effect a constitutional settlement. From January 1968 to January 1969 the British Government maintained a 'Senior British Official' to work and advise the local Anguilla Council and recommend some possible solutions to the problem. In March 1969 following the ejection from the island of Mr William Whitlock, Parliamentary Under Secretary of State for Foreign and Commonwealth Affairs, British Security Forces occupied Anguilla. Her Majesty's Commissioner was installed under temporary provisions. One of his tasks was to work out, if possible, an agreement which would satisfy all parties, including the Anguillians. There were further negotiations and eventually in 1971 agreement was reached on interim arrangements for the island's administration.

In July 1971 the British Parliament passed the Anguilla Act 1971, which authorised the making of orders in Council to secure peace, order and good government and appointment of a Commissioner to exercise the appropriate functions. The Anguilla Act also provided that when legislation was introduced into the Associated State legislature for the termination of the State's association with Britain, then Anguilla might be formally separated from the State.

Following the passing of the Anguilla Act, the Anguilla Administration Order in Council was made in August 1971 under the terms of which Her Majesty's Commissioner carried on the direct administration of the island, working in close consultation and co-operation with an elected Council. Those arrangements lasted until February 1976 when a new Constitution was established, under the terms of the Anguilla (Constitution) Order 1976 which replaced the Anguilla (Administration) Order 1971.

On 19th December 1980 Anguilla was formally separated from the State of St Kitts-Nevis-Anguilla.

Government

A new Constitution came into operation on 1st April 1982 and was amended in 1990. Executive power is vested in the Governor, who is appointed by Her Majesty The Queen. Save for his special responsibilities (External Affairs, Defence, International Financial Services, Internal Security including the Police and the Public Service) and his reserve powers in respect of legislation, the Governor discharges his executive powers on the advice of an Executive Council comprising a Chief Minister, three Ministers, with two *ex-officio* members (Attorney-General and Deputy Governor). This in effect means that for most practical purposes, the body politic has control over internal affairs.

GOVERNOR
Mr B G J Canty, OBE, JP

Deputy Governor: Hon Colville L Petty (Acting)
Chief Minister and Minister of Home Affairs, Agriculture and Tourism: Hon Emile Gumbs
Minister of Finance and Economic Development: Hon Osbourne Fleming
Minister of Social Services and Lands: Hon Eric Reid
Minister of Communications, Public Utilities and Works: Hon Kenneth Harrigan
Attorney General: Hon Kurt DeFreitas

ELECTED MEMBERS OF THE HOUSE OF ASSEMBLY
Mr Victor Banks
Mr Albert Hughes
Mr Hubert Hughes

Bermuda

Capital: Hamilton

The Bermudas or Somers Islands derived their names from the Spanish seaman Juan Bermudez, who sighted the group before 1515, but no settlement was made until 1609, when Sir George Somers, who was shipwrecked on his way to Virginia, colonised the islands. Bermuda is situated in the Western Atlantic Ocean about 917 km (570 miles) east of Cape Hatteras, North Carolina, latitude, 32° 18″N longitude, 64° 46″W. The Territory has a total area of 53.3 sq km (20.59 square miles) of which 5.9 sq km (2.30 square miles) are at present leased to the United States Government for military bases. The United States bases include a large airfield which is used by both military and commercial traffic.

The Bermudas consist of about 150 islands and islets, roughly in the form of a fishhook, along the southern rim of the oval plateau summit, about 35 km (22 miles) from east to west and 23 km (14 miles) from north to south, of a steep submarine volcanic mountain which is reputed to be between 4,200 m and 4,500 m in height. The ten principal islands are connected by bridges and form a chain about 35 km (22 miles) long between its north-east and south-west extremities. These islands vary in width but the main island, which is about 23 km (14 miles) long, has an average width of about 1.6 km, it comprises approximately 3,642 hectares (9,000 acres) of land, the highest point being only 78 m above the sea. All the other islands and areas reclaimed for the United States bases aggregate about 1,716 hectares (4,240 acres). There are no rivers or lakes.

The City of Hamilton, the capital since 1815, with a population of 3,000, is situated on the main island. The Town of St. George's on the Island of St. George's was formerly the capital. It has a population of 1,647.

The climate is generally humid with a mean annual temperature of 21°C (70°F) and average maximum and minimum temperatures of 32°C (90°F) and 9°C (47°F) respectively. The coldest and hottest months are February and August. The average annual rainfall is 1,453 mm.

Birth and death records show the civil population at the end of 1990 at 59,588. In 1990 there were 912 live births, 462 deaths, and 884 marriages.

Bermuda has a high population density—an estimated 2,777 people per square mile in 1990. The official language is English but there is a small minority of Portuguese speaking people.

The Department of Health and Social Services provides medical services and facilities including Child Health Clinics, School Health Services and Clinics, and a Clinic for Sexually Transmitted Diseases. Comprehensive Family Planning Services and Dental Services for children are also provided. There are also Health Visitors and District Nurses. Health Education by means of group talks and through use of the media are an important part of the service to the community.

The Department of Social Services is responsible for child protection, which includes foster care and adoption; financial assistance; probation; and residential care and rehabilitation for young people with behavioural problems. The Department also operates a Day Care Centre for pre-school children. Among the services sponsored by voluntary organisations are: a physical abuse centre; a hostel for alcoholics; education and counselling for adolescent unmarried mothers; children's institutions; Meals-on-Wheels; Marriage Guidance Council; physically handicapped children; emergency housing for young women and Big Brothers and Sisters; and support therapy for Aids patients and their relatives.

There are two hospitals—the King Edward the Seventh Memorial Hospital, a general hospital with 233 beds in private, semi-private, and public wards. KEMH is accredited by The Canadian Council on Hospital Accreditation. It is fully air-conditioned and completely equipped with modern, up-to-date facilities. The geriatric ward accommodates 92 geriatric and rehabilitation patients. There are 205 registered nurses and 30 enrolled nurses, 12 resident doctors and 47 doctors and 27 dentists on the attending staff.

There are specialists and consultants in anaesthesiology, gynaecology, internal medicine, neurology, orthopaedics, paediatrics, ophthalmology, pathology, psychiatry, radiology, laboratory medicine, surgery and urology in both the general and specialised fields. There are well-equipped laboratories, ECG, EEG, and physiotherapy departments. A blood transfusion unit with a blood bank is run in conjunction with the Department of Pathology. Complete alcoholism services and a chronic renal dialysis service are offered and there are ultra-sonographic diagnostic facilities available. Four ambulances are stationed at the Hospital. There is an excellent emergency department staffed 24 hours a day for the treatment of emergencies and accidents. A coffee shop is operated by the Women's Hospital Auxiliary (The Pink Ladies). St. Brendan's Hospital is a 175-bed hospital for the mentally ill with both in-patient and out-patient facilities in addition to out-patient clinics available for psychiatric patients. Assistance is also given by the nursing department, the occupational therapy department, and mental social workers. There are four full-time psychiatrists. There is also a cafe, library and offices as well as a new day-care centre, including industrial and occupational therapy. Lefroy House is operated as a geriatric unit.

There are 9 registered trade unions, the principal one being The Bermuda Industrial Union (BIU), The Bermuda Public Service Association (BPSA), the Amalgamated Bermuda Union of Teachers (ABUT) and The Bermuda Federation of Musicians and Variety Artists (BFMVA).

Vegetable production is the most important branch of agriculture in Bermuda but only a small percentage of the overall food consumption is produced. Egg production covers about 35 per cent of total requirements, milk about 100 per cent, potatoes 56 per cent, other vegetables 50 per cent, citrus fruit and bananas 50 per cent.

The area of arable land, always small, is diminishing owing to the encroachment of building development. Of the total acreage of 620, some 372 acres are used for commercial vegetation production; 105 are planted out to bananas and citrus and about 5 acres for flowers. There are 55 acres of pasture, 35 for forage and 48 acres are fallow.

Bermuda has almost 300 registered fishermen. The fishing industry has historically been centred around reef-dwelling species such as groupers, snapper, progy and spiny lobsters. Jacks and tuna have been secondary catches. Due to a recent decline in catches of the grouper species, fishermen now make better use of species such as wahoo, tuna, parrotfish, surgeonfish, gwelly, chub and shark. Pot fishing was banned in 1990 and a new pot is being designed for lobster fishing. Most of the catch from local waters is distributed to hotels and restaurants. In the absence of a local fish market, most fishermen process and sell their own catch.

The Government provides duty exemption for equipment and machinery used in the agricultural and fisheries industries. Fishermen must qualify for this concession through submission of catching and effort statistics.

Tourism is the major industry and source of revenue. Responsibility for the promotion of tourism, under the Minister of Tourism, rests with the Department of Tourism which has its head office in Bermuda; representation in London, and branch offices in New York, Boston, Atlanta, Chicago and Toronto. The Minister for Tourism has the final decision on matters of policy, but consults an advisory board in dealing with advertising and public relations, special events, overseas communications, etc. Another side of the Department's local operation is the maintenance and operation of Fort St Catherine, Gates Fort, The Featherbed Alley Printing Shop, Alexandra Battery and Fort Scaur, as attractive and interesting places to visit.

In 1990, 416,049 tourists visited Bermuda including those arriving by air and cruise ship. The origin of visitors remained the same—86 per cent of those arriving were from the USA, 7.0 per cent were from Canada, 3.7 per cent were from the UK and the remainder were from other countries. The degree of satisfaction of visitors, based on a survey of departing tourists, remained extremely high. The reasons they say they like Bermuda are: friendliness and hospitality of Bermudians; the fact that Bermuda is clean, quiet, restful and peaceful; and Bermuda's great scenic beauty.

Seventy-seven per cent of Bermuda's visitors arrive by air. The air gateways in the USA are Baltimore, Washington DC, Boston, Newark, New York, Philadelphia, Tampa, White Plains, Raleigh Durham and Atlanta. Eastern, Delta, American Airlines, Continental, US Air and Pan American Airways operate USA/Bermuda services. British Airways operates a service between London/Baltimore/Bermuda, and, a service between London/Bermuda/Tampa. Air Canada operates frequent services to Bermuda from Toronto and Halifax.

Bermuda has three ports, Hamilton, St George's and Freeport. The main ship traffic, passenger and cargo is centred on the Port of Hamilton which is also the Capital. Hamilton can accommodate vessels up to 26 feet in draught and 650 feet in length. It has approximately 2,500 feet of berthing space and shed space of some 42,000 square feet. A container park of some 5½ acres and an additional 650 feet of quay was completed in late 1973.

St George's, the former Capital of Bermuda, also has modern port facilities and handles cruise ships and a small amount of cargo traffic. Cruise ship facilities at Ordnance Island can accommodate vessels up to 650 feet in length and 28 feet draught. Pennos Wharf, 750 feet in length provides facilities for vessels up to 29 feet draught and shed space of some 15,000 square feet. On the north side of St George's Island Esso Bermuda own and operate an oil terminal for the reception of oil products and for bunkers. Vessels up to 34 feet draught can be accepted.

Freeport has a commercial berth 800 feet in length and a depth of water alongside of 34 feet (MLWOST) (1977). There are reception facilities for bulk cement and a bunkering station is operated by the Shell Company of Bermuda.

There are two main lights, Gibb's Hill Lighthouse—height 354 feet situated in the centre of the islands—and St David's Lighthouse—height 208 feet situated at Bermuda's eastern extremity.

Bermuda Harbour Radio situated at Fort George provides communications facilities as a coast radio station and for port and channel control. It also co-ordinates search and rescue operations.

The only airfield is at the United States Naval Air Station, which was originally constructed during the last war solely for military purposes. In 1948 this base, known as Kindley Field, was opened to civil aircraft in accordance with the provisions of a treaty agreement between the Government of the United States of America and the United Kingdom. The base itself is leased to the United States Government for 99 years. Civil aircraft are handled in a sub-leased area at the western end of the airfield which has been extended to accommodate Jumbo Jets. Both military and civil aircraft use the same runways and technical facilities of air traffic control, communications, weather and navigation aids.

There are 224 km of central and local government roads, most of which are surfaced; they include 6 km reserved for cyclists and pedestrians. There are also many surfaced estate roads and unsurfaced private roads.

International company business makes a significant contribution to the economy. In 1990, 7,002 international companies in the insurance and investment field were registered in Bermuda. They employed over 2,000 people, nearly 60 per cent of them Bermudians.

Prior to 1946, local listeners relied on broadcasts from North America and England. The Bermuda Broadcasting Company formed in 1943 and started commercial broadcasting under the call-sign ZBM, three years later. A second station under the call sign ZBM-2 was opened in 1953, and in 1962, an FM station was opened. A second broadcasting company, Capital Broadcasting, using the call-sign ZFB, also formed in 1962. In 1971, ZFB inaugurated a second FM station, producing stereophonic transmissions. In July, 1981, a third broadcasting station, St George's Broadcasting Company opened with the call sign VSB. To date, VSB has three AM facilities.

Bermuda's first commercial television ZBM-TV began operations in January 1958 on VHF Channel 10. Capital Broadcasting Company operated on Channel 8 from 1965, was acquired by Bermuda Broadcasting Company in 1982, and ceased broadcasting in 1984. In the fall of 1988, ZFB was reactivated on Channel 7, with syndicated programming. DeFontes Broadcasting Company operate on Channel 13. Bermuda uses the North American NTSC System M television broadcasting standard.

A telecommunications licence was offered to Bermuda Cablevision Limited in December 1985 and they began service of an island-wide cable television system in July 1988.

Income tax and estate duty are not levied in Bermuda but legislative approval was given in 1967 for the introduction of a property tax.

Bermuda was allocated several satellite channels by the International Telecommunications Union.

	Out-turn Fiscal Year 1991/92 BD$millions
Government Revenue	
Main Categories:	
Customs duties	130.5
Employment tax	29.2
International Companies tax	21.47
Land tax	19.65
Hotel Occupancy tax	12.1
Hospital levy	48.8
Vehicle Licences	11.7
Passenger departure taxes	14.5
Stamp duties	13.3
Immigration	10.42
Post Office	8.46

	Categories of expenditure as a % of total expenditure for 1991/92
Government Expenditure	
Main Categories:	
Education	14.2%
Health, Social Services & Housing	20.7%
Finance	11.6%
Works & Engineering	9.1%
Labour & Home Affairs	1.3%
Tourism	8.0%
Transport	5.6%
The Environment	3.3%
Youth, Sport & Recreation	1.2%
Community & Cultural Affairs	1.0%
Telecommunications	1.0%
Judicial, Legal, Legislative	2.0%
Administration	1.9%

Budget—Fiscal Year 1992	
Total Revenue	361,600
Total Expenditure	322,526
Budget Surplus	39,074

Retail Price Index

1987	149.6
1988	163.1
1989	167.7
1990	169.6

Education

The general administration of education is the responsibility of the Minister of Education who is assisted by a Permanent Secretary and an Advisory Board.

Education is compulsory between the ages of 5 and 16, and government assistance is given by the payment of grants, where necessary, of school fees. Free elementary education was introduced on 1st May 1949 and free secondary education in September, 1965. There are 18 primary schools with enrolment in each ranging from 91–416 students; 14 secondary schools (of which five are private, including two denominational schools and one run by the United States Armed Forces in Bermuda) which enrol 178–603 students each; four special schools at the primary and secondary levels which cater to 190 blind, deaf, speech impaired and multiple handicapped children; a Day Training Centre for children 5–14 years; an Opportunity Workshop which caters to severely handicapped persons aged 14–21, and 11 pre-school nurseries. Private schools do not receive Government aid, and charge fees.

Physical facilities at the Government schools are excellent. The teacher/pupil ratio in Government schools excluding administrative personnel, is 1 to 17 in primary schools and 1 to 11 in secondary schools.

All secondary schools, both public and private, are engaged in the Bermuda Secondary School Certificate (BSSC) programme. A five-year course of study leads to a certificate which, at the highest level of award will be equivalent to GCE 'O' Level.

All of Bermuda's secondary schools provide the opportunity to take 'O' level GCE or the equivalent. 'A' Level programmes are not taught in Bermuda's secondary schools. The Bermuda College, the only tertiary institution in Bermuda, offers a course equivalent to the first two years of North American universities and instruction at the GCE 'A' Level. The College also provides full and part-time education and training for persons over the compulsory school age.

The Minister of Education is also responsible for Bermuda's libraries. The main branch in Hamilton was opened in 1839 and there are branches in Somerset and St. George's. Total bookstock is 150,000 volumes. Included in the central facility is a reading room and a Reference Library. The Bermuda Archives, established under the Bermuda Archives Act, 1974, is legally responsible for the preservation of national documents, and also has the task of filing all Government records. The Central Government Microfilm Unit forms part of the Bermuda Archives. One of its largest projects was the microfilming of two local newspapers.

History

According to the Spanish navigator and historian Ferdinand d'Oviedo, who sailed close to the islands in 1515, they were discovered by Juan Bermudez. A 17th century French cartographer gives the date of their discovery as 1503 and there is evidence that the islands were known as 'La Bermuda' by 1510. The Spaniards do not seem to have taken any steps to form a settlement and the islands were still entirely uninhabited when in 1609 Admiral Sir George Somers' ship *The Sea Venture* was wrecked upon one of the reefs while carrying a party of colonists to Virginia. Reports of the beauty and fertility of the land caused the Virginia Company to seek an extension of their charter so as to include the islands within their dominion. This was granted by King James I in 1612 and the first emigrants went out in that year. Shortly afterwards the Virginia Company sold the islands for £2,000 to a new body of adventurers called 'The Governor and Company of the City of London for the Plantation of the Somers Islands', and for a considerable time afterwards the islands bore that name. In 1684 the charter of the Bermuda Company of London was annulled and government passed to the Crown.

As in the West Indies, slavery was permitted from the colony's earliest days, but following William Wilberforce's crusade in England it was abolished absolutely in Bermuda in 1834.

Later in the nineteenth century, following the inauguration of steamship services, Bermuda, in addition to enjoying a profitable agricultural export trade in vegetables, gradually became noted for its climate and charm. Slowly the tourist trade grew, many visitors coming annually to escape the rigorous North American winters and, as larger and faster ships were built and hotels erected, it finally became the colony's most important business. Since the Second World War, the tourist season has become virtually year-round, with the greatest influx of visitors coming during the long summer season.

The year 1959 was the 350th anniversary of the settlement of Bermuda. Throughout the year a comprehensive programme of functions and celebrations was carried out, and a special Crown piece was issued by the Royal Mint. His Royal Highness Prince Philip, Duke of Edinburgh, paid a flying visit in April 1959.

The Parliamentary Election Act, passed in December 1962, marked an important step in the political evolution of Bermuda. Throughout its history, members of the House of Assembly had been elected by the privileged few who could meet a freehold voting qualification (5,500 in 1962). The new act enfranchised everyone over the age of 25, thus creating a potential electorate of 22,000, while retaining for property-owners the privilege of an extra vote.

Bermuda's first political party, the Progressive Labour Party, was formed shortly before the elections held in May 1963 but the majority of seats were won by independent candidates. In the following year however most of the independent members formed a second party, the United Bermuda Party.

In November 1963 the Legislature appointed a Joint Select Committee to consider constitutional change. In an interim report the Committee recommended the abolition of the additional Property Vote and reduction of the voting age from twenty-five to twenty-one years. These changes became law early in 1966.

In its second report, published in November 1965, the Joint Select Committee made detailed recommendations for constitutional change. This report was accepted by the Legislature and subsequently a Constitutional Conference was convened in London in November 1966. In addition to the Governor and the Attorney-General, a representative delegation consisting of eighteen members of the Legislature attended. A new Constitution providing responsible internal self-government came into force on 8th June 1968, following a General Election on 22nd May, which resulted in the United Bermuda Party winning a majority of the seats in the House of Assembly. The progressive Labour Party became the official opposition.

The United Bermuda Party have been returned to power in six subsequent elections—1972, 1976, 1980, 1983, 1985 and 1989. The Progressive Labour Party are the official opposition. The National Liberal Party has only one elected representative and there are two Independent members of the House of Assembly.

Constitution

Under a Constitution introduced on 8th June 1968, there are provisions relating to the protection of fundamental rights and freedoms of the individual; the powers and duties of the Governor; the composition, powers, and procedure of the Legislature; the Cabinet; the Judiciary; the Public Service and Finance.

Her Majesty, Queen Elizabeth II, is represented by His Excellency the Governor who retains responsibility for external affairs, defence, internal security and the Police.

The Legislature consists of Her Majesty, The Senate, and The House of Assembly. Five members of the Senate are appointed by the Governor on the advice of the Premier; three by the Governor on the advice of the Opposition Leader; and three by the Governor acting in his own discretion. The Senate itself elects its President and Vice-President. The House of Assembly, consisting of 40 members elected under universal adult suffrage from 20 constituencies, elects a Speaker and a Deputy Speaker, and sits for a five-year term.

The Cabinet is headed by the Premier and at least six other members of the Legislature. The Governor appoints the majority leader in the House of Assembly as Premier who, in turn, nominates other members of the Cabinet. The Ministers are assigned responsibility for Government Departments and other business and are, in some cases, assisted by Parliamentary Secretaries.

The Cabinet is presided over by the Premier. The Governor's Council enables the Governor to consult with the Premier and two other members of the Cabinet nominated by the Premier on matters for which the Governor has responsibility. The Secretary to the Cabinet, who is also Head of the Civil Service, acts as Secretary to the Governor's Council.

Commonwealth citizens, over the age of 21 years, are qualified to vote in local elections if they possess Bermudian status, or if they were registered as electors on 1st May 1976. Candidates for election must qualify as electors and must possess Bermudian status.

Land policy

In 1982/83 properties were re-valued and the scale of land tax adjusted accordingly. There is a continuing programme of personal service of proposals each month on all affected owners for the amendment and updating of the 1977 Valuation List to take into account all new, altered and demolished properties.

Since 1975 a re-survey of all real estate in Bermuda has been completed and the Land Valuation Office now holds a plan for every property together with full survey details, and each valuation unit is readily identifiable within any particular complex of buildings and by grid reference to the Ordinance Survey plans for Bermuda.

In conjunction with the Accountant General's Department a Computer Master File results in:

(*a*) automatic reconciliation of the Land Tax Register with the Valuation List;

(*b*) earlier incorporation into the Land Valuation List and the Land Tax register of alterations of values and consequential Land Tax;

(*c*) availability of user and accommodation statistics for forward planning purposes.

Government (July 1991)
Governor and Commander-in-Chief: Sir Desmond Langley, KCVO, MBE
Deputy Governor: J P Kelly, MBE

THE CABINET
The Premier: The Hon John W D Swan, KBE, JP, MP
Deputy Premier and Minister of the Environment: The Hon Mrs Ann F Cartwright DeCouto, JP, MP
Minister of Labour and Home Affairs: The Hon Sir John H Sharpe, CBE, JP, MP
Minister of Health, Social Services and Housing: The Hon Quinton L Edness, JP, MP
Minister of Finance: Dr The Hon David J Saul, JP, MP
Minister of Telecommunications: Senator The Hon Charles T M Collis, JP
Minister of Education: The Hon Gerald D E Simons, JP, MP
Minister of Youth, Sport and Recreation: The Hon Harry W Soares, JP, MP
Minister of Community and Cultural Affairs: The Hon Leonard O Gibbons, JP, MP
Minister of Transport: The Hon Ralph O Marshall, JP, MP
Minister of Works and Engineering: Dr The Hon Clarence R Terceira, JP, MP
Minister of Tourism: The Hon Clarence V Woolridge, JP, MP
Minister of Management and Information Services: The Hon Michael J Winfield, JP

THE SENATE
President: Senator The Hon Albert Jackson, MBE, JP
Vice President: Senator Dr Norma A Cox Astwood
Senator The Hon Charles T M Collis, JP
Senator Maxwell Burgess
Senator W Alex Scott
Senator J C H Johnson, JP
Senator The Hon M J Winfield JP
Senator Ira P Philip, JP
Senator the Rev Trevor E Woolridge
Senator N Cindy Trimm
Senator Pamela F Gordon

THE HOUSE OF ASSEMBLY
His Honour the Speaker: The Hon David E Wilkinson, JP, MP
Deputy Speaker: Ernest D DeCouto, JP, MP
Forty Elected MPs
Clerk to the Legislature: James Smith
Assistant Clerks: Mrs Muriel Roach; Mr Clerk Somner

Local Government
There are two municipalities—The City of Hamilton (incorporated 1793 and made a city by act of legislation in 1897) which is governed by a corporation; and the town of St George (incorporated 1797) one of the oldest settlements in the Western Hemisphere and the capital of Bermuda until 1815. Charges for dock facilities and water are the Hamilton corporation's main source of revenue but both governing bodies derive revenue from rents and municipal taxes.

HAMILTON
Mayor: The Wor Cecil Dismont, MBE, JP
Secretary of the Corporation: H A Leseur, MBE

ST GEORGE'S
Mayor: The Wor Henry Hayward, JP
Secretary of the Corporation: Mrs Lily Oatley

Parish Councils are appointed annually to advise on the administration of general parochial affairs of the Poor Law by the parishes of St George's, Hamilton, Smith's, Devonshire, Pembroke, Paget, Warwick, Southampton and Sandys.

The systems of law applicable in Bermuda are the common law, the doctrines of equity and all English Acts of general application which were in force on the 11th July 1612. These systems are subject to Acts passed in Bermuda since that date in any way altering, modifying or amending those laws or doctrines. The Public Acts and Statutory Instruments made thereunder were reprinted in 1971, with a volume containing tables and indexes. There exists also an edition of private acts in two volumes.

CIVIL ESTABLISHMENT
Secretary to the Cabinet: Kenneth A Richardson, CBE, AIMP, JP
Financial Secretary: Dr I W Hughes, MBE
Permanent Secretary for Health, Social Services and Housing: Edward Dyer, CPSM, SRN, RMN
Permanent Secretary for Education and Libraries: Dr Marion Robinson
Permanent Secretary for Home Affairs: Ernest D Owen
Collector of Customs: Gerry Ardis
Auditor: L T Dennis, CA
Permanent Secretary, Ministry of the Environment: Dr James Burnett-Herkes
Director of Civil Aviation: James Pitman
Chief Education Officer: Dean Furbert
Chief Medical Officer: Dr John Cann
Chief Immigration Officer: Neville Smith
Law Officers: Attorney General: Walter Maddocks, *Solicitor General:* Andre Garneau, QC, JP
Registrar of the Supreme Court: Mrs Norma Wade, JP
Director of Marine & Port Services: Capt. Kenneth Hallam
Registrar-General: Mrs Marlene Christopher
Director of Planning: Erwin Adderley
Commissioner of Police: Clive Donald, CPM (G), QPM
Postmaster-General: Clevelyn Crichlow
Director of Public Transportation: Herman Basden

Director of Tourism: Gary Phillips
Permanent Secretary of Works and Engineering: Stanley Oliver

JUDICIARY
The Court of Appeal:
President: The Hon Sir Denys Roberts, KBE, SPMB
Members: The Hon Mr Justice Harvey DaCosta, CMG
The Hon Mr Justice Kenneth Henry
The Hon Sir Alan Huggins
The Hon Mr Justice Telford Georges, PC
Chief Justice: The Hon Sir James R Astwood, Jr, KBE, JP

PUISNE JUDGES
The Hon Mr Justice Austin Ward, QC, JP
The Hon Mr Justice Martyn Ward, JP
The Hon Mr Justice David Hull, JP
Senior Magistrate: The Wor William Francis, LLB, JP
Magistrates: The Wor John F W Judge, QC; The Wor Kenneth Brown

British Antarctic Territory

The British Antarctic Territory was designated by an Order-in-Council which came into force on the 3rd March 1962, and, with the exception of the island of South Georgia and the South Sandwich Islands, consists of the area previously known as the Falkland Islands Dependencies. The territory lies between longitudes 20° and 80°W., south of latitude 60°S. Within these bounds lie the South Orkney Islands, the South Shetland Islands, the Antarctic Peninsula and all adjacent islands, and the land mass extending to the South Pole, a total land area of about 1,709,400 sq km (660,000 square miles).

The majority of the islands in the territory are rugged with many glaciers. The Antarctic Peninsula is mountainous, the highest peak being Mount Jackson about 3,129 m (10,430 feet). There is a snow-covered plateau which extends along the peninsula but declines from 2,100 m (7,000 feet) in the south to about 1,200 mm (4,000 feet) in the north. The main continental area is covered by ice and fringed by floating ice shelves, generally about 240 m (800 feet) thick. The territory has a rigorous polar climate.

The territory has no indigenous inhabitants, and the British population consists of scientists and technicians who man the British Antarctic Survey scientific stations. During the winter of 1990 the total number was 70. In the summer months when relief personnel arrive, together with summer field workers, this figure may almost treble. The exact number of other nationals working in the area is not known. The main scientific stations and smaller field stations are situated on various islands and parts of the mainland.

The British stations are resupplied and restaffed between November and April each year, by the Survey's Royal Research Ships *Bransfield* and *James Clark Ross*. Four aircraft assist with the annual relief and provide support for field parties. The advance base, Fossil Bluff, which is now occupied during the summer only, is supplied entirely by air from Rothera station.

In addition to normal radio communication, satellite communications link the four main stations and the ships to the British Antarctic Survey headquarters in Cambridge.

Until the year ended 30th June 1962, British Antarctic Territory finances (including BAS finances) were embodied in those of the Falkland Islands Dependencies. Thereafter administration of the BAT remained in Port Stanley until 1989 when it was transferred to the Foreign and Commonwealth Office in London. However, from 1st April 1967 responsibility for the British Antarctic Survey was transferred from the Commonwealth Office to the Department of Education and Science, and the Survey and the Territory were separately financed from 1st July 1967. The following table shows revenue and expenditure for the years 1989–92:

		Revenue	*Expenditure*
1989–90	British Antarctic Survey	£546,000	£29,525,000
	British Antarctic Territory	£121,143	£65,763
1990–91	British Antarctic Survey	£922,730	£45,301,000
	British Antarctic Territory	£267,997	£103,778
1991–92	British Antarctic Survey	£250,000 (estimated)	£24,180,000 (estimated)
	British Antarctic Territory	£158,020 (estimated)	£152,055 (estimated)

History

The main island group of the South Shetland Islands was discovered and taken possession of by Captain W Smith in 1819, whilst the South Orkney Islands owe their discovery to Captain G Powell in 1821.

The Antarctic Peninsula was discovered in 1820 by Edward Bransfield, RN, and taken into the possession of Great Britain by John Biscoe in 1832. The penetration of what is now known as the Weddell Sea and the final discovery of the continental land masses to the south and east of the Antarctic Peninsula can be attributed to many great explorers—Cook, Weddell, Ross and Bruce to name but a few. Many of the islands within the territory were used as temporary bases for the early sealing and whaling expeditions, but at Deception Island in the South Shetland Islands a more permanent and more active whaling station was in operation from 1906 to 1931. During this time a magistrate was in permanent residence for the summer months.

In the 1943–44 season, under the code name of 'Operation Tabarin', the first of what are now known as the British Antarctic Survey stations were established at Deception Island and Port Lockroy. By 1956 the number of occupied stations had increased to 12 but, as field work has been completed in many areas and the use of aircraft has increased mobility, the number has now been reduced to 5.

The locations of the occupied stations are:

Signy—Signy Island, South Orkney Islands 60° 43′ S., 45° 36′ W.
Faraday—Argentine Islands, Graham Coast, Graham Land, 65° 15′ S., 64° 16′ W.
Rothera—Adelaide Island 67° 34′ S., 68° 07′ W.
Fossil Bluff—George VI Sound 71° 20′ S., 68° 17′ W. (summer only).
Halley—Caird Coast 75° 36′ S., 26° 43′ W. (on moving ice) (closes 1991–92 season).
Halley 5—Caird Coast 75° 35′ S., 26° 15′ W (on moving ice).

Stations were also maintained by the Survey at Grytviken, South Georgia (54° 17′ S., 36° 29′ W.) and on the neighbouring Bird Island (54° 00′ S., 38° 03′ W.). These were evacuated in April 1982, following the South Atlantic conflict, but work was resumed at Bird Island at the end of September 1982.

Other bases which have been established, but are at present unoccupied, are:

Admiralty Bay, King George Island, South Shetland Islands.
Anvers Island, Palmer Archipelago.
Cape Geddes, Laurie Island, South Orkney Islands.
Danco Coast, Graham Land.
Deception Island, South Shetland Islands.
Detaille Island, Loubet Coast, Graham Land.
Hope Bay, Trinity Peninsula, Graham Land.
Horseshoe Island, Marguerite Bay, Graham Land.
Port Lockroy, Wiencke Island, Palmer Archipelago.
Prospect Point, Graham Coast, Graham Land.
Stonington Island, Marguerite Bay, Graham Land.
View Point, Duse Bay, Trinity Peninsula, Graham Land.

(The unoccupied Adelaide Island station was made available to the Government of Chile, from 1983 onwards, as a base for its summer air operations.)

Until 30th June 1989 the territory was administered by the High Commissioner, resident in Stanley, Falkland Islands. On 1st July 1989 the administration was moved from Stanley to the Foreign and Commonwealth Office, London. The office of Commissioner for the Territory is held by the Head of South Atlantic and Antarctic Department and the post of Administrator is held by the Head of Polar Regions section in South Atlantic and Antarctic Department.

Base Commanders are appointed Magistrates for the territory whilst the courts of the territory are presided over by either a Senior Magistrate or Judge of the Supreme Court.

A Court of Appeal was set up on the 1st July 1965 for the purpose of hearing and determining appeals from the courts of the territory.

HIGH COMMISSIONERS
1962 Sir Edwin Arrowsmith, KCMG
1964 Sir Cosmo Haskard, KCMG, MBE

1971 Mr E G Lewis, CMG, OBE
1975 Mr N A I French, CMG, MVO
1976 Mr J R W Parker, CMG, OBE
1980 Sir Rex Hunt, KT, CMG
1985 Mr G W Jewkes, CMG
1988 MR W H FULLERTON, CMG

DIRECTORS, BRITISH ANTARCTIC SURVEY
1958 Sir Vivian Fuchs, FRS
1973 Dr R M Laws, CBE, FRS
1987 Dr D J Drewry

COMMISSIONERS
1989 Mr C L de Chassiron
1989 (W. e. f. October)
Mr M S Baker-Bates

ADMINISTRATORS
1989 Dr J A Heap

Antarctic Treaty

Britain was one of the original 12 signatories to the Antarctic Treaty, which came into force in 1961. The Treaty covers the area south of latitude 60° S. and lasts indefinitely, although it is open to review after 1991. Its objectives are to promote scientific and technical co-operation in the Antarctic; to demilitarise the area, reserve it for peaceful use and establish it as a nuclear free zone; to set aside disputes over territorial sovereignty in the area and prevent new territorial claims.

Twenty-seven additional states have since acceded to the Treaty and 14 of these have achieved Consultative Party status, along with the original signatories. The Consultative Parties meet biennially for the purpose of exchanging information, consulting together on matters of common interest pertaining to Antarctica, and formulating, considering and recommending to their Governments measures in furtherance of the principles and objectives of the Treaty.

British Indian Ocean Territory

The British Indian Ocean Territory, a British dependency since 1965, comprises the Chagos Archipelago which lies about 3,380 km (2,100 miles) east of Mombasa in Kenya. The islands of the Chagos have been British territory for over 170 years, having been ceded with Mauritius and Seychelles to Britain by France in 1814. Thereafter, for administrative convenience, they were administered from Mauritius, some 1,930 km (1,200 miles) distant, until 1965 when they were detached to form, with three island groups formerly administered by Seychelles, the new dependency. The last three groups—Aldabra, Desroches and Farquhar—became part of Seychelles when it became an independent republic within the Commonwealth in 1976.

In 1966 it was agreed to make the Territory available for the defence purposes of the United States and Britain. The Crown purchased the Chagos Archipelago in 1967 and they remain Crown property, administered from London by a Commissioner who is assisted by the officer in charge of the Royal Navy complement on Diego Garcia, the largest island and site of the joint British-United States naval support facility. An independent judiciary is represented by a Chief Justice, a senior magistrate and a principal legal adviser who performs the functions of an Attorney-General. All three are resident in Britain.

The Archipelago

The British Indian Ocean Territory covers some 54,400 square kilometres (21,000 square miles) of ocean, but the Chagos Islands, which form an archipelago of six main island groups situated on the Great Chagos Bank, have a land area of only 60 square kilometres (23 square miles). Diego Garcia, the most southerly of the Islands, is nearly 1,770 km (1,100 miles) east of Mahé (the main island of Seychelles) and consists of a V-shaped sand cay almost enclosing a large, deep lagoon. Its land area is about 44 square km (17 square miles). The other main island groups are those of Peros Banhos and Salomon. Uninhabited, they consist of small sand cays lying on large and roughly circular atolls; Peros Banhos, with 29 islands, has a land area of 10.4 square km (4 square miles), and Salomon, with 11 islands, has a land area of 5.2 square km (2 square miles).

The islands have a typical tropical maritime climate. The average temperature on Diego Garcia is 27°C (81°F) with the average maximum and minimum being 29°C (84°F) and 25°C (77°F) respectively. Rainfall is between 2,290 and 2,540 mm (90 and 100 inches) a year.

The Chagos Archipelago, which is an area of great natural beauty, is an outstanding example of mid-ocean island and reef development. Unlike other Indian Ocean reefs the Chagos reefs have not been affected by the damaging influences of siltation and pollution due to their isolated position and the lack of tourist related developments. The islands display a wide variety of flora and fauna and offer sanctuary to several endangered species including the coconut crab. They constitute the main Indian Ocean breeding grounds for the hawksbill turtle, and green turtles also nest in the area. The islands are a major breeding station for pelagic seabirds.

Wildlife in the Territory is protected under the Wildlife Protection Ordinance 1970 and the Wildlife Protection regulations 1984. The Territory is included in the United Kingdom's ratification of the Convention on International Trade in Endangered Species of Wild Fauna and Flora (CITES) and also the Bonn Convention.

History

By the eighteenth century, the Indian Ocean and its African, Arabian and Indian coasts had become a centre of rivalry between the Dutch, French and British East Indian companies for dominance over the spice trade and over the routes to India and the Far East. France, which had already colonised Réunion in the middle of the seventeenth century, claimed Mauritius in 1715 and sent its first settlers there in 1721; it subsequently took possession of the Seychelles group and the islands in the Chagos Archipelago. (Although the latter were not commercially important they had a strategic value because of their position astride the trade routes.) During the Napoleonic Wars, Britain captured Mauritius and Réunion from the French. Under the Treaty of Paris 1814, Britain restored Réunion to France, and France ceded to Britain Mauritius and its dependencies, which comprised Seychelles and various other islands including the Chagos archipelago. All these dependencies continued to be administered from Mauritius until 1903 when the Seychelles group was detached to form a separate Crown Colony. The Chagos Islands were administered as a dependency of Mauritius until, with the full agreement of the Mauritius Council of Ministers, they were detached to become part of the British Indian Ocean Territory in 1965. At the same time Britain paid a grant of £3 million to Mauritius in recognition of the detachment of the Chagos Islands.

As with Seychelles until 1903, the connection of the Chagos Islands with Mauritius was one of administrative convenience and followed French practice before 1814. The Islands were very loosely administered and there was little contact between them and Mauritius largely due to the great distance between the two territories. The Islands had no economic relevance to Mauritius other than as a supplier of copra oil and an employer of contract labour for the plantations.

Resettlement of the Population from the Chagos Archipelago

The Chagos Islands were exploited for copra from the late eighteenth century onwards. After emancipation in the nineteenth century some of the former slaves on the islands became contract employees, most of them coming from Mauritius. Some of the contract workers chose to remain on the islands and had children who also stayed. In 1965, therefore, there were several generations of people born in the Archipelago, mainly on Diego Garcia. Because the islands and the copra plantations were owned by a private company, the workers and their families had no legal right to remain and had no property; they were employees with permission to reside there at the discretion of the owners on whom they depended for their livelihood.

Following the decision to make the islands available for defence purposes and their purchase by the Crown in 1967, the plantations were run down as their commercial future could not be assured and the plantation workers were offered the choice of returning to Mauritius or Seychelles. Since most had maintained close ties with Mauritius, the majority, some 1,200 people settled there, the final arrivals taking place in 1973. To assist the resettlement programme, Britain made £650,000 available to the Mauritius Government.

Subsequently, following lengthy negotiations on further financial assistance involving both the British and Mauritius Governments and representatives of the former plantation workers, agreement was finally reached in July 1982. Under this, Britain made an *ex gratia* payment of £4 million for their resettlement in Mauritius, this money to be administered by a trust established by the Mauritius Government. For its part, the latter agreed to make land available for resettlement worth £1 million and in September 1986, 93 houses built on land provided by the Maritius Government were handed over to ex-islander families.

Defence arrangements

At the time of the establishment of the British Indian Territory, Britain made clear to Mauritius (and Seychelles) its intention to make the Territory available for the construction of defence facilities by Britain and the United States. An Exchange of Notes providing for this, for an initial period of 50 years, was signed by Britain and the United States in December 1966; the agreement also provided an administrative framework under which the two Governments would consult together and apportion costs of the defence facilities constructed.

Following several surveys of islands in the Territory, Britain and the United States announced in December 1970 that a British-United States naval commmunications facility would be constructed on Diego Garcia, an arrangement formalised by a further Exchange of Notes in October 1972. Under the agreement, the US Government was given the right to construct, maintain and operate a limited naval communications facility on the island, with Britain assisting in manning the facility. It was to consist of transmitting and receiving services, an anchorage, an airfield, associated logistic support and supply, and personnel accommodation, the aim being to provide a link in United States defence communications and to furnish improved communications support in the Indian Ocean for both British and United States ships and aircraft. It began operating in 1973.

In 1974 Britain approved US proposals for the development of the naval communications facility on Diego Garcia into a support facility of the US Navy involving improvements to the anchorage and the airfield as well as to shore facilities, these to be completed by 1978. These plans were incorporated in 1976 in a new agreement.

With Britain's approval, the United States began additional improvements to the naval support facility in 1980 and in 1981 as part of a long-term programme of strengthening its military capabilities in the Indian Ocean: these improvements still continue and provide for the pre-positioning of equipment available for use in any rapid deployment of substantial US forces in the region during an emergency. Other construction projects include improving the services and utilities on the island such as refuelling arrangements, the expansion of the storage, warehousing, maintenance and wharf installations, and the upgrading of the runway and other airfield support facilities. Work, financed by the United States has included a joint venture between British and US construction companies. In September 1991, there were about 2,000 United States and British military personnel and 1,500 civilian personnel stationed in the Territory.

The improvements to the joint defence facility have been regarded by successive British Governments as a means of maintaining peace and stability in the area and of protecting vital Western interests and trade routes, including the supply of oil from the Gulf.

Commissioner: T G Harris
Administrator: R G Wells

British Virgin Islands

Capital: Road Town

The British Virgin Islands are situated approximately 96.5 km (60 miles) east of Puerto Rico and straddle latitude 18° 25′ N. and longitude 64° 30′ W. The territory covers an area of 153 sq km (59 square miles) and consists of 36 islands, the largest being Tortola (54 sq km), Anegada (39 sq km), Virgin Gorda (21 sq km) and Jost Van Dyke (9 sq km). With the exception of Anegada, the islands represent a projection of Puerto Rico and the United States Virgin Islands archipelago. Anegada, a flat coral feature consisting entirely of limestone, is the northernmost of the islands in the Caribbean and is surrounded by dangerous reefs. The other islands are hilly. Virgin Gorda rises to a central peak 411 m high while Sage Mountain on Tortola reaches a height of 534 m. There are no rivers and the vegetation is mostly light bush.

The islands lie within the Trade Wind belt and possess a pleasant and healthy sub-tropical climate. The average temperature in winter ranges from 22°–28°C (71°–82°F) and in summer from 26°–31°C (78°–88°F) although the summer heat is tempered by sea breezes and there is usually a drop of 10°F at night. The average rainfall is 1,250 mm. Excellent beaches for bathing and swimming are to be found on all the major islands and there are very good facilities for yachting, diving and fishing. There are some twenty-six hotels and several guest houses, about half of which are in Road Town, Tortola and the remainder scattered over the other islands. Charter boat services are available on Tortola and Virgin Gorda.

Tourism is the mainstay of the local economy contributing an estimated 45 per cent of all identified current and capital receipts from the rest of the world, i.e., National Income. Holiday visitors arrivals for 1990 are estimated at 317,670 of whom 176,613 were overnight visitors. The charter yacht sub-sector accounted for 55 per cent of the latter. Visitor expenditure in 1990 was estimated at US$132.1 million, an increase of 9 per cent over the 1989 figure of US$124.7 million. The tourism sector is also the largest employer with an identified workforce of 2,576 in 1989, and tourism generates much of the activity in the other sectors of the economy.

The preliminary census count from the 1991 Population and Housing Census shows the total number of residents as 16,749. About 40 per cent of the population are immigrants from the Commonwealth Caribbean, most being from St Kitts/Nevis and St Vincent. A further 10 per cent are from North America and Europe; the fastest growing immigrant group is from the Dominican Republic.

The principal town and port is Road Town on Tortola (which has a population of 13,568). The great majority of the people—over 90 per cent—are of African stock. English is the official language. The population is largely of Christian Protestant persuasion, the Methodists being the largest denomination: Anglican (Episcopal), Church of God, Adventist, Baptist and Roman Catholic are the other main denominations. Peebles Hospital, the only public hospital in the territory, is situated in Road Town and provides 50 beds. There is one private hospital, also in Road Town, with 8 beds, specializing in cosmetic surgery. A government operated home for the elderly caters for 25 people. The expenditure for health services for 1991 was estimated at US$5.7 m.

Primary and secondary education is provided free of charge to all and illiteracy is negligible. Fifteen primary schools and one comprehensive secondary school (the BVI High School) are directly maintained by the Government. Secondary education programmes are also offerea at all age schools in Virgin Gorda and Anegada. There are also private primary and pre-primary schools. On 31st December, 1990 a total of 2,710 pupils were enrolled in all primary and pre-primary schools. Enrolment in secondary school programmes numbered 1,146 on the same date. They provide education to Caribbean Examination Council (CXC) Basic and Proficiency levels, and to a lesser extent to the GCE 'O' level. Although there are no sixth forms students can now register at the newly created British Virgin Islands Community College for GCE Advance Level courses. Scholarships tenable at universities in the Caribbean, USA, Canada and United Kingdom are available to the majority of students who qualify for places. There is also a Student Loan Scheme financed through the Caribbean Development Bank with emphasis on technical, craft and tourism training in the region.

Expenditure on education in 1991 was estimated at US$6.1 million or 12 per cent of the recurrent budget.

There is a public library in Road Town and library deposit stations in the out islands. The system shows a bookstock in excess of 40,000 volumes, and also offers a variety of information via other media. The National Documentation Centre was instituted in the Department in 1987 and exchanges information with other centres in the Caribbean region via actual document delivery and access to computer data bases.

There are two direct steamship services, one from the United Kingdom, and one from the United

States. A total of 1,139 cargo ships called in 1988 and gross tonnage of cargo landed rose from 47,004 in 1988 to 56,683 in 1989. Three launches maintain daily passenger and mail service with St Thomas (United States Virgin Islands). There are airports suitable for small aircraft on Beef Island, Virgin Gorda and Anegada. Scheduled air services operated by LIAT, Air BVI, Eastern Metro Express and American Airlines, from Beef Island Airport provide direct communication with the United States Virgin Islands, Puerto Rico, the Eastern Caribbean and the United States. A cargo airline, Four Star Air Cargo, also flies in to Beef Island. The territory possesses approximately 113 km (70 miles) of motorable roads. An external telephone service links Tortola with Bermuda and the rest of the world, and cable communications also exist to all parts of the world. International Direct Dialling is now available. A 10 kW medium wave radio broadcasting station, ZBVI, is located on Tortola, and two FM radio stations came on the air early in 1988 providing mainly US based musical programmes. BVI Cable TV operates a cable television service to provide subscribers with good quality reception of twelve television channels. Electricity at an average price of US$0.186 per Kwh is available all over the islands of Tortola and Virgin Gorda, and a limited supply at subsidized prices provided in Anegada.

For 1989, the total value of merchandise exports is estimated at US$2.7 million, the major items being fresh fish, construction aggregates, rum, fruit and vegetables. Except for rum which is marketed mainly to the US and Canada, exports are confined mainly to the US Virgin Islands. The major industry is tourism which contributes considerably to the Territory's Gross National Product. With tourism included, exports of goods and non-factor sources were estimated at US$88,100,000 for 1983. Lesser industries include one distillery for the manufacture of rum, one major plant making hollow concrete blocks and three stone crushing plants. One printery and two joinery establishments operate in the territory. The chief imports are building materials, foodstuffs, machinery, motor cars and beverages. For 1989 total value of imports was estimated at US$11.5 million.

The Pay-As-You-Earn system introduced in January 1982 and amended in 1987, provides for income tax at 3 cents on the dollar for the first US$2,500 of gross income; 6 cents on every dollar of the next US$5,000; 10 cents on every dollar of the next US$7,500 of gross income; 15 cents on every dollar of the next US$10,000 and 20 cents on the dollar for every dollar beyond US$25,000. Companies pay a flat rate of 15 per cent on taxable profits.

Since 1959, the British Virgin Islands has used the currency of the United States of America for all official purposes. There are no exchange controls and funds may be freely transferred both in and out of the Territory. British Virgin Islands silver and gold coins ranging in value from 5c to $5.00 and $25.00 to $100.00 respectively, are specially minted for issue from time to time. Although these are legal tender, they are not normally in day-to-day use.

History

The Virgin Islands were discovered in 1493 by Christopher Columbus who named them Las Virgenes in honour of St Ursula and her companions. In the early years of European settlement in the West Indies the group appears to have been a haunt of buccaneers and pirates.

In 1672 the Governor of the Leeward Islands, Colonel Stapleton, formally annexed the island of Tortola, demolished the fort and forced the inhabitants to move to St Kitts. In 1680 a few planters moved with their families from Anguilla in the Leewards to Virgin Gorda, starting a stream which by 1717 had raised the European population of that island to 317 and that of Tortola to 159. In 1773, on their second petition, the planters were granted civil government and constitutional courts with a completely elected House of Assembly (12 members) and a partly elected and partly nominated Legislative Council or 'Board' which met for the first time on 1st February 1774.

The islands became part of the Colony of the Leeward Islands in 1872 and continued as such with various constitutions until 1st July 1956 when the Leeward islands were defederated and the presidencies of Antigua, St Kitts, Montserrat and the Virgin Islands became separate colonies. The Islands continued to be administered by the Governor of the Leeward Islands until January 1960 when this office was abolished and the Administrator of the Virgin Islands became directly responsible to the Colonial Office. In August 1971, by Order in Council, the title of Administrator was changed to Governor. The territory did not, unlike the other former Leeward Islands, become part of the West Indies Federation which was dissolved in 1962.

Constitution

Under the new constitution, which came into effect on 1st June 1977, the Governor remains responsible for defence and internal security, external affairs and the Public Service. He continues to have reserved legislative powers necessary in the exercise of his special responsibilities, but on other matters is normally bound to act in accordance with the advice of the Executive Council. At the first general election, in 1979, held under the new Constitution membership of the Council changed to consist of a Speaker, nine elected members and the Attorney-General as an *ex-officio* member. The voting age is 18. Members are elected from single member constituencies and the Governor appoints as Chief Minister the person who, in his opinion, is best able to command a majority in the Legislative Council.

Justice is administered in the territory by the Eastern Caribbean Supreme Court, arrangements having been made for this Court to serve the Virgin Islands. A resident puisne judge was first appointed in 1983 and presides over the High Court, Admiralty and associated courts. The Court of Appeal sits twice a year, in January and June. There is also a Magistrate's Court, appeals from which lie to the Court of Appeal. Appeals from decisions of the latter go to the Judicial Committee of the Privy Council.

Land policy

Commonwealth citizens who are not deemed to belong to the territory and all aliens are required to obtain a licence before they may acquire an interest in land. Applications are, however, readily granted, usually on condition that the applicant undertakes an appropriate development project on the land within a certain period.

About 60 per cent of the total land area is in private ownership; Crown lands are estimated at 15,121 acres and are normally leased for a period of not exceeding 99 years. Rental is based either on tender or on 5 per cent of the unimproved value of the land which is reviewed at intervals of 10 years.

Government

A General Election was held on 12th November 1990. The Virgin Islands Party won 6 seats and secured control of the Legislative Council under its leader, Hon H Lavity Stoutt, as Chief Minister. The Opposition Leader is Hon Cyril B Romney.

Governor: Peter Penfold, OBE

EXECUTIVE COUNCIL

Chairman: The Governor
Attorney-General (ex-officio): Hon Donald Trotman
Chief Minister and Minister of Finance: Hon H Lavity Stoutt
Minister for Health, Education and Welfare: Hon C Louis Walters, MBE
Minister for Communications and Works: Hon T B Lettsome
Deputy Chief Minister and Minister for Natural Resources and Labour: Hon R T O'Neal, OBE
Clerk: Mrs Phyllis Shirley, MBE

LEGISLATIVE COUNCIL

Speaker: Hon Keith L Flax
Attorney-General (ex-officio): Hon Donald Trotman
Elected Members: Hon H Lavity Stoutt; Hon Omar W Hodge; Hon Oliver Cills; Hon C Louis Walters, MBE; Hon Ralph T O'Neal, OBE; Hon Terence Lettsome; Hon Prince Stoutt; Hon E Walwyn Brewley
Leader of the Opposition: Cyril B Romney
Clerk: Allington Hodge

CIVIL ESTABLISHMENT

Governor: Peter Penfold, OBE
Deputy Governor: E Georges, OBE
Financial Secretary: Glenroy Forbes (Ag)
Permanent Secretaries: S Gordon, MBE; Mrs L Smith; Miss E Smith; Miss I Smith (Ag)

JUDICIAL

Judge: Hon Justice L Williams
Magistrate: William Alexander
Registrar General: Antoinette McKain (Ag)
Registrar of Lands: Miss Juliette Penn

LEGAL

Attorney General: Hon Donald Trotman
Parliamentary Counsel: Mahindra Gooneratne
Assistant Parliamentary Counsel: Noel Vanterpool
Senior Crown Counsel: Davidson Baptiste
Crown Counsel: Miss Sheila George, Rafiq Khan

AUDIT

Chief Auditor: Theodore Fahie

AGRICULTURE

Chief Agricultural Officer: Jammi S Kumar

TREASURY AND CUSTOMS

Accountant General: Miss Gwen Frett
Comptroller of Customs: Mrs Kather Smith (Ag)

INLAND REVENUE

Commissioner of Inland Revenue: Arnold Lettsome (Ag)

MEDICAL AND HEALTH

Chief Medical Officer: D Orlando Smith, MBE
Surgeons: D Orlando Smith and Mrs Joyce Frett
Chief Nursing Officer: Mrs Rita Frett-Georges

PUBLIC WORKS DEPARTMENT

Chief Engineer: Kenrick Burgess

PUBLIC UTILITIES

Chief Engineer, Water and Sewerage Department: Gary Penn
General Manager: BVI Electricity Corporation: Ronnie Skelton

TOWN AND COUNTRY PLANNING DEPARTMENT

Chief Physical Planning Officer: Louis Potter

EDUCATION

Chief Education Officer: Elroy Turnbull
Principal, BVI High School: Elmore Stoutt

PUBLIC LIBRARY

Chief Librarian: Mrs Bernadine Louis

INFORMATION
Chief Information Officer: Sandra Ward (Ag)

POLICE
Commissioner of Police: John B Rutherford

PRISON
Superintendent of Prisons: Ashford Frett

FIRE AND RESCUE SERVICES
Chief Fire Officer: Leando Stoutt (Ag)

PORT AUTHORITY
General Manager: Darius Charlemagne

CIVIL AVIATION
Director of Civil Aviation: Milton Creque

LAND SURVEYS
Chief Surveyor: Ruel Campbell

LABOUR
Chief Labour Officer: Wendell Potter

IMMIGRATION
Chief Immigration Officer: Miss Marion Romney

SOCIAL DEVELOPMENT DEPARTMENT
Chief Social Development Officer: Mrs Edith Penn

Cayman Islands

Capital: George Town

Location, Topography and Climate

The Cayman Islands consist of Grand Cayman, Cayman Brac and Little Cayman, and they lie in the Caribbean Sea between latitudes 19° 15′ and 19° 45′ North and longitudes 79° 44′ and 81° 27′ West. Their total area is about 259 sq km (100 square miles).

All the islands are low lying and do not reach a height of more than 18 m above sea level except in Cayman Brac where the eastern end rises to 42 m. The principal island, Grand Cayman, is about 290 km (180 miles) west-north-west of Jamaica and just under 805 km (500 miles) south of Miami; it is about 35 km (22 miles) in length, with a breadth varying between six and 13 km; very low lying, it is difficult to sight from the sea. Most of the west end of the island is taken up by the North Sound, a shallow bay, 93 sq km (36 square miles) in area, protected by a reef. North Sound provides a safe haven for small craft. Cayman Brac is distinguished from the other islands by its central limestone bluff. The coasts are for the most part rockbound and protected by coral reefs enclosing a few fair harbours. Grand Cayman has the magnificent Seven Mile Beach. There are no rivers. Over 180 species of birds have been recorded in the islands.

The Cayman Islands are cool from November to March, the prevailing winds being from the north-east; temperatures range from 23°C (74°F) to 28°C (82°F) but have dropped as low as 11°C (52°F). From May to October the winds come mostly from the east-south-east and the temperatures range about five degrees higher, with the highest average temperature in the last five years being 29.1°C (84.4°F). Mosquitoes were a problem, but they are now controlled by the efforts of the Mosquito Research and Control Unit set up in 1965. The rainfall at George Town averages about 1,275 mm a year. The hurricane season lasts from June to November, and the islands have occasionally been hit, eg 1876, 1903, 1909, 1917, 1932, 1944 and 1988. In October 1952 they narrowly escaped severe damage, catching the edge of a hurricane whose centre passed only 64 km (40 miles) to the west of Grand Cayman. In August 1980 Hurricane 'Allen' passed the islands causing extensive damage to property in Cayman Brac and some damage in the other two islands. In September 1988 Hurrican 'Gilbert' passed 48 km (30 miles) south of Grand Cayman causing extensive damage to vegetation and destruction of property, although the islands escaped the devastation experienced elsewhere.

Population

The official and spoken language of the Cayman Islands is English. The population at the 1989 census was 25,355. Grand Cayman's main areas of population are: George Town, the capital, 12,921; West Bay, 5,632; Bodden Town, 3,407; East End, 1,064; and North Side, 857. Cayman Brac has four main settlements—Stake Bay, West End, Creek and Spot Bay; the total population of these is 1,441. Little Cayman has a permanent population of less than 50. The population figures are taken from the 1989 census, which revealed a 52 per cent increase since the 1979 census. Since 1891 a census has been taken eight times at intervals ranging from nine to 20 years. In 1990, 490 births, 109 deaths and 274 marriages were registered.

Health

Government medical services are provided at a hospital, an extended care unit, five district clinics and a new $900,000 dental clinic which opened in 1991 in Grand Cayman and, on Cayman Brac, at a hospital and a new $130,000 dental clinic which was opened in 1989. The 1991 Budget provided CI$10.4 million for personal health services. George Town Hospital has 52 beds and an eight-bed extended care unit at the Pines Retirement Home, and the Faith Hospital, Cayman Brac, has 10 beds. In 1990, Government approved $1.5 million for the construction of new surgical, trauma and intensive care facilities at the George Town Hospital, as well as for developing master plans for that hospital and the Faith Hospital on Cayman Brac. Included in this budget, also, were plans for an 18-bed extension to the hospital on Cayman Brac and the design drawings for a new hospital for George Town. There are 23 government medical officers, and 19 doctors in full-time private practice, with additional 16 visiting specialists. In addition to two government dental officers there are three dentists in private practice in George Town, two orthodontists and two periodontists. Tropical diseases are virtually absent from the islands, and immunisation coverage for children continues to be intensively pursued, exceeding the targets set by the World Health Organisation.

In recognition of the Islands' location on trans-shipment routes, the Government has invested heavily in preventive and rehabilitative anti-drug programmes through the schools, the health services, at the work place, and in the support of efforts by community service groups. Emphasis has also been placed on intensive surveillance and monitoring by law enforcement and customs agencies, in conjunction with international intelligence networks.

An important indicator of the Islands' development has been the provision of modern public water supply and sewerage schemes in recent years. The capital is currently served by a piped water system, introduced in 1988, and plans were approved in 1991 for the construction of a one million gallon reservoir and the laying of 90,000 metres of pipeline to serve most of the district of Bodden Town. This will advance considerably the ultimate goal towards providing a public water supply for all districts in Grand Cayman. Provision for West Bay was underway in 1990 with the award of a franchise to the private company which now serves the Seven Mile Beach area. Government's total sewerage and water provisions investment so far totals just under $20 m.

Communications

George Town is a port of registry with a total of 551 vessels on the register at 31st May 1991. An important achievement for the Islands in 1991 was the grant of Category 1 status to the Cayman Shipping Registry as a member of the Red Ensign Group of shipping registries, comprising the UK and its dependencies with significant registries. During 1990, 20 cargo vessels made 305 calls at the port, transporting 136,600 short tons of general cargo, much of it containerised. The islands are not served by a passenger line, and sea communications are maintained by several Caymanian-owned or registered vessels which ply regularly from the ports of Miami and Tampa, Florida, and from Kingston, Jamaica and Costa Rica.

Cayman Airways, the government-owned airline, offers regular services from Miami, Houston, Tampa, Atlanta, New York and Jamaica. Northwest, Pan American and American Airlines also make daily scheduled flights between Miami and Grand Cayman, with Air Jamaica providing regular links with Jamaica.

The Owen Roberts International Airport, Grand Cayman, has a 2,100 m runway and a CI$10 million new terminal opened in January 1985. The Gerrard Smith Airport, Cayman Brac, has a runway of 1,800 m used by Cayman Airways' Boeing 737 jets, and a CI$3.47 m new terminal and fire station, upgraded to international standards, opened in December 1988. A private airstrip capable of taking light aircraft is in use in Little Cayman. There are about 254 km (158 miles) of motorable roads in Grand Cayman and Cayman Brac, in which all districts are connected with roads of high standard, and there is an 11 km stretch of motorable road in Little Cayman.

The internal and international telephone, telegraph and telex services provided by Cable & Wireless (West Indies) Ltd. continue to expand. International Direct Dialling out of the islands was introduced in 1983, providing direct dialling to 110 countries all over the world. The total of 146 telex subscribers is still among the world's highest per capita, but has recently fallen as a result of the popularity of facsimile transmission, used by over 1,000 subscribers.

Economy

The Cayman Islands economy is vibrant, characterised by a GDP and GNP (1990) of CI$596 million and CI$539 m, respectively. Per capita income, ranking ahead of the Caribbean as well as Canada and the UK, was calculated at CI$21,800 (US$27,250). The 1989 census, which for the first time included income, indicated an average income of CI$369 per week (CI$439 for men and CI$293 for women). There is widespread home ownership. Of the 8,115 private residential households, 31 per cent owned their house outright, while 22 per cent owned their homes with a mortgage. The average household size was 3.1 (down from 3.8 in the 1979 census). The Cayman Islands currency consists of six notes, $1, $5, $10, $25, $50 and $100; and four coins: 25c, 10c, 5c and 1c. The Cayman Islands dollar is linked to the United States dollar at the rate of CI$1 = US$1.20.

The offshore finance industry and tourism are the mainstays of the economy. Few inhabitants engage in fishing and agriculture, and only a small minority are seamen, their numbers much reduced from the times when a third of the population was away at sea.

The islands have had a trade union law since 1942 but no more than three unions have been registered. A Labour law, the first comprehensive measure on this subject, was enacted in 1987, and establishes a code governing minimum terms and conditions of employment, including vacation time, unfair dismissal, allocation of gratuities, and the health and safety of employees. A few light industries have been established, mostly allied to construction or tourism. The Cayman Islands Chamber of Commerce, set up in 1965, has a membership of over 500.

To reduce the dependence on imported foodstuffs the Government is placing greater emphasis on promoting the development of agriculture, and in 1990 unveiled a CI$5 m, five-year development plan for the sector. In conjunction with this, the Agricultural and Industrial Development Board provides loans at reasonable rates of interest. The plan is expected to intensify the Department of Agriculture's research efforts, which include experiments with varieties of fruit, vegetables and grasses to establish which are best suited to local conditions. In view of the constraints imposed by the availability and quality of suitable land, continued emphasis will be placed on new methods such as hydroponics. To provide assistance and support to farmers in the implementaion of the plan, a special unit was established in 1991. The livestock population in the Islands in 1990 comprised 1,900 head of cattle, mostly for beef production, 264 pigs, 257 goats and 1,800 chickens (layers).

About 80 per cent of imports come from the United States. Income from tourism and the financial sector allows the islands to cope with a trade imbalance shown by these import and export figures for 1984–90:

	Total imports CI$ millions	*Exports CI$ millions*
1984	118	1
1985	122.7	1.5
1986	134	2.2
1987	162.6	1.8
1988	187.8	1.9
1989	215.6	2.1
1990	239.7	3.1

1990 was a most active year in terms of capital development projects, with $9.74 m of an approved $15.5 m capital development budget spent during the year. Heading the list of development projects completed during the year was the $4.74 m Community College, with further buildings in the project under consideration. Other school building projects in 1990 were the George Town Primary School assembly hall/hurricane shelter, completed in April 1991, and valued at $373,000; a $250,000 industrial arts classroom facility at the Cayman Brac High School, which began use in November 1990; and the opening of a new infant school in West Bay in September 1990, the four phases of which are estimated to cost $4.94 m. Phase I, valued at over $931,964, is soon scheduled for completion.

Plans for new construction for schools included a new infant school for George Town, expected to start in 1991; a new science block at the Cayman Islands High School, and a new $1.77 m library/learning resources centre at the Cayman Islands Middle School.

Another major construction project during 1990 was the second-storey construction of Broadcasting House, estimated to cost $459,000, with completion scheduled in early 1991. New offices for the Immigration Department at an estimated cost of $542,000 were completed in 1991, completing Phase II of a three-part programme expected to have a total value of over $900,000 on completion. In medical facilities, a new $900,000 dental clinic opened in 1991.

Construction work commenced in 1990 to convert an existing building into the new home for the National Archives, estimated to cost $388,000 at completion in mid-1991. Hurrican shelters throughout Grand Cayman were also upgraded in a two-year programme commencing in 1989, providing standby generators, storage rooms for the 17 shelters, at a cost of $700,000. A communications bunker was also constructed during 1990 to house Government's new state-of-the-art communications network.

The islands maintained a stable economic position during 1990, and the financial sector continued to expand. The number of banks and trust companies licensed increased from 528 to 546. By the end of the year, 360 licences granted under the Insurance Law were in force, 20 of which were issued during the 12-month period. The value of land and leases transferred during the year amounted to CI$118.49 m. Financial and business services were shown to be the most important sector, representing 31 per cent of the GDP, but when the parts of other industry groups relevant to tourism are added together it is this industry which makes the largest contribution to the economy. There were 614,870 visitors to the islands in 1990, including 361,702 cruise ship passengers. Of the 6,128 beds available for tourists, 3,220 were in hotels and 2,908 were in apartments, guest houses and cottages.

Government's estimated 1991 recurrent revenue was CI$101.8 m, and recurrent expenditure was CI$97.04 million.

There is no income tax, estate or excise duty. The principal sources of government revenue are import duty, stamp duty, company and other licence fees. The only form of direct taxation, a poll tax of CI$10 on males between 18 and 60 years, was abolished in 1985. Import duty ranges from duty free (on many basic foods) to 20 per cent on most other goods and 27.5 per cent on motor vehicles.

Stamp duty is payable on specified instruments and documents. The rate varies from 10 cents on cheques to 7.5 per cent on the transfer of property with a market value of up to CI$250,000, and 10 per cent on transactions in excess of that figure. CI$11.3 m was collected in stamp duty in 1990, just short of the previous year's figure of CI$11.85 m.

Education

Education is compulsory for children between the ages of four and 16 years and is provided free for Caymanian children at the Government's nine primary schools, one middle school, two high schools, one special education school and one adult traning centre for the handicapped. Fees are payable for non-Caymanian children at these schools and for all attending six private schools, three of which offer secondary as well as primary education. All the latter are church-sponsored. Enrolment in all schools in 1990 was 4,412, of whom 1,162 were in the private schools. Government expenditure on education in 1990 was in excess of CI$10 m, with an estimated budget of CI$13.4 m in 1991.

A highlight for education for the year was a review of education, expected to result in major changes in the system, following a public consultation exercise in 1991.

The Media

The Cayman Islands is served by one daily and a weekly newspaper, a monthly periodical and there is a Government-owned radio station. An addition to the local media in 1990 was a weekly one and a half hour local programme by a fledgling private television company, transmitting via satellite.

The daily, *The Caymanian Compass*, is issued Monday to Friday by the Cayman Free Press Ltd. The newspaper's circulation is 6,000 per day. In October 1990 it completed 25 continuous years' service since the launching of its predecessor publication, *The Caymanian Weekly*, in 1965.

Cayman Free Press also publishes annually *The Cayman Islands Yearbook and Business Directory*, aimed primarily at the business community, and *Key to Cayman*, a glossy, colourful portrayal of the Islands as a tourist resort, and *The Cayman Islands Map and Visitors' Guide*.

The weekly newspaper, *The New Caymanian*, was launched in June 1990, and is published mid-week.

The monthly periodical, *Newstar*, is published by a small group of Caymanians, Star Communications, Ltd. The company also publishes the *Cayman Islands Who's Who & Business Guide*, co-sponsored by the Department of Tourism.

Other local publications include the *Cayman Horizons*, founded in 1983 by Progressive Publications Ltd. The periodical, published every two months and mainly aimed at tourism promotion, serves as the official in-flight periodical of Cayman Airways, with a circulation of 20,000 per issue.

History

Cayman Brac and Little Cayman were sighted by Christopher Columbus on 10th May 1503 during his last voyage to the West Indies, though the islands are shown in approximately their correct position on maps published prior to this date. The Spaniards first called the group Las Tortugas because of the large numbers of turtles they saw in the surrounding waters, but by 1530 they were generally referred to as the Caimanas or Caymanes*. The Caymans, frequently visited by Spanish, English and French ships for revictualling, are mentioned in a 1661 document as being part of the territory of Jamaica, previously captured from the Spaniards by a Cromwellian army and in 1670 the Treaty of Madrid recognised Britain's possession of these and other West Indian islands. The Cayman Islands were subsequently colonised mainly from Jamaica, though some English and Scottish seamen shipwrecked on the Cuban coast also made their way to the islands, which, owing to their remoteness, were for long a favourite refuge for fugitives of one kind or another. The earliest record shows a population of 176 people in 1774, and an 1802 report said Grand Cayman had a population of 933.

By the end of the 18th century the ruthless exploitation of turtles had so far reduced their numbers that their virtual extermination in Cayman waters became inevitable, and the Caymanians, who had few other resources, were obliged to go further afield in search of new turtling grounds. They first turned to the uninhabited cays of Cuba but by 1839 their operations had been extended to the Nicaraguan and Hondurean coasts (*vide* Thomas Young: *Narrative of a Residence on the Mosquito Shore, During the Years* 1839, 1840 *and* 1841). This source of supply ceased in 1967 when all permits to fish in territorial waters were withdrawn by the Nicaraguan Government.

In 1832 representative government was established in the Cayman Islands with the forming of the Legislative Assembly.

The islands of Cayman Brac and Little Cayman were permanently settled only in 1833, when several families from Grand Cayman established themselves on Cayman Brac. They lived in isolation until 1850 when, then numbering 36, they built themselves a boat. As late as 1877 there was no administrative connection between Grand Cayman and the two lesser islands. In 1877 a Justice of the Peace was appointed in Cayman Brac but not until 1887 were any more formal links established.

The islands were favourably located for trade with passing shipping in the days of sail, and Caymanians achieved a considerable reputation as builders of small schooners; but as the 19th century advanced the islands became more and more cut off from the outside world, a state of affairs which lasted effectively until the 1940s and the era of air transportation. The result was extensive emigration to Nicaragua and the settlement of the Bay Islands (at one time British but now part of Honduras) and later emigration to Florida.

The ending of the constitutional link with Jamaica in 1962 set the Cayman Islands on their present successful course. Over the last 20 years the Government of the Cayman Islands has pursued policies aimed at developing the infrastructure, education and health services and fostering the growth of the Islands' two main industries: tourism and finance.

A notable event in July 1986 was the signing in Grand Cayman by representatives of the Cayman, United Kingdom and United States governments of a Mutual Legal Assistance Treaty, under which

---

* Cayman derives from a Carib work covering crocodilians in general and there is sufficient evidence that the islands were so named by the Spaniards because of the large numbers of crocodiles (almost certainly the largely-marine *Crocodylus acutus*) they found on shore. Dampier (*Voyages and Discoveries*, 1676) reported many crocodiles on Grand Cayman, which he carefully distinguished from alligators he had encountered elsewhere during his travels, noting that 'both kinds are called Caymanes by the Spaniards; therefore probably they reckon them for the same'. Incorrect identification probably accounts for later reports of 'alligators' on the islands (eg by Dr Hirst in 1910 and by observers during a hurricane in the 1930s). According to Dampier both crocodiles and alligators were commonly used as a source of fresh meat. Slaughter by ships' crews would account for the subsequent disappearance of crocodiles from the islands, which offered only limited areas of suitable cover. Specimens of *Crocodylus acutus* have been taken on Little Cayman at least as recently as 1939 (*vide* Chapman Grant, *The Herpetology of the Cayman Islands*, Institute of Jamaica, 1940).

information can be exchanged between the US and Cayman for the investigation and suppression of a specific range of crimes, including drug trafficking but excluding tax offences. The treaty was ratified by the US Senate in October 1989 and came into effect on 30th March 1990.

Constitution

When Jamaica achieved independence on 6th August 1962, the office of Governor of Jamaica, and consequently also of Governor of the Cayman Islands, disappeared. The Cayman Islands chose to remain under the British Crown. The 1959 Constitution was accordingly amended by Order in Council to provide for the assumption by the Administrator of most of the powers and responsibilities formerly exercised by the Governor. In November 1971 the title 'Administrator' was changed to that of 'Governor' by an Order in Council made by Her Majesty The Queen.

A revised constitution was introduced by the Cayman Islands (Constitution) Order 1972 which came into operation on 22nd August 1972. A constitutional review will take place in early 1991.

While the constitution requires the Governor, in general, to exercise his functions in accordance with the advice of the Executive Council, consisting of three official and four elected members, it provides for him to be responsible in his discretion for defence, external affairs, internal security, the police and certain matters relating to the public service.

The Governor assigns responsibility for business, or departments of the Government, to Members of the Executive Council.

The Legislative Assembly comprises the Speaker, three official members and 12 elected members. A Speaker was appointed in October 1990 and the Governor handed over the presidency on 15th February 1991.

A constitutional amendment made by the Privy Council in December 1987, resulting from a private member's motion in the Assembly, made a number of changes in qualifications for voters and election to the Assembly. The aim of the changes was to avoid the social instability which might result if Caymanians felt they were at political disadvantage in relation to newcomers to the Islands.

A review of the Constitution commenced in January 1991 with a subsequent report in June to the Legislative Assembly. The report was referred to a Select Committee of the whole House, which had invited public representations in mid-1991. It was anticipated that the Cayman Islands Legislative Assembly would make its recommendations to the British Government by November 1991. The report recommends moving to a ministerial system, with the creation of a post of chief minister, an additional seat in Executive Council (which now comprises four elected and three official members), the appointment of three parliamentary secretaries, the establishment of an office of leader of the opposition, and the inclusion of a bill of rights in the Constitution. Elections are held every four years, the next being scheduled in 1992.

Land Policy

There is no restriction on sale of land to non-Caymanians.

Governor: HE Mr A J Scott, CVO, CBE

EXECUTIVE COUNCIL

The Governor (Chairman)

The Hon T C Jefferson, OBE, JP (Financial Secretary)

The Hon R W Ground, QC (Attorney General)

The Hon J L Hurlston, MBE, JP (Administrative Secretary)

The Hon W N Bodden, OBE (Tourism, Aviation, Trade)

The Hon B O Ebanks, OBE (Education, Environment, Recreation, and Culture)

The Hon D E Miller (Health and Social Services)

The Hon L A Pierson (Communications, Works and Agriculture)

LEGISLATIVE ASSEMBLY

President: The Speaker

Appointed Members: The three Official Members

Elected Members: 12, representing six electoral districts and elected every four years

The Hon Norman Bodden (George Town)

Roy Bodden (Bodden Town)

Truman Bodden (George Town)

McKeeva Bush (West Bay)

The Hon Benson Ebanks (West Bay)

John Jefferson (West Bay)

Capt Mabry Kirkconnell (Sister Islands)

Gilbert McLean (Sister Islands)

John McLean (East End)

The Hon Ezzard Miller (North Side)

The Hon Linford Pierson (George Town)

Haig Bodden (Bodden Town)

CIVIL ESTABLISHMENT

Governor: HE Mr A. J. Scott, CVO, CBE

Chief Justice: Hon Sir Denis Malone

Financial Secretary: Hon T C Jefferson, OBE, JP

Attorney General: Hon R W Ground, QC

Administrative Secretary: Hon J L Hurlston, MBE, JP

Principal Secretaries: K Gomez, MBE, O Rankine, Mrs J Basdeo, JP, Mrs J Manderson, H Watler

District Commissioner, Islands: J M Ryan, MBE, JP

Puisne Judges: D Schofield, JP; G E Harre, JP

Commissioner of Police: A Ratcliffe

Chief Fire Officer: K. Nixon, MBE, QFSM
Director of Civil Aviation: S Hislop, MBE
Director of Tourism: R Selzer
Director of Planning: Miss Christine Ballard
Director, Port Authority: E Bush
Director, Water Authority: R Beswick
Director, Mosquito Research and Control Unit: Dr John Davies
Chief Education Officer: Miss Andrea Bryan
Chief Medical Officer: Dr B Martin-Smith
Chief Engineer: D Ebanks
Postmaster General: Miss C Sterling
Collector of Customs: C Powery
Registrar General: D Solomon (Ag)
Superintendent of Insurance: G Connolly
Inspector of Banks and Trusts: J Atkinson
Accountant General: R Bicknell
Chief Immigration Officer: J Bostock
Registrar of Lands: C Fenton
Chief Agricultural and Veterinary Officer: Dr A Benjamin
Director of Legal Studies: R I Finlay
Director of Prisons: D Marsden
Director of Training: J Philipson
Director of Broadcasting: L Banks
Director of Social Services: Mrs A Martins
Clerk of the Legislative Assembly: Mrs G Myrie
Senior Information Officer: Miss P Ebanks
Archivist: Dr P Pedley
Statistician: Mrs P Basset
Chief Marine Surveyor: A Macnaughton
Auditor-General: N Treen
Sports Co-ordinator: C Branche
Manager, Computer Sciences: K Bishop
Organisation and Methods Officer: P Gough

Falkland Islands

Capital: Stanley

The Falkland Islands are situated in the South Atlantic and lie 772 km (480 miles) north-east of Cape Horn. There are two large islands, the East and West Falklands, and numerous smaller islands. They cover about 12,173 sq km (4,700 square miles). The coastline is deeply indented and affords many good anchorages. The relief, except in Lafonia, is hilly and the maximum height above sea-level is in East Falkland where Mount Usborne rises to 693 m (2,312 feet). There are no large inland waters. Peculiar to the treeless, moorland scenery are the 'stone runs', long 'rivers' of angular, quartzite boulders.

The Falkland Islands are in the same latitude south as London is north but they have more hours of sunshine and less rainfall. There are marked climatic differences. The main feature of the Falklands' weather is the strong winds, which occur particularly in the spring. Climatic figures for Stanley are:

Mean annual temperature	5.5°C (42°F)
Mean annual wind speed	31.5 km.p.h. (17 knots)
Mean annual rainfall	625 mm (25 inches)
Annual maximum temperature around	21.1°C (70°F)
Annual minimum temperature around	−5.5°C (22°F)

On 5th March 1991, the date of the last census, the population was 2,121. This figure shows an increase of 205 (10.7 per cent) since the last census of 1986. The population is almost exclusively of British birth or descent.

Stanley, the capital, is the only town. In the Camp (the countryside outside Stanley) the largest settlement is at Goose Green on East Falkland where there are 38 residents.

There are three churches in Stanley; the Cathedral of the Anglican diocese of the Falkland Islands under the Archbishop of Canterbury; St Mary's Catholic Church; and the United Free Church. Also represented in the Islands are the Baha'i Faith, Jehovah's Witnesses, Lutherans, Southern Baptists, Seventh Day Adventists and Evangelists.

In 1990/91 there were 342 children receiving education which is free and compulsory for 5–15 year olds throughout the colony. There are no facilities for higher education, but there is provision for secondary education to GCSE level in a range of subjects at Stanley Senior School. Arrangements exist for pupils to progress to GCE 'A' level at a boarding school in the United Kingdom. A total of 25 students attended British universities, polytechnics, and sixth-form colleges in 1990/91. Outside Stanley education of younger pupils is carried on either in small settlement schools or by travelling teachers supported by two-way radio and correspondence work. At the beginning of 1991, six travelling teachers, five settlement teachers and three radio teachers with 62 pupils were supported by Government in rural areas. Most of the older pupils from the rural areas attend the Senior School; their parents pay a small contribution towards their board and lodging in the School Hostel. In Stanley, the Junior School has 147 pupils and 12 teachers and the Senior School 132 pupils and 15 teachers. A heated swimming pool was opened in Stanley in November 1989, and a new Senior School is under construction adjacent to the pool. The School, which will also include community sports facilities, is due to be completed in mid-1992.

Total operating expenditure on education and training from the Colony's funds was £1,378,650 in 1990/91. In addition, the new Senior School, to be named Falkland Islands College, will cost about £12 million.

The Falkland Island Government Medical Department is responsible for the provision of medical care and for public health and sanitation in the Colony. There are no private medical facilities, care being provided free of charge and funded by a 1 per cent levy on income; 1.5 per cent if self-employed. In 1991/92 the Medical Department had an establishment of: six registered medical practitioners; one dentist; one pharmacist; one physiotherapist; three laboratory and X-ray technicians; one matron and 15 registered nurse/midwives; and eight locally trained nurses. Following a fire which destroyed the King Edward VII Memorial Hospital in Stanley in 1984, a new hospital was built and came into operation in mid-1987. Specialist advice and assistance is available from the Royal Army Medical Corps, and the Royal Air Force provide an aeromedical evacuation service to the UK for the seriously ill. There is a routine and emergency flying doctor service to outlying settlements. Total expenditure on the medical department in 1990/91 was £1,643,110.

An international telephone and facsimile system provides a link between the outlying settlements, Stanley and the rest of the world.

Ships make the round trip to the United Kingdom about once a month. Internal civil transport communications are maintained by sea with the commercially run MV 'Monsunen' and MV 'Forrest', and a few small private vessels. There are plans for a ferry service to link East and West Falkland. There is also an internal air service, the Falkland Islands Government Air Service responsible for moving passengers, mail and small freight packages around the islands. Travellers also use horses, motor cycles or Land Rovers when moving between neighbouring settlements. Tarred roads exist only in Stanley and within the environs of the Mount Pleasant Airport Complex. Unsurfaced tracks connect most settlements on the main East and West Islands. The road between the capital and Mount Pleasant Airport is unsurfaced for most of its length. A camp tracks programme continues to fund the construction of all-weather tracks within the islands and about 110 km of tracks were completed by early 1991. There is no inland waterway or rail service.

The British Government announced on 8th December 1982 its response to the recommendations made in the updated economic survey of the islands by Lord Shackleton. £31 million over six years were earmarked for the development of the islands' economy; to be used, amongst other things, to establish a Falkland Islands Development Corporation, improve the harbour complex and roads, develop inshore fisheries and other industries based on local resources, including the manufacture of yarn and knitted garments.

The Falkland Islands Development Corporation was established on 14th June 1984. The FIDC's function is 'to encourage and assist in the economic development of the Falkland Islands'. More particularly the Corporation is committed to increasing employment opportunities by encouraging diversification of the economy and increasing the long term capacity of the Falkland Islands to develop and to improve community facilities.

A new dairy and a hydroponic market garden have been established with assistance from the Corporation. A variety of smaller projects are in the process of being established and these include a poultry unit for egg production, a photographic processing business and the development of sites for commercial and light industrial projects.

The Corporation has also played a large part in the acquisition of large absentee-owned farms and their subsequent subdivision and sale as family-sized farms to Falkland Islanders. The Corporation continues to monitor the progress of the subdivided units and to afford assistance with agricultural grants.

Five tourist lodges have been established. The Corporation also makes grants and loans to small businesses.

The Falkland Islands economy was formerly based on agriculture and a substantial proportion of the islands work force was either directly or indirectly employed on the land. However, since the establishment of the interim conservation and management zone around the islands and the consequent introduction on 1st February 1987 of a licensing regime for vessels fishing within the zone, the economy has diversified and income from the associated fishing activities has significantly increased Government revenue.

Almost all agricultural lands are devoted to the production of wool, with a little dairy farming to meet the islanders' own needs. A few crops are grown to provide winter fodder.

The chief imports are provisions, vehicles, machinery, alcoholic beverages, timber, clothing and hardware.

Direct taxation is in the form of income tax, individuals paying a tax on income (after deductions) of 20 per cent on the first £20,000 and 25 per cent on the remainder. From 1st January 1991, company tax rates are as follows:

—on all profits, whether distributed or undistributed—25 per cent

—a further 10 per cent is payable on any part of the Company's profits when the Company pays to a person not ordinarily resident or to a Company not resident in the Falkland Islands. Arrangements have been concluded with the United Kingdom, Denmark and Switzerland for the avoidance of double taxation. There is no general customs tariff and import duties are confined to spirits, beer and tobacco.

Public Finance tables are as follows:

	Ordinary Revenue £	*Ordinary Expenditure* £	*Capital Expenditure financed from* *Int. Sources* £	**Ext. Sources* £
1986–87	22,774,680	21,968,150	1,736,263	606,586
1987–88	32,691,910	24,041,730	6,884,540	224,640
1988–89	41,122,773	21,099,205	11,481,479	27,694
1989–90	42,035,173	26,806,704	11,252,850†	—
1990–91†	40,044,890	23,962,810	17,987,710	—
1991–92†	39,088,780	25,132,900	14,011,500	—

*Represents local costs financed from external sources, (excludes development expenditure met direct from the UK/FI £31 million development grant).
†Estimated

History

Navigators of several countries including Captain John Davis in 1592 and Sir John Hawkins in 1594, have been credited with first sighting the Falkland Islands. However, of the various claims to priority of discovery, only that of the Dutch sailor Sebald Van Weert is conclusively authenticated. Both the Spanish and English claims rest on imprecise evidence. The first known landing was in 1690 by Captain John Strong who gave the Islands their English name after Viscount Falkland, the Treasurer of the Navy. In 1764 Antoine-Louis de Bougainville established a small French settlement at Port Louis in the East Falkland which was handed over to Spain in 1767 on the payment of about £24,000. In 1765 Captain Byron took possession of the West Falkland and the following year Captain MacBride established a British settlement at Port Egmont on Saunders Island, whence it was driven out by the Spaniards in 1770. This action on the part of Spain brought that country and Britain to the verge of war. The Spaniards restored the settlement to the British in 1771, but the settlement was withdrawn on economic grounds in 1774. The Spaniards also abandoned their settlement at Soledad (Port Louis) in 1811.

In 1820 the Buenos Aires Government (which had formally declared its independence of Spain in 1816) sent a ship to the islands to proclaim its sovereignty. A settlement was established at Soledad in 1826 under the leadership of Louis Vernet, whom Buenos Aires appointed Governor, despite British protests. Five years later however, a United States warship, the Lexington, destroyed the fort at Soledad as a reprisal for the arrest of three American vessels by Vernet, who was attempting to establish control over sealing in the islands. The Commander of the Lexington declared the Falklands free of all government and they remained without visible authority until 1832, when Buenos Aires appointed a Civil and Military Governor *ad interim* who sailed to the Falklands at the end of that year. Shortly after his arrival there was mutiny among the soldiers and the newly appointed Governor was murdered. In January 1833 a British warship, HMS Clio, commanded by Captain Onslow visited the settlement, where he found that the Argentine Commander of the Buenos Aires schooner of war was attempting to establish order. Onslow claimed the Right of Sovereignty over the islands and requested the Commander and his force to leave. They departed, under protest, taking with them the majority of the settlers, and the British occupation of the islands was resumed.

In 1841 a civil Lieutenant-Governor was appointed, who took over the following year from the naval officer then in charge of the islands. In 1843 an Act of Parliament placed the civil administration on a permanent footing and the Lieutenant-Governor's title was changed to Governor. In 1844, following a decision taken the previous year, the seat of government was removed from Port Louis to Port William, where the settlement was named Stanley.

A grant-in-aid was approved in 1841 and continued until 1880. A grant-in-aid for a mail service continued until 1884–85, since when, apart from a few years following the Argentine invasion in 1982, the territory has been self-supporting. The development of the islands has been closely linked with the growth of the Falkland Islands Company formed in 1851 and until April 1991 the largest single landowner on the islands. In April 1991 the Falkland Islands Company sold to the Falkland Islands Government its four farms which together covered 27 per cent of the total land area of the islands. Only about four per cent of land is now owned by overseas interests. The Falkland Islands Company is now a trading company with interests in construction and services to the fishing industry.

The Falkland Islands were illegally invaded by Argentine military forces on 2nd April 1982. A British task force was immediately dispatched and, following a conflict in which over 1,000 British and Argentine lives were lost, the Argentines surrendered on 14th June, 1982.

Land policy

All the land in the Colony is held freehold. A policy of gradual subdivision of the larger farms into smaller family units has been actively pursued over the last 10 years. Certain areas are Crown reserves.

Constitution

The present Constitution of the Falkland Islands came into force on 3rd October 1985. The Governor is advised by an Executive Council consisting of three elected members of the Legislative Council and two *ex-officio* members, the Chief Executive and the Financial Secretary. The Legislative Council consists of eight elected members and the same two *ex-officio* members. Universal adult suffrage was introduced in 1949 and in 1977 the voting age was lowered from 21 to 18 years. The last general election was held on 11th October 1989.

Judicial system

The judicial system consists of Summary Courts of magistrates and a Magistrate's Court presided over by a (legally qualified) Senior Magistrate. Above them is a Supreme Court consisting of a non-resident Chief Justice. A Court of Appeal which was set up in 1965 sits in London. There is also provision for further appeals to the Judicial Committee of the Privy Council. There is an Attorney-General and a Crown Counsel. A firm of solicitors has set up a private practice.

HISTORICAL LIST OF GOVERNORS
(*For full list see* 1979 *edition*)

1970 E G Lewis, CMG, OBE
1975 N A I French, CMG, MVO
1976 J R W Parker, CMG, OBE
1980 R M Hunt, CMG (later (1982) Sir Rex Hunt, Kt, CMG)
1985 G W Jewkes, CMG
1988 W H Fullerton, CMG

EXECUTIVE COUNCIL
The Governor: H E Mr W H Fullerton, CMG
The Chief Executive: R Sampson
The Financial Secretary: D Howatt
H T Rowlands, CBE; R E Binnie; T J Peck, MBE, CPM
Clerk: A Livermore, CPM

CIVIL ESTABLISHMENT
Governor: H E Mr W H Fullerton, CMG
First Secretary to the Governor: R C Huxley
Chief Executive: R Sampson
Financial Secretary: D Howatt
Attorney-General: D G Lang, QC
Chief Police Officer: Supt K Greenland
Collector of Customs: L J Halliday
Senior Magistrate: (Vacant)
Chief Medical Officer: Dr J R Diggle
Chief Education Officer: Mrs P M Rendell
Superintendent of Posts & Telecommunications: J Stephenson
Director of Public Works: B Jarvis Hill
Director of Agriculture: O Summers
Director of Fisheries: A J Barton
Director of Civil Aviation: G W Cheek
General Manager, Falkland Islands Development Corporation: M V Summers

MILITARY ESTABLISHMENT
Commander British Forces Falkland Islands: Air Vice-Marshal P G Beer, CBE, LVO, RAF

Gibraltar

Gibraltar is a narrow peninsula jutting southwards from the south-west coast of Spain to which it is connected by a sandy isthmus about one mile long and half a mile wide. The name derives from the Arabic *jebel Tariq* (Tariq's mountain), after the Berber leader Tariq ibn Ziyad, who landed at or near Gibraltar in AD711. The territory consists of a long, high mountain known as the Rock and a sandy plain to the north of it, raised only a few feet above sea level, called the North Front. The total area of the territory is 6.5 sq km (2.5 square miles). Eight km (5 miles) across the bay to the west lies the Spanish port of Algeciras and 32 km (20 miles) across the Straits, to the south, is Africa. The Mediterranean lies to the east. The distance to Britain is approximately 2,252 km (1,400 miles) by sea.

The top of the Rock is a sharp, knife-edge ridge extending for about 2.4 km from the north escarpment, sloping gradually to the south for about 1.6 km, to terminate at the southern extremity, Europa Point, in perpendicular cliffs about 30 m (100 feet) high. Its greatest elevation is 418 m (1,396 feet). The whole upper length of the eastern face is inaccessible and the steep upper half of the western slopes is uninhabited.

Potable water consumed in Gibraltar is derived from desalinators (with a maximum production of over 500,000 gallons a day), and from wells. Water is also imported by tanker when required. Water from the various sources is blended and stored in large reservoirs inside the Rock.

The climate in Gibraltar is temperate. During the winter months the prevailing wind is from the west, often north-west and occasionally south-west. Snow or frost is extremely rare. The mean minimum and maximum temperatures during this period are 10.8°C (50°F) and 16.1°C (61°F) respectively.

The normal pattern is for summer to have a slight preponderance of winds from the east. A warm breeze laden with moisture known as the 'Levanter' strikes the eastern face of the Rock, condenses in the sky above and causes a cloud pall to hang over the city and bay. During this period the climate is humid and relaxing. The mean minimum and maximum temperatures in the summer are 19.3°C (68°F) and 27.0°C (80°F) respectively.

Population

In 1990 the population totalled 30,861 civilians of which 20,531 were Gibraltarians (males 9,803; females 10,728); 5,550 were other British (males 2,575; females 2,975); 4,780 were non-British (males 3,623; females 1,157). These figures exclude visitors and transients.

There were 531 births and 279 deaths in 1990.

Total expenditure on Medical and Health Services during the year ending 31st March 1990 was £12,102,072. The number of beds available in hospitals in 1990 was 252 and there were 4,878 admissions during the year.

The Economy

Approximately 2.8 per cent of the male wage-earners in Gibraltar are employed in one or other of the United Kingdom Departments (ie Ministry of Defence and the Department of the Environment) or by the Gibraltar Government. For many years the Ministry of Defence's (MOD) presence and related activities have been the backbone of Gibraltar's economy. Since 1988, however, increasing emphasis has been placed on the development of Gibraltar as a centre for financial services; in part this is to compensate for the gradual reduction in the MOD's involvement. In the private sector the main sources of employment are the tourist and related industries, the Finance Centre, the construction industry, hotel and catering services, and the retail and wholesale traders.

There are a number of relatively small industrial concerns engaged in the bottling of beer, mineral waters etc, mainly for local consumption. A major concern is a building components factory, based on Danish technology, and supplier of pre-fabricated components to meet the requirements of the local construction industry.

Retail Price Indices

1987	405.59
1988	418.08
1989	436.75
1990	436.19
1991	496.81

Indices are as at April of each year.

Over 43 per cent of Gibraltar's non-fuel imports orginate from the United Kingdom. Other sources include Spain, Japan, the Netherlands and USA. Foodstuffs accounted for around £20 million or 15 per cent of total imports in 1988. Exports are mainly re-exports of petroleum and petroleum products supplied to shipping.

	Imports (c.i.f.) £m.	*Exports (f.o.b.) £m.*
1985	113.2	47.9
1986	111.7	44.3
1987	141.0	51.7
1988	144.8	46.1
1989	200.5	76.1

Communications

Major world trade routes pass close to Gibraltar. Its port provides efficient, multiple services within the shipping industry such as ship and yacht repairs, ship chandlery, building, cleaning and surveying. Increasing use is made of the port for transshipment purposes and for crew changes (conveniently serviced by the airport which is half a mile from the port) as well as for ship and yacht registration.

The Port of Gibraltar offers protected berths to merchant shipping both at alongside berths or in the Anchorage; 3,395 vessels entered the Port in 1990 with an aggregate gross tonnage of 58 million Gross Register Tons.

Gibraltar has two marinas offering nearly 300 berths and a range of chandlery services of a high standard. Yacht repair facilities are available at the marinas and the Gun Wharf Yacht Centre.

Gibraltar Airport is situated at North Front in the area adjacent to La Linea, Spain and approximately 1.6 km from the centre of town. The runway is 1,829 metres long. Air Traffic Control, meteorological facilities, maintenance and the operation of Gibraltar Airport are the responsibility of the RAF who have an agreement with GB Airways for the handling, by the latter, of all civil aircraft. The administration, maintenance and security of the Air Terminal building, however, is carried out by the Gibraltar Airport Services Limited—a joint venture between the Government of Gibraltar and British Airport Services Limited. There are regular services operated by GB Airways (an associate company partly owned by British Airways and Bland Group of Companies, Gibraltar) Dan Air, Air UK Leisure, Air 2000 (operated by British Midland) and Britannic Airways direct from London to Gibraltar. GB Airways also provides a regular service between Manchester and Gibraltar.

The total number of telephones at the end of 1990 stood at 16,759.

The number of originated effective calls during 1990 was as follows:

Local Traffic	21,900,000
Operator Assisted	18,000
IDD Calls	2,436,206

During the year there was a net increase in the number of exchange lines connected of 1,037. The total number of exchange lines at the end of the year stood at 10,750; there were 621 applicants on the waiting list. The local Telephone Service is operated by Gibraltar Nynex Communications Limited, a joint venture company between The Government of Gibraltar and Nynex International Company from the United States of America. The Company was formed on 8th May 1990.

In 1990, a new Digital System X Exchange became operational with an initial capacity of 14,000 lines.

Gibraltar has a total of 49.9 km of road and a few bus services, but no railways.

The Media

GBC Radio (Radio Gibraltar) broadcasts in English and Spanish for 24 hours daily, an average of five hours weekly being devoted to commercial broadcasting. In addition to live and locally recorded programmes, use is made of BBC transcriptions and BBC World Service relays. GBC Television operates for 17 hours every weekday and 12 hours at weekends offering a combination of BBC WSTV and local programmes.

There were 7,340 licensed TV sets at the end of December 1990. There are no separate radio receiving licences as these are included in the television licence.

Trade and Finance

Gibraltar has always been valued for its strategic location. Today, although a British European Territory of the EC under Article 227 (4) of the Treaty of Rome, Gibraltar is exempted from community regulations on Value Added Tax, Common Customs Tariff and Commonwealth Agricultural Policy.

Gibraltar controls its own direct and indirect tax system—the liberal tax regime makes it an ideal investment base since it is able to offer competitive offshore facilities coupled with a modern European legal and professional framework often missing in other offshore centres.

The rate of tax applicable to a company is 35 per cent with effect from 1st July 1987. The rates applicable to individuals resident in Gibraltar with effect from 1st July 1987 are the following:

the first £1,500 of taxable income 20 per cent
the next £5,500 of taxable income 30 per cent
the next £5,500 of taxable income 35 per cent
the next £3,500 of taxable income 40 per cent
the next £3,500 of taxable income 45 per cent
the remainder of taxable income 50 per cent

All imports, with a few exceptions such as foodstuffs, drugs and medical preparations and certain basic building materials, are subject to import duty. Rates of duty range from 10 per cent to 45 per cent. A drawback is allowed to certain goods warehoused in a Government store and subsequently exported from Gibraltar and on components or other materials used in the manufacture of or the assembly of the goods in Gibraltar and exported on a commercial basis.

Estate Duty

Although Gibraltar has no equivalent to the previous UK capital transfer tax, it still retains the old estate duty, which stands at 5 per cent for an estate of £20,000 and rises gradually to a maximum of 25 per cent after £100,000. There is marginal relief in respect of an estate falling between the relevant percentages of the scale.

Estate duty is payable on all property whether settled or otherwise which passes on death. On the death of a person who is domiciled in Gibraltar, estate duty is payable on all real and personal property situated in Gibraltar and on the deceased's world-wide personal property. Under the Estate Duties Ordinance, estate duty is not payable in respect of real property situated outside Gibraltar even if the deceased was domiciled in Gibraltar. This property is, however, taken into account in the aggregation of the estate of the deceased to determine the amount of duty payable. Conversely duty is payable on the estate of a person who is not domiciled in Gibraltar on assets situated in Gibraltar (except shares and loans in an exempt or qualifying company and certain property deposited with banks or building societies). Relief is granted in certain cases where, on the death of one party to a marriage, estate duty has been paid or is payable in respect of settled property. There is also relief in respect of deaths in quick succession within five years on an estate consisting of land or business.

Gifts inter vivos of any property, made within a period of three years or more prior to death, render that property free from estate duty.

No duty is payable in respect of any property passing on the death of a non-resident person (not being property in the form of securities or other documents of title relating to property otherwise situated in Gibraltar) which is held on deposit in Gibraltar in any bank or building society. A non-resident person does not include any person who, immediately prior to his death, was treated as liable to taxation in Gibraltar by any rules made from time to time by the Governor in Council.

Stamp Duty

Stamp duty is levied on legal documents transferring title to assets. It is payable on every document relating to assets situated in Gibraltar and in respect of documents executed in Gibraltar relating to assets wherever situated.

In transfers and conveyances, the ad valorem stamp duty is charged on a sliding scale, reaching a maximum of 63 pence per £50 or part thereof where the consideration exceeds £500. Stamp duty is also levied on legal charges at a rate of 13 pence per £100.

The Stamp Duties (Amendment) Ordinance 1988 has recently limited the amount of duty in respect of capital loan issues, transfers and issues of debentures to £5,000 if the duty has been paid in advance of the issue and in one single payment. This concession was introduced to encourage major international banks to use Gibraltar as a centre for debenture issues. Furthermore, the said Ordinance exempted persons not ordinarily resident in Gibraltar from stamp duty in respect of a mortgage or a cash deposit held in a bank or building society in Gibraltar. There are also certain exemptions from stamp duty for unit trusts, life assurance policies and exempt companies, discussed later.

Life assurance policies, including annuities issued by an exempt insurance company, are not liable to any stamp duty in Gibraltar, even if they be executed and kept within Gibraltar. Any mortgage, charge or assignment of such policies is also free from stamp duty.

Unit trusts have been afforded stamp duty exemption in relation to issue and transfer of units on payment of an annual flat fee of £1,000.

All exempt and qualifying companies and non-resident trusts are relieved of liability to pay stamp duty in respect of any assets transferred by them. Furthermore, no stamp duty (other than nominal duty on authorised capital as referred to below) is payable on any document relating to the issue, allotment, renunciation, transfer, assignment or disposition of shares in exempt or qualifying companies. This exemption from stamp duty was enacted by the Finance Ordinance 1987. Nominal duty at ½% is payable on the authorised capital of exempt and qualifying companies. Stamp duty is only payable by exempt and qualifying companies and non-resident trusts if it relates to the transfer of immovable property in Gibraltar.

Education

Education in Gibraltar is free and available to all and the medium of instruction in the schools is English. Education is compulsory, between the ages of 5 and 15, and scholarships are made available for study at universities, colleges of higher education and other higher education establishments in Britain. There are 12 primary schools, one of which caters mainly for Jewish children, one special school for severely handicapped children, and two single-sex comprehensive schools. The Government also operates two nurseries, an occupational therapy centre for handicapped adults and a College of Further Education, taking full-time and day-release students for vocational courses.

Additionally, there are two Service primary schools and one independent primary school. Church of England children of civilian parents are admitted to the Services Schools by special arrangement between the Government and the Services Education Authority. Government primary schools are co-educational and divided into 'First Schools' catering for 4 + to 8 and 'Middle Schools' for children aged 8 to 12.

In September 1990 there were 1,340 pupils enrolled in Gibraltar First Schools, 1,365 in Middle Schools, 232 in private and 561 in Service Schools. There were also 22 pupils enrolled in the Special School for severely handicapped children from 2 to 18 years of age.

At secondary level, there were 906 pupils in Girls (Westside) School and 976 pupils in the Boys (Bayside) School. There were also 114 full-time and 550 part-time students attending the Gibraltar College of Further Eduation, bringing the total number of fulltime pupils in all educational institutions to 5,516.

Government expenditure on education for 1989/90 amounted to £7,620,143.

A lending library is maintained by the Gibraltar Government in the cultural centre—John Mackintosh Hall—to which the British Council also makes a contribution. At the Gibraltar Garrison Library, established in 1739, a reference section and lending library are available to members. The Museum contains exhibits of historical interest connected with Gibraltar.

History

It is clear from fossil remains discovered in the caves, that the Rock of Gibraltar was frequented by Neanderthal man and prehistoric animals; and, from the earliest recorded history, that the Bay of Gibraltar has sheltered ships and sailors from the very beginning of man's maritime adventure. Heracles, Calpe or Jebel Tariq, as the Rock has been known over the millennia, was one of the legendary Pillars of Hercules, long recognised as one of the boundaries of the then known world.

The cultural and administrative centre of the area for many centuries was the city of Carteia about a mile away at the head of the Bay, founded by the Phoenicians about 950 BC on the site of an earlier Iberian settlement. The decline of Phoenicia about 570 BC led to the occupation of Southern Spain by the erstwhile colonists, the Carthaginians, who held Carteia until it was taken for Rome—about 190 BC. During the Punic Wars, it was from Carteia that Julius Caesar marched to defeat the rival Roman army under Pompey's sons Cnaeus and Sextus at the famous battle of Munda (45 BC), not much more than a day's march from the Rock. Roman Carteia, which included Gibraltar (then known as Calpe) within its boundaries, was very prosperous and powerful having, among many other privileges, its own mint.

In later years, after the fall of Rome and a period of occupation by the Vandals, the Visigoths ruled Spain, and Carteia became one of the earliest Christian communities in Iberia. According to Spanish religious historian De La Concepción, it was the See of the Bishop of Carteia-Calpe until the Bishopric was removed first to Algeciras and later to Cadiz.

It was not until the Arab invasion of Spain under Tarik Ibn Zeyad in 711 AD that the Rock became a separate entity under the new name of Jebel Tariq (the mountain of Tariq—whence is derived the modern 'Gibraltar').

Its natural defences made it an ideal base for military operations and it played an important role throughout the nearly eight centuries of Arab occupation of Spain. In the internecine wars between the various caliphates in Arab Spain, Gibraltar changed hands several times. It acquired greater importance in 1160 AD, when the Almohad monarch Abd el Mumen developed the small town at the northern end of the Rock erecting a mosque, palaces, an elaborate water system with reservoirs, a windmill on the summit and well-designed defences.

In 1309, however, part of a Spanish force besieging Algeciras made a surprise attack on Gibraltar which capitulated after a short defence. The Arab inhabitants were expelled and allowed to go to Africa. The Spanish King Ferdinand and his successors had the defences rebuilt, with a tower or keep dominating the town, and developed a port area between the town and the sea as a haven for his galleys.

The period of Spanish occupation did not last long as in 1333 it was recaptured by the forces of the Marinid Sultan of Fez, Abul Hassan, after a siege of four and half months during which the garrison were reduced to eating the leather from their shields, belts and shoes, despite having been supplied at times by bags of flour hurled into the town by catapults on the ships. Gibraltar was developed and heavily re-fortified by Abul Hassan and his successors as a 'City of Islam'. Most of the Moorish structures still remaining, the Castle, defence walls, bath and the large mosque (now part of the Cathedral of St Mary the Crowned), were constructed in this period.

Dissension between the various caliphates in Spain and between these and those in Africa led eventually to the final recapture of the Rock by Spain after over seven centuries of Islamic domination.

This was on 29th August 1462, the feast of St Bernard of Clairvaux, who consequently became the patron saint of Gibraltar.

During the two hundred and forty-two years of subsequent Spanish occupation the Rock was fortified and developed as a naval base, at first against the Mediterranean and Barbary pirates and the fleets of Islam, and later in support of Spain's territorial expansion as it exploited its American empire and extended its hold on the Netherlands, Central Europe and Italy.

Disputes as to who should take the crown of Spain when Charles II died in 1701 led to the war of the Spanish succession, in which Britain and Holland joined Austria and the Holy Roman Empire in support of the Austrian claimant, the Arch-Duke Charles. Sir George Rooke, Vice Admiral of England, arrived in the Bay of Gibraltar on 21st July 1704 at the head of an Anglo-Dutch fleet which was carrying a military force composed of English and Dutch marines with a number of Spaniards and Catalans under Prince George of Hesse Darmstadt.

Some 2,300 English and Dutch marines were set ashore on the isthmus. A line half a cannon shot from the Rock was set up, cutting off all communication with the mainland and the garrison was summoned to surrender to their lawful King Charles III. A defiant reply was returned but, after three days in which the town was bombarded by the fleet, the sailors landed and captured the southern part of the Rock. The Spanish Governor then made an honourable capitulation. The gates were opened for the marines and the small Spanish garrison marched out with their arms. The Prince of Hesse Darmstadt proclaimed the town for Charles who was, however, ultimately unsuccessful in his bid for the Spanish throne. A strong counter-attack by the Spaniards in 1705 was successfully repelled.

In 1713, after the Archduke Charles had unexpectedly inherited the greater Crown of the Holy Roman Empire, the war was brought to a close by the Treaties of Utrecht, one of which, between Britain and Spain, settled the succession to the throne of Spain on the French claimant as Philip V, after securing that the Crowns of Spain and France could never be united in one person. In article X of this treaty Gibraltar was ceded to the Crown of Britain in the following terms:—'The Catholic King does hereby for himself, his heirs and successors yield to the Crown of Great Britain the full and entire propriety of the Town and Castle of Gibraltar, together with the port, fortifications and posts thereunto belonging and he gives up the said propriety, to be held and enjoyed absolutely with all manner of right for ever, without exception or impediment whatsoever....and in case it shall hereafter seem meet to the Crown of Great Britain to grant, sell or by any means to alienate therefrom the propriety of the said town of Gibraltar, it is hereby agreed and concluded that the preference of having the same shall always be given to the Crown of Spain before any other.' The Rock's defences, improved and developed as a British fortress, enabled it to resist two further sieges: the 13th siege in 1727 by the forces of Spain and France was followed by the Treaty of Seville which confirmed Utrecht. In the 14th and last or 'Great Siege' as it is more usually known, the garrison under the tireless and heroic leadership of the Governor, General George Augustus Eliott, outnumbered by four to one, successfully defended the Rock against the Spanish and French besieging forces, and the specially designed 'unsinkable and unburnable floating batteries', for three years seven months and twelve days (13th September 1779 to 12th March 1783). The Great Siege was followed in September 1783 by the Treaty of Versailles which also confirmed Britain's title to Gibraltar.

Gibraltar's strong defences, strategic position and ample harbour made it of great value to Britain and it played a most important part in Britain's maritime development. It was to Gibraltar that the damaged *Victory* was towed for repair after the Battle of Trafalgar carrying the body of Admiral Nelson and it was through Gibraltar that much of Britain's assistance to Spain in its struggle against Napoleon was provided during the Peninsular War.

The value of the Rock was also proved during the two World Wars when, in addition to providing repair and supply facilities for British and allied navies, it was an important convoy centre, air base and a key point in large anti-submarine operations. It now offers base facilities to the forces of the North Atlantic Treaty Organisation. The outstanding event of the second World War was the evacuation of almost the entire civil population in July—November 1940 in which some 16,700 people were sent to England and Northern Ireland and small groups also to Madeira and Jamaica. A repatriation scheme begun in 1944 was not completed until 1951.

In September 1963 the United Nations Special Committee on Decolonisation (the Committee of 24) considered the possible application to Gibraltar of the United Nations general policy on decolonisation, and Spain, which from time to time over the years had claimed the return of Gibraltar, seized the opportunity to begin a campaign for its return. A delegation from Gibraltar led by the Chief Minister appeared before the Committee and made it clear that Gibraltar already enjoyed a very large measure of self-government, that further constitutional changes were under discussion and that the ultimate aspiration of the people of Gibraltar was to achieve full internal self-government through free association with Britain. The suggestion that the sovereignty of Gibraltar should be discussed with Spain was vigorously resisted and on the return of the delegation from New York virtually the whole population took part in a massive demonstration of welcome and support.

On 17th October 1964 the Spanish Government of General Franco began a progressive series of restrictive measures against Gibraltar accompanied by a hostile and abusive press and radio campaign against the Gibraltarians.

Throughout subsequent talks the British Government made it clear that it had no doubt about its sovereignty over Gibraltar, and would protect the interests of its inhabitants. They also proposed that the legal issues in the dispute should be referred to the International Court of Justice at the Hague. This proposal was rejected by Spain. A referendum was held in 1967 in which all persons over 21, registered as Gibraltarians and ordinarily resident in Gibraltar, were qualified to vote, the total number being 12,762. 12,182 valid votes were cast of which 12,138 favoured retention of the link with Britain and 44 voted in favour of Spain.

During the period between 1964 and 1969 the Spanish Government progressively increased its restrictions against Gibraltar. All trade between Spain and Gibraltar was prohibited; some 2,000 female Spanish workers were prohibited by the Spanish Government from working in Gibraltar from 1966; vehicular traffic across the frontier was impeded from October 1964 and finally prohibited altogether in October 1966; in June 1969, Spain finally closed the frontier and thus deprived over 4,000 Spanish frontier workers of their jobs in Gibraltar; the Algeciras-Gibraltar passenger ferry service was withdrawn later that month; Spain completed Gibraltar's isolation by cutting telephone and telegraph links in October 1969. The British Government did not respond in kind.

Restrictions were also placed on the movement of British and NATO military planes through Spanish air space and prohibited areas of air space were created in the vicinity of Gibraltar's airport.

Throughout the period Spanish restrictions were in force the British Government honoured its commitment to sustain and support the people of Gibraltar, providing generous financial and technical aid for comprehensive development schemes particularly in the fields of housing, education, the port, public utilities and medical services. In addition it gave firm political support at the United Nations and in dealing with the Spanish Government.

In 1973 Gibraltar became part of the European Economic Community as a British dependent territory in Europe under article 227(4) of the Treaty of Rome, but was excluded at the request of the Government of Gibraltar from the Customs area of the Community, the Common Agricultural Policy, and the requirement to introduce Value Added Tax.

In 1977 and 1978 talks on Gibraltar were held between the British and Spanish Governments, Gibraltarian leaders attending as members of the British delegation. Official working parties were established to consider specific problems but no progress was made. Telephone communications were, however, restored by Spain at the end of 1977.

On 10th April 1980, agreement was reached at Lisbon between the British Foreign and Commonwealth Secretary and the Spanish Foreign Minister that Spain would remove all restrictions and negotiations would then be started in a spirit of goodwill, with a view to overcoming all the differences between Spain and Britain about Gibraltar. It was envisaged that all practical steps necessary for its implementation would be completed by 1st June 1980.

Although the British Government had completed its preparations for the re-opening of direct communications by then, the Spanish government was unable to give a firm date for its implementation. In December 1982, however, the Spanish authorities partially lifted their restrictions to allow Spaniards, Gibraltarians living in Gibraltar and the Campo area, British passport holders resident in Gibraltar, and immediate relatives to cross the border. At a meeting held in Brussels on 27th November 1984, the British and Spanish Foreign Ministers agreed to implement the Lisbon Statement by not later than 15th February 1985. The border was opened on 5th February and the negotiations (known as the Brussels Process) provided for in the Lisbon declaration began.

The 1981 British Nationality Act, which became effective on 1st January 1983 entitles British Dependent Territories Citizens who fail to be considered as United Kingdom Nationals for European Community purposes by reason of a connection with Gibraltar to be registered as British Citizens on application.

On 2nd December 1987 in an arrangement encompassing several distinct and separate agreements, the British and Spanish Foreign Ministers made a Joint Declaration on Gibraltar Airport (the Airport Agreement). The most controversial part of this deal was the suspension of the provisions of the first phase of the EC aviation liberalisation package (the 1987 Aviation Liberalisation Regulation) to Gibraltar until the Gibraltar Parliament agrees to the implementation of the Airport Agreement. On 10th November 1987 there was a mass demonstration in Gibraltar led by the entire House of Assembly against the proposed deal. Gibraltar's suspension continued when the second phase of the EC package was completed in June 1990.

After 38 years of virtually unopposed rule, the Association for the Advancement of Civil Rights (AACR) was defeated in the elections of 25th March 1988 by the Gibraltar Socialist Labour Party (GSLP). (Between 1969 and 1972 the Integration with Britain Party, supported by the Isola Group, held the majority in the House of Assembly.) The latter was committed by its manifesto to oppose the Airport Agreement and the Brussels Process of which it forms a part. The GSLP was reelected to power in 1992.

Constitution

Under the Gibraltar Constitution Order in Council 1964, there was a Gibraltar Council, a Council of Ministers and a Legislative Council consisting of a speaker appointed by the Governor, 11 elected members and two ex-officio members, the Attorney-General and the Financial Secretary. At Constitutional talks held in Gibraltar in July 1968, agreement was reached with local leaders on the lines of certain constitutional changes. These were incorporated in the new 1969 Constitution which is contained in the Gibraltar Constitution Order 1969, and which came into effect on 11th August 1969. This replaced the Legislative Council by a House of Assembly consisting of a Speaker, 15 elected members, the Attorney-General and the Financial and Development Secretary and formalised the devolution of responsibility for certain defined domestic matters to Ministers appointed from among the elected members of the Assembly. It also made provision for the abolition of the City Council, which dealt with municipal affairs and public utilities. The Governor retains direct responsibility for matters relating to defence, external affairs and internal security. He has the power to intervene in the conduct of domestic affairs in support of this responsibility; and has certain powers of intervention in the interests of maintaining financial and economic stability.

Executive authority is exercised by the Governor, who is also Commander-in-Chief. In the exercise of his functions relating to matters not dealt with by Ministers the Governor, whilst retaining the usual reserved powers, normally acts in accordance with the advice of the Gibraltar Council (which consists of the Chief Minister, the Deputy Fortress Commander, the Deputy Governor, the Attorney-General, the Financial and Development Secretary and four other Ministers appointed by the Governor after consultation with the Chief Minister). There is a Council of Ministers composed of all the Ministers and presided over by the Chief Minister.

The preamble to the Order in Council (to which the new Constitution is an annex) contains the following:

> 'whereas Gibraltar is part of Her Majesty's dominions and Her Majesty's Government has given assurances to the people of Gibraltar that Gibraltar will remain part of Her Majesty's dominions unless and until an Act of Parliament otherwise provides, and furthermore, that Her Majesty's Government will never enter into arrangements under which the people of Gibraltar would pass under the sovereignty of another state against their freely and democratically expressed wishes;....'

The Constitution also contains a Chapter providing for the protection of fundamental rights and freedoms on the lines of similar Chapters in the constitutions of various other territories within the Commonwealth.

GOVERNORS OF GIBRALTAR

(1977 Edition shows complete list of Governors of Gibraltar since the Great Siege of 1779–1783).

1969 Admiral of the Fleet Sir Varyl Begg, GCB, DSO, DSC

1973 Marshal of the Royal Air Force Sir John Grandy, GCB, KBE, DSO

1978 General Sir William Jackson, GBE, KCB, MC

1982 Admiral Sir David Williams, GCB

1985 Air Chief Marshal Sir Peter Terry, GCB, AFC

GIBRALTAR COUNCIL

The Governor

Ex-officio Members

The Deputy Governor

The Deputy Fortress Commander

The Attorney-General

The Financial and Development Secretary

COUNCIL OF MINISTERS

The Hon Joseph J Bossano *(Chief Minister with overall responsibility for the economy)*

The Hon Michael Feetham *(Minister for Trade and Industry)*

The Hon Joseph L Baldachino *(Minister for Housing)*

The Hon Joseph Pilcher *(Minister for GSL and Tourism)*

The Hon Robert Mor *(Minister for Labour and Social Security)*

The Hon Maria Isabel Montegriffo *(Minister for Medical Services and Sports)*

The Hon Juan Carlos Perez *(Minister for Government Services)*

The Hon Joseph L Moss *(Minister for Education, Culture and Youth Affairs)*

HOUSE OF ASSEMBLY

The Attorney-General: The Hon Kenneth Harris, QC

The Financial and Development Secretary: The Hon Peter Brooke

CIVIL ESTABLISHMENT

GOVERNOR AND COMMANDER-IN-CHIEF

Admiral Sir Derek Reffell, KCB

Military Assistant: Wing Commander D Thompson

Aide-de-Camp: Lt J Young

Deputy Governor: The Hon A Carter

Attorney General: The Hon Kenneth Harris, QC

Financial and Development Secretary: The Hon Peter Brooke

Administrative Secretary: E Montado

Accountant General: S Bensadon

Commissioner of Income Tax: J L Hernandez

Principal Auditor: W Crisp

Director of Education: J Alcantara

Director of Labour and Social Security: J J Capurro

Head of Public Works: M Perez

Commissioner of Police: J Canepa, QPM, CPM

Captain of the Port and Shipping Master: Capt J W Prior

City Electrical Engineer: A Aguilera

Director of Postal Services: E R Howes, ED

Superintendent of Prison: A Enriles
General Manager Gibraltar Tourism Agency: J Viale
Chief Fire Officer: L Edmonds

JUDICIARY
Chief Justice: The Hon Mr Justice Kneller
Additional Judge of the Supreme Court: J E Alcantara, OBE

Hong Kong

Location, Topography and Climate

The usual translation of Hong Kong is 'fragrant harbour'. Kowloon, the peninsula on the mainland opposite Hong Kong Island, means 'nine dragons' so named after the nine peaks of the range of hills to its immediate North.

Hong Kong lies on the South East coast of China, adjoining the province of Guangdong, between latitudes 22° 9′ and 22° 35′ North and longitudes 113° 50′ and 114° 30′ East, on the estuary of the Pearl River, the biggest river in South China.

It consists of the Island of Hong Kong (80 sq km), Kowloon (39 sq km) and the New Territories (954 sq km) which includes the large island of Lantau (over 140 sq km). The total land area is slightly over 1,000 sq km. The greater part is steep mountains covered with scrub and tussock with little flat land for agriculture or building. The coastline is deeply indented, and there are no navigable rivers. Man-made reservoirs provide several large fresh-water lakes. The highest mountains are Tai Mo Shan (975 m) and Lantau Peak (934 m). Victoria Peak on Hong Kong Island in 584 m. Country Parks cover 40 per cent of total land area.

The climate is sub-tropical and governed by monsoons, the winter being cool and dry and the summer hot and humid. Temperature ranges from a mean minimum of 13.6°C in January to a mean maximum of 31.5°C in July. Relative humidity varies from over 90 per cent in fog in spring and at times during early morning hours in summer, to less than 20 per cent after intense cold surges in the cool season. The mean annual rainfall is 2 214.3 mm of which over 80 per cent falls in May to October.

Population

In 1941 the population was 1,639,000. By the 1961 census it was 3,133,000, by the 1986 by-census 5,431,000 and at the end of 1990 was estimated at 5,859,000. Much of the increase in population has been due to immigration, also to natural increase. In 1990 the excess of births over deaths was 0.7 per cent. Based on the 1986 by-census, it is estimated that about 60 per cent of the population were born in Hong Kong. Most people have family origins in Guangdong or other coastal provinces of South China.

English is widely spoken and has equal legal status with Chinese. The lingua franca is Cantonese, but other coastal dialects such as Chao Zhu, Hokkien, Hakka and Shanghainese as well as Mandarin are also spoken. The principal religious influences are Buddhism, Taoism and Confucianism. There are over 250,000 Protestants and about the same number of Roman Catholics, and small communities of Jews and Sikhs.

The seat of Government is in the District of Victoria on Hong Kong Island. Hong Kong has two regions: based on the 1986 by-census, the urban area consisting of Hong Kong Island and Kowloon housing a population of about 3,320,000 and the New Territories housing about 1,677,000. In addition to these there are over 362,000 people in temporary accommodation. The whole territory is divided for administrative purposes into 19 districts. To avoid the densities of population of Hong Kong Island and Kowloon, several New Towns are being built in the New Territories. In 1990, the largest of these are Tsuen Wan/Kwai Chung (714,000), Sha Tin (492,000), Tuen Mun (384,000) and Tai Po (177,000). Further building continues. Most industry is located in Kowloon and the New Territories; most of the port facilities, including container terminals, are in the Tsuen Wan/Kwai Chung area.

Vietnamese Migrants

1991 was a difficult year for Hong Kong in dealing with the Vietnamese migrant problem.

By the end of 1991 there were 60,221 Vietnamese migrants. The huge influx of new arrivals posed not only major accommodation problems for Hong Kong but also created heavy community pressure for an end to the policy of first asylum. Despite all these difficulties, the Hong Kong Government still believes that the Comprehensive Plan of Action (CPA), agreed internationally by over 75 countries at the Geneva Conference in June 1989, remains the right approach to solve the Vietnamese migrant issue. It has been the failure to implement the CPA in full which has so far prevented a humane resolution of the problem.

The fourth meeting of the International Conference on Indo-Chinese Refugees (ICIR) Steering Committee which met in Geneva on 30th April/1st May 1991, reaffirmed that all participating Governments remained fully committed to all the provisions of the CPA, including existing cut-off dates, screening procedures and the return to Vietnam of all non-refugees. The Steering Committee also agreed to further consultations on alternative and additional measures to bring about a greatly accelerated return of non-refugees to Vietnam.

At talks in Hanoi in September 1991 between officials of the Vietnamese, British and Hong Kong Governments and representatives of the United Nations High Commissioner for Refugees (UNHCR) and of the International Organisation for Migration, Vietnam indicated that she was willing to accept the return from Hong Kong, in accordance with international practices, of all Vietnamese found not to be refugees. On 17th October, agreement was reached on the modalities for returning the "double-backers",* and on 29th October, Britain, Hong Kong and Vietnam signed a Statement of Understanding on the principles of an Orderly Repatriation Programme for all non-refugees in Hong Kong. Under this agreement, as a first step, all Vietnamese migrants arriving in Hong Kong after 29th October would be screened immediately, and those who, after screening and appeal, were found not to be refugees, would be returned to Vietnam without delay. Later, all non-refugees who had arrived in Hong Kong before 29th October would also be returned to Vietnam. Discussion of the modalities for this continue between the three parties.

On 9th November 1991, 59 Vietnamese illegal immigrants were repatriated from Hong Kong to Vietnam. This group was made up of "double-backers". Before their return, all had been screened, using procedures monitored by the UNHCR, and found to be non-refugees.

This operation was the first stage towards the implementation of the Orderly Repatriation Programme, which was agreed by the Vietnamese, British and Hong Kong Governments in October 1991. The Programme offers a way towards a humane and durable solution to the Vietnamese migrant problem. It is also in accordance with the provisions of the Comprehensive Plan of Action (CPA), which was agreed and came into effect in June 1989 at the second International Conference on Indo-Chinese Refugees (ICIR), and normal international practices.

Health

The standard of health is relatively high and the incidence of most infectious diseases is low. Expectation of life is 80 years for females and 74 for males. As at end 1990 there were 14 government, 20 government-assisted and 11 private hospitals and 43 institutions with over 25,000 beds (4.3 per 1,000 of the population). New hospital construction will increase these by about 7,560 by 1995. Hospital treatment is at nominal charge and emergency treatment is free. The overseeing of public hospital services has been taken over by the Hospital Authority, a statutory body, in 1991. There are 55 out-patient clinics provided by the government and 94 by the assisted charity organisations. Comprehensive family health services include antenatal and postnatal care, and immunisation against TB, diphtheria, whooping cough, tetanus, poliomyelitis, measles, rubella, mumps and hepatitis B. The principal causes of death are cancer, heart disease and cerebro-vascular disease.

Communications

Hong Kong's harbour is sheltered and has deep water. It has excellent facilities for loading and discharging cargoes in any form including containerisation, roll-on roll-off and break bulk. The marine services that modern shipping requires are readily available. In 1990 nearly 20,363 ocean-going and 99,460 rivertrade vessels called at Hong Kong and loaded and discharged 89 million tonnes of cargo, of which 50 per cent was containerised. Over 200 shipping agencies handle the vessels linking Hong Kong with the principal ports of the world. Hong Kong is a centre of ship-owning, financing and management. At the end of 1990 members of the Hong Kong Shipowners' Association controlled 69.8 m dead weight tonnes. Frequent ferry services cross the harbour and serve the principal islands. In 1990 ferries also carried about 13.2 million passengers between Hong Kong and Macau and 3.6 million between Hong Kong and China.

The Kowloon-Canton (Guangzhou) railway links Hong Kong with the Chinese railway system. In 1990 it carried 3.3 m tons of freight and 2 m head of livestock into Hong Kong and 1.1 m tons of freight into China. Cross-border passenger traffic during the year in both directions was 28 m. The section within Kong Kong is operated by the Kowloon-Canton Railway Corporation (KCRC), a statutory body. The 34 km of line is double-tracked and electrified. In addition to the China traffic it provides frequent high capacity passenger services. By the end of 1990 it was carrying about 491,000 passengers a day. The KCRC also operates an electrified Light Rail Transit System in the North Western New Territories servicing Tuen Mun and Yuen Long. It opened in 1988 and by the end of 1990 was carrying about 240,000 passengers a day on its 23 km of tracks, and was being extended. The urban areas of Hong Kong Island, Kowloon and Tsuen Wan/Kwai Chung are served by a Mass Transit Railway (MTR). By the end of 1990 it had 43 km of track including two separate harbour crossings, and was carrying about 2 m passengers a day. It too is being extended. It is operated by the Mass Transit Railway Corporation (MTRC), a statutory body.

Hong Kong's road system covers about 1,484 km. It includes two 4-lane tunnels beneath the harbour linking the island and mainland. The system is under continuous expansion. By 1990 road traffic to China in both directions amounted to 13,450 vehicles a day of which over 95 per cent were goods vehicles. Bus services are provided by the Kowloon Motor Bus Company, the China Motor Bus

* Those non-refugees who having returned voluntarily to Vietnam once, thereby benefiting from repatriation assistance from the UNHCR, entered Hong Kong illegally a second time, accompanied by members of their families.

Company, and the Lantau Bus Company. In 1990 these companies carried an average of 3.5 m passengers a day.

Hong Kong's airport is at Kai Tak in Kowloon, 5 km from the city centre, with a runway of 3,390 m. It is the major regional centre of air transport and services, and 46 international airlines operate regular services to and from it. In 1990 18.7 m passengers and 802,000 tons of freight passed through the Kai Tak terminals. Both passenger and freight terminals are being expanded.

In 1989 the Governor announced plans to build a new international airport, with room for two runways, on Chek Lap Kok for completion by about 1997. When fully developed, it will be able to operate 24 hours a day and will be able to handle 80 million passengers a year. Building the new airport and the associated road and rail links will be the largest infrastructure project ever undertaken in Hong Kong.

The Hong Kong Government estimate that the cost of airport core projects, including all the infrastructure projects amounts to £7.6 billion. The Hong Kong Government estimate that some 40 per cent of the cost will be met by the private sector by taking on commercially attractive projects and financing. The private sector wanted to see firm support from China before they would commit substantial funding so on 30th June 1991 an agreement was reached. A Memorandum of Understanding (MOU) was signed by the British Prime Minister and the Chinese Premier in Peking on 3rd September.

The MOU clearly states China's support and sets out that China will indicate to investors that contracts will be honoured after 1997.

The Economy

Hong Kong's economy is based on: its harbour which is the best natural deep water harbour in South China; trade and entrepot trade, mostly with China; large-scale manufacture of imported materials for export to world-wide markets; highly developed services, including financial services and tourism; and excellent communications of all sorts. It is the hub of regional business and communications. Agricultural land is limited and is used for intensive production of vegetables, flowers, poultry, pigs and fish farming. There is a large ocean-going fishing fleet. Much of imported food is bought from China, as is a substantial proportion of the water supply.

The Hong Kong Government has followed a consistent policy of free trade, free enterprise, conservative budgeting, and low taxation. The Hong Kong dollar note issue is 100 per cent backed by the Foreign Exchange Fund. Since 1983 the Hong Kong dollar has had an exchange rate fixed at 7.80 to the US$.

Hong Kong is one of the largest trading territories in the world—in 1990 the 11th largest. A wide range of sophisticated goods are produced for export by sea or air to a large spread of markets including the United States, China, and Europe. Some Hong Kong manufacturers also operate in neighbouring areas of China. In 1990 the largest exports are of clothing and accessories, miscellaneous manufactured articles (mainly jewellery, goldsmiths' and silversmiths' wares), photographic and optical goods, clocks and watches, electrical machinery and appliances, textiles, recording and office machinery. The tables below show the value of Hong Kong's overseas trade and the direction of imports, exports and re-exports.

VALUE OF OVERSEAS MERCHANDISE TRADE

	Unit	*1988*	*1989*	*1990*
Imports	HK$Million	498,798	562,781	642,530
Exports (excluding re-exports)	HK$Million	217,664	224,104	225,875
Re-exports	HK$Million	275,405	346,405	413,999

DIRECTION OF MERCHANDISE TRADE BY PERCENTAGE

	1979	*1989*	*1990*
Imports from:			
China	17.6	34.9	36.8
Japan	22.5	16.6	16.1
Taiwan	7.0	9.2	9.0
U.S.A.	12.1	8.2	8.1
Republic of Korea	2.9	4.5	4.4
United Kingdom	5.1	2.3	2.2
Exports (excluding re-exports) to:			
U.S.A.	33.6	32.2	29.4
China	1.1	19.3	21.0
Federal Republic of Germany*	11.4	7.0	8.0
United Kingdom	10.7	6.5	6.0
Japan	4.8	5.8	5.3

	1979	*1989*	*1990*
Re-exports to:			
China	6.6	29.9	26.8
U.S.A.	10.0	20.8	21.2
Japan	12.4	6.4	5.9
Federal Republic of Germany*	2.3	3.9	5.7
Taiwan	8.6	4.8	5.1
Republic of Korea	4.1	3.8	3.1

* In connection with the unification of Federal Republic of Germany (FRG) and German Democratic Republic (GDR) in October 1990, the trade figures for FRG in 1990 and previous years have been revised by adding those of the previous GDR. This is to ensure comparability of these trade figures with those after the German unification.

Hong Kong is a major centre of financial services, in which it is assisted by its position in the time zone and by excellent communications. At the end of 1990 locally incorporated banks and 138 overseas banks were operating in Hong Kong. In addition 155 overseas banks had representative offices. There is a mature foreign exchange market and a large and active stock exchange. Hotels (about 33,000 rooms) and restaurants are well developed, and in 1990, 5.9 m visitors went to Hong Kong.

In the 1980s, the economy of Hong Kong had grown at an average of over 7 per cent a year in real terms of GDP (2.7 per cent in 1989), bringing great improvement to the standard of living. In 1990, the per capita Gross Domestic Product was estimated to be HK$95,409 and the average daily wage rate was HK$184. Continuing the slow-down in 1989, the Gross Domestic Product showed a moderate growth rate of 2.8 per cent in real terms over 1989. The labour market remained generally tight (unemployment rate stayed at a low level of 1.3 per cent during 1990) and the economy was still operating close to capacity. After a weak performance in the latter part of 1989, domestic demand generally improved in 1990. Domestic exports recorded little change in 1990 as domestic exports to the United States, the United Kingdom and Japan continued to decline. On the other hand, growth in re-exports remained strong.

Development and Development Plans

In other sections of this chapter there are references to development and development plans in the fields of health, communication and education. The rapid growth of Hong Kong's wealth, and rise in the numbers and expectation of the population, require development planning to be continuous. Plans for all sectors are announced or up-dated each year in the Governor's address to the Legislative Council in the autumn, and the Budget speech of the Financial Secretary each spring. These must often have long lead-times as most land for development must first be created by levelling the mountains or reclamation from the sea.

Housing for the growing population has always been a major preoccupation of the government. Nearly three million people, over half the population, live in government housing operated by the Housing Authority, a statutory body. Under a long-term housing strategy being carried out by the Housing Authority, all the people in Hong Kong who need homes will be adequately housed by the turn of the century. To achieve this objective, some 670,000 more flats will be built, 400,000 of them by the Housing Authority and the rest by the private sector. The road and rail systems for the new international airport will provide fast communications between the island of Lantau and the Urban Area, and will open up land that hitherto was difficult of access. This may have considerable implications for the demography of the territory in the next century.

Education and Culture

Primary and junior secondary education are free and compulsory. The policy target is for subsidised places in senior secondary courses to be provided for 85 per cent of the 15-year-old population by 1991, with places for a further 10 per cent in craft and technical institutions. As for Secondary Six, courses of which lead up to matriculation requirements for tertiary institutions, the provision target is for one public sector Secondary Six place for every three public sector Secondary Four places two years previously. A full range of bachelor and higher degrees are offered at the University of Hong Kong and at the Chinese University of Hong Kong, including medical degrees. The Baptist College is another degree awarding tertiary institution, offering courses at undergraduate and postgraduate level. The Hong Kong Polytechnic, in addition to a wide range of diploma courses, also awards bachelor and some higher degrees, as does the City Polytechnic of Hong Kong. A third university, the Hong Kong University of Science and Technology, opened in October 1991. Lingnan College introduced degree courses in July 1991. A substantial increase in tertiary education is planned in response to popular and economic demand and to counteract loss of qualified people by emigration. In 1989 there were first degree places for eight per cent of the relevant age group. Under plans announced in 1989 the target figure for 1995 is 18 per cent. The Hong Kong University and Polytechnic Grants Committee advises the government on the development of higher education and administers government grants for tertiary institutions; its membership includes overseas academic and local business representation.

Hong Kong is an important cultural centre of European, Chinese and other Asian arts including music, drama, dance and visual arts. The Hong Kong Arts Festival, which is an international event, is held annually. In addition, a Festival of Asian Arts is held every two years. There is an Academy for Performing Arts. A large film industry produces for both Chinese and English-speaking audiences.

The Media

There is a thriving press in Hong Kong with more than 60 daily newspapers, of which 15 are in the English language. In addition several hundred periodicals are published. About 100 international news agencies, papers and broadcasting companies have offices in Hong Kong, providing both local and regional coverage. Ninety-seven per cent of households have a television set. Two private television companies (Television Broadcasts Ltd and Asia Television Ltd) broadcast both Chinese and English-language services. Radio Television Hong Kong (RTHK), which is owned by the Government, uses the transmission services of the two commercial stations to broadcast 12 hours each week of its own public affairs television in Chinese and English. Through the same services it broadcasts 8 hours daily of curriculum-based educational programmes for schools.

The first Hong Kong-based satellite television operator, Hutchvision Hong Kong Limited, has started to broadcast its Star TV Service to the entire Asia region. Star TV will eventually provide up to 7 channels, predominantly in English but also including Japanese and Mandarin. Sound broadcasting in Chinese and English is operated by RTHK (7 channels) by the Hong Kong Commercial Broadcasting Company (3 channels) and by Metro Broadcast Corporation Ltd (3 channels). FM and AM services are provided.

History

Under the Qing dynasty foreigners were not allowed to trade except through designated middle-men in Canton (Guangzhou) where foreign merchants were restricted to a small area. Following 50 years of friction about these restrictions and the way they were applied, and more notoriously and immediately about trade in opium, there was war. This resulted in the formal cession to Britain of Hong Kong Island in 1842 (the Treaty of Nanjing). It became a free port open to all. Following further war Kowloon was also ceded to Britain in 1860 (the Convention of Peking), and in 1898 the New Territories were added by a 99-year lease expiring on 30th June 1997 (the second Peking Convention). Hong Kong grew steadily as a centre of trade with China and as a British naval base.

In the late 1940s and early '50s, with civil war, revolution and social and economic upheaval in China, immigrants poured into Hong Kong. They brought new manufacturing and entrepreneurial skills from Shanghai, and it was they who started manufacture for export in Hong Kong. Soon afterwards trade was disrupted by the United Nations embargo on trade with China in 1950, and also by successive upheavals in China itself such as the Great Leap Forward in the 1950s and the Cultural Revolution in the 1960s. Under these pressures export to world markets of goods manufactured in Hong Kong replaced trade with China as the basis of the economy. It expanded with remarkable speed and success, as did also a variety of services. When trade with China revived in the 1970s Hong Kong was already established as a major centre of manufacture, and of international commerce, finance and communications, with large investment made in it by the United States, Japan and Britain.

Chinese interests are overseen by The New China News Agency which is directed by a senior diplomat. These redeveloped economic links with China have been additional to the continuing links with other countries built up over the last 40 years, and to their continuing investment and presence in Hong Kong.

The Future: The Sino-British Joint Declaration and The Basic Law

With the New Territories Lease due to expire in 1997, Britain and China began negotiations in 1982. These resulted in 1984 in the signature of the Joint Declaration. This provided that on 1st July 1997 China would resume the exercise of sovereignty over all Hong Kong, and that until then Britain would be responsible for its administration. Thereafter Hong Kong would become a Special Administrative Region of China (SAR) in which the basic policies set out in the Joint Declaration and its Annex I would be applied for 50 years after 1997. These policies would be stipulated in a Basic Law which would be promulgated under the Constitution of China. In the Joint Declaration and Annex I the Chinese Government pledged itself not to introduce socialism, and that Hong Kong's present social, economic, financial, fiscal and legal systems, freedoms, and associated way of life would continue. What this involved was set out in considerable detail. Defence and Foreign Affairs would be reserved to the Central Government, but the SAR would have a high degree of autonomy with a government composed of local inhabitants. The present public and judicial services would continue, including the employment of expatriates except in a few top posts reserved for Hong Kong Chinese citizens. The Joint Declaration was registered at the United Nations by both governments. A Sino-British Joint Liaison Group of officials meets regularly in Hong Kong, London and Peking to consult on implementation of the Joint Declaration. In 1985 China appointed a mixed Sino-Hong Kong committee to draft the Basic Law which would effectively be the Constitution of the SAR. The Committee published successive drafts to solicit opinions in Hong Kong in both 1988 and in 1989, occasioning lively debate. The final version of the Basic Law was promulgated by the National People's Congress of China in April 1990.

The Basic Law provides that the Chief Executive of the SAR will be a Hong Kong resident of long standing elected by an Election Committee and appointed by the Central Government for a five year term. The Election Committee is to consist of 800 members elected by Hong Kong functional sectors. The ultimate aim is stated to be election by universal suffrage. The Basic Law also lays down procedures for the transition in 1997, though some detail remains to be settled. The stated aim of both Governments is a smooth transition. Many Hong Kong people or their parents are refugees from China and they received the announcement in 1982 of negotiations for return to China with some alarm. This was followed by relief at the terms of the Joint Declaration. This faded during the prolonged and very public process of drafting the Basic Law and strident controversy over its terms. Confidence was further and more deeply shaken by events in Peking in June 1989. There has been a significant increase in emigration, and particularly emigration of qualified people. To encourage key people to stay in Hong Kong, and work for the success of the future SAR, in 1990 the British Government passed the British Nationality (Hong Kong) Act providing for the grant of United Kingdom citizenship with consequent right of entry and abode in the United Kingdom at will, to 50,000 Hong Kong people (plus their immediate dependants) to be selected on a points system, without prior residence qualification in the United Kingdom.

The Hong Kong Government has also brought in a Bill of Rights which became law in June 1991. This gives effect in local law to the International Covenant on Civil and Political Rights as applied to Hong Kong and makes it justiciable in Hong Kong courts.

Constitutional Development

The Government of Hong Kong is directed by a Governor appointed by the Secretary of State, with Executive and Legislative Councils appointed or elected, as provided for in Letters Patent and Royal Instructions. An Urban Council, partly elected, is charged with the provision of municipal, including cultural, services in the urban area. A Regional Council with a mix of elected and appointed members similarly provides for the New Territories. District Boards with majorities elected on universal adult franchise provide for consultation and participation in the administration of the 19 districts.

The size, representative character, and effective power of the Legislative Council have grown in the last 20 years. By 1989 it consisted of 56 members, of which 3 were ex officio, 27 were appointed (including 7 government officials), and 26 elected either by functional constituencies (constituencies of different professions) or electoral colleges composed of the members of District Boards and the Urban and District Councils. The Council was assisted by a large official staff. The Joint Declaration provided that all members of the Legislative Council would be selected by election, the form of election being unspecified and left for definition in The Basic Law. Though historically there has been little public interest in constitutional reform, it has grown sharply since the Joint Declaration. Debate has focused on the proportion of Legislative Councillors to be elected by direct election. The first direct election for 18 seats out of 60 was held in the elections of 1991.

The 1991 Elections

The Hong Kong Government conducted an extensive voter registration drive last year from mid-August to 20th November to prepare for the 1991 District Board, Municipal and Legislative Council (LegCo) elections. They used the media, distributed voter registration forms widely and conducted household visits. As a result the 1990 Final Register numbered 1,855,443, an increase of 257,936 over the 1989 figure of 1,597,507 and amounting to just over 50 per cent of the eligible electorate. This year's figure, following a last minute rush to register in time for the LegCo elections, was 1.9 million out of an eligible electorate of 3.67 million.

The *District Board* elections were successfully held on 3rd March. Voter turnout at 32.47 per cent was higher than most predictions and was 2 per cent up on the turnout in 1988; 272 members were elected to the 19 District Boards, including 81 who were unopposed. Of the 215 incumbent members who stood for election, 180 were re-elected. Elections to the *Municipal Councils* took place in May, 15 to the Urban Council and 12 to the Regional Council. Nineteen incumbent members were re-elected and two thirds (18) have overt political affiliations. The United Democrats did best, winning 14 of the seats.

The Legislative Council elections were held on 12th and 15th September. Elections for the 21 functional constituency seats took place on 12th September; 12 of the 21 seats were unopposed and 13 of the successful candidates were incumbents. Turnout rate was 47 per cent of registered voters. For the direct elections on 15th September all 18 seats were contested. The turnout rate was 39 per cent (of a registered electorate of 1.9 million). This was lower than many had expected, but higher than for any previous election in Hong Kong. The United Democrats and their other 'Liberal' allies did well, winning 16 of the 18 directly-elected seats and altogether 22 of the 39 elected seats. The other 17 elected members form a broad conservative group. Now, for the first time, LegCo will have a majority of elected members: 39 out of 60.

The Basic Law now states that in 1997 a third of the 60 members will be directly elected, progressing by the year 2003 to half, the other half being elected by functional constituencies. The ultimate aim is stated to be for all members to be elected by universal suffrage.

LIST OF GOVERNORS
For a full historical list see the 1978 edition
1964 Sir David Trench, GCMG, MC
1971 Sir Crawford Murray MacLehose, GBE, KCMG, KCVO (later (1982) Lord MacLehose of Beoch)
1982 Sir Edward Youde, GCMG, GCVO, MBE
1987 Sir David Wilson, GCMG (later (1992) Lord Wilson of Tillyorn)

EXECUTIVE COUNCIL (Position as at 1.8.1991)
(Presided over by the Governor)
The Chief Secretary (*ex-officio*)
The Commander, British Forces (*ex-officio*)
The Financial Secretary (*ex-officio*)
The Attorney-General (*ex-officio*)

Official Member: Barrie *Wiggham*, CBE
Appointed Members:
Baroness *Dunn*, DBE
Selina *Chow*, OBE
Rita *Fan* Lai-tai, OBE
Edmund *Ho* Sing-ting
Hui Yin-fat, OBE
Allen *Lee* Peng-fei, CBE
William *Purves*, CBE, DSO
Rosanna *Tam* Yick-ming, OBE
Wang Gungwu, CBE
Andrew *Wong* Wang-fat, OBE

LEGISLATIVE COUNCIL
The Governor (*President*) (*ex-officio*)
The Chief Secretary (*ex-officio*)
The Financial Secretary (*ex-officio*)
The Attorney-General (*ex-officio*)

Appointed Members:
John *Swaine* (*Deputy President*)
Allen *Lee*
Selina *Chow*
Martin *Barrow*
Miriam *Lau*
Lau Wah-sum
Peggy *Lam*
Rita *Fan*
Moses *Cheng* Mo-chi
Dr *Lam* Kui-chun
Steven *Poon*
Henry *Tang* Ying-yen
Vincent *Cheng* Hoi-chuen
Felice *Lieh-Mak*
Marvin *Cheung* Kin-tung
Timothy *Ha* Wing-ho
Edward *Chen* Kwan-yiu
Eric *Li* Ka-cheung

Elected Members:
James *McGregor*
Ngai Shiu-kit
Chim Pui-chung
Cheung Man-kwong
Simon *Ip* Sik-on
Samuel *Wong* Ping-wai
Edward *Ho* Sing-ting
Howard *Young*
Leung Kam-ho
Martin *Lee* Chu-ming
Man Sai-cheong
Yeung Sum
Huang Chen-ya
Szeto Wah
Li Wah-ming
Lau Chin-shek
Conrad *Lam* Kui-shing
Fung Kin-kee
James *To* Kun-sun
Emily *Lou* Wai-hing
Andrew *Wong* Wang-fat
Lee Wing-tat
Chan Wai-yip, Albert *Ng* Ming-yum
Tai Chin-wah
Fung Chi-wood
Tik Chi-yuen

JUDICIARY (Position as at 1.8.1991)
Chief Justice: The Hon Sir Ti Liang Yang
Justices of Appeal: The Hon Sir Derek Cons; The Hon Mr Justice Silke; The Hon Mr Justice Fuad; the Hon Mr Justice Kempster; The Hon Mr Justice Clough; The Hon Mr Justice Hunter CBE; The Hon Mr Justice Power; The Hon Mr Justice Penlington, OBE, AE; The Hon Mr Justice Macdougall
Judges of the High Court: The Hon Mr Justice Liu; The Hon Mr Justice Bewley; The Hon Mr Justice Rhind; The Hon Mr Justice Mayo; The Hon Mr Justice Hooper; The Hon Mr Justice Jones; The Hon Mr Justice Barnes; The Hon Mr Justice Nazareth, CBE; The Hon Mr Justice Mortimer; The Hon Mr Justice Wong; The Hon Mr Justice Sears; The Hon Mr Justice Godfrey; The Hon Mr Justice Barnett; The Hon Mr Justice Duffy; The Hon Mr Justice Ryan; The Hon Mr Justice Bokhary; The Hon Mr Justice Saied; The Hon Mr Justice Kaplan; The Hon Mr Justice Gall
Registrar, Supreme Court: Mr Julian Betts, JP

CIVIL ESTABLISHMENT

GOVERNOR AND COMMANDER-IN-CHIEF
Sir David Wilson, GCMG
Chief Secretary: Sir David Ford, KBE, LVO
Commander, British Forces: Maj-Gen Peter Royson Duffell, CBE, MC
Financial Secretary: Hamish Macleod
Political Adviser: William G Ehrman
Secretary for the Civil Service: Barrie Wiggham, CBE
Secretary for Security: Alistair Asprey, OBE, AE
Secretary for Economic Services: Mrs Anson Chan
Secretary for Home Affairs: Peter *Tsao* Kwang-yung, CBE, CPM
Secretary for Education and Manpower: John *Chan* Cho-chak, LVO, OBE
Secretary for Planning, Environment and Lands: Graham Barnes, CBE

Secretary for Works: Kenneth *Kwok* Wai-kai, OBE
Secretary for Monetary Affairs: David Nendick, CBE
Secretary for Recreation and Culture: James *So* Yiu-cho, OBE
Secretary for Trade and Industry: Chau Tak-hay
Secretary for Transport: Michael *Leung* Man-kin
Commissioner of Police: Li Kwan-ha, CBE, QPM, CPM
Attorney-General: Jeremy Fell Mathews, CMG
Secretary for the Treasury: Yeung Kai-yin
Secretary for Constitutional Affairs: Michael *Suen* Ming-yeung
Secretary for Health and Welfare: Mrs Elizabeth *Wong* Chien Chi-lien, ISO
Commissioner, London Office: John Yaxley, CBE
Director of Education: Li Yuet-ting

For the convenience of people unfamiliar with Chinese names the name which is the equivalent of a surname has been printed in italics.

Montserrat

Capital: Plymouth

Montserrat is part of the Leeward Islands group of the Lesser Antilles in the Eastern Caribbean, latitude 16° 45′ North, longitude 62° 10′ West, and has an area of 102 sq km (40 sq miles). It is entirely volcanic and there are seven active soufriere (hot springs) areas, one—Galways—readily accessible by road to tourists. The island is dominated by the three mountain ranges, Silver Hills in the North (397 m) Centre Hills (729 m) and Soufriere Hills with Chances Peak, (900 m) in the South. A feature of the terrain is the ravines (ghauts) and there are two waterfalls. The coastline is rugged and offers no all weather harbour although there are several anchorages in the western lee of the island sheltered from the prevailing trade winds.

There is no well defined rainy season, although normally the first six months of the year are drier than the second half of the year. The average rainfall is 1,475 mm. The coolest time of the year when temperatures have been as low as 18.5°C (65°F) is between the months of December and March. The hottest time of the year is between June and November which is also the hurricane season. Although in the hurricane belt Montserrat experiences serious hurricanes very infrequently. It was badly hit by Hurricane Hugo in 1989.

The Population

Latest census (1980) figures show a total population of 11,606 of which 1,478 live in Plymouth, the capital. This relatively low figure reflects the considerable emigration that took place in the fifties; but the population is now considered stable. The number of births in 1989 was 152; the number of deaths 137. The infant mortality rate was 1.1 per cent per 1,000.

Montserratians are predominantly of African descent. The language is English. Anglican, Methodist, Roman Catholic, Pentecostal and Seventh Day Adventists are the main religious denominations. Irish names abound, reflecting the island's history. There is a notable expatriate element of North American retired persons.

The unit of currency is the East Caribbean Dollar (EC$), pegged at 2.70 to the US dollar, fluctuating with the British sterling between 4.1 and 4.6 for 1 Pound Sterling in 1991. There are three main commercial banks on the island. A 1.75 per cent tax is levied on the export of foreign currency.

Self-sufficiency is the Government's primary agricultural strategy and towards this end development of capital intensive agro-based industries is encouraged. The following are some of the preferred areas of investment: processing of tropical fruits, production of poultry, beef, pork and eggs for local consumption, ornamental plant production and spring water bottling. Only about half the 9,000 acres suitable for agricultural use is being farmed at present.

A feature of the island is the large number of sheep and goats (5,000 in 1989) which provide the traditional stew 'Goat Water'. There are good cattle (2,500) and some pigs (1,500) and poultry (6,000). Donkeys (200) are used for transport in the hills.

Fisheries resources are under-exploited due to the absence of a sheltered harbour for larger fishing vessels. The local catch was estimated in 1989 at 130 metric tons.

The light industrial sector in Plymouth includes electronic assembly, the manufacture of plastic bags, garments, automotive products, tapestries and tile production. With the assistance of CIDA, under its Small Project Implementation Facility Programme (SPIFP), a commercial Agro Processing Facility is being established.

Government currently promotes investment in a number of selected areas including:—data processing, spring water bottling, hotel/villa/condominium development and poultry production. Increased private sector investment is highly desirable.

Although tourist arrival figures are small (28,000 in 1989) the industry is of major importance (earning EC$23m in 1989). The local form of tourism, so called 'villa tourism' also generates considerable activity in the local construction industry. Tourism is up-market. There are two medium-size hotels. Major resort hotels are planned for Bransby Point near Plymouth and at Little Bay in the north near the white sand beach at Rendezvous Bay. There is a golf course at Belham Valley.

A highly reliable supply of electricity is available: 210/220 volts, AC 60 cycles single phase for domestic use and 400/440 volts, 60 cycles, three phase for commercial usage. The installed power capacity far exceeds current demand. The industrial electricity rate is US$0.13 per kwh, plus fuel surcharge.

Water is available for both commercial and domestic use. The commercial water rate is US$3.70 per 1,000 imperial gallons. A fixed charge is added based on the value of the property served.

Montserrat was devastated by the passage of Hurricane Hugo in September 1989 which caused £20,000,000 worth of damage. The major hotels have reopened and the tourist industry has recovered.

Financial Services Centre

A Financial Services Centre has been set up to deal with the regulation and supervision of all banks (locally operated and offshore banks) registered in Montserrat.

The process of revising and improving the banking administrative, regulatory and supervisory systems is well advanced. A Regional Financial Services Adviser has been appointed by the British Foreign and Commonwealth Office to assist with this work in the British Caribbean Dependent Territories.

New ordinances for the regulation of both locally operated and offshore banks are soon to be introduced as well as new ordinances regulating offshore trusts, insurance and company management. At that time the existing moratorium on the issuance of offshore banking licences will be terminated and a full functioning Financial Services Centre operating in conformity with international standards will be put in place.

Communications

There is one seaport located in the capital Plymouth. The estimated number of cargo vesels in 1989 was 850 discharging over 120,000 tons of cargo (the bulk of the increased cargo tonnage was a direct result of hurricane rebuilding materials). Cruise ship passengers amounted to approximately 6,500. Blackburne Airport is 13 km from Plymouth on the other side of the island. International travellers transit the international airport in Antigua 20 minutes flying time from Montserrat. Blackburne has a 990 m runway, modern air traffic control systems, a tower, rebuilt in 1989, and a terminal. There are plans for a new runway with a different alignment to accommodate large aircraft.

Leeward Islands Air Transport Service (LIAT) operates four scheduled flights from Antigua to Montserrat and return daily. Two of these flights are operated by DASH 8 37 seaters and three by 19 seater Twin Otters. There is one flight a day to St Kitts.

International and internal telephone services are provided by Cable and Wireless which has recently invested heavily in modern digital equipment. Direct dial and fax services to the rest of the world are available.

Radio Montserrat is a Government-operated station. An FM service, GEM Radio, with repeater stations throughout the region operates commercial services. Radio Antilles is being restored to provide limited regional services to the region. This was extended to 200,000 watts at the end of 1990. Television is received via satellite and transmitted by cable. There is also a local TV station which will be restored to provide limited local programmes, and others, via satellite.

Education, Health and Community Services

There are 2 Day-Care Centres, 9 nursery schools and one nursery class at Lees, 12 Primary Schools and a Comprehensive Secondary School with 3 campuses, and a Technical College. Schools are run by Government, the churches and the private sector. In 1989 there were 330 pupils at nursery schools, 1,439 at Primary Schools, 900 at the Government Secondary School and one denominational Secondary School combined, and 41 students at the Technical Training College.

There is an Extra Mural Department of the University of the West Indies in Plymouth with about 216 students, 14 part time teachers and 1 full time teacher.

The privately owned American University of the Caribbean (AUC) was closed for the 1989/90 academic year due to massive damages inflicted on its facilities by Hurricane Hugo, but it has now reopened.

There is a 67 bed Government general hospital with an Infirmary. Government provides free medical and dental services, in certain circumstances, and a public sanitation service.

The Government operates a Social Security Scheme, a Government library service, and there is Government support for youth and sports organisations, cultural activities and the Montserrat National Trust. There are many church and charitable organisations.

The Economy

The work force in 1990 totalled 5,700, of which 350 were in agriculture, 250 in manufacturing and mining, 129 in utilities, 2,000 in construction, 600 in trade and tourism, 325 in communications and transport, 175 in banking and real estate, 1,800 in Government, community services and other household and personal services.

The gross Revenue and Expenditure of Government for 1986–1989 were:

	1986	*1987*	*1988*	*1989*
	EC$M	*EC$M*	*EC$M*	*EC$M*
Current Revenue	25,843	22,776	32,065	35,049
Capital Revenue	7,798	3,730	8,122	9,195
Revenue Total	33,641	26,506	40,187	44,244
	1986	*1987*	*1988*	*1989*
	EC$M	*EC$M*	*EC$M*	*EC$M*
Current Expenditure	25,156	27,276	30,060	32,900
Capital Expenditure	6,701	4,618	8,550	6,900
Total Expenditure	31,857	31,894	38,610	44,041
Gross Domestic Product	114,091	129,000	146,331	160,964
Gross Fixed Capital Formation	37,785	46,205	64,449	70,893

The capital budget is largely funded through overseas aid—from Britain and Canada in particular—and from other regional and international aid and lending organisations.

The maximum income tax rate is 30 per cent for individuals. The rate for companies is 40 per cent. Property tax is levied on the assessed market value at the rate of 1.5 per cent for land and 0.75 per cent for buildings.

Economic climate

This politically stable Dependent Territory with its own Ministerial system and a resident British Governor as the Representative of The Queen, offers an enticing commercial potential to small and medium sized foreign companies who will fit in with the island's modest size and population.

The Government of Montserrat actively encourages private investment both local and foreign. Investment incentives include tax holidays ranging from 5 to 15 years. Exemptions from local customs duties are also available. Tourism is the largest supplier of foreign exchange and one of the most important sectors of the economy. The Government encourages investment in tourism projects. Under the Hotels Aids Ordinance investors in the hotel industry are permitted exemptions from customs duties on materials and equipment used in hotel construction and operation.

Land Policy

It is obligatory for all non-Montserratians to obtain an alien land holding licence from the Government before they obtain any interest in land in the Territory. There are designated development areas in which non-nationals can acquire property. All other areas are restricted to nationals.

The Government participates in many regional organisations including:

Organisation of East Caribbean States
Caribbean Community
Caribbean Centre for Development Administration
Caribbean Labour Administrative Centre
Seismic Research Centre
Caribbean Food and Nutrition Institute
Environmental Health Institute
Eastern Caribbean Supreme Court
Leeward Islands Air Transport
Caribbean Research and Development Institute
University of the West Indies
Caribbean Conservation Association
OECS High Commission Office in Canada
Regional Laboratory Testing Organisation
Caribbean Examination Council

History

Montserrat was discovered by Christopher Columbus in November 1493, on his second voyage to the New World. The serrated profile of the islands reminded him of the locale of the Abbey of Montserrat in the Spanish highlands near Barcelona.

In 1632 Sir Thomas Warner sent a group of English and Irish from overcrowded St Christopher to settle on Montserrat. Further Irish immigrants arrived during the century from Virginia, driven out because of their Roman Catholic religion. They grew tobacco and indigo, then came cotton and later sugar. Through the years the planters were much harassed by the French and Carib Indian raids.

The island was stormed and taken by the French in 1664 and 1667 but was restored to England in 1667 by the Peace of Breda.

In 1671 the Leeward Islands were separated from Barbados and put under the rule of a Captain-General and Commander-in-Chief.

In 1678 Sir William Stapleton, Captain-General and Commander-in-Chief of the Leeward Islands, recorded the population of Montserrat as:

	Men	*Women*	*Children*	*Total*
English	346	175	240	761
Scottish	33	6	13	52
Irish	769	410	690	1,869
Total	1,148	591	943	2,682
Slaves	500	300	292	1,092

The first slaves from Africa arrived in Montserrat in the mid seventeenth century and reached as many as 9,500 in 1805, at which time the European population had dropped to 1,000.

The French under Cassard with 3,000 men raided Montserrat in 1712. They burned and pillaged to the extent of £203,500 damage, for which a special clause was inserted into the Treaty of Utrecht. The last capture of Montserrat by the French was in 1782, when de Bouille took most of the Leewards, but it was restored to England in 1783 by the Treaty of Versailles. During the Napoleonic Wars a French fleet under La Grange attacked the Leewards in 1805 and demanded ransom, of which Montserrat paid £7,500.

On 1st August 1834 slavery was abolished. The planters of Montserrat were paid compensation of £103,556 for 6,401 slaves. Added to the cessation of slavery and the apprentice system, the falling price of sugar in the late 19th century did much to discourage planters, who found it very difficult to run estates profitably; the rugged topography and a shortage of capital made it equally difficult to modernise estate agriculture. Between 1890 and 1936 Montserrat's economy had, in addition, to sustain a series of devastating earthquakes and hurricanes. All these factors combined to cause the demise of estate agriculture.

In 1857 Joseph Sturge, of Birmingham, England, formed the progenitor of the Montserrat Company Ltd., which bought abandoned estates, planted limes and made Montserrat lime juice famous. This company did much to up-grade the prosperity of the islands. They sold plots of land to the peasants, in the conviction that a settled people makes the soundest community. Much of Montserrat today is owned by small holders. In the 1870's the company also endowed and operated a school for the children of workers, which previously had been provided by church and private schools with the aid of grants from the National Society in England.

The Anglican Church was disestablished in January 1875, and received no more financial aid from the Government. The three main sects were, and still are, Anglican, Roman Catholic and Methodist, but Seventh Day Adventists are on the increase.

The Leeward Islands Act 1871 inaugurated the Federal Colony of the Leeward Islands, including the Presidencies of the British Virgin Islands, St. Christopher, Nevis and Anguilla, Montserrat and Dominica. Each Presidency was headed by a Commissioner or Administrator who was responsible to the Governor of the Federal Colony of the Leeward Islands.

The Federation of the Leeward Islands was abolished on 1st July 1956 when Montserrat became a Colony in its own right and from 1960 until 1971 an Administrator was the Queen's Representative in Montserrat.

When the Federation of the West Indies was created on 3rd January, 1958, all the British West Indian territories entered as separate units, Montserrat being one. Unfortunately, the Federation had but a short life and broke up with the secession of Jamaica in 1962. Since then Montserrat has been separately administered. On 3rd November 1971 HM The Queen approved the appointment of a Governor to replace the Administrator.

Constitution

The Constitution of 1989 provides for execution of Government through the Governor who is appointed by Her Majesty The Queen, an Executive Council and a Legislative Council. The Executive Council has the general control and direction of the government of the Territory. It is presided over by the Governor and there are two ex-officio members, the principal law officer (Attorney-General) and the Financial Secretary, and four official members (the Chief Minister, and three other Ministers).

The Governor appoints as Chief Minister the member of the Legislative Council who, in his judgement, is most likely to command a majority in the Legislative Council. The other official members of the Executive Council are appointed by the Governor on the advice of the Chief Minister. Ministers may be assigned responsibility for any Government business (including financial matters) except external affairs, defence, internal security, the audit of public accounts and the public service.

The Legislative Council is presided over by the Speaker (first elected in 1975) and comprises, besides the Speaker, two ex-officio members, seven elected members and two nominated members. There is a Deputy Speaker elected from within the Council. Elections are by universal adult suffrage from the age of 18.

A new Constitution was introduced in December 1989 which consolidated previous UK and local legislation. It included a statement on the fundamental rights and freedoms of the individual and transferred responsibility for international finance to the Governor.

A puisne judge of the Eastern Caribbean Supreme Court serves Montserrat as an itinerant judge. The appointment, dismissal and disciplinary control of public officers is vested in the Governor in his discretion, acting after consultation with the Public Service Commission.

Government

At the general election held on 25th August 1987, the People's Liberation Movement won four seats in the Legislature, a further two being won by the National Development Party, with the seventh retained by the Progressive Democratic Party.

GOVERNOR
His Excellency Mr D G P Taylor

EXECUTIVE COUNCIL
President: His Excellency The Governor
Chief Minister and Minister of Finance and Economic Development: Hon Ruben Meade
Minister of Communication and Works: Hon David Brandt
Minister of Education, Health and Community Services: Hon Lazelle Howes
Minister of Agriculture, Trade, Land and Housing: Hon Charles Kirnan
Attorney-General (ex-officio): Hon Stanley Moore
Financial Secretary (ex-officio): Hon C T John, OBE
Secretary to Executive Council: Miss K Russell

LEGISLATIVE COUNCIL
Speaker: Hon Dr H A Fergus, OBE, PHD
Attorney-General (ex-officio): Hon Stanley Moore
Financial Secretary (ex-officio): Hon Charles John, OBE
Nominated Member and Deputy Speaker: Hon Frank Edwards
Nominated Member: Hon Kenneth Allen

ELECTED MEMBERS WITH DISTRICTS
Hon Lazelle Howes (Plymouth District)
Hon B B Osborne, OBE (Southern District)
Hon Charles T Kirnan (North-Western District)
Hon Ruben T Meade (Central District)
Hon D Brandt (Windward District)
Hon N Tuitt (Eastern District)
Hon Ruby-Wade Bramble (Northern District)

CIVIL ESTABLISHMENT
Governor: D G P Taylor
Permanent Secretary (Administration): Miss Florence Daley, OBE

CHIEF MINISTER'S OFFICE AND MINISTRY OF FINANCE & ECONOMIC DEVELOPMENT
Financial Secretary: C T John, OBE
Permanent Secretary (Chief Minister): Miss I Bramble
Director of Development: Mrs Angela Greenaway (*Ag*)
Comptroller of Customs: R A Jemmotte
Accountant General: R Ryan
Comptroller of Inland Revenue: L Dyett
Postmaster: Mrs C Roach

TOURISM OFFICE
Director of Tourism: Mrs Leona Midgette

MINISTRY OF AGRICULTURE, TRADE, LANDS AND HOUSING
Permanent Secretary: S A W Maloney
Director of Agriculture: F Michael
Veterinary Officer: G Swanston
Chief Surveyor/Registrar of Lands: B Burke (*Ag*)

MINISTRY OF COMMUNICATIONS AND WORKS
Permanent Secretary: Mr M Cassell
Director of Public Works: K F Sparkes, OBE
Airport Manager: J O'Garro

MINISTRY OF HEALTH EDUCATION AND COMMUNITY SERVICES
Permanent Secretary: J Bass (Education, Health and Community Services)
Director of Education: Mrs M Fenton
Director of Health Services: L L Lewis, FRCS
Principal Community Development Officer: Mrs M Bass
Principal Librarian: Miss J Grell

LEGAL
Attorney-General: Hon Stanley Moore
Magistrate/Registrar: H Sergeant

AUDIT
Auditor General: Lorenzo Cassell

POLICE
Commissioner of Police: S Charles, MBE

PUBLIC SERVICE COMMISSION
Chairman: K Allen
Members: S. St. A Meade, OBE, Mrs E Edwards

JUDICIAL
Eastern Caribbean Supreme Court Puisne Judge (Montserrat Circuit): Justice A J Redhead

Pitcairn, Henderson, Ducie and Oeno Islands

The small volcanic island of Pitcairn 4.35 sq km (1.75 sq miles) is situated in the Pacific Ocean 25° 04′ S.; 130° 06′ W. roughly mid-way between Panama and New Zealand and 2,172 km (1,350 miles) east-south-east of Tahiti. It is a rugged island rising to 330 m (1,100 feet) and even at Bounty Bay, the only landing place, access from the sea is difficult. The climate is equable. Mean monthly temperatures vary from 19°C (66°F) in August to 24°C (75°F) in February; the average annual rainfall is 2,000 mm (80 inches), fairly evenly spread throughout the year. Moderate north-easterly winds predominate with short east to south-east gales occurring between April and September.

The early history of Pitcairn is uncertain but archaeological remains prove it was inhabited by Polynesians some six hundred years ago, at least for short periods. Modern history began with its discovery by Carteret in 1767, and its occupation by Fletcher Christian and eight of the *Bounty* mutineers, accompanied by twelve Tahitian women and six men, in 1790. Although an American vessel called at the island in 1808 it was not until the visit of HMS *Briton* and HMS *Tagus* in 1814 that the story of the Pitcairn settlement became widely known. The first decade had been marked by jealousies and violence and by 1800 the only adult male survivor was John Adams, who guided and led the small community until his death in 1829. In 1814 the population numbered 40; and by 1831 it had increased to 86 of whom 79 were born on the island. Concern for the future led to evacuation to Tahiti in 1831 but within six months the Pitcairners were back home, less twelve who had died during the absence. In 1856 the population had reached 194 and the island was again abandoned, a new home having been provided by the British Government on Norfolk Island off the east coast of Australia. By 1864, however, 43 Pitcairners had found their way back and since then the island has been permanently settled, the population reaching a peak of 233 in 1937. Since 1978 the population has been stable at between 50 and 60; at 31st December 1990 it was 52.

Pitcairn is a British settlement under the British Settlements Act 1887, but the islanders count their recognition as a colony from 1838 when Captain Eliott of HMS *Fly* gave them a constitution with universal adult suffrage, compulsory education and a code of law. In 1893 a parliamentary form of government was adopted and in 1898 the island was brought under the jurisdiction of the High Commissioner for the Western Pacific in Suva, which for the next twenty years was exercised through the British Consul in Tahiti. A further change in the constitution in 1904 restored the simpler pattern of 1838 which was retained as the basis for the wider reforms of 1940, whereby provision for local government by an elected Council and limited jurisdiction for an Island Court were given force of law by Order in Council. In 1952, the Pitcairn Order in Council transferred responsibility for administration to the person of the Governor of Fiji following the separation of the offices of Governor and High Commissioner. When Fiji became independent on 10th October 1970, a new order then transferred this responsibility to the British High Commissioner in New Zealand who is concurrently Governor of Pitcairn, Henderson, Ducie and Oeno Islands. The Local Government Ordinance constitutes a Council of ten members of whom six are elected, three are nominated (one by the elected members and two by the Governor) and one is an *ex officio* member, the Island Secretary. The Council is presided over by the Island Magistrate who is elected triennially. All other members hold office for one year. Liaison between the Governor and Council is effected by a Commissioner in the office of the British Consulate-General, Auckland.

Land is held under a system of family ownership, based upon the original division of the island by Fletcher Christian and his companions. Alienation to foreigners is not forbidden by law but, as a general rule, the only rights to pass are to their descendants by marriage to a Pitcairn Islander. The control of entry for the purposes of settlement further protects the customary tenure of land.

New Zealand decimal currency is in everyday use in Pitcairn. There is no taxation. Pitcairn is dependent on its own revenue generation, primarily derived from the sale of postage stamps, but continues to receive some British aid funds for special projects. Revenue in 1990/91 was approximately NZ$794,900 and expenditure NZ$697,500. Development works have largely been concentrated on telecommunications, power supply, improvements to the boat harbour and jetty at Bounty Bay and a tractor for roadworks and transportation. In 1983, for example, the Island Council purchased a 43 ft aluminium longboat and a Royal New Zealand Air Force C130 Hercules landed an 11 ton bulldozer onto the Island. During 1985, major modifications were made to the jetty and a cadastral survey was carried out over part of Pitcairn using British aid funds. A radio/telephone link via New Zealand with the rest of the world was also commissioned. A second aluminium longboat constructed in the United Kingdom was delivered in December 1987; in 1990 this vessel was shipped to New Zealand where alterations were made to the engine and transmission.

Free primary education is provided on the island under the direction of a qualified schoolteacher recruited from New Zealand. Scholarships provided by the Pitcairn Island Government are available for students to receive post primary education or specialist training in other fields in New Zealand. When a registered medical practitioner is not on the island a trained nurse, usually the wife of the Pastor, looks after the general health of the community, assisted if necessary by surgeons of passing ships when available. Government meets two-thirds of transport and hospital costs (or full costs in the case of pensioners) if a patient has to be transferred to New Zealand. The islanders have been adherents of the Seventh Day Adventist Church since 1887.

Pitcairn is on the direct shipping line between the Panama Canal and New Zealand and 54 ships and 11 yachts called there during 1990. Since mid-1968 passenger ships have ceased to call regularly at Pitcairn Island, and sea communications are now maintained by container vessels running between New Zealand and Panama which make scheduled calls at approximately three-monthly intervals. Transport between ship and shore is by diesel launch.

Gardening and fishing play an important part in community life. The fertile soil of the valleys produces a wide variety of tropical and sub-tropical crops which are used for subsistence and money income is earned by the sale of postage stamps and handicrafts. A cooperative store was established in 1967. A re-afforestation scheme was introduced in 1963 with emphasis on the planting of *miro* trees, which provide the wood used in making handicrafts.

The uninhabited islands of Henderson, lying 169 km (105 miles) east-north-east of Pitcairn, Oeno, 121 km (75 miles) north-west, and Ducie 471 km (293 miles) east, form part of the settlement. The first two islands are visited regularly by the Pitcairn Islanders.

Governor: D J Moss, CMG (resident, Wellington, New Zealand)
Island Magistrate: Mr J Warren, Adamstown, Pitcairn Island
Education Officer: Mr A Washington, Adamstown, Pitcairn Island

St Helena and St Helena Dependencies (Ascension and Tristan da Cunha)

Capital: Jamestown

St Helena lies in the South Atlantic Ocean, latitude 16°S., longitude 5° 45′W., 1,131 km (703 miles) south-east of Ascension and about 1,931 km (1,200 miles) from the south-west coast of Africa. It is 16.9 km (10.5 miles) long and 10.5 km (6.5 miles) broad, covering an area of 122 sq km (47 square miles.)

St Helena is rugged and mountainous and of volcanic origin. The highest peak, Diana's Peak, rises to 810 m. The only inland waters are small streams, few of them now perennial, fed by springs in the central hills. These streams and rainwater are sufficient for domestic water supplies and a few small irrigation schemes.

The cool South Atlantic trade winds blow throughout the year. The climate is mild and varies little, the temperatures in Jamestown, on the coast, ranging in summer between 14°C (57°F) and 32°C (90°F), and in winter between 14°C (57°F) and 26°C (79°F). It is cooler inland.

Rainfall figures (in millimetres) over four years, obtained from stations in the Eastern and Western districts of the country, the high slopes approaching Jamestown and Jamestown itself, are as follows:

	1987	*1988*	*1989*	*1990*
Hutts' Gate	614	767	950	1141.5
Plantation	761	975	851	915.6
Briars	317	563	453	366.2
Jamestown	214	295	250	242.7

The last census was on 22nd February 1987 when the total population was 5,664.

The language of the island has always been English, and the British way of life is firmly established. The majority of the population belongs to the Anglican Communion.

The total number of births during 1990 was 65 and the birth rate per 1,000 was 14.1.

The total number of deaths during 1990 was 35.

St Helena has a very mild climate. There is no industrial pollution of the atmosphere. There were no endemic diseases of note but the population is unusually susceptible to epidemic afflictions and minor ailments, both of which may be attributable to the island's isolation.

Three medical officers and a dentist are borne on the territory's establishment; there are no private medical practitioners on the island. A modern hospital of 40 beds provides for the routine and emergency needs of the population. Regular visits by the medical officers and midwife and district nurse to seven country clinics supply the out-patient needs of the population including the supervision of child welfare and ante-natal care.

Jamestown, the capital, is the only town and has a population of 1,332.

The 1987 census provided the following details concerning occupation:

	Males	*Females*	*Total*
Professional, technical and related workers	53	167	220
Managerial, administrative and clerical workers	143	180	323
Sales workers	71	132	203
Farmers, fishermen, etc.	121	16	137
Craftsmen, craftswomen, production process workers, etc.	354	17	371
Other Workers	865	397	1,262
	1,607	909	2,516

At the end of March 1991, 484 St Helenians were employed on Ascension Island, 223 on the Falklands and 108 in the United Kingdom.

There is only one Trade Union, the St Helena General Workers' Union, with a membership at December 1985 of 175.

The main crops are maize, potatoes, and vegetables.

The livestock population in 1988 was: donkeys 312: cattle 1,134; sheep 1,513; goats 1,354; pigs 599; poultry 10,931, horses 6.

Fish of many kinds are seasonally plentiful in the waters around St Helena and since the opening of a cold store in 1977 local demand has been met. Exports of frozen skipjack and tuna began in 1979 and of salt-dried skipjack in 1981. During 1990, 91,574 kg of fish were exported at a value of £69,595.

Fish and coffee were the only exports during the financial year ending 31st March 1990.

The timber resources of the island are small and most timber for construction purposes has to be imported. However, a timber-impregnation plant was provided in 1977 from Development Aid funds and much greater use is being made of locally grown timber. There are no minerals of any kind.

The main imports in 1989/90 were: motor vehicles £74,867; fuel oils and motor spirits £284,903; motor spares plus tyres and tubes £173,756; flour £46,573; meat (including hams and bacon) and meat preparations £234,844; liquor (including beer and stout) £270,388; sugar £31,621; margarine and lard £36,490; cheese £4,979; milk (canned and powders) £19,963; rice £42,664; vegetables (fresh, dried and canned) £91,201; confectionery £46,467; food preparations £75,109; paper, including stationery, £31,613; animal feed £91,928; cigarettes and tobacco £130,021; clothing and footwear £126,441; building materials including timber and cement £94,937; electrical equipment £38,907; other machinery and parts £41,409. Total imports for 1989/90 were valued at £4,970,393 of which 67.6 per cent were supplied from the United Kingdom and 31.8 per cent from South Africa.

The St Helena Growers' Co-operative Society is the only one on the island. It is both a consumer and a marketing society and provides consumer goods such as seeds, implements, and feeding stuffs to its members, and markets their produce, mainly vegetables, locally.

The only port in St Helena is Jamestown, which is an open roadstead with a good anchorage for ships of any size. Navigation lights are installed on the beacons at Ladder Hill and Mundens Point.

There is no airport or airstrip in St Helena and no railway. The total bitumen-sealed road surface is 98 km. In addition there are about 20 km of earth roads only usable in dry weather by motor vehicles. All roads have steep gradients and sharp curves.

The St Helena Shipping Company provides a passenger/cargo service from the United Kingdom and South Africa, which is subsidised by Britain at over £1m each year.

Aid in 1989/90 totalled £24.171m of which British aid programme comprises Budgetary Aid £3.904m, Shipping Subsidy £1.685m, Development Aid £2.189m and Technical Co-operation (TC) £1.985m, and Replacement Ship £14.408m which together meet the reasonable needs of the island.

An amended Income Tax Ordinance came into force in 1990. The rate for individuals is:— First £2,000–10 per cent, the next £2,000–20 per cent. Thereafter–25 per cent. Allowable deductions are:—

Personal single	£1,200
Married couple	1,800
1st Child	300
2nd Child	200
Thereafter	75 per child
Other Dependants	200
Every claimant who is a seaman	250

In respect of Life Insurance Policy upon the life of a claimant or his wife an allowance of the actual amount of the premium paid up to a maximum of £30 or the amount of £30 if the premium exceeds £30.

All sums paid by the claimant in respect of contribution to any Superannuation Schemes accepted by the Commissioners as an established Scheme.

With-holding tax is payable by non-residents on incomes accruing in or deriving from the Colony at a rate of 25 per cent.

Estate Duty is charged on the estates of deceased persons at varying rates.

Import duties are confined to a small range of goods. There are also taxes on motor vehicles and shops.

Locally raised revenue and expenditure for the two years 1988/89 and 1989/90 were as follows:

	Revenue £	*Expenditure* £
1988/89	2,379,000 (including grant in aid of £3,544,000)	5,923,000
1989/90	2,411,000 (including grant in aid of £3,904,000)	6,363,000

Currency: St Helena pounds (equivalent to £ sterling).

Education is compulsory and free for all children between the ages of five and fifteen. The standard of work at the Prince Andrew School is geared to 'GCSE' and 'A' Level requirements of the London University General Certificate of Education. A major project has been implemented to rationalise and revitalise St Helena's education system to enable it to provide for future manpower and development requirements. It involved changing from a two tier selective system with four small secondary schools, to a three tier comprehensive system with one large new upper school also available for adult education and community use. At the Islanders' request the new school is named after Prince Andrew who visited the Island for its 150th Anniversary (as a British colony) celebrations in April 1984. The project includes additional teacher training, curriculum development, expatriate teachers and initial running costs, from the TC and Budgetary Aid allocations. Part-time Further Education studies in several academic subjects up to 'GCSE' and 'A' Level requirements are provided free of charge. The literacy rate is 97 per cent.

There is a free public library in Jamestown financed by the Government and managed by a committee and a mobile library service to certain country districts.

History

The then uninhabited Island of St Helena was discovered on 21st May 1502 by the Portuguese navigator Joao da Nova Castella, on his homeward voyage from India. He named it in honour of Saint Helena, mother of the Emperor Constantine the Great, whose festival falls on that day in the Eastern Church calendar. The existence of the island appears to have remained unknown to other European nations until 1588 when it was visited by Captain Cavendish on his return from a voyage round the world. Soon afterwards St Helena became a port of call for ships of various nations voyaging between the East Indies and Europe. In 1633 the Dutch formally annexed it but made no attempt to occupy it. In 1659 it was annexed and occupied on behalf of the East India Company but the first official authorisation of the Company's occupation occurs in a charter dated 1661. In January 1673 the Dutch seized the island but were driven out again in May by the English navy. A charter to occupy and govern St Helena was issued by Charles II to the East India Company in December 1673 and it remained under that company until April 1834 when it was brought under the direct government of the Crown by an Act of Parliament of 1833. Napoleon Bonaparte was exiled in St Helena from 1815 until his death in 1821. Longwood House, in which he lived, is an important Napoleonic museum.

Constitution

The present Constitution came into force on 1st January 1989. Executive and legislative authority is reserved to Her Majesty but is ordinarily exercised by others in accordance with the provisions of the Constitution. The Constitution provides for there to be a Governor Commander-in-Chief of St Helena and its Dependencies (Ascension Island and Tristan da Cunha). There is a Legislative Council for St Helena, consisting of the Speaker, three *ex-officio* members (the Chief Secretary, the Financial Secretary and the Attorney General) and twelve elected members. The elected members choose five of their own number to be the Chairmen of the Council Committees. An Executive Council advises the Governor who, ordinarily, must follow such advice. The Executive Council consists of the *ex-officio* members of the Legislative Council and the five Chairmen of Council Committees. Although a member of both the Legislative Council and the Executive Council, the Attorney General does not vote on either. Executive and legislative functions for the Dependencies are exercised by the Governor.

Land policy

Individuals may hold leases or freeholds. Immigrants require a licence to hold land. The Crown is an important landowner and it is Government policy to release land, by lease or sale, for residential, agricultural and commercial purposes. Commonage grazing areas are made available by the Government to private stock owners.

Government

EXECUTIVE COUNCIL

The Governor (President)
Chief Secretary (*ex-officio*)
Financial Secretary (*ex-officio*)
Attorney General (*ex-officio*)
The Chairmen of Council Committees

LEGISLATIVE COUNCIL

Speaker
Chief Secretary (*ex-officio*)
Financial Secretary (*ex-officio*)
Attorney General (*ex-officio*)
12 Elected Members
Clerk of Councils (Miss P I D Lawrence)

JUDICIARY

Chief Justice: Sir John Farley Spry, Kt.

Justices of the Peace:
J R H Beadon; Mrs G P Musk; C A Lawrence, MBE; Mrs J Thomas; Mrs L M Crowie; D W Fagan; C P Yon; Miss J J Corker; P D Francis; Mrs I F George; G F Sim; A E D Clarke, MBE; Mrs J P Flagg; C R Timm.

CIVIL ESTABLISHMENT

Governor and Commander-in-Chief: A N Hoole, OBE
Chief Secretary: M S Hone, MBE
Financial Secretary: C M Rosling
Attorney General: D J Jeremiah
Deputy Secretary: Mrs E Yon
Chief Personnel Officer: Mrs S I Ellick
Chief Agricultural and Forestry Officer: V Hart
Chief Auditor: P J Sharman
Chief Education Officer: B A George
Chief of Police: G F Henry
Postmaster: R A Legg
Chief Medical Officer: N M Nichol
Chief Employment and Social Services Officer: Vacant
Chief Engineer: D Johnston
Chief Finance Officer: D W Wade
Chief Development Officer: R I Ellick

ASCENSION

The small island of Ascension lies in the South Atlantic Ocean 7° 55′S., 14° 20′W; 1,131 km north-west of St Helena, with an area of 88 sq km (34 sq miles).

It was discovered by a Portuguese expedition on Ascension Day 1501. The island was uninhabited until the arrival of Napoleon, the exiled French Emperor, on St Helena in 1815, when a small British naval garrison was placed on Ascension. Ascension remained under the supervision of the British Admiralty until it was made a dependency of St Helena in 1922.

Ascension is a barren rocky peak of purely volcanic origin, destitute of vegetation except above 450m on Green Mountain (875m). The mountain supports a small farm producing vegetables and fruit. About 170 pigs and 1,000 sheep are raised for meat. The island is famous for green turtles, which land here from December to May to lay their eggs in the sand. It is also a breeding ground of the Sooty Tern, or Wideawake, vast numbers of which settle on the island every eight months to lay and hatch their eggs. All wildlife except rabbits and cats is protected by law. Shark, Barracuda, Tuna, Bonito and other fish are plentiful in the surrounding ocean.

The population at 30th June 1991 was 1,067 (excluding British military personnel). Most of the population, excluding St Helenians, are expatriate personnel of Ascension Island Services, Cable and Wireless PLC, the BBC and the US Base. The population varies and is largely determined by the employment offered by these employers.

Ascension forms part of the Anglican diocese of St Helena. Some of the inhabitants are Roman Catholics.

In 1990 there were 907 road vehicles on Ascension. The St Helena Shipping Company serves the island with a two monthly passenger/cargo service between Cardiff in the UK and Cape Town, South Africa.

The island is an important communications centre, being a relay station for cables between South Africa and Europe operated by the South Atlantic Cable Co. The BBC operates a relay station on the island and a local broadcasting station has been established. The costs of administering Ascension Island are at present borne collectively by the User Organisations.

The budget of the financial year ending 31st March 1991 estimated revenue of £316,600 and expenditure of £384,200.

Cable and Wireless provide an international telecommunications service, via satellite and submarine cable, to all parts of the world. Ascension Island Services took over the running of the island's schools, power, water and medical services from Cable & Wireless in April 1984.

In 1942 the government of the USA, by arrangement with the British government, established a wartime air base, which it subsequently reoccupied by agreement with the British government in 1956, in connection with the extension of the long-range proving ground for guided missiles, centred in Florida. A further agreement in 1965 allowed the USA to develop tracking facilities on the island in support of the National Aeronautics and Space Administration's 'Apollo' space programme. These developments ceased in 1990.

Ascension was used as a staging post by the British military task force on its way to the Falkland Islands in April 1982, and it has continued to provide a key link in British supply lines to the South Atlantic.

Administrator: B N Connelly
Justices of the Peace: R A Lawrence, E A Scipio, S A Youde, G F Thomas and Mrs A George.

TRISTAN DA CUNHA

Tristan da Cunha is a small island in the South Atlantic Ocean, lying about midway between South America and South Africa. It is volcanic in origin and nearly circular in shape, covering an area of 38 square miles and rising in a cone to 6,760 feet. The climate is typically oceanic and temperate. Rainfall averages 66 inches per annum on the coast.

Possession was taken of the island in 1816 during Napoleon's residence in St Helena, and a garrison was stationed there. When the garrison was withdrawn, three men, headed by Corporal William Glass, elected to remain and became the founders of the present settlement. Because of its position on a main sailing route the colony thrived until the 1880s, but with the replacement of sail by steam, the island ceased to occupy a position on a main shipping route and a period of decline set in. No regular shipping called and the islands suffered at times from a shortage of food. Nevertheless, attempts to move the inhabitants to South Africa were unsuccessful. The islanders were engaged chiefly in fishing and agricultural pursuits.

The United Society for the Propagation of the Gospel maintained a missionary teacher on the island from 1922; a number of missionaries had also served on the island prior to this. In 1932 the missionary was officially recognised as Honorary Commissioner and Magistrate. Tristan da Cunha was transferred in 1955 from the Diocese of St Helena to the Archdiocese of Cape Town, and since 1981 the Chaplain (Rector) has been sent out from South Africa. There is a small Roman Catholic Community.

By Letters Patent dated 12th January 1938 Tristan da Cunha and the neighbouring uninhabited islands of Nightingale, Inaccessible and Gough were made dependencies of St Helena, though as a matter of practical convenience the administration of the group continued to be directly supervised by the Colonial Office. All islands support large and important breeding colonies of seabirds, notably albatrosses, rockhopper penguins, and species of petrel and shearwater; there are substantial rookeries of Amsterdam Island fur seal and smaller numbers of elephant seals. The islanders maintain huts on Nightingale Island and make annual visits there by longboat for guano and to crop young seabirds.

In 1942 a meteorological and wireless station was built on the island by a detachment of the South African Defence Force and was manned by the Royal Navy for the remainder of the war. The coming of the Navy re-introduced the islanders to the outside world, for it was a naval chaplain who recognised the possibilities of a crawfish industry on Tristan da Cunha. In 1948 a Cape Town based fishing company was granted a concession to fish the Tristan da Cunha waters. Many of the islanders found employment with the fishing company. In 1950 the office of Administrator was created: the Administrator is also the Magistrate. The Island Council received legislative sanction through a Bye-Laws Ordinance enacted in 1952.

On 10th October 1961 a volcanic cone erupted close to the settlement of Edinburgh and it was necessary to evacuate the island. The islanders returned to Tristan da Cunha in 1963, but a few have since re-settled in the United Kingdom. The Administration has been fully re-established and the Island Council reformed. The population at August 1991 was 297 plus a very small number of expatriates which include a doctor and a chaplain.

The present Island Council was elected in 1991 in accordance with the Island Council Ordinance 1985. The Council consists of the Administrator, three appointed members and eight elected members, of whom at least one must be a woman.

The Island is isolated and scheduled visits are restricted to about six calls a year by vessels from Cape Town, usually crawfish trawlers, and an annual call of the RMS *St Helena* from the United Kingdom. There is no airfield. A wireless station on the island is in daily contact with Cape Town. A local broadcasting service was introduced in August 1966 and a closed-circuit television system in 1983, although this was phased out during 1989 in favour of a video lending library. A radio-telephone service was established in 1969.

Electricity was introduced in 1969 to all the islanders' homes.

Although some revenue is received from the sale of stamps, the island community is still mainly dependent upon fishing for their livelihood. The company holding the fishing concession has built a new fish-freezing factory and the shore-based fishing industry is now developed following the construction of a harbour. The working population find employment in the industry and the Departments of the Administration.

Development aid has provided a harbour, a modern hospital and school, new roads, improved the sewage system, telecommunications and developments in the field of agriculture. Development aid ended in April 1980; since then the island has financed its own projects.

The United Kingdom continues to provide a modest amount of manpower aid, which comprises the services of the Administrator and a doctor. An optician visits every four years and a dentist every two. There is an annual presentation of books under the Books Presentation Programme, and the award of a scholarship for UK training when the requirement arises.

Administrator: Philip Johnson

South Georgia and the South Sandwich Islands

South Georgia lies some 1,126 km (700 miles) ESE of the Falkland Islands. Between its furthest points it is about 161 km (100 miles) long and 32 km (20 miles) wide. The total area, including offlying islands, is 3,755 sq km (1,450 square miles). The Island is barren with very steep, glacier-covered mountains. The highest point is Mount Paget (2,887 m). The north coast of the Island features several large bays providing sheltered anchorages. Principal amongst these are Stromness Bay, Cumberland West Bay, Cumberland East Bay and Royal Bay.

The South Sandwich group is situated 483 km (300 miles) to the SE of South Georgia. The islands form an arc between 56° 18′ and 59° 28′S. and between 26° 14′ and 28° 11′W. Most of the islands are volcanic and some, like Zavodovski, Visokoi, Candlemas, Saunders and Bellingshausen are active. Weather conditions in the area are generally poor making the islands difficult to approach. During the summer, the British Antarctic Survey Royal Research vessels call in at South Georgia.

The territory has no indigenous or permanent population.

No resources on the islands are being exploited, but the waters around the islands have been fished intensively. International efforts to conserve good stocks of fish and to regulate fishing are co-ordinated under the Convention for the Conservation of Antarctic Marine Living Resources to which the United Kingdom is a signatory. A major offshore biological programme is in progress to establish an understanding of the marine ecosystem in the area.

History

South Georgia was probably discovered by the London merchant Antoine De la Roche in 1675 and was finally annexed in 1775 by Captain James Cook RN, who, in the same year took possession of the South Sandwich Islands. South Georgia developed as a centre for whaling activities from 1904 onwards, and shore stations were established which continued in operation until 1965. From 1969 until 1982, when the island was briefly occupied illegally by Argentine military forces, the British Antarctic Survey team of 22 members manned the station at King Edward Point. Four members of a biological team are now stationed on Bird Island, and a military garrison is maintained at Grytviken.

Constitution

South Georgia and the South Sandwich Islands, formerly known as the Falkland Islands Dependencies and administered from the Falkland Islands until 1985, constitute a separate British dependent territory with its own laws and revenues. New and separate constitutions for the Falkland Islands and for South Georgia and the South Sandwich Islands came into force on 3rd October 1985. It provides for a Commissioner who shall be the officer for the time being administering the Government of the Falkland Islands. The present Civil Establishment is:—

Commissioner: W H Fullerton, CMG
Assistant Commissioner: R C Huxley
Financial Secretary: D Howatt
Attorney General: D G Lang, QC
Chief Police Officer: K D Greenland
Collector of Customs: L J Halliday

JUDICIARY
Magistrate: Garrison Commander
Harbour Master: Varies

Turks and Caicos Islands

Capital: Grand Turk

The Turks and Caicos Islands lie to the south-east of the Bahamas between latitudes 21° and 22°N, and longitudes 71° and 72° 30″W. The Turks Islands are said to derive their name from a species of cactus (*echinocactus myriostigma*) whose scarlet flowers resemble a Turkish fez. There are a number of theories on how the Caicos Islands got their name, one being that the name is derived from the Spanish name 'Cayos' for cays. The territory is made up of two groups of islands separated by a deep water channel about 35 sq km (22 miles) wide known as the Turks Islands passage. The Turks Islands lie to the east of the passage and the Caicos Islands to the west. The Turks Islands consist of two inhabited islands, Grand Turk and Salt Cay, six uninhabited cays and a large number of rocks. The principal islands of the Caicos group are South Caicos, East Caicos, Middle (or Grand) Caicos, North Caicos, Providenciales and West Caicos. Geographically the islands are a part of the Bahamas chain and have the same flat characteristics, there being no land above 75 m (250 feet). The total land area is estimated at 500 sq km (193 square miles).

The unit of currency is the US Dollar.

The climate is good. The south-east trade winds blow constantly throughout the year, giving an equable and healthy climate. Rainfall is variable and tends to be higher in the Caicos Islands; on Grand Turk the annual average is about 525 mm (21 inches). The temperature ranges throughout the year from 15°C (60°F) to 30°C (90°F). Severe hurricanes occurred in 1866, 1873, 1888, 1908, 1926, 1928, 1945 and 1960.

The population at the latest census (May 1990) was 12,350 (provisional) including 885 overseas visitors. The majority of the population are of African descent. The natural increase is currently estimated at 2.1 per cent. Religion is Christian, the main denominations being Baptist, Methodist and Anglican. English is the official and spoken language.

There are 14 Government Primary Schools, two private primary schools, four Government High Schools and one private High School.

In September 1990 there were 1,412 enrolments in the Primary Schools and 929 in the four Government High Schools. All education is free except at the private primary school and the private secondary school. However students are charged 50 per cent of the cost of books. Primary education is compulsory.

The main seaports are Grand Turk, Salt Cay, Providenciales, and Cockburn Harbour on South Caicos. There are regular mail and freight services from Miami.

Grand Turk, South Caicos, North Caicos and Providenciales have a number of metalled roads. Middle Caicos has a network of roads, albeit unpaved.

Grand Turk, South Caicos, Providenciales and North Caicos have international airports. There are three airstrips on other islands. From Spring 1991, Cayman Airways operates three flights a week from Miami. Turks Air and Caicos Caribbean Airlines operate non-scheduled freight services between Miami and the Islands.

Cable & Wireless (West Indies) Ltd provide all inhabited islands with equal access to national and international public telecommunications services. These include international direct dialling, facsimile, telex, packet switched international database access and leased circuits. A 24-hour operator assistance service is available. Digital telephone exchanges are installed on Grand Turk, Providenciales (2) and South Caicos and are linked together by a digital microwave radio system. An Intelsat standard 'B' earth station located on Grand Turk provides circuits to the USA, Bermuda and the United Kingdom.

The Government operate a radio broadcasting service to the Islands from Grand Turk for 105 hours a week on 1460 KHZ am band.

There is a General Hospital which was opened in 1953. It has a 16 bed male/female/paediatric/general block, a maternity ward comprising 4–5 antenatal beds, 5 post natal beds and 2 beds for labour and a geriatric block with 12 beds. There is a well equipped operating theatre, and a good laboratory with an X-ray room adjacent. The laboratory performs routine haematology, serology, bacteriology, and some chemical pathology including a blood chemistry screen. Some immunological testing (Elisa for HIV) is undertaken. Specimens for histology are sent to Nassau for examination. The X-ray Department can perform routine X-rays as well as IVP's oral cholecystograms and barium studies. The hospital renovation and rehabilitation project was recently completed. There are four Medical Officers all with GP experience including the CMO and an FRCS Surgeon. There are clinics throughout the islands staffed by nurses. These clinics are located in Salt Cay, South Caicos, Middle Caicos and North Caicos which are visited periodically by Medical Officers except Providenciales where an MO is stationed full time. Patients who are seriously ill are transferred to the Grand Turk Hospital where good medical and surgical care is offered.

There is practically no agriculture carried on in Turks Islands and South Caicos, but in the rest of the Caicos Islands corn, beans and other crops are normally grown in sufficient quantity to satisfy local needs. In the past the principal occupation of the population of the Turks Islands group and of South Caicos was the production of salt by solar evaporation. However, because of difficulties in finding markets, all operations were closed down. The principal natural resource of the Islands is its fishery, mainly spiny lobster (*panullirus argus*) and conch (*strombus gigas*). Most of the catch is exported to the United States. In 1987/88 exports of lobster totalled 266,478 lbs valued at US$1,380,233 and of conch 837,605 lbs valued at US$2,273,793. In 1990/91 exports of marine products were valued at $3,347,106. There is also some potential for development of a scale fishery and for mariculture.

Offshore finance, in all its ramifications, including captive insurance, is beginning to rival tourism and property development as the Islands main attraction and source of revenues. The offshore finance centre, which is fully supervised and regulated but offers attractive confidentiality, is on Grand Turk.

There are currently approximately 1,000 rooms available in Grand Turk, Providenciales, North, Middle and South Caicos and on Salt Cay. These include the 600 room Club Mediterranee resort opened on Providenciales in 1984. There is a Ramada Hotel on Providenciales. A number of other hotel projects are at various stages of planning. Scuba diving and water sports are the main attractions for tourists, together with the unspoilt nature of the islands. There were 48,800 tourist arrivals in 1990.

History

Although tradition ascribes discovery of the islands to Ponce de Leon in 1512, the most recent historical research claims that Grand Turk was Columbus' first landing place in the West Indies. An historical symposium on the subject was held in Miami in December 1989, and further gatherings are planned in the run up to the Quincentennial in 1992 when the Turks and Caicos Islands hope to establish their claim.

The first European occupation was by Bermudians who, beginning at least as early as 1678, came regularly for salt about March, remaining until around November when the salt raking season was over. They sometimes stayed throughout the year.

The Caicos Islands were settled by Loyalist planters from the Southern States of America after the War of Independence. After the abolition of slavery in 1838 the planters left the islands, their former slaves remaining in possession. In the meantime the islands were placed under the Bahamas Government, but in 1848 in answer to a petition from the inhabitants a separate charter was granted divorcing them from the control of the Bahamas; this provided for an elective Legislative Board and a President administering the Government. After a period of severe financial stringency, the Legislative Council in 1873 petitioned Her Majesty that the Islands might be annexed to the Colony of Jamaica and from 1874 to July 1959 they were one of its dependencies.

An Order in Council of 1873, which annexed the Islands to Jamaica, made provision for the constitution of a Legislative Board for the Turks and Caicos Islands. The Commissioner was ex-officio President of the Board, which had full legislative and budgetary powers, but ordinances required the assent of the Governor of Jamaica before becoming law. Laws passed by the Legislature of Jamaica did not apply to the Dependency unless they were made applicable in express terms.

On 20th February 1958 royal assent was given to the Cayman Islands and Turks and Caicos Islands Act, 1958, by which Her Majesty was empowered to make provision by Order in Council for the Government of the Cayman Islands and the Turks and Caicos Islands.

Constitutional development 1959–1976

The Turks and Caicos Islands (Constitution) Order in Council 1959, provided for a new constitution which was brought into operation on 4th July 1959. Under it the office of Governor of the Islands was constituted (the Governor of Jamaica was also Governor of the Islands) and the office of Commissioner replaced by the office of Administrator. The former Legislative Board was replaced by a Legislative Assembly consisting of the Administrator as President, two or three official members appointed by the Governor, two or three nominated non-official members appointed by the Governor and nine members elected on a constituency basis by universal adult suffrage; and an Executive Council was introduced consisting of the Administrator, two official members, one nominated member and two elected members (elected by the nominated and elected members of the Assembly from among the elected members of the Assembly).

On 6th August 1962, when Jamaica attained independence at the wish of the local inhabitants, the Islands became a Crown Colony and the post of Governor was abolished. A new Constitution then came into force, basically the same as that of 1959, but with the powers formerly exercised by the Governor to be exercised by the Administrator.

In 1964 talks were held between representatives of the Government of the United Kingdom, the Bahamas and the Turks and Caicos Islands concerning a closer association between the Bahamas and the Turks and Caicos Islands. As a result of these talks the Turks and Caicos Islands (Constitution) Order in Council 1965 (which came into operation on 5th November 1965) provided that the Governor of the Bahamas should also be Governor of the Turks and Caicos Islands. The office of Administrator, Turks and Caicos Islands, remained in being.

On 18th June 1969 a new Constitution came into force which provided for an Administrator and a State Council. The State Council consisted of a Speaker, three official members, not less than two, nor more than three nominated members and nine elected members. The Council sat in public under its Speaker when dealing with legislation and in private under the Administrator when dealing with executive matters.

However, in the light of the independence of the Commonwealth of the Bahamas, the powers previously held by the Governor and Commander-in-Chief of the Bahamas Islands were transferred to the Governor, a Supreme Court and a Court of Appeal of the Turks and Caicos Islands. Thus the office of Administrator was abolished and replaced by that of Governor, Turks and Caicos Islands.

The Constitution of the State Council was altered by the inclusion of Chief Secretary and Financial Secretary in place of the Treasurer and one additional official member. The Constitution (Amendment) Order 1973 came into operation on 25th April 1973.

A new Constitution was introduced on 30th August 1976 through the Turks and Caicos Islands (Constitution) Order 1976. It provided for a separate executive advisory to the Governor with provision for a Chief Minister and not more than three ministers with responsibility for the business of government exercised in accordance with policies decided by Executive Council. On 24th July 1986, however, the Ministerial Government was suspended and the future constitutional position was considered by a Constitutional Commission. Following the implementation of a number of recommendations of the Constitutional Commission, a General Election under the Multi X voting system was held on 3rd March 1988 and the islands returned to Ministerial Government.

Land policy

All land in the Islands is the subject of registered title, providing details such as proprietorship, charges, and leases.

The disposal of private land is not subject to any control but stamp duty is payable on registration of a disposition. Disposal of Crown Land is subject to a land policy the principal feature of which is that it will be sold or leased only to people who belong to the Islands, save in the most exceptional circumstances. These circumstances will usually involve a major commercial development expected to result in substantial benefits of employment and Government revenues. The disposal of Crown Land for residential or commercial development will almost always be on terms of a conditional purchase lease. This allows a set time for the development, usually three years, with reversion to the Crown if the development is not completed and the grant of freehold title if it is.

Proposals for developments should be addressed in the first place to the Chief Ministers Office, Grand Turk, Turks and Caicos Islands, who will then provide further guidance as necessary.

GOVERNMENT

At the general election held on 3rd April 1991 the Progressive National Party won eight seats in the Legislature and five were won by the People's Democratic Movement.

GOVERNOR
HE Mr M J Bradley, CMG, QC

EXECUTIVE COUNCIL
President: HE The Governor
Chief Minister, Minister of Tourism: Hon C W Misick
Minister of Natural Resources: Hon A Smith
Minister of Fisheries, Works and Immigration: Hon A Durham
Minister of Communications and Transportation: Hon M Misick
Minister of Health and Education: Hon R Hall
Chief Secretary: Mr Mark Forrester
Attorney-General: Mr G Gatland
Financial Secretary: Mr A Robinson, MBE

LEGISLATIVE COUNCIL
Speaker: Hon Mrs E Saunders
Deputy Speaker: Hon A Grant

ELECTED MEMBERS WITH DISTRICTS
Hon O O Skippings (Grand Turk (S) & Salt Cay)
Hon D H Taylor (Grand Turk (S) & Salt Cay)
Hon L Wilson (Grand Turk (S) & Salt Cay)
Hon C W Misick (Grand Turk (N))
Hon A Grant (Grand Turk (N))
Hon Mrs A Smith (Grand Turk (N))
Hon R Hall (Middle & North Caicos)
Hon G Hinson (Middle & North Caicos)
Hon M Misick (Middle & North Caicos)
Hon H Ewing (Providenciales)
Hon W Swann (Providenciales)
Hon A Durham (South Caicos)
Hon Mrs E Saunders (South Caicos)

NOMINATED MEMBERS
Hon L Astwood (PDM)
Hon Mrs R Gardiner (PNP)
Hon C Ewing (Governor)

LEADER OF THE OPPOSITION
Hon D H Taylor

CIVIL ESTABLISHMENT

The Governor: H E Mr M J Bradley, CMG, QC
Chief Secretary: Mr Mark Forrester

Deputy Chief Secretary, Providenciales: M Capes
Attorney General: G Gatland
Financial Secretary: A Robinson, MBE
Secretaries to Ministries: J Taylor, S W Garland, MBE, G Lewis, L W Jennings, R Robinson
District Commissioners: South Caicos: J Mills; Middle Caicos: Mrs D Arthur; North Caicos: Mrs E Gardiner; Salt Cay: Mrs P Simmons
Director of Education: Mrs L Williams
Chief Immigration Officer: T Saunders
Director of Civil Aviation: T A Swann
Director of Planning: O Williams
Chief Medical Officer: Dr H Malcolm
Chief Dental Officer: Dr St L Astwood
Chief Surveyor: T Smith
Chief Engineer: W Robson
Registrar of Lands: Mrs A Williams
Commissioner of Police: S E Williams
Fisheries Officer: Christopher Hall
Collector of Customs: B Mearns (Acting)
Magistrate: M Jackson
Registrar of Companies: R H Checkley
Postmistress: Miss A Garland
Chief Justice: Lindsay Irwin Worrell, GCM, QC
Chairman, Public Service Commission: Mr A F Williams, OBE

Australian External Territories

NORFOLK ISLAND

Norfolk Island was uninhabited when discovered by Captain James Cook in 1774. It is situated in the South Pacific Ocean at latitude 29° 02′S., and longitude 167° 57′E., and is in the form of an irregular ellipse. Its total area is 34.5 sq km and its 32 km coastline consists mainly of almost inaccessible cliffs rising from the water's edge. The climate is mild and subtropical. The average annual rainfall is 1,350 mm.

After serving as a penal station from 1788 to 1814 and from 1825 to 1855, Norfolk Island was abandoned. In 1856, 194 descendants of the Bounty mutineers, having become too numerous to subsist on Pitcairn Island, accepted an invitation given by Queen Victoria to settle on Norfolk Island and the island was created a distinct and separate settlement under the jurisdiction of the Governor of the colony of New South Wales. In 1897 it became a dependency of New South Wales and remained so until 1914 when, pursuant to the Norfolk Island Act 1913, it became a Territory of Australia.

In 1978 the Australian Government announced it would develop for the island a form of elected Government which would be responsible for raising the necessary revenues under its own system of law.

Under the Norfolk Island Act 1979, Norfolk Island progressed to responsible legislative and executive government, enabling it to run its own affairs to the greatest practicable extent. Wide powers are exercised by the Norfolk Island Legislative Assembly and by an Executive Council comprising the executive members of the Legislative Assembly who have ministerial type responsibilities. The Act preserves the Commonwealth's responsibility for Norfolk Island as a Territory under its authority. The Act indicates the Parliament's intention that consideration will be given to an extension of the powers of the Legislative Assembly and the political and administrative institutions of Norfolk Island within five years.

In 1985, and again in 1989 legislative and executive responsibility for a range of additional matters was formally transferred to the authority of the Norfolk Island Government.

The main economic activities are connected with the tourist industry. There are regular sea and air services to the Island.

The resident population of the Territory was 1,977 at 30th June 1986. In 1990/91 there were 28,891 tourist arrivals on the Island.

CORAL SEA ISLANDS TERRITORY

The Coral Sea Islands are situated east of Queensland between the Great Barrier Reef and longitude 156° 06′E and between latitude 12° and 24°S. The Territory comprises the islands in a sea area of approximately 780,000 sq km. The islands are largely formed of sand and coral. Some have grass or scrub cover, but most are extremely small, with no permanent fresh water. A meteorological station, staffed by four people, has operated on Willis Island since 1921. The remaining islands are uninhabited.

In the 19th century many ships were wrecked in the area, and the reefs and islands are often named after the ships which foundered there. There are beacons on the Frederick and Saumarez Reefs and a lighthouse on Bougainville Reef. Surveyors have found that the sand cays can shift many metres within a few days, and ships' captains are reluctant to rely solely on charts for this reason. There are occasional tropical cyclones in the area. Meteorological data are relayed to the mainland from automatic weather stations located on Cato Island, Flinders Reef, Frederick Reef, Holmes Reef, Lihou Reef and Marion Reef.

Six species of sea turtle nest in the Coral Sea Islands Territory, including the largest species in the world, *Dermochelys coriacea,* which is regarded as one of the most endangered of the world's sea turtles. There are at least 24 bird species in the Territory; many of these are protected under the Australia–Japan and Australia–China agreements on endangered and migratory birds. In 1982 the Lihou Reef and Coringa–Herald National Nature Reserves were declared to protect the wildlife in the Territory.

There have been a number of scientific expeditions to the region since 1859, and many specimens of flora and fauna are now housed in Australian herbariums and museums.

In 1969, the Coral Sea Islands became a Territory of the Commonwealth under the Coral Sea Islands Act. The Department of the Arts, Sport, the Environment, Tourism and Territories in Canberra, is responsible for the administration of the Territory, and liaises with other interested organisations such as the Bureau of Meteorology and the Australian National Parks and Wildlife Service. The area is visited regularly by the Royal Australian Navy.

AUSTRALIAN ANTARCTIC TERRITORY

By Order in Council of the 7th February 1933 that part of His Majesty's dominions in the Antarctic Seas which comprised all the islands and territories other than Terre Adélie (which is a French possession occupying an area between 142° and 136° longitude E.) which are situated south of the 60th parallel of S. latitude and lying between the 160th and 45th meridians of E. longitude was placed under the authority of the Commonwealth of Australia. An Act was passed in June 1933 by the Commonwealth Parliament declaring acceptance of the territory, by the name of the Australian Antarctic Territory, as a territory under the authority of the Commonwealth Government, and the Order in Council was brought into operation on the 24th August 1936 by a Proclamation issued by the Governor-General on that date. The Department of the Arts, Sport, the Environment, Tourism and Territories administers the Territory on behalf of the Commonwealth Government and the laws operating there are derived from three sources; laws of the Commonwealth expressly applying to the Territory, the laws of the Australian Capital Territory insofar as they are capable of being applied, and ordinances made specifically for the Territory.

The area of the Australian Antarctic Territory is estimated at 6,043,728 sq km of land and 75,756 sq km of ice shelf. The Territory has no permanent inhabitants.

Australia has three permanent stations in the Australian Antarctic Territory. On 13th February 1954 a scientific station, named Mawson, was set up on MacRobertson Land for the conduct of meteorological and other research. A second Antarctic station, named Davis, was established in the Vestfold Hills area, some 650 km east of Mawson on 13th January 1957. Australia assumed custody of the US 'Wilkes' Station on Budd Coast in 1959. On 19th February 1969 this station was closed and the scientific programmes were transferred to a new station named Casey about 3 km away. The Australian Government also conducts research programmes in various other areas of the Territory, including permanently established bases which are only occupied over the Antarctic summer.

Australia is a party to the Antarctic Treaty which was signed in Washington on 1st December 1959 and entered into force on 23rd June 1961, and to other international agreements under this Treaty.

HEARD ISLAND AND THE McDONALD ISLANDS

The islands, about 4,100 km south-west of Perth, comprise all the islands and rocks lying within the area bounded by the parallels 52° 30′ and 53° 30′ South latitude and the meridians 72° and 74° 30′ East longitude. Sovereignty was transferred by the United Kingdom to the Commonwealth Government on 26th December 1947 and they have been administered by the Commonwealth of Australia since then. An Australian station was established on Heard Island in the 1947/48 austral summer. The station has not been permanently occupied since March 1955 but the Australian Government has conducted research programmes on the island from time to time since then. The Heard Island and McDonald Islands Act 1953 provides for the administration of these islands as one Territory of the Commonwealth of Australia. The laws operating there are derived from three sources: laws of the Commonwealth expressly applying to the Territory, the laws of the Australian Capital Territory insofar as they are capable of being applied, and ordinances made specifically for the Territory. The islands are administered by the Department of Arts, Sport, the Environment, Tourism and Territories.

COCOS (KEELING) ISLANDS

The Cocos (Keeling) Islands, two separate atolls comprising some twenty-seven small coral islands with a total area of about 14 sq km, are situated in the Indian Ocean at latitude 12° 05′S. and longitude 96° 53′E. They lie some 2,750 km north-west of Perth and 3,700 km west of Darwin, while Johannesburg is some 7,075 km further distant to the south-west and Colombo is some 2,240 km to the north-west of the group.

The main islands are West Island, which is about 10 km from north to south and generally 1 km wide, on which are the aerodrome and most of the European community and Home Island, on which the Cocos Malay community live. None of the other islands (Direction Island, South Island, Horsburgh Island, North Keeling Island) is inhabited.

The islands of the atoll are low-lying, flat and thickly covered by coconut palms and other vegetation and surround a lagoon which has an anchorage in the northern part but which is extremely difficult for navigation.

The climate is equable and pleasant, usually being under the influence of the south-east trade winds for about three-quarters of the year. However, winds vary at times, and meteorological reports from the Territory are particularly valuable to those engaged in forecasting for the eastern Indian Ocean. The temperature varies between 19°C (68°F) and 31°C (88°F), and the average rainfall is about 2,000 mm.

The islands were discovered in 1609 by Captain William Keeling of the East India Company and were uninhabited and remained so until 1826 when the first settlement was established on the main atoll by an Englishman, Alexander Hare, who left the Islands in 1831. In the meantime a second settlement was formed on the atoll by John Clunies Ross, a Scottish seaman and adventurer, who assumed control of Hare's establishment and later brought in more labourers. In 1857 the islands were annexed to the Crown and formally declared part of the British dominions, and in 1878 responsibility for their supervision was transferred from the Colonial Office to the Government of Ceylon and then, in 1886, to the Government of the Straits Settlements. By indenture in 1886 Queen Victoria granted all land in the islands above high water mark to John Clunies Ross and his heirs and successors in perpetuity. In 1946 when the islands became a dependency of the Colony of Singapore, a Resident Administrator responsible to the Governor of Singapore was appointed.

On 23rd November 1955 the Cocos Islands were placed under the authority of the Commonwealth of Australia. The transfer was effected by an Order-in-Council made by Her Majesty Queen Elizabeth the Second under the Cocos Island Act, 1955, of the United Kingdom and by the Cocos (Keeling) Islands Act 1955 of the Commonwealth of Australia.

Responsibility for the administration of the Territory rests with the Minister for the Arts, Tourism and Territories.

The first Official Representative was appointed on 23rd November 1955 to take charge of the local administration of the Territory.

In 1975 the Australian Government up-graded the level of its presence in the Territory and appointed an Administrator to take over the duties formerly carried out by the Official Representative. Under the Administration Ordinance 1975 of the Territory, the Administrator is given such powers and functions in relation to the Territory as are delegated to him by the Minister under the Cocos (Keeling) Islands Act 1955 or are otherwise conferred on him under that Act or by or under any other law of the Territory.

Following the purchase in September 1978 by the Australian Government of the bulk of Mr John Clunies Ross's interests in the Islands, the Cocos Islands Co-operative Society Limited was established in January 1979. The Co-operative Society now owns and operates the supermarket and hostel, and undertakes contract work for the government authorities and Shell Company (Pacific Islands) Limited.

In July 1979 the Cocos (Keeling) Islands Council was established with a wide range of functions in the Home Island village area and to advise the Administrator on all matters affecting the Territory.

On 6th April 1984 the Cocos Malay community, in an Act of Self Determination which took the form of a referendum observed by the United Nations, chose to integrate with Australia. As a result, Cocos residents acquired the full rights, privileges and obligations of all Australian citizens. The powers and functions of the Cocos (Keeling) Islands Council have been expanded to give it greater responsibility. The electors of the Territory now have full voting rights in relation to the Australian Parliament.

A Memorandum of Understanding between the Commonwealth, the Cocos (Keeling) Islands Council and the Cocos Co-operative Society was signed on 7th March 1991. This document outlines the steps to be taken toward the extension of mainland equivalent living standards and levels of services to the Island community. It is expected that most of the measures contained in the document will be in place by 1st July 1992.

There is an airport on West Island. A regular air charter service (usually weekly) is operated for the Commonwealth by Australian Airlines between the Islands, Christmas Island and Perth. The Territory is also serviced by ship every 6–8 weeks. The Islands are linked by telephone, telex and facsimile communications via satellite with the mainland. The Administration provides non-commercial broadcasting stations for TV and radio.

The Territory's own postal service opened on 3rd September 1979, and includes a philatelic bureau. In 1990/91 12 houses were completed under the Home Island Development Plan.

At 30th June 1991 the Territory's population totalled 603 of whom 453 were residents of Home Island and 150 were residents of West Island.

CHRISTMAS ISLAND

Christmas Island, the summit of a submarine mountain, is situated in the Indian Ocean, at latitude 10° 25′S., and longitude 105° 40′E. It is 1,312 km from Singapore and 2,623 km from Perth; the nearest point on the Australian coast is North West Cape, Western Australia, which is 1,408 km to the south-east.

The area of the island is 135 sq km and consists of a central plateau of about 150–250 m with several prominent rises up to 360 m. The plateau descends to the sea in a series of steep slopes alternating with terraces, the last terminating in a sea cliff of 3 to 45 m, which is continuous round the island except in a few places, and the chief of which is Flying Fish Cove, where the main settlement is located and which is also the principal anchorage. Most of the island is covered with tropical rain forest. The climate is healthy and pleasant; from May to December the prevailing winds are from the south-east and from December to April (the wet season) they blow between north and west.

Christmas Island was annexed by Great Britain in 1888. In 1891 George Ross of the Cocos (Keeling) Islands and John Murray were granted a 99-year lease of the Island. In 1897 the lease was transferred to the Christmas Island Phosphate Company Limited. The Island was incorporated for administrative purposes within the Straits Settlements in 1900, and the laws of Singapore were generally applied. Christmas Island was occupied by Japanese forces from 31st March 1942 until the end of World War II.

The Straits Settlements (Repeal) Act 1947 of the United Kingdom ended the existence of the Straits Settlements. Subsequently the Singapore Colony Order-in-Council of 1946 decreed that the Island of Singapore and its dependencies, the Cocos (Keeling) Islands and Christmas Island, be governed and administered as a separate colony known as the Colony of Singapore.

From 1st January 1958 Christmas Island was administered as a separate British Crown Colony until 1st October 1958 when it became a Territory of the Commonwealth of Australia under the Christmas Island Act 1958.

From 1st October 1958 until 30th April 1968 Australia was represented in the Territory by Official Representatives appointed by the Minister of State for External Territories under the Administration Ordinance 1958.

In April 1968, the Administration Ordinance 1968 allowed the Governor-General to appoint an Administrator of the Territory to manage the Territory on behalf of the Commonwealth. Today responsibility for the administration of the Territory rests with the Minister for the Arts, Sport, the Environment, Tourism and Territories.

The Island's population at census was 1,271 in August 1991 which comprises mainly ethnic Chinese residents, with the remainder being mostly Malays and Australians. In January 1981, the Migration Act enabled residents to become Australian residents and citizens. The Christmas Island Administration (Miscellaneous Amendment) Act 1984 extended to the Territory a number of mainland benefits such as social security, health and education benefits and enfranchisements of Australian citizens on the Island. Amongst other things, the Taxation Laws Amendment Act 1985 extended full income tax liability which was progressively introduced over four years from July 1985.

On 28th September 1985, Christmas Island elected its first Assembly under the Christmas Island Assembly Ordinance 1985 and the Christmas Island Assembly (Election) Regulations. Three elections were held, with each term being for one year, until 3rd November 1987 when the Government dissolved the Assembly. The Administrator was appointed to act as the Assembly, until 10th December 1990 when a new Christmas Island Assembly was elected under the Christmas Island Assembly (Amendment) Ordinance 1990.

The Christmas Island Services Corporation (CISC) was formed on 26th October 1984 as a body responsible for functions normally associated with municipal Government. The Christmas Island Assembly has responsibility for directing CISC

The Island's economy was traditionally based almost entirely on the mining and extraction of phosphate. In December 1986 the Phosphate Mining Corporation of Christmas Island (PMCI) operations were closed by the Government. The appointment of a Liquidator on 11th November 1987 was to wind up PMCI and on 31st December 1987 formal operations ceased and all staff were laid off from that date. All employees received redundancy award entitlements and those who chose to relocate prior to 21st March 1988 additionally received a resettlement benefit. A Mining Joint Venture of Saley Investments and Clough Engineering was accepted as the preferred tenderer for the recommencement of phosphate mining operations on Christmas Island in July 1990.

In 1980 the well preserved South Western portion of Christmas Island was proclaimed the Christmas Island National Park under the National Parks and Wildlife Conservation Act 1975. On 20th December 1989 the Park was extended to include a total of 62 per cent of the land area of the Island. Significant marine habitats are also included in the Park.

The Government has actively encouraged private sector investments into new activities on the Island, to secure an economic future which is not dependent on mining. As the Government has long recognised the need to diversify the Island's employment, tourism was found to be an obvious alternative to mining considering the Island's unique flora and fauna. In April 1986 initial plans were announced for a hotel and casino complex. A lease was signed in May 1989 and construction is now well underway. The grand opening of the resort is expected to be held in October 1992.

In September 1990 the first auction of commercial premises was held on Christmas Island. Another property auction is planned for November 1991.

THE TERRITORY OF ASHMORE AND CARTIER ISLANDS

Ashmore Islands (known as Middle, East and West Islands) and Cartier Island are situated in the Indian Ocean some 850 km and 790 km west of Darwin respectively. The Islands lie at the outer edge of the continental shelf. They are small and low and are composed of coral and sand. Vegetation consists mainly of grass and scrub. The Islands have no permanent inhabitants.

Great Britain took formal possession of the Ashmores in 1878 and Cartier Island was annexed in 1909. By Imperial Order in Council of 23rd July 1931, the Islands were placed under the authority of the Commonwealth of Australia. The Islands were accepted by Australia through the Ashmore and Cartier Islands Acceptance Act 1933, under the name of the Territory of Ashmore and Cartier Islands. By amendments to the Act in 1938 the Territory was annexed to, and deemed to form part of, the Northern Territory. With the granting of self-government to the Northern Territory on 1st July 1978, the administration of the Territory became a direct responsibility of the Commonwealth Government.

Responsibility for the administration of the Territory rests with the Minister for the Arts, Sport, the Environment, Tourism and Territories.

On 1st October 1989 the Ashmore and Cartier Islands Acceptance Amendment Act 1985 came into effect. The Act applies the laws of the Northern Territory, as in force from time to time, to the Territory as far as they are applicable.

The Islands of Ashmore Reef abound with birdlife. Turtles are plentiful at certain times of the year and beche-de-mer is abundant. In recognition of the environmental significance of the area the Reef was in 1983 given the status of a national nature reserve under the Australian National Parks and Wildlife Conservation Act 1975. Regular visits are made to the Reef by officers of the Australian National Parks and Wildlife Service.

An Agreement between Australia and Indonesia allows Indonesian traditional fishermen to continue to fish in designated Australian waters including some waters of the Territory. In 1985, the Australian Government decided to place caretakers in the Territory during the Indonesian fishing season, from March to November each year, to monitor the activities of Indonesian fishermen and undertake tasks on behalf of Australian Government organisations.

Aerial surveillance of the Territory is undertaken by the Royal Australian Air Force and by chartered civil aircraft. Periodic visits are made to the Islands by ships of the Royal Australian Navy.

The Jabiru and Challis oil fields are located within the adjacent area of the Territory.

SELF GOVERNING COUNTRIES IN FREE ASSOCIATION WITH NEW ZEALAND

COOK ISLANDS

The fifteen islands of the Cook Group (Rarotonga, Mangaia, Atiu, Mauke, Mitiaro, Aitutaki, Palmerston Atoll (Avarau), Penrhyn (Tongareva), Suwarrow (Suvorov), Manihiki (Humphrey Island), Rakahanga (Rierson Island), Pukapuka (Danger Islands), Nassau, Manuae and its twin islet Te Au o tu (Hervey Islands and Takutea) have a total area of approximately 240.87 sq km (24,087 hectares) and lie between 8° and 23°S latitude and 156° and 167°W longitude. The estimated population in 1987 was 18,500.

Various islands of the Group were placed under British protection between 1888 and 1901.

Until 1901 British authority was represented by a Resident, who was paid by the Government of New Zealand and reported direct to the Governor. The first British Resident succeeded in 1891 in arranging for the establishment of an Elective Federal Parliament to make laws for the whole Group. Each island, however, continued to enjoy self-government in such purely local affairs as it could properly manage for itself. The Federal Executive Council or Government was composed of the Arikis, who were also the principal landowners. A Supreme Court was established. All laws and administrative acts were subject to the approval of the Resident, who was also a Deputy and Judicial Commissioner for the Western Pacific and Chief Justice of the High Court of the Cook Islands.

In 1900 a petition from leading islanders requested the abolition of the Federal Parliament and the annexation of the islands by New Zealand. An Imperial Order in Council was accordingly made on 13th May 1901, and on 11th June 1901 the Cook Islands were declared to lie within the boundaries of New Zealand. The administration and laws continued in force subject to the provisions of the Cook Islands Government Act passed in that year.

In 1915 an Act was passed by the New Zealand Parliament consolidating the laws relating to the Cook Islands and Niue Island and providing for the appointment of a member of the Executive Council of New Zealand as the Minister for the Cook Islands charged with the administration of the government of the Islands. By the Cook Islands Amendment Act, 1932, the administration of Niue Island was transferred to the Minister of External Affairs.

The 1915 Act also made provision for the constitution of Island Councils for the establishment of public schools, Courts of Justice, Native Land Courts, etc. The Island Territories Act, 1943, established a Ministry of Island Territories and charged the Minister with the administration of the government of any territory outside of New Zealand which may at any time be a dependency or mandated territory of New Zealand, or otherwise be under the jurisdiction of the Government or Parliament of New Zealand.

The enactment of the Cook Islands Amendment Act, 1957, marked a major step forward in the constitutional development of the Cook Islands. The most important provision of the Act was the replacement of the Legislative Council by a reconstituted Legislative Assembly of the Cook Islands consisting of fourteen members elected by universal suffrage by the electors of the various islands—seven members elected by the various island councils, one European member and four officials nominated by the Administration. In 1962 the New Zealand Government placed before the Legislative Assembly four possible schemes for political development—complete independence, full self-government, integration with New Zealand or ultimate integration into a Polynesian Federation—and asked them to decide which course they would most favour. The Assembly chose full self-government with continuing association with New Zealand.

In 1963 three constitutional advisers were appointed to hold discussions with the Assembly on the form of the Cook Islands Constitution, and in November 1964 a draft Constitution, having already been accepted by the Legislative Assembly, was enacted by the New Zealand House of Representatives. In order to put this constitution before the people of the Cook Islands, general elections were held on 20th April 1965 to elect a new Legislative Assembly equipped with a special mandate to accept or decline the constitution. They were conducted in the presence of a United Nations Mission which observed the elections at the invitation of the New Zealand Government.

The elections were won by Mr Albert Henry's Cook Islands Party which gained fourteen of the twenty-two seats in the new Legislative Council. The Cook Islands Party had already accepted the principle of full internal self-government and continuing association with New Zealand. Mr Henry informed the New Zealand Government, however, that his party wished to propose a number of amendments to the draft constitution. The most important of these were:

(*a*) An amendment to the existing electoral regulations on residential qualifications. This enabled Mr Henry (who had not been eligible to stand at the elections) to be elected to the Assembly in a by-election; and (*b*) An amendment to form a House of Arikis or Upper House on which the Arikis from all the islands would be represented.

The Cook Islands now have complete control of their own affairs in free association with New Zealand, but with the added special feature that they can at any time move into full independence by a unilateral act if they so wish. New Zealand will continue to be responsible for external affairs and defence in consultation with the Cook Islands Premier while the Cook Islands retain this special relationship.

Mr Geoffrey Henry became Premier following the General Election of January 1989.

An international airport at Rarotonga was opened in 1973 and has helped stimulate the tourist industry in the islands. The economy is based on agriculture, which is the main export revenue earner. Citrus fruit is processed on the islands and exported to New Zealand. Other crops include bananas, coconuts and pineapples.

Premier: Hon Geoffrey Henry
New Zealand Representative: Mr T Caughley

NIUE

Niue is situated at 169°W. 19°S. and has an area of 262.65 sq km (26,265 hectares). The estimated total population in February 1989 was 2,145. In contrast, more than 12,000 Niueans live in New Zealand.

The island was discovered by Captain Cook in 1774. British sovereignty was proclaimed over the island in 1900 and in 1901 Niue was annexed to New Zealand. Members of the Assembly are elected by universal suffrage and represent the fourteen villages on the island, while there are six common roll seats. There is a New Zealand representative appointed in accordance with the Constitution who acts as the channel of communication between the Government of Niue and the Government of New Zealand. The executive authority of Niue, vested in Her Majesty in right of New Zealand, is exercised by the Cabinet consisting of the Premier and three other members of the Niue Assembly. The Hon Sir Robert R Rex is Premier.

Niue attained self-government in 1974 in free association with New Zealand, which continues to have responsibility for foreign affairs and defence. The inhabitants of Niue retain their New Zealand citizenship, and New Zealand maintains financial and other aid to the islands. New Zealand aid in 1988 totalled NZ$9.25 million while Niue's exports to New Zealand (its main trading partner) were worth NZ$59,558.

Niue is linked with New Zealand and neighbouring Pacific islands by a weekly air service and a monthly shipping service.

Premier: Hon Sir Robert Rex
New Zealand Representative: Mr Kurt Meyer

PART VI

SOURCES AND NOTES FOR THE FOLLOWING TABLES

General Notes

Percentages or index numbers for three- or four-year periods are averages of the annual percentages or index numbers.

0 or 0.0 means zero or less than half the value of the final digit shown in the other figures in the column.

a. 1989, or period ending 1989 (where column heading is 1990, 1987–1990, 1981–90).

b. 1988, or period ending 1988.

c. Year from, or period ending, 1980 to 1987.

d. Year, or period ending, before 1980.

e. Year, not stated in source, earlier than specified in column heading.

Abbreviations

CMEA	Council for Mutual Economic Assistance
DAC	Development Assistance Committee of the OECD
FAO	Food and Agriculture Organisation of the United Nations
GDP	Gross Domestic Product
GNP	Gross National Product
ILO	International Labour Organisation
IMF	International Monetary Fund
OECD	Organisation for Economic Co-operation and Development
OPEC	Organisation of Petroleum Exporting Countries
SDRs	Special Drawing Rights
UN	United Nations
UNCTAD	United Nations Conference on Trade and Development
UNESCO	United Nations Educational, Scientific and Cultural Organisation
WHO	World Health Organisation

Table 1: Area and Population

Area: Total
Source: The Times Atlas of the World

Area: Arable land and land under permanent crops; Permanent pasture
Source: FAO *Production Yearbook 1990*
Note: Many of the figures are described as FAO estimates.
Arable land includes temporary meadows for mowing or pasture; in principle excludes fallow land resulting from shifting cultivation.
Land under permanent crops excludes land under trees grown for wood or timber.
Permanent meadows and pastures are land used for five years or more for herbaceous food crops, either cultivated or growing wild.

Population: Total
Source: World Bank Atlas 1991

Population: Rate of growth
Source: World Bank Atlas 1991

Crude birth rate; Crude death rate; Age distribution
Source: UN *Demographic Yearbook 1989*

Table 2: Basic Economic Statistics

Gross National Product
Source: World Bank Atlas 1991

Percentage of economically active population employed in agriculture
Source: FAO *Production Yearbook 1990*

Females as percentage of labour force
Source: ILO. *Yearbook of Labour Statistics 1989*

Composition of Gross Domestic Product
Source: World Bank: *World Development Report 1991* except as otherwise indicated.
Note: h. From UNCTAD. *Handbook of International Trade and Development Statistics 1989 Supplement.* It should be noted that there are some discrepancies between figures from the two sources.

Food production per capita
Source: FAO *Production Yearbook 1990*

Energy consumption per capita
Source: UN *Energy Statistics Yearbook 1989*

Investment as percentage of GDP
Source: IMF: *International Financial Statistics*

Exports and imports of goods and non-factor services as percentage of GDP
Source: IMF: *International Financial Statistics*

Average rate of inflation
Source: IMF: *International Financial Statistics*
Notes: Based on retail price index.

Table 3: Composition and Terms of Trade
Contribution to export earnings of agricultural goods, fuel and minerals; food and fuels as percentage of imports
Source: UNCTAD *Handbook of International Trade and Development Statistics 1989*
Notes: Food and agricultural raw materials: SITC 0+1+4+22+2 less (22+27+28).
Fuels: SITC 3.
Ores and metals: SITC 27+28+67+68.

Terms of trade
Source: IMF: *International Financial Statistics*
Note: Unit value index for exports as percentage of unit value index for imports.

Table 4: Current Account Balance, External Debt, Reserves and Aid Receipts
Current account balance as percentage of GDP
Source: IMF: *International Financial Statistics; World Bank Atlas 1991*
Note: Current account balances exclude exceptional financing.

External debt and debt services
Source: World Bank: *World Development Report 1991; World Debt Tables 1990–91 edition*
Note: Medium- and long-term debt is debt with an original or extended maturity of over one year.

IMF quota
Source: IMF: *International Financial Statistics*

Use of IMF credit
Source: IMF: *International Financial Statistics*
Note: Drawing from General Resources Account.

External reserves, coverage in terms of months of imports
Source: IMF: *International Financial Statistics*
Notes: External reserves are holdings by national monetary authorities of foreign exchange, SDRs, and gold, plus positions in the IMF. The gold component of reserves has been valued throughout at $US350 per ounce—somewhat below the average market price of gold in recent years.
Reserve figures for most countries are for dates from March to June 1989.
Import figures are for the latest four complete quarters shown in terms of US dollars in the source. For some countries, imports are for the year running to the second quarter of 1989, but for several they are for the year 1985. Consequently the import figures cannot necessarily be taken as representative of present levels.

Receipts of official development assistance
Sources: OECD: *Geographical Distribution of Financial Flows to Developing Countries 1986/89*
Notes: Official development assistance (ODA) is defined as financial flows to developing countries and multilateral institutions provided by official agencies, administered with promotion of development and welfare as the objective, and with 'grant element' for each transaction of at least 25 per cent as compared with a loan bearing interest at 10 per cent per annum. Flows are disbursements, net of payments of past ODA loans.
Members of the Development Assistance Committee of the OECD (DAC), besides the United Kingdom, Canada, Australia and New Zealand, are Austria, Belgium, Denmark, Finland, France, the Federal Republic of Germany, Ireland, Italy, Japan, the Netherlands, Norway, Sweden, Switzerland and the United States.
Figures do not include ODA provided by non-DAC Commonwealth countries or by CMEA countries.
Per capita figures for countries of small population are only approximate because of rounding in the data used.

l. Net disbursements of ODA to bilateral recipients and multilateral institutions (1983–85).
m. Net disbursements to independent Commonwealth countries—i.e. excluding disbursements to dependent territories (1983–85).
n. Contributions to multilateral institutions (1983–85).
o. Total net disbursements, as in l, per head of population of donor country (1983–85).

Table 5: Social and Education Statistics
Infant mortality; Life expectancy at birth
Source: UN *Demographic Yearbook 1989*

Nutrition
Source: FAO *Production Yearbook 1990*

Access to safe drinking water
Source: WHO: *World Health Statistics Annual 1989*

Health care
Source: UNCTAD *Handbook of International Trade and Development Statistics 1989 Supplement*

Primary school enrolment
Source: UNESCO *Statistical Yearbook 1989*
Note: Gross enrolment of all ages at primary level as a percentage of children of school-age as defined in each country and reported to Unesco. While many countries consider primary school age to be 6–11 years, others use different age groups. Consequently, gross enrolment may exceed 100 per cent if some pupils are younger or older than the country's definition of primary school age.

Daily newspaper circulation
Source: UNESCO *Statistical Yearbook 1989*

Table 1 **Area and Population of Commonwealth Countries**

	Area			Population				Age distribution, 1989 (percentage of population)	
	Total ('000 square kilometres)	Arable land and land under permanent crops, 1989 ('000 hectares)	Permanent pasture, 1989 ('000 hectares)	Total, 1990 ('000)	Annual growth, 1980–90 (per cent)	Crude birth rate, 1989 or 1985–90 (per '000)	Crude death rate, 1989 or 1980–90 (per '000)	Under 15 years of age	70 years of age or older
AFRICA									
Botswana	575	1380	33000	1304	3.4	47.3	11.7	40.3	1.2
The Gambia	10.7	178	90	861	3.3	46.8	21.3	43.8	2.7
Ghana	238.3	2720	5000	15028	3.4	44.3	13.1	n.a.	n.a.
Kenya	582.6	2428	3810	24031	3.9	53.9	11	30.7	1.2
Lesotho	30.3	320	2000	1744	2.7	40.8	12.4	40	4
Malawi	94.1	2409	1840	8754	3.4	48.3	25	46.2	1.4
Mauritius	1.9	106	7	1082	1.0	18.5	5.4	30.2	2.9
Namibia	824.3	662	52906	1781	3.2	44	12.2	n.a.	n.a.
Nigeria	923.9	31355	40000	108542	3.4	49.8	15.6	n.a.	n.a.
Seychelles	.4	6	n.a.	69	.7	23.9	8.4	35.1	2.9
Sierra Leone	72.3	1801	2204	4151	2.4	48.2	23.4	n.a.	n.a.
Swaziland	17.4	164	1180	788	3.4	46.8	12.5	46.8	2.2
Tanzania	939.8	5250	35000	27318	3.1	50.5	14	47.8	2.1
Uganda	236.6	6705	5000	18794	3.2	50.1	15.4	n.a.	n.a.

Zambia	752.6	5268	30000	8452	3.7	51.2	13.7	48.9	1.7
Zimbabwe	390.3	2810	4856	9709	3.4	41.7	10.2	44.9	1.6
ASIA, PACIFIC, AUSTRALASIA									
Australia	7682.3	48934	417992	17052	1.5	14.9	7.2	22.3	7.1
Bangladesh	144	9292	600	115593	2.6	42.2	15.5	42.3	1.7
Brunei Darussalam	5.8	7	6	266	3.3	28.5	3.2	36.2	1.6
India	3166.8	168990	12038	853094	2.1	31.3	10.9	36.3	2.3
Kiribati	.7	37	n.a.	66	1.9	21.9	6.5	41	2
Malaysia	333	4880	27	17891	2.6	28.6	5.6	37.8	2.2
Maldives	.3	3	1	215	3.5	41.2	7.6	45.1	1.5
Nauru	.02	n.a.	n.a.	n.a.	n.a.	19.8	4.5	n.a.	n.a.
New Zealand	265.2	507	13667	3392	.8	17.5	8.2	23.4	7.1
Pakistan	803	20730	5000	122626	3.3	30.3	8.1	44.5	3
Papua New Guinea	462.8	388	84	3874	2.5	38.7	12.1	40.5	1
Singapore	.6	1	n.a.	2723	1.2	17.8	5.2	23.1	3.5
Solomon Islands	29.8	57	39	320	3.5	42.0	10	47.3	1.9
Sri Lanka	65.6	1901	439	17217	1.5	20.7	5.8	34.7	2.6
Tonga	.7	48	4	95	.6	28.9	3.5	40.8	2.5
Tuvalu	.2	n.a.	n.a.	n.a.	n.a.	n.a.	n.a.	n.a.	n.a.
Vanuatu	14.8	144	25	158	2.9	45	20	45.5	1.4
Western Samoa	2.8	n.a.	n.a.	168	.6	n.a.	n.a.	n.a.	n.a.

Table 1 **Area and Population of Commonwealth Countries** (contd.)

	Area			Population				Age distribution, 1989 (percentage of population)	
	Total ('000 square kilometres)	Arable land and land under permanent crops, 1989 ('000 hectares)	Permanent pasture, 1989 ('000 hectares)	Total, 1990 ('000)	Annual growth, 1980–90 (per cent)	Crude birth rate, 1989 or 1985–90 (per '000)	Crude death rate, 1989 or 1980–90 (per '000)	Under 15 years of age	70 years of age or older
EUROPE AND MEDITERRANEAN									
Cyprus	9.3	156	5	701	1.1	18.6	8.2	25.7	7.1
Malta	.3	13	n.a.	353	−.5	16.5	7.8	23.8	6.3
United Kingdom	244.8	6736	11197	57438	.2	13.6	11.5	18.9	10.5
WESTERN HEMISPHERE									
Antigua & Barbuda	.4	8	4	76	.6	13.1	4.4	n.a.	n.a.
Bahamas	13.9	10	2	253	1.9	20.2	5.4	34.3	2.8
Barbados	.4	33	4	257	.3	15.7	8.9	25.1	8.2
Belize	23	56	48	187	2.8	37.3	4.1	44.5	4
Canada	9922.4	45960	33000	26521	.9	14.5	7.3	20.9	7.4
Dominica	.8	17	2	82	1.2	21.8	5.5	39.8	4.7
Grenada	.3	13	1	85	.7	24.5	6.8	38.6	4.9
Guyana	215	495	1230	796	.5	28.3	7.3	40.8	2.2
Jamaica	11.4	269	190	2456	1.2	21.9	5	38.4	4.6
St. Christopher-Nevis	.3	14	1	51	−1.2	23	10.5	33.8	6.3

St. Lucia	.6	18	3	150	2.0	21.3	5.5	44.4	3.7
St. Vincent & the Grenadines	.4	11	2	116	1.0	24.5	5.9	43.7	3.6
Trinidad & Tobago	5.1	120	11	1281	1.7	22.5	6.6	33.6	3.5

Table 2 **Basic Economic Statistics for Commmonwealth Countries**

	Gross national product				Percentage of economically active population employed in agriculture, 1990	Females as percentage of labour force, 1988	Composition of gross domestic product, 1987 (percentage)				Food production per capita, change 1979–80 to 1988–90 (percent)	Energy consumption per capita, 1989 (kilograms oil equivalent)	Investment as percentage of GDP, 1988–90 average	Exports of goods and non-factor services as percentage of GNP, 1988–90 average	Imports of goods and non-factor services as percentage of GNP, 1988–90 average	Average annual rate of inflation, 1984 to 1990 (percent)
	Total, 1990 (US$ million)	Per capita, 1990 (US$)	Annual growth, real, 1980–90 (percent) GNP	GNP per capita			Agriculture	Industry, mining, construction	(of which, manufacturing)	Services						
AFRICA																
Botswana	2561	2040	9.9	6.3	62.8	40.3[c]	3	57	4	40	−20.7	n.a	24c	77	84.2	9.7
The Gambia	229	260	3	−.3	81	46.3[c]	23[hc]	8[hc]	4[hc]	69[hc]	−14.1	74	14.7[d]	21[c]	82.1	23.4[a]
Ghana	5824	390	2.8	−.6	50	51.2[c]	49	17	10	34	7.8	76	12.4[b]	18[b]	16.1[b]	29.8
Kenya	8958	370	4.2	.3	77	n.a.	31	20	12	49	−.2	74	25.1[a]	11.9	24.1	8.9
Lesotho	832	470	1.8	−.9	79.6	32.3[d]	24	30	14	46	−26.8	n.a.	53.5	19[a]	129[a]	13.1
Malawi	1662	200	3.3	−.1	75.4	46.2[d]	35	19	11	45	−18.8	28	19.3	22	33.9	18.3
Mauritius	2422	2250	6.4	5.4	22.7	34.2[a]	13	32	24	56	−2.7	307	30.6	49.1	65.1	7.4
Namibia	1150[c]	1020[c]	2.9[c]	.2[c]	35.1	21.9[d]	11	38	5	50	−6.6	n.a.	n.a.	n.a.	n.a.	n.a.
Nigeria	31285	270	.2	−3	64.8	24.1[d]	31	44	10	25	15.7	135	8.9[a]	31.3	16.1	22.4
Seychelles	318	4670	3.2	2.5	n.a.	36.9[d]	6[hc]	16[hc]	9[hc]	78[hc]	n.a.	652	19.9[a]	12.5	60.3	2.2
Sierra Leone	981	240	.9	−1.5	62.3	35.6[d]	46	11	6	42	−14.6	53	7.8[b]	13.9	17.8	87.3
Swaziland	645	820	4.5	1.1	66.3	55.4[d]	21[hc]	25[hc]	17[hc]	53[hc]	−4.4	n.a.	29.4[c]	74.4[a]	91.1[a]	13.3[a]
Tanzania	2779	120	2.3	−.7	80.8	47.4[d]	66	7	4	27	−12	26[b]	21.2[b]	7.3[b]	21.2[b]	32.6[b]
Uganda	3814	220	4.1	.8	80.9	n.a.	67	7	5	26	−13.7	19	4.8[d]	6.9[a]	12	123.9
Zambia	3391	420	.7	−2.9	68.9	35.7[c]	13	47	24	40	−7.4	138	15.8[b]	44.8	34.8	50.7[a]
Zimbabwe	6313	640	2.6	−.8	68.2	39.2[c]	13	39	25	49	−3.3	487	20.2[c]	28.4[b]	28[c]	13.3
ASIA, PACIFIC, AUSTRALASIA																
Australia	290522	17080	3.2	1.7	5	39.9[a]	4	32	15	64	−10	5069	25.5	14.8	16.5	7.2
Bangladesh	22579	200	3.7	1	68.5	5.0[c]	44	14	7	41	−5.2	48	n.a.	7	17	9.9
Brunei Darussalam	3317[c]	14120[b]	−.7	−4	n.a.	30.7[c]	2[hc]	56[hc]	8[hc]	41[hc]	n.a.	9647	n.a.	n.a.	n.a.	n.a.
India	294816	350	5.4	3.2	66.5	26.9[c]	30	29	18	41	18.7	215	23.5[a]	5.5	7.4	8.0

Kiribati	54	760	3.6	1.7	n.a.	43.3[d]	n.a.	n.a.	n.a.	n.a.	n.a.	106	n.a.	39[c]	103[c]	n.a.
Malaysia	41524	2340	5.1	2.5	32.1	31.6[c]	20[hc]	40[hc]	22[hc]	41[hc]	62.8	966	26.3[a]	67.6	60.6	1.8[a]
Maldives	96	440	10	6.6	n.a.	21.7[c]	31[hc]	16[hc]	7[hc]	53[hc]	n.a.	139	n.a.	53.7	126.5	n.a.
Nauru	n.a.	n.a.	n.a.	n.a.	n.a.	8.8[d]	n.a.	n.a.	n.a.	n.a.	n.a.	4100	n.a.	n.a.	n.a.	n.a.
New Zealand	43185	12680	1.4	.6	9.2	41.7[b]	8	28	17	64	5.6	3543	22[a]	23.7	22.2	9.8
Pakistan	42649	380	6.3	2.9	49.7	3.7[c]	27	24	16	49	5.7	187	18.5	12.3	17.6	6.5
Papua New Guinea	3372	860	1.9	−.5	67.1	38.7[d]	28	30	10	42	4.4	206	23.3[a]	40.1	42.8	5.2
Singapore	33512	12310	7	5.7	1	37.8[a]	0	37	26	63	−13.5	3485	37.1[a]	160.7	181.2	1.4
Solomon Islands	187	580	7	3.4	n.a.	n.a.	44[hc]	9[hc]	4[hc]	45[hc]	−10.1	170	25.6[b]	42.9	61	12.2
Sri Lanka	7971	470	3.9	2.4	51.7	25.5[c]	26	27	16	47	−6.3	77	22.4	22.4	32	11.6
Tonga	100	1010	2.1	1.5	n.a.	21.5[b]	41[hc]	10[hc]	5[hc]	49[hc]	8.1	263	n.a.	10.4	64.7	10.5
Tuvalu	n.a.	n.a.	n.a.	n.a.	n.a.	n.a.	n.a.	n.a.	n.a.	n.a.	n.a.	n.a.	n.a.	n.a.	n.a.	n.a.
Vanuatu	167	1060	2.4	−.5	n.a.	43.4[d]	42[hc]	15[hc]	5[hc]	43[hc]	−20.9	136	29.3[c]	16.3[b]	50.5[a]	7.6
Western Samoa	121	730	2	1.2	n.a.	15.6[d]	38[hc]	26[hc]	16[hc]	36[hc]	n.a.	250	n.a.	10.8	66.1	8.8
EUROPE AND MEDITERRANEAN																
Cyprus	5633	8040	6	4.9	20.6	35.8[a]	7[hc]	28[hc]	15[hc]	64[hc]	2	1767	27.7	16.1	44.1	3.8
Malta	2342	6630	3.1	3.6	3.8	23.6[a]	4[hc]	36[hc]	25[hc]	60[hc]	9.2	1436	28[a]	42.6	76.3	.2
United Kingdom	923959	16070	2.7	2.5	2	38.8[c]	2	37	20	62	9.4	3520	19.3	19.3	24.4	5.8
WESTERN HEMISPHERE																
Antigua & Barbuda	363	4600	5.2	4.7	n.a.	n.a.	4[hc]	18[hc]	3[hc]	78[hc]	n.a.	1221	34.5[c]	7.3[b]	74.5[b]	2.5[c]
Bahamas	2913	11510	3.6	1.7	6.2	44.5[c]	4[hd]	16[hd]	0	80[hd]	n.a.	1784	28[c]	80[c]	74[c]	4.9
Barbados	1680	6540	1.7	1.4	6.6	47.2[a]	6[hc]	16[hc]	8[hc]	78[hc]	−22.3	1125	16.6[b]	11.8	40.4	3.9
Belize	373	1970	5.3	2.5	n.a.	22.7[c]	18[hc]	18[hc]	10[hc]	64[hc]	n.a.	326	20.9[c]	39	63.9	2.6[a]
Canada	542774	20540	3.3	2.4	3.3	43.4[a]	4[b]	40[b]	23[b]	56[b]	6.6	7639	22.5	25	24.3	4.4
Dominica	160	1940	4.3	3	n.a.	34.1[c]	27[hc]	13[hc]	6[hc]	61[hc]	n.a.	256	36.6[c]	36.3[a]	72.2	3.5[a]
Grenada	199	2120	5.8	5.1	n.a.	39.1[d]	15[hc]	14[hc]	4[hc]	71[hc]	n.a.	302	30.4[c]	48[c]	57.1[b]	2.9[a]
Guyana	293	370	−2.7	−3.2	22.2	29.9[a]	26[hc]	28[hc]	13[hc]	46[hc]	−13.7	n.a.	50.1	75.1	93[b]	23.3[b]
Jamaica	3606	1510	.7	−.4	27	38.8[c]	5	45	18	50	−15.6	597	27[a]	30.7[a]	55[a]	17.1

Table 2 **Basic Economic Statistics for Commmonwealth Countries** (contd.)

	Gross national product				Percentage of economically active population employed in agriculture, 1990	Females as percentage of labour force, 1988	Composition of gross domestic product, 1989 (percentage)				Food production per capita, change 1979–80 to 1988–90 (percent)	Energy consumption per capita, 1989 (kilograms oil equivalent)	Investment as percentage of GDP, 1988–90 average	Exports of goods and non-factor services as percentage of GNP, 1988–90 average	Imports of goods and non-factor services as percentage of GNP, 1988–90 average	Average annual rate of inflation, 1984 to 1990 (percent)
	Total, 1990 (US$ million)	Per capita, 1990 (US$)	Annual growth, real, 1980–90 (percent) GNP	GNP per capita			Agriculture	Industry, mining, construction	(of which, manufacturing)	Services						
St. Christopher-Nevis	133	3330	4.8	6	n.a.	41.0[c]	11[hc]	23[hc]	14[hc]	67[hc]	n.a.	500	70.1[c]	70[c]	96[c]	2.3[a]
St. Lucia	286	1900	6.3	4.2	n.a.	55.2[c]	12[hc]	18[hc]	7[hc]	71[hc]	n.a.	372	30.9[c]	79[c]	96[c]	3.1
St. Vincent & the Grenadines	184	1610	6.9	5.7	n.a.	35.9[d]	16[hc]	20[hc]	8[hc]	63[hc]	n.a.	252	27.6[c]	70[c]	81[c]	2.2[c]
Trinidad & Tobago	4458	3470	−4.3	−6	7.5	33.8[a]	3	41	8	56	−34	3952	22.9[a]	35.7	26.5	9.9

Table 3 **Composition and Terms of Trade of Commonwealth Countries**

	Contribution to export earnings of agricultural goods, fuels and minerals, 1987–89 average (per cent of total by value)			Food and fuels as percentage of imports, 1987–89 average		Terms of trade (period averages, 1985 = 100)			
	Food and materials	Fuels	Ores and Metals	Food and beverages	Fuels	1969–72	1974–77	1986–89	1990
AFRICA									
Botswana	n.a.	n.a.	n.a.	n.a.	n.a.	n.a.	n.a.	n.a.	n.a.
The Gambia	85[c]	n.a.	0	n.a.	n.a.	n.a.	n.a.	n.a.	n.a.
Ghana	80c	3[c]	11[c]	10[c]	31[c]	n.a.	n.a.	n.a.	n.a.
Kenya	63[c]	23[c]	2[c]	8[c]	36[c]	138	116	97	86[a]
Lesotho	n.a.	n.a.	n.a.	n.a.	n.a.	n.a.	n.a.	n.a.	n.a.
Malawi	94[c]	0	0	8[c]	16[c]	172	150	84[b]	81[b]
Mauritius	64[c]	0	0	27[c]	17[c]	105	150	137	146
Namibia	n.a.	n.a.	n.a.	n.a.	n.a.	n.a.	n.a.	n.a.	n.a.
Nigeria	4[c]	95[c]	0	17[c]	1[c]	n.a.	n.a.	n.a.	n.a.
Seychelles	12[c]	81[c]	0	20[c]	24[c]	n.a.	n.a.	n.a.	n.a.
Sierra Leone	32[c]	1[c]	36[c]	24[c]	27[c]	n.a.	n.a.	n.a.	n.a.
Swaziland	n.a.	n.a.	n.a.	n.a.	n.a.	n.a.	n.a.	n.a.	n.a.
Tanzania	80[c]	3[c]	6[c]	10[c]	26[c]	n.a.	n.a.	n.a.	n.a.
Uganda	99[c]	0	0	n.a.	n.a.	n.a.	n.a.	n.a.	n.a.
Zambia	3[c]	0	92[c]	6[c]	21[c]	n.a.	n.a.	n.a.	n.a.
Zimbabwe	48[c]	1[c]	18[c]	5[c]	15[c]	n.a.	n.a.	96[c]	n.a.

ASIA, PACIFIC, AUSTRALASIA									
Australia	40	21	18	6	5	133	127	100	111[a]
Bangladesh	25	1	0	30	14	n.a.	n.a.	74	79[a]
Brunei Darussalam	0	96	0	19[c]	2[c]	n.a.	n.a.	n.a.	n.a.
India	27	4	7	9[c]	37[c]	151	115	115	120[a]
Kiribati	n.a.	n.a.	n.a.	n.a.	n.a.	n.a.	n.a.	n.a.	n.a.
Malaysia	37	20	3	12[c]	11[c]	82	78	90[c]	n.a.
Maldives	n.a.	n.a.	n.a.	n.a.	n.a.	n.a.	n.a.	n.a.	n.a.
Nauru	n.a.	n.a.	n.a.	n.a.	n.a.	n.a.	n.a.	n.a.	n.a.
New Zealand	70	1	6	7	6	116	103	114	123
Pakistan	27	1	0	14	18	119	104	110	92
Papua New Guinea	41	0	46	20[c]	20[c]	n.a.	n.a.	n.a.	n.a.
Singapore	11	13	3	8	16	n.a.	n.a.	93	92
Solomon Islands	90	1	0	17[c]	24[c]	n.a.	n.a.	88[b]	n.a.
Sri Lanka	46	7	1	18[c]	21[c]	157	118	93	78
Tonga	87	0	2	29[c]	14[c]	n.a.	n.a.	n.a.	n.a.
Tuvalu	n.a.	n.a.	n.a.	n.a.	17[c]	n.a.	n.a.	n.a.	n.a.
Vanuatu	99[c]	0	0	28[c]	14[c]	n.a.	n.a.	n.a.	n.a.
Western Samoa	92	0	0	23[c]	17[c]	n.a.	n.a.	n.a.	n.a.
EUROPE AND MEDITERRANEAN									
Cyprus	33	5	2	14	13	122	110	113[c]	n.a.
Malta	5	0	2	14	7	131	108	109[b]	n.a.

Table 3 **Composition and Terms of Trade of Commonwealth Countries** (contd.)

	Contribution to export earnings of agricultural goods, fuels and minerals, 1987–89 average (per cent of total by value)			Food and fuels as percentage of imports, 1987–89 average		Terms of trade (period averages, 1985 = 100)			
	Food and materials	Fuels	Ores and Metals	Food and beverages	Fuels	1969–72	1974–77	1986–89	1990
United Kingdom	9	11	3	12	7	101	85	97	99
WESTERN HEMISPHERE									
Antigua & Barbuda	n.a.	n.a.	n.a.	n.a.	n.a.	n.a.	n.a.	n.a.	n.a.
Bahamas	2	85	1	4[c]	84[c]	n.a.	n.a.	n.a.	n.a.
Barbados	28	19	0	16[c]	14[c]	n.a.	n.a.	n.a.	n.a.
Belize	79[c]	0	0	25[c]	17[c]	n.a.	n.a.	n.a.	n.a.
Canada	20	10	9	6	5	94	104	100	n.a.
Dominica	58[c]	0	0	29[c]	9[c]	n.a.	n.a.	n.a.	n.a.
Grenada	84	0	0	31[c]	12[c]	n.a.	n.a.	n.a.	n.a.
Guyana	64[c]	0	21[c]	n.a.	n.a.	n.a.	n.a.	n.a.	n.a.
Jamaica	34	2	43	19[c]	33[c]	n.a.	n.a.	n.a.	n.a.
St. Christopher-Nevis	43	5	1	24[c]	11[c]	n.a.	n.a.	n.a.	n.a.
St. Lucia	68[c]	0	0	23[c]	10[c]	n.a.	n.a.	n.a.	n.a.
St. Vincent & the Grenadines	88	0	0	35[c]	9[c]	n.a.	n.a.	n.a.	n.a.
Trinidad & Tobago	5	66	1	21	8	64	81	64	62

Table 4 **Current Account Balance, External Debt, Reserves and Aid Receipts of Commonwealth Countries**

		External debt and debt service								Receipts of official development, 1987–89 average					
			Public and publicly guaranteed medium and long term debt, 1989		Debt service on public and publicly guaranteed debt, 1989, as percentage of										
	Current account balance as percentage of GNP, 1988–90 average	Total external debt, 1989 ($ US million)	($ US million)	as percentage of GNP	GNP	exports of goods and non-factor services	IMF quota (SDR million)	Use of IMF credit, August 31, 1991 (per cent of quota)	External reserves, coverage in terms of months of imports, end-1989	Net total ($ US million)	Net bilateral from Commonwealth countries ($ US million)	Net bilateral from other DAC countries ($ US million)	Net from OPEC countries and agencies ($ US million)	From other multilateral agencies ($ US million)	Total per head of population ($ US)
AFRICA															
Botswana	15.9	513	509	41[b]	6.1[b]	3.6	22.1	n.a.	26.3[a]	153.9	11.6	93.3	−.9	49.9	128.3
The Gambia	11.4[a]	342	292	147.5	9.3	10.9	17.1	186.4	1.7	126.1	43.3	46.2	−4.6	41.3	157.6
Ghana	−2.3	3,078	2,312	45	8.5	19.2	204.5	273.6	3.1[a]	563.7	147.5	169.7	3.7	242.8	40.3
Kenya	−6.1[a]	5,690	4,633	58.4	8.1	33.3	142.0	249.4	1.6[a]	983.3	211.9	569.2	2.9	199.3	43.5
Lesotho	2.0	324	312	37.5	2.7	2.8	15.1	70	1.4[a]	115.4	11.6	55.9	−.7	48.7	67.9
Malawi	−4.1[b]	1,394	1,246	79.9	6.1	28	37.2	215.1	2.6	366	70.4	125.9	0	169.6	45.8
Mauritius	−4.4	832	737	36.3	7	9.8	53.6	44.6[a]	4.4	110.5	29.9	51.2	−.2	29.7	100.5
Namibia	n.a.	n.a.	n.a.	n.a.	n.a.	n.a.	70	n.a.	n.a.	n.a.	n.a.	n.a.	n.a.	n.a.	n.a.
Nigeria	6.5	32,832	32,074	116.6	6.5	21.3	849.5	n.a.	1.6[a]	1,320.9	17.9	1,028.7	0	274.3	12.0
Seychelles	−8.3	168	133	47.6	8.6	11.9	3.0	n.a.	.7	14.4	−3.1	11.4	−.9	7.1	144.0
Sierra Leone	−.3[b]	1,057	512	57.6	.4	8.8[b]	57.9	125.9	.3	104.4	8	63.3	5.1	28	26.8
Swaziland	5.5	281	260	40.3	5.3	4.8	24.7	n.a.	3.3[a]	27.2	−4.8	23.8	−.3	8.5	38.9
Tanzania	−12.2	4,918	4,517	171	3.3	16.6	107.0	77.3	1.2[a]	913.6	87.3	653.1	−.5	173.7	37.0
Uganda	−.3[b]	1,808	1,488	36.8	5.2	81.2	99.6	221.2	.4	363.8	45.1	112	14	192.8	22.5
Zambia	−9.6[a]	6,874	4,095	82.2	3.4	12.3	270.3	237.4	1.9[a]	460.6	106.6	256.3	−.5	98.2	61.4
Zimbabwe	.9[c]	3,088	2,635	45.8	8.2	25.6	191.0	2.5[a]	1.8[a]	375.3	128.5	171.6	−2	77.1	40.4
ASIA, PACIFIC, AUSTRALASIA															
Australia	−5.7	n.a.	n.a.	n.a.	n.a.	n.a.	1,619.2	n.a.	3.7	−709.0[l]	−361.0[m]	n.a.	n.a.	−201.0[n]	−44.4[o]
Bangladesh	−3.0	10,712	9,926	49.4	2.4	19.9	287.5	161.1	2.3	1669.3	194.5	755.9	−19.9	738.9	15.3

Brunei Darussalam	n.a.	n.a.	n.a.	n.a.	n.a.	n.a.	n.a.	n.a.	n.a.	n.a.	n.a.	n.a.	n.a.	n.a.	9.6[a]
India	−2.6[b]	62,509	56,253	21.5	2.4	26.3	2,207.7	87.8	2.7	4,247.4	273.8	1,967.9	−8.7	2,014.4	5.2
Kiribati	n.a.	n.a.	n.a.	n.a.	n.a.	n.a.	2.5	n.a.	n.a.	17.4	8.2	5.7	n.a.	3.4	174.0
Malaysia	.3	18,576	15,837	44	11.7	14.6	550.6	n.a.	3.9	530.1	256.7	251	−1.9	24.2	31.4
Maldives	9.2[a]	67	54	60	10.8	8[b]	2.0	n.a.	2.4[a]	n.a.	n.a.	n.a.	n.a.	n.a.	n.a.
Nauru	n.a.	n.a.	n.a.	n.a.	n.a.	n.a.	n.a.	n.a.	n.a.	6.2	.1	6.1	n.a.	n.a.	7.3[a]
New Zealand	−3.5[a]	n.a.	n.a.	n.a.	n.a.	n.a.	461.6	n.a.	4	−72.0[(l)]	−12.0[(m)]	n.a.	n.a.	−12.0[(n)]	22.0[(o)]
Pakistan	−3.4[a]	18,509	14,807	37.5	4.5	23.2	546.3	98.4	1	1,718.4	90.6	848.1	−31.7	811.4	16.2
Papua New Guinea	−10.7[a]	2,496	2,328	69.2	15.8	34.3	65.9	65	3.3	498.5	338.8	71.3	−.3	88.7	134.7
Singapore	7.0	n.a.	n.a.	n.a.	n.a.	n.a.	92.4	n.a.	4.8	1,577.2	280.6	1,320.2	.1	−23.7	606.6
Solomon Islands	−17.2[a]	102	100	57.1	5.6	9	5.0	3.2	4	61.9	23.4	15.2	.2	23	206.3
Sri Lanka	−4.6[a]	5,101	4,341	62.6	5.9	17.8	223.1	115.5	.8	622.5	125.8	338.1	−.2	158.8	37.7
Tonga	−14.8[b]	45	44	43.2	1.9	2.3[b]	3.3	n.a.	n.a.	24.8	10.4	9	−.1	5.5	248.0
Tuvalu	n.a.	n.a.	n.a.	n.a.	n.a.	n.a.	n.a.	n.a.	n.a.	15.5	13.4	1.2	n.a.	.9	1633.2[a]
Vanuatu	1.5	32	22	17.5	1.9	3.1	9.0	n.a.	6.8[a]	51	21.8	16.9	n.a.	12.3	510.0
Western Samoa	5.4[a]	74	72	65.6	6.2	15	6.0	3.5	8.4	32.1	10.7	10.4	.5	10.6	160.5
EUROPE AND MEDITERRANEAN															
Cyprus	−1.2[a]	1,998[b]	1,280[b]	30.8[b]	6.6[b]	12[b]	69.7	n.a.	5.5	179.3	−4.1	107.7	4.8	70.9	256.1
Malta	1.8[a]	411	80	4	1.8	2.1	45.1	n.a.	10.7	n.a.	n.a.	n.a.	n.a.	n.a.	n.a.
United Kingdom	−3.4	n.a.	n.a.	n.a.	n.a.	n.a.	6,194.0	n.a.	2.3	−1,711.0[(l)]	−413[(m)]	n.a.	n.a.	−689[(n)]	30.2[(o)]
WESTERN HEMISPHERE															
Antigua & Barbuda	−43.4[c]	n.a.	n.a.	n.a.	n.a.	n.a.	5.0	n.a.	1.5[a]	20.7	5.1	14.1	−.1	1.6	207.0
Bahamas	−5.7	195[b]	147[b]	5.6[b]	2.0[b]	3.3[b]	66.4	n.a.	2.0[a]	1,080.8	25.3	1,044.4	n.a.	11.2	5,404.0
Barbados	−1.2[a]	746[b]	566[b]	36.2[b]	4.5[b]	8.9[b]	34.1	3[a]	2	15.9	−9.1	14.9	−.7	10.9	53.0
Belize	−3.4[a]	134	126	40.3	5.6	8	9.5	7.8[a]	3.5[a]	30.4	8	13.4	n.a.	9	152.0
Canada	−3.2	n.a.	n.a.	n.a.	n.a.	n.a.	2,941.0	n.a.	1.7	1,737.0[(l)]	−324[(m)]	n.a.	n.a.	−600[(n)]	67.8[(o)]
Dominica	−15.0	n.a.	n.a.	n.a.	n.a.	n.a.	4.0	88	1.2	20.8	12.3	−.6	−.3	9.3	208.0
Grenada	−88.3	78	68	37.2	1.4	7.7[b]	6.0	2.3[a]	2.3[a]	17.4	6.9	−.5	−.7	11.8	174.0

Table 4 **Current Account Balance, External Debt, Reserves and Aid Receipts of Commonwealth Countries** (contd.)

		External debt and debt service								Receipts of official development, 1987–89 average					
			Public and publicly guaranteed medium and long term debt, 1989		Debt service on public and publicly guaranteed debt, 1989, as percentage of										
	Current account balance as percentage of GNP, 1988–90 average	Total external debt, 1989 ($ US million)	($ US million)	as percentage of GNP	GNP	exports of goods and non-factor services	IMF quota (SDR million)	Use of IMF credit, August 31, 1991 (per cent of quota)	External reserves, coverage in terms of months of imports, end-1989	Net total ($ US million)	Net bilateral from Commonwealth countries ($ US million)	Net bilateral from other DAC countries ($ US million)	Net from OPEC countries and agencies ($ US million)	From other multilateral agencies ($ US million)	Total per head of population ($ US)
Guyana	−24.4[c]	1,713	987	429.1	12.2	11.4	49.2	181	.4[c]	46.8	12.7	9.3	n.a.	24.8	58.5
Jamaica	−3.8[a]	4,322	3,636	112.5	18.8	26.4	145.5	205.5	1	331.9	59.7	206	−4.7	70.9	138.3
St. Christopher-Nevis	−18.3[a]	n.a.	n.a.	n.a.	n.a.	n.a.	4.5	n.a.	n.a.	15.2	4.8	7.1	n.a.	3.3	361.9
St. Lucia	−8.4[a]	n.a.	n.a.	n.a.	n.a.	n.a.	7.5	n.a.	2.0[c]	23.6	12.5	3.7	n.a.	7.4	236.0
St. Vincent & the Grenadines	−2.8[a]	51	49	32.5[b]	2.5[b]	3.8[b]	4.0	n.a.	n.a.	15	2.5	3.4	−.1	9.2	150.0
Trinidad & Tobago	1.8	2,012	1,680	46.2	6.4	12.3	170.1	158.2	2.5	36.9	−6.2	17.6	n.a.	25.5	30.8

Table 5 **Social and Education Statistics for Commonwealth Countries**

	Infant mortality rate 1989 (per '000)	Life expectancy 1990	Nutrition		Access to safe drinking water, 1988 (per cent of population)		Population per physician 1989	Primary school enrolment ratios 1988		Daily newspaper circulation per '000 population, 1986
			Calories per capita per day, 1987–89	Protein 1986–89 (grams per capita per day)	Urban	Rural		Males	Females	
AFRICA										
Botswana	67	68	2,368	72.9	100.0	33.0	24,300	111[b]	117[b]	16
The Gambia	142.8	44	2,351	56.2	n.a.	n.a.	22,000	76	47	6
Ghana	89.5	56	2,246	48.6	95.8	54.8	11,940	78[b]	63[b]	35[c]
Kenya	72	60	2,159	58.6	n.a.	n.a.	14,840	98[b]	93[b]	13
Lesotho	100	57	2,326	65.8	n.a.	40.0	19,880	101[c]	125[c]	29
Malawi	150.5	48	2,098	60.8	66.0	49.0	46,900	73[b]	59[b]	2
Mauritius	23	70	2,823	67.3	100.0	98.0	3,960	105[b]	107[b]	71
Namibia	106	58	n.a.	n.a.	n.a.	n.a.	n.a.	n.a.	n.a.	13
Nigeria	105	52	2,306	49.5	36.3	n.a.	7,450	n.a.	77[c]	n.a.
Seychelles	n.a.	71	2,340	63.5	95.0	n.a.	4,000	n.a.	n.a.	46
Sierra Leone	154.3	42	1,841	38.4	86.0	20.0	16,440	64[c]	44[c]	3
Swaziland	118	57	2,612	62.2	38.0	n.a.	7,280	105[b]	103[b]	16[d]
Tanzania	105.6	50	2,209	55.0	50.0	38.0	20,237	67[b]		4
Uganda	102.7	49	2,136	48.1	45.0	12.0	24,876	76[c]	63[c]	2
Zambia	79.8	54	2,054	56.4	48.0	n.a.	11,700	102[c]	92[c]	14
Zimbabwe	72.1	64	2,288	56.5	53.0	13.5	5,030	130	126	24

ASIA, PACIFIC, AUSTRALASIA										
Australia	8.7	77	3,186	97.4	100.0	n.a.	447	106[b]	105[b]	264
Bangladesh	112.2	52	1,996	42.9	25.0	66.0	7,333	76	64	7
Brunei Darussalam	n.a.	76	2,824	77.6	90.0		1,456	n.a.	n.a.	n.a.
India	95	61	2,196	53.2	79.0	85.0	4,850	113[c]	81[c]	28
Kiribati	n.a.	57	2,956	70.1	n.a.	n.a.	4,400	n.a.	n.a.	n.a.
Malaysia	24.1	70	2,754	57.9	100.0	65.6	2,860	102[c]	102[c]	85[d]
Maldives	49.9	61	n.a.	n.a.	91.0	17.0	49,000	n.a.	n.a.	8
Nauru	n.a.	n.a.	n.a.	n.a.	n.a.	n.a.	700	n.a.	n.a.	n.a.
New Zealand	10	75	3,389	102.8	100.0	n.a.	579	107[b]	106[b]	328
Papua New Guinea	58.8	55	n.a.	n.a.	54.0	n.a.	14,141	75[b]	64[b]	12
Pakistan	103.9	56	2,197	60.1	84.0	28.0	3,298	51[b]	28[b]	13[d]
Singapore	7.4	74	3,249	91.1	100.0	n.a.	900	118[c]	113[c]	357
Solomon Islands	n.a.	65	2,191	53.4	90.9	59.8	5,190	n.a.	n.a.	n.a.
Sri Lanka	24	71	2,299	46.3	82.0	35.0	5,760	105[c]	102[c]	31
Tonga	n.a.	67	2,980	71.9	100.0	100.0	3,625	n.a.	n.a.	n.a.
Tuvalu	n.a.	n.a.	n.a.	n.a.	n.a.	n.a.	1,750	n.a.	n.a.	n.a.
Vanuatu	n.a.	65	2,552	65.8	45.0	n.a.	5,741	n.a.	n.a.	n.a.
Western Samoa	n.a.	66	n.a.	n.a.	n.a.	n.a.	3,795	n.a.	n.a.	n.a.
EUROPE AND MEDITERRANEAN										
Cyprus	12	76	n.a.	n.a.	100.0	100.0	754	106[b]	106[b]	124
Malta	n.a.	73	3,238	97.9	100.0	100.0	500	109[b]	105[b]	n.a.

Table 5 **Social and Education Statistics for Commonwealth Countries** (contd.)

	Infant mortality rate 1989 (per '000)	Life expectancy 1990	Nutrition		Access to safe drinking water, 1988 (per cent of population)		Population per physician 1989	Primary school enrolment ratios 1988		Daily newspaper circulation per '000 population, 1986
			Calories per capita per day, 1987–89	Protein 1986–89 (grams per capita per day)	Urban	Rural		Males	Females	
United Kingdom	9.1	76	3,181	89.6	100.0	100.0	870	105[c]	106[c]	421
WESTERN HEMISPHERE										
Antigua & Barbuda	n.a.	74	2,295	76.8	63.0	17.0	3,750	n.a.	n.a.	81[d]
Bahamas	28.4	69	2,791	81.2	100.0	n.a.	1,460	n.a.	n.a.	163
Barbados	n.a.	75	3,247	103.2	100.0	100.0	2,400	113[c]	108[c]	155
Belize	21.2	68	2,660	73.7	n.a.	n.a.	3,261	n.a.	n.a.	49[d]
Canada	7.3	77	3,462	99.8	100.0	100.0	455	106[b]	104[b]	225
Dominica	n.a.	76	2,820	68.5	77.0	n.a.	8,000	n.a.	n.a.	n.a.
Grenada	n.a.	70	2,657	68.8	85.0	n.a.	1,961	n.a.	n.a.	n.a.
Guyana	29.7	65	2,739	68.6	100.0	60.0	3,360	112[c]		80
Jamaica	18	73	2,622	64.7	99.0	93.0	7,412	104[c]	106[c]	59[d]
St. Christopher-Nevis	n.a.	70	2,614	75.5	100.0	100.0	1,920	n.a.	n.a.	44[d]
St. Lucia	23.7	72	2,582	71.3	70.0	n.a.	1,956	n.a.	n.a.	30
St. Vincent & the Grenadines	n.a.	70	2,618	59.1	75.0	n.a.	2,700	n.a.	n.a.	n.a.
Trinidad & Tobago	11.4	72	2,913	70.4	100.0	93.0	3,820	99[b]	100[b]	146

Area and Population of British Dependent Territories

Territory	Area Including inland waters (km^2)	Estimated population in thousands mid-1989	Annual rate of increase 1985–89 %
Anguilla	96	8	1.3
Ascension	88	n.a.	n.a.
Bermuda	53	58	.9
British Indian Ocean Territory	78	3	0
British Virgin Islands	153	13	1.3
Cayman Islands	259	22	1
Falkland Islands	12,173	2	0
Gibraltar	6	31	1.8
Hong Kong	1,045	5,769	1.4
Montserrat	102	13	2.3
Pitcairn Island	5	n.a.	n.a.
St Helena	122	7	2.8
Tristan Da Cunha	104	0	n.a.
Turks and Caicos Islands	430	9	1.4

Source: UN Demographic Yearbook 1989

Commonwealth Immigration into Britain

Until 1962 Britain freely admitted citizens of other Commonwealth countries for residence and a quarter of the world's population was thus entitled to enter and settle in Britain at will. In the early 1950s increasing numbers began to exercise this right with the result that by 1961 (in which year it was estimated 170,000 immigrants from other Commonwealth countries entered Britain) it became clear that the rate of flow of Commonwealth immigrants was exceeding Britain's capacity to absorb them. It was therefore decided that immigration would have to be controlled.

Commonwealth Immigrants Acts 1962 and 1968

Part I of the 1962 Act, subjected to control all Commonwealth citizens except, broadly speaking, those born in the United Kingdom and those holding passports issued by a United Kingdom authority.

During 1967 there was a rapid increase in the number of citizens of the United Kingdom and Colonies of Asian origin coming to this country from East Africa. In order to prevent the immigration policy from being undermined by this influx of people not subject to control under the 1962 Act, the Government introduced the 1968 Act, which extended immigration control to certain citizens of the United Kingdom and Colonies who held United Kingdom passports issued abroad, unless they—or one of their parents or grandparents—were born or naturalised in the United Kingdom or acquired citizenship of the United Kingdom and Colonies by adoption or registration in the United Kingdom or by registration in what was at the time an independent Commonwealth country.

At the time of the 1968 Act a scheme was introduced under which special vouchers were issued to heads of households whose exemption from immigration control had been ended by the Act and who wished to settle in the United Kingdom. The dependants of a voucher holder were entitled to accompany him to, or join him in, the United Kingdom under the normal rules of immigration control. These arrangements have continued following the introduction of the Immigration Act 1971.

Immigration Acts 1971 and 1988

The Immigration Act 1971 came into force on 1st January 1973 and replaced all previous immigration legislation. It introduced a single system of immigration control which applies both to Commonwealth citizens and to foreign nationals. It provides for control of entry into the United Kingdom from overseas, and for the control after entry of people who do not have the right of abode in the United Kingdom. The system of control set up by the 1971 Act was amended and updated by the Immigration Act 1988.

The right of abode

Under section 2 of the 1971 Act (which was amended by the British Nationality Act 1981) all British citizens and certain Commonwealth citizens have the right of abode. This means that they are entirely free from United Kingdom immigration control. Persons who are not British citizens have the right of abode if immediately before 1st January 1983 they were:

(*a*) Commonwealth citizens with a parent who at the time of their birth or legal adoption was a citizen of the United Kingdom and Colonies who had that citizenship by birth in the United Kingdom; or

(*b*) Commonwealth citizens who were then or had previously been the wife of a man with the right of abode.

A person claiming to have the right of abode must establish this at the point of entry by means of either a United Kingdom passport describing him as a British citizen or a citizen of the United Kingdom and Colonies having the right of abode in the United Kingdom, or a certificate of entitlement to the right of abode which may be obtained from a British post overseas or from the Home Office.

Entry clearance

The possession of a visa is mandatory for nationals of Bangladesh, Ghana, India, Nigeria, Pakistan, Sri Lanka and Uganda, coming to the United Kingdom except for those who benefit from a visa exemption. Under the visa exemption scheme persons who are settled in the United Kingdom and have not been away for more than 2 years or persons who have been granted leave to stay for more than 6 months and who travel from the United Kingdom and return within the period of their original leave are not required to present a visa. They will, however, be liable to examination at the port of entry to confirm that they qualify for re-admission. Visitors and others granted leave of 6 months or less are not visa exempt.

In addition, citizens of all other Commonwealth countries must obtain an entry certificate if seeking admission to the UK as a spouse, dependant or fiancé(e), or for certain other long term purposes. Either form of entry clearance can be obtained from British Diplomatic Missions overseas and entry clearance holders are likely to be admitted to Britain without difficulty when they arrive. Those who are not obliged to obtain entry clearance may nevertheless apply if they wish to travel with a similar assurance about their eligibility. If the holder of an entry clearance should be refused leave to enter he has a right of appeal exercisable in the United Kingdom except in occasional cases where refusal follows a personal decision of the Home Secretary that the presence in the United Kingdom of the person concerned would not be conducive to the public good.

Extensions of stay

Applications for extensions of stay may be made to the Immigration and Nationality Department, Home Office, Lunar House, Wellesley Road, Croydon CR9 2BY.

Employment

People who do not have the right of abode and who are seeking to enter the United Kingdom for employment are in general required to have work permits before setting out. There are some exceptions—for example ministers of religion; representatives of overseas newspapers; Commonwealth citizens who have a grandparent born in the United Kingdom; self-employed people such as writers and artists—but for these an entry clearance is obligatory and anyone seeking to come for employment should first make enquiries of a British High Commission or Consulate overseas.

Work permits are issued by the Department of Employment for a specific job with a particular employer who must himself apply to the Department. A work permit holder may be given leave to enter the United Kingdom for the period stated on the permit, subject to a condition requiring him to obtain the approval of the Department of Employment if he wishes to change his job. His stay may be extended if he is still in approved employment. After 4 years he may be granted settlement and he will then be free to take any employment.

Young Commonwealth citizens aged 17 to 27 inclusive who want to spend a working holiday in the United Kingdom before settling down in their own countries may come without work permits, provided that the employment (which may be part-time for most of the holiday or full-time for only part of the holiday) is incidental to the holiday. The maximum time allowed for working holidays is 2 years.

The spouse and children under 18 of work permit holders are admitted for the same period as the head of the household provided that they hold a valid entry clearance issued for that purpose, but they are not subject to any restriction on the taking of employment. No other dependants can be admitted before the head of the family has been accepted for settlement.

Students

Students are given leave to enter for an appropriate period depending on the length of the course of study and their means with a condition restricting their freedom to take employment. They are not permitted to take full time employment but they may work during their vacations and spare time if the conditions attached to their stay do not preclude this and they first obtain the approval of the Department of Employment.

The wife and children under 18 of a person admitted as a student are given leave to enter for the period of his authorised stay if he can maintain and accommodate them without working or recourse to public funds. Their freedom to take employment is not normally restricted unless the student himself is prohibited from taking employment, in which case the prohibition will extend to the wife and children.

A student who requires a visa to enter the United Kingdom (see 'Entry Clearance' above) but who did not enter the United Kingdom with a visa endorsed as a student or prospective student will not be granted leave to remain as a student unless he is to undertake postgraduate medical or dental training.

Visitors

Visitors are normally given leave to enter for a period of up to a maximum of 6 months on conditions prohibiting their taking employment. Those admitted as business visitors may transact business during their stay.

Au pair

An unmarried girl aged 17 to 27 inclusive and without dependants who is a national of certain European countries including Cyprus and Malta may be admitted for a period of up to 2 years where an arrangement has been made for her to live *au pair* with a resident English-speaking family.

Fiancé(e)s

A man or woman may be admitted to the United Kingdom for marriage to a person settled here provided they hold a current entry clearance granted for that purpose. A person holding a valid entry clearance as a fiancé(e) will normally be admitted for a 6 month initial period and advised to apply to the Immigration and Nationality Department for an extension of stay once the marriage has taken place. An entry clearance will be refused unless the entry clearance officer is satisfied that the primary purpose of the intended marriage is not to gain admission to the United Kingdom, and that the parties have already met and intend to live together permanently as husband and wife, and that adequate maintenance and accommodation will be available to the fiancé(e) before marriage and to the couple and their dependants thereafter without recourse to public funds.

Dependants

Spouses of persons already settled in the United Kingdom also require entry clearance. A person holding an entry clearance issued to them as the spouse of a person settled in the United Kingdom should normally be admitted for an initial period of 12 months so long as there has been no change in the applicant's circumstances since the entry clearance was issued and no false representations were given or material facts withheld from the entry clearance officer to obtain the entry clearance. Shortly before the end of that 12 month probationary period, the spouse may apply for the conditions attached to his or her stay in this country to be removed.

Entry clearance will be refused unless the entry clearance officer is satisfied that the marriage was not entered into primarily to obtain admission to the United Kingdom, that the couple intend to live permanently with each other and have met, that adequate accommodation will be available for the couple without recourse to public funds in accommodation of their own or which they occupy themselves, and that they will be able to maintain themselves and their dependants adequately without recourse to public funds.

Unmarried children of people settled here who are aged under 18 may be admitted for settlement if both parents or the sole surviving parent or a parent with sole responsibility for the child's upbringing, are settled in the United Kingdom. Children aged 18 or over must qualify for admission in their own right unless there are most exceptional compassionate circumstances. Special consideration may be given to fully dependent unmarried daughters under 21 who formed part of the family unit overseas and have no close relatives in their country to turn to. A widowed mother of any age, a widower over 65, or a married couple of whom either is over 65, will normally be admitted if they are wholly or mainly dependent upon children settled in the United Kingdom who are able and willing to support them without recourse to public funds, providing they are without close relatives in their own country to turn to. In exceptional circumstances other dependants of persons settled in the United Kingdom may be admitted.

The appeals system

The Immigration Act 1971 makes provision for a system of immigration appeals, with a right of appeal to an adjudicator and a further right of appeal, with leave, to the Immigration Appeal Tribunal. There are rights of appeal against refusal of a certificate of entitlement or an entry clearance. If a person claiming to have the right of abode holds either a United Kingdom passport or a certificate of entitlement but his claim is not accepted when he arrives here he will have a right of appeal. A person who does not have the right of abode and who is refused leave to enter the United Kingdom will be able to appeal against the refusal; but unless he holds a current work permit, or entry clearance he will have to exercise his right of appeal from overseas. A person whose application for an extension of stay or a variation of his entry conditions is refused has a right of appeal if his application was made in time and a person whose stay is curtailed or whose conditions are varied on the initiative of the Home Office also has a right of appeal. There is also a right of appeal for anyone against whom it has been decided to make a deportation order (except when this is on the recommendation of a court, in which case an appeal lies to a higher court against the recommendation). The 1988 Immigration Act, with certain exceptions, restricted the right of appeal in deportation cases where the person has overstayed or broken conditions of stay and has been in the United Kingdom less than 7 years to the facts of the case (ie whether or not he has overstayed or broken his conditions of stay). There is no right of appeal where the decision has been taken on security or political grounds, but a special advisory procedure applies in these cases.

Statistics

During the 12 months ending 31st December 1990, 3,340 Commonwealth citizens were admitted to the United Kingdom with work permits for 12 months or more; 2,820 as dependants of work permit holders; 1,390,000 as ordinary visitors; 8,270 were accepted for settlement on arrival, and 23,420 for settlement on removal of time limit (after some period in the United Kingdom). These figures were published as Cm 1571 in July 1991.

Table Showing Differences in Time between Commonwealth Countries

Figures in horizontal columns indicate difference of time between the country shown in left-hand margin and the countries shown (in vertical columns) at the head of the table.

Figures to the left of the diagonal must be added and figures to the right of the diagonal must be subtracted.

Source: Time Zone Chart of the World—published by the Admiralty 1987.

Summer Time (Daylight Saving)

Since 1918, most cities and towns in Canada have adopted daylight saving for varying periods in the summer months.

In Britain the statutory period of Summer Time is defined in the Summer Time Acts of 1922 and 1925, but under the Summer Time Act 1947 the statutory dates may be varied by Order in Council. Since 31st October 1971, Summer Time has been used for the period between 3rd Saturday in March and the 4th Saturday in October.

Some Australian States use daylight saving schemes.

Source: Time Zone Chart of the World, Published by the Admiralty 1987

	Time Zone Letter	Time Zone Number
	TZL	TZN
Western Samoa	X	+11
Canada (Pacific Time) (W. of 120°W.)	U	+8
Canada (Mountain Time) (102°W. to 120°W.)	T	+7
Canada (Central Time) (85°W. (north) or 90° (south) to 102°W.), Belize	S	+6
Canada (Eastern Time) (Ontario and Quebec) (68°W. to 85°W. (north) or 90° (south)), Jamaica, Bahamas	R	+5
Canada (Atlantic Time) (E. of 68°W.), Barbados, Antigua & Barbuda, Dominica, Grenada, St Christopher and Nevis, St Lucia, St Vincent and the Grenadines, Trinidad and Tobago	Q	+4
Canada (Newfoundland)	—	+3½
Guyana	P	+3
United Kingdom (GMT), Sierre Leone, Ghana, The Gambia	Z	0
United Kingdom (Summer Time), Nigeria, Malta	A	−1
Cyprus, Malawi, Zambia, Lesotho, Botswana, Swaziland, Zimbabwe, Namibia	B	−2
Tanzania, Uganda, Kenya	C	−3
Mauritius, Seychelles	D	−4
Maldives, Pakistan	E	−5
India, Sri Lanka	—	−5½
Bangladesh	F	−6
Western Australia, Malaysia, Singapore, Brunei	H	−8
South Australia, Northern Territory	—	−9½
Australia (Other States including Australian Capital Territory), Papua New Guinea	K	−10
Solomon Islands, Vanuatu	L	−11
Nauru, New Zealand, Kiribati, Tuvalu	M	−12
Tonga	—	−13

Western Samoa	Canada (Pacific Time)	Canada (Mountain Time)	Canada (Central Time)	Canada (Eastern Time)	Canada (Atlantic Time)	Canada (Newfoundland)	Guyana	United Kingdom (GMT)	United Kingdom (Summer Time)	Cyprus, Malawi, Zambia	Tanzania, Uganda, Kenya
+11	+8	+7	+6	+5	+4	+3½	+3	0	−1	−2	−3
	3	4	5	6	7	7½	8	11	12	13	14
3		1	2	3	4	4½	5	8	9	10	11
4	1		1	2	3	3½	4	7	8	9	10
5	2	1		1	2	2½	3	6	7	8	9
6	3	2	1		1	1½	2	5	6	7	8
7	4	3	2	1		½	1	4	5	6	7
7½	4½	3½	2½	1½	½		½	3½	4½	5½	6½
8	5	4	3	2	1	½		3	4	5	6
11	8	7	6	5	4	3½	3		1	2	3
12	9	8	7	6	5	4½	4	1		1	2
13	10	9	8	7	6	5½	5	2	1		1
14	11	10	9	8	7	6½	6	3	2	1	
15	12	11	10	9	8	7½	7	4	3	2	1
16	13	12	11	10	9	8½	8	5	4	3	2
16½	13½	12½	11½	10½	9½	9	8½	5½	4½	3½	2½
17	14	13	12	11	10	9½	9	6	5	4	3
19	16	15	14	13	12	11½	11	8	7	6	5
20½	17½	16½	15½	14½	13½	13	12½	9½	8½	7½	6½
21	18	17	16	15	14	13½	13	10	9	8	7
22	19	18	17	16	15	14½	14	11	10	9	8
23	20	19	18	17	16	15½	15	12	11	10	9
24	21	20	19	18	17	16½	16	13	12	11	10

Mauritius, Seychelles	Maldives	India, Sri Lanka	Bangladesh	Western Australia	South Australia	Australia (Other States)	Solomon Islands	New Zealand	Tonga	Time Zone Letter	Time Zone Number	
−4	−5	−5½	−6	−8	−9½	−10	−11	−12	−13	TZL	TZN	
15	16	16½	17	19	20½	21	22	23	24	X	+11	Western Samoa
12	13	13½	14	16	17½	18	19	20	21	U	+8	Canada (Pacific Time)
11	12	12½	13	15	16½	17	18	19	20	T	+7	Canada (Mountain Time)
10	11	11½	12	14	15½	16	17	18	19	S	+6	Canada (Central Time)
9	10	10½	11	13	14½	15	16	17	18	R	+5	Canada (Eastern Time)
8	9	9½	10	12	13½	14	15	16	17	Q	+4	Canada (Atlantic Time)
7½	8½	9	9½	11½	13	13½	14½	15½	16½	—	+3½	Canada (Newfoundland)
7	8	8½	9	11	12½	13	14	15	16	P	+3	Guyana
4	5	5½	6	8	9½	10	11	12	13	Z	0	United Kingdom (GMT)
3	4	4½	5	7	8½	9	10	11	12	A	−1	United Kingdom (Summer Time)
2	3	3½	4	6	7½	8	9	10	11	B	−2	Zambia
1	2	2½	3	5	6½	7	8	9	10	C	−3	Tanzania, Uganda, Kenya
	1	1½	2	4	5½	6	7	8	9	D	−4	Mauritius
1		½	1	3	4½	5	6	7	8	E	−5	Maldives, Pakistan
1½	½		½	2½	4	4½	5½	6½	7½	—	−5½	India
2	1	½		2	3½	4	5	6	7	F	−6	Bangladesh
4	3	2½	2		1½	2	3	4	5	H	−8	Australia (Western)
5½	4½	4	3½	1½		½	1½	2½	3½		−9½	Australia (South)
6	5	4½	4	2	½		1	2	3	K	−10	Australia (Other States)
7	6	5½	5	3	1½	1		1	2	L	−11	Solomon Islands
8	7	6½	6	4	2½	2	1		1	M	−12	Nauru, New Zealand
9	8	7½	7	5	3½	3	2	1			−13	Tonga

National Days of Commonwealth Countries

The principal national days celebrated in Commonwealth countries are listed below, (a) in alphabetical order, (b) in date order:

(a)	Antigua and Barbuda	1 November	Independence Day
	Australia	26 January	National Day
	The Bahamas	10 July	Independence Day
	Bangladesh	26 March	Independence Day
	Barbados	30 November	National Day
	Belize	21 September	Independence Day
	Botswana	30 September	National Day
	Britain	(1) June	The Queen's Official Birthday
	Brunei	1 January	Independence Day
	Canada	1 July	National Day
	Cyprus	1 October	Independence Day
	Dominica	3 November	Independence Day
	The Gambia	18 February	Independence Day
	Ghana	6 March	Independence Day
	Grenada	7 February	Independence Day
	Guyana	23 February	National Day
	India	26 January	Republic Day
	Jamaica	(2) August	Independence Day
	Kenya	12 December	Independence Day
	Kiribati	12 July	Independence Day
	Lesotho	4 October	Independence Day
	Malawi	6 July	Independence Day
	Malaysia	31 August	Malaysia Day
	Maldives	26 July	National Day
	Malta	31 March	National Day
	Mauritius	12 March	National Day
	Namibia	21 March	Independence Day
	Nauru	31 January	Independence Day
	New Zealand	6 February	National Day
	Nigeria	1 October	Republic Day
	Pakistan	23 March	National Day
	Papua New Guinea	16 September	Independence Day
	Saint Christopher and Nevis	19 September	Independence Day
	Saint Lucia	22 February	Independence Day
	St. Vincent and the Grenadines	27 October	Independence Day
	Seychelles	5 June	National Day
	Sierra Leone	27 April	Independence Day
	Singapore	9 August	National Day
	Solomon Islands	7 July	Independence Day
	Sri Lanka	4 February	Independence Commemoration Day
	Swaziland	6 September	Independence and National Day
	Tanzania	26 April	Union Day
	Tonga	4 June	Independence Day
	Trinidad and Tobago	31 August	Independence Day
	Tuvalu	1 October	Independence Day
	Uganda	9 October	Independence Day
	Vanuatu	30 July	Independence Day
	Western Samoa	1 June	Independence Day
	Zambia	24 October	Independence Day
	Zimbabwe	18 April	Independence Day

The second Monday in March is observed throughout the Commonwealth as Commonwealth Day.

(1) variable: second Saturday in June. (2) variable: first Monday in August.

(b)

1 January	Brunei	Independence Day
26 January	Australia	National Day
26 January	India	Republic Day
31 January	Nauru	Independence Day
4 February	Sri Lanka	Independence Commemoration Day
6 February	New Zealand	National Day
7 February	Grenada	Independence Day
18 February	The Gambia	Independence Day
22 February	Saint Lucia	Independence Day
23 February	Guyana	National Day
6 March	Ghana	Independence Day
12 March	Mauritius	National Day
21 March	Namibia	Independence Day
23 March	Pakistan	National Day
26 March	Bangladesh	Independence Day
31 March	Malta	National Day
18 April	Zimbabwe	Independence Day
26 April	Tanzania	Union Day
27 April	Sierra Leone	Independence Day
4 June	Tonga	Independence Day
(1) June	Britain	The Queen's Official Birthday
1 June	Western Samoa	Independence Day
5 June	Seychelles	National Day
1 July	Canada	National Day
6 July	Malawi	Independence Day
7 July	Solomon Islands	Independence Day
10 July	The Bahamas	Independence Day
12 July	Kiribati	Independence Day
26 July	Maldives	National Day
30 July	Vanuatu	Independence Day
(2) August	Jamaica	Independence Day
9 August	Singapore	National Day
31 August	Malaysia	Malaysia Day
31 August	Trinidad and Tobago	Independence Day
6 September	Swaziland	Independence and National Day
16 September	Papua New Guinea	Independence Day
19 September	Saint Christopher and Nevis	Independence Day
21 September	Belize	Independence Day
30 September	Botswana	National Day
1 October	Cyprus	Independence Day
1 October	Nigeria	Republic Day
1 October	Tuvalu	Independence Day
4 October	Lesotho	Independence Day
9 October	Uganda	Independence Day
24 October	Zambia	Independence Day
27 October	St. Vincent and the Grenadines	Independence Day
1 November	Antigua and Barbuda	Independence Day
3 November	Dominica	Independence Day
30 November	Barbados	National Day
12 December	Kenya	Independence Day

The second Monday in March is observed throughout the Commonwealth as Commonwealth Day.

(1) variable: second Saturday in June.

(2) variable: first Monday in August.

British Parliamentary and Non-Parliamentary Papers of Commonwealth Interest (1991)

Listed below are publications issued by, or on sale from, Her Majesty's Stationery Office, relating to the affairs and interests of Commonwealth countries. This list covers the period January to December, 1991. Earlier publications are listed in previous editions of this work.

Dates within brackets denote year of publication or date placed on sale. If the date of a report, conference etc. is the same year as publication, the date is not repeated within brackets.

GENERAL

1. Development and aid

The Caribbean Development Bank (Further Payments) Order 1991 (SI 1991/717) (0110137175) £0.60

The International Development Association (Ninth Replenishment) Order 1991 (SI 1991/462) (0110134621) £0.60

International Monetary Fund. Occasional paper 80. Domestic public debt of externally indebted countries by Pablo Guidotti and Manmohan Kumar. Washington: IMF (1557752087) £6.75

International Monetary Fund. World economic and financial surveys. World economic outlook, May 1991. A survey by the staff of the International Monetary Fund. Washington: IMF (1557752109) £20.00

Organisation for Economic Co-operation and Development. Competition and economic development. Paris: OECD (9264033475) £18.00

Organisation for Economic Co-operation and Development. Financing and external debt of developing countries: 1990 survey. Paris: OECD. (9264134948) £19.50

Organisation for Economic Co-operation and Development. Geographical distribution of financial flows to developing countries: disbursements, commitments economic indicators: 1986/1989. Paris: OECD (92 6403345 9) £32.00

Organisation for Economic Co-operation and Development. Trade, investment and technology in the 1990s. Paris: OECD (9264134808) £16.00

Organisation for Economic Co-operation and Development. Development Centre Studies. The diffusion of advanced telecommunications in developing countries by Christiano Antonelli (9264135782) £10.00

Organisation for Economic Co-operation and Development. Development Centre studies. Financial systems and development: what role for the formal and informal financial sectors? by Dimitri Germidis, Denis Kessler, Rachel Meghir. Paris: OECD (9264134727) £20

Organisation for Economic Co-operation and Development. Development Centre Studies. Rebalancing the public and private sectors: developing country experience. O Bouin and A Michelet. Paris: OECD (9264134409) £18.00

Organisation for Economic Co-operation and Development. Development Centre studies. The tying of aid by Catrinus J Jepma. Paris: OECD (926413459x) £7.00

United Nations. Department of International Economic and Social Affairs. Overcoming obstacles to institutional development in the least developed countries. (9211043697) £6.00

United Nations. Department of International Economic and Social Affairs. World economic survey 1991: current trends and policies in the world economy. New York: UN (9211091209) £37.00

Wilton Park Papers No. 34 The international economy: sources of instability and business and government responses by Nicholas Hopkinson. Based on Wilton Park Conference 358, 12–16 November 1990 (0117016101) £7.50

Foreign Affairs Committee session 1989/90 minutes of proceedings (Wednesday 6 December 1989–Wednesday 24 October 1990) HC 681 (0100204708) £4.10

Foreign Affairs Committee. 1st Report, session 1990/91: UK policy towards South Africa and the other states of the region.
Chairman: David Howell
Vol I: Report, together with the proceedings of the Committee (HC53–I) (0102748918) £14.80
Vol II: Minutes of evidence with appendices (HC 53–II) (0102747911) £32.00

Foreign Affairs Committee, 1st Report, session 1990/91: United Kingdom policy towards South Africa and the other states of the region: observations by the government. Foreign and Commonwealth Office, 4 April 1991 (Cm 1525) (0101152523) £2.35

Foreign and Commonwealth Office. Foreign and Commonwealth Office, including Overseas Development Administration: the Government's expenditure plans 1991/92 to 1993/94. (Cm 1502) (0101150229) £8.10

2. Overseas Services

The Commonwealth Yearbook 1991 (0115917098) £21.50
The Diplomatic Service List 1991 (011 591708x) £18.00
The London Diplomatic List (incorporating Directory of International Organisations) 2 issues per year. June 1991 (011591739x) £3.75

3. Migration and Citizenship

Home Office. Control of immigration: statistics, United Kingdom 1990 (Cm 1571) (0101157126) £15.80
Home Office. Statement of changes in immigration rules, 30 September 1991 (Cm 1672) (0101167229) £0.60
Immigration Appeal Tribunal. Immigration appeals: selected determinations of the Immigration Appeal Tribunal on appeals under the Immigration Act 1971: and selected reports of decisions of the House of Lords, the Court of Appeal and the High Court. Quarterly 1991. Annual subscription £54.00
Office of Population Censuses and Surveys. Series MN 16 International migration: migrants entering or leaving the United Kingdom and England and Wales, 1989. Chiefly tables. (0116913193) £7.50
Organisation for Economic Co-operation and Development. Demographic change and public policy. Migration: the demographic aspects. Paris: OECD (9264134395) £15.00

4. Miscellaneous

Agreement between the governments of the United Kingdom of Great Britain and Northern Ireland, Canada, Australia, New Zealand and India, and the government of the Tunisian Republic concerning Commonwealth war cemeteries, graves and memorials in Tunisia. Tunis, 2 May 1990. Treaty series no. 91 (1991) (Cm 1721). The Agreement entered into force 1 October 1991 (0101722125) £3.25
The Air Navigation (Overseas Territories) (Amendment) (No.2) Order 1991 (SI 1991/1697) (0110146972) £3.00
Convention on environmental impact assessment in a transboundary context. Espoo, Finland, 25 February 1991. Miscellaneous no. 15 (1991) (Cm 1645) (0101164521) £3.70
Environment Committee. 3rd Report. Climatological and environmental effects of rainforest destruction: report with appendix, together with the proceedings of the Committee, the minutes of evidence and appendices. Chairman: Sir Hugh Rossi (HC 40-i and HC 48-i) (010 202491x) £22.00
Environmental policies for cities in the 1990s. Paris: OECD (9264134352) £12.00
The Extradition (Designated Commonwealth Countries) Order 1991 (SI 1991/1700) (0110147006) £1.00
Organisation for Economic Co-operation and Development. Environmental policy: how to apply economic instruments. Paris: OECD (9264135685) £15.00
Organisation for Economic Co-operation and Development. Development Centre seminars. Environmental management in developing countries. Paris: OECD. Papers from a conference held 3–5/10/1990. (9264035036) £28.00
Schedule to the International Whaling Convention, 1946: revised to include the amendments adopted at the 41st Annual Meeting of the International Whaling Commission held in San Diego, June 1989. Treaty series no. 1 (1991) (Cm 1354). In continuation of Treaty series no. 76 (1984) (Cmnd 9372) (0101135424) £3.75
The state of the environment. Paris: OECD. 2 vols (9264134425) £22.00
United Nations. International Narcotics Control Board. Report of the International Narcotics Control Board for 1990. New York: UN (9211480825) £8.00
United Nations Environment Programme. United Nations Environment Programme: 1989 annual report of the Executive Director. New York: UN (9280712195) £30.00
Wilton Park papers 43. Fighting drugs trafficking in the Americas and Europe by Nicholas Hopkinson. Based on Wilton Park Conference 366 with the Institute for European-Latin American Relations (IRELA). 3–7 June 1991. Fighting the Drugs Trade: Prospects for co-operation between Europe and the Americas (0117016497) £8.00

REGIONAL

Australia

Agreement between the government of the United Kingdom of Great Britain and Northern Ireland and the government of Australia providing for the reciprocal recognition and enforcement of judgements in civil and commercial matters. Canberra, 23 August 1990. Australia no. 1 (1990) (Cm 1394). The Agreement is not in force (010113942x) £1.90

Agreement on social security between the government of the United Kingdom of Great Britain and Northern Ireland and the government of Australia. London 1 October 1990. Australia no. 2 (1991) (Cm 1589). The Agreement is not yet in force (0101158920) £3.25

Films co-production agreement between the government of the United Kingdom of Great Britain and Northern Ireland and the government of Australia. Canberra 12 June 1990. Treaty series no. 90 (1991) (Cm 1758) (0101175825) £1.90

Bahamas

Agreement between the government of the United Kingdom of Great Britain and Northern Ireland and the government of the Bahamas concerning the investigation of drug trafficking and confiscation of the proceeds of drug trafficking. Nassau, 28 June 1988. Treaty series no. 13 (1991) (Cm 1448). The Agreement entered into force on 24 October 1990. Previously published as Bahamas no. 1 (1988) (Cm 475) (010144822) £1.90

Bermuda

The Merchant Shipping Act 1988 (Bermuda) Order 1991 (SI 1991/1703) (0110147030) £3.45

Brunei

Agreement between the government of the United Kingdom of Great Britain and Northern Ireland and the government of His Majesty the Sultan and Yang Di-Pertuan of Brunei Darussalam concerning air services. London, 23 November 1990. Treaty series no.23 (1991) (Cm 1481). The Agreement entered into force on 23 November 1990 (0101148127) £4.10

The Caribbean

The Caribbean Territories (Abolition of Death Penalty for Murder) Order 1991 (SI 1991/988) (0110139887) £0.60

Cayman Islands

Exchange of notes between the government of the United Kingdom of Great Britain and Northern Ireland and the government of the United States of America extending the treaty between the United Kingdom of Great Britain and Northern Ireland and the United States of America concerning the Cayman Islands relating to mutual legal assistance in criminal matters, signed at Grand Cayman on 3 July 1986, to Anguilla, British Virgin Islands and Turks and Caicos Islands. Washington 9 November 1990 Treaty series no. 49 (1991) (Cm 1624). The Agreement entered into force on 9 November 1990. (0101162421) £0.70

Gibraltar

The Registrar of British Ships (Gibraltar) (Revocation) Order 1990 (SI 1990/2587) (0110056612) £0.55

Hong Kong

Foreign and Commonwealth Office. Annual report on Hong Kong 1990. Miscellaneous no. 6 (1991) (Cm 1527) (0101152728) £2.75

Namibia

Namibia Act 1991: chapter 4. Complete text as at date of Royal Assent (28.2.1991) (0118054953) £1.00

New Zealand

Exchange of notes between the government of Great Britain and Northern Ireland and the government of New Zealand amending the agreement concerning air services signed in London on 4 October 1982. Wellington, 12 February 1991. Treaty series no. 87 (1991) (Cm 1754) (0101175426) £1.00

Nigeria

Agreement between the government of the Federal Republic of Nigeria and the government of the United Kingdom of Great Britain and Northern Ireland for the promotion and protection of investments. Abuja, 11 December 1990. Treaty series no. 66 (1991) (Cm 1661). The Agreement entered into force on 11 December 1990 (0101166125) £1.90

Exchange of notes between the government of the United Kingdom of Great Britain and Northern Ireland and the government of the Federal Republic of Nigeria concerning certain commercial debts (the United Kingdom/Nigeria Debt Agreement no.3 (1991)) Lagos 10 June 1991. Treaty series no. 86 (1991) (Cm 1753). The Agreement entered into force on 10/06/91 (0101175329) £1.90

Saint Helena

Committee of Public Accounts. 13th Report. A new ship for St Helena. Chairman: Robert Sheldon. (HC 57) (0102057915) £8.75

Sierra Leone

Exchange of notes between the government of the United Kingdom of Great Britain and Northern Ireland and the government of the Republic of Sierra Leone concerning certain commercial debts (the United Kingdom/Sierra Leone debt agreement no. 4 (1986). Freetown 22 May 1987) Freetown 6 March 1991 Treaty series no. 69 (1991) (Cm 1671). The Agreement entered into force on 6 March 1991 (0101167121) £1.90

Tanzania

Exchange of notes between the government of the United Kingdom of Great Britain and Northern Ireland and the government of the United Republic of Tanzania concerning certain commercial debts: (the United Kingdom/Tanzania Debt Agreement no.3 (1990)). Dar es Salaam 4 March 1991. Treaty Series no. 61 (1991) (Cm 1649). The Agreement entered into force on 4 March 1991 (010 1164920) £1.90

Trinidad and Tobago

Exchange of notes between the government of the United Kingdom of Great Britain and Northern Ireland and the government of the Republic of Trinidad and Tobago concerning certain commercial debt (the United Kingdom/Trinidad and Tobago debt Agreement no. 2 (1990)). Port of Spain, 9 October 1990. Treaty series no. 84 (1991) (Cm 1751). The Agreement entered into force on 9 October 1990. (0101175124) £1.90

PART VII

The Overseas Development Administration

The Overseas Development Administration (ODA) is responsible for Britain's overseas aid to developing countries, and, jointly with the Diplomatic Wing of the Foreign and Commonwealth Office (FCO), the programme of assistance to Eastern Europe and the Soviet Union. ODA spends over £1,600 million a year on development aid in partnership with over 120 developing countries.

The ODA is part of the FCO and is headed by the Minister for Overseas Development, the Rt Hon Lynda Chalker, appointed in July 1989. ODA employs some 1,700 staff including administrators, professional advisers and scientists. Its headquarters is divided between London and East Kilbride in Scotland. Staff in London deal with bilateral and multilateral aid programmes, while those at East Kilbride are responsible for a number of other areas including the recruitment and administration of personnel under the ODA's overseas manpower programmes. British High Commissions and Embassies in developing countries help to implement the aid programme. In addition, the ODA itself has five regional offices—known as Development Divisions—two in Africa and the others in South East Asia, the Caribbean and the Pacific. The Development Divisions provide on the spot professional and technical advice on the planning and execution of aid in their regions.

The ODA also gives special emphasis to applied research to help developing countries achieve sustainable management of their renewable natural resources. Much of this practical scientific work is carried out for the ODA by the Natural Resources Institute (NRI), based at Chatham, which is recognised as a world centre of excellence in its field. Although most of its work is for the ODA, it also carries out contracts for multilateral agencies and other organisations. Key activities of the NRI include assessment of land and water resources, pilot scale development projects, applied research in the fields of pest control, crop and animal processing, storage and marketing and assessment of the environmental consequences of development projects.

Over half of the British aid programme is spent bilaterally, ie provided directly for the benefit of individual countries. The rest is channelled through multilateral agencies such as the World Bank, the European Community and the UN agencies. Britain gives a high proportion—about 80 per cent—of its bilateral aid to the poorer countries in the world, and about three-quarters goes to Commonwealth countries and the remaining dependencies, reflecting their political and cultural links with Britain. The largest recipients of British bilateral aid in recent years have been India, Kenya, Malawi, Bangladesh, Tanzania, Ghana, Nigeria, Sudan and Pakistan.

Virtually all our bilateral aid to the poorest countries is now in the form of grants, rather than loans which they may have difficulty in repaying. In addition, Britain has waived repayment of old official aid debts for most of these countries. Agreements to cancel such debts have now been signed with 23 countries and represent total reduction in debt service repayments for all these countries of over £1 billion. Britain has also consistently taken the lead in promoting debt forgiveness amongst the Paris Club of Creditor Countries in favour of the poorest, most heavily indebted countries.

Bilateral aid is spent on a range of different activities. Firstly, finance is provided for projects, eg to increase agricultural production; to develop power and water supplies; to build roads; to support forestry or other environmental conservation or to develop educational and health services. Secondly, ODA finances the supply of essential materials and equipment to keep existing investments running. This is particularly important for countries trying to overcome shortages of foreign exchange and debt problems. Thirdly, ODA has a substantial technical co-operation programme, designed to develop human skills and improve local institutions by providing British expert advice or special training. Other activities carried out under the bilateral programme include scientific research of benefit to developing countries, support for British voluntary organisations and volunteers and emergency aid for refugees and disaster relief.

Further information is available from ODA's Information Department, located at 94 Victoria Street, London SW1E 5JL (Tel: 071-917 0503).

Commonwealth Telecommunications Organisation

The first submarine telegraph cables linking what are now independent Commonwealth countries were laid by cable companies as commercial ventures and Governments were not directly concerned. However, because the cable companies were unwilling to meet the expense of laying a cable across the Pacific from Canada to Australia, the Governments of Britain, Canada, New Zealand and some of the Australian States agreed—largely as a result of the advocacy over many years of Sandford Fleming of the Canadian Pacific Railways—to subscribe money for a Pacific Telegraph Cable and to set up a representative Pacific Cable Board to construct and manage the cable, which was laid in 1902.

In 1927 on the recommendation of an Imperial Wireless and Cable Conference, the various cable and wireless interests which then served the Commonwealth, including the Pacific Cable Board, were merged and a single operating Company later to be known as Cable and Wireless Ltd was set up. A representative Imperial Communications Advisory Committee was established to lay down the policy which should be followed by the Company.

In 1945 a Commonwealth Telecommunications Conference recommended that the assets of Cable and Wireless Ltd in the various Commonwealth countries should be nationalised. The recommendation was accepted by the Commonwealth Governments concerned, and in 1948 a Commonwealth Telegraphs Agreement was drawn up to promote and co-ordinate the telecommunications services of the Commonwealth. Under the agreement, which was signed by the Governments of Britain, Canada, Australia, New Zealand, South Africa, India and Southern Rhodesia, the partner Governments agreed to operate their external telecommunications co-operatively with the advice of a Commonwealth Telecommunications Board in London, on which each was to be represented. The partner Governments introduced special external telecommunications accounting arrangements known as the first wayleave scheme. The 1948 Agreement was somewhat modified by a second Commonwealth Telegraphs Agreement signed in 1963.

On the recommendation of a Commonwealth Telecommunications Conference held in 1965 and 1966 the partnership was re-constituted and the Commonwealth Telecommunications Board was replaced by a new Commonwealth Telecommunications Organisation with a Constitution which provides for periodical Commonwealth Telecommunications Conferences at which any independent Commonwealth Government may be represented; a Commonwealth Telecommunications Council of serving telecommunications officials meeting at least once a year and carrying on its business between meetings by correspondence; and a secretariat, the Commonwealth Telecommunications Bureau (*q.v.*), in London.

The Commonwealth Telecommunications Board was accordingly dissolved on 31st March 1969 by an Order in Council made under the Commonwealth Telecommunications Act 1968. The Commonwealth Telegraphs Agreements were at the same time terminated and a new financial agreement between the Partner Governments in respect of the wayleave scheme, the Commonwealth Telecommunications Organisation Financial Agreement 1969, became operative.

The wayleave scheme continued in effect until 30th March 1973 under the direction of the Commonwealth Telecommunications Council. During that period arrangements for a new 'unified accounting scheme' were developed. The new scheme, to be known as the Commonwealth Telecommunications Financial Arrangements (CTFA) came into effect on 1st April 1973 through the signing of a Commonwealth Telecommunications Organisation Financial Agreement 1973 and an Agreement terminating the 1969 Financial Agreement.

The CTFA provided for similar accounting arrangements for external traffic as those operated under the wayleave schemes but overlaid those arrangements with a cost-sharing scheme based on the use each partner made of Commonwealth facilities. At the same time, the level of central co-ordination regarding operating practices was reduced. Unfortunately, the scheme proved too complex to accommodate all the new technologies being introduced during the late 1970's and early 1980's and arrangements were duly made to introduce a more flexible scheme.

Following the Commonwealth Telecommunications Conference in Nicosia in 1982 a new financial agreement replacing the 1973 Agreement was opened for signature in London on 30th March 1983 (for those Governments 'Partners' to the previous agreement) and entered into force on 1st April. Under the

Agreement the more developed national bodies assisted the less developed through preferential adjustments to accounting rate divisions or account settlements for inter-Commonwealth traffic and through donations to a common fund for a Programme for Development and Training (PDT).

In 1990 the preferential accounting arrangements were cancelled on the recommendation of The Commonwealth Telecommunications Conference in Nicosia and the Partner Governments agreed to concentrate all available funds on the Programme for Development and Training. This Programme as well as providing specialist training also provides expert assistance to tackle particular problems.

The present Partnership consists of the Governments of Australia, Bangladesh, Barbados, Botswana, Canada, Cyprus, The Gambia, Ghana, Guyana, India, Jamaica, Kenya, Lesotho, Malaysia, Malawi, Malta, Mauritius, New Zealand, Nigeria, Papua New Guinea, Seychelles, Sierra Leone, Sri Lanka, Swaziland, Tanzania, Trinidad and Tobago, Uganda, the United Kingdom, Vanuatu and Zambia. Moreover the following countries are able to participate in certain of the current arrangements through the auspices of Cable and Wireless: Antigua, Dominica, Grenada, Maldives, St Christopher and Nevis, St Lucia, St Vincent, Solomon Islands and Tonga.

Commonwealth Telecommunications Bureau

Claireville House, 26–27 Oxendon Street, London, SW1Y 4EL
General Secretary: Graham H Cunnold (Tel: 071-930-5516; Tlx: 27328; FAX: 071-930 4248)
Head of Accounts and Personnel: G B Pegg (071-930 5514)
Head of Collaborative Arrangements: J E Wilson-Law (071-930 5512)
Head of Council and ODG Support: G C Wood (071-930 5513)

The Commonwealth Telecommunications Bureau is the Secretariat of the Commonwealth Telecommunications Organisation.*

The Bureau was incorporated in Britain on 8th May 1968 by the Commonwealth Telecommunications Act 1968 and from 1st April 1969 it took over from the Commonwealth Telecommunications Board the administration of the Commonwealth Telecommunications Organisation's financial arrangements. The Bureau signed a headquarters agreement with the British Government on 30th March 1983 giving international status to the organisation and to the Bureau.

The Bureau under the direction of the General Secretary contributes to the achievement of the purposes of the Commonwealth Telecommunications Organisation by providing effective support to the Conference, the Council, its groups and committees and by assisting them in the performance of their respective functions and tasks. Its role includes the administration of the financial and other collaborative arrangements concluded by Partners and participation in the activities of the Council and its committees.

The implementation of the collaborative arrangements and the execution of the activities of the Commonwealth Telecommunications Organisation and its organs require the participation of the National Bodies and of the Bureau staff in a complementary but balanced manner. Accordingly, the Bureau is expected to have such expertise and resources as are necessary to ensure that it can perform its functions in the most efficient manner and to contribute in the most meaningful and practicable way to the development, implementation and administration of the collaborative arrangements and to the carrying out of the concomitant activities.

*See p. 524

INDEX

INDEX

A

B

C

H

I

J

K

T

U